FROMMER'S

COMPREHENSIVE TRAVEL GUIDE

FLORIDA '95

by Rena Bulkin,
Dan Levine & Nicole Faff,
Bill Goodwin,
Patricia Tunison Preston &
John J. Preston

MACMILLAN TRAVEL
U.S.A.

MACMILLAN TRAVEL

A Prentice Hall Macmillan Company
15 Columbus Circle
New York, NY 10023

ISBN 0-671-88616-9
ISSN 1044-2391

Design by Robert Bull Design
Maps by Geografix Inc.

Special Sales
Bulk purchases (10 + copies) of Frommer's Travel Guides are available to corporations at special
discounts. The Special Sales Department can produce custom editions to be used as premiums
and/or for sales promotion to suit individual needs. Existing editions can be produced with
custom cover imprints such as corporate logos. For more information write to: Special Sales,
Prentice Hall Travel, 15 Columbus Circle, New York, NY 10023.

Manufactured in the United States of America

CONTENTS

LIST OF MAPS

INVITATION TO THE READERS

In researching this book, we have come across many fine establishments, the best of which we have included here. We are sure that many of you will also come across appealing hotels, inns, restaurants, guesthouses, shops, and attractions. Please don't keep them to yourself. Share your experiences, especially if you want to comment on places that have been included in this edition that have changed for the worse. You can address your letters to the appropriate author (see inside back cover for a list):

Frommer's Florida '95
c/o Macmillan Travel
15 Columbus Circle
New York, NY 10023

A DISCLAIMER

Readers are advised that prices fluctuate in the course of time, and travel information changes under the impact of the varied and volatile factors that affect the travel industry. Neither the author nor the publisher can be held responsible for the experiences of readers while traveling. Readers are invited to write to the publisher with ideas, comments, and suggestions for future editions.

SAFETY ADVISORY

Whenever you're traveling in an unfamiliar city or country, stay alert. Be aware of your immediate surroundings. Wear a moneybelt and keep a close eye on your possessions. Be particularly careful with cameras, purses, and wallets, all favorite targets of thieves and pickpockets.

CHAPTER 1

GETTING TO KNOW FLORIDA

Lured by the promise of sunny skies and sandy beaches, millions of visitors flee bleak northern winters every year to bask in Florida's warmth. But though thousands of miles of pristine shoreline are its undeniable drawing card, America's Sunshine State offers much more than just a beach vacation.

Its lush tropical landscape, dotted with fish-filled lakes and springs, abounds in wildlife that will thrill the naturalist in you. Unspoiled marshes, mangroves, and mud flats provide habitats for great egrets, wood storks, ibis, bald eagles, flamingos, roseate spoonbills, pelicans, hawks, and herons among other shore birds; dolphins, otters, and manatees frolic in diverse waterways; and in the summer months, huge loggerhead turtles lumber ashore to lay their eggs in the sand. Dense forests of cypress draped in Spanish moss contrast with gracefully swaying palms and displays of brilliant bougainvillea, azaleas, hibiscus, crape myrtles, and fragrant jasmine and magnolias. Southwest of Miami is a vast primeval prairie that sweeps across 2,100 square miles of spectacular wilderness—Everglades National Park. The Keys, a string of coral reef islets, offer topography ranging from upland jungle and mangrove swamp to a 21-mile underwater garden filled with over 600 species of tropical fish. The world's largest stand of sand pines is in Ocala National Forest, a 366,000-acre wilderness. Citrus groves line the banks of the Indian River. And Sanibel Island, which along with nearby Captiva Island comprises a national wildlife refuge, is considered one of the world's best shelling sites.

Sports fans can cheer their favorite major-league baseball teams as they head into each season with spring training here, while thousands of football fans descend on Miami for the Orange Bowl each year and on Jacksonville for the Gator Bowl. And that's just the beginning. Florida offers every manner of spectator sport, from major golf and tennis tournaments to such local favorites as jai alai and greyhound racing. And, of course, there's Daytona Beach, mecca for auto-racing enthusiasts. In addition, it would be hard to name an active sport not readily available in the Sunshine State. You'll find details in each chapter.

Finally, Florida is America's most popular family vacation destination, offering a host of kid-pleasers—most notably Walt Disney World, but also including water parks such as Wet 'n Wild, alligator and crocodile parks, Universal Studios, Busch Gardens, Sea World and Marineland, and Lion Country Safari.

1. HISTORY

THE FLOWERY LAND On April 2, 1513—more than a century before the Pilgrims landed at Plymouth Rock— Juan Ponce de León, in search of the fabled "fountain of youth," spied the beaches and lush greenery of Florida's Atlantic coast. The conqueror and colonial governor of Puerto Rico laid anchor just south of present-day Cape Canaveral, rowed ashore, and confidently claimed the land

DATELINE

- **1513** Ponce de León makes landfall near Cape Canaveral, becoming first European to step on Florida soil.
- **1565** Pedro Menéndez de Avilés
  (continues)

for the Spanish Crown. Observing that the land was "very pretty to behold with many refreshing trees," he named it La Florida, or "the Flowery Land."

Eight years later, with a fighting force of 200 conquistadors, missionary priests, and a writ from the Spanish king promising him de facto ownership of any profits his endeavor might produce, he returned to conquer and colonize Florida. His party landed at Charlotte's Bay, near present-day Fort Myers, said a prayer of thanksgiving, and began building homes. But the fledgling settlement's prayers went unanswered. It was ferociously attacked with arrows and stones by hostile indigenous tribes. Ponce de León was wounded by an arrow and, along with other survivors, retreated to Cuba where he died. He was buried on Puerto Rico. Ponce de León's fate proved a harbinger of the difficulties the Spanish would encounter in Florida. Over the next 50 years, five expeditions pursuing rumors of golden cities attempted and failed to establish a colonial foothold on the peninsula.

It wasn't until 1565 that Pedro Menéndez de Avilés, arriving with 1,000 settlers and a priest, established St. Augustine, the first permanent European settlement in North America. In the years that followed, Franciscan friars created a chain of missions on Native American lands throughout Florida. Though the missions' ostensible aim was converting the tribes and instructing them in European trades and agricultural methods, they only succeeded in wreaking havoc among them. Many tribesmen died taking up primitive arms against Spanish steel and firepower, and many more were drafted into slavery. But the greatest toll was in deaths from European infectious diseases against which Native Americans had no immunities. By the middle of the 16th century, three-quarters of Florida's original inhabitants had been wiped out.

THE BRITISH ARE COMING Though their colony survived, life was difficult for the Spanish settlers who were beset by the same combination of harsh climate (those Florida hurricanes), hostile natives, famine, fire, and disease that undid earlier expeditions. St. Augustine was attacked time and again by pirates and armies of the rival French and British empires. Florida gained importance in the defense of Spain's commercial coastal route, but it never produced bounteous wealth for Spain as settlements in Mexico, the Caribbean, and South America had done. When the British captured the important Spanish port of Havana, Cuba, in the French and Indian War (1754–63), they offered to exchange Havana for the rights to Florida. Forced to choose, the Spanish reluctantly agreed.

During their two decades as stewards of Florida (1763–84), the British brought zeal and resources to the territory's development that far exceeded Spanish efforts. They began establishing Florida as a major agricultural center. Stately plantations, producing indigo, rice, and oranges, rose up along the Atlantic coast and the St. Johns River. St. Augustine bustled with activity. East Florida British Gov. James Grant captured the upbeat tenor of the times in a letter to a friend: "There is not so gay a Town in America as this is at present, the People [are] Musick and Dancing mad."

Bolstered by stipends from the British Parliament, Florida remained loyal to King George III during the American Revolution and, in fact, became a haven for Tories from the northern colonies. But when the newborn United States prevailed over England in 1783, the Treaty of Paris acknowledged Spain's wartime assistance by returning Florida to Spanish control.

SPANISH SETTLEMENT, SEMINOLE WARS & STATEHOOD

Florida remained in Spanish hands for the next four decades (1784–1821), but it was clear from the beginning that this regime was living on borrowed time. To attract settlers, the Spanish offered land grants to anyone willing to immigrate to the colony, and as English-speaking homesteaders from the United States began to stream into Florida, its Spanish character underwent a subtle shift. In 1791, Thomas Jefferson wrote cagily to President Washington: "I wish 10,000 of our inhabitants would accept the invitation. It would be a means of delivering to us peaceably what must otherwise cost us a war. In the meantime, we may complain of the seduction of our inhabitants just enough to make the Spanish believe it is a very wise policy for them."

This maneuvering over control of Florida between the two nations broke into open conflict with the outbreak of the War of 1812 and the First Seminole War of 1818. Andrew Jackson's unopposed marches through Florida during these two conflicts convinced Spain that it had no choice but to negotiate a graceful departure. In 1821, Spain ceded Florida to the United States.

The new territorial government aggressively set about encouraging the growth of its charge. Tallahassee, once a thriving Apalachee settlement, was chosen as the capital. Streets were laid in Cowford, a cattle crossing on the St. Johns River, and the village was renamed Jacksonville in honor of "Old Hickory." Florida's population, numbering 8,000 in 1821, had quadrupled by the 1830s. But one major obstacle to settlement yet remained—the Seminoles.

The Seminoles had migrated into the peninsula from Georgia toward the end of the 18th century, and by the 1820s, much of Florida's richest farmland—which the territorial government was eager to open to white homesteaders—lay in their hands. After a series of compromise treaties that left both sides dissatisfied, the federal government threw down the final gauntlet with the Indian Removal Act of 1830, stipulating that all eastern tribes be removed to reservations west of the Mississippi. The spark that ignited the Second Seminole War (1835–42) was provided by a young warrior named Osceola. At a treaty conference at Payne's Landing in 1832, he strode up to the bargaining table, slammed his knife into the papers on it, and pointing to the quivering blade, proclaimed, "The only treaty I will ever make is this!" Guerilla warfare thwarted the U.S. Army's attempts to remove the Seminoles for almost eight years. But finally, the Seminole population in Florida dwindled to fewer than 100 survivors who took refuge deep in the impenetrable swamps of the Everglades, where some of their descendants still live today. With the Seminoles out of the way, the Territorial General Legislature petitioned Congress for statehood, and on March 3,

(continues)

DATELINE

Civil War to take place in Florida.
- **1887** Florida legislature passes Jim Crow measures mandating separation of races.
- **1895** Henry Morrison Flagler's Florida East Coast railroad incorporated; catastrophic freeze forces citrus industry to move south.
- **1912** Flagler's railroad reaches Key West.
- **1915** Miami Beach incorporated.
- **1925** Miami's population explodes to 300,000 as real estate boom peaks.
- **1926–29** Collapse of land boom, two destructive hurricanes, fruit-fly infestation, and national stock-market crash leaves Florida's economy in ruins.
- **1942** German U-boats sink U.S. ships off Florida coast throughout the summer; thousands of servicemen arrive in Florida's new military bases.
- **1950** Booming tourism brings 4.5 million visitors to the state; first rocket launched from Cape Canaveral.
- **1959** Cubans fleeing Castro begin arriving in Florida.
- **1964** Civil rights protests rock St. Augustine.

DATELINE

- **1969** *Apollo XI's* historic journey to the moon launched from Kennedy Space Center.
- **1971** Walt Disney World opens.
- **1974** Big Cypress Swamp National Preserve created, a harbinger of Florida's growing environmental awareness.
- **1982** Epcot (Experimental Prototype Community of Tomorrow) opens at Walt Disney World.
- **1990** Universal Studios, theme park and working film studio, opens its doors.
- **1992** Hurricane Andrew slams into the Gold Coast, causing $1 billion in damages.

1845, President John Tyler signed a bill making Florida the 27th state in the Union.

Florida grew rapidly over the next 15 years. Cotton, cattle ranching, and forest industries thrived; railroads began to appear; and visitors from the north arrived to enjoy the state's sunny winters. By 1860, Florida's population had jumped to 140,000, 40% of whom were slaves. Then came the Civil War.

REBELS & RECONSTRUCTION In 1861, Florida became the third state to secede from the Union, and the modest progress it had achieved as a state came to a standstill. The stars and bars flew from every flagpole. Only one major battle of the Civil War was fought on Florida soil, however, when Confederate forces met federal troops seeking to advance on and destroy Florida farms at Olustee, on February 20, 1864. The Rebels routed the Yanks, and, in the months that followed, successfully continued to defend interior Florida against Union attack. When Robert E. Lee surrendered at Appomattox, Tallahassee was the only southern capital still in Confederate hands, but this was little consolation to Floridians, who had lost some 5,000 of their own during the strife.

Florida's fledgling cities and industries emerged from the Civil War relatively unscathed, but residents did not escape the social and political turmoil of Reconstruction. The Emancipation Proclamation released nearly half of Florida's population from slavery, and intense wrangling ensued between northern reformers and Floridians over the role blacks would play in postwar society. Blacks enjoyed some initial gains. Local elections of 1868 saw 19 blacks ride the Union victory to seats in the Florida legislature, and schools for black children were founded. But as elsewhere in the South, the traditional political power base of white Democrats soon regained the upper hand.

THE GILDED AGE Florida emerged from the rigors of Reconstruction to rebuild the state's economy and usher in an era of rapid growth and development. North-central Florida enjoyed the benefits of a booming citrus industry. Cigar factories sprang up in Tampa. Large tracts of swamp in the peninsula's interior were drained for agricultural use, and this newly arable land was sold to eager arriving immigrants. Many of these arrivals were recently freed African Americans, who by the 1890s accounted for 47% of the state's population. State planners recognized that the expansion of the railroads was the requisite catalyst for economic growth. Industrialists Henry Plant and William Chipley built railroads that connected Tampa and Pensacola to the developed regions in Florida's northeast. To ensure the profitability of their new railroads, both men invested heavily in the isolated cities at the end of the line. Plant's posh Tampa Bay Hotel still graces the city's skyline as the home of the University of Tampa.

But the man who revolutionized Florida tourism was the flamboyant Henry Morrison Flagler, a partner in John D. Rockefeller's Standard Oil Company. Visiting Florida in the early 1880s, he envisioned the sunny Atlantic coast state as a winter playground for millionaires—a southern Newport. He bought up and knit together the short rail lines that extended south from Jacksonville and laid track as far as West Palm Beach, incorporating it all under the Florida East Coast Railway Company. In 1896, Flagler's trains chugged into the infant hamlet of Miami, and by 1912 the rail line extended south to Key West. In Palm Beach, Flagler built his own mansion, Whitehall, as well as two palatial hotels, the Poinciana and the Breakers. And in St.

Augustine, his fabulous Ponce de Leon Hotel (today Flagler College), complemented by two other deluxe hostelries, the Alcazar and the Cordova, also drew moneyed visitors.

THE 20TH CENTURY: FLORIDA BOOMS . . . Florida entered the 20th century with a diversified economy centered on ranching, citrus, timber, and tourism. Prosperity was everywhere. The expanded rail system vastly improved mail service around the state; telephones and electricity reached most of rural Florida; a crude passenger airline began operating flights between St. Petersburg and Tampa, the first such outfit in the world; and an extensive road system accommodated the rapid growth of the automobile.

Congress passed the Eighteenth Amendment in 1919, and the Florida legislature, reflecting the staid attitudes of the rural population, quickly made Prohibition Florida law. But no such attitude ruled the increasingly cosmopolitan and sophisticated Gold Coast. People arrived in droves for holidays in Palm Beach and Miami, and illegal speakeasies rose up to serve them. Wild chases between lawmen and "rum runners" became commonplace. Florida quickly became one of the loosest environments of the Roaring '20s. The state was in a celebratory mood. As Henry Flagler had envisioned decades earlier, real estate was going through the roof. Millions of immigrants, speculators, and builders descended on the state, and new communities sprang up seemingly overnight. Miami Beach, for example, went from a barren strip of sand to a sprawling resort city with over 50 hotels in a decade. Land that had been available free to anyone who wanted it after the city's incorporation in 1915 was going for tens of thousands of dollars in 1925. The mayors of Miami, Miami Beach, Hialeah, and Coral Gables proclaimed their county "The most Richly Blessed Community of the most Bountifully Endowed State of the most Highly Enterprising People of the Universe."

. . . AND GOES BUST Quite suddenly the bubble burst. A July 1926 issue of the *Nation* provided the obituary for the land boom: "The world's greatest poker game, played with building lots instead of chips, is over. And the players are now . . . paying up." Construction stopped dead, and many newcomers who had arrived in Florida to jump on the bandwagon returned to their homes in the north. Two hurricanes, the first to hit the state in over a decade, pummeled the Gold Coast in 1926 and 1928, catastrophically damaging both the resort areas and the interior farmlands of the southern peninsula. A fruit-fly infestation crippled the citrus industry. The 1929 stock-market crash that precipitated the Great Depression seemed almost an afterthought to Florida's ruined economy. Within a few years, the announcers at Tampa radio station WDAE were giving wry notice of the state's suffering by changing the station's slogan "Wonderful Days and Evenings" to "We Don't Always Eat."

President Franklin D. Roosevelt's New Deal programs helped the state begin to climb back on its feet. The Works Progress Administration (WPA) put 40,000 unemployed Floridians back in the labor force building the automobile causeway from the mainland to Key West and a bridge across the Panhandle's Ocklockonee Bay, among other public projects. By 1936 the tourist trade had revived somewhat, and the state began attracting a broader range of visitors than ever before. But the event that finally lifted Florida—and the nation—out of the Depression was World War II. Following the Japanese attack on Pearl Harbor in 1941, scores of army bases and training facilities were expanded or opened all over Florida. Thousands of U.S. servicemen did part of their hitch in the state, and hotels were filled to capacity with military personnel. The war came right to Florida's shores—in 1942, German subs sank a U.S. tanker, the *Pan Massachusetts,* and over two dozen other Allied ships in plain sight of Florida's beaches. When the war ended, many soldiers returned to settle in the Sunshine State, and in the 1940s Florida's population nearly doubled.

POSTWAR PROSPERITY Florida shared the bullish economy of the 1950s with the rest of the nation. Its population grew a whopping 78.7% during the decade, making it America's 10th most populous state, and tourists came in droves, nearly 4.5

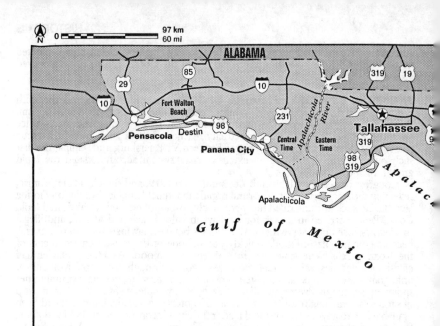

FLORIDA

GEORGIA

Amelia Island

Jacksonville
Jacksonville Beach

Lake City

St. Augustine
St. Augustine
Beach

Gainesville

Ocala
National
Forest
Ocala

De Land

Daytona Beach

NASA-Kennedy
Space Center

Cedar
Key
Homosassa
Springs

Orlando
Bee Line
Expwy.

Cape
Canaveral
Merritt Island

arpon Springs

Kissimmee

Melbourne

Tampa   Lakeland

Winter
Haven

earwater

St.
Petersburg

Tampa
Bay

Vero Beach

Bradenton

Fort Pierce

Sarasota

Jensen Beach

Lake
Okeechobee

Riviera Beach
West Palm Beach
Palm
Beach

Captiva Island

Cape
Coral

Fort Myers

Delray Beach
Boca Raton
Pompano
Beach

Sanibel Island

Big Cypress
Swamp

Everglade Pkwy.
(Alligator Alley)

Fort Lauderdale
Dania
Hollywood

Naples

Big Cypress
National
Preserve

Miami
Beach

Marco
Island

Everglades City

Miami

Ten
Thousand
Islands

Everglades
National
Park

Homestead

Flamingo

Biscayne Bay

Florida Bay

Key Largo

Florida Keys

Long Key
Marathon

Key West

Atlantic Ocean

St. Johns River

Suwannee River

Caloosahatchee River

Kissimmee River

Florida's Turnpike

million in 1950 alone. One reason for the influx was the advent of the air conditioner, which made life in Florida infinitely more pleasant.

A brand-new industry came into being at Cape Canaveral in 1950—the government-run space program. Cape Canaveral became NASA's headquarters for the Apollo rocket program that eventually blasted Neil Armstrong heavenward toward his famous "great step"—a happening in bizarre accordance with sci-fi writer Jules Verne's 1865 novel *From the Earth to the Moon*, which foretold that mankind would first reach for the moon from this latitude of Florida.

Beginning in 1959, great numbers of Cuban immigrants fleeing Fidel Castro's socialist revolution began arriving on Florida's shores. Most of these exiles had led middle- or upper-class lives in Cuba, and collectively they created a remarkable American success story, planting an indelible stamp on the business and cultural life of the city. Other exile communities, most notably Haitians, have been arriving in Florida's cities in recent years and are jostling for a piece of the economic pie. But the state's most important new arrival since Flagler was a cute rodent, in 1971.

THE MOUSE THAT ROARED   In the 1960s, Walt Disney began secretly buying up central Florida farmland and laying plans for the world's most spectacular theme park. Walt Disney World would soon turn the sleepy citrus-growing town of Orlando into the fastest-growing city in the state and attract so many visitors that they would outnumber residents. WDW continued to grow and expand, adding Epcot, Disney-MGM Studios, and other adjuncts (described in detail in Chapter 9). Today, not just Orlando but the entire state abounds in theme parks.

Florida has become the state "where everyone is from somewhere else"—even Mickey came from California. At the forefront of this influx of outsiders are retirees. A steady stream of seniors from the Northeast have settled in the Miami area, while an equally large contingent from the Midwest has made the lower Gulf Coast its home. In nearly a third of Florida's 67 counties, seniors now account for more than a third of the population. Silver-haired politicians have organized their peers into a force to be reckoned with in state politics and have won seniors a level of social services rarely found elsewhere. Elderly newcomers have plunged into Florida retirement with youthful enthusiasm, returning to school, taking up sports again (as in the Kids and Kubs Senior Baseball League), and enjoying Florida's balmy air and sunshine.

In the 1990s, Floridians have taken steps to protect their state's natural beauty and resources, including major initiatives to protect the Everglades and control the spread of tacky commercial districts. As they deal with challenges to Florida's continuing vitality—challenges both man-made and natural (such as 1992's Hurricane Andrew, which nearly annihilated South Dade County and left 250,000 homeless)—there is every reason for optimism. Florida's siren song beckons us to its shores throughout our lives. We come as children to the Magic Kingdom, return as young adults for spring break shennanigans and to view baseball spring training, as adults with our own children in tow, and finally as retirees.

2. THE REGIONS IN BRIEF

Northeast Florida   The northeast section of the state contains the oldest permanent settlement in America—St. Augustine, where Spanish colonists arrived and settled more than four centuries ago. Today, its history comes to life in a quaint historic district. St. Augustine is bordered to the north by Jacksonville, an up-and-coming sunbelt metropolis with miles of oceanfront beach and beautiful marine views along the St. Johns River. And to the south is Daytona Beach, home of the Daytona International Speedway and spring break mecca for the college crowd.

The Panhandle   Florida's narrow Panhandle features flat farmland, moss-draped forests of pine and live oak, and mile after mile of dazzling beaches formed by

IMPRESSIONS

The commodities of this land [Florida] are more than are yet knowen to any man. . . . it flourisheth with meadow, pasture ground, with woods of Cedar and Cypres, and other sorts, as better can not be in the world.
—VOYAGE OF SIR JOHN HAWKINS, 1565, QUOTED BY RICHARD HAKLUYT

. . . with the approach of the long and bitter winter, I could see why Florida is a golden word. . . . I found that more and more people lusted toward Florida and that thousands had moved there and more and more thousands wanted to and would . . . the very name Florida carried the message of warmth and ease and comfort. It was irresistible.
—JOHN STEINBECK, *TRAVELS WITH CHARLEY*, 1962

---

powdery, pure-white quartz washed down from the Appalachian Mountains by rivers flowing into peaceful backwater bays. With roots running deep into the antebellum South, Northwest Florida still has a distinctly Old South flavor made Sunbelt-sophisticated by Northerners who settled the area from the beach resorts of Pensacola to the state's tree-shrouded capital, Tallahassee.

Central Florida   Once a flat expanse of farmland, citrus groves, and scrub pine forests, Central Florida was transformed forever when Walt Disney World came to town in 1971. Today it's the state's theme park hub, and Orlando its fastest-growing city. Another brand of excitement is offered at the Kennedy Space Center, launch site for all manned U.S. space missions since 1968.

The West Coast   Halfway down the west coast of Florida lies Tampa Bay, lined with miles of sandy beaches. Beside the bay flourishes one of the fastest-growing metropolitan areas in the country, Tampa and St. Petersburg. Just south lies Bradenton, where you'll find the headquarters of the world's most famous orange juice company (Tropicana), and Sarasota, a shopping and performing arts mecca.

Southwest Florida   Some of America's wealthiest families have winter homes in the sophisticated riverfront towns of Fort Myers and Naples, and on Boca Grande, Sanibel, Captiva, Marco, and others of the 10,000-plus islands that make Southwest Florida unique. The white beaches bordering these narrow barrier islands are famous for the seashells that wash ashore in such great quantity that visitors often return home with a back ailment known as "the Sanibel stoop." A few miles away on its own man-made island, tiny Everglades City provides a back door to the alligators, birds, and mangrove swamps of the nation's second-largest national park.

Indian River Country   Just north of glittering Palm Beach, a sleepy atmosphere prevails in towns like Jupiter, Port St. Lucie, and Vero Beach. Nature lovers will enjoy the area's citrus groves and unspoiled beaches, still bypassed for the most part by developers.

The Southeast Coast   The palm-dotted sands of Florida's "Gold Coast" are lined with beachfront hotels and posh resorts. Just north of Miami, the coast extends through Fort Lauderdale, Boca Raton, and Palm Beach, which has been famous for many years as a playground for the rich and famous.

Miami and Miami Beach   Long a resort haven, Miami is a sophisticated, cosmopolitan city that boasts striking art deco architecture, gorgeous beaches, and glittering nightlife. It's also a major population center for Latin American immigrants, especially a thriving Cuban community. Southwest of the city lie the vast swamplands of Everglades National Park, teeming with unusual wildlife.

The Keys   From the southern tip of Florida, U.S. 1 travels through a hundred-mile string of islands with the Atlantic on one side and the Gulf of Mexico on the other. The chain extends down from Key Largo and John Pennecamp State Park to Key West, which lies only 90 miles from Cuba and is the southernmost point in the United States. Though many of the islands don't have spectacular beaches, the Keys offer other visitor attractions—excellent deep-sea fishing and snorkeling, blazing tropical sunsets, a wildlife refuge full of tiny deer, and Key West's laid-back, bohemian atmosphere.

3. FAMOUS FLORIDIANS

Marjory Stoneman Douglas   One of the state's most respected historians and conservationists.

Faye Dunaway   Winner of the 1976 Best Actress Oscar for *Network,* she also starred in *Bonnie and Clyde* and *Mommie Dearest.*

Henry Flagler   Railroad tycoon Flagler was largely responsible for developing Florida as a tourist destination by building a railroad that served the state's east coast and erecting luxurious resort hotels along it.

Zora Neale Hurston   Author of *Their Eyes Were Watching God* and *Jonah's Gourd Vine,* this Florida-born novelist was one of the major talents of the Harlem Renaissance in the 1920s.

Sidney Poitier   One of America's most distinguished actors, Poitier has appeared in such films as *Guess Who's Coming to Dinner?;* he was the winner of the 1963 Best Actor Oscar for his role in *Lilies of the Field.*

Marjorie Kinnan Rawlings   Her Pulitzer Prize–winning novel *The Yearling* (1939) captured the flavor of life in rural Florida.

Janet Reno   President Bill Clinton named this former Miami prosecutor to be the nation's first female attorney general in 1993.

John Ringling   Circus entrepreneur Ringling built a home overlooking Sarasota Bay, and the area has served as the winter headquarters of the Ringling Brothers and Barnum & Bailey Circus ever since.

Ben Vereen   A major Broadway star, Vereen won a 1973 Tony for his performance in *Pippin.*

4. SPORTS & RECREATION

With thousands of lakes, more than 100 rivers, and endless miles of coastline, Florida offers opportunities galore for fishing, sailing, canoeing, diving, waterskiing—just about any sort of water sport you can imagine. We'll detail the sports and recreation highlights of each city and town that's covered in the chapters that follow.

For brochures, calendars, schedules, and guides, contact the **Florida Sports Foundation,** 107 W. Gaines St., Tallahassee, FL 32399 (tel. 904/488-8347).

BASEBALL: SPRING TRAINING   In February and March, throngs of baseball fans head down to Florida to see their favorite teams getting ready for the upcoming season. Teams used to return year after year to the same Florida towns for spring training, but as "Grapefruit League" games have become more lucrative, competition for the honor of hosting a major-league team has become fierce and many clubs are in the process of choosing new venues.

If you'd like to plan a vacation around spring training, call the Florida Sports Foundation (listed above) or main office of **Major League Baseball,** 350 Park Ave., New York, NY 10022 (tel. 212/339-7800), to find out where your favorite team will be playing. And don't wait until you're in Florida to purchase tickets—almost all games sell out weeks in advance.

5. FOOD & DRINK

A BOUNTY OF SEAFOOD   Just a glance at a map will show you that Florida has hundreds of miles of coastline, so it should come as no surprise that seafood is a major attraction all across the state. Some waterfront restaurants even operate their own fishing boats, so you're guaranteed super-fresh offerings. You'll feast on snapper, swordfish, amberjack, triggerfish, pompano, grouper, clams, gulf shrimp, oysters, blue crab, and sweet deep-sea scallops.

Some of Florida's abundant seafood specialties will be new to your palate. The local **lobsters** are smaller and sweeter than the Maine variety, with most of their meat concentrated in the tail rather than in the claws. You should also try **conch,** a chewy shellfish that's often served in deep-fried fritters, in chowder, or in a spicy salad marinated in lime juice. And you're sure to fall in love with the taste of Florida's succulent **stone crabs.**

If you have the chance to eat in a **fish camp,** don't pass it up. These rustic, informal eateries are usually located right on the river or ocean and serve the very freshest of fish at unbelievably low prices.

CITRUS FRUITS & OTHER PRODUCE   Florida's farms and citrus groves produce billions of dollars' worth of oranges, grapefruit, and tangerines each year. Bags of grapefruit and fresh, sweet oranges are sold at roadside stands throughout the state. But that's not all. Tomatoes, coconuts, kumquats, and tangy lemons and limes grow here, along with more exotic fruits like mangoes, hearts of palm, and papaya. Florida chefs are adept at using local produce in creative sauces and garnishes. A favorite regional dish is **key lime pie,** made with the tiny yellowish limes that grow only in Florida. It's best when it's made with an old-fashioned graham cracker crust and served chilled.

AND OTHER CUISINES   Southern and Cajun culinary influences have found their way into Florida's kitchens, so you may find traditional favorites like catfish, hush puppies, frogs' legs, Créole-style blackened fish, gumbo, cheese grits, turnip greens, and southern fried chicken on many menus. As Florida's Asian population has increased, so has the number of restaurants across the state offering authentic Chinese, Thai, Japanese, Indian, and Vietnamese dishes. And Caribbean specialties have become popular too, from Bahamian conch fritters to fruity cocktails made with rum from the islands.

But Latin American and South American cuisines have had the most profound effect on Florida. Especially if you're visiting Miami, you should try one of the Cuban restaurants in Little Havana, which serve specialties like *pan cubano* (crusty white Cuban bread), *arroz con pollo* (succulent roast chicken served with yellow rice), roast suckling pig, plantains, and *café cubano,* rich (and very strong) black coffee. Find a place that serves *tapas,* Spanish-style appetizers served in small portions, and try several dishes at once.

6. RECOMMENDED BOOKS & FILMS

BOOKS

GENERAL

Allman, T. D. *Miami: City of the Future.* Atlantic Monthly Press, 1987.
Buchanan, Edna. *The Corpse Had a Familiar Face: Covering Miami, America's Hottest Beat.* Random House, 1987.
Capitman, Barbara Baer. *Deco Delights: The Beauty and Joy of Miami Beach Architecture.* Dutton, 1988.
Didion, Joan. *Miami.* Simon & Schuster, 1987.
Douglas, Marjory Stoneman. *The Everglades: River of Grass.* Pineapple Press, 1988.
Hatton, Hap. *Tropical Splendor: An Architectural History of Florida.* Knopf, 1987.
Pulitzer, Roxanne. *The Prize Pulitzer: The Scandal That Rocked Palm Beach.* Random House, 1988.

Rieff, David. *Going to Miami: Exiles, Tourists, and Refugees in the New America.* Little, Brown, 1987.

HISTORY

Muir, Helen. *Miami, USA.* Banyan Books, 1987.
Rothchild, John. *Up for Grabs: A Trip through Time and Space in the Sunshine State.* Viking, 1985.

FICTION

Hemingway, Ernest. *To Have and Have Not.* Macmillan, 1988.
Hiaasen, Carl. *The Tourist Season.* Putnam Publishing Group, 1988.
Hurston, Zora Neale. *Their Eyes Were Watching God.* University of Illinois Press, 1978.
Pratt, Theodore. *The Barefoot Mailman.* Mockingbird Books, 1980.
Rawlings, Marjorie Kinnan. *The Yearling.* Macmillan, 1985.
———. *Cross Creek.* Macmillan, 1987.
Willeford, Charles. *Miami Blues.* Ballantine, 1987.

FILMS

Dozens of films have been set in Florida. A few of the very best are the 1964 James Bond thriller *Goldfinger,* part of which was filmed in the spectacular Fontainebleau Hilton in Miami Beach; *Body Heat,* starring William Hurt and Kathleen Turner; Jonathan Demme's *Married to the Mob; Absence of Malice,* starring Paul Newman and Sally Field; and of course, the steamy classic *Key Largo,* with legendary screen stars Bogart and Bacall.

CHAPTER 2

PLANNING A TRIP TO FLORIDA

After you've chosen the Sunshine State as your destination, you'll find that doing a little homework before you go can save a lot of time and trouble later. This chapter pulls it all together for you: information sources, the best time of year to go, how to get there, and selecting an itinerary—all the advance-planning details that can help you enjoy a smooth, successful trip.

1. INFORMATION & MONEY

INFORMATION Contact the **Florida Department of Commerce, Division of Tourism,** 107 W. Gaines St., Suite 501D, Tallahassee, FL 32399-2000 (tel. 904/487-1462), whose helpful staff will gladly answer your questions. Be sure to ask for a *Florida Events Calendar* and their *Florida Vacation Guide,* a free guide to all the state's attractions that can help you choose which area of the state you want to visit.

For the lowdown on Walt Disney World, call or write **Walt Disney World Company,** P.O. Box 10000, Lake Buena Vista, FL 32830-1000 (tel. 407/824-4321).

Once you've chosen a specific destination within Florida, get in touch with the local visitor information office or chamber of commerce. We've listed each of the local offices in the chapters that follow.

MONEY Vacationers on a tight budget have always known that Florida offers some terrific travel bargains, especially in the off-season. (See "When to Go," later in this chapter, for details.)

A Note on Currency for British Travelers

British visitors will need to convert their pounds into U.S. dollars when visiting Florida. Here's how pounds break down into U.S. dollars (subject to market changes, of course).

THE U.S. DOLLAR & THE BRITISH POUND

U.S.$	£	U.S.$	£
.07	.05	8.94	6
.14	.10	10.43	7
.35	.25	11.92	8
.74	.50	13.41	9
1.05	.75	14.90	10
1.49	1	22.35	15
2.98	2	29.80	20
4.47	3	44.70	30
5.96	4	74.50	50
7.45	5	149.00	100

WHAT THINGS COST IN MIAMI	U.S. $
Taxi from the Miami airport to a downtown hotel	16.00
Local telephone call	.25
Double room at the Grand Bay Hotel (deluxe)	265.00
Double room at the Cavalier Hotel (moderate)	145.00
Double room at the Driftwood Resort Motel (budget)	70.00
Lunch for one at SoBe (moderate)	10.00
Lunch for one at the News Café (budget)	8.50
Dinner for one, without wine, at the Pavillon Grill (deluxe)	45.00
Dinner for one, without wine, at Thai Toni (moderate)	23.00
Dinner for one, without wine, at Versailles (budget)	12.00
Pint of beer	2.75
Coca-Cola in a restaurant	1.25
Cup of coffee	.85
Roll of ASA 100 film, 36 exposures	5.65
Admission to Miami Metrozoo	5.00
Movie ticket	7.00

Traveler's Checks   If you don't want to carry large sums of cash with you, traveler's checks are a good bet. They are accepted by most hotels, restaurants, and shops, and can be exchanged for cash at any bank. **American Express** (tel. toll free 800/221-7282) traveler's checks are widely accepted and can be purchased at many banks across the country. If you purchase them at an American Express office, there's a 1% commission fee (banks often charge more), but checks are free for members of AAA and cardholders who purchase checks by phone. **Citicorp** (tel. toll free 800/645-6556) and **Bank of America** (tel. 415/624-5400; collect calls are accepted) are other major issuers of traveler's checks. Record the number of each check you purchase, and ask these companies about refund hotlines; you'll be able to recover your money if your checks are lost or stolen.

2. WHEN TO GO — CLIMATE & EVENTS

You'll find that a Florida vacation offers terrific value for your money, especially if you time your visit so that it doesn't coincide with the peak tourist season.
For the southern half of the state, the high season is January to mid-April; each

winter countless visitors migrate south to escape northern winters. If you're willing to brave the humidity of a South Florida summer, you'll be rewarded with incredible bargains on accommodations and smaller crowds of tourists. In northern Florida, the reverse is true: Tourists flock here in the summer.

If you want to time your visit to Walt Disney World to avoid crowds, keep in mind that Orlando area attractions are packed during any holiday (especially Christmas) and when school is not in session during the summer. See Chapter 9 on Orlando for details.

CLIMATE Odds are, whenever you visit Florida, you're going to find sunny skies and warm temperatures.

Spring brings tropical showers and the first waves of humidity. **Summer** is hot and *very* humid, so if you're in an inland city you may not want to schedule anything too taxing when the sun is at its peak. Coastal areas, however, reap the benefits of ocean breezes.

Fall is a great time to visit—the really hottest days are behind you and the crowds have thinned out a bit. August through November is, however, tropical storm season—you may remember Hurricane Andrew, the August 1992 storm that caused billions of dollars' worth of damage to South Florida. But be assured that it's highly improbable you'll be in any danger from such a storm. The National Weather Service tracks hurricanes and gives local residents ample warning if there's any need to evacuate coastal areas.

Winter gets a bit nippy (sometimes downright cold) in northern Florida; although snow is pretty rare, a flake or two has been known to fall. But it's the peak season for the southern half of the state. When the rest of the country is bracing itself for icy winds, "snowbirds" are heading for Southwest Florida, Miami, Palm Beach, and the Keys to bask in the sun.

Average Temperatures [°F] in Selected Florida Cities

	Jan	Feb	Mar	Apr	May	Jun	July	Aug	Sept	Oct	Nov	Dec
Key West	69	72	74	77	80	82	85	85	84	80	74	72
Miami	69	70	71	74	78	81	82	84	81	78	73	70
Tampa	60	61	66	72	77	81	82	82	81	75	67	62
Orlando	60	63	66	71	78	82	82	82	81	75	67	61
Tallahassee	53	56	63	68	72	78	81	81	77	74	66	59

FLORIDA
CALENDAR OF EVENTS

JANUARY

☐ **Florida Citrus Bowl Football Classic,** Orlando. This annual college game takes place at the Florida Citrus Bowl Stadium. Call 407/849-2020 for information, 407/839-3900 for tickets. January 1.

☐ **Hall of Fame Bowl,** Tampa. Two of the nation's top college teams meet at Tampa Stadium in this highly rated annual football game. Call 813/874-2695 for details. January 1.

✪ *ORANGE BOWL Featuring two of the year's toughest college teams, this football game kicks off the month. Other activities include a marathon, a powerboat regatta, and the Three Kings Parade.*
    Where: *Orange Bowl, Miami.* ***When:*** *New Year's Day.* ***How:*** *Tickets*

are available starting March 1, through the Orange Bowl Committee, P.O. Box 350748, Miami, FL 33135 (tel. 305/371-4600).

☐ **Circus Festival,** Ringling Complex, Sarasota. A giant salute to the circus, with performers, arts and crafts, and music. Call 813/366-5258 for details. First week of January.

☐ **Art Deco Weekend,** South Beach, Miami. Held along the beach between 5th and 15th Streets, this festival celebrates the whimsical architecture that has made South Beach one of America's most unique neighborhoods with bands, food stands, and other activities. Call 305/672-2014 for details. A weekend in mid-January.

☐ **Taste of the Grove Food and Music Festival,** Peacock Park, Coconut Grove, Miami. An excellent chance for visitors to sample menu items from some of the city's top restaurants. The party is a fund-raiser. For details, call 305/444-7270. A weekend in mid-January.

☐ **Goodland Mullet Festival,** Goodland. Eat fresh mullet, dance the "buzzard lope," and particpate in the Men's Best Legs Contest at Stan Gober's Idle Hour Seafood Restaurant in Goodland, an old Florida fishing village near Marco Island. Call 813/394-3041 for details. Third weekend of January.

☐ **Manatee County Fair,** Manatee County Fairgrounds, Palmetto. A week-long celebration and sampling of the Bradenton area's produce—from citrus fruits and tomatoes to ornamental plants, cattle, and seafood. Call 813/722-1639 for details. Third weekend of January.

☐ **Key Biscayne Art Festival,** Cape Florida State Park. More than 200 artists come together in this high-quality adjudicated show—all for charity. Call 305/361-2531 for details. Late January.

✪ *SUPERBOWL The National Football League's two toughest teams go head to head in Miami for the championship. Contact the Superbowl Host Committee for information about related area activities.*

Where: Joe Robbie Stadium, Greater Miami North. When: January 29, 1995. How: Tickets are available through the Superbowl Host Committee, 200 S. Biscayne Blvd., Suite 2360, Miami, FL 33131 (tel. 305/373-4678).

FEBRUARY

☐ **Edison Pageant of Light,** Fort Myers. Arts and crafts shows, a five-kilometer race, pageants, and a spectacular finale, the Parade of Lights. Call 813/334-2550, or toll free 800/237-6444, for more information. First two weeks of February.

✪ *SPEEDWEEKS Sixteen days of events get underway with the Rolex 24 (a 24-hour endurance road race for sports cars), which draws international entries. Following that, top names in NASCAR stock-car racing compete in the Busch Clash, Arca 200, Gatorade Twin 125-Mile Qualifying Races, International Race of Champions (IROC), Florida 200, and Goody's 300, culminating in the Daytona 500 by STP, which is always held on the Sunday before the third Monday in February.*

Where: Speedway, Daytona Beach. When: First three weeks of February. How: Call 904/253-7223 for ticket information. For the Daytona 500 especially, tickets must be purchased far—even as much as a year—in advance; they go on sale on January 1 of the prior year.

✪ *FLORIDA STATE FAIR Just about anything that grows under the sun in Florida's 67 counties—from blue-ribbon livestock to fine foods and wines—is on display at this gathering, along with craft demonstrations, circus acts, carnival rides, horse shows, rodeos, alligator wrestling, and entertainment by top country-western stars.*

Where: Florida State Fairgrounds, Tampa. When: Second week of February. How: Contact the Florida State Fair Authority, P.O. Box 11766, Tampa, FL 33680 (tel. 813/621-7821).

✪ *GASPARILLA PIRATE INVASION AND PARADE* Ever since 1904, this has been Tampa's number-one annual event. In a spirit akin to Mardi Gras, the city's leading business executives don the pirate garb of José Gaspar—the legendary rogue of the high seas—and sail into the harbor on a triple-masted galleon flanked by a flotilla of 2,000 escort boats. This signals the start of a month-long program of parades, concerts, fiestas, races, and art festivals.
Where: Downtown Tampa, Bayshore Boulevard, and Harbour Island. *When:* Early February. *How:* Contact the Tampa/Hillsborough Convention & Visitors Association, 111 Madison St., Tampa, FL 33602–4706 (tel. 813/223-1111, or toll free 800/44-TAMPA).

☐ **Coconut Grove Art Festival.** The state's largest art festival, and the favorite event of many locals. Almost every medium is represented, including, unofficially, the culinary arts. For details, call 305/447-0401. Mid-February.

☐ **GTE Suncoast Classic,** Cheval Polo and Golf Club, Tampa. The top players on the Senior PGA tour tee off for this tournament. Call 813/971-1726 for details. Mid-February.

✪ *MIAMI FILM FESTIVAL* This festival has made an impact as an important screening room for Latin American cinema. Fashioned after the San Francisco model, this annual event is relatively small, well priced, and easily accessible to the general public.
Where: Miami. *When:* 10 days in mid-February. *How:* Contact the Film Society of Miami, 7600 Red Rd., Miami, FL 33157 (tel. 305/377-FILM).

☐ **Grand Prix of Miami.** An auto race that rivals the big ones at Daytona, this high-purse, high-profile event attracts the top Indy car drivers and large crowds. For information and tickets, contact Miami Motorsports, 7254 SW 48th St., Miami, FL 33155 (tel. 305/379-5660). Late February.

MARCH

✪ *FLORIDA STRAWBERRY FESTIVAL AND PARADE* If strawberry shortcake, milkshakes, sundaes, and cobblers tempt your sweet tooth, don't miss this one. Held annually since 1930, it also offers music by top country stars, rides, and amusements. Plant City is the "winter strawberry capital of the world."
Where: Florida Strawberry Festival Fairgrounds, Fla. 574, off Exit 10 of I-4 in Plant City, 25 miles east of Tampa. *When:* First week of March. *How:* Contact the Florida Strawberry Festival, P.O. Drawer 1869, Plant City, FL 34289-1869 (tel. 813/752-9194).

✪ *SANIBEL SHELL FAIR* A four-day celebration on Sanibel Island for seashell lovers and collectors, held since 1937. The fair features exhibits of seashells from around the world along with related activities and sale of unusual shell art.
Where: Sanibel Community Center, Sanibel Island. *When:* Begins the first Thursday in March. *How:* The fair is open free to the public; admission is charged to the Shell Show. Call 813/472-2155 for details.

☐ **Bike Week/Camel Motorcycle Week,** Daytona Beach. The rallying point for an international gathering of motorcycle enthusiasts. Major races (featuring road racers, motocrossers, and dirt trackers) at the Speedway include the Daytona 200 by Arai Motorcycle Classic, the Daytona Supercross by Honda, and the Camel Pro Grand National Kickoff. Call 904/253-7223 for details. 10 days in early March.

☐ **Central Florida Fair,** Central Florida Fairgrounds, Orlando. Rides, entertainers, livestock exhibits, a monkey show, and lots of food booths. Tickets cost $5 for adults, $2 for children 6 to 10, free for children under 6. Call 407/295-3247 for details. 11 days in early March.

- **Medieval Fair,** Ringling Museum, Sarasota. Arts and crafts, street music, jousting, and a live chess match. Call 813/355-5101 for details. Three days in early March.
- **Sidewalk Art Festival,** Park Avenue, Winter Park. This major arts festival draws artists and artisans from all over North America. Call 407/623-3234 or 407/644-8281 for details. Third weekend of March.

✪ *FESTIVAL OF THE STATES* *For more than 70 years this festival has been considered "the South's largest civic celebration," as St. Petersburg plays host to award-winning high school bands from around the country. Other events include a windsurfing competition, fishing tournament, regatta, air show, jazz fest, and antique-car rally.*
   Where: Downtown St. Petersburg. When: 17 days in late March and early April. How: Contact the Suncoasters of St. Petersburg, Inc., P.O. Box 1731, St. Petersburg, FL 33731 (tel. 813/898-3654).

✪ *SPRINGTIME TALLAHASSEE* *One of the South's largest celebrations, this festival features parades, arts and crafts, balloon rallies, food festivals, road races, and live music from bluegrass to blues.*
   Where: Tallahassee. When: Four weeks, beginning in late March. How: Call 904/224-1373 for details.

- **Arts & Crafts Spring Festival,** St. Augustine. A juried show in the downtown plaza. Call 904/829-8175 for details. Palm Sunday (March 27).
- **The Players Championship (TPC),** Tournament Players Club, Ponte Vedra Beach. This major golf event takes place at the toughest course on the PGA tour, and its 17th hole, located on an island, is the most photographed hole in golf. Average attendance is 150,000. Call 904/285-7888 for details. Late March.
- **Spring Speedway Spectacular,** Daytona Beach. This car show and swap meet features a wide variety of collector vehicles. In addition, displays include automotive toys and memorabilia, auto-themed art, and a crafts sale. Admission is charged. Call 904/255-7355 for details. Late March or early April.
- **Calle Ocho Festival,** Miami. One of the world's biggest block parties. More than a million people attend this salsa-filled blowout which is held along 23 blocks of Little Havana's SW 8th Street. For information, call 305/644-8888. Second Sunday in March.

APRIL

- **Jazz Festival,** Sarasota. A gathering of international jazz greats. Call 813/366-1552 for details. First week of April.
- **Fort Walton Beach Seafood Festival.** An annual seafood-eating frenzy. Call toll free 800/322-3319 for more information. Mid-April.
- **Fun 'n Sun Festival,** Clearwater. A tradition since 1953, this festival includes a band competition, parades, boat regatta, and sportsfest. Call 813/462-6531 for details. Last two weeks of April.

MAY

- **Artworks!,** St. Petersburg. This event includes live theater, art shows, antique auto shows, outdoor concerts, and the Fiesta de la Riba, a Spanish-themed festival commemorating Salvador Dali's birthday. Call 813/821-4069 for details. All of May.
- **Riverwalk Arts & Crafts Festival,** Jacksonville. A local biggie, with lots of food, crafts booths, and live entertainment. Admission is free. Call 904/396-4900 for details. Mother's Day (May 8).
- **Miami International Festival,** Exhibition Center, Coconut Grove. Food, folklore, and dance from around the world are featured. Call 305/279-1538 for more information.

JUNE

- ☐ **Billy Bowlegs Festival,** Fort Walton Beach. An annual week-long party named for William Augustus Bowles, self-proclaimed "King of Florida" and notorious buccaneer. Events include a pirate flotilla, treasure hunts, fishing competitions, and contests for kids. Call toll free 800/322-3319 for details. First week of June.
- ☐ **Fiesta of Five Flags,** Pensacola. This annual extravaganza combines a commemoration of the 1559 arrival of Spanish conquistador Tristan De Luna with parades, a Spanish fiesta, a children's treasure hunt, a billfish tournament, and much, much more. For more information, call 904/433-6512. First week of June.
- ☐ **Music Festival,** Sarasota. A world-class presentation of chamber and symphonic music. Call 813/953-4252 for details. First three weeks of June.

✪ *COCONUT GROVE GOOMBAY FESTIVAL A Bahamian bacchanalia with dancing in the streets, this bash is billed as the largest black-heritage festival in America. It celebrates Miami's Caribbean connection.*
*   **Where:** Coconut Grove, Miami. **When:** Early June. **How:** Call 305/372-9966 for festival details.*

✪ *CROSS & SWORD Florida's Official State Play tells the story of the founding of St. Augustine, using drama, dance, music, stage combat, and spectacular special effects. Admission is $10 for adults, $8 for seniors, $4 for students, and free for children under 5.*
*   **Where:** In the 1,500-seat outdoor amphitheater of Anastasia State Park, Fla. A1A South, St. Augustine. **When:** Performances from about mid-June through late August, Monday through Saturday at 8:30pm. **How:** Call 904/471-1965 for details.*

- ☐ **Spanish Night Watch Ceremony,** St. Augustine. Actors in period dress lead a torchlight procession through the Spanish Quarter and reenact the closing of the city gates, with music and pageantry. Call 904/824-9550 for details. Third Saturday in June.

JULY

- ☐ **Independence Day celebrations,** throughout the state. In honor of the nation's birthday, virtually every city, town, and theme park has something special going on. Celebrations include parades, barbecues, games, concerts, dancers, and of course—fireworks. July 4.
- ☐ **Suncoast Offshore Grand Prix,** Sarasota. This boat-racing event offers powerboats, parades, live theater, boat shows, exhibits, and fireworks. Call 813/955-9009 or 813/366-9255 for details. Week of July 4.
- ☐ **Pepsi 400,** the Speedway, Daytona Beach. This race marks the halfway point in the NASCAR Winston Cup Series for stock cars. Call 904/253-7223 for details. First Saturday in July.
- ☐ **Boca Grande Chamber Tarpon Tournament,** off the Lee coast, Boca Grande. This two-day fishing contest, the world's richest, has cash prizes totaling $175,000. Call the event hotline: 813/964-2995, or toll free 800/237-6444. First weekend in July.
- ☐ **Silver Spurs Rodeo,** Silver Spurs Arena, Kissimmee. A major event on the professional rodeo circuit. Call 407/847-5000 for information, 407/67-RODEO for tickets. A weekend in early July.

✪ *FLORIDA INTERNATIONAL FESTIVAL This highly acclaimed week-long musical event takes place every other year (in odd-numbered years). It features concerts by some of the top classical and pop musicians from all over the world, as well as preconcert lectures, jazz bands, ballet, and special concerts for children. The festival is also the "summer home" of the London Symphony Orchestra.*
*   **Where:** Daytona Beach (Peabody Auditorium, Ocean Center, and other*

venues). **When:** *Late July and/or early August.* **How:** *Call 904/257-7790 for details and ticket information.*

AUGUST

☐ **Miami Reggae Festival.** Jamaica's independence is celebrated with a dozen top bands playing for much of the city's sizeable Rastafarian community. Call 305/891-2944 for details. First Sunday in August.

SEPTEMBER

☐ **Riverside Arts Festival,** Riverside Park, Jacksonville. More than 100 artists—sculptors, painters, wood carvers, ceramists, and others—set up booths to sell their works. There are food vendors, too. Call 904/389-2449. Two days early in September.

☐ **Miami Boat Show,** Convention Center, Coconut Grove. Almost 250,000 boat enthusiasts come here every year. Call 305/579-3310 for details. Second or third week of September.

☐ **Festival Miami,** Coral Gables. This program of performing and visual arts, sponsored by the University of Miami, is centered in and around Coral Gables. For a schedule of events, contact the University of Miami School of Music, P.O. Box 248165, Coral Gables, FL 33146. Call 305/284-3941 for details. Three weeks in September.

☐ **King of the Beach Volleyball Tournament,** Daytona Beach. The action takes place in front of the Marriott Hotel. The top eight male players in the world compete, and a 3,000-seat stadium is erected on the beach. Admission is charged. Call 904/255-0981 for details. Late September or early October.

OCTOBER

☐ **Walt Disney World Village Boat Show.** Central Florida's largest in-the-water boat show features the best of new watercraft. Call 407/824-4321 for details. A three-day weekend in early October.

☐ **AMA/CCS Motorcycle Championship,** Speedway, Daytona Beach. Road-racing stars of tomorrow compete. Events include a program of AMA/CCS "Races of Champions" National Championship Sprints for a variety of road-racing classes, as well as the season-ending U.S. Endurance Championship event and the season finales for the Honda CBR 900RR Series and the Harley-Davidson Twin Sports Series. Call 904/253-7223 for ticket information. Three days in mid-October.

☐ **Jacksonville Jazz Festival,** Metropolitan Park, Jacksonville. This three-day nonstop-music event, featuring major artists and superstars, bills itself as the "world's greatest free jazz concert." Food and crafts booths, too. Call 904/353-7770 for details. Three days in Mid-October.

☐ **Jazz Festival,** Clearwater. This extravaganza features performances by top-name musicians. Call 817/461-0011 for details. Four days in mid-October.

✪ JOHN'S PASS SEAFOOD FESTIVAL *This rustic waterfront village west of St. Petersburg hosts one of Florida's most popular seafood festivals—with music, arts and crafts, and enormous quantities of fresh fish and seafood.*
    Where: *St. John's Pass Village and Boardwalk, Madeira Beach.* **When:** *Last weekend of October.* **How:** *Contact the Gulf Beaches Chamber of Commerce, 501 150th Ave., Madeira Beach, FL 33108 (tel. 813/392-7373).*

☐ **Halloween Horror Nights,** Universal Studios, Orlando. The studios and attractions are transformed into a gigantic "spooktacular" nighttime party, featuring a haunted sound stage, psychopath maze, special shows, and ghouls and goblins roaming the studio streets. Special admission is charged. Call 407/363-8000 for details. Weekends up to October 31.

☐ **Guavaween,** Ybor City. A Halloween parade, with costumes, music, food, and a giant street party. Call 813/248-3712 for information. Last Saturday in October.

☐ **Walt Disney World Oldsmobile Golf Classic.** Top PGA tour players compete for a total purse of $1 million at WDW golf courses. The event is preceded by the world's largest golf tournament, the Oldsmobile Scramble, on the same courses. Admission for the Scramble is free; daily ticket prices for the Golf Classic range from $8 to $15. Call 407/824-4321 for details.

NOVEMBER

☐ **Frank Brown International Songwriters' Festival,** Perdido Key. Composers gather at various beach venues on both sides of the Florida-Alabama line to perform their country-music hits. For details, call 904/492-4660. First week in November.

☐ **Florida Seafood Festival,** Battery Park, Apalachicola. Thousands gorge themselves on the reputedly aphrodisiac oysters and other briny morsels that make this little town famous. Call 904/653-8051 or 904/653-9419 for details. First weekend in November.

☐ **Fort Myers Beach Sand Sculpting Contest.** There are two divisions: the masters, and a local competition that is broken down into family, business, etc., categories. Over 50,000 people attend this event. Call 813/463-6451, or toll free 800/782-9283, for details. Four to six days in early November.

☐ **Coral Gables International Festival of Craft Arts.** Traditional and contemporary handcrafted arts are displayed along Alhambra Plaza and Ponce de Leon Boulevard. Call 305/445-9973 for details. Usually the second week of November.

☐ **Blue Angels Homecoming Air Show,** Pensacola Naval Air Station. Thrilling flight exhibitions by the world-famous Blue Angels. Call 904/452-2583 for details. Usually the second weekend in November.

☐ **Kahlúa Cup International Yacht Races,** Clearwater. This event draws international craft. Call 813/447-6000 for details. Second weekend in November.

☐ **Walt Disney World Festival of the Masters.** One of the largest art shows in the South takes place at the Village Marketplace. It features top artists, photographers, and craftspeople, all winners of juried shows throughout the country. No admission charge. Call 407/824-4321 for details. Second weekend in November.

☐ **Jacksonville Light Parade.** Boaters decorate their craft with colored lights and parade down the St. Johns River. This event also features fireworks, ice skating exhibitions, marching bands, and live entertainment. Call 904/396-4900. November 26.

☐ **Daytona Beach Fall Speedway Spectacular.** Featuring the Annual Turkey Rod Run, this is the Southeast's largest combined car show and swap meet, with thousands of street rods and classic vehicles on display and for sale. It takes place at the Speedway, but you'll see these fabulous cars all over town. Admission is charged. Call 904/255-7355 for details. Thanksgiving weekend.

☐ **Fall Arts & Crafts Festival,** St. Augustine. More than 140 artists display quality works for purchase. Call 904/829-8175 for details. Thanksgiving weekend.

☐ **Florida Classic Football Game,** Tampa Stadium, Tampa. One of the longest-running college football competitions. Call 813/874-2695 for information. Last weekend of November.

☐ **Miami Book Fair International.** One of the city's leading cultural attractions. Last year's show drew hundreds of thousands of visitors, including foreign and domestic publishers, and authors from around the world. Call 305/754-4931 for details.

DECEMBER

☐ **Edison/Ford Homes Holiday House,** Fort Myers. Thousands of lights and the sound of music hail the Christmas season at the adjacent riverside homes of Thomas Edison and Henry Ford, 2350 McGregor Blvd. (tel. 813/334-3614). First week in December.

☐ **Grand Illumination Ceremony,** St. Augustine. A torchlight procession from Government House through the Spanish Quarter featuring reenactments of British colonial customs, encampments, 18th-century music, crafts demonstrations, and cannon firings. Call 904/824-9550 for details. First Saturday in December.

☐ **Luminary Trail,** Sanibel and Captiva Islands. Miles of glowing paper-bag lanterns and twinkling white lights strung from trees and buildings turn these subtropical islands into winter wonderlands. For details, call 813/472-1080. First weekend in December.

☐ **Second Christmas Reenactment,** DeSoto State Archeological Site, Tallahassee. Commemorates Hernando DeSoto's first Christmas mass. Call 904/922-6007 for details. Early December.

☐ **Christmas Boat-A-Cade,** Madeira Beach. For over 25 years this has been a holiday highlight in the St. Petersburg area, with lighted and decorated boats parading at night in Boca Ciega Bay. Call 813/392-0665 for details.

☐ **Walt Disney World Christmas Festivities.** All Disney parks offer special embellishments and entertainments throughout the holiday season, with Nativity pageants, Christmas parties (tickets required), Candlelight Caroling Processions, and fireworks. Call 407/824-4321 for details.

☐ **World Karting Association Enduro World Championships,** the Speedway, Daytona Beach. The biggest karting event in the country. Call 904/253-7223 for details. Between Christmas and New Year's.

☐ **Gator Bowl,** Jacksonville. Call 904/630-3906 for information about the game, 904/353-3309 to charge tickets, or 904/353-1188 to find out about postgame festivities at Jacksonville Landing. Between Christmas and New Year's.

☐ **The King Mango Strut,** Coconut Grove. This Miami parade, from Commodore Plaza to Peacock Park, encourages everyone to wear wacky costumes and join the floats in a spoof on the King Orange Jamboree Parade (held the following night). Comedians and musical entertainment follow in the park. December 30.

○ *THE KING ORANGE JAMBOREE PARADE* *Ending the year, this special New Year's Eve event may be the world's largest nighttime parade, and is followed by a long night of festivities.*
Where: Along Biscayne Boulevard, Miami. When: December 31. How: For information and tickets (which cost $7.50 to $13), call 305/642-1515.

☐ **Citrus Bowl Parade/New Year's Citrus Eve,** Orlando. The impressive parade has lavish floats, some from Disney and Sea World (call 407/423-2476 for details). The official New Year's Eve celebration of the Citrus Bowl at Sea World includes headliner concerts, a laser and fireworks spectacular, and special shows throughout the park; admission is charged (call 904/255-7355 for details). December 31.

☐ **New Year's Eve celebrations,** throughout the state. Most cities, towns, and theme parks have special festivities to welcome in the New Year, including a spectacular fireworks display and other hoopla at Walt Disney World (call 407/824-4321 for details). December 31.

3. HEALTH & INSURANCE

HEALTH Florida doesn't present any unusual health hazards. The one thing you should protect yourself against is **sunburn.** Don't underestimate the strength of the sun's rays down here, even in the middle of winter. Limit the amount of time you spend in the sun, especially during the first couple of days of your trip. Bring along sunscreen with a high protection factor and apply it liberally. Wear a hat when you're outside, drink lots of water, and try to avoid exposure to the sun from 11am to 2pm, when the sun's rays can really fry fair skin.

Pack an adequate supply of any prescription drugs you need in your carry-on luggage, and bring copies of your prescriptions with you. If you have a serious condition or allergy, consider wearing a Medic Alert identification bracelet; contact the **Medic Alert Foundation** (tel. toll free 800/432-5378).

INSURANCE Before you leave home, call your credit- and charge-card companies to investigate whether they offer any sort of travel coverage that's already free to you as a cardholder. Many companies offer personal accident insurance or rental-car insurance at no extra charge, and they may also be able to help you get refunds if there's a problem with an airline ticket or hotel room that's paid for with your credit or charge card. Your current homeowner's policy may offer you some protection against off-premises theft as well.

If you still feel that you need to purchase extra travel insurance, contact **Travel Guard International** (tel. 715/345-0505, or toll free 800/826-1300), which offers policies that protect you against trip cancellation and include provisions for medical coverage and lost luggage as well. Prices start at $52 for one week of coverage. Other companies to consider include **Travelers Insurance Co.** (tel. 203/277-2318, or toll free 800/243-3174) and **Mutual of Omaha** (tel. toll free 800/228-9792), both of which offer similar protection.

4. WHAT TO PACK

It's not difficult to pack for a Florida vacation. Few places require jackets and ties; dress is casual in all but the poshest resorts and restaurants. (But bring at least one dressy outfit for a special night out.) Light cotton clothing is the order of the day, so pack lots of T-shirts and shorts. Unless you're visiting in the hottest months of summer, bring along a couple of sweaters or a jacket to keep you warm if the nights get nippy—or if the ever-present Florida air conditioning gets to you.

Useful additions to any traveler's suitcase include a travel alarm, sunscreen, a fold-up umbrella, mosquito repellent (especially if you're planning nature walks), and a small plastic container of Woolite. And don't forget your bathing suit and sunglasses!

5. TIPS FOR THE DISABLED, SENIORS, SINGLES, FAMILIES & STUDENTS

FOR THE DISABLED Write or call the **Florida Department of Commerce, Division of Tourism,** Visitor Inquiry Services, 107 W. Gaines St., Suite 501D, Tallahassee, FL 32399 (tel. 907/487-1462), for a free copy of their services directory for the physically challenged. It offers valuable information on accessibility at tourist facilities throughout the state.

Wilderness Inquiry (tel. 612/379-3858, or toll free 800/728-0719) operates adventure tours for people with disabilities.

Walt Disney World does everything possible to facilitate disabled guests. Its many services are detailed in the "Guidebook for Guests with Disabilities." To obtain a free copy, contact Guest Letters, P.O. Box 10,040, Lake Buena Vista, FL 32830-0040 (tel. 407/824-4321).

Some nationwide resources include the following: **Mobility International USA** (tel. 503/343-1284) offers accessibility information and has many interesting travel programs for the disabled. They also publish a quarterly newsletter called *Over the Rainbow* ($10 per year to subscribe). Help is also available from the **Travel Information Service** (tel. 215/456-9603). The **Society for the Advancement of Travel for the Handicapped** (tel. 212/447-7284) sends out information sheets on specific subjects for a small charge. And **Evergreen Travel Service** (tel. 206/776-1184, or toll free 800/435-2288) offers tours designed for the visually impaired, the elderly, and the mentally or physically disabled.

In addition, both **Amtrak** (tel. toll free 800/USA-RAIL) and **Greyhound** (call your local office) offer special fares and services for the disabled. Call at least a week in advance of your trip for details.

FOR SENIORS   Florida has always been a popular destination for seniors, and all kinds of establishments all over the state offer senior-citizen discounts. Don't be shy about asking if these are available; mention the fact that you're a senior citizen when you first make your travel reservations. Always carry some kind of identification, such as a driver's license, that shows your birthdate.

Contact the **American Association of Retired Persons**, 601 E St. NW, Washington, DC 22049 (tel. 202/434-2277), which offers group travel opportunities, plus discounts on airfares, car rentals, and accommodations.

Saga International Holidays, 222 Berkeley St., Boston, MA 02116 (tel. toll free 800/343-0273), offers group tours designed for travelers over 60.

Elderhostel, 75 Federal St., Boston, MA 02110 (tel. 617/426-8056), brings people together, sometimes on college campuses, for one- to three-week courses of study with plenty of time for relaxation and recreation. Prices include tuition, accommodations (usually in dormitories), and all meals. You must be at least 60 years old to register, although you can bring along an under-60 companion. To find out about their current offerings in Florida, write or call the main offices.

In addition, both **Amtrak** (tel. toll free 800/USA-RAIL) and **Greyhound** (call your local office) offer discounted senior fares.

FOR SINGLES   Singles are often at a disadvantage when it comes to travel, since most offers are based on double occupancy. **Travel Companion**, P.O. Box P-833, Amityville, NY 11701-0833 (tel. 516/454-0880), matches single travelers with compatible partners. For a fee, you'll be listed in the organization's records, and you'll receive a list of potential companions (you can request companions of the same sex or the opposite sex).

FOR FAMILIES   Florida is a great family destination—and the presence of major kids' attractions like Walt Disney World means that most Florida hotels and restaurants are willing and eager to cater to families traveling with children. In the pages that follow, you'll find lots of recommendations for hotels with kids' programs and babysitting services—and many that let children under 18 stay free in their parents' room. If you call ahead before dining out, you'll see that most restaurants have some facilities for children, such as booster chairs and low-priced kids' menus.

From the moment you begin planning your family's vacation to Florida, try to get your kids involved in and excited about the trip. (If you're headed to Walt Disney World, that shouldn't be too hard.) Set up ground rules before you leave about issues like bedtime and spending money.

Remember to pack a special toy or some other prized possession that will help your children feel at home even in strange surroundings. If you're traveling with an infant, pack enough baby food to last you through the trip and the first day or two until you've settled in and found the local supermarket.

Contact **Travel with Your Children**, 45 W. 18th St., New York, NY 10011 (tel. 212/206-0688), to subscribe to the *Family Travel Times*, a newsletter about traveling with children. It's packed with useful information, and readers can call in for advice during certain periods each week.

FOR STUDENTS   It's worth your while to bring along your valid high school or college identification. Presenting it can open the door to discounted admission to museums and other attractions.

6. ALTERNATIVE/ADVENTURE TRAVEL

OUTDOOR ADVENTURES   All Florida Adventure Tours, 8263B SW 107th Ave., Miami, FL 33173 (tel. toll free 800/338-6873), offers recreational and educational tours that emphasize local history and environmental education.

Florida Outback Safaris, 6446 SW 42nd St., Davie, FL 33314 (tel. 305/792-7393, or toll free 800/423-9944), offers camping, canoeing, tubing, snorkeling, marine biology programs, and excursions in Florida's Everglades and Keys.

Rock Rest Adventures, Rte. 2, Box 424, Pittsboro, NC 27312 (tel. 919/542-5502), offers five- to seven-day canoeing, kayaking, and camping adventures in Florida's Everglades and Keys.

Camping, snorkeling, and other adventurous trips can be arranged through **Wilderness Southeast,** 711 Sandtown Rd., Savannah, GA 31410 (tel. 912/897-5108).

North American Canoe Tours, Inc., P.O. Box 5038, Everglades City, FL 33929 (tel. 813/695-4666 November to April, 203/739-0791 May to October), offers one-week guided camping expeditions via motorized canoe through the Everglades.

CYCLING TRIPS **Vermont Bicycle Touring,** P.O. Box 711, Bristol, VT 05443 (tel. toll free 800/537-3850), offers deluxe Florida bike tours for cyclists at all fitness levels.

SWIMMING WITH DOLPHINS The **Dolphin Research Center,** Mile Marker 59, Overseas Highway, Grassy Key, FL 33050 (tel. 305/289-1121), an educational/research facility, offers guided walking tours of its premises four times a day Wednesday through Sunday; the cost is $7.50 for adults, $5 for children 4 to 12, free for children under 4.

The organization's **Dolphin Insight Program,** held three times a week, allows visitors to touch and interact with the dolphins but not get into the water with them. The cost is $75 per person, advance reservations are required, and it's recommended that children be at least 12 to participate.

Especially popular is **Dolphin Encounter,** a program that allows visitors to actually swim with dolphins. Advance reservations are required, and the center starts taking them the first day of the month for dates available the following month (for example, call March 1 to make April reservations). The cost is $90 per person; children must be at least 5 years old, and those under 12 must be accompanied by a paying adult.

7. GETTING THERE

BY PLANE

THE MAJOR AIRLINES Most major carriers offer service into the Sunshine State, so taking the time to make a few phone calls and do some comparison-shopping can pay off—call all the airlines until you find the best deal available.

Delta Air Lines (tel. toll free 800/221-1212), the official airline of Walt Disney World, offers more than 255 flights daily to 17 cities throughout the state, including Orlando (its Florida hub), Fort Lauderdale, Tampa/St. Petersburg, and Miami.

Other airlines serving the Sunshine State include: **American Airlines** (tel. toll free 800/433-7300), **Continental Airlines** (tel. toll free 800/525-0280), **TWA** (tel. toll free 800/221-2000), **Northwest** (tel. toll free 800/225-2525), **United** (tel. toll free 800/241-6522), and **USAir** (tel. toll free 800/428-4322).

AIRFARES Because Florida is such a popular destination, you'll have a wide choice of flights on many different carriers, and there's usually no shortage of promotional fares, especially in the off-season. If possible, avoid flying during holiday periods, when fares can more than double from their usual levels.

Your best bet for securing a low fare is to book your flight well before your departure—you can often find great deals if you buy your ticket 30 days in advance. Ask the airline for the *lowest* fare, and *keep asking questions*. Find out if you can get a better deal by flying in midweek or staying over a Saturday night. Remember, too, that many of the best deals are nonrefundable, so you may have to stick with the travel dates you've chosen.

BY TRAIN

Amtrak offers train service to Florida, with two daily trains that leave from New York, heading down the East Coast to Miami and Tampa—the **Silver Meteor** and the **Silver Star.** Travel time from New York is about 26 hours, but you can catch these trains as they make intermediate stops in Philadelphia, Washington, and Savannah. Depending on availability, round-trip fare from New York to Miami for midweek travel ranges from $160 to $230 and up. In addition, the **Palmetto** offers daily service from New York to Jacksonville.

If you want to travel to Florida by train while still bringing your own car, consider taking Amtrak's **Auto Train,** which runs daily from Lorton, Virginia, to Sanford, Florida (just northeast of Orlando). You'll travel in comfort while your car is secured in an enclosed car carrier. At press time, the round-trip fares were $175 for adults, $88 for children 15 and under, and $290 for a car.

In April 1993, Amtrak inaugurated regularly scheduled transcontinental rail service on the **Sunset Limited,** which runs three times weekly. The train leaves Los Angeles and crosses Arizona, New Mexico, Texas, Louisiana, Mississippi, and Alabama before it reaches its final destination in Florida 68 hours later. There are 52 stops along the way, including Orlando, Fort Lauderdale, and Miami. The train features reclining seats, a sightseeing car with large windows, and a full-service dining car. Round-trip coach fares begin at $259; sleeping accommodations are available for an extra charge.

For detailed information on schedules and fares (including Amtrak's "All Aboard America" fares), call Amtrak, (tel. toll free 800/USA-RAIL).

BY BUS

If you have the time for a leisurely trip, **Greyhound** offers low fares to a number of destinations in Florida. Service is available from almost anywhere in the country, and fares vary according to the point of origin. Discounted fares may be available if you can purchase your ticket in advance or if you travel in midweek. Consult your local directory for the office nearest you.

BY CAR

Countless visitors drive to Florida each year, and the state is easily reached by Interstate highway.

I-95 goes straight down the U.S. East Coast, from Maine down to Miami; it enters Florida at the Georgia border. **I-75** begins in northern Michigan and heads down through Ohio, Kentucky, Tennessee, and Georgia, before entering Florida; it then leads down to Tampa, Fort Myers, and Naples on the southwestern coast of Florida, then turns east to Fort Lauderdale. **I-10** traverses the southern part of the country, connecting southern California with Arizona, New Mexico, Texas, Louisiana, Mississippi, and Alabama before it enters Florida near Pensacola. It then cuts across the northern part of the state, heading toward Jacksonville. If you enter the state on a major highway, you'll come across a state Welcome Center.

Before taking a major trip, have a mechanic check out your car to be sure it's in good shape. If you're a member of the **American Automobile Association (AAA),** call them and ask about travel insurance, towing services, and free trip-routing plans that are available to you with membership.

PACKAGE TOURS

BY PLANE   Delta Air Lines' (tel. toll free 800/872-7786) offers numerous "Dream Vacations" packages—usually including round-trip airfare, accommodations, and a rental car with unlimited mileage—to major Florida destinations. For instance, dozens of packages—from budget to luxury—are available for stays in Walt

FROMMER'S SMART TRAVELER: AIRFARES

1. Call *all* the airlines that serve your destination—and check the Sunday *New York Times* travel section—to find the best fare.
2. Try to make your reservation 30 days in advance to take advantage of the lowest fares.
3. Keep checking fares as your departure date nears; airlines would rather fill a seat than have it fly empty, so they may cut fares dramatically in the days just before a flight leaves.
4. Investigate the cost of charter flights.
5. Avoid high-season travel, especially holidays. You can often get lower fares if you're willing to take midweek flights.
6. Always ask for the lowest fare, not just a discount fare.
7. Ask your airline about package deals that include accommodations and rental cars as well as airfare. Many of the major carriers have such deals, and most of them are excellent values. In Florida, Delta Dream Vacations are especially notable.

Disney World. At this writing, the rate for four nights midweek at the WDW All-Star resorts (see Chapter 9 for details)—including round-trip airfare from New York City, a rental car with unlimited mileage, complimentary transport to all WDW parks, unlimited admission to all Disney parks, a free Disney character breakfast, and all the benefits accruing to Disney resort guests—is just $629 per person. There are reduced rates for children under 12.

Other good sources for Florida packages include: **Continental Airlines Grand Destinations** (tel. toll free 800/634-5555), **American Airlines Flyaway Vacations** (tel. toll free 800/433-7300), **TWA Getaway Vacations** (tel. toll free 800/GET-AWAY), **United Airlines** (tel. toll free 800/328-6877), **American Express** (tel. toll free 800/241-1700), and your **travel agent.**

In Orlando, the **Walt Disney World Central Reservations Office** (tel. 407/W-DISNEY) has numerous packages.

BY SHIP   **Premier Cruise Lines** (tel. toll free 800/473-3262), known as the "Big Red Boat," offers three- and four-night luxury ocean cruises to The Bahamas in conjunction with three- or four-day Orlando theme-park vacations. Cruises depart from and return to Port Canaveral, 45 minutes from Walt Disney World. You can add the island segment before or after your stay in Orlando. Participating hotels include Disney resorts. Ships are equipped with swimming pools, Jacuzzis, health clubs, jogging tracks, movie theaters, beauty salons, casinos, and nightclubs. Looney-Tunes characters (Bugs Bunny, among others) are your on-board hosts. The package price includes all meals on board ship, a rental car with unlimited mileage for seven days, round-trip airfare to/from Orlando, and admission to varied attractions. Rates depend on stateroom and hotel category and the season you're traveling.

See Chapters 5 and 7 for cruises from Miami and Palm Beach, respectively, to The Bahamas.

8. GETTING AROUND

BY PLANE   Most major Florida cities are connected by intrastate airline routes, and fares for these short hops tend to be reasonable. Try the toll-free numbers listed in "Getting There," above, to book flights within Florida.

BY TRAIN   You'll find that train travel from destination to destination isn't terribly feasible in Florida, and it's not a great deal less expensive than flying.

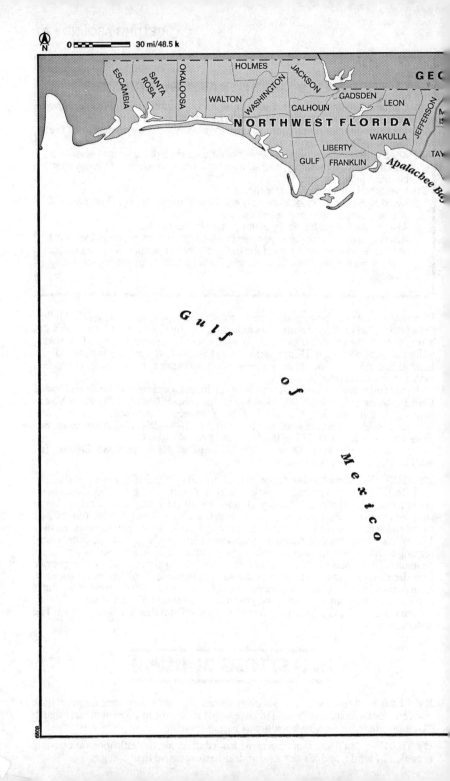

0 ▭▭▭ 30 mi/48.5 k

ESCAMBIA
SANTA ROSA
OKALOOSA
HOLMES
JACKSON
WALTON
WASHINGTON
GADSDEN
LEON
CALHOUN
GEO
NORTHWEST FLORIDA
WAKULLA
JEFFERSON
M
IS
LIBERTY
GULF
FRANKLIN
TAY
Apalachee Ba

Gulf

of

Mexico

FLORIDA COUNTIES AND REGIONS

IA

HAMILTON
COLUMBIA
BAKER
NASSAU
DUVAL
SUWANNEE
UNION
BRAD-FORD
CLAY
ST. JOHNS
FAYETTE
GILCHRIST
NORTH FLORIDA
ALACHUA
PUTNAM
FLAGLER
DIXIE
LEVY
MARION
VOLUSIA
CITRUS
SUMTER
LAKE
SEMINOLE
HERNANDO
CENTRAL FLORIDA
ORANGE
PASCO
BREVARD
PINELLAS
HILLSBOROUGH
POLK
OSCEOLA
Tampa Bay
INDIAN RIVER
MANTEE
HARDEE
OKEECHOBEE
ST. LUCIE
TAMPA BAY AREA
HIGHLANDS
SARASOTA
DE SOTO
MARTIN
GLADES
Lake Okeechobee
CHARLOTTE
PALM BEACH
LEE
HENDRY
SOUTH FLORIDA
SOUTHWEST FLORIDA
COLLIER
BROWARD
DADE
MONROE

Atlantic

Ocean

Florida Bay

FLORIDA KEYS

BY BUS Taking the bus, however, is fairly easy, as **Greyhound** offers extensive service, even to the smaller cities and towns. Fares are reasonable, and bus travel is more comfortable than you might expect. Ask for a regional timetable at any local office.

BY RENTAL CAR Most visitors opt for the freedom and flexibility of driving. If you're flying into Florida and want to rent a car, you'll have to sort out the maze of rental offers available.

Many packages are available that include airfare, accommodations, and a rental car with unlimited mileage. If you compare these prices with the cost of booking an airline ticket and renting a car yourself, you may find that these offers are a good deal.

If you opt to rent a car on your own, call several rental companies to compare prices, and if you're a member of any organization (the AARP or AAA, for example), check to see if you're entitled to discounts. Every major rental company is represented in Florida, including **Alamo** (tel. toll free 800/327-9633), **Avis** (tel. toll free 800/331-1212), **Budget** (tel. toll free 800/527-0700), **Hertz** (tel. toll free 800/654-3131), **National** (tel. toll free 800/227-7368), and **Thrifty** (tel. toll free 800/367-2277).

SUGGESTED ITINERARIES

IF YOU HAVE 10 DAYS IN SOUTHERN FLORIDA

Day 1: Tour Miami's art deco district. Then head downtown to stroll through Bayside Marketplace, a beautiful shorefront development full of retail shops and eateries.

Day 2: Visit the Miami Seaquarium and spend the rest of the day on the beach in Key Biscayne. Take in the sizzling Coconut Grove nightlife after dark.

Day 3: Head for Miami Metrozoo and Coral Castle, then treat yourself to an authentic Cuban dinner in Little Havana.

Day 4: Start out early in the morning and drive south of Miami to Everglades National Park. Tour the park and return to your Miami hotel for the night.

Day 5: Leave Miami and start heading south through the Keys. Pass through Key Largo, and visit John Pennekamp Coral Reef State Park, where you can go diving or take a glass-bottom-boat ride to view brilliantly colored tropical fish. Check into a hotel on Islamorada, 72 miles south of Miami.

Day 6: Enjoy a day of deep-sea fishing.

Day 7: Continue south to Key West and check into a hotel. Take the Conch Tour Train to get your bearings.

Day 8: Tour the Hemingway Home and Museum by day, and hit a few of the island's famous watering holes by night.

Day 9: Abandon yourself to the slow pace of Key West and relax.

Day 10: Drive back to Miami for your flight home.

IF YOU HAVE 10 DAYS IN CENTRAL FLORIDA

Day 1: Spend the day in the granddaddy of all Orlando attractions, the Magic Kingdom.

Day 2: Tour Epcot, then dance your night away at Pleasure Island.

Day 3: Head for Universal Studios or Disney-MGM Studios and learn how movie magic is created.

Day 4: Take a day trip 40 miles east to tour the John F. Kennedy Space Center. Return to your Orlando hotel.

Day 5: Spend the day at Sea World.

Day 6: Leave Orlando, driving southwest. Stop and tour Cypress Gardens, near Winter Haven, before continuing on to your hotel in Tampa.

Day 7: Give yourself a break from all this structured sightseeing and hit the beach.

Day 8: Tour Busch Gardens, a 300-acre theme park designed to resemble turn-of-the-century Africa.

Day 9: Stroll around downtown Tampa, and take the People Mover to Harbour Island for shopping and waterfront dining.

Day 10: Take in the Salvador Dalí Museum in nearby St. Petersburg, and spend part of the day exploring Tampa's Latin Quarter, Ybor City.

IF YOU HAVE 8 DAYS IN NORTHEAST FLORIDA

You might combine some of this itinerary with the Orlando/Central Florida attractions detailed above, heading northeast on I-4 to Daytona Beach instead of proceeding to Tampa on Day 6.

Day 1: Hit the "World's Most Famous Beach" and bask in the sun.

Day 2: Catch a race or car show at the Daytona International Speedway (many events require advance tickets, so call ahead as far in advance as possible; see Chapter 10 for details). If no race is on, tour the facility.

Day 3: Drive to DeLand for an eco-tour, a two-hour nature cruise along the Saint Johns River in an open-air pontoon; pack a picnic lunch and make a day of it.

Days 4–6: Continue north to St. Augustine, where you can relax at a plush resort or stay at a charming bed-and-breakfast. Spend leisurely days touring the quaint historic district and browsing in boutiques. Drink some water from the Fountain of Youth. There's beach here, too.

Day 7: Head north to Jacksonville. Spend the morning at Jacksonville's delightful zoo. Have lunch at the Sand Dollar, where you can watch a passing parade of boats and shore birds on the river. After lunch, check out Jacksonville Landing, browse in the shops, stroll the Riverwalk, and have dinner at a Landing restaurant.

Day 8: Tour Kingsley Plantation in the morning, Fort Caroline National Memorial and the adjacent Theodore Roosevelt Area (a stunning nature preserve) in the afternoon (bring a picnic lunch). This is best done on a Saturday or Sunday when ranger-guided tours are offered.

9. WHERE TO STAY

For a free hotel/motel directory, contact the **Florida Hotel/Motel Association,** 200 W. College Ave., Tallahassee, FL 32301 (tel. 904/224-2888).

IN WALT DISNEY WORLD Accommodations within Disney World range from the deluxe Grand Floridian Resort to the Fort Wilderness Campground. To find out about any of the Disney properties, contact the **Walt Disney World Central Reservations Office,** P.O. Box 10100, Lake Buena Vista, FL 32830-0100 (tel. 407/W-DISNEY).

CAMPING You can enjoy the great outdoors, keep accommodations costs down, and still stay near most of Florida's top attractions if you choose to stay at a KOA campground. RV sites are available, or you can pitch a tent; the campgrounds have restrooms, showers, food markets, and other facilities. For more information, contact **KOA Florida Camping,** P.O. Box 30558, Billings, MT 59114 (tel. toll free 800/848-1094).

In addition, many of Florida's state parks and recreation areas have tent and RV campsites. To order a guide to them all, contact the **Florida Department of Natural Resources,** Division of Recreation and Parks, MS #535, 3900 Commonwealth Blvd., Tallahassee, FL 32399-3000 (tel. 904/488-9872). Also ask for a separate list of entrance and camping fees.

HOSTELS **Hostelling International/American Youth Hostels** (tel. 202/783-6161) offers low-cost accommodations throughout the state at rates of about $15 per person per night for nonmembers. Rates for members ($25 annually for adults, $10 for those under 18, $15 for those over 54) are even lower and include discounts on other travel services. There are HI/AYH properties in St. Augustine's historic district, Miami's art deco district, and downtown Orlando overlooking Lake Eola (about a 35-minute drive from Walt Disney World). All Florida hostels have family rooms, which can be reserved in advance. Call for additional locations and information.

FAST *FACTS*
FLORIDA

Area Code Florida is so large that it needs four area codes: For southeastern Florida (including Fort Lauderdale, Miami, and the Florida Keys) it's 305, for east-central Florida (including the Orlando area) it's 407, for most of the west coast (including Tampa/St. Petersburg, Sarasota, and Fort Myers) it's 813, and for northern Florida (including Pensacola and Tallahassee in the west to Jacksonville, St. Augustine, and Daytona Beach in the east) it's 904.

Banks Banks are usually open Monday through Friday from 9am to 3 or 4pm, though many have Automatic Teller Machines (ATMs) that offer 24-hour banking. Each ATM network has a toll-free number you can call to locate machines in a given city. The toll-free number for Cirrus, one of the most popular networks, is 800/424-7787.

Business Hours Most offices throughout the state are open Monday through Friday from 9am to 5pm. Shopping malls are generally open until 8 or 9pm Monday through Saturday, and until 5pm on Sunday.

Camera/Film You'll certainly want to take pictures on your trip to Florida, so don't forget to pack your camera and film (be sure to take film that will work well for outdoor shots). If you've forgotten film or you need a few extra rolls, head for the nearest supermarket or drugstore, where you can find good prices on name brands. You'll spend a fortune if you buy film at shops or kiosks near major tourist attractions.

Car Rentals See "Getting Around," earlier in this chapter.

Climate See "When to Go," earlier in this chapter.

Drugstores Eckerd Drugs and Walgreens are two major chains; you'll see branches all over the state.

Emergencies Call **911** anywhere in the state to summon the police, the fire department, or an ambulance.

Liquor Laws You must be 21 to purchase or consume alcohol in Florida. This law is strictly enforced, so if you look young, carry some identification with you. Minors can usually enter bars where food is served.

Newspapers/Magazines Most cities of any size have a local daily paper, but the well-respected *Miami Herald* is generally available all over the state, with regional editions available in many areas.

Safety Whenever you're traveling in an unfamiliar city, state, or country, stay alert. Be aware of your immediate surroundings. Wear a moneybelt and keep a close eye on your possessions. Be particularly careful with cameras, purses, and wallets, all favorite targets of thieves and pickpockets. Always lock your car doors and the trunk when your vehicle is unattended, and don't leave any valuables in sight. See also the "Safety" section in the "For Foreign Visitors" chapter for specific information on car and driving safety.

Taxes The Florida state sales tax is 6%. In addition, most municipalities levy a special tax on hotel and restaurant bills; see individual city chapters for details.

Telephone Beware of the astronomical cost of making phone calls—even local calls—from your hotel room. It's much safer to make collect calls, to use a credit card, or to go in search of a pay phone.

Time Most of Florida observes eastern standard time, but most of the section west of the Apalachicola River is on central standard time, one hour behind the rest of the state.

Tipping Waiters and bartenders usually expect a 15% tip, and you might leave even more if you got exceptional service. Porters should be tipped about $1 per bag, taxi drivers get 15%, and parking valets should get $1. Leave $1 or $2 in your hotel room for each day you've stayed for the housekeeping staff when you check out.

Tourist Information See "Information and Money," earlier in this chapter, for the tourist office serving the entire state; for local offices, which will have more detailed information on your particular destination, see the individual city chapters that follow.

CHAPTER 3

FOR FOREIGN VISITORS

1. PREPARING FOR YOUR TRIP

2. GETTING TO & AROUND THE U.S.

- **FAST FACTS: FOR THE FOREIGN TRAVELER**

- **THE AMERICAN SYSTEM OF MEASUREMENTS**

Although American fads and fashions have spread across Europe and other parts of the world so much that the United States may seem like familiar territory before your arrival, there are still many peculiarities and uniquely American situations that any foreign visitor will encounter.

In this chapter we will point out to you many of the perhaps unexpected differences from what you are used to at home, and explain some of the more confusing aspects of daily life in the United States.

1. PREPARING FOR YOUR TRIP

ENTRY REQUIREMENTS

DOCUMENT REQUIREMENTS Canadian citizens may enter the United States without passports or visas; they need only proof of residence.

British subjects and citizens of New Zealand, Japan, and most western European countries traveling on valid passports may not need a visa for holiday or business travel to the United States for less than 90 days, providing that they hold a round-trip or return ticket and that they enter the United States on an airline or cruise line participating in the visa waiver program. (Note that citizens of these visa-exempt countries who first enter the United States may then visit Mexico, Canada, Bermuda, and/or the Caribbean islands and then reenter the United States by any mode of transportation, without needing a visa. Further information is available from any U.S. embassy or consulate.)

Citizens of countries other than those stipulated above, including citizens of Australia, must have two documents: (1) a valid passport with an expiration date at least six months later than the scheduled end of their visit to the United States; and (2) a tourist visa, available without charge from the nearest U.S. consulate.

To obtain a visa, the traveler must submit a completed application form (either in person or by mail) with a 1½-inch square photo and must demonstrate binding ties to a residence abroad. Usually you can obtain a visa at once or within 24 hours, but it may take longer during the summer rush from June to August. If you cannot go in person, contact the nearest U.S. embassy or consulate for directions on applying by mail. Your travel agent or airline office may also be able to provide you with visa applications and instructions. The U.S. embassy or consulate that issues your visa will determine whether you will be issued a multiple- or single-entry visa and any restrictions regarding the length of your stay.

MEDICAL REQUIREMENTS No inoculations are needed to enter the United States unless you are coming from, or have stopped over in, areas known to be suffering from epidemics, particularly cholera or yellow fever.

If you have a disease requiring treatment with medications containing narcotics or drugs requiring a syringe, carry a valid signed prescription from your physician to allay any suspicions that you are smuggling drugs.

CUSTOMS REQUIREMENTS   Every adult visitor may bring in free of duty: one liter of wine or hard liquor; 200 cigarettes or 100 cigars (but no cigars from Cuba) or three pounds of smoking tobacco; $100 worth of gifts. These exemptions are offered to travelers who spend at least 72 hours in the United States and who have not claimed them within the preceding six months. It is altogether forbidden to bring into the country foodstuffs (particularly cheese, fruit, cooked meats, and canned goods) and plants (vegetables, seeds, tropical plants, and so on). Foreign tourists may bring in or take out up to $10,000 in U.S. or foreign currency with no formalities; larger sums must be declared to Customs on entering or leaving.

INSURANCE

There is no national health system in the United States. Because the cost of medical care is extremely high, we strongly advise every traveler to secure health coverage before setting out.

You may want to take out a comprehensive travel policy that covers (for a relatively low premium) sickness or injury costs (medical, surgical, and hospital); loss or theft of your baggage; trip-cancellation costs; guarantee of bail in case you are arrested; costs of accident, repatriation, or death. Such packages (for example, "Europe Assistance" in Europe) are sold by automobile clubs at attractive rates, as well as by insurance companies and travel agencies.

MONEY

CURRENCY & EXCHANGE   The U.S. monetary system has a decimal base: one American **dollar ($1)** = 100 **cents** (100¢).

Dollar bills commonly come in $1 ("a buck"), $5, $10, $20, $50, and $100 denominations (the last two are not welcome when paying for small purchases and are not accepted in taxis or at subway ticket booths). There are also $2 bills (seldom encountered).

There are six denominations of coins: 1¢ (one cent or "penny"), 5¢ (five cents or "a nickel"), 10¢ (ten cents or "a dime"), 25¢ (twenty-five cents or "a quarter"), 50¢ (fifty cents or "a half dollar"), and the rare $1 piece.

Note: The "foreign-exchange bureaus" so common in Europe are rare even at airports in the United States, and nonexistent outside major cities. Try to avoid having to change foreign money, or traveler's checks denominated other than in U.S. dollars, at a small-town bank, or even a branch in a big city; in fact, leave any currency other than U.S. dollars at home—it may prove more nuisance to you than it's worth.

TRAVELER'S CHECKS   Traveler's checks denominated in U.S. dollars are readily accepted at most hotels, motels, restaurants, and large stores. But the best place to change traveler's checks is at a bank. Do not bring traveler's checks denominated in other currencies.

CREDIT & CHARGE CARDS   The method of payment most widely used is credit and charge cards: VISA (Barclaycard in Britain), MasterCard (EuroCard in Europe, Access in Britain, Chargex in Canada), American Express, Diners Club, Discover, and Carte Blanche. You can save yourself trouble by using "plastic money" rather than cash or traveler's checks in most hotels, motels, restaurants, and retail stores (a growing number of food and liquor stores now accept credit/charge cards). You must have a credit or charge card to rent a car. It can also be used as proof of identity (often carrying more weight than a passport) or as a "cash card," enabling you to draw money from banks that accept it.

SAFETY

GENERAL   While tourist areas are generally safe, crime is on the increase everywhere, and U.S. urban areas tend to be less safe than those in Europe or Japan. Visitors should always stay alert. This is particularly true of large U.S. cities. It is wise to ask the city's or area's tourist office if you're in doubt about which neighborhoods are safe. Avoid deserted areas, especially at night. Don't go into any city park at night unless there's an event that attracts crowds—for example, New York City's concerts in the parks. Generally speaking, you can feel safe in areas where there are many people and many open establishments.

Avoid carrying valuables with you on the street, and don't display expensive cameras or electronic equipment. Hold on to your pocketbook, and place your billfold in an inside pocket. In theaters, restaurants, and other public places, keep your possessions in sight.

Remember also that hotels are open to the public, and in a large hotel, security may not be able to screen everyone entering. Always lock your room door—don't assume that once inside your hotel you are automatically safe and no longer need be aware of your surroundings.

DRIVING Safety while driving is particularly important. Question your rental agency about personal safety, or ask for a brochure of traveler safety tips when you pick up your car. Obtain written directions, or a map with the route marked in red, from the agency showing how to get to your destination. And, if possible, arrive and depart during daylight hours.

Recently more and more crime has involved cars and drivers. If you drive off a highway into a doubtful neighborhood, leave the area as quickly as possible. If you have an accident, even on the highway, stay in your car with the doors locked until you assess the situation or until the police arrive. If you are bumped from behind on the street or are involved in a minor accident with no injuries and the situation appears to be suspicious, motion to the other driver to follow you. *Never* get out of your car in such situations. You can also keep a pre-made sign in your car which reads: PLEASE FOLLOW THIS VEHICLE TO REPORT THE ACCIDENT. Show the sign to the other driver and go directly to the nearest police precinct, well-lighted service station, or all-night store.

If you see someone on the road who indicates a need for help, do *not* stop. Take note of the location, drive on to a well-lighted area, and telephone the police by dialing 911.

Park in well-lighted, well-traveled areas if possible. Always keep your car doors locked, whether attended or unattended. Look around you before you get out of your car, and never leave any packages or valuables in sight. If someone attempts to rob you or steal your car, do *not* try to resist the thief/carjacker—report the incident to the police department immediately.

Also, make sure that you have enough gasoline in your tank to reach your intended destination, so that you're not forced to look for a service station in an unfamiliar and possibly unsafe neighborhood—especially at night.

You may wish to contact the local tourist information bureau in your destination before you arrive, as they may be able to provide you with a safety brochure. (See "Information and Money," in Chapter 2, and the individual city units for specific tourist organization names and addresses.)

2. GETTING TO & AROUND THE U.S.

GETTING TO THE U.S. Travelers from overseas can take advantage of the **APEX (Advance Purchase Excursion) fares** offered by all the major international carriers. Aside from these, attractive values are offered by Icelandair on flights from Luxembourg to New York and by Virgin Atlantic Airways from London to New York/Newark.

British travelers should check out **British Airways** (tel. 081/897-4000 in the U.K.), which offers direct flights from London to Miami and Orlando, as does **Virgin Atlantic Airways** (tel. 02/937-47747 in the U.K.). Canadian readers might book flights on **Air Canada** (tel. toll free 800/776-3000), which offers service from Toronto and Montréal to Miami and Tampa.

The visitor arriving by air, no matter what the port of entry, should cultivate patience and resignation before setting foot on U.S. soil. Getting through Immigration control may take as long as two hours on some days, especially summer weekends. Add the time it takes to clear Customs and you'll see that you should make very generous allowance for delay in planning connections between international and domestic flights—an average of two to three hours at least.

In contrast, travelers arriving by car or by rail from Canada will find border-crossing formalities streamlined to the vanishing point. And air travelers from Canada, Bermuda, and some places in the Caribbean can sometimes go through Customs and Immigration at the point of departure, which is much quicker and less painful.

For further information about travel to Florida, see "Getting There," in Chapter 2.

GETTING AROUND THE U.S. By Air Some large American airlines (for example, American Airlines, Delta, Northwest, TWA, and United) offer travelers on their transatlantic or transpacific flights special discount tickets under the name **Visit USA,** allowing travel between any U.S. destinations at minimum rates. They are not on sale in the United States, and must, therefore, be purchased before you leave your foreign point of departure. This system is the best, easiest, and fastest way to see the United States at low cost. You should obtain information well in advance from your travel agent or the office of the airline concerned, since the conditions attached to these discount tickets can be changed without advance notice.

By Train Long-distance trains in the United States are operated by Amtrak, the national rail passenger corporation. International visitors can buy a **USA Railpass,** good for 15 or 30 days of unlimited travel on Amtrak. The pass is available through many foreign travel agents. Prices in 1994 for a 15-day pass were $208 off-peak, $308 peak; a 30-day pass cost $309 off-peak, $389 peak. (With a foreign passport, you can also buy passes at some Amtrak offices in the United States, including locations in Boston, Chicago, Los Angeles, Miami, New York, San Francisco, and Washington, D.C.) Reservations are generally required and should be made for each part of your trip as early as possible.

However, visitors should be aware of the limitations of long-distance rail travel in the United States. With a few notable exceptions (for instance, the Northeast Corridor line between Boston and Washington, D.C.), service is rarely up to European standards: Delays are common, routes are limited and often infrequently served, and fares are rarely significantly lower than discount airfares. Thus cross-country train travel should be approached with caution.

By Bus The cheapest way to travel the United States is by bus. Greyhound, the sole nationwide bus line, offers an **Ameripass** for unlimited travel for 7 days (for $250), 15 days (for $350), and 30 days (for $450). Bus travel in the United States can be both slow and uncomfortable, so this option is not for everyone.

By Car Travel by car gives visitors the freedom to make—and alter—their itineraries to suit their own needs and interests. And it offers the possibility of visiting some of the off-the-beaten path locations, places that cannot be reached easily by public transportation. For information on renting cars in the United States, see "Getting Around," in Chapter 2, and "Automobile Organizations" and "Automobile Rentals" in "Fast Facts: For the Foreign Traveler," below.

 FOR THE FOREIGN TRAVELER

Automobile Organizations Auto clubs will supply maps, suggested routes, guidebooks, accident and bail-bond insurance, and emergency road service. The major auto club in the United States, with 955 offices nationwide, is the **American Automobile Association (AAA).** Members of some foreign auto clubs have reciprocal arrangements with the AAA and enjoy its services at no charge. If you belong to an auto club in your home country, inquire about AAA reciprocity before you leave. You may be able to join the AAA even if you're not a member of a reciprocal club; to inquire, call the AAA (tel. toll free 800/336-4357). The AAA can provide you with an **International Driving Permit,** validating your foreign license.

(Note that the AAA is actually an organization of regional auto clubs; in Florida, look under "AAA Automobile Club South" in the White Pages of the telephone directory.)

In addition, some automobile-rental agencies now provide many of these same services. Inquire about their availability when you rent your car.

Automobile Rentals   To rent a car you need a major credit or charge card. A valid driver's license is required, and you usually need to be at least 25. Some companies do rent to younger people but add a daily surcharge. Be sure to return your car with the same amount of gas you started out with; rental companies charge excessive prices for gasoline. All the major car-rental companies are represented in Florida (see "Getting Around," in Chapter 2).

Business Hours   Banks are open weekdays from 9am to 3 or 4pm, although there's 24-hour access to the automatic tellers (ATMs) at most banks and other outlets. Generally, **offices** are open weekdays from 9am to 5pm. **Stores** are open six days a week, with many open on Sunday, too; department stores usually stay open until 9pm at least one day a week.

Climate   See "When to Go," in Chapter 2.

Currency   See "Money" in "Preparing for Your Trip," above.

Currency Exchange   You'll find currency-exchange services in major airports with international service. Elsewhere, they may be quite difficult to come by. In New York, a very reliable choice is **Thomas Cook Currency Services, Inc.**, which has been in business since 1841 and offers a wide range of services. It sells commission-free foreign and U.S. traveler's checks, drafts, and wire transfers; it also does check collections (including Eurochecks). The rates are competitive and the service excellent. Thomas Cook maintains several offices in New York City, including a major one at 630 Fifth Ave. (tel. 212/757-6915); at the JFK airport International Arrivals Terminal (tel. 718/656-8444); and at La Guardia Airport in the Delta terminal (tel. 718/533-0784).

In Florida, there are **currency-exchange desks** in the Orlando and Tampa airports, and an office of BankAmerica International in Concourse E of the Miami International Airport, which is open 24 hours a day.

Drinking Laws   See "Liquor Laws" in "Fast Facts: Florida," in Chapter 2.

Electricity   The United States uses 110–120 volts A.C., 60 cycles, compared to 220–240 volts A.C., 50 cycles, as in most of Europe. In addition to a 100-volt transformer, small appliances of non-American manufacture, such as hairdryers and shavers, will require a plug adapter, with two flat, parallel pins.

Embassies and Consulates   All embassies are located in the national capital, Washington, D.C.; some consulates are located in major U.S. cities, and most nations have a mission to the United Nations in New York City. There is no consular representation in Florida for Australia, New Zealand, or the Republic of Ireland, but there are British and Canadian consulates in Miami (see below).

The embassy of **Australia** is at 1601 Massachusetts Ave. NW, Washington, DC 20036 (tel. 202/797-3000). The nearest Australian consulates are in the Quaker Tower, 321 N. Clark St., Suite 2930, Chicago, IL 60610 (tel. 312/645-9440); and in the International Bldg., 636 Fifth Ave., New York, NY 10111 (tel. 212/245-4000). Other Australian consulates are in Honolulu, Houston, Los Angeles, and San Francisco.

The embassy of **Canada** is at 501 Pennsylvania Ave. NW, Washington, DC 20001 (tel. 202/682-1740). There's a Canadian consulate in Florida at 200 S. Biscayne Blvd., Suite 1600, Miami, FL 33131 (tel. 305/579-1600). Other Canadian consulates are in Atlanta, Buffalo (N.Y.), Chicago, Cleveland, Dallas, Detroit, Los Angeles, Minneapolis, New York, San Francisco, and Seattle.

The embassy of the **Republic of Ireland** is at 2234 Massachusetts Ave. NW, Washington, DC 20008 (tel. 202/462-3939). The nearest Irish consulates are: Chase Bldg., 535 Boylston St., Boston, MA 02116 (tel. 617/267-9330); 400 N. Michigan Ave., Chicago, IL 60611 (tel. 312/337-1868); and 515 Madison Ave., New York, NY 10022 (tel. 212/319-2555). There's another Irish consulate in San Francisco.

The embassy of **New Zealand** is at 37 Observatory Circle NW, Washington, DC 20008 (tel. 202/328-4800). The only New Zealand consulate in the U.S. is in Los Angeles.

The embassy of the **United Kingdom** is at 3100 Massachusetts Ave. NW, Washington, DC 20008 (tel. 202/462-1340). In Florida, there's a British consulate at 1001 S. Bayshore Dr., Miami, FL 33131 (tel. 305/374-1522). Other British consulates are in Atlanta, Chicago, Houston, Los Angeles, and New York.

Emergencies   Call **911** to report a fire, call the police, or get an ambulance. This is a toll-free call (no coins are required at a public telephone).

If you encounter traveler's problems, check the local telephone directory to find an office of the **Traveler's Aid Society,** a nationwide, nonprofit, social-service organization geared to helping travelers in difficult straits. Their services might include reuniting families separated while traveling, providing food and/or shelter to people stranded without cash, or even emotional counseling. If you're in trouble, seek them out.

Gasoline (Petrol)   One U.S. gallon equals 3.8 liters or .85 Imperial gallons. There are usually several grades (and price levels) of gasoline available at most gas stations, and their names change from company to company. The unleaded ones with the highest octane rating are the most expensive (most rental cars take the least expensive "regular" unleaded gas); leaded gas is the least expensive, but only older cars can use this anymore, so check if you're not sure. Note that the price is often lower if you pay in cash instead of by credit or charge card. Also, many gas stations now offer lower-priced self-service gas pumps—in fact, some gas stations, particularly at night, are all self-service.

Holidays   On the following legal national holidays, banks, government offices, post offices, and many stores, restaurants, and museums are closed: January 1 (New Year's Day), the third Monday in January (Martin Luther King Day), the third Monday in February (Presidents Day, Washington's Birthday), the last Monday in May (Memorial Day), July 4 (Independence Day), the first Monday in September (Labor Day), the second Monday in October (Columbus Day), November 11 (Veterans' Day/Armistice Day), the last Thursday in November (Thanksgiving Day), and December 25 (Christmas). Also, the Tuesday following the first Monday in November is Election Day, and is a legal holiday in presidential-election years (next in 1996).

Languages   Major hotels may have multilingual employees. Unless your language is very obscure, they can usually supply a translator on request. Especially in southern Florida, many people are fluent in Spanish.

Legal Aid   The foreign tourist, unless positively identified as a member of the Mafia or of a drug ring, will probably never become involved with the American legal system. If you are pulled up for a minor infraction (for example, of the highway code, such as speeding), never attempt to pay the fine directly to a police officer; you may wind up arrested on the much more serious charge of attempted bribery. Pay fines by mail, or directly into the hands of the clerk of the court. If accused of a more serious offense, it's wise to say and do nothing before consulting a lawyer. Under U.S. law, an arrested person is allowed one telephone call to a party of his or her choice. Call your embassy or consulate.

Mail   If you want your mail to follow you on your vacation and you aren't sure of your address, your mail can be sent to you, in your name, **c/o General Delivery** at the main post office of the city or region where you expect to be. The addressee must pick it up in person and must produce proof of identity (driver's license, credit card, passport, etc.).

Generally to be found at intersections, mailboxes are blue with a red-and-white stripe and carry the inscription U.S. MAIL. If your mail is addressed to a U.S. destination, don't forget to add the five-figure postal code, or ZIP (Zone Improvement Plan) Code, after the two-letter abbreviation of the state to which the mail is addressed (CA for California, FL for Florida, NY for New York, and so on).

Domestic **postage rates** are 19¢ for a postcard and 29¢ for a letter. Check with any local post office for current international postage rates to your home country.

Newspapers/Magazines   National newspapers include the *New York Times, USA Today,* and the *Wall Street Journal.* National news weeklies include *Newsweek, Time,* and *U.S. News & World Report.* All over Florida, you'll be able to purchase the *Miami Herald,* one of the most highly respected dailies in the country.

Radio and Television   Audiovisual media, with four coast-to-coast networks—ABC, CBS, NBC, and Fox—joined in recent years by the Public

Broadcasting System (PBS) and the Cable News Network (CNN), play a major part in American life. In big cities, televiewers have a choice of about a dozen channels (including the UHF channels), most of them transmitting 24 hours a day, without counting the pay-TV channels showing recent movies or sports events. All options are usually indicated on your hotel TV set. You'll also find a wide choice of local radio stations, each broadcasting particular kinds of talk shows and/or music—classical, country, jazz, pop, gospel—punctuated by news broadcasts and frequent commercials.

Safety   See "Safety" in "Preparing for Your Trip," above.

Taxes   In the United States there is no VAT (Value-Added Tax) or other indirect tax at a national level. Every state, and each city in it, has the right to levy its own local tax on all purchases, including hotel and restaurant checks, airline tickets, and so on. In Florida, the statewide sales tax is 6%.

Telephone, Telegraph, Telex, and Fax   The telephone system in the United States is run by private corporations, so rates, especially for long-distance service and operator-assisted calls, can vary widely—even on calls made from public telephones. Local calls in the United States usually cost 25¢ (they're 25¢ throughout Florida).

Generally, hotel surcharges on long-distance and local calls are astronomical. You're usually better off using a **public pay telephone,** which you'll find clearly marked in most public buildings and private establishments as well as on the street. Outside metropolitan areas, public telephones are more difficult to find. Stores and gas stations are your best bet.

Most **long-distance and international calls** can be dialed directly from any phone. For calls to Canada and other parts of the United States, dial 1 followed by the area code and the seven-digit number. For international calls, dial 011 followed by the country code, city code, and the telephone number of the person you wish to call.

Note that all calls to area code 800 are toll free. However, calls to numbers in area codes 700 and 900 (chat lines, bulletin boards, "dating" services, etc.) can be very expensive—usually a charge of 95¢ to $3 or more per minute, and they sometimes have minimum charges that can run as high as $15 or more.

For **reversed-charge or collect calls,** and for **person-to-person calls,** dial 0 (zero, *not* the letter "O") followed by the area code and number you want; an operator will then come on the line, and you should specify that you are calling collect, or person-to-person, or both. If your operator-assisted call is international, ask for the overseas operator.

For local **directory assistance** ("information"), dial 411; for **long-distance information,** dial 1, then the appropriate area code and 555-1212.

Like the telephone system, **telegraph** and **telex** services are provided by private corporations like ITT, MCI, and above all, Western Union, the most important. You can bring your telegram in to the nearest Western Union office (there are hundreds across the country), or dictate it over the phone (a toll-free call, 800/325-6000). You can also telegraph money, or have it telegraphed to you, very quickly over the Western Union system. (Note, however, that this service can be very expensive. The service charge can run as high as 15% to 25% of the amount sent.)

Most hotels have **fax** machines available for guest use (be sure to ask about the charge to use it), and many hotel rooms are even wired for guests' fax machines. You'll probably also see signs for public faxes in the windows of local shops.

Telephone Directory   There are two kinds of telephone directories available to you. The general directory is the so-called **White Pages,** in which private and business subscribers are listed in alphabetical order. The inside front cover lists the emergency number for police, fire, and ambulance, and other vital numbers (like the Coast Guard, poison-control center, crime-victims hotline, and so on). The first few pages are devoted to community-service numbers, including a guide to long-distance and international calling, complete with country codes and area codes.

The second directory, printed on yellow paper (hence its name, *Yellow Pages*), lists all local services, businesses, and industries by type of activity, with an index at the back. The listings cover not only such obvious items as automobile repairs by make of car, or drugstores (pharmacies), often by geographical location, but also restaurants by type of cuisine and geographical location, bookstores by special subject and/or language, places of worship by religious denomination, and other information that the tourist might otherwise not readily find. The *Yellow Pages* also include city plans or detailed area maps, often showing postal ZIP Codes and public transportation routes.

Time The United States is divided into four **time zones** (six, if Alaska and Hawaii are included). From east to west, these are: eastern standard time (EST), central standard time (CST), mountain standard time (MST), Pacific standard time (PST), Alaska standard time (AST), and Hawaii standard time (HST). Always keep changing time zones in mind if you're traveling (or even telephoning) long distances in the United States. For example, noon in New York City (EST) is 11am in Chicago (CST), 10am in Denver (MST), 9am in Los Angeles (PST), 8am in Anchorage (AST), and 7am in Honolulu (HST).

Most of Florida observes eastern standard time, though the western part of the Panhandle region is on central standard time (its clocks are set an hour earlier). **Daylight saving time** is in effect from the last Sunday in April through the last Saturday in October (actually, the change is made at 2am on Sunday) except in Arizona, Hawaii, part of Indiana, and Puerto Rico. Daylight saving time moves the clock one hour ahead of standard time.

Tipping This is part of the American way of life, on the principle that you must expect to pay for any service you get (many service personnel receive little direct salary and must depend on tips for their income). Here are some rules of thumb:

In **hotels,** tip bellhops $1 per piece and tip the chamber staff $1 per day. Tip the doorman or concierge only if he or she has provided you with some specific service (for example, calling a cab for you or obtaining difficult-to-get theater tickets).

In **restaurants, bars, and nightclubs,** tip the service staff 15% of the check, tip bartenders 10% to 15%, tip checkroom attendants $1 per garment, and tip valet-parking attendants $1 per vehicle. Tip the doorman only if he has provided you with some specific service (such as calling a cab for you). Tipping is not expected in cafeterias and fast-food restaurants.

Tip **cab drivers** 15% of the fare.

As for **other service personnel,** tip redcaps at airports or railroad stations $1 per piece and tip hairdressers and barbers 15% to 20%.

Tipping ushers in cinemas, movies, and theaters and gas-station attendants is not expected.

Toilets Foreign visitors often complain that public toilets are hard to find in most U.S. cities. True, there are none on the streets, but the visitor can usually find one in a bar, restaurant, hotel, museum, department store, or service station—and it will probably be clean (although the last-mentioned sometimes leaves much to be desired). Note, however, a growing practice in some restaurants and bars of displaying a notice that "toilets are for the use of patrons only." You can ignore this sign, or better yet, avoid arguments by paying for a cup of coffee or soft drink, which will qualify you as a patron. The cleanliness of toilets at railroad stations and bus depots may be more open to question, and some public places are equipped with pay toilets, which require you to insert one or more coins into a slot on the door before it will open.

THE AMERICAN SYSTEM OF MEASUREMENTS
LENGTH

1 inch (in.)	=	2.54cm				
1 foot (ft.)	=	12 in.	=	30.48cm	=	.305m
1 yard	=	3 ft.	=	.915m		
1 mile (mi.)	=	5,280 ft.	=	1.609km		

To convert miles to kilometers, multiply the number of miles by **1.61** (for example, 50 mi. × 1.61 = 80.5km). Note that this conversion can be used to convert speeds from miles per hour (m.p.h.) to kilometers per hour (km/h).

To convert kilometers to miles, multiply the number of kilometers by **.62** (for example, 25km × .62 = 15.5mi.). Note that this same conversion can be used to convert speeds from kilometers per hour to miles per hour.

CAPACITY

1 fluid ounce (fl. oz.)	=	.03 liter	
1 pint	=	16 fl. oz.	= .47 liter
1 quart	=	2 pints	= .94 liter
1 gallon (gal.)	=	4 quarts	= 3.79 liter
	=	.83 Imperial gal.	

To convert U.S. gallons to liters, multiply the number of gallons by **3.79** (example, 12 gal. × 3.79 = 45.58 liters.)

To convert U.S. gallons to Imperial gallons, multiply the number of U.S. gallons by **.83** (example, 12 U.S. gal. × .83 = 9.95 Imperial gal.).

To convert liters to U.S. gallons, multiply the number of liters by **.26** (example, 50 liters × .26 = 13 U.S. gal.).

To convert Imperial gallons to U.S. gallons, multiply the number of Imperial gallons by **1.2** (example, 8 Imperial gal. × 1.2 = 9.6 U.S. gal.).

WEIGHT

1 ounce (oz.)	=	28.35 grams		
1 pound (lb.)	=	16 oz.	= 453.6 grams	= .45 kilograms
1 ton	=	2,000 lb.	= 907 kilograms	= .91 metric ton

To convert pounds to kilograms, multiply the number of pounds by **.45** (example, 90 lb. × .45 = 40.5kg).

To convert kilograms to pounds, multiply the number of kilos by **2.2** (example, 75kg × 2.2 = 165 lb.).

AREA

1 acre	=	.41 hectare	
1 square mile (sq. mi.)	=	640 acres	= 2.59 hectares
	=	2.6km	

To convert acres to hectares, multiply the number of acres by **.41** (example, 40 acres × .41 = 16.4ha).

To convert square miles to square kilometers, multiply the number of square miles by **2.6** (example, 80 sq. mi. × 2.6 = 208km²).

To convert hectares to acres, multiply the number of hectares by **2.47** (example, 20ha × 2.47 = 49.4 acres).

To convert square kilometers to square miles, multiply the number of square kilometers by **.39** (example, 150km² × .39 = 58.5sq. mi.).

TEMPERATURE

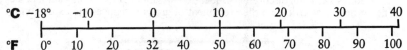

°C	−18°	−10	0	10	20	30	40
°F	0° 10 20	32 40	50	60 70	80	90	100

To convert degrees Fahrenheit to degrees Celsius, subtract 32 from °F, multiply by 5, then divide by 9 (example, 85°F − 32 × 5 ÷ 9 = 29.4°C).

To convert degrees Celsius to degrees Fahrenheit, multiply °C by 9, divide by 5, and add 32 (example, 20°C × 9 ÷ 5 + 32 = 68°F).

SETTLING INTO MIAMI

Florida's second-largest city, with almost two million residents, and famous for its white sand beaches, glittering waters, and sun-filled days, Miami attracts more than eight million visitors annually. The unique influence of its complex mix of cultures creates exciting opportunities to explore.

The unofficial capital of the Gold Coast, the city is less than 100 years old. Until the end of the 19th century, much of the Florida peninsula had never even been surveyed, and Miami itself was nothing more than a small trading post and the ruins of a U.S. Army camp, once known as Fort Dallas. The arrival in 1891 of an adventurous widow from Cleveland, Julia Tuttle, changed all that. Sensing the potential of the area, she set out to create a full-blown town. Realization of her dream depended on access to the area, and at first the railroad magnates whom she approached were less than enthusiastic. However, in 1896, when Henry Flagler's first train steamed into town, Tuttle became the only woman in American history to have started a major city.

It wasn't long before Miami's irresistible combination of surf, sun, and sand prompted America's wealthy to build elaborate winter retreats overlooking Biscayne Bay. Miami became chic, and following World War I, middle-class interest in the region prompted spectacular growth; the population grew from 30,000 to 100,000 in just five years. The building boom of the Roaring Twenties is directly responsible for the city's distinctive neighborhoods of today.

During the last decade the city has experienced startling changes in demographics as well as a new spurt of economic growth. The influx of refugees, predominantly from Cuba and Haiti, has swelled the city's Caribbean population and influenced all aspects of living, from art and architecture to food, music, and fashion.

Miami is a city still discovering its identity—a vibrant, brash young adult of a city. The air here is electric with the excitement of growth, change, and expansion.

1. ORIENTATION

ARRIVING

A hundred years ago Miami was a hard place to reach. But no longer: Today airlines fight perpetual price wars to woo tourists to the Sunshine State. In fact, fares are so

WHAT'S SPECIAL ABOUT MIAMI

Beaches
☐ Over a dozen miles of white sandy beaches, edged with coconut palms on one side and a clear, turquoise-blue ocean on the other.

Water Sports
☐ Parasailing, jet skiing, sailing, boating, windsurfing.

Food
☐ America's freshest citrus and seafood.
☐ Miami Regional—the area's unique cuisine.

Nightlife
☐ Music—everything from rock to reggae, and irresistible Latin rhythms.

Festivals
☐ Party from Calle Ocho to Goombay.

Architecture
☐ Miami Beach's art deco district—the largest collection of buildings on the National Register of Historic Places.
☐ The cityscape of downtown Miami, one of the prettiest in the world.

---

competitive that, unless you are visiting from an adjacent state, flying to Miami will almost always be your most economical option. But take a look at your alternatives, too. An overland journey to Florida's Gold Coast is both a more scenic and a more flexible way to travel. Greyhound offers several types of bus passes, and Amtrak offers a host of rail services.

BY AIR   Originally carved out of scrubland in 1928 by Pan American Airlines, **Miami International Airport (MIA)** has emerged as the 9th-busiest airport in the United States, and the 11th busiest in the world. It's also one of the most streamlined, making it a wonderful place to land. Since the airport is easy to negotiate, and located only six miles west of downtown, it's likely that domestic passengers can get from the plane to their hotel room in about an hour. International arrivals must pass through Customs and Immigration, a process that can double your time in the airport.

The route down to the baggage-claim area is clearly marked. You can change money or use your Honor or Plus System ATM card at Barnett Bank of South Florida, located near the exit.

Like most good international airports, MIA has its fair share of boutiques, shops, and eateries. Unless you're starving, or forgot to get a gift for the person picking you up, bypass these overpriced establishments. The airport is literally surrounded by restaurants and shops; if you can wait to get to them, you'll save a lot of money.

Note that if you're exiting Miami on an international flight, the excellent duty-free selection in the departure lounge shouldn't be missed.

If you're renting a car at the airport (see "Getting Around," below), you'll have to take one of the free shuttles to the rental site. Buses and vans, clearly marked with rental-car logos, circle the airport regularly, and stop at the wave of a hand. Signs at the airport's exit clearly point the way to various parts of the city.

Taxis line up in front of a dispatcher's desk outside the airport's arrivals terminals. Cabs are metered and will cost about $14 to Coral Gables, $16 to downtown, and $18 to South Miami Beach. Tip 10% to 15%.

Group limousines (multipassenger vans) also circle the arrivals area looking for fares. Destinations are posted on the front of each van, and a flat rate is charged for door-to-door service to the area marked. SuperShuttle (tel. 871-2000) is one of the largest airport operators, charging between $10 and $17 per person for a ride within Dade County. Their vans operate 24 hours a day and accept American Express, MasterCard, and VISA.

Private limousine arrangements can be made in advance through your local travel agent. A one-way meet-and-greet service should cost about $50.

Public transportation is not a recommended way to get to your hotel, or anywhere, for that matter. Buses heading downtown leave the airport only once per hour (from the arrivals level), and connections are spotty at best.

BY TRAIN If you're traveling to Miami by train (see "Getting There," in Chapter 2), you'll pull into Amtrak's Miami terminal at 8303 NW 37th Ave. (tel. 835-1205). Unfortunately, none of the major car-rental companies has an office at the train station; you'll have to go to the airport (see "Getting Around," below). Hertz (tel. toll free 800/654-3131) will reimburse your cab fare from the train station to the airport provided you rent one of their cars.

Taxis meeting each Amtrak arrival are plentiful. The fare to downtown is about $14; the ride takes less than 20 minutes.

BY CAR No matter where you start your journey, chances are you'll reach Miami by way of **I-95.** This north-south Interstate is the city's lifeline and an integral part of the region. The highway connects all of Miami's different neighborhoods, the airport, and the beach; and it connects all of South Florida to the rest of America. Every part of Miami is easily reached from I-95, and well-lit road signs clearly point the way. Take time out to study I-95's placement on the map. You'll use it as a reference point time and again. For a detailed description of the city's main arteries and streets, see "City Layout," below.

BY BUS Greyhound buses pull into a number of stations around the city including: 99 NE 4th St. (downtown); 16250 Biscayne Blvd., North Miami Beach; and 7101 Harding Ave., Miami Beach. Consult your local directory for the office nearest you.

INFORMATION

In addition to the data and sources listed below, foreign visitors should see Chapter 3 for entry requirements and other pertinent information.

The **Greater Miami Convention and Visitors Bureau,** 701 Brickell Ave., Miami, FL 33131 (tel. 305/539-3063, or toll free 800/283-2707), is the best source of any kind of specialized information about the city. Even if you don't have a specific question, be sure to phone ahead for their free magazine, *Destination Miami,* which includes several good, clear maps. The office is open Monday through Friday from 9am to 5pm.

For information on traveling in the state as a whole, contact the **Florida Division of Tourism (FDT),** 126 W. Van Buren St., Tallahassee, FL 32399 (tel. 904/487-1462), open Monday through Friday from 8am to 5pm. Europeans should note that the FDT maintains an office in England at 18/24 Westbourne Grove, 4th Floor, London W2 5RH (tel. 071/727-1661).

In addition to information on some of South Miami Beach's better hotels, the **Miami Design Preservation League,** 1001 Ocean Dr. (P.O. Bin L), Miami Beach, FL 33119 (tel. 305/672-2014), offers a free, informative guide to the art deco district, and several books on the subject. They're open Monday through Saturday from 10am to 7pm.

Greater Miami's various chambers of commerce also send maps and information about their particular parcels. These include: **Coconut Grove Chamber of Commerce,** 2820 McFarlane Rd., Miami, FL 33133 (tel. 305/444-7270); **Coral Gables Chamber of Commerce,** 50 Aragon Ave., Coral Gables, FL 33134 (tel. 305/446-1657); **Florida Gold Coast Chamber of Commerce,** 1100 Kane Concourse (Bay Harbor Islands), Miami, FL 33154 (tel. 305/866-6020), which represents Bal Harbour, Sunny Isles, Surfside, and other North Dade waterfront communities; **Greater Miami Chamber of Commerce,** Omni International, 1601 Biscayne Blvd., Miami, FL 33132 (tel. 305/539-3063, or toll free 800/283-2707); and **Miami Beach Chamber of Commerce,** 1920 Meridian Ave., Miami Beach, FL 33139 (tel. 305/672-1270).

The following organizations represent dues-paying hotels, restaurants, and attractions in their specific areas. These associations can arrange accommodations and tours, as well as provide discount coupons to area sights: **Miami Beach Resort Hotel Association,** 407 Lincoln Rd., Miami Beach, FL 33139 (tel. 305/531-3553, or toll free 800/531-3553), and **Sunny Isles Beach Resort Association,** 3909 Sunny Isles Blvd., Suite 307, Sunny Isles, FL 33160 (tel. 305/947-5826, or toll free 800/327-6366).

CITY LAYOUT

Miami may seem confusing at first, but it quickly becomes easy to negotiate. The small cluster of buildings that make up the downtown area is at the geographical heart of the city. You can see these sharp stalactites from most anywhere, making them a good reference point. In relation to Miami's downtown, the airport is west, the beaches are east, Coconut Grove is south, and the rest of the country is north.

FINDING AN ADDRESS Miami is divided into dozens of areas with official and unofficial boundaries. To make map-reading easier, all the addresses listed in this book are followed by an area listing, indicating which part of the city it's in.

Street numbering in the **City of Miami** is fairly straightforward, but you must first be familiar with the numbering system. The mainland is divided into four sections— NE, NW, SE, and SW—by the intersection of Flagler Street and Miami Avenue. First Street and First Avenue begin near this corner, and, along with Places, Courts, Terraces, and Lanes, the numbers increase from this point. Hialeah streets are the exception to this pattern; they are listed separately in map indexes.

Establishment addresses are often descriptive; 12301 Biscayne Boulevard is located at 123rd Street. It's also helpful to remember that avenues generally run north-south, while streets go east-west.

Getting around the barrier islands of **Miami Beach** is somewhat easier than moving around the mainland. Street numbering starts with 1st Street, near Miami Beach's southern tip, and increases to 192nd Street, in the northern part of Sunny Isles. Collins Avenue makes the entire journey from head to toe. As in the City of Miami, some streets in Miami Beach have numbers as well as names. When they are part of listings in this book, both names and numbers are given.

You should know that the numbered streets in Miami Beach are not the geographical equivalents of those on the mainland. The 79th Street Causeway runs into 71st Street on Miami Beach.

MAPS It's easy to get lost in sprawling Miami, so a reliable map is essential. If you aren't planning on moving around too much, the tourist board's maps, located inside their free publication *Destination Miami,* may be adequate. But if you really want to get to know the city, it pays to invest in one of the large, accordion-fold maps, available at most gas stations and bookstores. The *Trakker Map of Miami* ($2.50) is a four-color accordion that encompasses all of Dade County, handy if you plan on visiting the many attractions in Greater Miami South.

Some maps of Miami list streets according to area, so you'll have to know which part of the city you're looking for before the street can be found. All the listings in this book include area information for just this reason.

NEIGHBORHOODS IN BRIEF

Much of Miami is sprawling suburbia. But every city has its charm, and aside from a fantastic tropical climate, and the vast stretch of beach that lies just across the bay, Miami's unique identity comes from extremely interesting cultural pockets within various residential communities.

Coral Gables Just over 70 years old, Coral Gables is the closest thing to "historical" that Miami has. It's also one of the prettiest parcels in the city. Created by George Merrick in the early 1920s, the Gables was one of Miami's first planned developments. Houses here were built in a "Mediterranean style" along lush tree-lined streets that open onto beautifully carved plazas, many with centerpiece fountains. The best architectural examples of the era have Spanish-style tiled roofs and are built of Miami oolite, a native limestone, commonly called "coral rock." Coral Gables is a stunning example of "boom" architecture on a grand scale—and a great area to explore. Some of the city's best restaurants are located here, as are top hotels and good shopping. See "Accommodations" and "Dining," later in this chapter, for listings.

Coconut Grove   There was a time when Coconut Grove was inhabited by artists and intellectuals, hippies and radicals. But times have changed. Gentrification has pushed most alternative types out, leaving in their place a multitude of cafés, boutiques, and nightspots. The intersection of Grand Avenue, Main Highway, and McFarlane Road, the area's heart, sizzles with dozens of interesting shops and eateries. Sidewalks here are often crowded with businesspeople, college students, and loads of foreign tourists—especially at night, when it becomes the best place to people-watch in all of South Florida.

Coconut Grove's link to The Bahamas dates from before the turn of the century, when the islanders came to the area to work in a newly opened hotel called the Peacock Inn. Bahamian-style wooden homes, built by these early settlers, still stand on Charles Street. Goombay, the lively annual Bahamian festival, celebrates the Grove's Caribbean link and has become one of the largest black heritage street festivals in America.

Miami Beach   To tourists in the 1950s, Miami Beach *was* Miami. Its huge self-contained resort hotels were worlds unto themselves, providing a full day's worth of meals, activities, and entertainment.

In the 1960s and 1970s people who fell in love with Miami began to buy apartments rather than rent hotel rooms. Tourism declined and many area hotels fell into disrepair.

But since the late '80s Miami Beach has witnessed a tide of revitalization. Huge beach hotels are finding international tourist markets, and are attracting large convention crowds. New generations of Americans are discovering the special qualities that made Miami Beach so popular to begin with, and are finding out that the beach now comes with a thriving, international, exciting city.

Note: North Miami Beach is a residential area on the mainland near the Dade-Broward county line. It is in no way connected to Miami Beach.

Surfside, Bal Harbour, and Sunny Isles   Lying just north of Miami Beach, on barrier islands, Surfside, Bal Harbour, and Sunny Isles are, for the most part, an extension of the beach community below it. Collins Avenue crosses town lines with hardly a sign, while hotels, motels, restaurants, and beaches continue to line the strip.

In exclusive Bal Harbour, fancy homes—tucked away on the bay—hide behind walls, gates, and security cameras. For tourists, it seems that—with some outstanding exceptions—the farther north you go, the cheaper lodging becomes. All told, excellent prices, location, and facilities make Surfside, Bal Harbour, and Sunny Isles attractive places to locate.

South Miami Beach—The Art Deco District   Officially part of the city of Miami Beach, the Miami Beach Architectural District of South Miami Beach contains the largest concentration of art deco architecture in the world. South Beach, or SoBe, as it is known, is an exciting renaissance community with pensioners, soon-to-be-monied young investors, perpetually poor artists, and the usual Miami smattering of ethnic groups. Everywhere you go there's an air of excitement; hip clubs and cafés are filled with working models and their photographers, musicians and writers, and in-the-know locals, vacationers, and others.

Key Biscayne   The first island in the Florida Keys chain is Miami's forested and fancy Key Biscayne. Located south of Miami Beach, off the shores of Coconut Grove, Key Biscayne is protected from the troubles of the mainland by the long Rickenbacker Causeway and a $1 toll. Key Biscayne is largely an exclusive residential community with million-dollar homes and sweeping water views. For tourists, this key offers great beaches, some top resort hotels, and several good restaurants. Hobie Beach, adjacent to the causeway, is the city's premier spot for sailboarding and jet skiing. On the island's southern tip is Bill Baggs State Park, offering great beaches, bike paths, and dense forests for picnicking and partying.

Downtown   Miami's downtown boasts one of the world's most beautiful cityscapes. If you do nothing else in Miami, make sure that you take your time studying the area's inspired architectural designs. The streets of downtown are

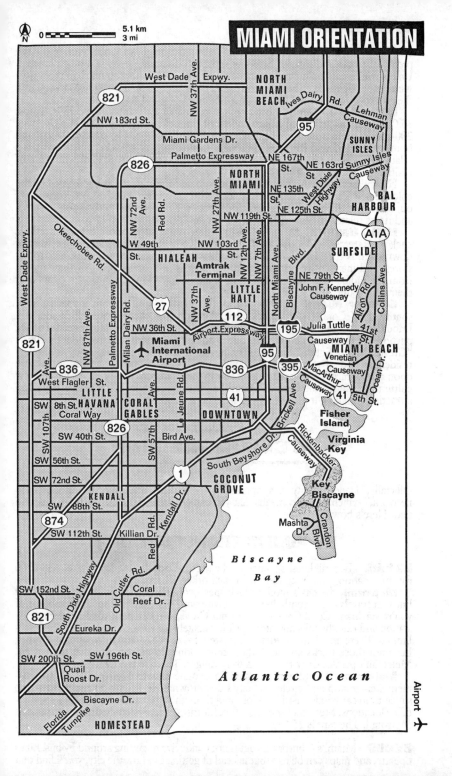

MIAMI ORIENTATION

5.1 km
3 mi

N

NORTH MIAMI BEACH
West Dade Expwy.
NW 37th Ave.
Ives Dairy Rd.
Lehman Causeway
821
NW 183rd St.
95
Miami Gardens Dr.
SUNNY ISLES
Palmetto Expressway
NE 167th St.
NE 163rd St.
Sunny Isles Causeway
826
NORTH MIAMI
NE 135th St.
West Dixie Highway
BAL HARBOUR
NW 72nd Ave.
Red Rd.
NW 27th Ave.
NW 119th St.
NE 125th St.
A1A
NW 103rd
North Miami Ave.
SURFSIDE
W 49th St.
HIALEAH
NW 12th Ave.
NW 7th Ave.
Biscayne Blvd.
Collins Ave.
Okeechobee Rd.
Amtrak Terminal
NE 79th St.
Alton Rd.
West Dade Expwy.
LITTLE HAITI
John F. Kennedy Causeway
27
NW 37th Ave.
112
Julia Tuttle Causeway
41st St.
NW 36th St.
Airport Expressway
195
MIAMI BEACH
NW 87th Ave.
Palmetto Expressway
Milan Dairy Rd.
Miami International Airport
95
Venetian Causeway
821
836
836
395
MacArthur Causeway
Ocean Dr.
West Flagler St.
NW Ave.
LeJeune Rd.
41
Brickell Ave.
Causeway
41
5th St.
LITTLE HAVANA
SW 8th St.
CORAL GABLES
DOWNTOWN
Fisher Island
SW 107th
Coral Way
826
SW 57th
Bird Ave.
Virginia Key
SW 40th St.
Rickenbacker Causeway
SW 56th St.
South Bayshore Dr.
SW 72nd St.
1
COCONUT GROVE
Key Biscayne
KENDALL
SW 88th St.
Red Rd.
Kendall Dr.
874
SW 112th St.
Killian Dr.
Mashta Dr.
Crandon Blvd.
Biscayne Bay
SW 152nd St.
South Dixie Highway
Old Cutler Rd.
Coral Reef Dr.
821
Eureka Dr.
SW 200th St.
SW 196th St.
Quail Roost Dr.
Atlantic Ocean
Biscayne Dr.
Florida Turnpike
HOMESTEAD

Airport ✈

unusually free of pedestrian traffic even during the height of lunch hour. You'll see plenty of stores and eateries here, but most sell discount goods and quick lunches. Unless you're bargain hunting for necessary items, there's not too much in the way of window-shopping. But the downtown area does have its mall (Bayside Marketplace), the Metro-Dade Cultural Center, and a number of good restaurants.

Little Haiti   During a brief period in the late 1970s and early 1980s, almost 35,000 Haitians arrived in Miami. Most of the new refugees settled in a decaying 200-square-block area north of downtown. Extending from 41st to 83rd Streets, and bordered by I-95 and Biscayne Boulevard, Little Haiti, as it has become known, is a relatively depressed neighborhood with over 60,000 residents, 65% of whom are of Haitian origin.

Northeast Second Avenue, Little Haiti's main thoroughfare, is highlighted by the colorful new Caribbean Marketplace, located at the corner of 60th Street. Keep an eye out for one of the many Haitian religious shops selling aromatic herbs, roots, incense, and items related to Santería and other voodoo ceremonies.

Little Havana   Miami's Cuban center is the city's most important ethnic enclave. Referred to locally as "Calle Ocho," SW 8th Street, located just west of downtown, is the region's main thoroughfare. Car-repair shops, tailors, electronics stores, and inexpensive restaurants all hang signs in Spanish. Salsa rhythms thump from the radios of passersby, while old men in guayaberas chain-smoke cigars over their daily game of dominoes.

Greater Miami South   To locals, South Miami is both a specific area, southwest of Coral Gables, and a general region that encompasses all of southern Dade County and includes Kendall, Perrine, Cutler Ridge, and Homestead. For the purposes of clarity, this book has grouped all these southern suburbs under the rubric "Greater Miami South." Similar attributes unite the communities: They are heavily residential, and all are packed with condominiums and shopping malls as well as acre upon acre of farmland. Tourists don't stay in these parts, as there is no beach and few cultural offerings. But Greater Miami South does contain many of the city's top attractions, making it likely that you'll spend some time here during the day.

2. GETTING AROUND

Officially, Dade County has opted for a "unified, multi-modal transportation network," which basically means that you can get around the city by train, bus, and taxi. Here's how:

BY PUBLIC TRANSPORTATION

BY RAIL   Two rail lines, operated by the Metro-Dade Transit Agency (tel. 638-6700 for information), run in concert with each other.

Metrorail, the city's modern high-speed commuter train, is a 21-mile elevated line that travels north-south, between downtown Miami and the southern suburbs. If you're staying in Coral Gables or Coconut Grove, you can park your car at a nearby station and ride the rails downtown. Unfortunately for visitors, the line's usefulness is limited. There are plans to extend the system to service Miami International Airport, but until those tracks are built, these trains don't go most places that tourists go. Metrorail operates daily from 6am to midnight. The fare is $1.25.

Metromover, a 1.9-mile elevated line, connects with Metrorail at the Government Center stop and circles the city's downtown area. Riding on rubber tires, the single-train car winds past 10 stations and through some of the city's most important office locations. Metromover offers a fun, futuristic ride. System hours are the same as Metrorail. The fare is 25¢.

BY BUS   Miami's suburban layout is not conducive to getting around by bus. Lines operate, and maps can be had, but instead of getting to know the city, you'll find that relying on bus transportation will only acquaint you with how it feels to wait at bus stops. You can get a bus map by mail, either from the Greater Miami Convention and Visitors Bureau (see "Information" in "Orientation," earlier in this chapter) or by writing the Metro-Dade Transit System, 3300 NW 32nd Ave., Miami, FL 33142. In Miami, call 638-6700 for public transit information. The fare is $1.25.

BY TAXI

If you're not planning on traveling much within the city, an occasional taxi is a good alternative to renting a car. If you plan on spending your holiday within the confines of South Miami Beach's art deco district, you may also wish to avoid the parking hassles that come with renting your own car. The taxi's meter drops at $1.10 for the first one-seventh of a mile, and rises 25¢ for each additional seventh of a mile. An average cross-city ride will cost about $10.

Major cab companies include **Metro** (tel. 888-8888) and **Yellow** (tel. 444-4444).

BY CAR

Tales circulate about vacationers who have visited Miami without a car, but they are very few indeed. If you're counting on exploring the city, even to a modest degree, private motor transportation will be essential to your plans. Unless you're going to spend your entire vacation at a resort, or are traveling directly to the Port of Miami for a cruise, a car is a necessity. Miami's restaurants, attractions, and sights are far from one another and any other form of transportation is impractical.

When driving across a causeway, or through downtown, allow extra time to reach your destination because of frequent drawbridge openings. Bridges open about every half hour, stalling traffic for several minutes. Don't get frustrated by the wait. The bridges keep the city's pace from becoming too fast and frenetic.

RENTALS It seems as though every car-rental company, big and small, has at least one office in Miami. Consequently, the city is one of the cheapest places in the world to rent a car. Many firms regularly advertise prices in the neighborhood of $89 per week for their bottom-of-the-line tin can—not an unreasonable sum for seven days of sun and fun.

Most rental firms pad their profits by selling an additional Loss/Damage Waiver (LDW), which usually costs an extra $8 to $10 per day. Before agreeing to this, however, check with your insurance carrier and credit- or charge-card companies. Many people don't realize that they are already covered by either one or both. If you're not, the LDW is a wise investment.

A minimum age, ranging from 19 to 25, is usually required of renters. Some rental agencies have also set maximum ages. If you are concerned that these limits may affect you, ask about rental requirements at the time of booking to avoid problems later.

National car-rental companies include: Alamo (tel. toll free 800/327-9633), Avis (tel. toll free 800/331-1212), Budget (tel. toll free 800/527-0700), Dollar (tel. toll free 800/822-1181), General (tel. toll free 800/327-7607), Hertz (tel. toll free 800/654-3131), National (tel. toll free 800/328-4567), and Thrifty (tel. toll free 800/367-2277). Literally dozens of other regional companies—some offering lower rates—can be found in the Miami *Yellow Pages* under "Automobile Renting and Leasing."

Finally, think about splurging for a convertible. Few things in life can match the feeling of flying along warm Florida freeways with the sun smiling on your shoulders and the wind whipping through your hair.

PARKING Always keep plenty of quarters, dimes, and nickels on hand in order to feed hungry meters. Parking is usually plentiful, but when it's not, be careful: Fines for illegal parking can be stiff.

In addition to parking garages, valet services are commonplace and often used. Expect to pay $3 to $5 for parking in Coconut Grove and on South Miami Beach's Ocean Drive on busy weekend nights.

LOCAL DRIVING RULES   Florida law allows drivers to make a right turn on a red light, unless otherwise indicated. In addition, all passengers are required to wear seat belts, and children under 3 years of age must be securely fastened in government-approved car seats.

BY BICYCLE

Miami's two best bicycling areas are vastly different from each other.

   Miami Beach   The hard-packed sand that runs the length of Miami Beach is one of the best places in the world to ride a bike. An excellent alternative to the slow pace of walking, biking up the beach is great for surf, sun, sand, exercise, and people-watching. You may not want to subject your bicycle to the salt and sand, but there are plenty of oceanfront rental places here. Most of the big beach hotels rent bicycles, as does **Cycles on the Beach,** 713 5th St. (tel. 673-2055). Located in South Miami Beach, the shop rents bicycles for $3 per hour. It's open daily from 10am to 9pm.

   Coral Gables and Coconut Grove   The beautiful and quiet streets of these neighborhoods beg for the attention of bicyclists. Old trees form canopies over wide, flat roads lined with grand homes and quaint street markers. Several bicycle trails are spread throughout these neighborhoods, including one that begins at the doorstep of **Dade Cycle,** 3216 Grand Ave., Coconut Grove (tel. 444-5997). It's open Monday through Saturday from 9:30am to 5:30pm and on Sunday from 10:30am to 5:30pm. MasterCard and VISA are accepted.

ON FOOT

With the exception of isolated pockets in Coconut Grove and South Miami Beach, Miami is not a walker's city because it's so spread out. Most attractions are too far apart to make walking feasible. In fact, most Miamians are so used to driving that they drive even when going just a few blocks.

FAST   MIAMI

   Airport   See "Arriving" in "Orientation," earlier in this chapter.
   American Express   For travel arrangements, traveler's checks, currency exchange, and other member services, Miami offices include: 330 Biscayne Blvd., downtown (tel. 358-7350); 9700 Collins Ave., Bal Harbour (tel. 865-5959); and 32 Miracle Mile, Coral Gables (tel. 446-3381). Offices are open Monday through Friday from 9am to 5pm and on Saturday from 9am until noon.
   To report lost or stolen traveler's checks, call toll free 800/221-7282.
   Area Code   The area code for Miami and all of Dade County is 305.
   Babysitters   Hotels can often recommend a babysitter or child-care service. If yours can't, try Central Sitting Agency, 1764 SW 24th St. (tel. 856-0550). Other child-minding agencies are listed in the *Yellow Pages* under "Sitting Services."
   Bookstores   Chain bookstores can be found in almost every shopping center in the city. A top bookseller in the city is Books & Books, 296 Aragon Ave. (tel. 442-4408), in Coral Gables.
   Buses   See "Getting Around," earlier in this chapter.
   Business Hours   Banking hours vary, but most **banks** are open Monday through Friday from 9am to 3pm. Several stay open until 5pm or so at least one day during the week, and many banks feature Automated Teller Machines (ATMs) for 24-hour banking.
   Most **stores** are open daily from 10am to 6pm; however, there are many exceptions. Shops in the Bayside Marketplace are usually open until 9 or 10pm, as are the boutiques in Coconut Grove. Stores in Bal Harbour and other malls are usually open one extra hour one night during the week (usually Thursday).
   As far as **business offices** are concerned, Miami is generally a 9am-to-5pm town.
   Car Rentals   See "Getting Around," earlier in this chapter.

Dentists The East Coast District Dental Society staffs an Emergency Dental Referral Service (tel. 285-5470). Michael H. Schenkman, D.D.S., in the Suniland Shopping Center, 11735 S. Dixie Hwy. (tel. 235-0020), features 24-hour emergency service and takes all major credit cards. All Dade Dental Associated, 11400 N. Kendall Dr., Mega Bank Building (tel. 271-7777), also offers round-the-clock care and accepts MasterCard and VISA.

Doctors In an emergency, call an ambulance by dialing 911 from any phone. No coins are required.

The Dade County Medical Association sponsors a Physician Referral Service (tel. 324-8717) Monday through Friday from 9am to 5pm.

Healthsouth Doctors' Hospital, 5000 University Dr., Coral Gables (tel. 666-2111), is a 285-bed acute-care hospital with a 24-hour physician-staffed emergency department.

Driving Rules See "Getting Around," earlier in this chapter.

Drugstores Walgreens Pharmacies are all over town, including 8550 Coral Way (tel. 221-9271), in Coral Gables; and 6700 Collins Ave. (tel. 861-6742), in Miami Beach. Their branch at 5731 Bird Rd. (tel. 666-0757) is open 24 hours, as is Eckerd Drugs, 1825 Miami Gardens Dr. NE (185th Street), North Miami Beach (tel. 932-5740).

Embassies/Consulates See "Fast Facts: For the Foreign Visitor," in Chapter 3.

Emergencies To reach the police, ambulance, or fire department, dial **911** from any phone. No coins are needed. Emergency hotlines include: Crisis Intervention (tel. 358-4357), Poison Information Center (tel. toll free 800/282-3171), and Rape Hotline (tel. 549-7273).

Eyeglasses Pearle Vision Center, 7901 Biscayne Blvd. (tel. 754-5114), in Coral Gables, can usually fill prescriptions in about an hour.

Hairdressers/Barbers The chain, Supercuts, 9803 Bird Rd. (tel. 553-4965), offers one of the lowest-priced shears in the city, while the salon at the Grand Bay Hotel, 2669 S. Bayshore Dr., Coconut Grove (tel. 858-9600), boasts one of the most costly pamperings around. Many other major hotels also have hair salons.

Hospitals See "Doctors," above.

Information Always check local newspapers for special things to do during your visit. The city's highest-quality daily, the *Miami Herald,* is an especially good source for current-events listings, particularly the "Weekend" section in Friday's edition. For a complete list of tourist boards and other information sources, see "Information" in "Orientation," earlier in this chapter.

Laundry/Dry Cleaning All Laundry Service, 5701 NW 7th St., west of downtown (tel. 261-8175), does dry cleaning and offers a wash-and-fold service by the pound in addition to self-service machines. It's open daily from 7am to 10pm. Clean Machine Laundry, 226 12th St., South Miami Beach (tel. 534-9429), is convenient to South Beach's art deco hotels. It's open 24 hours daily. Coral Gables Dry Cleaning, 250 Minorca Ave., Coral Gables (tel. 446-6458), has been dry cleaning, altering, and laundering since 1930. They offer a life-saving same-day service. Open Monday through Friday from 7am to 6:30pm and on Saturday from 8am to 3pm.

Libraries The Main Library in the Dade County system is located downtown at 101 W. Flagler St. (tel. 375-2665). It's open Monday through Wednesday and on Friday and Saturday from 9am to 6pm, on Thursday from 9am to 9pm, and during the school year also on Sunday from 1 to 5pm.

Liquor Laws Only adults 21 years of age or older may legally purchase or consume alcohol in the state of Florida. Minors are usually permitted in bars that serve food. Liquor laws are strictly enforced; if you look young, carry identification. In addition to specialty shops, beer and wine are also sold in most supermarkets and convenience stores. The City of Miami's liquor stores are closed on Sunday. Liquor stores in the City of Miami Beach are open all week.

Lost Property If you lost it at the airport, call the Airport Lost and Found office (tel. 876-7377). If you lost it on the bus, Metrorail, or Metromover, call Metro-Dade Transit Agency (tel. 638-6700). If you lost it somewhere else, phone the Dade County Police Lost and Found (tel. 375-3366). You may also wish to fill out a police report for insurance purposes.

Luggage Storage/Lockers   In addition to the baggage check at Miami International Airport (see "Arriving," in "Orientation," earlier in this chapter), most hotels offer luggage-storage facilities. If you're taking a cruise from the Port of Miami, bags can be stored in your ship's departure terminal.

Mail   Miami's Main Post Office, 2200 Milam Dairy Rd., Miami, FL 33152 (tel. 599-0166), is located west of Miami International Airport. Letters addressed to you and marked "General Delivery" can be picked up here. Conveniently located post offices include 1300 Washington Ave. (tel. 531-7306), in South Miami Beach; and 3191 Grand Ave. (tel. 443-0030), in Coconut Grove. Holders of American Express cards or traveler's checks can receive mail, free, addressed c/o American Express, 330 Biscayne Blvd., Miami, FL 33133.

Maps   See "City Layout" in "Orientation," above.

Money   In addition to paying close attention to the details below, foreign visitors should also see "Fast Facts" in Chapter 3 for monetary descriptions and currency-exchange information.

U.S. dollar **traveler's checks** are the safest, most negotiable way to carry currency. They are accepted by most restaurants, hotels, and shops, and can be exchanged for cash at banks and check-issuing offices. For American Express offices, see "American Express," above.

Most banks offer **Automated Teller Machines (ATMs),** which accept cards connected to a particular network. Citicorp Savings of Florida, 8750 NW 36th St., and at other locations (tel. 599-5555), accepts cards on Cirrus, Honor, and Metroteller networks. For additional bank locations, dial toll free 800/424-7787 for the Cirrus network, toll free 800/843-7587 for the Plus network.

Banks making **cash advances** against MasterCard and VISA cards include Barnett Bank (tel. toll free 800/342-8472), First Union Bank (tel. 593-6200), and NCNB National Bank (tel. 538-5421).

Newspapers/Magazines   The well-respected *Miami Herald* is the city's best-selling daily. It is especially known for its mammoth Sunday edition, and its excellent Friday "Weekend" entertainment guide. There are literally dozens of specialized Miami magazines geared toward tourists and natives alike. Many are free, and can be picked up at hotels, restaurants, and in vending machines all around town. The best entertainment freebie is the weekly tabloid *New Times.* But keep an eye out for *Welcome, Key, Miami Beach News, Coral Gables News, Florida Sports,* and others. *South Florida* is the area's best glossy for upscale readers.

Photographic Needs   Drugstores and supermarkets are probably the cheapest places to purchase film. You'll pay loads more for the same product at specialized kiosks near tourist attractions. One Hour Photo in the Bayside Marketplace (tel. 377-FOTO) charges $16 to develop and print a roll of 36 pictures. Open Monday through Saturday from 10am to 10pm and on Sunday from noon to 8pm. Coconut Grove Camera, 3317 Virginia St. (tel. 445-0521), features 30-minute color processing and maintains a huge selection of cameras and equipment. They rent, too.

Police   For emergencies, dial 911 from any phone. No coins are needed. For other matters, call 595-6263.

Radio/TV   About five dozen **radio** stations can be heard in the Greater Miami area. On the AM dial, 610 (WIOD), 790 (WNWS), 1230 (WNJO), and 1340 (WPBR) all specialize in news and talk. WDBF (1420) is a good Big Band station, and WPBG (1290) features golden oldies. The best rock stations on the FM dial include WZTA (94.9), WGTR (97.3), and the progressive rock station WVUM (90.5). WKIS (99.9) is the top country station, and public radio (PBS) can be heard either on WXEL (90.7) or WLRN (91.3).

In addition to cable **television** stations, available in most hotels, all the major networks and a couple of independent stations are represented. They include: Channel 4, WTVJ (NBC); Channel 6, WCIX (CBS); Channel 7, WSVN (Fox); Channel 10, WPLG (ABC); Channel 17, WLRN (PBS); Channel 23, WLTV (independent); and Channel 33, WBFS (independent).

Religious Services   Miami houses of worship are as varied as the city's population and include: St. Hugh Catholic Church, 3460 Royal Rd., at the corner of Main Highway (tel. 444-8363); Temple Judea, 5500 Granada Blvd., Coral Gables (tel. 667-5657); Bryan Memorial United Methodist, 3713 Main Hwy. (tel. 443-0880);

Christ Episcopal Church, 3481 Hibiscus St. (tel. 442-8542); and Plymouth Congregational Church, 3400 Devon Rd., at Main Highway (tel. 444-6521).

Restrooms   Stores rarely let customers use the restrooms, and many restaurants offer their facilities for customers only. Most malls have bathrooms, as do many of the ubiquitous fast-food restaurants. Many public beaches and large parks provide toilets; in some places you have to pay, or tip an attendant. Most large hotels have clean restrooms in their lobbies.

Safety   Whenever you're traveling in an unfamiliar city or country, stay alert. Be aware of your immediate surroundings. Wear a moneybelt and don't sling your camera or purse over your shoulder. It's your responsibility to be aware and alert, even in the most heavily touristed areas. See also "Safety" in Section 1 of Chapter 3.

Shoe Repair   There are dozens of shoe- and leather-repair shops around the city. Check the Miami *Yellow Pages* for the location nearest you, or visit Miller Square Shoe Repair, 13846 SW 56th St. (tel. 387-2875). It's open Monday through Friday from 9am to 7pm and on Saturday until 6pm.

Taxes   A 6% state sales tax is added on at the register for all goods and services purchased in Florida. In addition, most municipalities levy special taxes on restaurants and hotels. In Surfside, hotel taxes total 8%; in Bal Harbour, 9%; and in the rest of Dade County, a whopping 11%.

In Miami Beach, Surfside, and Bal Harbour, the resort (hotel) tax also applies to restaurants with liquor licenses.

Taxis   See "Getting Around," earlier in this chapter.

Telephone, Telex, and Fax   Find out how much it costs to use the direct-dial telephone in your hotel room before you pick up the receiver. Hotel surcharges are often astronomical, and even a local call can cost 75¢ or more! You can often save yourself a lot of money by using one of the hotel's public telephones in the lobby.

Most large Miami hotels have telex and/or facsimile (fax) machines; their numbers are included in this book with the appropriate listings. You should know that many hotels charge several dollars per page even to *receive* fax messages! Beware of the Hotel Copy service, and other high-price fax services.

Time   Miami, like New York, is in the eastern standard time zone. Between April and October, eastern daylight saving time is adopted, and clocks are set one hour ahead. America's eastern seaboard is five hours ahead of Greenwich mean time. To find out what time it is, call 324-8811.

Tipping   Waiters and bartenders expect a 15% tip, as do taxi drivers and hairdressers. Porters should be tipped 50¢ to $1 per bag, and parking valets should be given $1. It's nice to leave a few dollars on your pillow for the hotel maid, and lavatory attendants will appreciate whatever change you have.

Transit Information   For Metrorail or Metromover schedule information, phone 638-6700. See "Getting Around," earlier in this chapter, for more information.

Weather   For an up-to-date recording of current weather conditions and forecast reports, dial 661-5065.

3. ACCOMMODATIONS

Miami is chock-full of hotels. Whether you're looking to locate on a quiet strip of beach or right in the heart of the hustle, accommodation possibilities seem endless. Hotels here offer a huge variety of locations and services, and they appeal to a multiplicity of personalities and pocketbooks.

You may already know that South Florida's tourist season is well defined, beginning in mid-November and lasting through Easter. From the season's commencement, hotel prices escalate until about February, after which they again begin to decline. During the off-season, hotel rates are typically 30% to 50% lower than their winter highs. Oceanfront rooms are also more accessible between Easter and November, as are shops, roads, and restaurants.

But timing isn't everything. In many cases, rates will also depend on your hotel's proximity to the beach and how much ocean you can see from your window. Small motels, a block or two from the water, can be up to 40% cheaper than similar properties right on the sand. When a hotel *is* right on the beach, it is probable that its oceanfront rooms will be significantly more expensive than similar accommodations in the rear. Still, despite their higher prices, oceanfront rooms can often be hard to get; if you desire one, a reservation is definitely recommended.

There are so many hotels in Miami—in every price range—that few regularly fill to capacity. Even during the height of the tourist season, you can usually drive right into the city and find decent accommodations fairly quickly. But be careful. If you have your sights set on one particular hotel, if you have to have an oceanfront room, or if you want to stay in an area where accommodations are not particularly plentiful, you should reserve your room in advance.

Hotel toll-free telephone numbers will save you time and money when inquiring about rates and availability. Some of the larger hotel reservations chains with properties in the Miami area include: Best Western (tel. toll free 800/528-1234), Days Inns (tel. toll free 800/325-2525), Holiday Inn (tel. toll free 800/327-5476), Howard Johnson (tel. toll free 800/446-4656), Quality Inns (tel. toll free 800/228-5151), Ramada Inns (tel. toll free 800/272-6232), and TraveLodge (tel. toll free 800/255-3050).

If, after inquiring about room availability at the hotels listed in this book, you still come up empty-handed (an extremely unlikely prospect), look for an availability along Miami Beach's Collins Avenue. There are dozens of hotels and motels on this strip—in all price categories—so a room is bound to be available.

To help you decide on the accommodations option that's best for you, hotels below are divided first by area, then by price, using the following guide: "Expensive," more than $130; "Moderate," $80 to $130; and "Budget," less than $80. Prices are for an average double room during the high season. Read carefully. Many hotels also offer rooms at rates above and below the price category they have been assigned. Most hotel rates are significantly lower between Easter and Thanksgiving.

Prices listed below *do not include state and city taxes,* which, in most parts of Miami, total 11% (see "Fast Facts: Miami," above). Be aware that many hotels make additional charges for parking and levy heavy surcharges for telephone use. Some, especially those in South Miami Beach, also tack on an additional service charge. Inquire about these extras before committing. Room rates include breakfast where noted.

MIAMI BEACH

You probably have never seen more hotels than the solid wall of high-rises that seems to go on forever along Collins Avenue. The buildings are so effective at blocking the ocean from the view of passersby that you hardly know you're driving along the coast. But reserve a room at one of these behemoths and you'll have some of the world's best beach at your doorstep.

Most of these big beach resorts are so encompassing that it's possible to spend your entire stay on the premises of a single hotel. But when you're ready to explore, Miami Beach is within easy reach of the art deco district and the mainland just across the bay.

EXPENSIVE

ALEXANDER ALL-SUITE LUXURY HOTEL, 5225 Collins Ave., Miami Beach, FL 33140. Tel. 305/865-6500, or toll free 800/327-6121. Fax 305/864-8525. Telex 808172. 150 suites. A/C MINIBAR TV TEL

$ **Rates:** Dec 17–Easter, $310–$660 one-bedroom suite; $420–$900 two-bedroom suite. Easter–Dec 16, $225–$495 one-bedroom suite; $325–$620 two-bedroom suite. Additional person $25 extra. Children under 18 stay free in parents' room. Packages available. AE, CB, DC, MC, V. **Parking:** $8.

⭐ One of the nicest offerings on Miami Beach, the Alexander is an all-suite hotel, featuring spacious one- and two-bedroom mini-apartments. All suites have a living room, a fully equipped kitchen, two bathrooms, and a balcony. The hotel itself is well decorated with fine sculptures, paintings, antiques, and tapestries, most of which were garnered from the Cornelius Vanderbilt mansion. The pretty hotel's two oceanfront pools are surrounded by lush vegetation; one of the "lagoons" is also fed by a cascading waterfall.

Dining/Entertainment: Dominique's, a gourmet restaurant for a top-drawer dinner, offers French cuisine featuring seafood, rack of lamb, rattlesnake, and Everglades alligator. There's also a piano lounge and a pool bar.

Services: Valet/laundry service, room service, turn-down service, currency exchange.

Facilities: Two heated freshwater swimming pools, four Jacuzzis, Sunfish and catamaran rentals, gift shop.

DORAL OCEAN BEACH RESORT, 4833 Collins Ave., Miami Beach, FL 33140. Tel. 305/532-3600, or toll free 800/223-6725. Fax 305/534-7409. 293 rms, 127 suites. A/C MINIBAR TV TEL

$ Rates: Dec 20–Apr, $210–$300 single or double; from $335 suite. May–Dec 19, $125–$200 single or double; from $240 suite. Additional person $20 extra. Weekend and other packages available. AE, CB, DC, DISC, MC, V. **Parking:** $9.

The 18-story Doral Resort stands guard over Collins Avenue with the proud self-confidence of a truly grand hotel. This is one of the beach's famous "big boys," and it's one of the city's luxury leaders. For an oceanfront resort, the hotel is relatively quiet. Its immediate neighbors are private apartment buildings and, except for its 18th-floor restaurant, the Doral offers practically no nightlife.

Still, the hotel features all the activities you'd expect from a top waterfront resort, including sailing, waterskiing, jet skiing, and windsurfing. The Seabreeze Restaurant, specializing in stir-fries, gourmet pizzas, and health-oriented edibles, sits adjacent to an outdoor, Olympic-size pool. The biggest benefit of locating here, however, is that guests are entitled to use the facilities of the Doral's affiliated hotels, which include six golf courses and one of the best health spas in America. A free shuttle bus connects this beach resort with the others.

Dining/Entertainment: Three restaurants, a nightclub, two lounges, and a pool bar.

Services: 24-hour room service, laundry service, car rental, complimentary transportation to other resorts, child care and complimentary child-activity center.

Facilities: Heated outdoor swimming pool, Jacuzzi, fitness center, two lighted tennis courts, games room.

EDEN ROC HOTEL AND MARINA, 4525 Collins Ave., Miami Beach, FL 33140. Tel. 305/531-0000, or toll free 800/327-8337. Fax 305/531-6955. Telex 807120. 306 rms, 45 suites. A/C TV TEL

$ Rates: Dec 22–Apr, $150–$200 single or double; from $600 suite. May–Dec 21, $130–$180 single or double; from $250 suite. Additional person $15 extra. Weekend and other packages available. AE, CB, DC, DISC, MC, V. **Parking:** $8.50.

Another long-time hotel on the beach, the Eden Roc is one of those big hostelries that helped give Miami Beach its flamboyant image. Accommodations here are more than a bit gaudy, but compared to other monoliths on the strip, the atmosphere is relatively laid-back.

Accommodations are unpretentious, unusually spacious, and priced better than those of other nearby deluxe properties. Rooms are alternately decorated in deep, dark colors, and lighter earth tones. Bathrooms are covered with marble and pretty mirrors.

The Eden Roc, with its huge crystal chandeliers and marble-and-brass decor, is a hotel that wants to show off. The circular pink pastel lobby is as fanciful as the entrance. And in the Porch Restaurant, the transparent glass sides of the lounge-side swimming pool, adjacent to the restaurant, give drinkers an underwater view of the frolicking swimmers.

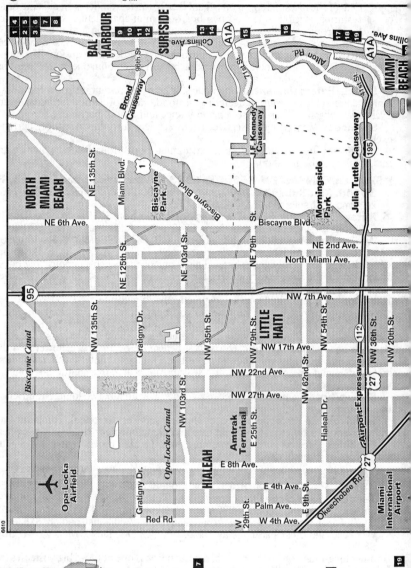

3.2 km
2 mi

FLORIDA

Miami

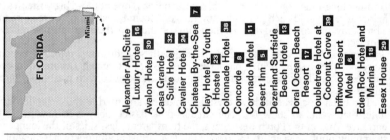

Alexander All-Suite
Luxury Hotel 16

Avalon Hotel 30

Casa Grande
Suite Hotel 32

Cavalier Hotel 24

Chateau By-the-Sea 7

Clay Hotel & Youth
Hostel 23

Colonnade Hotel 38

Concorde 8

Coronado Motel 11

Desert Inn 5

Dezerland Surfside
Beach Hotel 13

Doral Ocean Beach
Resort 17

Doubletree Hotel at
Coconut Grove 39

Driftwood Resort
Motel 6

Eden Roc Hotel and
Marina 18

Essex House 29

Fontainebleau Hilton 19

Golden Sands

MIAMI AREA ACCOMMODATIONS

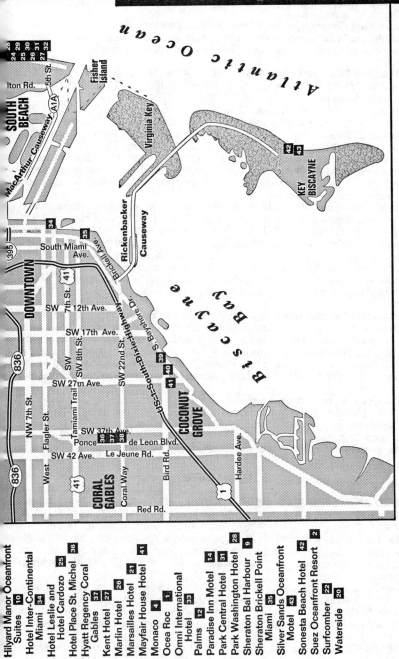

Atlantic Ocean

Fisher Island

Iton Rd.

5th St.

SOUTH BEACH

MacArthur Causeway (A1A)

Virginia Key

Rickenbacker Causeway

395

South Miami Ave.

Brickell Ave.

DOWNTOWN

41

SW 7th St.

SW 12th Ave.

SW 17th Ave.

SW 8th St.

SW 22nd St.

S. Bayshore Dr.

836

SW 27th Ave.

NW 7th St.

West Flagler St.

Tamiami Trail

US 1 South-Dixie Highway

39

40

41

COCONUT GROVE

Biscayne Bay

SW 37th Ave.

36
37
38

Ponce de Leon Blvd.

SW 42 Ave.

Le Jeune Rd.

836

41

CORAL GABLES

Coral Way

Bird Rd.

Red Rd.

Hardee Ave.

1

Airport

KEY BISCAYNE

42
43

24 28
25 29
25 30
26 31
27 32

34

35

Hilyard Manor Oceanfront Suites **10**
Hotel Inter-Continental Miami **34**
Hotel Leslie and Hotel Cardozo **25**
Hotel Place St. Michel **36**
Hyatt Regency Coral Gables **37**
Kent Hotel **27**
Marlin Hotel **26**
Marsailles Hotel **21**
Mayfair House Hotel **41**
Monaco **4**
Ocea Roc **1**
Omni International Hotel **33**
Palms **12**
Paradise Inn Motel **14**
Park Central Hotel **31**
Park Washington Hotel **28**
Sheraton Bal Harbour **9**
Sheraton Brickell Point Miami **35**
Silver Sands Oceanfront Motel **43**
Sonesta Beach Hotel **42**
Suez Oceanfront Resort **2**
Surfcomber **22**
Waterside **20**

Dining/Entertainment: Three lounges, two restaurants (one fancy, one casual), a coffee shop, and a deli.

Services: Concierge, laundry, room service, car-rental desk.

Facilities: Two outdoor swimming pools (one freshwater, one saltwater), water-sports concession, games room, beauty salon, shopping arcade.

FONTAINEBLEAU HILTON, 4441 Collins Ave., Miami Beach, FL 33140. Tel. 305/538-2000, or toll free 800/HILTONS. Fax 305/534-7821. Telex 519362. 1,146 rms, 60 suites. A/C TV TEL

$ Rates: Dec 16–Apr, $180–$250 single; $190–$275 double; from $330 suite. May–Dec 15, $130–$205 single; $150–$225 double; from $300 suite. Additional person $20 extra. Children stay free in parents' room. Weekend and other packages available. AE, CB, DC, DISC, MC, V. **Parking:** $9.

Far and away the most famous hotel in Miami, the Fontainebleau (pronounced "fountain-blue") has built its reputation on garishness and excess. For most visitors, the massive structure, with its free-form swimming pool and waterfall, is a spectacle more tourist attraction than hotel.

Since opening its doors in 1954, the hotel has hosted presidents, pageants, and movie productions—including the James Bond thriller *Goldfinger*. The sheer size of the Fontainbleau, with its full complement of restaurants, stores, recreational facilities, and over 1,100 employees, makes this a perfect hotel for conventioneers. Unfortunately, the same recommendation cannot be extended to individual travelers. The lobby is terminally crowded, the staff is overworked, and lines are always long. Still, this is the one and only Fontainebleau, in many ways the quintessential Miami hotel. Facilities are terrific and, for all its shortcomings, this is one place you'll never forget.

Dining/Entertainment: Four large restaurants include the Trop Art Cafe, which serves breakfast, lunch, and dinner. There are a half dozen or so other cafés and coffee shops (including two by the pool), as well as a number of cocktail lounges, including the Poodle Lounge, which offers live entertainment and dancing nightly. Club Tropigala (see "Evening Entertainment," in Chapter 5), just off the lobby, features a "Las Vegas–style" floor show with dozens of performers and not one, but two orchestras.

Services: Room service, house doctor, limousine service, complimentary child care during holidays and summer, laundry service.

Facilities: Shopping arcade with 28 shops, games room, two outdoor swimming pools (one freshwater, one saltwater), three whirlpool baths, seven lighted tennis courts, award-winning health spa, special activities for children.

MODERATE

DEZERLAND SURFSIDE BEACH HOTEL, 8701 Collins Ave., Miami Beach, FL 33154. Tel. 305/865-6661, or toll free 800/331-9346, 800/331-9347 in Canada. Fax 305/866-2630. Telex 4973649. 225 rms. A/C TV TEL

$ Rates: Dec 26–Mar, $85–$125 single or double. Apr–Dec 25, $60–$75 single or double. Additional person $8 extra. Children under 19 stay free in parents' room. Special packages and group rates available. AE, CB, DISC, MC, V. **Parking:** Free.

Designed by car enthusiast Michael Dezer, Dezerland is an unusual place—part hotel and part 1950s automobile wonderland. Visitors are welcomed by a 1959 Cadillac stationed by the front door, and a '55 Thunderbird hardtop sits in the lobby. A dozen other mint-condition classics are scattered about the floors, while walls are decorated with related '50s and '60s memorabilia.

Billed as "America's largest '50s extravaganza," this unique Quality Inn member features rooms that are named after some of Detroit's most famous models. Dezerland is located directly on the beach and features a mosaic of a pink Cadillac at the bottom of its surfside swimming pool.

Dining/Entertainment: American Classics restaurant and a lobby lounge with nightly entertainment.

Services: Laundry, babysitting.
Facilities: Adjacent tennis courts, gift shop featuring '50s memorabilia.

BUDGET

THE CHATEAU BY-THE-SEA, 19115 Collins Ave., Sunny Isles, Miami Beach, FL 33160. Tel. 305/931-8800, or toll free 800/327-0691. Fax 305/931-6194. 167 rms, 92 efficiencies. A/C TV TEL

$ Rates: Apr 16–Dec 17, $39–$60 single or double; $49–$70 efficiency. Dec 18–Feb 6 and Mar–Apr 15, $61–$88 single or double; $71–$98 efficiency. Feb 7–28, $63–$93 single or double. AE, DC, MC, V.

Looking very much like a misplaced Swiss chalet, the two-story Chateau stands-out in Sunny Isles for its good-quality accommodations under sloping, shingled roofs. Most rooms have two double beds, big walk-in closets, a refrigerator, and a safe; some have radios. Although the functionalist furnishings are decoratively uninspiring, the newest beds and bureaus are placed in the higher-priced rooms. The hotel sports one of the strip's most appealing swimming pools, which is located beachfront. There's also shuffleboard, a sauna, an oceanfront bar, and a lilliputian golf course.

THE GOLDEN SANDS, 6910 Collins Ave., Miami Beach, FL 33141. Tel. 305/866-8734, or toll free 800/932-0333, 800/423-5170 in Canada. Fax 305/866-0187. Telex 6974107. 80 rms, 20 efficiencies. A/C TV TEL

$ Rates: Dec–Mar, $50–$60 single; $57–$77 double; $80 efficiency. Apr–Nov, $43 single; $47–$57 double; $60 efficiency. Additional person $10 extra. Children stay free in parents' room. AE, MC, V. **Parking:** $5.

Despite the motel's lack of attention to detail and disorderly grounds, excellent rates and good services make the Golden Sands one of the best deals in Miami Beach. Located on the corner of 69th Street, directly on the ocean, the hotel sports a large pool area with outdoor weights, an indoor lounge, and an inexpensive restaurant. Bright, well-kept rooms, most with two double beds, have extra-clean baths, refrigerators, large closets, and contemporary floor lamps. The motel caters to a primarily German clientele.

PARADISE INN MOTEL, 8520 Harding Ave., Miami Beach, FL 33141. Tel. 305/865-6216. Fax 305/865-9028. 48 rms, 48 efficiencies. A/C TV TEL

$ Rates: Dec 22–Jan 14 and Mar 7–Apr 15, $42 single; $48 double; from $54 efficiency. Jan 15–Mar 6, $46 single; $52 double; from $60 efficiency. Apr 16–July 1 and Sept 2–Dec 21, $30 single; $33 double; from $37 efficiency. July 2–Sept 1, $32 single; $35 double; from $39 efficiency. Children under 13 stay free in parents' room. AE, CB, DC, DISC, MC, V.

 FROMMER'S SMART TRAVELER: HOTELS

1. Always remember that at any time of year a hotel room is a perishable commodity: If it's not sold, the revenue is lost forever. Therefore, it is a fact that rates are linked to the hotel's occupancy level. If it's 90% occupied, the price goes up; if it's 50% occupied, the price goes down. So always try negotiating by stating *your* price.
2. In summer, ask about summer discounts. At this time of year, hotels in Miami are very negotiable. Downtown hotels are less elastic.
3. Many hotels offer big discounts or package rates on weekends (Friday through Sunday night). If you're staying on a weekend, always ask about these. Downtown hotels are more elastic.
4. Before selecting a hotel, always ask about parking charges. Charges can be as much as $10—a big difference if you're planning on staying a while.

★ It's amazing how inexpensive simple, clean, and perfectly acceptable accommodations can be just one block from the ocean in Miami Beach. Nothing fancy here, but all rooms in this red-shingle-roofed motel have color television and air conditioning. The motel features free parking and laundry facilities, and it's a two-minute walk from public tennis courts and the huge beachfront North Shore Park. Harding Avenue runs parallel to Collins Avenue.

THE WATERSIDE, 2360 Collins Ave., Miami Beach, FL 33139. Tel. 305/538-1951. Fax 305/531-3217. 100 rms. AC TV TEL

$ Rates: Dec 16–Apr, $75–$90 single or double. May–Dec 15, $40–$60 single or double. Additional person $10 extra. Children stay free in parents' room. AE, DC, MC, V.

Across Collins Avenue from the beach, the Waterside is a medium-size bilevel motel popular with European tourists. The new owners, French-born Gérard and Maryse Meulien, recently sold their hotel in Marseille to give their full attention to the completely renovated Waterside. This blue-and-white motel wraps around a large swimming pool and features simple, well-kept rooms with free parking and excellent rates.

SOUTH MIAMI BEACH

I love to stay in South Miami Beach. Hotels here are not stuffy, nor are they too fancy. They are well located, pretty, and surrounded by well-priced restaurants and some of Miami's best nightlife options.

Ocean Drive, an inviting 10-block strip inside Miami's historic art deco district is, hands down, the beach's best esplanade. Fronting the Atlantic Ocean, this historic street is lined with squat, ice cream–colored hotels and coconut palms taller than most of the buildings.

Collins Avenue, just one block back, runs parallel to Ocean Drive. This pretty stretch of the street is not on the water, but staying here—or even farther from the beach—usually means lower room rates and easier parking.

EXPENSIVE

CASA GRANDE SUITE HOTEL, 834 Ocean Dr., South Miami Beach, FL 33139. Tel. 305/672-7003. Fax 305/673-3669. 31 studios and suites. A/C TV TEL

$ Rates: Nov–May, $175 studio; $225–$250 one-bedroom suite; $350 two-bedroom suite. June–Oct, $150 studio; $200–$225 one-bedroom suite; $325 two-bedroom suite. AE, DISC, MC, V. **Parking:** $14.

Ever since South Miami Beach began its pastel renaissance almost 10 years ago, style watchers have been waiting for a truly terrific hotel to open on Ocean Drive. It finally has! The Casa Grande Suite Hotel, located just steps from the drive's News Cafe epicenter, is not only the best hotel on Ocean, it's one of the best in South Beach.

Like most every other hotel on the beach, parking is difficult and services are few—there's no concierge, or a business center. What Casa Grande does offer is some of the largest rooms on the beach, well dressed in South Seas style, and outfitted with full kitchens, beautifully tiled baths, reed rugs, mahogany beds, and CD/stereos. Add large closets, interesting art, high-end furnishings and fixtures, and you have the most desired hotel on the beach.

Services: Overnight laundry and dry cleaning.
Facilities: Access to nearby pool and tennis courts.

HOTEL IMPALA, 1228 Collins Ave., South Miami Beach, FL 33139. Tel. 305/673-2021, or toll free 800/646-7252. Fax 305/673-5984. 14 studios, 3 suites. A/C MINIBAR TV TEL

$ Rates (including continental breakfast): Nov–May, $175 studio; from $250 suite. June–Oct, $150 studio; from $200 suite. AE, DISC, MC, V.

When the ultra-stylish Mediterranean Revival–style Hotel Impala opened in November 1993, it immediately became one of South Miami Beach's two top hotels. Filled with eclectic furnishings and original artwork, the highly detailed "boutique hotel" was opened by John Jones, the vice president of both Ultimo and Giorgio Armani in

Chicago, and Wallace Tutt, the contractor on Gianni Versace's new Ocean Drive villa. It's no surprise, then, that the upscale Impala boasts a unique "designer look." Guest rooms are decorated with an unusual combination of woods, marble, iron, and glass, and fitted with imported linens, VCRs, CD/stereos, voice-mail telephones with dataports, and grand showers and bathtubs. Some of the standard studios are smaller than their high prices would indicate, but suites, featuring oversize glass-wrapped showers and small balconies, are worth the extra bucks.

Facilities here are few—no swimming pool, no tennis courts, no health club, no business center, and no beach—the Atlantic is one block away. And only time will tell if the Impala will make good on its promise of grand-luxe service—surely a trump card in relatively serviceless South Beach.

Dining/Entertainment: The Sasa Restaurant, located on the hotel's ground floor, is as stylish as the Impala itself, and features neo-Neapolitan cooking. Light, healthful twists on tradition translate into heavy doses of seafoods, lean meats, and a liberal use of vegetables. Main courses range from $11 to $38.

Services: Concierge, evening turn-down, overnight laundry.

THE MARLIN, 1200 Collins Ave., South Miami Beach, FL 33139. Tel. 305/673-8770, or toll free 800/338-9076. Fax 305/673-9609. 10 rms, 7 suites. A/C TV TEL

$ Rates: $200 studio; $225 one-bedroom suite; $240 deluxe one-bedroom suite; $310 two-bedroom suite. AE, CB, DC, DISC, MC, V.

Opened in early 1992 after extensive renovations and a complete exterior make-over, this hotel is visually one of the most outstanding on the beach. The hotel's proprietor, former Island Records owner Chris Blackwell, has attracted a rock-'n'-roll clientele that has made an instant hit out of the high-profile Marlin. The hotel's beautifully lit powder-blue exterior gives way to a far less grand interior filled with gaily painted but rather small and simple rooms and suites.

Although the relatively high prices might not be warranted by the quality of the rooms themselves, contemporary touches and an in-the-know staff give guests a sense of being someplace special. In addition to a kitchenette, every Jamaican-style room is outfitted with a TV, VCR, CD player, and a host of tropical toiletries. Deluxe one-bedroom suites have two bathrooms. Room service is provided by Shabeen, the hotel's in-house Caribbean restaurant.

MODERATE

AVALON HOTEL, 700 Ocean Dr., Miami Beach, FL 33139. Tel. 305/538-0133, or toll free 800/933-3306. Fax 305/534-0258. 60 rms. A/C TV TEL

$ Rates (including continental breakfast): Oct 15–May 15, $110–$150 single or double. May 16–Oct 14, $70–$125 single or double. Additional person $10 extra. 10% discount for stays of seven days or more. Weekly packages available. AE, MC, V. **Parking:** $6.

The Avalon is an excellent example of classic art deco digs right on the beach. Occupying a pretty parcel that wraps around the corner of 7th Street, the hotel is striking both inside and out. Rooms are well decorated in traditional '30s style, and all are equipped with compact refrigerators, cable televisions, and individually controlled air conditioning. The hotel's modest lobby is occupied by a casual restaurant, best for sandwiches at lunch either inside or on the outdoor patio.

The experienced management, known for their excellent inns in Newport, Rhode Island, run this hotel with an even hand. If the Avalon is full, don't hesitate to accept a room in their other property, the Majestic, located across the street.

Dining/Entertainment: The lobby restaurant is a top pick in the area for an informal lunch or a relaxing snack. By night, the menu gets fancier, prices get higher, and the cozy bar becomes a romantic place to pass the time.

Services: Like other hotels on the strip, reception can arrange car rental, babysitting, hairstyling, and other services.

CAVALIER HOTEL AND CABANA CLUB, 1320 Ocean Dr., Miami Beach, FL 33139. Tel. 305/534-2135, or toll free 800/338-9076. Fax 305/531-5543. Telex 204978. 43 rms, 2 suites. A/C TV TEL

$ Rates (including continental breakfast): Oct–Apr, $135–$160 single or double; $180 suite. May–Sept, $105–$130 single or double; $160 suite. 10% service charge additional. AE, DC, DISC, MC, V.

★ This architectural masterpiece, built in 1936, was one of Ocean Drive's first art deco renovations. Completely restored in 1987, the Cavalier now sports central air conditioning, beautifully restored period furnishings, and an ultra-contemporary atmosphere recalling less-hurried times.

Popular with fashion-photography crews, rooms here are luxuriously carpeted, and guests are pampered with fluffy towels, fresh mineral water, and a newspaper every morning. Still, this place is no stuffed shirt. Like other area hotels, there are no parking attendants, no porters, and not a single tie in sight. The Cavalier is on the best strip on the beach, within walking distance of the area's most noted restaurants and clubs. Still, it's easy to get a quiet night's sleep here as the lobby is devoid of bars, bands, or restaurants.

A full continental breakfast buffet, including fresh fruit and croissants, is served in the breakfast room each morning.

Services: Reception can make arrangements for hair cutting, massage, limousine, and laundry services.

ESSEX HOUSE, 1001 Collins Ave., Miami Beach, FL 33139. Tel. 305/ 534-2700, or toll free 800/55-ESSEX. Fax 305/532-3827. 38 rms, 12 suites. A/C TV TEL

$ Rates (including continental breakfast): Oct–May, $100–$145 single or double; from $300 suite. June–Sept, $75–$125 single or double; from $250 suite. 10% service charge additional. Minimum stay two nights on weekends, three nights on holidays. AE, MC, V.

This art deco delight is one of South Beach's plushest gems. Now a TraveLodge affiliate, the pretty Essex House is the result of a painstaking restoration, a textbook example of the famous "Streamline Moderne" style, complete with large porthole windows, original etched glasswork, ziggurat arches, and detailed crown moldings. The solid oak bedroom furnishings are also original and, like many other details in this special hotel, were painstakingly restored.

Murphy's homey, personal touches include teddy bears on the beds, "touch-sensitive" lamps, and an extremely attentive staff. The Essex also features 24-hour reception, a high-tech piano in the lobby/lounge, and a state-of-the-art security system.

Located just one block from the ocean, this hotel is both romantic and spick-and-span clean. Smoking is not permitted in any of the rooms and, according to the hotel staff, children are "inappropriate" here.

Dining/Entertainment: The hotel's lobby/lounge is sort of an all-purpose room serving light lunches, afternoon tea, and evening cocktails. Pianists sometimes entertain.

Services: Limousine, babysitting, laundry service, evening turn-down.

HOTEL LESLIE AND HOTEL CARDOZO, 1244 and 1300 Ocean Dr., Miami Beach, FL 33139. Tel. 305/534-2135, or toll free 800/338-9076. Fax 305/531-5543. Telex 204978. 69 rms, 8 suites. A/C TV TEL

$ Rates (including continental breakfast): Oct–Apr, $105–$135 single or double; $225 suite. May–Sept, $85–$105 single or double; $190 suite. 10% service charge additional. AE, DC, DISC, MC, V.

★ Operated by Tecton Management, the Leslie and the Cardozo were among the first properties on Ocean Drive to undergo extensive renovation.

Designed by noted architect Albert Anis in 1937, the Leslie is one of the area's smallest and quietest hotels. The light and airy beds and bureaus that dominate the hotel's art nouveau interior are a departure from the building's distinct art deco design. Still, the modern furniture and whimsical wall hangings look right in place.

The 40-room Cardozo is equally cozy but, by contrast, contains original walnut furniture and a new, as yet unnamed lobby restaurant and bar. It was here that Frank Sinatra filmed the 1950s movie *Hole in the Head;* today the hotel's soft pastels still grace the background of many fashion shoots.

These hotels are among the best in Miami. Guests in each are pampered with free morning newspapers and a hearty continental breakfast buffet.

Services: Reception can make arrangements for hair cutting, massage, babysitting, limousine, and laundry services.

PARK CENTRAL HOTEL, 640 Ocean Dr., Miami Beach, FL 33139. Tel. 305/538-1611. Fax 305/534-7520. 80 rms. A/C TV TEL

$ Rates (including continental breakfast): Dec–Apr, $120–$165 single or double. May–Nov, $80–$125 single or double. Additional person $10 extra. AE, DISC, DC, MC, V.

The Park Central is an architectural masterpiece, and one of the prettiest art deco hotels on the beach. Built in 1937, and reestablished 50 years later by New York developer Tony Goldman, the hotel competently combines the sophisticated style of a bygone era with the excitement and services of a modern-day hotspot. The smallish rooms are comparable, both in size and appointments, to others on the block, all with color TVs and direct-dial phones.

Dining/Entertainment: The Borroco restaurant, in the lobby's rear, serves competent Italian food at moderate to high prices. Sip a cocktail in the lobby; it's a great place to see and be seen, especially on weekend nights when it's quite crowded.

Services: If you're staying in the hotel, Borroco delivers. Limousine, laundry, and other services can be arranged at reception.

BUDGET

CLAY HOTEL & YOUTH HOSTEL, 1438 Washington Ave., Miami Beach, FL 33139. Tel. 305/534-2988. Fax 305/673-0346. 180 beds.

$ Rates: $26–$31 single; $29–$35 double; $10–$14 per person in a multishare. Sheets $2 extra. Weekly rates available. MC, V.

A member of the International Youth Hostel Federation (IYHF), the Clay occupies a beautiful 1920s-style Spanish Mediterranean building at the corner of historic Espanola Way. Like other IYHF members, this hostel is open to all ages and is a great place to meet like-minded travelers. The usual smattering of Australians, Europeans, and other budget travelers make this place the best clearinghouse of "inside" travel information in Miami. Even if you don't stay here, you might want to check out the ride board and make some friends.

Understandably, rooms here are basic. Reservations are essential for hotel rooms year-round, and recommended from December through April for all accommodations. The above rates reflect accommodations with and without air conditioning.

KENT HOTEL, 1131 Collins Ave., Miami Beach, FL 33139. Tel. 305/531-6771. Fax 305/531-0720. 56 rms. A/C TV TEL

$ Rates (including continental breakfast): Oct 15–May 15, $65–$80 single or double. May 16–Oct 14, $45–$70 single or double. Weekly discounts available. AE, MC, V.

The well-located Kent is an excellent example of the way hotel prices drop dramatically when you get away from Ocean Drive. Typically art deco, the squat Kent is not fancy, and is elegant only in a historical kind of way. Still, the hotel is comfortable and full of character. Breakfast is served both inside and on the porch, and street parking is always available.

MARSEILLES DECO BEACH HOTEL, 1741 Collins Ave., Miami Beach, FL 33139. Tel. 305/538-5711, or toll free 800/327-4739. Fax 305/673-1006. 104 rms, 6 suites. A/C TV TEL

$ Rates (including continental breakfast): Dec 21–Easter, $65–$70 single or double, $70 single or double with kitchenette; $75 suite. Easter–Dec 20, $45–$50 single or double, $50 single or double with kitchenette; $55 suite. Additional person $5 extra. Children under 8 stay free in parents' room. AE, DC, MC, V. **Parking:** $4.

A skyscraper by local standards, this pretty and basic hotel is not one of the area's fanciest, but it is well located, well run, and extremely well priced. The hotel's furnishings have recently been updated, and all rooms come equipped with a refrigerator and remote-control television. The Marseille's lobby café, a casual eatery with light American food, is welcoming, but a short walk in almost any direction will put you right in the middle of some of the area's hottest nightspots and eateries.

PARK WASHINGTON HOTEL, 1020 Washington Ave., Miami Beach, FL 33139. Tel. 305/532-1930. Fax 305/672-6706. 35 rms, 15 suites. A/C TV TEL

$ Rates: Nov–Apr, $59–$79 single or double; $139–$180 suite. May–Oct, $49–$69 single or double; $129–$170 suite. Additional person $10 extra. Children stay free in parents' room. AE, MC, V.

The Park Washington, a newly refurbished, large hotel offers some of the best values in South Beach. Located three blocks from the ocean, this hotel is trying to make a name for itself by offering good-quality accommodations at incredible prices. It's not too fancy here. But unlike many other hotels in the area that accept long-term residents, this hostelry is strictly geared toward tourists.

Originally designed in the 1930s by Henry Hohauser, one of the beach's most famous architects, the new Park Washington reopened only in 1989. Most of the rooms have original furnishings, and include color TVs, direct-dial telephones, refrigerators, and individual air conditioning and heating. Single rooms have single beds.

The Park Washington recently incorporated the adjacent deco Taft House and Kenmore hotels into its burgeoning real estate portfolio. The three properties are connected by unified landscaping, consistent quality, and an honest value-oriented philosophy.

THE SURFCOMBER, 1717 Collins Ave., Miami Beach, FL 33139. Tel. 305/532-7715, or toll free 800/336-4264. Fax 305/532-7280. 194 rms. A/C TV TEL

$ Rates (including continental breakfast): Dec 15–Apr 15, $70–$110 single or double. Apr 16–Dec 14, $60–$100 single or double. Additional person $10 extra. Kitchenettes $5 per day extra. Children under 15 stay free in parents' room. Monthly and seasonal rates, and senior discounts available. AE, CB, DISC, DC, MC, V.

Family-owned since 1949, the Surfcomber has been one of the art deco district's traditional standbys since the beginning. Well located and fronting 150 feet of beach, the hotel has been undergoing continual renovations for years. Some rooms are definitely more desirable than others, but all feature direct-dial phones and in-room movies. Refrigerators are available upon request.

Hotel services include a coffee shop, a gift shop, a health-food restaurant, and an outdoor bar alongside an Olympic-size heated swimming pool.

SURFSIDE, BAL HARBOUR & SUNNY ISLES

The residents of Surfside, Bal Harbour, and Sunny Isles like to think of their towns as more exclusive and sedate than the overpopulated, frenetic Miami Beach to the south. In reality, though, these towns are so similar to Miami Beach that most of their hotels use Miami Beach in their addresses. However, they're significantly farther than Miami Beach from Coconut Grove and downtown. On the plus side, the beaches here are just as good as Miami Beach's, and hotel prices are some of the lowest in Miami.

EXPENSIVE

SHERATON BAL HARBOUR BEACH RESORT, 9701 Collins Ave., Bal Harbour, FL 33154. Tel. 305/865-7511, or toll free 800/325-3535. Fax 305/864-2601. Telex 519355. 625 rms, 50 suites. A/C MINIBAR TV TEL

$ Rates: Dec 12–Apr, $240–$300 single or double; May–Sept, $165–$235 single or double; Oct–Dec 11 $250–$320 single or double. Suites $500 year-round. Additional person $25 extra. Children under 18 stay free in parents' room. Weekend and other packages, and senior discounts available. AE, CB, DC, DISC, MC, V. **Parking:** $9.

This hotel has the best location in Bal Harbour, on the ocean and across the street

FROMMER'S COOL FOR KIDS: HOTELS

Doral Ocean Beach Resort (see p. 55) The Doral provides child care and a complimentary children's activity center.

Fontainebleau Hilton Hotel (see p. 58) Offering play groups and child care during holiday periods, the Fountainebleau has a waterfall swimming pool that's a child's dream come true.

Sonesta Beach Hotel (see p. 67) The Sonesta offers a "Just Us Kids" program and a free, supervised play group for children 5 to 13. Experienced counselors lead morning field trips as well as daily beach games and evening activities.

from the swanky Bal Harbour Shops. It's one of the nicest Sheratons I've seen, with large, well-decorated rooms and a two-story glass-enclosed atrium lobby. A spectacular staircase wraps itself around a cascading fountain full of wished-upon pennies.

One side of the hotel caters to corporations, complete with ballrooms and meeting facilities, but the main sections of the hotel are relatively uncongested and removed from the convention crowd. A full complement of aquatic playthings can be rented on the beach, including sailboats and jet skis.

Dining/Entertainment: Four restaurants and lounges.

Services: Room service, laundry, currency exchange.

Facilities: Two swimming pools, two tennis courts, water-sports concession, gift shop.

MODERATE

THE PALMS, 9449 Collins Ave., Surfside, FL 33154. Tel. 305/865-3551, or toll free 800/327-6644, 800/843-6974 in Canada. Fax 305/861-6596. 120 rms, 50 efficiencies. A/C TV TEL

$ Rates: Dec 16–Easter, $115–$135 single or double; from $185 suite. Easter–Dec 15, $85–$90 single or double; from $130 suite. Additional person $10 extra. Children stay free in parents' room. Weekly rates available. AE, MC, V. **Parking:** Free.

The Palms is stereotypical Miami Beach. The majority of the guests here are retired. The lobby activity board advertises times for the day's shuffleboard tournaments, and nightlife usually centers around a singer who performs Eddie Fisher standards.

The hotel's management is intent on widening the hotel's popularity, and staying here can be really fun. Rooms are basic but comfortable; many have balconies overlooking the large pool and adjacent waterside bar. Located in the Surfside/Bal Harbour area of Miami Beach, the Palms is recommended for any traveler who wants to stay on the ocean—but still stay on a budget.

BUDGET

CORONADO MOTEL, 9501 Collins Ave., Surfside, FL 33154. Tel. 305/866-1625. 41 rms. A/C TV TEL

$ Rates: Jan 16–Mar 14, $69–$90 single or double. May–Dec 14, $44–$69 single or double. Dec 23–Jan 2, $75–$125 single or double. The rest of the year, $59–$80 single or double. Additional person $8 extra in winter, $5 extra in summer. Children stay free in parents' room. AE, CB, DC, DISC, MC, V.

Just one block from the Bal Harbour shops, the Coronado offers good budget accommodations with an excellent oceanfront location. The motel seems a bit lax when it comes to security, and is not the prettiest in the land—dwarfed by larger properties on either side. On the plus side, the freshwater pool is heated in the winter, and there's a refrigerator in every room. The motel is on the corner of 95th Street.

DESERT INN, 17201 Collins Ave., Sunny Isles, FL 33160. Tel. 305/947-0621, or toll free 800/327-6361, 800/223-5836 in Canada. 54 rms, 50 efficiencies. A/C TV TEL

$ Rates: Dec 19–Jan and Apr, $55–$80 single or double. Feb–Mar, $69–$90 single or double. May–Dec 18, $40–$70 single or double. Efficiencies $10 extra. Additional person $10 extra. Children under 14 stay free in parents' room. MC, V.

The Desert Inn stands out for its life-size horse-drawn covered wagon sculpture in front and its free tennis court out back. In between are a kidney-shaped pool, laundry facilities, minigolf, shuffleboard, a dining room, patio bar, and typical double rooms and efficiencies. There's also an outdoor beach shower and a large children's pool. The parking lot is surrounded by gates for additional security.

DRIFTWOOD RESORT MOTEL, 17121 Collins Ave., Sunny Isles, FL 33160. Tel. 305/944-5141, or toll free 800/327-1263. 118 efficiencies. A/C TV TEL

$ Rates: Dec 20–Jan 10, $62–$88 efficiency for one or two. Jan 11–31, $58–$78 efficiency for one or two. Feb–Apr 11, $78–$98 efficiency for one or two. Apr 12–May 2, $52–$80 efficiency for one or two. May 3–Dec 19, $33–$65 efficiency for one or two. Additional person $10 extra. Children under 12 stay free in parents' room. AE, DC, MC, V.

The Driftwood's dated but clean rooms are all efficiencies, equipped with either stoves or microwaves, and utensils. The motel's basic, budget-quality rooms are just steps from two shuffleboard courts, laundry facilities, and a parking lot. The homely lobby encompasses a restaurant serving surf-and-turf meals. The motel is located smack in the middle of Motel Row; its pool directly overlooks the ocean, and is surrounded by plenty of lounge chairs which can be rented for $2 per day.

HOTEL HILLYARD, 9541 Collins Ave., Surfside, FL 33154. Tel. 305/866-7351, or toll free 800/327-1413, 800/453-4333 in Canada. Fax 305/864-3045. Telex 808165. 2 rms, 28 suites. A/C TV TEL

$ Rates: Dec 18–Jan 18 and Mar 20–May 1, $56 single or double; $66–$86 suite. Jan 19–Mar 19, $66 single or double; $76–$94 suite. May 2–June 22 and Sept 3–Dec 17, $42 single or double; $47–$66 suite. June 23–Sept 2, $46 single or double; $52–$72 suite. AE, CB, DC, DISC, MC, V.

This U-shaped motel is typical of the area in price and architecture. It's been around a long time, and it shows. Atypical, however, is the emphasis on well-stocked suites, complete with bedroom, kitchen, living room, and dining area. The units are well equipped with plates, pots, a toaster, and even an ironing board. Oceanfront corner room no. 36 is best. There's a small, heated swimming pool and laundry facilities.

OCEAN ROC, 19505 Collins Ave., Sunny Isles, FL 33160. Tel. 305/931-7600, or toll free 800/327-0553. Fax 305/866-5881. 70 rms, 25 efficiencies. A/C TV TEL

$ Rates: Jan 15–Mar 15, $60 single or double. Mar 16–Apr 15 and Dec 15–Jan 14, $42–$56 single or double. Apr 16–Dec 14, $32–$40 single or double. Efficiencies $6 extra. Additional person $6 extra. Children stay free in parents' room. Special rates for longer stays. AE, CB, DC, MC, V. **Parking:** Free.

The Ocean Roc is the last motel on Collins Avenue before the Dade County line. Its simple, three-story, rectangular shape allows for only eight oceanfront rooms, while the others have ocean views and sweeping parking-lot vistas. Rooms are basic, most with two double beds. In the 1960s the motel's angled exterior lines probably looked futuristic. Today it's a bit outdated, but the prices can hardly be beat. There's no beach—the ocean comes right up to the pool deck where guests can lounge on $2-per-day rental chairs and children can frolic in the wading pool. The motel has a small coffee shop and laundry facilities on the premises.

SUEZ OCEANFRONT RESORT, 18215 Collins Ave., Sunny Isles, FL 33160. Tel. 305/932-0661, or toll free 800/327-5278, or 800/432-3661 in Florida. Fax 305/937-0058. 150 rms. A/C TV TEL

$ Rates: Jan 19–Apr, $65–$93 single or double. July–Sept 2 and Nov–Dec 19, $50–$72 single or double. Dec 20–Jan 3, $62–$93 single or double. Jan 4–18, $59–$85 single or double. May–June and Sept 3–Oct, $45–$67 single or double. Kitchenette units $15 extra. Additional person $10 extra. Children under 16 stay free in parents' room. AE, DC, MC, V.

Guarded by an undersized replica of Egypt's famed Sphinx, the campy Suez offers nice rooms and lounges and some of the best motel facilities on the beach—all at highly competitive rates. Following a fairly strict orange-and-yellow motif, the motel is more reminiscent of a fast-food restaurant than ancient Egypt. The grass umbrellas over beach lounges and the Spanish-Mediterranean–style fountains in the courtyard add to the confused decor. The motel's lush grounds encompass three shuffleboard courts, two large swimming pools, a small sauna, one lighted tennis court, and half a basketball court. There's also a kiddie pool and a beachfront children's playground.

Most rooms have two double beds, clock radios, and hairdryers, while others with kitchenettes have gas stoves, sinks, and dishes. The motel's large restaurant overlooks the ocean and features a nightly $16 all-you-can-eat buffet.

KEY BISCAYNE

This first island in Florida's Keys chain is the water-sports capital of Miami. Palms sway over busy beaches while windsurfers, jet-skiers, and sailboats ply the waters just off shore. There are only a handful of hotels here, though several more are planned. All are on the beach, and room rates are uniformly high. There are no budget listings here, but if you can afford it, Key Biscayne is a great place to stay. The island is far enough from the mainland to make it feel like a secluded tropical paradise, yet close enough to downtown to take advantage of everything Miami has to offer.

EXPENSIVE

SILVER SANDS OCEANFRONT MOTEL, 301 Ocean Dr., Key Biscayne, FL 33149. Tel. 305/361-5441. 50 efficiency apts, 4 cottages. A/C TV TEL

$ Rates: Oct 22–Dec 17, $79–$149 standard apt. Dec 18–Apr 22, $115–$139 standard apt. Apr 23–Sept 3, $79–$89 standard apt. Sept 4–Oct 21, $72–$89 standard apt. Year-round, $149–$215 oceanfront apt. Additional person $10 extra. AE, MC, V. **Parking:** Free.

The modest Silver Sands motel seems out of place on its million-dollar parcel, sandwiched between two luxury high-rises. The owners know that this is a special place, so room rates are not particularly low. Still, the rooms are priced well below the name-brand accommodations next door.

Accommodations here are basic—they probably haven't changed much since the 1960s. The standard efficiency apartments have small kitchenettes, and visitors can decide between a room facing the courtyard or one overlooking the parking lot (there's no view from either). The oceanfront apartments are some of the most sought-after rooms in Miami, popular with those in-the-know. Although they're not particularly cheap, they are as close to the ocean as you can get without getting wet, and the whispering surf assures a good night's sleep. The motel's duplex cottages offer more room and larger kitchens. They're a nice alternative to regular hotel rooms, but pale next to the oceanfront accommodations.

Dining/Entertainment: The Sandbar Restaurant, with a deck right on the beach, is one of Miami's most attractive hidden treasures.

Facilities: Olympic-size heated swimming pool.

SONESTA BEACH HOTEL, 350 Ocean Dr., Key Biscayne, FL 33149. Tel. 305/361-2021, or toll free 800/SONESTA. Fax 305/361-3096. Telex 519303. 269 rms, 16 suites, 15 villas. A/C MINIBAR TV TEL

$ Rates: Dec 18–Apr, $245–$329 single or double; from $550 suite. June–Sept, $155–$250 single or double; from $465 suite. May and Oct–Dec 17, $205–$260 single or double; from $505 suite. Year-round, $395–$900 villa (five-night minimum). Additional person $35 extra. Children stay free in parents' room. Packages available. AE, CB, DC, DISC, MC, V. **Parking:** $4.50.

The Sonesta's dominating modern oceanfront pyramid is the sort of structure most communities tend to protest against when building plans are put forward, since it permanently changes the nature of the town. But now that it's done, enjoy! This place is definitely deluxe, and its balconied beachfront rooms are some of the best in Miami. Accommodations are excellent, but it's the hotel's spectacular location that justifies its high prices.

Services aside, the nicest thing about the Sonesta is its lack of pretension. No one ever forgets that this is a beach resort, lending these lodgings a sort of casual luxuriousness.

The hotel's luxurious villas come with a full kitchen (complete with beverages and breakfast foods), laundry facilities, daily chamber service, and a large, private heated pool. Parents with kids will appreciate the hotel's "Just Us Kids" program, a free, supervised play group for children 5 to 13. Experienced counselors lead morning field trips as well as daily beach games and evening activities.

Dining/Entertainment: The hotel's four restaurants include the Rib Room, and Two Dragons, with Japanese and Chinese cuisine, plus a snack shop/deli. Desires nightclub features daily happy hours and dancing at night.

Services: Room service, laundry service, currency exchange, car rental, complimentary children's programs.

Facilities: Olympic-size heated swimming pool, 10 tennis courts (3 lighted), water-sports concession, bicycle rentals, beauty salon, three gift shops, travel agency, health club (with Jacuzzi, sauna, and steam rooms).

COCONUT GROVE

This intimate enclave hugs the shores of Biscayne Bay just south of U.S. 1. The Grove offers ample nightlife, excellent restaurants, and beautiful surroundings. Unfortunately, all the hotels are expensive. But even if you don't stay here, you'll surely want to spend a night or two exploring the area.

EXPENSIVE

DOUBLETREE HOTEL AT COCONUT GROVE, 2649 S. Bayshore Dr., Coconut Grove, FL 33133. Tel. 305/858-2500, or toll free 800/528-0444. Fax 305/858-5776. 172 rms, 18 suites. A/C TV TEL

$ Rates: Jan–Mar, $129 single; $139–$189 double; from $209 suite. Apr–Dec, $119 single; $129–$139 double; from $149 suite. Additional person $10 extra. AARP and AAA discounts; weekend and other packages available. AE, CB, DC, DISC, MC, V. **Parking:** $8.

Doubletree hotels are known as business hotels. And although this property is a good choice for working travelers, its superior location and relatively reasonable rates make it an excellent choice for vacationers as well.

Standard rooms are not particularly fancy, but they're more than adequate. Suites are large and pretty and feature floor-to-ceiling windows. On higher floors, guests are treated to sweeping views of Biscayne Bay and Coconut Grove.

Dining/Entertainment: The Café Brasserie, just off the lobby, offers an excellent breakfast buffet and relaxed all-day dining. There are bars both inside and poolside.

Services: Laundry service, complimentary welcoming chocolate-chip cookies, complimentary van service to local shops.

Facilities: Outdoor heated swimming pool, two lighted tennis courts; sailing, fishing, and boat docks just across the street.

GRAND BAY HOTEL, 2669 S. Bayshore Dr., Coconut Grove, FL 33133. Tel. 305/858-9600, or toll free 800/327-2788. Fax 305/858-1532. Telex 441370. 132 rms, 49 suites. A/C MINIBAR TV TEL

$ Rates: Oct–May, $220–$275 single or double; from $300 suite. June–Sept, $175–$245 single or double; from $300 suite. Additional person $15 extra. Packages available. AE, CB, DC, MC, V. **Parking:** $8.

⭐ The Grand Bay opened in 1983 and immediately won praise as one of the fanciest hotels in the world. Designed by the Nichols Partnership, a local architectural firm, and outfitted with the highest-quality interiors, this stunning pyramid-shaped hotel is a masterpiece both inside and out.

Rooms are luxurious, featuring high-quality linens; comfortable, overstuffed love seats and chairs; a large writing desk; and all the amenities you'd expect in deluxe accommodations. Bathrooms have hairdryers, robes, telephones, and more towels than you'll know what to do with. Original art and armfuls of fresh flowers are generously displayed throughout.

There is no check-in counter here; guests are escorted to a goldleaf-trimmed antique desk and encouraged to relax with a glass of champagne while they fill out the forms. The Grand Bay consistently attracts wealthy high-profile people, and it basks in its image as a rendezvous for royalty, socialites, and superstars. Indeed, the list of rich and famous who regularly walk through the lobby is endless. Guests come here to be pampered, to see and be seen.

Dining/Entertainment: The hotel's Grand Café is one of the top-rated restaurants in Miami. Drinks are served in the Ciga Bar and the Lobby Lounge, where a traditional afternoon tea is served from 3 to 6pm.

Services: 24-hour room service, 24-hour concierge, complimentary welcoming champagne, limousine service, same-day laundry and dry cleaning.

Facilities: Outdoor freshwater pool, health club, beauty salon, gift shop.

MAYFAIR HOUSE HOTEL, 3000 Florida Ave., Coconut Grove, FL 33133. Tel. 305/441-0000, or toll free 800/433-4555. 182 suites. A/C MINIBAR TV TEL

$ Rates: Dec 16–May, $230–$525 suite for one or two; from $600 penthouse suite. June–Dec 15, $180–$445 suite for one or two; from $600 penthouse suite. Additional person $35 extra. Packages available. AE, DC, DISC, MC, V. **Parking:** $9.50.

Situated inside Coconut Grove's posh Mayfair Shops complex, the all-suite Mayfair House is about as centrally located as you can get. Each guest suite has been individually designed, and no two are identical. All are extremely comfortable, and some suites are even opulent. Most of the more expensive accommodations include a private, outdoor, Japanese-style hot tub. Top-floor terraces offer good views, and all are hidden from the street by leaves and latticework.

The hotel contains several no-smoking suites and about 50 rooms with antique pianos. Since the lobby is in a shopping mall, recreation is confined to the roof, where a small swimming pool, sauna, and snack bar are located.

Dining/Entertainment: There is a relaxed café in the lobby. The Mayfair Grill is more formal, and there's also a rooftop snack bar.

Services: 24-hour room service, twice-daily maid service, complimentary glass of champagne upon arrival, discount shopping card for stores below, laundry service, child care.

Facilities: Rooftop pool and Jacuzzi, beauty salon, travel agency, shopping arcade.

CORAL GABLES

Coconut Grove eases into Coral Gables, which extends north toward Miami International Airport. The Gables, as it's affectionately known, was one of Miami's original planned communities, and it's still one of the city's prettiest. Staying here means being close to the shops along Miracle Mile as well as to some of Miami's nicest homes. Like other wealthy communities, Coral Gables doesn't offer much in the way of budget accommodations, but if you can afford it, hotels here are great places to stay.

EXPENSIVE

COLONNADE HOTEL, 180 Aragon Ave., Coral Gables, FL 33134. Tel. 305/441-2600, or toll free 800/533-1337. Fax 305/445-3929. 140 rms, 17 bilevel suites. A/C MINIBAR TV TEL

$ Rates: May–Dec, $215–$245 single or double; from $445 suite. Jan–Apr, $265–$305 single or double; from $445 suite. Packages available. AE, CB, DC, DISC, MC, V. **Parking:** $8.50.

The Colonnade occupies part of a large, historic building, originally built by Coral Gables's inventor, George Merrick. Faithful to its original style, the hotel is a successful amalgam of new and old, with emphasis on the former. An escalator brings guests from street level to the hotel's grand rotunda entrance. The lobby is just down the hall, but pause for a moment and admire the pink-and-black marble floor, domed roof, and stylish column supports. This is the most eye-catching feature of Mr. Merrick's original building.

Guest rooms are outfitted with historic photographs, marble counters, gold-finished faucets, and understated furnishings worthy of the hotel's rates. Champagne upon arrival and morning coffee or tea are complimentary.

Dining/Entertainment: The Aragon Café is one of the area's most celebrated restaurants, while the hotel's Doc Dammers Saloon is probably the best happy-hour haunt for the 30-something crowd. There is frequent live entertainment.

Services: 24-hour room service, child care, car rental, complimentary shoe shine, same-day dry-cleaning and laundry service, evening turn-down service.

Facilities: Heated outdoor swimming pool, Jacuzzi, hot tub, rooftop fitness center.

HYATT REGENCY CORAL GABLES, 50 Alhambra Plaza, Coral Gables, FL 33134. Tel. 305/441-1234, or toll free 800/233-1234. Fax 305/443-7702. 242 rms, 50 suites. A/C MINIBAR TV TEL

$ Rates (including buffet breakfast): $145–$235 single; $165–$260 double; from $200 suite. Additional person $25 extra. Packages and senior discounts available. AE, CB, DISC, DC, MC, V. **Parking:** $8.50 valet, $7 self-parking.

High on style, comfort, and price, this Hyatt is part of Coral Gables's Alhambra, an office-hotel complex with a Mediterranean motif. The building itself is gorgeous, designed with pink stone, arched entrances, grand courtyards, and tile roofs. Inside you'll find overstuffed chairs on marble floors, surrounded by opulent antiques and chandeliers. The hotel opened in 1987, but like many historical buildings in the neighborhood, the Alhambra attempts to mimic something much older, and much farther away.

Rooms are a good size and are well appointed, outfitted with everything you'd expect from a top hotel—terry robes and all. Most furnishings are antique.

Dining/Entertainment: A restaurant serving decent, high-priced food is augmented by a good lounge and nightclub.

Services: 24-hour room service, laundry service, babysitting on request.

Facilities: Health club with Nautilus equipment, heated outdoor swimming pool, Jacuzzi, two saunas, gift shop.

MODERATE

HOTEL PLACE ST. MICHEL, 162 Alcazar Ave., Coral Gables, FL 33134. Tel. 305/444-1666, or toll free 800/247-8526. Fax 305/529-0074. 24 rms, 3 suites. A/C TV TEL

$ Rates (including continental breakfast): $109 single; $125 double; $165 suite. Additional person $10 extra. Children under 12 stay free in parents' room. Senior discounts available. AE, CB, DC, MC, V. **Parking:** $7.

It's always a pleasure to stay in this unusual cultured gem in the heart of Coral Gables. The accommodations and hospitality are straight out of old-world Europe, complete with dark wood-paneled walls, cozy beds, beautiful antiques, and a quiet elegance that seems startlingly out of place in hip, future-oriented Miami. Everything here is charming, from the parquet floors to the paddle fans; one-of-a-kind furnishings make each room special. Guests are treated to fresh fruit baskets upon arrival, evening turn-down service, and complimentary continental breakfast each morning.

Hotel Place St. Michel is small, but in no way is it insignificant. Popular with visiting literati and cognoscenti, the hotel may well be the most romantic spot in the region. The ground-floor restaurant has an equally committed clientele and is widely regarded as one of Miami's finest French restaurants.

DOWNTOWN

Understandably, most downtown hotels cater primarily to business travelers. But this hardly means that tourists should overlook these well-located, good-quality accommodations. Miami's downtown is small, so getting around is relatively easy. Locating here means staying between the beaches and the Grove, and being within minutes of the Bayside Marketplace and the Port of Miami.

Although business hotel prices are often high, and less prone to seasonal markdowns, quality and service are also of a high standard. Look for weekend discounts, when offices are closed and rooms often go empty.

EXPENSIVE

HOTEL INTER-CONTINENTAL MIAMI, 100 Chopin Plaza, Miami, FL 33131. Tel. 305/577-1000, or toll free 800/332-4246. Fax 305/577-0384. Telex 153127. 612 rms, 34 suites. A/C MINIBAR TV TEL
$ Rates: Jan 16–May, $199–$259 single; $229–$289 double; from $329 suite. June–Sept, $159–$219 single; $189–$249 double; from $450 suite. Oct–Jan 15, $179–$239 single; $209–$269 double; from $450 suite. Additional person $20 extra. Weekend and other packages available. AE, CB, DC, MC, V. **Parking:** $10.

The Hotel Inter-Continental Miami is both an architectural masterpiece and, arguably, the financial district's swankiest hotel. Both inside and out, the hotel boasts more marble than a mausoleum. The five-story lobby features a marble centerpiece sculpture by Henry Moore and is topped by a pleasing skylight. Plenty of plants, palm trees, and brightly colored wicker chairs add charm and enliven the otherwise stark space. Brilliant building and bay views add luster to already posh rooms that are outfitted with every convenience known to hoteldom.

Dining/Entertainment: The hotel's three restaurants cover all price ranges and are complemented by two full-service lounges.

Services: 24-hour room service, concierge, laundry service, currency exchange, mobile phone, car rental.

Facilities: Heated outdoor swimming pool, access to an off-premises health spa, jogging track, gift shop, travel agency, guest laundry room.

OMNI INTERNATIONAL HOTEL, 1601 Biscayne Blvd., Miami, FL 33132. Tel. 305/374-0000, or toll free 800/THE-OMNI. Fax 305/374-0020. Telex 515005. 489 rms, 46 suites. A/C MINIBAR TV TEL
$ Rates: Jan–Apr, $150–$170 single; $165–$185 double; from $225 suite. May–Dec, $140–$160 single; $155–$175 double; from $225 suite. Additional person $20 extra. Senior discounts, weekend and other packages available. AE, CB, DC, DISC, MC, V. **Parking:** $10.

One of downtown's best-known megahotels, this glass-and-chrome structure offers contemporary accommodations overlooking the Venetian Causeway and Biscayne Bay. Built in 1977 atop a large multistory shopping mall, the hotel has undergone several renovations and is still one of the luxury leaders in Miami's ever-growing hotel marketplace.

Rooms are traditionally decorated with modest but comfortable furnishings and deluxe fittings like bathroom telephones. But the Omni's most important asset is the 150-plus shopping complex below, a convenience that includes a popular multiplex cinema.

Dining/Entertainment: The Fish Market, the hotel's flagship lobby-level restaurant, is an excellent, elegant place for seafood. A coffee shop offers simpler meals and snacks. Lobby and poolside lounges are also offered.

Services: 24-hour room service, child care, currency exchange, car rental, laundry, free beach shuttle, turn-down service.

Facilities: Fifth-floor heated outdoor pool, beauty salon, gift shop; shopping mall below.

SHERATON BRICKELL POINT MIAMI, 495 Brickell Ave., Miami, FL

33131. Tel. 305/373-6000, or toll free 800/325-3535. Fax 305/374-2279. Telex 6811701. 584 rms, 14 suites. A/C TV TEL

$ Rates: Jan–Apr, $149–$159 single; $159–$179 double; from $305 suite. May–Dec, $119–$139 single; $129–$159 double; from $295 suite. Additional person $20 extra. Children under 18 stay free in parents' room. Senior discounts, weekend and other packages available. AE, CB, DC, DISC, MC, V. **Parking:** $7.50.

This downtown hotel's waterfront location is its greatest asset. Nestled between Brickell Park and Biscayne Bay, the Sheraton is set back from the main road and surrounded by a pleasant bayfront walkway.

Just as clean and reliable as other hotels in the Sheraton chain, the Brickell Point has a pretty location and good water views from most of the rooms, as well as all the amenities you'd expect from a hostelry in this class. The dozens of identical rooms are both well furnished and comfortable.

Dining/Entertainment: Ashley's serves continental and American cuisine overlooking Biscayne Bay. The Coco Loco Club is an indoor/outdoor bar with a good happy-hour buffet and comedy nights.

Services: Room service, car rental, weekday laundry service.

Facilities: Outdoor heated swimming pool, gift shop.

CAMPING

LARRY AND PENNY THOMPSON PARK, 12451 SW 184th St., Miami, FL 33177. Tel. 305/232-1049.

$ Rates: $14–$20 per site (for up to four people). MC, V.

This inland park encompasses over 270 acres and includes a large freshwater lake for swimming and fishing. Laundry facilities and a convenience store are also on the premises. The tent area is huge, and not separated into tiny sites.

From downtown, take U.S. 1 south to SW 184th Street. Turn right and follow the signs for about four miles. The park entrance is at 125th Avenue.

LONG-TERM STAYS

If you plan on visiting Miami for a month, a season, or more, think about renting a room in a long-term hotel in South Miami Beach, or a condominium apartment in Miami Beach, Surfside, Bal Harbour, or Sunny Isles. Rents can be extremely reasonable, especially during the off-season. And there's no comparison to a tourist hotel in terms of the amount of space you get for the same buck. A short note to the chamber of commerce in the area where you're looking will be answered with a list of availabilities (see "Information" in "Orientation," earlier in this chapter).

Many area real estate agents also handle short-term (minimum of one month) rentals. These include: **Century 21 Realty,** 3100 NW 77th Court, Miami, FL 33122; and **Keys Company Realtors,** 100 N. Biscayne Blvd., Miami, FL 33152 (tel. 305/371-3592).

4. DINING

One of the best things about traveling is finding new restaurants and sampling new foods. Packed with an enormous array of foreign and inventive restaurants, Miami will not disappoint. Dozens of different specialty kitchens represent a world of cuisines, and all are available in a variety of price ranges. In addition to Chinese, French, Thai, and Italian eateries, there are, not surprisingly, many area dining rooms specializing in Cuban, Caribbean, and Latin American food. In fact, Miami boasts some of the best cooking those regions have to offer; high demand and good prices attract some of the world's best chefs and ingredients.

Be sure to sample Miami's own regional American fare. Based on the California model, these inventive dishes rely heavily on seafood and citrus and are exemplified by creative recipes and fresh, local ingredients.

Keep an eye out for flavorful tropical fruits like mangoes, papayas, and Surinam cherries. Shellfish, including rock shrimp, clams, oysters, and bay and deep-sea scallops (the former are smaller and sweeter) are also regular menu items.

Most hotels in Miami do not include breakfast in their room rates, but many in South Miami Beach do. These are usually good-sized buffets with fresh fruit, cold cuts, rolls, croissants, coffee, and fresh-squeezed orange juice. At lunch, many business-oriented restaurants offer main courses priced well below those served at dinner. Restaurants often serve dinner until midnight or later.

To help you choose where to eat, restaurants below are divided first by area, then by price, using the following guide: "Very Expensive," more than $40 per person; "Expensive," $30 to $40 per person; "Moderate," $20 to $30 per person; "Inexpensive," $10 to $20 per person; and "Budget," less than $10 per person.

These categories reflect the price of the majority of dinner menu items and include an appetizer, main course, coffee, dessert, tax, and tip. Wine is not included. Whenever a special lunch menu is available—typically half the price of a full-course dinner—I have noted it in the heading of each listing.

MIAMI BEACH
VERY EXPENSIVE

THE DINING GALLERIES, in the Fontainebleau Hilton Hotel, 4441 Collins Ave. Tel. 538-2000.
  Cuisine: CONTINENTAL. **Reservations:** Recommended.
$ **Prices:** Sun brunch $25.50 per person. AE, CB, DC, MC, V.
  Open: Sun brunch 10am–3pm.
Ensconced deep inside Miami Beach's showiest hotel, the Dining Galleries' overindulgence seems somehow appropriate. *Note:* At press time the Dining Galleries restaurant was only open for Sunday brunch. (The restaurant was damaged during Hurricane Andrew; repairs are still being made.)

DOMINIQUE'S, in the Alexander All-Suite Luxury Hotel, 5225 Collins Ave. Tel. 865-6500.
  Cuisine: FRENCH/CONTINENTAL. **Reservations:** Recommended, especially at dinner.
$ **Prices:** Appetizers $8–$11; main courses $20–$30. AE, CB, DC, MC, V.
  Open: Daily 7am–11pm.
Dominique's is one of Miami Beach's best restaurants. Exorbitant and elegant, with heavy antique furniture and Oriental rugs, it boasts a good view of the Atlantic.

The menu spotlights a variety of wild-game appetizers that are not just novel, but tasty, too. They include such unusual dishes as buffalo sausage, tender alligator scaloppine, and fresh diamondback-rattlesnake salad. Still, it's the more traditional dishes like marinated rack of lamb chops and prime steak that keeps the regulars returning. Service is good, and the heavy French food, the menu's main feature, is consistently excellent. Jackets are requested for men at dinner.

THE FORGE RESTAURANT, 432 Arthur Godfrey Rd. (41st St.). Tel. 538-8533.
  Cuisine: AMERICAN. **Reservations:** Required.
$ **Prices:** Appetizers $6–$9; main courses $18–$25. AE, DC, MC, V.
  Open: Dinner only, Sun–Thurs 5pm–midnight, Fri–Sat 5pm–3am.
English oak paneling and Tiffany glass suggest high prices and haute cuisine, and that's exactly what you can expect from the remodeled Forge. Each elegant dining room possesses its own character, and features high ceilings, ornate chandeliers, and high-quality, conservative European artwork.

The Forge's huge American menu has a northern Italian bias, evidenced by a long list of creamy pasta appetizers. Equal attention is given to fish, veal, poultry, and beef dishes, many of which are prepared on the kitchen's all-important oak grill. Look for appetizers like oak-grilled tomatoes with mozzarella, or a simple oak-grilled main course of meat or fish. Finally, it's important to note that the Forge has one of Miami's

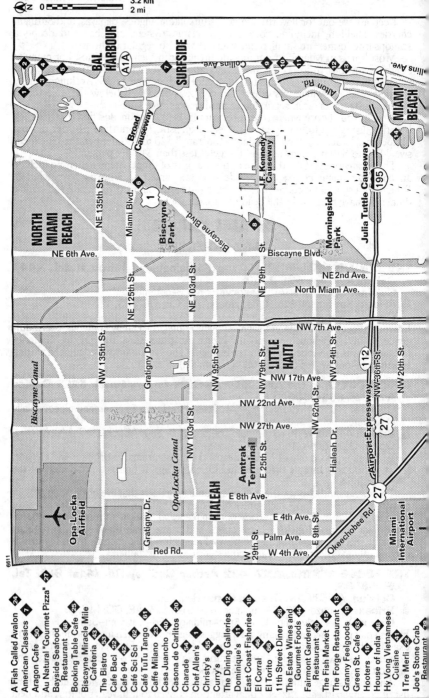

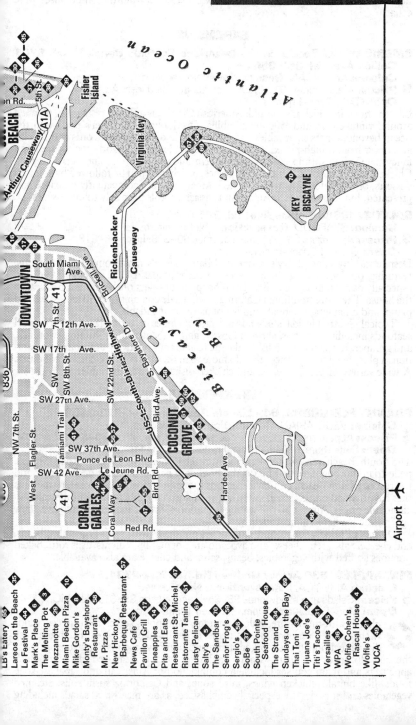

MIAMI AREA DINING

Atlantic Ocean

BEACH

Arthur Causeway A1A
on Rd.
5th St.
Fisher Island

Virginia Key

Rickenbacker Causeway

KEY BISCAYNE

DOWNTOWN
South Miami Ave.
41
SW 7th St.
7th-12th Ave.

SW 17th   Ave.
SW   SW 8th St.
SW 22nd St.
SW 27th Ave.
Brickell Ave.
S. Bayshore Dr.
US-1—South-Dixie-Highway
Bird Ave.

Biscayne Bay

836

NW 7th St.
West
Flagler St.
Tamiami Trail
SW 37th Ave.
Ponce de Leon Blvd.
SW 42 Ave.   Le Jeune Rd.
41
COCONUT GROVE
Bird Rd.
Hardee Ave.
1

CORAL GABLES
Coral Way
Bird Rd.
Red Rd.
95

Airport

LB's Eatery 65
Lareos on the Beach 55
Le Festival 44
Mark's Place 6
The Melting Pot 3
Mezzanotte
Miami Beach Pizza 10
Mike Gordon's 8
Monty's Bayshore Restaurant 58
Mr. Pizza 2
New Hickory Barbeque Restaurant 57
News Cafe 43
Pavillon Grill 17
Pineapples 66
Pita and Eats
Restaurant St. Michel 47
Ristorante Tanino 51
Rusty Pelican 67
Salty's 5
The Sandbar 70
Señor Frog's 59
Sergio's 56
SoBe 47
South Pointe Seafood House
The Strand 34
Sundays on the Bay 69
Thai Toni 32
Tijuana Joe's 26
Titi's Tacos 37
Versailles 45
WPA 38
Wolfie Cohen's Rascal House 4
Wolfie's 24
YUCA 49

best wine lists, encompassing about 280 pages selected from the on-premises wine cellar.

EXPENSIVE

AMERICAN CLASSICS, in the Dezerland Surfside Beach Hotel, 8701 Collins Ave. Tel. 865-6661.

Cuisine: AMERICAN. **Reservations:** Not required.
$ Prices: Main courses $11–$20; lunch about a third less. AE, MC, V.
Open: Daily 7am–11pm.

Like the hotel in which it's located, American Classics is a theme restaurant, planned around vintage cars and '50s memorabilia. Overlooking the hotel's pool, and the ocean beyond, diners sit at tables and booths made of dismantled Fords and Buicks, and order from a high-priced, like-minded menu. Simple seafood specials are given fancy names like shrimp scampi Duesenberg and American Graffiti surf and turf. Chicken and steak round off the main dishes, which can then be followed by assorted desserts, or "tailgaters," as they're called. Meals here are competently prepared and presented, but like the hotel, American Classics appeals primarily to enthusiasts.

SALTY'S, 10880 Collins Ave. Tel. 945-6065.

Cuisine: SEAFOOD. **Reservations:** Not required.
$ Prices: Appetizers $5–$11; main courses $9–$28; lunch $6–$18.
Open: Daily 11:30am–midnight.

Despite its silly name, Salty's is one of Miami Beach's most romantic restaurants, featuring outdoor dining on a covered waterfront patio. The eatery's large bar, especially popular at sunset, offers good happy-hour selections without a bad seat in the house. The more traditional seafaring motif inside contains over 50 tables, a grand piano, and a hanging rowboat, and is not as recommendable.

Typical South Florida surf-and-turf fare includes a veritable survey of local seafoods including scallops, shrimp, lobster, and crab, as well as salmon, swordfish, and grouper. Extremely fresh fish make the restaurant's relatively uninspired preparations a plus; avoid messy sauces that do more to mask than enhance natural goodness. A wide variety of pastas, steaks, and chicken dishes are also available.

INEXPENSIVE

GRANNY FEELGOODS, 649 Lincoln Road Mall. Tel. 673-0408.

Cuisine: VEGETARIAN. **Reservations:** Not required.
$ Prices: Appetizers $2–$5; main courses $3–$9; smoothies $3–$4. AE, MC, V.
Open: Sun–Thurs 7:30am–10pm, Fri–Sat 7:30am–11pm.

The South Beach renaissance has finally reached north to Lincoln Road Mall, a pedestrian thoroughfare that marks the boundary between the art deco district and the rest of Miami Beach. Granny Feelgoods is one of almost half a dozen restaurants that have opened on this street in the last year, and is notable for healthful meals and affordable prices. Almost all the seating is outdoors, on the mall itself, and live "new age" music is offered almost nightly.

Dozens of salads, soups, and sandwiches are made with fresh vegetables, beans, and cheese. Salsa, feta cheese, and avocado are popular ingredients, as is tofu. Baked potatoes stuffed with vegetables, beans, salsa, and cheese are also available.

PINEAPPLES, 530 Arthur Godfrey Rd. Tel. 532-9731.

Cuisine: AMERICAN. **Reservations:** Not accepted.
$ Prices: Salads and sandwiches $5–$6; main courses $8–$10. AE, MC, V.
Open: Mon–Fri 8:30am–10pm, Sat–Sun 10am–10pm.

Half health-food store, half restaurant, Pineapples serves fresh juices, sandwiches, and a variety of menu items, either to take out or eat in. In the busy dining section, an overworked staff distributes huge menus to patrons sitting at the half dozen or so plain wooden tables set atop a clean red-tile floor. Both appetizers and main courses include a combination of American and Japanese-style foods, like buffalo chicken wings, miso soup, and California sushi rolls. Steamed vegetables and stir-fries are especially emphasized, as are meal-sized salads including

FROMMER'S SMART TRAVELER: RESTAURANTS

1. Go ethnic—the city has some great inexpensive ethnic dining.
2. Eat your main meal at lunch when prices are lower—and you can taste the cuisine at the gourmet hot spots for a fraction of the dinner prices.
3. Watch the booze—it can add greatly to the cost of any meal.
4. Look for early-bird specials, which are commonplace in and around the city.
5. Keep an eye out for fixed-price menus, two-for-one specials, and other money-saving deals.

vegetable, chicken, pasta, pineapple, and more. The restaurant is located in the middle of a row of boutiques on the south side of bustling Arthur Godfrey Road.

BUDGET

CURRY'S, 7433 Collins Ave. Tel. 866-1571.
   Cuisine: AMERICAN. **Reservations:** Not accepted.
$ Prices: Meal $8–$11. MC, V.
   Open: Dinner only, daily 5–10pm.
Established in 1937, this large dining room on the ocean side of Collins Avenue is one of Miami Beach's oldest restaurants. Neither the restaurant's name nor the Polynesian wall decorations are indicative of the menu's offerings, which are straightforwardly American and reminiscent of the area's heyday. Broiled and fried-fish dishes are available, but the best selections, including steak, chicken, and ribs, come off the open charcoal grill perched by the front window.
   Prices are incredibly reasonable here, and all include an appetizer, soup, or salad, as well as a potato or vegetable, dessert, coffee or tea.

MIAMI BEACH PIZZA, 6954 Collins Ave. Tel. 866-8661.
   Cuisine: ITALIAN. **Reservations:** Not accepted.
$ Prices: Large cheese pizza $9.50; pasta $5–$6. MC, V.
   Open: Mon–Thurs 11am–midnight, Fri–Sat 11am–1am, Sun noon–midnight.
New York–style pizza is delivered free to most Miami Beach hotels. The cheesy pies are inexpensive and good. Other menu items include veal parmigiana, chicken cacciatore, meatball sandwiches, beer, and soda.

FROMMER'S COOL FOR KIDS: RESTAURANTS

American Classics *(see p. 76)* This is a theme restaurant, planned around vintage cars and '50s memorabilia. If you think your child would like to eat dinner inside a 1950s automobile, this is the place to go. The "surf and turf" menu is rounded off by a good assortment of desserts, or "tailgaters."

The Melting Pot *(see p. 88)* In this fondue joint diners dip chunks of bread into pots of sizzling cheese. It's definitely a fun way to eat, for kids as well as adults. But save room for dessert—chunks of pineapple, bananas, apples, and cherries are served with a creamy chocolate fondue for dipping.

Señor Frog's *(see p. 93)* This place is both fun and filling, featuring a house mariachi band and excellent food. The restaurant is right in the heart of Coconut Grove, so you can walk around and see the sights before or after dinner.

SOUTH MIAMI BEACH — THE ART DECO DISTRICT
EXPENSIVE

CAFFÈ MILANO, 850 Ocean Dr. Tel. 532-0707.
Cuisine: ITALIAN. **Reservations:** Recommended.
$ Prices: Appetizers $8–$15; main courses $10–$15 for pasta, $11–$14 for carpacci, $12–$23 for meat/fish dishes; lunch about 30% less. AE, MC, V.
Open: Lunch Wed–Mon 11am–5pm; dinner daily 7pm–midnight.
In South Miami Beach, Italian restaurants seem to change as fast as the seasons, but, hopefully, the Milano is here to stay. Even on a nice night the restaurant's requisite sidewalk seating might be passed up for a table in the bustling dining room where hardwood floors and original abstract art can make you feel as if you're eating in a Soho gallery.

The eccentric young proprietors own two restaurants in Milan, and staff this kitchen with trained Italian chefs. Prosciutto, bresaola (air-dried beef), and other meat antipasti precede a good pasta menu (tortelli are recommended) and an unusual selection of carpacci (thinly sliced raw or warmed meats). Fish, chicken, and veal dishes are conservatively prepared according to traditional Italian recipes.

The pretty marble bar that lines an entire wall of the restaurant stocks a full line of beverages, including 15 grappas.

I TRE MERLI, 1437 Washington Ave. Tel. 672-6702.
Cuisine: ITALIAN. **Reservations:** Recommended.
$ Prices: Appetizers $7–$10; pasta $10–$13; meat/fish dishes $16–$21. AE, CB, DC, MC, V.
Open: Dinner only, Sun–Thurs 6pm–1am, Fri–Sat 6pm–2am.
Immediately trendy upon opening in 1982, South Miami Beach's I Tre Merli is the spitting image of its popular sibling restaurant in New York's Soho. Under an unusually high ceiling are exposed red-brick walls lined with thousands of bottles of house-label wine. A second-floor loft overlooks the main dining room, where about 20 of the most coveted (and congested) tables are located.

The rather mainstream, strictly Italian menu augments all the traditional highlights like gnocchi (potato dumplings), spaghetti vongole (with clams), and veal scaloppine, with a few offbeat offerings like penne with artichokes, and shrimp and salmon with caviar sauce. While the food is not outstanding, it's good. And despite the restaurant's popularity, service is unhurried, as the staff knows that the ability to linger is what ultimately lures the patrons.

JOE'S STONE CRAB RESTAURANT, 227 Biscayne St. Tel. 673-0365.
Cuisine: SEAFOOD. **Reservations:** Not accepted.
$ Prices: $31.95 for jumbo crab claws, $23.95 for large claws. AE, CB, DC, MC, V.
Open: Lunch Tues–Sat 11:30am–2pm; dinner Sun–Thurs 5–10pm, Fri–Sat 5–11pm (until 11pm on Miami Heat home-game nights). **Closed:** Late May to early Oct.
Open since 1913 and steeped in tradition, this restaurant may be the most famous in Florida, as evidenced by long lines to get in. Other menu items are available, but to go to Joe's and not order stone crab is unthinkable. In fact, the restaurant is so identified with this single crustacean that it closes for the six months that the crabs are out of season. Stone crabs are available at other restaurants around Miami, but they just don't seem to taste as good as they do at the place where they were invented. If jumbo claws are available, splurge. Be warned: The wait can be long, and many readers have complained that the host gives preference to those who "tip" in advance. Lines are shortest Monday through Wednesday. The restaurant is at the corner of Biscayne Street and Washington Avenue. No shorts allowed.

MEZZANOTTE, 1200 Washington Ave. Tel. 673-4343.
Cuisine: ITALIAN. **Reservations:** Recommended.

$ Prices: Appetizers $7; main courses $12–$14 for pasta, $15–$25 for meat and fish. AE, CB, DC, MC, V.
Open: Dinner only, Sun–Thurs 6pm–midnight, Fri–Sat 6pm–2am.

Papparazzo charm is in full swing at this trendy-to-the-max corner bistro. Who cares if better food can be had at any number of places up the street? This is the place where the fashionable can see and be seen. The food is decent; traditional antipasti are followed by good veal chops, competent pastas, and simple meat dishes.

The large room is undivided for the best sightlines and easy table-hopping. An entire wall is mirrored so that no one's back is to the crowd, and a whip of neon around the ceiling keeps everyone bright enough to be seen. You might pass on dessert, but order a cappuccino; it's a small price to pay to linger.

SOUTH POINT SEAFOOD HOUSE, Washington Ave. Tel. 673-1708.
Cuisine: SEAFOOD. **Reservations:** Recommended.
$ Prices: Appetizers $5–$11; main courses $14–$34; lunch about half price. AE, DC, MC, V.
Open: Lunch Mon–Sat 11:30am–3pm; dinner Mon–Thurs 5–11pm, Fri–Sat 5pm–midnight, Sun 5–10:30pm; brunch Sun 11am–3pm.

The best thing about this restaurant is its location in South Pointe Park, at the southernmost tip of South Miami Beach. Here you can sit in front of Government Cut and watch the cruise and cargo ships slowly ease their way in and out of the Port of Miami.

The South Point Seafood House is casual, with several small dining rooms and lots of window seats. Appetizers include Florida alligator (which is not an endangered species) and bacon-wrapped shrimp, as well as raw-bar selections. Fish, in various guises, is the house specialty, but the kitchen gets marks for its tender steak and veal, too.

MODERATE

CASONA DE CARLITOS, 2232 Collins Ave. Tel. 534-7013.
Cuisine: ARGENTINEAN. **Reservations:** Not required.
$ Prices: Appetizers $7–$9; main courses $8–$10 for pasta, $9–$16 for meat and fish; lunch about half price. AE, CB, DC, DISC, MC, V.
Open: Sun–Thurs noon–midnight, Fri–Sat noon–1am.

Except for its unusually large size, the outside of this corner storefront is rather unassuming. The dining room inside is not very fancy either, opting instead for a casual atmosphere that complements the unpretentious, traditional kitchen. Menus are available in English, Spanish, German, French, and Portuguese, and they contain dozens upon dozens of traditional dishes.

Shrimp ceviche and a delicately marinated eggplant are two of the more unusual appetizers. These can be followed by baked fish smothered in a bleu-cheese sauce, chicken oreganato in wine sauce, or any one of a number of grilled meats and homemade pastas. The restaurant is located on the corner of 23rd Street, across from the Holiday Inn.

FAIRMONT GARDENS RESTAURANT, in the Fairmont Hotel, 1000 Collins Ave. Tel. 531-0050.
Cuisine: ITALIAN/CONTINENTAL. **Reservations:** Recommended, especially on weekends.
$ Prices: Appetizers $4–$6; main courses $10–$12 for pasta, $14–$16 for meat and fish. AE, CB, DC, MC, V.
Open: Dinner daily 6pm–midnight. (Happy hour Mon–Fri 4–7pm.)

The Fairmont's fancy, tropical outdoor courtyard is adjacent to a far less extravagant hotel, one block from the ocean in the art deco district. Brightly colored angled canvas canopies provide a light and airy roof over a multilevel, pastel-colored dining area. Indoor tables are also available, but are far less desirable on warm nights.

Traditional hot and cold appetizers are bolstered by island-inspired selections like hearts of palm salad and a house lobster ravioli. Main dishes are equally adventurous, highlighted by boneless chicken served with sweet red pimientos and flamed in cognac and cream, conservatively prepared steaks, and a variety of fresh fish and pasta dishes. The Fairmont features live music (often calypso) nightly.

A FISH CALLED AVALON, in the Avalon Hotel, 700 Ocean Dr. Tel. 532-1727.
   Cuisine: MIAMI REGIONAL. **Reservations:** Recommended.
$ Prices: Appetizers $6–$10; main courses $14–$22. AE, MC, V.
   Open: Dinner only, Sun–Thurs 6–11pm, Fri–Sat 6pm–1am.
There's something about this well-placed Ocean Drive restaurant that's almost surreal; dramatic paintings are softened by intimate specular light, and mellow pastels counterpoint huge, imposing windows. White linen cloths and matching chair covers highlight each table's centerpiece—a single tropical Siamese fighting fish swimming around in a small glass bowl.

   The menu changes nightly, but the emphasis is always on fresh local fish, grilled or roasted, served with creative seasonal sauces. Steak and chicken are always on the menu, as are soups like chilled mango-peach and cream of carrot.

   The Avalon's bar, a dramatically beautiful, intimately low-key lounge gets marks as one of the best little places to drink on the strip.

LAREOS ON THE BEACH, 820 Ocean Dr. Tel. 532-9577.
   Cuisine: CUBAN. **Reservations:** Recommended.
$ Prices: Appetizers $2–$9; main courses $7–$15; lunches $4–$7. AE, MC, V.
   Open: Sun–Thurs 11:30am–midnight, Fri–Sat 11:30am–1:30am.
Miami musical goddess Gloria Estefan has teamed with her favorite Cuban chef to create this ultra-stylish ethnic restaurant right in the heart of South Beach hustle. The restaurant's 1950s Cuba-meets-postmodern decor means a suspended ceiling with blue neon cloudlike cut-outs, and faux-finish walls decorated with vintage magazine covers. About two dozen well-dressed tables are arranged in front of a small bandstand where a lively salsa band regularly performs. There's also a beautiful bar that's less active than it should be, and excellent sidewalk seating.

   Few aficionados believe Lareos to be the best Cuban restaurant in Miami—downscale Versailles in Little Havana, and upscale Yuca in Coral Gables often take that honor. But for the uninitiated, this trendy beach bistro takes you on a culinary island tour that's sure to please.

   All the favorites are represented, including ropa vieja (a stringy beef stew), fabada asturiana (a hearty black-bean and sausage soup), palomilla (thinly sliced beef served with onions and parsley), and a number of tapas (Spanish-style hors d'oeuvres served in grazing-size portions). Some of the more unusual preparations include liver steaks and lobster Créole.

SOBE, 560 Washington Ave. Tel. 531-7170.
   Cuisine: INTERNATIONAL. **Reservations:** Recommended.
$ Prices: Appetizers $4–$9; main courses $7–$17. AE, DISC, MC, V.
   Open: Dinner only, Sun–Thurs 6pm–midnight, Fri–Sat 6pm–1am.
One of the newest darlings of South Beach's culinary scene, SoBe is a stylish, modern restaurant with good sightlines, a long bar, and an open kitchen specializing in a small selection of well-prepared appetizers and main courses. Winning starters include spicy fried calamari and seared tuna. Recommendable main courses—many of which are low in fat and cholesterol—include shrimp pasta with tarragon and red onion; and chicken with rosemary, asparagus, eggplant, and endive. Chicken, swordfish, and a variety of roasts are prepared on an exhibition rôtisserie. Burgers, steaks, and fish are also served.

THE STRAND, 671 Washington Ave. Tel. 532-2340.
   Cuisine: AMERICAN. **Reservations:** Recommended on winter weekends.
$ Prices: Appetizers $4–$7; main courses $5–$9 for burgers and sandwiches, $9–$18 for meat and fish. AE, DC, MC, V.

Open: Dinner only, Sun–Thurs 6pm–midnight, Fri–Sat 6pm–1am.

Not just another hot spot for trendies and young professionals, the Strand actually has culinary integrity, offering a well-planned menu punctuated by high-quality and fresh ingredients. Candlelit tables and a large, open-room layout are conducive to both intimate dining and table-hopping. And, happily, this old standby is still a good place to see and be seen. The menu changes nightly, but both food and service are very consistent, and a number of well-priced and light items are always on offer and excellent homemade mousses and cakes are always freshly prepared. The house wine list contains some good vintages, including several selections below $20.

THAI TONI, 890 Washington Ave. Tel. 538-8424.
Cuisine: THAI. **Reservations:** Recommended on weekends.
$ Prices: Appetizers $6–$7; main courses $7–$13 ($15–$18 for fish). AE, MC, V.
Open: Dinner only, Sun–Thurs 5:30–11pm, Fri–Sat 5:30pm–midnight.

One of the best restaurants in Miami, Thai Toni sparkles with ultra-contemporary decor, traditional service, and really top-notch food. The most spectacular item on the menu, to both eye and palate, is the hot-and-spicy fish, a whole snapper fileted tableside and fried with a bold, spicy red sauce. Other top picks have tropical twists, like beef curry with coconut milk and avocado, and a tender, boneless crispy duck served with mushrooms, baby corn, water chestnuts, cashews, and a light wine sauce.

The casual atmosphere is complemented by taped jazz and the option of floor-cushion seating at traditional low tables.

WPA, 685 Washington Ave. Tel. 534-1684.
Cuisine: AMERICAN. **Reservations:** Not accepted.
$ Prices: Appetizers $4–$7; main courses $9–$17; lunch $5–$9. AE, MC, V.
Open: Sun–Thurs noon–2am, Fri–Sat noon–4am.

Opened during the recession of 1992, WPA, named for Roosevelt's most famous economy-stirring New Deal program, serves huge portions of American standards at refreshingly low prices. Perpetually packed, the pretty restaurant is decorated with giant 1940s-style murals, and sturdy, functional furnishings. Whether you order a salad, sandwich, pasta or pizza, plates are uniformly tasty and huge. Fish, chicken, and beef dishes are served with mountains of french fries, and the full bar serves strong drinks in equally large tumblers. WPA is an intelligently concocted restaurant that's worth every one of the accolades it has received.

INEXPENSIVE

BOOKING TABLE CAFE, 728 Ocean Dr. Tel. 672-3476.
Cuisine: INTERNATIONAL. **Reservations:** Not accepted.
$ Prices: Salads and sandwiches $5–$7; meat and fish dishes $9–$11; breakfast $3–$6. AE, MC, V.
Open: Sun–Thurs 8am–2am, Fri–Sat 24 hours.

Unlike many Ocean Drive restaurants, which seem to put more emphasis on style than substance, this indoor/outdoor café next to the Colony Hotel boasts some of the best food on the strip. Despite the glass brick and European-style marble tables, the Booking Room's decor is considerably more low-key than its neighbors.

The colorful menu has everything from soups, sandwiches, and salads to lobsters and steaks. Breakfasts are popular, and include anything from a simple croissant to eggs, waffles, and quiche. The fish is particularly recommended during lunch and dinner, and like most of the other offerings, it's extremely well priced. Cappuccino, drinks, and a small, well-chosen list of wines are also available.

11TH STREET DINER, 11th St. and Washington Ave. Tel. 534-6373.
Cuisine: AMERICAN. **Reservations:** Not accepted.
$ Prices: Appetizers $3–$6; main courses $5–$14; lunch $3–$6. AE, MC, V.
Open: Mon–Wed 7am–2am, Thurs–Sun 24 hours.

This authentic 1950s-style curved-steel diner was moved here wholesale in 1993 and opened with considerable hype. The result is a greasy spoon with attitude that's especially popular with after-midnight SoBe hipsters. Despite nostalgic offerings like Philly cheese steaks, Coney Island hot dogs, California Cobb salads, and southern fried chicken, meals are positively '90s priced. Portions are huge, however, and the atmosphere is surprisingly satisfying.

TIJUANA JOE'S, 1201 Lincoln Rd. Tel. 674-1051.
Cuisine: MEXICAN. **Reservations:** Not accepted.
$ Prices: $5–$14. AE, MC, V.
Open: Dinner only, daily 5pm–midnight.

South Beach's best Mexican restaurant is not a phony American margarita chain, it's this simple corner Tex-Mex cantina. There is no separate bar here, just a dozen or so plastic tablecloth-topped tables, with white wooden chairs and a traditional menu. It's often crowded, as the place has caught on. Fajitas are the house specialty, and there is live Mexican music Tuesday through Saturday.

TITI'S TACOS, 900 Ocean Dr. Tel. 672-8484.
Cuisine: MEXICAN. **Reservations:** Accepted.
$ Prices: Appetizers $4–$8; main courses $7–$12. AE, MC, V.
Open: Daily 11am–2am.

Titi's Tacos, a small, colorfully tiled Mexican kitchen located smack-dab in the middle of trendland, serves decent south-of-the-border meals amid above-average surroundings. Enchiladas, tacos, and burritos are always preceded by chips and salsa, and often accompanied by a margarita. Titi's gets marks for its more complicated preparations which include chicken mole (a chile-based chocolate sauce), and sautéed shrimp- and jalapeno-topped beef steak. The restaurant is especially recommendable for lunch, as the dinnertime din from the bar next door is almost deafening.

WOLFIE'S, 2038 Collins Ave. Tel. 538-6626.
Cuisine: JEWISH DELICATESSEN. **Reservations:** Not required.
$ Prices: Omelets and sandwiches $2–$6; other dishes $5–$12. MC, V.
Open: Daily 24 hours.

Wolfie's originally opened in 1947 and quickly became a popular spot. The decor is simple—two wood-paneled rooms, lined on one side by a glass-enclosed display case—and the food is New York traditional. The bowl of pickles and basket of assorted rolls and miniature danishes on each table tells you that this is the real thing. Meals include cold smoked-fish platters, overstuffed sandwiches, stuffed cabbage, chicken-in-a-pot, and other favorites. Wolfie's is a relic of the past, but like other South Beach monuments, it has recently received a lease on life from the area's fashionable late-night crowd.

BUDGET

AU NATURAL "GOURMET" PIZZA, 1427 Alton Rd. Tel. 531-0666.
Cuisine: PIZZA. **Reservations:** Not required.
$ Prices: Large pizza $9–$19. No credit cards.
Open: Sun–Thurs 11am–midnight, Fri–Sat 11am–1am.

California-style pizza has reached the glitterati of South Miami Beach, with concoctions like pesto-and-ricotta, or smoked-salmon and cream cheese. Other designer pies include the Mediterranean, with sautéed eggplant, artichoke hearts, and prosciutto, and barbecued chicken with marinated mesquite-smoked poultry. Au Natural also delivers pints of Brices Yogurt and Ben & Jerry's ice cream.

NEWS CAFE, 800 Ocean Dr. Tel. 538-NEWS.
Cuisine: AMERICAN. **Reservations:** Not required.
$ Prices: Continental breakfast $2.75; salads $4–$8; sandwiches $5–$7. AE, MC, V.
Open: Daily 24 hours.

Of all the chic spots around trendy South Miami Beach, the News Café is tops. Excellent and inexpensive breakfasts and café fare are served at about 20 perpetually congested tables. Most of the seating is outdoors, and terrace tables are the most coveted. This is the meeting place for Ocean Drive's multitude of fashion photography crews and their models—who, incidentally, also occupy most of the area's hotel rooms. Delicious, often health-oriented dishes include yogurt with fruit salad, various green salads, imported cheese and meat sandwiches, and a choice of quiches. Coffee (including espresso) and a variety of black and herbal teas are also available.

SURFSIDE, BAL HARBOUR & SUNNY ISLES
INEXPENSIVE

WOLFIE COHEN'S RASCAL HOUSE, 17190 Collins Ave. Tel. 947-4581.
Cuisine: JEWISH/DELICATESSEN. **Reservations:** Not required.
$ Prices: Omelets and sandwiches $4–$6; other dishes $5–$14. No credit cards.
Open: Daily 7am–1:45am.

Almost 40 years young and still going strong, this historic, nostalgic culinary extravaganza is one of Miami Beach's greatest traditions. Simple tables and booths as well as plenty of patrons fill the airy, 425-seat dining room. The menu is as huge as the portions, which include corned beef, schmaltz herring, brisket, kreplach, chicken soup, and other authentic Jewish staples. Take-out service is available.

BUDGET

MY PIZZA, 18120 Collins Ave., Sunny Isles. Tel. 932-6915.
Cuisine: ITALIAN. **Reservations:** Not required.
$ Prices: Sandwiches $3.50–$5; pastas $4–$8; large pizza $12. CB, DISC, MC, V.
Open: Daily 11:30am–midnight.

Dark-wood walls and red-and-white-checked tablecloths surround the restaurant's open kitchen. My Pizza specializes in New York–style Sicilian and Neapolitan pies. Good pastas, subs, and calzones are also available. Best of all, they deliver—from 71st Street to the Dade County line—for $1.

KEY BISCAYNE
EXPENSIVE

RUSTY PELICAN, 3201 Rickenbacker Causeway. Tel. 361-3818.
Cuisine: CONTINENTAL. **Reservations:** Recommended.
$ Prices: Appetizers $4–$8; main courses $16–$20; lunch about half price. AE, CB, DC, MC, V.
Open: Lunch Mon–Sat 11:30am–4pm; dinner Sun–Thurs 5–11pm, Fri–Sat 5pm–midnight; brunch Sun 10:30am–4pm.

The Pelican's private tropical walkway leads over a lush waterfall into one of the most romantic dining rooms in the city, located right on beautiful blue-green Biscayne Bay. The restaurant's windows look out over the water onto the sparkling stalactites of Miami's magnificent downtown. Inside, quiet wicker paddle fans whirl overhead and saltwater fish swim in pretty tableside aquariums.

The restaurant's surf-and-turf menu features conservatively prepared prime steaks, veal, shrimp, and lobster. The food is good, but the atmosphere is even better, especially at sunset when the western view is especially awesome.

SUNDAYS ON THE BAY, 5420 Crandon Blvd. Tel. 361-6777.
Cuisine: AMERICAN. **Reservations:** Recommended for Sun brunch.
$ Prices: Appetizers $6–$7; main courses $15–$24; lunch about half price; Sun brunch $18.95. AE, CB, DC, MC, V.
Open: Lunch Mon–Sat 11:30am–5pm; dinner Sun–Wed 5pm–2am, Thurs–Sat 5pm–2:30am; brunch Sun 10:30am–3:30pm.

Steak, chicken, pasta, veal—it's all on the menu here. But fish is the specialty, and all the local favorites—grouper, tuna, snapper, and so on—are broiled, boiled, or fried to your specifications. Competent renditions of classic shellfish dishes such as oysters Rockefeller, shrimp scampi, and lobster Fra Diavolo are also recommendable. Sunday is a fantastically fun tropical bar, with an upbeat, informal atmosphere. Sunday brunches are particularly popular, when a buffet the size of Bimini attracts the city's late-rising in-crowd.

The lively bar stays open all week until 2:30am, and live reggae music is featured Thursday through Saturday from 9pm and all day Sunday.

INEXPENSIVE

BAYSIDE SEAFOOD RESTAURANT AND HIDDEN COVE BAR, 3501 Rickenbacker Causeway. Tel. 361-0808.
Cuisine: SEAFOOD. **Reservations:** Not accepted.
$ Prices: Raw clams or oysters $7 per dozen; appetizers, salads, and sandwiches $4.50–$6; platters $7–$13. AE, MC, V.
Open: Sun–Thurs noon–10:30pm, Fri–Sat noon–midnight.

Known by locals as "The Hut," this ramshackle restaurant and bar is a laid-back eating and drinking place with an especially pleasant outdoor tiki hut and terrace. Good soups and salads make heavy use of local fish, conch, clams, and other seafood. Chicken wings, hamburgers, and sandwiches are also available, as is a long list of finger foods to complement the drinks and the view. On weekends, the Hut features their house band playing live reggae and calypso.

THE SANDBAR, in the Silver Sands Motel, 301 Ocean Dr. Tel. 361-5441.
Cuisine: AMERICAN. **Reservations:** Not accepted.
$ Prices: Main courses $7–$11; lunch about half price. AE, MC, V.
Open: Breakfast Sat–Sun 8–11am; lunch daily 11:30am–3:30pm; dinner daily 5–10pm.

The Sandbar is a Miami institution, boasting Key Biscayne's best beach location at any price. Situated oceanfront, in a motel that would hardly get a second look if it were anywhere else, the restaurant features fish, burgers, and salads, and a deck right on the beach. It's extremely informal—patrons regularly dine barefoot, having just come off the beach. Eggs and omelets are served for breakfast on the weekends; otherwise, grouper sandwich, the house specialty, should be ordered.

DOWNTOWN

VERY EXPENSIVE

PAVILLON GRILL, in the Inter-Continental Hotel, 100 Chopin Plaza. Tel. 577-1000.
Cuisine: MIAMI REGIONAL. **Reservations:** Recommended.
$ Prices: Appetizers $7–$12; main courses $18–$24. AE, CB, DC, MC, V.
Open: Dinner only, Mon–Sat 6:30–10:30pm.

Private club by day, deluxe restaurant by night, the Pavillon Grill maintains its air of exclusivity, with leather sofas and an expensive salon setting. Dark-green marble columns divide the spacious dining room, while well-spaced booths and tables provide comfortable seating and a sense of privacy. The menu features both heavy club-room fare and lighter dishes prepared with a masterful Miami Regional hand. Prices here are rounded off to the highest dollar and spelled out in lieu of numerals—a practice that seems a touch pretentious, until your food arrives.

Standouts include the chilled trout appetizer, stuffed with seafood and basil, and an unusual grilled shrimp cocktail with pineapple relish and a citrus-flavored lobster mayonnaise. Skillfully prepared, adventurous dishes include boneless quail Louisiana, stuffed with oysters and andouille sausage. Meat, fish, and chicken dishes are abundant, as are a host of creative pastas, including an artichoke, garlic, truffles, and a cheese-stuffed ravioli that redefines the limits of these Italian tiny turnovers. The Hotel Inter-Continental is located adjacent to the Bayside Marketplace.

EXPENSIVE

THE FISH MARKET, in the Omni International Hotel, 1601 Biscayne Blvd. Tel. 374-0000.

Cuisine: SEAFOOD. **Reservations:** Recommended.
$ Prices: Appetizers $6–$8; main courses $17–$22. AE, CB, DC, MC, V.
Open: Lunch Mon–Fri 11:30am–2:30pm; dinner Mon–Sat 6–11pm.
One of the city's most celebrated seafood restaurants is this understated, elegant dining room right in the heart of the city. Located in an unassuming corner, just off the Omni International Hotel's fourth-floor lobby, the restaurant is both spacious and comfortable, featuring high ceilings, reasonable prices, and a sumptuous dessert-table centerpiece.

Don't overlook the appetizers here, which include a meaty Mediterranean-style seafood soup and a delicate yellowfin tuna carpaccio. Local fish, prepared and presented simply, is always the menu's main feature; sautéed or grilled, it's this guide's recommendation. The Omni International Hotel is just north of downtown at the corner of 16th Street.

MODERATE

EAST COAST FISHERIES, 360 W. Flagler St. Tel. 373-5516.
Cuisine: SEAFOOD. **Reservations:** Recommended.
$ Prices: Appetizers and grazing $4–$8; main courses $9–$15, most under $14; lunch from $7. AE, DISC, MC, V.
Open: Daily 11:30am–10pm.
East Coast Fisheries is a no-nonsense retail market and restaurant, offering a terrific variety of the freshest fish available. The dozen or so plain wood tables are surrounded by refrigerated glass cases filled with snapper, salmon, mahi-mahi, trout, tuna, crabs, oysters, lobsters, and the like. The menu is absolutely huge, and features every fish imaginable, cooked the way you want it—grilled, fried, stuffed, Cajun style, Florentine, hollandaise, blackened. It's a pleasure to walk around and ask questions about the many local fish before choosing. Service is fast. But good prices and an excellent product still mean long lines on weekends. Highly recommended. The restaurant is located on the Miami River, at the edge of West Flagler Street.

LAS TAPAS, in the Bayside Marketplace, 401 Biscayne Blvd. Tel. 372-2737.
Cuisine: SPANISH. **Reservations:** Not required.
$ Prices: Tapas $4–$7; main courses $12–$19; lunch about half price. AE, CB, DC, DISC, MC, V.
Open: Sun–Thurs 11am–midnight, Fri–Sat 11am–1am.
Occupying a large corner of downtown's Bayside Marketplace, glass-wrapped Las Tapas is a pretty and fun place to dine in a laid-back, easy atmosphere.
Tapas, small dishes of Spanish delicacies, are the featured fare here. Good chicken, veal, and seafood main dishes are on the menu, but it's more fun to taste a variety of the restaurant's tapas. The best include shrimp in garlic, smoked pork shank with Spanish sausage, baby eel in garlic and oil, and chicken sauté with garlic and mushroom.

An open kitchen in front of the entrance greets diners with succulent smells. The long dining room is outlined in red Spanish stone and decorated with hundreds of hanging hams. Bayside Marketplace is on Biscayne Bay in the middle of downtown.

BUDGET

HOOTERS, in the Bayside Marketplace, 401 Biscayne Blvd. Tel. 371-3004.
Cuisine: AMERICAN. **Reservations:** Not accepted.
$ Prices: Meals $5–$12. AE, MC, V.
Open: Mon–Thurs 11am–midnight, Fri–Sat 11am–1am, Sun 11am–10pm.
Hooters' hiring policy seems to mean buxom waitresses in midriff tops, giving it a reputation as one of the most sexist restaurants in Florida. Despite this (or because of it, depending on your perspective), the casual second-floor restaurant does offer good, inexpensive meals, and a great terrace overlooking the Bayside Marketplace and

Biscayne Bay. Large chicken, fish, and meat burgers are served with massive quantities of beer. Local fraternity brothers are a common sight here, huddled around mountains of chicken wings and full pitchers. Hooters is on the second floor of the Marketplace's north pavilion.

There is a second location in Coconut Grove's Cocowalk, 3015 Grand Ave. (tel. 442-6004).

LITTLE HAVANA

Southwest 8th Street, also known as Calle Ocho, is the center of Little Havana, home to a large number of Cuban immigrants. In addition to shops and markets, this area contains some of the world's best Cuban and Latin American restaurants, treasures that help make the city a wonderful place to visit.

Most restaurants list menu items in English for the benefit of "norteamericano" diners. Here's a sample of what you can expect:

Arroz con pollo: Roast chicken served with pimento-seasoned yellow rice.

Picadillo: A rich stir-fry of ground meat, brown gravy, peas, pimentos, raisins, and olives.

Platanos: A deep-fried, soft, mildly sweet banana.

Pan cubaño: This is the famous long, white crusty Cuban bread that should be ordered with every meal.

Ropa vieja: Literally meaning "old clothes," this is a delicious stringy beef stew.

Cafe cubano: Very strong black coffee, served in thimble-size cups with lots of sugar—a real eye-opener.

Palomilla: Similar to American minute steak, thinly sliced beef usually served with onions, parsley, and a mountain of french fries.

Camarones: Shrimp.

Paella: A Spanish dish of chicken, sausage, seafood, and pork mixed with saffron rice and peas—very good.

Fabada asturiana: A hearty black-bean and sausage soup.

Tapas: A general name for Spanish-style hors d'oeuvres; served in grazing-size portions.

MODERATE

CASA JUANCHO, 2436 SW 8th St. Tel. 642-2452.
   Cuisine: SPANISH/CUBAN. **Reservations:** Recommended; not accepted Fri–Sat after 8pm.
$ Prices: Tapas $6–$8; main courses $11–$20; lunch about half price. AE, CB, DC, MC, V.
   Open: Sun–Thurs noon–midnight, Fri–Sat noon–1am.

Casa Juancho offers an ambitious menu of excellently prepared main dishes and tapas. Except for a few outstanding main dishes like roast suckling pig, baby eels in garlic and olive oil, and Iberian-style snapper, diners would be wise to stick exclusively to tapas, smaller dishes of Spanish "finger food." Some of the best include mixed seafood vinaigrette, fresh shrimp in hot garlic sauce, and fried calamari rings.

The several dining rooms are decorated with traditional Spanish furnishings and are enlivened nightly by strolling Spanish musicians.

INEXPENSIVE

HY VONG VIETNAMESE CUISINE, 3458 SW 8th St. Tel. 446-3674.
   Cuisine: VIETNAMESE. **Reservations:** Not required.
$ Prices: Appetizers $2–$3.50; main courses $8–$12. No credit cards.
   Open: Dinner only, Tues–Sun 6–11pm. **Closed:** Two weeks in Aug.
Similar in style, if not taste, to Thai food, Vietnamese cuisine combines the best of Asian and French cooking with spectacular results. The food at Hy Vong is terrific. Appetizers include small, tightly packed Vietnamese spring rolls, and kimchee, a spicy, fermented cabbage. Star main dishes include pastry-enclosed chicken with a watercress cream-cheese sauce, and fish in a tangy mango sauce.

The dining room itself is just a small, sparsely decorated, wood-paneled room. Located in the heart of Little Havana, it attracts an interesting and mixed crowd.

BUDGET

VERSAILLES, 3555 SW 8th St. Tel. 444-0240.
   Cuisine: CUBAN. **Reservations:** Not accepted.
$ Prices: Soup and salad $2–$5; main courses $5–$8. DC, MC, V.
   Open: Mon–Thurs 8am–2am, Fri 8am–3:30am, Sat 8am–4:30am, Sun 9am–2am.

Versailles is the area's most celebrated diner, especially after 10pm. The restaurant sparkles with glass, chandeliers, and mirrors, and moves at a quick pace to please patrons at tables and counters and in take-out lines. If you want inexpensive, authentic Cuban cuisine, look no further. Nothing fancy here—just straightforward food from the home country. The menu is a veritable survey of Cuban cooking and includes specialties like Moors and Christians (flavorful black beans with white rice), ropa vieja, and fried whole fish.

NORTH DADE
VERY EXPENSIVE

CHEF ALLEN'S, 19088 NE 29th Ave., North Miami Beach. Tel. 935-2900.
   Cuisine: MIAMI REGIONAL. **Reservations:** Not required.
$ Prices: Appetizers $7–$10; main courses $20–$27. AE, MC, V.
   Open: Dinner only, Sun–Thurs 6–10:30pm, Fri–Sat 6pm–midnight.

If one needs any evidence that Miami Regional cuisine is strongly influenced by California cooking, look no further than Chef Allen's. Owner/chef Allen Susser, of New York's Le Cirque fame, has built a classy but relaxed restaurant with art deco furnishings, a glass-enclosed kitchen, and a hot-pink swirl of neon surrounding the dining room's ceiling.

The delicious homemade breadsticks are enough to hold you, but don't let them tempt you away from an appetizer that may include lobster and crab cakes served with strawberry-ginger chutney, or baked Brie with spinach, sun-dried tomatoes, and pine nuts. Served by an energetic, young staff, favorite main dishes include crisp roast duck with cranberry sauce, and mesquite-grilled Norwegian salmon with champagne grapes, green onions, and basil spaetzle. Local fish dishes, in various delectable guises, and homemade pastas are always on the menu. An extensive wine list is well chosen and features several good buys. The restaurant is on the mainland at 190th Street, near the Dade County Line.

EXPENSIVE

MARK'S PLACE, 2286 NE 123rd St., North Miami. Tel. 893-6888.
   Cuisine: MIAMI REGIONAL. **Reservations:** Recommended.
$ Prices: Appetizers $6–$9; main courses $10–$15 for pasta and pizza, $16–$20 for meat and fish; lunch about half price. AE, MC, V.
   Open: Lunch Mon–Fri noon–2:30pm; dinner Mon–Thurs 6–10:30pm, Fri–Sat 6–11pm, Sun 6–10pm.

Attracting an upscale but leisurely crowd, this restaurant's claim to fame is its owner/chef, Mark Militello, an extraordinarily gifted artist who works primarily with fresh, natural, local ingredients. A smart, modern bistro, Mark's Place shines with off-white walls, an aquamarine ceiling, contemporary glass sculptures, and a friendly, open kitchen. Each table has its own pepper mill, and fresh, home-baked bread.

Mark's inspired food is often unusual, and rarely misses the mark. Appetizers include oak-grilled mozzarella and prosciutto, curry-breaded fried oysters, and an unusual petite pizza topped with smoked chicken and Monterey Jack cheese. The best main dishes are braised black grouper, Florida conch stew, or flank steak in a sesame marinade. Try one of Mark's suggestions. Desserts like Icky Sticky Coconut Pudding are equally unusual, and baked with the same originality as the rest of the menu.

MODERATE

MIKE GORDON'S, 1201 NE 79th St. Tel. 751-4429.
   Cuisine: SEAFOOD. **Reservations:** Not accepted.
$ Prices: Appetizers $3–$6; main courses $13–$17; lunch about half price. AE,
   CB, DC, MC, V.
   Open: Daily noon–10pm.

Over 40 years have passed and this Miami institution is now managed by Mike
Gordon's sons, but it still offers seafood as fresh as the fish market next door. This is a
traditional pier restaurant in a Cape Cod kind of way, with dark-wood beams, ceiling
fans, and pelicans playing on the docks outside. The huge menu features lobster, crab,
and an usual array of meaty local fish, traditionally prepared and served with drawn
butter and french fries. The best part of this dining experience is the restaurant's
interesting location, directly on the Intracoastal Waterway. Even if you have
reservations, it's likely you'll have to wait for a table. But the bar is long, and there are
few better places in Miami to pass the time. The restaurant is located at the foot of the
mainland side of the 79th Street Causeway.
   A second restaurant has opened in the Four Ambassadors building, 801 S.
Bayshore Dr., Coconut Grove (tel. 577-4202).

INEXPENSIVE

**THE MELTING POT, in Sunny Isles Plaza shopping center, 3143 NE
   163rd St., North Miami Beach. Tel. 947-2228.**
   Cuisine: FONDUE. **Reservations:** Not required.
$ Prices: Main courses $9–$10 for cheese fondue, $11–$16 for meat and fish
   fondues. AE, MC, V.
   Open: Dinner only, Sun–Thurs 5:30–11pm, Fri–Sat 5:30pm–midnight.

Dipping your own chunks of bread into pots of sizzling cheese is certainly a different
dining experience. This traditional dish is supplemented by combination meat-and-
fish dinners, which are served with one of almost a dozen different sauces. The
Melting Pot's variation on Swiss fondue is a good alternative dinner decision. But best,
perhaps, is dessert: chunks of pineapple, bananas, apples, and cherries that you dip
into a creamy chocolate fondue. No liquor is served here, but the wine list is extensive,
and beer is available. The restaurant is located on the north side of 163rd Street,
between U.S. 1 and Collins Avenue.
   A second Melting Pot is located at 9835 SW 72nd St. (Sunset Drive), Kendall (tel.
279-8816).

CORAL GABLES & ENVIRONS
VERY EXPENSIVE

CHRISTY'S, 3101 Ponce de Leon Blvd. Tel. 446-1400.
   Cuisine: AMERICAN. **Reservations:** Required.
$ Prices: Appetizers $4–$7; main courses $17–$25; lunch about half price. AE,
   CB, DC, MC, V.
   Open: Lunch Mon–Fri 11:30am–4pm; dinner Mon–Thurs 4–11pm, Fri 4–
   11:45pm, Sat 5–11:45pm, Sun 5–11pm.

Decorated in an elegant, Victorian style, Christy's is one of Coral Gables's most
expensive trendy establishments. Frequented by a power-tie crowd, this New
American eatery is known primarily for its generous cuts of thick, juicy steaks and
ribs. "Big" appears to be the chef's chief instruction—the prime rib is so thick that
even a small cut weighs about a pound. New York strip, filet mignon, chateaubriand
. . . it's all on the menu here, and all steaks are fully aged without chemicals or
freezing. Main dishes are served with a jumbo Caesar salad and a baked potato.
Seafood, veal, and chicken dishes are also available.

EXPENSIVE

THE BISTRO, 2611 Ponce de Leon Blvd. Tel. 442-9671.
   Cuisine: FRENCH. **Reservations:** Not required.

$ Prices: Appetizers $5–$10; main courses $16–$26; lunch $4–$14. AE, CB, DC, MC, V.
Open: Lunch Mon–Fri 11:30am–2pm; dinner Mon–Thurs 6–10:30pm, Fri–Sat 6–11pm.

The Bistro's intimate atmosphere is heightened by soft lighting, 19th-century European antiques and prints, and an abundance of flowers atop crisp white tablecloths.

Co-owners Ulrich Sigrist and André Barnier keep a watchful eye over their experienced kitchen staff, which regularly dishes out artful French dishes with an international accent. Look for the terrine maison, a country-style veal-and-pork appetizer that's the house specialty. Common French bistro fare like escargots au Pernod and coquilles St-Jacques are prepared with uncommon spices and accoutrements, livening a rather typical continental menu. Especially recommended is the roast duck with honey-mustard sauce and the chicken breasts in a mild curry sauce, each served with fried bananas and pineapple.

CAFFÈ BACI, 2522 Ponce de Leon Blvd. Tel. 442-0600.
Cuisine: ITALIAN. **Reservations:** Recommended for dinner.
$ Prices: Appetizers $6–$9; main courses $14–$20 for pasta, $16–$24 for meat and fish; lunch about half price. AE, CB, DISC, DC, MC, V.
Open: Lunch Mon–Fri noon–3pm; dinner Sun–Thurs 6–11pm, Fri–Sat 6–11:30pm.

The most stylish bistro in Miami comes in the form of this tiny, classy restaurant with great food at reasonable prices. Soft pink pastel walls, covered with Roman architectural prints, reflect off a pretty, tin-can-shaped gold-metal ceiling. A typical meal, served by courteous, professional waiters, might start with fresh tuna carpaccio, or a marinated medley of artichoke hearts, mushrooms, tomatoes, and zucchini. Main courses include homemade pastas with sweet Italian sausages, porcini (mushrooms), basil and tomato sauces, as well as a number of succulent, marinated meats and fish topped with tomato and cream sauces and any number of aromatic herbs.

If you have difficulty choosing from the terrific menu—and you will—trust suggestions made by the boisterous proprietor, Domenico Diana.

CHARADE, 2900 Ponce de Leon Blvd. Tel. 448-6077.
Cuisine: FRENCH/SWISS. **Reservations:** Recommended.
$ Prices: Appetizers $9–$11; main courses $19–$30; lunch about half price. AE, CB, DC, MC, V.
Open: Lunch daily 11:30am–3pm; dinner Sun–Thurs 6–11pm, Fri–Sat 6pm–midnight.

A historic Coral Gables low-rise is the setting for this restaurant with soft piano music, a romantic courtyard, and excellent French/Swiss cuisine. More formal than Kaleidoscope, its cousin in Coconut Grove (see below), Charade has a gentleman's club feel with wooden ceilings and furniture and old-world portraits on the walls.

Like many imaginative continental restaurants, eating here is a real culinary experience. Masterful main dishes include shrimp-and-chicken jambalaya; duckling with orange, kiwi, ginger, and Grand Marnier; and chateaubriand.

LE FESTIVAL, 2120 Salzedo St. Tel. 442-8545.
Cuisine: FRENCH. **Reservations:** Required for dinner.
$ Prices: Appetizers $5–$8; main courses $16–$20; lunch about half price. AE, CB, DC, MC, V.
Open: Lunch Mon–Fri 11:45am–2:30pm; dinner Mon–Thurs 6–10:30pm, Fri–Sat 6–11pm. **Closed:** Sept–Oct.

Le Festival's contemporary, sharp pink awning hangs over one of Miami's most traditional Spanish-style buildings, hinting at the unusual combination of cuisine and decor that awaits inside. In fact, the snazzy, modern dining rooms, which are enlivened with New French features and furnishings, belie the traditional features that are the highlights of a well-planned menu.

Shrimp and crab cocktails, fresh pâtés, and an unusual cheese soufflé are star starters. Both meat and fish are either simply seared with herbs and spices, or doused in the wine-and-cream sauces that have made the French famous. Dessert can be a delight with a modest amount of foresight. Grand Marnier and chocolate soufflés are individually prepared, and must be ordered at the same time as the main courses. A wide selection of other homemade sweets should also entice you to leave room for dessert.

Le Festival is located five blocks north of Miracle Mile, in an area slightly removed from other Coral Gables restaurants.

RESTAURANT ST. MICHEL, in the Hotel Place St. Michel, 162 Alcazar Ave. Tel. 444-1666.
   Cuisine: FRENCH/MEDITERRANEAN. **Reservations:** Recommended.
$ **Prices:** Appetizers $6–$8; main courses $14–$16 for pasta, $18–$25 for meat and fish. AE, CB, MC, V.
   Open: Lunch Mon–Sat 11am–5pm; dinner Sun–Thurs 5–10:30pm, Fri–Sat 5–11:30pm; brunch Sun 11am–2:30pm.

⭐ One of the most subtly sensuous restaurants in Miami is, appropriately, in the city's most romantic hotel. Art deco chandeliers, hardwood floors, delicate antiques, and flowers re-create the feeling of a quaint 1930s Parisian café.
The creative menu complements the artful decor with its metropolitan French coast cuisine. Duck consommé Oriental and pan-fried blue-crab cakes highlight the hors d'oeuvres, while prosciutto-stuffed veal chops, and an excellent couscous lead the winning main dishes. Goose, rabbit, venison, and other unusual meats often grace the tables, topped with tangy fruit sauces and spicy wine creations. A special six-course dinner is prepared and priced nightly.

YUCA, 177 Giralda. Tel. 444-4448.
   Cuisine: CUBAN/AMERICAN. **Reservations:** Recommended.
$ **Prices:** Appetizers $7–$13; main courses $19–$29. AE, CB, DC, MC, V.
   Open: Lunch Mon–Sat noon–4pm; dinner Sun–Thurs 6–11pm, Fri–Sat 6pm–midnight.

⭐ One of Miami's most celebrated ethnic eateries, Yuca features an exciting menu that combines traditional Cuban ingredients with the latest international influences. Fun is always the dish of the day, and not just because of the restaurant's catchy name, an anagram for Young Upscale Cuban-American. While the kitchen is strictly gourmet, one can't help but think that the colorful menu and decor were created with tongue firmly in cheek. Star dishes include barbecued ribs with a tangy guava sauce, and plantain-coated dolphin (fish) with a tamarind sauce.

MODERATE

EL CORRAL, 3545 Coral Way. Tel. 444-8272.
   Cuisine: NICARAGUAN. **Reservations:** Not required.
$ **Prices:** Appetizers $3–$5; main courses $9–$15 (served two for the price of one Mon–Thurs 5–7pm). AE, MC, V.
   Open: Mon–Fri 11:30am–11pm, Sat–Sun noon–11pm.
This untraditional Nicaraguan steakhouse serves punchy marinated beef filets, along with plantains, rice, and beans from the barrio. Antojitos, Nicaragua's answer to appetizers, include homemade sausages with salad and plantains, fried pork with Créole sauce, and a wonderful deep-fried cheese. Aside from a couple of obligatory fish and chicken listings, the long main-course menu focuses strictly on beef in various guises. Tender filet tips are served under a sauce of butter, brandy, cream, and Roquefort cheese. And a center-cut tenderloin is matched with pickled onions and marinara sauce.

Most Nicaraguans don't even think of eating dinner before 9 or 10pm, so El Corral entices hungry others with a great two-for-the-price-of-one main-dish "early-bird" special, Monday through Thursday from 5 to 7pm. It's a good deal for vacationing carnivores on a budget.

RISTORANTE TANINO, 2312 Ponce de Leon. Tel. 446-1666.
   Cuisine: ITALIAN. **Reservations:** Not required.
$ **Prices:** Main courses $6–$9 at lunch, $9–$12 at dinner for pasta, $12–$18 for meat, fish, and poultry. AE, CB, DC, DISC, MC, V.

Open: Lunch Mon–Fri 11:30am–3pm; dinner daily 6–11pm.

⭐ Restaurants in the Gables come and go. But, hopefully, Ristorante Tanino is here to stay. The beautiful, petite exterior houses an equally intimate dining room, where great Italian cuisine is remarkably underpriced. Lunch offers the best deals, with daily $8 specials that include a linguine frutti di mori, a robust lasagne, and a particularly well-done penne with eggplant and tomato sauce. All are served with soup or salad. Specials would easily sell for twice the price in New York. Dinner is à la carte, and the well-chosen menu is also kindly priced. Pastas, like fettuccine Alfredo with smoked salmon, are as good as or better than similar dishes served elsewhere at twice the cost. Other meals include chicken breast with prosciutto, onion, and basil; peppers stuffed with a bread-and-veal mixture and topped with tomato sauce; and saltimbocca. Good cooking and a good value.

INEXPENSIVE

HOUSE OF INDIA, 22 Merrick Way. Tel. 444-2348.

Cuisine: INDIAN. **Reservations:** Not required.
$ **Prices:** Appetizers $1–$5; main courses $7–$10; lunch buffet (served Mon–Fri 11:30am–3pm and Sat noon–3pm) $6.95. AE, MC, V.
Open: Mon–Thurs 11:30am–10pm, Fri–Sat 11:30am–11pm, Sun 5–10pm.

The House of India's curries, kormas, and kebabs are some of the city's best, but the restaurant's well-priced all-you-can-eat lunch buffet is unsurpassed. All the favorites are on display, including tandoori chicken, naan bread, and various meat and vegetarian curries, as well as rice and dal (lentils). If you've never had Indian food before, this is an excellent place to experiment, since you can see the food before you choose it. Veterans will know that this is high-quality cooking from the subcontinent.

The restaurant is not fancy, but nicely decorated with hanging printed cloths, and traditional music. It's located one block north of Miracle Mile.

NEW HICKORY BARBECUE RESTAURANT, 3170 Coral Way. Tel. 443-0842.

Cuisine: BARBECUE. **Reservations:** Not accepted.
$ **Prices:** Appetizers $2–$4; main courses $4–$11. MC, V.
Open: Tues–Thurs and Sun 11am–10pm, Fri–Sat 11am–midnight.

The best barbecue joints are always the same kind of sites—wooden picnic tables on sawdust floors, and an intense smokey stink that permeates every crack and punctuates every conversation. New Hickory is no exception. Barbecuing here for almost 40 years, the restaurant has a loyal following of carnivores who return for beef, pork, and lamb ribs that are slowly smoked over hickory wood. Steaks, chicken, shrimp, and fish are also available. Onion rings, french fries, coleslaw, and baked beans round out the menu, along with a small selection of domestic beers on tap.

BUDGET

BISCAYNE MIRACLE MILE CAFETERIA, 147 Miracle Mile. Tel. 444-9005.

Cuisine: SOUTHERN AMERICAN. **Reservations:** Not accepted.
$ **Prices:** Main courses $3–$4. No credit cards.
Open: Lunch Mon–Sat 11am–2:15pm; dinner Mon–Sat 4–8pm, Sun 11am–8pm.

No bar, no music, and no flowers on the tables—just great southern-style cooking at unbelievably low prices. The menu changes, but roast beef, baked fish, and barbecued ribs are typical dishes, few of which exceed $4.

As the name says, food is picked up cafeteria style and brought to one of the many unadorned Formica tables. The restaurant is always busy.

CAFE 94, 94 Miracle Mile. Tel. 444-7933.

Cuisine: CUBAN. **Reservations:** Not required.
$ **Prices:** Breakfast/lunch $2–$5. No credit cards.
Open: Mon–Sat 7am–4pm.

This Cuban coffee shop is a great place to try the island's specialties. Daily lunch specials cost less than $5 and usually include grilled chicken or steak, rice, black beans, and plantains. Cuban-style sandwiches are also available, as are hearty American-style breakfasts. Café 94 occupies a narrow storefront in the heart of the Gables' main shopping thoroughfare.

ESTATE WINES & GOURMET FOODS, 92 Miracle Mile. Tel. 442-9915.
Cuisine: EUROPEAN/AMERICAN. **Reservations:** Not required.
$ **Prices:** $4–$6. No credit cards.
Open: Mon–Fri 10am–8pm, Sat 10am–6pm.
This storefront, in the heart of Coral Gables's main shopping strip, is primarily a wine shop. But Magdalena A. von Freytag, one of the friendliest storekeepers in Miami, also serves gourmet meals to a handful of lucky lunchers. Deliciously thick soups are served with pâtés, salads, and sandwiches around an overturned barrel that can only accommodate a handful of diners. I hesitate to write about this find for fear of spoiling it. Magdalena's only advertisement is word of mouth, and knowledgeable locals are her dedicated regulars.

SERGIO'S, 3252 Coral Way. Tel. 529-0047.
Cuisine: CUBAN/AMERICAN. **Reservations:** Not accepted.
$ **Prices:** Appetizers $3–$4; main courses $5–$7; lunch $2–$5. AE.
Open: Sun–Thurs 6am–midnight, Fri–Sat 24 hours.
Located across from Coral Gables's Miracle Center Mall, Sergio's stands out like a Latin-inspired International House of Pancakes, with red-clothed tables, neon signs in the windows, and video games along the back wall.

From ham-and-eggs breakfasts to grilled-steak-sandwich lunches and dinners, Sergio's is not a place for vegetarians. The family-style restaurant specializes in native Cuban-style dishes, as well as grilled chicken, fajitas, and a variety of sandwiches. Low prices and late-night dining keep it popular with the locals.

COCONUT GROVE
EXPENSIVE

CAFÉ SCI SCI, 3043 Grand Ave. Tel. 446-5104.
Cuisine: ITALIAN. **Reservations:** Not required.
$ **Prices:** Appetizers $7–$11; main courses $12–$17 for pasta, $16–$23 for meat and fish; lunch about half price. AE, MC, V.
Open: Lunch Tues–Sun noon–3pm; dinner Sun–Thurs 3pm–12:30am, Fri–Sat 3pm–1am.
The original Sci Sci café (pronounced "shi shi") was a turn-of-the-century Naples eatery and a meeting place for international artists and intellectuals. That restaurant also claims that it was the site where gelato—the silky-smooth Italian ice cream—was perfected. Like its namesake, Café Sci Sci in the Grove is also an inviting place to lounge and linger. Their solid marble floors and columns combine with ornate decor and furnishings to create one of the area's most stunning European-style cafés. Visually and gastronomically, this restaurant is a pleasing combination of old and new.

The large menu offers both hot and cold antipasti, including carpaccio, sautéed mussels, ham and melon, and fried mozzarella with marinara sauce. Pasta dishes feature such winning combinations as homemade black fettuccine with vodka, tomato, cream, and black pepper; tortellini filled with smoked cheese in Gorgonzola sauce; and paparddina rustiche-wide noodles with shrimp, saffron, peas, and cream. Meat, fish, and chicken dishes also combine traditional and contemporary styles. The pace here is relaxed, as every order is freshly prepared. The restaurant is at the Groves' primary intersection, at the top of Main Highway.

KALEIDOSCOPE, 3112 Commodore Plaza. Tel. 446-5010.
Cuisine: NEW AMERICAN. **Reservations:** Recommended.
$ **Prices:** Appetizers $6–$10; main courses $12–$15 for pasta, $14–$20 for meat and fish; lunch about half price. AE, CB, DC, DISC, MC, V.
Open: Lunch Mon–Fri 11:30am–3pm; dinner Mon–Sat 6–11pm, Sun 5:30–10:30pm.

⭐ Kaleidoscope is one of the few restaurants in the heart of Coconut Grove that would still be recommended if it were located somewhere less exciting. The atmosphere is elegantly relaxed, with attentive, low-key service, comfortable seating, and a well-designed terrace overlooking the busy sidewalks below. Dishes are well prepared and pastas, topped with meaty sauces like seafood and fresh basil, or pesto with grilled yellowfin tuna, are especially tasty. The linguine with salmon and fresh dill is perfection. The appetizers are tempting, but even hearty eaters should be warned that the main courses are large, and all are preceded by a house salad.

MODERATE

GREEN STREET CAFE, 3110 Commodore Plaza. Tel. 567-0662.
Cuisine: CONTINENTAL. **Reservations:** Not accepted.
$ **Prices:** Appetizers $2–$4; main courses $6–$12; breakfast $3–$6. AE, MC, V.
Open: Sun–Thurs 6:45am–11:30pm, Fri–Sat 6:45am–1am.
Green Street is located at the "100% corner," the Coconut Grove intersection of Main Highway and Commodore Plaza that 100% of all tourists visit. This enviable location—loaded with outdoor seating that's great for people-watching—relieves the pressure on Green Street to turn out great meals. But despite its great location, the food here is well above average. Continental-style breakfasts include fresh croissants and rolls, cinnamon toast, and cereal. Heartier American-style offerings include eggs and omelets, pancakes, waffles, and French toast. Soup, salad, and sandwich lunches mean overstuffed chicken, turkey, and tuna-based meals. Dinners are more elaborate, and involve several decent pasta dishes, along with fresh fish, chicken, and burgers, including one made of lamb.

MONTY'S BAYSHORE RESTAURANT, 2560 S. Bayshore Dr. Tel. 858-1431.
Cuisine: SEAFOOD. **Reservations:** Not required.
$ **Prices:** Chowder $3; appetizers and sandwiches $6–$8; platters $7–$12; main courses $15–$20. AE, CB, DC, MC, V.
Open: Sun–Thurs 11am–11pm, Fri–Sat noon–midnight.
Monty's comes in three parts: a lounge, a raw bar, and a restaurant. Between them, they serve everything from steak and seafood to munchies like nachos, potato skins, and buffalo chicken wings. This is a fun kind of place, usually with more revelers and drinkers than diners. Sitting at the outdoor dockside bar can be a pleasant way to spend an evening. There's live music nightly, as well as all day on the weekends (see "The Bar Scene" in "Evening Entertainment," in Chapter 5).

SEÑOR FROG'S, 3008 Grand Ave. Tel. 448-0999.
Cuisine: MEXICAN. **Reservations:** Recommended on weekends.
$ **Prices:** Main courses $9–$12. AE, CB, DC, MC, V.
Open: Mon–Sat 11:30am–2am, Sun 11:30am–1am.
⭐ You know you're getting close to Señor Frog's when you hear laughing and singing spilling out of the restaurant's courtyard. Filled with the college-student crowd, this restaurant is known for a raucous good time, its mariachi band, and powerful margaritas. The food at this rocking cantina is as good as its atmosphere, featuring excellent renditions of traditional Mexican-American favorites. The mole enchiladas, with 14 different kinds of mild chiles mixed with chocolate, is as flavorful as any I've tasted. Almost everything is served with rice and beans and, like all good Mexican places, portions are so large, few diners are able to finish.

INEXPENSIVE

CAFÉ TU TU TANGO, 3015 Grand Ave., in Cocowalk. Tel. 529-2222.
Cuisine: SPANISH/INTERNATIONAL. **Reservations:** Not accepted.
$ **Prices:** Appetizers $3–$6; main dishes $4–$8. AE, MC, V.
Open: Sun–Wed 11:30am–midnight, Thurs 11:30am–1am, Fri–Sat 11:30am–2am.
When the Cocowalk Mall opened a few years ago, this small, colorful shopping center was full of vibrant boutiques and unique restaurants. Economic pressures have since weeded out the unusual in favor of the more ordinary, but one particularly

worthwhile eatery remains—Café Tu Tu Tango. Located on the mall's second floor, the restaurant is designed to look something like a disheveled artist's loft. Seating is either inside, or outdoors overlooking bustling Coconut Grove.

Flamenco and other Latin-inspired tunes compliment a menu with a decidedly Spanish flair. Hummus spread on rosemary flat bread and baked goat cheese in marinara sauce are two very recommendable starters. Main courses include roast duck with dried cranberries, toasted pine nuts, and goat cheese; and Cajun chicken eggrolls filled with corn, Cheddar cheese, and tomato salsa. Pastas, ribs, fish, and pizzas round out the eclectic offerings.

SOUTH MIAMI
INEXPENSIVE

EL TORITO, in The Falls shopping center, 8888 Howard Dr. Tel. 255-6506.
  Cuisine: MEXICAN. **Reservations:** Not required.
$ Prices: Appetizers $4–$5.50; main courses $6–$9. AE, MC, V.
  Open: Daily 11am–midnight.
Red clay tile, Mexican artifacts, and three-dimensional murals create an authentic south-of-the-border atmosphere only found in American restaurant chains. It's nice though. And seeing how it's pretty difficult to mess up Mexican "cuisine," especially when it's prepared by authentic Latinos, the food is pretty good too. All the hits are here, including enchiladas, tacos, chimichangas, and tostadas. It's pretty cheap, and very unlikely that you'll leave hungry.

A second El Torito is located in the Miami International Mall, 10633 NW 12th St. (tel. 591-0671).

BUDGET

LB'S EATERY, 5813 Ponce de Leon Blvd. Tel. 661-8879.
  Cuisine: AMERICAN. **Reservations:** Not accepted.
$ Prices: Salads and sandwiches $3–$4.50; main courses $5–$8. DISC, MC, V.
  Open: Mon–Thurs 11am–10pm, Fri–Sat 11am–11:30pm.
High-quality, low-priced meals are served cafeteria style in this popular, no-nonsense eatery. A good selection of salads include chicken, tuna-apple, and a variety of green combinations. Sandwiches are built on breads or croissants, and include almost every known variation. For a main course, look for lasagne, chicken, roast beef, and vegetarian selections like ratatouille. Five nightly dinner specials include a main dish, salad, and garlic bread, and start under $5. There are no waiters here—order at the counter and wait to be called. Despite its listing in this category, LB's is technically in Coral Gables, a half block from the University of Miami stadium, across from the Metrorail tracks.

SPECIALTY DINING
HOTEL DINING

The **Aragon Cafe** in the Colonnade Hotel (tel. 448-2600) is highly recommended as one of the best restaurants of its kind in Miami, with an atmosphere as elegant as the cuisine (see the entry in "Coral Gables," above). In the Fontainebleau Hilton, the **Dining Galleries** (tel. 538-2000) has a pleasantly overdone decor and a menu emphasizing meat and fish (see the entry in "Miami Beach" above). The elegant and opulent **Dominique's** (tel. 865-6500), in the Alexander All-Suite Luxury Hotel, spotlights a variety of wild-game appetizers such as alligator scaloppine as well as such dishes as tender, marinated rack of lamb and prime steak (see entry in "Miami Beach"; jackets required for men).

In the downtown area are two excellent choices. Just off the Omni International's fourth-floor lobby is **The Fish Market** (tel. 374-0000), with one of the best seafood menus in town. The **Pavillon Grill** (tel. 577-1000), in the Inter-Continental, is a deluxe restaurant with an imaginative and adventurous cuisine. (See the entries in "Downtown," above.) For a more laid-back choice, try the **Restaurant St. Michel** (tel. 444-1666), in the Hotel Place St. Michel, where a creative French coast cuisine is complemented by an artful deco decor (see the entry in "Coral Gables and Environs," above).

BREAKFAST/BRUNCH

The Fontainebleau Hilton's famous Sunday brunch is served in the **Dining Galleries** (tel. 538-2000). Eggs cooked to order, carved meats, and fresh-baked breads served buffet style ensure that no one leaves hungry. Right in the heart of South Miami's art deco district, the **News Cafe,** 800 Ocean Dr. (tel. 538-NEWS), offers an inexpensive and excellent breakfast of both traditional and health-oriented yogurt dishes. **Sundays on the Bay,** 5420 Crandon Blvd. (tel. 361-6777), in Key Biscayne, is a fun, tropical eatery with an upbeat, informal atmosphere. Sunday brunch here is highly popular, so reservations are recommended, but still expect a wait.

LATE NIGHT

Most (but not all) **7-Eleven** food stores are open around the clock, including the downtown store at 2 SE 7th St. (tel. 358-5409), the South Miami Beach branch at 1447 Alton Rd. (tel. 672-1520), and the store at 51 Harbor Dr., Key Biscayne (tel. 361-6857).

In South Miami Beach, the **News Cafe** (tel. 538-NEWS) and **Wolfie's** (tel. 538-6626) both stay open until the wee hours (see the entries in "South Miami Beach," above). **Versailles** (tel. 444-0240) is Little Havana's most celebrated diner, busy and brisk until 2am (see the entry in "Little Havana," above).

DINING COMPLEXES

The **Bayside Marketplace Food Court,** 401 Biscayne Blvd. (tel. 577-3344), is not a single eatery. It's a restaurant shopping mall with more than 30 stalls and stands to choose from, representing a myriad of international cuisine. Choices range from bagel sandwiches and burgers to grilled chicken, Chinese stir-fry, Créole conchs, and Middle Eastern kebabs. Few dishes top $7. Plenty of public tables means that your entire party can be satisfied by different delights and still eat together.

Many of the counters here specialize in dessert, including Bimini Bay Brownies, the Cookie Bar, Everything Yogurt, and The Fudgery, making the Food Court an excellent stop, even if it's not mealtime. For more information on stores in the Bayside Marketplace, see "Savvy Shopping," in Chapter 5. The Food Court is located on the entire second level of the Marketplace's main pavilion. It's open Monday through Thursday from 10am to 10pm, on Friday and Saturday from 10am to 11pm, and on Sunday from 11am to 8pm. Some eateries open later.

PICNIC FARE

Publix is one of Miami's largest supermarket chains, with locations that include 18330 Collins Ave., Sunny Isles (tel. 931-9615); 2551 LeJeune Rd., Coral Gables (tel. 445-2641); and 4870 Biscayne Blvd., Greater Miami North (tel. 576-4318). Small groceries can be very convenient, and are literally located all over Miami. Ask at your hotel for the closest.

Compass Market, 860 Ocean Dr., South Miami Beach (tel. 673-2906), located on 8th Street just behind the Compass Café, is an upscale, downstairs marketplace that features gourmet food items like goat cheese, sun-dried tomatoes, and roasted peppers. High-end snacks and cooking supplies are also available. Sandwiches and bagels are sold from their deli counter, along with hot coffee, sparkling cider, bottled water, and other beverages.

CHAPTER 5

WHAT TO SEE & DO IN MIAMI

Many of Miami's attractions were built in the 1940s and 1950s, designed to cash in on the growing tourist-oriented economy. Like the Fontainebleau hotel along Collins Avenue, the city's still-extant showplaces are time capsules—relics of an earlier age.

With few exceptions, Miami's best sights are outdoors. The city's beautiful buildings and beaches tend to be far away from each other, so driving is definitely in order. Miami is relatively easy to negotiate; you can't get too lost.

Miami has always been a city of dreams, a place for tourists to relax and recuperate. Miami's single most common attribute is its ability to entertain. The city's top tourist destinations highlight curiosities in architecture, plants, animals, and human beings. And leaping lizards! They're extremely entertaining.

SUGGESTED ITINERARIES

IF YOU HAVE ONE DAY In the morning, drive to Miami Beach's art deco district and take an informal tour of the area. Spend some time on the beach along Ocean Drive, and eat lunch in a nearby café. In the afternoon, head to Miami's Seaquarium, on Key Biscayne, then drive through the sparkling city at sunset.

IF YOU HAVE TWO DAYS Spend the first day as outlined above. Miami's art deco district, in particular, should not be missed.

On your second day, drive down to Greater Miami South to visit one or more of the attractions listed below, such as Monkey Jungle or Coral Castle. Alternatively, visit the Miami Metrozoo, or go downtown to shop and stroll in the Bayside Marketplace.

IF YOU HAVE THREE DAYS Spend your first two days as outlined above.

On your third day visit historical Miami. Start with a tour of Villa Vizcaya, one of the city's first estates. Visit the Barnacle in Coconut Grove, then drive through Coral Gables, and stroll around the grounds of the grand Biltmore Hotel and the Venetian Pool. If there's time, head north to the Spanish Monastery Cloisters, America's oldest standing structure.

IF YOU HAVE FIVE OR MORE DAYS Spend Days 1–3 as outlined above.

On your fourth and fifth days, take time out from sightseeing and head for the beach. Play golf or tennis, fish, sail, waterski, or even place a bet at the horse or dog races. Relax at a sidewalk café in Coconut Grove, or spend an evening dining in an elegant restaurant or dancing into the wee hours. With an extra day, you can drive up to Fort Lauderdale, down to the Everglades (see "Easy Excursions from Miami," below), visit Key West (see Chapter 6), or even hop on a one-day cruise to Freeport or Nassau in The Bahamas (see "Easy Excursions from Miami," below).

1. THE TOP ATTRACTIONS

CENTRAL MIAMI

THE ART DECO DISTRICT

⭐ Miami's best sight is not a museum or an amusement park, but a part of the city itself. Located at the southern end of Miami Beach, the art deco district is a whole community made up of outrageous, fanciful 1920s and 1930s architecture that shouldn't be missed.

MIAMI METROZOO, SW 152nd St. and SW 124th Ave., south of Coral Gables. Tel. 251-0403.

Rarely does a zoo warrant mention as a city's "Top Attraction," but Miami's Metrozoo is different. This huge 290-acre complex is completely cageless; animals are kept at bay by cleverly designed moats. Star attractions include two rare white Bengal tigers. Especially appealing for both adults and children is PAWS, a newly designed petting zoo. The elephant ride is particularly fun.

Admission: $5 adults, $2.50 children 3–12, free for children under 3. Reduced rates for Florida residents.

Open: Daily 9:30am–5:30pm (ticket booth closes at 4pm). **Directions:** From U.S. 1, take the SW 152nd Street exit west three blocks to the Metrozoo entrance.

MIAMI SEAQUARIUM, 4400 Rickenbacker Causeway (south side), Key Biscayne. Tel. 361-5705.

Visitors walk around the 35-acre oceanarium, admiring the various mammals' beauty, creativity, and intelligence. One entertaining exhibit stars Flipper, the original dolphin from the television series. Other performances are highlighted by the antics of a trained killer whale.

Miami Seaquarium is a profit-making enterprise and admission is steep. Still, their shows are entertaining, and they help visitors gain insight into these interesting marine mammals.

Admission: $17.95 adults, $14.95 seniors over 65, $12.95 children under 13.

Open: Daily 9:30am–6pm (ticket booth closes at 4:30pm). **Directions:** From downtown Miami, take I-95 south to the Rickenbacker Causeway.

VILLA VIZCAYA, 3251 S. Miami Ave., just south of the Rickenbacker Causeway, north Coconut Grove. Tel. 250-9133.

⭐ You already know that South Florida is wacky, and this place proves it. Sometimes referred to as the "Hearst Castle of the East," this magnificent villa was built in 1916 as a winter retreat for James Deering, former vice-president of International Harvester. The industrialist was fascinated by 16th-century art and architecture, and his ornate mansion—which took 1,000 artisans five years to build—became a celebration of these designs.

Pink marble columns, topped with intricately designed capitals, reach up toward hand-carved European-style ceilings. Antiques decorate 34 of the 70 rooms, which are filled with baroque furniture and Renaissance paintings and tapestries. The spectacularly opulent villa wraps itself around a central courtyard. Outside, lush formal gardens, accented with statuary, balustrades, and decorative urns, front an enormous swath of Biscayne Bay.

Admission: $8 adults, $4 children 6–12, free for children under 6.

Open: Daily 9:30am–5pm; gardens open until 5:30pm (ticket booth closes at 4:30pm). **Closed:** Christmas Day. **Directions:** Take I-95 south to Exit 1 and follow the signs to Vizcaya.

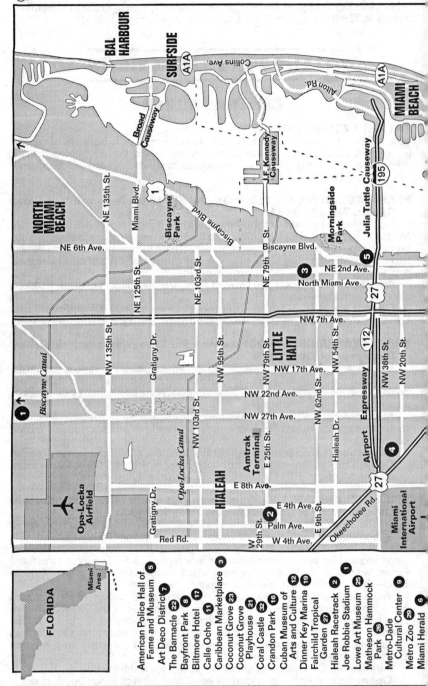

2 mi
3.2 km

BAL
HARBOUR

SURFSIDE
(A1A)

Collins Ave.

MIAMI
BEACH

(A1A)

Broad
Causeway

J.F. Kennedy
Causeway

Alton Rd.

Julia Tuttle Causeway

(195)

NORTH
MIAMI
BEACH

NE 135th St.

Miami Blvd.

Biscayne
Park

Biscayne Blvd.

1

Morningside
Park

NE 6th Ave.

NE 125th St.

NE 103rd St.

Biscayne Blvd.

NE 2nd Ave.

3

North Miami Ave.

5

(27)

NW 7th Ave.

NW 135th St.

Gratigny Dr.

NW 95th St.

NW 79th St.

LITTLE
HAITI

112

Biscayne Canal

NW 17th Ave.

NW 54th St.

NW 36th St.

NW 20th St.

1

NW 22nd Ave.

NW 27th Ave.

NW 62nd St.

Airport Expressway

NW 103rd St.

Hialeah Dr.

4

Opa-Locka Canal

HIALEAH

Amtrak
Terminal

E 25th St.

27

Opa-Locka
Airfield

E 8th Ave.

Gratigny Dr.

E 4th Ave.

Miami
International
Airport

W
29th St.

2

Palm Ave.

E 9th St.

Red Rd.

W 4th Ave.

Okeechobee Rd.

FLORIDA

Miami
Area

American Police Hall of
  Fame and Museum 5
Art Deco District 7
The Barnacle 22
Bayfront Park 8
Biltmore Hotel 17
Calle Ocho 11
Caribbean Marketplace 3
Coconut Grove 23
Coconut Grove
  Playhouse 21
Coral Castle 33
Crandon Park 16
Cuban Museum of
  Arts and Culture 12
Dinner Key Marina 19
Fairchild Tropical
  Garden 27
Hialeah Racetrack 2
Joe Robbie Stadium 1
Lowe Art Museum 25
Matheson Hammock
  Park 26
Metro-Dade
  Cultural Center 9
Metro Zoo 29
Miami Herald 6

MIAMI AREA ATTRACTIONS

Atlantic Ocean

BEACH

Collins

5th St.

Fisher Island

Virginia Key

Key Biscayne

Arthur Causeway A1A

n Rd.

14

15

16

8

South Miami Ave.

95

9

SW 12th Ave.

SW 17th Ave.

SW 27th Ave.

NW 7th St.

SW 42 Ave.

West

Flagler St.

Tamiami Trail

41

10

11

12

7th St. 41

SW 8th St.

SW 22nd St.

South Dixie Highway

US 1

Brickell Ave.

Rickenbacker Causeway

DOWNTOWN

13

Biscayne Bay

S. Bayshore Dr.

19

20 21 22

Bird Ave.

23

COCONUT GROVE

18

17

SW 37th Ave.

Ponce de Leon Blvd.

Le Jeune Rd.

CORAL GABLES

Coral Way

Red Rd.

Bird Rd.

24

25

Hardee Ave.

1

26 27 28 29

30 31 32

Airport

6612

Miami Jai-Alai Fronton 4
Miami Seaquarium 15
Monkey Jungle 30
Orange Bowl 10
Orchid Jungle 31
Parrot Jungle 28
Rickenbacker Causeway 14
South Bayshore Drive 20
University of Miami 24
Venetian Pool 18
Villa Vizcaya 13

GREATER MIAMI SOUTH

Many of Miami's tourist attractions are located in Howard, Perrine, Homestead, and other communities south of downtown. The best way to visit these attractions is via U.S. 1, a major highway that extends all the way down into the Keys. You can't get lost—blaring billboards point the way to all attractions listed. Think about combining several of the following sights, put your car's top down, turn the music up, and prepare yourself for wacky times!

CORAL CASTLE, 28655 S. Dixie Hwy., Homestead. Tel. 248-6344.
There's plenty of competition, but Coral Castle is probably the zaniest attraction in Florida. In 1917, the story goes, a crazed Latvian, jilted by unrequited love, immigrated to South Florida and spent the next 25 years of his life carving massive amounts of stone into a roofless, prehistoric-looking "castle." It was a monumental task that may remind you, in a light-hearted way, of the Great Pyramids or Stonehenge. If you're in the area, especially with kids in tow, take an hour to visit this monument of one man's madness.
Admission: $7.75 adults, $6.50 seniors, $5 children 6–12, free for children under 6.
Open: Daily 9am–5pm. **Directions:** Take U.S. 1 to SW 286th Street in Homestead.

MONKEY JUNGLE, 14805 SW 216th St., Greater Miami South. Tel. 235-1611.
See rare Brazilian golden lion tamarins! Watch the "skin diving" Asian macaques! Yes folks, it's primate paradise! Visitors are protected, but there are no cages to restrain the antics of these monkeys as they swing, chatter, and play their way into your heart! Where else but in Florida would an attraction like this still be popular after 60 years? Screened-in trails wind through acres of "jungle," and daily shows feature the talents of the park's most progressive pupils.
Admission: $10.50 adults, $9.50 seniors, $5.35 children 4–12, free for children under 4.
Open: Daily 9:30am–6pm (tickets sold until 5pm). **Directions:** Head south on U.S. 1 to 216th Street, about 20 minutes from downtown.

PARROT JUNGLE AND GARDENS, 11000 SW 57th Ave., Greater Miami South. Tel. 666-7834.
Not just parrots, but hundreds of magnificent macaws, prancing peacocks, cute cockatoos, and fabulous flamingos fly in this 50-year-old park. Alligators, tortoises, and iguanas are also on exhibit. But it's the parrots you came for, and it's parrots you get! With brilliant splashes of color, these birds appear in every shape and size. Continuous shows in the Parrot Bowl Theater star roller-skating cockatoos, card-playing macaws, and more stunt-happy parrots than you ever thought possible! Other attractions include a wildlife show, Primate Experience, a children's playground, and a petting zoo.
Admission: $11 adults, $8 children 3–12, free for children under 3.
Open: Daily 9:30am–6pm. **Directions:** Take U.S. 1 south, turn left onto SW 57th Avenue, and continue straight for 2½ miles.

PRESTON B. BIRD AND MARY HEINLEIN FRUIT AND SPICE PARK, 24801 SW 187th Ave., Homestead. Tel. 247-5727.
Miami's early settlers were terrific horticulturalists. It was the weather that originally brought them here, and plant lovers experimented with unusual tropical breeds that couldn't thrive elsewhere in America. This 20-acre living plant museum is an example of these early experiments. You'll be amazed by the unusual varieties of fruit growing on dozens of strange-looking trees with unpronounceable names.
You are free to sample anything that falls to the ground on any day you visit, but you'd be wise to wait until Saturday or Sunday, when an excellent and informative tour guide can tell you what it is before you put it in your mouth.
Admission: $1. Tours, $1.50 adults, $1 children.

Open: Daily 10am–5pm. Tours: By group reservation. Access for the disabled.
Directions: Take U.S. 1, turn right on SW 248th Street, and go straight for five miles
to SW 187th Avenue.

2. MORE ATTRACTIONS

AMERICAN POLICE HALL OF FAME AND MUSEUM, 3801 Biscayne Blvd., Miami. Tel. 573-0070.

It's somehow appropriate that America's police museum should open on Miami's Biscayne Boulevard, one of the most crime-filled strips in one of the country's most notorious cities. Inside this museum, dedicated to the history of America's police force, is a combination of reality and fantasy that's part thoughtful tribute
and part Hollywood-style drama. Just past the police car that's featured in the motion
picture *Blade Runner* is a mock prison cell, in which visitors can take pictures of
themselves "doing 5 to 10." On the educational side, would-be criminals can learn
how detectives find clues from evidence found at crime scenes. There are also displays
of execution devices, including a guillotine and an electric chair. On the serious side is
a memorial to the more than 3,000 police officers who have lost their lives in the
line of duty.

Admission: $6 adults, $3 children under 12.
Open: Daily 10am–5:30pm. **Directions:** Drive north from downtown until you
see the building with the real police car affixed to its side.

THE BARNACLE, 3485 Main Hwy., Coconut Grove. Tel. 448-9445.

The former home of naval architect and early settler Ralph Middleton Munroe is
now a museum in the heart of Coconut Grove, one block south of Commodore Plaza.
The house's quiet surroundings, wide porches, and period furnishings are a good
illustration of the way Miami's privileged class lived in the days before skyscrapers and
luxury hotels. Enthusiastic and knowledgeable state park employees and innumerable
period objects offer a wealth of historical information.

Admission: $2.
Open: Tours given Thurs–Mon at 9am, 10:30am, 1pm, and 2:30pm. **Directions:** From downtown Miami, take U.S. 1 south to South Bayshore Drive and
continue to the end; turn right onto McFarlane Avenue and left at the traffic light onto
Main Highway; the museum is five blocks along on the left.

BASS MUSEUM OF ART, 2121 Park Ave., at the corner of 21st St., South Miami Beach. Tel. 673-7530.

The Bass is the most important visual arts museum in Miami Beach. European
paintings, sculptures, and tapestries from the Renaissance, baroque, rococo, and
modern periods make up the bulk of the small permanent collection. Temporary
exhibitions alternate between traveling shows and rotations of the Bass's stock, with
themes ranging widely, from 17th-century Dutch art to contemporary architecture.

Built from coral rock in 1930, the Bass sits in the middle of six landscaped,
tree-topped acres. Be sure to visit the funky outdoor fountain made up of bathtubs,
sinks, and shower bases donated by the Formica Corporation, one of the museum's
latest acquisitions.

Admission: $2 adults, $1 students, free for children under 16. Tues admission is
by donation.
Open: Tues–Sat 10am–5pm, Sun 1–5pm (second and fourth Wed of each month,
1–9pm). **Closed:** Holidays.

THE BILTMORE HOTEL, 1200 Anastasia Ave., Coral Gables.

This grand hotel is one of Miami's oldest properties. Its 26-story tower is a replica
of the Giralda Bell Tower of the Seville Cathedral in Spain. The enormous cost of
operating this queen has forced the hotel through many hands in recent years.

Bankruptcy shut the hotel in 1990, but the Biltmore may once again be open by the time you visit. If it is, go inside and marvel at the ornate marble and tile interior.

CRIMINAL JUSTICE BUILDING, Civic Center, 1351 NW 12th St., at the corner of NW 13th Ave., downtown. Tel. 547-4888.

Okay, you've seen it in the newspaper, you've seen it on TV, but so far the infamous Miami crime scene has eluded you. If you really want to see the city's judicial system in process, stop into the city's main courthouse, right behind the Miami city jail, for some real-life drama. You're free to come and go as you wish, so check out a few courtrooms before settling on a case.

Admission: Free.

Open: Mon–Fri 9am–4:30pm.

CUBAN MUSEUM OF ARTS AND CULTURE, 1300 SW 12th Ave., at the corner of SW 13th St., Little Havana. Tel. 858-8006.

This unique museum displays significant works of art and memorabilia important for the promotion and preservation of the Cuban culture. The collection of paintings and drawings only adds up to about 200, but they're well selected, and representative of a wide range of styles. The museum has also been designated as the official repository for the mementos of Agustino Acosta, the famous Cuban poet.

Admission: $2 adults, $1 students and seniors.

Open: Daily noon–6pm. **Directions:** From downtown, head west on SW 7th Street and turn left on 12th Avenue; the museum is six blocks ahead on the right.

FAIRCHILD TROPICAL GARDENS, 10901 Old Cutler Rd., Coral Gables. Tel. 667-1651.

These large botanical gardens feature both rare and exotic plants. Tropical cycads, palms, and other unique species create a scenic, lush environment. On the hourly tram tour you can learn what you always wanted to know about the various flowers and trees.

Admission (including tram tour): $7 adults, free for children under 13.

Open: Daily 9:30am–4:30pm. **Directions:** From U.S. 1 south, turn left on LeJeune Road, follow it straight to the traffic circle, and take Cutler Road 2½ miles to the park.

METRO-DADE CULTURAL CENTER, 101 W. Flagler St., downtown.

In addition to the Dade County Public Library, the Metro-Dade Cultural Center houses both a historical museum and a fine arts center.

The primary exhibit at the **Historical Museum of Southern Florida** (tel. 375-1492) is "Tropical Dreams," a state-of-the-art, chronological history of the last 10,000 years in South Florida. The hands-on displays, audiovisual presentations, and hundreds of artifacts are really quite interesting.

The **Center for Fine Arts** (tel. 375-1700) features an eclectic mix of modern and contemporary works by such artists as Eric Fischl, Max Beckman, Jim Dine, and Stuart Davis.

Admission (to both museums): $5 adults, $2.50 seniors 65 and over, $2 children 6–12, free for children under 6.

Open: Mon–Wed and Fri–Sat 10am–5pm, Thurs 10am–9pm, Sun noon–5pm.

Directions: From I-95 north, take the NW 2nd Street exit, turn right, and continue east to NW Second Avenue; turn right and park at the Metro-Dade Garage (50 NW Second Ave.). From I-95 south, exit at the Orange Bowl–NW 8th Street exit and continue south to NW 2nd Street; turn left onto NW 2nd Street and go 1½ blocks to NW Second Avenue, turn right, and park at the Metro-Dade Garage (50 NW Second Ave). Bring the parking ticket to the lobby for validation.

ORCHID JUNGLE, 26715 SW 157th Ave. (Homestead), at 272nd St., just off U.S. 1. Tel. 247-1990.

Bathed in rich colors and heavenly scents, visitors wind their way on a self-guided tour through what may be the world's largest outdoor orchid garden. Besides orchids, you'll see rare foliage plants and beautiful palms. Many kinds of orchids are for sale in the unique gift shop.

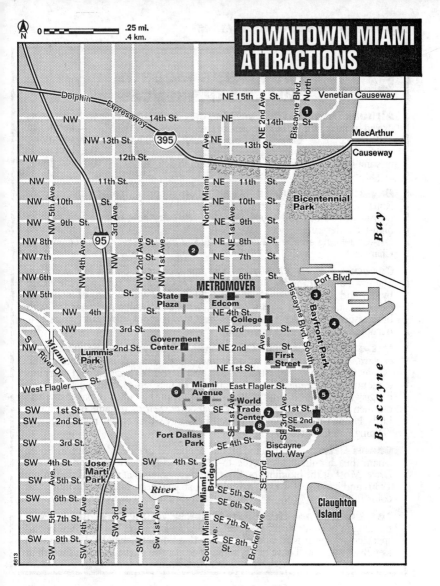

DOWNTOWN MIAMI ATTRACTIONS

0 | .25 mi.
| .4 km.

N

Dolphin Expressway

NW 14th St.
NW 13th St.
NW 12th St.
NW 11th St.
NW 10th St.
NW 9th St.
NW 8th
NW 7th
NW 6th
NW 5th
NW 4th
NW 3rd St.
NW 2nd St.
Lummis Park
West Flagler St.

NE 15th St.
NE 14th St.
NE 13th St.
NE 12th St.
NE 11th St.
NE 10th St.
NE 9th St.
NE 8th St.
NE 7th St.
NE 6th St.

Biscayne Blvd. North
Venetian Causeway
MacArthur Causeway

Bicentennial Park

Bay

Port Blvd.

METROMOVER

State Plaza
Edcom
NE 4th St.
College
NE 3rd St.
Government Center
NE 2nd St.
First Street
NE 1st St.

Miami Avenue
East Flagler St.
World Trade Center
Fort Dallas Park
Biscayne Blvd. Way

SW 1st St.
SW 2nd St.
SW 3rd St.
SW 4th St.
Jose Marti Park
SW 5th St.
SW 6th St.
SW 7th St.
SW 8th St.

Miami River

Miami Ave. Bridge

SE 2nd St.
SE 3rd St.
SE 4th St.
SE 5th St.
SE 6th St.
SE 7th St.
SE 8th St.

Bayfront Park

Biscayne Blvd. South

Challenger Seven Memorial

Biscayne

Claughton Island

6813

FLORIDA

Downtown Miami

Bayfront Park ❸
Bayside Marketplace ❹
Challenger Seven Memorial ❺
CenTrust Tower ❽
Gusman Philharmonic Hall ❼
Metromover ❻
Miami Arena ❷
Omni Shopping Mall ❶
Metro-Dade Cultural Center ❾

FROMMER'S FAVORITE
MIAMI EXPERIENCES

Airboat Through the Everglades   You've seen these wide, flat boats driven by huge fans in the rear. Airboat rides, offered by the Miccosukee Indian Village (see "Easy Excursions from Miami," below) and other organizations, are fantastic half-hour, high-speed tours through some of America's most pristine lands. Birds scatter as the boats approach, and when you slow down, alligators and other animals appear.

Bayside Marketplace   Miami's best shopping mall is this outdoor Rouse Company development, located on the water in the heart of the city's downtown. About 100 shops and carts sell everything from plastic fruit to high-tech electronics (see "Savvy Shopping," below). Upstairs, a mammoth fast-food eating arcade is a great place for a meal or snack (see "Dining," in Chapter 4).

Coconut Grove at Night   The intersection of Grand Avenue, Main Highway, and McFarlane Road is the heart of Coconut Grove, a sedate village by day and a busy meeting place by night. Sizzling with dozens of interesting cafés, boutiques, and nightspots, the Grove's sidewalks are crowded with businesspeople, students, and tourists. On weekends, sidewalk tables stay occupied until long after midnight.

Little Havana   Miami's Cuban center is the city's most important ethnic enclave. Located just west of downtown, Little Havana is centered around "Calle Ocho," SW 8th Street. This busy street is exciting and warrants exploration. Car-repair shops, tailors, electronics stores, and restaurants all hang signs in Spanish, salsa rhythms thump from the radios of passersby, and old men in guayaberas chain-smoke cigars over their daily game-of dominoes. Little Havana is also home to some of the city's best ethnic restaurants (see "Dining," in Chapter 4).

Ocean Drive   The beauty of the celebrated art deco district in South Miami Beach culminates on the 15-block beachfront strip known as Ocean Drive. Most of the buildings on this stretch are hotels that were built in the late 1930s and early 1940s. Even if you're not staying here, take a stroll along this colorful street.

The View from the Rickenbacker Causeway   Almost every building in Miami's sleek, 21st-century skyline is a gem. The best view of this spectacular cluster is from the causeway that connects mainland Miami with Key Biscayne. You'll have to pay a toll of $1 for the privilege, but it's worth it.

Admission: $5 adults, $4 students 13–17 and seniors, $1.50 children 6–12, under 6 free.
   Open: Daily 10am–5pm. **Closed:** Thanksgiving and Christmas. **Directions:** From Downtown, follow U.S. 1 South about 25 miles. Turn right on 272nd St. (Epmore Dr.). Then turn right on 157th Ave. Orchid Jungle is ½ mile on the right.

SPANISH MONASTERY CLOISTERS, 16711 W. Dixie Hwy., at the corner of 167th St., North Miami Beach. Tel. 945-1462.
   The Spanish Monastery Cloisters were first erected in Segovia, Spain in 1141. Newspaper magnate William Randolph Hearst purchased the monastery, and had it dismantled and shipped to Miami. It took workers 5 years to figure out how to reassemble it. Visitors will find a collection of medieval art inside.
   Admission: $4 adults, $2.50 seniors, $1 children 7–12, free for children under 7.
   Open: Mon–Sat 10am–4pm, Sun noon–4pm. **Directions:** From downtown,

take U.S. 1 north and turn left onto 163rd Street; make the first right onto West Dixie Highway and the Cloisters are three blocks ahead on right.

3. COOL FOR KIDS

Florida's vacationland has always been family oriented, and offers a host of programs and activities exclusively for children. Several beachfront resort hotels provide excellent supervised activities for kids, including the Sonesta Beach Hotel on Key Biscayne, and the Fontainebleau and Doral hotels in Miami Beach (see "Accommodations," in Chapter 4). Information on these and other family packages is available from the Miami Convention and Visitors Bureau (see "Information" in "Orientation," in Chapter 4).

TOP CITY ATTRACTIONS

For details of attractions listed here, see "The Top Attractions," above.

The Miami Metrozoo This completely cageless zoo offers such star attractions as a monorail "safari" and a newly designed petting zoo. Especially fun for kids are the elephant rides.

Monkey Jungle A zoo filled with monkeys, gorillas, and chimpanzees. Special shows are offered daily.

Parrot Jungle For its roller-skating cockatoos, card-playing macaws, and lots of stunt-happy parrots.

Miami Seaquarium Especially for performances given by Flipper, the original dolphin from the television series.

MORE ATTRACTIONS

MIAMI MUSEUM OF SCIENCE AND SPACE TRANSIT PLANETARIUM, 3280 S. Miami Ave., Coconut Grove. Tel. 854-4247 for general information, 854-2222 for planetarium show times.

The Museum of Science features over 140 hands-on exhibits which explore the mysteries of the universe. Live demonstrations and collections of rare natural-history specimens make a visit here fun and informative.

The adjacent Space Transit Planetarium projects astronomy and laser shows. Most interesting, perhaps, is the in-house observatory, free and open to the public on weekend evenings.

Admission: Science museum, $6 adults, $4 children 3–12 and seniors, free for children under 3; planetarium, $5 adults, $2.50 children and seniors; combination ticket, $9 adults, $5.50 children and seniors.

Open: Science museum, daily 10am–6pm. Call for planetarium show times. **Closed:** Thanksgiving and Christmas Days. **Directions:** Take I-95 south to Exit 1 and follow the signs; alternatively, ride the Metrorail to the Vizcaya Station.

VENETIAN POOL, 2701 DeSoto Blvd., at Toledo St., Coral Gables. Tel. 460-5356.

Miami's most unusual swimming pool, dating from 1924, is hidden behind pastel stucco walls, and is honored with a listing in the National Register of Historic Places. The free-form lagoon is fed by underground artesian wells and shaded by three-story Spanish porticos, and features soft fountains and waterfalls. During the summer months, the pool's 800,000 gallons of water are drained and refilled nightly, ensuring a cool, clean swim. Visitors are free to swim and sunbathe here, year-round, just as Esther Williams and Johnny Weissmuller did decades ago.

Admission: $4 adults, $3.50 children 13–17, $1.60 children under 12.

Open: June–Aug, Mon–Fri 11am–7:30pm, Sat–Sun 10am–4:30pm; Sept–Oct and Apr–May, Tues–Fri 11am–5:30pm, Sat–Sun 10am–4:30pm; Nov–Mar, Tues–Fri 11am–4:30pm, Sat–Sun 10am–4:30pm.

4. ORGANIZED TOURS

Like the tourist attractions, many of Miami's organized tours are interestingly offbeat. They are also fun and generally well priced. Always call ahead to check prices and times. Reservations are usually suggested.

WALKING TOURS   If you're lucky enough to be in Miami on a Saturday, don't miss the fascinating look at the city's historic art deco district conducted by the **Miami Design Preservation League,** headquartered at the Art Deco Welcome Center, 1001 Ocean Dr., in South Miami Beach (tel. 672-2014). Tourgoers meet at 10:30am on Saturday at the welcome center for a 1½-hour walk through some of America's most exuberant architecture; the cost is $6 per person. The Design Preservation League led the fight to designate this area a National Historic District, and is proud to share the splendid results with visitors.

TROLLEY TOURS   Old Town Trolley of Miami's distinctive orange-and-green "trolley" buses cruise the city's streets and causeways in a continuous 90-minute loop. You can stay aboard for the entire trip, or disembark at any one of half a dozen stops and reboard at your convenience. Trolleys depart daily, every 30 minutes from 10am to 4pm, and tickets ($16 for adults, $7 for children) are valid all day. Tours are completely narrated, and depart from the Bayside Marketplace and a dozen other locations. Call 374-8687 for information.

BOAT TOURS   More adventure than tour, a relaxing cruise aboard *Heritage Miami II* (tel. 442-9697), a topsail schooner and Miami's only "tall ship," is a fun way to see the city. The two-hour cruises pass by Villa Vizcaya, Coconut Grove, and Key Biscayne, and put you in sight of Miami's spectacular skyline. Cruises depart from the Bayside Marketplace Marina, 401 Biscayne Blvd. (downtown), September through May, daily at 1:30 and 6:30pm, and on Saturday and Sunday also at 11am and 9pm. The cost is $10 for adults and $5 for children under 12. Call beforehand to make sure the ship is running on schedule.

Biscayne National Park includes almost 200,000 acres of mangrove shoreline, barrier islands, and living coral reefs—all protected by the federal government. Tours of the area aboard the 52-foot glass-bottom **Biscayne National Park tour boats** cross the aquatic wilderness for a fish-eye view of some of America's most accessible coral reefs. Tours depart on Saturday and Sunday at 10am and 1:30pm from the east end of SW 328th Street in Homestead, and reservations are required (tel. 247-2400). The charge is $16.50 for adults and $8.50 for children under 12. Family snorkeling and canoe rentals are also offered.

Operated by *River Queen* **Sightseeing,** in the Eden Roc Yacht & Charter Center, 4525 Collins Ave. (at 45th Street), Miami Beach (tel. 538-5380), the *River Queen* is an authentic Mississippi River–style paddlewheel boat that cruises up Indian Creek and out into Biscayne Bay. There are three daily sightseeing tours, at 10am, 1pm, and 4pm. The charge is $10 for adults and $5 for children under 12; pickup at your hotel can be arranged.

HELICOPTER TOURS   Seeing Miami from the air is the ultimate photo opportunity! **Dade Helicopter,** 950 MacArthur Causeway (tel. 374-3737), offers helicopter rides ranging from 7 to 20 minutes, and costing $50 to $120 per person (children under 12 ride for half price; children under 2 are free). The helipad is located on the south side of the MacArthur Causeway, between the mainland and Miami Beach.

5. SPORTS & RECREATION

SPECTATOR SPORTS

Miami's spectacular sports scene includes several major professional franchises, including football and basketball, and an eclectic variety of international games including cricket, soccer, and jai alai. Check the sports sections of the *Miami Herald* for a daily listing of local events, and the paper's Friday "Weekend" section for comprehensive coverage and in-depth reports.

BASEBALL   The **University of Miami Hurricanes** (tel. 284-2655, or toll free 800/GO-CANES in Florida) play about 50 home games in the 5,000-seat Mark Light Stadium, on the university's Coral Gables campus. The season lasts from February to May, with both day and evening games scheduled. Admission is $3 to $10, and the box office is open Monday through Friday from 8am to 6pm and on Saturday from 8am to 2pm.

BASKETBALL   The NBA's **Miami Heat** made their debut in 1988, and, predictably, are one of Miami's hottest sports draws. With games played at the Miami Arena, 721 NW First Ave., the approximately 41-home-game season lasts from November to April; most games begin at 7:30pm. Tickets cost $9 to $29, and are available through the box office (tel. 577-HEAT), open Monday through Friday from 10am to 4pm (until 8pm on game nights); tickets are also available through Ticketmaster (tel. 358-5885).

DOG RACING   Greyhound racing is Miami's most popular spectator sport. The dogs circle the oval at speeds averaging 40 miles per hour. Similar to the horsetrack, betting is simple and track workers are willing to give you a hand. Note that racing is during the winter months only.

   The fun, high-stakes **Flagler Greyhound Track,** 401 NW 38th Court, at NW 33rd Street (tel. 649-3000), features some of America's top dogs. The track hosts the $110,000 International Classic, one of the richest races on the circuit. Races are held Monday through Saturday at 7:30pm, with matinees on Tuesday, Thursday, and Saturday at 12:30pm. General admission is $1, $3 to the clubhouse; parking costs 50¢.

   An average crowd of 10,000 fans wager a collective $1 million nightly at the **Hollywood Greyhound Track,** 831 N. Federal Hwy., at Pembroke Road, in Hallandale (tel. toll free 800/959-9404), which is considered by experts to be one of the best dog tracks in the country. If you've never been to a dog track before, arrive a half hour early for a quick introduction to greyhound racing, shown on the track's television monitors. The season is late December to late April, with post times Monday through Saturday at 7:30pm and on Sunday at 7pm; there are also matinees on Monday, Wednesday, and Saturday at 12:30pm. General admission is $1, $2 to the clubhouse; parking costs $1.

FOOTBALL   The NFL's **Miami Dolphins** (tel. 620-5000) franchise is Miami's most recognizable team and followed by thousands of "dolfans." During the season, about six home games are played at Joe Robbie Stadium, 2269 NW 199th St., Greater Miami North. Most games start at 1pm and tickets cost about $30. The box office is open Monday through Friday from 10am to 6pm; tickets are also available through Ticketmaster (tel. 358-5885).

   The **University of Miami Hurricanes** (tel. 284-2655, or toll free 800/GO-CANES in Florida) play at the famous Orange Bowl, 1501 NW 3rd St., from September through November. The stadium is seldom full, and games here are really exciting. If you sit high up, you'll also have an excellent view over Miami. Tickets cost $5 to $12, and the box office is open Monday through Friday from 8am to 6pm, and prior to all home games. Call for the schedule.

HORSE RACING   Wrapped around an artificial lake, suburban **Gulfstream Park,** U.S. 1 and Hallandale Beach Boulevard, Hallandale (tel. 944-1242), is both pretty and popular. Large purses and important races are commonplace, and the track is often crowded. The season is January 4 to March 16, with post times Tuesday through Sunday at 1pm. Admission is $2 to the grandstand, $4.50 to the clubhouse; parking costs $1 and up.

   You've probably seen the pink American flamingos at **Hialeah Park** (tel. 885-8000) on "Miami Vice," and indeed this famous colony is the largest of its kind. Hialeah Park, listed on the National Register of Historic Places, is one of the most beautiful in the world, featuring old-fashioned stands and acres of immaculately manicured grounds. Races are held from mid-November through mid-May; call for post times. Admission is $2 to the grandstand, $4 to the clubhouse; children under 18 enter free with a paying adult. The grandstand entrance is at East Second Avenue and 32nd Street; parking costs $1.50 and up. The park is open for sightseeing year-round, Monday through Saturday from 10am to 4pm.

JAI ALAI Sort of a Spanish-style indoor lacrosse, jai alai is popular around these parts and is regularly played in two Miami-area frontons. Players use woven baskets (*cestas*) to hurl balls (*pelotas*) at speeds that sometimes exceed 170 miles per hour. Spectators, who are protected behind a wall of glass, place bets on the evening's players.

America's oldest fronton, the **Miami Jai Alai Fronton,** 3500 NW 37th Ave., at NW 35th Street (tel. 633-6400), dates from 1926 and schedules 13 games per night. It's open year-round (except for a four-week recess in the fall), with the first games Monday and Wednesday through Saturday at 7pm; there are matinees on Monday, Wednesday, and Saturday at noon. Admission is $1 to the grandstand, $5 to the clubhouse.

SOCCER Representing yet another attempt to make soccer a viable spectator sport, the **Miami Freedom** plays its games April through August in Milander Stadium, 4800 Palm Ave., Hialeah (tel. 446-3136). Tickets cost $8.50 for adults, $3 for children under 15. The box office is open Monday through Friday from 9am to 5pm; call for the current schedule.

RECREATION

The climate in this southern city is perfectly suited for recreation, and there are a host of opportunities.

It should come as no surprise that the lion's share of participatory sports options here are water related. **Penrod's Beach Club,** 1 Ocean Dr., South Miami Beach (tel. 538-1111), offers a pool, a Jacuzzi, and jet ski, waverunner, windsurfer, and parasail rentals. It's open Sunday through Thursday from 10am to 2am and on Friday and Saturday from 10am to 5am.

BEACHES In short, there are two distinct beach alternatives: Miami Beach and Key Biscayne. It's all explained below.

Miami Beach's Beaches Collins Avenue fronts 10 miles of white sandy beach and blue-green waters from 1st to 192nd Streets. Although most of this stretch is lined with a solid wall of hotels, beach access is plentiful, and you're free to frolic along the entire strip. There are lots of public beaches here, complete with lifeguards, toilet facilities, concession stands, and metered parking (bring lots of quarters). Miami Beach's beaches are both wide and well maintained. Except for a thin strip close to the water, most of the sand here is hard-packed—the result of a $10-million Army Corps of Engineers Beach Rebuilding Project meant to protect buildings from the effects of eroding sand.

In general, the beaches on this barrier island become less crowded the farther north you go. A wooden boardwalk runs along the hotel side of the beach from 21st to 44th Streets—about 1½ miles—offering a terrific sun and surf experience without getting sand in your shoes. Aside from the "Best Beaches" listed below, Miami Beach's public, lifeguard-protected beaches include: 21st Street, at the beginning of the boardwalk; 35th Street, popular with an older crowd; 46th Street, next to the Fontainebleau Hilton Hotel; 53rd Street, a narrower, more sedate beach; 64th Street, one of the quietest strips around; and 72nd Street, a local old-timers spot.

Key Biscayne's Beaches If Miami Beach is not private enough for you, Key Biscayne might be more of what you had in mind. Crossing Rickenbacker Causeway ($1 toll) is almost like crossing into The Bahamas. The five miles of public beach here are blessed with softer sand, and are less developed and more laid-back than the hotel-laden strips to the north.

The "Best Beaches" The following are the "best" beaches for various recreational activities:

Bill Baggs Cape Florida State Park, on the south end of Key Biscayne, has barbecue grills and picnic tables shaded by a tall forest of trees, making it the **best picnic beach.** On weekends the place really hops, primarily with partying families playing games, listening to music, and cooking up a storm. The adjacent narrow, soft-sand beach is home to the picturesque Cape Florida Lighthouse, which has operated here since 1825. Admission is $2 per vehicle, $1 per passenger.

For the **best surfing beach,** the 1st Street Beach, at the bottom of Ocean Drive in South Miami Beach, has Miami's "gnarliest" waves—but there's no lifeguard.

My choice for the **best party beach** is the Crandon Park Beach, on Crandon Boulevard in Key Biscayne. It has three miles of oceanfront beach, 493 acres of park, 75 grills, three parking lots, several soccer and softball fields, and a public 18-hole championship golf course. The beach is particularly wide and the water is usually so clear that you can see to the bottom. Admission is $2 per vehicle. It's open daily from 8am to sunset.

The competition is fierce for the **best swimming beach,** but my favorite is the chic Lummus Park Beach, which runs along Ocean Drive from about 6th to 14th Streets in South Miami Beach's art deco district. It's pretty, has plenty of metered parking, and is close to a number of restaurants with excellent happy hours.

For the **best windsurfing beach,** Hobie Beach, beside the causeway leading to Key Biscayne, isn't really a beach but a quiet inlet with calm winds and a number of windsurfer-rental places.

Bal Harbour Beach, Collins Avenue at 96th Street, just a few yards north of Surfside Beach, is the **best shell-hunting beach.** There's a vita course, good shade, and usually plenty of colorful shells—but no lifeguard.

BOATING/SAILING Sailboats and catamarans are available through the beachfront concessions desk of several top resorts. They are listed under the appropriate hotels in Chapter 4. Other private rental places include the following:

The 50-horsepower, 18-foot powerboats at **Beach Boat Rentals,** 2380 Collins Ave., Miami Beach (tel. 534-4307), rent for some of the best rates on the beach: $45 for one hour, $120 for four hours, $175 for eight hours (MasterCard and VISA are accepted). Cruising is exclusively in and around Biscayne Bay, as ocean access is prohibited. Renters must be over 21 years old and must present a current passport or driver's license. The rental office is at 23rd Street, on the inland waterway in Miami Beach. It's open May to October, daily from 9am to 6pm, and (weather permitting) November to April, daily from 9am to 5pm.

At **Club Nautico of Coconut Grove,** 2560 S. Bayshore Dr., Coconut Grove (tel. 858-6258), you can rent high-quality powerboats for fishing, waterskiing, diving, and cruising in the bay or on the ocean. All boats are Coast Guard equipped with VHF radios and safety gear. They charge $150 and up for four hours, $249 and up for eight hours. There are two other Club Nautico locations, in the Crandon Park Marina, 400 Crandon Blvd., Key Biscayne (tel. 361-9217), and in the Miami Beach Marina, Pier E, 300 Alton Rd., South Miami Beach (tel. 673-2502). They're open daily from 8am to 5:30pm, weather permitting.

FISHING Bridge Fishing This is popular in Miami—you'll see people with poles over almost every waterway.

Surf Casting Some of the best surf casting in the city can be had at **Haulover Beach Park,** at Collins Avenue and 105th Street, where there's a bait-and-tackle shop right on the pier. **South Pointe Park,** at the southern tip of Miami Beach, is another popular fishing spot, and features a long pier, comfortable benches, and a great view of the ships passing through Government Cut.

Deep-Sea Fishing A number of deep-sea-fishing opportunities are also available, including the **Kelley Fishing Fleet,** Haulover Marina, 10800 Collins Ave. (at 108th Street), Haulover (Miami Beach) (tel. 945-3801). Half-day, full-day, and night fishing aboard diesel-powered "party boats" lure in fish like snapper, sailfish, and mackerel. The fleet's emphasis on drifting is geared toward trolling and bottom fishing, although they also schedule two-, three-, and four-day trips to The Bahamas. Reservations are recommended. Trips depart daily at 9am, 1:45pm, and 8pm. Half-day and night fishing trips cost $19.75 for adults and $12.75 for children; full-day trips are $29.75 for adults and $18.75 for children. Rod and reel rental is $4.25.

Although there's no shortage of private charter boats here, the **Helen C,** at the Haulover Marina, 10800 Collins Ave., Haulover (Miami Beach) (tel. 947-4081), under

Capt. Dawn Mergelsberg, is a good pick since she puts individuals together to get a full boat. The *Helen C* is a twin-engine 55-footer, equipped for big-game "monster" fish like marlin, tuna, dolphin, and bluefish. The cost is $60 per person, and she sails daily from 8am to noon and 1 to 5pm. Call for reservations.

GOLF   In addition to the two below, there are dozens of golf courses in the Greater Miami area, many of which are open to the public. Contact the Greater Miami Convention and Visitors Bureau (see "Information" in "Orientation," in Chapter 4) for a complete list of courses and costs.

The **Bayshore Golf Course,** 2301 Alton Rd., Miami Beach (tel. 532-3350), has an 18-hole green and a lighted driving range for night swings. Greens fees are $40 per person before 11am, $31 after 11am, and $23 after 2pm (Florida residents pay $5 less). It's open daily from 6:30am to dusk.

The **Key Biscayne Golf Course,** 6700 Crandon Blvd., Key Biscayne (tel. 361-9129), is the number-one ranked municipal course in the state and one of the top five in the country. The park is situated on 200 bayfront acres, and offers a pro shop, rentals, lessons, carts, and a lighted driving range. Greens fees from Thanksgiving to Easter are $55 to $73 per person; from Easter to Thanksgiving, $45 per person. These prices include carts, which are required until 1pm. The course is open daily from dawn to dusk.

HEALTH CLUBS   At the **Barcado Beach Club Gymnasium,** on the ground floor of Roney Plaza, 2377 Collins Ave. (between 23rd and 24th Streets), Miami Beach (tel. 531-7357), there are some bicycles and Universal-type pulley systems, but the workout room is primarily a free-weight facility. Not fancy, it's well equipped and visitors have free access to a nearby swimming pool. Admission is $6 per day. It's open Monday through Friday from 7am to 10pm, on Saturday from 9am to 8pm, and on Sunday from 9am to 1pm.

JET SKIING   At **Tony's Jet Ski Rentals,** 3601 Rickenbacker Causeway, Key Biscayne (tel. 361-8280), you can rent jet skis, Yamaha waverunners, and Kawasaki two-seaters. The city's largest rental shop, Tony's is located on a private beach in the Miami Marine Stadium lagoon. The cost is $45 and up per hour; waverunners rent for $65 per hour. It's open daily from 10am to 6:30pm.

SCUBA DIVING/SNORKELING   In 1981, the government began a wide-scale project designed to increase the number of habitats available to marine organisms. One of the program's major accomplishments has been the creation of nearby artificial reefs, which have attracted all kinds of tropical plants, fish, and animals.

Several dive shops around the city offer organized weekend outings, either to these reefs or to one of over a dozen old shipwrecks around Miami's shores. Check "Divers" in the *Yellow Pages* for rental equipment, and for a full list of undersea tour operators.

Anything Underwater Dive Charters, 3391 SW 25th Terrace, Miami (tel. 445-4930 or 478-2885), offers regularly scheduled full- and half-day dives. Experienced guides and quality equipment are provided to adventurers. Reservations are required. You pay $35 per person and rentals are additional. Call for sail times.

SKATING   **Skate 2000,** Ocean Drive at 12th Street, South Miami Beach (tel. 538-8282), helps you keep up with the beach crowd by renting in-line skates and the associated safety accessories. Rentals are $8 per hour, $24 per day. The company also offers skating lessons and skating tours of South Beach for $12 and $10, respectively.

TENNIS   In addition to hotel tennis facilities, about 500 public courts are available free or for a minimal charge. Some of the best tennis courts are located in Miami Beach. For information on courts closest to you, contact the **Metro-Dade County Parks and Recreation Department** (tel. 857-6868), weekdays between 8am and 5pm.

The **Flamingo Park Center,** 1245 Michigan Ave., at 12th Street, South Miami Beach (tel. 673-7761), is the city's largest facility, with 13 clay and 14 hard courts. Open Monday through Friday from 9am to 8pm and on Saturday and Sunday from 9am to dusk. The **Bayshore Golf Course,** 2301 Alton Rd., Miami Beach (tel. 532-3350), has two hard courts and is open daily during daylight hours.

WINDSURFING   Sailboards Miami, Rickenbacker Causeway, Key Biscayne (tel. 361-SAIL), operates out of big yellow trucks on Hobie Beach (see "Beaches," above), the most popular windsurfing spot in the city. Rentals are by the hour or day, and lessons are given throughout the day. You pay $15 per hour, $45 per day; a two-hour lesson and rental package is $39. It's open daily from 9am to 6pm.

6. SAVVY SHOPPING

With few exceptions, Miami's main shopping areas are not streets, but malls—a reminder of the city's strong suburban bent. Most, like Dadeland Mall and the Mall at 163rd Street, are unabashedly straightforward about their identities; others, like the Bal Harbour Shops and Bayside Marketplace, are more coyly named, as they shy away from the "mall's" middle-class connotations. South Florida's gaggle of galleries has created stiff competition, a situation that keeps shoppers happy with good values and lots of choices.

THE SHOPPING SCENE

SHOPPING AREAS   Almost every major street in Miami is lined with an infinite variety of small stores, restaurants, motels, and fast-food joints. Some of the city's best shops and shopping areas are outlined below under "Shopping A to Z," but you're bound to make your own finds. Keep your eyes open and stop at shops that interest you.

   Coconut Grove   Downtown Coconut Grove is one of Miami's few pedestrian-friendly zones. Centered around Main Highway and Grand Avenue, and branching onto the adjoining streets, the Grove's wide, café- and boutique-lined sidewalks provide hours of browsing pleasure. You can't escape Miami's ubiquitous malls, however—there's one near this cozy village center (see "Mayfair Shops," below). Coconut Grove is best known for its dozens of avant-garde clothing stores, funky import shops, and excellent sidewalk cafés.

   Coral Gables—Miracle Mile   Actually only a half mile, this central shopping street was an integral part of George Merrick's original city plan. Today the strip's importance seems slightly more historical than commercial. Lined primarily with small, '70s storefronts, the Miracle Mile, which terminates at the Mediterranean-style City Hall rotunda, also features several good and unusual restaurants (see "Dining," in Chapter 4), and is worth a stop on your tour of Coral Gables.

   South Miami Beach—Lincoln Road   The Lincoln Road Mall is an eight-block pedestrian zone, near the north end of Miami Beach's art deco district. The hip but struggling area stretches from Washington Avenue to Alton Road, and is the center of the city's most exciting art scene. The buildings that are not empty contain a unique assortment of art galleries, antiques stores, and furniture shops, as well as the studios of the Miami City Ballet. Surrounding streets, including Washington and Collins Avenues, are rife with funky thrift stores, eateries, and T-shirt shops.

HOURS, TAXES & SHIPPING   For most shops around the city **open hours** are Monday through Saturday from 10am to 6pm and on Sunday from noon to 5pm. Many stay open late (usually until 9pm) one night of the week (usually Thursday). Shops in trendy Coconut Grove are open until 9pm Sunday through Thursday, and even later on Friday and Saturday nights. Department stores and shopping malls keep longer hours, staying open from 10am to 9 or 10pm Monday through Saturday and noon to 6pm on Sunday.

   The 6% Florida state **sales tax** is added to the price of all nonfood purchases.

   Most Miami stores can wrap your purchase and **ship** it anywhere in the world via the United Parcel Service (UPS). If they can't, you can send it yourself, either through UPS (tel. 238-0134) or through the U.S. Mail (see "Fast Facts: Miami," in Chapter 4).

BEST BUYS   Locally produced and widely distributed goods are easily Miami's best buys. Not surprisingly, local seafood and citrus products are some of the city's most important exports. Other high-quality items are available in Miami, but fruit and fish are the region's specialties, and nowhere will you find them fresher.

Downtown Miami is the best district to visit for discounts on all types of goods, from watches and jewelry to luggage and leather. Inexpensive electronics and discount clothing can also be found, often from shops with a heavy Hispanic influence. Look around Flagler Street and Miami Avenue for all kinds of cluttered bargain stores. Most of the signs around here are printed in both English and Spanish, for the benefit of locals and tourists alike.

Citrus Fruit   There was a time when it seemed as though almost every other store was shipping fruit home for tourists. Today such stores are a dying breed, but a few high-quality operations still send the freshest oranges and grapefruit. **Todd's Fruit Shippers,** 221 Navarre Ave. (tel. 448-5215), can take your order over the phone, and charge it to American Express, MasterCard, or VISA. Boxes are sold by the bushel or fraction thereof, and start at about $20.

Seafood   **East Coast Fisheries,** 360 W. Flagler St., downtown (tel. 373-5516), a retail market and restaurant (see "Dining," in Chapter 4), has shipped millions of pounds of seafood worldwide from its own fishing fleet. They're equipped to wrap and send 5- or 10-pound packages of stone crab claws, Florida lobsters, Florida Bay pompano, fresh Key West shrimp, and a variety of other local delicacies to your door via overnight mail.

Miami's most famous restaurant is **Joe's Stone Crab,** located at 227 Biscayne St., South Miami Beach (tel. 673-0365, or toll free 800/780-CRAB). Joe's makes overnight air shipments of stone crabs to anywhere in the country. Joe's is only open during crab season (from October through May).

SHOPPING A TO Z
ART & ANTIQUES

The best collection of antiques shops in the city is located in the art deco district of South Miami Beach. They are usually open Tuesday through Saturday afternoons. A full list of offerings with their specific operating hours can be obtained free from the **Art Deco Welcome Center,** 1001 Ocean Dr., South Miami Beach (tel. 672-2014). Good choices are:

DECOLECTABLE, 233 14th St., South Miami Beach. Tel. 674-0899.
   This store sells art deco furniture, radios, clocks, and lighting.

GALLERY ANTIGUA, Boulevard Plaza Building, 5318 Biscayne Blvd. Tel. 759-5355.
   One of the more unusual specialty shops, featuring African-American and Caribbean art, Gallery Antigua frequently offers individual original works as well as complete art installations.

ONE HAND CLAPPING, 432 Espanola Way, South Miami Beach. Tel. 532-0507.
   This is another excellent find, featuring a broad range of art, antiques, and collectibles from this and previous centuries. A special collection of art deco antiques from the 1940s and '50s are sold.

BEACHWEAR

In addition to stores in all of the area shopping malls, try the following:

TOO COOL OCEAN DRIVE, 504 Ocean Dr., South Miami Beach. Tel. 538-5101.
   If it has to do with the beach, it's here: swimsuits, T-shirts, shorts, thongs, floats, beach chairs, towels, umbrellas, tanning lotions, and more.

BOOKS

B. DALTON, in the Bayside Marketplace, 401 Biscayne Blvd., downtown. Tel. 579-8695.

Like others in the chain, this B. Dalton has a wide selection of general-interest books.

A second bookshop is located in the Omni International Mall, 1601 Biscayne Blvd., downtown (tel. 358-1895).

BOOKS & BOOKS, 296 Aragon Ave., Coral Gables. Tel. 442-4408.

This is one of the best bookshops to be found anywhere. It's not particularly big, but B&B stocks an excellent collection of new, used, and hard-to-find books on all subjects. They have a particularly strong emphasis on art and design, as well as alternative literature, and the shop hosts regular, free lectures by noted authors and experts. For a recorded listing of upcoming events, dial 444-POEM.

A second Books & Books is located at 933 Lincoln Rd. in South Miami Beach (tel. 532-3222).

BOOKWORKS II, 6935 Red Rd. Tel. 661-5080.

This is one of Miami's most upscale bookshops, located between Coconut Grove and Coral Gables. Bookworks has long featured works from both national and local publishers.

DOUBLEDAY BOOK SHOP, in the Bal Harbour Shops, 9700 Collins Ave. Tel. 866-2871.

Located in one of the city's most upscale shopping centers, this Doubleday is known for its good variety of titles, and a particular emphasis on books of local interest.

DOWNTOWN BOOK CENTER, 247 SE 1st St., downtown. Tel. 377-9939.

Downtown Books is the city's best commerical area store, and is a great place to browse. This long-established shop is known for both its good service and its wide selection.

They have a second location at 215 NE Second Ave. (tel. 377-9938).

WALDENBOOKS, in the Omni International Mall, 1601 Biscayne Blvd. Tel. 358-5764.

Waldenbooks is a good place for the latest titles, as well as good classics and light beach reading.

DEPARTMENT STORES

Department stores are often the primary "anchors" for Miami's many malls. The biggest include:

BURDINES, 22 E. Flagler St., downtown. Tel. 835-5151.

One of the oldest and largest department stores in the state, Burdines specializes in high-quality, middle-class home furnishings and fashions.

Additional stores are located in the Dadeland Mall and at 1675 Meridian Ave. in Miami Beach. All stores can be reached at the number above. Check the telephone directory for additional locations.

SEARS ROEBUCK & COMPANY, in the Aventura Mall, 19505 Biscayne Blvd., Aventura. Tel. 937-7500.

This common store has all the usual fashions and furnishings, plus appliances, insurance, and financial services.

It's also located at 3655 Coral Way (tel. 460-3400), next to the Miracle Center just east of Coral Gables.

DISCOUNT STORES & OUTLETS

FASHION   Over 100 retail outlets are clustered in Miami's mile-square Fashion District just north of downtown. Surrounding Fashion Avenue (NW Fifth Avenue), and known primarily for swimwear, sportswear, high-fashion children's clothing, and glittery women's dresses, Miami's fashion center is second in size only to New York's. The district features European- and Latin-influenced designs with tropical hues and subdued pastels. Most stores offer high-quality clothing at a 25% to 70% discount and on-site alterations. Most are open Monday through Friday from 9am to 5:30pm.

HOUSEWARES Miami's design district shops are also some of the best in the country. Strongly influenced by Latin American markets, outlets feature the latest furniture and housewares, all at discount prices. Not all stores are open to the public, but those that are offer incredible bargains to the savviest of shoppers. The district runs north along NE Second Avenue, beginning at 36th Street.

ELECTRONICS

BEYOND, in the Bayside Marketplace, 401 Biscayne Blvd. Tel. 592-1904.

Beyond features the latest in consumer electronics. Futuristic portable stereos, televisions, telephones, and the like are all offered at reasonable rates.

Other stores are located at Cocowalk, Dadeland, Aventura, and The Falls shopping malls.

SPY SHOPS INTERNATIONAL, INC., 2900 Biscayne Blvd. Tel. 573-4779.

Farther up the street, this store sells real-life James Bond–style gadgets like night-vision binoculars, bulletproof briefcases, "bug" detectors, and other expensive gizmos. This is a serious store, not a museum, so look like you intend to buy.

FOOD & DRINK

EPICURE MARKET, 1656 Alton Rd., South Miami Beach. Tel. 672-1861.

This is the place to go for prime meats, cheeses, and wines. Cooked foods include strictly gourmet hors d'oeuvres, pâtés, and desserts. The shop also sells homemade breads and soups, along with a variety of freshly made hot items that are ready to heat and serve.

THE ESTATE WINES & GOURMET FOODS, 92 Miracle Mile, Coral Gables. Tel. 442-9915.

This exceedingly friendly storefront in the middle of Coral Gables's main shopping street offers a small but well-chosen selection of vintages from around the world. Every third Thursday from 6 to 8pm, the store's knowledgeable owner hosts a wine tasting and lecture, at which vineyard representatives are present. Tastings cost $10, and are open to the public.

GIFTS & SOUVENIRS

DAPY, in the Bayside Marketplace, 401 Biscayne Blvd., downtown. Tel. 374-3098.

Gift shops are located all over town and in almost every hotel, but Dapy's tops if you're in the market for high-tech watches, rubber coasters, Technicolor trash cans, oversize calculators, Lucite televisions, and the like. If it's cool, it's here. New Wave Japanese and European fads and gifts cost from just a few cents to hundreds of dollars.

JEWELRY

THE SEYBOLD BUILDING, 3601 NE 1st St., downtown. Tel. 377-0122.

This is the best place in Miami for discount diamonds and jewelry. The building is located right in the middle of downtown, and houses a large variety of retail shops.

LINGERIE

LINGERIE BY LISA, 3000 McFarlane Rd., Coconut Grove. Tel. 446-2368.

Coconut Grove's best lingerie shop features a huge selection of bras, panties, teddies, and camisoles. Located on the corner of Main Highway, this store includes lots of items you'll never see in a national catalog. On weekends, a live model poses in the window.

LUGGAGE

BENTLEY'S, in the Bayside Marketplace, 401 Biscayne Blvd., downtown. Tel. 372-2907.
Carrying a large selection of luggage and travel-related items, this store also features leather cases and business accessories. Bentley's also makes expert repairs.

MALLS

There are so many shopping centers in Miami that it would be impossible to mention them all, but here's a list of the biggest and the best:

AVENTURA MALL, 19501 Biscayne Blvd., Aventura. Tel. 935-4222.
Enter this large, insulated indoor mall, located at Biscayne Boulevard and 197th Street near the Dade-Broward county line, and it's easy to imagine you're on the outskirts of Omaha—or anywhere else in America for that matter. Over 200 generic shops are complemented by the megastores JC Penney, Lord & Taylor, Macy's, and Sears. Parking is free.

BAL HARBOUR SHOPS, 9700 Collins Ave., Bal Harbour. Tel. 866-0311.
There's not much in the way of whimsy here, just the best-quality goods from the fanciest names. Ann Taylor, Fendi, Krizia, Rodier, Gucci, Brooks Brothers, Waterford, Cartier, H. Stern, Tourneau . . . the list goes on and on. The Bal Harbour Shops are the fanciest in Miami. With Neiman Marcus at one end and Saks Fifth Avenue at the other, the mall itself is a pleasant open-air emporium, with covered walkways and lush greenery. The Bal Harbour Shops are located at 97th Street, just opposite the tall Sheraton Bal Harbour hotel. Parking is $1.

BAYSIDE MARKETPLACE, 401 Biscayne Blvd., downtown. Tel. 577-3344.
Miami's successful Rouse Company development has taken over a stunning location—16 beautiful waterfront acres in the heart of downtown—and turned it into a lively and exciting shopping place. Downstairs, about 100 shops and carts sell everything from plastic fruit to high-tech electronics (some of the more unique specialty shops are listed in this section). The upstairs eating arcade is stocked with dozens of fast-food choices, offering a wide variety of inexpensive international eats (see "Dining," in Chapter 4). Some restaurants stay open later than the stores, which close at 11pm Monday through Saturday and at 8pm on Sunday. Parking is $1 per hour.

DADELAND MALL, 7535 N. Kendall Dr., Kendall. Tel. 665-6226.
The granddaddy of Miami's suburban mall scene, Dadeland features more than 175 specialty shops, anchored by five large department stores—Burdines, JC Penney, Jordan Marsh, Lord & Taylor, and Saks Fifth Avenue. Sixteen restaurants serve from the adjacent Treats Food Court. The mall is located at the intersection of U.S. 1 and SW 88th Street, 15 minutes south of downtown. Parking is free.

THE FALLS, 8888 Howard Dr., in the Kendall area. Tel. 255-4570.
Tropical waterfalls are the setting for this outdoor shopping center with dozens of moderately priced, slightly upscale shops. Miami's only Bloomingdale's is here, as are Polo Ralph Lauren, Caswell-Massey, and over 60 other specialty shops. The Falls is located at the intersection of U.S. 1 and 136th Street, about three miles south of Dadeland Mall. Parking is free.

THE MALL AT 163RD STREET, 1421 NE 163rd St., North Miami Beach. Tel. 947-9845.
This aptly named three-story megamall, between U.S. 1 and I-95 in Greater Miami North, is protected by the world's first Teflon-coated fiberglass roof. Beneath it are 150 "Middle American" shops, including Burdines, Mervyn's, and Marshalls

WHAT TO SEE & DO IN MIAMI

department stores. The customer-service center dispenses maps and tourist information as well as wheelchair loans and $1 stroller rentals. Parking is free.

MAYFAIR SHOPS IN THE GROVE, 2911 Grand Ave., Coconut Grove. Tel. 448-1700.

The small and labyrinthine Mayfair Shops complex, just a few blocks east of Commodore Plaza, conceals several top-quality shops, restaurants, art galleries, and nightclubs. The emphasis is on chic, expensive elegance, and intimate, European-style boutiques are featured. Valet parking is $5.

MARKETS

THE OPA-LOCKA/HIALEAH FLEA MARKET, 12705 NW 42nd Ave. (LeJeune Rd.), near Amelia Earhart Park. Tel. 688-0500.

Featuring over 1,000 merchants, this flea market sells everything from plants and pet food to luggage and linen. This indoor/outdoor weekend market is one of the largest of its kind in Florida. There are no real antiques here. Almost everything is brand new (of suspect quality and origin) and dirt cheap.

It's open from 5am to 6pm Friday through Sunday. Admission and parking are free.

PERFUMES & BEAUTY SUPPLIES

PERFUMANIA, in the AmeriFirst Building, 1 SE Third Ave., downtown. Tel. 358-3224.

Perfumania sells designer fragrances at 20% to 60% below normal retail prices. The shop is in the heart of downtown Miami.

Other locations include 223 Miracle Mile, Coral Gables (tel. 529-0114); and 1604 Washington Ave., South Miami Beach (tel. 534-7221).

SAFETY EQUIPMENT

SPY SHOPS INTERNATIONAL, INC., 350 Biscayne Blvd., downtown. Tel. 374-4779.

Leave it to Miami to nurture a chain of stores specializing in electronic surveillance and countersurveillance equipment, nonlethal protection devices, day and night optical devices, and other protective devices. Stun guns belting out 90,000 volts of electricity, and Greenguard, a chemical spray that temporarily disables an attacker, are also sold. Other neat gadgets include portable doorknob alarms and shaving cream safes—the bottom untwists, revealing a dry space for hiding cash and valuables.

TOYS

FUNWORLD TOYS & HOBBIES, 145 E. Flagler St., downtown. Tel. 374-1453.

This large store features all the hits, including Legos, Sega electronics, Mattel cars and toys, and remote-control boats, cars, and airplanes. Fisher Price and other toddlers' toys are also available.

7. EVENING ENTERTAINMENT

One of the most striking aspects of the city is the recent growth of world-class music, dance, and theater. Miami proudly boasts an opera company and a symphony orchestra, as well as respected ballet and modern dance troupes.

South Florida's late-night life is abuzz, with South Miami Beach at the center of the scene. The **art deco district** is the spawning ground for top international acts including Latin artist Julio Iglesias, controversial rappers 2 Live Crew, jazz man Nestor Torres, and rockers Expose, Nuclear Valdez, and of course, Gloria Estefan and the Miami Sound Machine. It's no secret that Cuban and Caribbean rhythms are extremely popular, and the sound of the conga, incorporated into Miami's club culture, makes dancing irresistible.

If you're not sure where to spend an evening, you can't go wrong by heading into downtown **Coconut Grove.** In the heart of this otherwise quiet enclave, music clubs blast their beats, and sidewalks are perpetually crowded with outdoor café tables. There's not a lot of professional entertainment in the Grove; the main show is always on the street, where crowds gather to see and to be seen.

New Times is the most comprehensive of Miami's free weekly newspapers. Available each Wednesday, this paper prints articles, previews, and advertisements on upcoming local events. Several **telephone hotlines**—many operated by local radio stations—give free recorded information on current events in the city. These include: Love 94 Concert Hotline (tel. toll free 800/237-0939), Song & Dance Concerts (tel. 947-6471), 24-Hour Cosmic Hotline (tel. 854-2222), and the UM Concert Hotline (tel. 284-6477). Other information-oriented telephone numbers are listed under the appropriate headings, below.

THE PERFORMING ARTS

Where noted, tickets can be purchased by phone through **Ticketmaster** (tel. 358-5885). The company accepts all major credit cards, and has phone lines open 24 hours. If you want to pick up your tickets from a Ticketmaster outlet, call for the location nearest you. Outlets are open Monday through Saturday from 10am to 9pm and on Sunday from noon to 5pm. There's a small service charge.

MAJOR PERFORMANCE HALLS

COLONY THEATER, 1040 Lincoln Rd., South Miami Beach. Tel. 532-3491.

After years of decay and a $1-million face-lift, the Colony has become an architectural showpiece of the art deco district. This multipurpose 465-seat theater stages performances by the Miami City Ballet and the Ballet Flamenco La Rosa, as well as various special events.

DADE COUNTY AUDITORIUM, 2901 W. Flagler St., downtown. Tel. 547-5414.

Performers gripe about the lack of space, but for patrons, this 2,500-seat auditorium is comfortable and intimate. It's home to the city's Greater Miami Opera, and stages productions by the Miami Ballet Company and the Concert Association of Florida.

GUSMAN CENTER FOR THE PERFORMING ARTS, 174 E. Flagler St., downtown. Tel. 374-2444.

Seating is tight, but the sound is good at this 1,700-seat downtown theater. In addition to providing a regular stage for the Philharmonic Orchestra of Florida and the Ballet Theatre of Miami, the Gusman Center also features pop concerts, plays, film festival screenings, and special events.

MAJOR CONCERT & PERFORMANCE HALL BOX OFFICES

Colony Theater, 1040 Lincoln Rd., South Miami Beach (tel. 532-3491).
Dade County Auditorium, 2901 W. Flagler St., downtown (tel. 547-5414).
Gusman Center for the Performing Arts, 174 E. Flagler St., downtown (tel. 374-2444).
Gusman Concert Hall, 1314 Miller Dr., Coral Gables (tel. 284-2438).
Jackie Gleason Theater of the Performing Arts (TOPA), 1700 Washington Ave., South Miami Beach (tel. 673-7300).

The auditorium itself was built as a movie palace, the Olympia Theater, in 1926, and its ornate interior is typical of the era, complete with fancy columns, a huge pipe organ, and twinkling "stars" on the ceiling.

GUSMAN CONCERT HALL, 1314 Miller Dr., Coral Gables. Tel. 284-2438.

Not to be confused with the Gusman Center, above, this roomy 600-seat hall gives a stage to the Miami Chamber Symphony and a varied program of university recitals.

JACKIE GLEASON THEATER OF THE PERFORMING ARTS [TOPA], 1700 Washington Ave., South Miami Beach. Tel. 673-7300.

It has become tradition for the American Ballet Theatre to open its touring season here during the last two weeks of January, after which TOPA is home to big-budget Broadway shows, classical music concerts, opera, and dance performances. This 2,705-seat hall has been newly renovated in order to improve the acoustics and sightlines.

MIAMIWAY THEATER, 12615 W. Dixie Hwy., North Miami. Tel. 893-0005.

Owned by actor Philip Michael Thomas of "Miami Vice" fame, this high-tech performing arts complex features a state-of-the-art sound system in a 435-seat theater. Although the stage is often dark, keep an eye out for interesting alternative productions as well as various live performances.

Admission: Depends on the production.

MINORCA PLAYHOUSE, 232 Minorca Ave., Coral Gables. Tel. 446-1116.

The Florida Shakespeare Theater calls Minorca "home." At other times, traveling dance and theater companies perform here. Performances are usually held Tuesday through Saturday evenings, as well as Wednesday, Saturday, and Sunday matinees throughout the year. The box office is open Monday through Saturday from 10am to 8pm and on Sunday from noon to 4pm.

Admission: Tickets, $18 and $20, $10 and $15 for students and seniors.

THE RING THEATRE, on the University of Miami Campus, 1380 Miller Dr., entrance no. 6, Coral Gables. Tel. 284-3355.

The university's Department of Theater Arts uses this stage for advanced student productions of comedies, dramas, and musicals. Faculty and guest actors are regularly featured, as are contemporary works by local playwrights. Performances are usually scheduled Tuesday through Saturday during the academic year only. The box office is open Monday through Friday from 10am to 5pm, and two hours before show time.

Admission: Tickets, $8–$20.

THEATER

ACME ACTING COMPANY, 955 Alton Rd., Miami Beach. Tel. 372-9077.

Miami's closest approximation to New York's Off Off Broadway is embodied in this single local troupe. Lively productions of contemporary plays are most often performed at the Colony Theater in South Miami Beach. Performances are Wednesday through Saturday at 8:15pm and on Sunday at 7:15pm.

Admission: Tickets, $15 Wed–Fri and Sun, $17 Sat, $13 students and seniors.

COCONUT GROVE PLAYHOUSE, 3500 Main Hwy., Coconut Grove. Tel. 442-4000.

The Grove Theater, as it was originally called, opened as a movie house in 1927. Thirty years later, real estate developer George Engle bought this beautiful Spanish rococo palace and, after a $1-million renovation, staged the American première of *Waiting for Godot*.

Today this respected playhouse is known for its original and innovative staging of both international and local plays. Dramas and musicals receive equal attention on the theater's main stage, while the house's second, more intimate Encore Room is well suited to alternative and experimental productions.

The theater's play season lasts from October through June. The box office is open

Tuesday through Saturday from 10am to 9pm and on Sunday and Monday from 10am to 6pm; tickets are also available through Ticketmaster. Main stage performances are Tuesday through Saturday at 8:15pm, with matinees on Wednesday, Saturday, and Sunday at 2pm. Encore Room performances are Tuesday through Saturday at 8:30pm, with matinees on Wednesday, Thursday, and Sunday at 2:15pm. Schedules differ during previews.
Admission: Tickets, $15–$37.50.

CLASSICAL MUSIC & OPERA

In addition to the local orchestras and operas described below, each year brings with it a slew of special events and touring artists. One of the most important and longest-running series is produced by the **Concert Association of Florida (CAF),** 555 17th St., South Miami Beach (tel. 532-3491). Known for almost a quarter of a century for their high-caliber, star-packed schedules, CAF regularly arranges the best classical concerts for the city. Season after season the schedules are punctuated by world-renowned dance companies and seasoned virtuosi such as Itzhak Perlman, and Andre Watts.

CAF does not have its own space. Performances are usually scheduled either in the Dade County Auditorium or the Jackie Gleason Theater of the Performing Arts (see "Major Performance Halls," above). The performance season lasts from October through April, and ticket prices range from $20 to $60.

GREATER MIAMI OPERA ASSOCIATION, 1200 Coral Way, Coral Gables. Tel. 854-1643.

The 50th Anniversary of the Miami Opera was in 1991. It regularly features singers from America's and Europe's top houses. All productions are sung in their original language and staged with projected English supertitles. Tickets become scarce when Plácido Domingo or Luciano Pavarotti (who made his American debut here in 1965) comes to town.

The opera's season runs roughly from January through April only, with performances four days per week. Most productions are staged in the Dade County Auditorium (see "Major Performance Halls," above).
Admission: Tickets, $13–$50; student and senior discounts available.

THE NEW WORLD SYMPHONY, 541 Lincoln Rd., South Miami Beach. Tel. 673-3331.

Alternating performances between downtown's Gusman Center for the Performing Arts and South Beach's Lincoln Theatre, this six-year-old orchestral academy is a major stepping-stone for gifted young musicians seeking a professional career. Accepting artists on the basis of a three-year fellowship, and led by artistic advisor Michael Tilson Thomas, the orchestra specializes in ambitious, innovative, energetic performances, and often features guest soloists and renowned conductors. The symphony's season lasts from October through May.
Admission: Tickets, $10–$40; student and senior discounts available.

FLORIDA PHILHARMONIC ORCHESTRA, Dade County Office, 836 Biscayne Blvd., downtown. Tel. toll free 800/226-1812.

South Florida's premier symphony orchestra, under the direction of James Judd, presents a full season of mainstream and pops programs interspersed with several children's and contemporary popular music dates. The Philharmonic performs downtown in the Gusman Center for the Performing Arts, the Jackie Gleason Theater, and the Dade County Auditorium (see "Major Performance Halls," above).
Admission: Tickets, $11–$35.

MIAMI CHAMBER SYMPHONY, 5690 N. Kendall Dr., Kendall. Tel. 858-3500.

Renowned international soloists regularly perform with this professional orchestra. The symphony performs October through May, and most concerts are held in the Gusman Concert Hall, on the University of Miami campus (see "Major Performance Halls," above).
Admission: Tickets, $12–$30.

DANCE

Several local dance companies train and perform in the Greater Miami area. In addition, top visiting troupes regularly pass through the city, stopping at the venues listed above. Keep your eyes open for special events and guest artists.

BALLET FLAMENCO LA ROSA, 1008 Lincoln Rd., South Miami Beach. Tel. 672-0552.

This year marks the ballet's sixth season in South Miami Beach. A professional company, Ballet Flamenco La Rosa combines other forms of dance with traditional flamenco works. Performances are usually held in South Miami Beach's Colony Theater.

Admission: Tickets, $15–$20.

MIAMI CITY BALLET, 905 Lincoln Rd. Mall, South Miami Beach. Tel. 532-4880.

★ Headquartered behind a storefront in the middle of the art deco district and directed by Edward Villella, this eight-year-old Miami company has quickly emerged as an important troupe, performing a repertoire of classical and contemporary works. The artistically acclaimed and innovative company features a repertoire of more than 60 ballets, many by George Balanchine, and more than 20 world premières. The City Ballet season runs from September through April, with performances at the Dade County Auditorium (see "Major Performance Halls," above).

Admission: Tickets, $17–$49.

MIAMI BALLET COMPANY [MBC], 2901 W. Flagler St. Tel. 667-5985.

Because MBC is an amateur troupe, performers put forth a lot of energy, fueled by the dream of going pro. Established in 1951, the company has a reputation for working with talented underage performers as well as guest dancers from around the world. Miami performances are in October, November, January, and May. The MBC usually performs in the Dade County Auditorium (see "Major Performance Halls," above).

Admission: Tickets, $11–$40.

BALLET THEATRE OF MIAMI, 1809 Ponce de Leon Blvd., Coral Gables. Tel. 442-4840.

The Ballet Theatre is a professional troupe, under the artistic direction of Lizette Piedra and Tony Catanzaro, formerly of the Boston Ballet. Beautifully staged performances of traditional and avant-garde dances have earned critical acclaim. Performances are held from October through June in the Gusman Center for the Performing Arts (see "Major Performance Halls," above).

Admission: Tickets, $12–$40.

THE CLUB & MUSIC SCENE

LIVE REGGAE

Lots of local clubs regularly feature live and recorded reggae. Some are authentic Jamaican joints, while others play the music to round out their island motifs. Check the local listings for the latest.

THE HUNGRY SAILOR, 3064½ Grand Ave., Coconut Grove. Tel. 444-9359.

This small, wood-paneled, English-style "pub" has Watneys, Bass, and Guinness on draft, and reggae regularly on tap. The club attracts an extremely mixed crowd. There's a short British menu and high-quality live music Tuesday through Saturday. It's open Sunday through Thursday from 11am to midnight and on Friday and Saturday from 11am to 2:30am.

Admission: Free Sun–Thurs, $5–$10 Fri–Sat.

SUNDAYS ON THE BAY, 5420 Crandon Blvd., Key Biscayne. Tel. 361-6777.

Terrific happy hours are followed by dockside disco nights. Sundays has a great party atmosphere, fantastic water views, and good tropical food (see "Dining," in Chapter 4). Open Sunday through Wednesday from 11am to midnight and Thursday through Saturday from 11am to 1am.

Sundays' sibling restaurant, Salty's (tel. 945-5115), also occupies a terrific location, in Haulover Park at Collins Avenue and 108th Street in Miami Beach.
Admission: Free.

ROCK/COUNTRY/FOLK

Rock clubs often overlap with dance spots (see below) which also sometimes offer live rock bands. For up-to-date listings, check the papers, **WGTR-FM Concertline** (tel. 284-6477), and the **ZETA Link** (tel. toll free 800/749-9490). Along with the venues listed below, free rock concerts are held every Friday throughout the winter in South Miami Beach's South Pointe Park. The shows feature the best local bands and start at 8pm.

Many area clubs book country bands and folk musicians, but not regularly enough to be included here. Check the free weekly *New Times,* and keep your eyes and ears open for current happenings.

CACTUS CANTINA GRILL, 630 6th St. (just west of Washington Ave.), South Miami Beach. Tel. 532-5095.

This Los Angeles–style cantina is one of South Beach's hottest finds. Gritty to the max, the Cactus features music that's live and loud almost every night. Styles range from jazz and blues to country, rockabilly, and soul. The new Coyote Room is open on Thursday and Friday, with original rock. A huge, excellent, and inexpensive Cal-Mex menu is complemented by killer margaritas and a well-stocked tequila bar. Highly recommended. Open daily from 5pm to 5am.
Admission: Free, except for the Coyote Room and special events.

FIREHOUSE FOUR, 1000 S. Miami Ave., downtown. Tel. 379-1923.

Miami's oldest fire station is now a popular restaurant and club. Live new rock music is featured on Friday or Saturday, and there's usually a spirited crowd nightly. The club sometimes hosts folk artists on Thursday. Open Monday through Thursday from noon to 11pm, and on Friday and Saturday from noon to 3am. (See "Happy Hours," below.)
Admission: Free–$5.

PENROD'S, 1 Ocean Dr., South Miami Beach. Tel. 538-1111.

South Miami Beach's jack-of-all-trades also books bands. Most weekdays there's straightforward rock music all day, and calypso tunes on weekends. Drink and snack specials are common in this multilevel, sports-oriented club. It's open daily from 10am to 1am.
Admission: Free.

THE SPOT, 218 Espanola Way, South Miami Beach. Tel. 532-1682.

New and red-hot, Mickey Rourke's Spot is yet another celeb-owned place in the city's trendiest quarter. Lines can be vicious, especially on weekends, but once inside, the crowd is mellower and surprisingly unpretentious. The large drinking room features a full bar and good music that's often even danceable. Open daily from 9pm to 5am.
Admission: Free.

JAZZ/BLUES

South Florida's jazz scene is very much alive with traditional and contemporary performers. Keep an eye out for guitarist Randy Bernsen, vibraphonist Tom Toyama, and flutist Nestor Torres, young performers who lead local ensembles. The **University of Miami** has a well-respected jazz studies program in their School of Music (tel. 284-6477), and often schedules low- and no-cost recitals. Frequent jazz shows are also scheduled at the **Miami Metrozoo** (see "The Top Attractions," above). The lineup changes frequently, and it's not always jazz, but the quality is good and concerts are included in the zoo admission.

Additionally, many area hotels feature cool jazz and light blues in their bars and lounges. Schedules are listed in newspaper entertainment sections. Finally, some of the rock clubs listed above also feature blues bands. Try calling the **Blues Hotline** (tel. 666-MOJO), and the **Jazz Hotline** (tel. 382-3938) for the most up-to-date bookings in Miami's jazz rooms.

Perhaps because the area itself is reminiscent of the Jazz Age, the bulk of the listings below are clustered in the art deco district of South Miami Beach, making it easy to plan an evening walking tour of some of the city's best clubs.

CAFE AVALON, in the Avalon Hotel, 700 Ocean Dr., at the corner of 7th St., South Miami Beach. Tel. 538-0133.

One of the beach's most stunning art deco hotels has jazz and other live music Thursday through Sunday in their lobby restaurant/bar. The café is open daily from dawn to midnight or 2am.

Admission: Free.

CLEVELANDER RESTAURANT, in the Clevelander Hotel, 1020 Ocean Dr., at 10th St., South Miami Beach. Tel. 531-3485.

Offering live jazz, rock, or reggae most nights, the Clevelander is another good choice along South Beach's most popular strip. It's open daily from 11am to 5am.

Admission: Free.

LET'S MAKE A DAIQUIRI, in the Bayside Marketplace, 401 Biscayne Blvd., downtown. Tel. 372-5117.

Right smack in the middle of the mall is this outdoor bar with one of the best views in town. Live jazz, rock, reggae, and calypso are featured almost nightly, and you don't even have to order a drink. It's open Sunday through Thursday from 9am to midnight, and on Friday and Saturday from 9am to 2am. The music ends an hour before closing.

Admission: Free.

SCULLY'S TAVERN, 9809 Sunset Dr., South Miami. Tel. 271-7404.

Excellent local bands, most often jazz and blues oriented, frequent Scully's, a sports-type bar with television monitors. There's live music Wednesday through Friday. Open Sunday through Thursday from 11am to 1am, and on Friday and Saturday from 11am to 3am.

Admission: Free.

TOBACCO ROAD, 626 S. Miami Ave., downtown. Tel. 374-1198.

Featuring live music nightly, Tobacco Road sports an eclectic menu of new and local jazz, rock, and blues. On weekends, two stages, one up and one down, heat up simultaneously. This is a great place to dance. It's open daily from noon to 5am.

Admission: Free–$6.

DANCE CLUBS

In addition to quiet cafés and progressive poolside bars, Miami Beach pulsates with one of the liveliest night scenes in the city. Several loud dance clubs feature live bands as well as DJ dancing.

THE KITCHEN CLUB, CLUB BEIRUT, AND REGGAE DIRECTORY, 100 21st St. at the beach, South Miami Beach. Tel. 538-6631.

The same space adopts different personas on alternate nights of the week. The Kitchen is a DJ dance joint featuring the newest wave grooves. Beirut is generally a live-music venue where cutting-edge bands are given a stage. Reggae Directory features new Jamaican sounds. Call for times and schedules.

Admission: Free–$10.

STUDIO ONE 83, 2860 NW 183rd St., Carol City. Tel. 621-7295.

This African-American–oriented disco with occasional Caribbean bands also features live jazz in the Jazz Room daily. Special live concerts are also booked. It's open daily from 5pm to 4am; there's a happy hour daily from 5 to 8pm.

Admission: Free–$5.

VAN DOME, 1532 Washington Ave., South Miami Beach. Tel. 534-4288.

South Beach's current star of the moment is an impressive New York–style dance club, located behind the carved stone walls of a former Jewish synagogue. Gothic styling and a wraparound second-floor ambulatory have attracted trendies, while an excellent sound system, late-night snack/raw bar, and quiet-enough tables combine to give this place some staying power. It's open Thursday through Saturday from 10pm to 5am.
Admission: $5–$15.

THE BAR SCENE

Besides the many music clubs listed above, Miami's bars and lounges are noted for their spirited happy hours. In addition, several unique "theme" bars offer fun and adventure.

HAPPY HOURS

Miami is a happy-hour heaven. For tourists and locals alike, few things are more relaxing than sitting down with food, drinks, and friends in a casual atmosphere.

Most hotel bars and many restaurants—especially in South Miami Beach and Coconut Grove—offer discounted drinks and food, served just around sunset. Some are in sight of spectacular waterfront views. Many establishments offering special happy hours are listed with the restaurants in Chapter 4. Others are listed in this section under various club headings, and the rest are listed below.

ALCAZABA, in the Hyatt Regency Hotel, 50 Alhambra Plaza, Coral Gables. Tel. 441-1234.

The Hyatt's Top-40 lounge exudes a Mediterranean atmosphere that mixes fantasy with reality. Tropical drinks and authentic tapas are on the menu. Happy hour, on Wednesday and Friday from 5 to 7pm and on Saturday from 9 to 11pm, offers half-price beer, wine, and well drinks plus a free buffet.

THE CLEVELANDER BAR, 1020 Ocean Dr., Miami Beach. Tel. 531-3439.

One of Ocean Drive's largest bars, the Clevelander is an art deco gem, featuring a 1930s-era "flying saucer" statue, and a curvy, neon-lit glass-brick bar that's packed most nights. Live bands perform nightly, outside by the large swimming pool and under the glass-wrapped South Beach Gym. Inside, another large bar is backed by a saltwater tank, and fronted by a busy pool table. It's open daily from 11am to 5am.

COCO LOCO'S, in the Sheraton Biscayne Bay Hotel, 495 Brickell Ave., downtown. Tel. 373-6000.

Coco's offers one of the best happy-hour buffets in town, with hot hors d'oeuvres like chicken wings, pasta, and pizza. On Friday there's an extra-special buffet, with a $2 plate charge. Happy hour is Monday through Friday from 5 to 8pm. On Friday and Saturday nights there's live Latin entertainment.

DOC DAMMERS SALOON, in the Colonnade Hotel, 180 Aragon Ave., Coral Gables. Tel. 441-2600.

A well-stocked mahogany bar and an easygoing 1920s motif are the hallmarks of this 30-something hangout. The light menu features dozens of upscale appetizers, gourmet pizzas, and alligator burgers. Happy hour is Monday through Friday from 5 to 8pm. Specials include $2.50 beer, wine, and drinks, plus a free buffet on Friday; look for $1-drink "Ladies' Nights."

FIREHOUSE FOUR, 1000 S. Miami Ave., downtown. Tel. 379-1923.

Burgers, fries, and crunchy conch fritters make great beer companions (see "Rock/Country/Folk," above). Happy hour is Monday through Friday from 5 to 8pm. Specials include $2 drinks and a free hot buffet.

MANGO'S TROPICAL CAFE, 900 Ocean Dr., South Miami Beach. Tel. 673-4422.

When critics accuse South Beach of becoming too commercial, they usually point to Mango's as evidence. Tailor-made for tourists, this Cuban-style honky-tonk caters to visitors who crave tropical drinks and live, loud Latin rhythms. An artificial waterfall splashes in back of an extensive bar, and the whole complex has a decidedly islandy open-air feel. There's a juice bar by the entrance, and dancing till the wee hours. Damn the critics—this place is fun!

MONTY'S RAW BAR, 2560 S. Bayshore Dr., Coconut Grove. Tel. 858-1431.

This tropical-looking, outdoor, pier-top bar offers the Grove's swingingest happy hour, with beautiful sea views and rocking island music. Fresh oysters, chowders, and fritters are available. Happy hour is Monday through Friday from 4 to 8pm.

SOUTH POINTE SEAFOOD HOUSE, South Pointe Park, 1 Washington Ave., South Miami Beach. Tel. 673-1708.

The mood is casual, and the scenery breathtaking with views overlooking the Atlantic Ocean and Government Cut. This is a great place to "kick back," especially on Friday when the cruise ships pass by on their way out to sea. Happy hour is Monday through Friday from 5 to 7pm. There's a free buffet.

TOBACCO ROAD, 626 S. Miami Ave., downtown. Tel. 374-1198.

Home of Miami's first liquor license, Tobacco Road still offers good music, great burgers (cheese, mushroom, chili), and wonderful homemade ice cream. Happy hour is Monday through Friday from 5 to 8pm. Specials include drink discounts and $1 appetizer plates.

THEME BARS

PENROD'S BEACH CLUB, 1 Ocean Dr., South Miami Beach. Tel. 538-1111.

Earning a listing here for its party-happy evenings and frequent special events, Penrod's is always chock-full of surprises. Almost every night it has a featured attraction, like drink and food specials, dance and bathing-suit contests, barbecues, laser shows, and live bands. Open daily from 10am to 1am.

Admission: Free.

MORE ENTERTAINMENT
SUPPER CLUBS

Since their heyday in the 1950s, Miami's many dinner shows fell upon difficult times. Today, however, they are experiencing a renaissance. Meals are served at all the establishments listed below, but you don't have to eat. After paying the cover charge, you can decide to just have drinks or coffee and dessert. Reservations are always recommended.

CLUB TROPIGALA, in the Fontainebleau Hilton Hotel, 4441 Collins Ave., Miami Beach. Tel. 538-2000.

Extravagant costumes on shapely showgirls are the hallmark of this glitzy hotel's tropical-theme nightclub. Musical reviews change, but all include huge casts, overdone production numbers, and two orchestras, on opposite sides of the room, alternating between Latin and Top-40 music. Shows are given on Wednesday, Thursday, and Sunday at 8:30pm, and on Friday and Saturday at 8 and 10pm. Jackets are required for men.

Admission: $13.50.

LES VIOLINS SUPPER CLUB, 1751 Biscayne Blvd., downtown. Tel. 371-8668.

What Club Tropigala is to the North American "snowbirds," Les Violins is to the Latin community. Garish, lavish, and utterly formal, the entertainment here features glittery costumes, spectacular floor shows, and strolling violinists. Somehow, however, it seems as though Les Violins is not fake or contrived. Rather, the club's intricately staged entertainment is performed with an entirely straight face. The dances amuse, and the sets are truly stunning. Except for Cuban desserts and Spanish wines, the cuisine is strictly continental. Highly recommended.

Shows are on Thursday at 8:30pm, on Friday at 9pm, on Saturday at 8:30 and 10:30pm, and on Sunday at 9pm. Jackets are required for men.

Admission: $15.

SEVEN SEAS DINNER SHOW, at the Holiday Inn Newport Pier Resort, 16701 Collins Ave., Sunny Isles. Tel. 940-7440.
It's not exactly the South Seas, but it's Miami's only Polynesian dinner theater, complete with live music, hula girls, and fire dancers. This all-inclusive tropical luau features an all-you-can-eat three-course meal with a heavy Chinese influence, tax, tip, and a souvenir island necklace. Shows are Wednesday through Sunday at 8pm.
Admission: $33–$40 for dinner and show.

MOVIES

Except for the annual Miami Film Festival (see "Florida Calendar of Events," in Chapter 2), foreign and independent screenings in the city are almost nonexistent. Most of Miami's libraries show classic films one day during the week (usually Wednesday), and are listed in the weekly *New Times,* and the *Miami Herald's* Friday magazine section. Hollywood-oriented cinemas are commonplace, and are located in all the malls. Some of the larger and better-located multiplexes include:
Bay Harbor 4 (tel. 866-2441), at 96th Street west of Collins Avenue in Miami Beach.
Cinema 10 (tel. 442-2299), in the Miracle Center, 3301 Coral Way, just east of Coral Gables.
Movies at The Falls (tel. 255-5200), U.S. 1 and SW 136th Street, in The Falls shopping center in Greater Miami South.
Omni 10 (tel. 358-2304), 1601 Biscayne Blvd., inside the Omni International Mall at 16th Street (downtown).

8. NETWORKS & RESOURCES

FOR STUDENTS Located in south Coral Gables, the large main campus of the **University of Miami** encompasses dozens of classrooms, a huge athletic field, a large lake, a museum, a hospital, and more. For general information, call the university (tel. 372-0120).
The school's main student building is the **Whitten University Center,** 1306 Stanford Dr. (tel. 284-2318). Social events are often scheduled here, and important information on area activities is always posted. The building houses a recreation area, a swimming pool, a snack shop, and a Ticketmaster outlet.
The **Ring Theatre,** on the University of Miami Campus, 1380 Miller Dr. (tel. 284-3355), is the main stage for the Department of Theater Arts' productions. Faculty and guest actors are regularly featured, as are contemporary works by local playwrights. See "The Performing Arts" in "Evening Entertainment," above, for more information.
The **Gusman Concert Hall,** 1314 Miller Dr. (tel. 284-2438, or 284-6477 for a recording), features performances by faculty and students of the university's School of Music, as well as concerts by special guests. See "Major Performance Halls" in "Evening Entertainment," above, for more information, and call for schedules and tickets.
For tickets to Miami Hurricanes basketball, football, and baseball home games, call the **U of M Athletic Department** (tel. 284-3822, or toll free 800/GO-CANES in Florida). See "Sports and Recreation," above, for more information.
The university's **Beaumont Cinema** (tel. 284-2211) features new and classic films. Call for ticket prices and screening schedules.

FOR GAY MEN & LESBIANS Miami has a significant gay community, supported by a wide range of services.
The **Gay and Lesbian Community Hotline** (tel. 759-3661), an interactive

recording that can be reached with a pushbutton phone, lists 14 categories of information of interest to the gay community. These include political issues, gay bars, special events, support groups, businesses serving the gay community, doctors and lawyers, help wanted, and others.

The **Gay Community Bookstore,** 7545 Biscayne Blvd. (tel. 754-6900), features quality literature, newspapers, videos, music, cards, and more. It's open Monday through Saturday from 11am to 9pm and on Sunday from noon to 6pm.

The *Weekly News* is the best local gay publication. It's available free at bookstores and gay bars throughout South Florida. Other local literature to look for include the magazines *David* and *Hot Shots*.

9. EASY EXCURSIONS FROM MIAMI

Miami's scenic surroundings make a short excursion a great idea. Whether you'd like to tour Everglades National Park, hop aboard a Caribbean cruise, or just relax on a beach in Key West (see Chapter 6), all are easily accessible to you. For information about the Greater Miami area, contact the **Greater Miami Convention and Visitors Bureau,** 701 Brickell Ave., Miami, FL 33131 (tel. 305/539-3063, or toll free 800/283-2707). The offices are open Monday through Friday from 9am to 5:30pm.

EVERGLADES NATIONAL PARK

Encompassing more than 2,000 square miles and 1.5 million acres, Everglades National Park covers the entire southern tip of Florida and is one of America's most unusual regions. Unlike Yosemite or Grand Canyon National Park, the Everglades' awesome beauty is more subtle. In fact, it is not its geological grandeur that, in 1947, led lawmakers to preserve this remarkable place. Rather, the Everglades is a wildlife sanctuary, set aside for the protection of its delicate plant and animal life. Don't misunderstand, this park is gorgeous—but its beauty may not be immediately obvious. At first glance, the Glades appear only to be a river of saw grass dotted with islands of trees. But stand still and look around: You'll notice deer, otters, and great white egrets. Follow a rustle and a tiny tree frog appears. Hawks and herons flutter about, while baby—and bigger—alligators laze in the sun. You're in one of the world's most unusual jungles; the longer you stay, the more you perceive. But beware of mosquitos! Wear protective clothing and don't forget your repellent.

INFORMATION   Part of the park was damaged by Hurricane Andrew in August 1992 and will remain closed indefinitely. For general information, as well as specific details, direct your inquiries to the Park Superintendent, Everglades National Park, P.O. Box 279, Homestead, FL 22020.

The **Tropical Everglades Visitor Association,** 160 U.S. 1, Florida City, FL 33034 (tel. 305/245-9180, or toll free 800/388-9669), is located at the turnoff from U.S. 1 to the main entrance to the park. You can pick up information about the surrounding area plus a good map. Open daily from 8am to 6pm.

GETTING THERE   From Miami, there are two ways to approach the park: either from the east, through the Main Visitor Center, or from the north, via the Tamiami Trail (U.S. 41).

The Main Visitor Center (tel. 305/242-7700) is located on the east side of the park, about 45 miles south of downtown Miami. From downtown Miami, take U.S. 1 south about 35 miles. Turn right (west) onto Fla. 9336 (follow the sign) and continue straight for about 10 miles to the park entrance. This is the park's official headquarters. There's a small building which houses audiovisual exhibits on the park's fragile ecosystems. It's open daily from 8am to 5pm, and admission is $5 per car to enter the park, $3 per person by bus.

The Tamiami Trail (U.S. 41) runs east-west from downtown Miami to the Gulf of Mexico, and follows the northern edge of the Everglades into Big Cypress National

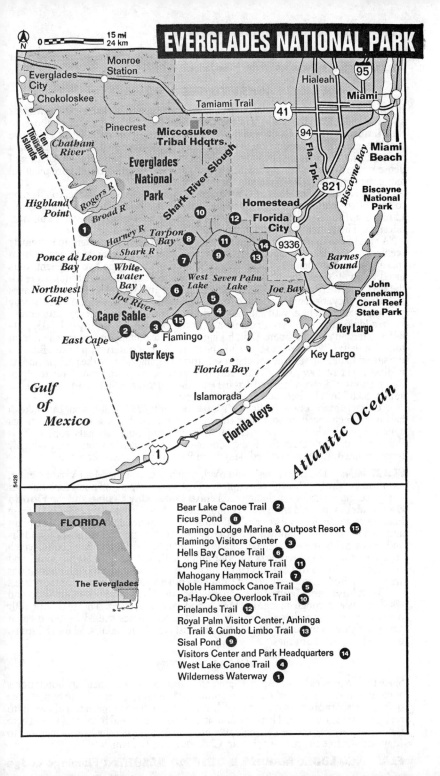

EVERGLADES NATIONAL PARK

0 15 mi
0 24 km
N

Everglades City
Chokoloskee
Ten Thousand Islands
Chatham River
Highland Point
Rogers R
Broad R
Harney R
Shark R
Ponce de Leon Bay
Northwest Cape
Cape Sable
East Cape
Oyster Keys

Monroe Station
Pinecrest
Tamiami Trail
Miccosukee Tribal Hdqtrs.
Everglades National Park
Shark River Slough
Tarpon Bay
Whitewater Bay
Joe River
Flamingo
West Lake
Seven Palm Lake
Joe Bay

Hialeah
Miami
Miami Beach
Biscayne Bay
Biscayne National Park
Homestead
Florida City
Barnes Sound
John Pennekamp Coral Reef State Park
Key Largo
Key Largo

Gulf of Mexico
Florida Bay
Islamorada
Florida Keys
Atlantic Ocean

41
94
95
821
9336
1

❶ ❷ ❸ ❹ ❺ ❻ ❼ ❽ ❾ ❿ ⓫ ⓬ ⓭ ⓮ ⓯

5428

FLORIDA

The Everglades

Bear Lake Canoe Trail ❷
Ficus Pond ❽
Flamingo Lodge Marina & Outpost Resort ⓯
Flamingo Visitors Center ❸
Hells Bay Canoe Trail ❻
Long Pine Key Nature Trail ⓫
Mahogany Hammock Trail ❼
Noble Hammock Canoe Trail ❺
Pa-Hay-Okee Overlook Trail ❿
Pinelands Trail ⓬
Royal Palm Visitor Center, Anhinga
   Trail & Gumbo Limbo Trail ⓭
Sisal Pond ❾
Visitors Center and Park Headquarters ⓮
West Lake Canoe Trail ❹
Wilderness Waterway ❶

Preserve. Along the way you'll pass a number of concerns offering airboat and other rides through the saw grass of the Everglades.

WHAT TO SEE & DO

If you just have one day to tour the park, take the single road that winds its way for about 38 miles from the **Main Visitor Center** at the park's entrance (see above) to the **Flamingo Visitor Center** in the southwest corner of the state. This scenic drive provides a beautiful introduction to the park. Along the way you'll pass through half a dozen distinct ecosystems, including a dwarf cypress forest, endless saw grass, and dense mangroves. Well-marked winding trails and elevated boardwalks are plentiful along the entire stretch; all contain informative signs.

At the **Royal Palm Visitor Center,** just beyond the main entrance, you'll come to two of the park's most famous paths: the Anhinga boardwalk, and the Gumbo Limbo Trail. You'll see snakes, fish, alligators, and a cross section of the park's unusual offerings. The center itself is open daily from 8am to 4:30pm.

A visit to the Everglades through the park's northern entrance offers an extremely scenic, but slightly more superficial tour of the wetlands. However, approaching from this angle is recommended if you want to take advantage of the two excellent tours listed below. It's also shorter than the all-day trip to Flamingo (see above). To reach the park's northern edge, follow the scenic Tamiami Trail (U.S. 41) for about 35 miles to Shark Valley, or the Miccosukee Indian Reservation, just beyond. Along the way you'll see several signs advertising airboat rides and other tourist-oriented attractions.

In addition to a small visitor center and bookstore, **Shark Valley** (tel. 305/221-8455) offers an elevated boardwalk, hiking trails, bike rentals, and an excellent tram tour that delves 7½ miles into the wilderness to a 50-foot observation tower. Built on the site of an old oil well, the tower gives visitors sweeping views of the park, including endless acres of saw grass. Tours run regularly, year-round, from 9am to 4pm. Reservations are recommended from December to March. The cost is $7.30 for adults, $3.65 for children, and $6.50 for seniors.

At the **Miccosukee Indian Village** (tel. 305/223-8380), you can take a half-hour, high-speed airboat tour through the rushes. Birds scatter as the boats approach, and when you slow down, alligators and other animals appear. This thrilling "safari" through the Everglades is one you will not soon forget—highly recommended. Rides are offered daily from 9am to 5pm, and cost just $7.

FLAMINGO   The Everglades' main road, which begins at the Main Visitor Center, terminates in the tiny "town" of Flamingo. This is the jumping-off point for a number of sightseeing excursions including the **White Water Bay Cruise** and the **Florida Bay Cruise.** Operated from the Flamingo Lodge Marina (tel. 305/253-2241), these boat tours cruise nearby estuaries and sandbars for an in-depth look at native plant and animal life. The White Water tour lasts about two hours and costs $12 for adults and $6 for children 6 to 12; free for children under 6. The Florida Bay Cruise, which goes out into open water, lasts an hour and a half, and costs $8.50 for adults and $4.50 for children 6 to 12. Tours run regularly year-round, and although reservations are not required, they are suggested from December to March. Phone for tour times.

The **Wilderness Tram Tour** departs from the Flamingo Lodge Gift Shop and winds its way through mangrove forests and coastal prairies. The two-hour tour operates from November to April only, and is sometimes stalled by flooding or particularly heavy mosquito infestation. The cost is $7.75 for adults, $4 for children 6 to 12. Phone for tour times.

WHERE TO STAY

Since the Everglades is so close to Miami, most visitors return to their city hotel rooms at night. If you want to stay in the park, however, Flamingo is not only the best, it's the *only* place. **Camping** is a good option here, though in the summer a ton of mosquito repellent is required gear. There are 300 sites made for cars and tents, and RVs. There is no electricity and showers are cold. Permits cost $4 to $8 per site from September to May and it's free the rest of the year. Checkout time is 10am.

FLAMINGO LODGE MARINA & OUTPOST RESORT, 1 Flamingo Lodge

Hwy. (P.O. Box 428), Flamingo, FL 33030. Tel. 305/253-2241, toll free 800/600-3813. Fax 813/695-3921. 102 rms, 24 cottages.

$ Rates: Nov–Apr, $74–$87 single or double, $87–$102 cottage; May–Oct, $59 single or double, $72 cottage. Extra person $10. AE, CB, DC, DISC, MC, V.

An attractive, well-appointed, and spacious motel, the Flamingo is located right in the center of the action. It's also the only lodging inside the Everglades park. Rooms are relatively simple and clean and overlook the Florida Bay. Lodge facilities include a restaurant and bar, freshwater swimming pool, gift shop, and coin-op laundry.

WHERE TO DINE

FLAMINGO RESTAURANT, in the Flamingo Visitor Center. Tel. 253-2241.

Cuisine: AMERICAN. **Reservations:** Not required.

$ Prices: Main courses $7–$17. AE, MC, V.

Open: Nov–Apr, breakfast daily 7–10:30am; lunch daily 11:30am–3pm; dinner daily 5–9pm. May–Oct, buffet dining 11:30am–9pm.

This is one of the best restaurants in South Florida, and the only one in the Everglades park area. The view from this multilevel eatery overlooking the Florida Bay is spectacular. The menu features several meat, poultry, and vegetarian dishes, but is noted for its well-prepared fresh fish selections.

CRUISING THE CARIBBEAN

Most people think that taking a cruise means spending thousands of dollars and booking a ship far in advance. It's true that some unusually big trips require serious advance planning, but most of the Caribbean-bound ships, sailing weekly out of the Port of Miami, are relatively inexpensive, can be booked without advance notice, and make for an excellent excursion. Usually all-inclusive, cruises offer exceptional value and unparalleled simplicity compared to other vacation options.

All the shorter cruises are well equipped for gambling, and casinos open as soon as the ship clears U.S. waters, typically 45 minutes after the ship leaves port. Usually, four full-size meals are served daily, with portions so huge they're impossible to finish. Games, movies, and other on-board activities ensure that you are always busy. Passengers can board up to two hours prior to departure for meals, games, and cocktails.

There are dozens of cruises to choose from. A full list of options can be obtained from the **Metro-Dade Seaport Department,** 1015 North America Way, Miami, FL 33132 (tel. 305/371-7678).

Most of the ships listed below offer two- and three-day excursions to The Bahamas. Cruise ships usually depart Miami on Friday night and return Monday morning. If you want more information, contact **The Bahamas Tourist Office,** 255 Alhambra Circle, Suite 425, Coral Gables, FL 33134 (tel. 305/442-4860). All passengers must travel with a passport or proof of citizenship for reentry into the United States.

CARNIVAL CRUISE LINES, 3655 NW 87th Ave., Miami, FL 33178. Tel. 305/599-2200, or toll free 800/327-9501.

One of the largest cruise ships in the world, Carnival's *Fantasy* made its debut in 1990. Several swimming pools, games rooms, and lounges surround a spectacular multistory foyer. The 70,000-ton ship can accommodate up to 2,600 passengers. The *Fantasy* sails from Miami on three-night cruises to Nassau in The Bahamas, departing on Friday at 4pm and returning on Monday at 7am. The cruise cost begins at $360 per person.

DOLPHIN CRUISE LINE, 901 South American Way, Miami, FL 33132. Tel. 305/358-5122, or toll free 800/222-1003.

One of the smallest ships sailing from Miami is Dolphin's intimate 590-passenger *Dolphin IV,* which not only sails to Nassau but also to uncrowded Blue Lagoon

Island, about 45 minutes away. Three-night cruises depart Miami on Friday at 4:30pm and return on Monday at 8am; four-night cruises depart on Monday at 4:30pm, returning on Friday at 8am. The charge is from $344 per person. The line often runs promotional price specials. Contact the line for details.

FANTASY CRUISES, 4770 Biscayne Blvd., Miami, FL 33137. Tel. 305/ 262-5411, or toll free 800/437-3111.

If you've never taken a cruise before, Fantasy Cruises' *Britanis* is a good way to get acquainted with the waves. It's very inexpensive, the food is excellent, and even with a full load of 922 passengers, it doesn't seem crowded. All sailing is done at night, so you arrive at your destination well rested. The *Britanis* sails on two-night cruises to Nassau in The Bahamas, departing on Friday at 4:30pm and returning to Miami on Sunday at 8am. This cruise begins at $220 per person.

NORWEGIAN CRUISE LINE, 95 Merrick Way, Coral Gables, FL 33134. Tel. 305/445-0866, or toll free 800/327-7030.

Norwegian Cruise Line's 1,534-passenger *Seaward* makes three-day jaunts to Nassau and Great Stirrup Cay, the cruise line's private island resort. As on other Caribbean-bound ships, passengers are not required to disembark at any destination. You can stay on board for food, drinks, and games. Cruises depart Miami on Friday at 4:30pm and return on Monday at 8am, and cost from $689 per person.

ROYAL CARIBBEAN CRUISE LINE, 1050 Caribbean Way, Miami, FL 33132. Tel. 305/539-6000, or toll free 800/327-6700.

Royal Caribbean has entered the three-night Caribbean cruise market with the *Nordic Empress,* which sailed on its maiden voyage in June 1990. Beautifully streamlined and stylized, this special ship is fully outfitted, and treats its 1,610 passengers to some of the world's swankiest seafaring. Cruises to Nassau and Coco Cay, the line's private island five hours away from Nassau, depart Miami on Friday at 5pm and return on Monday at 9am. The fare begins at $515 per person.

CHAPTER 6

THE FLORIDA KEYS

- **WHAT'S SPECIAL ABOUT THE FLORIDA KEYS**
1. **THE UPPER KEYS: KEY LARGO TO MARATHON**
2. **THE LOWER KEYS: BIG PINE KEY TO COPPITT KEY**
3. **KEY WEST**

Although the Keys appear not to have had any permanent inhabitants during early times, several native groups visited the area, including Calusas, Seminoles, and the warlike Caribs. Juan Ponce de León, the Spanish explorer who is credited with "discovering" Florida, found the Keys in 1513—he called them Los Martieres (The Martyrs) because they looked like men in distress. The Keys remained largely undeveloped until Florida was "transferred" from Spain to the United States in 1819. The entire island of Key West was purchased by an American promoter, John W. Simonton, and developed into a mercantile and "wrecking" center, luring fishermen and shipwreck salvagers; by 1825, 28 salvage vessels were operating. By 1874, Key West had become the largest city in the state of Florida, attracting Bahamians, Cubans, and migrating North Americans. The establishment of iron-pile lighthouses from Key Largo to Key West, as well as better navigational methods, were a blow to Island wreckers/salvagers.

Before the new century was very old, Key West's fortunes began to wane, but with the extension of Henry Flagler's railroad to Key West in 1912 came an economic resurgence. Trade and tourism thrived until 1935, when a powerful hurricane in the Middle Keys destroyed the rail line.

The Overseas Highway (U.S. 1) was completed in 1938 on the old railroad bed. Soon after, President Franklin Roosevelt ordered the other Keys made more habitable. The Civilian Conservation Corps (CCC), a Depression-era WPA organization that was not conservation-minded at all, was put in charge and the Keys were opened to development with a "dredge and fill" philosophy that is anathema to today's ecological thinking. Inland waterways were created and sanctioned, allowing otherwise landlocked homeowners to dock their boats in their backyards. Chemical-based mosquito-abatement programs were instituted, coral reefs were slashed, trees were chopped, and towns began to sprout up along the hundred-mile highway.

Luckily, modern-day environmental activism and governmental protection has saved most of the Keys from this kind of devastating development. Surrounding what are known as the "Mainland" Keys, through which the Overseas Highway runs, are dozens of small islands known locally as the "Backcountry." Largely uninhabited, most of these islands are federally protected national wildlife refuges. Other areas are under the protection of a private organization, the Nature Conservancy. A rich variety of indigenous plants and animals live here, including many endangered species. Eagles, egrets, and Key deer are some of the most visible, as are gumbo limbo trees (with peeling red bark), mangroves, royal poincianas, banyans, and aloe.

The Florida Keys are surrounded by the world's third-largest barrier reef, precious living corals that support a complex and delicate ecosystem. About three miles wide, the reef contains a unique variety of stony and soft corals that can take years to grow just one inch. They are home to a variety of interdependent species including sponges, anemones, jellyfish, crabs, rays, sharks, turtles, snails, lobsters, and of course, thousands of varieties of fish.

Unfortunately, the Keys' reefs and the wildlife that inhabits them are in danger of destruction both from pollution washing down through the Everglades and from the garbage, anchors, and lines of unaware tourists and boaters. When you visit the Keys, do your part to save them; be environmentally conscious of this vulnerable habitat.

WHAT'S SPECIAL ABOUT THE FLORIDA KEYS

Celebrations

☐ Sunsets—celebrated each evening in Key West's Mallory Square, where tourists and locals join with jugglers, artists, acrobats, vendors, and mimes to herald the evening.

☐ Big-game fishing in Islamorada, ritualized with tournaments that are held several times a year.

☐ Old Island Days, a full schedule of special events that lasts all summer long, making Key West even more special.

Natural Habitats

☐ Key deer, three-foot-tall miniatures, unique to Big Pine Key, where they enjoy protected status from the U.S. government.

☐ The coral reef that surrounds the Keys, the third-largest barrier reef in the world, supporting a dazzling array of life, including sharks, rays, lobsters, and seemingly endless varieties of fish.

☐ Indian Key and Lignumvitae Key, two small islands a mile from the Islamorada developments, allowing tourists a glimpse of the "real" Keys, before "modernization"—now state botanical sites, these keys sustain a complex and diverse ecosystem that's as fragile as it is unusual.

Don't disturb nesting birds or feed any animals. Fishermen should catch and release, and divers and snorkelers should be aware that simply touching coral can damage and even kill it. I am convinced that the Keys are one of America's greatest treasures, and feel certain that if you take your time exploring these extraordinary gems, you, too, will become their advocate.

SEEING THE FLORIDA KEYS

Sure, you can fly to Key West from Miami (costing anywhere from $99 to $298 round-trip), but one of the best things about the Florida Keys is the car journey there. Unless you're really pressed for time, driving is the way to go. U.S. 1 (the Overseas Highway) skips over 42 bridges and across 31 islands through some of the most beautiful terrain in the world. Separating the Gulf of Mexico from the Atlantic Ocean, much of the stretch is wide, with water vistas where on either side you can see as far as the horizon. At other times the road is clogged with shopping centers and billboards advertising restaurants, rest stops, and attractions. A good portion of U.S. 1 is a narrow, two-lane highway; some sections open up to four lanes. The legal speed limit is 55 m.p.h. (35 m.p.h. in commercial areas), and on a good day you can make the trip to Key West from Miami in four hours. But don't rush. The scenery is beautiful, and there are plenty of places to stop along the way.

You should know that gasoline prices rise rapidly the farther south you go, but then descend slightly when you arrive on Key West. If you can, fill up in Miami.

FINDING AN ADDRESS Along the way, you'll find that most addresses are given by Mile Marker (MM), small green signs on the right side of the road that announce the distance from Key West. The markers begin with number 126, just south of the Florida mainland. The zero marker is in Key West, at the corner of Whitehead and Fleming Streets. Listings in this chapter are organized first by price, then by location, from north to south. Addresses are often accompanied by a MM designation to help you determine its location on (or near) U.S. 1.

FISHING IN THE KEYS Fishing is a highly popular activity in the Keys, as this is one of the world's most fertile sportfishing grounds. There are three different kinds of fishing: Deep-sea fishing is for big-game fish like marlin, sailfish, tuna, and amberjack.

THE FLORIDA KEYS

0 | 9 mi
0 | 14 km

Gulf of Mexico

Everglades National Park

905

Key Largo

Key Largo

1

Florida Bay

Tavernier
Tavernier Key
Plantation Key
Upper Matecumbe Key
Windley Key
Islamorada
Lower Matecumbe Key

Straits

of

Florida

Fiesta Key
Long Key

Overseas
Conch Key
Duck Key
Grassy Key

Hawk Channel

Marathon Airport
Key Vaca
Marathon
931
Boot Key

Pigeon Key

Bahia Honda
Big Pine Key
Spanish Harbor Key
Little Torch Key

Great White Heron
Nat'l Wildlife Refuge

940

942

Summerland Key
Cudjoe Key

939

Sugarloaf Channel

Sugarloaf Key

Intracoastal Waterway

Waterway

941
Stock Island

Key West
Key West Intl. Airport

FLORIDA

The Florida Keys

John Pennekamp Coral Reef State Park ①
Bahia Honda State Park (Big Pine Key) ⑥
Dolphin Research Center ④

Long Key State Recreation Area ③
National Key Deer Refuge ⑦
Seven-Mile Bridge ⑤
Theater of the Sea ②

5432

Reef fishing is for "eating fish" like snapper and grouper. Backcountry fishing, on the gulf side of the islands, is for the most skillful fishermen, who stalk bonefish, tarpon, and other prey.

Saltwater fishing licenses are mandatory, unless you're fishing from the land, a pier, or a sanctioned bridge. Licenses, which cost about $20 per week for nonresidents, can be purchased from almost any bait or boat shop, many of which are listed in this chapter.

If your catch will not be eaten or mounted, you are encouraged to "catch and release" to preserve the area's declining fish population.

1. THE UPPER KEYS: KEY LARGO TO MARATHON

48–105 miles SW of Miami

GETTING THERE **By Bus** Greyhound runs three buses a day, in each direction, between Key West and Miami, stopping in the Upper Keys along the way. The company no longer operates a single nationwide telephone number, so consult your local directory for the office nearest you.

By Car From Miami, take the Florida Turnpike south along the east coast to Exit 4, Homestead/Key West. This is the Turnpike Extension that meets U.S. 1 in Florida City. Islamorada is about an hour south.

If you're coming from Florida's west coast, take Alligator Alley to the Miami Exit, then turn south onto the Turnpike Extension.

ESSENTIALS The telephone area code is 305.

Information There are several tourist offices offering specialized information for their particular parcel of land.

The **Key Largo Chamber of Commerce,** 105950 Overseas Hwy., Key Largo, FL 33037 (tel. 305/451-1414), is open daily from 9am to 6pm.

The **Islamorada Chamber of Commerce,** in the Little Red Caboose, Mile Marker 82.5 (P.O. Box 915), Islamorada, FL 33036 (tel. 305/664-4503, or toll free 800/322-5397), also offers maps and literature on the Upper Keys.

The **Greater Marathon Chamber of Commerce,** 3330 Overseas Hwy., Mile Marker 48.7, Marathon, FL 33050 (tel. toll free 800/842-9580), is located in a squat pink building on the right-hand side of the road (facing Key West).

I slamorada, the unofficial capital of the Upper Keys, was one of the first of these islands to claim permanent settlers. Located behind the town library, Islamorada's original natural swimming hole still exists, though it has been "enhanced" with an artificial beach and picnic tables.

Marathon, the Upper Keys' other main population center, began in 1908 as the construction headquarters for the overseas railroad. Located just north of the world-famous Seven-Mile Bridge, right in the middle of the key chain, Marathon is a

IMPRESSIONS

I've a notion to move the capital to Key West and just stay.
—U.S. PRESIDENT HARRY S TRUMAN

I want to get to Key West and get away from it all.
—ERNEST HEMINGWAY

curious mixture of modern tract-home community, tourist resort, and old fishing village.

In between Islamorada and Marathon are about 35 miles of highway, alternating between wetlands, strip malls, nesting grounds, resort hotels, blue waters, and billboards.

WHAT TO SEE & DO

SIGHTS & ATTRACTIONS

JOHN PENNEKAMP CORAL REEF STATE PARK, U.S. 1, Mile Marker 102.3, Key Largo. Tel. 451-1202.

The Keys' largest and most popular park is chock-full of activities, and definitely worth a stop on your way down the coast. In addition to camping (see "Where to Stay," below), visitors can participate in a plethora of daytime activities, such as swimming, sailing, and canoeing. The 188-square-mile park has a couple of winding nature trails where self-guided walkers can explore forests of mangroves and subtropical hardwoods. A boardwalk trail leads to an observation tower. Canoe trails wend their way through mangroves and natural tidal creeks, and a special snorkeling area is made even more distinctive by an authentic reconstruction of an early Spanish shipwreck.

The park's visitor center houses a 30,000-gallon saltwater marine aquarium surrounded by various educational exhibits. There are a few beach areas where visitors can sunbathe and swim, and a dive shop offering daily scuba and snorkeling reef excursions and boat rentals. They also rent scuba gear, sailboats, windsurfers, and canoes. Two-hour glass-bottom-boat tours take riders over coral reefs.

Admission: $3.75 per vehicle, $1.50 per pedestrian or bicyclist; glass-bottom-boat tours, $14 adults, $9 children under 12; sailing and snorkeling tours, $38 per person, including equipment; scuba dives, $32.50 per person, not including equipment; reef boat rental, $22–$30 per hour.

Open: Daily 8am–5pm; phone for tour and dive times.

THEATER OF THE SEA, Overseas Hwy., Mile Marker 84.5, Islamorada. Tel. 664-2431.

Established in 1946, the Theater of the Sea is one of the world's oldest marine zoos. Although facilities here seem a bit tired, and sea mammal acts have fallen from political correctness, the theater's dolphin and sea lion shows can be both entertaining and informative, especially for children. Sharks, sea turtles, and other local creatures are also on display. Under the pretense of "education," the park offers visitors the opportunity to swim with the dolphins in their supervised oceanwater lagoon. Reservations for this pricy "Dolphin Adventure" must be made in advance.

Admission: $12.25 adults, $6.75 children; Swim with the Dolphins, $75 per person.

Open: Daily 9:30am–4pm.

INDIAN KEY AND LIGNUMVITAE KEY, off Indian Key Fill, Overseas Hwy., Mile Marker 79. Tel. 664-4815.

Most of the Florida Keys that are not connected by the Overseas Highway are protected as wildlife preserves and closed to casual visitors. Indian Key and Lignumvitae Key are two worthy exceptions, which allow tourists a glimpse of the "real" keys, before modern development. These two small islands, preserved and managed by the Florida Department of Natural Resources, are located about one mile from the Islamorada highway. Named for the lignum vitae ("Wood of Life") trees found there, Lignumvitae Key supports a virgin tropical forest that's typical of the kind of vegetation that once thrived on most of the Upper Keys. Now a state botanical site located on the gulf side of Islamorada, the key sustains a complex and diverse ecosystem that's as fragile as it is unusual.

Indian Key, located on the Atlantic side of Islamorada, is a 10-acre historic site that was occupied by Native Americans for thousands of years. It was also the original seat of Dade County before the Civil War. An 1840 rebellion by Native Americans almost wiped out the island's once-growing population, leaving the ruins to posterity.

Three-hour boat tours to these islands depart Indian Key Fill Thursday through Monday at 8:30am for Indian Key and at 1:30pm for Lignumvitae Key. In summer, tours operate Friday through Sunday only. The tour fee for each island is $7 for adults and $3 for children under 12. Reservations are suggested.

LONG KEY STATE RECREATION AREA, Overseas Hwy., Mile Marker 68, Long Key. Tel. 664-4815.

Located just north of Marathon Key, this is a great place to explore the natural habitats of the Upper Keys. Unique nature trails lead hikers through miles of wilderness where indigenous flora and fauna flourish. A specially marked canoe trail is particularly fun, guiding explorers through wild wetlands. Boat rentals are available in the park. In addition, the recreational area also offers a clean beach for year-round swimming and fishing, and several picnic areas.

DOLPHIN RESEARCH CENTER, Overseas Hwy., Mile Marker 59, Marathon Shores. Tel. 289-0002.

This nonprofit organization, dedicated to the increased understanding and appreciation of marine mammals, runs regularly scheduled tours to help visitors learn about and interact with dolphins and other sea creatures. In the basic tour, visitors can see families of dolphins, imprisoned in natural saltwater lagoons, respond to human commands and perform various tricks. The more in-depth DolphInsight program—a half-day presentation offered Wednesday, Saturday, and Sunday afternoons—includes a guided tour of the facility and open-air workshops on dolphin physiology and basic training techniques. Visitors are given the opportunity to touch and communicate with dolphins using a variety of hand signals. The center also operates a swim-with-the-dolphins program, called Dolphin Encounter, for which reservations are required up to a month in advance.

Admission: $7.50 adults, $5 children 4–12, free for children under 4. DolphInsight Program, $75 per person; Dolphin Encounter, $90 per person.

Open: Tours given daily at 10am, 12:30pm, 2pm, and 3:30pm.

MUSEUM OF NATURAL HISTORY, Overseas Hwy., Mile Marker 50.5, Marathon. Tel. 743-9100.

Located at Crane Point Hammock, a woody park directly across from the K-Mart shopping center, this small museum displays dozens of local historical artifacts, including shell tools and pottery from pre-Columbian native tribes and booty from one of America's oldest shipwrecks. Other exhibits focus on the Keys' natural habitats, including a coral-reef tank, where visitors can see sharks, lobster, and tropical fish, and a touch tank, where you can handle rays, starfish, and other safe sea creatures. A special children's section of the museum has several informative interactive displays, including tropical aquariums, a miniature railway station, and a small saltwater lagoon. Outside, visitors are encouraged to wander through the museum's quarter-mile nature trail which winds through rare tropical palm hammock.

Admission: $5 adults, $4 seniors 65 and older, $1 students, free for children 12 and under.

Open: Mon–Sat 9am–5pm, Sun noon–5pm.

SEVEN-MILE BRIDGE, Overseas Hwy., Mile Markers 40–47.

The Keys' most celebrated span rests on 546 concrete piers, and rises to a 72-foot crest, the highest point in the Keys. The first bridge was constructed here in 1910, built to carry Henry Flagler's railroad track that ran all the way to Key West. Most of the bridge blew away in a hurricane on September 2, 1935; you can still see portions of the original trackbed running for miles adjacent to the modern span, which was constructed 10 years later.

Heading south on the Overseas Highway, slow down just before the bridge and turn right off the road, onto the unpaved parking lot at the foot of the bridge. From here you can walk along the old bridge that goes for almost four miles before abruptly dropping off into the sea. The first half mile of this "ghost bridge" is popular with area fishermen who use shrimp as bait to catch barracuda, yellowtail, and a host of other fish. Near the end of the bridge is the University of Miami's Institute of Marine Science, a research facility that's not open to the public.

ORGANIZED TOURS

BY BOAT   Traveling aboard the 39-foot sailing yacht *Amantha,* built in 1946, is one of the best ways to see Florida Bay. The daily four-hour tour circumnavigates several uninhabited keys, passes under the old Seven-Mile Bridge, and skirts the historic buildings of Pigeon Key. Captains Ken Carter and Joan Pellegrino not only point out the sites, they also show you the rigging of their ship, offer sailing tips, and let first-timers try their hand at the sails. Contact **Sail *Amantha,*** Overseas Highway, Mile Marker 48, Marathon (tel. 743-9020), for departure times. Tour prices are $30 for adults, $15 for children under 16.

BY PLANE   The **Flight Department,** 9850 Overseas Hwy., Marathon Airport, (tel. 305/743-4222), has half-hour tours over the reef that give you a bird's-eye view of the islands and the coral that surrounds them. Passengers can choose their itinerary from several different flight plans. Tours cost $75 per flight for up to three passengers.

FISHING CHARTERS   Located at the south end of the Holiday Isle Docks (see "Where to Stay," below), **Robbie's Partyboats and Charters,** Overseas Highway, Mile Marker 84.5, on Islamorada (tel. 664-8070 or 664-4196), offers day and night deep-sea and reef-fishing trips on 60- and 70-foot party boats. Big-game-fishing charters are also available, and "splits" are arranged for solo fishermen. Party-boat fishing costs $25 for a half day, $40 for a full day, and $30 at night. Charters run $375 for a half day, $550 for a full day; splits begin at $65 per person.

One of the largest marinas between Miami and Key West, **Bud n' Mary's Fishing Marina,** Overseas Highway, Mile Marker 79.8, on Islamorada (tel. 305/664-2461, or toll free 800/742-7945), is packed with sailors offering guided backcountry fishing charters. Stalking tarpon, bonefish, trout, redfish, snook, and snapper is not for impatient novices. Deep-sea- and coral-fishing trips are also arranged.

The marina also offers snorkel and scuba trips to nearby Alligator Reef, as well as glass-bottom-boat tours.

Charters cost $375 to $450 for a half day, $575 to $650 for a full day, and splits begin at $125 per person. Snorkel and scuba trips run $20 to $35; the glass-bottom-boat tour, $15.

The ***Bounty Hunter,*** 9500 Overseas Hwy., Mile Marker 48, Marathon (tel. 743-2446), offers full-day reef and Everglades trips to Florida's most deserted beaches. For years Capt. Brock Hook's huge sign has boasted NO FISH, NO PAY. You're guaranteed to catch *something.* Shark, barracuda, sailfish, and other trips are arranged.

WHERE TO STAY
VERY EXPENSIVE

JULES' UNDERSEA LODGE, Overseas Hwy., Mile Marker 103.2 (P.O. Box 3330), Key Largo, FL 33037. Tel. 305/451-2353. Fax 305/451-4789. 2 rms. A/C TV TEL
$ Rates (including breakfast and dinner): $195–$295 per person double. DISC, MC, V.
Originally built as a research lab in the 1970s, this small underwater compartment opened as a single-room hotel in November of 1986. As expensive as it is unusual, the lodge is popular with diving honeymooners and other active and romantic couples. You don't need to be a scuba specialist to stay here; guests use tethered breathing lines in lieu of air tanks. The underwater suite consists of a bedroom and galley, and sleeps up to six. Facilities include a stereo and VCR, and dinner (which is included) is delivered to your door in a waterproof container. Needless to say, this novelty is not for everyone. Phone for further information and a brochure.

CHEECA LODGE, Overseas Hwy., Mile Marker 82 (P.O. Box 527),

Islamorada, FL 33036. Tel. 305/664-4651, or toll free 800/327-2888. Fax 305/664-2893. 203 rms, 64 suites. A/C MINIBAR TV TEL

$ Rates: Dec 21–May 2, $225–$475 single or double; from $300 suite. May 3–Dec 20, $150–$375 single or double; from $250 suite. AE, CB, DC, DISC, MC, V.

Cheeca's blue-and-white plantation-style buildings surround Islamorada's most lushly landscaped gardens, tennis courts, pools, and golf courses. Located on 27 beachfront acres, this well-maintained resort offers guests a full range of activities and a high standard of accommodation.

While the guest rooms are not particularly plush, they are roomy, with large, comfortable beds, contemporary baths, VCRs, and balconies, many of which overlook the water. The resort works hard to educate their guests about environmental issues, and takes pains to protect their particularly lovely parcel. A unique kids' program, led by specially trained counselors, combines nature lessons with fun activities that sometimes include parents as well.

Dining/Entertainment: The Atlantic's Edge restaurant is well known in these parts for excellently prepared seafood served in elegant surroundings. The more casual Ocean Terrace Grill has indoor and outdoor seating overlooking the pool and ocean. The Light Tackle Lounge is open daily and offers live entertainment on weekends.

Services: Room service, concierge, children's programs, free snorkeling lessons, water aerobics, massages.

Facilities: Six lighted tennis courts, nine-hole golf course, water-sports rentals, ocean beach, two swimming pools, saltwater lagoon, 525-foot fishing pier, sports shop, boutique, diving and fishing trips, four hot tubs, nature trail, champagne and sunset cruises, parasailing, fishing, diving, bicycle rentals.

MODERATE

CONCH KEY COTTAGES, off the Overseas Hwy., Mile Marker 62.3 (RR1, Box 424), Marathon, FL 33050. Tel. 305/289-1377, or toll free 800/330-1577. 10 units. A/C TV

$ Rates: Dec 12–May 15 and July 16–Sept 7, $86–$121 one-bedroom apt; $155 one-bedroom beachfront unit; $144–$190 two-bedroom cottage. May 16–July 15, $75–$109 one-bedroom apt; $144 one-bedroom beachfront unit; $121–$178 two-bedroom cottage. Sept 8–Dec 11, $63–$86 one-bedroom apt; $121 one-bedroom beachfront unit; $115–$144 two-bedroom cottage. Additional person $5 extra. Weekly rates available. DISC, MC, V.

Occupying its own private island, just off the Overseas Highway, Conch Key Cottages sounds a lot more romantic than they look. An eclectic variety of accommodations range from waterside bungalows to mangrove-fronting mobile homes. It should be no surprise that the one-bedroom beachfront units are most recommendable, featuring their own private stretch of natural, private beach. All units contain kitchens, pets are welcome, and the cottages' owner tells me that a swimming pool is going in by the summer of 1994.

FARO BLANCO MARINE RESORT, Overseas Hwy., Mile Marker 48.5, Marathon, FL 33050. Tel. 305/743-9018, or toll free 800/759-3276. 170 rms, 20 condos. A/C TV TEL

$ Rates: Dec 20–Apr, $65–$119 single or double in the cottages, $99–$185 single or double on a houseboat, $175 single or double in the lighthouse; $225 condominium. May–Dec 19, $55–$99 single or double in the cottages, $79–$145 single or double on a houseboat, $135 single or double in the lighthouse; $198 condominium. Additional person $10 extra. AE, MC, V.

Spanning both sides of the Overseas Highway, and all on waterfront property, this huge, two-shore marina and hotel complex offers something for every taste. Camp-style cottages, each with a small bedroom and kitchen, are the least expensive accommodations; they're very basic, most with two single beds and slightly fading interiors. The rectangular houseboats, which float in a relatively quiet marina, look like buoyant mobile homes and are uniformly clean, fresh, and recommendable. The complex's large, first-class condominium apartments, located in a cluster of tall towers, each have three bedrooms, two baths, a living room, and a fully stocked kitchen. Finally, there are two unusual rental units located in a lighthouse on the pier; circular staircases, unusually shaped rooms and showers, and nautical decor make this quite an unusual place to stay, but some guests might find that it literally cramps their style.

There are several restaurants on the property, including Kelsey's, the resort's top eatery, which serves seafood, beef, veal, and poultry dishes. The Upper Deck Restaurant, which overlooks the bay, is a good choice for an afternoon snack or cocktail. Angler's serves burgers, sandwiches, and salads but is best known for its weekday-afternoon happy hours and nightly live entertainment.

INEXPENSIVE

HOLIDAY ISLE RESORT, Overseas Hwy., Mile Marker 84, Islamorada, FL 33036. Tel. 305/664-2711 or 305/664-3611, or toll free 800/327-7070. 180 rms, 19 suites.
$ Rates: Dec 18–Apr 17, $95–$180 single or double; from $150 suite. Apr 18–Dec 17, $65–$125 single or double; from $120 suite. AE, DC, DISC, MC, V.
A huge resort complex encompassing five restaurants, lounges, and shops, and four distinct, if not distinctive hotels, the Holiday Isle is one of the biggest resorts in the Keys. The company's marketing strategy is decidedly downscale, attracting a spring break–style crowd year-round. Their Tiki Bar claims the invention of the Rum Runner drink (151-proof rum, blackberry brandy, banana liquor, grenadine, and lime juice), and there's no reason to doubt it. Hordes of partiers are attracted to the resort's almost nonstop merrymaking, live music, and beachfront bars. As a result, some of the accommodations here can be noisy—a plus to some.

El Captain and Harbor Lights, two of the least expensive hotels on the property, are both austere and basic. The Holiday Isle Hotel is located near the Tiki Bar at ground zero, while Howard Johnson's, which is a little farther from the action, is a shred more civilized. Small efficiency kitchens are available in most of the hotels.

BREEZY PALMS RESORT, Overseas Hwy., Mile Marker 80 (P.O. Box 767), Islamorada, FL 33036. Tel. 305/664-2361 or 664-2371. Fax 305/664-2572. 39 rms, 23 efficiencies.
$ Rates: Dec 16–Apr 20, $75–$90 single or double; from $105 apt. Apr 21–Dec 15, $65–$80 single or double; from $95 apt. Efficiencies available. Additional person $10 extra. AE, DISC, MC, V.
Family owned and operated, this simple, shingle-roofed, pastel hotel gets mention for its ideal location, directly on the ocean. It offers modest accommodations, a large swimming pool, a sheltered harbor with plenty of dock space, a boat ramp, volleyball and shuffleboard courts, and barbecue pits on the beach. Complimentary coffee is served each morning.

BUDGET

OCEAN VIEW, Overseas Hwy., Mile Marker 84, Islamorada, FL 33036. Tel. 305/664-2321. 6 rms. TV
$ Rates: Dec 18–Apr 17, $55–$60 single or double. Apr 18–Sept 6, $45–$50 single or double; Sept 7–Dec 17, $35–$40 single or double. AE, DISC, MC, V.
Located across from the Holiday Isle Resort, this place is as basic as can be, but it's also the least expensive you'll find. Units have small kitchenettes, and are located adjacent to a sports bar and package store.

CAMPING

JOHN PENNEKAMP CORAL REEF STATE PARK, Overseas Hwy., Mile Marker 102.3 (P.O. Box 487), Key Largo, FL 33037. Tel. 305/451-1202. 47 campsites.
$ Rates: $24–$26 per site. MC, V.
One of Florida's most celebrated state parks (see "What to See and Do," above), Pennekamp offers 47 relatively secluded campsites, half available by advance reservation, the rest distributed on a first-come, first-served basis. Campers are not allowed to

stay more than 14 days, and to hold reservations after 5pm the park must be notified of late arrival by phone on the check-in date. The park opens at 8am and closes at sundown, and pets are not allowed.

KOA FIESTA KEY RESORT, Overseas Hwy., Mile Marker 70, Long Key, FL 33001. Tel. 305/664-4922. 375 campsites.
$ Rates: $32–$55 per site, depending on location. AE, DISC, MC, V.
Although the campsites are too close to one another, the waterfront location is nice, as are the immaculately maintained grounds. Like most KOA campgrounds, this one is family oriented, offering many facilities and activities for children. In addition to ocean swimming, there is a recreation hall, shuffleboard courts, and a playground. There's also a restaurant and pub. The higher-priced camping spaces are wooded.

LONG KEY STATE RECREATION AREA, Overseas Hwy., Mile Marker 67.5 (P.O. Box 776), Long Key, FL 33001. Tel. 305/664-4815. 60 campsites.
$ Rates: $25 per site for one to four people. Additional person (over four) $1 extra. MC, V.
This is one of the area's most popular camping grounds; so I suggest making reservations 60 days in advance. All sites are located oceanside.

WHERE TO DINE
VERY EXPENSIVE

ATLANTIC'S EDGE, in the Cheeca Lodge, Overseas Hwy., Mile Marker 82, Islamorada. Tel. 664-4651.
Cuisine: SEAFOOD. **Reservations:** Recommended.
$ Prices: Appetizers $4–$9; main courses $17–$32; fixed-price meals $25 and $29. AE, CB, DC, DISC, MC, V.
Open: Dinner only, daily 5:30–10pm.
If you caught it, they'll cook it. If yours got away, the restaurant will prepare one of their fresh fish—blackened, grilled, braised, or steamed. One of the nicest restaurants in the Upper Keys, Atlantic's Edge offers elegant beachfront dining in a warm, window-wrapped dining room. Caribbean-influenced meals might start with a salad of avocado, grilled pineapple, black beans, and plantains, or a cup of roasted corn and stone crab soup. Onion-crusted Florida snapper (served with braised artichokes) and gulf shrimp on creamy polenta (with braised cabbage) are excellent examples of the kitchen's capabilities. There is also a well-stocked raw bar.

MODERATE

LAZY DAYS OCEANFRONT BAR AND SEAFOOD GRILL, Overseas Hwy., Mile Marker 80.5, Islamorada. Tel. 664-5256.
Cuisine: AMERICAN/SEAFOOD. **Reservations:** Not accepted.
$ Prices: Appetizers $4–$8; main courses $10–$13; lunch $5–$8. AE, DISC, MC, V.
Open: Tues–Sun 11:30am–10pm.
It's hard to miss this "Miami Vice"–colored, glass-enclosed, rectangular restaurant on stilts. Located on your left (heading toward Key West), Lazy Days is set slightly back from the road behind willowy palms. Opened in 1992, the restaurant is refreshingly bright, boasting a single large dining room (with additional outdoor terrace seating), with blond-wood floors and the requisite mounted marlin.
Some of the more tempting appetizers include steamed clams with garlic and bell peppers; and nachos with seasoned beef, beans, cheese, and jalapeños. Lunch selections include chowders, salads, and a large selection of sandwiches, including charcoal-grilled fish, spicy Caribbean jerk chicken, and sausages with green peppers and onions. Dinners rely heavily on fish, though Caribbean- and Italian-style foods are also served. Most main courses come with baked potatoes, vegetables, a tossed salad, and French bread.

MANNY & ISA'S KITCHEN, Overseas Hwy., Mile Marker 81.6, Islamorada. Tel. 664-5019.

Cuisine: SPANISH-AMERICAN. **Reservations:** Not accepted.
$ Prices: Appetizers $3–$4; main courses $9–$17; lunch $3–$8. AE, MC, V.
Open: Wed–Mon 11am–9pm.

I love this place. Opened a dozen or so years ago as a small shop selling key lime pies and conch chowder exclusively, this pint-size café-style restaurant has expanded its menu and become a very popular local hangout. There are fewer than 10 tables here, and a moderate-length menu packed with Florida-influenced Spanish-American specialties such as pork chops with black beans and rice, lobster enchiladas with lobster chunks in a Spanish sauce, and sandwiches. Of course they still serve conch chowder and key lime pie.

PAPA JOE'S, Overseas Hwy., Mile Marker 79.7, Islamorada. Tel. 664-8109.

Cuisine: AMERICAN. **Reservations:** Not required.
$ Prices: Appetizers $4–$8; main courses $10–$13; lunch $5–$8. AE, MC, V.
Open: Wed–Mon 11am–10pm.

From the road, this wooden landmark—under a big palm tree and yellow-and-white tiki-style sign—looks like the ultimate island eatery. It's well weathered and right on the water but, unfortunately, there are no outdoor tables. Inside, it's so dark that it feels like night even on the brightest days.

Whatever the fresh catch is, order it sautéed—on either a platter or a bun—and you won't be disappointed. The usual variety of burgers, salads, sandwiches, meat, and chicken are also available. The raw bar is particularly appealing, and a full range of drinks is served.

SID & ROXIE'S GREEN TURTLE INN, Overseas Hwy., Mile Marker 81.5, Islamorada. Tel. 664-9031.

Cuisine: SEAFOOD/AMERICAN. **Reservations:** Not required.
$ Prices: Appetizers $4–$6; main courses $10–$18; lunch $5–$11. AE, DC, DISC, MC, V.
Open: Tues–Sun noon–10pm.

An Islamorada landmark since 1947, the Green Turtle comes from an age when dark interiors were a mark of elegance. It's a family kind of place, where broiled surf-and-turf dinners come with soup, potatoes, and a salad. Soups, breads, and pies are all made on the premises, and served by career waitresses who have been here for years. In addition to prime beef and fresh-caught fish, the restaurant offers alligator steak, shrimp, and chicken dishes. Look for the giant turtle and you'll know you've found the place.

EVENING ENTERTAINMENT

WOODY'S SALOON AND RESTAURANT, Mile Marker 82, Islamorada. Tel. 664-4335.

The "hottest" local bar in the Upper Keys, Woody's is a lively blue-collar place serving up mediocre pizzas and live bands almost every night of the week. The house band, Big Richard and the Extenders, has been playing here for years, and will probably do so for years to come. There are also pool tables, video games, and more than an occasional karaoke night.

2. THE LOWER KEYS: BIG PINE KEY TO COPPITT KEY

110–140 miles SW of Miami

GETTING THERE By Bus Greyhound runs three buses a day, in each direction, between Key West and Miami, stopping in the Lower Keys along the way. The company no longer operates a single nationwide telephone number, so consult your local directory for the office nearest you.

By Car From Miami, take the Florida Turnpike south along the east coast to Exit

4, Homestead/Key West. This is the Turnpike Extension that meets U.S. 1 in Florida City. Big Pine Key is about two hours south.

If you're coming from Florida's west coast, take Alligator Alley to the Miami exit, then turn south onto the Turnpike Extension.

ESSENTIALS   The telephone area code is 305.

The **Lower Keys Chamber of Commerce,** Overseas Highway, Mile Marker 31, Big Pine Key, FL 33043 (tel. 305/872-2411, or toll free 800/872-3722), offers information on area sights, restaurants, and hotels.

Big Pine, Sugarloaf, Summerland, and the other Lower Keys are less developed and more inviting than their Upper Key neighbors. The Lower Keys have mercilessly been preserved for nature and, indeed, are one of America's most important unaffected habitats—a last frontier that hopefully will always remain far from the reach of land developers and tourist-hungry profiteers. Unlike their neighbors to the north and south, the Lower Keys are devoid of rowdy spring break–style crowds, have few T-shirt and trinket shops, and fewer late-night bars. What they do have is a divine beauty that's truly awe-inspiring. Don't hurry to Key West. Stay overnight in the Lower Keys, rent a boat, and explore the reefs—you won't be disappointed.

WHAT TO SEE & DO

SIGHTS & ATTRACTIONS

LEDA-BRUCE GALLERYS, Overseas Hwy., Mile Marker 30.2, Big Pine Key. Tel. 872-0212.

A contemporary art gallery? Is this a sign that the Lower Keys are getting Hamptons hip? Well, not exactly. Owners Leda and Bruce Seigal are longtime residents of the Keys and famous in these parts for both their art and their eccentricities. In this concrete building, just past the island's only traffic light (when heading toward Key West), the couple displays some of the best works from the Keys' most important artists. In short, this is the finest gallery between Miami and Key West. It's a great place to browse, and the friendly owners are usually on hand to chat.

Admission: Free.

Open: Tues–Sat 10am–6pm.

NATIONAL KEY DEER REFUGE, Key Deer Blvd., near Mile Marker 30, Big Pine Key. Tel. 872-2239.

Speed-limit signs on Big Pine Key direct motorists to slow down to 35 m.p.h., a measure enacted to help preserve the key deer, a three-foot-tall miniature native to these woods, which are the only lands in the Keys that have fresh water. Except for their toy size and endangered status, these deer are much like their better-known mainland counterparts. They freeze when staring into headlights, and usually try to avoid the traffic on U.S. 1. You'll probably drive straight through Big Pine without spotting one of these cute creatures, unless you specifically look for them at the Deer Refuge, where there's a well-marked hiking trail.

When heading toward Key West, turn right at Big Pine Key's only traffic light onto Key Deer Boulevard (take the left fork immediately after the turn). The National Key Deer Refuge trailhead is about two miles ahead on your left.

BAHIA HONDA STATE PARK, Overseas Hwy., Mile Marker 29.5, Big Pine Key. Tel. 872-2353.

The best park in the Lower Keys, Bahia Honda rivals John Pennekamp Park (see "The Upper Keys," above) for facilities, character, and the sheer beauty of its wilderness. Spread out across 635 acres, the park offers large stretches of white sandy beach, deep waters close to shore that are perfect for snorkeling and diving, and miles of trails packed with unusual plants and animals. There are guided trail walks, fishing charters, daily snorkeling excursions, and shaded beachside picnic areas with tables and grills. Docking and camping facilities are available; see "Where to Stay," below, for complete information.

Admission: $3.75 per vehicle, $1 per pedestrian or bicyclist, free for children under 6; $2 boat-ramp fee.

SUGARLOAF BAT TOWER, next to Sugarloaf Airport by Mile Marker 17.

Standing silently alone—surrounded by nothing—the squat, wooden Sugarloaf Bat Tower was constructed in 1929 in an effort to attract bats that would in turn eat the ever-present mosquitoes that plague most of the keys. The bats never came, however, and the failed "Bat Motel" remains to beguile passersby who have no idea what it is.

To reach the tower, turn right at the Sugarloaf Airport sign and turn right again, onto the dirt road that begins just before the airport gate; the tower is about 100 yards ahead.

BOAT RENTALS

Several shops rent powerboats for fishing and reef exploring. Most also rent tackle, sell bait, and have charter captains available. Rental shops include **Bud Boats,** at the Old Wooden Bridge Fishing Camp & Marina, Big Pine Key (tel. 743-6316); **Jaybird's Powerboats,** Overseas Highway, Mile Marker 33, Big Pine Key (tel. 872-4132, or 872-2351); and **T.J.'s Sugarshack,** at the Sugarloaf Lodge Marina, Overseas Highway, Mile Marker 17, Sugarloaf Key (tel. 745-3135).

ORGANIZED TOURS

Fantasy Dan's Airplane Rides, Overseas Highway, Mile Marker 17, Sugarloaf Key Airport (tel. 745-2217), offers 15-minute and half-hour rides over the reefs and keys. Tours usually include a buzzing of Key West and the mangrove forests of uninhabited smaller islands. Flights require a minimum of two people and cost $25 per person for 15 minutes, $35 per person for a half hour.

WHERE TO STAY

VERY EXPENSIVE

LITTLE PALM ISLAND, Overseas Hwy., Mile Marker 28.5 (P.O. Box 1036), Little Torch Key, FL 33042. Tel. 305/872-2524, or toll free 800/343-8567. Fax 305/872-4843. 30 suites. A/C MINIBAR

$ Rates: Dec 21–May, $465–$795 suite for two. June–Dec 20, $330–$695 suite for two. Special honeymoon packages available. AE, DC, MC, V.

Little Palm Island is the name of the resort that occupies the entire five acres of Little Munson Island, a former fishing camp that once accommodated Presidents Roosevelt, Truman, Kennedy, and Nixon, among other power elite. It's still an "in" spot; Vice-President Albert Gore stayed here during Thanksgiving 1991. The resort's top-of-the-line accommodations appeal to rich recluses—Hollywood glitterati need not apply. The island is only accessible by boat and privacy is the name of the game here, so much so that the resort's 30 secluded suites don't even have telephones (although that should hardly make a difference in this cellular world) or TVs.

The hotel's suites are well spaced about the property, hidden behind ample tropical plants and bushes including coconut palms, bougainvillea, oleander, and hibiscus, with private sun decks with hanging hammocks. Rooms are outfitted with ceiling fans, wicker and rattan furnishings, coffee makers, refrigerators, and outdoor showers. The Mexican-tile baths have whirlpool tubs and the contemporary amenities you'd expect from a top hotel.

Dining/Entertainment: The Little Palm Restaurant is a formal restaurant serving international cuisine. The Palapa Pool Bar offers refreshments and light snacks all day.

Services: Room service, laundry, massage, airport transportation.

Facilities: Swimming pool, complimentary water-sports rentals (including sailboats, windsurfers, canoes, kayaks, and snorkeling and fishing gear), sauna, boutique, fully equipped dive shop.

MODERATE

THE BARNACLE, U.S. 1 (P.O. Box 780A), Big Pine Key, FL 33043. Tel. 872-3298. 5 rms. A/C TV TEL

$ Rates (including breakfast): Dec 15–May 15, $90–$100 single or double. May 16–Dec 14, $75–$85 single or double. No credit cards.

It makes a difference that the Barnacle's owners, Woody and Joan Cornell, were once innkeepers in Vermont. They know what amenities travelers are looking for, and go out of their way to fulfill special requests. Their Big Pine Key home has only five bedrooms, each with its own personality. Three are located upstairs, in the main house—their doors open into the home's living room which contains a small Jacuzzi-style tub. For privacy, the remaining two rooms are best; each has its own entrance and is out of earshot of the common areas. Accommodations are standard, not luxurious. All rooms have queen-size beds, small refrigerators, and private baths. There is no abundance of fluffy towels, no fru-fru soaps and toiletries. The property has its own private, sandy beach where you can float all day on the inn's rafts, rubber boat, or kayak. The house is located directly on a shallow-water beach, and beach towels, chairs, and coolers are also provided for guests' use.

DEER RUN BED AND BREAKFAST, Long Beach Dr. (P.O. Box 431), Big Pine Key, FL 33043. Tel. 305/872-2015. 3 rms.

$ Rates (including breakfast): $85–$110 single or double.

Sue Abbott's small, smoke-free B&B is a real find, and a pleasure for those wanting an intimate look at the Lower Keys. Located directly on the beach, the neat three-room bed-and-breakfast is truly homey—the kind of a place where you'd stay if you had friends in the Keys. One upstairs and two downstairs bedrooms are comfortably furnished with queen-size beds, good closets, and touch-sensitive lamps. Breakfast, which is served in a pretty, enclosed deck, is cooked to order by Sue herself.

PARMER'S PLACE COTTAGES, Barry Ave., near Mile Marker 28.5, Little Torch Key (P.O. Box 445, Big Pine Key, FL 33043). Tel. 305/872-2157. 40 rms, 8 efficiencies.

$ Rates: Oct–Apr, $80–$85 single or double; $90 efficiency. May–Sept, $60–$65 single or double; $75 efficiency. Additional person $12.50 extra. AE, DISC, MC, V.

One of my favorite places in the Lower Keys, this downscale resort offers modest but comfortable cottages in a variety of configurations. Every unit is different: Some face the water while others are a few steps away. Some have small kitchenettes and others hold just a bedroom. Most cottages contain two separate units that can be combined into one for large families. Rooms are sparsely decorated and very clean, though guests who choose daily maid service will incur a small additional charge (otherwise there's only light housekeeping during your stay). Parmer's has been a fixture here for almost 20 years, and is well known for its charming hospitality and very informative staff.

SUGARLOAF LODGE, Overseas Hwy., Mile Marker 17 (P.O. Box 148), Sugar Loaf Key, FL 33044. Tel. 305/745-3211. 55 rms, 10 efficiencies. A/C TV TEL

$ Rates: Dec 19–Apr, $85–$95 single or double; $100 efficiency. May–Aug, $65–$80 single or double; $85 efficiency. Sept–Dec 18, $55–$65 single or double; $70 efficiency. Additional person $10 extra. AE, CB, DC, DISC, MC, V.

On one hand, this is just a motel: plain rooms, color TV, good parking, swimming pool—you get the idea. But its ideal location in the heart of the Lower Keys and its immediate proximity to the backcountry reefs really make the Sugarloaf Lodge special. There are two wings to this sprawling property, which surround a lagoon where the motel's mascot dolphin lives. Efficiency rooms outfitted with small, fully equipped kitchenettes are also available. The motel is close to tennis courts and a miniature golf course, and adjacent to T.J.'s Sugarshack, an excellent marina from which you can fish or sightsee on the reef (see "Boat Rentals" in "What to See and Do," above). There's a restaurant and lounge serving meals and drinks all day.

CAMPING

BAHIA HONDA STATE PARK, Overseas Hwy., Mile Marker 29.5 (P.O. Box 782), Big Pine Key, FL 33043. Tel. 305/872-2353. 80 campsites, 6 cabin units.

$ Rates: Camping, $25 per site for one to four people; additional person (over four) $1 extra. Cabins, Dec 15–Sept 14, $125 per cabin for one to four people; Sept 15–Dec 14, $97 per cabin; additional person (over four) $6 extra. MC, V.

One of the best parks in the whole state of Florida, Bahia Honda is as loaded with facilities and activities as it is with campers. Don't be discouraged by its popularity—this park encompasses over 600 acres of land, and some very private beaches (see "What to See and Do," above, for complete information).

If you're lucky enough to get one, the park's cabins represent a very good value. Each holds up to eight guests, and comes complete with linens, kitchenettes, and utensils.

KOA CAMPGROUND, Overseas Hwy., Mile Marker 20, Sugarloaf Key (P.O. Box 469, Summerland Key, FL 33042). Tel. 305/745-3549. 350 campsites.

$ Rates: $33–$43 per site. Additional person $7 extra.

Although it's a bit too popular with RV travelers, this campground offers excellent facilities for tent campers as well, including a large swimming lagoon, swimming pool, hot tub, pub, laundry facilities, and showers.

WHERE TO DINE

MODERATE

ISLAND REEF, Overseas Hwy., Mile Marker 31.3, Big Pine Key. Tel. 872-2170.
   Cuisine: AMERICAN. **Reservations:** Not accepted.
$ Prices: Breakfast $3–$7; lunch $2–$8; dinner $9–$14. AE, DISC, MC, V.
   Open: Breakfast/lunch daily 6:30am–2:30pm; dinner daily 5–9:30pm.

This colorful ramshackle restaurant seems almost as old as the Keys themselves. It's extremely popular with locals, and the conversations you'll overhear tend toward today's catch and tomorrow's weather. There are only about a dozen tables, as well as six stools at a small diner-style bar.

Breakfasts tend toward fresh-fruit platters and French toast, while lunches mean simple sandwiches and tasty island chowders. Dinner specials change nightly; sometimes it's roast chicken with stuffing or leg of lamb, and other times it's prime rib or baked dolphin fish. It's always as good as the atmosphere.

BALTIMORE OYSTER HOUSE, Overseas Hwy., Mile Marker 30, Big Pine Key. Tel. 305/872-2314.
   Cuisine: SEAFOOD. **Reservations:** Not required.
$ Prices: Appetizers $4–$10; main courses $6–$14. AE, MC, V.
   Open: Mon–Sat noon–10pm.

Happily, the Baltimore Oyster House, which has had its ups and downs over the years, is up again. An old-timer on Big Pine, this house serves oysters, fresh shrimp, mussels, and clams, all priced by the pound. Crawdads (suck the head, dip the tail) are also available, as are fresh fish (like dolphin, salmon, and snapper), steak, chicken, and salads.

The restaurant's nautical-diner interior features fish nets on the ceiling and a full bar. The single-story, free-standing restaurant is located on your left (heading toward Key West), right in the middle of town.

MONTE'S, Overseas Hwy., Mile Marker 25, Summerland Key. Tel. 745-3731.
   Cuisine: SEAFOOD. **Reservations:** Not accepted.
$ Prices: Appetizers $2–$4; main courses $9–$13; lunch $2–$7. No credit cards.
   Open: Tues–Sat 10am–10pm, Sun noon–9pm.

If the food wasn't both excellent and fresh, then this place would close, because nobody goes to Monte's for its atmosphere: plastic place settings on plastic-covered picnic-style tables in a plastic-enclosed dining patio. Monte's has been open for 16 years because the food is very good and incredibly fresh; in fact, you can choose by sight the very fish you eat. Today's catch may include shark, tuna, lobster, stone crabs, and a variety of different size shrimp. In addition to grilling and frying fresh fish, the restaurant prepares several dishes including clam chowder, spiced crayfish pie, and even barbecued spareribs.

MANGROVE MAMA'S RESTAURANT, Overseas Hwy., Mile Marker 20, Sugarloaf Key. Tel. 745-3030.
   Cuisine: SEAFOOD/AMERICAN. **Reservations:** Not required.
$ **Prices:** Appetizers $3–$9, main courses $13–$19, lunch $2–$9; brunch $5–$7. CB, DC, MC, V.
   Open: Lunch daily 11:30am–3pm; dinner daily 5:30–10pm.
One of the few structures to survive the infamous 1935 hurricane, Mangrove Mama's (formerly Eddie's Fish Basket) is truly a Lower Keys institution. It's a dive, in the best sense of the word—a leap into another time, when the corner bar was the town's epicenter and "haute cuisine" was a foreign term. The restaurant is a mere shack that used to have a gas pump as well as a grill. A handful of simple tables, both inside and out, are shaded by banana trees and often occupied by locals.
   It's not surprising that fish is the menu's mainstay, though chowders, salads, and large omelets (including one filled with shrimp, scallops, and crabmeat) are also served. Grilled teriyaki chicken and club sandwiches are available, as are meatless chef's salad (with bleu cheese, boiled eggs, and vegetables), baked stuffed shrimp with crabmeat stuffing, and spicy barbecued baby back ribs.

BUDGET

MAXIMILLIONS DINER, at Sugarloaf Lodge, Overseas Hwy., Mile Marker 17, Sugarloaf Key. Tel. 745-3741.
   Cuisine: AMERICAN. **Reservations:** Not accepted.
$ **Prices:** Breakfast $2–$5; lunch $4–$7; dinner $5–$8. AE, DC, DISC, MC, V.
   Open: Breakfast/lunch daily 7:30am–2:30pm; dinner Sun–Thurs 5–9pm, Fri–Sat 5–10pm.
It's just a simple, small-town restaurant that could be anywhere—if it weren't for the mounted marlin and view of the dolphin pool. It's hard to believe that this huge dining room ever fills to capacity, though the adjacent wood-paneled bar is often hopping with local fishermen.
   Breakfasts here include the usual variety of egg dishes, served with corned-beef hash, sausage, ham, or steak. Pancakes and French toast are also available. At lunch and dinner, you can get a variety of hot and cold sandwiches including chicken and steak, fish, burgers, and other traditional American foods. In deference to their dolphin, the diner never serves tunafish.

3. KEY WEST

150 miles SW of Miami

GETTING THERE   By Plane   Several major airlines fly nonstop from Miami to Key West, and charge $99 to $298 round-trip, depending on date of travel and ticket restrictions. These include: **American Eagle** (tel. toll free 800/443-7300) and **USAir Express** (tel. toll free 800/428-4322). Planes fly into Key West International Airport, South Roosevelt Boulevard (tel. 305/296-5439), on the southeastern corner of the island.

By Bus   Greyhound runs three buses a day, in each direction, between Key West and Miami. The company no longer operates a single nationwide telephone number, so consult your local directory for the office nearest you.

By Car   From Miami, take the Florida Turnpike south along the east coast to Exit 4, Homestead/Key West. This is the Turnpike Extension that meets U.S. 1 in Florida City. Key West is about 2½ hours south.

If you're coming from Florida's west coast, take Alligator Alley to the Miami exit, then turn south onto the Turnpike Extension.

The journey will take you across 42 toll-free bridges, including Seven-Mile Bridge, reputedly the longest segmental bridge in the world.

ESSENTIALS   The telephone area code is 305.

The **Florida Keys & Key West Visitors Bureau,** P.O. Box 1147, Key West, FL 33041 (tel. 305/296-2228, or toll free 800/FLA-KEYS), offers a free vacation information kit for the asking. The **Key West Chamber of Commerce,** 402 Wall St. (P.O. Box 984), Key West, FL 33040 (tel. 305/294-5988, or toll free 800/527-8539), also offers general as well as specialized information and is open Monday through Friday from 8am to 5pm and on Saturday and Sunday from 8:30am to 5pm.

Key West is just four miles long and two miles wide, so getting around is easy. The "Old Town," centered around **Duval Street,** is the island's meeting ground and collective watering hole. It's also the location of most of the island's bars, restaurants, and sights. Many of the surrounding streets are filled with some of America's most beautiful Victorian/Bahamian-style homes.

Located about 150 miles from Miami, at the terminus of U.S. 1, Key West is the most distant member of Florida's key chain. Accessible only by boat until 1912, when Henry Flagler's railroad reached it, Key West's relative isolation from the North American mainland has everything to do with its charm.

During the first half of the 19th century, many locals made their living as "wreckers"—helping themselves to the booty of ships overturned in the shallows offshore. Since that time, the key has been home to an untold number of outlaws, drifters, writers, musicians, and other miscreants and eccentric types.

Today, in addition to artists and intellectuals, the island supports a healthy mix of Cubans and Caribbeans, and one of the largest gay populations in America. On Duval Street, smart boutiques stand next to old gin-joint dives and laid-back strollers fill the sidewalks. Key West is known for its terrific weather (about 10° cooler than Miami during the height of summer), quaint 19th-century architecture, and a friendly, easygoing atmosphere.

WHAT TO SEE & DO

Key West is famous for its relaxed atmosphere. Literally at the end of the road, this distant metropolitan hideaway has somehow eluded conventional domestication. Although it was tamed long ago by gourmet ice cream and chocolate-chip cookie shops, Key West has reached legend status for the way its residents jealously guard the island's independent identity. Tales of old-time pirating and modern-day renegades abound. And natives, who call themselves "conchs" (pronounced "conks"), have mockingly declared seccession from the United States in favor of their independent "Conch Republic."

Accordingly, the best thing to do on the island is to take a long stroll down Duval Street and stop in at the many open-air bars. Meet some locals, have a few drinks, and end up at the Mallory Docks by sunset. While strolling around, you might even want to visit some of the historical houses and fascinating museums below.

SIGHTS & ATTRACTIONS

AUDUBON HOUSE AND GARDENS, 205 Whitehead St. Tel. 294-2116.

Named for the famous naturalist John James Audubon, who visited here in 1832, this restored three-story house features the master artist's original etchings and a large collection of lithographs. The house also holds a collection of Dorothy Doughty's porcelain birds and the period furnishings of its former owner, Capt. John Geiger, who was once one of the wealthiest men in Key West. Friendly docents are eager to answer questions, and admission includes a self-guided-tour brochure of the home and the lush tropical gardens that surround it.

Admission: $6 adults, $5 seniors, $2 children 6–12, free for children under 6.
Open: Daily 9:30am–5pm.

THE CURRY MANSION, 511 Caroline St. Tel. 294-5349.

Built in 1855 by Florida's first millionaire, William Curry, this lovely conch-style mansion has been lovingly restored and filled with innumerable antiques. Listed in the National Register of Historic Places, the manor is a tribute to the early days of Key West. A self-guided tour of the house includes original parlors, several bedrooms, the dining room, and the carriage entrance. Also open to view is the master bedroom and dressing room, as well as the porches and surrounding grounds. Part of the mansion also operates as a bed-and-breakfast (see "Where to Stay," below, for complete information).

Admission: $5 adults, $1 children 4–12, free for children under 4.
Open: Daily 10am–5pm.

EAST MARTELLO MUSEUM AND GALLERY, 3501 S. Roosevelt Blvd. Tel. 296-3913.

There are several museums in Key West dedicated to the island's history, but for variety, this is one of the best. Housed in a pre–Civil War fort that was built to protect the nation's southernmost flank, the museum exhibits various historical artifacts illustrating the Keys' history of shipwrecks, pirates, sponging, and cigar making.

In addition to displays of historical interest, the museum exhibits many works by local artists, including dozens by native Mario Sanchez, whose crude and colorful wood carvings depict scenes from his Key West boyhood.

Admission: $5 adults, $1 children 5–15, free for children under 5.
Open: Daily 9:30am–5pm.

ERNEST HEMINGWAY HOUSE MUSEUM, 907 Whitehead St. Tel. 294-1575.

From 1931 to 1961 the author shared these quarters with 50-odd six-toed cats, and lived here while writing *For Whom the Bell Tolls, Death in the Afternoon,* and several other novels. Hemingway, it is said, usually awoke early and wrote in the loft of his poolhouse. If his work was progressing well, he would continue without a break for hours. "If the words are coming hard," Hemingway once said, "I often quit before noon."

Built in 1851, the writer's beautiful stone Spanish Colonial house was one of the first on the island to be fitted with indoor plumbing and a built-in fireplace. The house was opened to the public in 1963, two years after Hemingway's death, and contains many personal possessions, as well as dozens of six-toed feline descendants.

Admission: $6 adults, $1.50 children.
Open: Daily 9am–5pm.

KEY WEST CEMETERY, Margaret and Angela Sts.

Both old and picturesque, this 21-acre cemetery in the center of the island is a Key West original. The island's rocky geological makeup forced residents to "bury" their dead above ground, in stone-encased caskets. Many memorials are emblazoned with nicknames, which are popular on this informal island. Look for headstones labeled "The Tailor," "Bean," "Shorty," and "Bunny." Many other headstones also reflect residents' not-so-serious attitudes toward life. "I Told You I Was Sick" is one of the more famous epitaphs, as is a tongue-in-cheek widow's inscription "At Least I Know Where He's Sleeping Tonight."

KEY WEST LIGHTHOUSE MUSEUM, 938 Whitehead St. Tel. 294-0012.

Many locals mourned when the Key West Lighthouse was opened in 1848; its bright warning to ships also signaled the end of the island's profitable shipwrecking businesses. When the lighthouse keeper died in 1908, his wife, Mary Bethel, took his place, becoming the first and only female lighthouse keeper in America. The technical

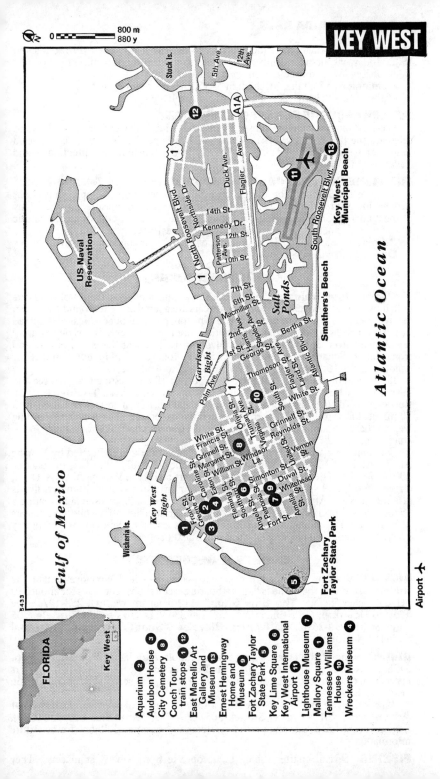

KEY WEST

0   800 m
       880 y

FLORIDA

Key West

Aquarium **2**
Audubon House **3**
City Cemetery **8**
Conch Tour
train stops **1** **12**
East Martello Art
Gallery and
Museum **13**
Ernest Hemingway
Home and
Museum **9**
Fort Zachary Taylor
State Park **5**
Key Lime Square **6**
Key West International
Airport **11**
Lighthouse Museum **7**
Mallory Square **1**
Tennessee Williams
House **10**
Wreckers Museum **4**

Gulf of Mexico

US Naval
Reservation

Wisteria Is.

Stock Is.

5th Ave.
12th Ave.

A1A

Duck Ave.
Flagler Ave.
Northside Dr.
North Roosevelt Blvd.

14th St.
Kennedy Dr.
12th St.
10th St.
Patterson Ave.

7th St.
6th St.
Macmillan St.
2nd Ave.
Harris Ave.
1st St.
George St.
Staples St.
Thompson St.
White St.

*Salt
Ponds*

Bertha St.
Flagler St.
Laird St.
Atlantic Blvd.
South St.

South Roosevelt Blvd.

Key West
Municipal Beach

Smathers's Beach

Atlantic Ocean

Key West
Bight

*Garrison
Bight*

Palm Ave.

White St.
Francis St.
Grinnell St.
Margaret St.
Eaton St.
William St.
Fleming St.
Southard St.
Angela St.
Petronia St.

Olivia St.
Truman Ave.
Windsor La.

Grinnell St.
Reynolds St.
Vernon St.
Simonton St.
Duval St.
Whitehead St.
United St.
Fort St.
Amelia St.
Virginia St.

Front St.
Greene St.
Caroline St.

Fort Zachary
Taylor State Park

Airport ✈

age of radar and sonar made the lighthouse obsolete; it was opened to tourists in 1972. Today, visitors can climb the 88 steps to the top for magnificent panoramic views of Key West and the ocean.

Admission: $5 adults, $1 children 5–15, free for children under 5.
Open: Daily 9:30am–5pm (last admission at 4:30pm).

MALLORY SQUARE SUNSET CELEBRATION.

Every evening, just before sunset, locals and visitors alike gather at the docks to celebrate the day gone by. This quaint Caribbean tradition is augmented by food vendors, jugglers, artists, acrobats, and mimes who compete for the attentions—and dollars—of tourists.

MEL FISHER'S TREASURE MUSEUM, 200 Greene St. Tel. 294-2633.

Some of the $400 million in gold and silver artifacts from the Spanish galleons *Atocha* and *Santa Margarita* are displayed in this tribute to treasure hunting. Many of the doubloons, emeralds, and solid gold bars are copies; but the cannons, historic weapons, and other less marketable finds are the real McCoy.

Admission: $5 adults, $1.50 children 6–12, free for children under 6.
Open: Daily 9:30am–5pm.

ORGANIZED TOURS

The **Conch Tour Train** (tel. 294-5161) is not a train at all, but a series of tram cars pulled by a "locomotive." These canopied cars are a familiar sight around Key West, and represent a good way to see the island. The tour passes about 60 local sites, spread out over some 14 miles of road. Reservations are not necessary. Trains depart every few minutes from 3850 N. Roosevelt Blvd. (on U.S. 1, near the island bridge) and from Mallory Square (at the end of Duval Street). Tours cost $14 for adults and $6 for children under 16, and are given daily from 9am to 4:30pm.

I'll bet you didn't know that there were at least 100 interesting things to see and hear about in Key West. The 90-minute tour on the **Old Town Trolley,** 1910 N. Roosevelt Blvd. (tel. 296-6688), will point them all out. The trolley travels in a 30-minute loop around the island, allowing riders to get on and off at will, reboarding free of charge. Tours leave daily from 9am to 4pm and cost $14 for adults, $6 for children under 12.

For something a little different, **Flights of Nostalgia** are operated by Vintage Air Tours, 5728 Major Blvd., Suite 316, Orlando (tel. 305/292-1323, or toll free 800/835-9323). The year is 1945 when passengers board the Vintage Airways' DC-3, a reconditioned 49-year-old aircraft that takes tourists on nostalgic 30-minute flights around the Keys. After take-off from Key West Airport, a flight attendant wearing a 1940s-style uniform brings glasses of champagne through the cabin while wartime hits play over the P.A. system. It's a fun flight that's certainly different from ordinary everyday experience. The cost of the flight is $20 per person.

SPORTS & RECREATION

BICYCLING   Key West is a great place to see by bicycle. It's relatively small, the streets are safe, and the island is flat as a board. Several shops rent bikes for about $10 per day. They include **The Bike Shop,** 1110 Truman Ave. (tel. 294-1073); the **Moped Hospital,** 601 Truman Ave. (tel. 296-3344); **Bubba's Fun Rentals,** 705 Duval St. (tel. 294-2618); and **Tropical Bicycles & Scooter Rentals,** 1300 Duval St. (tel. 294-8136).

DIVING   One of the area's largest scuba schools, **Key West Pro Dive Shop,** 3128 N. Roosevelt Blvd. (tel. 305/296-3823, or toll free 800/426-0707), offers instruction on all levels, and dive boats take participants to scuba and snorkel sites on nearby reefs.

Wreck dives and night dives are two of the more unusual offerings of **Lost Reef Adventures,** 261 Margaret St. (tel. 305/296-9737, or toll free 800/952-2749). Regularly scheduled runs and private charters can be arranged. Phone for departure information.

FISHING   Several charter fishing boats operate from Key West marinas. They include Capt. Jim Brienza's 25-foot *Sea Breeze,* docked at Oceanside Marina, 25 Arbutus Dr. (tel. 294-6027); Captain Henry Otto's 43-foot *Sunday,* docked at A&B Lobster House and Marina, 9 Geiger Rd. (tel. 294-7052), and a host of deep-sea vessels docked at **Garrison Bight Marina,** Eaton Street and Roosevelt Boulevard (tel. 296-9969).

WHERE TO STAY
VERY EXPENSIVE

MARRIOTT'S CASA MARINA RESORT, 1500 Reynolds St., Key West, FL 33040. Tel. 305/296-3535, or toll free 800/228-9290. Fax 305/296-9960. 312 rms. 71 suites. A/C MINIBAR TV TEL

$ Rates: Dec 19–Apr 24, $250–$325 single or double; from $325 suite. Apr 25–Dec 18, $170–$235 single or double; from $235 suite. Additional person $25 extra. Children under 18 stay free in their parents' room. AE, CB, DC, DISC, MC, V.

Built in the 1920s by railroad tycoon Henry Flagler, Casa Marina was Key West's first grand hotel, popular with movie stars and socialites. Falling in stature after the 1935 hurricane, the hotel was opened in the early 1940s to World War II military personnel, and run by the U.S. Navy. During the Cuban Missile Crisis in the early 1960s, President Kennedy again moved troops into the hotel, and installed antiaircraft missile launchers on the beach.

Casa Marina is a nice place, encompassing several low-rise structures and a huge swath of oceanfront, but it's not grand on the scale of Palm Beach's Breakers, or the Boca Raton Resort and Club—other Flagler-inspired projects created to lure film stars and land speculators. The lobby is the hotel's masterpiece, outfitted with saloon-style swinging doors, bronze paddle fans, French doors, peacock chairs, and dark woods from floor to ceiling.

Guest rooms, which are located in several Spanish-Mediterranean-style three-story wings, are comparatively modest and straightforward, comparable to business-oriented Marriotts elsewhere. The most expensive accommodations have balconies overlooking the ocean, while those at the lower end of the price spectrum face inland. Most of the rooms are similar, if not identical, making them popular with groups.

Dining/Entertainment: Flagler's, the hotel's top restaurant, features Caribbean-inspired decor and fresh local seafood. There's a breakfast buffet and Sunday brunch served outdoors on the patio. The adjacent lounge offers regular live entertainment. The Sun Pavilion, a beachfront eatery, serves breakfast, lunch, dinner, late-night snacks, and drinks all day.

Facilities: Private beach with 80-foot swimming pier, two swimming pools, outdoor whirlpool, health club with sauna, three lighted tennis courts, water-sports center, beauty salon, gift shops.

Services: Room service, concierge, business center, evening turn-down, laundry, overnight shoeshine, massage.

THE PIER HOUSE, 1 Duval St., Key West, FL 33040. Tel. 305/296-4600, or toll free 800/327-8340. Fax 305/296-7568. 142 rms. 13 suites. A/C MINIBAR TV TEL

$ Rates: Dec 21–Apr 19, $275–$400 single or double; from $450 suite; additional person $35 extra. Apr 20–Dec 20, $205–$330 single or double; from $300 suite; additional person $20 extra. AE, CB, DC, DISC, MC, V.

This is the best hotel in Key West, period. The Pier House's excellent location, at the foot of Duval Street just steps from Mallory Docks and stumbling distance from most every bar, is the envy of the island. Set back from the busy street, on a short strip of beach, the hotel is a welcome oasis of calm, offering luxurious rooms, top-notch service, and even a full-service spa.

Accommodations vary tremendously, from relatively simple business-class rooms to indulgently romantic guest quarters, complete with integrated stereo systems and whirlpool tubs. Every room has either a balcony or a patio.

Dining/Entertainment: Long a part of Key West history, it's said that Tennessee Williams was a frequent guest at the Pier House Restaurant, the hotel's primary eatery. Old Havana Docks is a popular, elevated drinkery, with a large deck that wraps around the hotel and overlooks the water.

Services: Room service, concierge, laundry.

Facilities: Spa treatments, water-sports rentals, swimming pool, beach.

THE REACH, 1435 Simonton St., Key West, FL 33040. Tel. 305/296-5000, or toll free 800/228-9290. Fax 305/296-2830. 150 rms. A/C MINIBAR TV TEL

$ Rates: Dec 21–Apr 28, $243–$450 single or double. Apr 29–Dec 20, $171–$350 single or double. Additional person $25–$30 extra. AE, CB, DC, DISC, MC, V.

The colossal, labyrinthine, pastel-colored Reach is one of the few hotels on the island with its own strip of sandy beach. The ample surrounding grounds also encompass huge palms, a large pool with plenty of lounge chairs, and a private pier for fishing and suntanning. Rooms are relatively straightforward, in the Hilton or Sheraton mold. Most are identical, with small, well-equipped baths, double beds with brightly printed spreads, remote-control TVs, and fully stocked minibars. All rooms have sliding glass doors that open onto balconies, some with ocean views. The hotel is located a short walk from the "far" end of Duval Street—a 15-minute walk away from the center of the action.

Dining/Entertainment: The Ocean Club serves fresh local seafood in a Mediterranean seaside setting. The beachfront Sand Bar, a fish-and-burger place, is not known for its culinary prowess, but offers one of the best settings on the island. For a quick bite, stop by A Little Something, the resort's deli and French bakery. Nightfall, a rooftop bar, offers regular entertainment and good sunset views.

Services: Room service, concierge, laundry.

Facilities: Heated swimming pool, sauna, health spa, steam room, sailboats, windsurfers.

SHERATON SUITES, 2001 S. Roosevelt Blvd., Key West, FL 33040. Tel. 305/292-9800, or toll free 800/325-3535. Fax 305/294-6009. 180 suites. A/C MINIBAR TV TEL

$ Rates (including breakfast): Dec–Apr 17, $235–$295 suite for one or two. Apr 18–Nov, $155–$225 suite for one or two. AE, DC, MC, V.

One of Key West's newest hotels, the Sheraton Suites is located on the beach side of the island, just across the street from Key West's best swimming and water-sports beach. Don't be discouraged by the hotel's faux-colonial architecture, which looks more "prefab" than the turn-of-the-century "rehab" look they were going for. The building looks new because it is, which translates into almost 200 good-size suites all containing separate living rooms with sofa beds, a comfortable dressing area, and nice baths. Interior decorations are excellent. Rooms are beautifully dressed and well planned—all the furnishings are in just the right places. The more expensive suites include whirlpool baths, minibars, microwave ovens, coffee makers, and two telephones.

Dining/Entertainment: The hotel's restaurant, the Jupiter Crab Company, serves three meals daily from 6:30am to 11pm.

Services: Room service, concierge, overnight laundry, complimentary daily newspaper, airport transportation, free shuttle to Old Town.

Facilities: Gift shop, bicycle rentals, scooter rentals.

EXPENSIVE

THE CURRY MANSION INN, 511 Caroline St., Key West, FL 33040. Tel. 305/294-5349, or toll free 800/253-3466. Fax 305/294-4093. 21 rms. A/C MINIBAR TV TEL

$ Rates (including continental breakfast): Dec 22–May 1, $180–$220 single or double. June 2–Oct 1, $125–$175 single or double. The rest of the year, $140–$160 single or double. Additional person $25 extra. AE, MC, V.

Dating from 1899, and listed on the National Register of Historic Places, the Curry Mansion is a popular sightseeing destination as well as a notable bed-and-breakfast (see "What to See and Do," above, for complete information). The lobby has beautiful hardwood floors, a tiled fireplace, and copious antiques which are liberally spread throughout the house. Although the B&B's rooms—most of which are located in an adjacent annex—are not as luxurious as the inn's proprietors, Al and Edith Amsterdam, like to profess, they are of moderate standard, and in unusual turn-of-the-century surroundings. There's a small swimming pool on the property; guests are treated to complimentary afternoon cocktails and are entitled to use the facilities of the Pier House Beach Club, located just one block away.

MARQUESSA HOTEL, 600 Fleming St., Key West, FL 33040. Tel. 305/292-1919, or toll free 800/869-4631. Fax 305/294-2121. 11 rms, 4 suites. A/C TV TEL

$ Rates: Dec 21–Apr 11, $185–$215 single or double; from $245 suite. June–Oct 27, $115–$140 single or double; from $150 suite. The rest of the year, $140–$160 single or double; from $185 suite. Additional person $15 extra. AE, MC, V.

The Marquessa would be Key West's most luxurious bed-and-breakfast, if only they served breakfast. Food notwithstanding, however, everything about this finely restored Victorian home is very much like an elegant B&B—one of the nicest I've ever seen. Beautifully appointed rooms are carefully prepared with dozens of special touches and extra-plush furnishings. Every accommodation is different, though most have gilded mirrors, tropical accents, original contemporary art, and plenty of fresh flowers. There's a helpful concierge, and newspapers are delivered daily to each door.

Dining/Entertainment: The adjacent Café Marquessa is a great place for lunch or dinner. Trendy South Florida foods are served in equally faddish surroundings.

Services: Room service, concierge, evening turn-down.

Facilities: Swimming pool.

MODERATE

LA PENSIONE, 809 Truman Ave., Key West, FL 33040. Tel. 305/292-9923. Fax 305/296-6509. 7 rms. A/C

$ Rates (including breakfast): Dec 25–May 15, $138–$148 single or double. May 16–Dec 24, $88–$98 single or double. 10% discount for readers who mention this guide. MC, V.

One of the island's newest bed-and-breakfasts, La Pensione opened in 1992, a lovely restoration of an 1891 Victorian home. Hoteliers Vince Cerrito and Joseph Rimkus have done a bang-up job creating a modestly priced charming inn that's thoroughly recommendable. Rooms are colorful and airy, featuring bright, flowery spreads and prints on well-chosen budget wicker and wood furnishings. There are big closets, king-size beds, and clock radios, but no telephones or TVs—an attraction for some guests.

Breakfast, which includes waffles and fresh fruit, is served in a pleasing downstairs dining room, which is adjacent to an equally nice living room and porch which guests are encouraged to use.

THE MERMAID AND THE ALLIGATOR, 729 Truman Ave., Key West, FL 33040. Tel. 305/294-1894. Fax 305/296-5090. 5 rms.

$ Rates (including full breakfast): Dec 25–May 1, $95–$165 single or double. May 2–Dec 24, $65–$105 single or double. AE, MC, V.

One of the prettiest restored buildings on the street, this inspired, eccentric inn is packed with American amenities and European charm. Every room is different, but all have shiny hardwood floors and special touches that may include four-poster beds and large bay windows. A full breakfast is served outside on a lovely deck in back of the house. There's off-street parking and a heated swimming pool.

SOUTHERNMOST POINT GUEST HOUSE, 1327 Duval St., Key West, FL 33040. Tel. 305/294-0715. Fax 305/296-0641. 3 rms, 3 suites. A/C TV TEL

$ Rates (including continental breakfast): Dec 20–Apr, $80–$110 single or double; from $130 suite. May–Dec 19, $55–$70 single or double; from $95 suite. Additional person $5–$10 extra. AE, MC, V.

Built in 1885, this well-kept, architecturally stunning home pays tribute to the romantic charm of old Key West. The rather sparse and antiseptically clean rooms are not as fancy as the house's ornate exterior. Each offers basic beds and couches, and some are decorated with stuffed deer heads bagged by owner Mona Santiago. The hotel itself occupies a prime location, at the "far" end of Duval Street just one block from the beach.

INEXPENSIVE

WICKER GUESTHOUSE, 913 Duval St., Key West, FL 33040. Tel. 305/296-4275, or toll free 800/880-4275. Fax 305/294-7240. 20 rms. A/C TV TEL

$ Rates: Dec–May, $69–$125 single or double. June–Nov, $40–$95 single or double. Additional person $10 extra. AE, DC, DISC, MC, V.

Occupying three separate buildings overlooking busy Duval Street, the Wicker offers some of the best-priced accommodations on the island. Pretty porches outline the traditional "conch" houses, and the rooms are predictably sparse. This cozy hotel is a welcome option in tab-happy Key West.

BUDGET

KEY WEST INTERNATIONAL HOSTEL, 718 South St., Key West, FL 33040. Tel. 305/296-5719. Fax 305/296-0672. 80 beds.

$ Rates: $13 for IYHF members. $16 for nonmembers. MC, V.

It's not the Ritz, but it's cheap. Very busy with European backpackers, this place is just a hair above camping out.

WHERE TO DINE

EXPENSIVE

BAGATELLE, 115 Duval St. Tel. 296-6609.
   Cuisine: SEAFOOD/TROPICAL. **Reservations:** Not required.
$ Prices: Appetizers $5–$9; main courses $15–$22; lunch $5–$13. AE, CB, DC, DISC, MC, V.
   Open: Lunch daily 11:30am–3pm; dinner daily 5:30–10pm.

Resembling a Mediterranean mansion, Bagatelle has pretty, dark-wood floors, a beautiful upstairs dining room with wooden schoolhouse chairs at clothed tables, and outdoor dining on a great porch overlooking Duval Street. It's very romantic, and made even more fanciful by a keyboardist at the grand piano.

A large lunch selection includes blackened chicken breast sandwich with crumbled bleu cheese, a variety of grilled fish, and a salad of mixed greens combined with avocados, walnuts, raisins, cheeses, and scallions. Your dinner should begin with the herb- and garlic-stuffed whole artichoke or the sashimilike seared rare tuna rolled in black peppercorns and served with garlic, soy, and sesame sauce. The best dishes are the local Florida fish selections such as shrimp-stuffed grouper crowned with shrimp- and lobster-cream sauce, and garlic-herb pasta combined with shrimp, lobster, fish, and mushrooms. The best chicken and beef dishes are tropically treated, grilled with papaya, ginger, and soy.

THE BUTTERY, 1208 Simonton St. Tel. 294-0717.
   Cuisine: FLORIDA REGIONAL. **Reservations:** Recommended.
$ Prices: Appetizers $7–$9; main courses $16–$24. AE, CB, DC, MC, V.
   Open: Winter, dinner only, daily 6–10pm. Summer, dinner only, daily 7–10pm.

Now almost 15 years old, the Buttery was once one of Key West's brightest culinary stars. Its facade has faded, but the chefs still turn out consistently good dishes, even if their innovations have recently been eclipsed in younger kitchens.

The restaurant's surprisingly downscale, dark dining rooms have a 1970s steak-house feel that's echoed by equally weighty preparations. Heavy creams douse tender steak filets, and local fruit sauces typically top the freshest of fish. Yellowtail is baked with sliced bananas, walnuts, and banana liqueur. Sea scallops are wrapped in bacon and brushed with roasted red-pepper hollandaise sauce. Some of the restaurant's more unusual appetizers include chilled spicy noodle salad with carrots, snow peas, shiitake mushrooms, and seafood; and pan-fried grouper with Chinese cabbage glazed with a combination of ginger, orange, and soy.

CAFE DES ARTISTES, 1007 Simonton St. Tel. 294-7100.

Cuisine: FRENCH. **Reservations:** Recommended.
$ Prices: Appetizers $5–$11; main courses $19–$25. AE, MC, V.
Open: Dinner only, daily 6–11pm.

Dark, quiet, and old-world elegant, the Café des Artistes has built quite a reputation in its more than 10 years of service. Parisian without pretension, the restaurant's beautiful surroundings include good-quality contemporary art, small shaded table lamps, and comfortable covered wooden chairs. During good weather you can choose to dine outside under the restaurant's retractable roof.

Cognoscenti suggest starting with duck-liver pâté, made with fresh truffles, and old cognac or Maryland crabmeat served with an artichoke heart and herbed tomato confit. Main courses are no simpler, and include cognac-based lobster flambé with saffron butter, mango, and basil, and wine-basted lamb chops rubbed with rosemary and ginger. There's a good wine selection, including an inspired choice of specials by the glass.

LOUIE'S BACKYARD, 700 Waddell Ave. Tel. 294-1061.

Cuisine: CARIBBEAN CONTEMPORARY. **Reservations:** Required.
$ Prices: Appetizers $6–$10; main courses $17–$28; brunch $25. AE, CB, DC, MC, V.
Open: Lunch Mon–Sat 11:30am–3pm; dinner Mon–Sun 6–10pm; brunch Sun 11:30am–3pm.

Louie's Backyard has come under fire in recent years for being overpriced and uneven. And while both these accusations are true, when the weather is nice and the food is good, Louie's is unbeatable. The restaurant's multilevel rear deck is built directly over the water, offering the most comfortable and romantic dining experience on the island. While the inside dining room is less desirable, it's incredibly charming, with pastel colors and large paddle fans that complement an authentic "conch" house feel.

Asian, North African, and Latin American ingredients and preparations are combined into an interesting contemporary Caribbean cuisine. Sliced, grilled chicken breast is served atop a tangy mixture of black beans, Mexican slaw, sour cream, guacamole, and served with a crispy flour tortilla. Local shrimp are marinated in conch-Créole sauce and tossed with spinach pasta, and grilled veal chops, basted with a Spanish wine sauce, are coupled with artichokes, plum tomatoes, and onions. Sunday brunches offer equally engaging recipes, including gingerbread pancakes and poached eggs.

SQUARE ONE, 1075 Duval St. Tel. 296-4300.

Cuisine: AMERICAN. **Reservations:** Recommended.
$ Prices: Appetizers $4–$8; main courses $14–$20. AE, DISC, MC, V.
Open: Dinner only, daily 6:30–10:30pm.

When queried recently about their favorite restaurants in Key West, a number of knowledgeable local diners put Square One as their top spot. In its four short years of operation, this classy medium-sized Los Angeles–style restaurant has gained an excellent reputation for food, service, and surroundings. The single dining room, which also accommodates a small bar and grand piano, is stylish without being showy, while a few outdoor tables overlook a courtyard fountain.

The food here is sophisticated but not complicated. Baked garlic with puréed feta cheese makes an excellent start to a meal that might include sautéed duck breast with peppered pineapple sauce, or perfectly grilled mahi-mahi or salmon. The nightly pasta special can be anything from lobster ravioli to rigatoni with capers, olives, and sun-dried tomatoes—it's always recommendable.

MODERATE

ANTONIA'S, 615 Duval St. Tel. 294-6565.

Cuisine: ITALIAN. **Reservations:** Recommended.
$ Prices: Appetizers $4–$9; main courses $11–$20. AE, DC, MC, V.
Open: Dinner only, daily 6–11pm.

It's hard not to like Antonia's, a festive Italian eatery that's fun and faithfully good. The Key West casual interior makes extensive use of aged woods that look as though they might have been culled from a turn-of-the-century sunken ship. Despite the restaurant's cordial, climate-controlled interior, large bay windows never let diners forget that bustling Duval Street is just a glance away.

Don't expect great Roman cooking and you won't be disappointed. Antonia's straightforward, down-home Italian-American cuisine is closer to Brooklyn than it is to Trastevere. Pastas include penne with eggplant and tomatoes, and angel hair with fresh tuna, tomato sauce, capers, and anchovies. Veal cutlets are filled with shiitake mushrooms and fontina cheese in marsala wine, and snapper is sautéed with shrimp and Italian greens, white wine, and olive oil. Good ports and sherries complement a selection of wines.

THE TWISTED NOODLE, 628 Duval St. Tel. 296-6670.
   Cuisine: ITALIAN. **Reservations:** Not required.
$ Prices: Appetizers $3–$5; main courses $6–$14. No credit cards.
   Open: Dinner only, daily 5–10:30pm.

This once-fading sanctuary of sanity in costly Key West received a new lease on life in 1992 when it was purchased by five young friends from Baltimore. The enthusiastic new owners are both friendly and knowledgeable about food. The chefs, who change the menu daily, might bake cheese-stuffed artichoke hearts, or toss chilled noodles with sesame sauce. Spinach fettuccine may be topped with mushroom-Alfredo sauce, and a variety of seafood and vegetables are regularly paired with pastas. Only beer and wine are served.

The pastel-colored restaurant, which is set back about half a block from Duval Street, has only about a dozen tables, many of which are set out in front under the open sky.

YO SAKE, 722 Duval St. Tel. 294-2288.
   Cuisine: JAPANESE. **Reservations:** Not required.
$ Prices: Sushi $2–$14; appetizers $5–$7; main dishes $12–$18. AE, DC, DISC, MC, V.
   Open: Dinner only, daily 6–11pm.

A hip black-and-white dining room and a business steady enough to keep the fish fresh make Yo Sake Key West's most recommendable sushi room. A wall of sharply designed booths, private tatami rooms, and the long sushi bar that's planted opposite them, are the most important statements in the restaurant's Japanese pop interior. In addition to the usual sushi and sashimi selections, the kitchen prepares a number of noodle dishes (soba and udon), shrimp and vegetable tempura, and stir-fried gingered pork with vegetables.

INEXPENSIVE

HALF SHELL RAW BAR, 920 Caroline St. Tel. 294-7496.
   Cuisine: SEAFOOD. **Reservations:** Not accepted.
$ Prices: Main courses $5–$10. No credit cards.
   Open: Mon–Sat 11am–11pm, Sun noon–11pm.

Located at the foot of Margaret Street, the Half Shell is the best place on the island for inexpensive, fresh-as-can-be seafood, in an authentic dockside setting. Decorated with "vanity" license plates from every state in the Union, the restaurant features a wide variety of freshly shucked shellfish and daily catch selections. Beer is the drink of choice here, though other beverages and a full bar are available. Seating is either at indoor varnished wooden tables, or out on the small but pretty deck overlooking the piers.

JIMMY BUFFETT'S MARGARITAVILLE CAFE, 500 Duval St. Tel. 292-1435.
   Cuisine: AMERICAN. **Reservations:** Not accepted.
$ Prices: Sandwiches $5–$6; fresh fish platter $10; margarita $4. AE, MC, V.
   Open: Sun–Thurs 11am–2am, Fri–Sat 11am–4am.

This large, friendly, and easygoing restaurant/bar is heavy on soups, salads, sandwiches, and local catches. A long bar runs the length of the laid-back dining room, in clear sight of an adjacent gift shop which often seems as busy as the bar. Live bands regularly perform, and Mr. Buffett himself has even been known to take the stage on a whim. It's very touristy, but recommended.

BUDGET

CROISSANTS DE FRANCE, 816 Duval St. Tel. 294-2624.
   Cuisine: FRENCH. **Reservations:** Not accepted.
$ **Prices:** Pastries $1–$3; lunch $3–$8. No credit cards.
   Open: Thurs–Tues 7:30am–11pm (lunch served until 3pm).
One of the few true cafés on Duval Street, this pleasant restaurant more than adequately fills its niche. The unusual combination of French charm in a tropical setting works well here, where diners can eat fresh-baked breads, rolls, and croissants on a pleasant, plant-packed porch.

   Breakfasts run the gamut from a simple croissant and coffee to a full European-style feast that includes breakfast with sliced ham, Swiss cheese, and French bread. Sandwiches, soups, salads, quiches, and crêpes are available until 3pm, after which only drinks and desserts are sold.

DUVAL DELI AND RESTAURANT, 724 Duval St. Tel. 294-3663.
   Cuisine: CONTINENTAL. **Reservations:** Not required.
$ **Prices:** Breakfast $3–$7; sandwiches $4–$6; pizza $6–$15. No credit cards.
   Open: Mon–Sat 8am–10:30pm.
Locals swear by the Duval Deli, a great, bright and clean soup-and-sandwich spot that has a flair for style as well as substance. Despite hokey names like "sexy bagel" (served with cream cheese, red onion, tomato, smoked salmon, and a hard-boiled egg) and "Hollywood Bowl" (a fresh fruit–topped bowl of granola), breakfasts and other meals are top-of-the-line. "Superstar" sandwiches include "Shirley Maclaine" (three kinds of cheese, veggies, and "Cosmic" dressing on a whole-wheat bun) and "Plain Jane" (peanut butter, jam, and banana). Gourmet pizzas are topped with tuna salad, peanut- and ginger-marinated chicken, and other untraditionals. Coffee, wine, and beer are served. The restaurant offers a 10% discount to any diner sporting a nightclub handstamp.

SHOPPING

Without a doubt, **Duval Street** is *the* strip for Key West shopping. The island is hardly a shopper's paradise, but among the T-shirt shops that line this key's most touristy strip are several excellent boutiques that are well worth checking out. The island's best bets are shops selling men's fashions, including **Coco Ibiza,** 601 Duval St. (tel. 444-4766); **Swept Away for Men,** 605 Duval St. (tel. 296-6654); and **Zero for Men,** 624 Duval St. (tel. 294-3899). Most Duval Street shops are open daily from 11am to 8pm.

EVENING ENTERTAINMENT
THE PERFORMING ARTS

THE RED BARN THEATER, 319 Duval St. Tel. 296-9911.
   Set back off Duval Street, the little red barn that now houses one of Key West's best stages was originally a carriage house connected to one of the island's oldest homes. The 100-seat Red Barn has gone through many changes since it was reborn in the 1940s as the home of the Key West Community Players. Renovated again in 1980, the theater now offers excellent local and visiting theatrical productions. Phone for current performance information.
   Admission: Tickets, $13–$25.

WATERFRONT PLAYHOUSE, Mallory Sq. Tel. 294-5015.
   Larger and prettier then the Red Barn, the Waterfront Playhouse attracts a variety of theatrical performances, including musicals, plays, and other stage shows. Performances are usually held from December through April. Call for show times.
   Admission: Tickets, $5–$15.

THE CLUB, MUSIC & BAR SCENE

Duval Street is the Bourbon Street of Florida. Between the T-shirt shops and clothing boutiques is bar after bar, serving stiff drinks to revelers who usually hop from one to another. Here's a run-down of the best:

CAPTAIN TONY'S SALOON, 428 Greene St. Tel. 294-1838.

Just around the corner from the beaten Duval path, Captain Tony's jealously retains its seasoned and quixotic pretourist ambience, complete with old-time regulars who really know what this island life is about. Smoky, small, and cozy, this saloon is owned by Capt. Tony Tarracino, a former Key West mayor who is known in these parts for his acerbic wit and unorthodox ways. The bar is well supported by locals who say that Hemingway drank, caroused, and even wrote here.

CRAZY DAIZY'Z, in La Concha Hotel, 430 Duval St. Tel. 296-2991.

A full bar and short list of domestic and imported beers are served in plastic cups from a well-aged marble bar. There are two big-screen TVs, and occasional live music (usually on the weekends). The bar is well located, in the middle of the Duval Street action. Sandwiches and conch chowder are served.

DURTY HARRY'S, 208 Duval St. Tel. 296-4890.

One of Duval's largest entertainment complexes, Durty Harry's features live rock bands almost every night (and most afternoons, too), and several outdoor bars. Upstairs at Rick's is an indoor/outdoor dance club that's very popular almost every night. The Red Garter, yet another related business on this property, is a pocket-size strip club popular with local bachelor parties and the few visitors who know about it.

FAT TUESDAYS, 305 Duval St. Tel. 296-9373.

Over 20 colorful, slushy, frozen slightly chemically alcoholic concoctions swirl in special see-through tanks behind the bar of this lively outdoor bar. Located on an elevated deck near the busiest end of Duval, Fat Tuesdays features live music daily and is popular with a rowdy college-age crowd.

HAVANA DOCKS, at the Pier House Resort, 1 Duval St. Tel. 296-4600.

The huge outdoor, top-floor terrace of the Pier House, Key West's best hotel, is a natural for visitors looking to celebrate the sunset in style. Great water views and live music make this one of the most popular places to toast at twilight.

HOG'S BREATH SALOON, 400 Front St. Tel. 296-4222.

Except for the fact that they sell lots of T-shirts, there's no relationship between this bar and its namesakes in California and around America. Once you realize that it's not part of a corporate chain—like Planet Hollywood or Hard Rock Café—the Hog's Breath becomes an inviting, fun place to hang out. Several outdoor bars, good live music, a raw bar, and decent food earn this place a top spot in this guide. There are daily happy hour specials from 5 to 7pm.

SLOPPY JOE'S, 201 Duval St. Tel. 294-5717.

Although this probably wasn't the place Ernest Hemingway made famous, the author figures prominently in this bar's logo. It can be debated whether Hemingway liked this place or not, but there's no argument that Sloppy Joe's turn-of-the-century wooden ceiling and cracked tile floors are Key West originals. Popular, loud, and rowdy, this large, raucous bar is crowded with tourists almost 24 hours a day. There's almost always live music, a full bar, and a rather uninspired selection of beers and wines.

208 TREE BAR, 208 Duval St. Tel. 296-4890.

Located right at the entrance to Durty Harry's (see above), this small, 12-seat bar only pours top-shelf liquors, and squeezes fresh limes and oranges into their margaritas and screwdrivers.

CHAPTER 7

THE GOLD COAST

1. JUPITER & NORTH PALM BEACH COUNTY

• **WHAT'S SPECIAL ABOUT THE GOLD COAST**

2. THE PALM BEACHES

3. BOCA RATON & DELRAY BEACH

4. FORT LAUDERDALE & ENVIRONS

The south-central coast of Florida, which is dominated by Palm Beach County, is one of the nation's richest residential regions. This "Gold Coast" is inhabited largely by wealthy retirees and other "snowbirds" from the north. Homes in Palm Beach are so grand, they are called "compounds." Residential sightseeing in Boca Raton is less satisfying, only because the nicest homes there are well hidden behind gates and shrubbery.

The region's recorded history dates back to 1835, when the U.S. Army cleared trails while battling native Seminole peoples. Few early settlers were attracted to these marshlands. Until the early 1870s, A. O. Lang, keeper of the Jupiter lighthouse, was the region's only known settler of European origin. Lang was later joined by a handful of families who, in 1878, planted thousands of coconuts which had been washed up on the shore by a wrecked Spanish ship.

The arrival of Henry Flagler's train in 1893 precipitated tremendous growth in the area. Along with architect Addison Mizner, who built one of the region's first hotels, Flagler parceled out much of southeastern Florida's land and encouraged the area's first developments.

SEEING THE GOLD COAST

All major tourist areas and roads along the Gold Coast hug the ocean, making it easy to navigate your way around. The closer you get to the water, the narrower and more picturesque the roads. Interstate 95 is a fast freeway, filled with commuters during rush hours. U.S. 1, which generally hugs the mainland side of the Intracoastal Waterway, is a narrower thoroughfare, choked with traffic lights and lined with an unending variety of shops and fast-food restaurants. Florida A1A, which is laid out over the barrier islands, is your best bet if you really want to see the various towns along the South Florida coast.

This chapter is arranged geographically from north to south. If you're driving up the coast from Miami, start with the last section.

---

1. JUPITER & NORTH PALM BEACH COUNTY

20 miles N of Palm Beach, 100 miles N of Miami

GETTING THERE   By Plane   The **Palm Beach International Airport** (tel. 407/471-7420) serves this area. Volunteer "Airport Ambassadors", are nearly always on hand to help visitors with information. Major domestic carriers using the airport include American (tel. toll free 800/433-7300), Continental (tel. 407/832-5200, or toll free 800/525-0280), Delta (tel. 407/655-5300, or toll free 800/221-1212), Northwest (tel. toll free 800/225-2525), TWA (tel. 407/655-3776, or toll free 800/221-2000), and United (tel. toll free 800/241-6522).

WHAT'S SPECIAL ABOUT
THE GOLD COAST

Palatial Homes
- [ ] The estates of Palm Beach and Boca Raton, some of the swankiest in the world—a cruise around these communities will make your jaw drop.

Historic Hotels
- [ ] The Breakers, the grand dame of South Florida hotels and a tourist attraction in its own right.
- [ ] The Spanish-Mediterranean–style main house of the Boca Raton Resort and Club, just the tip of a 350-acre complex that straddles both sides of the Intracoastal Waterway.

Top Shops
- [ ] A short stretch of Palm Beach's Worth Avenue, lined by some of the world's most exclusive shops, galleries, and restaurants.

- [ ] The Gardens Mall in Palm Beach Gardens, a 1.2-million-square-foot shopping complex boasting five major department stores and more than 200 other shops—a shopper's paradise.

Best Beaches
- [ ] Blowing Rocks Preserve, on Jupiter Island, just one of many wonderfully picturesque beaches here, made beautiful by a cluster of large rock formations.
- [ ] Dozens of swimming beaches from deserted to lively, guaranteeing plenty of sun, surf, and sand whatever your style.

By Train Amtrak (tel. toll free 800/USA-RAIL) trains from New York stop in West Palm Beach on their way to Miami. The local station is at 201 S. Tamarind Ave., West Palm Beach (tel. 407/832-6169).

By Bus Greyhound can get you to the Palm Beaches from almost anywhere. The company no longer operates a single nationwide telephone number, so consult your local directory for the office nearest you.

By Car If you're driving up or down the Florida coast, you'll probably reach the Palm Beach area on I-95, a highway that extends all the way from Maine to Miami. Visitors on their way to or from Orlando should take the Florida Turnpike, a toll road that runs almost directly from this county's beaches to Walt Disney World. Finally, if you're coming from Florida's west coast, you can take either Fla. 70, which runs north of Lake Okeechobee to Fort Pierce, or Fla. 80, which runs south of the lake to Palm Beach.

ESSENTIALS The **telephone area code** is 407.
For information, maps, and an Arts and Attractions Calendar, contact the **Palm Beach County Convention and Visitors Bureau,** 1555 Palm Beach Lakes Blvd., Suite 204, West Palm Beach, FL 33401 (tel. 407/471-3995, or toll free 800/554-PALM).

Slate-blue water, warmed in winter and cooled in summer by the powerful Atlantic Gulf Stream, is North Palm Beach County's greatest asset. Like the rest of the county, North Palm is teeming with playful dolphins, majestic sea turtles, and giant marlin. Because it's farther from Miami, however, this region is less populated than areas to the south, offering welcome relief from crowded beaches and freeways. Several good hotels and restaurants make Jupiter and the surrounding area a happy medium between the barren lands to the north and the populous areas to the south.

WHAT TO SEE & DO

North Palm is best known for the giant **sea turtles** that lay their eggs on the sand from May through August. These endangered marine animals return here annually, from as far as South America, to lay their clutch of about 115 eggs each. Nurtured by the warm sand, but preyed upon by birds and other predators, only about one or two from each nest survive to maturity.

The **Gumbo Limbo Nature Center** (tel. 338-1473), which offers turtle expeditions in season, recommends that visitors take part in an organized program (rather than go on their own) in order to minimize any disturbance to the turtles. The Jupiter Beach Resort (tel. 746-2511) and the Marinelife Center of Juno Beach (tel. 627-8280) also sponsor guided expeditions to the turtle egg-laying sites.

Actor Burt Reynolds is famous in Palm Beach County, and his name is associated with a number of businesses and attractions. You'll probably see advertisements for the **Burt Reynolds Ranch and Mini Petting Farm** (tel. 747-5390). However, this is a mediocre attraction where visitors can wander around old movie sets and see domesticated farm animals. The ranch is located two miles west of the Florida Turnpike on Jupiter Farms Road and is open daily from 10am to 5pm; admission is free, $10 for tours.

THE GARDENS MALL, PGA Blvd., Palm Beach Gardens. Tel. 622-2115.
South Florida is acquiring a reputation as the land of the "megamall," and this 1.2-million-square-foot shopping complex is one of the reasons why. Anchored by five major department stores—Macy's, Sears, Bloomingdale's, Burdines, and Saks Fifth Avenue—this two-story mammoth is rounded out by almost 200 other shops and decorated with marble floors, a glass ceiling, and art deco accents. The mall's fairly standard food court offers a large variety of world cuisines to suit many different tastes.

JUPITER INLET LIGHTHOUSE, U.S. 1 and Alternate Fla. A1A, Jupiter. Tel. 747-6639.
Owned by the U.S. Coast Guard, this is the oldest extant structure in Palm Beach County. Congress appropriated funds for its construction in 1853, and the lights went on in 1860. The Loxahatchee Historical Society sponsors tours of the lighthouse every Sunday, enabling visitors to explore the cramped interior, which includes a small museum in the structure's base.
Admission: $3, which includes entrance to the Historical Society Museum and Pioneer Home.
Open: Sun 1–4pm only.

LOXAHATCHEE HISTORICAL SOCIETY MUSEUM, 805 U.S. 1 N., in Burt Reynolds Park, Jupiter. Tel. 747-6639.
The museum's primary exhibit, "History Shaped by Nature," consists of various historical artifacts from ancient times up to today relating to Jupiter and its vicinity. The displays are arranged chronologically, from Seminole Indian utensils to Burt Reynolds's boots.
There are also guided tours of nearby historical sites—ask for a current schedule.
Admission: $3 adults, $2 seniors, $1 children.
Open: Tues–Fri 10am–4pm, Sat–Sun 1–4pm.

MARINELIFE CENTER OF JUNO BEACH, Loggerhead Park, 1200 U.S. 1, Juno Beach. Tel. 627-8280.
An indoor/outdoor attraction located in a public beachfront park, the Marinelife Center is a combination ecology museum and nature trail, focusing on life in and close to the sea. Visitors can learn about the unique ecosystem of South Florida's shores through hands-on exhibits and informative placards. Outdoor trails wind through dune vegetation, and live (although endangered) sea turtles (which nest nearby during the summer) are always on display.
Admission: Free; donations accepted.
Open: Tues–Sat 10am–4pm, Sun noon–3pm.

BEACHES & PARKS

As you head north from populated Palm Beach, Jupiter and North Palm Beach are the first bits of land you encounter, where castles and condominiums give way to open space and public parkland.

BLOWING ROCKS PRESERVE, Fla. A1A, Jupiter Island.

This wonderfully picturesque beach owes its beauty to a cluster of large rock formations. Although swimming is not recommended, Blowing Rocks is popular for fishing. There's a small parking lot, but no beach facilities. The preserve is a 10-minute drive from downtown Jupiter.

BURT REYNOLDS PARK, U.S. 1 N., Jupiter.

Surrounded by the Intracoastal Waterway, this rocky beach is well known to boaters and water-sports enthusiasts. There are picnic shelters, as well as boat slips for short-term visitors.

CARLIN COUNTY PARK, State Rd. (Fla. A1A), Jupiter.

Located just north of Indiantown Road, this busy park has a large oceanfront area complete with picnic tables, restrooms, a snack bar, tennis courts, a fitness track, and hiking trails.

JOHN D. MACARTHUR BEACH STATE PARK, 10900 State Rd. (Fla. A1A), Singer Island.

One of the area's largest parks, MacArthur has more than 8,000 feet of oceanfront beach, a nature center, and acres of park overlooking bucolic Lake Worth Cove. To reach the park from the mainland, cross the Intracoastal on Blue Heron Boulevard and turn north.

SCUBA DIVING & SNORKELING

North Palm's year-round, warm, clear waters make this area great for scuba diving and snorkeling. Several coral reefs are accessible by swimming from the water's edge, while others, farther offshore, are accessible by means of boats that make daily dive runs. Diving equipment can be rented and information can be obtained on the area's reefs from several local dive shops, including: **Gulf Stream Diver II**, 1030 U.S. 1, Suite 105, North Palm Beach (tel. 627-8966, or toll free 800/771-3903); **Seafari Sport and Dive Shop**, 304 N. Old Dixie Hwy., Jupiter (tel. 747-6115); and **Subsea Aquatics**, 1870 U.S. 1, Jupiter (tel. 744-6674).

WHERE TO STAY

VERY EXPENSIVE

PGA NATIONAL RESORT, 400 Ave. of the Champions, Palm Beach Gardens, FL 33418. Tel. 407/627-2000, or toll free 800/633-9150. Fax 407/622-0261. 335 rms, 60 suites. A/C MINIBAR TV TEL **Directions:** From I-95, exit onto PGA Boulevard west and continue for approximately two miles to the resort entrance.

$ Rates: Dec 20–May 2, $265–$375 single or double; from $500 suite. May 3–30 and Sept 20–Dec 19, $195–$300 single or double; from $425 suite. May 31–Sept 19, $99–$175 single or double; from $240 suite. AE, DC, DISC, MC, V.

A resort in the fullest sense of the word, the PGA National is a 2,340-acre estate that encompasses five golf courses, 19 tennis courts, five racquetball courts, three swimming pools, mineral spas, workout rooms, and a private beach fronting a 26-acre, water-sports-filled lake. Originally known for its well-conditioned 18-hole golf courses, the resort has since added a full-service spa, which offers a variety of pamperings, including massage therapies, algae wraps, and facials. Heated mineral pools contain healing salts from both the Pyrenees Mountains and the Dead Sea. Staff experts offer comprehensive fitness evaluations, as well as courses and lectures on menu planning and healthy living.

Other resort facilities include top-of-the-line exercise equipment, croquet, and tennis courts. Special children's programs are offered.

PGA's welcoming Mediterranean-style lobby features terra-cotta tile floors topped with large area rugs and light, plush furniture. The newly renovated guest rooms, which extend into three separate wings, are equally well furnished, with dark carpets, bright contemporary prints, crown moldings, and oak cabinets. Every room has a private terrace or balcony. Conveniences include soft terrycloth robes, in-room safes, hairdryers, and contemporary white tile and marble baths.

Dining/Entertainment: There are six restaurants on the premises. The Citrus Tree, a casual eatery, specializes in low-calorie and low-fat spa cuisine, and offers both indoor and outdoor seating. The dark and richly decorated Explorers Restaurant is the resort's top dining room, open for dinner only.

Services: 24-hour room service, concierge, evening turn-down, overnight shoeshine, laundry, car rental, babysitting service.

Facilities: Five 18-hole golf courses, 19 clay tennis courts (12 lighted), three swimming pools, private beach on a 26-acre lake, water-sports rentals, five indoor racquetball courts, aerobics studio, mineral spas, salon.

EXPENSIVE

JUPITER BEACH RESORT, 5 N. Fla. A1A (at Indiantown Rd.), Jupiter, FL 33477. Tel. 407/746-2511. Fax 407/747-3304. 194 rms, 28 suites. A/C MINIBAR TV TEL

$ Rates: Jan–Apr, $160–$475 single or double; from $500 suite. May and Oct–Dec, $140–$375 single or double; from $400 suite. June–Sept, $120–$325 single or double; from $350 suite. Additional person $20–$30 extra. AE, DC, DISC, MC, V.

Just a few miles north of Palm Beach, this bright retreat is suitable for couples and families looking for a high-quality beachfront vacation. Oceanfront accommodations are the most expensive, but on the other side one can enjoy beautiful sunsets. Nearly all rooms have two double beds, and all have private balconies, sheer drapes, and beds with rattan headboards and print spreads.

The lobby and public areas have a Mediterranean feel, decorated in green marble, and feature arched doorways, wooden chandeliers, and plush pastel furniture.

Dining/Entertainment: Sinclair's Restaurant, founded by restaurateur Gordon Sinclair, serves an eclectic mix of continental, southwestern, and Caribbean cuisine. Bananas, situated just off the lobby, features live entertainment several nights a week. Three other pool and beach bars serve snacks and refreshments throughout the day.

Services: Room service, concierge, supervised children's programs, overnight shoeshine, laundry, free transportation to local shopping areas, summer turtle-watch program.

Facilities: Swimming pool, tennis court, exercise room, boutique, dive shop, water-sports rentals, coin laundry, games room.

INEXPENSIVE

BARREN'S LANDING MOTEL, 18125 Ocean Blvd. (Fla. A1A), Jupiter, FL 33477. Tel. 407/746-8757. 10 rms. A/C TV **Directions:** From U.S. 1, exit onto Ocean Boulevard (Fla. A1A) east, just south of the Jupiter inlet; the hotel is on your right, on the corner of Love Street.

$ Rates: Dec 15–Apr, $75 single or double. May–Dec 14, $45 single or double. No credit cards.

There are relatively few rooms in this single-story, Intracoastal-front motel, and many of them are rented to "snowbirds" for weeks or months at a time. Some rooms have twin beds, while others have doubles; most offer foldout sofas or daybeds for larger parties. Nearly all rooms have small kitchenettes, which include a refrigerator, sink, microwave, and dishes. There are no phones in the rooms. A swimming pool is available on the premises.

WELLESLEY INN, 34 Fisherman's Wharf, Jupiter, FL 33477. Tel. 407/ 575-7201, or toll free 800/444-8888. Fax 407/575-1169. 105 rms, 12 suites. A/C TV TEL

$ Rates: Dec 25–Apr 15, $85 single or double; from $105 suite. Apr 16–Dec 24, $55 single or double; from $65 suite. AE, CB, DC, DISC, MC, V.

Behind a neocolonial facade, complete with white columns, arched windows, and a tall, tiled fountain, are 105 modestly decorated guest rooms, each with plain bedspreads, small tables, and compact dressers. Some rooms do not have complete closets, but rather a small railing for hanging clothes and few amenities. The minisuites are actually large double rooms, while the larger maxisuites are outfitted with sofa beds, refrigerators, and microwave ovens. There's a small swimming pool on the premises. The inn is conveniently located—near the Intracoastal Waterway and Fla. A1A.

WHERE TO DINE
VERY EXPENSIVE

ST. HONORE, 2401 PGA Blvd., Palm Beach Gardens. Tel. 655-1510.
   Cuisine: FRENCH/CONTINENTAL **Reservations:** Recommended.
$ Prices: Appetizers $10–$22; main courses $22–$35. AE, CB, DC, MC, **V.**
   Open: Breakfast/lunch daily 8:30am–2:30pm; dinner daily 6–10:30pm.
A French restaurant with a continental flair, St. Honoré is located upstairs in the Harbour Shops, a small shopping center in Palm Beach Gardens. Picturesque and romantic, the restaurant's decor includes lovely wood-beamed ceilings, pastel-colored tablecloths, and comfortable, oversize old-fashioned chairs. There's an intimate bar lined with teak, rattan stools, and small, salmon-colored marble tables. Beyond the French doors is an outdoor patio with potted plants and covered with a wooden trellis.

   Some of the more imaginative dishes include roasted salmon with pesto, seafood fettuccine, sautéed veal sweetbreads with candied ginger, and beef tenderloin in muscat-raisin sauce. A typical starter is lobster bisque made with mango. The restaurant makes its own pastries and desserts, and offers a nice wine list.

EXPENSIVE

BACKSTAGE, 1061 E. Indiantown Rd. (just west of U.S. 1), Jupiter. Tel. 747-9533.
   Cuisine: AMERICAN. **Reservations:** Required.
$ Prices: Appetizers $5–$8; main courses $13–$22. AE, CB, DC, MC, V.
   Open: Lunch Mon–Fri 11:30am–2:30pm; dinner Sun–Thurs 5–9:30pm, Fri–Sat 5pm–midnight.
Partly owned by Burt Reynolds, Backstage is a rather formal dining spot featuring tiered seating and black lacquered tables illuminated by tiny stage lights. The walls are decorated with black-and-white photographs of film stars and media personalities.

   The menu emphasizes such American-style dishes as blackened prime rib, herb-roasted chicken, Florida lobster, and veal in champagne sauce. Appetizers include Cajun fried shrimp, stuffed mushrooms, and frogs' legs. Live jazz is performed during most meals.

HARPOON LOUIE'S, 1065 Fla. A1A Service Rd., Jupiter. Tel. 744-1300.
   Cuisine: SEAFOOD/TROPICAL. **Reservations:** Not required.
$ Prices: Appetizers $3–$9; main courses $14–$22; breakfast $3–$7; lunch $5–$7. AE, CB, DC, DISC, MC, V.
   Open: Mon–Fri 11am–10pm. Sat–Sun 8am–10pm.
A tropical island–kind of eatery filled with low rattan tables and floral cushions, this is the kind of place found in southern Florida and southern California that may surprise tourists from other parts of the country. Somewhat fancy, but quite informal, this waterfront restaurant offers indoor dining as well as a large outdoor deck equipped with heatlamps and glass-topped tables—a beautiful place to enjoy a piña colada or a Palm Beach punch while relishing the majestic views of the lighthouse just across the water.

   At lunch, you might want to choose only an appetizer, like smoked Irish salmon with brown bread, Jamaican chicken wings, or fried Florida alligator. There's also a selection of salads, soups, and seafood-topped pizzas. Jamaican-style chicken and pastas are available at dinner, but you would do better to choose one of the many seafood dishes like phyllo-wrapped grouper with lobster-basil sauce, fried coconut shrimp, or the fish of the day (grilled, broiled, or blackened).

MODERATE

JUPITER CRAB, 1511 Dixie Hwy., Jupiter. Tel. 747-8300.
  Cuisine: SEAFOOD. **Reservations:** Not accepted.
$ Prices: Appetizers $3–$9; salads and sandwiches $4–$11; main courses $13–$21. AE, DISC, MC, V.
  Open: Sun–Thurs 11:30am–10pm, Fri–Sat 11:30am–11pm.

Jupiter Crab's saltwater decor—lifeboats, fishing nets, and the like—might not be enough to make you forget that the restaurant is actually located on a busy intersection, but the food will. Take your seat at one of the captain's-style tables, located outside, inside on the ground floor, and on the second-story loft that overlooks it.

Few come here for steak—seafood is the food of choice, and the choices are many. Appetizers include selections from the raw bar—clams or oysters—and soups that almost always include clam chowder, oyster stew, and crab bisque. Other traditionals include oysters Rockefeller, clams casino, and fried calamari. Lunches are strictly soup, salad, and sandwich affairs; lobster or crab salad is augmented by a seafood-topped Caesar, and sandwiches are filled with grilled meats and fish. Dinners are a bit more substantial, and include an excellent selection of crabs (six different types at last count), including Maryland soft shell, blue point, and Alaskan King legs. A variety of fresh fish is always available, as is a host of "turf" items like pork chops, ribs, and chicken.

LOG CABIN RESTAURANT, 631 N. Fla. A1A, Jupiter. Tel. 746-6877.
  Cuisine: AMERICAN. **Reservations:** Not accepted.
$ Prices: Appetizers $1–$8; main courses $4–$16. AE, CB, DC, DISC, MC, V.
  Open: Daily 7am–9:30pm.

This restaurant is really housed in a log cabin. When you step up onto the wide porch and enter through the front door, you'll find yourself in a warm, snug home that's actually quite beautiful. Furnishings include antique clocks, sleds, framed yellowed newspaper articles, old bottles, and moonshine jugs, many of which hang from the vaulted ceiling. To reach the dining room, stay to the left; for the bar, go to your right.

Menu offerings include large portions of pit-smoked barbecued ribs, beef, and chicken, as well as deep-fried seafood. Standard favorites such as chili, beef stew, meatloaf, and burgers are also available. Traditional desserts—including pecan pie and sweet-potato pie—are homemade.

NO ANCHOVIES!, 2650 PGA Blvd., Palm Beach Gardens. Tel. 622-7855.
  Cuisine: ITALIAN. **Reservations:** Not accepted.
$ Prices: Appetizers $3–$7; pizza and pasta $7–$9; main courses $10–$17. AE, DC, MC, V.
  Open: Dinner only, Sun–Thurs 5:30–10:30pm, Fri–Sat 5:30–11pm.

Some of Florida's best restaurant finds are located in strip malls, a fact of sprawling suburbia that shouldn't discourage you from a potentially excellent meal. No Anchovies! is exactly this kind of a place—cheery and welcoming in an otherwise canned setting. The new Italian restaurant is comfortably spacious, featuring green plaid booths, an exhibition kitchen, and oversize posters of the most important Italian spices: garlic, onion, basil, and peppers.

An equally colorful menu offers a large variety of pastas, which you then match with your favorite sauce—pesto, spicy tomato, or marinara. Pizza is prepared in a wood-burning oven, and marinated chicken and other meats are roasted with oak. A special children's menu is also available for kids under 10.

PARKER'S LIGHTHOUSE, in the Harbour Shops, 180 Rue de la Mer, Palm Beach Gardens. Tel. 627-0000.
  Cuisine: SEAFOOD/CONTINENTAL. **Reservations:** Recommended.
$ Prices: Appetizers $3–$11; main courses $11–$20; lunch $5–$12. AE, DC, DISC, MC, V.

Open: Mon–Thurs 11:30am–10pm, Fri–Sat 11:30am–10:30pm; Sun brunch 11am–2:30pm, dinner 4:30–9pm. (Bar, Sun–Thurs until midnight, Fri–Sat until 1am.)

Architecturally, this is one of the most unusual restaurants I've ever visited. Under a towering central skylight, designed to resemble a lighthouse, are three floors—the top two connected by a spiral staircase. The first floor contains the restaurant's glass-enclosed kitchen, fitted with red carpeting and nautical decor. The second floor, which is for dining, has tables situated next to glass walls; diners are treated to magnificent views of the luxury yacht harbor. The top floor has a wood-paneled lounge, built around a Z-shaped bar that serves drinks and snacks until late. Wraparound windows offer panoramic harbor views.

The restaurant emphasizes fresh seafood appetizers and main dishes, although Caesar salad with grilled chicken, prime rib, Thai-style chicken, and a small selection of sandwiches are also available.

SCHOONERS, 1001 N. Fla. A1A, at Love St. Jupiter. Tel. 746-7558.
　　Cuisine: SEAFOOD/AMERICAN. **Reservations:** Not required.
$ Prices: Appetizers $3–$7; main courses $11–$18; lunch $3–$10. AE, MC, V.
　　Open: Lunch daily 11am–4:30pm; dinner daily 5–9:30pm.

Schooners is especially recommended for warm afternoons when you can sit outside on the restaurant's large covered patio. Inside is a dark bar and dining room featuring such nautical decor as fish nets, boating lights, and schools of mounted fish.

The lunch menu includes burgers, deep-fried fish, and a large assortment of sandwiches. Dinners begin with an extensive choice of starters, from steamed mussels to honey-dipped chicken wings. An even longer list of main dishes reads like a veritable survey of seaside American cooking, from fresh fish to pastas and prime New York strip steak.

Fishermen and other locals comprise most of the Schooners' clientele; they know a good and friendly place when they see one.

WATERWAY CAFE, 2300 PGA Blvd., Palm Beach Gardens. Tel. 694-1700.
　　Cuisine: SEAFOOD/AMERICAN. **Reservations:** Not required.
$ Prices: Appetizers $5–$9; main courses $11–$20; lunch $6–$8. AE, MC, V.
　　Open: Mon–Thurs 11:30am–10pm, Fri–Sat 11:30am–11pm, Sun 4–11pm. (Bar, open later.)

Large, open, bright, and cheery, the Waterway Café is yet another good choice, overlooking the Intracoastal Waterway. Wooden crew boats, sporting Ivy League insignia, hang from the ceiling. Large, leafy plants, which adorn the well-polished light-wood floors, are highlighted by the sun that streams in through a domed skylight. Additional tables outdoors enable diners to see the restaurant's boat slips and floating tiki bar, which is equipped with lifevests for tipsy drinkers.

Raw oysters and clams are recommended for those who like them. Other good lunch choices include chilled poached salmon, crab cakes, and an assortment of sandwiches, salads, and pastas. Dinners are equally straightforward. Conch fritters and peel-and-eat shrimp make great starters, perhaps followed by shrimp, dolphin (fish), sea-scallop casserole, or stir-fried steak and shrimp. Pasta dishes are always available, as are salads and burgers. Plan to save room for the delectable Mississippi mud pie.

INEXPENSIVE

CHILI'S GRILL & BAR, 65 U.S. 1, at Indiantown Rd., Jupiter. Tel. 576-6900.
　　Cuisine: SOUTHWESTERN. **Reservations:** Not accepted.
$ Prices: Appetizers $4–$6; main courses $6–$15; lunch $3–$10. AE, DISC, MC, V.
　　Open: Sun–Thurs 11:30am–11pm, Fri–Sat 11:30am–midnight.

A chain restaurant in the Bennigan style, Chili's southwestern cuisine offers diners a welcome break from the usual Florida emphasis on fish. Brightly tiled table tops, copper lamps, green window shutters, and lots of plants hint at America's Southwest.

But the enormous bar, which offers regular drink specials and televised sports, was clearly designed for the restaurant's local patrons.

The restaurant offers the same menu all day. The best appetizers are the fried mozzarella sticks, fried whole onions (served with an unusual seasoned sauce), and spicy buffalo chicken wings. Recommended main dishes include vegetarian soft tacos, chicken Caesar salad, and fajitas (my favorite), which are served with an audible sizzle. Go elsewhere for dessert.

EVENING ENTERTAINMENT
THE PERFORMING ARTS

BURT REYNOLDS INSTITUTE FOR THEATER TRAINING, 304 Tequesta Dr., Tequesta. Tel. 746-8887.
Founded in 1979, this institute offers an apprenticeship program for promising young actors from across the country. Well-known professionals perform with the students in comedies, dramas, and musicals. There are both matinee and evening performances; call for a current schedule.
Admission: Tickets, $15–$20.

JUPITER DINNER THEATER, 1001 E. Indiantown Rd., at Fla. A1A, Jupiter. Tel. 746-5566.
Year-round productions include Broadway musicals and hit comedies. Original works are occasionally staged here, and top theater and film performers often appear in the cast. Dinner precedes the show; phone to find out what's on the menu.
Admission: Tickets, $40–$75.

THE CLUB & MUSIC SCENE

BACKSTAGE, 1061 E. Indiantown Rd. (just west of U.S. 1), Jupiter. Tel. 747-9533.
I recommended Backstage as a restaurant (see "Where to Dine," above), but it's also a good place for drinks and entertainment; live jazz or dance music is featured almost every night of the week. Open daily from 5pm to midnight.
Admission: Free.

CLUB SAFARI, in the Marriott Hotel, 4000 RCA Blvd., Palm Beach Gardens. Tel. 662-8888.
I'm always skeptical about dance clubs in hotels, but this one is more hip than most, even if the safari theme is taken a bit too far. The huge, sunken dance floor is surrounded by vines and lanky, potted trees. Nearby, a large Buddha statue blows steam and smoke while waving its burly arms. Fake rocks are everywhere, sometimes concealing flame-shooting pots. There is DJ music, a large video screen, and a cover charge on the weekends. It's open Tuesday through Friday from 5pm to 3am and on Saturday and Sunday from 8pm to 3am.
Admission: Free Tues–Thurs, $3 Fri–Sun.

JOX SPORTS CLUB, 200 N. U.S. 1, Jupiter. Tel. 744-6600.
The players are not just on television here—in this participatory-sports bar the patrons are encouraged to shoot hoops as well as pool. It's not just a jock joint, though. There's DJ dancing, several fully stocked bars, and a friendly atmosphere. Open Sunday through Thursday from 8pm to 2am and on Friday and Saturday from 8pm to 3am.
Admission: Free.

WATERWAY CAFE, 2300 PGA Blvd., Palm Beach Gardens. Tel. 694-1700.
Two large bars inside and one floating on the water in back make the Waterway a great place for an afternoon or evening drink. There's usually live reggae every Sunday afternoon and Wednesday evenings (see "Where to Dine," above, for additional information). Open on Monday, Tuesday, and Thursday from 11:30am to 11pm; on Wednesday, Friday, and Saturday from 11:30am to 1am; and on Sunday from 4 to 11pm.

2. THE PALM BEACHES

26 miles N of Miami, 193 miles E of Tampa

GETTING THERE   By Plane   The **Palm Beach International Airport** (tel. 407/471-7420) is easy to negotiate and a pleasure to use. Volunteer "Airport Ambassadors," recognizable by their distinctive teal-green shirts and jackets, are nearly always on hand to help visitors with free information. Major domestic carriers using the airport include American (tel. toll free 800/433-7300), Continental (tel. 407/832-5200, or toll free 800/525-0280), Delta (tel. 407/655-5300, or toll free 800/221-1212), Northwest (tel. toll free 800/225-2525), TWA (tel. 407/655-3776, or toll free 800/221-2000), and United (tel. toll free 800/241-6522).

By Train   Amtrak (tel. toll free 800/USA-RAIL) trains from New York stop in West Palm Beach on their way to Miami. The local station is at 201 S. Tamarind Ave., West Palm Beach (tel. 407/832-6169).

By Bus   Greyhound can get you to the Palm Beaches from almost anywhere. The company no longer operates a single nationwide telephone number, so consult your local directory for the office nearest you.

By Car   If you're driving up or down the Florida coast, you'll probably reach the Palm Beach area on I-95, a highway that extends all the way from Maine to Miami. Visitors on their way to or from Orlando should take the Florida Turnpike, a toll road that runs almost directly from this county's beaches to Walt Disney World. Finally, if you're coming from Florida's west coast, you can take either Fla. 70, which runs north of Lake Okeechobee to Fort Pierce, or Fla. 80, which runs south of the lake to Palm Beach.

ESSENTIALS   The **telephone area code** is 407.

The **Palm Beach County Convention and Visitors Bureau,** 1555 Palm Beach Lakes Blvd., Suite 204, West Palm Beach, FL 33401 (tel. 407/471-3995, or toll free 800/554-PALM), distributes an informative brochure, and will answer questions about visiting the Palm Beaches. Ask for a map as well as a copy of their Arts and Attractions Calendar, a day-by-day guide to art, music, stage, and other events in the county.

Palm Beach is an island, both literally and figuratively. Located just across the Intracoastal Waterway from West Palm Beach on the mainland, this area boasts one of the highest concentrations of expensive mansions and estates in the world. It's really astonishing to drive around Palm Beach and see so many elegant homes. Palm Beach has been the traditional winter home of America's super-rich—the Kennedys, the Rockefellers, the Trumps, well-to-do heirs and heiresses, and top-echelon CEOs. For tourists, a visit here means marvelous restaurants, great golfing, and spectacular sightseeing.

West Palm Beach, by contrast, is somewhat more work-oriented. With the exception of some wonderful (but expensive) golfing communities, the mainland is less extravagant and more commercial than its richer offshore counterpart.

WHAT TO SEE & DO

DREHER PARK ZOO, 1301 Summit Blvd., West Palm Beach. Tel. 533-0887, or 547-9453 for a recorded message.

More than 500 different animals inhabit this 23-acre zoo. Several endangered species are on display, including the Florida panther and the mouse-sized marmoset. It's worth going just for the unusual reptile exhibit.

Admission: $5 adults, $3.50 children, $4.50 seniors, free for children under 3.

Open: Daily 9am–5pm (last admission at 4:30pm).

PALM BEACH & BOCA RATON

0   1.6 km
2 mi.

FLORIDA

Palm Beach &
Boca Raton

Ann Norton Sculpture
  Gardens **8**
Bethesda-by-the-Sea
  Church **4**
Dreher Park Zoo **11**
Flagler Memorial
  Bridge **2**
Flagler Museum **3**
Lion Country Safari **13**
Morikami Museum **12**
Norton Gallery of Art **6**
Palm Beach Kennel
  Club **9**
Palm Beach Polo
  & Country Club **1**
Royal Palm Bridge **5**
Society of the Four Arts **7**
South Florida Museum **10**

Bee-Line Hwy

Palm
Beach
Gardens

786

786

N. Palm Beach

811

850

Northlake Blvd

Lake Park

Park
Ave.

Lake
Worth

Blue-Heron-Blvd

Riviera
Beach

8th-St.

Palm
Beach
Shores

702

45th-St.

702

710

Lake
Mangonia

1

WEST
PALM
BEACH

Lakes
Blvd.

2

704

Okeechobee

Blvd.

704

Clear
Lake

3

4

PALM
BEACH

7

5

704

98

Benoist-Farms-Rd

Jenks-Rd

Belvedere

9

Rd.

6

8

7

Haverhill

Palm
Beach

Southern-Blvd

West-Palm-Beach-Canal

13

Palm
Beach
International
Airport

10

11

1

Forest-Hill-Blvd

882

Lake Clarke Shores

A1A

809

95

441

Greenacres
City

Palm
Springs-Lake
Worth

10th
Ave. N.

Lake-Worth-Rd

Jog-Rd

Palm Beach
Co. Park
Airport

Osborne
Lake

Dixie-Hwy.

Olive-Ave.

Lantana-Rd

812

6th-Ave.

S. Palm
Beach

Atlantis

Lantana

Hypoluxo-Rd

Range-Line-Rd

Manalpan

Boynton
Beach

Ocean
Ridge

804

Boynton-Beach-Blvd

804

Briny
Breezes

Gulf Stream

441

809

1

12

Delray
Beach

Atlantic-Ave

806

Military-Trail

Congress-Ave

Linton-Blvd

95

Clint-Moore-Rd

Highland
Beach

Jog-Rd

Intracoastal Waterway

Atlantic Ocean

808

Boca Raton
Municipal
Airport

BOCA
RATON

798

Airport

5434

HENRY MORRISON FLAGLER MUSEUM, Coconut Row, Palm Beach. Tel. 655-2833.

Henry Flagler probably had a greater influence on South Florida's development than any other individual. Cofounder of the Standard Oil Company, the future-oriented businessman built the railroad that would eventually link Jacksonville with Key West.

The museum that now bears his name was originally a mansion called Whitehall, built by Flagler in 1901 for his third wife, Mary Lily Kenan. In 1960 one of his granddaughters had the house restored to its original turn-of-the-century condition, including many of the home's original furnishings. "The Rambler," Mr. Flagler's beautifully outfitted personal railroad car dating from 1886, is also on display.

Admission: $5 adults, $2 children.
Open: Tues–Sat 10am–5pm, Sun noon–5pm.

LION COUNTRY SAFARI, Southernmost Blvd. W., West Palm Beach. Tel. 793-1084.

More than 1,300 animals from around the world are enclosed in this 500-acre wildlife preserve. Keep your windows rolled up as you drive through this cageless zoo, which more or less faithfully reproduces the native habitats from various continents. Originally established to provide entertainment, Lion Country Safari has changed its goal with the times; now it's a protected breeding ground for endangered species. An adjacent amusement park is still intended as fun, and all the rides are included in the price of admission. Picnics are encouraged, and camping is available (tel. 793-9797 for overnight reservations).

Admission: $11.95 adults, $9.95 children 3–15, free for children under 3.
Open: Daily 9:30am–5:30pm (last vehicle admitted at 4:30pm).

NORTON GALLERY OF ART, 1451 S. Olive Ave., West Palm Beach. Tel. 832-5194.

This gallery houses one of Palm Beach's best collections of French impressionist and post-impressionist paintings, as well as renowned American and Chinese works, making the Norton an especially good rainy-day destination. Call for information on current events and shows.

Admission: Free; $5 donation suggested.
Open: Tues–Sat 10am–5pm, Sun 1–5pm.

THE RAPIDS GOLF, SLIDE AND BANKSHOT, Military Trail (north of 45th St.), West Palm Beach. Tel. 842-8756.

From March through September, this "family entertainment complex" cools visitors off with four gigantic water slides, an artificial river, a huge Jacuzzi, and dozens of waterfalls. There's also a 19-hole miniature golf course, and the requisite games room.

Admission: $13, $8 after 4pm.
Open: Daily 10am–8pm. **Closed:** Oct–Feb.

SOCIETY OF THE FOUR ARTS, Four Arts Plaza, Palm Beach. Tel. 655-7226.

There's always something going on in this cultural complex that includes a museum, library, and auditorium. Art exhibits change monthly, and concerts, lectures, and movies are regularly scheduled. The society's gardens are great for strolling, too. Phone to find out what's going on when you're in town.

Admission: Free; donation requested. Concerts, $20; lectures, $15; films, $2.50.
Open: Mon–Sat 10am–5pm, Sun 2–5pm. **Closed:** May–Nov.

SOUTH FLORIDA SCIENCE MUSEUM AND PLANETARIUM, 4801 Dreher Trail N., West Palm Beach. Tel. 832-1988.

Natural phenomena and physics are taught through hands-on exhibits which demonstrate the qualities of light, sound, energy, and the like. The complex encompasses an observatory, planetarium, and aquarium with several large tanks containing many marine species. On Friday and Saturday nights there are laser light shows set to rock music (separate admission).

Admission: $5 adults, $4.50 seniors, $2 children 4–11, free for children under 4.

Open: Museum, Sat–Thurs 10am–5pm, Fri 10am–10pm; planetarium, shows Mon–Thurs at 2pm, Fri at 2 and 7pm, Sat–Sun at noon and 2pm; observatory, Fri 8–10pm, weather permitting.

SIGHTSEEING/DAY CRUISES

A cruise along the Intracoastal Waterway lets you take an unobstructed peek at the area's grand mansions. The *Star of Palm Beach,* operating from 900 E. Blue Heron Blvd., Singer Island (tel. 848-7827), offers water tours of Palm Beach. Daily sightseeing as well as lunch, dinner, and theme cruises are offered, some with live entertainment. Costs range from $8 to $30.

The *Viking Princess,* Port of Palm Beach (tel. 407/845-7447, or toll free 800/841-7447), offers half-day brunch and dinner ocean cruises, as well as one-day excursions to The Bahamas. A breakfast buffet and five-course dinner are served on the way to and from the island. Evening cruises cost $40 to $50, brunch trips cost $60, and the Bahama island voyage costs $80.

SPORTS & RECREATION
Spectator Sports

GREYHOUND RACING Greyhounds, the world's fastest dogs, have been racing at the **Palm Beach Kennel Club,** 1111 N. Congress Ave., at Belvedere Road, in West Palm Beach (tel. 683-2222), since 1932. Able to reach speeds of more than 40 miles an hour, the dogs chase a fake rabbit around the track while punters place bets to win, place, or show. There is racing year-round; call for post times. Admission is 50¢ to $2, free on Sunday.

JAI ALAI Jai alai, a Spanish cross between lacrosse and handball, is popular in South Florida. Players use woven baskets, called *cestas,* to hurl balls, called *pelotas,* at speeds that sometimes exceed 170 miles per hour. Spectators, who are protected behind a wall of glass, place bets on the evening's players.

Games are played from September through July in West Palm Beach at the **Palm Beach Jai Alai Fronton,** 1415 45th St., in West Palm Beach (tel. 844-2444). Admission is 50¢ to $5 and the games begin Tuesday at 6:30pm, Wednesday through Saturday at 1 and 6:30pm, and on Sunday at 1pm.

POLO The **Palm Beach Polo and Country Club,** 13198 Forest Hill Blvd., West Palm Beach (tel. 798-7000, or toll free 800/327-4204), is one of the world's premier polo grounds. This posh West Palm Beach club attracts some of this aristocratic sport's best players. Matches are open to the public and celebrities are often in attendance. Star-watchers have spotted Prince Charles, the Duchess of York, Sylvester Stallone, and Ivana Trump here, among others. General admission is $6; box seats cost $24. Matches are held on Sunday at 3pm, December to March.

Participatory Sports

BEACHES Most of Palm Beach's best beachfront real estate is now part of someone's private estate, raising the public beaches here to an almost sacred stature. **Palm Beach Municipal Beach,** located on Fla. A1A, just south of West Palm's Royal Park Bridge, is small, undeveloped, and undercelebrated. **Phipps Ocean Park,** located on Ocean Boulevard between the Southern Boulevard and Lake Avenue causeways, is large and lively, encompassing over 1,300 feet of groomed and guarded oceanfront. There are picnic and recreation areas here as well as plenty of parking.

BICYCLING Palm Beach is great for biking. It's flat, and there are several trails that take you places that cars just can't go. The **Palm Beach Bicycle Trail Shop,** 223 Sunrise Ave. (tel. 659-4583), rents bicycles for $6.50 an hour or $20 a day, and they will be happy to direct you to the trails.

GOLF There's good golfing here, but many of the private club courses are maintained exclusively for the use of their members. Ask at your hotel, or contact the

Palm Beach Convention and Visitors Bureau (tel. 407/471-3995) for information on which clubs are available for play.

From May to October or November, close to a dozen private golf courses open their greens to visitors who are staying in a Palm Beach County hotel. This "Golf-A-Round" program is free (carts are additional), and reservations can be made through most major hotels.

The **Palm Beach Public Golf Course,** 2345 S. Ocean Blvd. (tel. 547-0598), a popular public 18-hole course, is a par 54 with greens that are between 100 and 235 yards from the tee. Open at 8am, the course is run on a first-come, first-served basis. There are no club rentals. Greens fees are $18 per person.

SCUBA DIVING & SNORKELING   Year-round warm waters, barrier reefs, and plenty of wrecks make South Florida one of the world's most popular places for diving. One of the best-known artificial reefs in this area is a vintage Rolls-Royce Silver Shadow which was sunk offshore in 1985.

Several local dive shops rent equipment and dispense information on the area's reefs. They include: **The Aqua Shop,** 505 Northlake Blvd., North Palm Beach (tel. 848-9042); **Atlantic Underwater,** 901 Cracker St., West Palm Beach (tel. 686-7066); **Dixie Divers,** 1401 S. Military Trail, West Palm Beach (tel. 969-6688); and **Ocean Sports Scuba Center,** 1736 S. Congress Ave., West Palm Beach (tel. 641-1144).

TENNIS   Several places offer tennis courts on a first-come, first-served basis. The following are in West Palm Beach:

Currie Park, 2400 N. Flagler Dr. (tel. 835-7025), another public park, has three lighted hard courts. There's no charge for their use.

The nine hard courts in the **South Olive Tennis Center,** 345 Summa St. (tel. 582-7218), are all lighted and open to the public. The center is located close to Dixie Highway, just south of Forest Hill Boulevard. Courts cost $3 per person per hour.

WHERE TO STAY
VERY EXPENSIVE

BREAKERS HOTEL, 1 S. County Rd., Palm Beach, FL 33480. Tel. 407/655-6611, or toll free 800/833-3141. Fax 407/659-8403. 562 rms, 53 suites. A/C MINIBAR TV TEL **Directions:** From I-95, exit onto Okeechobee Boulevard east, and turn north onto South County Road; the hotel is just ahead on your right.

$ Rates: Dec 17–Apr 10, $285–$480 single or double; from $465 suite. Apr 11–May 27 and Oct–Dec 16, $200–$440 single or double; from $420 suite. May 28–Sept, $125–$270 single or double; from $300 suite. Additional person $25 extra. AE, CB, DC, DISC, MC, V.

The grand dame of South Florida hostelries, and a tourist attraction in its own right, the Breakers was Palm Beach's first major hotel, built by railroad magnate Henry Flagler in the early 1900s. After two fires, a couple of rebuilds, and a handful of additions and face-lifts, the hotel has been transformed into the celebrated structure you see today, complete with its trademark sandstone exterior and twin belvedere towers. Architect Leonard Schultze designed this elaborate masterpiece to resemble an Italian palace, crowned with hand-painted frescoed ceilings inside and a Florentine fountain out front. The grand gilded lobby, dripping with crystal chandeliers, is dressed with rich green tapestry-covered furnishings, and features floor-to-ceiling French doors that open into a huge inner courtyard bubbling with its own fountains.

Although the hotel's guest rooms can't compare to the opulence of the public areas, accommodations are fine indeed, trimmed with little glass wall sconces and custom-framed artwork. In addition to the expected amenities, all accommodations include in-room safes and clock radios. The light marble bathrooms have a telephone, hairdryer, scale, and plush robes. There's also a separate vanity area.

The hotel's top floors have been renovated into the Flagler Club. These special concierge floors offer guests additional features and amenities. Rooms have more formal taffeta furnishings, large closets, and beautiful oak armoires. All contain marble baths with curtained showers, gold fixtures, hairdryers, and a phone. Included is access to the concierge lounge, a bright, attractive room with French doors leading to a small outdoor deck. A complimentary continental breakfast, afternoon tea, before-dinner hors d'oeuvres, and late-night desserts are served here.

Dining/Entertainment: There are five restaurants in the hotel. The window-walled Circle Dining Room serves breakfast daily in a beautiful setting with painted ceiling scenes of Italian cities and Monte Carlo and a huge, outstanding center skylight. The large Florentine Room has beamed ceilings and formal touches while live music plays to dinner guests. The Fairways Café and the Beach Club offer light snacks and refreshments. The Beach Club Patio surrounds an indoor (though unused) pool and serves lunch daily as well as a Sunday buffet brunch attracting many locals.

Services: 24-hour room service, concierge, supervised children's activities, business center, evening turn-down, overnight shoeshine, massages.

Facilities: Two golf courses, 20 tennis courts (11 lighted), heated swimming pool, private beach, putting green, water-sports and bicycle rentals, children's playground, health club, shopping arcade, croquet, shuffleboard, beach volleyball courts.

THE OCEAN GRAND, 2800 S. Ocean Blvd., Palm Beach, FL 33480. Tel. 407/582-2800, or toll free 800/432-2335. Fax 407/547-1557. 210 rms, 12 suites. A/C MINIBAR TV TEL **Directions:** From I-95, take the Sixth Avenue exit east and turn left onto Big Sea Highway; then turn east onto Lake Avenue and north onto South Ocean Boulevard, and the hotel is just ahead on your right.

$ Rates: Dec 15–Apr 14, $295–$485 single or double; from $750 suite. May 1–26 and Oct–Dec 14, $225–$385 single or double; from $600 suite. May 27–Sept, $145–$270 single or double; from $500 suite. Additional person $25 extra. AE, MC, V.

Opened in 1990, this premier lodging is one of the newest additions to an ever-growing list of prestigious Palm Beach retreats. Guests are welcomed by an elegant cream-marble lobby tastefully decorated with antique European furnishings and original art. In both the lobby and the adjoining lounge, intimate tables and love seats are separated from one another by lofty palms and towering white columns.

Ocean views can be enjoyed from almost every guest room in the house. Each room has its own private balcony and is decorated in cool oceanic colors. Armoires hide a stereo system, TV, VCR, and minibar. Most rooms also have king-size beds and safes, with hairdryers, scales, and bathrobes in the good-size gray-and-white marble bathrooms. The hotel's "Club" rooms are a bit larger, and include access to a club lounge, where continental breakfast, afternoon refreshments, and evening cocktails are served gratis. Suites include an additional sitting room, oversize balconies, and two bathrooms.

A year-round "Kid's Club" offers supervised activities for children 3 to 12. In the morning, indoor and outdoor events include water sports, crab races, scavenger hunts, puppet shows, and arts and crafts. In the afternoon, the club opens up to the entire family, offering bike rides, fishing tournaments, and excursions to nearby Lion Country Safari (see "What to See and Do," above).

Dining/Entertainment: The hotel's signature restaurant, simply called "The Restaurant," serves an eclectic variety of dishes utilizing local ingredients and European cooking methods. The more casual Ocean Bistro serves breakfast, lunch, and dinner outdoors, overlooking the Atlantic. The elegant and comfortable Living Room lounge is one of the best places in town for an intimate cocktail. A live jazz trio performs here on Friday and Saturday evenings, and a pianist plays every afternoon.

Services: 24-hour room service, concierge, evening turn-down, complimentary transportation to Worth Avenue, bicycle rentals, aerobics classes, overnight laundry and shoeshine, babysitting, massage.

Facilities: Three tennis courts, swimming pool, sauna, whirlpool, water-sports rentals, gym and health spa (offering body treatments and facials), beauty salon, gift shop.

RITZ-CARLTON, PALM BEACH, 100 S. Ocean Blvd., Manalapan, FL 33462. Tel. 407/533-6000, or toll free 800/241-3333. Fax 407/588-4555. 214 rms, 56 suites. A/C MINIBAR TV TEL **Directions:** From I-95, take Exit 45 (Hypoluxo Road) east; after a mile, turn left onto Federal Highway (U.S. 1), continue north for about one mile, and turn right onto Ocean Avenue; cross the

Intracoastal Waterway, turn right onto South Ocean Boulevard, and the hotel is just ahead on your left.

$ Rates: Dec 13–May 1, $310–$500 single or double; $550–$600 Club-level single or double; from $870 suite. May 2–26 and Oct 3–Dec 12, $235–$385 single or double; $450–$490 Club-level single or double; from $700 suite. May 27–Oct 2, $130–$230 single or double; $230–$330 Club-level single or double; from $525 suite. AE, DC, DISC, MC, V.

Like most of the members of the upscale Ritz-Carlton chain, the Palm Beach hostelry occupies an architecturally grand building with a prominent sandstone facade. Visitors enter an elegant and dramatic lobby dominated by a pink-marble fireplace. The lobby bar is outfitted with antique coffee tables, tapestry-covered furniture, and gold candelabra. Afternoon tea is served daily, but is best Wednesday through Saturday, when a jazz trio entertains.

Three towers of rooms are decorated in organic colors. Furnishings include marble writing desks and gilded mirrors; among other luxuries are marble baths with separate showers and tubs, double vanities, wall safes, three telephones, terrycloth robes, and private balconies. The hotel's Club level, popular with business travelers, offers concierge service and a lounge where complimentary continental breakfasts, midafternoon snacks, and evening cordials are served.

Dining/Entertainment: The elegant Dining Room serves continental-style dinners in ornate surroundings. Other restaurants on the property include the Grill, open for dinner only; the Restaurant, which serves all day; and the poolside Ocean Café and Bar, which is open from lunch until late. Cocktails are also served in the lobby lounge, and live entertainment is usually scheduled somewhere on the property every day of the week.

Services: 24-hour room service, concierge, complimentary airport transportation, evening turn-down, overnight laundry and shoeshine, babysitting, massage.

Facilities: Seven tennis courts, heated swimming pool, sauna, whirlpool, steam room, health club, scuba and snorkeling concessions, beauty salon, gift shop, bicycle rentals.

EXPENSIVE

CHESTERFIELD HOTEL DELUXE, 363 Coconut Row, Palm Beach, FL 33480. Tel. 407/659-5800, or toll free 800/243-7871. Fax 407/659-6707. 57 rms, 8 suites. A/C TV TEL **Directions:** From I-95, exit onto Okeechobee Boulevard east, cross the Intracoastal Waterway, and turn right on Coconut Row; the hotel is ahead, on your left, just past Australian Avenue.

$ Rates: Dec 14–Apr 2, $185–$265 single or double; from $375 suite. Apr 3–Dec 13, $75–$125 single or double; from $175 suite. AE, CB, DC, MC, V.

Less ostentatious than most of its expensive rivals, the intimate Chesterfield is packed with a discreet old-world charm. Its location, just one block from Worth Avenue, has made it popular with in-the-know visitors since the 1920s. Behind a light stucco exterior, enlivened with arched windows and colorful flags, is an overly designed lobby composed of contrasting furnishings and fabrics. The Chesterfield's English country manor style is evident in the wood-paneled library, just off the lobby. Dark wooden bookshelves filled with volumes are not just for show; guests are encouraged to browse and to borrow. Afternoon tea is served here daily from 3 to 5pm.

Lemon-yellow hallways with gold-leaf mirrors and ornately framed paintings lead to Laura Ashley rooms with brass knockers on the doors. Heavy wooden furniture and plush red carpets give each room a warm feeling. Baths are marble, and other pleasant touches such as thick terrycloth robes, armfuls of fresh flowers, and fluffy towels give the rooms a special homey feel.

Dining/Entertainment: Butler's, the hotel's primary dining room, serves respectable French favorites all day; reservations are essential for dinner. The Leopard lounge, named for the print that predominates here, serves light meals and cocktails throughout the day. There's live music here most evenings and on Sunday afternoons.

Services: 24-hour room service, concierge, complimentary transportation to local attractions, overnight laundry and shoeshine.

Facilities: Swimming pool, whirlpool.

PALM BEACH HISTORIC INN, 365 S. County Rd., Palm Beach, FL 33480. Tel. 407/832-4009. Fax 407/832-6255. 9 rms, 4 suites. A/C TV TEL
$ Rates (including continental breakfast): Dec 16–Apr, $125–$150 single or double; from $225 suite. May–Dec 15, $60–$75 single or double; from $95 suite. AE, DC, DISC, MC, V.

Built in 1923, the Palm Beach Historic Inn is a Palm Beach landmark located within walking distance of Worth Avenue and several good restaurants. The small lobby is filled with antiques, books, magazines, and an old-fashioned umbrella stand that evokes a homey B&B feel. All the rooms are one flight up, on the second floor, and each is uniquely decorated, outfitted with either a double, a queen-size, or two twin beds. When making reservations, be sure to state what size bed you prefer, as even some higher-priced suites are outfitted only with twin beds.

Every room is full of frill. Floral prints, sheer curtains, bed ruffles, and a plethora of lace can sometimes be overwhelming, masking rather than complimenting beautiful antique writing desks and dressers. Happily, there are also fluffy bathrobes, an abundance of towels, and plenty of good-smelling toiletries. The friendly innkeepers, Barbara and Harry Kehr, offer a complimentary afternoon drink, and extra-large continental breakfasts that include fruit, yogurt, muffins, juice, and coffee or tea—delivered to your room with the morning paper.

PLAZA INN, 215 Brazilian Ave., Palm Beach, FL 33480. Tel. 407/832-8666, or toll free 800/233-2632. Fax 407/835-8776. 50 rms, 1 suite. A/C MINIBAR TV TEL **Directions:** From I-95, exit onto Okeechobee Boulevard east, cross the Intracoastal Waterway, turn right onto Coconut Row, then left onto Brazilian Avenue; the hotel is just ahead on your left.
$ Rates (including breakfast): Dec 15–Apr, $135–$195 single or double; from $250 suite. May–Dec 14, $75–$95 single or double; from $125 suite. Additional person $15 extra. AE, MC, V.

⭐ From the moment you arrive at this luxurious bed-and-breakfast, you're overcome with the feeling that you're visiting good friends at their summer home. A bright and shiny ground-floor entrance hall is made even warmer by a beautiful antique writing table, a grand piano, and lovely pastel wallcoverings.

Each and every individually decorated room exudes charm. Several contain carved four-poster beds, hand-crocheted spreads, lace curtains, and pastel-colored taffeta shower curtains; every room is dressed with the same meticulous attention to detail found throughout the inn.

Dining/Entertainment: A full cooked-to-order breakfast that includes fresh fruit, breakfast breads, and hot main dishes is served each morning in a delightful dining room designed with lace-covered tables, fresh flowers, and crystal chandeliers. Except for breakfast, no other meals are served in the hotel. The cozy Stray Fox Pub, a comfortable little bar with mahogany tables, serves cocktails throughout the evening.
Services: Concierge.
Facilities: Heated swimming pool, Jacuzzi.

MODERATE

BEACHCOMBER SEA CAY MOTOR APARTMENTS, 3024 S. Ocean Blvd. (Fla. A1A), Palm Beach, FL 33480. Tel. 407/585-4646, or toll free 800/833-7122. Fax 407/547-9438. 46 rms, 4 suites. A/C TV TEL **Directions:** From I-95, exit onto Lake Worth Road east, stay to the right and take Lake Avenue over the Intracoastal Waterway, then turn right onto South Ocean Boulevard; the hotel is just ahead on your left.
$ Rates: Dec 20–Jan 14, $60–$100 single or double; from $110 suite. Jan 15–Apr 11, $75–$130 single or double; from $140 suite. Apr 12–Oct, $42–$75 single or double; from $75 suite. Nov–Dec 19, $45–$95 single or double; from $115 suite. Additional person $10 extra. Weekly rates available. AE, DISC, MC, V.

Because it's bright pink, this squat, two-story motel stands out among the high-rise buildings that surround it. For more than 35 years the Beachcomber has been bringing sanity to tab-happy Palm Beach, offering a good standard of accommodation at reasonable prices. It's located directly on the beach, a short drive from Worth Avenue shops and local attractions.

Every room has two double beds, large closets, and distinctive furniture with tropical accents. The most expensive rooms have balconies overlooking the ocean, or contain small kitchenettes; suites have both. The motel offers coin-operated laundries, shuffleboard, a huge saltwater pool, and a sun deck overlooking the Atlantic Ocean.

HEART OF PALM BEACH HOTEL, 160 Royal Palm Way, Palm Beach, FL 33480. Tel. 407/655-5600, or toll free 800/523-5377. Fax 407/832-1201. 88 rms, 2 suites. A/C MINIBAR TV TEL **Directions:** From I-95, exit onto Okeechobee Boulevard east and continue over the Royal Park Bridge onto Royal Palm Way; the hotel is ahead, on your right, just past South County Road.

$ Rates: Dec 15–Apr, $99–$189 single or double; from $225 suite. May–Dec 14, $59–$119 single or double; from $99 suite. Additional person $10 extra. AE, CB, DC, MC, V.

Centrally located, the Heart of Palm Beach Hotel is within walking distance of Worth Avenue's shops and just half a block from the beach. Both of the hotel's buildings are distinctively decorated: one with white bedspreads and ivory lacquered furniture, the other with lighter wicker furnishings and colorful, contemporary prints. Some rooms have balconies, some have patios, and all have clean, tiled baths with modern amenities. A nice outdoor pavilion area, at pool-side, has a barbecue for guests' use. The hotel's staff is particularly outgoing when it comes to helping guests plan outings and itineraries.

Dining/Entertainment: The Town Tavern serves a selection of sandwiches, pastas, salads, and cocktails, and is open daily from morning to night.

Services: Room service, concierge.

Facilities: Heated swimming pool, complimentary covered parking.

PALM BEACH HAWAIIAN OCEAN INN, 3550 S. Ocean Blvd. (Fla. A1A), Palm Beach, FL 33480. Tel. 407/582-5631, or toll free 800/457-5631. Fax 407/582-5631. 58 rms, 8 suites. A/C MINIBAR TV TEL **Directions:** From I-95, exit onto Lantana Road east, turn right onto Federal Highway (U.S. 1) and then left onto Ocean Avenue; cross the Intracoastal Waterway, turn left onto Ocean Boulevard (Fla. A1A), and the inn is about a mile ahead, on your right.

$ Rates: Dec 15–Jan 14, $96–$110 single or double; from $115 suite. Jan 15–Apr, $100–$110 single or double; from $134 suite. May–Dec 14, $70–$80 single or double; from $109 suite. Additional person $5 extra. AE, CB, DC, DISC, MC, V.

This rather basic wooden motel is a good pick for those who want to save money, but still want to locate right on Palm Beach's beach. Most rooms have dark-wood paneling with pastel prints, two twin beds, and eclectic 1950s furnishings. Bathrooms are all covered with white tile and have standing showers instead of bathtubs.

Clearly, the best part about this place is its oceanfront swimming pool and large wooden sun deck that extends to the sand. Beach umbrellas and rafts are available for rent. The motel's restaurant, open for breakfast, lunch, and dinner, will deliver directly to your room.

INEXPENSIVE

HIBISCUS HOUSE, 501 30th St., West Palm Beach, FL 33407. Tel. 407/863-5633. 6 rms, 2 suites. A/C TV TEL **Directions:** From I-95, exit onto Palm Beach Lakes Boulevard east and continue four miles until you come to a dead end, turn left onto Flagler Drive and go about 20 blocks to 30th Street. Turn left on 30th and go two blocks to the inn; it will be on your right.

$ Rates (including breakfast): Dec–Apr, $75 single or double; $90 suite. May–Nov, $65 single or double; $80 suite. No credit cards.

S Inexpensive bed-and-breakfasts are truly a rarity in this part of South Florida, making the Hibiscus House a real find. Discreetly located a few miles from the coast in a quiet residential neighborhood, this 1920s-era B&B regularly hosts guests from around the world.

Each room is named for its predominant color scheme. Hence, the Red Room has cardinal walls and matching floral-print bedspreads and curtains; the Peach Room has a charming four-poster bed, 19th-century-style furniture, and polished pine floors.

Every accommodation features its own private terrace or balcony. There are plenty of pretty public areas as well, many of which are filled with antiques. One little sitting room has walls of windows and comes complete with playing cards and board games for guests' use. The backyard has been transformed into a planted courtyard with a swimming pool and sun loungers.

A filling two-course breakfast is served each morning, either in the inside dining room or outside in the gazebo.

WHERE TO DINE
VERY EXPENSIVE

CAFE L'EUROPE, in the Esplanade, 150 Worth Ave., Palm Beach. Tel. 655-4020.
   Cuisine: CONTINENTAL. **Reservations:** Required.
$ **Prices:** Appetizers $7–$17; main courses $20–$32; lunch $7–$17. AE, CB, DC, MC, V.
   Open: Lunch Mon–Sat 11:30am–3pm; dinner daily 6–10:30pm. (The Caviar Bar stays open later.)

It should come as no surprise that Palm Beach has several terrific restaurants, and this is definitely one of them. Located on the upper level of the Esplanade, a two-story Spanish-style shopping arcade, this formal restaurant is romantically decorated with tapestried café chairs surrounding the linen-topped tables set with crystal and china. Brick archways, wood-paneled walls, and terra-cotta floors are capped with lofty ceilings.

However, it's the food you've come for, and the chef won't disappoint. Lunch might include crispy, Chinese-style lettuce leaves wrapped around minced squab, water chestnuts, bamboo shoots, and rice; poached filet of salmon; Mediterranean salad (feta cheese, ham, Greek olives, eggs, and vegetables); or a giant bleu-cheese burger. Other dinnertime appetizers include snails in garlic butter, baked chèvre (goat cheese) salad with raspberry-walnut dressing, and chilled gazpacho with avocado. Main courses are equally as adventurous, and include salmon filet rolled in a pecan crust, grilled veal medallions rubbed with tarragon, and rack of lamb served with minted couscous. A pastry chef bakes chocolate cakes and fruit tarts here daily.

The Caviar Bar has five or more different caviars always available. Located adjacent to the dining room, it features a large marble bar and small European-style café tables. Visit it for light seafood dishes, dessert, and gourmet coffees.

EXPENSIVE

BICE, 313½ Worth Ave., Palm Beach. Tel. 835-1600.
   Cuisine: ITALIAN. **Reservations:** Recommended.
$ **Prices:** Appetizers $7–$14; main courses $17–$22 for pasta, $19–$28 for meat and fish; lunch $9–$13. AE, DC, MC, V.
   Open: Lunch daily noon–3pm; dinner 6–10pm.

Good, trendy food and mood have made Bice (pronounced "Be-chay") one of the most talked about eateries in Palm Beach. Located at the end of a shop-lined walk, between Worth and Peruvian Avenues, the restaurant would look something like a Venetian villa, if it weren't in such great shape. The beautiful light-orange stucco building is wrapped with large French doors that open on all sides. The elegant dining area combines contemporary-style light-wood furnishings with a warm green carpet that wouldn't be out of place in an old-world gentlemen's club. In warm weather, the best seats are outdoors, at green marble tables that surround a tiled fountain.

Local seafood and air-shipped meats are prepared according to a not so traditional northern Italian kitchen. Spicy shrimp cakes with basil olio and sautéed peppers and onions is a most winning appetizer, as is beef carpaccio with arugula salad. Recommendable pastas are orecchiette with broccoli, garlic, sun-dried tomatoes, peppers, and parmesan cheese; and roasted veal ravioli with sundried porcini mushroom sauce. While there are no stand-outs in the meat and fish department, everything is competently prepared and guaranteed fresh. Order grilled salmon, striped sea bass, sirloin steak, or veal chops, depending on your mood.

CHARLEY'S CRAB, 456 S. Ocean Ave., Palm Beach. Tel. 659-1500.
Cuisine: SEAFOOD. **Reservations:** Required.
$ Prices: Appetizers $5–$10; main courses $18–$25; lunch $6–$12. AE, DC, DISC, MC, V.
Open: Lunch Mon–Sat 11:30am–4pm; dinner Sun–Thurs 5–10pm, Fri–Sat 5–11pm; brunch Sun 10:30am–2:30pm.

Sort of legendary in these parts, Charley's Crab is well known as the place to go for the best and freshest local seafood. Price is as high as the quality, however, and unless you're prepared, you'll be thinking about this dinner bill all the way home.

All the usual fishes are served here—salmon, pompano, dolphin (fish)—as are baked clams, oysters Rockefeller, and mini crab cakes. Steak, lamb, and chicken dishes are also available. Main dishes are accompanied by different side dishes each evening—if parmesan roasted potatoes are on today's menu, order them. The restaurant also features a good raw bar with a variety of shellfish, and a well-selected wine list with picks from California and around the world. There's live entertainment Wednesday through Saturday nights.

CHUCK & HAROLD'S CAFE, 207 Royal Poinciana Way, Palm Beach. Tel. 659-1440.
Cuisine: SEAFOOD/AMERICAN. **Reservations:** Recommended.
$ Prices: Appetizers $3–$8; main courses $14–$28; lunch $5–$12. AE, CB, DC, DISC, MC, V.
Open: Mon–Thurs 7:30am–midnight, Fri–Sat 8am–1am, Sun 8am–11pm.

Nestled between a popular row of restaurants and shops, this is one of the best places in town to people-watch. Chuck & Harold's serves consistently good food to a loyal clientele of both tourists and locals. Dining is either inside, in one of two spacious, palm-filled dining rooms, or outdoors on the patio, where reservations are essential.

When seated, diners are immediately presented with a basket of crispy crackers, served with a tangy hummus spread. Tuscan black-bean soup, chilled gazpacho, and pineapple, tomato, and Gorgonzola salad are the most recommendable appetizers. Main dishes include fresh grilled or broiled fish, boiled lobster, and various homemade pasta and chicken dishes. If you happen to visit during stone crab season, order them here. Ecologically harvested, only one claw is removed from each crab; then it's returned to the ocean where it will grow another one. Crab claws are served steamed or chilled, and served with a traditional honey-mustard sauce.

One final hint: Unless you're still hungry, don't order dessert; complimentary cookies are served at the end of each meal.

TABOO, 221 Worth Ave., Palm Beach. Tel. 835-3500.
Cuisine: CONTINENTAL. **Reservations:** Recommended.
$ Prices: Appetizers $7–$11; main courses $7–$25; lunch $5–$15. AE, MC, V.
Open: Daily 11:30am–1am.

Kind of trendy, kind of classic, Taboo stands out among other snazzy Worth Avenue eateries, offering excellent food in pleasantly familiar surroundings. Lots of greenery, a glowing fireplace, and contemporary southwestern charm make Taboo as inviting and comfortable as its food is appealing. Variety is always the chef's special, with extensive lunch and dinner offerings that are often calorie- and cholesterol-conscious.

California-style individual-size gourmet pizzas are topped with delicacies like barbecued chicken, goat and mozzarella cheeses, and sweet roasted red peppers. Other lunch choices include scallops with roasted garlic, portobello mushrooms, and arugula; and a delicious sandwich of sweet peppers and goat cheese. The best dinner starter is fresh tuna marinated in ginger and lime, a sort of one-item ceviche. Dinner choices change nightly, and may include grilled swordfish topped with olive-caper sauce or sautéed chicken breast covered with green apples and a brandy-based cream sauce. Grilled veal served on the bone, Maine lobster, and various chicken dishes are also usually available. Desserts are made on the premises, and there's a nice wine selection.

MODERATE

BIMINI BAY CAFE, 104 Clematis St., West Palm Beach. Tel. 833-9554.

Cuisine: SEAFOOD/CONTINENTAL. **Reservations:** Not required.
$ Prices: Appetizers $3–$7; main courses $11–$17; lunch $3–$8. AE, DISC, MC, V.
Open: Sun–Thurs 11am–1am, Fri–Sat 11am–2am.

Popular with local, young urban professionals, Bimini Bay is busiest on weekdays soon after work lets out. From your table on the café's large wooden outdoor deck, you can see all the way across the Intracoastal Waterway to Palm Beach. The decor is *Casablanca* style; there are also lots of hanging plants, modern white-paper lamps, and neon lights.

Hot Maryland crab dip, baked Brie with fruit, and artichoke-spinach dip are the restaurant's specialty appetizers. Lunch here usually means soup, salad, or sandwiches; a good selection of each is always on offer. Dinner expands to include seafood dishes, pasta, chicken, and steak. Malibu mixed grill, which combines two fresh fish selections, is recommendable, as is the grilled chicken Alfredo with linguine. There's live music Thursday through Saturday nights.

CAFE PROSPECT, 3111 S. Dixie Hwy., West Palm Beach. Tel. 832-5952.

Cuisine: CONTINENTAL. **Reservations:** Recommended.
$ Prices: Appetizers $3–$9; main courses $14–$20; lunch $3–$8. MC, V.
Open: Lunch Tues–Fri 11:30am–2pm; dinner Tues–Sun 5–10pm.

You wouldn't expect to find such a charming restaurant located in an otherwise ordinary Dixie Highway strip mall. But Café Prospect is a pleasant surprise, with a smell of fresh garlic and spices, as arresting as the atmosphere of this relaxed, homelike place. The intimate restaurant has a pseudo–art deco decor with accents that include Asian-style screens, bright wall prints, ballooned floral drapes, and glass bricks. There's no printed menu; the day's offerings are marked on a chalkboard and usually include several fresh fish selections, soups, salads, and sandwiches. Every dish is made to order.

E. R. BRADLEY'S SALOON, 111 Bradley Place, at Royal Poinciana Way, Palm Beach. Tel. 833-3520.

Cuisine: AMERICAN. **Reservations:** Recommended.
$ Prices: Appetizers $2–$11; main courses $11–$17; lunch $4–$8. AE, MC, V.
Open: Mon–Fri 11am–3am, Sat–Sun 10am–3am.

Named after Edward Riley Bradley, an avid gambler who opened a casino here in 1898, this restaurant has just enough rough edges to keep it from seeming contrived. A bar runs the length of the restaurant, and just in case that's not enough, a second bar is located at the eatery's far end. Lattice ceilings are dotted with gently whirling fans. During warmer weather, there's outdoor dining at marble-top tables with woven placemats.

At lunch, you'd do well to stick with a meal of appetizers like baked Brie with bread and fruit, and a mountain of nachos served with guacamole, cheese, and black beans. A variety of salads are available, as are unusually large sandwiches and burgers. The grilled fish and steaks are always available during dinner, but I suggest the manicotti, or the angel-hair pasta with shrimp and mussels. The restaurant is located on the corner of Royal Poinciana Way.

TESTA'S, 221 Royal Poinciana Way, Palm Beach. Tel. 832-0992.

Cuisine: CONTINENTAL. **Reservations:** Not required.
$ Prices: Appetizers $5–$12; main courses $11–$35; lunch $3–$13. AE, DC, DISC, MC, V.
Open: Daily 7am–midnight.

A family-owned restaurant, Testa's has been a Palm Beach fixture since 1921—an eon for a young city like this. A large outdoor patio, protected from passersby by a squat row of groomed hedges, is a great spot for people-watching any time of the year. Inside, wooden booths with pink-clothed tables furnish the main room, while a second Garden Room is notable for its roof, which can be removed during fine weather.

The restaurant's friendly staff is one of the reasons for its continued success. The menu is vast, and the staff won't rush you into choosing—it really can be difficult to decide between appetizers like crabmeat- and cheese-stuffed potato skins, eggplant provençal, or just garlic bread. A long list of seafood, steak, chicken, and pasta dishes is available, as are a host of desserts. Especially if you're traveling with a family, Testa's is thoroughly recommendable.

INEXPENSIVE

HAMBURGER HEAVEN, 314 S. County Rd., Palm Beach. Tel. 655-5277.
   Cuisine: AMERICAN. **Reservations:** Not accepted.
$ **Prices:** Salads and sandwiches $3–$6; burgers and dinners $5–$15; breakfast $3–$5. No credit cards.
   Open: Mon–Sat 7:30am–8pm.

Hamburger Heaven hasn't changed much since it began flipping burgers in 1945. A central U-shaped bar, surrounded by low stools, is encircled by old-fashioned Formica booths which line the walls. A large sailboat-studded ocean mural covers one entire wall, a refreshing change from all the other overly decorated, and overpriced, restaurants in this area.

As you might have guessed, burgers are the main food sold here, but daily dinner specials widen the variety. Tuesday means chicken and dumplings, Friday is for pasta with tomato-basil sauce, and Saturday is homemade meatloaf day. Rice pudding, cakes, and pies are always available. A full egg menu is offered at breakfast.

NARCISSUS, 200 Clematis St., West Palm Beach. Tel. 659-1888.
   Cuisine: CONTINENTAL. **Reservations:** Not required.
$ **Prices:** Appetizers $3–$6; main courses $7–$12; lunch $5–$7. AE, MC, V.
   Open: Lunch Mon–Fri 11am–3pm; dinner Mon–Thurs 4pm–midnight, Fri 4pm–1am; Sat–Sun noon–midnight.

This little restaurant always seems to be in vogue, popular with Palm Beach's younger set, who sit at tables on the front patio under yellow umbrellas. Inside, black lacquer-topped tables are matched with red café chairs, and booths are covered with contemporary geometric patterns.

A large selection of specialty salads and sandwiches includes Mandarin chicken salad and tuna pizza melt sandwich. Fresh snapper, grouper, swordfish, or tuna is always available, as are a selection of pasta dishes and homemade chicken pot pie. There's live entertainment here nightly during the high season.

BUDGET

GREEN'S PHARMACY, 151 N. County Rd., Palm Beach. Tel. 832-9171.
   Cuisine: AMERICAN. **Reservations:** Not accepted.
$ **Prices:** Breakfast $2–$5; burgers and sandwiches $3–$5. AE.
   Open: Mon–Sat 7:30am–4:30pm, Sun 7am–1pm.

This neighborhood corner pharmacy offers one of the best meal deals in Palm Beach. Both breakfast and lunch are served coffee-shop style, at a Formica bar above a black-and-white checkerboard floor.

Breakfast specials include eggs and omelets served with home-fries, bacon, sausage, or corned-beef hash. Cold cereal, oatmeal, and bagels are also available. At lunch, the grill serves up burgers and sandwiches, as well as ice-cream sodas and milkshakes.

SHOPPING

Palm Beach's **Worth Avenue** is a must, even if you have no desire to go shopping. The Rodeo Drive of the East Coast, Worth Avenue is lined with one of the world's most impressive collections of posh shops, interesting art galleries, and upscale restaurants. The four blocks between South Ocean Boulevard and Coconut Row, are home to the stores of Louis Vuitton, Cartier, Polo Ralph Lauren, and Chanel, among others. Victoria's Secret, The Limited Express, and several other less-impressive chains have snuck in here, too. Most of the street's stores are open Monday through Saturday from 10am to 5pm.

The Esplanade, 150 Worth Ave., Palm Beach, is a particularly nice mini-mall in the heart of the high-rent district. This two-story Spanish arcade is filled with specialty shops and restaurants. Big-name shops and department stores like Saks Fifth Avenue, Banana Republic, and Liz Claiborne surround Mediterranean-style gardens.

The **Palm Beach Mall,** Palm Beach Lakes Boulevard (tel. 683-9186), located just east of I-95, is where you go when you really need to buy something. Recently renovated with tropical fountains, plants, and skylights, this mall features several department stores, including Mervyn's, JC Penney, Sears, Burdines, and Lord & Taylor.

EVENING ENTERTAINMENT

There are several showrooms in the Palm Beaches, offering everything from live theater and classical concerts to heavy-metal rock. The **ArtsLine** (tel. 820-4567, ext. 2787, or toll free 800/882-ARTS) offers up-to-date recorded information on cultural events and goings-on in Palm Beach County. Tickets to many area events can be charged to your credit card over the phone through Ticketmaster (tel. 966-3309).

THE MAJOR ALL-PURPOSE AUDITORIUMS

RAYMOND F. KRAVIS CENTER FOR THE PERFORMING ARTS, 701 Okeechobee Blvd., West Palm Beach. Tel. 833-8300. Fax 407/833-3901.

This stunning, $55-million center opened in late 1992. It's quite an architectural achievement, featuring a large, curved glass facade. Inside are three different performance spaces: The elegant, 2,200-seat main concert theater and adjacent 300-seat "black box" theater between them hold over 300 performances a year. Music, theater, and dance performances are staged almost every night of the week. Phone for a current schedule.

A new restaurant has opened at the Kravis Center. The Colonnade specializes in seafood and is open for lunch daily from 11:30am to 2:30pm, and for dinner nightly from 5 to 11pm. Reservations are suggested.

WEST PALM BEACH AUDITORIUM AND MUNICIPAL STADIUM, 1610 Palm Beach Lakes Blvd. Tel. 683-6012.

Many concerts, sporting events, and festivals are held here. Musical guests include popular rap stars and country greats. The complex is located half a mile east of Exit 53 off I-95, and on the corner of Congress Avenue.

THE PERFORMING ARTS

Theaters

QUEST THEATER INSTITUTE, INC., 444 24th St., at Spruce St., West Palm Beach. Tel. 832-9328.

Palm Beach's only African American–oriented theater is also one of the city's most active, offering a wide range of professional, multicultural works. Past performances have included *Ain't Misbehavin'* and *A Raisin in the Sun*. The theater operates year-round.

Admission: Tickets, $18 adults, $10 students and seniors, $5 children under 12.

ROYAL POINCIANA PLAYHOUSE, 70 Royal Poinciana Plaza. Tel. 659-3310.

Broadway and Off Broadway plays and musicals are staged here throughout the year. The playhouse promotes itself as "the most glamorous theater in the country," and this may be so. It's pretty, all right, and top names regularly perform. Musical concerts are produced here as well.

Admission: Tickets, $30–$45.

Classical Music, Opera, and Dance

FLORIDA PHILHARMONIC ORCHESTRA, at the Kravis Center, 701 Okeechobee Blvd., West Palm Beach. Tel. 930-2997.

The Kravis Center is the primary Palm Beach performance hall for the Florida Philharmonic (see "The Major All-Purpose Auditoriums," above). Under the baton of James Judd, this professional symphony orchestra performs from September through May.
Admission: Tickets, $15–$37.

GREATER PALM BEACH SYMPHONY, Royal Poinciana Playhouse, Palm Beach. Tel. 655-2703.

Performing throughout Palm Beach County, the symphony performs orchestra concerts and chamber music recitals in several area halls including the Breakers Hotel and the Kravis Center. The symphony usually plays 12 to 14 concerts from November through April.
Admission: Tickets, $25–$100.

PALM BEACH OPERA, 415 S. Olive Ave., West Palm Beach. Tel. 833-7888.

Three operas are performed each season, one each in December, January, and March. They're usually staged at the Kravis Center, and often feature world-famous soloists.
Admission: Tickets, $18.50–$75.

MIAMI CITY BALLET, West Palm Beach Auditorium, 1610 Palm Beach Lakes Blvd., West Palm Beach. Tel. 488-7134.

This young professional company regularly performs in four Florida cities. Works by resident choreographer Jimmy Gamonet de Los Heros are staged, as are the dances of George Balanchine, Martha Graham, and others. The season runs from July through April.
Admission: Tickets, $19–$50.

THE CLUB & MUSIC SCENE

AU BAR, 336 Royal Poinciana Way, Palm Beach. Tel. 832-4800.

Friends tell me that they never charged admission before William Kennedy Smith was accused of raping a girl he took home from here. Publicity from that affair was good for business, and now everyone knows about this luxurious bar that was once the mainstay of Palm Beach's young jet-set. Richly upholstered chairs and glass-top tables surround a tiny dance floor. The large marble-top bar is garnished with hanging crystal and a huge floral bouquet. Dress to kill. Au Bar is open Tuesday through Sunday from 8pm to 3am.
Admission: Free Sun and Tues–Thurs, $10 Fri–Sat.

CRUZANS, 2224 Palm Beach Lakes Blvd., West Palm Beach. Tel. 686-5613.

On the other end of the haughty spectrum from Au Bar, Cruzans is about as basic as it gets, looking like spring break all year long. It's huge, and has three bars, six pool tables, and a large-screen TV. There are drink and theme specials every night of the week, including ladies' nights, bikini contests, and "red hot" male reviews. Music is not the only thing that throbs here. Open on Tuesday and Wednesday from 8pm to 3am, on Thursday from 5pm until 3am, on Friday from 5pm to 4am, and on Saturday from 8am until 4am.
Admission: Varies depending on what's on; call for the latest.

E. R. BRADLEY'S SALOON, 111 Bradley Place, Palm Beach. Tel. 833-3520.

Casual restaurant by day, busy bar by night, Bradley's is the kind of place where revelers literally dance on the bar—ducking to avoid the ceiling fans. A two-cocktail minimum happy-hour buffet is offered Monday through Friday from 4 to 6:30pm and on Saturday and Sunday from 4 to 5pm. Bradley's is open Monday through Friday from 11am to 3am and on Saturday and Sunday from 10am to 3am.

RESPECTABLE STREET CAFE, 518 Clematis St., West Palm Beach. Tel. 832-9999.

This happening spot in downtown West Palm Beach has remained popular for more than five years. The café's plain storefront exterior belies its funky high-ceilinged interior, decorated with large black booths, psychedelic wall murals, and a large checkerboard-tile dance floor. The young, alternative crowd dances to both live and recorded music. Open Wednesday through Saturday from 9pm to 4am.

Admission: $2–$5.

ROXY'S, 323 Clematis St., West Palm Beach. Tel. 833-1003.

It's one of the best neighborhood joints—complete with a long bar, low stools, a pool table, antique taps, and T-shirted locals. Go across the Intracoastal to mingle with the wannabe glitterati. Open daily from 9am to 3am.

---

3. BOCA RATON & DELRAY BEACH

26 miles S of Palm Beach, 38 miles N of Miami

GETTING THERE By Plane The **Palm Beach International Airport** (tel. 407/471-7420) serves the Boca Raton area, and is a pleasure to fly in or out of. Helpful "Airport Ambassadors" in their teal-green shirts and jackets, are on hand to offer information. Major domestic carriers servicing the airport include American (tel. toll free 800/433-7300), Continental (tel. 407/832-5200, or toll free 800/525-0280), Delta (tel. 407/655-5300, or toll free 800/221-1212), Northwest (tel. toll free 800/225-2525), TWA (tel. 407/655-3776, or toll free 800/221-2000), and United (tel. toll free 800/241-6522).

By Train Amtrak (tel. toll free 800/USA-RAIL) trains departing from New York stop in West Palm Beach on their way to Miami. The local station is at 201 S. Tamarind Ave., West Palm Beach (tel. 407/832-6169).

By Bus Greyhound can get you to Boca from almost anywhere. The company no longer operates a single nationwide telephone number, so consult your local directory for the office nearest you.

By Car If you're driving up or down the Florida coast, you'll probably reach Boca Raton on I-95, a highway that runs all the way from Maine to Miami. Visitors on their way to or from Orlando should take the Florida Turnpike, a toll road that runs almost directly from this county's beaches to Walt Disney World. Finally, if you're coming from the state's west coast, you can either take Fla. 70, which runs north of Lake Okeechobee to Fort Pierce, or Fla. 80, which runs south of the lake to Palm Beach.

ESSENTIALS The **telephone area code** is 407.

The **Palm Beach County Convention and Visitors Bureau,** 1555 Palm Beach Lakes Blvd., Suite 204, West Palm Beach, FL 33401 (tel. 407/471-3995, or toll free 800/554-PALM), distributes an informative brochure, and will answer your questions about visiting Boca Raton and Delray Beach.

Boca Raton was named by the Spanish conquistadors who landed here with Ponce de León—"Boca de Raton" means mouth of the rat. It is widely believed that the sailor's "rats" were actually the large and dangerous rocks that protrude from the water in Boca's protected harbor.

Not much happened here until the 1920s, when architect Addison Mizner built the Cloister Inn, a stunning Mediterranean Revival–style hotel that's still the architectural basis for all of Boca Raton. It wasn't until the 1960s that Boca really began to boom, growing around a new IBM manufacturing plant and other high-tech industries. The city's strict building codes and plethora of low-density developments make Boca popular with moneyed ex–New Yorkers.

Many of Boca's residents would shudder if you mention Delray Beach in the same breath, much less the same guidebook heading. Delray grew up completely separately, founded in 1894 by a midwestern postmaster who sold off five-acre lots through

Michigan newspaper ads. Delray is named after a suburb of Detroit. For tourists, however, there's no reason why Boca and adjacent Delray should be explored independently. Budget-conscious travelers would do well to eat and sleep in Delray, and dip into Boca for sightseeing purposes only.

WHAT TO SEE & DO

BOCA RATON MUSEUM OF ART, 801 W. Palmetto Rd., Boca Raton. Tel. 392-2500.

In addition to a relatively small but well-chosen permanent collection that's strongest in 19th-century European oils, the museum stages a wide variety of temporary exhibitions by local and international artists. Lectures and films are offered on a regular basis; phone for details.

Admission: Free; donations requested.
Open: Mon–Fri 10am–4pm, Sat–Sun noon–4pm.

CHILDREN'S SCIENCE EXPLORIUM, in the Royal Palm Plaza, Suite 15, 131 Mizner Blvd., Boca Raton. Tel. 395-8401.

Here, 30 interactive exhibits teach children—and elders—about how things work in the world we live in. There are displays on electrical fields, gravitational forces, recycling, and computer technology. Even if you're not in a museum mood, you might want to visit the Explorium's unusual gift shop for freeze-dried astronaut food, hologram cards, and other unique presents you just can't get at home.

Admission: $2, free for children under 3.
Open: Tues–Sat 10am–5pm, Sun noon–5pm.

SPORTS & RECREATION

BEACHES Before South Florida was completely overrun with buildings, the state set aside lands dedicated to protection and preservation. Happily, many of these properties are on the waterfronts in Boca Raton and Delray Beach. Some are left alone and remain in a relatively natural state; others are groomed and lifeguarded.

The **Delray Beach Public Beach** is on Ocean Boulevard at the east end of Atlantic Avenue. This pretty beach is groomed and cleaned for the comfort of bathing and sunning beachgoers. There's limited parking along Ocean Boulevard.

At **Red Reef Park**, a fully developed 67-acre oceanfront park in Boca Raton, the beach has year-round lifeguard protection and good snorkeling around the rocks and reefs that lie just offshore. There's a small picnic area with grills, tables, and restrooms. The park is on Fla. A1A half a mile north of Palmetto Park Road, and is open daily from 8am to 10pm.

Spanish River Park, North Ocean Boulevard (Fla. A1A), Boca Raton, two miles north of Palmetto Park Road, is a huge oceanfront park that has a large grassy area, making it one of the best for picnicking. Facilities include picnic tables, grills, restrooms, and a bilevel 40-foot observation tower. Walk through tunnels under the highway to nature trails that wind through fertile grasslands.

GOLF From May to October or November, close to a dozen private golf courses open their greens to visitors staying in a Palm Beach County Hotel. This "Golf-A-Round" program is free (carts are additional), and reservations can be made through most major hotels. Ask at your hotel, or contact the Palm Beach Convention and Visitors Bureau (tel. 407/471-3995) for information on which clubs are available for play.

The private 18-hole, par-61 course at the **Boca Raton Executive Country Club,** 7601 E. Country Club Blvd. (tel. 997-9410), is usually open to the public. A driving range is also on the property as well as a pro shop and a restaurant. A PGA professional gives lessons, and rental clubs are available. From Yamato Road east, turn left onto Old Dixie Highway; after about a mile, turn left onto Hidden Valley Boulevard, and continue straight to the club. Greens fees are $14 to $26.

The **Boca Raton Municipal Golf Course,** 8111 Golf Course Rd. ·(tel. 483-6100), is located just north of Glades Road, half a mile west of the Florida Turnpike. This public 18-hole, par-72 course covers approximately 6,200 yards.

There's a snack bar, and a pro shop where clubs can be rented. Greens fees are $10 to $20 for 9 holes and $14 to $21 for 18 holes.

TENNIS The snazzy **Delray Beach Tennis Center,** 201 W. Atlantic Ave. (tel. 243-7360), has been recently spruced up for a Virginia Slims tournament. There are 19 lighted courts. Phone for rates and reservations.

The 17 public lighted courts at **Patch Reef Park,** 2000 NW 51st St. (tel. 997-0881), are available on a first-come, first-served basis. It's recommended that you call ahead to see if courts are available. The fee for nonresidents is $5.75 per person per hour. Courts are available Monday through Saturday from 8am to 10pm and on Sunday from 8am to dusk. To reach the park from I-95, exit at Yamato Road west and continue past Military Trail to the park.

WHERE TO STAY
VERY EXPENSIVE

BOCA RATON RESORT AND CLUB, 501 E. Camino Real Dr. (P.O. Box 5025), Boca Raton, FL 33431. Tel. 407/395-3000, or toll free 800/448-8355. Fax 407/391-3183. 963 rms, 37 suites, 70 golf villa apts. A/C MINIBAR TV TEL **Directions:** From I-95 north, exit onto Palmetto Park Road east, turn right onto Federal Highway (U.S. 1), and then left onto Camino Real to the resort.

$ Rates: Jan–Apr, $220–$390 single or double; from $375 suite; from $380 golf villa apt. May 28–Sept, $110–$210 single or double; from $170 suite; from $150 golf villa apt. May 1–27 and Oct–Dec, $170–$350 single or double; from $305 suite; from $285 golf villa apt. AE, DC, MC, V.

The Spanish-Mediterranean–style main house of the Boca Raton Resort and Club used to be all there was to this now-grand retreat. Built in 1926, and originally named the Cloister Inn by southeastern Florida's seminal architect, Addison Mizner, the hotel has grown substantially over the years. Today, Boca's best resort straddles both sides of the Intracoastal Waterway, occupying over 350 acres of land. Its romantic European architecture is mixed with modern buildings and additions.

Rooms in the historic Cloisters building have fine arched doorways, high beamed ceilings, refined wood furnishings, and Oriental carpets covering terra-cotta floors. The Boca Beach Club building is the most contemporary in feel, with high glass walls, light marble floors, and pastel-and-white decor. Guests can also choose to lodge in one of three other structures: the modern, 27-story Tower; the service-oriented Palm Court Club, complete with its own private concierge service; or in the Golf Villas, which has patios and balconies overlooking the hotel's 18-hole golf course. Each building has its own charm and style, offering guests options for varying tastes.

Each room in every building comes with bathrobes, hairdryers, at least two phones, full-length mirrors, and in-room safes. Also, no matter where you stay here, you're guaranteed to receive top-notch service from an experienced and attentive staff.

Dining/Entertainment: Nine restaurants and three lounges are spread throughout the property. The Top of the Tower, a formal Italian restaurant, is located, appropriately enough, on the 27th floor of the Tower building, offering extraordinary views of Boca Raton and surrounding areas. Only dinner is served here. Nick's Fishmarket, located at the Boca Beach Club, is known for excellently prepared seafood served in graceful surroundings. Or stop for an afternoon coffee at the Cappuccino Bar in the Cloister.

Services: 24-hour room service, concierge, business center, fitness classes, supervised children's programs, evening turn-down, laundry, overnight shoeshine.

Facilities: Three fitness centers, five swimming pools, two golf courses, 34 tennis courts (9 lighted), water-sports and bicycle rentals, snorkeling and scuba instruction, croquet, volleyball, basketball courts.

EXPENSIVE

BOCA BRIDGE HOTEL, 999 E. Camino Real, Boca Raton, FL 33432. Tel. 407/368-9500, or toll free 800/327-0130. Fax 407/362-0492. 96 rms, 25 suites. A/C TV TEL

$ Rates: May–Dec 20, $70–$105 single; $80–$115 double; from $140 suite. Dec 21–Apr, $140–$175 single; $150–$185 double; from $280 suite. Additional person $10 extra. AE, DISC, MC, V. **Parking:** Free.

The Boca Bridge is a welcome oasis in tab-happy Boca Raton. A tall hotel, bathed in "Boca Pink," the Boca Bridge fronts the Intracoastal Waterway, but is still close enough to the ocean to allow for good views of the Atlantic from east-facing floors. Intelligently, every room is located at least four stories up, allowing views from every room. To its further advantage, each room contains a small balcony with outdoor chairs that's actually usable. Inside, wide hallways dressed with ornate wall sconces, lead to particularly large rooms and suites that are tastefully outfitted with striped bedspreads and green tapestried furniture. Baths are well stocked, and include hairdryers and lighted vanities. Suites have marble entryways and plenty of closet space.

Dining/Entertainment: The Top of the Bridge Supper Club and Lounge—located you know where—is actually a rather nice place to eat. Boca doesn't boast the best skyline in the world, but the view from here is pretty good. There's live entertainment and dancing Wednesday through Saturday nights, and a buffet brunch is served on Sunday from 11am to 3pm. The hotel's other restaurant, Watercolor's Cafe, is located downstairs, on the waterfront. The pretty little indoor/outdoor restaurant serves three meals daily, from 7am to 10pm.

Services: Room service, overnight laundry, complimentary valet parking.
Facilities: Health club, swimming pool, sauna.

SEAGATE HOTEL & BEACH CLUB, 400 S. Ocean Blvd., Delray Beach, FL 33483. Tel. 407/276-2421, or toll free 800/233-3581. Fax 407/243-4714. 70 suites. A/C TV TEL **Directions:** From I-95, exit onto Atlantic Avenue east, turn right onto Ocean Boulevard (Fla. A1A), and continue one block to the hotel.

$ Rates: Feb–Apr 18, $145–$241 one-bedroom suite; $285 two-bedroom suite; $625 penthouse. Apr 19–Nov 19, $59–$79 one-bedroom suite; $109 two-bedroom suite; $325 penthouse. Nov 20–Jan, $94–$145 one-bedroom suite; $190 two-bedroom suite; $425 penthouse. Additional person $15 extra. Children under 18 stay free in parents' suite. AE, CB, DC, MC, V.

At the Seagate, an all-suite hotel, the ample rooms containing large kitchenettes are split between two adjacent buildings located directly across the street from the beach. Except for the fact that one of the buildings is closer to the swimming pool, it hardly matters which one you choose. Suites in both are painted in earthy pastels, and stocked with light-wood and wicker furniture; there are large closets, safes, and alarm clocks. Kitchenettes come chef-ready, prestocked with all the utensils and cookware you need. Fresh coffee, homemade muffins, and newspapers are available in the hotel's lobby every morning.

The Beach Club part of the hotel is located across the street. There are no accommodations here, just facilities that include a heated saltwater pool, chaise longues, towels, a restaurant, and cocktail service on the sand.

Dining/Entertainment: The Beach Club Restaurant, an American eatery, is open for lunch and dinner. There's a small bar here, too. The adjacent Patio Bar is far less formal, serving snacks, burgers, and drinks.

Services: Room service, children's activities during peak season, water aerobics.
Facilities: Water-sports rentals, locker rooms.

MODERATE

THE COLONY, 525 E. Atlantic Ave. (P.O. Box 970), Delray Beach, FL 33447. Tel. 407/276-4123, or toll free 800/552-2363. 93 rms. A/C TEL **Directions:** From I-95, exit onto Atlantic Avenue east; the hotel is about one mile ahead on your left.

$ Rates (including breakfast and dinner): Jan 10–Apr 5, $110–$190 single or double. Additional person $30 extra. AE, MC, V. **Closed:** May–Dec.

This three-story hotel, well located right on Delray's main street, is open during the "season" only. Not much has changed at the Colony since the hotel debuted in 1926; in fact, the furniture and decor may very well have been here since opening day. The spacious lobby is filled with rattan tables and chairs that often host senior-citizen card games. But the hotel is also popular with families who appreciate the many planned activities and meals that are offered here. Rooms are quite modest, and contain old-fashioned switchboard-type phones.

Guests have full access to the hotel's beachfront club, which offers a heated saltwater swimming pool, private beach, and various activities like putting and shuffleboard tournaments. Prices include both breakfast and dinner—not gourmet quality, but with good variety.

RAMADA INN, 2901 N. Federal Hwy., Boca Raton, FL 33431. Tel. 407/395-6850, or toll free 800/272-6232. Fax 407/368-7964. 100 rms, 32 suites. A/C TV TEL **Directions:** From I-95, exit onto Glades Road east; after two miles, turn left onto Federal Highway (U.S. 1) and the hotel is about a mile ahead on your left.

$ Rates: Dec 16–Apr, $85–$115 single or double; from $120 suite. May–July, $54–$75 single or double; from $75 suite. Aug–Dec 15, $49–$70 single or double; from $65 suite. AE, CB, DC, MC, V. **Parking:** Free.

Although the Ramada chain is most closely associated with business travel, this four-story pink concrete hotel is both well located and welcoming to vacationers. Rooms here are just as bright as the hotel's large, white marble lobby. There's nothing particularly fancy, but accommodations are both comfortable and modern. Suites are not much larger than regular rooms—the main difference is that they contain pull-out sofa beds. There's a large heated pool. The hotel's Garden Café, located adjacent to the lobby, serves lunch and dinner and offers live entertainment on weekends.

SEA AIRE, 1715 S. Ocean Blvd., Delray Beach, FL 33483. Tel. 407/276-7491. 3 studios, 8 apts, 5 villas. A/C TV TEL

$ Rates: Apr 20–Nov, $45 studio; $50–$63 apt; $68–$75 villa. Dec, $101 studio; $105–$115 apt; $120–$135 villa. Jan, $107 studio; $110–$121 apt; $126–$155 villa. Feb–Apr 19, $125 studio; $130–$142 apt; $147–$190 villa. No credit cards.

Located on the ocean just north of Linton Boulevard, Sea Aire is a no-frills motel filled with return guests who stay for weeks and months at a time. The motel's squat white buildings surround a thick grassy area that's punctuated by a pear-shaped pool.

Not surprisingly, the Sea Aire's best accommodations are their most expensive—stand-alone villas that are both modern and bright. They feature lots of windows, and nicer carpets and furnishings than the other rooms on the property. All units have fully stocked kitchens and most contain standard mismatched motel furniture. A bar of soap and a few towels are the only bath amenities; pack your own shampoo and other essentials. Likewise, you might want to stow a beachchair as the pool lounges are not allowed on the sand.

SHORE EDGE MOTEL, 425 N. Ocean Blvd. (Fla. A1A), Boca Raton, FL 33432. Tel. 407/395-4491. 16 rms. A/C TV TEL **Directions:** From I-95, exit onto Palmetto Park Road east, turn left onto Ocean Boulevard (Fla. A1A), and continue four blocks to the motel.

$ Rates: Jan–Mar, $75–$95 single or double. Apr and Dec, $55–$75 single or double. May–Nov, $45–$55 single or double. AE, MC, V.

Located slightly north of downtown Boca Raton, this is a great choice for those who wish to be near the beach, but want to avoid exorbitant resort rates. Despite its name, the Shore Edge is not on the sand, but across the street from a public beach. It's the quintessential South Florida motel: a small, pink, single-story structure surrounding a modest swimming pool and courtyard.

Although the rooms are a bit on the small side, they're very neat, outfitted with patterned curtains and framed artwork. The higher-priced accommodations are larger and come with full kitchens. The motel's owners, Lauren and Don Manuel, are terrific hosts, and are more than willing to share their knowledge of the surrounding area with you.

INEXPENSIVE

RIVIERA PALMS MOTEL, 3960 N. Ocean Blvd., Delray Beach, FL 33483. Tel. 407/276-3032. 21 rms, 13 efficiencies. A/C TV

$ Rates: Dec 15–Jan, $50 single or double; from $55 efficiency. Feb–Apr 15, $60 single or double; from $65 efficiency. Apr 16–Dec 14, $40 single or double; from $45 efficiency. Weekly rates available. No credit cards.

In Florida, competition among hotels is tough, rates are competitive, and you usually get what you pay for. This place is no exception—it's plain, simple, and relatively inexpensive. Behind the motel's two-story, cream-colored exterior are large rooms filled with a mixed bag of 1950s-era furnishings. Efficiencies come with full kitchens complete with dishes and silverware. There are no phones in the rooms. A large swimming pool is surrounded by a nice courtyard with sunning lounges, patio tables, barbecue grills, and (of course) shuffleboard courts.

WHERE TO DINE
VERY EXPENSIVE

LA VIEILLE MAISON, 770 E. Palmetto Park Rd., Boca Raton. Tel. 391-6701 or 737-5677.
Cuisine: CONTINENTAL. **Reservations:** Required.
$ Prices: Appetizers $5–$13; main courses $18–$35; fixed-price dinners $38 and $49. AE, CB, DC, MC, V.
Open: Dinner only, daily 6–9:30pm (call for seating times).

In a rustic, old house with dark floral carpeting, French country crystal and silver, and original European art, lucky diners are treated to great food in a particularly romantic setting. Several small downstairs rooms, each with just one or two quiet tables, make you feel as if you're dining at home—if home is Versailles. Upstairs is larger and livelier, and the food is just as agreeable.

Begin with warm bell-pepper soup served with a dollop of sour cream, or an unusual open-face ravioli filled with duck confit and sage butter. You might choose to continue with salmon wrapped in rice paper, or try roast rack of lamb with thyme and goat cheese. Desserts are just as fine, and may include lemon crêpe soufflé with raspberry sauce, or crispy meringue with vanilla ice cream and chocolate sauce. The labels from the restaurant's vast, award-winning wine cellar could (and does) fill a thick book.

EXPENSIVE

BISTRO L'EUROPE, 346 Plaza Real, in Mizner Park, Boca Raton. Tel. 368-4488.
Cuisine: CONTINENTAL. **Reservations:** Recommended.
$ Prices: Appetizers $5–$9; main courses $17–$22; lunch $4–$13. AE, DC, MC, V.
Open: Lunch Mon–Sat 11:30am–3pm; dinner Mon–Thurs 6–10pm, Fri–Sat 6–11pm.

Although the restaurant is not small, it's somehow intimate, made cozy with a tricolored hardwood floor and fine wall murals of neighborhood scenes.

Tasty lunches run the gamut from Italian pastas to Mandarin-style stir-fries and healthful spa cuisine. A light Alfredo sauce is served over penne pasta with Gorgonzola cheese, asparagus, and mushrooms. Blackened chicken breast is served on toasted sourdough bread with mozzarella. And braised mahi-mahi is served with yellow squash and zucchini. Dinners, which are slightly more formal, might begin with tricolored caviar pie, or escargots in garlic-chablis butter. Main courses include sea shell pasta with pesto and chicken, and wienerschnitzel with potatoes and leaf spinach. A full range of desserts are also available, including fresh-baked fruit tarts, bread pudding, and mixed sorbets.

JOE MUER SEAFOOD, 6450 N. Federal Hwy., Boca Raton. Tel. 997-6688.
Cuisine: SEAFOOD. **Reservations:** Recommended.
$ Prices: Appetizers $4–$12; main courses $13–$24; lunch $4–$12. AE, MC, V.
Open: Lunch Mon–Fri 11:30am–3:30pm; dinner daily 4:30–10pm.

This enormous dining room seems to stretch on forever, interrupted only by a forest of flowers and plants. It tends to get a bit noisy here, but lots of diners seem to like it that way.

The restaurant has become justifiably famous for its oversize seafood dishes that are not just well prepared, but beautifully presented. The usual selection of ocean fish can be grilled, broiled, poached, sautéed, or blackened—any way you like it. Other fresh seafood choices include Michigan smelts, crabmeat-stuffed shrimp, and Lake Heron perch. Frogs' legs, filet mignon, and rack of lamb are also available. The nice wine list emphasizes California grapes.

MODERATE

BACI, 344 Plaza Real, in Mizner Park, Boca Raton. Tel. 362-8500.
   Cuisine: ITALIAN. **Reservations:** Recommended.
$ Prices: Appetizers $5–$12; main courses $12–$17; lunch $5–$15. AE, MC, V.
   Open: Lunch daily 11:30am–2:30pm; dinner Sun–Thurs 5–11pm, Fri–Sat 5pm–midnight.

Yet another good restaurant located in Mizner Park, Baci offers indoor and outdoor seating, as well as a huge bar for drinks and appetizers. White patio tables with black director's chairs surround a tiled fountain and tall Floridian palms. Inside, bulky matte-black modern furnishings and a massive granite bar create a curious art deco industrial look. A contemporary Italian-style café, this eatery is both loud and crowded on weekends, popular with Boca's see-and-be-seen crowd.

Lunch selections include a variety of salads like salmon, tuna, and sliced duck breast, most of which are made with designer greens like arugula, radicchio, and escarole. Pastas, pizza, and assorted sandwiches round out the rest of the menu. The gnocchi al verde (potato dumplings with spinach-pistachio pesto) is particularly recommendable, as are the individual-size gourmet pizzas, topped with oak-grilled chicken, goat cheese, and the like. The dinner menu includes many of the same lunch items as well as a special lasagne of the day (like whole-wheat pasta with broccoli, Italian sausage, and sun-dried tomatoes). The accede-roasted baby chicken with cornbread stuffing and the grilled rabbit with grappa-soaked cherries are also recommendable. There's a great selection of Italian wines.

BOSTON'S ON THE BEACH, 40 S. Fla. A1A, Delray Beach. Tel. 278-3364.
   Cuisine: SEAFOOD/AMERICAN. **Reservations:** Not required.
$ Prices: Appetizers $3–$7; main courses $9–$18; lunch $3–$8. AE, MC, V.
   Open: Mon–Sat 6:30am–1am, Sun 6:30am–midnight.

Somewhat of a legend in Delray Beach, Boston's is well known to regulars who have been coming here for years. Eclectic, low-budget wall decorations include street signs and framed sport prints. Informal and casual, the restaurant is most crowded around happy hour, daily between 4 and 6pm.

Omelets, pancakes, eggs Benedict, and French toast are served for breakfast, while traditional salads and sandwiches make up the bulk of the lunch selections. Some of the more unusual lunch and dinner offerings include bacon-wrapped scallops, smoked fish, and calamari-topped linguine. Crab legs, shrimp, raw clams, and oysters are also always available, as are a host of steak and chicken dishes.

The restaurant is located across the highway from the Delray public beach. There is outdoor seating on a covered porch, and inside, around wooden tables.

FIFTH AVENUE GRILL, 821 SE Fifth Ave., Delray Beach. Tel. 265-0122.
   Cuisine: FLORIDA REGIONAL. **Reservations:** Accepted only for large parties.
$ Prices: Appetizers $3–$9; main courses $14–$26; lunch about half price. AE, DISC, MC, V.
   Open: Lunch daily 11:30am–4pm; dinner daily 5–11pm.

Once you've had your fill of pastel-saturated, tropically inspired restaurants, the dark, romantic Fifth Avenue Grill seems particularly welcoming. Sitting here, it's possible to forget for a moment that you're in South Florida and imagine that you've been transported to a château in a foreign country. Until you read the menu.

The Fifth Avenue Grill is essentially an American seafood and steakhouse serving lobster tails and certified Angus filet mignons. Every main course includes a trip to the salad bar, and is accompanied by a cheese-stuffed baked potato, fried shoestrings, or brown rice. Some hearty eaters start with a cup of Bermuda onion soup, a sweeter twist on the French favorite. The restaurant's Florida roots are made apparent in the kitchen, where local fish like grouper is broiled and topped with sweet banana sauce and roasted almonds.

MAX'S GRILL, 404 Plaza Real, in Mizner Park, Boca Raton. Tel. 368-0080.

Cuisine: AMERICAN. **Reservations:** Accepted only for large parties.
$ Prices: Appetizers $5–$7; main courses $12–$20; lunch $5–$12. AE, CB, DC, MC, V.
Open: Lunch Mon–Fri 11:30am–2:30pm; dinner Mon–Thurs 5:30–10:30pm, Fri–Sat 5–11pm, Sun 5–10pm; brunch Sat 11:30am–2:30pm; Sun 11:30am–3pm.

One of Mizner Park's best restaurants, Max's is Boca's quintessential contemporary Florida restaurant. Most everything on the menu is prepared with fresh, local ingredients, including meatloaf in a wild-mushroom/cabernet sauce and grilled salmon with leek-cucumber glaze and tricolor spätzle. Lunch items include spinach salad with mushrooms, pistachio–goat cheese torta, and grilled yellowfin tuna steak.

Wrapped with enormous plate-glass windows that look out onto Mizner Park, the high-ceilinged dining room features black booths and tables with dark-wood accents and a large, open kitchen that welcomes the gaze of diners. Outdoor dining is also available on black tables with white plastic patio chairs.

INEXPENSIVE

BANANA BOAT RESTAURANT, 739 E. Ocean Ave., Boynton Beach. Tel. 732-9400.

Cuisine: SEAFOOD/AMERICAN. **Reservations:** Not required.
$ Prices: Appetizers $2–$7; main courses $11–$20; lunch $4–$11; weekend brunch $5–$7. AE, MC, V.
Open: Mon–Fri 11am–2am, Sat–Sun 9am–2am.

Skimpily clad waitresses serve lunch and dinner to frat boys and others in Mediterranean-style dining rooms. It's actually pretty nice both indoors and outside on a wooden patio that overlooks the Intracoastal Waterway. There's often a live band; if not, dance disks are spinning. The location, drinks, and entertainment are good; few people come here just for the food. In addition to a raw bar, chicken Caesar salads, fried fish, and a variety of sandwiches are always for sale. Hot dinner dishes include fresh fish, shrimp, and terriyaki steak. They also serve weekend brunch with omelets and waffles.

LUNCH ONLY

WOLLEY'S, 25 Royal Palm Plaza, Boca Raton. Tel. 392-2977.

Cuisine: AMERICAN. **Reservations:** Not accepted.
$ Prices: Main courses $3–$6. No credit cards.
Open: Mon–Sat 9am–6pm, Sun 11am–4pm.

This tiny café, rather sterile in atmosphere, but a good place to stop for a quick bite, serves well-prepared sandwiches and salads made fresh in their adjacent gourmet-food store. The eatery's little outdoor tables topped with large umbrellas are a pleasant place to sit. Try the frozen yogurt special: a whole baked apple topped with sliced bananas, frozen yogurt, and nuts; or perhaps toasted waffles topped with yogurt and fresh fruit.

SHOPPING

Mizner Park, on Federal Highway in Boca Raton (tel. 362-0606), is the area's most celebrated shopping arcade. There are just a handful of specialty shops here, nestled next to a few good restaurants. Each shopfront faces a grassy island with blue and green gazebos, potted plants, and garden benches. It's extremely popular with strollers who continue to stream in until late in the evening. The park entrance is between Palmetto Park Road and Glades Road.

Royal Palm Plaza, Federal Highway (U.S. 1), between Palmetto Park Road and Camino Real (tel. 395-1222), is another quaint Boca shopping center. Called the "Pink Plaza" for its distinctive architecture, Royal Palm features two-story buildings with terra-cotta roofs, central fountains, white stone benches, and large banyan trees. Specialty stores, boutiques, restaurants, and the Royal Palm Dinner Theater make this a popular place to shop.

A large number of antiques shops are clustered together on **Atlantic Avenue** in downtown Delray Beach. Most of the stores here are open Monday through Wednesday and on Friday and Saturday from 10am to 5pm, plus Thursday from 10am to 9pm. You can pick up the "Delray Beach Antique Shop Guide" at almost any of the stores on the street.

EVENING ENTERTAINMENT

THE PERFORMING ARTS

BOCA RATON SYMPHONIC POPS, 100 NE First Ave., Boca Raton. Tel. 393-7677.

This 85-member orchestra plays jazz, swing, pop, and classical music, often with well-known guest stars. During the winter months the Pops plays at Florida Atlantic University; in the summer, at the Boca Raton Hotel. Call for an events schedule.
Admission: Tickets, $10–$35.

CALDWELL THEATRE COMPANY, 7873 N. Federal Hwy., Boca Raton. Tel. 832-2989 or 241-7380.

The resident company of this 305-seat theater presents professional-quality contemporary and classical plays, comedy, and musicals. There are usually four different productions staged between September and May, and one running through July and August.
Admission: Tickets, $20–$25.

DELRAY BEACH PLAYHOUSE, 950 NW 9th St., Delray Beach. Tel. 272-1281.

Plays and musicals performed by local amateurs are sometimes really quite good. There are usually six different productions in winter and one in the summer, often in July. Call to see what's on.
Admission: Tickets, $13–$19.

LITTLE PALM THEATER, 137 SE 1st St., Boca Raton. Tel. 394-0206.

Now in its 17th year, this popular children's theater performs every Saturday morning at 9:15am at the Royal Palm Dinner Theater (see below). Classic children's stories and fairy tales are the usual fare. Casts are composed of volunteer actors, both children and adults. Every six weeks the Little Palm takes its production to Boynton Beach at 128 E. Ocean Ave. Call for details. The box office is open only on Saturday from 8:30 to 9:15am.
Admission: $6 general admission.

ROYAL PALM DINNER THEATER, 303 Mizner Blvd., Boca Raton. Tel. 392-3755.

Hit Broadway musicals and comedies are the main fare at this shoebox-size dinner theater in Boca Raton. Music concerts are sometimes performed here as well. Phone for prices and showtimes. The box office is open on Sunday and Monday from 10am to 5pm, and Tuesday through Saturday from 10am to 7pm.

THE CLUB & MUSIC SCENE

BOSTON'S ON THE BEACH, 40 S. Fla. A1A, Delray Beach. Tel. 278-3364.

One of the first places in the area to give reggae bands a stage, Boston's is still one of the best, especially on Monday nights when it gets quite crowded. It's not always

Caribbean music, however, and the club's popularity on any given day depends on who's playing. Boston's is also a good choice for happy hour, Monday through Friday from 4 to 7pm. It's open Monday through Saturday from 6:30am to 1am and on Sunday from 6:30am to midnight.

CLUB BOCA, 7000 W. Palmetto Rd., Boca Raton. Tel. 368-3333.
Because it's a little far from the beach, Club Boca is relatively devoid of tourists, but extremely popular with those in-the-know. The club is huge, and features live music six nights a week. Food is available. It's open Monday to Thursday from 9pm to 3am and on Friday and Saturday from 10pm to 4am.
Admission: $5.

DIRTY MOE'S, 395 NE Spanish River Blvd., Boca Raton. Tel. 395-3513.
Big and casual, Moe's has been around for a while—and looks like it. There's a long wooden bar in each of two large rectangular rooms. One has a small elevated stage where bands usually perform Wednesday through Sunday. Glossy, wooden pizza-parlor tables are filled with beer drinkers who also hang around the bar's pool tables. The second room is quieter, and food is served. Open Sunday through Tuesday from 11:30am to midnight and Wednesday through Saturday from 11:30am to 2am.
Admission: $3–$5 when bands play.

---

4. FORT LAUDERDALE & ENVIRONS
10 miles N of Miami

GETTING THERE By Plane The **Fort Lauderdale/Hollywood International Airport** (tel. 305/357-6100) is small, extremely user-friendly, and located just 15 minutes from downtown. Major domestic carriers servicing the airport include American (tel. toll free 800/433-7300), Continental (tel. 407/832-5200, or toll free 800/525-0280), Delta (tel. 407/655-5300, or toll free 800/221-1212), Northwest (tel. toll free 800/225-2525), and United (tel. toll free 800/241-6522).

By Train Amtrak (tel. toll free 800/USA-RAIL) trains departing from New York do not stop in Fort Lauderdale. Passengers de-train in West Palm Beach, 201 S. Tamarind Ave. (tel. 407/832-6169), or in Miami.

By Bus Greyhound can get you to Fort Lauderdale from almost anywhere in the country. The company no longer operates a single nationwide telephone number, so consult your local directory for the office nearest you.

By Car If you're driving up or down the Florida coast, you'll probably reach Fort Lauderdale on I-95, a highway that runs all the way from Maine to Miami. Visitors on their way to or from Orlando should take the Florida Turnpike, a toll road that runs from just north of Fort Lauderdale to Walt Disney World.

ESSENTIALS The **telephone area code** is 305.
The **Greater Fort Lauderdale Convention & Visitors Bureau,** 200 E. Las Olas Blvd., Suite 1500, Fort Lauderdale, FL 33301 (tel. 305/765-4466), distributes an excellent visitors guide with information on events and sightseeing in Broward County.

Fort Lauderdale Beach, a two-mile strip along Fla. A1A, gained fame in the 1950s as a spring break playground for partying college students. Not amused, the city's elders have long since ushered the mayhem elsewhere, and continue to work hard to bolster the town's image among other, more respectable (and presumably, richer) visitors. Self-promoted as "The Venice of America," for its 300 miles of navigable waterways, Fort Lauderdale is riddled with artificial canals that permit thousands of residents to anchor boats in their backyards. Boating is not just a hobby in Fort Lauderdale, it's a lifestyle—and the reason many residents have chosen to live here.

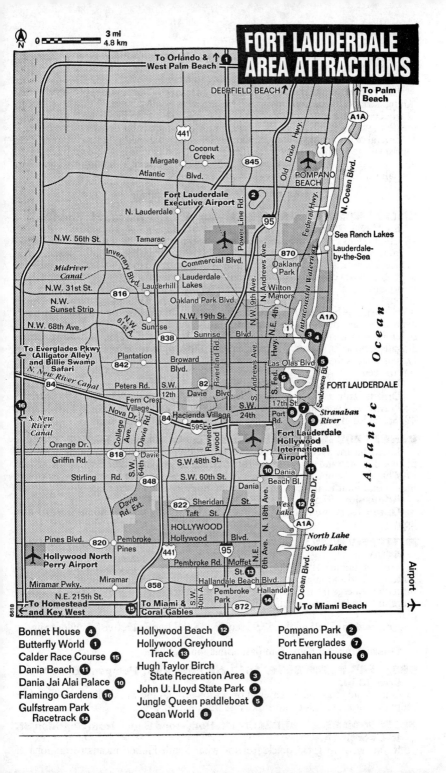

FORT LAUDERDALE AREA ATTRACTIONS

Bonnet House **4**
Butterfly World **1**
Calder Race Course **15**
Dania Beach **11**
Dania Jai Alai Palace **10**
Flamingo Gardens **16**
Gulfstream Park Racetrack **14**

Hollywood Beach **12**
Hollywood Greyhound Track **13**
Hugh Taylor Birch State Recreation Area **3**
John U. Lloyd State Park **9**
Jungle Queen paddleboat **5**
Ocean World **8**

Pompano Park **2**
Port Everglades **7**
Stranahan House **6**

Mega-yachts, unique to South Florida (and Monaco), are built here by Broward Marine, and the organizers of the Whitbread Round the World Race chose Fort Lauderdale as the April stop in their 1994 challenge.

Hollywood, founded in the 1920s as the "dream city" of developer Joseph Wesley Young, attracts an interesting mix of Montrealers and Manhattanites who speak in Québécois and New Yorkese. The city's three-mile paved beach Broadwalk is its greatest asset, and the strip around which most of the action occurs.

Several of the listings below are actually in Lauderdale-by-the-Sea, a charming little tourist village just north of Fort Lauderdale. Centered around an 876-foot fishing pier, and fronting a long strip of white sand, the hamlet has several hotels and restaurants in a small six-block area that's largely devoid of traffic.

WHAT TO SEE & DO

BILLIE SWAMP SAFARI, HC-61, Box 46, Clewiston, FL 33440. Tel. 813/983-6102, or toll free 800/949-6101.

Chief James E. Billie opened his Seminole Indian Reservation to visitors in March 1993. It was developed not as a tourist trap but as a place where people can learn how Native Americans live. Alligator wrestling is demonstrated to show how the Seminoles kept gators alive—and hence, fresh—during their ancient three-day hunts. An informative snake show features live poisonous snakes, and a short airboat ride through the swamps takes visitors through the sawgrass that has long been a Seminole home area. The best feature of this new attraction is the 90-minute Jeep safari through cypress domes, deep-swamp wetlands, and virgin hammocks. There are about 20 different animal species, and guides point out tracks of the Florida panther, bears, alligators, bobcats, snakes, whitetailed deer, wild hog, tortoises, and more. Surprisingly, nighttime is the best time to tour this area—that's when most of the animals come out to feed.

Admission: Jeep safari, $30; airboat rides, $15.

Open: Daily 9am–9pm. **Directions:** From Fort Lauderdale, take I-95 south to I-595 west, and continue west on I-75 to Alligator Alley (Fla. 84); exit at Mile Marker 49, Snake Road (look for the signs), turn right, and follow the signs.

BONNET HOUSE, 900 N. Birch Rd., Fort Lauderdale. Tel. 563-5393.

Listed on the National Register of Historic Places, Bonnet House is a 35-acre plantation home and estate dating from the turn of the century. Located in the middle of a highly developed beach area, the house is still occupied by a member of the family that built it. It's open to the public by reservation only.

Admission: $7.50 adults, $5 seniors and students.

Open: Tours given May–Nov, Tues–Fri at 10am, 11am, and noon, Sun at 1 and 2pm.

BUTTERFLY WORLD, 3600 W. Sample Rd., Coconut Creek. Tel. 977-4400.

Truly a unique sightseeing destination, Butterfly World houses thousands of butterflies and moths in and around a screened aviary. Visitors can actually watch butterflies emerge from their cocoons, and see dozens of exotic live varieties. Dozens more are mounted in an adjacent museum. The gift shop sells butterfly-attracting plants.

Admission: $8.95 adults, $7.95 seniors, $5 children 3–12, free for children under 3.

Open: Mon–Sat 9am–5pm (last admission at 4pm).

GOODYEAR BLIMP BASE, 1500 NE Fifth Ave., Pompano Beach. Tel. 946-8300.

One of only four blimp bases in operation around the world, this one offers free tours to visitors. Call for tour times and information.

HOLLYWOOD BEACH BROADWALK, Hollywood Beach from Sheridan St. to Georgia St.

If you want to get a quick feel for what South Florida means to millions of retirement-age "snowbirds," be sure to visit this lengthy paved beach path. Three miles long and 27 feet wide, the sandside Broadwalk is packed with French Canadians and others who take daily ritualistic strolls past the path's gift shops, cafés, and restaurants. Part of the pavement is dedicated to bicyclers who loudly proclaim their rights to wayward walkers.

HUGH TAYLOR BIRCH STATE RECREATION AREA, 3109 E. Sunrise Blvd., Fort Lauderdale. Tel. 546-4521.

Located between busy Fla. A1A and the Intracoastal Waterway just off Sunrise Boulevard, this pristine park was once the private home of Hugh Taylor Birch, a Chicago attorney who purchased the land in 1893. Birch donated his estate for use as a public park, preserving it from the growing development of the surrounding area. Today you can rent canoes and paddle your way through the park's freshwater lagoon, or take a self-guided walk on a nature trail that leads through a tropical hardwood forest of medicinal plants. The park's varied wildlife includes hawks, ducks, turtles, raccoons, gray squirrels, rabbits, opossums, and a variety of nonpoisonous snakes. Shaded picnic areas, playgrounds, and barbecue grills are also located throughout the park.

Admission: $1 per pedestrian, $3.60 per car (for up to eight people).
Open: Daily 8am–sundown.

INTERNATIONAL SWIMMING HALL OF FAME, 1 Hall of Fame Dr., Fort Lauderdale. Tel. 462-6536.

This huge, two-story ode to aquatics is the world's largest repository of swimming memorabilia, and includes films, books, interactive video displays, and seemingly endless archives relating to aquatic sports. A plethora of Olympic memorabilia from over 100 countries includes gold medals won by some of the sport's brightest stars. Home to the 1992 U.S. Olympic Diving Team, as well as a training facility for swimmers, the complex also houses two Olympic-size swimming pools.

Admission: $3 adults, $2 students and seniors.
Open: Daily 9am–7pm.

MUSEUM OF DISCOVERY & SCIENCE, 401 SW 2nd St., Fort Lauderdale. Tel. 467-MODS.

Opened in 1991, this $32-million museum houses seven interactive exhibit areas on two floors. "Florida EcoScapes" is an "ecology mountain" comprising numerous aquaria, terraria, and simulated habitats demonstrating the diversity of nature. "KidScience," with its musical staircase and colorful carpeted maze, appeals to the natural curiosity of kids 3 to 5. "Space Base" teaches about the development of technology leading to flight and the exploration of space; "Choose Health" uses interactive exhibits to focus on wellness and nutrition issues; "Sound" teaches about auditory physical properties, as well as its reception and storage; and "No Place Like Home" uses a huge cutaway model of a house to increase consumer awareness about the environmental effects of everyday living. The traveling exhibit hall features changing exhibits from all over the country.

The museum also contains the only IMAX theater in Florida. Its five-story-high screen with state-of-the-art sound shows specially produced short films about humans and nature. Stop by the museum's new café, serving sandwiches and drinks.

Admission: Museum, $6 adults, $5 children 3–12 and seniors 65 and older, free for children under 3; IMAX theater, $5 adults, $4 children 3–12 and seniors 65 and older, free for children under 3; combination ticket, $8 adults, $7 children 3–12 and seniors 65 and older, free for children under 3.
Open: Mon–Fri 10am–5pm, Sat 10am–8:30pm, Sun noon–5pm.

PARKS & BEACHES

Not all beaches are created equal—they offer different facilities and attract different crowds. Here's a run-down on the county's best from south to north:

Hallandale Beaches attract the retirement-aged folks who live in the condominiums that surround them. Close to Gulfstream and Hallandale Racetracks, the beaches here are less crowded after post time.

Hollywood Beach is really special, primarily because of its three-mile-long Broadwalk. Sometimes described as "Venice Beach without the weirdos," Hollywood is packed with French-Canadian vacationers who attend senior-citizen dances and shows at the beach's Theater Under the Stars.

North Beach State Park is known for its Sea Turtle Hatchery, which helps migrating turtles when they come ashore each November. There are no lights on this beach during hatching season so as not to confuse the turtles.

Dania's beaches have the best waves in the county, and are popular with surfers. **John Lloyd State Park** is best, as surf most everywhere else is usually flat.

The **Fort Lauderdale Beach Promenade** has undergone a $20-million renovation—and it looks marvelous. Once popular with spring-break revelers, this beach is backed by an endless row of hotels and is popular with tourists and locals alike.

Pompano Beach is famous for fishing and diving. A coral reef is located close to shore, and divers can walk right to the dive site. While Pompano is very family oriented, it also has an authentic fishermen's charm. You kind of feel as if you should be hanging a line and drinking a beer.

Lighthouse Point and Hillsboro Beach are the upscale, pretty parcels of millionaires. They're worth a look.

Finally, there's **Deerfield Beach,** dotted with boulders and coves. There is a well-paved walkway with beach showers and good facilities. The sands here are quieter than most, since the residential streets of Deerfield Beach are located east of busy Fla. A1A.

SPORTS & RECREATION

BASEBALL The **Fort Lauderdale Yankee Stadium,** 5301 NW 12th Ave. (tel. 776-1921), is the winter home of the New York Yankees and features major-league spring-training games during February and March. The Minor League Fort Lauderdale Yankees take over the stadium from April through August.

GREYHOUND RACING Greyhounds, the world's fastest dogs, reach speeds of more than 40 m.p.h. while chasing a fake rabbit around a track. As with the horses, bettors can wager to win, place, or show. There's racing year-round at the **Hollywood Greyhound Track,** 831 N. Federal Hwy., Hallandale (tel. 454-9400). Call for post times.

HORSE RACING The **Pompano Harness Track,** 1800 SW 3rd St., Pompano Beach (tel. 972-2000), Florida's only harness track, features racing and betting from October to early September.

There are lots of horse tracks in Florida, and while **Gulfstream Park,** 901 S. Federal Hwy. in Hallandale (tel. 454-7000), might not be the prettiest, it's one of the biggest and best-known thoroughbred tracks in the state.

JAI ALAI Jai alai, a Spanish cross between lacrosse and handball, is popular in South Florida. Players use woven baskets, called *cestas,* to hurl balls, called *pelotas,* at speeds that sometimes exceed 170 miles per hour. Spectators, who are protected behind a wall of glass, place bets on the evening's players. **Dania Jai-Alai,** 301 E. Dania Beach Blvd., Dania (tel. 428-7766), is one of the nicest frontons in the United States.

PARASAILING You've seen parasailers cruising over Fort Lauderdale's beaches, hanging from a parachute that's pulled by a boat. If this is your idea of fun, go to **Watersports Unlimited, Inc.,** 301 Seabreeze Blvd., Fort Lauderdale (tel. 467-1316). The cost is $30 to $50 per person, and reservations are essential. They're open daily from 9am to 5pm.

WATER SPORTS Located right on the Intracoastal Waterway, **Bill's Sunrise Watersports,** 2025 E. Sunrise Blvd., Fort Lauderdale (tel. 462-8962), has a wide variety of water-sports equipment. The year-round concession, open daily from 9am to 5:30pm, rents jet skis, waverunners, 13-foot cigarette boats, 18-foot powerboats, and 24-foot party boats. Waterskiing is available December through April. Phone for up-to-date rates.

ORGANIZED TOURS

Operated by *Jungle Queen Cruises,* Bahia Mar Yacht Center, Fla. A1A, Fort Lauderdale (tel. 462-5596), this Mississippi River–style steamer, one of Fort Lauderdale's oldest attractions, is a sightseeing attraction in its own right. It's a popular sight as it cruises up the New River. Each three-hour tour takes visitors past Millionaires' Row, Old Fort Lauderdale, the new downtown, and the Port Everglades cruise-ship port. Tours are given daily at 10am and 2pm, and cost $8 for adults and $5.45 for children.

Visitors can learn about historical and modern-day Fort Lauderdale aboard the cute "old-style" trolleys operated by **South Florida Trolley Tours** (tel. 768-0700). The charge is $10 for adults, $6 for children 6 to 12, and free for children under 6. The trolleys pick up passengers at most major hotels. Phone for tour times.

Water taxis serve the dual purpose of transportation and entertainment around this city of canals. **Water Taxi of Fort Lauderdale** (tel. 565-5507) operates service on demand, like a shared land taxi, carrying up to 48 passengers. Route maps are available from most area hotels. Service operates daily from 10am to midnight or 2am. The cost is $6 per person per trip, $14 for a full day.

WHERE TO STAY

VERY EXPENSIVE

MARRIOTT'S HARBOR BEACH RESORT, 3030 Holiday Dr., Fort Lauderdale, FL 33316. Tel. 305/525-4000, or toll free 800/222-6543. Fax 305/766-6165. 624 rms, 35 suites. A/C TV TEL

$ Rates: Dec 19–Jan 8, $249–$365 single or double. Jan 9–May 7, $249–$330 single or double. May 8–Dec 18, $189–$245 single or double. Year-round, from $500 suite. AE, CB, DC, DISC, MC, V.

Located on 16 oceanfront acres, this premier resort features luxurious accommodations that are every bit as good as the hotel's ideal location. Every spacious room opens onto a private balcony, the most expensive of which overlook the hotel's exclusive strip of beach. Lavish gardens surround several bubbling fountains and an oversize 8,000-square-foot swimming pool.

Dining/Entertainment: Sheffield's, a classy continental restaurant, requires both jackets and reservations (see "Where to Dine," below). Kinoko is less formal, and serves Japanese hibachi-style dinners that are prepared at your table. The Oceanview, Sea Breeze Grill, and Cascades are three other casual restaurants serving breakfast, lunch, dinner, and late-night drinks.

Services: 24-hour room service, concierge, complimentary golf at off-premises club, massage, babysitting.

Facilities: Swimming pool, five clay tennis courts, beach cabañas, whirlpool, sauna, exercise room, water-sports rentals.

EXPENSIVE

LAGO MAR RESORT AND CLUB, 1700 S. Ocean Lane, Fort Lauderdale, FL 33316. Tel. 305/523-6511, or toll free 800/255-5246. Fax 305/523-6511. 44 rms, 132 suites. A/C TV TEL **Directions:** From Federal Highway (U.S. 1), turn east onto the SE 17th St. Causeway, then right onto Mayan Drive; turn right again onto South Ocean Drive, left onto Grace Drive, and left again onto South Ocean Lane to the hotel.

$ Rates: Dec 15–Apr, $155–$180 single or double; from $245 suite. May–Oct 25, $85–$95 single or double; from $120 suite. Oct 26–Dec 14, $100–$115 single or double; from $145 suite. AE, CB, DC, MC, V.

Lago Mar, Spanish for "lake to ocean," occupies its own little island between Lake Mayan and the Atlantic. The resort offers oversize rooms that are sparsely decorated with eclectic furnishings and textured wallpaper with pastel accents. In addition to balconies, all suites are equipped with either a full kitchen, or a microwave and a refrigerator. Newly remodeled executive suites are smarter and more modern than other rooms.

Dining/Entertainment: The Palm Garden Room serves three meals daily.

Reservations are required for dinner and there's live entertainment six nights a week. The Sea Grape Terrace, also serving from morning to night, is less formal, and has a wonderful outdoor patio sheltered by white, vined trellises. The Soda Shop and Ocean Grill are open for lunch and snacks, while the Lago Mar Bar and Lounge and the Promenade Bar are open late for cocktails.

Services: Room service, concierge, supervised children's programs during holiday periods.

Facilities: Two swimming pools, four tennis courts, miniature golf course, volleyball courts, shuffleboard, children's playground, water-sports rentals, games room, fitness center, apparel shops.

PIER 66 HOTEL AND MARINA, 2301 SE 17th St. Causeway, Fort Lauderdale, FL 33316. Tel. 305/525-6666, or toll free 800/327-3796, 800/432-1956 in Florida. Fax 305/728-3541. 384 rms, 8 suites. A/C MINIBAR TV TEL

$ Rates: Dec 16–Apr 15, $159–$279 single or double; from $650 suite. Apr 16–May and Oct–Dec 15, $129–$249 single or double; from $620 suite. June–Sept, $109–$209 single or double; from $590 suite. Additional person $15 extra. AE, DC, DISC, MC, V.

A Fort Lauderdale landmark since 1954, the Pier 66 Resort and Marina recently received a much-needed face-lift. The resort's new entrance is impressive—an atrium-style lobby, complete with high ceilings over beige marble floors. Floor-to-ceiling windows are positioned to get the most out of the 22-acre property, where walkways lead through lush, tropical gardens and two swimming-pool waterfalls.

While leisure travelers might be disappointed by this resort's emphasis on groups and business travelers, for services and amenities Pier 66 is hard to beat. Accommodations are roomy, with either a king-size bed or two double beds, and spacious walk-in closets. Baths are also large, and are outfitted with a nice amenities package, phone, and hairdryer. All rooms also come with balconies, clock radios, voicemail messaging, and access to over 100 movies.

The resort's spa, aptly called Spa 66, offers massages, facials, and other pampering services. There is a large fitness center with Stairmasters, Lifecycles, treadmills, Nautilus equipment, and free weights.

Dining/Entertainment: Six restaurants and lounges are located on the property. The Mariner's Grill, located in the lobby, serves breakfast, lunch, and dinner. Cafe 66 is the resort's best waterfront restaurant. The Pelican Lounge serves free cocktails, and the Pier Top Lounge, located on the top floor of the tower, is open daily for drinks and revolves 360° every 90 minutes.

Services: 24-hour room service, concierge, business center, free beach shuttle, overnight laundry and dry cleaning.

Facilities: Two lighted tennis courts, two swimming pools, boat rentals, 40-person whirlpool, 142-slip marina, full-service salon, resort store, spa.

MODERATE

BANYAN MARINA APARTMENTS, 111 Isle of Venice, Fort Lauderdale, FL 33301. Tel. 305/524-4430. Fax 305/764-4870. 10 apts. A/C TV TEL

$ Rates: Dec–Apr, from $120 apt. May–Nov, from $75 apt. Weekly and monthly rates available. MC, V.

Peter and Dagmar Neufeldt's Banyan Marina Apartments represents one of the best accommodation values in South Florida. Wrapped around a 75-year-old banyan tree, this well-maintained two-story inn is located directly on an active waterway, halfway between Fort Lauderdale's downtown and the beach. The accommodations—one-and two-bedroom apartments—are all decorated differently. Some have modern art deco accents, some are outfitted with blond woods, and others have more contemporary ivory laminates and brass highlights. Livability is the key here. There's a small pool just off the center courtyard, and boat dockage for eight yachts.

LAUDERDALE COLONIAL, 3049 Harbor Dr., Fort Lauderdale, FL 33316.

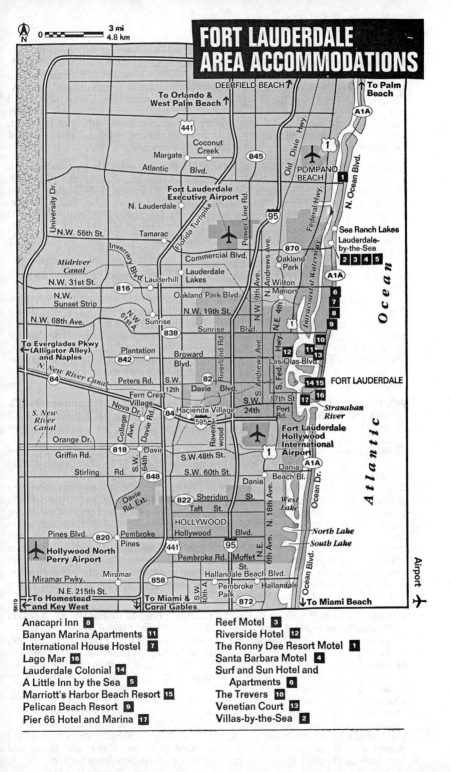

FORT LAUDERDALE AREA ACCOMMODATIONS

Anacapri Inn **8**
Banyan Marina Apartments **11**
International House Hostel **7**
Lago Mar **16**
Lauderdale Colonial **14**
A Little Inn by the Sea **5**
Marriott's Harbor Beach Resort **15**
Pelican Beach Resort **9**
Pier 66 Hotel and Marina **17**

Reef Motel **3**
Riverside Hotel **12**
The Ronny Dee Resort Motel **1**
Santa Barbara Motel **4**
Surf and Sun Hotel and Apartments **6**
The Trevers **10**
Venetian Court **13**
Villas-by-the-Sea **2**

Tel. 305/525-3676. Fax 305/463-3787. 12 rms, 8 suites. A/C TV TEL
$ Rates: Dec 15–Apr, $90–$100 single or double; from $105 suite. May–Dec 14, $53–$64 single or double; from $75 suite. Additional person $15 extra. MC, V.

Listed here for its good Intracoastal waterfront location and above-average quality, this affordable motel is relatively straightforward, offering basic rooms, suites, and efficiencies surrounding a central courtyard. Although every room in this compact black-and-white motel is different, all are simply decorated with light furniture, wall-to-wall carpeting, refrigerators, and tea/coffee-making facilities. There's a heated swimming pool, barbecue area, and laundry facilities for guest use.

A LITTLE INN BY THE SEA, 4546 El Mar Dr., Lauderdale-by-the-Sea, FL 33308. Tel. 305/772-2450. Fax 305/938-9354. 30 rms, 7 suites. A/C TV TEL
$ Rates (including continental breakfast): Dec 18–Apr 13, $79–$125 single or double; from $129 suite. Apr 14–Sept, $39–$89 single or double; from $89 suite. Oct–Dec 17, $49–$89 single or double; from $99 suite. Additional person $10 extra. AE, DC, MC, V.

Co-owned by a Broadway set designer, A Little Inn by the Sea is meticulously designed both inside and out. You enter the inn via glass doors which open into a central courtyard containing a trickling fountain, soft classical music, café tables, and lots of plants. It's not hard to imagine that you're on a tropical island as you walk through the courtyard or past the pool that sits directly on the beach.

Rooms are equally well dressed, with complimentary wall and furniture coverings. Many come with small kitchenettes that are well stocked with cooking and dining necessities. Some rooms include a romantic mesh canopy over the bed, and sofas in a tasteful sitting area. Additional pluses are large closets and tiled baths. A continental breakfast is served in the courtyard, and consists of coffee or tea, fresh fruits and juice, and muffins or pastries. A Little Inn by the Sea is recommendable for those who can do without the all-night services of a hotel, and don't wish to pay for a plethora of resort-style activities.

PELICAN BEACH RESORT, 2000 N. Atlantic Blvd., Fort Lauderdale, FL 33305. Tel. 305/568-9431, or toll free 800/525-6232. Fax 305/565-2622. 47 rms, 12 suites. A/C TV TEL **Directions:** From Fla. A1A, turn east onto Atlantic Boulevard, just north of Sunrise Boulevard.
$ Rates: Dec 16–Apr, $95–$115 single or double; $115–$135 efficiency; from $145 suite. May–Dec 15, $60–$70 single or double; $70–$85 efficiency; from $90 suite. Additional person $10 extra. AE, CB, DC, DISC, MC, V.

The sprawling, family-owned and -operated Pelican Beach Resort encompasses seven dissimilar buildings, each of which possesses distinctive style and charm. Guest rooms, which are connected to one another by wooden decks and tropical walkways, are cleanly decorated with tile floors, pastel-colored walls, and vertical blinds. Suites are truly special, as they come with spa bathtubs, huge standing showers, and even binoculars. Efficiencies are equipped with small kitchens outfitted with dishes, coffee makers, and refrigerators. Although it's located directly on the beach, the hotel also offers a particularly striking swimming pool that glows by night with fiber-optic light.

A large, complimentary breakfast, served each morning from 7 to 10am, makes this hotel a particularly good value.

RIVERSIDE HOTEL, 620 E. Las Olas Blvd., Fort Lauderdale, FL 33301. Tel. 305/467-0671, or toll free 800/325-3280. Fax 305/462-2148. 110 rms, 7 suites. A/C TV TEL **Directions:** From I-95, exit east onto Broward Boulevard, turn right onto Federal Highway (U.S. 1), and then go left onto Las Olas Boulevard.
$ Rates: Dec 23–Apr 15, $95–$145 single or double; from $175 suite. Apr 16–Dec 22, $70–$99 single or double; from $125 suite. Additional person $10–$15 extra. AE, CB, DC, MC, V.

One of the oldest hotels in South Florida, the 1936 Riverside is packed with prewar charm. Located on Fort Lauderdale's main street, sandwiched between contemporary restaurants and shops, the hotel is a welcome celebration of a bygone era. A lobby containing wicker furnishings, paddle fans, and a fireplace that crackles even on the hottest days leads into nicely decorated guest rooms with oak furnishings and intricately tiled baths. There is a concierge and evening turn-down service.

VILLAS-BY-THE-SEA, 4456 El Mar Dr., Lauderdale-by-the-Sea, FL 33308. Tel. 305/772-3550, or toll free 800/247-8963. Fax 305/772-3835. 148 rms. A/C TV TEL

$ Rates: Feb–Apr 11, $100–$130 single or double; from $145 apt. Apr 12–Dec 19, $65–$85 single or double; from $95 apt. Dec 20–Jan, $85–$115 single or double; from $130 apt. Weekly and monthly rates available. AE, CB, DC, MC, V.

Hotel rooms, efficiencies, and apartments are located in six different buildings clustered on a single block of this charming northern Fort Lauderdale village. Every room has been recently redecorated with light contemporary furniture, ceramic tile floors, and modern amenities. Each well-maintained pastel-colored building has its own small, tropical courtyard containing a swimming pool or sunbathing facilities.

There are five heated swimming pools on the grounds as well as a Jacuzzi, barbecue grills, tennis courts, a beach bar, a restaurant, and an outdoor fitness area. The hotel is justifiably popular with international tourists, many of whom stay here for months at a time.

INEXPENSIVE

ANACAPRI INN, 1901 N. Federal Hwy. (U.S. 1), Fort Lauderdale, FL 33305. Tel. 305/563-1111. Fax 305/568-3304. 120 rms. A/C TV TEL

$ Rates: Dec 15–Jan and Apr, $59 single or double. Feb–Mar, $64 single or double. May–Nov, $49 single or double. Additional person $10 extra. AE, MC, V.

Inside the large pink buildings that comprise the Anacapri are 10 dozen pleasant enough simply decorated rooms that are reliably comfortable and clean. Although the accommodations here won't win any awards for style, they are well located, within five minutes of most of the city's major attractions. There's a swimming pool and a café/bar offering happy-hour specials on weekdays and live jazz on weekends.

RONNY DEE RESORT MOTEL, 717 S. Ocean Blvd., Pompano Beach, FL 33062. Tel. 305/943-3020. 35 rms. A/C TV

$ Rates: Dec 16–Jan 7, $47–$55 single or double; from $65 apt. Jan 8–31 and Apr 1–15, $43–$50 single or double; from $60 apt. Feb–Mar, $56–$65 single or double; from $75 apt. Apr 16–Dec 15, $29–$32 single or double; from $37 apt. Additional person $6 extra. MC, V.

The bad news is that this family-owned motel is located on busy Fla. A1A; the good news is that it's just 100 yards from the beach, and amazingly inexpensive. Popular with European guests, this two-story yellow motel, wrapped around a central swimming pool, is outfitted with suburban-style wood-paneled guest rooms that are filled with an eclectic mix of furniture and small refrigerators. There are no in-room telephones; payphones are located in a public area, near a large games room that contains a pool table, a VCR, books, and assorted games. Ping-Pong and shuffleboard are also available.

Complimentary coffee and doughnuts are served each morning in the motel lobby.

SANTA BARBARA MOTEL, 4301 El Mar Dr., Lauderdale-by-the-Sea, FL 33308. Tel. 305/491-5211, 305/566-1164 at night. 13 rms. A/C TV

$ Rates: Dec 18–Jan 20, $42–$66 single or double; from $76 apt. Jan 21–Apr 10, $42–$75 single or double; from $88 apt. Apr 11–May 1, $38–$53 single or double; from $65 apt. May 2–Nov 1, $34–$38 single or double; from $46 apt. Nov 2–Dec 17, $36–$46 single or double; from $55 apt. CB, DC, MC, V.

One of the best values in Lauderdale-by-the-Sea, this small two-story motel offers little more than clean, basic, spacious, homey rooms, a small swimming pool, and cordial proprietors Bev and Gil Wilson.

SURF AND SUN HOTEL AND APARTMENTS, 521 N. Atlantic Blvd., Fort Lauderdale, FL 33304. Tel. 305/564-4341, or toll free 800/248-0463. Fax 305/522-5174. 23 rms. A/C TV TEL

$ Rates: Dec 21–Jan, $53 single or double; $66 efficiency; from $86 apt. Feb–Apr 19, $59 single or double; $74 efficiency; from $93 apt. Apr 20–Dec 20, $36 single or double; $42 efficiency; from $53 apt. Additional person $6 extra. AE, DISC, MC, V.

Nobody stays here to lounge in the rooms, which tend to be a bit dark and musty. But you can't beat the location—directly across from Fort Lauderdale's new $20-million beach promenade and within walking distance of several restaurants, bars, and shops. Accommodations are almost austere, though rooms do contain refrigerators. There's a small courtyard with wooden lounges for sunbathing.

THE TREVERS, 552 N. Birch Rd., Fort Lauderdale, FL 33304. Tel. 305/564-9601, or toll free 800/533-4744. Fax 305/564-5618. 14 rms. A/C TV TEL

$ Rates: Apr 16–Dec 17, $36–$52 single or double. Dec 18–Jan 1 and Jan 30–Apr 15, $67–$88 single or double. Jan 2–29, $50–$73 single or double. Additional person $11 extra. AE, DC, DISC, MC, V.

The most outstanding feature of the Trevers is its location, just half a block from the Fort Lauderdale beach and the newly renovated beachside shopping strip. Behind the hotel's bright pink-and-white exterior are just over a dozen rather basic musty rooms outfitted with mismatched furniture. All come with refrigerators and microwave ovens. Bathrooms are predictably small, and are equipped only with soap and towels. Additional persons sharing a room cost $11, while dogs are $25 additional.

VENETIAN COURT, 71 Isle of Venice, Fort Lauderdale, FL 33301. Tel. 305/525-8444, or toll free 800/780-0987. Fax 305/524-2520. 16 rms, 6 suites. A/C TV TEL

$ Rates: May–Dec 15, $35–$45 single or double; $70 two-bedroom suite. Dec 16–Jan 15, $55–$75 single or double; $120 two-bedroom suite. Jan 16–Apr, $60–$81 single or double; $126 two-bedroom suite. DC, MC, V.

Fort Lauderdale's maze of canals is one of the most attractive features of this South Florida city. Venetian Court, positioned canalfront on Isle of Venice, takes full advantage of its somewhat hidden location, offering magnificent views of yachts and area mansions. The hotel itself wraps around a small swimming pool and barbecue area. Inside, contemporary furnishings offer a pleasant surprise, as do spacious walk-in closets, nice pluses in a moderately priced hotel. Studios have refrigerators and microwave ovens, and all other accommodations have full kitchens. There's a boat dock and laundry facilities on the property.

BUDGET

INTERNATIONAL HOUSE HOSTEL, 3811 N. Ocean Blvd., Fort Lauderdale, FL 33308. Tel. 305/568-1615. 84 beds.

$ Rates: $15 per person.

Bare-bones budgeteers will appreciate this motel-style hostel, where international guests in their 20s share rooms by the half dozen. There are bunk beds and televisions in most rooms, and some come with kitchenettes. Private rooms are available for traveling couples. There's beach access across the street, a large swimming pool, and laundry facilities. Look for the colorful flags of the world flying outside the motel.

WHERE TO DINE

EXPENSIVE

CAFE ARUGULA, 3110 N. Federal Hwy., Lighthouse Point. Tel. 785-7732.

Cuisine: AMERICAN. **Reservations:** Recommended.

$ Prices: Appetizers $6–$8; main courses $15–$29. AE, DC, DISC, MC, V.

Open: Dinner only, Sun–Thurs 5:30–10pm, Fri–Sat 5:30–10:30pm.

Celebrity restaurateur Dick Cingolani was one of the first to bring imaginative American "Cuisine" to Fort Lauderdale. Today, the Café Arugula remains one of the city's most celebrated restaurants. Amid comfortable surroundings which include soft lighting, plush furnishings, and properly distanced tables, both the kitchen and the dining room are clearly influenced by international trends that include the best of the Caribbean, California, and the Mediterranean. Mussels are wrapped with Cajun smoked ham, escargots mixed with chorizo (Mexican sausage), and red snapper is drenched with cilantro-lime butter and rolled in ground pecans. Desserts are equally interesting and inviting, and include such specialties as raspberry crème brûlée and bitter Mexican chocolate torte.

CHARLEY'S CRAB, 3000 NE 32nd Ave., Fort Lauderdale. Tel. 561-4800.
   Cuisine: SEAFOOD. **Reservations:** Recommended.
$ Prices: Appetizers $5–$8; main courses $15–$22. AE, DC, DISC, MC, V.
   Open: Sun–Thurs 11:30am–10pm, Fri–Sat 11:30am–11pm.
The Fort Lauderdale outpost of this popular, upscale South Florida seafood chain is every bit as good—and almost as expensive—as its more celebrated Palm Beach sibling.
   All the usual fish are served here—salmon, pompano, dolphin (fish)—as are baked clams, oysters Rockefeller, and mini crab cakes. Steak, lamb, and chicken dishes are also available. Main courses are accompanied by different side dishes each evening, and if parmesan roasted potatoes is on the day's menu, order it. The restaurant also features a good raw bar with a variety of shellfish, and a well-selected wine list with picks from California and around the world.

DOWN UNDER, 3000 E. Oakland Park Blvd., Fort Lauderdale. Tel. 564-6984.
   Cuisine: CONTINENTAL. **Reservations:** Recommended.
$ Prices: Appetizers $5–$8; main courses $15–$22. DC, DISC, MC, V.
   Open: Lunch daily 11:30am–2pm; dinner daily 6–10pm.
There's nothing Australian about this superior, elegant riverside bistro that's named for its location—below an overpass that crosses the Intracoastal Waterway. Decorated with antiques, dark woods, and a jungle of hanging plants, the restaurant is much more appealing than its rather austere exterior would suggest.
   While meals here were once thought refreshingly novel, the restaurant's California/Louisiana cuisine is no longer considered to be on the culinary edge. Chicken and fish in light spicy sauces are best bets and, together with a slightly sentimental atmosphere, make the Down Under one of the city's most romantic restaurants.

SEA WATCH, 6002 N. Ocean Blvd., Fort Lauderdale. Tel. 781-2200.
   Cuisine: SEAFOOD/AMERICAN. **Reservations:** Recommended.
$ Prices: Appetizers $3–$7; main courses $12–$31; lunch $6–$10. AE, MC, V.
   Open: Lunch daily 11am–3:30pm; dinner daily 5:30–11pm.
Located a short drive north of downtown Fort Lauderdale, Sea Watch is a good bet on your way up or down the coast. The restaurant's nautical decor borders on being pirate-like—in a tropically, romantic sort of way. Is that a clear description? Guests walk on a creaky wood-plank floor on their way to the tables, which are situated on a covered patio and surrounded by tall swaying palms and a lush garden. Less adventurous mates sit inside, surrounded by stained-glass windows and dark paintings.
   Fresh seafood is prepared even more imaginatively than the restaurant's decor. Canadian sea scallops are grilled with red-pepper sauce, and crab cakes are served with avocado butter and a tangy smoked pepper sauce. The bounteous bouillabaisse—lobster, shrimp, scallops, clams, mussels, swordfish, and grouper in a garlic-saffron tomato broth—would win no awards in Paris, but would certainly turn some culinary heads. Other good choices include grilled chicken breast, roast prime rib, and beef tenderloin. Hamburgers and salads are also always offered, as is a decent wine list.

SHEFFIELD'S, in Marriott's Harbor Beach Resort, 3030 Holiday Dr., Fort Lauderdale. Tel. 525-4000.
   Cuisine: CONTINENTAL. **Reservations:** Recommended.
$ Prices: Appetizers $8–$9; main courses $20–$32. AE, DC, DISC, MC, V.
   Open: Dinner only, daily 5:30–10:30pm.
When you're ready to abandon South Florida's trendy light salads and rare braised fish, visit Sheffield's, a handsome, clubby, intimate restaurant inside an equally fancy

but decidedly more casual hotel. Four small dark-wood dining rooms are decorated with plush heavy furnishings, etched-glass dividers, and plenty of cozy nooks. The restaurant's celebrated English-manor-house comfort is augmented by a conservative and knowledgeable career service staff and heavy continental menu.

Appetizers like escargots with garlic butter and Camembert cheese, French forest morels with brandied-cream sauce, and chilled roast duck medallions with pinot noir and currant sauce are sure to raise cholesterol levels, but at these prices, who's noticing? The main dishes are just as divine, and include a classical beef Wellington, salmon with champagne beurre blanc, mesquite-grilled veal chops, Long Island duckling, and rack of lamb with mint-cabernet sauce. Desserts like chocolate pâté and Brie cheesecake don't disappoint either, but fitting it all in is another matter.

MODERATE

ARUBA BEACH CAFE, 1 Commercial Blvd., Lauderdale-by-the-Sea. Tel. 776-0001.
   Cuisine: SEAFOOD/AMERICAN. **Reservations:** Required for parties over 6.
$ **Prices:** Appetizers $3–$7; main courses $7–$15; lunch $3–$10. AE, DC, DISC, MC, V.
   Open: Daily 11am–11pm. (Bar, open until 1am).
Brightly colored wicker chairs, a lively bar, indoor/outdoor seating, and large plate-glass windows overlooking a particularly beautiful stretch of beach combine to make this contemporary restaurant one of Fort Lauderdale's most atmospheric. The ambience is as easy as the menu, which is replete with salads, sandwiches, and the requisite local seafood offerings. Two of the best lunchtime dishes are blackened fish and herb-roasted chicken with new potatoes. Oversize evening main courses include coconut-fried shrimp served with yogurt-lime dipping sauce, grilled Cuban steak served with pickled onions, and seafood fettuccine marinara with shrimp, scallops, and swordfish. Any time of day you'd be well advised to start with the smoked fish dip served with seasoned flat bread, or a selection from the fresh raw bar.

BURT & JACK'S, Berth 23, Port Everglades. Tel. 522-5225.
   Cuisine: AMERICAN. **Reservations:** Recommended.
$ **Prices:** Appetizers $7–$9; main courses $15–$29. AE, DC, DISC, MC, V.
   Open: Dinner only, Sun–Thurs 5–10pm, Fri–Sat 5–11:30pm.
Despite the fact that this restaurant is partly owned by actor Burt Reynolds, it's not a celebrity glamour spot filled with papparazzi and star seekers. Instead, Burt & Jacks is a highly respected surf-and-turf restaurant, serving excellent aged New York steaks, prime rib, Maine lobster, local fish, and large salads.

The restaurant is unusually located deep inside Fort Lauderdale's cruise-ship port; follow the signs to the ships.

FISHERMAN'S WHARF, 222 Pompano Beach Blvd., Pompano Beach. Tel. 941-5522.
   Cuisine: AMERICAN. **Reservations:** Not required.
$ **Prices:** Appetizers $5–$9; main courses $11–$16; lunch $4–$7. AE, MC, V.
   Open: Lunch daily 11am–2pm; dinner Sun–Thurs 4:30–10pm, Fri–Sat 4:30–11pm.
Fisherman's Wharf's casual atmosphere has everything to do with its location—on the sand, at the foot of Pompano Beach Pier. A double dining room outfitted with heavy wooden tables and chairs is centered around a busy bar, complete with a nonstop popcorn machine. The rear room, which looks very much like a glass box with good water views, holds a small stage where live bands perform every night but Sunday. Outside is a separate tiki bar and barbecue shack.

Just as you'd expect, lunches include clam chowder, Cobb salad, blackened-fish sandwiches, burgers, and fresh fish selections. Dinner, which is more formal, adds filet mignon with mushroom caps, mussels marinara over linguine, and fancier fish dishes. Special children's selections are always available.

HOUSTON'S, 1451 N. Federal Hwy., Fort Lauderdale. Tel. 563-2226.
   Cuisine: STEAKHOUSE. **Reservations:** Not required.
$ **Prices:** Appetizers $2–$5; main courses $8–$16; lunch $5–$8. AE, MC, V.

Open: Mon–Thurs 11:30am–11pm, Fri–Sat 11:30am–midnight, Sun 11:30am–10pm.

Most South Florida restaurants, it seems, are decorated in one of two ways: with new bright tropical colors, or in a 1950s family style with dark-wood walls, brick archways, and shuttered windows. Houston's is out of the latter mold—dim and romantic. Oil-burning lamps illuminate a tiered dining room that's furnished with large, overstuffed chairs arranged around white-clothed tables and booths.

Houston's is not a chi-chi New York–style Soho eatery, it's an upscale Texas-style steak-and-seafood house that's the best place in town for red meats. In addition to the requisite burger, prime rib, and filet mignon, a number of well-prepared chicken and fish dishes are always available.

The restaurant's bar, located adjacent to the dining room, is a pretty place to drink, as evidenced by the early-evening happy-hour crowds.

MISTRAL, 201 Fla. A1A, Fort Lauderdale. Tel. 463-4900.
   Cuisine: SOUTH FLORIDA REGIONAL. **Reservations:** Accepted only for large parties.
$ **Prices:** Appetizers $4–$8; main courses $8–$16. AE, DISC, MC, V.
   Open: Mon–Thurs 11am–11pm, Fri–Sat 11am–midnight. (Bar stays open later.)

Is South Miami Beach coming north? Opened in June 1993, Mistral is exactly the kind of breezy nouvelle spa eatery that has taken over in South Florida's trendier quarters. Located across from the beach on Fort Lauderdale's newly remodeled Fla. A1A, Mistral features wraparound doors that remain open during warmer afternoons and evenings, and European-style sidewalk dining. Indoors, white fresco nymphs float on coral-colored walls, surrounding tables with white cloths and cast-iron chairs softened with floral cushions. Terra-cotta tile floors and large, contemporary prints round out the decor.

Every meal begins with a large basket of warm breadsticks. Lunches might continue with a Mediterranean-influenced roasted vegetable salad marinated in garlic olive oil, or a California/Neapolitan-style pizza topped with marinated shrimp and scallops. Tapas, small Spanish-style plates, are served in the evening, and might include stuffed mussels, clams, or marinated olives. Meals might continue with grilled chicken breast layered with eggplant, tomato, zucchini, spinach, and goat cheese; or a decent bouillabaisse. The restaurant gets a good bar crowd, and live jazz plays on Friday and Saturday night from 10pm to 1am.

SHOOTERS, 3033 NE 32nd Ave., Fort Lauderdale. Tel. 566-2855.
   Cuisine: SEAFOOD/INTERNATIONAL. **Reservations:** Recommended.
$ **Prices:** Appetizers $3–$7; main courses $9–$16; lunch $4–$8. AE, CB, DC, DISC, MC, V.
   Open: Daily 11:30am–1am. (Bar open until 2am Fri and 3am Sat.)

If you want great museums, go to New York. But if it's great bars you're looking for, it's hard to beat South Florida. Shooters is one of those convivial bar/restaurants that give this area its great reputation for fun dining. An elevated, open-air dining room has great sightlines over a couple of large bars, located directly on the Intracoastal. Boaters tie up right in front.

Of course, the food can't beat the atmosphere, but nobody seems to care. Large portions, ordered from an equally large menu, include individual-size pizzas, seafood salads, sandwiches, and burgers. Heartier meals include grilled, blackened, broiled, or sautéed fresh fish, plus chicken, pasta, and steak. Shooters is best at night, when it's filled with warm-weather partiers.

INEXPENSIVE

COUNTRY HAM N' EGGS, 4405 El Mar Dr., Lauderdale-by-the-Sea. Tel. 776-1666.
   Cuisine: AMERICAN. **Reservations:** Not accepted.
$ **Prices:** Breakfast $2.50–$3; lunch/dinner $5–$8. No credit cards.
   Open: Daily 6:30am–9pm.

Europeans love this campy coffee shop, where breakfast is served all day at bright-yellow booths and Formica tables. After 10:30am the menu is expanded to include a variety of sandwiches, homemade meatloaf, and burgers. The restaurant is located one block from the ocean in the cozy hamlet of Lauderdale-by-the-Sea.

MANGOS, 904 E. Las Olas Blvd., Fort Lauderdale. Tel. 523-5001.
   Cuisine: CONTINENTAL. **Reservations:** Not required.
$ **Prices:** Appetizers $3–$6; salads and sandwiches $4–$6; main courses $8–$16. AE, MC, V.
   Open: Sun–Mon 11:30am–midnight, Tues–Thurs 11:30am–1am, Fri 11:30am–2am, Sat 11:30am–3am.

A relaxed brasserie-style restaurant serving light meals throughout the day, Mangos features both indoor and outdoor seating at the corner of Las Olas Boulevard and SE Ninth Avenue in the heart of downtown Fort Lauderdale. The same eclectic menu is served all day, and includes everything from salads to sandwiches to country-style pork chops, mahi-mahi, and seafood au gratin. The restaurant's soups are reputed to be the best in town, and with the exception of a certain bisque served at Sheffield's, the reputation is bang-on.

   Mangos has a large bar and stage, and features live bands most nights. Phone to see what's on.

PIER RESTAURANT, 2 E. Commercial Blvd, Lauderdale-by-the-Sea. Tel. 776-1690.
   Cuisine: SEAFOOD/AMERICAN. **Reservations:** Not accepted.
$ **Prices:** Sandwiches and burgers $3–$5. No credit cards.
   Open: Daily 7am–4pm.

Located on the near end of the Lauderdale-by-the-Sea pier, this tiny eatery is little more than a luncheonette on the beach, occupying one of the region's most enviable locations. The built-in outdoor wooden picnic tables are the best seats, shaded from the sun but in full view of the suntanners. The menu, which is printed on wooden signs posted above the low Formica bar, features American standards like bacon and eggs, pancakes, patty melts, and milkshakes.

SHOPPING

There are three places every visitor to Fort Lauderdale should know about. The first is **Antique Row,** a strip of U.S. 1 around North Dania Beach Boulevard (in Dania, about one mile south of Fort Lauderdale/Hollywood International Airport) that holds about 200 antiques shops. Although most are a bit overpriced, if you're persistent, there are bound to be some good finds in furniture, silver, china, glass, linens, and more. The shops are closed Sunday.

   The **Fort Lauderdale Swap Shop,** 3291 W. Sunrise Blvd. (tel. 791-7927), is one of the world's largest flea markets, containing endless acres of vendors as well as a mini–amusement park, a 12-screen drive-in movie theater, weekend concerts, and even a free circus complete with elephants, horse shows, high-wire acts, and clowns. This is truly one of the best flea markets anywhere. It's open daily and admission is free.

   Sawgrass Mills, Sunrise Boulevard and Flamingo Road, Fort Lauderdale (tel. 846-2300), bills itself as the world's largest outlet mall, offering more than 225 brand-name off-price stores including Macy's, Saks Fifth Avenue, Ann Taylor, Spiegel, and Levi's. Merchandise is priced up to 75% below retail for discontinued or slightly irregular products. It's truly a unique shopping experience.

EVENING ENTERTAINMENT
THE PERFORMING ARTS

BROWARD CENTER FOR THE PERFORMING ARTS, 201 SW Fifth Ave., Fort Lauderdale. Tel. 522-5334.

   Opened in 1991, this stunning new $52-million multitheater complex contains both a 2,700-seat auditorium and a smaller 595-seat theater. The center attracts top opera, symphony, dance, and Broadway productions, as well as more modest size shows.

OFF BROADWAY, E. 26th St., Fort Lauderdale. Tel. 566-0554.

As the name says, this theater specializes in smaller, independent, and sometimes offbeat productions of contemporary plays. The stage operates year-round.

THE OPERA GUILD. Tel. 462-0222.
For more than 40 years this sometimes world-class society has been dazzling audiences with a wide-ranging series of shows that has featured such top names as Pavarotti and Domingo. The season runs from December through April, usually in the Broward Center for the Performing Arts (see above).

PARKER PLAYHOUSE, 707 NE 8th St. Tel. 764-0700.
Fort Lauderdale's best theater series, Parker productions regularly attract big-name shows with nationally known actors. This is a really good, "insider" kind of place, well supported by the community. It's small, and offers great sightlines from every seat.

PHILHARMONIC ORCHESTRA OF FLORIDA. Tel. 561-2997.
When this innovative South Florida–based company comes to Fort Lauderdale, they usually perform in the Broward Center for the Performing Arts (see above). Their season runs from October to May.

SINFONIA VIRTUOSI AND CHORUS OF FLORIDA. Tel. 561-5882.
Classical, romantic, baroque, and contemporary music is performed under the direction of James Brooks-Bruzzese. Individual tickets are usually available to the series which runs from November through May.

THE BAR, CLUB & MUSIC SCENE

CAFE 66, at the Pier 66 Resort and Marina, 301 SE 17th St. Causeway. Tel. 525-6666.
There's always something happening at this busy waterfront bar—sometimes it's live rock, sometimes a dance contest. Pier Top, a revolving restaurant and bar in the hotel's penthouse, attracts an older crowd that can appreciate a good sunset.

CROOCO'S, 3339 N. Federal Hwy., Oakland Park. Tel. 566-2406.
One of the largest bars in Florida, this giant sports disco and rock 'n' roll club encompasses numerous bars, several dance floors, a basketball court, a baseball batting cage, and one of the biggest TV screens you've ever seen.

DO DA'S AMERICAN COUNTY SALOON & DANCEHALL, 700 S. Fla. 7, Fort Lauderdale. Tel. 792-6200.
Line dancing is in, and this is where they do it best. Couples two-step till the wee hours on the large, polished dance floor. Free dance lessons are offered on Monday and Tuesday nights. It's open on Monday and Tuesday from 5pm to 2am, Wednesday through Friday from 5pm to 4am, and on Saturday from 6pm to 4am.
Admission: Free Mon–Thurs, $3.50 Fri–Sat.

ELBO ROOM, 241 South Atlantic. Tel. 463-4615
This is the beachfront dive that was once almost synonymous with spring break. It's still a lively—and sometimes rowdy—place, packed with college kids and wet T-shirt contestants.

MAI-KAI, 3599 N. Federal Hwy., Fort Lauderdale. Tel. 563-3272, or toll free 800/262-4524.
Polynesian for "good food," Mai Kai is not just a touristy Hawaiian dinner show, it's a lively night of unusual entertainment and fun foods. Grass-skirted dancers have been hula-ing here twice nightly since time immemorial. Tropical drinks at the terrifically tacky Molokai bar are a bit pricy, but the selection is lengthy and the "rain forest" atmosphere unparalleled. A la carte dinners are also served (steaks, ribs, seafood, and a variety of Polynesian pork dishes), and cost from $16 per person. Shows are given nightly at 7:15 and 10pm.
Admission: $8 per person.

PARROT LOUNGE, 911 Sunrise Lane, Fort Lauderdale. Tel. 563-1493.
Turn toward the bar and you'll see fun-loving, friendly locals getting drunk on piña coladas and beer. Turn toward the wall and you'll see photographs of the same locals

getting drunk on piña coladas and beer. A cluttered sports bar, the Parrot Lounge is the kind of place where most customers are known to the staff by name, and if you're new here, you'll soon be asked yours. Good music plays loud, but not too loud to miss the football commentary coming from the television sets.

Sunrise Lane is located just off Sunrise Boulevard on the ocean side of the Intracoastal Waterway in a little shopping area called "The Village." It's open Monday through Saturday from 11am to 2am and on Sunday from noon to 2am.

SQUEEZE PROGRESSIVE DANCETERIA, 2 S. New River Dr. Tel. 522-2151.

A long-lasting club spinning straightforward dance beats to a 20-something crowd, it's open Tuesday through Saturday from 9pm to 2am.

Admission: $5.

CHAPTER 8

INDIAN RIVER COUNTRY

1. **STUART/JENSEN BEACH**
- **WHAT'S SPECIAL ABOUT INDIAN RIVER COUNTRY**
2. **PORT ST. LUCIE/FORT PIERCE**
3. **VERO BEACH**

The Intracoastal Waterway that runs between the Florida mainland and the barrier island, called Hutchinson Island, is known as the Indian River. The channel gives this area its name. You've probably heard of Indian River grapefruit, and indeed, this is one of the most fertile citrus-growing regions in the world. Indian River Country prides itself on environmentally conscious construction that's reminiscent of what so much of South Florida *used* to be. No massive growth here. Vast areas of pristine oceanfront remain undeveloped, with beautiful vistas that are unobscured by the condominiums, hotels, and other tropical skyscrapers that mar much of the lands to the south. This is the old Florida. Sandy stretches of coastline pay homage to bluff plants and native animals.

With that said, I must admit that Hutchinson Island, a 20-mile-long barrier island just across the Intracoastal Indian River, is indeed dotted with a handful of high-rises (and pricy beach clubs), but there are not yet enough of them to spoil the wilderness. Here, you can expect to find relatively uncrowded beaches, where the tanners are locals and the tourists are few. Small-town museums and charming antiques shops compete with historical markers and unspoiled beaches for the attentions of visitors.

SEEING INDIAN RIVER COUNTRY

All the major roads in Indian River Country run north-south, making sightseeing easy. The best drive, either to or from Miami, is along Fla. A1A (also called the Dixie Highway), which hugs the ocean along most of the coast. U.S. 1 (also called Federal Highway), doesn't cross the Intracoastal to the barrier islands, making it a slightly faster (but less interesting) way to see Florida's east coast. It's hard to get too lost while wandering around the Indian River Country's roads—the ocean is always to the east.

---

1. STUART/JENSEN BEACH

130 miles SE of Orlando, 105 miles N of Miami

GETTING THERE By Plane The **Palm Beach International Airport** (tel. 407/471-7420), located about 25 miles to the south, is the closest gateway to the Stuart area. See Chapter 7 on the Gold Coast for complete information.

By Train Amtrak (tel. toll free 800/USA-RAIL) trains departing from New York stop in West Palm Beach, about 25 miles to the south, and in Okeechobee, about 30 miles to the west. The West Palm station is located at 201 S. Tamarind Ave., West Palm Beach (tel. 407/832-6169). The Okeechobee station is located at 801 N. Parrot Ave., off U.S. 441 N. (tel. 813/763-1114).

WHAT'S SPECIAL ABOUT INDIAN RIVER COUNTRY

Fishing

☐ Edible and game species that inhabit the ocean, rivers, inlets, and lakes, with world-class bottom fishing and inshore trolling.

☐ Big-game ocean fishing—so good that the town of Stewart bills itself the "Sailfish capital of the World."

Water Sports

☐ Boating and sailing, popular activities year-round, as well as windsurfing at Sebastian Inlet State Park.

☐ Good snorkeling and diving at several offshore reefs and dive sites, with old wrecks make for particularly fine diving.

Beaches

☐ Over 26 miles of Atlantic coastline and an average year-round temperature of 73°, making this a great place for swimming and sunning.

Marine Marvels

☐ Endangered loggerhead turtles, crawling onto the sand from May through August to lay their eggs; local environmental groups lead educational "turtle watches."

By Bus   Greyhound can get you to the Stuart area from almost anywhere. The company no longer operates a single nationwide telephone number, so consult your local directory for the office nearest you.

By Car   If you're driving up or down the Florida coast, you'll probably reach the Stuart area on Interstate 95, a highway that runs all the way from Maine to Miami. Visitors on their way to or from Orlando should take the Florida Turnpike, a toll road that runs almost directly from this region's beaches to Walt Disney World. Finally, if you're coming from the state's west coast, you'll probably take Fla. 70, which runs north of Lake Okeechobee to Fort Pierce, located just up the road from Stuart.

ESSENTIALS   The **telephone area code** is 407.
  The **Stuart/Martin County Chamber of Commerce,** 1650 S. Kanner Hwy., Stuart, FL 34994 (tel. 407/287-1088), is the region's main source for information. The **Jensen Beach Chamber of Commerce,** 1901 NE Jensen Beach Blvd., Jensen Beach, FL 34957 (tel. 407/334-3444), offers specialized information on their sparkling strip of sand.

The Stuart/Jensen Beach area has never been highly developed. From 1960 to the mid-1970s, the county's population swelled from a mere 6,000 residents to a whopping 37,000, evidence of South Floridians' desire to leave the metropolises of Miami and Palm Beach for quieter, less-known beaches. Despite the growth, it's still pretty quiet around these parts. Once populated primarily with pineapple plantations, the towns of Martin County—which include Stuart, Jensen Beach, Port Salerno, and Hobe Sound—are now home to citrus plantations, modest homes, and a handful of tourist-oriented hotels and sights. Strict building codes keep these communities free from high-rise condominiums and endless strip malls. Downtown Stuart has recently been spruced up with lovely landscaped walkways and attractive storefronts. Many historical buildings in both Stuart and Fort Pierce have been lovingly restored, making a stroll around these beachfront towns a worthy stop on your exploration of the Southeast Florida coast.

WHAT TO SEE & DO

MUSEUMS

COURTHOUSE CULTURAL CENTER, 80 E. Ocean Blvd., Stuart. Tel. 287-6676.

This historical former courthouse is now the region's principal center for the arts. It functions primarily as a historical museum and art gallery with changing exhibitions, many of local interest. A helpful staff dispenses information on area events and activities.

Admission: Free; $2 donation suggested.
Open: Mon–Fri 10am–4pm, Sat 11am–3pm.

ELLIOTT MUSEUM, 825 NE Ocean Blvd., Hutchinson Island, Stuart. Tel. 225-1961.

A treasure trove of early Americana, this museum was built by inventor Harmon Parker Elliott in 1961, in honor of his father and partner, Sterling Elliott. A series of exhibits illustrate life from the Civil War through the 1920s. An apothecary, a barbershop, a blacksmith forge, a clock and watch shop, and other old-fashioned, life-size dioramas are displayed with collections of dolls, teas, spices, and even fishing tackle.

The inventor and his father claimed 222 patents between the two of them. Although none changed the world, a display dedicated to the Elliotts' inventions are the museum's highlight. They include an envelope-addressing machine and a mechanical knot-tier.

Admission: $3.50 adults, 50¢ children 6–13, free for children under 6.
Open: Daily 11am–4pm.

GILBERT'S BAR HOUSE OF REFUGE, 301 MacArthur Blvd., Stuart. Tel. 225-1875.

The oldest structure in this area dates from 1875, when it functioned as a rescue center, caring for shipwrecked sailors. Restored to its original splendor in 1975–76, Gilbert's is listed on the National Register of Historic Places, and operates as a historical museum displaying an unusual collection of marine artifacts, life-saving equipment, and related objects.

Admission: $1 adults, 50¢ children 6–13, free for children under 6.
Open: Tues–Sun 11am–4:15pm.

STUART HERITAGE MUSEUM AT THE STUART FEED STORE, 161 NW Flagler Ave., Stuart. Tel. 220-4600.

In 1901, when the Stuart Feed Store was the territory's most important general store, the region's inhabitants would come from miles around to buy feed for their animals and supplies for themselves, as well as catch up on all the local news. Native Seminole peoples shopped and traded here as well. Today, the former shop is a museum of local history, an ode to the pioneers who first worked the lands around Stuart.

Mrs. Catherine M. Lewis, the small museum's very friendly docent, is a storehouse of information and the museum's most valuable treasure. A member of the Stuart Heritage Committee, Mrs. Lewis loves to inform visitors about goings-on in this area, in the past and the present. Ask her about the museum's collection of antiques, which includes old soda fountains, meat grinders, and other settlers' tools.

Admission: Free.
Open: Mon–Sat 10am–4pm.

BEACHES & PARKS

Bathtub Beach, on Hutchinson Island, Stuart, is one of the best oceanside parks in the county. In addition to calm waters, protected by coral reefs, visitors can explore the region on dune and river trails. The reef here is very close to shore, and great for snorkeling. Bathtub Beach is popular with young families, especially on warmer weekends. To reach the park, cross the Intracoastal Waterway on Ocean Boulevard and turn right, onto MacArthur Boulevard. The beach is located about a mile ahead, on your left, just past the House of Refuge Museum.

Jaycee Park, on SE Ocean Boulevard, between Hutchinson Island and the mainland, is split between a picnic-area island, and a park that's popular with sports enthusiasts. When you cross the Intracoastal Waterway on Ocean Boulevard, the first island you reach is the picnic area. Continue over the next bridge to the park that's best known for fishing and windsurfing.

WHERE TO STAY
VERY EXPENSIVE

INDIAN RIVER PLANTATION, 555 NE Ocean Blvd., Hutchinson Island, FL 34996. Tel. 407/225-3700, or toll free 800/947-2148. Fax 407/225-3948. 200 rms, 54 suites. A/C TV TEL **Directions:** From U.S. 1, turn east onto Monterey Road, then right onto East Ocean Boulevard; the resort is located past the second bridge, on your right.

$ Rates: Feb 6–Apr 10, $195–$245 single or double; from $285 suite. Jan 2–Feb 5, Apr 11–May 29, and Sept 30–Dec 15, $160–$200 single or double; from $230 suite. May 30–Sept 29, $130–$160 single or double; from $210 suite. Dec 16–31, $160–$245 single or double; from $285 suite. AE, CB, DC, DISC, MC, V.

The Indian River Plantation is the biggest thing ever to happen to this otherwise sleepy island. To those who don't care about the region's unadulterated natural habitats, this large resort appears to be southern Hutchinson Island's reason to be. Occupying a former pineapple plantation, the resort offers a multitude of family-oriented activities amid lush surroundings. The white lattice-and-wicker lobby is filled with a bountiful harvest of plants, and large windows that look over the hotel's swimming pool and tiki bar.

Generously sized standard rooms continue the floral motif, with colorful spreads and draperies. Simple rattan furnishings are enlivened with special extras that include clock radios, ceiling fans, two phones, small refrigerators, and contemporary bathrooms complete with hairdryers. All rooms, whether ocean-view or oceanfront, have large windows and balconies. Some come with complete kitchen facilities.

The resort's activities revolve around tennis, golfing, and boating. Sportfishing, scuba diving, and various other water sports are also available. The Indian River Plantation is an excellent place for families with kids. The resort's Pineapple Bunch Children's Camp sponsors daily activities for children, teens, and families, like hayrides, bonfires, poolside games, marshmallow cookouts, golf and tennis lessons, arts and crafts, and beach walks. From May through August, sea turtles crawl onto the sand to lay their eggs, and local environmental groups lead educational "turtle watches."

Dining/Entertainment: Five restaurants, three lounges, and two tiki bars ensure that you'll never go hungry or thirsty. Scalawags, a seafood restaurant, is the resort's top dining room, and is popular with locals. The less-formal Emporium serves breakfast, lunch, and all-day snacks like frozen yogurt. There's live music nightly, in at least two bars.

Services: 24-hour room service, concierge, complimentary movies, bicycle and sports-equipment rentals, overnight laundry and dry cleaning.

Facilities: 18-hole golf course, luxury sightseeing boat, full-service marina, 13 tennis courts (5 lighted), four heated swimming pools, two Jacuzzis, fitness center, shopping arcade.

MODERATE

HUTCHINSON INN, 9750 S. Ocean Dr. (Fla. A1A), Jensen Beach, FL 34957. Tel. 407/229-2000. A/C TV TEL **Directions:** From I-95, take the Stuart exit east to County Rd. 76 and continue to Fla. A1A north; the hotel is about four miles ahead on your right.

$ Rates (including continental breakfast): Dec–Apr, $80–$125 single or double;

from $165 suite, May–Nov, $60–$100 single or double; from $145 suite. Additional person $10–$20 extra. MC, V.

It may not look like much from the road, where only the tennis court is visible, but your entrance is soon greeted by striking white gazebos dotting thick green lawns and regal brick walkways leading to a proud, pastel two-story retreat. Located directly on the beach, the Hutchinson Inn is a quiet hideaway, a 15-minute drive from anywhere. It's hard to top it for charm, from its tiny lobby with its green canopy to the little love birds that live below the stairs leading to your room.

Rooms are lightly decorated with rattan dressers, tables, and chairs. Most are good size and all have alarm clocks and tiled baths. Sofas convert into pull-out beds, and several rooms can be joined to accommodate large families.

Facilities and services are few, but there is a large pool and a good swimming beach, and freshly baked cookies are served each evening before bedtime. On Saturday afternoons, guests are invited to join in a complimentary barbecue.

INEXPENSIVE

CORAL REEF MOTEL, 2680 NE Indian River Dr., Jensen Beach, FL 34957. Tel. 407/334-1474. 8 efficiencies. A/C TV
$ Rates: Jan–Mar, $40–$50 single or double. May–Nov, $30–$35 single or double. Apr and Dec, $35–$40 single or double. MC, V.

John and Marie Hascup manage this little motel enviably located right in the town of Jensen Beach. The architecture is typically 1950s, but most every other part of the motel is far more up-to-date. The Hascup's attention to cleanliness and detail makes the Coral Reef a good option for inexpensive accommodations in the area. Beyond a soft gravel driveway is a well-kept yard with barbecue grills that guests are welcome to use. Every room contains an efficiency-style kitchenette, and is loaded with linens, towels, pots, pans, dishes, glasses, and silverware. Rooms have either two twin or two double beds; be sure to specify your needs when making reservations.

WHERE TO DINE
MODERATE

ASHLEY RESTAURANT, 61 SW Osceola St., Stuart. Tel. 221-9476.
Cuisine: CONTINENTAL. **Reservations:** Not required.
$ Prices: Appetizers $2–$7; main courses $6–$14; breakfast $3–$5; lunch $4–$7. MC, V.
Open: Breakfast Sun 8am–1pm; lunch Tues–Fri 11am–2pm; dinner Tues–Sat 5–10pm.

Fun and bright, the Ashley is an eclectic mix of tile, glass, and color. Ultra-contemporary wall prints hang under an unusual aqua-colored beamed ceiling, while stained-glass windows throw their colored light onto ornate gold bars that protect the kitchen from mealtime gazers.

Happily, the French-inspired food, accented with local citrus and seafood, is just as snappy as the surroundings. Simple lunches tend toward chicken, shrimp, and fruit crêpes; croissant sandwiches; and a variety of burgers. Dinner, the meal of choice here, might start with smoked salmon, crab-stuffed avocado, or escargots bobbing in burgundy. Imaginative pasta, meat, seafood, and poultry dishes might include duck breast in a caramel-orange sauce, or broiled local grouper.

Weekend breakfasts are especially recommended, when fresh-fruit crêpes and homemade quiches tempt you away from your usual cereal and eggs.

THE BLACK MARLIN, 53 W. Osceola St., Stuart. Tel. 286-3126.
Cuisine: FLORIDA REGIONAL. **Reservations:** Not accepted.
$ Prices: Appetizers $4–$8; salads and sandwiches $4–$10; main courses $8–$19. AE, MC, V.
Open: Sun–Thurs 4pm–midnight, Fri–Sat 4pm–2am.

Sporting the look and feel of an English pub, the Black Marlin luckily stays away from English cuisine, opting instead for a medley of regional flavors. The "salmon BLT" is typical of the dishes here—grilled salmon on a toasted bun topped with bacon, lettuce, tomato, and cole slaw. Designer pizzas are topped with shrimp, roasted red peppers, and the like, and main dishes, all of which are served with vegetables and potatoes, include fried lobster tail with a honey-mustard sauce, and a charcoal-grilled chicken breast served on radicchio with caramelized onions.

The Black Marlin is pretty; fully half of the floor space is occupied by a beautifully polished wood bar, and true to its name, a huge black marlin is mounted on the back brick wall.

CHUCK MUER'S KEY WEST, 1405 NE Indian River Dr., Jensen Beach. Tel. 220-3000.

Cuisine: SEAFOOD/AMERICAN. **Reservations:** Not required.

$ Prices: Appetizers $3–$8; sandwiches and salads $6–$12; main courses $8–$20. AE, CB, DC, DISC, MC, V.

Open: Sun–Thurs 11:30am–10pm, Fri–Sat 11:30am–11pm.

Probably the largest, and most "happening," restaurant in Jensen Beach, Chuck Muer's Key West is still a sleepy bodega by big-city standards. Situated waterfront, with large decks overlooking the Indian River, the restaurant features a long, wave-shaped bar and fake tropical fish and surf boards that dangle from the beamed ceiling like misplaced Christmas ornaments.

Meals here might begin with lightly fried Cheddar cheese–stuffed jalapeño peppers called "Armadillo eggs," or cold marinated conch salad with peppers, onion, tomato, and fresh herbs. Main dishes include fresh fish (grilled, broiled, or sautéed), a 16-ounce rib-eye steak, and Jamaican jerk chicken. Their large salads and sandwiches are not necessarily for smaller appetites. Bimini seafood salad is made with grilled shrimp and scallops atop mixed greens, peppers, and assorted vegetables. The turkey club sandwich is prepared in a pita with avocado and pineapple and served with fresh fruit.

GUYTANO'S GRILLE, 2220 E. Ocean Blvd., Stuart. Tel. 286-7550.

Cuisine: FLORIDA REGIONAL. **Reservations:** Not required.

$ Prices: Appetizers $3–$9; main courses $5–$11. AE, DC, DISC, MC, V.

Open: Mon–Thurs 11:30am–10pm, Fri–Sat 11:30am–11pm, Sun 4–10pm.

Located on the mainland, just across from Hutchinson Island, Guytano's two large dining rooms are some of the finest in town. High ceilings and white stucco walls are made lively with jazz music, slowly twirling ceiling fans, plants, and ultra-contemporary lighting.

Meals are both beautifully presented and delicious—a winning combination anywhere. Chef and owner Guy M. Ciccone presides over a skilled kitchen that creates such mouth-watering appetizers as sautéed eggplant crusted with breadcrumbs and escarole soup with tiny meatballs and ricotta raviolini. Lunches might include wood-grilled shrimp salad with artichokes, mozzarella, roasted peppers, and endive; or veal sausages served on Italian bread layered with red peppers, red onion, and tomato sauce. Pastas are all handmade, and might include black-pepper tagliolini with grilled chicken, Gorgonzola cream, and pine nuts. Other recommendable dishes are jumbo lump crab cakes sautéed in mustard sauce, and veal milanese with sautéed sweet peppers.

ISLAND REEF, 10900 S. Ocean Dr., Jensen Beach, Hutchinson Island. Tel. 229-2600.

Cuisine: FLORIDA/CARIBBEAN. **Reservations:** Not required.

$ Prices: Appetizers $2–$8; main courses $8–$16; lunch $5–$11; brunch $2–$7. AE, DISC, MC, V.

Open: Lunch Mon–Sat 11:30am–2:30pm; dinner Sun–Thurs 5–9:30pm, Fri–Sat 5–10pm; brunch Sun 11:30am–2:30pm.

A wooden walkway over a tropics-inspired rock fountain transports you through a miniature fern gully into this beachfront restaurant. Fortunately, the handsome interior is not as calculated as the Disney-inspired entranceway. High wood-beamed ceilings and hardwood floors sandwich a well-stocked raw bar, and a wall of windows overlooks a huge outdoor dune-top patio with the most coveted seats in the house.

The island-themed lunch menu features fresh fish covered with tropical spices and sauces—shrimp tempura with coconut butter and fruit juices is but one example. But wise diners would do well to ask for the sauce on the side, or stick to more traditional orders like salads and sandwiches. The same goes for dinner, when you should enjoy reading the adventurous menu, then think of simpler things. The grouper baked in a banana leaf (sans curry-cream sauce) is very recommendable, as is the charcoal-grilled chicken with tropical fruit juices, cilantro, lemongrass, and salsa. But shrimp and scallops with angel-hair pasta in pepper-vodka-cream sauce and other complicated Caribbean-style preparations stretch the limits of the cooking staff.

Sunday brunches include many traditional North American plates with a twist. Try French toast topped with almond slivers or a breakfast burrito filled with eggs, chili beef, bell peppers, onions, cheese, and salsa.

SCALAWAGS RESTAURANT, 555 NE Ocean Blvd., Hutchinson Island. Tel. 225-3700.

Cuisine: SEAFOOD/STEAKS. **Reservations:** Recommended.
$ Prices: Appetizers $4–$10; main courses $15–$21; Wed seafood buffet $19.75; Sun brunch $17.50. AE, DISC, MC, V.
Open: Dinner Wed 5–10pm, Thurs–Tues 6–10pm; buffet brunch Sun 10am–2:30pm.

Scalawags Restaurant's Wednesday-night seafood buffet is the best deal in town. Tables upon tables, filled with the area's freshest assortment of seafood and landfood, are presented for this weekly all-you-can-eat feast. Here's what $19.75 will get you: jumbo shrimp, split crab legs, oysters, clams, salads, salmon, prime rib, blackened dolphin, steamed scrod, baked flounder, sautéed shrimp and scallops, fettuccine Alfredo, and an assortment of desserts.

The restaurant's Sunday brunch buffet offers a similarly sized gluttonous abundance of food. Create-your-own omelet and fill your plate again and again with assorted salads, smoked salmon, pâtés, stuffed flounder, eggs Benedict, and more. There's also a large table filled with desserts, and champagne and mimosas flow freely.

A regular menu of seafood, steaks, and pasta is served the rest of the week.

INEXPENSIVE

CHINA STAR, 1501 S. Federal Hwy., Stuart. Tel. 283-8378.

Cuisine: CHINESE. **Reservations:** Not required.
$ Prices: Appetizers $1–$4; combination platters $5–$8; main dishes $4–$11. AE, DISC, MC, V.
Open: Mon–Thurs 11am–10pm, Fri–Sat 11am–11pm, Sun 11:30am–10pm.

China Star would look like a miniature White House misplaced on Federal Highway if it weren't for the telltale Chinese-red trim around the restaurant's doors and windows. There are few surprises inside, where red walls are adorned with the requisite Oriental prints and landscape murals. And why does almost every Chinese restaurateur decorate with fish tanks?

The food is straightforward and good—a rave from this spoiled New Yorker. A la carte selections are listed under the usual beef, poultry, pork, and seafood headings, and include jade scallop, moo goo gai pan, vegetable egg foo yung, and cashew chicken (my favorite). Combination platters come with fried rice, an eggroll, and wonton or egg drop soup.

BUDGET

NATURE'S WAY CAFE, 25 SW Osceola St., in the Post Office Arcade, Stuart. Tel. 220-7306.

Cuisine: VEGETARIAN. **Reservations:** Not accepted.
$ Prices: Sandwiches/salads $3–$6; juices/shakes $1–$3. No credit cards.
Open: Mon–Fri 10am–4pm, Sat 11am–3pm.

One large room with little tables and a few strategically placed bar stools overlooking the sidewalk is all there is to this pleasantly decorated, white-tiled eatery. A sort of health-food deli, Nature's Way offers an assortment of prepared salads, make-your-own vegetarian sandwiches, and frozen yogurts. There's also a healthy assortment of shakes, fresh juices, and homemade muffins. If it's a particularly nice day, you might ask them to pack your lunch so you can picnic in a park or on the beach.

PICNIC SUPPLIES

In addition to **Nature's Way Café,** listed above, try **Plantation Pantry,** 650 NE Ocean Blvd., on Hutchinson Island, Stuart (tel. 225-1100), for some of the region's best take-away foods. Located across the road from the Indian River Plantation, and just behind a gas station, the shop looks much like any other quick-stop market. But usual it's not: In addition to a full deli making both hot and cold sandwiches, there's a large selection of gourmet treats such as smoked salmon and trout, homemade quiches, lasagnes, and freshly made jams and jellies. For dessert, get a piece of their locally produced fudge, which comes in an incredibly wide variety of flavors.

SHOPPING

You may already have realized that the Hutchinson Island area is no Paris or Milan, but that doesn't mean there's nothing to buy. This area's specialty is food, a tempting mix of tropical and southern flavors that, with surprisingly little effort, can be exported home.

The **Monterey Farmer's Market,** 642 SE Monterey Rd., in Bruner Plaza, Stuart (tel. 287-1588), sells all types of locally grown produce, including the famous Indian River grapefruit and oranges. They ship anywhere in North America.

Mrs. Peter's, at the Stuart Heritage Museum, 161 NW Flagler Ave., Stuart (tel. 287-3154), sells some of the most succulent smoked foods you've ever eaten. Their motto is "We Smoke Everything But Mermaids," and they've been doing so since 1931. Old-fashioned–style hand-smoked kingfish, amberjack, turkey breast, and other meats are sold and shipped from here. Order forms are available for other smoked specialties.

Mrs. Peter's has a second location at 1500 Fla. 707, Rio/Jensen Beach (tel. 334-2184).

EVENING ENTERTAINMENT

Even the tourist office of this relatively sleepy region refrains from boasting too loudly about Stuart's cultural evenings. Still, there *are* some things to do when the sun goes down; and you might be lucky enough to arrive on a particularly lively night. Phone the following listings to find out what's on.

THE PERFORMING ARTS

The Barn Theater, 2400 E. Ocean Blvd., Stuart (tel. 287-4884), is a good-quality community theater, presenting five shows per season, September to June.

The **Lyric Theater,** 216 SE Flagler Ave., Stuart (tel. 220-1942), a beautiful 1920s-era 600-seat hall, hosts a variety of shows and films throughout the year. Programs run the gamut from amateur plays to top-name theatrical shows and concerts, sometimes from the rock music world. Phone for the latest.

THE BAR SCENE

The bar at the **Black Marlin,** 53 W. Osceola St., Stuart (tel. 286-3126), is visited by fun-loving local professionals and tourists alike. The bar takes up half the small restaurant, and on Thursday, Friday, and Saturday night it's filled three deep. Open Sunday through Thursday from 4pm to midnight, and on Friday and Saturday from 4pm to 2am.

Younger and wilder revelers go to **Shuckers,** in the Island Beach Resort, 9800 S. Ocean Dr., Jensen Beach (tel. 229-1224). It's a crazy place filled with beer signs and sports banners and a huge circular wood bar in the center. There are a couple of pool tables and video games, as well as a small dance floor where the crowd goes wild to thumping DJ-ed hits. Shuckers is open Monday through Saturday from 10am until 2am, and on Sunday from 10am to midnight.

Higher rollers and locals alike go to **Scalawags Lounge,** 555 NE Ocean Blvd., at the Indian River Plantation, Stuart (tel. 225-3700), a fancy bar located inside the region's best hotel. The view from the upstairs lounge is so nice that you almost don't feel guilty about drinking so early in the afternoon. Stick around for the live musical entertainment that's offered almost every night.

2. PORT ST. LUCIE/FORT PIERCE

7 miles N of Stuart, 10 miles W of the ocean

GETTING THERE   By Plane   The **Palm Beach International Airport** (tel. 407/471-7420), located about 30 miles to the south, is the closest gateway to the Port St. Lucie/Fort Pierce area. See Chapter 7 on the Gold Coast for complete information.

By Train   Amtrak (tel. toll free 800/USA-RAIL) trains departing from New York stop in West Palm Beach, about 30 miles to the south, and in Okeechobee, about 30 miles to the west. The West Palm Beach station is located at 201 S. Tamarind Ave. (tel. 407/832-6169). The Okeechobee station is located at 801 N. Parrot Ave., off U.S. 441 N. (tel. 813/763-1114).

By Bus   Greyhound can get you to the Port St. Lucie/Fort Pierce area from almost anywhere. The company no longer operates a single nationwide telephone number, so consult your local directory for the office nearest you.

By Car   If you're driving up or down the Florida coast, you'll probably reach the Port St. Lucie/Fort Pierce area on Interstate 95, a highway that runs all the way from Maine to Miami. Visitors on their way to or from Orlando should take the Florida Turnpike, a toll road that runs almost directly from this region's beaches to Walt Disney World. Finally, if you're coming from the state's west coast, you'll probably take Fla. 70, which runs north of Lake Okeechobee right into Fort Pierce.

ESSENTIALS   The **telephone area code** is 407.
   The **Stuart/Martin County Chamber of Commerce,** 1650 S. Kanner Hwy., Stuart, FL 34994 (tel. 407/287-1088, or toll free 800/524-9704), is the region's main source of information.

Port St. Lucie and Fort Pierce seem to thrive on sportfishing. Seemingly endless piers jut out along the Intracoastal Waterway and the Fort Pierce Inlet for both river and ocean runs. It's hard not to wax nostalgic about how Miami used to look when you drive along the region's relatively quiet streets, two-lane roads ruled by small pubs and raw bars. Here visitors can enjoy adventures like diving and snorkeling, as well as more passive pastimes like beachcombing and sunbathing.
   Driving along Fla. A1A on Hutchinson Island, you'll discover several secluded beach clubs interspersed with 1950s-style homes, a few small inns, dozens of grungy single-story raw bars, and even a few high-rise condominiums. Much of this island is government-owned, kept undeveloped for the public's enjoyment. On the other side of the Intracoastal, along the road that hugs the river, you'll find attractive modest homes with small motorboats moored to private docks. Farther inland, fronting busy U.S. 1, are strip shopping malls and chain restaurants.

WHAT TO SEE & DO

Florida is full of unique museums, but none is more curious than the **UDT–SEAL Museum,** 3300 N. Fla. A1A, Fort Pierce, on Hutchinson Island (tel. 489-3597 or 595-1570), a most peculiar tribute to the secret forces of the U.S. Navy—frogmen and their successors, the SEAL teams. Chronological displays trace the history of these clandestine divers, and detail their most important achievements. The best exhibits are those that display equipment used by the navy's most elite members. Needless to say, this is the only museum of its type in the world. Admission is $2 for adults, $1 for children, free for kids under 5. It's open Tuesday through Saturday from 10am to 4pm and on Sunday from noon to 4pm.

Jai alai, sort of a Spanish-style indoor lacrosse popular around South Florida, is regularly played in the **Fort Pierce Jai Alai Fronton,** 1750 S. King's Hwy., Fort Pierce (tel. 464-7500, or toll free 800/524-2524 in Florida). Players use woven baskets (called *cestas*) to hurl balls (*pelotas*) at speeds that sometimes exceed 170 miles per hour. Spectators, who are protected behind a metal screen, place bets on the evening's players. Admission is $2.50 for reserved seats, $1 for general admission. Games are played from November through April on Wednesday, Saturday, and Sunday at noon and 7pm, on Monday, Thursday, and Friday at 7pm only.

WHERE TO STAY
EXPENSIVE

CLUB MED–THE SANDPIPER, 3500 Morningside Blvd., Port St. Lucie, FL 34952. Tel. 407/335-4400, or toll free 800/CLUB-MED. Fax 407/335-9497. 600 rms. A/C TV TEL **Directions:** From U.S. 1, turn west onto Westmoreland Boulevard, then turn left onto Pine Valley Road and the resort entrance is straight ahead.

$ Rates (including three meals per day): Feb–Apr, $175–$225 per person double. May–Jan, $150–$255 per person double. Weekly rates available. AE, MC, V.

Club Med, a pioneer of the all-inclusive resort, is represented in South Florida by this large, three-story lodge secluded on 500 acres on the shores of Port St. Lucie. To me, Club Med always conjures up images of a carefree paradise on a distant tropical island. Except for the fact that this place is not too far away, it very much lives up to my ideal. All meals and activities are included in the club's basic price, and guests are completely spoiled during their stay. This is not a singles' getaway. The resort is very family-oriented, and offers lots of programs just for children. In addition to golf and tennis, adults can waterski, sail, or cruise on the river. A free minibus shuttles guests 20 minutes to the beach.

The resort's simple rooms are decorated in bright ethnic colors, and feature small balconies, tiled floors, and modern amenities. All rooms come with in-room safes, large closets, and mini-refrigerators.

Dining/Entertainment: All-you-can-eat buffets are served in the main dining room three times a day. In addition, La Fontana restaurant serves late breakfasts and Italian cuisine at dinner, and the French-style Riverside is open for dinner only. There's a variety of nightly entertainment around the resort.

Services: Room service, concierge, overnight laundry.

Facilities: Two golf courses, driving range, 19 tennis courts, waterskiing, volleyball courts, fitness center, water-sports rentals, billiards, five swimming pools, wading pool, aerobics classes, workshops, boutique, cinema.

MODERATE

HARBOR LIGHT INN, 1160 Seaway Dr., Fort Pierce, Hutchinson Island, FL 34949. Tel. 407/468-3555, or toll free 800/433-0004. 21 rms. A/C MINIBAR TV TEL

$ Rates: Dec 20–Apr, $78–$120 single or double. May–Dec 19, $58–$95 single or double. Additional person $10 extra. AE, CB, DC, DISC, MC, V.

Fronting the Intracoastal Waterway, the Harbor Light is a good choice for boating and fishing enthusiasts, offering 15 boat slips and two private fishing piers. The hotel itself carries on this nautical theme with pierlike wooden stairs and ropelike railings. While not exactly captain's quarters, the rooms, simply decorated with pastel colors and small wall prints, are adequate. Higher-priced rooms either have waterfront balconies or small kitchenettes that contain a coffee maker, refrigerator, oven, and a toaster. The inn also offers a swimming pool with a large deck for sunbathing.

BUDGET

EDGEWATER MOTEL AND APARTMENTS, 1156 Seaway Dr., Fort Pierce, Hutchinson Island, FL 34949. Tel. 407/468-3555, or toll free 800/433-0004. 14 rms, 7 efficiencies. A/C TV TEL
$ Rates: Dec 20–Apr, $47 single or double; from $80 efficiency. May–Dec 19, $37 single or double; from $60 efficiency. AE, DISC, MC, V.

This budget alternative to the Harbor Light Inn, next door, offers modestly decorated rooms garnished with an eclectic mix of furniture. There's a private swimming pool, and guests have access to the adjacent fishing pier and boat docks.

Efficiencies contain small kitchens, and are available on a daily or weekly basis.

WHERE TO DINE

MODERATE

P.V. MARTIN'S, 5150 N. Fla. A1A, Fort Pierce. Tel. 569-0700.
Cuisine: AMERICAN. **Reservations:** Recommended.
$ Prices: Appetizers $3.50–$8; main courses $9–$19; lunch $4–$11. AE, MC, V.
Open: Lunch Mon–Sat 11am–3:30pm; dinner Sun–Thurs 5–9pm, Fri–Sat 5–9:30pm; brunch Sun 10:30am–2:30pm.

This relatively elegant eatery, with an eclectic American menu, is my top pick in Fort Pierce. The restaurant's wood floors, beamed ceilings, tile-top tables, and rattan chairs would be nice anywhere, but here they look out through floor-to-ceiling windows onto sweeping ocean vistas. By night, the room is warmed by a huge central stone fireplace, and on weekends there's live entertainment in the adjacent bar.

Surf-and-turf dinners run the gamut from crab-stuffed shrimp and grouper baked with bananas and almonds, to Brie- and asparagus-stuffed chicken breast and barbecued baby back ribs. An excellent selection of appetizers includes escargots in mushroom caps and a succulent fried softshell crab (available in season).

Lunches can be lighter, and include sandwiches, burgers, and stuffed potato skins. But prime rib, seafood-topped pasta dishes, and other meatier meals are always available.

INEXPENSIVE

CAFE COCONUTS, 4304 NE Ocean Blvd., Hutchinson Island. Tel. 225-6006.
Cuisine: AMERICAN. **Reservations:** Not required.
$ Prices: Appetizers $4–$7; main courses $8–$15; lunch $3–$9. MC, V.
Open: Daily 11:30am–midnight.

Located in the Island Shoppes shopping center on Fla. A1A, this large restaurant's three separate dining rooms are all packed with simple, pink-clothed tables. Pink and blue "Miami Vice"–toned walls are covered with oceanic prints and posters, as is the bar, which occupies much of the restaurant's principal room.

A wide variety of salads and sandwiches are matched by an equally extensive selection of meat and fish dishes, including seafood and steak, and chicken. Despite their healthfulness, the restaurant's "low-calorie suggestions" are also some of their tastiest. Try the charcoal-broiled chicken or the broiled fresh catch-of-the-day.

THEO THUDPUCKER'S RAW BAR AND SEAFOOD RESTAURANT, 2025 Seaway Dr., Fort Pierce. Tel. 465-1078.
Cuisine: SEAFOOD. **Reservations:** Not accepted.
$ Prices: Appetizers $2–$6; main courses $8–$14; lunch $4–$7. No credit cards.
Open: Mon–Thurs 11:30am–9:30pm, Fri–Sat 11:30am–11pm, Sun 1–9:30pm.

Nobody comes here for luxurious ambience. Located in a little building by the beach, wallpapered with maps and newspapers, Thudpucker's pretends only to be what it is: a straightforward fresher-than-now chowder bar. Prominently placed signs attest to the food's purity: "Both clams and oysters are packed with ice and are not opened until you place your order. Please be patient." Chowder and stews, often made with sherry and half-and-half, make excellent starters or light meals. The most recommendable (and filling) dinner dishes are sautéed scallops, onions, green peppers, and tomatoes; deviled crabs; and deep-fried Okeechobee catfish.

BUDGET

CAPTAIN'S GALLEY, 827 N. Indian River Dr., Fort Pierce. Tel. 466-8495.
  Cuisine: SEAFOOD/AMERICAN. **Reservations:** Not accepted.
  $ Prices: Appetizers $2–$3; main courses $9; breakfast/lunch $2–$5. MC, V.
  Open: Mon–Sat 7am–9pm, Sun 7am–noon.
Anywhere else, this might be just another coffee shop. But here, just over the Intracoastal at the north end of Hutchinson Island, it's a local institution. Dressed up with printed window valances and hanging plants, the Captain's Galley is busiest during breakfast, when locals catch up on the previous day's events and plan for the coming one over eggs, toast, and home-fries. Lunch specials usually include a variety of burgers and a small selection of salads and sandwiches. And dinner is for seafood, when the Galley serves up scampied shrimp, the day's fish, or land specialties like strip steak and chicken français.

EVENING ENTERTAINMENT

Café Coconuts, 4304 NE Ocean Blvd., on Hutchinson Island (tel. 225-6006), is recommended here for its bars and entertainment. There are three different drinking rooms: The circular bar downstairs is surrounded by televisions and has a kind of nautical theme. A second bar is more intimate, located on a small patio; and the third is upstairs, and outdoors, in a beach setting with high white bar tables that keep your feet off the floor. There's live music on the weekends. Admission is free, and it's open daily from 11:30am to 2am.

3. VERO BEACH

85 miles SE of Orlando, 175 miles N of Miami

GETTING THERE By Plane The **Palm Beach International Airport** (tel. 407/471-7420), located about 100 miles to the south, is the closest gateway to the Vero Beach area. See Chapter 7 on the Gold Coast for complete information.

By Train Amtrak (tel. toll free 800/USA-RAIL) trains departing from New York stop in West Palm Beach, about 30 miles to the south, and in Okeechobee, about 30 miles to the west. The West Palm Beach station is located at 201 S. Tamarind Ave. (tel. 407/832-6169). The Okeechobee station is located at 801 N. Parrot Ave., off U.S. 441 N. (tel. 813/763-1114).

By Bus Greyhound can get you to the Vero Beach area from almost anywhere. The company no longer operates a single nationwide telephone number, so consult your local directory for the office nearest you.

By Car If you're driving up or down the Florida coast, you'll probably reach the Vero Beach area on Interstate 95, a highway that runs all the way from Maine to Miami. Visitors on their way to or from Orlando should take the Florida Turnpike, a toll road that runs almost directly from this region's beaches to Walt Disney World. Finally, if you're coming from the state's west coast, you'll probably take Fla. 70, which runs north of Lake Okeechobee right into Fort Pierce.

ESSENTIALS The **telephone area code** is 407.
  The **Indian River County Tourist Council,** 1216 21st St., Vero Beach, FL 32961 (tel. 407/567-3491), offers information on the entire county.

Vero Beach is located at the southern tip of the Indian River area. Much of the Vero Beach area belongs to the Indian River Citrus District and is responsible for 75% of the total grapefruit crop grown in the state of Florida. The warm climate that originally attracted so many citrus farms has also attracted many residents, and the area is growing. Native Floridians who want to escape from the intense development in the southern cities are moving north to Vero Beach. Residents who used to know Miami and Fort Lauderdale before the days of massive high-rises and overcrowding desire to reclaim the home-town feel they have lost. And that's exactly what you'll find in this area with its laid-back, relaxed atmosphere, nicely reflected in the moderate rates for accommodations just across from the beach. In addition, many water-sports enthusiasts are drawn to the area to enjoy offshore diving and snorkeling as well as surfing and windsurfing, and baseball buffs are drawn here in the summer to catch some action from the Vero Beach Dodgers as they participate in exhibition games during their spring training.

WHAT TO SEE & DO
MUSEUMS

INDIAN RIVER CITRUS MUSEUM, 2140 14th Ave. Tel. 770-2263.

Even if you've never heard of the Indian River, it's likely you know of Indian River citrus. Known by connoisseurs as some of the best in the world, oranges and grapefruit from this region are prized for their flavor and juiciness. Now comes the fruit's latest honor: its own museum. The Indian River Citrus Museum exhibits artifacts relating to the history of the citrus industry, from its initial boom in the late 1800s to the current day. Displays include old photographs, dated farm tools, antique citrus labels, and original harvesting equipment. There's also an unusual gift shop that alone is worth visiting.

Admission: $1 donation.
Open: Tues-Sat 10am-4pm, Sun 1-4pm.

McCLARTY TREASURE MUSEUM, 13180 N. Fla. A1A. Tel. 589-2147.

When the treasure of a Spanish fleet that sank off this coast in 1715 was recovered, the hunters chose to cash in, leaving only replicas to this museum. So what if the gold and coins are not original? Suspend your disbelief and imagine what it must have been like to uncover this hoard of riches. Various Native American artifacts are also on display.

Admission: $1.
Open: Daily 10am-4pm.

FLORIDA EAST COAST RAILWAY DEPOT EXHIBITION CENTER, 2336 14th Ave. Tel. 778-3435.

Railroads built South Florida, and this station, established in 1903, was one of the first to be constructed in the area. From its pioneer-day beginnings through the Depression and two world wars, this depot welcomed thousands of passengers to this little piece of beachside paradise. Now no longer in use, the station house has been restored to its early condition, moved to the city-owned park, and opened as a museum. Inside are railroad artifacts, historical exhibits, and other displays of local interest. The museum also offers historical walking tours on most Wednesdays at 11am and 1pm; reservations are required.

Admission: Free.
Open: Wed 10am-3pm, Sat 10am-noon, Sun 2-4pm.

DODGERTOWN, 3901 26th St. (P.O. Box 2887), Vero Beach, FL 32961. Tel. 407/569-4900.

An entire sports and recreation complex has opened around the stadium that's the winter home of baseball's Los Angeles Dodgers. The 450-acre complex encompasses two golf courses, a conference center, country club, movie theater, and recreation room. Exhibition games are played here during the winter months at Holman's Stadium. If you want something more filling than a Dodger Dog, visit the Country Club Restaurant, where fans often report sightings of their favorite players.

Admission: Complex, free; stadium, $5-$10.
Open: Daily 8am-11pm. **Directions:** From I-95, follow County Rd. 60 east for

five miles to 43rd Avenue, turn left, continue to 26th Street, and turn right; the entrance is straight ahead.

SPORTS & RECREATION

BEACHES   Most of Vero's beachfront is open to the public—an all-too-unusual situation that you should take advantage of. The beach at the end of Beachland Boulevard is one of the most popular and convenient. Others are best for sports and picnicking. Here's the lowdown:

Jaycee Beach Park, on Ocean Drive and Mango Road in Vero Beach, is a small park with a nice beach area, picnic facilities, public restrooms, showers, and even a restaurant.

Riverside Park, east of Barber Bridge at the end of Memorial Island Drive, is, appropriately enough, located directly on the Indian River. There are tennis and racquetball courts here, as well as a jogging course, boat ramps, and picnic pavilions.

South Beach Park, on South Ocean Drive, at the end of Marigold Lane, is a busy, developed beach with picnic tables, restrooms, and showers. This is one of the best swimming beaches, and lifeguards are on duty here.

FISHING   Captain Jack Jackson works seven days a week out of **Vero's Tackle and Sportshop,** 51 Royal Palm Blvd. (tel. 567-6550), taking fishers on private river and big-game excursions. Captain Jackson provides all the equipment along with his 25-foot boat. Half-day jaunts on the Indian River cost $150 per person and require a minimum of two people. Deep-water ocean excursions last a whole day and cost $400 per person.

GOLF   There are two courses at **Dodgertown,** on the corner of 43rd Avenue and 26th Street (tel. 569-4800): an 18-hole championship course at the Dodger Pines Country Club, and a challenging 9-hole run located adjacent to the complex's baseball stadium. Club rentals are available and lessons are offered by PGA professionals. Greens fees are $11 to $20.

The **Whisper Lakes** public course, at U.S. 1 and 53rd Street (tel. 567-3321), represents the best driving deal in town. Here you can play 9 or 18 holes of golf or just hit a practice bucket on the driving range. Clubs rent for $3; greens fees are $5 for 9 holes, $10 for 18 holes. Carts are an additional $2.

MINIATURE GOLF   Duffers with kids in tow might visit **Safari Golf and Games,** 455 Oslo Rd. (also known as 9th St. S.W. or Route 606; tel. 562-6492), a deluxe miniature playland that offers not one, but two 18-hole miniature golf courses complete with waterfalls and caves. There are also baseball and softball batting cages, as well as the requisite games room, outfitted with video games, billiards, and hard-to-find Skeeball and air-hockey games. Admission is $4.50 for adults, $3.50 children 5 to 12, free for kids 4 and under. It's open Monday through Thursday from 11am to 9:30pm, on Friday and Saturday from 11am to 11pm, and on Sunday from noon to 9:30pm.

TENNIS   The 10 tennis courts (6 lighted) can each be rented for $3 per person per hour at the **Memorial Island Tennis Club,** on Royal Palm Boulevard at the east end of Barber Bridge (tel. 231-4787). Reservations are accepted up to 24 hours in advance. The club also has two racquetball courts at reasonable rates.

WHERE TO STAY
EXPENSIVE

THE DAYS RESORT, 3244 Ocean Dr., Vero Beach, FL 32963. Tel. 407/231-2800, or toll free 800/245-3297. 102 rms, 8 efficiencies. A/C TV TEL
$ Rates: Dec 15–Apr, $79–$125 single or double; from $120 efficiency. May–Dec 14, $59–$99 single or double; from $100 efficiency. AE, MC, V.

The recently renovated Days Resort opens with a simple but pretty lobby dominated by a grand chandelier that hangs over an Oriental rug. Bright hallways are made cheerier with brilliant-colored carpets and fresh coats of paint. Most of the hotel's rooms have two double beds, and look exactly as you'd expect a large chain hotel room to look. They are far from extraordinary, but are clean and have all the necessities. The simple baths offer few amenities, and guests' clothes are meant to be hung on a small rod near the door rather than in a closet.

What the resort lacks in amenities and decor it makes up for in location and services. The hotel is situated directly on the beach, and has a large swimming pool just steps from the sand. Room service is offered from the hotel restaurant, which is open Monday through Saturday from 7am to 10pm and on Sunday from 7am to 3pm.

GUEST QUARTERS SUITE RESORT, 3500 Ocean Dr., Vero Beach, FL 32963. Tel. 407/231-5666, or toll free 800/841-5666. Fax 407/234-4866. 55 suites. A/C MINIBAR TV TEL

$ Rates: Dec 23–Apr, $185–$225 one-bedroom suite; $245–$275 two-bedroom suite. May–Dec 22, $95–$125 one-bedroom suite; $145 two-bedroom suite. AE, CB, DC, DISC, MC, V.

Vero's best all-suite hotel is located directly on the beach, close to local restaurants and shops. First-class accommodations are located in a modern, pastel-colored, four-story building. What the nearly identical suites lack in character, they make up for in content. All are nicely decorated with pastel wallpapers and bedspreads. Rooms are equipped with small refrigerators and coffee makers, two phones, and modern baths that include hairdryers.

Dining/Entertainment: The Lanai Room is open daily from 10am to 10pm, and serves breakfast, lunch, and dinner. The Seabreeze pool bar is open daily for snacks and cocktails.

Services: Room service, concierge, laundry.

Facilities: Swimming pool, whirlpool; tennis, golf, and racquetball are nearby.

MODERATE

THE DRIFTWOOD RESORT, 3150 Ocean Dr., Vero Beach, FL 32963. Tel. 407/231-0550. 100 rms. A/C TV TEL

$ Rates: Dec 21–Jan 1 and Feb–Maundy Thurs (before Easter), $55–$110 single or double; from $130 two-bedroom suite. The rest of the year, $80–$160 single or double; from $160 two-bedroom suite. AE, MC, V.

South Florida, 1930—world traveler and vacation visionary Waldo Sexton began construction on a coastal hideaway built from local cypress logs. Originally planned as a private estate, the Driftwood was opened to the public after several travelers stopped to inquire about renting a room here. Today the hotel's rooms and public areas are filled with knickknacks collected by Waldo Sexton from throughout the world, including many bells.

All the guest rooms are different. Some feature terra-cotta–tiled floors and lighter furniture while others have a more rustic feel with hardwood floors and antiques. Each accommodation has its own bath, and few frills.

ISLANDER MOTEL, 3101 Ocean Dr., Vero Beach, FL 32963. Tel. 407/231-4431, or toll free 800/952-5886. 16 rms. A/C TV TEL

$ Rates: Dec 19–Jan 20, $64–$75 single or double. Jan 21–Apr 20, $94–$99 single or double. Apr 21–Dec 18, $54–$65 single or double. AE, DISC, MC.

Resident owners Robert and Winifred Carter run one of the most comfortable and welcoming inns in the area. Well located in downtown Vero Beach, this aqua-colored motel is just a short walk to the beach, restaurants, and shops. Every guest room has either a king-size bed or two double beds, plus a small refrigerator. Accommodations are outfitted in a Caribbean motif with brightly printed curtains, matching bedspreads, and white rattan furniture. There's a heated pool and a barbecue area in the handsomely landscaped central courtyard, along with a small walk-up café.

VERO BEACH INN, 4700 N. Fla. A1A, Vero Beach, FL 32963. Tel. 407/231-1600, or toll free 800/227-8615. 105 rms, 3 suites. A/C TV TEL

Directions: From I-95, exit east on Fla. 60, continue all the way to the ocean, and turn left onto Fla. A1A; the hotel is one mile ahead, on your right.

$ Rates: Feb 8–Apr 14, $90–$100 single or double; from $125 suite. Apr 15–Feb 7, $65–$75 single or double; from $90 suite. Additional person $6 extra. AE, CB, DC, DISC, MC, V.

One of my more unusual picks is this slightly eccentric inn located just north of downtown Vero Beach. Overgrown exterior plantings give this brick mansion a mildly mysterious look, intensified by tall white columns and black iron railings. The rooms are very comfortable, combining mauvey earthtones and modern amenities. I particularly like the inn's unusual swimming pool, which is partly enclosed by the hotel and partly open to the sky.

The hotel itself rests right on the beach, and is a short drive to nearby shops, restaurants, and attractions. Its restaurant, the Silver Sands Cafe, has ocean and pool views, and Runyon's Lounge features live entertainment on the weekends.

CAMPING

SUNSHINE TRAVEL PARK, County Rd. 512 and I-95, Sebastian, FL 32978. Tel. 407/589-7828. 300 sites.
$ Rates: $26.50 per site.
A kind of Club Med for campers, this RV resort features a heated pool, shuffleboard, miniature golf, and a full schedule of activities.

VERO BEACH KOA RV PARK, 8850 U.S. 1, Wabasso, FL 32970. Tel. 407/589-5665. 120 sites. **Directions:** From I-95, take County Road 512 east, then turn south on U.S. 1 to the campground.
$ Rates: $16.95–$19.95 per site.
This campground is two miles from the ocean and the Intracoastal Waterway. There's running water at most campsites, as well as showers and a shop, and hook-ups for RVs.

WHERE TO DINE
EXPENSIVE

THE BLACK PEARL, 1409 Fla. A1A. Tel. 234-4426.
   Cuisine: CONTINENTAL. **Reservations:** Recommended.
$ Prices: Appetizers $3–$5; main courses $14–$17. AE, MC, V.
   Open: Dinner only, daily 6–10pm.
It's unusual that such a small, unassuming little restaurant should handmake everything they serve, but that's exactly what they do here, where you can be wooed by seductive smells even before you walk through the front door. There's just a single, romantic dining room which features bright prints on crisply clean pastel walls. Full wine racks and black art deco accents round out the decor.

The restaurant's small list of appetizers may include feta cheese and spinach fritters, chilled leek-and-watercress soup, or oysters baked with crabmeat and butter. Equally creative main courses recently included Cajun pasta (topped with shrimp, scallops, and sausage), sautéed crabmeat-stuffed veal covered with hollandaise sauce, and rib-eye steak, blackened, with a crown of tomatoes. There's a good wine list, and a better dessert selection, baked daily in the restaurant's kitchen.

OCEAN GRILL, 1050 Sexton Plaza. Tel. 231-5409.
   Cuisine: AMERICAN. **Reservations:** Accepted only for large parties.
$ Prices: Appetizers $2–$9; main courses $11–$20; lunch $6–$11. AE, CB, DC, DISC, MC, V.
   Open: Lunch Mon–Fri 11:30am–2:30pm; dinner daily 5:45–10pm.
The Ocean Grill was founded in 1941 by some of the area's earliest developers. Now something of a historical landmark in these parts, the restaurant is justifiably proud of its long service in South Florida. The grill's dark-wood interior and distinct musty aroma attest to its authenticity. The dining room is filled with Spanish antiques that include a massive iron chandelier that hangs above one of the world's largest solid, red mahogany tables. Winters are best, when a fire roars from an imposing stone fireplace. But summers are nice too, especially when you sit by the great glass windows that open onto the ocean.

It doesn't matter what main course you choose, as long as you accompany it with an order of onion rings. At lunch, it might be a deviled-crab sandwich, hot thinly sliced roast beef on a toasted French roll, or spinach salad with hot bacon dressing. Dinners mean fresh fish, which is available broiled, fried, or Cajun style; grilled pork chops with homemade jalapeño applesauce; and a roast duckling that's deserving of the restaurant's self-congratulatory "gold seal."

MODERATE

CHARLEY BROWN'S, 1410 S. Fla. A1A. Tel. 231-6310.
Cuisine: AMERICAN. **Reservations:** Recommended.
$ Prices: Burgers and sandwiches $5–$9; main courses $10–$15. AE, MC, V.
Open: Dinner only, daily 5–10pm.

I'm usually not one for corporate restaurants, but this dark, wood-and-fern chain eatery gets high marks for its unusually large salad bar that rivals any I've seen. For a reason I don't quite understand, many diners order hot dishes to accompany the copious salad bar. Fish is blackened, baked, or charcoal-broiled; chicken is barbecued or grilled; and beef is served as prime rib, or shish kebab style on a skewer with onions, tomatoes, green peppers, and mushrooms.

WALDO'S, in the Driftwood Resort, 3150 Ocean Dr. Tel. 231-7091.
Cuisine: SEAFOOD/AMERICAN. **Reservations:** Not accepted.
$ Prices: Appetizers $2–$6; main courses $10–$13; sandwiches and salads $5–$7. AE, MC, V.
Open: Mon–Sat 7am–10pm, Sun 8am–10pm.

Everyone who hears that you went to Vero Beach will ask if you went to Waldo's. The restaurant is not famous for its food, which is good but not great. Waldo's is known for its unusual setting: picnic tables set outdoors, directly overlooking the beach. Sandwiches are the best bet, whether you choose a turkey club, broiled chicken, or a burger. Dinners are just slightly more elaborate, and include Danish-style barbecued ribs and Cajun seafood kebabs.

SHOPPING

Ocean Boulevard and **Cardinal Drive** are Vero's two main shopping streets, both of which are near the beach and lined with specialty boutiques.

Some of the more distinctive shops in town include **Hale Indian River Groves,** 615 Beachland Blvd. (tel. 231-1752), a shipper of local citrus and jams since 1947; and **Bodi and Sol,** 3349 Ocean Dr. (tel. 231-5151), a shop selling contemporary women's clothing, with pastel prints and other tropical colors.

EVENING ENTERTAINMENT

CENTER FOR THE ARTS, 3001 Riverside Park Dr. Tel. 231-0707.

Vero Beach's boosters are justifiably proud of their newly completed cultural center. In addition to being beautifully designed and landscaped, the center actually attracts important events in its lecture hall, museum, and 250-seat Leohardt Auditorium. Volunteer docents give tours of the galleries Wednesday through Sunday from 1:30 to 3:30pm. Call for scheduled exhibitions and performances. The center is open October to April, Friday through Wednesday from 10am to 4:30pm and on Thursday from 10am to 8pm; May to September, on Tuesday, Wednesday, Friday, and Saturday from 10am to 4:30pm, on Thursday from 10am to 8pm, and on Sunday from 1 to 4:30pm.

Admission: Museum, free; auditorium prices vary, depending on the performance scheduled.

RIVERSIDE THEATER, on Riverside Park Dr., just past the drawbridge. Tel. 231-6990.

Plays, musicals, children's shows, summer workshops, and various celebrity events are scheduled here from October through May. During the summer months, there's usually only one major performance. Call for schedules and tickets.

Admission: Tickets, $5–$30.

ORLANDO & WALT DISNEY WORLD

Orlando was a sleepy southern village ringed with sparkling lakes, pine forests, and citrus groves until Walt Disney waved his pixie-dusted paintbrush over 43 square miles of swampland in 1971 and turned it into a Magic Kingdom. He literally "animated" the area, sparking a building boom in hotels and restaurants to serve massive numbers of Walt Disney World visitors. And scores of additional attractions soon arose to take advantage of the tourist traffic Disney had generated. The world's most famous mouse has changed Central Florida forever. Many national firms have moved their headquarters to this thriving sunbelt region, and it has also become one of the fastest-growing high-technology centers in the country.

For the tourist, the city and its environs are so attraction-rich that unless you stay for several weeks, you can't possibly see everything in one trip. The original Magic Kingdom—a fantasyland of animated characters, rides, dazzling parades, and nightly fireworks—has been augmented by half a dozen additional Disney attraction areas and over 20 Disney resorts and official hotels. And scores of non-Disney attractions—most notably Sea World, Universal Studios, Cypress Gardens, and the Kennedy Space Center—also compete for your tourist dollar. This is one destination that requires advance planning for optimum enjoyment.

1. ORIENTATION

ARRIVING

BY PLANE The **Orlando International Airport** (tel. 407/825-2001), 25 miles from Walt Disney World, is a thoroughly modern and user-friendly facility with centrally located information kiosks. Delta, the official airline of Walt Disney World, offers service from 200 cities and has a Fantastic Flyer program for kids. Other carriers include Aero Costa Rica, Aeropostal, Air Jamaica, All Nippon Airways, America West, American, American Trans Air, British Airways, ComAir, Continental, Icelandair, KLM, Kiwi, LeisureAir, LTU, Mexicana, Northwest, Spirit, Transbrasil, TWA, United, USAir, Valuejet, and Virgin Atlantic.

Since advance-purchase fares are almost always the lowest available, it's a good idea to book your flight as far in advance as possible.

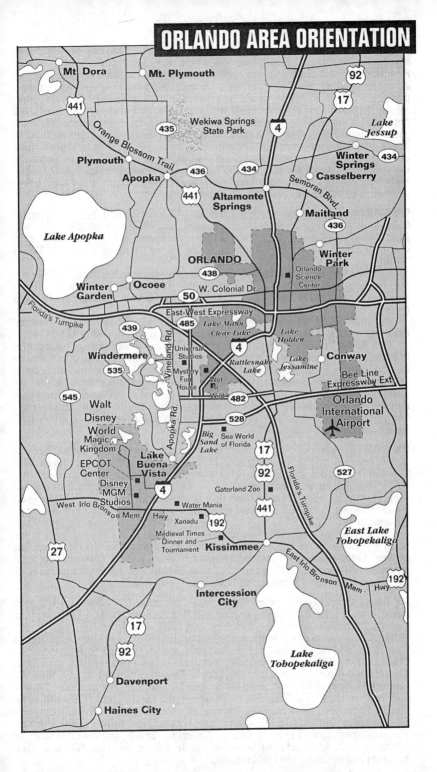

ORLANDO AREA ORIENTATION

Mt. Dora
Mt. Plymouth
441
435
Wekiwa Springs State Park
92
17
Lake Jessup
Orange Blossom Trail
4
Plymouth
436
434
Winter Springs
434
Apopka
Semoran Blvd
Casselberry
441
Altamonte Springs
Maitland
436
Lake Apopka
ORLANDO
438
Winter Park
Orlando Science Center
Winter Garden
Ocoee
50
W. Colonial Dr.
Florida's Turnpike
East-West Expressway
485
Lake Mann
Clear Lake
Lake Holden
439
4
Windermere
Universal Studios
Rattlesnake Lake
Lake Jessamine
Conway
535
Vineland Rd.
Mystery Fun House
Wet 'n Wild
482
Bee Line Expressway Ext.
545
Apopka Rd.
528
Orlando International Airport
Walt Disney World
Magic Kingdom
Big Sand Lake
Sea World of Florida
17
EPCOT Center
Lake Buena Vista
92
527
Disney MGM Studios
4
Gatorland Zoo
Florida's Turnpike
West Irlo Bronson Mem.
Water Mania
441
East Lake Tobopekaliga
Hwy
Xanadu
192
27
Medieval Times Dinner and Tournament
Kissimmee
East Irlo Bronson Mem. Hwy
192
Intercession City
17
92
Lake Tobopekaliga
Davenport
Haines City

When you call to reserve your flight, also inquire about **money-saving packages.** For instance, Delta Dream Vacations, in several price ranges, include round-trip air transport, accommodations (state and hotel room tax included), an air-conditioned intermediate rental car with unlimited mileage or round-trip airport transfer, a "Magic Passport" which provides unlimited admission to all WDW parks for the length of your stay, one breakfast (which can be a character breakfast), and entry into a selected theme park one hour before regular opening time. Since the packages utilize Walt Disney World Resorts, you get all the advantages accruing to guests at these properties (see "Accommodations," below). If you put all those components together on your own, the cost would be much, much higher. Delta also has Orlando packages for which WDW tickets are optional. For details, call toll free 800/872-7786 or consult your local travel agent. Note: Delta is the only airline authorized to use Disney resorts in its packages.

BY TRAIN Amtrak trains (tel. toll free 800/USA-RAIL) pull into the station in Orlando at 1400 Sligh Blvd., between Columbia and Miller Streets (about 23 miles from Walt Disney World). There's also a Kissimmee station at 316 Pleasant St., at the corner of Dakin Avenue and Thurman Street (about 15 miles from Walt Disney World).

A limited number of discount-fare seats are set aside on each train; the sooner you reserve, the greater the savings. Many people reserve fares months in advance. There may be some restrictions on travel dates for discounted fares around very busy holiday times.

To inquire about Amtrak's money-saving packages—including hotel accommodations, car rentals, tours, etc., with your train fare—call toll free 800/321-8684.

The Auto Train Amtrak's Auto Train offers the convenience of having a car in Florida without driving it there. The Auto Train begins in Lorton, Va. (about a four-hour drive from New York, two hours from Philadelphia) and ends up at Sanford, Fla. (about 23 miles northeast of Orlando). Once again, reserve early for the lowest fares. The Auto Train departs Lorton and Sanford at 4:30pm daily, arriving at the opposite destination at 9am the next morning. Note: You have to arrive one or two hours before departure time so they can board your car. Call toll free 800/USA-RAIL for details.

BY BUS Greyhound buses connect the entire country with Orlando. They pull into a terminal at 555 N. Magruder Blvd. (John Young Pkwy.), between West Colonial Drive and Winter Garden Road, a few miles west of downtown Orlando (tel. 407/292-3440), or in Kissimmee at 16 N. Orlando Ave., between Emmett and Mabbette Streets, about 14 miles from Walt Disney World (tel. 407/847-3911). There is van transport from the Kissimmee terminal to most area hotels and motels. From Orlando, a taxi ($25 to $30 to Walt Disney World–area hotels) is the only viable option. Greyhound's fare structure tends to be complex, but the good news is that when you call to make a reservation, the agent will always give you the lowest-fare options. Once again, advance-purchase fares booked 3 to 21 days prior to travel represent vast savings. For fare and scheduling information, check your phone book for a local Greyhound listing, or call toll free 800/231-2222.

BY CAR Orlando is 436 miles from Atlanta, 1,312 miles from Boston, 1,120 miles from Chicago, 1,009 miles from Cleveland, 1,170 miles from Dallas, 1,114 miles from Detroit, 1,105 miles from New York City, and 1,261 miles from Toronto.

From Atlanta, take I-75 south to the Florida Turnpike to I-4 west. From Boston, New York, and other points in the Northeast, take I-95 south to I-4 west. From Chicago, take I-65 south to Nashville, then I-24 south to I-75 south to the Florida Turnpike to I-4 west. From Cleveland, take I-77 south to Columbia, S.C., then I-26 east to I-95 south to I-4 west. From Dallas, take I-20 east to I-49 south to I-10 east to I-75 south to the Florida Turnpike to I-4 west. From Detroit, take I-75 south to the Florida Turnpike to I-4 west. From Toronto, take Canadian Rte. 401 south to Queen Elizabeth Way south to I-90 (New York State Thruway) east to I-87 (New York State Thruway) south to I-95 over the George Washington Bridge, and continue south on I-95 to I-4 west. AAA and some other automobile club members can call local offices for maps and optimum driving directions.

TOURIST INFORMATION

Contact the **Orlando/Orange County Convention & Visitors Bureau,** 8445 International Dr. (in the Mercado Shopping Village), Orlando, FL 32819 (tel. 407/363-5871). They can answer all your questions and will be happy to send you maps, brochures (including the informative *Official Visitors Guide,* the *Area Guide* (to local restaurants), the *Official Accommodations Guide,* and the "Magicard" (good for discounts of 10% to 50% on accommodations, attractions, car rentals, and more). Discount tickets to attractions other than Disney parks are sold on the premises, and the multilingual staff can also make dining reservations and hotel referrals. The bureau is open daily except Christmas from 8am to 8pm.

For general information about Walt Disney World, and a copy of the informative *Walt Disney World Vacation Guide,* write or call the **Walt Disney World Co.,** P.O. Box 10000, Lake Buena Vista, FL 32830-1000 (tel. 407/824-4321).

If you're driving, you can stop at a Walt Disney World information facility in Ocala, Fla., at the intersection of I-75 and Fla. 200, about 90 miles north of Orlando (tel. 904/854-0770). Here you can purchase tickets and Mickey ears, get help planning your park itinerary, and make hotel reservations.

And at the Orlando International Airport, arriving passengers can stroll over to Greetings from Walt Disney World Resort (tel. 904/825-2301), a shop and information center on the third floor in the main lobby just behind the Northwest counter. This facility sells WDW park tickets, makes dinner show and hotel reservations at Disney properties, and provides brochures and assistance. It's open daily from 7am to 10pm.

Also contact the **Kissimmee–St. Cloud Convention & Visitors Bureau,** 1925 U.S. 192 (P.O. Box 422007), Kissimmee, FL 34742-2007 (tel. 407/847-5000, or toll free 800/327-9159). They'll send maps, brochures, discount books, and the *Kissimmee–St. Cloud Vacation Guide* which details the area's accommodations and attractions.

CITY LAYOUT

Orlando's major artery is **I-4,** which runs diagonally across the state from Tampa to Daytona Beach. Exits from I-4 take you to Walt Disney World, Sea World, International Drive, U.S. 192, Kissimmee, Lake Buena Vista, Church Street Station, downtown Orlando, and Winter Park. The **Florida Turnpike** crosses I-4 and links up with I-75 to the north. **U.S. 192,** a major east-west artery, stretches from Kissimmee (along a major motel strip) to **U.S. 27,** crossing I-4 near the Walt Disney World entrance road. Farther north, a toll road called the **Beeline Expressway** (Fla. 528) goes east from I-4 past Orlando International Airport to Cape Canaveral.

Walt Disney World property is bounded roughly by I-4 and Fla. 535 to the east (the latter also north), World Drive (the entrance road) to the west, and U.S. 192 to the south. EPCOT Center Drive (Fla. 536, the south end of International Drive) and Buena Vista Drive cut across the complex in a more-or-less east-west direction; the two roads cross at Bonnet Creek Parkway. Excellent highways and explicit signs make it very easy to find your way around.

Note: The Disney parks are actually much closer to Kissimmee than to downtown Orlando.

NEIGHBORHOODS IN BRIEF

Walt Disney World A city unto itself, WDW sprawls over more than 26,000 acres containing theme parks, resorts, hotels, shops, restaurants, and recreational facilities galore (copious details below).

Lake Buena Vista On the eastern end of Disney property, Lake Buena Vista is a hotel village/marketplace owned and operated by Walt Disney World. However, though Disney owns all the real estate, many of the hotels, and some shops and restaurants, in this area are independently owned. It's a charming area of manicured lawns and verdant thoroughfares with traffic islands shaded by towering oak trees.

International Drive [Fla. 536]   This attractive area extends 7 to 10 miles north of the Disney parks between Fla. 535 and the Florida Turnpike. It, too, centers—for a long way—on a wide thoroughfare with a tree-shaded traffic island. It contains numerous hotels, restaurants, shopping centers, and the Orange County Convention Center, and offers easy access to Sea World and Universal Studios. (*Note:* Locally, this road is always referred to as I-Drive.)

Kissimmee   South of the Disney Parks, Kissimmee centers on U.S. 192/Irlo Bronson Memorial Highway, a strip as archetypical of American cities as Main Street. It's lined with budget motels, lesser attractions, and every fast-food restaurant you can name.

Downtown Orlando   Reached via I-4 east, this burgeoning sunbelt metropolis is 17 miles northeast of Walt Disney World. Though many tourists never venture downtown, it does have a number of attractions, including noteworthy nightlife.

WHEN TO GO

Orlando is essentially a theme-park destination, and its busiest seasons are whenever kids are out of school—summer (early June to about August 20), holiday weekends, Christmas season (mid-December to mid-January), and Easter. Obviously, the whole experience is more enjoyable when the crowds are thinnest and the weather most temperate. Best times are the week after Labor Day until Thanksgiving, the week after Thanksgiving until mid-December, and the six weeks before and after school spring vacations. The worst time is summer, when crowds are very large and the weather hot and humid.

2. GETTING AROUND

FROM THE AIRPORT   Orlando International Airport is 25 miles from Walt Disney World. **Mears Transportation Group** (tel. 407/423-5566) buses ply the route from the airport to all Disney resorts and official hotels, as well as most other area properties. The comfortable, air-conditioned shuttle vans operate around the clock, departing every 15 to 25 minutes. Rates vary with your destination: The round-trip cost for adults is $19 between the airport and downtown Orlando or International Drive, $23 for Walt Disney World/Lake Buena Vista, $35 for Kissimmee/U.S. 192. Children 4 to 11 pay $14, $17, and $28, respectively; children 3 and under ride free.

Note: It's always a good idea to ask about transportation options between the airport and your hotel when you make your reservations, or if you're renting a car, for driving directions from the airport.

BY BUS   **Disney shuttle buses** serve all Disney resorts and official hotels, offering unlimited complimentary transportation via bus, monorail, ferry, and water taxi to all three parks from two hours prior to opening until two hours after closing; also to Disney Village Marketplace, Typhoon Lagoon, Pleasure Island, Fort Wilderness, and other Disney resorts. Disney hostelries offer transportation to other area attractions as well, though it's not complimentary. Almost all area hotels and motels also offer transportation to Walt Disney World and other attractions, but it can be pricey.

Mears Transportation Group (tel. 407/423-5566) operates buses to all major attractions, including Cypress Gardens, Kennedy Space Center, Universal Studios, Sea World, Busch Gardens (in Tampa), and Church Street Station, among others. Call for details.

BY TAXI   Taxis line up in front of major hotels, and at smaller hostelries the front desk will be happy to call you a cab. Or call **Yellow Cab** (tel. 699-9999). The charge is $2.45 for the first mile, $1.40 per mile thereafter.

BY CAR Though you can get to and around Walt Disney World and other major attractions here without a car, it's always handy to have one. All the major car-rental companies are represented here and maintain desks at the airport. Some handy phone numbers: **Alamo** (tel. toll free 800/327-9633), **Avis** (tel. toll free 800/331-1212), **Budget** (tel. toll free 800/527-0700), **Dollar** (tel. toll free 800/800-4000), **Hertz** (tel. toll free 800/654-3131), and **Thrifty** (tel. toll free 800/367-2277).

FAST ORLANDO

Area Code The telephone area code for most of Central Florida is 407.

Babysitters In this child-oriented town, almost every hotel provides babysitting services, and several hostelries have marvelous child-care facilities with counselor-supervised activity programs on the premises. Disney properties use KinderCare sitters (tel. 827-5444), so you can be sure they've been very carefully checked out. Rates for in-room service are $8 per hour for one child, $9 per hour for two children, $11 per hour for three children, $14 per hour for four children. There's a four-hour minimum, the first half hour of which is travel time for the sitter, and 24-hour advance notice is required.

Doctors and Dentists Inquire at your hotel desk, or call the Dental Referral Service (tel. 628-4363) from 5:30am to 6pm daily; they can tell you the nearest dentist who meets your needs. Check the *Yellow Pages* for 24-hour emergency services.

Disney has first-aid centers in all three major parks. There's also a very good 24-hour service in the area called HouseMed (tel. 648-9234). HouseMed doctors, who can dispense medication, make "house calls" to all area hotels. HouseMed also operates the Medi-Clinic, a walk-in medical facility (not for emergencies) at the intersection of I-4 and U.S. 192, open daily from 9am to 9pm (same phone); call for directions from your hotel. See also "Hospital Emergency Wards" and "Pharmacies," below.

Emergencies Dial 911 to contact the police or fire department or to call an ambulance. The 24-hour emergency hotline for the Poison Control Center is 897-1940.

Hairdressers Many hotels have on-premises hairdressers. If yours doesn't, check out the better hotel listings below to find one.

Hospital Emergency Wards Sand Lake Hospital is at 9400 Turkey Lake Rd., about two miles south of Sand Lake Road (tel. 351-8550). Take Exit 27A (the Sea World exit) off I-4, make a left at the stop sign at the end of the exit ramp, and bear right onto Turkey Lake Road; the hospital is ahead on your left.

Kennels All the major theme parks offer animal-boarding facilities at reasonable fees. At Walt Disney World, there are kennels at Fort Wilderness, Epcot, the Magic Kingdom, and Disney–MGM Studios. If you're traveling with a pet, don't leave it in the car, even with a window cracked, while you enjoy the park—many pets have perished this way in the hot Florida sun. Note: Where hotel listings mention that pets are accepted, there's always a charge.

Newspapers/Magazines The *Orlando Sentinel* is the major local newspaper, but you can also purchase papers of major cities (most notably the *New York Times*) in most hotel gift shops. Also informative is a city magazine called *Orlando*.

Pharmacies Walgreen Drug Store, 1003 W. Vine St. (U.S. 192), just east of Bermuda Avenue (tel. 847-5252), operates a 24-hour pharmacy. They can deliver to hotels for a charge ($10 from 7am to 5pm, $15 at all other times).

Post Office The main post office in Lake Buena Vista is at 12541 Fla. 535 near TGI Friday's in the Crossroads Shopping Center (tel. 828-2606). It's open Monday through Friday from 9am to 4pm and on Saturday from 9am to noon.

Religious Services Hotel desks invariably keep a list of local churches and synagogues. You can also check the *Yellow Pages*.

Safety Whenever you're traveling in an unfamiliar city, stay alert. Be aware of your immediate surroundings. It's a good idea to keep your valuables in a safety-deposit box (inquire at your hotel's front desk), though many hotels nowadays are equipped with in-room safes. Keep a close eye on your valuables when you're in a public place—restaurant, theater, even airport terminal. And don't leave valuables in your car, even in the trunk.

Tax   The hotel tax in Orlando is 10% and in Kissimmee it's 11%, both including a state sales tax that's charged on all goods except most grocery-store items and medicines.

Time   Call 646-3131 for the correct time and temperature.

Weather   Call 851-7510 for a weather recording.

3. ACCOMMODATIONS

You'll find a wealth of hotel options in the Walt Disney World area. Stunningly landscaped multifacility resorts are the rule, but there's something to suit every taste and pocketbook. Of course, reserve as far in advance as possible—the minute you've decided on the dates of your trip.

In some hotel listings below, I've mentioned concierge levels. If you're not familiar with this concept, it involves a "hotel within a hotel" where guests enjoy a luxurious private lounge that's the setting for complimentary continental breakfast, hot and cold hors d'oeuvres at cocktail hour, late-night cordials and pastries, and other special services. Rooms are usually on high floors with upgraded decor.

Also mentioned under "Facilities" are counselor-supervised child-care/activity centers. These are, for the most part, creatively run facilities where kids enjoy Disney movies, video games, arts and crafts, and outdoor activities. Some centers provide meals and/or have beds where a child can go to sleep while you're out on the town. Check the individual hotel listings for these facilities and call to find out exactly what's offered.

Note: Consider the cost of parking or shuttle buses to and from Disney and other theme parks in determining your hotel choice. It can add up to quite a bit.

DISNEY HOSTELRIES & OFFICIAL HOTELS

There are 14 Disney-owned properties (hotels, resorts, villas, wilderness/homes, and campsites) and 9 privately owned "official hotels," a goodly selection of which are described in this section. All are within the Walt Disney World complex.

In addition to their proximity to the parks, there are a number of advantages to staying at a Disney property or official hotel. At all Disney resorts and official hotels these include:

- Unlimited complimentary transportation via bus, monorail, ferry, and water taxi to/from all three parks from two hours before opening until two hours after closing. Unlimited complimentary transport is also provided to/from Disney Village Marketplace, Typhoon Lagoon, Pleasure Island, Fort Wilderness, and other Disney resorts. Three hostelries—the Polynesian, Contemporary, and Grand Floridian—are stops on the monorail. This free transport can save a lot of money. It also means that you're guaranteed admission to all parks, even during peak times when parking lots sometimes fill up.
- Free parking at WDW parking lots (other visitors pay $5 a day).
- Reduced-price children's menus in almost all restaurants, and character breakfasts and/or dinners at many hostelries.
- TVs equipped with the Disney Channel and Walt Disney World information stations.

- A guest services desk where you can purchase tickets to all WDW theme parks and attractions and obtain general information.
- Use of—and in some cases, complimentary transport to—the five Disney-owned golf courses and preferred tee times at them (these can be booked up to 30 days in advance).
- Access to most recreational facilities at other Disney resorts.
- Service by the Mears airport shuttle.

Additional perks at Disney-owned hotels, resorts, villas, and campgrounds (but not at "official" hotels) include charge privileges at restaurants and shops throughout Walt Disney World; early admission, prior to the public opening, to the Magic Kingdom on specific days; and dining and show reservations (including Epcot restaurants) which can be made on the premises.

WALT DISNEY WORLD CENTRAL RESERVATIONS OFFICE To reserve a room at Disney hotels, resorts, and villas; official hotels; and Fort Wilderness homes and campsites, contact the Central Reservations Office, P.O. Box 10100, Lake Buena Vista, FL 32830-0100 (tel. 407/W-DISNEY), which is open seven days a week between 8:30am and 10pm. Have your dates and credit or charge card ready when you call.

The CRO can recommend accommodations that will suit your specific needs as to price, location (perhaps you wish to be closest to Epcot, Magic Kingdom, or Disney–MGM Studios), and facilities such as counselor-supervised child-care centers, on-premises sports and recreational facilities, a kitchen, and so on.

Be sure to inquire about their numerous package plans which include meals, tickets, recreation, and other features. The right package plan can save you both money and time, and a comprehensive plan is helpful in computing the cost of your vacation in advance.

The CRO can also give you information about various park ticket options and make dinner-show reservations for you at the *Hoop-de-Doo Revue* and the *Polynesian Luau Dinner Show* when you book your room.

OTHER RESERVATIONS & PACKAGES **Delta,** the official airline of Walt Disney World, is the only airline permitted to use Disney resorts and campgrounds in its packages. They offer accommodations in different price ranges at your choice of a number of resorts. For details, call toll free 800/872-7786.

American Express Vacations is also officially authorized to use Disney resorts in its packages. For details, call toll free 800/241-1700.

Most **hotels** listed below also offer packages; inquire when you call. And **your travel agent** may also offer interesting packages.

DISNEY RESORTS

Very Expensive

DISNEY'S BEACH CLUB RESORT, 1800 EPCOT Resorts Blvd., (off Buena Vista Dr.; P.O. Box 10100), Lake Buena Vista, FL 32830-0100. Tel. 407/W-DISNEY or 407/934-8000. Fax 407/354-1866. 584 rms. 24 suites. A/C MINIBAR TV TEL

$ Rates: $210–$290 single or double, depending on view and season. Additional person $15 extra. Children under 18 stay free in parents' room. Inquire about packages. AE, MC, V. **Parking:** Free self- and valet parking.

With its pristinely white-trimmed sky-blue exterior, palm-fringed entranceway, sandy beach, and manicured gardens, the Beach Club evokes a luxurious Victorian Cape Cod resort. Charming rooms, furnished in bleached woods, are decorated in seafoam green with peach and coral accents. Beach umbrellas, seashells, and ocean waves adorn bedspreads, and wall sconces are seahorse-shaped. Some rooms have widow's walk balconies. Amenities include ceiling fans, extra phones in the bath, remote-control cable TVs, clock radios, safes, and game tables. Note: The Beach Club is within walking distance of Epcot.

Dining/Entertainment: The very elegant Ariel's, a seafood restaurant named for the *Little Mermaid* character, is open for dinner nightly (see "Dining," below, for details). In the adjoining Martha's Vineyard Lounge, international wines are offered by the glass. Ideal for family dining is the Cape May Café, serving buffet character breakfasts hosted by Admiral Goofy, and authentic New England clambake buffet dinners. The Rip Tide Lounge, off the lobby, features an array of California wines, wine coolers, and frosty concoctions. Beaches & Cream, adjoining the video-game arcade and central to both the Yacht and Beach Clubs, looks like an old-fashioned ice-cream parlor; light fare, plus sundaes, floats, and shakes are featured. Also central to both properties is Hurricane Hanna's Grill, for light fare, ice-cream sundaes, and specialty drinks.

Services: 24-hour room service, babysitting, guest services desk, complimentary daily newspaper, boat transport to MGM theme park.

Facilities: Large swimming pool, Jacuzzi, quarter-mile beach, boat rentals, two tennis courts, state-of-the-art health club, volleyball/croquet/bocci ball courts, two-mile jogging trail, coin-op washers/dryers, full-service unisex hair salon, shops, full business center, large video-game arcade, Sandcastle Club (a counselor-supervised child-care/activity center). Stormalong Bay, a 790,000-gallon free-form swimming pool-cum-waterpark, sprawls over three acres between the Yacht and Beach Clubs and flows into the lake; it includes a 150-foot serpentine water slide.

DISNEY'S GRAND FLORIDIAN BEACH RESORT, 4401 Floridian Way (P.O. Box 10100), Lake Buena Vista, FL 32830-0100. Tel. 407/W-DISNEY or 407/824-3000. Fax 407/354-1866. 878 rms, 26 suites. A/C MINIBAR TV TEL

$ Rates: $230–$325 standard single or double, depending on view and season; $410–$440 single or double on the concierge floors; $500–$1,450 suite. Additional person $15 extra. Children under 18 stay free in parents' room. Inquire about packages. AE, MC, V. **Parking:** Free self- and valet parking.

The Grand Floridian, right near the Magic Kingdom, is magnificent from the moment you step into its opulent five-story lobby under triple-domed stained-glass skylights. Here, a pianist entertains during afternoon tea, and an orchestra plays big-band music every evening. Sunny rooms are decorated in muted greens and pinks and furnished with Victorian-style convertible sofas and bleached oak two-poster beds. In-room amenities include remote-control cable TVs, safes, alarm-clock radios, and ceiling fans. In the bath, you'll find an extra phone, hairdryer, and terry robe. And private latticed balconies or verandas overlook formal gardens, the pool, or a 200-acre lagoon.

Dining/Entertainment: Victoria & Albert's, Orlando's finest restaurant, is described below (see "Dining"). The lovely Grand Floridian Café, with elegantly draped Palladian windows overlooking formal gardens, serves American fare at all meals. The festive exposition-themed 1900 Park Fare is the setting for buffet character breakfasts and dinners. Entered via a Victorian rotunda, Flagler's has a 19th-century garden ambience. At dinner, the fare is northern Italian; weekends, the restaurant is used for buffet breakfasts. At the gazebolike Narcoossee's, grilled meats and seafood are prepared in an exhibition kitchen; it's open for lunch and dinner daily. The 24-hour Gasparilla Grill, adjoining the video-game arcade, offers light fare and continental breakfasts to Nintendo noshers. Cozily intimate and very Victorian, Mizner's Lounge features an international selection of ports, brandies, and appetizers. The Garden View Lounge off the lobby is the setting for ultra-elegant afternoon teas; evenings, champagne cocktails are a specialty. And frozen drinks and snacks are available from the octagonal Summerhouse Pool Bar.

Services: 24-hour room service, nightly turn-down with Belgian chocolates, babysitting, on-premises monorail, boat transport to the Magic Kingdom and the Polynesian Resort, free trolley transport around the hotel grounds, shoeshine, massage, guest services desk, complimentary daily newspaper.

Facilities: Large swimming pool, kiddie pool, whirlpool, two tennis courts, boat

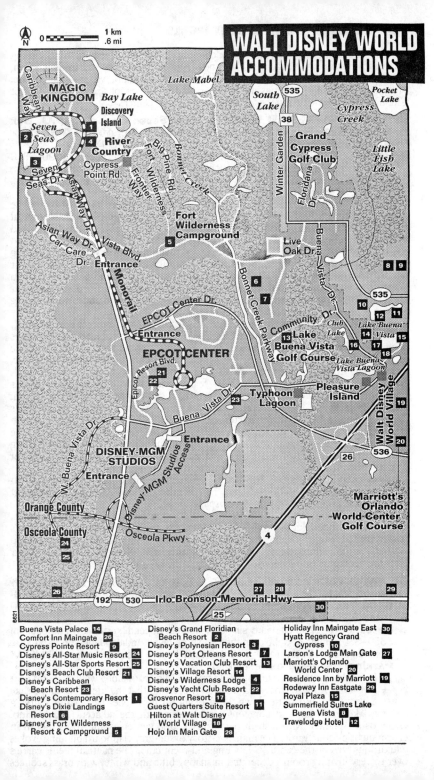

WALT DISNEY WORLD ACCOMMODATIONS

0   1 km
     .6 mi

Buena Vista Palace **14**
Comfort Inn Maingate **26**
Cypress Pointe Resort **9**
Disney's All-Star Music Resort **24**
Disney's All-Star Sports Resort **25**
Disney's Beach Club Resort **21**
Disney's Caribbean
  Beach Resort **23**
Disney's Contemporary Resort **1**
Disney's Dixie Landings
  Resort **6**
Disney's Fort Wilderness
  Resort & Campground **5**

Disney's Grand Floridian
  Beach Resort **2**
Disney's Polynesian Resort **3**
Disney's Port Orleans Resort **7**
Disney's Vacation Club Resort **13**
Disney's Village Resort **16**
Disney's Wilderness Lodge **4**
Disney's Yacht Club Resort **22**
Grosvenor Resort **17**
Guest Quarters Suite Resort **11**
Hilton at Walt Disney
  World Village **18**
Hojo Inn Main Gate **28**

Holiday Inn Maingate East **30**
Hyatt Regency Grand
  Cypress **10**
Larson's Lodge Main Gate **27**
Marriott's Orlando
  World Center **20**
Residence Inn by Marriott **19**
Rodeway Inn Eastgate **29**
Royal Plaza **15**
Summerfield Suites Lake
  Buena Vista **8**
Travelodge Hotel **12**

rentals, waterskiing, croquet, volleyball, children's playground, jogging trails, fishing excursions, white sand beach, full business center, full-service unisex hair salon, coin-op washers/dryers, shops, state-of-the-art health club, video-game arcade, organized children's activities in summer and peak seasons, the Mouseketeer Clubhouse (a counselor-supervised child-care activity center).

DISNEY'S POLYNESIAN RESORT, 1600 Seven Seas Dr. (P.O. Box 10100), Lake Buena Vista, FL 32830-0100. Tel. 407/W-DISNEY or 407/824-2000. Fax 407/354-1866. 841 rms, 12 suites. A/C TV TEL

$ Rates: $195–$268 single or double, depending on view and season; $290–$310 single or double on the concierge floors; $342–$1,050 suite. Additional person $15 extra. Children under 18 stay free in parents' room. Inquire about packages. AE, MC, V. **Parking:** Free self- and valet parking.

Designed to complement Adventureland in the Magic Kingdom (and just below the Magic Kingdom itself), the 25-acre Polynesian Resort is fronted by lush tropical foliage, waterfalls, palms, and koi ponds. At night, lava rock walkways are illuminated by flaming torchiers. A private white sand beach looks out on a 200-acre lagoon. And the skylit lobby is a virtual rain forest of tropical plantings, with a waterfall cascading into a stream stocked with goldfish. Large, beautiful rooms, most with balconies or patios, have canopied beds, bamboo and rattan furnishings, and walls hung with Gauguin prints. All overlook tropical gardens or the lagoon. In-room amenities include alarm-clock radios, remote-control cable TVs, and wood-bladed ceiling fans.

Dining/Entertainment: The French Polynesian–themed Papeete Bay Verandah is the setting for Minnie's Menehune Character Breakfast (a daily buffet). It also serves à la carte Polynesian dinners (enhanced by a three-piece island band and dancer). The exotic Tambu Lounge, specializing in Polynesian drinks and nightly piano bar music, adjoins. The Coral Isle Café serves American fare from 7am to 11pm. Captain Cook's Snack Bar, a classic ice-cream parlor, features an array of snack fare and a make-your-own-sundae bar. Tangaroa Terrace, a sunny plant-filled dining room, serves à la carte and buffet breakfasts daily. Luau Cove is the setting for Mickey's Tropical Luau (a Polynesian/character show for children) and the Polynesian Luau Dinner Show. Snack Isle, adjoining the video-game arcade, serves light fare. And the Barefoot Pool Bar, also featuring island drinks and light fare, has a beautiful setting on the beach overlooking the lagoon. A pianist entertains nightly on the second floor of the lobby.

Services: Room service, babysitting, on-premises monorail, boat transport (to the Magic Kingdom, Discovery Island, Fort Wilderness, and River Country), guest services desk, complimentary daily newspaper.

Facilities: Two swimming pools (one of them immense, with waterfalls, grottoes, and a water slide), kiddie pool, boat rental, waterskiing, volleyball, children's playground, 1½-mile jogging trail, fishing excursions, unisex hair salon, coin-op washers/dryers, shops, large video-game arcade, the Neverland Club (a Peter Pan–themed counselor-supervised child-care/activity center).

DISNEY'S YACHT CLUB RESORT, 1700 EPCOT Resorts Blvd., (off Buena Vista Dr.; P.O. Box 10100), Lake Buena Vista, FL 32830-0100. Tel. 407/W-DISNEY or 407/934-7000. Fax 407/354-1866. 625 rms, 10 suites. A/C MINIBAR TV TEL

$ Rates: $210–$290 standard single or double, depending on view and season; $350–$390 single or double on the concierge level. Additional person $15 extra. Children under 18 stay free in parents' room. Inquire about packages. AE, MC, V. **Parking:** Free self- and valet parking.

Legend has it that the ship of world traveler Old Stormalong went aground on a lagoon here, and the area was so beautiful that he decided to forsake adventuring and settle down. And beautiful it is! The Yacht Club shares a 25-acre lake, facilities, and gorgeous landscaping with the adjacent Beach Club. Grounds are planted with lush tropical foliage, and gardenias and roses bloom in charming brick courtyards. The main five-story oyster-gray clapboard building evokes a luxurious turn-of-the-century New England yacht club. The nautical theme carries over to very inviting rooms, decorated in snappy blue and white, with brass sconces

FROMMER'S COOL FOR KIDS: HOTELS

All Disney Properties and Official Hotels (see p. 233–246) These hostelries offer many advantages for kids, including proximity to Walt Disney World parks, complimentary transportation between the hotel and the parks, and reduced-price children's menus and Disney character appearances in hotel restaurants. Extensive facilities might include lakefront beaches, boating, waterskiing, bike rentals, playgrounds, video-game arcades, swimming pools with waterfalls and slides, and/or organized children's activities.

Disney's Fort Wilderness Resort and Campground (see p. 242) All of the above and more is offered here—plus you get to go camping.

Residence Inns (see pp. 249 and 252) Not only do they have swimming pools, children's playgrounds, and other recreational facilities but also accommodations with fully equipped kitchens—a potential money-saver for families. Rates include breakfast. The Meadow Creek Drive Residence Inn has an extensive recreation department offering free children's activities. The Lake Cecile hostelry has on-premises barbecue grills and picnic tables and offers boating and waterskiing on a scenic lake.

Holiday Inn Sunspree Resort Lake Buena Vista (see p. 250) This Holiday Inn has a special check-in desk for kids and on-premises mascots to welcome them. Rooms are equipped with kitchenettes. Kids under 12 eat free in their own restaurant where movies and cartoons are shown. Numerous organized children's activities are free.

Holiday Inn Maingate East (see p. 251) The children's facilities here are identical to those at the Lake Buena Vista counterpart.

and ship lights, maps on the walls, and crisp floral-chintz drapes and bed ruffles. French doors open onto porches or balconies. Amenities include ceiling fans, extra phones in the bath, remote-control cable TVs, alarm-clock radios, safes, and game tables. The fifth floor is a concierge level.

Dining/Entertainment: The plush Yachtsman Steakhouse, open for dinner nightly, features an exhibition kitchen where select cuts of steak, chops, and fresh seafood are grilled over oak and hickory. The nautically themed Yacht Club Galley serves American regional fare at all meals. The Crew's Cup Lounge, its walls hung with Ivy League rowing-team memorabilia, serves up light fare and frosted mugs of international ales and beers; sporting events are aired on the TV. The cozy Ale and Compass Lounge, a lobby bar with a working fireplace, features specialty coffees and cocktails. The seasonal Sip Ahoy Snack Bar serves the secluded pool. And a brass quartet entertains nightly on the mezzanine level. (See also the Beach Club restaurants and bars, above.)

Services: 24-hour room service, babysitting, guest services desk, complimentary daily newspaper, boat transport to MGM theme park, tram transport to Epcot.

Facilities: Yacht Club facilities are identical to those of the Beach Club (see above).

Expensive

DISNEY'S CONTEMPORARY RESORT, 4600 N. World Dr. (P.O. Box 10100), Lake Buena Vista, FL 32830-0100. Tel. 407/W-DISNEY or 407/824-1000. Fax 407/354-1866. 1,036 rms, 17 suites. A/C TV TEL

$ Rates: $195–$235 standard single or double; $250–$270 single or double on the concierge level. Additional person $15 extra. Children under 17 stay free in parents' room. Inquire about packages. AE, MC, V. **Parking:** Free self- and valet parking.

The Contemporary—centering on a sleek 15-story A-frame tower flanked by two garden wings—occupies 26 acres bounded by a natural lake and the Disney-made Seven Seas Lagoon. The monorail whizzes right through the hotel. Rooms are decorated in shades of tan with splashes of color. Furnishings and lighting fixtures are art deco, there are ceiling fans overhead, and walls display cheerful Matisse prints. In-room amenities include alarm-clock radios, remote-control cable TVs, two phones, and safes. The 14th floor of the tower is the concierge level.

Dining/Entertainment: The Concourse Grill, a large coffee shop, serves all meals. The Contemporary Cafe features all-you-can-eat prime rib/shrimp buffet dinners and morning character breakfasts. The Outer Rim, a bar/lounge with gorgeous views of Bay Lake, offers piano bar and other live entertainment evenings. A no-frills cafeteria adjoins the video-game arcade on the first floor; next to it is a children's theater where Disney movies are shown nightly. And in peak season the Sand Bar dispenses specialty drinks poolside.

Services: 24-hour room service; guest services desk; daily newspaper delivery to rooms; babysitting; boat transport to Discovery Island, Fort Wilderness, and River Country; direct monorail link to the Polynesian Resort.

Facilities: Two swimming pools, kiddie pool, white sand beach with volleyball court, shuffleboard, boat rentals, full-service unisex hair salon, six tennis courts (lessons available), shops, Delta Airlines desk, coin-op washers/dryers, full business center, extensive health club, sauna/massage/tanning rooms, vast 24-hour video-game arcade, the Mouseketeer Clubhouse (a counselor-supervised child-care/activity center).

DISNEY'S VACATION CLUB RESORT, 1510 N. Cove Rd., (off Community Dr.; P.O. Box 10100), Lake Buena Vista, FL 32830-0100. Tel. 407/W-DISNEY or 407/827-7700. Fax 407/354-1866. 709 villas. A/C TV TEL
$ **Rates:** $190–$205 deluxe rooms; $240–$260 one-bedroom vacation home; $345–$365 two-bedroom vacation home; $755 three-bedroom Grand Villa. Rates are for any number of people. Range reflects high and low seasons. Inquire about packages. AE, MC, V. **Parking:** Free self-parking.

Its architecture evocative of Key West at the turn of the century, the Vacation Club is a time-share property. However, you can rent accommodations here when they're not in use by the owners. The 156-acre property is beautifully landscaped: Tree-lined brick walkways are edged by white picket fences, palms sway softly in the breeze, shore birds swoop lazily over lagoons, and the air is scented with honeysuckle. Accommodations, in two- and three-story tin-roofed clapboard buildings painted in pale pastels, offer lovely water, woodland, or fairway views. All but deluxe rooms have fully equipped kitchens and furnished patios, and amenities including bedroom ceiling fans, full laundry rooms (washers/dryers/ironing boards/irons), large-screen remote-control cable TVs with VCRs in the living room (smaller sets in the bedrooms), phones in each bedroom and living room, and AM/FM clock radios in all bedrooms. Many units contain whirlpool tubs in the master suite, and Grand Villas have stereo systems.

Dining/Entertainment: The Key West–themed Olivia's Cafe serves all meals; it offers al fresco seating on a patio overlooking the Trumbo Canal. At the Gurgling Suitcase pool bar, you can watch the sunset over piña coladas. Good's Food To Go, offering take-out sandwiches and light fare, adjoins.

Services: Babysitting, guest services desk, ferry service to Disney Village Marketplace and Pleasure Island, free bus transport around the grounds, food shopping (for a minimal charge).

Facilities: Two tennis courts, white sand play area, four swimming pools, whirlpool, kiddie pool, bicycle rental, boat rentals, children's playground, extensive health club, sauna, shuffleboard, horseshoes, volleyball, complementary use of washers/dryers, general store, small video-game arcade. The Community Hall, a recreation center, shows Disney movies nightly and offers various activities.

DISNEY'S VILLAGE RESORT, 1901 Buena Vista Dr. (P.O. Box 10100), Lake Buena Vista, FL 32830-0100. Tel. 407/W-DISNEY or 407/827-1100. Fax 407/354-1866. 324 suites, villas. A/C TV TEL

$ Rates: $185–$200 Club Suite; $250–$270 one-bedroom Vacation Villa (for up to four people); $300–$320 two-bedroom Vacation Villa (for up to six people); $335–$355 Treehouse Villa (for up to six people); $355–$375 two-bedroom Fairway unit (for up to eight people); $750 two-bedroom Grand Vista home; $825 three-bedroom Grand Vista home. Range reflects view and season. Inquire about packages. AE, MC, V. **Parking:** Free self-parking.

Sprawled over 265 Arcadian acres of lakes, woodlands, and streams adjacent to the Disney Village Marketplace, the Village Resort is a great choice for golfers and families. Peacocks roam the grounds, and your accommodations might overlook a verdant golf course or a forest of towering pines. Octagonal Treehouse Villas, elevated on stilts, have large outdoor patios and balconies amid the treetops. Decorated in earth tones, with knotty-pine furnishings, these rustic two-story lodgings offer fully equipped kitchens, dining areas, full living rooms, three bedrooms, and two baths. Amenities include remote-control cable TVs and phones on each floor and AM/FM alarm-clock radios in all bedrooms. Similarly equipped Fairway Villas, just off the golf course, are elegant ski-lodgey cedar town houses with rough-hewn slanted pine paneling and beamed cathedral ceilings. The most inexpensive accommodations are one-bedroom Club Suites. Bordering a lake, they're attractively decorated in forest green, rust, and tan, with cathedral ceilings, pine furnishings, and Ralph Lauren–look striped and plaid fabrics. They have kitchenettes and balconies or porches. One- and two-bedroom Vacation Villas are two-story town houses with big picture windows overlooking woodlands or waterways and Early American bleached-pine furnishings. All have country kitchens, dining areas, large living rooms, and patios. And for total luxury there are two- and three-bedroom Grand Vista homes that sleep six to eight people. They're beautiful residential accommodations with full kitchens, two big screened porches (one set up for dining), upscale furnishings, marble whirlpool tubs in the bath, and homey touches such as live plants, shelves of books, and objets d'art. Each has its own electric golf cart, bicycles, and barbecue grill.

Dining/Entertainment: Disney Village Marketplace restaurants are close by.

Services: Room service (7am to 11pm), babysitting, guest services desk, free bus transport around the property, free grocery delivery from the Gourmet Pantry (meat, poultry, fresh vegetables, and more).

Facilities: 18-hole par-72 championship golf course, three tennis courts, golf/tennis pro shops, six swimming pools, five whirlpool spas, kiddie pool, bicycle rental, eight miles of bike trails, boat rentals, health club, seven children's playgrounds, 3.4-mile jogging course with 32 exercise stations, coin-op washers/dryers, outdoor barbecue grills and picnic tables scattered throughout the property, two video-game arcades. A foot bridge connects to Disney's Village Marketplace.

DISNEY'S WILDERNESS LODGE, 901 Timberline Dr. (P.O. Box 10100), Lake Buena Vista, FL 32830-0100. Tel. 407/W-DISNEY or 407/824-3200. Fax 407/354-1866. 697 rms, 25 junior suites, 6 suites. A/C TV TEL

$ Rates: $149–$195 single or double, depending on view and season; $250–$270 junior suite; $480–$580 suite. Additional person $15 extra. Children under 18 stay free in parents' room. Inquire about packages. AE, MC, V. **Parking:** Free self- and valet parking.

Evocative of rustic turn-of-the-century national park lodges, this gorgeous new Disney resort is on the southwest shore of Bay Lake just east of the Magic Kingdom, surrounded by towering oak and pine forests. Its imposing lobby, supported by 55-foot bundled lodgepole-pine columns, centers on a massive floor-to-ceiling stone fireplace. From the lobby, a geothermal spring flows under a picture-window wall into Silver Creek, which itself empties into beautiful 340-acre Bay Lake. Outside, "volcanic" meadow landscaping is punctuated by bubbling craters, babbling brooks, a cascading waterfall, and spewing geysers. Guest rooms are decorated in muted shades of forest green, with mahogany woodwork and coffee-hued walls, the latter adorned with tribal friezes and landscape paintings of the Northwest. Equipped with remote-control cable TVs, alarm-clock radios, ceiling fans, and safes, they have patios or balconies.

Dining/Entertainment: Artist's Point, with large windows overlooking Bay Lake and dramatic western landscape murals adorning interior walls, specializes in hickory-, oak-, and mesquite-grilled steak, seafood, and wild game; open for all meals, it also has lakeside terrace seating. Trappers and explorers are honored in the adjoining Territory Lounge. The cheerful Whispering Canyon Cafe serves coffee-shop fare at breakfast and dinner. The fly-fishing-themed Roaring Fork, adjacent to the video-game arcade, serves snack fare around the clock. And the Trout Pass Bar provides light fare and drinks poolside. Five-minute geyser shows take place in the meadow periodically throughout the day, and nightly electric water pageants can be viewed from the shores of Bay Lake.

Services: Room service, guest services desk, babysitting, Mears airport shuttle, boat transport to the Magic Kingdom, free bus transport around the property.

Facilities: Immense swimming pool, kiddie pool with water slide, hot and cold spa pools, boat rentals, children's playground/recreation area, bicycle rental, two-mile jogging/bike trail, large video-game arcade, gift shop, Cub's Den (a counselor-supervised activity center for children 3 to 12).

Moderate

DISNEY'S CARIBBEAN BEACH RESORT, 900 Cayman Way (off Buena Vista Dr.; P.O. Box 10100), Lake Buena Vista, FL 32830-0100. Tel. 407/W-DISNEY or 407/934-3400. Fax 407/354-1866. 2,112 rms. A/C MINIBAR TV TEL

$ Rates: $89–$119 single or double. Additional person $12 extra. Children under 17 stay free in parents' room. Inquire about packages. AE, MC, V. **Parking:** Free self-parking.

Opened in 1988, the Caribbean Beach occupies 200 palm-fringed acres stunningly landscaped with lush tropical foliage. Accommodations surround a large, duck-filled lake in five "villages," each with metal-roofed stucco buildings architecturally evocative of the Caribbean. Room interiors are charming, utilizing pleasing color schemes such as dusty rose and mint. All have attractive oak furnishings and exquisite floral-print cotton chintz bedspreads. In-room amenities include coffee makers, ceiling fans, and remote-control cable TVs. All rooms have verandas, many of them overlooking the lake. In addition, 16 beautifully landscaped public courtyards furnished with umbrella tables dot the property.

Dining/Entertainment: The festive Farmers Market Food Court, a garden setting with trellises and brightly colored Chinese kites overhead, has counters offering diverse fare. The nautically themed Captain's Tavern specializes in fresh fish and prime rib. And Banana Cabaña, featuring light fare and frozen tropical drinks, serves the main pool.

Services: Room service (pizza only), guest services desk, babysitting, complimentary shuttle around the grounds.

Facilities: Video-game arcade, shops, boat rentals, bicycle rental, coin-op washers/dryers. The main swimming pool replicates a Spanish-style Caribbean fort with pirate's cannons and stone walls; it has a water slide, kiddie pool, and whirlpool. In addition, there are nice-sized pools, children's playgrounds, and lakefront white sand beaches in each village. A 1.4-mile promenade—popular for jogging—circles the lake. An arched wooden bridge leads to Parrot Cay Island where there's a short nature trail, an aviary of tropical birds, a picnic area, and a playground.

DISNEY'S DIXIE LANDINGS RESORT, 1251 Dixie Dr. (off Bonnet Creek Pkwy.; P.O. Box 10100), Lake Buena Vista, FL 32830-0100. Tel. 407/W-DISNEY or 407/934-6000. Fax 407/934-5777. 2,048 rms. A/C TV TEL

$ Rates: $89–$121 for up to four people. Children under 18 stay free in parents' room. Inquire about packages. AE, MC, V. **Parking:** Free self-parking.

Nestled on the banks of the Disney-made Sassagoula River and dotted with bayous, Dixie Landings shares its magnificently landscaped 325-acre site with the Port Orleans Resort (described below). Themed after the Louisiana countryside, it's divided into "parishes" with accommodations housed in stately colonnaded plantation homes or rustic Cajun-style dwellings. Rooms in the former are elegantly decorated in Federalist blue and gold, with brass-trimmed maple furnishings. Cajun rooms, on the other hand, feature bed frames made of bent branches, patchwork quilts, and calico-print drapes. In-room amenities throughout include remote-control cable TVs, ceiling fans, and alarm-clock radios.

Dining/Entertainment: Boatwright's Dining Hall, patterned after a 19th-century boat-building factory, serves Cajun fare at breakfast and dinner. The Colonel's Cotton Mill, a food court, occupies a rustic setting under a 50-foot massively beamed pine ceiling. Muddy Rivers, a poolside bar in a ramshackle structure, serves drinks and light fare; it has a very pleasant shaded porch cooled by ceiling fans. Off the lobby, the Cotton Co-op lounge, with plush leather couches before a blazing fireplace, is designed to suggest a cotton-trading commodity house. Monday-night football games are aired on a large-screen TV here, and Tuesday through Saturday comedians and singers entertain.

Services: Room service (pizza only), guest services desk, babysitting, boat transport (to Port Orleans, Village Marketplace, and Pleasure Island).

Facilities: Six large swimming pools, coin-op washers/dryers, children's playground, vast video-game arcade, bicycle rental, boat rentals, 1.7-mile riverfront jogging path, Fulton's General Store. Facilities on Ol' Man Island, a woodsy 3½-acre recreation area, include an immense rustically themed free-form pool with waterfalls cascading from a broken bridge and a waterslide entered via a pump house, a playground, kiddie pool, spa, sun deck, and fishin' hole (rent bait and poles and angle for catfish and bass).

DISNEY'S PORT ORLEANS RESORT, 2201 Orleans Dr. (off Bonnet Creek Pkwy.; P.O. Box 10100), Lake Buena Vista, FL 32830-0100. Tel. 407/W-DISNEY or 407/934-5000. Fax 407/934-5353. 1,008 rms. A/C TV TEL

$ Rates: $89–$121 for up to four people. Children under 18 stay free in parents' room. Inquire about packages. AE, MC, V. **Parking:** Free self-parking.

⑤ This beautiful resort, themed after turn-of-the-century New Orleans, shares a site on the banks of the "mighty" Sassagoula River, with Dixie Landings, described above. Cheerful three-story buildings, painted in variegated pastels with shuttered windows and lacy wrought-iron balconies, house lovely rooms. Decorated in mocha, rust, and teal, they have pretty cherrywood furnishings, swagged draperies, and art nouveau sconces. A handsome armoire conceals your remote-control cable TV, and in-room amenities include ceiling fans and alarm-clock radios. Accommodations buildings are fronted by lovely flower gardens opening onto fountained courtyards. Landscaping throughout the property is a delight, with stately oaks, formal boxwood hedges, azaleas, and jasmin.

Dining/Entertainment: The very New Orleansy Bonfamille's Café, enclosing a fountained courtyard, is open for breakfast and dinner, the latter featuring Créole specialties. At the festive Sassagoula Floatworks and Food Factory, food-court vendors serve up varied fare from 6am to midnight daily. Scat Cat's Club, a cocktail lounge off the lobby, features family-oriented live entertainment. And the poolside Mardi Grog's offers cool and fruity libations and light snacks.

Services: Room service (pizza only), guest services desk, babysitting, boat transport (to Dixie Landings, Village Marketplace, and Pleasure Island).

Facilities: Olympic-size Doubloon Lagoon swimming pool, surmounted by an enormous sea serpent–shaped water slide; whirlpool; kiddie pool; coin-op washers/dryers; vast video-game arcade; bicycle rental; boat rentals; 1.7-mile riverfront jogging path; shops.

Inexpensive

DISNEY'S ALL-STAR MUSIC RESORT, 3499 W. Buena Vista Dr. (at World Dr. and Osceola Pkwy.; P.O. Box 10100), Lake Buena Vista, FL 32830-0100. Tel. 407/W-DISNEY or 407/939-6000. Fax 407/354-1866. 1,920 rms. A/C TV TEL

$ Rates: $69–$79 single or double, depending on view and season. Additional person $8 extra. Children under 18 stay free in parents' room. Inquire about packages. AE, MC, V. **Parking:** Free self-parking.

Nestled among pristine pine forests southwest of MGM Studios, this brand-new Disney property—part of a 246-acre complex that also includes the adjacent All-Star Sports Resort (see below)—offers numerous facilities and visitor perks at low prices. Its 10 buildings are musically themed around country, jazz, rock, calypso, or Broadway show tunes, with oversize "icons" in public areas such as three-story cowboy boots, conga drum–shaped stairways, and a walk-through neon-lit jukebox. Small ponds dot the property, and building courtyards are attractively landscaped in appropriate themes (New Orleans–style gardens in the jazz section, a wildflower-filled meadow in the country-western area, and so on). Attractive rooms, with ecru walls and red-accented blue carpets have musically themed bedspreads, paintings, and wall friezes. They're equipped with remote-control cable TVs, AM/FM alarm-clock radios, and safes.

Dining/Entertainment: The cheerful Intermission Food Court, adorned with music paraphernalia and memorabilia, has stations for barbecue, pizza, pastas, and more; it's open for all meals. The adjoining Singing Spirits Bar serves the food court and pool area.

Services: Room service (pizza only), babysitting, guest services desk, Mears airport shuttle.

Facilities: Two large swimming pools, kiddie pool, children's playground, jogging trail, coin-op washers/dryers, large retail shop, car-rental desk, vast video-game arcade.

DISNEY'S ALL-STAR SPORTS RESORT, 3499 W. Buena Vista Dr. (at World Dr. and Osceola Pkwy.; P.O. Box 10100), Lake Buena Vista, FL 32830-0100. Tel. 407/W-DISNEY or 407/939-5000. Fax 407/354-1866. 1,920 rms. A/C TV TEL

$ Rates: $69–$79 single or double, depending on view and season. Additional person $8 extra. Children under 18 stay free in parents' room. Inquire about packages. AE, MC, V. **Parking:** Free self-parking.

Adjacent to and sharing facilities with the above-listed All-Star Music Resort, this 82-acre sports-themed section of Disney's exciting new economy complex opened in May 1994. The rooms are housed in 10 T-shaped buildings with football, baseball, basketball, tennis, and surfing themes. For instance, the turquoise surf buildings have waves along their rooflines, surfboards mounted on exterior walls, and a courtyard encompassing a swimming pool. Public-area "icons" include oversize tennis-ball-can stairways and four-story football helmets and whistles. Cheerful rooms, with coffee-colored walls and painted dark-green furniture, feature sports-action–motif bedspreads, paintings, and wall friezes. They're equipped with remote-control cable TVs, alarm-clock radios, and safes.

Dining/Entertainment: The End Zone Food Court, filled with sports memorabilia, has stations for barbecue, pizza, pastas, and more. It's open for all meals. The adjoining Team Spirits bar serves the food court and pool area.

Services: Room service (pizza only), babysitting, guest services desk, Mears airport shuttle.

Facilities: Two large swimming pools, kiddie pool, children's playground, jogging trail, coin-op washers/dryers, large ice rink–themed shop, car-rental desk, vast video-game arcade.

A Disney Campground

DISNEY'S FORT WILDERNESS RESORT AND CAMPGROUND, 3520 N. Fort Wilderness Trail (P.O. Box 10100), Lake Buena Vista, FL 32830-0100. Tel. 407/W-DISNEY or 407/824-2900. Fax 407/354-1866. 784 campsites, 408 wilderness homes. AC TV

$ Rates: $35–$52 campsite, depending on season, location, number of people, size, and extent of hookup; $180–$195 wilderness home. Inquire about packages. AE, MC, V. **Parking:** Free self-parking at your campsite or wilderness home.

This woodsy 780-acre camping resort makes an ideal venue for family vacations. Secluded campsites—most set up for tent campers, the others for trailers—offer

110/220-volt outlets, barbecue grills, picnic tables, and children's play areas. Another option here is a wilderness home, a rustic one-bedroom cabin with a piney interior. Accommodating two adults and up to four children, these have cozy living rooms with Murphy beds, fully equipped eat-in kitchens, and on-premises picnic tables and barbecue grills. Amenities include remote-control cable TVs, phones, and clock radios. Guests here enjoy a lot of extras, including extensive recreational facilities and a nightly campfire program hosted by Chip 'n' Dale and featuring Disney movies, cartoons, and sing-alongs.

Dining/Entertainment: The rustic Trails End in Pioneer Hall is open for cafeteria-style breakfasts, lunches, and dinners daily (some noteworthy buffets here), and late-night pizza, with live entertainment during the evening meal. Adjoining it is Crockett's Tavern, a cozy full-service restaurant filled with Davy Crockett memorabilia. It features Texas fare at dinner. There's also a snack bar in the Meadow Recreation Complex adjacent to the video-game arcade, another near the beach. In summer, guests enjoy a dazzling electrical water pageant from the beach, nightly at 9:45pm. And the rambunctious *Hoop-Dee-Doo Musical Revue* takes place in Pioneer Hall nightly (details in "Evening Entertainment," below).

Services: Guest services desk, babysitting, boat transport (to Discovery Island, the Magic Kingdom, and the Contemporary Resort).

Facilities: Comfort station in each campground area (with restrooms, private showers, ice machines, telephones, and laundry rooms), two large swimming pools, white sand beach, Circle D Ranch horseback riding (trail rides), petting farm, pony rides, fishing, three sand volleyball courts, ball fields, tetherball, shuffleboard, bike rentals, boat rentals, 1.5-mile jogging path, two tennis courts, shops, kennel, car-rental desk, two video-game arcades, two 18-hole championship golf courses.

LAKE BUENA VISTA/OFFICIAL HOTELS

These properties, designated "official" WDW hotels, are located on and around Hotel Plaza Boulevard, a delightful thoroughfare with a wide traffic island shaded by lofty oaks. Guests at these hotels enjoy many privileges (see above). And the location is a big plus—close to the Disney parks and within walking distance of Disney Village Marketplace and Crossroads shops and restaurants, as well as Pleasure Island nightlife.

Expensive

BUENA VISTA PALACE, 1900 Buena Vista Dr. (just north of Hotel Plaza Blvd.; P.O. Box 22206), Lake Buena Vista, FL 32830. Tel. 407/827-2727, or toll free 800/327-2990. Fax 407/827-6034. 898 rms, 130 suites. A/C MINIBAR TV TEL

$ Rates: $130–$235 standard single or double, $219–$250 Crown Level single or double; $245–$290 one-bedroom suite; $390–$455 two-bedroom suite. Range reflects view and season. Additional person $15 extra. Children under 18 stay free in parents' room. Inquire about packages and weekend rates. AE, CB, DC, DISC, MC, OPT, V. **Parking:** Free self-parking, $6 per night valet parking.

Entered via a balconied 15-story atrium lobby ascending to a stained-glass skylight, this 27-acre waterfront resort flies the flags of all Epcot countries at its entrance. The rooms are decorated in earth tones with dark oak furnishings. All but a few have balconies or patios, many of them overlooking Lake Buena Vista. Amenities include remote-control cable TVs (with Spectravision movie options), alarm-clock radios, safes, bedroom and bath phones, and ceiling fans. Luxurious residential-style one- and two-bedroom suites—with living rooms, dining rooms, and private balconies or patios (microwave ovens and refrigerators are available on request)—are housed in a peach stucco art deco building on the property's Recreation Island; it connects to a tower building via tropically landscaped walkways. Crown rooms on the 10th floor comprise a concierge level.

Dining/Entertainment: Arthur's 27, offering breathtaking panoramic views of WDW parks and nightly fireworks from its 27th-floor location, is the hotel's elegant premier restaurant, serving continental fare at dinner enhanced by selections from a vast, award-winning wine cellar. An adjoining lounge offers live jazz and piano-bar entertainment and dancing. The Australian-themed Outback Restaurant, with a three-story indoor waterfall, specializes in steak, lobster, and fresh seafood grilled over an open pit; it's open for dinner only. Minnie, Goofy, and Pluto host Sunday-morning buffet breakfasts in the Watercress Cafe. Open 6am to midnight daily, it specializes in Florida cuisine. The 24-hour Watercress Bake Shop, for incredible desserts and Häagen-Dazs ice-cream sundaes, adjoins. The festive Laughing Kookaburra Good Time Bar boasts a selection of 99 beers and offers happy hour international hors d'oeuvres buffets and live bands for dancing nightly. The gazebo-style Lobby Lounge in the atrium serves premium wines by the glass, gourmet teas and coffees, and pastries; come by for piano-bar entertainment in the evening. The Recreation Island Pool Snack Bar offers light fare and tropical drinks. And Courtyard Pastries and Pizza, an outdoor ice-cream parlor/snack bar, serves breakfast and light fare at umbrella tables on a fountained plaza where the shuttle buses to Disney parks pull up.

Services: 24-hour room service, babysitting, guest services desk (sells tickets, and arranges transportation, to all nearby attractions; tickets to WDW parks available at the Disney shop), complimentary newspaper at guest services, shoeshine/shoe repair, nightly bed turn-down, complimentary transport to/from all WDW parks, Mears airport shuttle.

Facilities: Two large swimming pools, whirlpool, kiddie pool, three tennis courts, golf privileges at WDW courses, boat rentals on property and at nearby Disney Village Marina, three-mile jogging path, volleyball, children's playground, car-rental desk, beauty salon, massage, full business center, fully equipped health club, sauna, shops, coin-op washers/dryers, large video-game arcade, Kids Stuff (a counselor-supervised child-care center, open summer and some major holidays only).

GUEST QUARTERS SUITE RESORT, 2305 Hotel Plaza Blvd. (just west of Apopka-Vineland Rd./Fla. 535), Lake Buena Vista, FL 32830. Tel. 407/934-1000, or toll free 800/424-2900. Fax 407/934-1008. 229 suites. A/C TV TEL
$ Rates: $139–$195 one-bedroom suite for one or two people, depending on view and season (additional person $20 extra; children under 18 stay free in parents' suite); $250–$395 two-bedroom suite. Inquire about packages and rates including breakfast. AE, CB, DC, DISC, JCB, MC, OPT, V. **Parking:** Free self-parking.

Entered via a small skylit atrium lobby with a large aviary of tropical birds, this all-suite hotel is a great choice for families. Large one-bedroom suites which can sleep up to six people are delightfully decorated in teal, mauve, and peach, utilizing light-wood furnishings and pretty floral-print fabrics. Accommodations include a full living room with a convertible sofa, dining area, and a separate bedroom. Among the in-room amenities are a wet bar, refrigerator, coffee maker, microwave oven, remote-control cable TVs with Spectravision options in the living room and bedroom, a smaller black-and-white TV in the bath, two phones, an alarm-clock radio, and a hairdryer.

Dining/Entertainment: Parrot Patch, a tropically themed restaurant/lounge, serves American fare at all meals. A pool bar serves the same menu as Parrot Patch. Scoops & Games is an ice-cream parlor–cum–video-game arcade off the pool area.

Services: Room service, babysitting, guest services desk (sells tickets to WDW parks and all other nearby attractions; also arranges transport to latter), complimentary transport to/from all WDW parks, Mears airport shuttle.

Facilities: Large swimming pool, whirlpool, kiddie pool, two tennis courts, golf privileges at WDW courses, boat rental at nearby Disney Village Marina, jogging path, volleyball, children's playground, car-rental desk, exercise room, shops, coin-op washers/dryers, video-game arcade.

HILTON AT WALT DISNEY WORLD VILLAGE, 1751 Hotel Plaza Blvd., (just east of Buena Vista Dr.), Lake Buena Vista, FL 32830. Tel. 407/827-4000, or toll free 800/782-4414. Fax 407/827-6380. 787 rms, 27 suites. A/C MINIBAR TV TEL
$ Rates: $119–$245 single or double (tower rooms $40 additional), depending on season. Additional person $20 extra. Children of any age stay free in parents'

room. Inquire about packages and weekend rates. AE, CB, DC, DISC, ER, JCB, MC, V. **Parking:** Free self-parking, $6 per night valet parking.

Heralded by a palm-fringed circular driveway leading up to an imposing waterfall and fountain, the Hilton occupies 23 beautifully landscaped acres including two large lakes. Accommodations, in a vast 10-story main building with a plant-filled skylit lobby, are done up in soft earth tones with teal/mauve accents and floral-print bedspreads. Amenities include remote-control cable TVs with HBO and Spectravision movie options, alarm-clock radios, coffee makers, and phones with two lines. The 9th and 10th floors comprise the Towers, a concierge level.

Dining/Entertainment: The Florida Fin Factory, a seafood restaurant, has an adjoining bar/lounge and raw bar. Benihana Japanese Steakhouse features teppanyaki dinners nightly; you can also enjoy appetizers such as calamari tempura, and/or tropical drinks, in the adjoining lounge. County Fair, a cheerful coffee shop, serves à la carte breakfasts, lunches, and dinners. The adjoining County Fair Buffeteria sets out a lavish buffet at breakfast. And the County Fair Terrace, with umbrella tables on a brick patio, offers light al fresco breakfasts and lunches while you wait for the shuttle bus to WDW. Rum Largo Poolside Cafe & Bar provides snack/lunch fare and exotic tropical drinks. John Ts Plantation Bar, off the lobby, evokes the antebellum South. It features light fare, exotic tropical drinks, and nighttime entertainment for dancing; major sporting events are aired on a large-screen TV. And kids love the Old Fashioned Soda Shoppe for pizzas, burgers, and hot dogs, not to mention malts, shakes, and sundaes; it even has video games. A cedar gazebo is the scene of frequent live poolside entertainment.

Services: Room service (6:30am to 1am), babysitting, concierge (sells tickets and arranges transport to all other nearby attractions/airport; WDW tickets available at Walt Disney World men's shop on the lobby level), nightly bed turn-down on request, complimentary transport to/from all WDW parks.

Facilities: Two very large swimming pools, two-tiered whirlpool in a tropical/rock-garden setting, children's spray pool, two tennis courts, golf privileges at (and free transportation to) WDW courses, boat rental at nearby Disney Village Marina, volleyball, water volleyball, badminton, children's playground, car-rental desk, full-service unisex beauty salon, full business center, fully equipped health club, sauna, shops, coin-op washers/dryers, large high-tech video-game arcade, Vacation Station Kids Hotel (a counselor-supervised child-care center).

Moderate

GROSVENOR RESORT, 1850 Hotel Plaza Blvd. (just east of Buena Vista Dr.), Lake Buena Vista, FL 32830. Tel. 407/828-4444, or toll free 800/624-4109. Fax 407/828-8192. 625 rms, 5 suites. A/C TV TEL

$ Rates: $99–$160 for up to four people, depending on view and season. Inquire about packages. AE, CB, DC, DISC, ER, JCB, MC, OPT, V. **Parking:** Free self-parking, $5 per night valet parking.

The British Colonial–themed Grosvenor, on 13 beautifully landscaped lakeside acres, centers on a 19-story peach stucco building fronted by towering palms. The recently renovated guest rooms have been attractively decorated in seafoam green or muted blue color schemes with splashy print bedspreads, light-oak furnishings, and marble-top desks. Amenities include remote-control cable TVs with VCRs (movie tapes can be rented), alarm-clock radios, coffee makers (tea and coffee supplied), safes, and hairdryers.

Dining/Entertainment: The elegant Baskervilles Restaurant has a Sherlock Holmes museum—and a re-creation of his Baker Street headquarters—on the premises. Windowed walls overlook the lake. Saturday nights, Baskervilles is the scene of mystery dinner theater productions. The restaurant also features buffet breakfasts and dinners (including a character breakfast every Tuesday, Thursday, and Saturday morning, and a character dinner every Wednesday night). A la carte American/continental selections are also an option at all meals. Moriarty's Pub, offering live entertainment in high season, adjoins. Crumpets Cafe, a food court, is open 24 hours. Barnacles Pool Bar serves tropical drinks and light fare. And at Cricket's Lounge, off the lobby, sporting events are aired on a large-screen TV.

Services: Room service (7am to midnight), babysitting, guest services (sells tickets and arranges transport to all nearby attractions; WDW park tickets are available at the Disney shop), free transport to/from all WDW parks, Mears airport shuttle.

Facilities: Two swimming pools, whirlpool, two tennis courts, golf privileges at (and free transportation to) WDW courses, boat rental at nearby Disney Village Marina, playground, lawn games, car-rental desk, business services, coin-op washers/dryers, shops, video-game arcade.

ROYAL PLAZA, 1905 Hotel Plaza Blvd. (between Buena Vista Dr. and Apopka-Vineland Rd./Fla. 535), Lake Buena Vista, FL 32830. Tel. 407/828-2828, or toll free 800/248-7890. Fax 407/827-6338. 386 rms, 10 suites. A/C TV TEL

$ Rates: $97–$197 for up to four people; $304–$550 suite. Range reflects view and season. Inquire about packages. AE, Barclaycard, CB, DC, DISC, ER, JCB, MC, OPT, V. **Parking:** Free self- and valet parking.

As we go to press, the 17-story Royal Plaza is completing a multi-million-dollar renovation and upgrade—adding two executive floors and a concierge level, and refurbishing all accommodations and public areas. The rooms are freshly decorated in teal, peach, and periwinkle, with grasspaper-covered walls and splashy print bedspreads. You can watch Magic Kingdom fireworks from your furnished balcony. Amenities include remote-control cable TVs with WDW channels, VCRs (movie tapes can be rented), alarm-clock radios, safes, and Mickey Mouse phones; refrigerators are available on request, and deluxe rooms have wet bars.

Dining/Entertainment: A new upscale restaurant and lounge, plus a lobby bar, are in the works at this writing. The Giraffe Lounge, a lively disco, plays high-energy music for dancing nightly. It also features complimentary happy-hour buffets. And a pool bar is open in season.

Services: Room service, babysitting, guest services (sells tickets and arranges transport to all nearby attractions; WDW park tickets are available at the Disney shop), free transport to/from all WDW parks, airport shuttle.

Facilities: Large L-shaped swimming pool, whirlpool, four tennis courts, golf privileges at WDW courses, boat rental at nearby Disney Village Marina, children's playground, sauna, fitness center, shuffleboard, Ping-Pong, car-rental desk, overnight film developing, video-camera rental, unisex hair salon, coin-op washers/dryers, shops, video-game arcade.

TRAVELODGE HOTEL, 2000 Hotel Plaza Blvd. (between Buena Vista Dr. and Apopka-Vineland Rd./Fla. 535), Lake Buena Vista, FL 32830. Tel. 407/828-2424, or toll free 800/348-3765. Fax 407/828-8933. 321 rms, 4 suites. A/C MINIBAR TV TEL

$ Rates: $99–$169 for up to four people, depending on room size and season. Inquire about packages. AE, CB, DC, DISC, ER, JCB, MC, OPT, V. **Parking:** Free self-parking.

This 12-acre lakefront property offers rooms and public areas more upscale than you might expect at a Travelodge. This is the company's flagship hotel. Designed to evoke a Barbados plantation manor house, it has a Carribean resort ambience with tropical foliage and bright floral-print fabrics and carpeting. Rooms are decorated in muted peach and beige with light bleached-wood furnishings, their walls adorned with floral friezes and lovely framed botanical prints. All accommodations have furnished balconies, many of them overlooking Lake Buena Vista. Amenities include remote-control cable TVs (with Spectravision movie options), alarm-clock radios, coffee makers, safes, and hairdryers. Free local phone calls are a plus.

Dining/Entertainment: Traders, with a wall of windows overlooking a densely wooded area, is open for breakfast and dinner, the latter featuring steak and seafood; a screened-in, plant-filled terrace adjoins. The Flamingo Cove Lounge, a cocktail bar featuring espresso and cappuccino cocktails, also has screened outdoor seating. The Parakeet Cafe, a casual cafeteria-style eatery, serves pizza, croissant sandwiches, and salads. And on the 18th floor, Toppers, a beautiful nightclub with windows all around, offers magnificent views of Lake Buena Vista and beyond. It's a great vantage point for watching nightly laser shows and fireworks. A DJ or live band plays top-40s dance music.

Services: Room service, babysitting, guest services (sells tickets and arranges transport to all nearby attractions; WDW park tickets are available at the Disney shop), free newspaper delivered to your room weekdays, free transport to/from all WDW parks, Mears airport shuttle.

Facilities: Large swimming pool, kiddie pool, golf privileges at WDW courses, boat rental at nearby Disney Village Marina, children's playground, car-rental desk, coin-op washers/dryers, shops, video-game arcade.

OTHER LAKE BUENA VISTA AREA HOTELS

All the hotels below are within a few minutes' drive of WDW parks.

VERY EXPENSIVE

HYATT REGENCY GRAND CYPRESS, 1 Grand Cypress Blvd. (off Fla. 535), Orlando, FL 32836. Tel. 407/239-1234, or toll free 800/233-1234. Fax 407/239-3800. 675 rms, 75 suites. A/C MINIBAR TV TEL

$ **Rates:** $185–$325 for up to five people in a room; $350–$420 in the Regency Club. Range reflects room size, view, and season. Inquire about packages. AE, CB, DC, DISC, ER, JCB, MC, V. **Parking:** Free self-parking, $7 per night valet parking.

This dazzling multifacility resort is in a class by itself. The tropical plantings of the atrium lobby comprise a small rain forest, with stone-bedded streams and live birds in brass cages. Outside, the Hyatt's gardeners have created an Edenic 1,500-acre botanic garden, dotted with babbling brooks, beautiful flower beds, charming outdoor sculpture, and rock gardens ablaze with bougainvillea and hibiscus. Colorful sailboats and swans glide serenely on 21-acre Lake Windsong. The accommodations are deluxe, with grasspaper wall coverings and teal carpeting complemented by lovely cotton chintz bedspreads and curtains. Oak armoires house remote-control cable TVs with Spectravision movie options. Amenities include alarm-clock radios, ceiling fans, safes, and, in the bath, hairdryers, cotton robes, bathroom scales, and fine toiletries. Three floors comprise the Regency Club, a concierge level.

Dining/Entertainment: The Cascade Grill, down a brass spiral staircase, centers on a 35-foot sculpture of a bronze mermaid backed by a waterfall. American fare is served at all meals. La Coquina, with exquisitely appointed tables amid potted palms and splashing fountains, has a wall of two-story windows overlooking Lake Windsong. It serves French regional fare at dinner nightly; a harpist entertains. The gardenlike Palm Cafe, a self-service buffeteria with both indoor seating and umbrella tables on a poolside patio, offers traditional breakfast fare and an array of sandwiches, salads, main courses, and desserts at lunch; evenings, it's transformed into Papa Geppetto's, featuring California-style pizzas. The western-motif White Horse Saloon specializes in aged Black Angus prime rib dinners; a country-western trio entertains while you dine. Swinging double doors lead to the White Horse Saloon. Papillon, a plush pool bar, is a *simpático* setting for frosty drinks and snacks. Also wonderfully situated is On the Rocks, nestled in a rock cave surrounded by waterfalls, for specialty drinks, snack fare, and ice-cream concoctions. In the lobby "rain forest," set amid cascading waterfalls, is Trellises, a bar/lounge where a jazz ensemble entertains evenings. The Rock Hyatt Club, adjoining the video-game arcade, offers movies, music, and games for teens 13 to 17.

Services: 24-hour room service, babysitting, concierge (sells tickets to WDW parks and other nearby attractions), free transportation around the grounds via shuttle buses and restored Victorian trolleys, hourly shuttle between the hotel and all WDW parks (round-trip fare is $4 per day), Mears airport shuttle.

Facilities: Half-acre swimming pool spanned by a rope bridge and flowing through rock grottoes (with 12 waterfalls and two steep water slides), three secluded whirlpools, white sand beach, 12 tennis courts, 45-hole/par-72 Jack Nicklaus–designed golf course, 9-hole pitch-and-putt golf course, golf and tennis instruction/pro shops, equestrian center, bicycle rental, boat rental, 4.7-mile jogging path, 45-acre

Audubon nature walk, racquetball/volleyball/shuffleboard courts, croquet, children's playground, car-rental desk, full-service unisex beauty salon, full business center, state-of-the-art health club, shops, helicopter landing pad, large high-tech video-game arcade, counselor-supervised child-care center/Camp Hyatt activity center, teen activities program.

EXPENSIVE

CYPRESS POINTE RESORT, 8651 Treasure Cay Lane (off Apopka-Vineland Rd./Fla. 535), Lake Buena Vista, FL 32830. Tel. 407/238-2300, or toll free 800/749-8651. Fax 407/238-2886. 104 suites. A/C TV TEL

$ Rates: $175 two-bedroom suite (for up to six people); $225 three-bedroom suite (for up to nine people). Inquire about packages. AE, CB, DC, DISC, MC, V.
Parking: Free self-parking.

This luxurious vacation-ownership resort, just minutes from Disney's main gate, is entered via a lobby filled with plants, cages of tropical birds, and an aquarium. The accommodations are simply gorgeous, with plushly furnished living rooms (equipped with large-screen remote-control cable TVs, videocassette players, and CD/cassette players), large dining areas, additional dining set-ups on screened patios, fully equipped kitchens, Jacuzzis for two in the master bedrooms, and baths for each bedroom. Amenities include full laundry rooms, TVs/phones/alarm-clock radios in the living room and two bedrooms, and ceiling fans in all rooms.

Dining/Entertainment: Breakfast and light lunches are available poolside from a cabaña bar. Local restaurants, many of which deliver to the hotel, are numerous.

Services: Guest services desk (sells tickets to WDW parks and other nearby attractions, most of them discounted; the round-trip fare to WDW parks is $6); airport shuttle, babysitting.

Facilities: Vast swimming pool with waterfall and "erupting volcano" whirlpool, sand volleyball court, basketball/shuffleboard courts, tennis court, children's playground/ball crawl, well-equipped health club, games room, organized resort activities, convenience store, small video-game room.

MARRIOTT'S ORLANDO WORLD CENTER, 8701 World Center Dr. (on Fla. 536 between I-4 and Fla. 535), Orlando, FL 32821. Tel. 407/239-4200, or toll free 800/621-0638. Fax 407/238-8777. 1,503 rms, 85 suites. A/C MINIBAR TV TEL

$ Rates: $149–$189 for up to five people in a room (range reflects season); pool-view rooms $10 additional per night (14-day advance-purchase rates $124–$154, subject to availability); $265–$2,400 suite. Inquire about packages and rates including full buffet breakfast. AE, CB, DC, DISC, ER, JCB, MC, OPT, V.
Parking: Free self-parking, $8 per night valet parking.

This sprawling 230-acre multifacility resort is just two miles from WDW parks. A grand palm-lined driveway, flanked by rolling golf greens, leads to the main building—a massive 27-story tower housing spacious guest rooms cheerfully decorated in pastel hues with bamboo and rattan furnishings. All have desks, sofa beds, large closets (in which you'll find an iron and ironing board), and patios or balconies. Amenities include alarm-clock radios, safes, remote-control cable TVs (with HBO, extensive pay-movie options, and video account review/message retrieval), and hairdryers in the bath. Step outside the tower and you'll find magnificently landscaped grounds, punctuated by rock gardens, shaded groves of pines and magnolias, and cascading waterfalls; swans and ducks inhabit over a dozen lakes and lagoons spanned by graceful arched bridges.

Dining/Entertainment: With its rich mahogany-and-cherry paneling and 18th-century furnishings, the luxurious Tuscany's, Marriott's premier restaurant, serves haute-cuisine Italian dinners. The Mikado Japanese Steak House is a serene setting for classic teppanyaki dinners overlooking rock gardens, reflecting pools, and a palm-fringed pond. The Garden Terrace, for family dining, is rather elegant with comfortable leather-upholstered furnishings amid lush tropical plantings; it's open for breakfast, lunch, dinner, and buffet Sunday brunch. JW's Steakhouse is one of my favorite places in town for sun-dappled breakfasts and lunches on a screened balcony that yields breathtaking views of the lagoon and golf greens—or for cozy dinners in the rustic pine interior. Champion's a *simpático* sports-themed bar, airs athletic events on 16 TV monitors and one large-screen TV; other amusements here include blackjack, pool tables, video games, air hockey, and, some nights, music for dancing. The Pagoda Lounge offers nightly piano-bar entertainment off the lobby and centers on an imposing Chinese black lacquer pagoda under a sloped skylight. You can relax over cocktails in plush armchairs and sofas amid tropical blooms or on a lovely outdoor veranda overlooking the pool. Palm's serves drinks and light fare, including pizza, poolside. In high season it's augmented by the Shrimp Shack, vending peel-and-eat shrimp, and the hexagonal open-air Pavilion, overlooking a pool and waterfalls and serving frozen drinks and snacks. Stachio's, adjoining the video-game arcade, serves light fare throughout the day.

Services: 24-hour room service, babysitting, concierge, shoeshine, newspaper delivered to your room weekdays, Mears transportation/sightseeing desk (sells tickets to all nearby attractions, including WDW parks; also provides transport, by reservation, to WDW, other attractions, and the airport), one-hour film developing.

Facilities: Three swimming pools, four whirlpools, large kiddie pool, eight tennis courts, 18-hole/par-71 Joe Lee–designed championship golf course, golf and tennis pro shops/instruction, 18-hole miniature golf course, two-mile jogging path, two volleyball courts, car-rental desk, full-service unisex beauty salon, extensive business center, state-of-the-art health club, coin-op washers/dryers, shops, video-game arcade, Lollipop Lounge (a counselor-supervised child-care/activities center). Inquire as well about organized children's activities—games, movies, nature walks, and more.

RESIDENCE INN BY MARRIOTT, 8800 Meadow Creek Dr. (just off Fla. 535 between Fla. 536 and I-4), Orlando, FL 32821. Tel. 407/239-7700, or toll free 800/331-3131. Fax 407/239-7605. 688 suites. A/C TV TEL

$ Rates (including full breakfast): $150–$199 one-bedroom suite (for up to four people); $180–$249 two-bedroom suite (for up to six people). Range reflects season. Inquire about packages. AE, CB, DC, DISC, ER, JCB, MC, V. **Parking:** Free self-parking.

⭐ This delightful all-suite hostelry occupies 50 magnificently landscaped acres, with neatly manicured lawns, duck-filled ponds, fountains, and flower beds shaded by tall palms, pine trees, live oaks, and magnolias. Guests enjoy a serene environment that offers the seclusion of a private community. And they can avail themselves of the extensive facilities at the adjoining Marriott Orlando World Center (see details above) with room-charge privileges. A lighted walkway connects the two properties via a gorgeous golf course. Accommodations are tastefully decorated in muted blue or green color schemes with soft peach and aqua accents. All offer fully equipped eat-in kitchens (some with washing machines and dryers), private balconies or patios, and large living rooms with sleeper sofas. Amenities include remote-control cable TVs (with HBO, Spectravision movie options, and VCRs; movie tapes can be rented), alarm-clock radios, two phones (kitchen and bedroom), ceiling fans, and safes. Two-bedroom units have two baths.

Dining/Entertainment: A full breakfast is available in the gatehouse each morning. A Pizza Hut is on the premises, local restaurants deliver food (there are menus in each room), and, of course, there are quite a few restaurants at the Marriott.

Services: Guest services (sells tickets—most of them discounted—and provides transport to all nearby theme parks and attractions; round-trip to Disney parks costs $4.50), babysitting, complimentary daily newspaper, free shuttle transport around the grounds, same-day film developing, free food-shopping service, Mears airport shuttle.

Facilities: Three large swimming pools (one with a rock waterfall), two whirlpools, sports court (basketball, badminton, volleyball, paddle tennis, shuffleboard), tennis court, children's playground, coin-op washers/dryers, shops, two small video-game arcades. A recreation department organizes numerous free children's activities on a daily basis in peak seasons, less frequently at other times. Note all the additional facilities available to guests here at the Marriott Orlando World Center (see above).

SUMMERFIELD SUITES LAKE BUENA VISTA, 8751 Suiteside Dr. (off Apopka-Vineland Rd./Fla. 535), Lake Buena Vista, FL 32836. Tel. 407/238-0777, or toll free 800/833-4353. Fax 407/238-0778. 150 suites. A/C TV TEL

$ Rates (including extended continental breakfast): $159–$199 one-bedroom suite (for up to four people); $179–$249 two-bedroom suite (for up to eight people). Range reflects season. Inquire about packages. AE, CB, DC, DISC, MC, V. **Parking:** Free self-parking.

This brand-new all-suite property, offering free transport to and from the nearby Disney parks, is an excellent choice for families. Accommodations surround a palm-fringed brick courtyard with umbrella tables, fountains, and gazebos. Spacious residential-style suites are attractively decorated in peach and teal with bleached-oak furnishings. They have fully equipped eat-in kitchens and comfortable living rooms, with a bath for each bedroom. Amenities include fully equipped laundry rooms, bedroom and kitchen phones, remote-control cable TVs in each bedroom and the living room, videocassette players (movies can be rented), and AM/FM alarm-clock radios.

Dining/Entertainment: Guests enjoy an extensive continental buffet breakfast in the pleasant dining room or at umbrella tables in the courtyard. An on-premises lobby deli (which sells light fare and liquor) also serves the pool area. Local restaurants, many of which deliver to the hotel, are numerous.

Services: Room service (pizza only), guest services desk (sells tickets to WDW parks and other nearby attractions, many of them discounted), shuttle to airport/ nearby attractions, free newspaper delivered to your room daily, complimentary grocery shopping, babysitting.

Facilities: Large swimming pool, whirlpool, kiddie pool, car-rental desk, full business services, exercise room, coin-op washers/dryers, shop, small video-game arcade.

MODERATE

HOLIDAY INN SUNSPREE RESORT LAKE BUENA VISTA, 13351 Fla. 535 (between Fla. 536 and I-4), Lake Buena Vista, FL 32821. Tel. 407/239-4500, or toll free 800/FON-MAXX. Fax 407/239-7713. 507 rms. A/C TV TEL

$ Rates: $89–$129 for up to four people, depending on season. Inquire about packages. AE, CB, DC, DISC, JCB, MC, V. **Parking:** Free self-parking.

About a mile from the Disney parks, this Holiday Inn caters to children in a big way. Kids "check in" at their own pint-size desk and receive a free fun bag containing a video-game token coupon and a small gift. And they're personally welcomed by animated raccoon mascots (Max and Maxine). Camp Holiday activities—magic shows, clowns, sing-alongs, arts and crafts, and much more—are free of charge for kids 2 to 12. And parents can arrange (by reservation) for Max to come tuck a child into bed. Accommodations are decorated in aqua, peach, and teal, with bleached-oak furnishings. All rooms have kitchenettes with refrigerators, microwave ovens, and coffee/tea makers. Amenities include remote-control cable TVs with videocassette players (tapes can be rented), alarm-clock radios, hairdryers, and safes. Open-air hallways add to the resort ambience.

Dining/Entertainment: Maxine's is the setting for buffet and à la carte breakfasts and dinners, the latter featuring steak and seafood. Max's Funtime Parlor offers nightly Bingo (with prizes) and karaoke; it also airs sporting events on a large-screen TV. Pinky's Diner serves light fare from 6am to midnight. Kids 12 and under eat all meals free, either in a hotel restaurant with their parents or in Kid's Kottage, a cheerful facility where movies and cartoons are shown on a large-screen TV and dinner includes a make-your-own-sundae bar. The Barefoot Bar and Grill serves snack fare (pizzas, nachos, burgers) and frozen drinks poolside.

Services: Room service, babysitting, guest services desk (sells tickets to all nearby attractions, including WDW parks), free scheduled transport to the Disney parks (there's a charge for transport to other nearby attractions), telephone grocery shopping, Mears airport shuttle.

Facilities: Large free-form swimming pool, two whirlpools, kiddie pool, fitness center, children's playground, coin-op washers/dryers, shops, car-rental desk, video-game arcade, Camp Holiday (a counselor-supervised child-care/activity center for ages 2 to 12, open from 8am to midnight; parents can rent beepers to keep in touch with the kids).

INEXPENSIVE

COMFORT INN, 8442 Palm Pkwy. (between Fla. 535 and I-4), Lake Buena Vista, FL 32830. Tel. 407/239-7300, or toll free 800/999-7300. Fax 407/239-7740. 640 rms. A/C TV TEL

$ Rates: $39–$69 for up to four people, depending on season. Inquire about packages. AE, CB, DC, DISC, MC, V. **Parking:** Free self-parking.

This is an ideally located, large, and attractively landscaped property with two small man-made lakes amid expanses of manicured lawn and lush greenery. And it offers free transport to/from Disney parks. The immaculate rooms are tastefully decorated in shades of mauve or rust. In-room amenities include cable TVs and safes. The Boardwalk Buffet, a sunny restaurant with windows all around, offers reasonably priced buffet meals at breakfast and dinner; kids under 12 eat free. The Comfort Zone, a bar/lounge, adjoins. And complimentary tea and coffee are served in the lobby every afternoon. The guest services desk sells tickets (most of them discounted) and provides transport to all nearby theme parks, dinner shows, and the airport. On-premises facilities include two swimming pools, coin-op washers/dryers, a snack-vending machine area, a gift shop, and a video-game arcade. Pets are permitted.

ON U.S. 192/KISSIMMEE

This very American stretch of highway dotted with fast-food eateries isn't what you'd call scenic, but it does contain many inexpensive hotels within one to eight miles of WDW parks.

MODERATE

HOLIDAY INN MAINGATE EAST, 5678 Irlo Bronson Hwy. (U.S. 192, between I-4 and Poinciana Blvd.), Kissimmee, FL 34746. Tel. 407/396-4488, or toll free 800/FON-KIDS. Fax 407/396-8915. 670 rms. A/C TV TEL

$ Rates: $75–$105 for up to four people, depending on season. Inquire about packages. AE, CB, DC, DISC, JCB, MC, V. **Parking:** Free self-parking.

Just a few miles from the entrance to the Magic Kingdom, the Holiday Inn Maingate, occupying 18 attractively landscaped acres, offers identical facilities to the Holiday Inn Sunspree Resort Lake Buena Vista (described above) including its own Camp Holiday and all the kid-pleaser features (here the welcoming mascots are Holiday and Holly Hound). There's even a small merry-go-round in the lobby. Accommodations, in two-story motel-style buildings enclosing courtyard swimming pools, are decorated in muted blue and peach. Once again, facilities and in-room amenities are identical to those at the Lake Buena Vista property. Pets are permitted here.

Dining/Entertainment: The Vineyard Cafe serves breakfast and dinner, the latter featuring steak and seafood. The Court Street Bar adjoins. The People's Choice, a food court, has six eateries, a pizza and pasta outlet, a deli, a soup and salad bar, and a bakery among them. Tropical Treasures Pool Bar serves up light fare and frozen tropical drinks. Kids 12 and under eat all meals free, either in a hotel restaurant with their parents or in the Gingerbread House, a cheerful facility where movies and cartoons are shown on a large-screen TV and dinner includes a make-your-own-sundae bar.

Services: Room service, babysitting, guest services desk (sells tickets to all nearby attractions, including WDW parks), free scheduled transport to the Disney parks (there's a charge for transport to other nearby attractions), telephone grocery shopping, Mears airport shuttle.

Facilities: Two Olympic-size swimming pools, two whirlpools, kiddie pool, children's playground, two tennis courts, sand volleyball, basketball court, coin-op washers/dryers, shops, car-rental desk, two video-game arcades, Camp Holiday (a counselor-supervised child-care/activity center for ages 3 to 12, open from 8am to midnight; parents can rent beepers to keep in touch with the kids).

RESIDENCE INN BY MARRIOTT ON LAKE CECILE, 4786 W. Irlo Bronson Memorial Hwy. (between Fla. 535 and Siesta Lago Dr.), Kissimmee, FL 34746. Tel. 407/396-2056, or toll free 800/468-3027. Fax 407/396-2909. 159 suites. A/C TV TEL

$ Rates (including extended continental breakfast): $109–$115 studio (for up to four people); $115–$119 studio double (for up to four people); $149–$169 bilevel penthouse (for up to six people). Range reflects season. Inquire about packages. AE, CB, DC, DISC, ER, JCB, MC, OPT, V. **Parking:** Free self-parking.

This all-suite hostelry has peacocks roaming its attractively landscaped grounds on the banks of beautiful 223-acre Lake Cecile. The accommodations, tastefully decorated in gray and mauve, have fully equipped eat-in kitchens and comfortable living room areas with sleeper sofas. All but studio doubles have wood-burning fireplaces (logs are supplied), and the cathedral-ceilinged penthouses have full baths upstairs and down. Many suites offer balconies overlooking the lake. Amenities include remote-control cable TVs (VCRs are available on request and movie tapes can be rented), alarm-clock radios, and in-room safes.

Dining/Entertainment: The lovely gatehouse lounge off the lobby, with comfy sofas facing a working fireplace, is the setting for an extended continental breakfast each morning. And an al fresco bar serves light fare and frosty drinks poolside on a canopied wooden deck with umbrella tables. Local restaurants deliver food (there are menus in each room).

Services: Guest services (sells tickets—most of them discounted—and provides transport to all nearby theme parks and attractions; a round-trip to the Disney parks costs $7), complimentary daily newspaper, free food-shopping service, Mears airport shuttle.

Facilities: Small swimming pool, whirlpool, sports court (basketball, volleyball, badminton, paddle tennis), children's playground, coin-op washers/dryers, 24-hour food shop, picnic tables, barbecue grills. Lake activities include fishing, jet skiing, bumper rides, and waterskiing, and you can rent pedalboats, canoes, and sailboats.

INEXPENSIVE

COLONIAL MOTOR LODGE, 1815 W. Vine St. (U.S. 192, between Bermuda and Thacker Aves.), Kissimmee, FL 34741. Tel. 407/847-6121, or toll free 800/325-4348. Fax 407/847-0728. 83 rms, 40 apts. A/C TV TEL

$ Rates (including continental breakfast): $24–$42 for up to four people; $49.95–$89.95 two-bedroom apt (for up to six people). Range reflects season. AE, CB, DC, DISC, MC, V. **Parking:** Free self-parking.

This well-run motor lodge is entered via a white colonial-style building with peach columns and shutters and a Federalist eagle over the door. The pleasantly furnished lobby is the setting for a complimentary continental breakfast each morning. Standard motel rooms decorated in rust and tan with whitewashed pine-paneled walls offer remote-control cable TVs with HBO and alarm clocks. Two-bedroom apartments, in two-story white buildings fronted by small gardens, represent a good choice for families. In addition to two full bedrooms, they have living rooms and fully equipped eat-in kitchens.

Facilities include two junior Olympic-size swimming pools and a kiddie pool. Adjacent to the Colonial are an International House of Pancakes and a shopping center with a dry cleaner and self-service laundry. The Black Angus, a steak-and-seafood restaurant, is across the street. And a supermarket, 7-Eleven, Hardy's, and Kentucky Fried Chicken are a block away. Guest services sells tickets to all Disney parks and nearby attractions (some of them discounted) and offers transportation to/from them and the airport. Transport to the Disney parks is $11 per person round-trip.

COMFORT INN MAINGATE, 7571 W. Irlo Bronson Memorial Hwy. (U.S. 192, between Reedy Creek Blvd. and Sherbeth Rd.), Kissimmee, FL

34747. Tel. 407/396-7500, or toll free 800/221-2222. Fax 407/396-7497.
281 rms. A/C TV TEL
$ Rates: $38–$74 single or double, depending on season; garden rooms $6–$10
additional. Additional person $8 extra. Children 18 and under stay free in parents'
room. AE, CB, DC, DISC, ER, JCB, MC, V. **Parking:** Free self-parking.
Just one mile from the Disney parks, this Comfort Inn houses clean, spiffy-looking
standard motel accommodations in two-story peach stucco buildings. More upscale
are the garden rooms, facing a lawn with a gazebo; decorated in teal, seafoam green,
and peach, they're equipped with small refrigerators, coffee makers, and hairdryers.
The Royal Palms Restaurant on the premises serves low-priced buffets and à la carte
meals. A comfortable bar/lounge adjoins. And right next door are a 7-Eleven and an
International House of Pancakes. The guest services desk sells tickets (most of them
discounted) and provides transport to all nearby attractions and the airport; the
round-trip to the Disney parks costs $7. Facilities include a medium-sized swimming
pool, children's playground, coin-op washers/dryers, and a small video-game arcade.

**ECONO LODGE MAINGATE EAST, 4311 W. Irlo Bronson Memorial Hwy.
(U.S. 192, between Hoagland Blvd. and Fla. 535), Kissimmee, FL
34746. Tel. 407/396-7100,** or toll free 800/ENJOY-FL. Fax 407/239-2636.
173 rms. A/C TV TEL
$ Rates: $29–$79 for up to four people, depending on season. AE, CB, DC, DISC,
JCB, MC, V. **Parking:** Free self-parking.
At this attractively landscaped Econo Lodge, accommodations are set well
back from the highway in rustic two- and three-story buildings with cedar
balconies and roofing. Well-maintained rooms are equipped with cable TVs
and safes; small refrigerators can be rented. The pool bar serves light fare, including
full breakfasts and lunches at umbrella tables under towering live oaks. The guest
services desk sells tickets (most of them discounted) and provides transport to all
nearby attractions and the airport; a round-trip to the Disney parks costs $12.
On-premises facilities include a large swimming pool, kiddie pool, volleyball,
shuffleboard, horseshoes, coin-op washers/dryers, picnic tables, barbecue grills, and a
small video-game arcade. This is one of six area hotels under the same ownership, all
of which can be booked via the above toll-free number.

**HOJO INN MAIN GATE, 6051 W. Irlo Bronson Memorial Hwy. (U.S. 192,
just east of I-4), Kissimmee, FL 34747. Tel. 407/396-1748,** or toll free
800/288-4678. Fax 407/649-8642. 358 rms, 9 family suites. A/C TV TEL
$ Rates: $60–$76 for up to four people, depending on season (children under 19
stay free in parents' room); $70–$86 efficiency unit with a kitchenette; $90–$106
family suite. Inquire about packages. AE, CB, DC, DISC, JCB, MC, V. **Parking:**
Free self-parking.
This Howard Johnson's hostelry, just two miles from the Magic Kingdom, offers
attractive accommodations decorated with quilted lavender bedspreads, royal-blue
carpeting, and beach-themed paintings. In-room amenities include cable TVs with
VCRs (movies can be rented) and safes. Efficiency units have fully equipped
kitchenettes. And family suites have both full kitchens and living rooms with
convertible sofas.
Facilities here include a medium-size swimming pool, whirlpool, kiddie pool,
children's playground, coin-op washers/dryers, small video-game arcade, car-rental
desk, and pool table. Adjoining the property is a large water park called Watermania
and a plant-filled International House of Pancakes. On the premises, a pool bar serves
light fare and drinks, and complimentary coffee and tea are served in the lobby
throughout the day. Guest services sells tickets to all Disney parks and nearby
attractions (some of them discounted) and offers transportation to/from them and the
airport. Transport to the Disney parks is $7 per person round-trip.

**LARSON'S LODGE KISSIMMEE, 2009 W. Vine St. (U.S. 192, at Thacker
Ave.), Kissimmee, FL 34741. Tel. 407/846-2713,** or toll free 800/624-
5905. Fax 407/846-8695. 200 rms. A/C TV TEL
$ Rates: $39–$79 for up to four people, depending on season; $49–$89 efficiency
unit with a kitchenette. AE, CB, DC, DISC, MC, V. **Parking:** Free self-parking.

⑤ This friendly family-run hostelry just eight miles from Walt Disney World has been operated by the Larsons since 1976. Standard motel units—decorated in teal and tan or teal and peach—have a vaguely southwestern look. They're equipped with remote-control cable TVs and in-room safes. More upscale are cheerful efficiency units which have living room areas and fully equipped kitchenettes.

The guest services desk sells tickets to all nearby theme parks, including WDW (many of them discounted), and a shuttle bus plies the route between the hotel and all WDW parks throughout the day (the round-trip fare is $10); transport is also available to other nearby attractions and the airport. On-premises facilities and amenities include a large swimming pool, a smaller free-form pool, kiddie pool, whirlpool, children's playground, tennis court, gift/sundries shop, coin-op washers/dryers, and video-game arcade. Guests get free tickets to Watermania, the water park at Larson's Lodge Main Gate (see below). Pets are permitted. A shopping center is close by, and the Black Angus restaurant, serving all meals (dinner features steak and seafood), is on the premises; there's nightly entertainment in its adjoining western-motif lounge.

LARSON'S LODGE MAIN GATE, 6075 W. Irlo Bronson Memorial Hwy. (U.S. 192, just east of I-4), Kissimmee, FL 34747. Tel. 407/396-6100, or toll free 800/327-9074. Fax 407/396-6965. 128 rms. A/C TV TEL
$ Rates: $39–$79 single or double, depending on season; $54–$94 efficiency unit with a kitchenette. Additional person $8 extra. Children under 18 stay free in parents' room. AE, CB, DC, DISC, MC, V. **Parking:** Free self-parking.

⑤ With its large, on-premises water park (Watermania), children's playground, and poolside picnic tables and barbecue grills, Larson's Lodge is a good choice for families. It has a cheerful on-site Shoney's restaurant. Accommodations are attractively decorated in peach and seafoam green with bleached-oak furnishings. They're equipped with remote-control cable TVs (VCRs and movie tapes can be rented), coffee makers, and in-room safes. Efficiency units have fully equipped kitchenettes, and a supermarket is just a few minutes away by car.

The guest services desk sells tickets to all nearby theme parks, including WDW (many of them discounted), and a shuttle bus plies the route between the motel and all WDW parks throughout the day (the round-trip fare is $8). Transport is also available to other nearby attractions and the airport. On-premises facilities include a large swimming pool and whirlpool, shops, coin-op washers/dryers, a small video-game arcade, and a pool table. Guests enjoy free use of the tennis court at Larson's Lodge Kissimmee and get free tickets to Watermania. Pets are permitted.

RODEWAY INN EASTGATE, 5245 W. Irlo Bronson Memorial Hwy. (U.S. 192, between Poinciana and Polynesian Isle Blvds.), Kissimmee, FL 34746. Tel. 407/396-7700, or toll free 800/423-3864. Fax 407/396-0293. 200 rms. A/C TV TEL
$ Rates: $31–$55 for up to four people, depending on view and season. Rates may be higher during major events. AE, CB, DC, DISC, ER, JCB, MC, V. **Parking:** Free self-parking.

The Rodeway's U-shaped configuration of two-story pink stucco buildings form an attractively landscaped courtyard around a large swimming pool. There are picnic tables and a children's play area on the lawn. Rooms are nicely decorated in teal, aqua, and mauve, with oak furnishings and grasspaper-look/bamboo-motif wall coverings.

The on-site Terrace Restaurant serves buffet breakfasts, and the comfy Half Time Lounge, where sporting events are aired on a seven-foot screen, has a pool table and dart boards. Other facilities include a small video-game arcade off the lobby, coin-op washers/dryers, and a gift shop. Guest services sells tickets to all Disney parks and nearby attractions (many of them discounted) and offers transportation to/from them and the airport. Transport to the Disney parks is $7.50 per person round-trip.

INTERNATIONAL DRIVE

Hostelries listed here are 7 to 10 miles north of the Walt Disney World parks and close to Universal Studios and Sea World.

EXPENSIVE

PEABODY ORLANDO, 9801 International Dr. (between the Beeline Expy. and Sand Lake Rd.), Orlando, FL 32819. Tel. 407/352-4000, or toll free 800/PEABODY. Fax 407/351-0073. 835 rms, 57 suites. A/C MINIBAR TV TEL

$ Rates: $190–$230 for up to three people; $250 for Peabody Club; $395–$1,300 suite. Children under 18 stay free in parents' room; seniors 50 and over get a $1 discount per year of age. Rates May–Sept 15 slightly reduced. Inquire about packages. AE, CB, DC, DISC, ER, JCB, MC, V. **Parking:** Free self-parking, $6 per night valet parking.

This deluxe 27-story resort hotel has some especially famous avian residents. Every morning at 11am, five fluffy ducks proudly parade along a red carpet to the beat of John Philip Sousa's *King Cotton* march, their journey culminating at a marble fountain in the lobby. But ducks are just a fillip here. The Peabody, in the grand tradition, pampers guests with sumptuous surroundings and attentive service. The luxurious rooms have bamboo and bleached-wood furnishings and walls hung with quality artworks. Amenities include two phones (bedroom and bath), remote-control cable TVs with Spectravision and laser-disc movie set-ups, and, in the bath, cosmetic lights, fine European toiletries, a hairdryer, and a small TV. The concierge-level Peabody Club occupies the top three floors. The Peabody is about 15 minutes by car from the WDW parks and very close to Sea World and Universal Studios.

Dining/Entertainment: Dux, the Peabody's elegant signature restaurant, features American regional cuisine dinners in a plush candlelit and crystal-chandeliered setting; it does not, however, serve duck. Capriccio, for sophisticated northern Italian fare, is open for dinner and champagne Sunday brunches. The B-Line Diner, a 24-hour art deco eatery, dishes up traditional American specialties. From the B-Line Express window, you can order cold take-out fare from the restaurant's menu. The Peabody Pool Bar serves cold, frothy specialty drinks and snacks. A singer and trio perform jazz, blues, and show tunes in the atrium Lobby Bar nightly. The lobby is also the setting for weekday afternoon English teas. The adjoining Mallards Lounge is a cozy gathering place; sports events are aired on the TV over the bar. And al fresco jazz concerts take place on the fourth-floor recreation level spring and fall.

Services: 24-hour room service, babysitting, 24-hour concierge, shoeshine, nightly bed turn-down on request, free newspaper delivered to your room daily, "Double Ducker" shuttle bus making runs between the hotel and all WDW parks throughout the day (unlimited daily round-trips cost $5), Mears transportation/sightseeing desk (sells tickets to all nearby attractions, including the WDW parks and dinner shows; also provides transport, by reservation, to attractions and the airport).

Facilities: Double-Olympic-length swimming pool, indoor and outdoor whirlpools, large kiddie pool with waterfall fountain, four tennis courts, golf privileges at four nearby courses, seven-mile jogging path, car-rental desk, Delta Airlines desk, full-service unisex beauty salon, full business center, state-of-the-art health club, shops, small video-game arcade, the Children's Hotel (a counselor-supervised child-care/activities center); hot-air balloon rides, deep-sea fishing, scuba lessons, and other amusements/excursions can be arranged.

MODERATE

SUMMERFIELD SUITES, 8480 International Dr. (between the Beeline Expy. and Sand Lake Rd.), Orlando, FL 32819. Tel. 407/352-2400, or toll free 800/833-4353. Fax 407/352-4631. 146 suites. A/C TV TEL

$ Rates (including extended continental breakfast): $139–$159 one-bedroom suite (for up to four people); $159–$199 two-bedroom suite (for up to six people). Range reflects room size and season. Inquire about packages. AE, CB, DC, DISC, MC, V. **Parking:** Free self-parking.

This delightful five-story cream stucco hotel is built around a nicely landscaped central courtyard. Spacious, neat-as-a-pin residential-style suites, very attractively decorated in peach and teal with bleached-oak furnishings, contain fully equipped eat-in kitchens, comfortable living rooms, big walk-in closets, and large dressing areas. Two-bedroom units have two baths, and all bedrooms have doors (ensuring privacy). Amenities include irons and ironing boards, phones (with two lines, computer hookup, and voice-mail messaging) in each bedroom and the kitchen, remote-control satellite TVs (with free HBO) in each bedroom and the living room (the latter with a VCR; rent movies downstairs), and alarm-clock radios in each bedroom. A large shopping center is across the street, the WDW parks are about 15 minutes away by car, Sea World and Universal Studios are close by, and numerous restaurants are in the area. This is a great choice for families.

Dining/Entertainment: An extensive continental buffet breakfast is served in a charming peach-walled dining room, and the cozy lobby bar is a popular gathering place evenings. A cabaña bar offers drinks and snacks poolside. And local restaurants deliver food to the premises.

Services: Babysitting, concierge/tour desk (sells tickets to the WDW parks and other nearby attractions), newspapers delivered to your room daily, transport between the hotel and all WDW parks (the round-trip fare is $7), shuttle available to the airport and nearby attractions, complimentary grocery shopping.

Facilities: Nice-size swimming pool, whirlpool, kiddie pool, car-rental desk, full business services, exercise room, coin-op washers/dryers, 24-hour shop, small video-game arcade.

INEXPENSIVE

FAIRFIELD INN BY MARRIOTT, 8342 Jamaica Court (off International Dr. between the Beeline Expy. and Sand Lake Rd.), Orlando, FL 32819. Tel. 407/363-1944, or toll free 800/228-2800. Fax 407/363-1944. 135 rms. A/C TV TEL

$ Rates (including continental breakfast): $29–$74 for up to four people. Range reflects season. AE, CB, DC, DISC, ER, MC, V. **Parking:** Free self-parking.

Jamaican Court, in a secluded area off International Drive, is a neatly landscaped complex of hotels and restaurants, including this handsome three-story tan stucco hostelry with blue roofing and doors. It has spiffy-looking rooms decorated in rust, tan, and Federalist blue with oak furnishings. In-room amenities include remote-control cable TVs with free HBO, AM/FM radios, alarm clocks, and phones equipped with 25-foot cords and modem jacks. Guests enjoy a few thoughtful extras here: 100-watt bulbs in the lamps, candies on your pillow at check-in, complimentary daily newspapers, and free local calls. A continental breakfast is served in the lobby each morning. In addition, there are many free-standing and hotel restaurants right in Jamaican Court, and several local eateries deliver food.

The guest services desk sells tickets (most of them discounted) and provides transport to all nearby theme parks and attractions and the airport; a round-trip to the Disney parks costs $10. There's a small swimming pool on the premises, and the lobby has a microwave oven for guest use.

4. DINING

Since most Orlando visitors spend the majority of their time in the Walt Disney World area, I've focused on the best choices throughout that vast enchanted empire. Also listed are a few worthwhile choices beyond the realm. Parents will be pleased to note that just about every restaurant in town offers a low-priced children's menu and usually provides some kind of kid's activity (mazes, coloring, paper dolls) as well. See also the listings for dinner shows in "Evening Entertainment," later in this chapter.

AT WALT DISNEY WORLD

EPCOT

An ethnic meal at one of the World Showcase pavilions is part of the Epcot experience. If you want to have lunch or dinner at a Future World or World Showcase restaurant, make reservations at Earth Center as soon as you enter the park in the morning. That will ensure optimum choice of dining time and cuisine. Guests at WDW-owned and official hotels can make reservations by phone up to three days in advance (ask the Central Reservations Office for details when you reserve, or call the guest services or concierge desk at your hotel). And during slower seasons, you can very often just walk up to an Epcot restaurant and make a reservation on the spot. All the establishments listed below offer lunch and dinner daily, serve alcoholic beverages, are in the "Expensive" category, do not permit smoking, and take American Express, MasterCard, and VISA.

Note: In addition to the places listed below there are plenty of lower-priced walk-in eateries throughout the park that don't require reservations; check your *EPCOT Center Guidebook* for details.

World Showcase

UNITED KINGDOM   The plank-floored **Rose & Crown,** entered via a cozy pub with a pungent aroma of ale, evokes Victorian England with servers in period costume and English and Scottish folk music. It also offers outdoor seating at umbrella tables overlooking the lagoon. The menu features items like Scotch egg and Stilton cheese, fish and chips, steak-and-kidney pie, and sherry trifle. Traditional afternoon tea, with scones and finger sandwiches, is served daily at 4pm.

FRANCE   Chefs de France is under the auspices of a world-famous culinary triumvirate: Paul Bocuse, Roger Vergé, and Gaston LeNôtre. A meal here might begin with a seafood cream soup with crab dumplings (Vergé), continue to a main course of broiled salmon in sorrel-cream sauce à la façon de Bocuse, and conclude with a soufflé Grand-Marnier (LeNôtre). The art nouveau/fin-de-siècle interior, under a coffered cherrywood ceiling, is agleam with brass candelabra chandeliers.

The   ✪ **Bistro de Paris,** upstairs from Chefs de France and serving dinner only, offers similar fare in a more serene country French setting.

MOROCCO   The palatial   ✪ **Restaurant Marrakesh**—with its exquisitely carved faux-ivory archways, hand-set mosaic tilework, and intricate cut-brass chandeliers suspended from a beamed ceiling painted with Moorish motifs—represents 12 centuries of Arabic design. Belly dancers perform while you dine on dishes like lamb couscous, chicken bastilla (a sweet pastry flavored with chopped almonds and cinnamon), and shish kebab. The Moroccan diffa (traditional feast) that lets you sample a variety of dishes is recommended.

JAPAN   The main dining area of the **Mitsukoshi Restaurant** is a teppanyaki steakhouse where diners sit at grill tables and white-hatted chefs perform samuraiike culinary moves—rapidly dicing, slicing, stir-frying, and propelling the cooked food onto your plate with amazing dexterity. Main courses feature shrimp, scallops, lobster, steak, and chicken. It's great fun watching the chef wield his knife and utensils. Dining areas are divided by shoji screens. Since you'll share a table with strangers, this makes for a convivial dining experience.

ITALY   Patterned after Alfredo De Lelio's celebrated establishment in Rome, ✪ **L'Originale Alfredo di Roma Ristorante** evokes a seaside Roman palazzo with beautiful trompe-l'oeil frescoes of 15th-century patrician villas on the walls. Exuberant strolling musicians create a festive ambience. De Lelio invented fettuccine Alfredo, and it remains an excellent choice here. Other recommendables are vodka-flavored ziti in a piquant tomato-cream sauce and chicken alla parmigiana served with an array of fresh vegetables. Don't pass up the sublime tira misu for dessert.

GERMANY   Lit by streetlamps, **The Biergarten** simulates a Bavarian village courtyard at Oktoberfest with autumnal trees, a working waterwheel, and geranium-filled flower boxes adorning Tudor-style houses. Oom-pah bands, singers, dancers, and a strolling accordionist entertain. Traditional fare includes goulash soup, sauerbraten with dumplings and red cabbage, and apple strudel for dessert. Wash it down with a 33-ounce stein of Beck's or a glass of Liebfraumilch.

CHINA   One of the most attractive of the World Showcase restaurants,   ✪ **Nine Dragons** has intricately carved rosewood paneling, lacquer screens embellished with cherry blossoms, and a beautiful dragon-motif ceiling. Window seats overlook the lagoon. You can choose Mandarin, Shanghai, Szechuan, Hunan, or Cantonese dishes ranging from Szechuan deep-fried shrimp in a Mao Tai liqueur-spiked fruit sauce to moo shoo pork. There are also dim sum appetizers and assorted Chinese pastries for dessert. Try the melon juice, plain or with rum or vodka.

NORWAY **Akershus** re-creates a 14th-century castle fortress that stands in Oslo's harbor. Its pristine white stone interior, with glossy oak floors, lofty pine and beamed cherrywood ceilings, and leaded-glass windows, features intimate dining niches divided by Gothic stone archways. The meal is an immense smörgåsbord including items like smoked pork with honey mustard, venison in cream sauce, gravlax, Norwegian tomato herring, cheeses, red cabbage, eggs nordique, cold meats, seafood, and salads. Order a "veiled maiden" for dessert and Norwegian beer.

MEXICO The ✪ **San Angel Inn** evokes a hacienda courtyard under a starlit sky in the shadow of a Yucatán pyramid, with the Popocatepetl volcano erupting in the distance. Tables are candlelit (even at lunch) and lighting is very low. Order an appetizer of queso fundido (melted cheese with Mexican pork sausage, served with homemade flour tortillas). Main-course specialties include mole poblano (chicken simmered with more than 20 spices and a hint of chocolate) and combination platters of enchiladas, chiles rellenos, and beef tacos.

Future World

LIVING SEAS PAVILION Dine "under the sea" at the enchanting ✪ **Coral Reef,** where all seating rings a 5.6-million-gallon coral-reef aquarium inhabited by more than 4,000 denizens of the deep. The strains of Debussy's *La Mer* and Handel's *Water Music* playing softly in the background help set the tone. The menu features (what else?) seafood—oysters Rockefeller, lobster bisque, sautéed mahi-mahi in lemon-caper butter, and seafood fettuccine Alfredo, along with steak and chicken dishes. Dessert options include Belgian chocolate mousse cake and key lime pie.

THE LAND The revolving **Garden Grill,** on the upper level of this pavilion, seats diners in comfortable semicircular booths. As you dine, your table travels past desert, prairie, farmland, and rain-forest environments. The fare is American. A meal here might consist of an appetizer of spicy chicken wings with bleu cheese dressing, a main course of Cajun-style jambalaya or southern fried chicken, and an oven-fresh fruit crisp with vanilla ice cream for dessert. Many menu selections feature produce grown in the pavilion's greenhouses.

THE MAGIC KINGDOM

There are dozens of eateries throughout the Magic Kingdom, but I enjoy a quiet full-service meal. To dine at any of the establishments listed below, make reservations at the restaurant itself when you enter the park in the morning. Guests at WDW-owned and official hotels can make reservations by phone up to three days in advance (ask the Central Reservations Office for details when you reserve, or call the guest services or concierge desk at your hotel). All the establishments listed below take American Express, MasterCard, and VISA. No Magic Kingdom restaurants serve alcoholic beverages or allow smoking.

FRONTIERLAND Highly recommended is the **Diamond Horseshoe Jamboree** in Frontierland, combining a light meal with a 40-minute western-themed musical revue (details in Section 5 of this chapter).

LIBERTY SQUARE The **Liberty Tree Tavern** is an 18th-century pub, with low beamed ceilings, peg-plank oak floors, and a vast brick fireplace hung with copper pots. Main courses range from New England pot roast served with mashed potatoes and vegetables to a traditional roast turkey dinner with all the trimmings. All-American desserts include apple pie topped with cinnamon ice cream. Open for lunch and dinner. Price range: Moderate to expensive.

CINDERELLA CASTLE **King Stefan's Banquet Hall** is a castle dining room complete with heraldic banners and candelabra chandeliers suspended from a vaulted ceiling. Oak tables are candlelit. The only anachronistic note: The background music is from Disney movies. The menu features hearty cuts of steak and prime rib, along with chicken and seafood dishes. Open for lunch and dinner. Price range: Expensive.

MAIN STREET Inspired by the Disney movie *Lady and the Tramp,* **Tony's Town Square Restaurant** is Victorian plush, with rich cherrywood beams and paneling, cut-glass mirrors, and globe lighting fixtures. There's additional seating in a plant-filled solarium. The menu is Italian, featuring pastas, pizzas, salads, and frittatas at lunch, and such main courses as steak with lobster and linguine at dinner. Open for breakfast, lunch, and dinner. Price range: Moderate to expensive.

DISNEY–MGM STUDIOS

There are over a dozen eateries in this Hollywood-themed park with names like the Studio Commissary and Starring Rolls Bakery. The two listed below are my favorites. Both require reservations, which should be made at the Hollywood Junction Red Car Station on Sunset Boulevard or at the restaurants themselves when you enter the park in the morning. Guests at WDW-owned and official hotels can make reservations by phone up to three days in advance (ask the Central Reservations Office for details when you reserve, or call the guest services or concierge desk at your hotel). Both serve lunch and dinner, have full bars, and take American Express, MasterCard, and VISA. Smoking is prohibited.

The **Hollywood Brown Derby,** modeled after the famed Los Angeles celebrity haunt where Louella Parsons and Hedda Hopper held court, evokes its West Coast counterpart with interior palm trees, derby-shaded sconces, and mahogany-paneled walls hung with hundreds of caricatures—every major star from Barbara Stanwyck to Rin Tin Tin. The Derby's signature dish is the Cobb salad, invented by owner Bob Cobb in the 1930s. A typical dinner: appetizer of pan-fried Maryland crabcakes served with spicy marinara sauce, a main course of smoked rack of lamb served with fresh vegetables and minted dried-fruit sauce, and grapefruit cake with vanilla icing (another house specialty) for dessert. Price range: Expensive.

The **Sci-Fi Dine-In Theater Restaurant** replicates a 1950s Hollywood drive-in movie theater. Diners sit in flashy convertible cars under a twinkling starlit sky, while friendly servers bring complimentary popcorn and food. While you eat, you can watch the movie screen, where a mix of zany newsreels (like *News of the Future*) is interspersed with cartoons, horror-movie clips, and coming attractions. Menu items have names like Terror of the Tides (deep-fried shrimp with french fries and coleslaw) and Monster Mash (oven-roasted turkey with all the trimmings). Finish up with the Cheesecake That Ate New York. Price range: Moderate.

AT DISNEY RESORTS

Very Expensive

VICTORIA & ALBERT'S, in Disney's Grand Floridian Beach Resort, 4401 Floridian Way. Tel. 824-2383.
    Cuisine: AMERICAN REGIONAL. **Reservations:** Required.
$ Prices: $80 per person prix fixe; $25 additional for the Royal Wine Pairing. AE, MC, V.
    Open: Dinner only, daily, with seatings at 6–6:45pm and 9–9:45pm.
        It's not often that one describes a dining experience as flawless, but at Victoria & Albert's, the World's most elite restaurant (Walt Disney World, that is) I experienced nothing less than idyllic perfection. The plushly furnished dining room is girded by a circular colonnade. Brocaded walls are hung with gilt-framed ink drawings, and an exquisite floral arrangement—above which a Chinoiserie chandelier is suspended from a beautifully painted dome—serves as an aesthetic centerpoint. A maid and butler provide deft and gracious service, and a harpist plays softly while you dine.

Dinner, a seven-course affair, changes nightly. On a recent visit, I began with an hors d'oeuvre of Florida lobster tail with aioli on mitzuma lettuce. It was supplanted by a more formal appetizer, vermouth-poached jumbo sea scallops served in a crisp rice-noodle basket on shallot-chive sauce and garnished with flying fish caviar and Chinese tat soi leaves. A shot of peppered vodka added piquancy to a velvety plum tomato bisque lightly topped with pesto-cream sauce. For a main course, I selected a fan of pinkly juicy sautéed Peking duck breast with wild rice and crabapple chutney. A salad of esoteric greens in an orange-sherry vinaigrette cleared the palate for the next course—English Stilton served with pine-nut bread, port wine, and a pear poached in burgundy, cognac, and cinnamon sugar. The conclusion: a sumptuous hazelnut and Frangelico soufflé, followed by coffee and chocolate truffles. There is, of course, an extensive wine list. I suggest that you opt for the Royal Wine Pairing, which pairs an appropriate wine with each course and lets you sample a variety of selections from the restaurant's distinguished cellars. Jackets are required for men, and no smoking is permitted. There is free self-parking and validated valet parking.

Expensive

ARIEL'S, at Disney's Beach Club Resort, 1800 EPCOT Resorts Blvd. Tel. 934-3357.
  Cuisine: SEAFOOD. **Reservations:** Recommended.
$ Prices: Appetizers $4.25–$8.95; main courses $17.95–$24. AE, MC, V.
  Open: Dinner only, daily 6–10pm.

Named for the *Little Mermaid* character, this exquisite restaurant overlooking Stormalong Bay is awash in seafoam green, peach, and coral. White-linened tables are elegantly appointed with fish and seashell-motif china, a prismed 2,000-gallon coral-reef tank is filled with tropical fish, and whimsical fish mobiles and glass bubbles dangle from a vaulted ceiling. You'll feel like you're dining in an underwater kingdom.

Appetizers include scrumptious New England silver dollar crabcakes served with a spicy tartar sauce and a Cajun-style shellfish gumbo. Recommended seafood dishes here include a traditional paella and Maine lobster sautéed with shiitake mushrooms and served atop a nest of tricolor angel-hair pasta with two sauces—a buttery lobster sauce and herbed cream. A few nonseafood options are offered as well. Desserts include a rich Chambord raspberry-chocolate cake, and an extensive award-winning wine list indicates which selections best complement your main course. There is free self- and valet parking.

Moderate

CAPE MAY CAFE, at Disney's Beach Club Resort, 1800 EPCOT Resorts Blvd. Tel. 934-3415.
  Cuisine: CLAMBAKE BUFFET. **Reservations:** Not accepted.
$ Prices: Buffet, $16.95 adults, $8.95 ages 6–11, free for kids under 6. Lobster is additional. AE, MC, V.
  Open: Dinner only, daily 5:30–9:30pm.

A hearty 19th-century-style New England clambake is featured nightly at this charming peach and seafoam-green restaurant, where sand sculptures, paintings of turn-of-the-century beach scenes, and furled striped beach umbrellas evoke an upscale seaside resort. Aromatic stews and chowders, steamed clams and mussels, corn on the cob, chicken, lobster, and redskin potatoes are cooked up in a crackling rockweed steamer pit that serves as the restaurant's centerpiece. And these traditional clambake offerings are supplemented by dozens of salads, hot dishes (barbecued baby back ribs, fried chicken, pasta dishes), and a wide array of oven-fresh breads and desserts. There's a full bar. There is free self- and valet parking.

WALT DISNEY WORLD VILLAGE MARKETPLACE/PLEASURE ISLAND

Located about 2½ miles from Epcot, off Buena Vista Drive, the Marketplace is a very pleasant complex of cedar-shingled shops and restaurants overlooking a scenic lagoon. Pleasure Island, a complex of nightclubs and shops, adjoins.

Note: You don't have to pay the entrance fee to Pleasure Island to dine at the Fireworks Factory or Portobello Yacht Club.

Expensive

PORTOBELLO YACHT CLUB, 1650 Lake Buena Vista Dr., Pleasure Island. Tel. 934-8888.

 Cuisine: NORTHERN ITALIAN. **Reservations:** Not accepted (arrive early to avoid a wait).
 $ Prices: Appetizers $5.95–$8.95; main courses $6.95–$8.95 at lunch, $12.95–$22.95 at dinner; pizzas $6.95–$7.95. AE, MC, V.
 Open: Daily 11:30am–midnight (dinner served from 4pm).

Occupying a Bermuda-style gabled house, the Yacht Club is nautically themed, its interior, though casual, evoking a luxury cruise ship. Inside, robin's-egg-blue walls are plastered with photographs of racing yachts, and shelves are lined with racing trophies. From the lively mahogany-paneled bar, you can watch oak-fired pizzas being prepared in an exhibition kitchen. Multipaned windows overlook Lake Buena Vista, as do tables on an awninged patio.

Those oak-fired pizzas have crisply thin crusts and toppings such as quattro formaggi—mozzarella, romano, Gorgonzola, and provolone—with sun-dried tomatoes. At dinner, you might select a main course of charcoal-grilled half chicken marinated in olive oil, garlic, and fresh rosemary and served with garlicky oven-roasted mashed potatoes and seasonal vegetables. Or choose a pasta dish such as bucatini with plum tomatoes, Italian bacon, garlic, and fresh basil. There's an extensive list of Italian and California wines. A dessert of crema bruccioto (white-chocolate custard with a caramelized sugar glaze) is recommended. There's free self-parking; valet parking is $4.

Moderate

CHEF MICKEY'S, at Walt Disney World Village. Tel. 828-3900.

 Cuisine: AMERICAN. **Reservations:** Recommended.
 $ Prices: Appetizers $3.95–$6.95; main courses $5.75–$10.25 at lunch, $9.75–$15 at dinner; breakfast fare $1.95–$6.25. AE, MC, V.
 Open: Breakfast daily 9–11am; lunch daily 11:30am–2pm; dinner daily 5–10pm.

Rustically attractive, Chef Mickey's plant-filled interior has ficus trees growing toward a skylight and exposed brick walls hung with signed photographs of Disney characters. About half the seats overlook Buena Vista Lagoon. One dining area has redwood-paneled walls and a beamed pine cathedral ceiling; another offers a view of white-hatted chefs at work in an exhibition kitchen. And should you have to wait for a table (only 20% of tables are alloted via reservations, with the rest reserved for walk-ins, but you can reserve up to 30 days in advance; walk-ins should arrive early to avoid a wait), you can do so in a lounge where kids can watch cartoons on a large-screen TV and adults can watch sporting events at the bar. Mickey turns out some pretty terrific food here, and, at dinner, he table-hops greeting patrons.

My favorite appetizer choice is light and fluffy crabcakes Boca. An excellent main course is the cheesy crisp-baked salmon lasagne served in a spinach/pine-nut sauce. Or you might opt for fork-tender barbecued ribs with grilled corn (served in the husk), a big slab of homemade cornbread, and coleslaw. Leave room for peach cobbler topped with vanilla-bean ice cream. Parking is free (use Lot A).

THE FIREWORKS FACTORY, 1630 Lake Buena Vista Dr., Pleasure Island. Tel. 934-8989.

 Cuisine: AMERICAN REGIONAL. **Reservations:** Recommended.
 $ Prices: Appetizers $4.95–$6.95; main courses $5.95–$8.95 at lunch, $13.95–$19.95 at dinner. AE, MC, V.
 Open: Daily 11:30am–11:30pm (dinner served from 4pm, with light fare and drinks served to 2am).

According to Disney legend, Capt. Merriweather Adam Pleasure, the mythological 19th-century ship merchant and adventurer who developed Pleasure Island, manufactured fireworks as a hobby in this "explosively" exuberant corrugated-tin warehouse. The Factory has big red pipes overhead and exposed brick or tin walls hung with neon signs and advertisements for fireworks. You can eat downstairs or enjoy the lively scene from a balcony level. This is a good choice for family dining.

Lunch or dinner, start off with a "3 and 3 combo" appetizer of fried catfish, applewood-smoked shrimp, and spicy chicken wings tossed in Louisiana hot sauce. Follow that up with a barbecue trio—smoked pork loin, sliced brisket, and shredded chicken—served with corn on the cob and fries. Dinner options include grilled citrus-soaked chicken served with New Orleans dirty rice and steamed Dungeness crab served with drawn butter, corn on the cob, and a baked potato. In addition to "dynamite" cocktails (try a 21 Rum Salute) and wines, the Fireworks Factory offers more than 45 varieties of domestic and imported beer, ale, and stout, including several microbrewery selections.

MEALS WITH DISNEY CHARACTERS

CAPE MAY CAFE, at Disney's Beach Club Resort, 1800 EPCOT Resorts Blvd. Tel. 934-8000.

The Cape May Café, a delightful New England–themed dining room, serves lavish buffet character breakfasts daily. Food tables are laden with quiches, waffles, hot and cold cereals, egg dishes, roast beef hash, bread pudding, fruit fritters, cheese blintzes, bacon and cheese crêpes, fresh-baked pastries and muffins, and many other goodies. Admiral Goofy and his crew—Chip 'n' Dale and Pluto (exact characters may vary)—are hosts. Adults pay $12.95 and children 3 to 11 are charged $7.95; kids under 3 eat free. Reservations are not accepted; arrive early to avoid a wait.

CHEF MICKEY'S, at Walt Disney World Village. Tel. 828-3830.

At Chef Mickey's, Mickey is on hand to greet dinner patrons each night from 5 to 10pm. Reservations are suggested, although only 20% of the tables are allotted via reservations, with the rest reserved for walk-ins. On the other hand, you can reserve up to 30 days in advance. Walk-ins should arrive early to avoid a wait. This is an especially appealing choice, since there's first-rate food for adults, and the menu also offers burgers, chicken bits, and other kid pleasers in the $3.25 to $3.75 range.

THE CONTEMPORARY CAFE, at Disney's Contemporary Resort, 4600 N. World Dr. Tel. 824-1000.

The Contemporary Cafe—an indoor formal garden with faux topiary, trelliswork, planter dividers, and tables under bright-yellow canvas umbrellas—is the setting for buffet character breakfasts from 8 to 11am daily. On hand to meet, greet, and mingle with guests are Goofy, Pluto, Chip 'n' Dale, Tigger, and Prince John (from *Robin Hood*). The prix-fixe buffet ($12.95 for adults, $7.95 for children 3 to 11, free for kids under 3) features a wide array of breakfast foods: eggs, potatoes, French toast, pancakes, bacon and sausage, apple cobbler, bread pudding, and much more. Reservations are not accepted; arrive early to avoid a wait.

EMPRESS LILLY, at Walt Disney World Village. Tel. 828-3900.

Five opulently Victorian dining rooms aboard the *Empress Lilly*, a plushly furnished triple-decker paddlewheeler docked on Lake Buena Vista, are used for morning character breakfasts. There are two seatings daily, at 8:30 and 10am (arrive at least 20 minutes ahead of time). A prix-fixe menu ($10.95 for adults, $7.95 for children 3 to 9, free for kids under 3) features sausage and eggs and a Mickey-shaped waffle. If you want a lighter meal, ask for a fruit and yogurt plate. Donald, Mickey, Minnie, and Pluto are on hand to greet the guests. Reservations are essential, and can be made any time in advance; do so as soon as you decide the dates of your trip.

LUAU COVE, at Disney's Polynesian Resort, 1600 Seven Seas Dr. Tel. W-DISNEY.

Luau Cove, an exotic open-air facility, is the setting for an island-themed character show called *Mickey's Tropical Luau* daily at 4:30pm. It's an abbreviated version of the Polynesian Luau Dinner Show described below in "Evening Entertainment," featuring Polynesian dancers along with Mickey, Minnie, Pluto, and Goofy. Your prix-fixe meal ($28 for adults, $21.50 for ages 12 to 20, $12.50 for ages 3 to 11, free for kids under 3) includes tropical fruit salad, a trio of main courses (seafood stir-fry,

FROMMER'S COOL FOR KIDS: RESTAURANTS

In a town where the major attractions are amusement parks, just about every restaurant is child-oriented. Some notables:

The Sci-Fi Dine-In Theater Restaurant (see p. 259) A drive-in movie theater where you sit in actual convertible cars. At Disney–MGM Studios.

Chef Mickey's (see pp. 261 and 262) Great food pleases mom and dad, and kids love the nightly appearances by Mickey Mouse. If you want to linger over dinner, the kids can retreat to a lounge where cartoons are shown.

Mickey's Tropical Luau (see p. 262) Not just a meal but a Polynesian floor show featuring Minnie, Mickey, Pluto, and Goofy along with a cast of South Sea Islanders. At Disney's Polynesian Resort in Luau Cove. Character breakfasts here, too.

Cape May Café Clambake Buffet (see p. 260) This old-fashioned nightly clambake at Disney's Beach Club Resort is fun for the whole family.

Hoop-Dee-Doo Musical Revue (see p. 297) I've never met anyone who didn't have a great time at this whoopin' and hollerin' country-music dinner show in Fort Wilderness's Pioneer Hall.

---

barbecued ribs, and teriyaki chicken), rice, coconut-almond bread with orange butter, and a Disney character ice-cream bar. Guests are presented with shell leis on entering. Reserve far in advance.

1900 PARK FARE, at Disney's Grand Floridian Beach Resort, 4001 Grand Floridian Way. Tel. 824-2383.

This exquisitely elegant Disney resort hosts character meals in the festive exposition-themed 1900 Park Fare. Big Bertha—a French band organ that plays pipes, drums, bells, cymbals, castanets, and xylophone—provides music. Mary Poppins, Winnie the Pooh, Goofy, Pluto, Chip 'n' Dale, and Minnie Mouse appear at elaborate buffet breakfasts served daily between 7:30am and noon. An assortment of fresh fruits, breakfast meats, egg dishes, home-fries, pancakes, French toast, waffles, fresh-baked pastries and muffins, bagels and cream cheese, hot and cold cereals, cheese blintzes, and fruit cobblers are featured. Adults pay $14.95, children 3 to 11 are charged $9.75, and kids under 3 eat free.

Mickey and Minnie appear at nightly buffets (featuring prime rib, stuffed pork loin, fresh fish, and more) from 5 to 9pm. Adults pay $17.95, children 3 to 11 are charged $9.75, and kids under 3 eat free. Reservations are essential for both meals.

PAPEETE BAY VERANDAH, at Disney's Polynesian Resort, 1600 Seven Seas Dr. Tel. 824-1391.

The Polynesian Resort hosts Minnie's Menehune Character Breakfast buffets daily from 7:30 to 10:30am in the French Polynesian-themed Papeete Bay Verandah. A wide selection of hot and cold breakfast foods is featured: omelets, French toast, biscuits, cereals, fresh-baked pastries, fresh fruits, and more. Adults pay $12.95, children 3 to 11 are charged $7.95, and kids under 3 eat free. Minnie, Goofy, and Chip 'n' Dale appear. Reservations are essential.

SOUNDSTAGE RESTAURANT, at Disney–MGM Studios, adjacent to the Magic of Disney Animation. Tel. 824-4321.

The characters from the movie *Aladdin*—the genie, Jafar, and Aladdin or Jasmin—plus Mickey in Moroccan garb, visit tables and sign autographs daily from

8:30 to 10:30am in this Middle Eastern–motif restaurant. A vast buffet—fresh and dried fruits, breakfast meats, eggs, pastries, muffins and bagels, cereals, waffles, and blintzes—evokes an Arab marketplace, and there's a magic lamp on every table. The cost is $12.95 for adults, $7.95 for kids 3 to 11, and free for kids under 3. Reservations are essential.

WATERCRESS CAFE, at the Buena Vista Palace, 1900 Buena Vista Dr. Tel. 827-2727.

The plant-filled Watercress Café—with large windows overlooking Lake Buena Vista—is the setting for Sunday-morning character breakfasts (8 to 10:30am) featuring Minnie, Goofy, and Pluto. You can order à la carte or buffet meals. The buffet costs $9.75 for adults, $4.95 for kids 4 to 12, and free for kids under 4. Reservations are not accepted; arrive early to avoid a wait.

INTERNATIONAL DRIVE: OUTSIDE WALT DISNEY WORLD

DUX, in the Peabody Orlando Hotel, 9801 International Dr. Tel. 345-4550.
   Cuisine: AMERICAN REGIONAL. **Reservations:** Recommended.
$ **Prices:** Appetizers $7.50–$13.25; main courses $22–$28.50. AE, CB, DC, DISC, ER, JCB, MC, OPT, V.
   Open: Dinner only, Mon–Sat 6–11pm.

Named for the hotel's signature ducks that parade ceremoniously into the lobby each morning to Sousa's *King Cotton* march, this is one of Central Florida's most highly acclaimed restaurants. Decorated in shimmery earth tones, its textured gold walls are hung with watercolors representing 72 ducks! Diners are comfortably ensconced in upholstered bamboo chairs and cushioned banquettes at candlelit, white-linened tables set with flowers. There's free self-parking and validated valet parking.

Chef Mike Mc Sweeney's menu changes seasonally. At a recent dinner, I started off with an appetizer of sautéed leeks, wild mushrooms, and sherried lobster meat wrapped in a phyllo-dough pocket. A main course of mesquite-grilled Gulf Coast snapper was served with applewood-roasted corn salsa, slices of grilled balsamic-marinated Chinese eggplant, and puréed Washington cherries in a red Zinfandel sauce. Another of baked Atlantic salmon came wrapped in a crispy grated-potato crust on a platter arrayed with haricots verts, ragoût of pearl onions, roasted garlic, wild mushrooms, and an edible flower garnish. Dessert was a sublime trilogy of crème brûlées: one topped with fresh raspberries and sprigs of mint, a second flavored with coffee beans, and a third with candied ginger. An extensive, award-winning wine list is available.

EXPENSIVE

MING COURT, 9188 International Dr., between Sand Lake Rd. and the Beeline Expy., just across from the Peabody Orlando Hotel. Tel. 351-9988.
   Cuisine: CHINESE REGIONAL. **Reservations:** Recommended.
$ **Prices:** Appetizers $1.95–$3.95 at lunch, $4.50–$7.95 at dinner; dim sum items $1.95–$3.50; main courses $4.50–$7.50 at lunch, $11.95–$18.95 at dinner. AE, CB, DC, DISC, JCB, MC, V.
   Open: Lunch daily 11am–2:30pm; dinner daily 4:30pm–midnight.

I was thrilled to find an Orlando restaurant whose culinary offerings are on a par with the finest Chinese haute cuisine of New York and California. The Ming Court is fronted by a serpentine "cloud wall" crowned by engraved sea-green Chinese tiles (it's a celestial symbol; you dine above the clouds here, like the gods). Its candlelit interior is stunningly decorated in soft earth tones. Glass-walled terrace rooms overlook lotus ponds filled with colorful koi, and a plant-filled area under a lofty skylight ceiling evokes a starlit Ming Dynasty courtyard. A musician plays classical Chinese music on a *zheng* (a long zither) at dinner.

The menu offers specialties from diverse regions of China. Begin by ordering a variety of appetizers such as wok-charred Mandarin pot stickers, crispy spring rolls stuffed with wood ear cabbage, and wok-smoked shiitake mushrooms topped with sautéed scallions. The main courses will open up new culinary vistas to even the most sophisticated diners. Lightly battered deep-fried chicken breast is served with a delicate lemon-tangerine sauce. Szechuan charcoal-grilled filet mignon is topped with a toasted onion/garlic/chili sauce and served with stir-fried julienne vegetables. And crispy stir-fried jumbo Szechuan shrimp is enhanced by a light fresh tomato sauce nuanced with saké, ginger, chili oil, scallion, garlic, and cilantro. At lunch, you can order dim sum items in addition to menu offerings. An extensive wine list includes everything from Pouilly-Fuissé to Chinese rice wines, plum wines, and saké. And as a concession to Western palates, the Ming Court features sumptuous desserts such as a moist cake layered with Mandarin oranges, key lime, and fresh whipped cream in orange-vanilla sauce. There's free self-parking.

MODERATE

B-LINE DINER, at the Peabody Orlando Hotel, 9801 International Dr. Tel. 345-4460.
Cuisine: AMERICAN. **Reservations:** Not accepted.
$ **Prices:** Appetizers $5.50–$8.25; main courses $3.25–$8.25 at breakfast, $6.75–$9.50 at lunch, $7.25–$17.25 at dinner. AE, CB, DC, DISC, ER, JCB, MC, OPT, V.
Open: Daily 24 hours.

This popular local eatery is of the nouvelle art deco diner genre, which is to say that it's an idealized version of America's ubiquitous roadside establishments. A high-gloss peach-and-gray interior gleams with chrome edging that adorns everything from a cove ceiling to peach Formica tables. A jukebox plays oldies tunes.

The menu, in the shape of a Wurlitzer jukebox, offers sophisticated versions of diner food such as turkey meatloaf served with mashed potatoes, fresh vegetables, and cranberry relish; spicy Jamaican jerk chicken wings; and sautéed pork medallions with Thai sauce and papaya salsa. Other items—such as grilled tuna with vegetable couscous and red pepper coulis, classic French onion soup, and a falafel sandwich—bear no relation to traditional diner fare. You may have noticed a glass display case of scrumptious fresh-baked desserts when you came in, everything from banana cream pie to white-chocolate/Grand Marnier mousse cake. There's a full bar. And kids get their own low-priced menu, a coloring/activities book, and crayons. There's free self-parking and validated valet parking.

5. WALT DISNEY WORLD ATTRACTIONS

Walt Disney World, attracting more than 13 million visitors annually, is one of the world's most popular travel destinations. And why not? It provides a welcome retreat into a star-spangled all-American fantasyland where wonderment, human progress, and old-fashioned family fun are the major themes. And these themes are presented in spectacular parades, dazzling fireworks displays, 3-D and 360° movies, and adventure-filled journeys through time and space. Though it's not inexpensive, you'll seldom hear people complain about not getting their money's worth at WDW. Disney delivers!

The Magic Kingdom opened in 1971. Later additions include Epcot, where guests take exhilarating voyages around the world and into the future; Disney–MGM Studios, centered on "Hollywood Boulevard" and providing a thrilling behind-the-scenes look at motion-picture and TV studios; Pleasure Island, an ongoing street festival in a six-acre complex of nightclubs and shops; the Walt Disney Village Marketplace, a charming lakeside enclave of shops and restaurants; Typhoon Lagoon, a 56-acre water park where you can catch the world's largest man-made waves or plummet down steep water flumes; River Country, a smaller water park; and Discovery Island, an utterly delightful nature preserve and aviary.

WDW ORIENTATION

TIPS FOR PLANNING YOUR TRIP   How you plan your time at Walt Disney World will depend on such factors as the ages of the children in your party, what you've seen on previous visits, your specific interests, and whether you're traveling at a peak time or off-season (when lines are shorter and you can cram more in). Planning, however, is essential. Unless you're staying for considerably more than a week, you can't possibly experience all the rides, shows, and attractions here, not to mention the vast array of recreational facilities. You'll only wear yourself to a frazzle trying—it's better to follow a relaxed itinerary, including leisurely meals and recreational activities, than to make a demanding job out of trying to see everything.

Information   Call or write the **Walt Disney World Co.,** P.O. Box 10000, Lake Buena Vista, FL 32830-1000 (tel. 407/824-4321), for a copy of the very informative *Walt Disney World Vacation Guide,* an invaluable planning aid. Inquire about any special events that will be on during your stay. Once you've arrived in town, guest services and concierge desks in all area hotels—especially Disney properties and official hotels—have up-to-the-minute information about what's going on in the parks. Stop by to ask questions and pick up literature. If your hotel doesn't have this information, call 824-4321. There are also **information locations** in each park—at City Hall in the Magic Kingdom, Earth Station in Epcot, and the Guest Services Building in Disney–MGM Studios.

Create an itinerary for each day   Read the *Vacation Guide* and the detailed descriptions in this book of every nook and cranny of Walt Disney World, and plan your visit to include all shows and attractions that interest you. It's a good idea to make a daily itinerary, putting these in some kind of sensible geographical sequence so you're not zigzagging all over the place. Familiarize yourself in advance with the layout of each park. Schedule in sit-down shows, recreational activities (a boat ride or swim late in the afternoon can be wonderfully refreshing), and at least some unhurried meals. (My suggested itineraries are given below.)

Buy tickets in advance   You can purchase four- or five-day passes (see details below) at the Orlando airport, at your hotel, or by contacting the Central Reservations Office (tel. 407/824-8000) prior to your trip (allow 21 days for processing your request). In the latter case there's a $2 postage-and-handling charge. Of course, you can always purchase tickets at any of the parks, but why stand on an avoidable line? Note: One-day tickets can be purchased only at park entrances.

In the Parks   Upon entering any of the three major Disney parks, you'll be given an **entertainment schedule** and a comprehensive **park guidebook,** which contains a map of the park and lists all attractions, shops, shows, and restaurants. If by some fluke you haven't obtained these, they're available at the information locations mentioned above. If you've formulated an itinerary prior to arrival, you already know the major shows (check show schedules for additional ideas) you want to see during the day and what arrangements you need to make. If you haven't done this, use your early arrival time, while waiting for the park to open, to figure out which shows to attend, and, where necessary, make reservations for them as soon as the gates swing open. Some restaurant reservations also need to be made first thing in the morning (see "Dining" and "Evening Entertainment," in this chapter, for details).

Leaving the Parks   If you leave any of the parks and plan to return later in the day, be sure to get your hand stamped on exiting.

Best Days to Visit   The busiest days at the Magic Kingdom and Epcot are Monday through Wednesday; at Disney–MGM Studios, Thursday and Friday. Surprisingly, weekends are the least busy at all parks. In peak seasons, especially, arrange your visits accordingly.

Arrive Early   Always arrive at the parks a good 30 to 45 minutes before opening time, thus avoiding a traffic jam entering the park and a long line at the gate. Early arrival also lets you experience one or two major attractions before big lines form. In high season parking lots sometimes fill up and you may even have to wait to get in. The longest lines in all parks are between 11am and 4pm.

Parking   Parking (free to guests at WDW resorts) otherwise costs $5 per day no matter how many parks you visit. Be sure to note your parking location before leaving your car. There are special lots for the handicapped at each park (call

824-4321 for details). Don't worry about parking far from the entrance gates; trams constantly ply the route.

The Easy Way   Staying at Disney hostelries simplifies many of the above tasks and procedures. See the full list of perks for Disney and "official" hotel guests above under "Accommodations."

OPERATING HOURS   Hours of operation vary somewhat throughout the year. The **Magic Kingdom** and **Disney–MGM Studios** are generally open from 9am to 7pm, with extended hours (sometimes as late as midnight) during major holidays and the summer months. **Epcot** hours are generally 9am to 9pm, once again with extended holiday hours. **Typhoon Lagoon** is open from 10am to 5pm most of the year (with extended hours during some holidays), 9am to 8pm in summer. **River Country** and **Discovery Island** are open from 10am to 5pm most of the year (with extended hours during some holidays), 10am to 7pm in summer.

Note: Epcot and MGM sometimes open a half hour or more before posted time. Keep in mind, too, that Disney hotel guests enjoy early admission to the Magic Kingdom on designated days for a full lineless hour.

TICKETS   There are several ticket options. Most people get the best value from four- and five-day passes. All passes offer unlimited use of the WDW transportation system. Prices quoted below include sales tax.

The **Four-Day Value Pass** provides admission for: one day at the Magic Kingdom, one day at Epcot, one day at Disney–MGM Studios, and one day at your choice of any of those three parks; you can use it on any four days following purchase. The cost is $132 for ages 10 and over, and $103.50 for children 3 to 9; free for kids under 3. (Note: Guests at Disney resorts can purchase a **Four-Day Super Pass** that allows them any combination of visits to the three major parks for the same price.)

The **Five-Day Around the World Pass** provides admission for: one day at the Magic Kingdom, one day at Epcot, one day at Disney–MGM Studios, and two days at your choice of one park each of the two additional days, including Typhoon Lagoon, River Country, Discovery Island, and Pleasure Island for a period of seven days beginning the first date stamped. It costs $179.60 for ages 10 and over, and $142.60 for children 3 to 9; free for kids under 3. (Note: Guests at Disney resorts can purchase a **Five-Day Super Duper Pass** that allows them any combination of visits to all Disney parks for the same price.)

A **one-day, one-park ticket for the Magic Kingdom, Epcot, or Disney–MGM Studios** is $36.95 for ages 10 and over, and $29.55 for children 3 to 9; free for kids under 3.

A **one-day ticket to Typhoon Lagoon** is $22.80 for ages 10 and over, and $17.50 for children ages 3 to 9; free for kids under 3.

A **one-day ticket to River Country** is $14.85 for ages 10 and over, and $11.65 for children ages 3 to 9; free for kids under 3.

A **one-day ticket to Discovery Island** is $10.05 for ages 10 and over, and $5.55 for children ages 3 to 9; free for kids under 3.

A **combined one-day ticket for River Country and Discovery Island** is $17.75 for ages 10 and over, and $13 for children ages 3 to 9; free for kids under 3.

If you're staying at any Walt Disney World Resort or hotel you are also eligible for a money-saving **Be Our Guest Pass** priced according to length of stay. It also offers special perks.

If you plan on visiting Walt Disney World more than one time during the year, inquire about a money-saving **annual pass.**

SUGGESTED ITINERARIES

You won't see all the attractions at any of the parks in a single day. Read through the descriptions, decide which are musts for you, and try to get to them. My favorite rides and attractions are starred. I stress once more—it's more enjoyable to keep a relaxed pace than to race around like a maniac trying to do it all.

A DAY IN THE MAGIC KINGDOM   Get to the park well before opening time, tickets in hand. When the gates open, head for the kiosk just outside Disneyana

Collectibles and make a reservation for a lunchtime show at the Diamond Horseshoe Jamboree. Then hightail it to Frontierland and ride Splash Mountain before long lines form. When you come off, it will still be early enough to beat the lines at another major attraction. Double back to Adventureland and do Pirates of the Caribbean. Then relax and take it slow. Complete whatever else interests you in Adventureland, and enjoy Frontierland attractions until it's time for your lunch show. After lunch, continue visiting Frontierland attractions as desired, or proceed to the Hall of Presidents and the Haunted Mansion in Liberty Square. By 2:30pm (earlier in peak seasons), you should snag a seat on the curb in Liberty Square along the parade route. After the parade, continue around the park taking in Fantasyland and Tomorrowland attractions. If Spectro Magic is on during your stay, don't miss it.

If you have little kids (age 8 and under) in your party, after making your lunch reservations for Diamond Horseshoe Jamboree, take the WDW Railroad from Main Street to Mickey's Starland to see the show. Work your way through Fantasyland until lunch. After lunch, visit the Country Bear Jamboree in Frontierland and proceed to Adventureland for the Jungle Cruise, Swiss Family Treehouse, and Tropical Serenade. Once again, stop in good time to get parade seats (in Frontierland). Little kids need to sit right up front to see everything. That's a long enough day for most little kids, and your best plan is to go back to your hotel for a nap or swim. If, however, you wish to continue, return to Frontierland and/or Fantasyland for the rides you didn't complete earlier.

A DAY AT EPCOT   As above, arrive early, tickets in hand. Make your first stop at Earth Station to make lunch reservations at the San Angel Inn Restaurant in Mexico for about 1pm. If you like, also make dinner reservations at the World Showcase restaurant of your choice. (Note: Disney hotel guests can make these in advance.) Then head for the lagoon and take the launch to Germany. While cruising the lagoon, check your show schedule and decide which shows to incorporate into your day. Don't stop in Germany. First take in Italy and the American Adventure (check show times for the latter) before working your way back counterclockwise through the Germany, China, and Norway pavilions. You should arrive in Mexico just about in time for a leisurely lunch, after which you can visit its attractions. After lunch, continue on the same side of the park, visiting the World of Motion, Horizons, Wonders of Life, the Universe of Energy, and CommuniCore East in Future World. Frankly, unless crowds are very light, you can't see everything in all these showcase pavilions and themed areas in one day. So rather than do it all, hit the highlights you don't want to miss. If you have only one day at Epcot, plan dinner in the park and stay for IllumiNations (usually at 9pm, but check your schedule). Otherwise, leave the park, have dinner elsewhere (see "Dining" and "Evening Entertainment" for suggestions), and see IllumiNations your second night.

If You Have Two Days   On your second day, make your first stop at Earth Station to make dinner reservations for the World Showcase restaurant of your choice. Check your show schedule and make your reservations early enough to allow time to find a seat on the lagoon at least a half hour before IllumiNations begins. Then take the launch across the lagoon to Morocco, walk to Japan, and after seeing its attractions (don't miss the show here), continue clockwise to Morocco, France, the United Kingdom, and Canada. Stop for a light early lunch at a casual restaurant, perhaps Au Petit Café in France or the Buffeteria in Canada (no reservations required at either). After lunch, visit Journey into Imagination, The Land, the Living Seas, Spaceship Earth, and CommuniCore West. Have an early dinner and watch IllumiNations.

A DAY AT DISNEY—MGM STUDIOS THEME PARK   Since showtimes change seasonally, you may have to revise this itinerary a bit when you visit. Upon entering the park, stop at the Hollywood Brown Derby (details in "Dining") and make reservations for a 1pm lunch. Then make a beeline for the new Twilight Zone Tower of Terror, as it will no doubt have the longest lines as the day progresses. Afterward, head over to the Magic of Disney Animation, followed by the Voyage of the Little Mermaid, the Backstage Studio Tour, and, if time allows, Inside the Magic, prior to lunch. After lunch, do the Great Movie Ride, Superstar Television, the Monster Sound Show, Indiana Jones Epic Stunt Spectacular, Jim Henson's Muppet Vision 3-D movie (not to be missed), and Star Tours, ending up at Beauty and the Beast in the Backlot Theater. You may have to make some adjustments to include the Aladdin's Royal Caravan parade (preferably in the afternoon); check your show schedule for times. In peak seasons, stay on for fireworks.

THE MAGIC KINGDOM

Centered around Cinderella Castle, the Magic Kingdom occupies about 100 acres, with 45 major attractions and numerous restaurants and shops in seven themed sections or "lands." From the parking lot, you have to take a short monorail or ferry ride to the Magic Kingdom entrance. During peak attendance times, arrive at the Magic Kingdom an hour prior to opening time to avoid long lines at these conveyances.

Upon entering the park, consult your *Magic Kingdom Guidebook* map to get your bearings. It details every shop, restaurant, and attraction in every land. Also consult your **entertainment schedule** to see what's on for the day.

If you have questions, all park employees are very knowledgeable, and **City Hall,** on your left as you enter, is both an information center, and, along with Mickey's Starland, a likely place to meet up with costumed characters. There's a stroller-rental shop just after the turnstiles to your right, and the Kodak Camera Center, near Town Square, supplies all conceivable photographic needs, including camera and Camcorder rentals and two-hour film developing.

MAIN STREET U.S.A.

Designed to replicate a typical turn-of-the-century American street, albeit one that culminates in a 13th-century castle, this is the gateway to the Kingdom. Don't dawdle on Main Street when you enter the park; leave it for the end of the day when you're heading back to your hotel.

WALT DISNEY WORLD RAILROAD & OTHER MAIN STREET VEHICLES   You can board an authentic 1928 steam-powered railroad here for a 15-minute journey clockwise around the perimeter of the park. There are stations in Frontierland and Mickey's Starland. There are also horse-drawn trolleys, horseless carriages, jitneys, omnibuses, and fire engines plying the short route along Main Street from Town Square to Cinderella Castle.

MAIN STREET CINEMA   Main Street Cinema is an air-conditioned hexagonal theater where vintage black-and-white Disney cartoons (including *Steamboat Willie* from 1928, in which Mickey and Minnie debuted) are aired continually on six screens. Viewers have to watch these standing—there are no seats.

PENNY ARCADE   At this old-fashioned penny arcade, hand-cranked Cail-o-scopes, old pinball games, Kiss-o-Meter, Gypsy fortune teller, and shooting gallery evoke pleasant childhood memories to those of a certain age and are a novelty to the Nintendo generation.

CINDERELLA CASTLE   At the end of Main Street, in the center of the park, you'll come to a fairyland castle, 180 feet high and housing a restaurant (King Stefan's Banquet Hall) and shops. Mosaic murals inside depict the Cinderella story, and Disney family coats of arms are displayed. Cinderella herself, dressed for the ball, often makes appearances in the lobby area.

ADVENTURELAND

Cross a bridge to your left and stroll into an exotic jungle of lush tropical foliage, thatch-roofed huts, and carved totems. Amid dense vines and stands of palm and bamboo, drums are beating and swashbuckling adventures are taking place.

SWISS FAMILY TREEHOUSE   This attraction is based on the 1960 Disney movie version of Johann Wyss's *Swiss Family Robinson,* about a shipwrecked family who created an ingenious dwelling in the branches of a sprawling banyan tree. Using materials and furnishings salvaged from their downed ship, the Robinsons created bedrooms, a kitchen, a library, and a living room. Visitors ascend the 50-foot tree for a close-up look into these rooms. Note the Rube Goldberg rope-and-bucket device with bamboo chutes that dips water from a stream and carries it to treetop chambers.

JUNGLE CRUISE   What a cruise! In the course of about 10 minutes, your boat sails through an African veldt in the Congo, an Amazon rain forest, the Mekong River in Southeast Asia, and along the Nile. Lavish scenery, with ropes of hanging vines, cascading waterfalls, and lush foliage (most of it real), includes dozens of Audio-Animatronic™ birds and animals—elephants, zebras, lions, giraffes, crocodiles, tigers, even fluttering butterflies. On the shore you'll pass an Asian temple cave guarded by snakes and a jungle camp taken over by apes. But the adventures aren't all on shore. Passengers are menaced by everything from water-spouting elephants to fierce warriors who attack with spears.

PIRATES OF THE CARIBBEAN   This is Disney magic at its best. You'll proceed through a long grottolike passageway to board a boat into a pitch-black cave where elaborate scenery and hundreds of Audio-Animatronic™ figures (including lifelike dogs, cats, chickens, and donkeys) depict a rambunctious pirate raid on a Caribbean town. To a background of cheerful "yo-ho-yo-ho" music, the sound of rushing waterfalls, squawking seagulls, and screams of terror, passengers view tableaux of fierce-looking pirates chasing maidens, swigging rum, looting, and plundering. This might be scary for kids under 5.

TROPICAL SERENADE   In a large hexagonal Polynesian-style dwelling, 250 tropical birds, chanting totem poles, and singing flowers whistle, tweet, and warble songs such as "Let's All Sing Like the Birdies Sing." Highlights include a thunderstorm in the dark (the gods are angry!), a light show over the fountain, and, of course, the famous "in the tiki, tiki, tiki, tiki, tiki room" song. You'll find yourself singing it all day. This is a must for young children.

FRONTIERLAND

From Adventureland, step into the wild and woolly past of the American frontier, where rough-and-tumble architecture runs to log cabins and rustic saloons, and the landscape is southwestern scrubby with mesquite, saguaro cactus, yucca, and prickly pear. Across the river is Tom Sawyer Island, reachable via log rafts.

SPLASH MOUNTAIN   Themed after Walt Disney's 1946 film *Song of the South*, Splash Mountain is an enchanting journey in a hollowed-out log craft along the canals of a flooded mountain, past 26 brilliantly colored tableaux of backwoods swamps, bayous, spooky caves, and waterfalls. Riders are caught up in the bumbling schemes of Brer Fox and Brer Bear as they pursue the ever-wily Brer Rabbit. The music from the film forms a delightful audio backdrop. Your log craft twists, turns, and splashes—sometimes plummeting in total darkness—culminating in a thrilling five-story splashdown from mountaintop to briar-filled pond at 40 miles per hour!

BIG THUNDER MOUNTAIN RAILROAD   This mining-disaster-themed roller coaster—its thrills deriving from hairpin turns and descents in the dark—is situated in a 200-foot-high redstone mountain with 2,780 feet of track winding through windswept canyons and bat-filled caves. You'll board a runaway train that careens through the ribs of a dinosaur, under a thundering waterfall, past spewing geysers and bubbling mudpots, and over a bottomless volcanic pool. Riders are threatened by flash floods, earthquakes, rickety bridges, and avalanches. Audio-Animatronic™ characters (such as the longjohn-clad fellow navigating the floodwaters in a bathtub) enhance the scenic backdrop, as does a wealth of authentic antique mining equipment.

DIAMOND HORSESHOE JAMBOREE   This 40-minute show provides an opportunity to sit down in air-conditioned comfort and enjoy a rousing western revue. The "theater" is a re-creation of a turn-of-the-century saloon. Owner/bartender Sam plays the washboard, tells silly jokes, and shoots at the audience (with a water gun). Lily (a Mae West type) and her troupe of dancehall girls do a can-can (which Sam, in drag, joins in). And the cowboys perform feats of fast fiddling and foot-stomping acrobatic dances. There are five shows daily; plan on going around lunchtime so you can eat during the show. The menu features deli or peanut butter and jelly sandwiches served with chips. (Make reservations when you enter the park just outside Disneyana Collectibles on the east side of Main Street in Town Square.) Seating is reserved, so you can arrive shortly before showtime.

COUNTRY BEAR JAMBOREE I've always loved the Country Bear Jamb-
oree, a 15-minute show featuring a troupe of fiddlin', banjo strummin', harmonica playin' Audio-Animatronic™ bears belting out rollicking country tunes and crooning plaintive love songs. A special holiday show plays throughout the Christmas season each year.

TOM SAWYER ISLAND Board Huck Finn's raft for a one-minute float across the river to the densely forested Tom Sawyer Island, where kids can explore the narrow passages of Injun Joe's Cave (complete with scary sound effects like whistling wind), a walk-through windmill, a serpentine abandoned mine, or Fort Sam Clemens. Narrow winding tree-lined paths create an authentic backwoods island feel. You might combine this attraction with a fried-chicken lunch at Aunt Polly's restaurant, which has outdoor tables on a porch overlooking the river.

FRONTIERLAND SHOOTIN' ARCADE Combining state-of-the-art electronics with a traditional shooting-gallery format, this vast arcade presents an array of 97 targets (slow-moving ore cars, buzzards, gravediggers) in a three-dimensional 1850s gold-mining town scenario. To keep the western ambience authentic, new-fangled electronic firing mechanisms loaded with infrared bullets are concealed in genuine Hawkins 54-caliber buffalo rifles. When you hit a target, elaborate sound and motion gags are set off. You get 25 shots for 50¢.

LIBERTY SQUARE

Serving as a transitional area between Frontierland and Fantasyland, Liberty Square evokes 18th-century America with Georgian architecture, Colonial Williamsburg–type shops, and neat flower beds bordering manicured lawns. You might encounter a fife-and-drum corps marching along Liberty Square's cobblestone streets.

THE HALL OF PRESIDENTS In this red-brick colonial hall, all American presidents—from George Washington to Bill Clinton (who recorded the voice for his character)—are represented by Audio-Animatronic™ figures. They dramatize important events in the nation's history, from the signing of the Constitution through the space age. The show begins with a film, projected on a 180° screen, about the importance of the Constitution. Maya Angelou narrates.

THE HAUNTED MANSION Its eerie ambience enhanced by inky dark-
ness, spooky music, and mysterious screams and rappings, this mansion is replete with bizarre scenes and objects: a ghostly banquet and ball, a graveyard band, a suit of armor that comes alive, luminous spiders, a talking head in a crystal ball, weird flying objects, and much more. At the end of the ride, a ghost joins you in your car. The experience is more amusing than terrifying, so you can take small children inside.

BOAT RIDES A steam-powered sternwheeler called the *Richard F. Irvine* and two Mike Fink Keel Boats (the *Bertha Mae* and the *Gullywhumper*) depart from Liberty Square for scenic cruises along the Rivers of America. Both ply the identical route and make a restful interlude for foot-weary parkgoers.

FANTASYLAND

The attractions in this happy "land"—themed after such Disney film classics as *Snow White* and *Peter Pan*—are especially popular with young visitors. A new attraction based on the Disney movie *The Lion King* is in the works at this writing. If your kids are 8 or under, you might want to make it your first stop in the Magic Kingdom. Note: Two rides here—Snow White's Adventures and Mr. Toad's Wild Ride—are a bit scary. If your under-5s frighten easily, skip them.

MAD TEA PARTY   This is a traditional amusement park ride à la Disney with an *Alice in Wonderland* theme. Riders sit in oversize pink teacups on saucers that careen around a circular platform. Believe it or not, this can be a pretty wild ride or a tame one—it depends on how much you spin, a factor under your control via a wheel in the cup.

MR. TOAD'S WILD RIDE   This ride is based on the 1949 Disney film *The Adventures of Ichabod and Mr. Toad,* which was itself based on the classic children's story *Wind in the Willows.* Riders navigate a series of dark rooms, hurtling into solid objects (a fireplace, a bookcase, a haystack) and through barn doors into a coop of squawking chickens. They're menaced by falling suits of armor, snorting bulls, and an oncoming locomotive in a pitch-black tunnel, and are sent to jail (for car theft), to hell (complete with pitchfork-wielding demons), and through a fiery volcano.

20,000 LEAGUES UNDER THE SEA   Based on the Jules Verne classic, this submarine voyage travels beneath the waters of Fantasyland's lagoon. Via portholes, you'll observe undersea vegetation and creatures—talking fish, seahorses, mermaids, and sea serpents among them. You'll also experience an underwater volcano and a storm at sea.

SNOW WHITE'S ADVENTURES   You might not remember that *Snow White,* originally a Grimm's fairy tale, was a little scary, and this boat ride in the dark concentrates on some of its more sinister elements—the evil queen, the cackling witch offering a poisoned apple to Snow White, skeletons in cages, and a crocodile lurching at riders. Even the trees are menacing.

CINDERELLA'S GOLDEN CAROUSEL   It's a beauty, built by Italian wood carvers in the Victorian tradition in 1917 and refurbished by Disney artists who added scenes from the Cinderella story. The band organ plays such Disney classics as "When You Wish Upon a Star."

DUMBO, THE FLYING ELEPHANT   This is a very tame kiddie ride in which the cars—baby elephants (Dumbos)—go around and around in a circle gently rising and dipping. But it's very exciting for wee ones.

IT'S A SMALL WORLD   You know the song—and if you don't, you will. It plays continually as you sail "around the world" through vast rooms designed to represent different countries. They're inhabited by appropriately costumed Audio-Animatronic™ dolls and animals, all singing "It's a small world after all . . ." in tiny doll-like voices. This cast of thousands includes Chinese acrobats, Russian kazatski dancers, Indian snake charmers, Arabs on magic carpets, African drummers, a Venetian gondolier, and Australian koalas. Cute. Very cute.

PETER PAN'S FLIGHT   Riding in Captain Hook's ship, passengers careen through dark passages while experiencing the story of *Peter Pan.* The adventure begins in the Darlings' nursery, and includes a flight over nighttime London to Nevernever Land, where riders encounter mermaids, Indians, a ticking crocodile, the lost boys, Tinkerbell, Hook, Smee, and the rest—all to the movie music "You Can Fly, You Can Fly, You Can Fly." It's fun.

SKYWAY   Its entrance close to Peter Pan's Flight, the Skyway is an aerial tramway to Tomorrowland, which makes continuous round-trips throughout the day.

MICKEY'S STARLAND

This small land, adjacent to Fantasyland, with a topiary maze of Disney characters and a block of Duckburg architecture, is accessible from Main Street via the Walt Disney World Railroad. It includes a Walk of Fame à la Hollywood, with Disney character "voiceprints" activated when you step on a star; a hands-on fire station; storefronts that come alive at the push of a button; Grandma Duck's Farm (a petting zoo); funhouse mirrors; a treehouse; and an interactive video area. And Mickey's house is here too, complete with living room TV tuned to the Disney Channel and his familiar outfits hanging on a clothesline in the yard.

The main attraction is **Mickey's Starland Show,** which is presented on a stage behind his house. The show, a lively musical, features the Goof Troop, Chip 'n' Dale, a perky hostess named CJ, and a vocal computer-control system called Dude. The story line: The show is about to start, but Mickey is missing! While CJ frantically searches for him, Goofy and his son, Max, accidentally get locked in the house. But it all works out in the end. The cheerful cartoon-inspired scenery, audience participation, and dramatic special effects are all designed to appeal to young viewers. After the show there's an opportunity to meet Mickey backstage.

TOMORROWLAND

This futuristic land focuses on space travel and exploration. But since Tomorrowland opened in the early 1970s, the Disney people recently decided that it was beginning to look like "Yesterdayland." So, at this writing, they're revamping the land to reflect the future as a galactic, science fiction–inspired community inhabited by humans, aliens, and robots.

Its major new attraction, **Extra"terror"estrial Alien Encounter,** scheduled to open in 1996, will feature an interplanetary "teletransporter" capable of beaming living beings between planets light years apart. But just as this revolutionary device is being marketed to earthlings by representatives from another planet, the demonstration goes awry, resulting in a shocking close encounter with a fearsome extraterrestial!

As we go to press, two other new attractions are in the works. In **Visionairium**—a fourth-dimension adventure that will combine Circle-Vision™, Audio-Animatronic™ figures, and high-tech special effects—guests will time-travel back to centuries past and forward to those yet to come. And **AstroOrbiter** will spin guests around in rockets amid whirling planets.

DELTA DREAMFLIGHT The history and wonder of aviation—from barnstorming to space shuttles—is captured in this whimsical fly-through adventure presented by the official airline of Walt Disney World. High-tech special effects and 70mm live-action film footage add dramatic 3-D–style verisimilitude. Guests travel from a futuristic airport up a hillside to witness a flying circus, parachutists, stunt flyers, wing walkers, crop dusters, and aerial acrobats. The action moves on to the ocean-hopping age of commercial flight, and finally your vehicle is pulled into a giant jet engine and sent into hypersonic flight through psychedelic tunnels of light for a journey to outer space at a simulated speed of 300 m.p.h.

WEDWAY PEOPLEMOVER A futuristic means of transportation, the PeopleMover has no engine. It works by electromagnets, emits no pollution, and uses little power. Narrated by a computer guide named Horack I, it offers an overhead look at Tomorrowland, including a pretty good preview of Space Mountain. If you're only in the Magic Kingdom for one day, this can be skipped.

WALT DISNEY'S CAROUSEL OF PROGRESS This recently revamped 22-minute show in a revolving theater features an Audio-Animatronic™ family in various tableaux demonstrating a century of development (beginning in 1900) in electric gadgetry and contraptions from Victrolas to virtual reality.

SKYWAY Its Tomorrowland entrance just west of Space Mountain, this aerial tramway to Fantasyland makes continuous round-trips throughout the day.

SPACE MOUNTAIN In a precursor to the concept of preshows, Space Mountain entertains visitors on its long lines with space age music, exhibits, and meteorites, shooting stars, and space debris whizzing about overhead. These "illusioneering" effects, enhanced by appropriate audio, continue during the ride itself, which is something like a cosmic roller coaster in the inky starlit blackness of outer space. The exit to Space Mountain is a moving sidewalk, past scenes of Audio-Animatronic™ figures that demonstrate the future uses of electronic media.

GRAND PRIX RACEWAY This is a great thrill for kids (including teens still waiting to get their driver's licenses) who get to put the pedal to the metal, steer, and *vroom* down a speedway in an actual gas-powered sports car. Maximum speed on the four-minute drive around the track is about 7 m.p.h., and kids have to be four feet four inches tall to drive alone.

PARADES, FIREWORKS & MORE

You'll get an *Entertainment Show Schedule* when you enter the park, which lists all kinds of special goings-on for the day. These include concerts (everything from steel drums to barbershop quartets), encounters with Disney characters, holiday events, and the three major happenings listed below.

THE 3 O'CLOCK PARADE You haven't really seen a parade until you've seen one at Walt Disney World. The spectacular daily parade kicks off at 3pm year-round on Main Street and meanders through Liberty Square and Frontierland. The route is outlined on your *Entertainment Show Schedule*. The only problem: Even in slow seasons you have to snag a seat along the curb a good half hour before it begins, and even earlier during peak travel times. (That's a long time to sit on a hard curb; consider packing inflatable pillows.) But the parade is worth a little discomfort. Disney characters from Mickey Mouse to Roger Rabbit are represented by 40-foot Macy's-style balloon figures, and there are elaborate floats, costumes, special effects, and a captivating cavalcade of acrobats, court jesters, stilt-walking harlequins, Mardi Gras and calypso bands, and storybook characters. Great music, too.

SPECTROMAGIC Along a darkened parade route (the same one as above), 72,000 watts of dazzling high-tech lighting effects (including holography) create a glowing array of pixies and peacocks, seahorses and winged horses, flower gardens and fountains. Roger Rabbit is the eccentric conductor of an orchestra producing a rainbow of musical notes that waft magically into the night air. There are dancing ostriches from *Fantasia,* whirling electric butterflies, flowers that evoke Tiffany glass, bejewelled coaches, luminescent ElectroMen atop spinning whirlyballs, and, of course, Mickey, surrounded by a sparkling confetti of light. And the music and choreography are on a par with the technology. Once again, very early arrival is essential to get a seat on the curb. SpectroMagic takes place nightly in summer, on selected nights during Christmas and Easter vacation times, and during other special celebrations. Consult your *Entertainment Show Schedule* for details.

FIREWORKS Like SpectroMagic, Fantasy in the Sky Fireworks, immediately preceded by Tinker Bell's magical flight from Cinderella's Castle, take place nightly in summer, on selected nights during Christmas and Easter vacation times, and during other special celebrations. Consult your *Entertainment Show Schedule* for details. Suggested viewing areas are Liberty Square, Frontierland, and Mickey's Starland.

EPCOT

In 1982, Walt Disney World opened its second major attractions park, the World's Fair–like Epcot (Experimental Prototype Community of Tomorrow). Its aims are described in a dedication plaque: "May Epcot entertain, inform and inspire. And, above all . . . instill a new sense of belief and pride in man's ability to shape a world that offers hope to people everywhere." Ever growing, Epcot today occupies 260 acres so stunningly landscaped as to be worth visiting for botanical beauty alone. There are two major sections, Future World and World Showcase.

Epcot is huge, and walking around it can be exhausting. Don't try to do it all in one day. Conserve energy by taking launches across the lagoon from the edge of Future World to Germany or Morocco. There are also double-decker buses circling the World Showcase Promenade and making stops at Norway, Italy, France, and Canada. Unlike the Magic Kingdom, Epcot's parking lot is right at the gate. Stop by **Earth Station** (Epcot's information center) when you come in to pick up an **Epcot Guidebook** and **entertainment schedule,** and, if you so desire, make reservations for lunch or dinner. Many Epcot restaurants are described in "Dining," earlier in this chapter. Strollers can be rented to your left at the Future World entrance plaza and in World Showcase at the International Gateway between the United Kingdom and France.

Since most people begin the day by touring Future World, the best way to beat the crowds is to head directly to World Showcase. As at the Magic Kingdom, arrive early, tickets in hand. Take a launch across to either side of the lagoon, and work your way down to the right or left, taking in World Showcase and Future World attractions on one side of the park. By the time you reach Future World in the afternoon, traffic there will be lighter. The second day, follow the same method and cover the other side of the park.

FUTURE WORLD

The northern section of Epcot (where you enter the park) comprises Future World, centered on a giant geosphere known as Spaceship Earth. Future World's 10 themed areas, sponsored by major American corporations, focus on discovery, scientific achievements, and tomorrow's technologies in areas running the gamut from energy to underseas exploration.

SPACESHIP EARTH Spaceship Earth, housed in a massive silvery "geosphere," is Epcot's most cogent symbol. Inside, a show narrated by Walter Cronkite takes visitors on a 15-minute journey through the history of communications. You board time-machine vehicles to the distant past, where an Audio-Animatronic™ Cro-Magnon shaman recounts the story of a hunt while others record it on cave walls. You advance thousands of years to ancient Egypt, where hieroglyphics adorn temple walls and writing is recorded on papyrus scrolls. By the 9th century B.C., the Phoenicians have developed a 22-letter alphabet, simplifying communications. The Greeks add vowels to the alphabet and refine its use as a tool to express new inner needs for speculative thought, art, and philosophy; the theater is born. Roman roads and the vast Islamic empire expand the network of communications, furthering knowledge of science, astronomy, and art. With the development of the Gutenberg printing press in 1456, man's increasing ability to disseminate ideas becomes a catalyst for the Renaissance which, in turn, spawns the Age of Invention. Technologies develop at a rapid pace, enlarging our communications spectrum via steam power, electricity, the telegraph, telephone, radio, movies, and TV. It's but a short step to the age of electronic communications. You are catapulted into outer space to see "spaceship earth" from a new perspective, returning via a kaleidoscopic passageway for a dazzling finale that places the audience amid interactive global networks. High-tech special effects, animated sets, and laser beams create an exciting experience in this "global neighborhood," and new shows demonstrate emerging technologies.

As you leave Spaceship Earth, you'll enter **Earth Station,** an electronic information center with guest-relations booths and touch-sensitive video monitors (where you can make reservations for Epcot restaurants). Staff here can answer all questions.

THE LIVING SEAS This United Technologies–sponsored pavilion contains the world's sixth "ocean," a 5.6-million-gallon saltwater aquarium (including a complete coral reef) inhabited by more than 4,000 sea creatures—sharks, barracudas, parrot fish, rays, and dolphins among them. While waiting on line, visitors pass exhibits tracing the history of undersea exploration, including a glass diving barrel used by Alexander the Great in 332 B.C. A 2½-minute multimedia preshow about today's ocean technology is followed by a seven-minute film demonstrating the formation of the earth and seas as a means to support life.

After the film, visitors enter hydrolators for a rapid descent to the ocean floor. Upon arrival, they board Seacabs that wind around a 400-foot-long tunnel to enjoy stunning close-up views of ocean denizens in a natural coral-reef habitat. The ride concludes in the Seabase Concourse, which is the visitor center of Seabase Alpha, a prototype ocean-research facility of the future. Here, informational modules contain numerous exhibits focusing on ocean ecosystems, harvestable resources grown in controlled undersea environments, marine mammals, earth systems, the study of oceanography from space, undersea exploration, and life in a coral-reef community. You can step into a diver's JIM Suit and use controls to complete diving tasks, and expand your knowledge of oceanography via interactive computers.

THE LAND Sponsored by Nestlé, this largest of Future World's pavilions highlights man's relation to food and nature in a variety of intriguing attractions.

Circle of Life: Under construction as we go to press, this new attraction—a 15-minute, 70mm motion picture based on the Disney feature *The Lion King*—will utilize a combination of live and animated characters. It will star Simba, Timon, and Pumbaa in a cautionary environmental tale. Timon and Pumbaa are building a monument to the good life called Hakuna Matata Village, but their project, as Simba points out, is damaging the savannah for other animals. Simba relates a story about how other creatures (humans) once nearly destroyed their beautiful planet, and how they finally learned from their mistakes and cleaned up the land, air, and water.

Living with the Land: A 13-minute boatride takes you through three ecological environments—a rain forest, an African desert, and windswept American plains—each populated by appropriate Audio-Animatronic™ denizens. New farming methods are showcased in real gardens. If you'd like a more serious overview, take a 45-minute guided walking tour of the growing areas, offered every half hour between 9:30am and 4:30pm. Sign up at the Broccoli & Co. shop near the entrance to Food Rocks.

Food Rocks: Audio-Animatronic™ rock performers transformed into culinary favorites—Pita Gabriel, the Peach Boys, Chubby Cheddar, and others—deliver an entertaining nutritional message.

JOURNEY INTO IMAGINATION In this wondrous pavilion, presented by Kodak, even the fountains are magical, with arching streams of water that leap into the air like glass rods. Its major attraction is:

Honey I Shrunk the Audience, a 3-D thriller based on the Disney hit film, is opening shortly after this book goes to press. While waiting to get in, you'll enjoy a charmingly narrated slide montage of Kodak moments. It's a real tearjerker.

Journey into Imagination Ride: Visitors board moving cars for a 14-minute ride, hosted by a red-bearded adventurer named Dreamfinder and his sidekick, Figment, a mischievous baby dragon with a childlike ability to dream. After a simulated flight across the nighttime sky, you enter the "Imaginarium," where whimsical tableaux featuring Audio-Animatronic™ characters explore creativity in the fine arts, performing arts, literature, science, and technology. The ride culminates at:

Image Works, housing dozens of hands-on electronic devices and interactive computers. Here you can activate musical instruments by stepping on hexagons of colored light, participate in a TV drama, draw patterns with laser beams, operate a giant kaleidoscope, and conduct an electronic philharmonic orchestra.

INNOVENTIONS The pair of crescent-shaped buildings to your right and left just beyond Spaceship Earth (formerly called CommuniCore East and CommuniCore West) contain numerous exhibits that are being revamped at this writing. Both buildings will soon house a major new and constantly evolving exhibit called Innoventions that will showcase cutting-edge and future products for home, work, and play. Guests will preview the latest developments in interactive TV, hand-held personal digital assistants, microdiscs, electronic games and toys, high-definition TV, voice-activated appliances, computerized home management, automobile navigation equipment, telephone technologies, group video games, and more. With new systems such as CD-ROM and interactive CDs, visitors will be able to "tour" the Egyptian Pyramids and choose preferred viewing angles. Leading manufacturers will sponsor many of the exhibit areas (there will be 15 major displays). There will also be live stage demonstrations and interactive hands-on displays.

The two-story **Epcot Discovery Center,** which will be located on the right side of Innoventions, will include an information resource area where guests can get answers to all their questions about Epcot attractions in particular and Walt Disney World in general. For instance, if after visiting The Land, you'd like to learn more about hydroponics, they can print out an information sheet on it. The Discovery Center will also house a shop called **Field Trips** featuring educational products and software.

WORLD OF MOTION Everything you always wanted to know about transportation—past, present, and future—is explored in this General Motors–sponsored vast wheel-shaped, gleaming stainless-steel pavilion.

World of Motion Show: The pavilion's highlight is this whimsical 15-minute ride that utilizes animated scenery, 70mm film, and a cast of 140 Audio-Animatronic™ characters to document civilization's eternal quest for movement. It begins with sore-footed cavemen, early attempts at riding animals (test-driving a zebra), and the invention of the wheel. Leonardo da Vinci is shown experimenting with ideas for flight, the era of railroads is represented by a train being held up by masked desperados, and an astonished horse looks on as a man cranks up a car. Just about every mode of transport is covered, from paddlewheelers to ocean liners, from wagon trains to barnstorming planes. You proceed—always to a cheerful background score called "It's Fun to Be Free"—to the widening travel opportunities presented by auto and air travel. And, this being WDW, the ride climaxes with a dizzying journey through computer-graphics space for a look at the future: spaceship transportation.

Transcenter: The other major attraction here is a behind-the-scenes look at General Motors' advanced engineering and manufacturing facilities, its prototype vehicles of the future, and its concerns in creating nonpolluting engines and fuel economy. Here you can test your knowledge of automotive signals, learn how robotics are used in automobile manufacturing, and sit down in the prototype models and examine the controls.

HORIZONS The theme of this pavilion is the future, which presents an unending series of new horizons. In the line area, designed as a futuristic transportation center, a public address system pages passengers bound for exotic destinations. You board sideways-facing gondolas for a 15-minute journey into the next millennium. The first tableau honors visionaries of past centuries (like Jules Verne) and looks at outdated visions of the future and classic sci-fi movies. You ascend to an area where an IMAX film projected on two 80-foot-high screens presents a kaleidoscope of brilliant micro and macro images—growing crystals, colonies in space, solar power, a space shuttle launching, DNA molecules, and a computer chip. You then travel to 21st-century cityscapes, desert farms, floating cities under the ocean's surface, and outer-space colonies populated by Audio-Animatronic™ denizens who use holographic telephones, magnetic levitation trains, and voice-controlled robotic field hands. For the return to 20th-century earth, you can select one of three futuristic transportation systems: a personal spacecraft, a desert hovercraft, or a mini-submarine.

WONDERS OF LIFE Housed in a vast geodesic dome fronted by a 75-foot replica of a DNA molecule, this Epcot pavilion offers some of Future World's most engaging shows and attractions. They include:

The Making of Me: Starring Martin Short, this captivating 15-minute motion picture combines live action with animation and spectacular in-utero photography to create the sweetest introduction imaginable to the facts of life.

Body Wars: You're miniaturized to the size of a single cell for a medical rescue mission inside the immune system of a human body. Your objective: to save a miniaturized immunologist who has been accidentally swept into the bloodstream. This motion-simulator ride takes you on a wild journey through gale-force winds (in the lungs) and pounding heart chambers.

Cranium Command: In this hilarious multimedia attraction, Buzzy, an Audio-Animatronic™ brain-pilot-in-training, is charged with the seemingly impossible task of controlling the brain of a typical 12-year-old boy. Cranium Command is a training center for brain pilots, in which Buzzy has to prove his ability at the helm. The boy's body parts are played by Charles Grodin, Jon Lovitz, Bob Goldthwait, Kevin Nealon and Dana Carvey (as Hans and Franz), and George Wendt.

Fitness Fairgrounds: This large area is filled with fitness-related shows, exhibits, and participatory activities, including a film called *Goofy About Health*

(Goofy has the "Unhealthy Livin' Blues" until he reforms) and Coach's Corner, where your tennis, golf, or baseball swing is analyzed by experts. You can also try working out on a video-enhanced exercise bike, get a computer-generated evaluation of your health habits, and take a video voyage to investigate the effects of drugs on your heart. There's much, much more. You could easily spend hours here.

UNIVERSE OF ENERGY Sponsored by Exxon, this pavilion, its roof glistening with solar panels, aims to better our understanding of America's energy problems via a 35-minute ride-through attraction with visitors seated in solar-powered "traveling theater" cars. On a massive screen in Theater I, an animated motion picture depicts the earth's molten beginnings, its cooling process, and the formation of fossil fuels. You move from Theatre I to travel back 275 million years into an eerie storm-wracked landscape of the Mesozoic Era, a time of violent geological activity. Here, you're menaced by giant Audio-Animatronic™ dragonflies, pteryodactyls, dinosaurs, earthquakes, and streams of molten lava before entering a steam-filled tunnel deep through the bowels of the volcano to emerge back in the 20th century in Theatre II. In this new setting, which looks like a NASA Mission Control room, a 70mm film projected on a massive 210-foot wraparound screen depicts the challenges of the world's increasing energy demands and the emerging technologies that will help meet them. Your moving seats now return to Theatre I where swirling special effects herald a film about how energy impacts our lives in areas such as mobility, communications, agriculture, health, education, and recreation. It ends on a dramatically upbeat note—a vision of an energy-abundant future.

WORLD SHOWCASE

Surrounding a 40-acre lagoon at the park's southern end is World Showcase, a permanent community of 11 miniaturized nations, all with authentically indigenous landmark architecture, landscaping, background music, restaurants, and shops. The cultural facets of each nation are explored in art exhibits, dance performances, and innovative rides, films, and attractions. And all employees in each pavilion are natives of the country represented.

CANADA Our neighbors to the north are represented by diverse architecture ranging from a mansard-roofed replica of Ottawa's Château Laurier (here called the Hôtel du Canada) to a rustic stone building modeled after a famous landmark near Niagara Falls. A Native American village signifies the culture of the Northwest, while the Canadian wilderness is reflected by a steep mountain (a Canadian Rocky), a waterfall cascading into a white-water stream, and a "forest" of evergreens, stately cedars, maples, and birch trees. Don't miss the stunning floral displays inspired by the Butchart Gardens in Victoria, B.C. The pavilion's highlight attraction is *O Canada!,* a dazzling 18-minute, 360° Circle-Vision™ film that reveals Canada's scenic splendor from sophisticated Montréal to the thundering flight of thousands of snow geese near the St. Lawrence. Other scenes (there are over 50) depict a chuckwagon race in the Calgary Stampede, the pine-covered mountains of Banff National Park, a fishing village off the Newfoundland coast, herds of reindeer in the Northwest Territory, and an aerial view of the majestic snow-covered Rockies. Canada pavilion shops carry sandstone and soapstone carvings, snowshoes, lumberjack shirts, duck decoys, fur-lined parkas, toy tomahawks and teepees, a vast array of Eskimo stuffed animals and Native American dolls, turquoise jewelry, and, of course, maple syrup.

UNITED KINGDOM Centered on Brittania Square—a formal London-style park, complete with copper-roofed gazebo bandstand and a statue of the Bard—the U.K. pavilion evokes Merry Olde England. Four centuries of architecture are represented along quaint cobblestone streets, troubadours and minstrels entertain in front of a traditional British pub, and a formal garden replicates the landscaping of 16th- and 17th-century palaces. High Street and Tudor Lane shops display a broad sampling of British merchandise: toy soldiers, Paddington bears, hobby horses, personalized coats of arms, Scottish clothing (cashmere and Shetland sweaters, golf wear, tams, knits, and tartans), shortbreads, Royal Doulton china, and Waterford crystal. A tea shop occupies a replica of Anne Hathaway's thatch-roofed 16th-century cottage in

Stratford-upon-Avon, while other emporia represent the Georgian, Victorian, Queen Anne, and Tudor periods.

FRANCE Focusing on La Belle Epoque (1870–1910)—a flourishing period for French art, literature, and architecture—this pavilion is entered via a replica of the beautiful cast-iron Pont des Arts footbridge over the Seine. It leads to a park inspired by Seurat's painting, *A Sunday Afternoon on the Island of La Grande Jatte*, with pleached sycamores, Bradford pear trees, flowering crape myrtles, and sculpted parterre flower gardens. A one-tenth replica of the Eiffel Tower looms above the grand boulevards. The highlight attraction is *Impressions de France.* Shown in a palatial (mercifully sit-down) theater à la Fontainebleau, this 18-minute film is a breathtakingly scenic journey through diverse French landscapes projected on a vast 200° wraparound screen. It takes you from charming farm and fishing villages to the sophistication of Paris and the Côte d'Azur. You soar over the French Alps, attend a traditional Brittany wedding, visit Versailles, and see vineyards at harvest time. Emporia in the covered shopping arcade have interiors ranging from a turn-of-the-century bibliothèque to a French château. Merchandise includes French art prints, cookbooks, cookware, fashions, wines, pâtés, Madeline and Babar books and dolls, and perfumes. A marketplace/tourism center revives the defunct Les Halles, where Parisians used to sip onion soup in the wee hours. The heavenly aroma of a boulangerie penetrates the atmosphere, and mimes, jugglers, and strolling chanteurs entertain.

MOROCCO This exotic pavilion is heralded by a replica of the Koutoubia Minaret, the prayer tower of a 12th-century mosque in Marrakesh. The Medina (old city), entered via a replica of an arched gateway in Fez, leads to Fez House (a traditional Moroccan home) and the narrow winding streets of the *souk*, a bustling marketplace where all manner of authentic handcrafted merchandise is on display. Here you can peruse or purchase pottery, brassware, sheepskin bags, baskets, hand-knotted Berber carpets, colorful Rabat carpets, prayer rugs, and wall hangings. There are weaving demonstrations in the *souk* throughout the day. The Medina's rectangular courtyard centers on a replica of the ornately tiled Najjarine Fountain in Fez, the setting for musical entertainment. The pavilion's Royal Gallery contains an ever-changing exhibit of Moroccan art, and the Center of Tourism offers a continuous three-screen slide show.

JAPAN Heralded by a flaming red *torii* (gate of honor) on the banks of the lagoon and the graceful blue-roofed Goju No To pagoda, this pavilion focuses on Japan's ancient culture. The pagoda, topped by a bronze spire with gold wind chimes and a water flame, was inspired by a shrine built at Nara in A.D. 700. In a traditional Japanese garden, cedars, yew trees, bamboo, "cloud-pruned" evergreens, willows, and flowering shrubs frame a contemplative setting of pebbled footpaths, rustic bridges, waterfalls, exquisite rock landscaping, and a pond of golden koi. The Yakitori House is based on the renowned 16th-century Katsura Imperial Villa in Kyoto, considered by many to be the crowning achievement of Japanese architecture. Exhibits ranging from 18th-century Bunraki puppets to Samurai armor take place in the moated White Heron Castle, a replica of the Shirasagi-Jo, a 17th-century fortress overlooking the city of Himeji. And the Mitsukoshi Department Store (Japan's answer to Macy's) is housed in a replica of the Shishinden (Hall of Ceremonies) of the Gosho Imperial Palace built in Kyoto in A.D. 794. It sells lacquer screens, kimonos, kites, fans, collectible dolls in traditional costumes, origami books, tea sets, Samurai swords, Japanese Disneyana, bonsai plants, pottery, even modern electronics. In the courtyard, artisans demonstrate the ancient arts of *anesaiku* (shaping brown rice candy into dragons, unicorns, and dolphins), *ikebana* (flower arranging), *sumi-e* (calligraphy), and *origami* (paper folding). Be sure to include a show of traditional Japanese music and dance at this pavilion in your schedule. It's one of the best in the World Showcase.

AMERICAN ADVENTURE Housed in a vast Georgian-style structure, *The American Adventure* is a 29-minute dramatization of U.S. history utilizing a 72-foot rear-projection screen, rousing music, and a large cast of lifelike Audio-Animatronic™ figures, including narrators Mark Twain and Ben Franklin. The "adventure" begins with the voyage of the *Mayflower* and encompasses major historic events. You view Jefferson writing the Declaration of Independence, the expansion of the frontier, Mathew Brady photographing a family about to be divided by the Civil War, the stock market crash of 1929, Pearl Harbor, and the *Eagle* heading toward the moon. John Muir and Teddy Roosevelt discuss the need for national parks, Susan B. Anthony speaks out on women's rights, Frederick Douglass on slavery, Chief Joseph on the situation of Native Americans. While waiting for the show to begin, you'll be entertained by the wonderful Voices of Liberty Singers performing American folk songs in the Main Hall. Formally symmetrical gardens complement the pavilion's 18th-century architecture, and a rose garden includes varieties named for American presidents. A shop called Heritage Manor Gifts sells American food products, patchwork baby quilts, Davy Crockett hats, books on American history, historically costumed dolls, classic political campaign buttons, and vintage newspapers with banner headlines like "Nixon Resigns!" An artisan in the shop makes jewelry out of coins.

ITALY One of the prettiest World Showcase pavilions, Italy lures visitors over an arched stone footbridge to a replica of Venice's intricately ornamented pink-and-white Doge's Palace. Other architectural highlights include the 83-foot campanile (bell tower) of St. Mark's Square, Venetian bridges, and a central piazza enclosing a version of Bernini's Neptune Fountain with a delightful statue of the sea god flanked by water-spewing dolphins. A garden wall suggests a backdrop of provincial countryside, and Mediterranean citrus, olive trees, cypress, and pine frame a formal garden. Gondolas are moored on the lagoon. Shops—some of them in a Tuscan-style open-air market—sell baskets, leather, Perugina chocolates, biscotti, cameo and filigree jewelry, Murano and Venetian glass, alabaster figurines, and inlaid wooden music boxes. A troupe of street actors perform a contemporary version of 16th-century Commedia del Arte in the piazza.

GERMANY Enclosed by towered castle walls, this festive pavilion is centered on a cobblestone *platz* with pots of colorful flowers girding a fountain statue of St. George and the Dragon. An adjacent clock tower is embellished with whimsical glockenspiel figures that herald each hour with quaint melodies. The pavilion's outdoor biergarten—where it's Oktoberfest all year long—was inspired by medieval Rothenberg. And 16th-century building facades replicate a merchant's hall in the Black Forest and the town hall in Frankfurt's Romsburg Square. Shops here carry Hummel figurines, crystal, glassware, cookware, cuckoo clocks, cowbells, music boxes, pewterware, German wines and specialty foods, toys, art reproductions, and books. An artisan demonstrates the molding and painting of Hummel figures; another paints exquisite detailed scenes on eggs.

CHINA Bounded by a serpentine wall that snakes around its outer perimeter, the China pavilion is entered via a vast triple-arched ceremonial gate inspired by the Temple of Heaven in Beijing. Passing through the gate, you'll see a half-size replica of this ornately embellished red-and-gold circular temple, built in 1420 during the Ming Dynasty. Gardens simulate those in Suzhou, with miniature waterfalls, fragrant lotus ponds, groves of bamboo, and weeping mulberry trees. The highlight attraction here is *Wonders of China,* a 20-minute, 360° Circle-Vision™ film that explores 6,000 years of dynastic and Communist rule and the breathtaking diversity of the Chinese landscape. Narrated by 8th-century Tang Dynasty poet Li Bai, it includes scenes of the Great Wall (begun 24 centuries ago!), a performance by the Beijing Opera, a Manchurian ice-sculpture festival, the Forbidden City in Beijing with 9,000 rooms in six palaces, Yangtze River gorges, rice terraces of Hunan Province, the Gobi Desert, and tropical rain forests of Hainan Island. Adjacent to the theater, an art gallery houses changing exhibits of Chinese art. A bustling marketplace offers an array of merchandise including silk robes, lacquer and carved-jade furniture, cloisonné vases, silk rugs and embroideries, stuffed pandas, kites, dolls, fans, pottery, wind chimes, and Chinese clothing. Note the towering stone elephant nearby: Legend has it that if you throw a stone on its back and it remains there, luck will follow you the rest of your days. Artisans here paint wooden ducks and demonstrate calligraphy.

NORWAY Centered on a picturesque cobblestone courtyard, this pavilion evokes ancient Norway. A *stavekirke* (stave church), styled after the 13th-century Gol

Church of Hallingdal, houses changing exhibits. A replica of Oslo's 14th-century Akershus Castle, next to a cascading woodland waterfall, is the setting for the pavilion's featured restaurant. Other buildings simulate the red-roofed cottages of Bergen and the timber-sided farm buildings of the Nordic woodlands. There's a two-part attraction here. **Maelstrom,** a boatride in a dragon-headed Viking vessel, traverses Norway's fjords and mythical forests to the music of *Peer Gynt*—an exciting journey during which you'll be menaced by polar bears prowling the shore and trolls who cast a spell on the boat and propel it backward into raging rapids. The watercraft crashes through a narrow gorge and spins into the North Sea where a violent storm, complete with crashing waves and lightning, is in progress. But the storm abates, and passengers disembark safely in a 10th-century Viking village to view the 70mm film **Norway,** which documents a thousand years of history. Featured images include *Oseberg bat* (a 1,000-year-old Viking ship), a fiery nighttime view of an oil rig silhouetted against 45-foot waves of the tumultuous North Sea, a small fishing village, festive national holiday celebrations in Oslo, and soaring jumps at the Holmenkollen ski resort. Shops feature hand-knit wool hats and sweaters, toys, pewterware, and jewelry made from Norwegian gemstones.

MEXICO You'll hear the music of marimba and mariachi bands as you approach the festive showcase of Mexico, fronted by a towering Mayan pyramid modeled on the Aztec Temple of Quetzalcoatl (God of Life) dating to the 3rd century A.D. Upon entering the pavilion, you'll find yourself in a museum of pre-Columbian artifacts. Down a ramp is a small lagoon, the setting for **El Rio del Tiempo,** where visitors board boats for eight-minute cruises through Mexico's past and present. Dance performances focusing on the cultures of Mayan, Toltec, Aztec, and Colonial Mexico are presented in film segments and by a folk-costumed Audio-Animatronic™ cast in vignettes ranging from a Day of the Dead skeleton band to children breaking a piñata. The show culminates in a Mexico City fiesta with exploding fiber-optics fireworks. Shops in and around the Plaza de Los Amigos (a "moonlit" Mexican *mercado*) display an array of leather wallets and handbags, baskets, sombreros, big paper flowers, piñatas, pottery, embroidered dresses and blouses, maracas, papier-mâché birds, worry dolls, turquoise jewelry, carved onyx animals, cut-tin candle lamps, weavings, and blown-glass objects (an artisan gives demonstrations). La Casa de Vacaciones, sponsored by the Mexican Tourist Office, provides travel information.

SHOWS & SPECTACULARS

As at Magic Kingdom, check your show schedule upon entering the park and plan to attend many of the below-listed performances.

WORLD SHOWCASE PAVILION SHOWS These international entertainments make up an important part of the Epcot experience. There are Chinese lion dancers, German oom-pah bands, Caledonian bagpipers, and Moroccan belly dancers. Be sure not to miss the Voices of Liberty singers at American Adventure and the traditional music and dance displays in Japan.

ILLUMINATIONS A backdrop of classical music by international composers, high-tech lighting effects, darting laser beams, fireworks, strobes, and rainbow-lit dancing fountains combine to create this awesome 16½-minute Epcot spectacular, presented nightly. Each nation is highlighted in turn—colorful kites fly over Japan, the giant Rockies loom over Canada, a gingerbread house rises in Germany, and so on. Don't miss it! Find a seat around the lagoon about a half hour before showtime.

SPLASHTACULAR This 20-minute futuristic musical extravaganza centering on Epcot's vast CommuniCore fountain, features a cast of lavishly costumed dancers, stilt walkers, space aliens, and Disney characters. Mickey and Minnie are the stars. Dazzling special effects include hundreds of laserlike jets of water crashing 150 feet skyward in a stunning aquatic dance. In a story line pitting good against evil, a wicked alien sorceress conjures up an intergalactic nemesis called TerrosaurX (he has metal-spike teeth and drools!). Towering 45 feet above the stage, he menaces hapless earthlings and steals their vibrant colors. But Mickey triumphs over the fearsome monster, and the show ends in a brilliantly Technicolor finale, complete with rainbows, bubbles, dancing butterflies, and fireworks.

THE MAGICAL WORLD OF BARBIE   At the America Gardens Theater in World Showcase, Barbie, Ken, Skipper, and the rest of their ever-exuberant doll family and friends come to life in a 30-minute around-the-world stage show. Amid lively music and dance numbers, Barbie and pals travel to the Australian outback, a Russian ballet theater, African jungle, and a fashion-show runway in Paris—always, of course, in appropriate outfits from their vast wardrobes. A must for Barbie-obsessed kids!

DISNEY-MGM STUDIOS

In 1989, WDW premiered its third "magical kingdom," Disney–MGM Studios, offering exciting movie and TV-themed shows and behind-the-scenes "reel-life" adventures. Its main streets include Hollywood and Sunset Boulevards, with art deco movie sets evocative of Hollywood's glamorous Golden Age. There's also a New York street lined with Gotham landmarks (the Empire State, Flatiron, and Chrysler Buildings) and typical New York characters including peddlers hawking knock-off watches. More important, this is a working movie and TV studio, where shows are in production even as you tour the premises.

Arrive at the park early, tickets in hand. Unlike the Magic Kingdom and Epcot, MGM's 110 acres of attractions can pretty much be seen in one day. The parking lot is right at the gate. If you don't get a *Disney–MGM Studios Guidebook* and/or **entertainment schedule** when you enter the park, you can pick them up at **Guest Services** (MGM's information center). First thing to do is check showtimes and work out an entertainment schedule based on highlight attractions and geographical proximity. My favorite MGM restaurants are described in the "Dining" section of this chapter. Strollers can be rented at Oscar's Super Service inside the main entrance.

THE TWILIGHT ZONE TOWER OF TERROR   In a thrilling journey to another dimension, you'll enter a once-grand but now-deserted (and haunted) Sunset Boulevard hotel and wend your way through a series of deceptive optical-illusion rooms to the boiler room. Here, you'll board the ride vehicle and rise past mysterious hotel hallways, beckoned by ghostly guests en route. The climax: The hotel "elevator" malfunctions in descent, sending you on a terrifying 13-story free-fall plunge into *The Twilight Zone!* Rod Serling narrates.

THE MAGIC OF DISNEY ANIMATION   You'll see Disney characters come alive at the stroke of a brush or pencil as you tour actual glass-walled animation studios and watch artists at work. Walter Cronkite and Robin Williams explain what's going on via video monitors, and they also star in a very funny eight-minute Peter Pan–themed film about animation. The tour also includes entertaining video talks by animators and a grand finale of magical moments from such Disney classics. This popular attraction should be visited early in the morning; long lines form later in the day.

BACKSTAGE STUDIO TOUR   This 25-minute tram tour takes you behind the scenes for a close-up look at the vehicles, props, costumes, sets, and special effects used in your favorite movies and TV shows. You'll see costumers at work in wardrobe, the house facade of "The Golden Girls," and carpenters building sets. All very interesting until the tram ventures into Catastrophe Canyon, where an earthquake in the heart of desert oil country causes canyon walls to rumble and riders are threatened by a raging oil fire, massive explosions, torrents of rain, and flash floods! Then you're taken behind the scenes to see how filmmakers use special effects to create such disasters. After the tram tour, visit Studio Showcase, a changing walk-through display of sets and props from popular movies.

VOYAGE OF THE LITTLE MERMAID   Hazy light, creating an underwater effect in the reef-walled theater, helps set the mood for this charming musical spectacular based on the Disney feature film. The show combines live and Audio-Animatronic™ performers with over 100 puppets, movie clips, and innovative special effects. Sebastian sings the movie's Academy Award–winning song

"Under the Sea"; the ethereal Ariel shares her dream of becoming human in a live performance of "Part of Your World"; and the evil Ursula belts out "Poor Unfortunate Soul" in which she tempts Ariel to part with her most precious possession, her voice. It all has a happy ending, as most of the young audience knows it will—they've seen the movie.

INSIDE THE MAGIC Movie and TV special effects and production facets are the focus of this behind-the-scenes walking tour of studio facilities. The tour is enhanced by entertaining videotaped narrations en route by Warren Beatty, Mel Gibson, George Lucas, and others. You'll see how a naval battle—complete with burning ships and undersea explosions—is created and how miniaturization was achieved in the movie *Honey, I Shrunk the Kids.* You'll also visit studio soundstages, view a short movie called *The Lottery* starring Bette Midler and learn how its special effects were achieved, and find out what goes on in video and audio post-production areas. The tour ends with a screening of coming Disney attractions in a sit-down theater.

JIM HENSON'S MUPPET VISION 3D This utterly delightful film starring Kermit and Miss Piggy combines Jim Henson's puppets with Disney Audio-Animatronics™ and special-effects wizardry, 70mm film, and cutting-edge 3-D technology. The coming-at-you action includes flying Muppets, cream pies, cannon balls, fiber-optic fireworks, bubble showers, even an actual spray of water. Statler and Waldorf critique the action (which includes numerous mishaps and disasters) from a mezzanine balcony. Kids in the first row interact with the characters. In the preshow area, guests view a hilarious Muppet video on overhead monitors and see an array of Muppet movie props.

THEATER OF THE STARS This 1,500-seat amphitheater is currently presenting a live Broadway-style production of *Beauty and the Beast,* based on the Disney movie version. Musical highlights range from the rousing "Be Our Guest" opening number to the poignant title song featured in a romantic waltz-scene finale complete with the release of white doves. A highlight is "The Mob Song" scene in a dark forest, in which villagers armed with pitchforks set out on a rampage to "kill the beast," setting up the emotional climax: Belle speaks the three magic words that heal the beast's heart and transform him into a handsome prince. Sets and costumes are lavish, production numbers spectacular. Arrive early to get a good seat. *Note: Beauty and the Beast* has been enjoying a long run here; a new show, based on a more recent Disney movie, may be in progress by the time you visit.

STAR TOURS A wild galactic journey based on the *Star Wars* trilogy (George Lucas collaborated on its conception), this action-packed adventure uses dramatic film footage and flight-simulator technology to transform the theater into a vehicle careening through space. On a voyage to the Moon of Endor, you encounter robots, aliens, and droids, among them our inexperienced pilot, RX-24. The spaceship lurches out of control, and passengers experience sudden drops, violent crashes, and oncoming laser blasts. The harrowing ride ends safely, and you exit into a "droid and baggage claim" area.

MONSTER SOUND SHOW Four volunteers are chosen from the audience to create sound effects for a short film starring Chevy Chase and Martin Short that includes thunder, rain, creaking doors, falling chandeliers, footsteps, ringing bells, and explosions. You see the film three times: first with professional sound, then without sound as volunteers frantically scramble to create an appropriate track, and finally with the sound effects they've provided. Errors in timing and volume make it all quite funny, as a knock at the door or crashing glass comes just a few seconds too late. David Letterman narrates a terrific video preshow. In a post-show area called Soundworks, guests can try their hand at creating sounds via interactive computers.

SUPERSTAR TELEVISION This 30-minute show takes guests through a broadcast day that spans TV history. During the preshow, "casting directors" choose volunteers from the audience to reenact 15 famous television scenes (arrive early if you want to snag a role). The broadcast day begins with a 1955 black-and-white "Today" show featuring Dave Garroway and continues through "Late Night with David

Letterman," including scenes from a classic "I Love Lucy" episode (the candy factory), "General Hospital," "Bonanza," "Gilligan's Island," "Cheers," and "The Golden Girls" among others. Real footage is mixed with live action, and though occasionally a star is born, there's plenty of fun watching amateur actors freeze up, flub lines, and otherwise deviate from the script.

THE GREAT MOVIE RIDE Audio-Animatronic™ replicas of movie stars enact some of the most famous scenes in filmdom on this thrilling ride through movie history: Bergman and Bogart's classic airport farewell in *Casablanca,* Rhett carrying Scarlett up the stairs of Tara for a night of passion, Brando bellowing "Stellllaaaa," Sigourney Weaver fending off slimy *Alien* foes, and many more. Action is enhanced by dramatic special effects. The setting for this attraction is a full-scale reproduction of Hollywood's famous Mann's Chinese Theatre, complete with hand- and footprints of the stars out front.

INDIANA JONES EPIC STUNT SPECTACULAR Visitors get an inside look at the world of movie stunts in this dramatic 30-minute show, which re-creates major scenes from the *Raiders of the Lost Ark* series. The show opens on an elaborate Mayan temple backdrop. Indiana Jones crashes dramatically onto the set via a rope, and as he searches with a torch for the golden idol, he encounters booby traps, fire and steam, and spears popping up from the ground, before being chased by a vast rolling boulder! The set is dismantled to reveal a colorful Cairo marketplace where a swordfight ensues and the action includes jumps from high places, virtuoso bullwhip maneuvers, lots of gunfire, and a truck bursting into flame. An explosive finale takes place in a desert scenario. Throughout, guests get to see how elaborate stunts are pulled off. Volunteers are chosen to participate as extras during the preshow.

PARADES, SHOWS, FIREWORKS & MORE A dazzling parade, ✪ **Aladin's Royal Caravan,** based on the movie, takes place once or twice daily (check your entertainment schedule for route and times). Its exotic cast includes a 26-foot genie on a bejeweled float, brass bands, amazing acrobats, scimitar dancers, golden camels, a giant out-of-control ape, magicians, a harem, and the grand entrance of Prince Ali and Princess Jasmine on Abu (transformed from a monkey into an elephant), followed by Aladdin's old nemesis, the villainous Jafar, now reduced to pushing the honey bucket behind them. Don't miss it! Find a curbside seat (or grab a bench near the Monster Sound Show) along the parade route a half hour before it begins.

The ✪ **Sorcery in the Sky** fireworks show is presented nightly during summer and peak seasons. Check your entertainment schedule to see if it's on.

The **Star Today** program features frequent appearances by stars such as Betty White, Howie Mandel, and Sally Struthers. They visit attractions, record their handprints in front of the Chinese Theater, and appear at question-and-answer sessions with park guests. Check your entertainment schedule to see if it's on.

The **Teenage Mutant Ninja Turtles** emerge from the sewers to demonstrate their radical moves, sing, and sign autographs in a "totally awesome" show on New York street several times each day.

A movie set replica serves as a playground in the *Honey, I Shrunk the Kids Movie Set Adventure.* Outsize props include 30-foot blades of grass, giant Legos, and a sliding pond made from an immense film reel.

Centering on a gleaming 14½-foot bronze Emmy, the **Academy of Television Arts & Sciences Hall of Fame Plaza,** adjacent to SuperStar Television, honors TV legends. Bronze sculptures of Carol Burnett, Sid Caesar, Red Skelton, Milton Berle, and other television luminaries are displayed.

TYPHOON LAGOON

Located off Lake Buena Vista Drive halfway between Walt Disney World Village and Disney–MGM Studios, this is the ultimate in water theme parks. Its fantasy setting is a palm-fringed tropical island village of ramshackle tin-roofed structures, strewn with cargo, surfboards, and other marine wreckage left by the "great typhoon." A storm-stranded fishing boat dangles precariously atop the 95-foot-high Mount Mayday, the steep setting for several major park attractions. Every half hour the boat's smokestack erupts, shooting a 50-foot geyser of water into the air. In summer, arrive no later than 9am to avoid long lines; the park is often filled to capacity by 10am and closed to later arrivals. Beach towels and lockers can be obtained for a minimal fee, and all beach accessories can be purchased at Singapore Sal's. Light fare is available at two restaurants, and there are picnic tables. Guests are not permitted to bring their own floatation devices into the park.

TYPHOON LAGOON   This large and lovely blue lagoon, the size of two football fields and surrounded by white sandy beach, is the park's main swimming area. Large surfing and bobbing waves crash against the shore every 90 seconds. A foghorn sounds to warn you when a wave is coming. Young children can wade in the lagoon's peaceful bay or cove.

CASTAWAY CREEK   Hop onto a raft or inner tube and meander along this 2,100-foot lazy river. Circling the lagoon, Castaway Creek tumbles through a misty rain forest, past caves and secluded grottoes. It has a themed area called Water Works where jets of water spew from shipwrecked boats, and a Rube Goldberg assemblage of broken bamboo pipes and buckets spray and dump water on passersby. There are exits along the route where you can leave the creek; if you do the whole thing, it takes about a half hour.

WATER SLIDES   Humunga Kowabunga consists of two 214-foot Mount Mayday water slides that drop you down the mountain before rushing into a cave and out again at 30 m.p.h. Three longer but less steep slides—Jib Jammer, Rudder Buster, and Stern Burner—take you on a serpentine route through waterfalls and bat caves, and past nautical wreckage at about 20 m.p.h. before depositing you in a bubbling catch pool; each offers slightly different views and thrills.

WHITE-WATER RIDES   Mount Mayday is also the setting for three white-water rafting adventures—Keelhaul Falls, Mayday Falls, and Gangplank Falls—all offering steep drops, coursing through caves, and passing lush scenery. Keelhaul Falls has the most winding spiral route, Mayday Falls the steepest drops and fastest water, while the slightly tamer Gangplank Falls uses large tubes so the whole family can ride together.

SHARK REEF   Guests are given free snorkel equipment (and instruction) for a 15-minute swim through this 362,000-gallon simulated coral-reef tank populated by about 4,000 rainbow parrotfish, queen angelfish, yellowtail damselfish, rock beauties, and other colorful denizens of the deep. There's a rock waterfall at one end. If you don't want to get in the water, you can observe the fish via portholes in a walk-through area.

KETCHAKIDDIE CREEK   Many of the above-mentioned attractions require guests to be at least four feet tall. This section of the park is a kiddie area exclusively for those *under* four feet. An innovative water playground, it has bubbling fountains to frolic in, mini-water slides, a pint-sized white-water tubing adventure, spouting whales and squirting seals, rubbery crocodiles to climb on, grottoes to explore, and waterfalls to loll under.

RIVER COUNTRY

One of the many recreational facilities at the Fort Wilderness Resort campground, this mini-water park is themed after Tom Sawyer's swimming hole. Kids can scramble over man-made boulders that double as diving platforms for a 330,000-gallon clearwater pool. Two 16-foot water slides also provide access to the pool. Attractions on the adjacent Bay Lake, which is equipped with ropes and ships' booms for climbing, include a pair of flumes—one 260 feet long, the other 100 feet—that corkscrew through Whoop-N-Holler Hollow; White Water Rapids, which carries inner tubers along a winding 230-foot creek with a series of chutes and pools; and the Ol' Wading Pool, a smaller version of the swimming hole designed for young children. There are poolside and beachside areas for sunning and picnicking, plus a 350-yard boardwalk nature trail. Beach towels and lockers can be obtained for a minimal fee. Light fare is available at Pop's Place.

To get here, take a launch from the dock near the entrance to the Magic Kingdom or a bus from its Transportation and Ticket Center.

DISCOVERY ISLAND

This lushly tropical 11½-acre zoological sanctuary—just a short boat ride away from the Magic Kingdom entrance, the Contemporary Resort, or Fort Wilderness—provides a tranquil counterpoint to Disney World dazzle. Plan to spend a leisurely afternoon strolling its scenic mile-long nature trail which, shaded by a canopy of trees, winds past gurgling streams, groves of palm and bamboo, ponds and lagoons filled with ducks and trumpeter swans, a bay that's a breeding ground for brown pelicans, and colonies of rose-hued flamingos. Peacocks roam free, and aviaries house close to 100 species of colorful exotic birds. Discovery Island denizens also include Patagonian cavies, alligators and caimans, Galapagos tortoises, small primates, and Muntjac miniature deer from Southeast Asia. Two different bird shows and a reptile show are scheduled several times throughout the day; they take place outdoors with seating on log benches. Guests can also look through a viewing area to see the nursery complex of the island's animal hospital, where baby birds and mammals are often hand-raised.

6. TWO TOP ORLANDO ATTRACTIONS

SEA WORLD

This popular 175-acre marine-life park, at 7007 Sea World Dr. (tel. 407/351-3600), explores the mysteries of the deep in a format that combines entertainment with wildlife-conservation awareness. Its beautifully landscaped grounds, centering on a 17-acre lagoon, include flamingo and pelican ponds (over 1,500 birds, primarily water fowl, make their home in the park) and a lush tropical rain forest. Shamu, a killer whale, is the star of the park.

MAJOR ATTRACTIONS   There are 10 major shows and attractions:

Mission: Bermuda Triangle   Combining a high-definition underwater adventure film with state-of-the-art flight-simulator technology, this attraction takes visitors aboard a scientific research submarine. Your "mission": to explore the 444,000-square-mile expanse of the Atlantic Ocean known as the Bermuda Triangle, in which thousands of people and hundreds of ships and planes have vanished without a trace. It's all very rational and scientific . . . until an underwater earthquake threatens the expedition!

Terrors of the Deep   This exhibit houses 220 specimens of venomous and otherwise scary sea creatures in a tropical-reef habitat. Immense acrylic tunnels provide close encounters with slithery eels, three dozen sharks, barracudas, lionfish, and poisonous pufferfish. A theatrical presentation focusing on sharks puts across the message that pollution and uncontrolled commercial fishing make humankind the ultimate "terror of the deep."

Manatees: The Last Generation?   Today the Florida manatee is in danger of extinction, with as few as 2,000 remaining. Underwater viewing stations, innovative cinema techniques, and interactive displays combine to create an exciting format for teaching visitors about the manatee and its fragile ecosystem. Also on display here are hundreds of other native fish as well as alligators, turtles, and shore birds, and there's a nursing pool for manatee mothers and their babies.

Sea World Theatre: Window to the Sea   A multimedia presentation takes visitors behind the scenes at Sea World and explores a variety of marine subjects. These include an ocean dive in search of the rare six-gilled shark, a killer whale giving birth, babies born at Sea World (dolphins, penguins, walruses), dolphin anatomy, and underwater geology.

Shamu: New Visions Sea World trainers develop close relationships with killer whales, and in this partly covered open-air stadium, they direct performances that are extensions of natural cetacean behaviors—twirling, waving tails and fins, rotating while swimming, and splashing the audience (sit pretty far back if you don't want to get soaked). The evening show here, called "Shamu: Night Magic," utilizes rock music and special lighting effects.

The Whale and Dolphin Discovery Show At Discovery Cove, a big partially covered open-air stadium, whales and Atlantic bottlenose dolphins perform flips and high jumps, swim at high speeds, twirl, swim on their backs, and give rides to trainers—all to the accompaniment of calypso music. Once again, these are extensions of natural behaviors which showcase the abilities of these creatures.

The Gold Rush Ski Show This wacky waterski exhibition features a cantankerous prospector and a talented team of cowboy waterskiers performing long-distance jumps, water ballet, flips, and backward and barefoot skiing. Their antics are accompanied by rollicking hoedown music and dance.

Penguin Encounter This display of hundreds of penguins and alcids (including adorable babies) native to the Antarctic and Arctic regions also serves as a living laboratory for protecting and preserving polar life. On a moving walkway, you'll view six different penguin species congregating on rocks, nesting, and swimming underwater. There's an additional area for puffins and murres (flying Arctic cousins of penguins).

Hotel Clyde and Seamore Two sea lions, along with a cast of otters and walruses, appear in this fishy "Fawlty Towers" comedy with a conservation theme.

Shamu's Happy Harbor This innovative three-acre play area provides facilities for kids to climb a four-story net tower with a 35-foot crow's-nest lookout, fire water cannons, operate remote-controlled vehicles, and navigate a water maze.

ADDITIONAL ATTRACTIONS The park's other attractions include: **Pacific Point Preserve,** a 2½-acre naturalistic setting that duplicates the rocky northern Pacific Coast home of California sea lions and harbor and fur seals; a **Tide Pool of touchables,** such as sea anemones, starfish, sea cucumbers, and sea urchins; a 160,000-gallon man-made **coral-reef aquarium,** home to 1,000 brightly hued tropical fish displayed in 17 vignettes of undersea life; a musical spectacular in the park's **Nautilus Theatre;** and **Stingray Lagoon,** where visitors enjoy hands-on encounters with harmless southern diamond and cownose rays.

A **Hawaiian dance troupe** entertains in an outdoor facility at Hawaiian Village; if you care to join in, grass skirts and leis are available. You can ascend 400 feet to the top of the **Sea World Sky Tower** for a revolving 360° panorama of the park and beyond (there's an extra charge of $3 per person for this activity). And at the 5.5-acre **Anheuser-Busch Hospitality Center** you can try free samples of Anheuser-Busch beers and snacks and stroll through the stables to watch the famous Budweiser Clydesdale horses being groomed (Anheuser-Busch owns Sea World).

The **Aloha! Polynesian Luau Dinner and Show,** a musical revue featuring South Seas food, song, and fire dancing, takes place nightly at 6:30pm. Park admission is not required. The cost is $29.65 for adults, $20.10 for children 8 to 12, $10.55 for kids 3 to 7, and free for kids under 3. Reservations are required (tel. 407/363-2559, or toll free 800/227-8048).

There are, of course, numerous **restaurants,** snack bars, and food kiosks throughout the park, offering everything from chicken and biscuits to mesquite-grilled ribs. Dozens of **shops** carry marine-related gifts, as well as wilderness/conservation-oriented items.

And visitors can take 90-minute behind-the-scenes **tours** of the park's breeding, research, and training facilities and/or attend a 45-minute presentation about Sea World's animal behavior and training techniques. The cost for either tour is $5.95 for ages 10 and over, $4.95 for children 3 to 9, and free for kids under 3.

ADMISSION A one-day ticket costs $32.95 for ages 10 and over, $28.95 for children 3 to 9; a two-day ticket is $37.95 for ages 10 and over, $33.95 for children 3 to 9; a one-year pass costs $59.95 for ages 10 and over, $49.95 for children 3 to 9; kids under 3 are free. Discounted admissions in conjunction with Cypress Gardens (see "Easy Excursions from Orlando," below) and Busch Gardens in Tampa (see Chapter 12) are also available; call for details or inquire at the gate. Parking costs $5 per vehicle, $7 for RVs and trailers.

OPEN   The park is open from 9am to 7pm 365 days a year, later during summer and holidays when there are also laser/fireworks spectaculars and additional shows at night. Call before you go.

DIRECTIONS   Take I-4 to the Bee Line Expressway (Fla. 528) and follow the signs.

UNIVERSAL STUDIOS

Universal Studios Florida, 1000 Universal Studios Plaza (tel. 407/363-8000), is a working motion-picture and television production studio. As you stroll along "Hollywood Boulevard" and "Rodeo Drive," you'll pass more than 40 full-scale sets and large props from famous movies.

MAJOR ATTRACTIONS   Thrilling rides and attractions utilize cutting-edge technology—such as OMNIMAX 70mm film projected on seven-story screens—to create unprecedented special effects. And on hand to greet visitors are Hanna-Barbera characters (Yogi Bear, Scooby Doo, Fred Flintstone, and others). While waiting on line, you'll be entertained by excellent preshows.
    Major attractions include:
Jaws   As your boat heads out to open water, an ominous dorsal fin appears on the horizon. What follows is a series of terrifying face-to-glistening-jaw attacks from a three-ton, 32-foot-long great white shark which tries to sink its teeth into passengers. And there's more trouble ahead. The boat is surrounded by a 30-foot wall of flame from burning fuel. I won't tell you how it ends, but here's a hint: The pungent stench of charred shark flesh adds verisimilitude!
E.T. Adventure   Visitors are given a passport to E.T.'s planet, which needs his healing powers to rejuvenate it. You'll soar with E.T. on a mission to save his ailing planet, through the forest and into space, aboard a star-bound bicycle—all to the accompaniment of that familiar movie theme music.
Back to the Future   The year is 2015. The incompetent but evil Biff has penetrated Doc Brown's Laboratory of Future Technology, imprisoned Doc, and taken off in the DeLorean. On a mission to save the time machine from Biff, visitors blast through the space-time continuum, plummeting into volcanic tunnels ablaze with molten lava, colliding with Ice Age glaciers, thundering through caves and canyons, and are briefly swallowed by a dinosaur, in a spectacular multisensory adventure.
Kongfrontation   It's the last thing the Big Apple needed. King Kong is back! As you stand in line in a replica of a grungy, graffiti-scarred New York subway station, CBS newsman Roland Smith reports on Kong's terrifying rampage. Everyone must evacuate to Roosevelt Island. So it's all aboard the Roosevelt Island tram. Cars collide and hydrants explode below, police helicopters hover overhead putting you directly in the line of fire, the tram malfunctions, and, of course, you encounter Kong—32 feet tall and 13,000 pounds. He emits banana breath in your face and menaces passengers, dangling the tram over the East River. A great thrill—or just another day in New York.
Earthquake, The Big One   You board a BART train in San Francisco for a peaceful subway ride, but just as you pull into the Embarcadero station there's an earthquake—the big one, 8.3 on the Richter Scale! As you sit helplessly trapped, vast slabs of concrete collapse around you, a propane truck bursts into flames, a runaway train comes hurtling at you, and the station floods (60,000 gallons of water cascade down the steps).
Ghostbusters   There are so many ghosts these days, Ghostbusters just has to sell franchises. Lewis Tully delivers a zany high-pressure sales pitch to the audience, and volunteers come up on stage and get slimed. Tully demonstrates flushing ghosts into the Ectoplasmic Container Chamber and discusses starter kits in three price

ranges. But the ghosts, of course, break loose from Gozer's Temple and demons lunge at the audience.

Wild, Wild, Wild West Show Stunt people demonstrate falls from balconies, gun and whip fights, dynamite explosions, and other oater staples.

The Beetlejuice Graveyard Revue Dracula, Wolfman, the Phantom of the Opera, Frankenstein and his bride, and Beetlejuice put on a funky—and very funny—rock music show with pyrotechnic special effects and MTV-style choreography.

The FUNtastic World of Hanna-Barbera This motion-simulator ride takes guests careening through the universe in a spaceship piloted by Yogi Bear to rescue Elroy Jetson. Prior to this wild ride, you'll learn about how cartoons are created. After it, in an interactive area, you can experiment with animation sound effects—boing! plop! Splash!

ADDITIONAL ATTRACTIONS On the **Nickelodeon Studios Tour,** a must for young kids, you can see the soundstages where Nick shows are produced, visit the kitchen where gak and green slime are made (touch and taste it, if you like), play typical show games, and try out new Sega video games. There's lots of audience participation, and a volunteer will get slimed.

Other park attractions include: a **Rocky and Bullwinkle character show,** with those scheming no-goodnik spies, Boris and Natasha; the **Gory, Gruesome, & Grotesque Horror Makeup Show** for a behind-the-scenes look at the transformation scenes from movies like *The Fly* and *The Exorcist;* a **tribute to Lucille Ball,** America's queen of comedy; **Fievel's Playland,** an innovative western-themed playground based on the Spielberg movie *An American Tail;* **"Murder She Wrote,"** which puts you on the set with Angela Lansbury and lets you make post-production executive decisions via computer; and **Alfred Hitchcock's 3-D Theatre,** a tribute to the "master of suspense" in which Tony Perkins narrates a reenactment of the famous shower scene from *Psycho,* and *The Birds,* as if it weren't scary enough, becomes an in-your-face 3-D movie.

Descendants of Lassie, Benji, Mr. Ed, and other animal superstars perform their famous pet tricks in the **Animal Actors Show.** During **Screen Test Home Video Adventure,** a director, crew, and team of "cinemagicians" put visitors on the screen in an exciting video production. And **Dynamite Nights Stunt Spectacular,** a nightly show, combines death-defying stunts with a breathtaking display of fireworks.

Over 25 **shops** in the park sell everything from Lucy collectibles to Bates Motel towels, and **restaurants** run the gamut from Mel's Drive-In (of *American Graffiti* fame), to the Hard Rock Café, to Schwab's.

ADMISSION A one-day ticket costs $35 for ages 10 and over, $28 for children 3 to 9; a two-day ticket is $55 for ages 10 and over, $44 for children 3 to 9; an annual pass (admission for a full year) is $87.50 for ages 10 and over, $70 for children 3 to 9; ages 2 and under enter free. Parking costs $5 per vehicle, $6 for RVs and trailers.

OPEN The park is open 365 days a year. Hours are basically 9am to 7pm, extended during summer and holidays. Call before you go.

DIRECTIONS Take I-4 east, making a left on Sand Lake Road, then a right onto Turkey Lake Road, and follow the signs.

---

7. MORE AREA ATTRACTIONS

KISSIMMEE

Kissimmee's sights are closest to the Walt Disney World area—about a 10- to 15-minute drive.

GATORLAND, 14501 S. Orange Blossom Trail (U.S. 441), between Osceola Pkwy. and Hunter's Creek Blvd. Tel. 855-5496.

Founded in 1949 with a handful of alligators living in huts and pens, Gatorworld today features 5,000 alligators and crocodiles on a 55-acre spread. Breeding pens, nurseries, and rearing ponds are situated throughout the park, which also displays monkeys, snakes, deer, goats, birds, sheep, Florida lake turtles, a Galápagos tortoise, and a bear. A 2,000-foot boardwalk winds through a cypress swamp and a 10-acre breeding marsh with an observation tower. Or you can take the free Gatorland Express Train around the park. There are three shows scheduled throughout the day: gator wrestling, gator jumping, and an informative snake show. An open-air restaurant, shop, and picnic facilities are on the premises.

Admission: $11.60 adults, $8.45 children 3–11, free for kids under 3. Parking is free.

Open: Daily 8am–dusk.

SPLENDID CHINA, Formosa Gardens Blvd. off W. Irlo Bronson Memorial Hwy. (U.S. 192), between Entry Point Blvd./Sherbeth Rd. and Black Lake Rd. Tel. 396-7111.

This 76-acre outdoor attraction features more than 60 miniaturized replicas of China's most noted man-made and natural wonders, spanning 5,000 years of history and culture. Visitors enter via a bustling commercial street in the "water city" of Suzhou (the Venice of the East) circa A.D. 1300 to view a short orientation film about China. Park highlights include: a half-mile-long copy of the 4,200-mile Great Wall; the Forbidden City's 9,999-room Imperial Palace, built in 1420; Tibet's sacred Potala Palace, former mountain home of the Dalai Lama; carved Buddhist grottoes with statuary dating from A.D. 477 to 898; the massive Leshan Buddha, carved out of a mountainside between A.D. 713 and 803; the Stone Forest of Yunan, a natural formation of towering limestone peaks; and the Mongolian mausoleum of Genghis Khan. Live shows (acrobats, martial-arts demonstrations, storytelling, dance, puppetry, and more) take place throughout the day on stages around the park and in a 900-seat open-air amphitheater; check your entertainment schedule. Over a dozen shops sell Chinese merchandise, and food concessions, a gourmet restaurant, and a Chinese cafeteria are on the premises. Two-hour guided walking tours, departing several times a day, cost $5 per person (children under 12 free), and one-hour golf-cart tours ($45 per six-person cart) depart every half hour. There is also recorded commentary at each attraction.

Admission: $23.55 for adults, $13.90 for children 5–12, free for kids under 5. Parking is free.

Open: Daily 9:30am–9:30pm.

WATER MANIA, 6073 W. Irlo Bronson Memorial Hwy. (U.S. 192), just east of I-4. Tel. 396-2626.

This conveniently located 36-acre water park offers a variety of aquatic thrill rides and attractions. You can boogie-board or body-surf in continuous wave pools, float lazily along an 850-foot river, enjoy a white-water tubing adventure, and plummet down spiraling water slides and steep flumes. Or dare to ride the Abyss, an enclosed tube slide that corkscrews through 300 feet of darkness, exiting into a splash pool. There's a rain forest–themed water playground for children. A miniature golf course and wooded picnic area—with arcade games, a beach, and volleyball—adjoin.

Admission: $19.95 adults, $17.95 children 3–12, free for kids under 3. Parking is $2.

Open: Daily. Hours vary seasonally (call before you go). **Closed:** Nov 29–Dec 25.

INTERNATIONAL DRIVE

Like Kissimmee's attractions, these are about a 10- to 15-minute drive from the Disney area.

RIPLEY'S BELIEVE IT OR NOT! MUSEUM, 8201 International Dr., 1½ blocks south of Sand Lake Rd. Tel. 363-4418.

It's always fun to peruse a Ripley collection of oddities, curiosities, and fascinating artifacts from faraway places. Among the hundreds of items and mannequins on display here are: a 1,069-pound man, a five-legged cow, a mosaic of the *Mona Lisa* created from 1,426 pieces of toast, torture devices from the Spanish Inquisition, a Tibetan flute made from human bones, a shrunken head, a painting on a grain of rice, and Ubangi women with wooden plates in their lips. Guests are greeted by a hologram of Robert Ripley.

Admission: $8.95 adults, $5.95 children 4–11, free for kids under 4.
Open: Daily 10am–11pm.

WET 'N WILD, 6200 International Dr., at Republic Dr. Tel. 351-WILD, or toll free 800/992-WILD.

When temperatures soar, head for this 25-acre water park and cool off jumping waves, careening down steep flumes, and running rapids. Among the highlights: **The Surge** (the longest, fastest multi-passenger tube ride anywhere in the United States with 580 feet of exciting banked curbs); **Surf Lagoon,** a vast pool with four-foot ocean waves; **Bomb Bay** (enter a bomblike casing 76 feet in the air for a speedy vertical flight straight down to a target pool); **Black Hole** (enter a spaceship and board a two-person raft for a 30-second, 500-foot, twisting, turning, space-themed reentry through total darkness propelled by a 1,000-gallon-a-minute blast of water!); **Raging Rapids,** a simulated white-water tubing adventure with a waterfall plunge; and **Lazy River,** a leisurely float trip. There are additional flumes, a challenging children's water playground, a sunbathing area, and picnic area. Food concessions are located throughout the park, lockers and towels can be rented, and you can purchase beach accessories at the gift shop.

Admission: $20.95 adults, $17.95 children 3–9, free for kids under 3. Parking is free.
Open: Daily. Hours vary seasonally (call before you go). **Directions:** Take I-4 east to Exit 30A and follow the signs.

ORLANDO

All of the following Orlando attractions are in close proximity to one another, making for a pleasant day's excursion. Loch Haven Park is about 35 minutes by car from the Disney area. Plan lunch at **Buckets,** 1825 N. Mills Ave., just across the street from Loch Haven Park museums (tel. 894-5197). It has tables overlooking Lake Rowena, some on an open-air deck, and serves American fare. You can probably also incorporate Winter Park sights in the same day.

HARRY P. LEU GARDENS, 1730 N. Forest Ave., between Nebraska St. and Corrine Dr. Tel. 246-2620.

At this delightful 56-acre botanical garden on the shores of Lake Rowena, meandering paths lead through forests of giant camphors, moss-draped oaks, palms, cycads, and camellias (one of the world's largest collections). Exquisite formal rose gardens display 75 varieties. Other highlights include orchids, azaleas, desert plants, beds of colorful annuals and perennials, a flowering tree garden (mimosa, cherry, plum, and others), and a 50-foot floral clock. The gardens were created by Orlando businessman Harry P. Leu, who donated his estate to the city in the 1960s. Free 20-minute tours of the Leu House, built in 1888, take place on the hour and half hour. The house is a veritable decorative arts museum filled with Victorian, Empire, and Chippendale pieces, among many other furnishings and objets d'art. It takes about two hours to see the house and gardens.

Admission: $3 adults, $1 children 6–16, free for kids under 6.
Open: Gardens, daily 9am–5pm. Leu House tours, Sun–Mon 1–3:30pm, Tues–Sat 10am–3:30pm. **Closed:** Christmas. **Directions:** Take I-4 east to Exit 43 (Princeton Street), follow Princeton Street east, make a right on Mills Avenue, turn left on Virginia Drive, and look for the gardens on your left.

ORANGE COUNTY HISTORICAL MUSEUM, 812 E. Rollins St., between Orange and Mills Aves., in Loch Haven Park. Tel. 897-6350.

Sharing a building with the Orlando Science Center (details below), this museum focuses on Florida history, beginning with prehistoric tooled animal bones from hunting cultures that existed here 12,000 years ago. Other exhibits include displays of Seminole pottery and clothing, items from a pioneer kitchen, artifacts from an 1892 courthouse, a chronicle of the citrus industry, and re-creations of a turn-of-the-century country store, a Victorian parlor, and the old *Orlando Sentinel* composing room. Also on the premises is Fire Station No. 3, a restored 1926 firehouse containing historic fire trucks, equipment, and memorabilia. The permanent collection is supplemented by changing exhibits of local, national, and international significance.

Admission: $2 adults, $1.50 seniors 55 and over, $1 children 6–12, free for kids under 6.

Open: Mon–Sat 9am–5pm, Sun noon–5pm. **Closed:** New Year's Day, Martin Luther King Day, Memorial Day, July 4th, Labor Day, Thanksgiving, and Christmas. **Directions:** Take I-4 east to Exit 43 (Princeton Street) and follow the signs to Loch Haven Park.

ORLANDO MUSEUM OF ART, 2416 N. Mills Ave., in Loch Haven Park off Hwy. 17-92. Tel. 896-4231.

The museum displays its permanent collection of 19th- and 20th-century American art, pre-Columbian artifacts dating from 1200 B.C. to A.D. 1500, and African objects on a rotating basis. These holdings are augmented by long-term loans focusing on Mayan archeology and arts of the African sub-Saharan region. "Art Encounter" is an interactive hands-on area for children, where they might weave on a giant loom, piece together a pre-Columbian pot, or play African instruments. And recent temporary exhibits have ranged from Hudson River School landscapes to works of Andy Warhol. Inquire about guided tours, workshops, gallery talks, and other activities. Museum shops and a restaurant are on the premises.

Admission: $4 adults, $2 children 4–11, free for kids under 4. Parking is free.

Open: Tues–Sat 9am–5pm, Sun noon–5pm. Art Encounter, Tues–Fri and Sun noon–5pm, Sat 10am–5pm. **Closed:** New Year's Day, Memorial Day, July 4, Labor Day, Thanksgiving, and Christmas. **Directions:** Take I-4 east to Exit 43 (Princeton Street) and follow the signs to Loch Haven Park.

ORLANDO SCIENCE CENTER, 810 E. Rollins St., between Orange and Mills Aves., in Loch Haven Park. Tel. 896-7151.

The Orlando Science Center specializes in hands-on interactive exhibits. In its Tunnel of Discovery you can pedal a bicycle to generate electricity, create a tornado, or learn about anatomy from an immense soft-sculpture doll named Stuffee. NatureWorks focuses on the flora and fauna of four Florida habitats—cypress swamp, sand pine scrub, sinkhole lake, and pine flatwood. In WaterWorks, young children can play with water-creature puppets, learn how water moves objects by building dams and canals, crawl under a glass-bottom turtle tank, and touch starfish and sponges. There are free planetarium shows and science demonstrations throughout the day. A café and gift shop are on the premises. Inquire about nighttime planetarium shows and laser-show rock concerts.

Admission: $6.50 adults, $5.50 children 3–11, free for kids under 3.

Open: Mon–Thurs and Sat 9am–5pm, Fri 9am–9pm, Sun noon–5pm. **Closed:** Thanksgiving and Christmas. **Directions:** Take I-4 east to Exit 43 (Princeton Street) and follow the signs to Loch Haven Park.

WINTER PARK

This lakeside town is a lovely place to spend an afternoon. Visit the Morse Museum, cruise the lakes, and browse in the posh boutiques that line Park Avenue. Plan to stay for dinner. A good choice is the plant-filled **Park Plaza Gardens,** 319 S. Park Ave., between Lyman and New England Avenues (tel. 645-2475). The fare is French, the prices on the upscale side. If you want a less expensive choice, there are plenty of options on the same street.

To get to Winter Park from Orlando (about a five-mile drive), continue east on I-4 to Fairbanks Avenue (Exit 45), turn right, and proceed about a mile, making a left on Park Avenue.

CHARLES HOSMER MORSE MUSEUM OF AMERICAN ART, 133 E. Welbourne Ave., at Center St. Tel. 644-3686.

This gem of a museum was founded by Hugh and Jeanette McKean in 1942 to display their peerless art collection, which includes 40 magnificent windows and 21 paintings by Louis Comfort Tiffany! In addition, there are non-Tiffany windows ranging from creations by Frank Lloyd Wright to 15th- and 16th-century German masters; leaded lamps by Tiffany and Emile Gallé; paintings by John Singer Sargent, Maxfield Parrish, and others; jewelry designed by Tiffany, Lalique, and Fabergé; photographic works by Tiffany and other 19th-century artists; and art nouveau furnishings. Also on display is Tiffany memorabilia. Because of space limitations, only a small portion of the collection can be shown at any given time; however, the works on display are wonderfully impressive.

Admission: $2.50 adults, $1 students of any age.

Open: Tues–Sat 9:30am–4pm, Sun 1–4pm. **Closed:** New Year's Day, Memorial Day, July 4, Labor Day, Thanksgiving, and Christmas.

SCENIC BOAT TOUR, on the lake at the eastern end of Morse Blvd. Tel. 644-4056.

For over half a century tourists have been boarding pontoons at this location for leisurely hour-long cruises on Winter Park's beautiful chain of natural lakes. The ride traverses area lakes, winding through canals built by loggers at the turn of the century and tree-shaded fern gullies lined with bamboo and lush tropical foliage. You'll view magnificent lakeside mansions, pristine beaches, cypress swamps, ancient trees draped with Spanish moss, and dozens of marsh birds—possibly even an American bald eagle. The captain regales passengers with local lore. It's an utterly delightful trip.

Admission: $5.50 adults, $2.75 children 2–11, free for kids under 2.

Open: Tours depart daily, every hour on the hour 10am–4pm (more often Dec 26 to early June). **Closed:** Christmas.

8. SPORTS & RECREATION

In addition to the listings below, check out the Friday "Calendar" section in the *Orlando Sentinel*. It lists numerous outdoor activities in the Orlando area ranging from bass-fishing trips to bungee jumping.

SPECTATOR SPORTS

The Orlando Centroplex administers six public sports and entertainment facilities in the downtown area. These include three major sporting arenas: the Florida Citrus Bowl, the Orlando Arena, and Tinker Field.

FLORIDA CITRUS BOWL, 1610 W. Church St., at Tampa St. Tel. 849-2020 for information, 839-3900 to charge tickets.

The Florida Citrus Bowl seats 70,000 people for major sporting events including the annual New Year's Day Citrus Bowl classic, college football games, NFL preseason games, mud and monster truck racing, motocross, and World Cup soccer games.

Admission: Ticket prices vary with the event. Parking is $5.

Open: Year-round. **Directions:** Take I-4 east to the East-West Expressway and head west to U.S. 441, make a left on Church Street, and follow the signs.

ORLANDO ARENA, 600 W. Amelia St., between I-4 and Parramore Ave. Tel. 849-2020 for information, 839-3900 to charge tickets.

This 15,500-seat arena is the home of the NBA **Orlando Magic** basketball team during their October–April season, the NHL **Tampa Bay Lightning** hockey team (same season), and the **Orlando Predators** (arena football, May–August). The McDonald's American Cup Gymnastic Competition takes place here every March, and the National Championship Finals Rodeo every November. In the past the arena has also hosted key events such as the NCAA Basketball Championship, U.S. Figure Skating Championships, and the NBA All-Star Weekend. Call to find out what's on when you're in town.

Admission: Ticket prices vary with the event. Tickets to Orlando Magic games (about $17–$45) have to be acquired far in advance; they usually sell out by September before the season starts. Parking costs $4 (for up-to-the-minute parking information, tune your car radio to 1620 AM).

Open: Year-round. **Directions:** Take I-4 east to Amelia Avenue, turn left at the traffic light at the bottom of the off-ramp, and follow the signs.

TINKER FIELD, 287 S. Tampa Ave., between Colonial Dr. (Fla. 50) and Gore St. Tel. 872-7593 for information and to charge tickets.

From April to September, the **Orlando Cubs** (the Chicago Cubs Class AA Southern League affiliate) play at Tinker Field, which adjoins the Citrus Bowl. Various other baseball and softball events take place here throughout the year. Call for details.

Admission: Tickets to Cubs games, $3–$5. Parking is $3.

Open: Year-round. **Directions:** Take I-4 east to the East-West Expressway, head west to U.S. 441, make a left on Church Street, and follow the signs.

RECREATION

Recreational facilities of every description abound in Walt Disney World and the surrounding area. These are especially accessible to guests at Disney-owned resorts, official hotels, and Fort Wilderness Resort and Campground, though many other large resort hotels also offer comprehensive facilities (see details in "Accommodations," above). The Disney facilities listed below are all open to the public, no matter where you're staying. For further information about WDW recreational facilities, call 407/824-4321. Guests at Disney properties can inquire when making hotel reservations or at guest services/concierge desks.

BIKING Bike rentals (single- and multispeed bikes for adults, tandems, and children's bikes) are available from the **Bike Barn** (tel. 824-2742) at Fort Wilderness Resort and Campground. Rates are $3 per hour, $8 per day ($1 additional for tandems).

BOATING At the **Walt Disney World Village Marketplace Marina** you can rent Water Sprites, canopy boats, Sun Kats, and 20-foot pontoon boats. For information, call 828-2204.

The **Bike Barn** at Fort Wilderness (tel. 824-2742) rents canoes ($4 per hour, $10 per day) and pedalboats ($5 per half hour, $8 per hour).

FISHING Fishing excursions on **Lake Buena Vista**—mainly for largemouth bass—can be arranged up to 14 days in advance by calling 407/824-2204. Equipment can be rented. No license is required. The fee is $70 for one person for two hours, $90 for two people, $110 for three to six people, $25 for each additional hour, those rates include gear, guide, and refreshments.

You can also rent fishing poles at the **Bike Barn** (tel. 824-2742) to fish in Fort Wilderness canals. No license is required.

GOLF Walt Disney World operates five championship 18-hole, par-72 golf courses and one 9-hole, par-36 walking course. All are open to the general public and offer pro shops, equipment rentals, and instruction. For tee times and information, call 407/824-2270 up to 7 days in advance (up to 30 days for Disney resort and "official-hotel" guests).

HAYRIDES The hay wagon departs from Pioneer Hall at **Fort Wilderness** nightly at 7 and 9:30pm for hour-long old-fashioned hayrides with singing, jokes, and games. The cost is $5 for adults, $4 for children 3 to 11, free for kids under 3. Children under 12 must be accompanied by an adult. No reservations—it's first-come, first-served.

HORSEBACK RIDING Disney's Fort Wilderness Resort and Campground offers 50-minute scenic **trail rides** daily, with four to six rides per day. The cost is $16 per person. Children must be at least 9 years old. For information and reservations up to five days in advance, call 407/824-2832.

TENNIS There are 22 lighted tennis courts located throughout the Disney properties. Most are free and available on a first-come, first-served basis. If you're willing to pay for court time, courts can be reserved at two Disney resorts: the Contemporary (up to two weeks in advance; $10 per hour) and the Grand Floridian (up to a month ahead of time; $12 per hour). There's a large pro shop at the Contemporary where equipment can be rented. To reserve a court or lesson time with resident pros, call 824-3578 at the Contemporary, 824-2433 at the Grand Floridian.

WATER PARKS/SWIMMING   See Walt Disney World listings for River Country and Typhoon Lagoon, as well as the parks listed in "More Area Attractions," above.

9. SAVVY SHOPPING

Just about every shop throughout Walt Disney World carries what I call "Disneyana": plush Mickey Mice, *Little Mermaid* T-shirts, etc. But you may be surprised at some of the other merchandise on display here.

THE MAGIC KINGDOM

MAIN STREET AREA   The vast **Disneyana Collectibles** carries limited-edition movie cels, antique Disney clocks and porcelain figures, collectible dolls, and items such as a 1947 Donald Duck cookie jar that today is worth $2,000! (Why did I ever let Mom throw out my old toys?)

In Town Square, **The Emporium** houses the park's largest selection of Disneyana, everything from Mickey-logo golf balls to Winnie the Pooh slippers. There's a wonderful collection of music boxes here. Note the Audio-Animatronic™ window displays.

Basically an old-fashioned candy store, **The Market House** also carries an interesting line of pipes and tobaccos, as well as Disney-themed kitchenware, including Mickey and Minnie corn picks, cupcake papers, ice-cube molds, and waffle irons.

Over at the **Harmony Barber Shop,** where nostalgic men's grooming items are sold (moustache wax, spice colognes, shaving mugs), a barbershop quartet performs on the hour all day (except at 3pm). The **House of Magic** is the place to acquire double-headed nickels, folding quarters, squirting calculators, invisible inks, and other items with which to amaze and impress your friends. And at the **Shadow Box** you can watch a silhouette artist create cut-out portraits of customers on black paper.

ADVENTURELAND   The exotic **Traders of Timbuktu** carries African masks and carved wooden and soapstone animals and cowhide drums from Kenya, among other ethnic wares. For the Indiana Jones look, check out the clothes at **Elephant Tales. Island Supply** offers nature-themed books, posters, toys, and more. The **Zanzibar Shell Shop** is the place for shell mobiles and hangings. The **House of Treasure** retails pirate merchandise: hats, Captain Hook T-shirts, ships in bottles, skull-and-crossbones keychains, and toy muskets and daggers. And rather fun is **Lafitte's Portrait Deck,** where you can have a costumed photo taken in any of six elaborate Disney sets.

FRONTIERLAND   Mosey into the **Frontier Trading Post** for western-look leather items, cowboy boots and hats, turquoise jewelry, western and Native American sculpture, and toy rifles. Similar wares are found at **Prairie Outpost & Supply.**

LIBERTY SQUARE   **Olde World Antiques** sells items ranging from an 18th-century pine hutch to 19th-century Staffordshire Chinoiserie willow-pattern platters. The adjoining **Silversmith** carries Revere-style silver and pewter butter dishes, candlesticks, bowls, trays, and picture frames, along with such valuable items as a 46-piece set of Benjamin Franklin sterling silverware in a cherrywood chest ($3,500).

Over at **Heritage House** you can purchase parchment copies of famous American documents as well as actual historic framed letters (one signed by President Andrew Johnson in 1864 was priced at $2,350).

FANTASYLAND It's always the holiday season at **Mickey's Christmas Carol,** supply central for Disney-motif ornaments, Mickey Christmas stockings, and charming Christmas-themed music boxes. The **King's Gallery,** inside Cinderella Castle, is cluttered with family crests, tapestries, suits of armor, and other medieval wares. An artisan demonstrates damascening, a form of metal engraving that originated in Damascus circa A.D. 600.

TOMORROWLAND Kids love browsing over **Space Port's** *Star Trek* and *Star Wars* merchandise and games, sonic-blaster guns, robots, alien masks, and astronaut-costumed Mickeys.

EPCOT

The most fascinating shops are found in **World Showcase** pavilions, which comprise an international bazaar selling everything from Berber rugs to Japanese kimonos.

In **Future World,** check out the **Centorium,** a vast Disneyana shop that also carries a wide variety of Epcot souvenirs and memorabilia.

DISNEY–MGM STUDIOS

There's some really interesting shopping here. **Sid Cahuenga's One-of-a-Kind** sells autographed photos of the stars, original movie posters, and star-touched items such as a bracelet that once belonged to Joan Rivers. Over at **Cover Story,** you can have your photograph put on the cover of your favorite magazine, anything from *Forbes* to *Psychology Today* to *Golf Digest.* Costumes are available. **Celebrity 5 & 10,** modeled after a 1940s Woolworth's, has movie-related merchandise: *Gone With the Wind* memorabilia, MGM Studio T-shirts, movie posters, Elvis mugs, and more. And major park attractions all have complementary merchandise outlets selling Indiana Jones adventure clothing, *Little Mermaid* stuffed characters and logo-wear, *Star Wars* souvenirs, and so on.

DISNEY VILLAGE MARKETPLACE

Just 2½ miles from Epcot, this complex of restaurants and shops on Buena Vista Lagoon makes for a very pleasant browse. About 20 shops, open daily from 9:30am to 10pm, carry a wide variety of giftware, Disneyana, resortwear (including many logo items), Christmas-year-round merchandise, jewelry, crystal, housewares, surfboarding gear, wines and spirits, and sports shoes. There's plenty of free parking.

10. EVENING ENTERTAINMENT

My hat's off to those of you who, after a long day of traipsing around amusement parks, still have the energy to venture out at night in search of entertainment. You'll find plenty to do. And this being kids' world, many evening shows are geared to families.

Check the "Calendar" section of Friday's *Orlando Sentinel* for up-to-the-minute details on local clubs, visiting performers, concerts, and events. It has hundreds of listings. A recent edition would have informed you of entertainment options including the Captain and Tenille, the Byrds, the Black Crowes, Itzhak Perlman, and Marie Osmond.

Tickets to many performances are handled by Ticketmaster. Call 839-3900 to charge tickets.

MAJOR CONCERT/PERFORMANCE HALLS

BOB CARR PERFORMING ARTS CENTRE, 401 W. Livingston St., between I-4 and Parramore Ave. Tel. 849-2020 for information, 839-3900 to charge tickets.

This 2,500-seat theater is the home of the Orlando Opera Company and the

Southern Ballet Theater, both of which perform during October to May seasons here. The facility also offers concerts and comedy shows (a recent year's performers included Patti LaBelle, B.B. King, Manhattan Transfer, and Crosby, Stills, and Nash). The Orlando Broadway Series here (September to May) features original-cast Broadway shows such as *Cats*, *Les Misérables*, and *Crazy For You*.

Admission: Concert prices vary with performers; ballet tickets, $12–$30; opera, $19–$41; Broadway Series, $20–$45. Parking costs $4.

Open: Year-round. **Directions:** Take I-4 east to Amelia Avenue, turn left at the traffic light at the bottom of the off-ramp, and follow the signs.

FLORIDA CITRUS BOWL, 1610 W. Church St., at Tampa St. Tel. 849-2020 for information, 839-3900 to charge tickets.

This 70,000-seat arena is the setting for major rock concerts starring such headliners as Paul McCartney, George Michael, Pink Floyd, Genesis, Guns n' Roses, and Metallica.

Admission: Ticket prices vary with the performer. Parking is $5.

Open: Year-round. **Directions:** Take I-4 east to the East-West Expressway, head west to U.S. 441, make a left on Church Street, and follow the signs.

ORLANDO ARENA, 600 W. Amelia St., between I-4 and Parramore Ave. Tel. 849-2020 for information, 839-3900 to charge tickets.

This 15,500-seat arena offers an array of family-oriented entertainment, including the Ringling Bros. and Barnum & Bailey Circus every January, the Tour of World Figure-Skating Champions in April or May, *Walt Disney's World on Ice* in September, and *Sesame Street Live* in October. It also hosts about 30 varied music and comedy concerts a year, featuring performers such as Elton John, Billy Joel, Bruce Springsteen, Bette Midler, and the Grateful Dead. Call to find out who's on when you're in town.

Admission: Ticket prices vary with the event. Parking costs $4.

Open: Year-round. **Directions:** Take I-4 east to Amelia Avenue, turn left at the traffic light at the bottom of the off-ramp, and follow the signs.

WALT DISNEY WORLD DINNER SHOWS

Three distinctly different dinner shows are hosted by Walt Disney World. Other nighttime park options include SpectroMagic, fireworks, and IllumiNations (details above in "Walt Disney World Attractions").

HOOP-DEE-DOO MUSICAL REVUE, Disney's Fort Wilderness Resort and Campground, 3520 N. Fort Wilderness Trail. Tel. W-DISNEY.

Fort Wilderness's rustic log-beamed Pioneer Hall is the setting for this two-hour foot-stompin', hand-clappin', down-home musical revue. It's a high-energy show, with 1890s costumes, corny vaudeville jokes, rousing songs, and lots of good-natured audience participation. And during the show, you'll chow down on an all-you-can-eat barbecue dinner including chips and salsa, salad, smoked ribs, country-fried chicken, corn on the cob, baked beans, loaves of fresh-baked bread with honey butter, and a big slab of strawberry shortcake for dessert. Beverages are included. Reservations required. If you catch an early show, stick around for the Electrical Water Pageant at 9:45pm, which can be viewed from the Fort Wilderness Beach.

Admission: $34 adults 21 and over, $25 ages 12–20, $17 children 3–11. Taxes and gratuities extra. Free self-parking.

Open: Daily, showtimes at 5, 7:15, and 9:30pm.

POLYNESIAN LUAU DINNER SHOW, at Disney's Polynesian Resort, 1600 Seven Seas Dr. Tel. W-DISNEY.

This delightful two-hour dinner show features a colorfully costumed cast of entertainers from New Zealand, Tahiti, Hawaii, and Samoa performing authentic hula, warrior, ceremonial, love, and fire dances on a flower-bedecked stage. There's even a Hawaiian/Polynesian fashion show. It all takes place in a heated open-air theater with candlelit tables and red-flame lanterns suggesting torchiers. The all-you-can-eat meal includes a tropical fruit-and-greens salad with creamy ranch dressing, a loaf of coconut-almond bread, fried rice with vegetables, seafood stir-fry, barbecued ribs, dessert, and beverages. Reservations required. There's also a 4:30pm version daily (see "Meals with Disney Characters" in "Dining," above).

Admission: $32 adults 21 and over, $24.50 ages 12–20, $16.50 children 3–11, free for children under 3. Taxes and gratuities extra. Free self- and valet parking.

Open: Daily, showtimes at 6:45 and 9:30pm.

ENTERTAINMENT COMPLEXES

PLEASURE ISLAND, in Walt Disney World, adjacent to Walt Disney World Village. Tel. 934-7781.

Opened in 1989, this Walt Disney World theme park is a six-acre complex of nightclubs, restaurants, shops, and movie theaters where, for a single admission price, you can enjoy a night of club-hopping till the wee hours. The park is designed to suggest an abandoned waterfront industrial district with clubs in "converted" ramshackle lofts, factories, and warehouses, but the streets are festive with brightly colored lights and balloons. You'll be given a map and show schedule when you enter the park; take a look at it and plan your evening around shows that interest you. You can feel perfectly secure sending your teenage kids here for the evening, though they must be 18 to get in unless accompanied by a parent or legal guardian. The on-premises clubs come and go. At this writing they include:

The Island Jazz Company: This big barnlike club—purported to be an abandoned waterfront carousel factory (pine walls are adorned with merry-go-round horses)—features contemporary and traditional live jazz. Performers are mostly locals, but about once a month there are big names such as Kenny Rankin, Lionel Hampton, Maynard Ferguson, the Rippingtons, and Manfredo Best. Light fare, international coffees, and a variety of foreign and domestic wines are available.

Mannequins Dance Palace: Housed in a vast three-story dance hall with a small-town moviehouse facade, Mannequins is supposed to be a converted theatrical mannequin warehouse (remember, you're still in Disney World). It's a high-energy club with a large rotating dance floor. A DJ plays contemporary tunes at an ear-splitting decibel level; high-tech lighting effects, with laser shows twice nightly, are part of the excitement. You must be 21 to get in.

Neon Armadillo Music Saloon: You guessed. This trilevel club is country, with neon beer signs, rustic tables mounted on beer barrels, and a spur-shaped neon chandelier. Live country bands play nightly, and dancers whirl around the floor doing the Texas two-step or cotton-eyed Joe (lessons are given from 7 to 8pm). Sometimes name stars come in and take the stage. The staff is in cowboy/cowgirl garb. A specialty at the bar is Jell-O shooters—Jell-O cubes laced with alcoholic beverages. You can also order southwestern fare.

Adventurers Club: The most unusual of Pleasure Island's clubs—and my personal favorite—occupies a multistory building that, according to Disney legend, was designed to house the vast library and archeological trophy collection of Island founder and compulsive explorer Merriweather Adam Pleasure. It's also headquarters for the Adventure Club, which Pleasure headed until he vanished at sea in 1941. The plushly furnished club is chock-full of artifacts: early aviation photos, hunting trophies, shrunken heads, even a mounted "yakoose" (half yak, half moose) that occasionally speaks. He's not the only one. In the eerie Mask Room, over 100 masks move their eyes, jeer, and make odd pronouncements. Also on hand are Pleasure's zany band of globe-trotting friends and club servants. Played by skilled actors who interact with guests and always stay in character, they include the Colonel (a British pukka sahib), Pamelia Perkins (the stuffy upper-class club president), Otis T. Wren (a curmudgeonly ichthyologist), Hathaway Brown (dashing aviator; "the earth was no magnet for him, the skies beckoned"), and Graves (the lugubrious butler), among others. Improvisational comedy shows take place throughout the evening in the main salon, and diverse 20-minute cabaret shows in the library. You could easily hang out here all night imbibing potent tropical drinks in the library and at the bar.

Comedy Warehouse: Housed in the island's former power plant, the Comedy Warehouse—another of my favorites—has a rustic interior with tiered seating. A very talented troupe performs improvisational comedy based on audience suggestions. There are five shows a night, and bar drinks are available. Arrive early. Tickets are distributed 30 minutes before showtime, and lines soon form.

Rock & Roll Beach Club: Once the laboratory where Pleasure developed a unique flying machine, this three-story structure today houses a dance club where live bands play oldies and top-40 tunes nightly. There are bars on all three floors. The first level contains the dance floor. The second and third levels offer air hockey, pool tables, basketball machines, pinball, video games, blackjack tables, foosball, a bowling machine, and a pizza and beer stand.

8 TRAX: This 1970s-style club, with about 50 TV monitors airing divers shows and videos over the dance floor, occupies three levels, all with bars. A DJ plays disco music, and guests engage in games of Twister.

Other Attractions: In addition, **live bands**—including occasional big-name groups—play the West End Plaza outdoor stage and the Hub Stage; check your schedule for showtimes. You can star in your own music video at **SuperStar Studios.** There are carnival games, a video-game arcade, a Velcro wall, and an Orbitron (originally developed for NASA, it lets you experience weightlessness). And every night features a midnight **New Year's Eve celebration** with fireworks and confetti. **Shops and eateries** are found throughout the park.

Admission: Free before 7pm, $15.85 after 7pm. Admission is included in the Five-Day Super Duper Pass. Free self-parking; valet parking is $4.

Open: Clubs, daily 8pm–2am; shops, daily 10am–1am.

CHURCH STREET STATION, 129 W. Church St., off I-4 between Garland and Orange Aves. in downtown Orlando. Tel. 422-2434.

Though not part of Walt Disney World, Church Street Station in downtown Orlando operates on a similar principle to Pleasure Island. Occupying a cobblestone city block lined with turn-of-the-century buildings—genuine ones—it, too, is a shopping/dining/nightclub complex offering a diverse evening of entertainment for a single admission price. There are 20 live shows nightly; consult your show schedule on entering. Stunning interiors are the rule here. It's worth coming by just to check out the magnificent woodwork, stained glass, and thousands of authentic antiques. Entry to restaurants, the Exchange Shopping Emporium, and the Midway game area is free. Highlights include:

Rosie O'Grady's Good Time Emporium: This 1890s saloon is filled with interesting antiques. The train benches came from an old Florida rail station, backbar mirrors from a Glasgow pub, and bank teller's cages from a 19th-century Pittsburgh bank. Dixieland bands, banjo players, singing waiters, and can-can dancers entertain nightly. Light fare is available. The house specialty drink is a rum-and-fruit concoction called the Flaming Hurricane.

Apple Annie's Courtyard: Adjoining Rosie's, this brick-floored establishment, domed by arched pine and cypress trusses from an early 19th-century New Orleans church, evokes a Victorian tropical garden. Patrons sip potent tropical fresh fruit and ice-cream drinks while listening to folk and bluegrass music.

Lili Marlene's Aviator's Pub & Restaurant: Its plush oak-paneled interior is embellished with World War I memorabilia, stained-glass transoms, and accoutrements from an 1850 Rothschild town house in Paris. And eclectic seating ranges from hand-carved oak pews that came from a French church to a place at a large drop-leaf mahogany table where Al Capone once dined. Model airplanes are suspended from a beamed pine ceiling with a stained-glass skylight. The menu features premium aged steaks, prime rib, and fresh seafood.

Phineas Phogg's Balloon Works: This whimsical bar, with hot-air balloons and airplanes over the dance floor, is a high-energy club playing loud, pulsating music. It doubles as a virtual ballooning museum housing photographs and artifacts from historic flights. Every Wednesday from 6:30 to 7:30pm beers cost just 5¢ here. No one under 21 is admitted.

Cheyenne Saloon and Opera House: This stunning trilevel balconied saloon, crowned by a lofty stained-glass skylight, is constructed of golden oak lumber from a century-old Ohio barn. Quality western art is displayed throughout, including many oil paintings and 11 Remington sculptures. Balcony seating, in restored church pews, overlooks the stage, the setting for entertainment ranging from country bands to clogging exhibitions. The menu features steaks, barbecued chicken and ribs, and hickory-smoked brisket, served with buttermilk biscuits and honey-and-bourbon baked beans.

The Orchid Garden Ballroom: This stunning space, with ornate white wrought-iron arches and Victorian lighting fixtures suspended from an elaborate oak-paneled ceiling, is the setting for an oldies dance club. A DJ plays rock 'n' roll classics like "Great Balls of Fire" and "Let's Go to the Hop," interspersed with live bands. As the evening progresses, so do the musical decades.

Crackers Oyster Bar: Brick columns, oak paneling, and a gorgeous antique oak-and-mahogany bar characterize this cozy late 1800s-style dining room. Fresh Florida seafood is featured, along with more than 50 imported beers. You can nibble on appetizers such as oysters Rockefeller, smoked fish dip served with carrot and celery sticks, and steamed mussels. Or opt for more serious dishes ranging from crab cakes remoulade to paella.

Other Attractions: In addition, the 87,000-square foot Exchange houses the carnivallike **Commander Ragtime's Midway of Fun, Food and Games** (including an enormous video-games arcade), a food court, and over 50 specialty shops. You can rent a **horse-drawn carriage** out front for a drive around the downtown area and Lake Eola. And **hot-air balloon flights** can be arranged (tel. 841-8787).

Admission: Free before 5pm, $16.90 after 5pm. There are several parking lots nearby (call for specifics); valet parking, at Church Street and Garland Avenue, is $5.

Open: Clubs, daily until 2am; shops, daily until 11pm. **Directions:** Take I-4 east to Exit 38 (Anderson Street), stay in the left lane, and follow the blue signs. Most hotels offer transportation to and from Church Street (and since you'll probably be drinking, I advise it).

11. EASY EXCURSIONS FROM ORLANDO

Two of Central Florida's major sights are within an hour's drive of the Disney parks.

CYPRESS GARDENS Founded in 1936, Cypress Gardens, Fla. 540 at Cypress Gardens Blvd., in Winter Haven (tel. 813/324-2111, or toll free 800/237-4826, 800/282-2123 in Florida), came into being as a 16-acre public garden along the banks of Lake Eloise, with cypress-wood-block pathways and thousands of tropical and subtropical plants. Today it has grown to over 200 acres, with ponds and lagoons, waterfalls, classic Italian fountains, topiary, bronze sculptures, manicured lawns, and—most notably—ancient cypress trees shrouded in Spanish moss forming a backdrop to ever-changing floral displays of 8,000 varieties of plants from 75 countries. Southern belles in Scarlett O'Hara costumes stroll the grounds or sit on benches under parasols in idyllic tree-shaded nooks. They symbolize Florida's old-fashioned southern hospitality. In the late winter and early spring, more than 40 varieties of bougainvillea, 60 of azalea, and 500 of roses burst into bloom. Crape myrtles, magnolias, and gardenias perfume the late-spring air, while brilliant birds of paradise, hibiscus, and jasmine brighten the summer landscape. And in winter, the golden rain trees, floss silk trees, and camellias of autumn give way to millions of colorful chrysanthemums and red, white, and pink poinsettias.

Strolling the grounds is, of course, the main attraction (there are over two miles of winding botanical paths, and half the park's acreage is devoted to floral displays), but this being Central Florida, it's not the only one. Four shows are scheduled several times each day. The world-famous **Greatest American Ski Team** performs on Lake Eloise in a show augmented by an awesome hang-gliding display. **Feathered Follies,** a bird show, stars members of the parrot family roller-skating, playing basketball, and otherwise mimicking humans. **Variété Internationale** features specialty acts from all over the world. And since visitors can't be here to observe all seasonal changes, a slide show called **Seasons of Cypress Gardens** provides an overview of the year's blooms.

And there's still more. An enchanting exhibit called **Wings of Wonder** surrounds visitors with hundreds of brightly colored free-flying butterflies in a 5,500-square-foot Victorian-style glass conservatory. **Electric boats** navigate a maze of lushly landscaped canals in the original botanical gardens area. You can ascend 153 feet to the Kodak™ **Island in the Sky** for a panoramic vista of the gardens and a beautiful chain of Central Florida lakes. **Carousel Cove,** with eight kiddie rides and arcade games, centers on an ornate turn-of-the-century–style carousel. It adjoins another kid pleaser, **Cypress Junction,** an elaborately landscaped model railroad that travels over 1,100 feet of track with up to 20 trains moving at one time. **Cypress Roots,** a museum of park memorabilia, displays photographs of famous visitors (Elvis on waterskis, Tiny Tim tiptoeing through the roses) and airs ongoing showings of *Easy to Love* starring Esther Williams (it was filmed here). A **radio museum** commemorates the age of radio with a display of hundreds of vintage radios, radio memorabilia, and recordings of radio shows and music from the 1920s to the 1950s. Wind up your visit with a relaxing 30-minute narrated **pontoon cruise** on scenic Lake Eloise, past virgin forest, bulrushes, and beautiful shoreline homes (there's a $3.50-per-person charge).

Dining options range from a food court to the Crossroads Restaurant, a cheerful full-service facility serving American fare; the latter also offers al fresco seating at umbrella tables on a terrace. And if you care to pack a basket, there are picnic tables. Over a dozen **shops** sell everything from quaint country-store merchandise to gardening books and paraphernalia.

Admission is $24.95 for ages 10 and over, $16.45 for children 3–9; free for kids under 3. There are discounts for seniors. Discounted admissions in conjunction with Sea World (see "Two Top Orlando Attractions," above) and Busch Gardens in Tampa (see Chapter 12) are also available; call for details or inquire at the gate. Parking is free.

Open: Cypress Gardens is open 365 days a year from 9:30am to 5:30pm, with extended hours during peak seasons.

Directions: Take I-4 west to U.S. 27 south, and proceed west on to Fla. 540. The park is 40 miles southwest of Walt Disney World.

JOHN F. KENNEDY SPACE CENTER Operated by NASA, the Kennedy Space Center (tel. 407/452-2121) has been the launch site for all U.S. manned space missions since 1968. Astronauts departed earth at this site en route to the most famous "small step" in history—man's first voyage to the moon.

At **Spaceport USA,** the visitor facility of the Kennedy Space Center, the past, present, and future of space exploration are explored on bus tours of the facility and in movie presentations and numerous exhibits. It takes at least a full day to see and do everything. Arrive early and make your first stop at Information Central (it opens at 9am) to pick up a schedule of events/map and for help in planning your day. Nearby are space-related exhibits and interactive computers at which you can access information about all 10 U.S. NASA centers.

On the two-hour **Red Tour** you'll board a double-decker bus to explore the complex. At the first stop—in a simulated launch-control firing room of the Flight Crew Training Building—visitors view a film about the *Apollo 11* mission. The countdown, launch, and planting of a flag on the moon are thrilling even at secondhand. The tour continues to Complex 39 Space Shuttle launch pads (where a stop is made for exploration) and the massive Vehicle Assembly Building where Space Shuttles are assembled. Nearby, visitors get a close-up look at an actual Apollo/Saturn V moon rocket, America's largest and most powerful launch vehicle. Also on view are massive six-million-pound Crawler Transporters that carry Space Shuttles to their launch pads. Tours depart at regular intervals beginning at 9:45am, with the last tour leaving two hours before dusk. Purchase tickets at the Ticket Pavilion as soon as you arrive. Note: Itinerary variations may occur subject to launch schedules.

Though most visitors are sated by the Red Tour, a second two-hour **Blue Tour** (same hours) visits Cape Canaveral Air Force Station. On this tour, you'll see where America's first satellites and astronauts were launched in the Mercury and Gemini programs, view launch pads currently being used for unmanned launches, visit the original site of Mission Control, and stop at the Air Force Space Museum which houses a unique collection of missiles and space memorabilia.

Satellites and You is a 50-minute voyage through a simulated future space station. In Disney-esque fashion, the attraction combines Audio-Animatronic™ characters with innovative audiovisual techniques to explain satellites and their uses.

In the **Galaxy Center** building, two spectacular IMAX films projected on 5½-story screens are shown continually throughout the day in twin theaters. In *The Dream Is Alive*—featuring in-flight footage from three Space Shuttle missions— viewers join astronauts in preflight training, aboard the Space Shuttle in orbit, and on a breathtaking launch and landing. The second film, *Blue Planet,* is an environmentally themed look at Spaceship Earth from the vantage point of outer space. The Galaxy Center also houses a NASA art exhibit; a walk-through replica of the future Space Station *Freedom,* a manned research laboratory that will be orbiting the earth by 1999; and an exhibit called Spinoffs from Space. This exhibit, hosted by hologram characters, displays some of the 30,000 spinoffs that have resulted from space program research, including improved consumer products ranging from football helmets to cordless tools.

The **Gallery of Spaceflight,** a large museum, houses hardware and models relating to significant space projects and offers interesting exhibits on lunar exploration and geology.

Spaceport Theater presents films on a variety of topical space-related subjects, such as what astronauts do inside the Space Shuttle, the evolution of the space program, and the history of Kennedy Space Center. The **Astronauts Memorial,** a 42½- by 50-foot black granite "Space Mirror" dedicated May 9, 1991, honors the 16 American astronauts who have lost their lives in the line of duty. Aboard *Explorer,* a full-size replica of a Space Shuttle orbiter, visitors can experience the working environment of NASA astronauts. And the **Rocket Garden** displays eight actual U.S. rockets.

If you'd like to see a launch, call Spaceport USA (tel. 407/452-2121 for current launch information, ext. 260 to make reservations; fax 407/454-3211). Tickets for viewing cost $7 for adults, $4 for children 3 to 11, free for kids under 3. You can reserve tickets up to seven days before a launch, but they must be picked up at least two days before the launch. A special bus takes observers to a site just six miles from the launch pad.

There are two **cafeterias** and a **gift shop** on the premises.

Admission: Free. Tickets for either bus tour cost $7 for adults, $4 for children 3 to 11, free for kids under 3. IMAX film tickets are $4 for adults, $2 for children 3 to 11, free for kids under 3. Parking is free.

Open: The center is open daily from 9am to dusk; closed Christmas.

Directions: Take the Beeline Expressway (Fla. 528) east, and where the road divides, go left on Fla. 407, make a right on Fla. 405, and follow the signs.

CHAPTER 10

NORTHEAST FLORIDA

1. JACKSONVILLE
- **WHAT'S SPECIAL ABOUT NORTHEAST FLORIDA**
2. ST. AUGUSTINE
3. DAYTONA BEACH

Few people realize that the first European settlements in America were not in Jamestown, Virginia (1607), or at Plymouth Rock (1620). Juan Ponce de León discovered and named the Florida coast in 1513, and by 1565 the Spanish had settled 1,000 people in St. Augustine and crushed a French attempt to stake a claim in nearby Jacksonville. In both of these popular beach-resort cities, you can visit sites that evoke the earliest European incursions into the New World. St. Augustine has a large and quaintly charming restored historic district and Spanish Quarter, where the lives of residents in centuries past is vividly evinced.

If you love marine scenery, you'll be enchanted by Jacksonville's abundance of shimmering blue waterways. To get a feel for a little-known facet of Florida history (a brief 16th-century French colony) and to explore beautiful unspoiled woodlands, tranquil marsh, and ancient Timucuan sites, be sure to visit Fort Caroline and take a guided nature walk through the adjoining Theodore Roosevelt Area.

Nearby Daytona Beach is famous for a more recent kind of history—automotive speed. It's the "World Center of Racing," home to the Daytona International Speedway. And, of course, the town is synonymous with spring-break vacation frenzy. Pack your favorite wet T-shirt and party on.

---

1. JACKSONVILLE

35 miles S of Georgia, 160 miles NE of Orlando, 400 miles N of Miami

GETTING THERE By Plane American, Continental, Delta, TWA, United, and USAir fly into the spiffy-looking **Jacksonville International Airport** (recently renovated to the tune of over $100 million) on the city's north side, about 12 miles from downtown. The First Coast Information Booth, on the lower level (tel. 904/741-4902), is open daily from 8am to 10pm.

By Train There's an Amtrak station in Jacksonville at 3570 Clifford Lane, off U.S. 1, just north of 45th Street (tel. toll free 800/USA-RAIL).

By Bus Greyhound buses connect Jacksonville with most of the country. They pull into a terminal at 10 N. Pearl St., between Bay and Forsyth Streets in the heart of downtown (tel. 904/356-5521).

By Car If you're coming from north or south, take I-95. From points west, take I-10.

Boasting the largest land mass of any city in the continental United States (840 square miles), this sunbelt metropolis is on its way to becoming one of the nation's first-tier cities. An important Atlantic seaport, it's the insurance and banking capital of the South and corporate headquarters to many Fortune 500 companies, with a

WHAT'S SPECIAL ABOUT NORTHEAST FLORIDA

Architecture
- ☐ Historic houses, constructed of *tabby* (a kind of primitive concrete made of sand, water, and crushed oyster shells) and a similar but natural shell rock called *coquina*.

Museums
- ☐ The Lightner Museum in St. Augustine, a vast collection of Victoriana in a converted turn-of-the-century Spanish Renaissance–style hotel.
- ☐ The Cummer Gallery of Art in Jacksonville, with a permanent collection comprising works from 2000 B.C. to the present.

Sports
- ☐ Daytona International Speedway, the "World Center of Racing."
- ☐ Dog races, an archetypical Florida experience, at the Daytona Beach Kennel.
- ☐ Jacksonville Jaguar games at the Gator Bowl.

Florida Wilderness and Wildlife
- ☐ Dolphins and dozens of sea birds offshore near St. Augustine.
- ☐ The Theodore Roosevelt Area at Fort Caroline National Memorial in Jacksonville.

For Kids
- ☐ Art Connections at the Cummer Gallery in Jacksonville, an innovative art-themed play area with holograms, computer art stations, and other hands-on exhibits.
- ☐ Jacksonville Museum of Science & History, focusing on science and North Florida history, with dozens of hands-on activities for children plus planetarium shows.
- ☐ Jacksonville Zoological Park, a lushly landscaped zoo.
- ☐ Marineland of Florida in St. Augustine, for close encounters with dolphins and other marine denizens.

downtown of gleaming glass skyscrapers stunningly mirrored on the waterfront. Rapid economic growth is bringing cosmopolitan trappings to town—good museums, fancy hotels, fine restaurants, and first-rate entertainment among them. But these urban advantages aside, Jacksonville will always have more to offer than big-city sophistication. In addition to 20 miles of pristine oceanfront beach, the St. Johns River bisects the city, creating breathtaking marine views against a landscape of pine wilderness and parkland. A downtown riverside "festival marketplace" called Jacksonville Landing is just one of many places where you can enjoy a passing parade of seagulls, sandpipers, pelicans, and boats over a leisurely lunch.

A BRIEF HISTORY In this modern city, you'll also learn about some of America's earliest history. The Timucuan peoples and their ancestors lived here peacefully from ancient times until 1562 when French admiral and Huguenot leader Jean Ribault sailed into the St. Johns River in search of wealth and religious freedom, and with the short-lived hope of challenging Spanish supremacy in Florida. Though the French did found a settlement here in 1564, it was destroyed by the Spanish a year later and the entire colony was massacred. Today you can visit a replica of the French fort. Spain and England spent the next few centuries battling over the area, until, in 1821, Florida became a territory of the United States. At that time, this sleepy town had about two dozen residents and served merely as a cattle crossing. By the 1840s, Jacksonville—named in 1822 for Florida's first territorial governor, Gen. Andrew Jackson—had established itself as a viable port town exporting cotton and timber. After the Civil War, it emerged as a winter resort, and by the end of the 19th century, with the arrival of a railway system, it was drawing 75,000 tourists to its beaches each year. The tourist boom was cut short by a yellow fever epidemic in 1888, followed by a massive fire in 1901 that destroyed 146 city blocks and 2,368 buildings, including most of the downtown district. A new town rose from the ashes, emerging briefly as a center of the movie industry. There were over 30 studios here in the early 20th century, and Oliver Hardy's first movie was shot in one of them. The industry had moved on to Los Angeles by the 1920s, but by this time World War I had brought a boom in shipbuilding and the downtown skyline was underway. After World War II, Jacksonville became a leading southern financial center. More recent developments, in the mid-1980s, include the creation of riverfront recreational areas such as Jacksonville Landing and the Riverwalk. And football fever hit the city big time in 1993 with the acquisition of a new NFL team, the Jacksonville Jaguars, sparking a $60-million renovation of the Gator Bowl. Today Jacksonville is a thriving business center and tourist mecca—well worth a few days' visit.

ORIENTATION

INFORMATION   Write, call, or visit the **Jacksonville and the Beaches Convention & Visitors Bureau,** 3 Independent Dr. (just north of Water Street, at Main Street), Jacksonville, FL 32202 (tel. 904/798-9148), for informative literature, maps, brochures, events calendars, and suggestions on accommodations, restaurants, and shopping. It's open Monday through Friday from 8am to 5pm.

CITY LAYOUT   Jacksonville is bisected by the St. Johns River, so getting around will usually involve crossing a bridge or two. I-295 forms a beltway around the city, I-95 is the major north-south artery, and J. Turner Butler Boulevard (providing access to Jacksonville and Ponte Vedra Beaches) is the major west-east artery. Florida A1A runs from Mayport south along Atlantic Beach, Neptune Beach, Jacksonville Beach, and Ponte Vedra Beach, all bordering the Atlantic Ocean. The Main Street bridge spans the St. Johns River leading to the heart of downtown at its northern end.

GETTING AROUND

ARRIVING   A taxi from the airport will cost about $20 to downtown, about $40 to $50 to beach hotels.

BY TAXI   Taxis charge $1.25 when the meter drops, and $1.25 for each additional mile thereafter.

BY BUS   The Jacksonville Transit Authority provides local bus service seven days a week from about 5am to 3am. The fare is 60¢ for adults, free for seniors and children under 42 inches accompanied by an adult. For route information, call 630-3100.

BY WATER TAXI   Weather permitting, water taxis ply the route between the Riverwalk and Jacksonville Landing from about 11am to 10pm (hours vary a bit seasonally). The fare is $2 one-way, $3 round-trip.

WHAT TO SEE & DO

ATTRACTIONS

ANHEUSER-BUSCH BREWERY, 111 Busch Dr. Tel. 751-8118.

On its free self-guided tours given throughout the day, Anheuser-Busch explains the beer-making process and traces the company's growth from its inception in 1852. You'll also learn about the history of beer and the famed Budweiser Clydesdales, which originally pulled a gleaming-red wagon along Pestalozzi Street in St. Louis in 1933 to celebrate the repeal of Prohibition. From observation windows you'll view vast grain-mashing tanks; the brew kettle where hops are blended with wort; fermenting tanks; lager tanks where beer rests for aging, classification, and natural carbonation; and the bottling, labeling, and packaging operation. And at the end, there's a brewski for you (two gratis 10-ounce cups actually) and a bowl of Eagle brand pretzels (another Busch product) which you can enjoy in a comfortable lounge. A gift shop carries a large variety of Anheuser-Busch and Clydesdale logo merchandise.

Admission: Free. Parking is free on the premises.
Open: Mon–Sat 9am–4pm. **Directions:** Take I-95 north to the Busch Drive exit.

CUMMER GALLERY OF ART, 829 Riverside Ave., between Post and Fisk Sts. Tel. 356-6857.

Founded in 1958 when Mrs. Ninah M. H. Cummer donated her art collection to the city, this stunning museum with its fountain courtyard has a permanent collection that encompasses works from 2000 B.C. to the present. It's especially rich in American impressionist paintings, while additional highlights include a large collection of 18th-century Meissen porcelain and 18th- and early 19th-century Japanese Netsuke ivory carvings. Other galleries contain 18th- and 19th-century American portraits and landscapes; Roman, Greek, and Egyptian antiquities; Italian Renaissance paintings; works by baroque masters such as Rubens and Bernini; 18th-century English paintings; and 16th- through 19th-century Dutch and Flemish paintings.

Take a stroll outside to view the Cummer's spectacular English, azalea, and Italian gardens, the last with beautiful fountains, reflecting pools, and statuary created after the famous garden of the Villa Gamberaia near Florence. The gardens are shaded by a 200-year-old live oak, and vine-covered brick archways frame a scenic vista of the St. Johns River beyond. Bring the kids—an extensive facility called Art Connections features child-size hands-on exhibits, including computer art stations where youngsters can experiment with color mixing, perspective, animation, and optical illusion. The Cummer's gift shop is filled with objets d'art and jewelry.

Admission: $3 adults, $2 seniors over 62, $1 students and children 5–18, free for children under 5. Parking is free in the lot across the street.

Open: Tues–Fri 10am–4pm, Sat noon–5pm, Sun 2–5pm. **Closed:** New Year's Day, Easter, July 4, Labor Day, Thanksgiving, Christmas Day; early closing day on New Year's Eve.

FORT CAROLINE NATIONAL MEMORIAL, 12713 Fort Caroline Rd., off Monument Rd. Tel. 641-7155.

This 16th-century fort on the St. Johns River was a French outpost in the European struggle for ascendancy in the New World. The French hoped to compete for gold and silver, and establish a haven for persecuted French Protestants (Huguenots). French admiral and Huguenot leader Gaspard de Coligny sent Jean Ribault on an exploratory expedition to the area in 1562. Ribault erected a column to claim the land for France and signify eventual return and settlement, then sailed home to gather colonists and supplies. He found France in the midst of a civil war, and, unable to secure support there, turned to Queen Elizabeth of England. At first she agreed to help him, but then changed her mind and threw him in jail. In 1564, while Ribault was still imprisoned, de Coligny sent René de Laudonnière to Florida with several hundred soldiers, artisans, and colonists. They founded a settlement here named La Caroline in honor of King Charles IX. The native Timucuans initially welcomed the colonists, but the relationship soon soured. By 1565, the settlers were discontented with their meager lifestyle, disappointed in their search for riches, and on the brink of starvation. They were ready to abandon the colony and return to France when Ribault sailed into the harbor that August with seven ships loaded with food, supplies, and 600 settlers. But the French colony's relief was short-lived.

Ribault's arrival was viewed with alarm by the Spanish throne, and Philip II sent Admiral Pedro Menéndez de Avilés to rout the French. Menéndez established a base of operations in nearby St. Augustine, and Ribault sailed down the coast to attack and destroy it. However, a hurricane devastated his fleet. Menéndez rushed to take advantage of the situation, storming the poorly guarded fort and massacring 140 settlers. Returning south with booty from Fort Caroline, Menéndez's troops encountered Ribault and the shipwrecked Frenchmen and slaughtered 350 of them. Ribault's head was cut into quarters which were displayed on lances at each corner of the Spanish fort. The French never again gained a foothold in Florida.

Today a slightly smaller reconstruction of Fort Caroline near the original site is under the auspices of the National Park Service, as is the nearby 600-acre **Theodore Roosevelt Area.** This beautiful woodland, rich in history and undisturbed since the

Civil War, contains natural salt- and freshwater marsh and dune scrub. On a two-mile hike along a centuries-old park trail, you'll see a wide variety of birds (including bald eagles, wood storks, and pelicans), wildflowers, and maritime hammock forest. After the trail crosses Hammock Creek, you're in ancient Timucuan country, where their ancestors lived as far back as 500 B.C. Here, you're walking on vast shell mounds, 15 to 20 feet deep, resulting from the disposal of oyster shells (oysters were a mainstay of this ancient people's diet). Farther along is a cabin in the wilderness that belonged to reclusive brothers Willie and Saxon Browne. They lived without electricity or running water, and supported their needs by hunting and fishing. Saxon died in 1953, and Willie stayed on alone. In 1969 he dedicated his property to the Nature Conservancy for safekeeping, so that people could come here and "learn about God." The land became part of the National Park System in 1988.

I strongly suggest the guided tours of the fort and Theodore Roosevelt Area; park rangers provide a wealth of fascinating information about history, flora, and fauna. Arrive at the fort early, allowing about half an hour to see two films on these attractions. If you can't fit a guided tour into your schedule, pick up trail maps and information at the Fort Caroline Visitor Center. Bring binoculars if you have them; hiking boots are recommended but not mandatory. There are picnic areas at the fort and the trailhead.

Admission: Free. Parking is free at both sites.

Open: Daily 9am–5pm; 30-minute ranger-guided tours of Fort Caroline given weekends, followed by 1½-hour guided nature walks through the Theodore Roosevelt Area (call ahead for tour times). **Closed:** Christmas Day. **Directions:** Take Atlantic Boulevard east, make a left on Monument Road, and turn right on Fort Caroline Road. The Theodore Roosevelt Area is entered from Mt. Pleasant Road, about a mile southeast of the fort; look for an inconspicuous sign on your left that says TRAILHEAD PARKING and follow the narrow dirt road to the parking lot.

IRENE PARFUMS LAB, INC., 1141 W. Adams St., at I-95. Tel. 358-3206.

This is where Irène Saltzman creates, manufactures, and sells her own line of intoxicating perfumes, some of which emulate ancient fragrances used by the Romans and Egyptians. On a tour of her lab, you can see the processes involved in creating and making perfumes and smell undiluted oils such as myrrh, jasmine, musk, and sandalwood. Irène also operates a gift shop (china, silver, antiques) and art gallery on the premises.

Admission: Free.

Open: Tours given Mon–Fri 10am–4pm. **Directions:** Drive to the end of Adams Street and pass I-95 (be careful not to get on it).

JACKSONVILLE ART MUSEUM, 4160 Boulevard Center Dr., between Beach and Atlantic Blvds. Tel. 398-8336.

Founded in 1924, this is Jacksonville's oldest museum. It moved to its current building in 1964 and was expanded in 1973. On permanent display is a notable pre-Columbian collection which spans a geographical range from northern Mexico to southern Peru and a time range from 3000 B.C. through A.D. 1500. Totally unrelated is the museum's collection of art from 1945 to the present, including works by Picasso, Louise Nevelson, Roy Lichtenstein, and other noted artists. An ongoing series of temporary exhibits ranges from a major Andrew Wyeth retrospective to "Annie Leibovitz: Photographs 1970–1990." Three Mayan stelae (monumental stones) from A.D. 849–870 grace the museum's outdoor sculpture garden which adjoins a pine-shaded picnic area.

Admission: Free. Parking is free on the premises.

Open: Tues–Wed and Fri 10am–4pm, Thurs 10am–10pm, Sat–Sun 1–5pm. **Closed:** New Year's Day, July 4, Thanksgiving, and Christmas Day.

JACKSONVILLE LANDING, 2 Independent Dr., between Main and Pearl Sts. on the St. Johns River. Tel. 353-1188.

This six-acre dining/shopping/entertainment complex on the waterfront was developed by the Rouse Company in 1987. Its vast two-story Main Building adjoins other structures to form a semicircle facing the river and girding a central fountain courtyard. The Main Building entrance takes you into King's Road Market, where open-air stalls display an array of produce. Upstairs, a 10,000-square-foot facility called Ostrich Landing houses video and arcade games. At Dawson & Buckles Market, also upstairs, pushcart vendors hawk trendy wares. There are over 65 shops in the complex, including all the mall regulars—Laura Ashley, The Limited, Banana Republic, Victoria's Secret, The Gap, B. Dalton—and specialty emporia selling items like silk flowers. Diners have a choice of seven full-service restaurants. And Founders Food Hall—a sunny second-floor fast-food court with indoor and outdoor seating overlooking the river—offers international specialties. The Landing is the scene of hundreds of special events annually ranging from arts festivals to baseball-card shows, and holidays and sporting events are celebrated with gusto. From March through the end of December, there are free outdoor rock, blues, country, and jazz concerts every Friday and Saturday night. Call the above number to find out what's going on at the Landing during your stay. Weather permitting, water taxis ply the route between Jacksonville Landing and the Riverwalk between about 11am and 10pm (hours vary a bit seasonally); the fare is $2 each way, $1 for children under 12.

Admission: Free. Parking is 35¢ per half hour for the first three hours, 70¢ each half hour thereafter, to a $7.50 maximum daily charge ($5 evenings after 6pm and Sat–Sun and holidays).

Open: Mon–Sat 10am–9pm, Sun noon–5:30pm; restaurants and cafés may have later hours. **Closed:** Christmas Day. **Directions:** Take I-95 north, cross the Main Street bridge and make a right on Newnan Street, turn right again at Coastline Drive, and continue straight ahead to the parking lot.

JACKSONVILLE MUSEUM OF SCIENCE & HISTORY, 1025 Museum Circle (Gulf Life Dr.), on the Riverwalk between Main St. and San Marco Blvd. Tel. 396-7062.

This children's museum focuses on science and northern Florida history. Permanent exhibits on the first floor include a small aviary of Florida songbirds, a 10,000-gallon aquarium of Florida fish, and "Defense in a Boneless World," an exhibit on protective devices used by starfish, sea urchins, fiddler crabs, scorpions, and lizards. A sinuous pathway called "The Ribbon of Life" explores the history and ecology of the St. Johns River area. Over 100 Florida animals and natural-history specimens can be seen in the Living World and Living Room. And in Kidspace, activities include face painting, a play telephone system, a puppet theater, miniature cars and gas pumps, and a water table (kids can operate a water wheel, dam the water, and test items to see if they sink or float).

On the second floor, kids utilize interactive stations to test their knowledge of nutrition and exercise, learn about electricity and motion, and gauge reaction time and muscle endurance. "Bridges, Bridges, Bridges" explores Jacksonville's many bridges; kids get to build a bridge as well as run cars over and steer boats under a video of one. An exhibit called "Currents of Time" traces Jacksonville history from the days of the Timucuans to the 1940s. And "Maple Leaf: Port at Last" displays artifacts from an ongoing excavation of the *Maple Leaf,* a paddlewheeler sunk by a Confederate mine in the St. Johns River in 1864.

Planetarium shows for adults and children are scheduled daily (call ahead for show times, and, at the same time, inquire about science demonstrations, special shows, workshops, and lectures). A pleasant window-walled cafeteria serves light fare and offers outdoor seating. Note the flock of exotic chickens that live just outside the museum on the Riverwalk. Use the parking lot across San Marco Boulevard (it's free for up to two hours; if you need to stay longer, get a sticker at the museum).

Admission: $5 adults, $4 seniors, $3 children 3–12, free for kids under 3.

Open: Mon–Fri 10am–5pm, Sat 10am–6pm, Sun 1–6pm, (Sept hours vary; call ahead for details). **Closed:** New Year's Day, Thanksgiving, Christmas.

JACKSONVILLE ZOOLOGICAL GARDENS, 8605 Zoo Rd., off Heckscher Dr. Tel. 757-4462 or 757-4463.

This lushly landscaped zoo, bordering the Trout River, exhibits over 700 mammals, birds, and reptiles—many of them in large, natural enclosures that simulate native habitats. At the entrance is Main Camp Safari Lodge, containing a 30,000-gallon shark aquarium. Walk through the vast Birds of the Rift Valley Aviary en route to the Plains of the Serengeti, an 18-acre African-veldt habitat housing over 72 animal species. Here lions inhabit Mahali Pa Simba ("the place of the lion" in Swahili), with ostriches, giraffes, rhinos, elephants, and antelopes as neighbors. Okavango Delta, a walk-through aviary of exotic birds on the St. Johns River, adjoins the junglelike Okavango Village, home to Nile crocodiles, blue duikers, Kirk's dik-diks, and South African crested porcupines; it also contains a petting zoo offering close encounters with domestic African animals such as pygmy goats and miniature horses. You can watch the ever-entertaining antics of chimps on an outdoor island, and see cute newborns at the baby animal nursery. Chilean flamingos grace a marshy lagoon, and a boardwalk traverses naturally occurring Florida wetlands.

During warmer months, visitors can view alligator and crocodile feedings at 2pm. Two on-premises eateries offer light fare. A miniature train rode around the zoo costs $1.50. And there are daily animal shows and frequent special events (storytelling, lectures, workshops); inquire when you come in. Strollers can be rented.

Admission: $4 adults, $3 seniors 65 and over, $2.50 children 3–12, free for kids under 3. Shows are free.

Open: Daily 9am–5pm. **Closed:** New Year's Day, Thanksgiving, and Christmas.
Directions: Take I-95 north to Hecksher Drive (Exit 124) and follow the signs.

THE RIVERWALK, on the south bank of the St. Johns River between Crawdaddy's Restaurant and the Friendship Fountain. Tel. 396-4900.

This 1.2-mile wooden zigzag boardwalk bordering the St. Johns River is one of Jacksonville's most popular recreational areas. Throughout the day it's filled with joggers, tourists, and folks sitting on benches watching the passing parade of river boats and shore birds. The downtown skyline across the river is reflected on the water. The Friendship Fountain, at the west end, is, at 200 feet in diameter, the nation's largest self-contained fountain; it's especially beautiful at night when illuminated by 265 colored lights. Farther along, you'll pass the Navy Memorial (a bronze statue of a sailor peering out at the river), another memorial honoring the men and women who served in Operation Desert Storm, the Maritime Museum (with interesting nautically themed exhibits, many of them on Jacksonville's shipping history and the *Titanic*; admission is free), the Jacksonville Historical Society (a small history museum; admission is free), dozens of exotic chickens that graze in front of the Museum of Science & History, and a bust of Ponce de León. The Riverwalk is the scene of seafood fests, food tastings, parties, parades, and arts and crafts festivals. It has food vendors, picnic tables, and restaurants. Weather permitting, water taxis ply the route between the Riverwalk and Jacksonville Landing (see "Getting Around," above).

Admission: Free.
Open: Daily 24 hours. **Directions:** Take I-95 north to the Prudential Drive exit, make a right, and follow the signs; look for Crawdaddy's Restaurant on your left.

ZEPHANIAH KINGSLEY PLANTATION, 11676 Palmetto Ave., just off Fla. A1A. Tel. 251-3537.

A winding three-mile road under a canopy of trees, with lushly tropical foliage on either side, is what remains of an elegant palmetto drive that led to the 19th-century plantation of Zephaniah Kingsley. Here, on the banks of the Fort George River, Kingsley lived from 1813 to 1839 with his Senegalese wife, Anna Madgigaine Jai, whom he had originally purchased as a slave in Havana. A man of contradictions, he was a Quaker who believed that "the coloured race were superior to us, physically and morally," yet made a fortune in the slave trade and utilized over 200 slaves to tend his 30,000 acres of Sea Island cotton, sugar cane, sweet potatoes, corn fields, and citrus orchards. To motivate his work force, he utilized a system whereby each slave was assigned daily tasks, upon completion of which he or she could enjoy any remaining daylight hours. Ambitious slaves used the free time to grow their own crops, improve their dwellings, or moonlight for money, and Kingsley's will contained provisions to enable them to buy their freedom after his death. When Florida changed from a Spanish colony to an American territory in 1821, Kingsley was appointed to the Legislative Council by President Monroe. In 1838, alarmed by rising sentiment against free blacks, he sent Anna and their four children to Haiti to live.

Visitors can tour the two-story residence, kitchen house, barn/carriage house, and the remains of 23 slave cabins. Plantation artifacts and documents are on display.

Today the plantation is under the auspices of the National Park Service, and rangers provide very interesting tours.

Admission: Free; donations appreciated.

Open: Daily 9am–5pm; 30-minute tours are scheduled throughout the day; call ahead for times. **Closed:** Christmas. **Directions:** Take I-95 north to Heckscher Drive and follow the signs.

SPORTS & RECREATION

Fish, swim, snorkel, sail, sunbathe, or stroll on the sand dunes along Jacksonville's ocean **beaches**—they're just 12 to 15 miles from downtown via Atlantic, Beach, or J. Turner Butler Boulevards. As home to the PGA Tour's world headquarters, the city has over a dozen major public **golf** courses, some of them top-rated, and as home to the international Association of Tennis Professionals, it also abounds with high-quality **tennis** courts.

You can go **fishing** off the Jacksonville Beach Pier, just south of Beach Boulevard at Sixth Avenue (tel. 246-6001); rods, reels, and bait can be rented on the premises, and no license is required. Or fish for red snapper, grouper, sea bass, small sharks, and amberjack 15 to 25 miles offshore in the Atlantic Ocean aboard the *King Neptune* (tel. 264-0104), a 65-foot air-conditioned deep-sea fishing boat. It departs at 8am daily from 4378 Ocean St., a half mile south of the Mayport Ferry. The price is $35 per person, including all bait and tackle. Light fare can be purchased on board.

Sawgrass Stables, 23900 Marsh Landing Pkwy., off Fla. A1A in Ponte Vedra Beach (tel. 285-3791), offers daily trail rides and riding lessons. Call for details.

The colossal 85,000-seat **Gator Bowl,** 1400 E. Duval St., at Haines Street (tel. 630-3900 for information, 353-3309 to charge tickets), one of the nation's largest stadiums, is the site of the annual Florida/Georgia football game every October and the Gator Bowl every New Year's Eve. It hosts additional college football games September through December, NFL pre-season football games, rodeos, and motorsports events. And beginning in the fall of 1995 it will be the home of the new Jacksonville Jaguars (NFL) which will play 10 games here between September and December. Call toll free 800/618-8005 for ticket information.

Adjacent to it, and under the same auspices, is the 10,600-seat **Jacksonville Veterans Memorial Coliseum,** 1145 E. Adams St. (same phone numbers), a venue for NHL exhibition games, Division I college basketball games, ice-skating exhibitions, wrestling matches, and gymnastics championships.

Gator Bowl tickets run $25 to $35 and should be purchased as far in advance as possible. Tickets to the Florida/Georgia game are in the $20 to $30 range. There's paid parking for ticketed events. (Note: During Gator Bowl games, water taxis ply the route between Jacksonville Landing and the stadium; the fare is $5 round-trip.)

The 8,000-seat **Wolfson Park,** 1201 E. Duval St. (tel. 358-2846 for information, 353-3309 to charge tickets), is home to the minor-league Class AA Jacksonville Suns baseball team, whose season runs from April to September. The park also hosts motorcycle races, equestrian shows, and other sporting events. Ticket prices vary according to the event. There's paid parking for ticketed events.

Take the kids for self-guided nature walks along three marked paths at **Tree Hill,** a 40-acre urban wilderness at 7152 Lone Star Rd., off Arlington Road (tel. 724-4646). Signs indicate woodpecker holes, aspects of wetland vegetation, types of lichen, species of trees and shrubs, how dead trees serve as habitats for insects and lizards, and other interesting natural phenomena. A small natural history museum, gardens, and a picnic area are on the premises. It's open Monday through Saturday from 8:30am to 5pm. Admission is $1 for adults, 50¢ for children under 18.

WHERE TO STAY

SOUTHPOINT/BAYMEADOWS

Moderate

RESIDENCE INN BY MARRIOTT, 8365 Dix Ellis Trail (off I-95 at the Baymeadows exit), Jacksonville, FL 32256. Tel. 904/733-8088, or toll free 800/331-3131. Fax 904/731-8354. 112 suites. A/C TV TEL

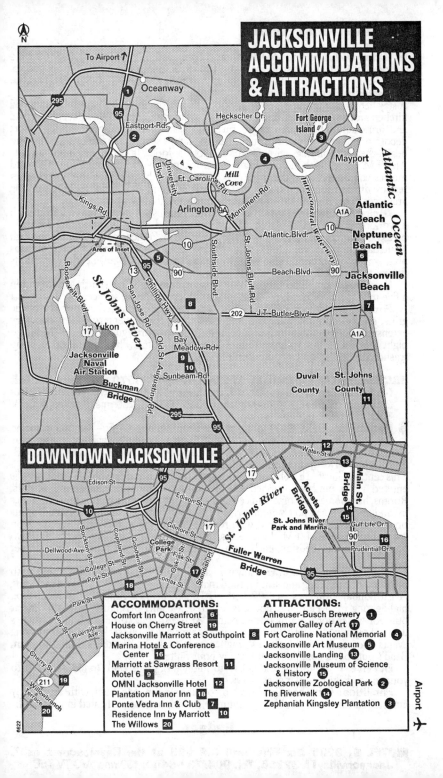

JACKSONVILLE ACCOMMODATIONS & ATTRACTIONS

N
To Airport ↑
Oceanway
295
95
Eastport Rd.
Heckscher Dr.
Fort George Island
Mayport
University Blvd.
Ft. Caroline Rd.
Mill Cove
Atlantic Ocean
Intracoastal Waterway
Kings Rd.
Arlington 9A
Monument Rd.
A1A
Atlantic Beach
Atlantic Blvd.
10
Neptune Beach
Area of Inset
10
95
90
Southside Blvd.
St. Johns Bluff Rd.
Beach Blvd.
90
Jacksonville Beach
Roosevelt Blvd.
St. Johns River
San Jose Rd.
Phillips Hwy.
13
202
J.T. Butler Blvd.
7
Yukon
17
Bay Meadow Rd.
A1A
Jacksonville Naval Air Station
Old St. Augustine Rd.
Sunbeam Rd.
9
10
Duval County
St. Johns County
Buckman Bridge
295
11
95

DOWNTOWN JACKSONVILLE

Edison St.
95
Water St.
12
13
Edison St.
17
Acosta Bridge
Main St. Bridge
10
Gilmore St.
17
St. Johns River
St. Johns River Park and Marina
14
15
Gulf Life Dr.
College Park
Fisk St.
Goodwin St.
Copeland St.
Dellwood Ave.
College St.
Post St.
Standish Pl.
Lomax St.
Fuller Warren Bridge
95
90
Prudential Dr.
16
18
17
Park St.
King St.
Riverside Ave.
Cherry St.
211
19
Willowbranch Terrace
20
Airport ✈

ACCOMMODATIONS:
Comfort Inn Oceanfront 6
House on Cherry Street 19
Jacksonville Marriott at Southpoint 8
Marina Hotel & Conference Center 16
Marriott at Sawgrass Resort 11
Motel 6 9
OMNI Jacksonville Hotel 12
Plantation Manor Inn 18
Ponte Vedra Inn & Club 7
Residence Inn by Marriott 10
The Willows 20

ATTRACTIONS:
Anheuser-Busch Brewery 1
Cummer Galley of Art 17
Fort Caroline National Memorial 4
Jacksonville Art Museum 5
Jacksonville Landing 13
Jacksonville Museum of Science & History 15
Jacksonville Zoological Park 2
The Riverwalk 14
Zephaniah Kingsley Plantation 3

6622

$ Rates (including extended continental breakfast): Mon–Thurs, $95–$109 suite for one; $100–$114 suite for two; $100–$130 penthouse for four to six people. Fri–Sun, about 40% less, subject to availability. AE, DC, DISC, ER, MC, V. **Parking:** Free self-parking.

A stay here is like having your own Jacksonville apartment, with a large fully equipped kitchen and comfortable living room area containing a convertible sofa, coffee table, and armchairs. Oak and bamboo furnishings, colorful floral-print fabrics, resort decorator colors (teal, peach, seafoam green), lamps shaped like fish or seashells, and beach-themed paintings give rooms a Florida look. In-room amenities include AM/FM alarm-clock radios, remote-control cable TVs with free HBO (VCRs and movies can be rented at the front desk), and ironing boards. Two-story penthouses feature dining rooms and two baths. Many rooms and all penthouses have working fireplaces. This is one of the few hotels in town that allows pets.

Dining/Entertainment: The comfortably furnished gatehouse—a lounge with a working fireplace, CD player, library, games, and toys—is the setting for daily breakfast buffets that include pancakes, waffles, or French toast. Monday through Thursday the gatehouse additionally offers complimentary evening buffets (perhaps pizza, tacos, or barbecue) plus beer, wine, and soft drinks. Many nearby restaurants deliver to the hotel.

Services: Complimentary daily newspaper, complimentary shuttle service within a five-mile radius of hotel, complimentary grocery-shopping service.

Facilities: Outdoor swimming pool and sun deck, three whirlpools, barbecue grills, sports court for volleyball and basketball, complimentary use of two very extensively equipped nearby health clubs and tennis courts, guest activities (Monday-night football parties, volleyball games, Bingo nights, many holiday events), coin-op washer/dryers, laptop computers on request.

JACKSONVILLE MARRIOTT AT SOUTHPOINT, 4670 Salisbury Rd. (off I-95 at J. Turner Butler Blvd.), Jacksonville, FL 32256. Tel. 904/296-2222, or toll free 800/228-9290. Fax 904/296-7561. 250 rms, 6 suites. A/C TV TEL

$ Rates: Sun–Thurs, $109 for up to four people in a room, Fri–Sat, $69 including full buffet breakfast for two; $175–$275 suite. Lower advance-purchase rates subject to availability. Inquire about golf packages. AE, CB, DC, DISC, ER, JCB, MC, V. **Parking:** Free self-parking.

This centrally located hotel, just minutes from the beach and downtown attractions, is entered via a plushly furnished marble-floored lobby with Chinoiserie accents. Rooms, handsomely decorated in celadon green or tan, feature mahogany furnishings in traditional styles, pretty floral-print bedspreads, and gilt-framed Oriental prints on the walls. They're equipped with remote-control cable TVs (with Spectravision movie channels), AM/FM clock radios, in-room irons and ironing boards, and two phones (desk and bedside, each with two lines). "King-bed rooms" have sleeper sofas.

Dining/Entertainment: Banyans, a softly lit resort-style restaurant with bleached-oak paneling and seating amid many large plants, serves all meals, including lavish Sunday brunches (see "Where to Dine," below); American regional fare, highlighting fresh Florida seafood, is featured. Weather permitting, you can dine at outdoor tables bordered by potted palms. At the *simpático* Beau's Lounge, there's dancing nightly. Additional diversions include blackjack on weeknights and sporting events aired on a large-screen TV. Light fare is available. Weekdays from 5 to 8pm, Beau's puts out a complimentary happy hour buffet.

Services: Room service (6:30am to midnight), gratis *USA Today* delivered to your room daily, 24-hour guest services.

Facilities: Gift shop, health club, outdoor swimming pool with attractively landscaped sun deck, pool bar (in summer), whirlpool, sauna, heated indoor pool.

Budget

MOTEL 6, 8285 Dix Ellis Trail (off I-95 at the Baymeadows exit), Jacksonville, FL 32256. Tel. 904/731-8400. 109 rms. A/C TV TEL

$ Rates: $27 single. Additional person $4 extra. Children under 17 stay free in parents' room. AE, CB, DC, DISC, MC, V. **Parking:** Free self-parking.

Accommodations at this centrally located branch of the budget Motel 6 chain are far back from the highway, so there's no traffic noise. Clean, attractive standard motel units contain satellite TVs with HBO movie stations. "King-bed rooms" have sofa beds. A small free-form pool is on the premises, a Denny's coffee shop is within walking distance, and dozens of restaurants are just a few minutes away by car. Pets are allowed.

THE RIVERWALK/JACKSONVILLE LANDING
Moderate

MARINA HOTEL & CONFERENCE CENTER, 1515 Prudential Dr. (on the Riverwalk), Jacksonville, FL 32207. Tel. 904/396-5100, or toll free 800/342-4605. Fax 904/396-7154. 307 rms, 18 suites. A/C TV TEL
$ Rates: Sun–Thurs, $79–$89 single; $99 double. Fri–Sat, $58 single; $68 double. $175–$365 suite. Additional person $10 extra. Children under 18 stay free in parents' room. High-end rates are for river views. Inquire about packages. AE, CB, DC, MC, V. **Parking:** Free self-parking.

This five-story hotel on the St. Johns River is appropriately nautical looking, from its ultramarine roofing to its enormous shiplike lobby with exposed pipes and corrugated-tin ceiling. Classical music is played in public areas. Rooms—half with river views—are very cheerful, with shell-motif bleached-oak furnishings, dusty-rose carpeting, Matisse-like paintings of beach scenes on the walls, and bright abstract bedspread fabrics. They're equipped with AM/FM alarm-clock radios and remote-control satellite TVs with Spectravision movie options.

Dining/Entertainment: The very pretty Café St. John, offering breakfast, lunch, and dinner, is festively decorated in bright colors with seating around a tiled fountain. It serves American fare, highlighting steaks and seafood. Equally pleasant is the lobby lounge, with indoor tables under white canvas umbrellas, where guests gather to watch Monday-night football; light fare and frozen tropical drinks are served.

Services: Room service, complimentary *USA Today* at front desk, complimentary morning coffee in lobby, airport shuttle ($8 each way), travel agency (handles airline tickets and car rentals).

Facilities: Two tennis courts, medium-size swimming pool/sun deck, small video-game arcade with pool table, gift/sundries shop.

OMNI JACKSONVILLE HOTEL, 245 Water St. (between Pearl and Hogan Sts.), Jacksonville, FL 32202. Tel. 904/355-OMNI, or toll free 800/THE-OMNI. Fax 904/350-0359. 350 rms, 4 suites. A/C MINIBAR TV TEL
$ Rates: Mon–Wed, $114–$124 single; $124–$135 double. Thurs–Sun, $99 single or double. Club Level $10 extra. Additional person $15 extra. Children under 18 stay free in parents' room. Inquire about packages. AE, CB, DC, DISC, MC, V. **Parking:** Self-parking, $6 Mon–Thurs, $4 Fri–Sun; valet parking, $8 per night.
Directly across the street from Jacksonville Landing shops, restaurants, and nightlife, the Omni, catering primarily to a corporate clientele, is also a great choice for tourists. Very attractive rooms are decorated in soft hues (muted greens, peach, tan, cream) with blond-wood furnishings. All offer remote-control cable TVs (with free HBO and pay-movie options) and AM/FM alarm-clock radios. Especially nice are corner rooms with king-size beds and sofas. The 15th and 16th floors comprise a Club Level where guests enjoy upscale amenities and services, along with use of a plush private lounge offering panoramic city views.

Dining/Entertainment: The garden-motif Juliette's Restaurant & Bistro, with seating overlooking the plant-filled atrium lobby, serves American-regional fare at all meals, including a Sunday jazz brunch. The elegant adjoining lounge offers complimentary hors d'oeuvres from 5 to 7pm weekdays, blackjack tables, and occasional live entertainment at night.

Services: Room service, complimentary shoeshine, concierge, car-rental desk.
Facilities: Rooftop river-view swimming pool/sun deck, small exercise room

(guests also have access to a state-of-the-art health club just across the street for a small fee), full business services, large gift/sundries shop.

BED & BREAKFAST

These charming B&Bs, in the historic Riverside district, are 10 minutes from downtown attractions.

HOUSE ON CHERRY STREET, 1844 Cherry St. (on the St. Johns River),
   Jacksonville, FL 32205. Tel. 904/384-1999. Fax 904/981-2998. 4 rms (all
   with bath). A/C TV
$ Rates (including full breakfast): $75–$90 single or double. Additional person $15
   extra. No small children accepted. MC, V. **Parking:** Free on premises.
This colonial-style wood-frame house nestles in a tree-shaded cul-de-sac on the St. Johns River. The entrance hall is strewn with Persian rugs and centers on a piecrust table used for lavish floral displays; a collection of 19th-century woven wool coverlets adorns the walls. French doors open to a delightful screened-in back porch furnished with rocking chairs; it overlooks an expanse of tree-shaded lawn (where guests play croquet) leading to the river. A full breakfast—fresh-baked muffins, croissants or breads, an entree (perhaps Gouda soufflé or eggs Benedict), fresh fruit, juice, and coffee—is served daily in a pleasant dining room furnished with antiques.

Rooms are exquisitely decorated. You might select the lovely river-view Rose Room, with a canopied four-poster bed, late 18th-century walnut armoire, shelves displaying objets d'art, and pretty floral-print wallpaper. A four-poster (with a hand-crocheted antique lace canopy) also graces the Duck Room, which has shelves of books, a beautiful wool-plaid-upholstered couch, and a bath with Victorian tub and duck-themed wallpaper. It, too, offers river views. Ducks are rather a theme here; hundreds of antique decoys are displayed in rooms and public areas. All accommodations offer adjacent sitting rooms, AM/FM alarm-clock radios, ceiling fans, and remote-control TVs. They're supplied with fresh flowers, books, and magazines.

Complimentary wine and hot and cold hors d'oeuvres are served daily at 6pm on the patio or in the dining room, and an upstairs refrigerator is stocked with free soft drinks, bottled water, and beer. There are bicycles for guest use. Genial owner/hosts Carol and Merrill Anderson are tennis buffs who referee U.S. Open matches. They keep a gentle pet greyhound—formerly a racing dog—named Streak. No smoking permitted.

PLANTATION MANOR INN, 1630 Copeland St. (between Oak and Park
   Sts.), Jacksonville, FL 32204. Tel. 904/384-4630. 8 rms (all with bath).
   A/C TV TEL
$ Rates (including full breakfast): $85–$135 single or double. Additional person $10
   extra. AE, DC, MC, V. **Parking:** Free on premises.
This three-story plantation-style home, fronted by a spacious colonnaded veranda, was built in 1905. Its interior features glossy pine floors and gorgeous cypress paneling, wainscotting, and carved moldings. Breakfast—breakfast meats, eggs, fresh fruit, juice, fresh-baked muffins and breads, and coffee—is served in a lovely dining room with a crystal chandelier above a lace-clothed table, swagged mint-green draperies, and a working fireplace. Or, weather permitting, you might take the morning meal on an enclosed brick patio, a delightful setting with ivied walls, · flower beds and pots of geraniums, outdoor statuary, and garden furnishings under the shade of a massive live oak tree. The patio also contains a lap pool and whirlpool spa. Another public area is a comfortable living room with a stunning cypress-framed ceramic-tile fireplace. And there's also a big furnished wraparound porch on the second floor with seating amid potted geraniums, hibiscus, and bougainvillea.

Accommodations are beautifully furnished with antiques. Yours might have an 1870s French bedroom suite, a king-size mahogany four-poster made up with a Laura Ashley rose-motif bedspread and ruffled pillow shams, an 18th-century Louis XVI–style bed with a lilac-motif spread, an Early American oak armoire and rolltop desk, Oriental silk rugs, or 19th-century cherrywood Mission pieces. There are wonderful curtain treatments throughout, all rooms are equipped with ceiling fans and clock radios, and residential touches include shelves of objets d'art, baskets filled with Victorian dried-flower arrangements, decorative fireplaces, and marvelous old paintings. Amenities include nightly turn-down with a chocolate mint and brandy, fresh fruit in every room, and a public refrigerator stocked with complimentary beer and soft drinks.

THE WILLOWS ON THE ST. JOHNS RIVER, 1849 Willow Branch Terrace, Jacksonville, FL 32205. Tel. 904/387-9152 or 904/389-6394. 2 rms (both with bath). A/C MINIBAR TV TEL

$ Rates (including full breakfast): $75–$85 per room. No small children accepted. No credit cards. **Parking:** Free on premises.

This charming riverside B&B occupies an ivy-covered Mediterranean-style stucco house on a tranquil tree-lined street. Inside, guests have access to a vast terra-cotta–floored living room with a beamed pecky-cypress ceiling, serpentine Moorish furnishings, a hand-painted German piano, and a working fireplace flanked by brass torchiers; French tapestries adorn its white stucco walls. A lacy black wrought-iron gate heralds the dining room, which overlooks the river. Full breakfasts—fresh fruit, juice, breakfast meats, homemade muffins and biscuits, a main course (perhaps French toast or cheese soufflé), and coffee—are served here on a handsome oak table. The back lawn, which faces on the river and contains a 50-foot swimming pool, is planted with magnolias, palms, pines, and live oaks. Guests can sit out on a porch or balcony portico, sipping complimentary wine and watching boats gliding along the river.

The jade-and-cream bedroom downstairs is Asian themed, with a Chinese carpet, silk embroideries, and chairs upholstered in a pagoda motif. A nonworking fireplace is used to display an arrangement of silk and dried flowers. The other, more ornate accommodation has a dusty-rose velvet sofa with throw pillows, a French floral-pattern rug on an oak floor, a Venetian-style candelabra chandelier ornamented with ceramic roses, and a suite of bedroom furnishings embellished with ormulu floral decorations. French doors open to a private balcony with Moorish-style Corinthian columns framing arched windows overlooking the river. Both rooms have beautifully tiled baths and refrigerators stocked with free beer, wine, and soft drinks. Charming hostess Mary Collins pampers guests with fruit, liqueurs, chocolates, and fresh flowers on arrival. No smoking permitted on premises.

PONTE VEDRA BEACH RESORTS

Originally an executive retreat for a titanium-mining company, Ponte Vedra Beach is one of Florida's ritziest areas. Officially, it's part of St. Augustine, but since the deluxe resorts described here are closer to Jacksonville, I've listed them in this section.

Expensive

MARRIOTT AT SAWGRASS RESORT, 1000 TPC Blvd. (off Fla. A1A between U.S. 210 and J. Turner Butler Blvd.), Ponte Vedra Beach, FL 32082. Tel. 904/285-7777, or toll free 800/457-GOLF or 800/228-9290. Fax 904/285-0906. 323 rms, 121 suites/villas. A/C MINIBAR TV TEL

$ Rates: $115–$189 single or double in standard rooms and villa rooms (additional person $20 extra; children under 17 stay free in parents' room); $175–$240 one-bedroom villa; $265–$460 two-bedroom villa; $325–$550 three-bedroom villa. Higher rates reflect peak season (mid-Feb to mid-Jun). Inquire about golf, tennis, and honeymoon packages. Lower advance-purchase rates subject to availability. AE, CB, DC, DISC, JCB, MC, V. **Parking:** Free self-parking, $8 per night valet parking.

Entered via a towering skylit atrium lobby, with a waterfall cascading into a lush tropical garden, this stunning 4,800-acre resort occupies a verdant landscape of golf greens, waterfalls, lakes, and lagoons spanned by graceful wooden bridges. Forests of ancient oaks and magnolias form a backdrop for prim manicured lawns and flower beds. The grounds are home to hundreds of blue herons, egrets, and other shore birds.

Rooms in the main building are cheerfully decorated in teal hues, with birch furnishings and splashy floral prints adding peach, mauve, and lavender accents. All are equipped with bedside and desk phones, clock radios, and remote-control cable TVs with Spectravision movie options. Rooms with king-size beds have sofas. One- and two-bedroom villas on or near a golf course offer fully equipped kitchens, living rooms with ceiling fans, and large furnished patios or balconies. And especially luxurious are one- to three-bedroom beachfront villas furnished in residential style with huge kitchens, living rooms with working fireplaces, full dining rooms, and large screened wooden decks.

Dining/Entertainment: The ultra-elegant Augustine Room is the resort's gourmet dining room (see "Where to Dine," below). The country club–like Café on the Green, a lovely plant-filled restaurant with a picture window overlooking the golf course, serves breakfast, lunch, dinner, and Sunday brunch. Adjoining it is Cascades, a multilevel, tropically themed piano bar below an indoor waterfall. The upscale Cabana Club restaurant at the beach serves nouvelle cuisine; it has an outdoor patio and an adjoining lounge featuring nightly music for dancing. The 100th Hole, a poolside bar, serves light fare and frozen tropical drinks; it has open-air seating on a wooden deck with umbrella tables. Champs, an on-premises dance club, is described in "Evening Entertainment," below.

Services: Room service, car-rental desk, complimentary shuttle to/from the beach and golf courses, newspaper delivery/nightly turn-down on request, airport transfer available.

Facilities: Two swimming pools (one Olympic size), kiddie pool, two whirlpools, pool/beach accessories shop, 21 tennis courts, two first-rate health clubs, five championship golf courses (with 99 holes, Marriott at Sawgrass is America's second-largest golf resort; two of its courses are top-ranked), golf/tennis pro shop and teaching pros/clinics, four driving ranges, six putting greens, gratis use of 2½-mile private beach at the nearby Cabana Club, on-premises rentals (windsurf boards, bicycles, fishing poles), lagoons stocked with wide-mouth bass for fishing, nature and biking trails, horseback riding, Sawgrass Village (a complex of boutiques and specialty shops), gift shop.

The Grasshopper Gang, a children's program, offers daily activities for ages 3 to 12, a recreation room, and a playground; open Monday through Saturday from 10am to 3pm, it costs $20 per child, lunch included. There's also a teen program for ages 13 to 15.

PONTE VEDRA INN & CLUB, 200 Ponte Vedra Blvd. (off Fla. A1A), Ponte Vedra Beach, FL 32082. Tel. 904/285-1111, or toll free 800/234-7842. Fax 904/285-2111. 182 rms, 20 suites. A/C MINIBAR TV TEL

$ Rates: Dec–Feb, $95–$115 single or double. Mar–May, $175–$195 single or double. June–Aug, $125–$145 single or double. Sept–Nov, $145–$165 single or double. Suite $70–$100 extra. Additional person $8 extra; children under 12 stay free in parents' room. Highest rates for oceanfront views, lowest for golf course views. Inquire about golf, tennis, spa, and other packages. AE, CB, DC, DISC, MC, V. **Parking:** Free self- and valet parking.

Here's a chance to pamper yourself at a luxurious 300-acre private country club and spa that has been "enjoyed by some of this country's finest families" since 1928. The Ponte Vedra Inn is ultra-elegant from the moment you drive up to its manicured front lawn that doubles as a putting green. Inside, a charming lobby adjoins the lodgelike Great Lounge, a sedate precinct under a beamed cypress ceiling with overstuffed sofas and armchairs and massive fireplaces at either end.

Spacious rooms—all with furnished patios or balconies—are individually decorated in beachy pastel colors (aqua, peach, mauve) and furnished with bleached-wood pieces. They're enhanced by lovely fabrics and aesthetically pleasing valence and cornice treatments. Some have four-poster or sleigh beds. In-room amenities include wet bars, coffee makers, safes, ceiling fans, AM/FM alarm-clock radios, and remote-control cable TVs with free HBO. You'll find a hairdryer, scale, luxury bath products, and plush terry robe in the bath, a cosmetic mirror and double sink in your large dressing room. Microwave ovens and small refrigerators are available on request.

Dining/Entertainment: Breakfast and dinner are served in the formal Gourmet Room, a genteel setting with beautifully appointed white-linened tables, candlelit at night. A traditional continental menu features steaks, chops, and seafood. The adjoining Audubon Lounge offers nightly piano bar entertainment. Steak and seafood are also on the menu at the casual turquoise-and-peach Florida Room, open for dinner only. The Golf Club Restaurant, with picture windows overlooking the greens and a lagoon, serves reasonably priced American fare at lunch; a bar/lounge adjoins. The Patio, open only for lunch March through October, serves salads, sandwiches, and frozen tropical drinks; it has outdoor seating at umbrella tables. And the elegant Seafoam Dining Room, with tiered ocean-view seating, features American/ continental lunches and dinners; a pianist entertains at dinner, and there's dancing on Friday and Saturday nights to a live trio in the adjoining Seahorse Lounge. The spa has its own little ocean-view restaurant serving light lunches to women enjoying "days of beauty." And the High Tides Lounge, with umbrella tables on a patio overlooking the ocean, offers light fare and frozen drinks.

Services: 24-hour room service, concierge, executive business center, nightly bed turn-down, shoeshine, complimentary newspaper each morning.

Facilities: Three outdoor swimming pools (one Olympic-size), kiddie pool, oceanfront whirlpool, two championship 18-hole golf courses, 15 tennis courts, golf/tennis pro shops and instruction, upscale gift/resortwear shop, flower shop, the Surf Shop (beach apparel/resortwear), beach rentals (catamarans, cabañas, boogie boards, umbrellas, bicycles), private sand beach and boardwalk, steam, sauna, extensive health club, sand volleyball court, library, planned activities for adults and children.

A gorgeous on-premises spa offers ocean-view massage rooms, all hair-salon services, herbal and seaweed wraps, facials, hydrotherapy, fitness training, waxing, manicures, pedicures, nutrition consultations, and much more; treat yourself to a "day of beauty."

A child-care facility called the Nursery provides care and activities for children 6 months to 6 years; the charge is $3 per child, $1 for each additional child. In summer there's a full youth camp program for children 4 to 12.

JACKSONVILLE BEACH

Inexpensive

COMFORT INN OCEANFRONT, 1515 N. 1st St. (off Fla. A1A), Jacksonville Beach, FL 32250. Tel. 904/241-2311, or toll free 800/654-8776. Fax 904/249-3830. 177 rms, 3 suites. A/C TV TEL

$ Rates (including continental breakfast): $59.50–$69.50 standard single or double, $65–$75 single or double with pool or ocean view, $75–$95 single or double oceanfront; $125–$135 suite. Additional person $10 extra. Children under 18 stay free in parents' room. AE, CB, DC, DISC, ER, JCB, MC, V. **Parking:** Free self-parking.

Fronted by 3,000 feet of pristine white sand beach, the Comfort Inn offers spiffy-looking accommodations and numerous facilities. Rooms are decorated in raspberry or seafoam-green color schemes, with bleached-wood or oak furnishings and paintings of beach scenes and shore birds on the walls. All have balconies (screened patios on the first level) and are equipped with remote-control cable TVs with pay movie options. Microwave/refrigerator units are available for $7 a night. An especially good deal here is a honeymoon suite with Jacuzzi tub, living room area, microwave oven (dishes and cooking utensils are supplied), refrigerator, and wet bar.

Dining/Entertainment: Continental breakfast and light fare are served in Lite Bites, a small poolside eatery. Kokomo's, a beautiful pine-paneled lounge with a window wall overlooking the ocean, features live music for dancing nightly April through Labor Day, as well as a pool table and dart boards. Complimentary hors d'oeuvres are served weekdays at happy hour. In season you can order light fare at

Kokomo's, and, weather permitting, there's outdoor seating at umbrella tables. An oceanside cabaña bar is also operational in peak season.

Facilities: Large pool with rock waterfalls and palm-fringed sun deck, secluded grotto whirlpool, small fitness room, gift/sundries shop/convenience store, multicourt sand volleyball park (scene of major tournaments), rentals (summer only; surfboards, boogie boards, bicycles, kayaks, windsurfers, beach chairs and umbrellas).

WHERE TO DINE
VERY EXPENSIVE

THE AUGUSTINE ROOM, in the Marriott at Sawgrass Resort, 1000 TPC Blvd. (off Fla. A1A between U.S. 210 and J. Turner Butler Blvd.), Ponte Vedra Beach. Tel. 285-7777.
　Cuisine: AMERICAN/CONTINENTAL. **Reservations:** Recommended.
$ Prices: Appetizers $7.95–$11.95; main courses $21.95–$31.95. AE, CB, DC, DISC, JCB, MC, V.
　Open: Dinner only, Tues–Sat 6:30–10pm.

The oak-paneled Augustine Room is Jacksonville's most formal dining room. Tables covered in ecru Belgian linen sparkle with fine china, crystal, silver, and vases of fresh flowers. Seating is in plush leather banquettes or Regency-style chairs, and ultra-suede walls are hung with hand-tinted etchings and lithographs of turn-of-the-century St. Augustine. Men are requested to wear jackets.

Freshly shucked baked oysters filled with backfin crabmeat and topped with mornay sauce and fresh-grated parmesan make a great beginning to your meal here. Another possibility is an enchilada stuffed with julienne of Maine lobster served with a crisp-fried smoked scallop wonton and crisscrossed with a spicy tomato coulis. A dish of sautéed jumbo shrimp was served atop a bed of nutmeg-flavored spinach and angel-hair pasta garnished with roasted pine nuts in basil-cream sauce. Also excellent was the rack of lamb—a fan of slices served with orange marmalade sauce, dauphinois potatoes, and an array of vegetables. Sorbet is served between courses. Desserts are fittingly sumptuous. You might opt for banana-strawberry mousse in a gingerbread-cinnamon horn served atop a strawberry-marbelized custard and garnished with rum-soaked strawberries and banana slices. The restaurant's extensive wine list is international in scope.

EXPENSIVE

THE CHART HOUSE, 601 Hendricks Ave., at Prudential Dr. (on the Riverwalk). Tel. 398-3353.
　Cuisine: STEAK/SEAFOOD/PRIME RIB. **Reservations:** Recommended. **Directions:** Take I-95N and make a right at the Prudential Drive exit, a left at Hendricks Avenue, and a right into the Marina complex.
$ Prices: Appetizers $4.25–$7.95; main courses $13.50–$23. AE, CB, DC, DISC, MC, V.
　Open: Dinner only, Sun–Thurs 5:30–10pm, Fri–Sat 5:30–11pm.

This beautiful restaurant, with a window wall overlooking the St. Johns River, was designed by a protégé of Frank Lloyd Wright named Kendrick Kellogg.
Like Wright, Kellogg highlights natural elements—a stone waterfall at the entrance, an arched cypress ceiling crossed by rough-hewn beams, and seating in roomy circular booths, enclosed by teakwood, amid ficus trees, ferns, and potted palms. Stone columns serve as a base for massive planters of cascading philodendrons. It's almost like dining outdoors. Candlelit tables are topped with laminated oak-framed world maps—a Chart House tradition. The Chart House is a national chain, but each location is different.

There are few appetizers on the menu, because your main-dish price includes—along with a basket of hot fresh-baked sourdough and cakey brown squaw breads—unlimited selections from an excellent and very extensive salad bar. If you want something additional before your main dish, try the New England clam chowder, a thick, creamy soup with big chunks of potato and clams. For a main course, I suggest baked grouper, lightly dredged in garlicky herbed breadcrumbs, or, if you're in a meatier mood, filet mignon with béarnaise sauce. The Chart House serves fresh seafood and midwestern corn-fed Grade-A beef, aged and cut on the premises. Main courses are accompanied by yummy Chart House rice tossed with toasted almonds and bits of pimiento and pineapple. For dessert, indulge in decadent mud pie—coffee mocha ice cream on a buttery chocolate cookie crust topped with fudge sauce, real whipped cream, and butter-toasted almonds. There's a full bar, and a sizable wine list, with premium wines available by the glass.

STERLING'S CAFE, 3551 St. Johns Ave., between Talbot and Ingleside Aves. Tel. 387-0700.
   Cuisine: AMERICAN/CONTINENTAL. **Reservations:** Recommended.
$ **Prices:** Appetizers $7.50–$7.95; main courses $6.75–$8.50 at lunch, $15.95–$23.95 at dinner; Sun jazz brunch $14.95 prix fixe. AE, CB, DC, DISC, MC, V.
   Open: Lunch Mon–Sat 11am–2:30pm; dinner Mon–Thurs 5:30–10pm, Fri–Sat 5:30–11pm; brunch Sun 11am–2:30pm.

This very *simpático* restaurant has a lovely interior. White-trimmed dark-cocoa walls are hung with stunning works of art, potted ivy topiaries grace beautifully appointed white-linened tables (candlelit at night), and a gorgeous flower arrangement adorns the bar. French doors lead to a lovely plant-filled fountain patio under a striped awning. There's also seating out front on a patio fronted by planters of rhododendrons. Soft jazz or classical music add to Sterling's sophisticated ambience.
   Begin your dinner with a sautéed black-bean cake served with piquant salsa, warm corn relish, and a dollop of guacamole. This is also your chance to try fried green tomatoes, here sautéed in golden cornmeal batter and topped with spicy hollandaise and warm crumbled Montrachet cheese. Pasta, tossed with a flavorful mix of seasonal mushrooms, sun-dried tomatoes, and prosciutto in sage-flavored marsala-cream sauce, is available as an appetizer or main course. Also scrumptious: chicken Tchoupitoulis—chicken breasts brushed with Cajun spices and sautéed with crunchy morsels of tasso, onions, mushrooms, potatoes, and peppers. Topped with béarnaise sauce, it was served with a couscous and broccoli soufflé. All main courses include chewy sourdough bread served with herbed extra-virgin olive oil and a superb house salad. Lunch features salads and sandwiches. And Sunday brunch, with live jazz, includes a salad buffet, fruit juices, fresh fruit, homemade muffins and cinnamon rolls, breads and pastries, coffee, and an alcoholic beverage, along with such main dishes as poached Norwegian salmon or eggs Benedict. Sterling's offers a good selection of domestic and imported wines—many available by the glass—to complement your meal. And desserts range from an ambrosial crème brûlée to apple-cream pie.

MODERATE

CAFE CARMON, 1986 San Marco Blvd., between Carlo St. and Naldo Ave. Tel. 399-4488.
   Cuisine: AMERICAN. **Reservations:** Not accepted.
$ **Prices:** Appetizers $4.95–$7.95; main courses $5.95–$7.95 at lunch, $7.50–$14.95 at dinner. AE, DC, DISC, MC, V.
   Open: Mon–Thurs 11am–11pm, Fri–Sat 11am–midnight; breakfast/brunch Mon–Fri 7–10am, Sat 8–10am, Sun 9am–3pm.

This comfy and casual restaurant is located in the heart of the San Marco shopping district. During the week it's a mecca for foot-weary shoppers, while on Friday and Saturday nights the place is jammed with post-movie and theatergoers who come in for cappuccino and dessert. The sunny interior is decorated in pristine black and white, with fans and schoolroom lights suspended from a lofty ceiling and stark gallery-white walls hung with attractive paintings. There's also café seating out front on a terra-cotta patio.
   At lunch or dinner, you can order delicious sandwiches (including a classic Reuben) and salads such as sautéed goat cheese with sun-dried tomatoes, toasted hazelnuts, cilantro, and mixed greens in a tangy vinaigrette. Dinner options also include penne pasta tossed with sautéed salmon in dill-flavored white wine cream sauce, boneless pork chop with pan-seared apples in praline-cream sauce, and

blackened fresh catch (often grouper) sautéed in cumin butter and white wine. Dinner courses are served with house salad, warm bread, and a side dish (perhaps red-skin potato salad or pasta primavera). Portions are huge, everything is made from scratch, and it's all first-rate. Leave room for dessert. The rich, moist carrot cake—a huge slab studded with raisins and walnuts, layered with praline cream, slathered with cream-cheese icing, and topped with toasted coconut—is the *ne plus ultra* of its genre. Premium wines are available by the glass. Great breakfast/brunch fare here, too.

CIAO GIANNI RISTORANTE, Jacksonville Landing. Tel. 353-2626.

Cuisine: ITALIAN. **Reservations:** Recommended.

$ Prices: Appetizers $4.95–$5.50 at lunch, $4.95–$6.95 at dinner; main courses $5.50–$8.95 at lunch, $10.95–$15.95 at dinner. AE, MC, V.

Open: Sun–Thurs 11am–10:30pm, Fri–Sat 11am–11pm (lunch menu available until 3:30pm).

This casual Jacksonville Landing restaurant is popular with locals, especially for dessert and espresso after shows at the nearby Civic Center (park in the Landing lot). Sunny during the day, candlelit at night, it has marble-top tables, cherrywood beams and columns, and interior leaded-glass windows. Owner/chef Giovanni Recupito, from Salerno, tosses pizzas and pastas in an open display kitchen. Italian music or light jazz enhance the ambience. In good weather, you can dine al fresco under a bright-yellow awning.

Appetizers of fried mozzarella, calamari, or zucchini come with chunky marinara sauce. Thin-crust pizza—perhaps quatro formaggi, topped with meunster, mozzarella, fontina, and romano cheeses—is another good beginning. Or you might request a scrumptious starter salad of fresh mozzarella with roasted red and green peppers in herbed vinaigrette. Among the pasta dishes, I like the fettuccine San Remo, tossed in cream sauce with an array of fresh fish and seafood—calamari, scallops, shrimp, scungilli, clams, and mussels—served with fresh-grated parmesan. Main dishes include a house salad and hot, garlicky herbed rolls. Non-pasta choices—such as grilled shrimp scampi or chicken sautéed with mushrooms, cream, and fresh tarragon—also include a side of pasta. You can get half orders of pasta for children, and lunch fare includes sandwiches such as eggplant parmigiana on Italian bread. There's a full bar, and the wine list highlights Italian and California selections, with house-label wines available by the glass. The dessert of choice is creamy zabaglione topped with fresh strawberries.

L&N SEAFOOD GRILL, Jacksonville Landing. Tel. 358-7737.

Cuisine: SEAFOOD/STEAK/PASTA. **Reservations:** Not accepted (but call ahead for preferred seating).

$ Prices: Appetizers $3.95–$6.95; main courses $4.50–$8.95 at lunch, $6.95–$15.95 at dinner. AE, CB, DC, DISC, MC, V.

Open: Lunch daily 11am–4pm; dinner Sun–Thurs 4–10pm, Fri–Sat 4–11:30pm.

A riverside seafood restaurant with wraparound windows offering scenic water views, L&N is a handsome place with seating in teak booths at green-and-white checkerboard-clothed tables, lots of leafy plants, and wood-bladed fans suspended from a dark-green pressed-tin ceiling. A shiplike effect is enhanced by teak paneling and columns and walls pristinely adorned with nautically themed prints and scientific illustrations of fish. Soft lighting emanates from halaphane lamps and sconces. You can enjoy drinks and fresh-shucked oysters at a marble-top bar in the black-and-white–tiled lounge. And there's outdoor seating on an awninged brick terrace bordered by flowering plants. Many boaters tie up at a dock just outside the restaurant. Parking is in the Jacksonville Landing lot.

Begin your meal with a sharp seafood cheese dip loaded with shrimp and served with blue- and white-corn tortilla chips. Or opt for plump oysters Rockefeller baked with a topping of herbed breadcrumbs, fresh spinach, garlic butter, and sherried cheese sauce. Dinner dishes include a crisp bottomless salad with homemade creamy ranch dressing and unlimited fresh-baked biscuits. Among your choices: baked shrimp stuffed with softshell crabmeat in a creamy mornay sauce, served with rice pilaf and crisply cooked fresh vegetables; wood-smoked chicken, tossed with penne pasta and slivers of sweet red peppers in a white wine–pesto sauce, topped with fresh-grated parmesan; and mesquite-grilled sirloin served with garlic butter and redskin potatoes.

Most of the above items are also available at lunch. Also recommendable at either meal is blackened chicken salad with honey-mustard dressing. Desserts range from ice-cream key lime pie on graham-cracker crust to ultra-rich butterscotch-pecan pie served in caramel sauce and topped with vanilla ice cream.

RIVER CITY BREWERY, 835 Gulf Life Dr., on the Riverwalk at Museum Circle. Tel. 398-2299.
 Cuisine: CALIFORNIA/NEW ORLEANS. **Reservations:** Not accepted.
$ **Prices:** Appetizers $2.50–$7.50; main courses $4.50–$6.50 at lunch, $10.95–$15.95 at dinner; burgers and salads $4.95–$5.95. AE, DC, DISC, MC, V.
 Open: Sun–Thurs 11am–10pm, Fri–Sat 11am–11pm; lounges and terrace open for light fare Sun–Tues to midnight, Wed–Sat to 2am.

Occupying a prime location on the south bank of the St. Johns River, this gorgeous restaurant brings big-city sophistication to Jacksonville's dining scene. Glass-walled to provide almost all tables with stunning waterfront and skyline views, its handsome knotty pine-paneled interior is embellished by a tasteful display of ship models and nautical antiques. There's additional seating on a large awninged wooden deck overlooking a boat-filled marina. After dinner, dance off calories in the cozy oak-and-pine downstairs lounge (blues, mellow rock, reggae; live Thursday through Saturday, DJ other nights); the lounge houses the restaurant's microbrewery, its copper mash tun and kettle forming part of the decor. Or enjoy after-dinner drinks in the clubby upstairs lounge, with a sofa and wing chairs in front of a blazing fireplace.

Chef Tim Felver and his pastry-wizard wife, Barbara, worked with Wolfgang Puck in Los Angeles and have catered meals for everyone from Philippe Rothschild to Madonna. Great beginnings here include Tim's black-bean cake sautéed in blue cornmeal and served with cilantro crème fraîche, salsa, and plump grilled shrimp; pan-fried herbed crab cakes with mango-tomatillo salsa and sun-dried tomato vinaigrette; and shrimp wonton and shiitake salad with pickled ginger, fresh field greens, and Japanese vinaigrette. Order them all and graze. A pasta dish of red-pepper fettuccine tossed with spicy Cajun chicken, tasso ham, and mushrooms in a zesty cream sauce was unforgettable. Other options range from hearty seafood jambalaya to grilled filet mignon with fresh asparagus, sautéed shrimp, and béarnaise sauce. For a lighter meal, choose a sandwich on crusty French bread—perhaps a blackened shrimp po-boy with melted Cheddar and homemade remoulade sauce, served with fries. Barbara bakes a variety of scrumptious breads every night, and her desserts—such as a cakey version of tira misu on a layer of thick Belgian chocolate, topped with vanilla Häagen Dazs—are ambrosial. A carefully chosen list of American and imported wines—not to mention those house microbrewery beers—are available to complement your meal. Sunday brunch, with live music, is in the planning stage at this writing.

Arrive off-hours to avoid a wait at this very popular restaurant. Be sure to validate your parking ticket. At lunch you can take a free water taxi to and from Jacksonville Landing.

SAND DOLLAR, 9716 Heckscher Dr., just north of the Maypont Ferry. Tel. 251-2449.
 Cuisine: SEAFOOD. **Reservations:** Accepted only for large parties.
$ **Prices:** Appetizers $3.50–$6.95; burgers and sandwiches $3.95–$5.50; main courses $6.75–$10.95 at lunch, $11.95–$20.95 at dinner. All-you-can-eat specials $14.95 Mon–Thurs after 4pm. MC, V.
 Open: Sun–Thurs 11am–10pm, Fri–Sat 11am–11pm (closes an hour earlier in winter).

This is the perfect place to stop for lunch en route to or from the Kingsley Plantation, the Jacksonville Zoo, or the Anheuser-Busch Brewery. The rustic interior, with rough-hewn pine dividers and overhead beams, is warmly inviting, and the view from a wall of windows—a passing parade of boats and shore birds along the St. Johns River—is thrillingly scenic. All tables offer great water views, and in summer you can dine on a riverside wooden deck. Many boats dock here for meals.

Fried seafood—oysters, shrimp, and deviled crab—is the specialty. Order a combination plate with a baked potato and coleslaw. Another good choice is the Fort

George roaster—grilled shrimp, served with new potatoes, fresh corn on the cob, and steamed cabbage. Or you might select a po-boy sandwich of fried shrimp or oysters on a hoagie bun with tartar sauce. Chicken, steaks, and burgers are available for non–seafood fanciers, and a children's menu offers $3.25 meals. The bar is a popular hangout for locals. Homemade desserts include mud and key lime pies.

INEXPENSIVE

CHILI'S GRILL & BAR, in the Baymeadows Commons Shopping Center, 9500 Baymeadows Rd., just west of Southside Blvd. Tel. 739-2476.
Cuisine: SOUTHWESTERN. **Reservations:** Not accepted.
$ Prices: Appetizers $3.95–$5.95; main courses $4.75–$9.95. AE, CB, DC, DISC, MC, V.
Open: Sun–Thurs 11am–11pm, Fri–Sat 11am–midnight.

Chili's is a national chain, based in Texas, offering superior "bowls of red" and other southwestern specialties. This branch is sunny and plant-filled, with seating in comfortable upholstered booths. Hanging lamps made from old copper chili pots illuminate ceramic-tiled tables, gray-green walls are adorned with framed posters and photographs of chili cookoffs, and slowly whirring fans are suspended from the forest-green ceiling. You can also eat in the lively bar area where the TV is always tuned to sporting events. Chili's is a great choice for family dining.

The same menu is offered all day. Chili is, of course, a specialty, available with or without beans. Equally popular are fabulous half-pound burgers, perhaps topped with cheese and chili and served with home-style fries. Another big item here: fried chicken with country gravy, homemade mashed potatoes (with skins), corn on the cob, and garlic toast. And should you want something lighter, there's a salad of grilled tuna mixed with greens, pico de gallo, sugary walnuts, and onions in ranch dressing. Save room for dessert—perhaps a brownie topped with vanilla ice cream, hot fudge, chopped walnuts, and whipped cream. A children's menu lists full meals for just $2.65.

BRUNCH

Banyan's, at the Jacksonville Marriott, 4670 Salisbury Rd., off I-95 at J. Turner Butler Boulevard (tel. 296-2222), offers a lavish buffet brunch, including unlimited champagne, every Sunday from 10:30am to 2pm. The table is laden with piles of peel-and-eat shrimp, assorted salads, broiled fresh fish, a chicken dish, breakfast meats, lyonnaise and new potatoes, pasta dishes, blintzes, bagels and lox, fresh fruits and vegetables, cheeses, juices, and tea and coffee. There's an omelet/waffle/French toast/pancake station, a roast meat–carving station, and a Caesar salad station. And the dessert display table offers homemade cobbler, ice cream, pies, cakes, and mousses. Banyan's is softly lit, with comfortable seating at white-linened tables, bleached-oak panels and columns, and many plants. Weather permitting, there are tables on a patio outside bordered by potted palms. A harpist entertains while you dine. The cost is $12.95 for adults, $10.95 for seniors 65 and over, $6.95 for ages 6 to 12, free for kids under 6. Reservations suggested.

EVENING ENTERTAINMENT

There's lots to do at night in this lively beach town. Check the papers for concerts and events at Jacksonville Landing and other entertainment venues. Also consider the *simpático* lounge at **River City Brewery** (details above).

THE PERFORMING ARTS

ALHAMBRA DINNER THEATRE, 12000 Beach Blvd., between Hodges and St. Johns Bluff Rds. Tel. 641-1212, or toll free 800/688-SHOUL.
The Alhambra presents entertaining professional productions of Broadway

shows—most of them musicals and comedies. Recent productions have included *Hello Dolly, Phantom of the Opera, A Chorus Line*, and *Man of La Mancha*. There are five to seven productions each year. The price of admission includes a full buffet dinner featuring a prime rib carving station, baked chicken dish, seafood Newburg, and an array of vegetables, salads, and desserts, as well as tea or coffee. A full bar and wine list are available. Tuesday through Sunday, the buffet dinner begins at 6:30pm, the show at 8:15pm; for the Saturday matinee, the buffet begins at 11:30am, the show at 1:15pm; and for the Sunday matinee, the buffet begins at 12:15pm, the show at 2pm.

Admission: $27.50 Sun–Fri, $29.50 Sat night, $24.50 Sat–Sun matinees; seniors 55 and over, active military, and children under 17 pay $2 less except on Fri–Sat nights.

CIVIC AUDITORIUM, 300 Water St., between Hogan and Pearl Sts. Tel. 630-0700 for information, 353-3309 to charge tickets.

This 3,200-seat facility on the St. Johns River is used for symphony concerts, ballet performances, headliner concerts (Julio Iglesias, Sade, the Black Crowes, Barry Manilow, David Copperfield, Megadeth) and theatrical productions. In addition to presenting Broadway shows such as *Cats* and *Les Misérables*, the Civic is the home of the acclaimed Jacksonville Symphony Orchestra; visiting performers have included everyone from flautist James Galway to violinist Itzhak Perlman. From the lobby, the waterfront setting provides a beautiful backdrop. Park in the adjacent lot; the charge varies with the event.

Admission: Ticket prices vary with the event.

ROCK, POP & FAMILY SHOWS

THE GATOR BOWL, 1400 E. Duval St., at Haines St. Tel. 630-3900 for information, 353-3309 to charge tickets.

This huge facility is the setting for major rock concerts featuring such superstars as Michael Jackson and the Rolling Stones.

Adjacent to it, and under the same auspices, is the 10,600-seat **Jacksonville Veterans Memorial Coliseum**, 1145 E. Adams St. (same phone numbers), another venue for many headliner concerts—Frank Sinatra, Garth Brooks, Reba McEntire, Luther Vandross, TLC—as well as family shows such as the circus and *Disney on Ice*. There's paid parking for ticketed events; rates vary with the event.

Admission: Ticket prices vary according to the event.

THE CLUB & BAR SCENE

CHAMPS, at the Marriott at Sawgrass Resort, 1000 TPC Blvd., off Fla. A1A, Ponte Vedra Beach. Tel. 285-7777.

This handsome mahogany-paneled club is popular with locals and visitors alike. Plushly furnished, it has a wall of windows overlooking a lagoon and even offers outdoor seating on a flagstone patio. A live band plays top-40 tunes for dancing Tuesday through Saturday nights. There's a nice-sized dance floor, and additional attractions include blackjack tables (you can't win money, but you can hone your skills). Champs serves complimentary hot and cold hors d'oeuvres weekdays during happy hour (5:30 to 7pm). At night it offers light fare—pizzas, quesadillas, blackened chicken salad—and a wide range of specialty drinks ranging from concoctions like a frozen sand castle (Kahlúa, cream of coconut, and pineapple juice) to liqueur-spiked coffees topped with whipped cream. It's open nightly until 12:30am. Parking is free on the premises.

Admission: Free.

CLUB CAROUSEL, 8550 Arlington Expy. (Hwy. 115/U.S. 90 Alt.), on the service road just south of Mill Creek Rd. Tel. 725-2582.

A 30,000-square-foot facility, with a 4,000-square-foot dance floor enhanced by high-tech laser/lighting effects and a revolving stage, the Club Carousel offers an eclectic mix of entertainment. Call ahead for hours and to find out what's on—"Hot Latin" night, country, "alternate-lifestyle" night, high-energy techno, female impersonators, international recording stars, top 40, or a mix of several of the above. Club

Carousel is open Monday and Wednesday through Saturday nights. There are also bars—and pool tables—at either end of the club, and a quieter bar is up front. You must be 18 to get in. There's free on-premises parking.

Admission: Usually $4, higher for some concerts.

THE COMEDY ZONE, in the Ramada Inn Conference Center, 3130 Hartley Rd., just above the junction of I-295 and San Jose Blvd. in Mandarin. Tel. 292-4242.

The Comedy Zone presents nationally known comics—the acts you see on comedy channels and the Leno and Letterman shows. Showtimes are Tuesday through Thursday at 8:30pm, on Friday and Saturday at 8 and 10pm, and on Sunday at 8pm. The first Monday of every month is amateur night. Light fare—pizzas and sandwiches—is available. You must be 18 to get in.

Admission: $5 Tues–Thurs and Sun, $8 Fri–Sat, $2 amateur night. In addition, there's always a one-drink minimum (average drink is $3.50; if you're under 21, you must purchase a $3 beverage coupon for soft drinks).

CRAZY HORSE SALOON, 5800 Phillips Hwy., a block south of University Blvd. Tel. 731-8892.

This large facility actually encompasses two clubs on its premises, the Crazy Horse and Masquerade. At the Crazy Horse—an archetypical urban cowboy club—a DJ plays country-western music, and every Tuesday night a cable show called "Hitkicker Country" is filmed on the dance floor. Neon beer signs adorn the walls; the crowd wears boots, jeans, and cowboy hats; and there are half a dozen pool tables off the dance floor. Lessons in line dancing are available for $5 on Monday and Thursday nights, while Tuesday nights there are lessons in western swing for more advanced dancers.

At Masquerade, a DJ plays top-40 tunes and progressive rock. There are good lighting effects on the dance floor, and a large video monitor backs the stage. The club is the scene of frequent contests—hot buns, wet T-shirts, hot legs, and the like—most offering $100 prizes. Dress is casual. You must be 21 to get into either part of the club.

Crazy Horse is open Monday through Saturday till 2am; Masquerade, Wednesday through Saturday till 2am. Parking is free on the premises.

Admission: $2, good for both clubs; Wed nights ladies are admitted free and enjoy free drinks from 9pm to midnight.

RAGTIME TAVERN AND TAPROOM, 207 Atlantic Blvd., off Fla. A1A. Tel. 241-7877.

This popular beach bar and restaurant features local groups playing live jazz and blues Thursday through Sunday nights. It's a *simpático* setting, with oak furnishings and exposed-brick walls hung, country-western style, with neon beer signs. Weekends, especially, the place is really jumping and the crowd is young, but it's lively rather than rowdy. Ragtime brews its own beer—lager, stout, red ale, and wheat beer—in a brewery on the premises. A fairly extensive menu highlights fresh Florida seafood and New Orleans specialties, but it also lists other items ranging from pasta dishes to fajitas. You must be 21 to get in on Friday or Saturday after 11pm. There are other clubs on this corner, so you can begin an evening at Ragtime and go bar-hopping. It's open on Thursday and Sunday till 11pm, on Friday and Saturday till 1am.

Admission: Free.

2. ST. AUGUSTINE

123 miles NE of Orlando, 344 miles N of Miami, 43 miles S of Jacksonville

GETTING THERE   By Plane   St. Augustine is about equidistant (a one-hour drive) from airports in Jacksonville and Daytona Beach.

By Train   The closest Amtrak station (tel. 800/USA-RAIL) is in Jacksonville (see Section 1 of this chapter for details).

By Bus Greyhound buses connect St. Augustine with most of the country. They pull into a very centrally located terminal at 100 Malaga St., near King Street (tel. 904/829-6401).

By Car If you're coming from north or south, take I-95 to U.S. 1 (Exits 92 to 95; ask when you reserve accommodations which is closest). From points west, take I-10 to I-95 South to U.S. 1.

With its 17th-century fort, horse-drawn carriages clip-clopping along narrow streets, old city gates, and reconstructed 18th-century Spanish Quarter, St. Augustine seems more like a picturesque European village than a modern American city. This is an exceptionally charming town, replete, like other coastal Florida destinations, with palm-fringed ocean beaches—but its primary lure is historic. Here Western civilization first took root in the New World.

A SHORT HISTORY The First Spanish Period Founded in 1565, 55 years before the Pilgrims landed at Plymouth Rock, St. Augustine was America's first city. Though Juan Ponce de León sighted—and named—the Florida coast as early as 1513, it was Pedro Menéndez de Avilés who established the Spanish supremacy that lasted for two centuries. He arrived with some thousand settlers and a priest, and named the town St. Augustine in honor of the saint whose feast day—August 28—coincided with his first sighting of the Florida coast. The newcomers settled in a Timucuan village called Seloy—site today of the Fountain of Youth and Mission de Nombre de Dios—and set about routing the French from nearby Fort Caroline and converting the natives to Christianity. Later, for reasons of military strategy, the colony moved to higher ground about a mile south, near the bayfront. Life was not easy. The fledgling town was beset by famine, fire, hurricanes, plagues, and attacks by Native Americans, pirates, and the rival British Empire. But St. Augustine survived, and its importance grew as it became increasingly vital to Spain's defense of her commercial coastal route. Between 1672 and 1695 the colonists constructed an impregnable fort, the Castillo de San Marcos. Though British troops attacked and burned the town in 1702 and 1740, the populace holed up in the Castillo and survived both onslaughts.

    Briefly British In 1763, the British finally gained control of St. Augustine when Spain ceded all of Florida to them in exchange for Havana and other territorial possessions after the French and Indian War. Rather than become British subjects, most of the 3,000 Spanish inhabitants sailed to Cuba. During the American Revolution, St. Augustine remained loyal to the Crown. The population increased in 1777 with the arrival of 1,400 Minorcan, Italian, and Greek indentured servants fleeing the tyranny of harsh servitude in New Smyrna, a town about 80 miles south of St. Augustine.

    The Second Spanish Regime In 1784, the Treaty of Paris returned Florida to Spain as a reward for its aid during the American Revolution. Once again the population shifted, as many prior Spanish residents returned and most of the English left. The Minorcans—whose previously British Balearic Island country had come under Spanish rule by this time—stayed on. The British loyalists left the city in a shambles. The inhabitants valiantly tried to rebuild, but by the beginning of the 19th century the Spanish Empire was already beginning to decline. When it became evident, after numerous incursions, that the Americans would eventually seize Florida anyway, the Spanish sensibly decided to sell it to them. The transfer took place peacefully in 1821, and the Spanish soldiers departed, never to return.

    From the Territorial Era to the Gilded Age American rule got off to a shaky start, as a massive yellow fever epidemic decimated the population. Many of St. Augustine's buildings by this time were run-down or in ruins. Nine years after American occupation, there were only 1,700 residents, a third of them slaves. In 1835 the city suffered two major disasters—a freeze that destroyed the orange crop and the onset of a seven-year Seminole War, during which Native Americans struggled to regain control of Florida. But as the focus of hostilities moved away from St.

Augustine, the town began to prosper by providing weapons and ships to its embattled neighbors. Roads were built with the profits, and the population grew, as did the pressure for statehood. In 1845, Florida entered the Union as the 27th state.

During the early days of statehood, with the Seminole Wars over, seasonal visitors from the chilly north began arriving in Florida to enjoy its warm winters. This growth in tourism was interrupted by the Civil War. In March 1862, St. Augustine surrendered to Union forces, and the city remained occupied until the end of the conflict. But almost immediately after the war, the snowbirds began to return. A most important visitor arrived in 1883—Standard Oil magnate Henry M. Flagler. Taken with St. Augustine's Spanish antiquity and mellow charm, he determined to develop the area as a fashionable resort for the wealthy. By the turn of the century, Flagler had revolutionized the tourism industry throughout Florida, building plush hotels and developing rail travel along its eastern coastline. Flagler spared no expense—his decorator was Louis Comfort Tiffany. Three of his deluxe hostelries—the Cordova (today the county courthouse), the Alcazar (today the Lightner Museum), and the Ponce de León (today Flagler College)—can still be seen.

St. Augustine Today It wasn't until well into the 20th century, however, that St. Augustine began to fully appreciate its unique heritage and architectural treasure trove. The Historic St. Augustine Preservation Board, formed in 1959, has been responsible for extensive restoration, preservation, and research into the city's past. Today's visitors can explore fascinating historic sites, relax on beautiful beaches, dine at waterfront fish camps and charming cafés, and reside in quaint antique-furnished bed-and-breakfast lodgings.

ORIENTATION

INFORMATION Before you go, write or call the **St. Augustine Chamber of Commerce,** 1 Riberia St., St. Augustine, FL 32084 (tel. 904/829-5681), which will send you a calendar of events, maps, and information on attractions, restaurants, and accommodations.

Upon arrival, make your first stop in town the **St. Augustine Visitor Information Center,** 10 Castillo Dr., at San Marco Avenue (tel. 904/825-1000). Here you can view a free visitor information video; pick up brochures about accommodations, restaurants, sights, and shops; and—most important—obtain a combined three-day ticket for sightseeing trains and trolleys along with discount tickets to major attractions (for details, see "Getting Around," below). While you're here, be sure to see *Dream of Empire,* a 52-minute film about a 16th-century St. Augustine family. Shown daily on the hour between 9am and 4pm, it costs $3 for adults, $2 for children 5 to 17, free for kids under 5. There's also a history museum on the premises. A knowledgeable staff can answer all your questions. There's inexpensive parking on the premises. The VIC is open daily: Memorial Day to Labor Day, 8:30am to 7:30pm; April to Memorial Day and the day after Labor Day to the end of October, 8:30am to 6:30pm; November to March, 8:30am to 5:30pm. Closed Christmas.

CITY LAYOUT St. Augustine is quite a small town, and you'll easily find your way around. It's bounded to the west by U.S. 1, to the east (along the coast of the Intracoastal Waterway and Matanzas Bay) by Avenida Menendez. The North Bridge leads to Fla. A1A North and Vilano Beach, the beautiful Bridge of Lions to Fla. A1A South and Anastasia Island. Florida 16 on the north side of town provides access to I-95. The heart of town is still the original plaza laid out in the 16th century, bounded east and west by Charlotte and St. George Streets, north and south by Cathedral Place and King Street. The old Spanish Quarter is farther north on St. George Street, between Cuna and Orange Streets.

GETTING AROUND

BY SIGHTSEEING TROLLEYS & TRAINS St. Augustine provides excellent transportation, via sightseeing trolleys and trains, to its numerous historic sites and tourist attractions. These vehicles travel around town along seven-mile loop routes, stopping at or near all attractions. It's easier than using a car, because you never have to worry about parking, which can be difficult at times (you can leave your car at the trolley or train lot, or take advantage of complimentary pickup and return to and from local hotels). Entertaining and informative on-board narrations enhance your touring.

Trolleys and trains are run by two separate (and equally recommended) companies, and these two firms have collaborated to offer a truly great deal. If you purchase your tickets at the **Visitor Information Center** (see "Information," in "Orientation," above) you can get a three-day ticket for both trolleys and trains at the same price you'd pay elsewhere for either separately—$10 for adults, $4 for children 6 to 12, free for children under 6. Both trolleys and trains depart from the VIC as well. While you're there, inquire about trolley and train tickets that include discount admissions to the attractions. There are numerous plans.

St. Augustine Historical Tours, 167 San Marco Ave., at Williams Street (tel. 829-3800, or toll free 800/397-4071), operates San Francisco–style green-and-white open-air trolleys between 8:30am and 5pm daily. You can park your car at their headquarters, which is also a stop on the tour and site of two tourist attractions. There are 16 stops on the route, and for the price of your ticket you can get off at any stop, visit the attractions, and step aboard the next vehicle that comes along. Several trolleys make a continuous circuit along the route throughout the day; you won't ever have to wait more than 15 to 20 minutes for a trolley to come along. Or you can ride the entire route, which is enhanced by entertaining live narration. It takes about an hour to complete.

St. Augustine Sightseeing Trains, 170 San Marco Ave., at Fla. A1A (tel. 829-6545, or toll free 800/226-6545), is almost identical to the above, but takes a different route and makes 19 stops. Its vehicles are red-and-blue open-air trains.

BY HORSE-DRAWN CARRIAGE   Colee's Carriage Tours (tel. 829-2818), operated by the Colee family, has been showing people around town in quaint surreys (some with fringed canopies), turn-of-the-century vis-a-vis, and broughams since 1877. The carriages line up at the bayfront, just south of the fort. Slow-paced, entertainingly narrated 45- to 50-minute rides (which include a 10-minute stop at Memorial Presbyterian Church) are offered from 9am to 9pm daily except Christmas. The cost is $9 per adult, $4 for children 5 to 11, free for kids under 5, with hotel and restaurant pickup available for an additional charge. Tours go past the Castillo, old town and Spanish Quarter sights, churches and historic homes, Flagler College, the Lightner Museum, and other notable landmarks and attractions. It makes for a delightful ride.

BY BOAT   The Usina family has been running **St. Augustine Scenic Cruises** (tel. 824-1806) on Matanzas Bay since the turn of the century. They offer 75-minute narrated tours aboard open-air sightseeing boats departing from the Municipal Marina just south of the Bridge of Lions. The tours are delightful. There are often dolphins cavorting on the bay, and you're likely to spot brown pelicans, cormorants, kingfishers, and other water birds. From the boat you'll see the Castillo, unspoiled saltwater marshes, oyster beds, the St. Augustine Lighthouse, the San Sebastian and North Rivers, the St. Augustine inlet to the Atlantic Ocean, and Vilano Beach waterfront homes, many of them with boats docked out front. Snacks and soft drinks are sold on board, and if the weather gets nippy outside you can retreat to enclosed seating below deck. Weather permitting, departures are at 11am, 1pm, 2:45pm, and 4:30pm daily except Christmas, with an additional tour at 6:15pm Labor Day to October 15 and April 1 to May 14; May 15 to Labor Day there are two additional tours, at 6:45 and 8:30pm. That's the current schedule, but call ahead—schedules can change. Adults pay $7.50, children 3 to 11 are charged $3, and kids under 3 ride free. If you're driving, allow a little time to find a parking space on the street.

BY CAR   There are a number of inexpensive parking lots in the historic district. Drive in on Hypolita Street off Avenida Menendez and look for a lot on your right. If it's full, continue on Hypolita and park in the lot across Cordova Street.

WHAT TO SEE & DO

St. Augustine's attractions are open seven days a week. In addition to over a dozen historic sites and museums, there's almost always some **special event** going on. It might be anything from a reenactment of Sir Francis Drake's raid on the town in 1586 to a very 20th-century beach festival.

There are numerous **golf** courses and 22 municipal **tennis** courts (inquire at the Visitor Information Center). The best **beaches** are St. Augustine Beach, about four miles out of town on Fla. A1A South (take the Bridge of Lions) and Vilano Beach on Fla. A1A North, right over the North Bridge. And the historic district is dotted with quaint shops.

AUTHENTIC OLD JAIL, 167 San Marco Ave., at Williams St. Tel. 829-3800.

This Victorian brick prison was built in 1890 with the financial assistance of Henry Flagler, and it served the county through 1953. It was recently restored, and fascinating tours are given here throughout the day by costumed guides assuming the roles of Sheriff Joe Perry and his wife, Lulu. Perry, 6′ 6″ tall and weighing 300 pounds, was sheriff here for 25 years, earning a reputation as a fearless law enforcer. Visitors are shown the Perrys' living quarters and the kitchen where Lulu cooked the inmates gruel for breakfast and one-pot meals (stews) for lunch and dinner. Downstairs are Spartan accommodations for women, painted black and provided with straw mattresses (no linens) on bunk beds. On the same floor are a maximum-security cell where murderers, horse thieves, and those convicted of grand theft were confined; a cell housing prisoners condemned to hang (they could see the gallows being constructed from their window); and an especially grim solitary confinement cell—pitch-dark with no windows, bed, or mattress. Minimum-security prisoners—bootleggers, debtors, petty thieves—were kept upstairs in quarters almost as bleak and lightless as those below. Adding to the general level of misery throughout was the fact that the cells were stiflingly hot in summer and freezing in winter, and the bugs were awful.

Additional exhibits include weapons seized from criminals, restraining devices, and an exact replica of the electric chair still used today in Florida. A snack bar and picnic tables are on the grounds.

Admission: $4.25 adults, $3.25 children 6–12, free for kids under 6. Parking is free on the premises.

Open: Daily 8:30am–5pm. **Closed:** Easter, Christmas Eve Day, and Christmas.

CASTILLO DE SAN MARCOS NATIONAL MONUMENT, 1 Castillo Dr., between Orange and Charlotte Sts. Tel. 829-6506.

In 1669—a year after English pirates had sacked St. Augustine—Mariana, Queen Regent of Spain, ordered colonists to construct an impregnable stone fort to stave off future British advances. The little town was of key importance to Spain in defending Florida's coastal commercial route along which its galleons, loaded with gold and silver from the mines of Mexico and Peru, sailed back to Cádiz. The Castillo, which took 23 years (1672–95) to build, was stellar in design, with a double drawbridge entrance over a 40-foot moat. The earth dug out from the moat created a small embankment, called a *glacis,* that prevented cannon balls from hitting the wall bases. Massive coquina (shell rock) walls enclosed a large courtyard lined inside with storage rooms, and diamond-shaped bastions in each corner—which enabled cannons to set up a deadly crossfire—contained domed sentry towers. Originally, the fort was white plaster with red trim, the colors of the Spanish flag, so that passing ships could recognize its nationality.

The Castillo was never captured in battle, and its coquina walls did not crumble when pounded by enemy artillery. In 1702, the English occupied St. Augustine for 50 days, and though they burned the town, its 1,500 residents holed up in the fort and remained safe. The fort also held up during a 27-day British bombardment in 1740. The British only gained possession when Spain ceded Florida to them in return for Havana after the French and Indian War in 1763. They held the fort (renaming it Fort St. Mark) through the American Revolution for 21 years, after which the Treaty of Paris returned Florida to Spain. The Castillo, like the rest of Florida, came under American rule in 1821, and in 1824 its name was changed to Fort Marion in honor of a Revolutionary War general. It was used to house Native American prisoners during the Seminole War of 1835–42, occupied briefly by Confederate troops during the

Civil War, and served as a military prison during the Spanish-American War. America's oldest—and best-preserved—masonry fortification was decommissioned as an active military base in 1900, designated a National Monument in 1924, and given back its original name in 1942.

Today the old storerooms house museum exhibits documenting the history of the fort, and visitors can also tour the vaulted powder magazine room, a dank prison cell, the chapel, and guard rooms. A walk around the upper-level gundeck is both historically evocative (imagine yourself a Spanish sentry scanning the sea for danger) and scenic. Most of the bronze and cast-iron cannons are at least 200 years old and could fire a ball over a mile. A self-guided tour map and brochure are provided at the ticket booth. In addition, subject to staff availability, interesting 20- to 30-minute ranger talks are given several times a day, and in summer there are occasional living-history presentations and cannon firings (call for times before you go).

Admission: $2 adults, free for children under 17 and seniors over 61.
Open: Daily 8:45am–4:45pm (sometimes later in summer). **Closed:** Christmas Day.

FLORIDA HERITAGE MUSEUM, 167 San Marco Ave., at Williams St. Tel. 829-3800.

Adjacent to the Authentic Old Jail (see above) and under the same auspices, this museum documents state and local history in exhibits focusing on the colorful life of Henry Flagler; his Florida and East Coast Railroad and Hotel Company, which played a key role in the development of Florida tourism; the Civil War; and the Seminole Wars. A replica of a Spanish galleon filled with weapons, pottery, and treasures complements display cases filled with actual gold, silver, and jewelry recovered from galleons sunk off the Florida coast. A typical wattle-and-daub hut of a Timucuan in a forest setting illustrates the lifestyle of St. Augustine's first residents. And additional exhibits include 17th- and 18th-century Spanish furnishings; an extraordinary collection of toys and dolls, mostly from the 1870s to the 1920s; textiles (with spinning and weaving demonstrations); and Florida shells. These permanent displays are augmented by changing exhibits. A gift shop is on the premises.

Admission: $4.25 adults, $3.25 children 6–12, free for kids under 6. Parking is free on the premises.
Open: Daily 8:30am–5pm. **Closed:** Easter, Christmas Eve Day, and Christmas Day.

FLORIDA PORTRAYED, 15 Hypolita St., between Charlotte and St. George Sts. Tel. 826-0415.

This small private museum has two floors of exhibits showing how Florida has been portrayed over the centuries. It includes photographs, paintings, prints, book illustrations, maps, souvenir plates and mugs, movie posters, promotional brochures, and postcards.

Admission: $3 adults, $1 children 6–16, free for kids under 6.
Open: Thurs–Mon 10am–5pm. **Closed:** May–June and Sept–Oct.

FOUNTAIN OF YOUTH, 155 Magnolia Ave., at Williams St. Tel. 829-3168.

This beautifully landscaped 25-acre archeological park, billed as North America's first historic site, is purported to be the Native American village of Seloy visited by Ponce de León upon his arrival in the New World. Today, 45-minute guided tours begin with a planetarium show about 16th-century celestial navigation during which the audience experiences a storm at sea.

The famed fountain itself is located in the Springhouse along with a coquina stone cross believed to date from Ponce de León's ostensible visit in 1513. Tableaux here depict a Timucuan village and the arrival of Ponce de León. Visitors get to drink a sample of the sulfury water—not terrifically delicious.

One of the most fascinating exhibits in the complex is a Timucuan burial ground discovered by a gardener planting orange trees in 1934. More than 100 Native American interments—both Christian and prehistoric—were unearthed by Smithsonian experts. The skeletal remains were once on display, but a reburial was performed in 1991 to pay respect to America's first inhabitants. Today you can view photographs of the excavation. Murals in this room portray St. Augustine from prehistoric through colonial times.

Also on the grounds are historic cannons, a 16th-century Timucuan dugout canoe, and a statue of 16th-century Timucuan chief Oriba—not to mention a picnic area and snack bar.

Admission: $4.50 adults, $3.50 seniors, $1.50 children 6–12, free for kids under 6. Parking is free on the premises.

Open: Daily 9am–5pm. **Closed:** Christmas.

GOVERNMENT HOUSE MUSEUM, 48 King St., at St. George St. Tel. 825-5033.

Government House—on the site of the 16th-century Spanish colonial governor's office—houses an exhibit entitled "The Dream, the Challenge, the City." It focuses on the cultural, economic, architectural, and archeological components of St. Augustine's rich heritage. Displays highlight Florida explorers, the struggles of the first Spanish settlement, the construction of the Castillo de San Marcos, and the varied inhabitants who have lived here throughout the centuries. Visitors can listen to a recording about the early days while looking at a scale model of the town. And many artifacts recovered from Spanish shipwrecks—coins, jewelry, and weapons—are on display.

Admission: $2 adults, $1 students and children 6–12, free for kids under 6. Park in the lot at the Visitor Information Center at San Marco Avenue and Castillo Drive.

Open: Daily 10am–4pm. **Closed:** Christmas.

LIGHTNER MUSEUM, 75 King St., at Granada St. Tel. 824-2874.

Henry Flagler's opulent Spanish Renaissance–style Alcazar Hotel, built in 1889, closed during the Depression, and stayed vacant until Chicago publishing magnate Otto C. Lightner bought the building in 1948 to house his vast collection of Victoriana. The former hotel makes a gorgeous museum, centering on an open palm courtyard with an arched stone bridge spanning a fish pond. The first floor houses a Victorian village, with shopfronts representing emporia selling hats, toys, china, and other period wares. A Victorian Science and Industry Room displays shells, rocks, minerals, and Native American artifacts in beautiful turn-of-the-century cases. Other exhibits include stuffed birds, an Egyptian mummy from 500 B.C., Italian cameos, steam engine models, and amazing examples of Victorian glassblowing. A room of automated musical instruments on this floor—a self-playing violin, organ grinder's street piano, roller organ, music boxes, and an 1874 German orchestrion among them—are best seen during daily concerts of period music at 11am and 2pm, which are enhanced by docent lectures.

On the second floor you'll find 18th- and 19th-century European porcelains, art nouveau glass by Louis Comfort Tiffany and contemporaries, intricately carved Oriental export furniture, and other decorative arts. You'll also see a malachite urn from the St. Petersburg Winter Palace of the tsar and a 19th-century Chickering grand piano that belonged to opera star Amelia Galli-Curci.

Victorian furnishings ranging from the British Raj to intricate Near Eastern mother-of-pearl inlay pieces are on the third floor, along with collections of buttons, stamps, coins, dolls, dollhouses, and textiles.

Take some time to look at the building itself, designed by Thomas Hastings and John Carrère, architects of the U.S. Senate Office Building and the New York Public Library. It's listed in the National Register of Historic Places. And on your way out, check out the gift shop's 19th-century antique and reproduction objets d'art. The charming plant-filled Courtyard Deli, open weekdays from 7am to 5pm, is on the premises.

Admission: $4 adults, $1 college students with ID and children 12–18, free for children under 12. Parking is free on the premises.

Open: Daily 9am–5pm. **Closed:** Christmas.

MARINELAND OF FLORIDA, 9507 Ocean Shore Blvd. (Fla. A1A), Marineland. Tel. 471-1111.

This beachfront marinelife park on the Atlantic Ocean came into being in 1938 as an underwater motion picture studio and tourist attraction. It was the first establishment to successfully maintain dolphins in a man-made environment and achieve a successful birth in captivity. In pre-Disney days, it was Florida's most popular commercial attraction. Today, Marineland features dolphin shows in a vast circular saltwater oceanarium as well as displays of penguins, flamingos, sharks, and sea lions. A second oceanarium is home to thousands of marine specimens representing more than 125 species. A marine science exhibit, which incorporates a video and eight large aquariums, examines the biology of underwater creatures. Native Florida species (gar, largemouth bass, sunfish, and crappie) can be viewed in the 35,000-gallon Wonders of the Spring aquarium—the world's largest freshwater exhibit. Over 6,000 rare and beautiful sea shells are on display at the Margaret Herrick Shell Museum. And a 20-minute 3-D film called *Sea Dream* is shown throughout the day in the Aquarius Theater. A full-service oceanfront restaurant, lounge, fast-food eatery, and snack bars are on the premises. And speaking of dining, you can view underwater feedings. Marineland is 18 miles south of St. Augustine.

Admission: $12 adults, $9.60 seniors 55 and over, $7 children 3–11, free for kids under 3. Parking is free.

Open: Daily 9am–5:30pm.

MISSION OF NOMBRE DE DIOS, San Marco Ave. and Old Mission Rd. Tel. 824-2809.

This serene setting overlooking the Intracoastal Waterway is believed to be the site of the first Indian Mission in the United States, founded in 1565. An arched bridge spans a lagoon, leading to a statue of Fr. Francisco López de Mendoza Grajales, chaplain of Menéndez de Avilés's fleet and founding pastor of the parish. A towering 208-foot gleaming stainless-steel cross—illuminated at night to create a "beacon of faith" visible to ships at sea—marks the site where the gospel was first preached in a permanent Christian settlement in the New World. Also on the grounds are a charming old mission-style vine-covered chapel built in 1915, the Shrine of Our Lady of La Leche, on the site of an original 1613 chapel. The mission is a popular destination of religious pilgrimages. Whatever your beliefs, it's a beautiful tree-shaded spot, ideal for quiet meditation.

Admission: Free; donations appreciated. Parking is free on the premises.

Open: Daily 7am–6pm.

MUSEUM OF WEAPONS AND EARLY AMERICAN HISTORY, 81-C King St., between Sevilla and Cordova Sts. Tel. 829-3727.

An eclectic assortment of historic artifacts and weapons from 1500 to 1900 are displayed in this private museum. Exhibits include Native American war clubs, spears, and arrowheads; historic pistols, rifles, and muskets; slave auction notices; a miniature Austrian pistol (about 1½ inches long) that really works; and Kentucky rifles that helped open the frontier. Among many Civil War items are an array of Confederate weapons, money, belt buckles, and buttons; a bible that stopped a bullet; a Florida Confederate flag that was taken in the Battle of Fredericksburg in 1862; and a Vicksburg, Mississippi, newspaper printed on the back side of wallpaper in 1863 during a paper shortage. Related antiques and reproductions and books on the Civil War are sold in the adjoining gift shop. Parking is free on the premises.

Admission: $3 adults, $2.50 seniors 62 and over, $1 children 6–12, free for kids under 6.

Open: Daily 9:30am–5pm. **Closed:** Christmas Day.

★ THE OLDEST HOUSE, 14 St. Francis St., at Charlotte St. Tel. 824-2872.

Archeological surveys indicate that a dwelling stood on this site as early as the beginning of the 17th century. Like the rest of the town, it was probably burned by the British in 1702. What you see today, called the Gonzáles-Alvarez House (for two of its prominent owners), evolved from a two-room coquina dwelling built between 1702 and 1727. Rooms are furnished to evoke various historical eras. There are several abandoned wells on the site, and Native American, Spanish, and British artifacts (some of them discovered in those wells) are displayed.

Tomás Gonzáles, a colonist from Tenerife in the Canary Islands, lived here with his fourth-generation St. Augustine wife, Francisca, from about 1727 through 1763, when Florida became a British colony and the town's 3,000 Spaniards were ordered to leave. Tomás worked as an artilleryman at the Castillo, supplementing his meager salary by fishing, hunting, and tending fruit trees and a vegetable garden out back. The Gonzáleses had 10 children, 6 of whom survived infancy. One of the original two rooms is simply furnished to represent this period. Possessions are scant (sleeping pallets and a chest or two), and artifacts include a few native clay bowls and olive jars used for cooking and storage; a brazier provided heat and served as a deterrent to mosquitoes (carriers of the dread yellow fever).

After the Gonzáleses' departure for Havana, Mary and Joseph Peavett (he was a paymaster for the British garrison) took possession. They added a second story, a front door, a fireplace, and glass window panes. The ambitious Mary operated a store and tavern on the premises, and she also worked as a midwife. In 1783, Florida became Spanish once again and now the British were forced to leave unless they publicly professed conversion to Catholicism. Joseph Peavett was already a Catholic, and Mary converted at the age of 56, shortly after Joseph's death in 1786. That same year she remarried, this time to 28-year-old John Hudson. Deemed a "profligate wastrel," Hudson ran up outrageous debts and got himself arrested for tearing down a government edict and making "the indecent gesture of wiping his backside" with it. After serving time in the Castillo, he was banished from St. Augustine and died in exile at the age of 33. A room upstairs with a tea-tray ceiling evokes the era of Mary's tenancy.

In 1790 the house was auctioned to pay the Hudsons' debts, and it became the property of Gerónimo Alvarez, a Spanish immigrant who owned a store and bakery close by. His wife, Antonia, died at the age of 25 in 1798 after bearing five children, only two of whom survived. Alvarez and his son Antonio went on to become important figures in local politics. The family and its descendants lived in the house for almost a century. A dining room of their period is re-created upstairs.

Admission also entitles you to explore the adjacent **Museum of Florida's Army,** which occupies a mid-18th-century building and details the state's military history from the days of the conquistadors to the present. And you can also check out exhibits in the **Manucy Museum of St. Augustine History,** where artifacts, maps, and photographs document the founding of St. Augustine, European struggles for supremacy in the New World, lifestyles of local inhabitants, the British and second Spanish periods, and the Flagler era.

Admission: $5 adults, $4.50 seniors 55 and over, $3 students, free for children 6 and under; $12 families. Parking is free on the premises.

Open: Daily 9am–5pm; tours depart on the hour and half hour, with the last tour leaving at 4:30pm. **Closed:** Christmas Day.

THE OLDEST STORE MUSEUM, 4 Artillery Lane, between St. George and Aviles Sts. Tel. 829-9729.

The C. F. Hamblen General Store was St. Augustine's one-stop shopping center from 1835 to 1960, and the museum on its premises today replicates the emporium at the turn of the century. On display are over 100,000 items sold here in that era, many of them gleaned from the store's attic. They include such diverse items as red-flannel underwear, high-button shoes, lace-up corsets, butter churns, gramophones, spinning wheels, sewing machines, 1890s bathing suits, snuff boxes, barrels of dill pickles (you can purchase one), and medicines that were 90% alcohol! Some 19th-century brand-name products shown here are still available today, among them Hershey's chocolate, Ivory soap, and Campbell's soups. A harness-maker's shop, blacksmith, gunmaker, cobbler, and ship's chandlery were on the premises, and vehicles sold here ran the gamut from steam-driven tractors to Model-T Fords. Itinerant dentists and doctors treated patients at the store as well. It all makes for fascinating browsing. Visitors are greeted by guides in 19th-century dress, and recordings at various exhibits provide a self-guided tour. An adjoining gift shop carries old-time merchandise.

Admission: $4 adults, $1.50 children 6–12, free for kids under 6.

Open: Mon-Sat 9am–5pm, Sun noon–5pm (in summer, Sun 10am–5pm). **Closed:** Christmas Day.

THE OLDEST WOODEN SCHOOLHOUSE, 14 St. George St., between Orange and Cuna Sts. Tel. 824-0192.

This red cedar and cypress structure, held together by wooden pegs and handmade nails, is more than two centuries old, with hand-wrought beams still intact. Its original hand-split cypress roof shingles were replaced by cedar ones after a hurricane. The floor is composed of tabby, an oyster shell–based concrete. Minorcan immigrant Juan Genoply acquired the house in 1788. He lived upstairs with his wife and three children and ran a school downstairs. His classroom is re-created today with animated pupils and teacher (a typical lesson is shown), complete with a dunce and a below-stairs "dungeon" for unruly children. There's a display of old schoolroom artifacts, such as 19th-century readers. Rules for teachers from 1872 state that although "men teachers may take one evening each week for courting purposes . . ." "women teachers who marry or engage in unseemly conduct will be dismissed." Visitors can see a kitchen outbuilding where teachers prepared their meals and a kitchen garden where they grew produce. Also on the grounds are the old school bell, an outhouse, and a wishing well under the shade of an ancient pecan tree. The last class was held here in 1864.

Admission: $1.50 adults, 75¢ children 6–12, free for kids under 6. Park in the pay lot on the corner of Orange Street and Avenida Menéndez.

Open: Daily 9am–5pm. **Closed:** Christmas Day.

PENA-PECK HOUSE, 143 St. George St., at Treasury St. Tel. 829-5064.

Built in the early 18th century for Royal Treasurer Juan Estaven de Pena, this is one of St. Augustine's oldest surviving Spanish colonial structures. The coquina house was a social center—scene of many gala parties. When the British took control of the town in 1763, the de Penas were forced to leave, and the house was rented to wealthy aristocrat John Moultrie, who added fireplaces, glazed windows, and an east wing. The house changed hands many times after that before it was purchased by New England doctor Seth S. Peck in 1837. He did extensive repairs and added a second floor. Members of his family lived here through 1931, hence many of his beautiful original furnishings and china can be seen here on guided tours given daily between 12:30 and 4pm. A shop on the premises sells handcrafted items.

Admission: $2.50 adults, $2 seniors over 55, $1.50 children 12–18, free for kids under 12.

Open: Mon–Sat 10:30am–4:30pm, Sun noon–4:30pm. **Closed:** Major holidays.

POTTER'S WAX MUSEUM, 17 King St., between Aviles and St. George Sts. Tel. 829-9056.

Over 170 wax figures are on display at Potter's, among them not only key figures in local Florida history (Ponce de León, Pedro Menéndez de Avilés, and Seminole leader Osceola) but international religious leaders, kings and queens, presidents and premiers, military leaders, writers, artists, composers, poets, and explorers. And, of course, there's the requisite torture section, here focusing on the Spanish Inquisition. The features of each wax figure have been carefully researched at the British Museum in London, and equal effort was spent determining authentic costuming. Francis Drake and de Soto, for instance, are clad in actual armor from their eras. Wax figures are also incorporated into a 12-minute film presentation shown continually throughout the day. And in a workshop up front, you can see a craftsperson at work on wax figures.

Admission: $5 adults, $4.25 for seniors 55 and over, $2.75 children 6–12, free for kids under 6.

Open: Daily 9am–5pm (to 9pm June 15–Labor Day). **Closed:** Christmas Day.

RIPLEY'S BELIEVE IT OR NOT! MUSEUM, 19 San Marco Ave., at Castillo Dr. Tel. 824-1606.

Housed in a converted 1887 Moorish Revival residence known as Warden Castle—complete with battlements, massive chimneys, and rose windows—this massive display comprises hundreds of oddities and fascinating artifacts from faraway places collected by Robert Ripley.

Among the exhibits are a Haitian voodoo doll that was owned by "Papa Doc" Duvalier, letters carved on a pencil with a chain saw by Ray "Wild Mountain Man"

Murphy (a man who lost several fingers to his hobby), an African mask made with human skin flayed from prisoners of war, a replica of the Eiffel Tower made of 110,000 toothpicks, a 2,000-year-old mummified Egyptian cat, and a Fiji Island cannibal fork. Other exhibits—such as the woman who sat on a nest of eggs until they hatched and a 17-inch dwarf who was imprisoned for treason in a parrot's cage—utilize mannequins. Videos and a film at various points document amazing people tricks (such as the man who banged nails into wood planks with his hands and pulled them out with his teeth), and odd things people of various cultures eat (grubs, tarantulas, human bone soup).

Admission: $7.50 adults, $4.25 children 5–12, free for kids under 5. Parking is free on the premises.

Open: Daily 9am–6pm (till 9pm mid-June to Labor Day).

ST. AUGUSTINE ALLIGATOR FARM, 999 Anastasia Blvd. (Fla. A1A), at Old Quarry Rd. Tel. 824-3337.

A St. Augustine attraction since 1893, the Alligator Farm today houses the world's most complete collection of crocodilians, a category that includes alligators, crocodiles, caiman, and gavial. To celebrate its 100th birthday in 1993, the farm opened a new exhibit called "Land of Crocodiles." Encompassing all 22 species—and most of the 28 subspecies—it is arranged zoogeographically, by continent.

Another notable exhibit is Gomek, at 1,800 pounds and almost 18 feet in length, the largest crocodile in captivity in the western hemisphere. Its species (*Crocodylus porosus*) has been known to attack, kill, and devour humans. Housed in a setting that simulates its native New Guinea habitat, Gomek can be viewed both above and below water. In addition to alligators and crocs, other creatures on display here include geckos, prehensile-tailed skinks, lizards, snakes, tortoises, spider monkeys, and exotic birds. There are ponds filled with a variety of ducks, geese, and swans, as well as a petting zoo with Nubian goats, Mouflon sheep, and Fallow deer. And in addition to official residents, numerous shore birds feed in the park's natural tropical foliage and alligator-filled lagoon. The birds seek out roosts above the alligators, because they afford them protection from tree-climbing predators.

There are entertaining and very educational 20-minute alligator and reptile shows hourly throughout the day, and spring through fall you can often see narrated feedings (the menu highlights nutria, which are large muskrats); be sure to check the show and feeding schedule when you enter the park.

The Alligator Farm makes for a delightful and informative outing. The grounds are beautiful, the animal inhabitants are treated with respect and dignity, and environmental awareness is stressed. For many years the farm has been involved in breeding endangered crocodilians. It also maintains a habitat planted with southern red cedars for the endangered Sweadner's hairstreak butterfly.

Admission: $8.95 adults, $8.05 seniors 65 and over, $5.95 children 3–10, free for kids under 3. Parking is free.

Open: Daily 9am–5pm (to 6pm June–Labor Day).

ST. AUGUSTINE'S RESTORED SPANISH QUARTER, entrance on St. George St., between Cuna and Orange Sts. Tel. 825-6830.

This two-block area south of the City Gate is St. Augustine's most comprehensive historic section, where the city's colonial architecture and landscape have been re-created. Docents and craftspeople in 18th-century attire are on hand to interpret the life of early inhabitants. It wasn't until 1959 that a commission was established to restore and preserve the city's heritage. What you see today is the result of extensive research and archeological investigation under the auspices of the Historic St. Augustine Preservation Board. About 90% of the buildings in the area are reconstructions, with houses named for prominent occupants. Unless otherwise indicated, the buildings described below date to the mid-18th century, the period re-created here. Highlights include:

The Spanish Colonial–style **Triay House**—with its highly pitched shingled gable roof and grape arbor overhanging the patio—belonged to Minorcan settlers, Francisco and María Triay. The property remained in their family through 1834.

Today it serves as an orientation center, where visitors learn about area history and archeological studies and view many of the artifacts uncovered in local digs.

The **Gómez House** was the home of Lorenzo Gómez, a foot soldier, and his Native American wife, Catalina. They lived in this sparsely furnished one-room cypress A-frame with three children, operating a store on the premises. Some of the items they would have sold—such as wine, blankets and fabrics, rosin (used heated for caulking), beans, jars of olives, and tobacco—can be seen here. There's a loft upstairs where the children slept in cold weather on straw-filled mattresses. Generally, whole families slept in the same room; privacy was not an issue for them. Like most people of this era, the Gómez family had little furniture. It all had to be handcrafted, which took time, and it was difficult to gather the requisite wood because of the danger of attack by local tribes. Cooking was done in the yard outdoors, where you'll also see a square coquina well (the family's water source) and a typical vegetable garden. Most residents of this old garrison town raised much of their own food.

The **Gallegos House,** built in 1720, was home to Martín Martínez Gallegos and his wife, Victoria, who lived here with three children and Juan Garcia, a retired infantryman in his 60s. The Gallegos family was more affluent than the Gómez family. Martín was an officer—an artillery sergeant stationed at the Castillo. Their two-room tabby (oyster-shell concrete) home has a built-in interior masonry stove, though most cooking was still done outside over a wood fire. An outdoor wooden trough served the Gallegos family as a sink, washing machine, and bathtub, with whelk shells used for dippers. In the yard is a three-barrel well (people dug a hole until they hit water and then inserted as many barrels as necessary to form a well). In addition to fruit trees, vegetables, and herbs, there's aloe growing in the walled garden; it was used for healing purposes. A craftsperson on the premises demonstrates lace making. Note the swinging rat shelf used to store food over the table; its motion scared rats away. Outside is a *matate* made of volcanic rock as well as a mortar and pestle—all used for grinding corn. It may interest you to know that hand-grinding corn for three hours produces enough for just one loaf of bread!

Nearby, a woodworker demonstrates how items such as furniture, kitchen implements, and religious artifacts were made in the 18th century. And farther along is a **blacksmith shop** where a craftsman turns out hand-wrought hardware using 18th-century methods. He can tell you about his work, his life (he lives above the shop), and everyday expressions deriving from his craft, such as "strike when the iron is hot."

The rectangular **Gonzáles House,** home of cavalryman Bernardo Gonzáles, is larger than many of its neighbors, indicating a prosperous owner. The architecture is typical of the first Spanish Period, with a flat roof constructed of hand-hewn boards laid across hand-hewn rafters. The house is used for spinning and weaving demonstrations utilizing a 1797 loom. Here you'll see the exquisite natural yarn colors created from berries, carrots, onionskins, plants like marigold and indigo, and crushed insects. The vegetable garden is supplemented by plants used for dyes.

The tabby **Geronimo de Hita y Salazar House** was home to a soldier with a large family. Today it is set up to represent a tavern with kegs of wine and beer and chairs ranged along the walls, as was the custom in the 1740s. A sparsely furnished typical soldier's bedroom adjoins.

The **DeMesa-Sánchez House** exemplifies two periods. Two rooms date to the residence of shore guard Antonio de Mesa in the late 1700s, while a second story was added in the 19th century. Furnishings reflect the comfortable lifestyle of Charles and Mary Jane Loring, who lived here during the American Territorial Period (1821–45). They even had a bathtub in the kitchen, the practice of bathing having recently come into vogue. The Lorings had servants and slaves to do rough work, and, unlike earlier residents, enjoyed some leisure. Mr. Loring might have used this time to attend horse races or pursue real estate interests; his wife might have played an instrument or done needlework. The house is made of coquina, which has been plastered over and painted pink. A docent costumed as Mr. Loring gives tours on the half hour, and there are quilting demonstrations on Thursday morning.

The **José Peso de Burgo and Francisco Pellicer House,** a wooden structure dating from the British Period (1763–83), was shared by two families. Peso de Burgo, a Corsican, was a merchant and shopkeeper; Francisco Pellicer, a Minorcan carpenter. The families had separate kitchens. Today a shop occupies the house, selling books and gift items relating to the period. Outbuildings here were used as slave quarters and for storage.

After you've left the Spanish Quarter, explore the quaint narrow streets nearby. They also contain many reconstructed and original historic buildings (indicated by markers), as well as charming boutiques and antique shops.

Admission: Ticket for all exhibit buildings, $5 adults, $3.75 seniors, $2.50 students 6–18, free for kids under 6; $10 maximum per family. Park in the lot at the Visitor Information Center at San Marco Avenue and Castillo Drive.

Open: Daily 9am–5pm. **Closed:** Christmas.

SPANISH MILITARY HOSPITAL, 3 Aviles St., at King St. Tel. 825-6808.
What you see today is a reconstruction of the Royal Hospital of Our Lady of Guadalupe, which occupied this site from 1791 to 1821. A docent in period dress explains exhibits, which include the grisly tools of 18th-century medicine (saws, implements for removing bullets, dental instruments, scalpels for bleeding—remember that all procedures were done without anesthesia), an apothecary's office where medicines were made, a herb garden with plants marked for medicinal uses, a typical ward, and a display on the history of medicine.

Admission: Free; donations appreciated. Parking is free on the premises.

Open: The hospital is run by volunteers, so days and hours vary; it's generally open daily from 9am to 5pm.

WHERE TO STAY

St. Augustine's accommodations include lovely bed-and-breakfast lodgings, most of them in beautifully restored historic homes. Generally, the B&Bs don't take young children.

HOTELS AT THE BEACH

LA FIESTA OCEANSIDE INN, 810 Fla. A1A Beach Blvd. (at F St.), St. Augustine Beach, FL 32084. Tel. 904/471-2220, or toll free 800/852-6390. Fax 904/471-0186. 36 rms. A/C TV TEL

$ Rates: Labor Day to early Feb, $40–$45 single or double; $65 ocean-view room or bridal suite. Early Feb to Labor Day, $60–$70 single or double; $90 ocean-view room or bridal suite. Additional person $5 extra. AE, CB, DC, DISC, MC, V.
Parking: Free.

La Fiesta's cheerful beachfront accommodations are housed in two-story tan stucco buildings with Spanish-style terra-cotta roofs and fragrant Confederate jasmine climbing the columns. They're decorated in soft, beachy hues, with white furnishings and prints of beach scenes adorning stucco walls. Eight offer ocean views, and two are ocean-view bridal suites equipped with extra-large tubs (ample for two), wet bars, small refrigerators, and king-size beds. The latter have very nice rattan and bamboo furnishings. All rooms are equipped with remote-control cable TVs.

Dining/Entertainment: The sunny Beachhouse Cafe serves breakfast daily from 7am to noon, with options ranging from hotcakes to eggs scrambled with sharp Cheddar and ham served with grits and homemade biscuits. You can also get sandwiches and award-winning Minorcan clam chowder here, and if you sample the alligator salad, you're given a certificate of membership in the Alligator Eating Society of America.

Facilities: Coin-op washer/dryers, boardwalk over the dunes, beach, children's playground, 60-foot pool, 18-hole beachfront miniature golf course, small video-game room, hair salon, picnic area with barbecue grill.

OCEAN GALLERY, 4600 Fla. A1A S. (between Dondonville Rd. and Trade Winds Lane), St. Augustine, FL 32084. Tel. 904/471-6663, or toll free 800/940-6665. 200 condo apts. A/C TV TEL

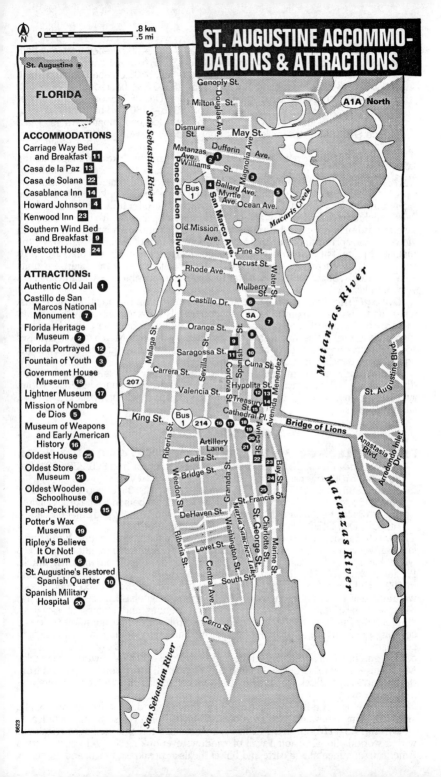

ST. AUGUSTINE ACCOMMO-DATIONS & ATTRACTIONS

0 | .8 km
.5 mi

FLORIDA

St. Augustine

ACCOMMODATIONS

Carriage Way Bed
and Breakfast **11**
Casa de la Paz **13**
Casa de Solana **22**
Casablanca Inn **14**
Howard Johnson **4**
Kenwood Inn **23**
Southern Wind Bed
and Breakfast **9**
Westcott House **24**

ATTRACTIONS:

Authentic Old Jail **1**
Castillo de San
Marcos National
Monument **7**
Florida Heritage
Museum **2**
Florida Portrayed **12**
Fountain of Youth **3**
Government House
Museum **18**
Lightner Museum **17**
Mission of Nombre
de Dios **5**
Museum of Weapons
and Early American
History **16**
Oldest House **25**
Oldest Store
Museum **21**
Oldest Wooden
Schoolhouse **8**
Pena-Peck House **15**
Potter's Wax
Museum **19**
Ripley's Believe
It Or Not!
Museum **6**
St. Augustine's Restored
Spanish Quarter **10**
Spanish Military
Hospital **20**

Genoply St.
Milton St.
Douglas Ave.
Dismure St.
May St.
Matanzas Ave.
Williams St.
Dufferin St.
Magnolia Ave.
A1A North
Bus 1
Ballard Ave.
Myrtle Ave.
Ocean Ave.
San Marco Ave.
Ponce de Leon Blvd.
Old Mission Ave.
Macaris Creek
Pine St.
Locust St.
Rhode Ave.
Water St.
Mulberry St.
Castillo Dr.
Matanzas River
5A
Orange St.
Malaga St.
Saragossa St.
Sevilla St.
Carrera St.
Spanish St.
Cordova St.
Cuna St.
207
Valencia St.
Hypolita St.
Treasury St.
Avenida Menendez
King St.
Bus 1
214
Cathedral Pl.
Aviles St.
Bridge of Lions
St. Augustine Blvd.
Artillery Lane
Cadiz St.
Bridge St.
Bay St.
Anastasia Blvd.
Arredondo Dr.
Weedon St.
Spanish St.
St. Francis St.
DeHaven St.
Maria Sanchez Lake
St. George St.
Charlotte St.
Marine St.
Riberia St.
Lovet St.
Washington St.
Central Ave.
South St.
Matanzas River
San Sebastian River
Cerro St.
San Sebastian River
San Sebastian River

$ Rates (per week, one-week minimum): Mar–Aug, $400 one-bedroom/one-bath apt; $425 two-bedroom/one-bath apt; $450–$645 two-bedroom/two-bath apt; $525–$775 three-bedroom/two-bath apt. Jan–Feb, $300 one-bedroom/one-bath apt; $325 two-bedroom/one-bath apt; $350–$500 two-bedroom/two-bath apt; $425–$625 three-bedroom/two-bath apt. Sept–Dec, $275 one-bedroom/one-bath apt; $295 two-bedroom/one-bath apt; $315–$460 two-bedroom/two-bath apt; $375–$560 three-bedroom/two-bath apt. Reduced monthly rates. Maid service $40–$45 extra for length of stay. MC, V. **Parking:** $10 length-of-stay charge.

Set on 44 attractively landscaped acres with gardens, lakes, and lagoons, the Ocean Gallery offers beautiful vacation homes with access to 17 miles of palm-fringed, white sandy beach. All its condos are decorated in upscale resort styles, complete with such residential touches as shelves of knickknacks; some have VCRs and/or CD and cassette players. Units offer fully equipped kitchens (including dishwashers, washer/dryers, and refrigerators with ice makers), full living and dining areas, and furnished balconies or patios. About half have beach views, but keep in mind that the more stunningly beautiful your ocean view, the higher the price. These are very spacious living quarters; one-bedroom units are 1,110 square feet, two-bedroom units 1,156 to 1,320 square feet, three-bedroom units 1,450 to 1,627 square feet. Book as far in advance as possible; the Ocean Gallery is very popular.

Dining/Entertainment: There are no restaurants on the premises, since most guests do their own cooking (a Publix supermarket is a few minutes away by car), but there are barbecue grills and picnic tables at the Clubhouse, and some units have their own outdoor grills. Restaurants are nearby. January through March, an on-premises social director organizes daily activities such as walks, bridge games, Bingo, crafts, aqua-robics, dancing, and cocktail parties.

Facilities: Five swimming pools, five whirlpools, four hard-surface tennis courts (lit for night play), two racquetball courts, two shuffleboard courts, exercise room, two saunas, small video-game room, clubhouse (equipped with games and a library), storage lockers.

A RESORT HOTEL

PONCE DE LEÓN GOLF & CONFERENCE RESORT, 4000 U.S. 1 N., St. Augustine, FL 32095. Tel. 904/824-2821, or toll free 800/228-2821. Fax 904/829-6108. 169 rms, 24 minisuites, 7 suites. A/C TV TEL

$ Rates: $85 single; $95 double; $95 minisuite for one, $105 for two; $145 suite for one, $155 for two. $10 higher June–July. Additional person $10 extra. Children under 18 stay free in parents' room. Inquire about golf, family, and other packages. AE, CB, DC, DISC, ER, JCB, MC, V. **Parking:** Free.

This lovely 350-acre resort—with a beautiful championship golf course bordering a large saltwater marsh/bird sanctuary—has been a St. Augustine tradition since 1916 when Henry Flagler built it to complement his ultra-luxurious in-town hotels. President Warren G. Harding came here to relax on the greens before his inauguration in 1921, and many famous golfers have played the course. Resort accommodations were added in 1952. The grounds, shaded by palms, magnolias, and centuries-old live oaks, vary neat flower beds with duck-filled lagoons and clumps of sawgrass. Traditionally furnished rooms are large and cheerful, with white faux-moiré silk wall coverings; teal, mauve, or raspberry carpeting; and pretty floral-print bedspreads in complementary colors. All feature furnished patios or balconies overlooking the golf course, and in-room amenities include remote-control cable TVs (with 35 channels). Minisuites—ideal for families—additionally offer small sitting rooms separated from sleeping areas by trellises, clock radios, in-room coffee makers, small refrigerators, and microwave ovens.

The hotel is just a five-minute drive from the historic district. Rooms and public areas are being renovated at this writing, and landscaping is also being upgraded.

Dining/Entertainment: Michael's, an attractive cathedral-ceilinged restaurant with a working fireplace and a wall of windows overlooking the golf course, serves American/continental à la carte and buffet meals at breakfast, lunch, and dinner. A lavish prime rib and seafood buffet is featured every Saturday night, and a pianist and guitarist entertain at extensive champagne buffet brunches every Sunday. The adjoining bamboo-furnished Bogie Lounge, also with golf course views, offers complimentary happy-hour hors d'oeuvres, nightly piano-bar entertainment, and light fare; patio seating is a plus in good weather. And Mulligan's off the Tee offers light fare to golfers.

Facilities: Donald Ross–designed par-72 championship golf course, 18-hole poolside putting green, golf pro shop, six hard-surface tennis courts (lit for night play), large cloverleaf-shaped swimming pool, sand volleyball court, shuffleboard, croquet, bocci ball, basketball, horseshoes, jogging trails, coin-op washer/dryers, planned activities (nature walks, movies, games, etc.) for children in summer.

MOTEL ACCOMMODATIONS

HOWARD JOHNSON, 137 San Marco Ave. (between Sebastian/Myrtle Aves. and Sanchez Ave.), St. Augustine, FL 32084. Tel. 904/824-6181. 70 rms, 7 suites. A/C TV TEL
$ Rates (including continental breakfast): $49–$79 for up to four Sun–Thurs; $59–$89 Fri–Sat; $99.95 during special events and holidays. $99–$129 Jacuzzi room; $159–$199 Jacuzzi suite. Children under 18 stay free in parents' room. AE, CB, DC, DISC, ER, JCB, MC, V. **Parking:** Free.

HoJo's terra-cotta–roofed mission-style building evokes the Spanish colonial period. Its standard motel rooms—decorated in teal and peach with bleached-wood furnishings—offer remote-control TVs.

On-premises facilities include a medium-size swimming pool and whirlpool surrounded by flower beds, coin-op washer/dryers, and a small video-games room. A garden courtyard planted with palms and hibiscus centers on a massive 500-year-old live oak draped in Spanish moss. Continental breakfast is served in a pleasant nook off the lobby. HoJo is just a few minutes from the historic district.

BED & BREAKFAST

Expensive

CASA DE SOLANA, 21 Aviles St. (at Cadiz St.), St. Augustine, FL 32084. Tel. 904/824-3555. 4 suites (all with bath). A/C TV
$ Rates (including full breakfast): $125 suite for one or two. Children under 12 not accepted. AE, DISC, MC, V.

This charming dormer-windowed colonial house was built in 1763 for Don Manuel Solana—a Spanish soldier. Like all of St. Augustine's early buildings (this is the city's seventh-oldest house), it was constructed of coquina stone, but in the mid-1800s the exterior was covered over with the pale-pink stucco you see today. The house is fronted by a lovely walled garden planted with jasmine and trumpet vines. And since it has been under the rule of three governments, British, Spanish, and American flags fly from the balcony.

Hostess Faye McMurry has been running a B&B in these historic precincts since 1982. Her homemade breakfasts—an egg dish (perhaps a quichelike sausage-and-cheese casserole), delicious fresh-baked muffins and breads, fruit juices, grits, and gourmet teas and coffees—are served in an elegant crystal-chandeliered dining room with Williamsburg-blue wainscotting and dark-wood beams overhead. Faye dons colonial dress for the occasion and sets her table with fine china and silver.

The rooms are nicely decorated with antique pieces, such as white wicker furnishings. Yours might have a four-poster, brass, art deco, or mahogany-rice bed, perhaps made up with a ribbon-and-lace quilt and pillow shams. Attractive window treatments (cornices, balloon curtains) and doors hung with vine wreaths enhance the homey ambience, as do decorative fireplaces. All accommodations are equipped with cable color TVs, radios, and clocks (a public phone is in the hallway), and you'll find a welcoming decanter of sherry in your room on arrival. Three suites have full living rooms (the fourth has a small parlor), and one has a balcony. Bicycles are available free of charge. And there's a baby grand in the dining room, scene of occasional impromptu nighttime sing-alongs. No smoking is permitted in the house. There's free parking at the Oldest House Museum, a block away.

WESTCOTT HOUSE, 146 Avenida Menendez (between Bridge and Francis Sts.), St. Augustine, FL 32084. Tel. 904/824-4301. 8 rms (all with bath). A/C TV TEL
$ Rates (including continental breakfast): $95–$135 single or double Sun–Thurs, $135 Fri–Sat. AE, MC, V.

Its bayfront location would make Westcott House a winner, even if it were not for its pristine and exquisitely furnished rooms. Everything here just gleams. Another of St. Augustine's elegant 19th-century houses, this two-story Victorian/Queen Anne wood frame is neatly painted pale peach with white trim and gray-blue shutters. A porch and second-story veranda—both furnished with white wicker rockers and hung with plants—overlook the boat-filled Matanzas Bay, as does a coquina-walled brick courtyard with ornate white garden furnishings under shade trees. All these make delightful venues for breakfast, which here consists of croissants and danish, fresh fruit, juices, bagels and cream cheese, dry cereal, and tea or coffee.

As for the above-mentioned rooms—some with bay windows and/or working fireplaces—they're simply stunning. A typical unit has a brass bed made up with a white quilt and lace dust ruffle, pretty floral-print wallpaper, and kelly-green chintz balloon curtains. Another, painted pale pink with plum trim, has Victorian furnishings, a fan chandelier overhead, a highly polished pine floor strewn with area rugs, and walls hung with attractive artwork and vintage photographs. And all offer in-room hairdryers, clocks, and remote-control cable TVs (discreetly concealed in armoires). On-premises amenities include a barbecue grill in the courtyard and bicycles for rent. Complimentary fresh fruit and peach or apricot brandy are available all day in the parlor, and guests are cosseted with terry bathrobes and fruit brandies and chocolates at nightly turn-down. Smoking is not permitted in the house. There's parking on the street or free in a nearby lot.

Moderate

CARRIAGE WAY BED AND BREAKFAST, 70 Cuna St. (between Cordova and Spanish Sts.), St. Augustine, FL 32084. Tel. 904/829-2467. 9 rms (all with bath) A/C TEL
$ Rates (including full breakfast): $59–$95 single or double Sun–Thurs, $69–$105 Fri–Sat. Children under 8 not accepted. DISC, MC, V. **Parking:** Free on premises.

Occupying an 1883 Victorian wood-frame house fronted by roses and hibiscus, the Carriage Way is in the heart of the historic district. Its rooms—charmingly decorated in soft pastel colors like pale peach, powder blue, and mint green—are furnished with quality antiques. One unit has an oak four-poster bed with carved pineapple posts made up with a white comforter, lacy dust ruffle, and eyelet-trimmed pillow shams. Others have brass, wicker, or even canopy beds. Accommodations are enhanced by beautiful dried-flower arrangements and wreaths, lovely curtains and window treatments, and aesthetically pleasing paintings. One guest room features a converted wood-burning fireplace (it burns Sterno); another, a cathedral ceiling with high triangular windows. Baths throughout have clawfoot tubs and are papered in pretty floral prints.

A console TV, books, magazines, and games are provided in a comfortable parlor. And a second-story veranda offers a nice view of the picturesque area (horse-drawn carriages frequently pass by). Breakfast, served in the dining room or al fresco on the front porch, includes eggs, breakfast meats, homemade fruit breads and muffins, fresh fruit, juice, and beverage. Hospitable owner/hosts Bill and Diane Johnson offer many complimentary extras: bicycles for touring the area; tea and coffee set out all day long in the dining room; decanters of crème de menthe, red wine, and sherry ever available on a buffet table in the entrance hallway; and a refrigerator stocked with iced glasses, beer, and soft drinks. A basket of complimentary sundries—toothpaste, sewing kit, razor—is available, and guests can also utilize the Johnsons' washer and dryer at no charge. On request, you can arrange romantic extras such as long-stemmed roses and/or champagne in your room, breakfast in bed, or a gourmet picnic lunch. No smoking is permitted in the house.

CASA DE LA PAZ, 22 Avenida Menendez (between Hypolita and Treas-ury Sts.), St. Augustine, FL 32084. Tel. 904/829-2915. 4 rms, 2 suites (all with bath). A/C TV

$ Rates (including full breakfast): $80–$95 single or double Sun–Thurs, $95–$120 Fri–Sat. Additional person $10 extra. Children under 8 not accepted. AE, DISC, MC, V. **Parking:** Free behind house and nearby.

⭐ This bayfront white stucco Mediterranean Revival B&B offers up an alluring package. Its exquisite country French rooms and public areas are *Architectural Digest* caliber, and owner/hostess Mavis Maki proffers warm hospitality. The inn (built in 1915) is entered via a lovely sun-drenched parlor furnished in white wicker, with thriving plants hanging in arched windows and potted palms adding Victorian nuance. French doors lead to a pristinely charming dining room—very 18th century, with white-trimmed, pale-yellow walls, and a Georgian-style chandelier over the table. Full breakfasts are served here each morning—egg casseroles, bagels, granola, fresh-baked fruit breads and muffins, juice, platters of fresh-cut fruit, and tea or coffee. Guests can relax in the living room, where furnishings are ranged around a wood-burning fireplace, and a large picture window overlooks Matanzas Bay. Water views can also be enjoyed from a second-story veranda. And a charming walled garden behind the house—planted with palms, camellias, gardenias, jasmin, hibiscus, and pots of geraniums—centers on a small swimming pool.

Rooms furnished with antiques are delightfully decorated in pastel colors such as eggshell green, pale yellow, and lavender. Glossy pine floors are strewn with Oriental rugs, lacy metal beds are made up with snowy-white quilts set off by charming floral-chintz pillow shams and dust ruffles, walls are hung with framed botanical prints and gorgeous dried-flower wreaths, and windows are adorned with white lace and swagged curtains. Live plants and ficus trees enhance the residential ambience. A remote-control cable TV is discreetly concealed in an armoire, and a clock is available. One suite has a working fireplace. Mavis stocks her guest rooms with an assortment of books and magazines, a decanter of sherry, and chocolates. Compli-mentary wine and champagne are available on request, gratis refreshments are served afternoons, and a refrigerator in the downstairs kitchen is stocked with soda, beer, and wine. There's a washer/dryer for guest use. No smoking is permitted in the house.

CASABLANCA INN, 24 Avenida Menendez (between Hypolita and Treasury Sts.), St. Augustine, FL 32084. Tel. 904/829-0928, or toll free 800/826-2626. Fax 904/826-1892. 2 rms, 10 suites (all with bath). A/C

$ Rates (including continental breakfast): Mon–Thurs, $59–$79 double; $65–$115 suite. Fri–Sun, $79–$100 double; $85–$135 suite. Children under 10 not accepted. AE, MC, V. **Parking:** Free on premises.

This 1914 Mediterranean-style white stucco house faces directly on the bay. Guests enjoy stunning water views from rocking chairs on the colonnaded portico or through large windows in the cozy parlor. And though over half the rooms and suites offer full marine vistas—and all have private balconies or porches—most divinely decadent are the two second-floor suites whose bayfront balconies are equipped with hammocks.

Owners and charming hosts Brenda and Tony Bushell have done a nice job decorating here. White-walled, carpeted rooms are furnished with turn-of-the-century American oak pieces and have beds (some of them four-posters) made up with down comforters and windows framed by pretty floral-chintz curtains. Homey touches might include a Victorian birdcage, dried-flower wreath, lamps with fringed shades, teddy bears, toy soldiers, or a grouping of antique dolls on your mantel. All offer a selection of books, fan chandeliers, and AM/FM alarm-clock radios. Suites have sitting room areas, and, in some cases, Jacuzzis. Guests can use the microwave and refrigerator in the kitchen and help themselves to complimentary beer, wine, soda, tea, coffee, chocolates, and cookies at all times. And a scrumptious breakfast—which can be enjoyed al fresco on the porch or in a glass-enclosed conservatory/reading room—includes thick slabs of French toast or a Minorcan baked eggs and sausage soufflé, fresh-fruit salad, fresh-baked danish, juice, and tea or coffee. The

Bushells play classical music in public areas. Bicycles are available free of charge. No smoking is permitted in the house.

SOUTHERN WIND BED & BREAKFAST, 18 Cordova St. (between Sara-gossa and Orange Sts.), St. Augustine, FL 32084. Tel. 904/825-3623. Fax 904/829-0946. 8 rms (all with bath). A/C TV

$ Rates (including full breakfast): $60–$129 single or double. Additional person $8 extra. Rooms on boat $150 per night, with a two-night minimum. AE, DISC, MC, V.
Parking: Free on premises.

Dennis and Jeanette Dean, originally from Los Angeles, were crusing on their yacht in 1988, docked in St. Augustine, fell in love with the town, and decided to stay on. Hence, the Southern Wind (it was the name of the boat), a charming two-story colonnaded house fronted by a flower-bordered lawn. A plant-filled porch and second-story veranda are furnished with white wicker rockers and armchairs. Inside, a cozy parlor with a lace-curtained bay window has wing chairs and sofas facing a fireplace. The eclectically furnished rooms are homey, offering a mix of antiques and flea-market finds. They have glossy pine floors, beds made up with ruffled pillow shams, and attractive window treatments such as balloon curtains. Most desirable are the Honeymoon Suite—which, like the parlor downstairs has a bay window—and a luxurious Jacuzzi suite. Guests are cosseted with fresh flowers and chocolates on arrival, and wine is served in the parlor every afternoon. Classical music is played in public areas. Breakfast consists of fresh fruit, fresh-baked fruit breads and muffins, bagels and cream cheese, juice, and a hot dish—perhaps baked eggs with ham and spices.

The Deans also have another B&B close by, the **Family Inn,** 34 Saragossa St. (same phone; $65–$105 double), a vine-covered cottage with a white picket fence. Rooms here offer wet bars, small refrigerators, coffee makers, and microwaves; dishes and utensils are supplied.

Inexpensive

THE KENWOOD INN, 38 Marine St. (at Bridge St.), St. Augustine, FL 32084. Tel. 904/824-2116. 10 rms, 4 suites (all with bath). A/C

$ Rates (including continental breakfast): $45–$65 single; $55–$85 double; $125 three-room suite for one or two. Additional person $10 extra. Children under 8 not accepted. DISC, MC, V.

The delightful Kenwood Inn wins points with me by playing classical music in its public areas. Originally built as a summer residence, this hip-roofed Victorian wood-frame house with graceful verandas—today invitingly painted in pale peach with white trim—has served as a boarding house or inn since the late 19th century. It's on the National Register of Historic Places.

Each room is uniquely decorated. The Colonial Room, for instance, is painted in Williamsburg blue and furnished with a canopied mahogany bed, a beautiful oak armoire, and rocking chairs. The very feminine Classic Rose Room has mint walls and white iron beds made up with rose-motif bedspreads, ruffled curtains, and pillow shams. Navy-blue paisley fabrics, an antique steamer trunk, a ship's desk, and nautical prints set the theme for the Captain's Room. Chintz plaids, balloon curtains, wing chairs, a king-size mahogany bed, and a working fireplace are assets of the Old English Room. The exquisite Country French Room (my favorite) has an 18th-century-reproduction headboard and sofas upholstered in striped chintz. And you don't have to be a newlywed to rent the lovely 1,000-square-foot Honeymoon Suite offering bay views along with an eat-in kitchen and separate living and sitting rooms. Throughout, highly polished pine-plank floors are strewn with Chinese and Persian rugs, fans whirr slowly overhead, and decorative touches include framed vintage photographs, botanical prints, dried-flower wreaths, and charming hand-painted fireplace screens. A private wraparound veranda with cushioned white wicker furnishings and rocking chairs is a plus for residents of two rooms upstairs. Some accommodations offer TVs.

Breakfast—coffee, juice, and freshly baked muffins, fruit breads, cinnamon strudels, and cakes—can be enjoyed in a lovely parlor with lace-curtained bay windows and a working fireplace; in a wicker-furnished sun room equipped with books, games, and a TV; or on the front porch. A small swimming pool, its sun deck planted with hibiscus, is a plus. And guests can also retreat to a secluded garden courtyard which has a fishpond and neat flower beds under the shade of a sprawling pecan tree. There's a refrigerator for guest use, and complimentary sherry, tea, and coffee are offered throughout the day. Smoking is not permitted in the house. Parking is on the street or free in a nearby lot.

WHERE TO DINE

For a small town, St. Augustine has a lot of excellent restaurants, many of them featuring fresh seafood. Local specialties include red-hot datil peppers, Minorcan clam chowder, alligator, and oysters.

EXPENSIVE

CATALINA'S GARDENS, 46 Avenida Menendez, between Cathedral Place and Treasury St. Tel. 824-7765.
  Cuisine: SEAFOOD/STEAK/PASTA. **Reservations:** Not required.
$ **Prices:** Appetizers $3.55–$6.25 at lunch, $3.95–$6.95 at dinner; main courses $4.95–$6.25 at lunch; $11.95–$18.95 at dinner. AE, MC, V.
  Open: Lunch Fri–Sun 11:30am–3pm; dinner Sun–Thurs 5–10pm, Fri–Sat 5–10:30pm.

Housed in a charming gable-roofed lime-green colonial-revival house (it dates to 1888), with dormer and Palladian windows, Catalina's Gardens is heralded by an imposing coquina archway over two centuries old. Inside, a cozy fire blazes in the lounge, which adjoins a bar and, via French doors, a plant-filled patio; weather permitting, you can dine al fresco. The candlelit dining rooms upstairs and down are intimate venues with seating at solid oak tables, many of them offering views of the bay. Background music ranges from mellow rock to Spanish guitar.

New England chowder—nuanced with Worcestershire and Tabasco and replete with chunks of clam and potatoes—makes a good beginning. Also available as an appetizer is crunchy tempura-battered coconut shrimp served with plum sauce, but it's so good that I suggest saving it for a main-course choice. Other possibilities range from prime rib au jus with creamy horseradish sauce to farm-raised salmon béarnaise, the latter not on the menu but a frequent special. Your main course comes with salad (select the Caesar) and roasted red bliss potatoes baked in butter, rosemary, and thyme. Limited main dishes, sandwiches, burgers, and salads are offered at lunch. For dessert there's mud pie—coffee and chocolate-chip ice cream layered with caramel and fudge and topped with fresh whipped cream and butter almonds. The key lime pie is also excellent.

Parking is on the street or in the bank lot on Charlotte Street directly behind the restaurant.

MODERATE

FIDDLER'S GREEN, 2750 Anahma Dr., at Ferroll Rd. on Vilano Beach. Tel. 824-8897.
  Cuisine: FLORIDIAN/SEAFOOD. **Reservations:** Recommended Sun–Fri, not accepted Sat. **Directions:** Head north on San Marco Avenue, cross the Vilano Bridge (Fla. A1A North), and bear right to Vilano Beach.
$ **Prices:** Appetizers $3.95–$5.50; main courses $8.95–$14.95. AE, CB, DC, DISC, MC, V.
  Open: Dinner only, Sun–Thurs 5–9pm, Fri–Sat 5–10pm.

Situated right on the Atlantic Ocean, the shiplike Fiddler's Green is appropriately entered via a kind of gangplank. Inside, rustic elegance is the keynote, an effect achieved with pecky cypress and cedar paneling, a beamed knotty-pine ceiling, two blazing coquina stone fireplaces, and a profusion of hanging plants. There's a warren of five gorgeous dining rooms, each with unique decorator schemes, varying from tropical to lodgelike to nautical. Most of the seating overlooks the grassy marsh and ocean beyond. Lighting is soft and romantic, and mellow jazz provides a simpatico musical backdrop.

Start your meal with peppery conch fritters fried in beer batter (ask for tarragon tartar sauce with them) or sautéed mushroom caps stuffed with finely chopped shrimp and artichokes in a brandied roasted red-pepper/cream sauce. For a main course, you can't go wrong with the Mariner—fresh catch of the day, lightly floured and sautéed in browned butter, lemon, and parsley. You can also order the daily catch crusted with sliced almonds and shredded coconut, baked, and topped with banana slices and creamy orange-curry sauce. Another noteworthy dish is chicken Anastasia, a roasted whole breast of chicken filled with a sherried apple/pecan/herb stuffing and glazed with raspberry-port sauce. All main courses come with fresh vegetables and a starch—perhaps coarsely mashed dolloped potatoes (mixed with onion, sour cream, and parsley, topped with old English Cheddar, and oven browned). You also get a very good house salad topped with kernels of popped wheat and a basket of fresh-baked squaw and sourdough breads. For dessert, try a "chimney sweep"—homemade espresso/chocolate-chip ice cream splashed with Kahlúa and crowned with fresh whipped cream. However, if the chocolate crème brûlée is on the menu, it's not to be missed. There's a carefully chosen and fairly extensive wine list. Free parking.

LA PARISIENNE, 60 Hypolita St., between Spanish and Cordova Sts. Tel. 829-0055.
   Cuisine: FRENCH. **Reservations:** Recommended.
$ Prices: Appetizers $5.50–$6.80; main courses $4.95–$6.50 at lunch, $12–$16.95 at dinner; breakfast items 75¢–$1.50. AE, DISC, MC, V.
   Open: Breakfast Sat–Sun 9am–11am; lunch Tues–Sun 11am–3pm; afternoon tea Tues–Sun 3–4pm; dinner Tues–Sun 5:30–9pm (6–9pm May–Aug).

This quaintly charming little restaurant does indeed evoke Paris in both ambience and cuisine, and its location in the heart of the picturesque historic district further enhances the illusion that you're dining in Europe. A trellised, plant-filled entrance-way leads to a lovely dining room with a rough-hewn beamed pine ceiling, lace-curtained windows, and wicker-seated ladderback chairs at crisply white-linened tables (candlelit at night). The restaurant is run by the Poncet family of Provence, who are expanding at this writing by adding an upstairs dining room.

Begin your dinner with a fan of rare duck slices over a salad of exotic lettuces in raspberry vinaigrette or a delicious velvety crab bisque. Recommendable main courses include a classic steak au poivre in cognac-cream sauce and roast rack of lamb coated with Dijon mustard and fresh garlic. Both are served with house salad and two side dishes—perhaps haricots verts and scalloped potatoes gratiné with Gruyère. The lunch menu offers traditional bistro fare—quiche Lorraine, croque monsieur (the Gallic answer to an American grilled ham-and-cheese sandwich), croissant sandwiches, and salad niçoise, among other selections. Fresh-baked baguettes are served with your meal, and an extensive international wine list is available.

Also visit La Parisienne for a delightful weekend breakfast of rich French coffee and flaky-buttery croissants—perhaps filled with apricots and crème pâtissière. Croissants are also served at afternon tea (which could as well be afternoon espresso or cappuccino), along with oven-fresh chocolate eclairs, praline ganaches, white-chocolate mousse cakes layered with raspberries, and fruit tarts.

RAINTREE, 102 San Marco Ave., at Bernard St. Tel. 824-7211.
   Cuisine: CONTINENTAL. **Reservations:** Recommended. **Transportation:** A complimentary courtesy car provides transportation from/to local hotels.
$ Prices: Appetizers $4.95–$7.95; main courses $8.95–$19.95; early dinner selections (served 5–6pm) $8.95–$10.95; children's dishes $5.95. AE, CB, DC, MC, V.
   Open: Dinner only, daily 5–10pm.

Occupying an 1879 Victorian house, this is one of St. Augustine's most romantic restaurants. Bamboo furnishings, dozens of plants and ficus trees, and a red-and-white-striped canvas awning create a cozy garden ambience, and cut-crystal lamps cast a soft glow on red-linened tables. Soft jazz enhances the ambience. Some seating is upstairs in a charming plant-filled room with swagged damask curtains and stained-glass panels; a model of a Bequian whaling boat serves as a room divider. And, weather permitting, you might opt for after-dinner drinks or dessert and coffee on the open-air porch, balcony, or lushly planted brick patio. Note the landscaping, which includes a gazebo, fountain, koi pond, and small aviary.

Truffle goose-liver pâté with toast points makes a heavenly appetizer. You can dine inexpensively here by ordering a crêpe dish, or in the same price category, a pasta dish such as linguine sautéed in herbed garlic butter tossed with sun-dried tomatoes, artichoke hearts, and black olives in sherry-cream sauce. More serious main courses include fresh fish of the day (I had grouper with sautéed mushrooms in a white wine–Dijon mustard–cream sauce), rack of lamb with port wine sauce, beef Wellington, and filet mignon béarnaise. All come with potatoes du jour (perhaps au gratin), fresh vegetables, a basket of hot fresh-baked breads, and a house salad of 17 varieties of leaf lettuce in a balsamic vinaigrette with crumbled Gorgonzola. The menu is augmented by many daily specials and complimented by an extensive, award-winning wine list. Desserts range from crêpes Suzette to a sinfully rich chocolate mousse served in a white-chocolate cup.

INEXPENSIVE

CREEKSIDE DINERY, 160 Nix Boat Yard Rd., off U.S. 1 (turn at Long John Silver). Tel. 829-6113.
> **Cuisine:** TRADITIONAL FLORIDIAN. **Reservations:** Not accepted.
> **$ Prices:** Appetizers $2.75–$5; main courses $4.50–$6 at lunch, $8–$14 at dinner. AE, DISC, MC, V.
> **Open:** Lunch Mon–Fri 11:30am–2:30pm; dinner Sun–Thurs 5–9pm, Fri–Sat 5–10pm.

This cozy restaurant occupies a dormer-windowed white frame house fronted by live oak, pecan, and magnolia trees. Guests wait for tables on a rose vine–covered porch furnished with wicker rocking chairs. The rough-hewn cedar interior is equally charming, with curtained multipaned windows, numerous plants and ficus trees, and seating under a peaked cathedral ceiling with fishnet draped over white-painted beams. Each candlelit table has a different cloth, creating a cheerful variegated effect. There's additional seating in a back room and on a screened patio overlooking a creek and boatyard. Big Band music from the '30s and '40s creates a perfect acoustic backdrop.

A good beginning here is hot-and-spicy shellfish chowder—a rich seafood stew to which datil peppers add considerable zest. The creamy chicken buttermilk bisque is also excellent. And I love garlicky, buttery oysters Creekside topped with oven-browned provolone cheese and herbed breadcrumbs. Among the main courses, a superb specialty is the catch of the day (mine was a marvelously tender fresh flounder) baked on an oak plank and topped with crunchy breadcrumbs and horseradish-spiked mustard sauce. It came with roasted potatoes and fresh stringbeans and butter beans seasoned with herb-garlic butter. Also fabulous: sautéed fresh shrimp Sebastian, served with a garlic- and cilantro-flavored tomato-cream sauce over angel-hair pasta. Steaks and chicken dishes (perhaps roast chicken glazed with rosemary-plum sauce) are also options. Main courses are served with a basket of soft garlicky breadsticks and a tasty house salad. The all-American wine list highlights selections from Florida vineyards. Leave room for a dessert called "the chocolate thing," basically an old-fashioned icebox cake made of chocolate cookie and whipped cream layers. Arrive early to avoid a wait.

GYPSY CAB COMPANY, 828 Anastasia Blvd. (Fla. A1A), between White and Comares Sts. Tel. 824-8244.
> **Cuisine:** URBAN ECLECTIC. **Reservations:** Not accepted. **Directions:** Take the Bridge of Lions to Anastasia Boulevard; the restaurant is on your left after a short drive.
> **$ Prices:** Appetizers $5–$7; main courses $5–$7 at lunch, $9–$15 at dinner. MC, V.
> **Open:** Lunch Mon and Wed–Sat 11am–3pm; dinner Sun–Mon and Wed–Thurs 5:30–10pm, Fri–Sat 5:30–11pm; brunch Sun 10:30am–3pm.

The concept seems more New York than St. Augustine. Gypsy Cab is funky, comfortable, and eclectic. Its decor—already too grandiose a word to describe so casual a setting—consists of glossy pine tables (candlelit at night), a bit of glass brick, a bit of trellising, a few neon signs, and a changing art exhibit on the walls. It all reflects the personality of offbeat owner Ned Pollack, whose arrival in town was less than auspicious. Driving through Florida with no particular destination in mind, he hit a car full of nuns in St. Augustine. No one was hurt, but while Ned's truck was being repaired, he decided he liked the place and stayed on.

The menu changes nightly. On my last visit appetizers included cheese spedini (lightly herb-breaded Swiss cheese that's sautéed and finished with lemon, garlic, parsley, and butter) and a hummus platter with pita bread. A main course of blackened salmon with herbed citrus butter came with an array of fresh veggies and sautéed rice tossed with minced onions, tomato, garlic, and herbs (you can, however, request homemade mashed potatoes instead). Other choices included New York strip steak with peppercorn Gorgonzola glaze and sautéed shrimp with fresh basil and artichoke hearts in a light, garlicky mornay sauce over angel-hair pasta. Lunch and brunch fare is similar, but offers sandwiches, salads, and egg dishes as well. There's a full bar, and rich fresh-baked desserts—such as creamy peanut butter pie on semisweet-chocolate crust—are topped with dollops of real whipped cream.

OSCAR'S OLD FLORIDA GRILL, 614 Euclid Ave., off Fla. A1A on the Intracoastal Waterway. Tel. 829-3794.

Cuisine: OLD FLORIDA/SEAFOOD. **Reservations:** Not accepted, but you can call ahead for priority seating (that means you get the first table available when you arrive). **Directions:** Go over the Vilano Bridge, veer left on Fla. A1A north and drive about 2½ miles, turning left at Compton's.

$ Prices: Appetizers $2.50–$6.95; main courses $3.95–$13.95. MC, V.

Open: Wed–Thurs 5–9pm, Fri 5–10pm, Sat noon–10pm, Sun noon–9pm.

Boats have been docking here for grub since the late 19th century when Frank and Catherine Usina served up oyster roasts to Henry Flagler, his Vanderbilt pals, and other hungry sailors in palmetto-thatched huts. The Usinas' old fish camp is today Oscar's, a rustic eatery housed in a 1909 roadhouse with pine-plank floors and a steeply pitched tin ceiling, its rough-hewn rafters twined with philodendrons and strings of tiny lights. Tables are covered with green-and-white-checkerboard plastic cloths, the walls hung with neon beer signs. In this very casual setting (wear your jeans), the mood ranges from convivial (strangers talk to one another) to rollicking—especially on Wednesday and Thursday nights when live bluegrass and country music groups perform from 6 to 9pm. That's definitely the time to visit, though I also love weekend lunches here, when you can sit outside at riverside picnic tables shaded by a grove of live oaks. A bait shop adjoins, and people frequently fish from the dock after lunch. Parking is free.

Like the atmosphere and the music, the menu lacks nothing in old Florida authenticity. Order up a large bucket of steamed oysters or a platter of fried shrimp, fresh fish, oysters, clam strips, or crab patties—all accompanied by french fries *and* hush puppies, homemade coleslaw, and homemade sauces (try the piquant pink sauce composed of mayonnaise and datil peppers). These fried items are also available as sandwiches. Other good choices are crab Oscar (crabmeat baked in a rich cream sauce) and grilled fish of the day served with linguine and cheese toast. Some side dishes merit attention, among them red beans and rice with country sausage and scallions, pan bread (unsweetened southern-style cornbread served in a cast-iron skillet), Minorcan clam chowder (a local specialty), and cheese grits. Because the owners wanted Oscar's to be a family-oriented operation, not a rowdy fish camp bar, only beer and wine are served. The graham cracker–crusted key lime pie and the rich sweet-potato pie are great desserts.

SALT WATER COWBOY'S, 299 Dondanville Rd., off Fla. A1A. Tel. 471-2332.

Cuisine: OLD FLORIDA/SEAFOOD/BARBECUE. **Reservations:** Not accepted, so arrive early to avoid a wait. **Directions:** Go over the Bridge of Lions and follow Fla. A1A south for about 10 minutes; look for the restaurant's billboard, and make a right onto Dondanville Road just before you see a 7-Eleven store.

$ Prices: Appetizers $2.95–$6.95; main courses $7.95–$13.95. AE, DISC, MC, V.

Open: Dinner only, Sun–Thurs 5–9pm, Fri–Sat 5–10pm.

Arrive early for dinner at Salt Water Cowboy's—not only because it's immensely popular and fills up quickly, but because you'll want to enjoy the spectacular view of the sun setting over a saltwater marsh. Designed to resemble a turn-of-the-century fish camp, this rambling Intracoastal Waterway restaurant has a rustic candlelit interior paneled with cedar lapwood and shingles. The unfinished wide-plank pine floors come from an old Jacksonville train station. And dozens of plants are suspended from rough-hewn cypress-log beams overhead. A mix of dining areas ranges from intimate booths in alcoves lit by driftwood sconces to an outdoor plant-filled deck shaded by live oaks and illumined by tiki torches. One room has a hibiscus theme; another, flamingos. The background music is great—ragtime, Dixieland, and banjo tunes played at a low decibel level.

Like its ambience, Cowboy's cuisine harks back to old Florida. Order up a smoked-fish appetizer with crackers and a glass of wine while you peruse the menu. For openers, there's a very rich and creamy chowder with big chunks of clam, potato, and celery. And garlicky oysters Dondanville are baked with a buttery topping of parmesan cheese and herbed breadcrumbs. A main course of fork-tender baby back ribs is a great choice; the ribs are smothered in a tangy barbecue sauce and served with fries and coleslaw. Another winner: oysters, scallops, or shrimp fried in light cornmeal batter. Scallops are also superb here, baked in a cream/shallot/white wine sauce and crisply gratinéed. And there's a first-rate spicy jambalaya served over seasoned rice with homemade cornbread. Main courses come with hot breads, a very good house salad, a baked potato, and a vegetable. Plan on dessert—creamy chocolate-almond pie on a chocolate cookie crust.

SUNSET GRILLE, 421 Beach Blvd. (Fla. A1A), at 15th St. Tel. 471-5555.

Cuisine: AMERICAN. **Reservations:** Not accepted. **Directions:** Take the Bridge of Lions and follow the signs to Fla. A1A/Beach Boulevard; the restaurant is on your right.

$ Prices: Appetizers $2.95–$6.95; main courses $1–$4.25 at breakfast, $2.50–$5.95 at lunch, mostly $5.95–$9.95 at dinner. DISC, MC, V.

Open: Breakfast Sat–Sun 7–11:30am; lunch daily 11am–5pm; dinner daily 5–10pm (limited late-night menu served till midnight).

This casual Key West–style restaurant, owned by four ostensibly Floridianized New Yorkers (they still air all Giants, Jets, Knicks, and Ranger games on a large-screen TV in the bar), is headquarters for local "dittoheads" and "parrotheads" (Rush Limbaugh and Jimmy Buffet fans, respectively, for the uninitiated). The Jimmy Buffet song "Floridays" is reproduced in its entirety on the dinner menu. The Sunset Grille is a kick-back kind of place, with ceiling fans whirring overhead, numerous plants, pickled-pine walls hung with photographs of sunsets and works of local artists, and a very lively bar. Tables—candlelit at night—are hand-painted in bright tropical colors with "Margaritaville" motifs: lizards, gators, fish, etc. And bar windows latch up and have stools outside so the beach and boating crowd (the ocean's across the street) can eat and drink in bathing attire. Sunday afternoon a live band plays oldies and the place is mobbed.

Everything is made from scratch. At lunch or dinner, you can dine lightly on deli sandwiches, burritos, two-alarm chili, or burgers. A more serious dinner might consist of an appetizer of fried clam strips or homemade conch fritters followed by blackened chicken (tell your waiter if you like it very black) or grilled fresh swordfish with a creamy herbed-shrimp sauce. Both come with a salad; baked potato, rice, or angel-hair pasta; and an array of lightly sautéed al dente vegetables. For dessert, choose the peanut butter pie on chocolate graham-cracker crust.

BUDGET

SCHMAGEL'S BAGELS, 69 Hypolita St., at Cordova St. Tel. 824-4444.

Cuisine: BAGEL SANDWICHES. **Reservations:** Not accepted.

$ Prices: Sandwiches $1.75–$4.50. No credit cards.

Open: Mon–Sat 8am–2pm, Sun 9am–2pm.

On sunny mornings I just love to sit outdoors at one of Schmagel's umbrella-shaded patio tables and peruse the morning paper over oven-fresh bagels and steaming coffee. It's a perfectly peaceful setting in the heart of the historic district. But even when it rains and I have to sit in one of the Formica booths inside, I can't resist Schmagel's authentically plump New York–style bagels. They come in 10 varieties—plain, whole wheat, sesame, onion, salt, cinnamon-raisin, blueberry, poppy seed, and garlic—or a combination of most of the above. Cream-cheese spreads come mixed with scallions, vegetables, honey pecans, strawberries, or walnuts and raisins. Of course, you can always order a traditional cream cheese and Nova or bagels filled with ham and swiss or homemade chicken salad. The menu also lists fresh soups du jour, soft drinks, and fresh-baked fruit muffins. There's metered parking in a lot across Cordova Street.

EVENING ENTERTAINMENT

MILL TOP TAVERN, 19½ St. George St., at Fort Alley. Tel. 829-2329.
Housed in an 18th-century mill building (the water wheel is still outside), this rustic tavern has a woody interior—rough-hewn beams, pecky cypress walls, and pine plank floors. Weather permitting, it's an open-air space, with glassless windows overlooking the Castillo. If it gets cold, the windows are covered with plastic and the room is heated. There's additional seating at picnic tables on an outdoor wooden deck and on a patio shaded by live oak and palm trees. Every Sunday and Monday a classic rock guitarist performs. Tuesday is Ladies Night (discounted drinks for women) and the music is contemporary rock. On Wednesday, jazz and blues are featured; Thursday it's bluegrass. And Friday and Saturday varies bluegrass, rock, blues, and country rock. A full menu—burgers, sandwiches, salads—is served till 11pm Monday through Saturday, till 9pm on Sunday, and there's a large selection of specialty drinks with names like "Sex on the Beach" and "Beam Me Up Scotty." Most of the crowd is thirtysomething. You must be 21 to get in after 9pm. There's live entertainment from 1pm to closing nightly. On-street parking is available.
   Admission: Free Sun–Thurs, $1 Fri–Sat.

PASSPORT JOE'S, 2665 Fla. A1A S., at 4th St. Tel. 471-6722.
This is your classic funky beach bar. In addition to live entertainment, sporting events (such as Monday-night football) are aired on TV monitors over the bar and on a large-screen TV on the patio. There are pool tables and dart boards, weekly dance competitions, beer-chugging contests, trivia games, ladies' nights, and karaoke nights (Monday and Saturday). On Sunday the music is provided by an acoustic guitarist and/or live bands. On Monday an acoustic guitarist and singer perform. On Tuesday (the only night 18- to 20-year olds are allowed in) live progressive bands are featured, and there's free beer. On Wednesday, Thursday, and Saturday a DJ plays high-energy dance music. And on Friday live bands play oldies. There's a full restaurant menu ranging from sandwiches to full Mexican and Caribbean dishes, steak, and seafood. Open Sunday through Thursday till 1am, on Friday and Saturday till 2am, with live entertainment from 9pm. To get there, take the Bridge of Lions, stay in the left lane and follow signs to the beaches, and proceed on Fla. A1A for about four miles; it's on your right. There's free parking on the premises.
   Admission: $1; Tues nights those under 21 pay $3 cover. Occasionally higher admission is charged for special events.

SCARLETT O'HARA'S, 70 Hypolita St., at Cordova St. Tel. 824-6535.
In the heart of St. Augustine's historic district, Scarlett O'Hara's offers a warren of cozy rooms with working fireplaces and shuttered windows in a rambling 19th-century wood-frame house. And if you want to get away from the crowd—and fairly loud music—you can sit out on the front porch or dine in a booth upstairs. Live rock, jazz, and R&B bands play Monday through Saturday, and though there's no dance floor, people get up and dance wherever. Sunday is karaoke night. Sporting events are aired on a large-screen TV in a tropically themed oyster bar. Sandwiches, seafood, Florida specialties (like fried gator with honey mustard), and munchies on the order of nachos and buffalo wings are served nightly through midnight. You must be 21 to get in after 9pm. There's nightly entertainment from 9pm to 12:30am. Parking is free in a lot across Cordova Street.
   Admission: Usually free; sometimes $1 Fri–Sat.

TRADE WINDS TROPICAL LOUNGE, 124 Charlotte St., between Cathedral Place and Treasury St. Tel. 829-9336.

Toni Leonard and her daughters, Janet and Julie, have been operating this funky-friendly local hangout for four decades. The ambience is nautical/tropical, with corrugated-tin roofing, a neon alligator and palm trees, bamboo wall coverings, a Gauguin-like mural, and a clutter of plants, seashells, buoys, and ship's lanterns suspended from fishnet overhead. The music is a mix of southern rock, oldies, folk, country, and blues. Toni gets a kick out of telling how she fired Jimmy Buffet before he was famous because she didn't think he had any talent (they're still friends). Most of the groups playing Trade Winds are local, but well-known oldies groups like the Platters, the Coasters, the Drifters, and the Byrds do occasional gigs here. And on Palm Sunday every year, all the musicians who've ever played the club come back for a music marathon. Light fare is available. You must be 21 to get in after 9pm. Trade Winds is also a *simpático* spot for weekday happy hour from 5 to 8pm. There's live entertainment nightly from 9pm to 1am. Parking is on the street or in the bank lot next door.

Admission: Free Sun–Thurs, $1–$2 Fri–Sat.

WHITE LION, 20 Cuna St., between Charlotte and St. George Sts. Tel. 829-2388.

The White Lion is a cozy two-story British-style pub, with beamed ceilings, pine-plank floors, candlelit tables, and a working fireplace. Sunday through Thursday evening (except in winter), an acoustical guitarist plays mellow rock from 7:30 to 10:30pm. On Friday and Saturday, jazz, rock, R&B, and bluegrass groups perform from 9:30pm to 1am. And weekends, weather permitting, a guitar player entertains on the large trellised outdoor patio. Even when there's no entertainment, this is a *simpático* hangout. A full menu featuring steaks, burgers, sandwiches, chili, and fish and chips is offered through 9pm nightly. Frozen daiquiris and margaritas, draft beer, and potent tropical drinks are specialties. Well drinks are half price during happy hour weekdays from 4:30 to 7:30pm. You must be 21 to get in after 9:30pm. The White Lion is open Sunday through Thursday till about 11pm, on Friday and Saturday to 1am. Use the parking lot on Charlotte Street, less than half a block away.

Admission: Free Sun–Thurs, $1–$5 Fri–Sat, depending on the entertainment.

---

3. DAYTONA BEACH

50 miles NE of Orlando, 260 miles N of Miami, 89 miles S of Jacksonville

GETTING THERE   By Plane   American, Continental, Delta, and USAir fly into **Daytona Beach International Airport** (tel. 904/248-8030). A taxi from the airport to most beach hotels runs between $8 and $12.

By Train   The closest Amtrak station (tel. toll free 800/USA-RAIL) is in De Land, 23 miles southwest of Daytona.

By Bus   **Greyhound** buses connect Daytona with most of the country. They pull into a very centrally located terminal at 138 S. Ridgewood Ave. (U.S. 1) between International Speedway Boulevard and Magnolia Avenue (tel. 904/255-7076, or toll free 800/231-2222).

From Orlando, **Daytona-Orlando Transit Service (DOTS)** (tel. 904/257-5411, or toll free 800/231-1965) provides van transport between the two cities. They offer 12 round-trips daily. One-way fare is $26 for adults, $46 round-trip; children under 12 are charged half price. The service brings passengers to the company's terminal at 1598 N. Nova Rd., at 11th Street, or, for an $8 to $21 fee, to beach hotels. In Orlando, the vans depart from the airport.

By Car   If you're coming from north or south, take I-95 and head east on International Speedway Boulevard (U.S. 92). From Tampa or Orlando, take I-4 east and follow the Daytona Beach signs to I-95 north to U.S. 92. From northwestern Florida, take I-10 east to I-95 south to U.S. 92.

The self-proclaimed "World's Most Famous Beach" is even more celebrated as the "Birthplace of Speed" and the "World Center of Racing." It has been a mecca for car-racing enthusiasts since the days when automobiles were called horseless carriages. Early automobile magnates Ransom E. Olds, Henry Ford, the Stanley brothers (of steamer fame), and Louis Chevrolet—along with motor-mad millionaires like the Vanderbilts, Astors, and Rockefellers—wintered in Florida and raced their vehicles on the hard-packed sand beach. The first competition, in 1902, was between Olds and gentleman racer Alexander Winton; they worked up to the then-impressive speed of 57 miles an hour. By 1904, a Daytona Beach event called the Winter Speed Carnival was drawing participants from all over the world, most of them wealthy sportsmen and financiers. Three years later, Fred Marriott wrapped a mile of piano wire around the boiler of his souped-up Stanley Steamer (to keep it from blowing up) and raced the course at a spectacular 197 m.p.h.! At the end of the stretch he crashed, just as spectacularly, into the pounding surf. He emerged uninjured, but after the accident the Stanley brothers quit racing their steam-driven cars, and gas engines became more prominent.

Many men who were to become famous for their skill with machinery first tested their ideas on the sands of Daytona Beach. Glenn Curtiss, the father of naval aviation, raced motorcycles here. And Sir Malcolm Campbell, a millionaire English sportsman, raced a car powered by an aircraft engine in 1928, reaching a speed of over 206 m.p.h.; in later years he set the ultimate beach speed record of 276.8 m.p.h. Most of these early beach events, by the way, were individual speed trials rather than actual races. The final speed trials were held in 1935.

The year 1936 ushered in the era of stock-car racing with a new beach racecourse, a host of daredevil drivers, and thousands of cheering fans. In 1947, driver and race promoter Bill France founded the National Association for Stock Car Auto Racing (NASCAR), headquartered at Daytona Beach. Today it's the world's largest motorsports authority, sanctioning the Daytona 500 and other major races at the International Speedway and tracks throughout the United States. The last stock-car race on the beach took place in 1958. A year later, France's dream of a multimotorsports facility, the Daytona International Speedway, was realized.

Of course, you don't have to be a racing aficionado to enjoy Daytona. It has 23 miles of sandy beach, and you can still drive and park—but not race—on the sand; maximum speed allowed is 10 m.p.h. The town is filled with college students during spring break—the annual beach blanket Babylon—and during Bike Week in February thousands of leather-clad motorcycle buffs make the scene. But barring spring break and major speedway events, Daytona is a laid-back beach resort, offering boating, tennis, golf, water sports, and the opportunity to stroll the sands, swim, and soak up some sunshine.

ORIENTATION

INFORMATION The **Daytona Beach Area Convention & Visitors Bureau,** 126 E. Orange Ave., just west of the Silver Beach Bridge (P.O. Box 910), Daytona Beach, FL 32115 (tel. 904/255-0415, or toll free 800/854-1234), can help you with information on attractions, accommodations, dining, and events. Call in advance for maps and brochures, or visit their office when in town. They also maintain a branch at the Speedway.

CITY LAYOUT Daytona Beach is surrounded by water. The Atlantic Ocean borders its east coast and the Halifax River flows north to south through the middle of the city. There are actually four little towns along its beach—**Ormond Beach** to the north, the centrally located **Daytona Beach** and **Daytona Beach Shores,** and **Ponce Inlet** at the southern tip, just above New Smyrna Beach.

Florida A1A (Atlantic Avenue) runs along the beach north to south. **U.S. 1** runs inland paralleling the west side of the Halifax River, and I-95 vaguely parallels it still farther west. **International Speedway Boulevard** is the main east-west artery.

GETTING AROUND

BY TROLLEY & BUS   VOTRAN, Volusia County's public transit system, runs **buses** throughout major areas of town Monday through Saturday between 6am and 7pm. Adults pay 75¢, children under 17 and seniors pay 35¢, and children under 6 accompanied by an adult ride free.

The company also operates turn-of-the-century-style **trolleys** between Granada Boulevard and Dunlawton Avenue along Fla. A1A Monday through Saturday from noon to 12:30am; fares are the same as bus fares. Call 904/761-7700 for routing information.

BY CAR   You can drive and park directly on the beach here. There's a $3 access fee between February 1 and Labor Day; the rest of the year it's free.

WHAT TO SEE & DO

In addition to the attractions listed below, the **Daytona Flea Market** is one of the world's largest, with 1,000 covered outdoor booths and 100 vendors in an air-conditioned building. Located on Tomoka Farms Road, a mile west of the Speedway at the junction of I-95 and U.S. 92 (tel. 252-1999), it's open year-round Friday through Sunday from 8am to 5pm (parking is free). And the **Dixie Queen Riverboat Company** (tel. 904/255-1997, or toll free 800/329-6225) offers year-round lunch, Sunday brunch, and dinner cruises—all with entertainment—as well as full-day trips to St. Augustine aboard a 150-passenger paddlewheeler. Cruises leave from 841 Ballough Rd. on the southwest side of the Seabreeze Bridge. Call for prices and departure times.

DAYTONA BEACH KENNEL CLUB, 2201 W. International Speedway Blvd., just west of Fentress Blvd. Tel. 252-6484.

This is a pleasant way to spend a day or evening, especially if you opt to watch the races over lunch or dinner in the upstairs restaurant. There are a variety of ways to bet on the greyhounds; if you've never done it before, pick up a free brochure that explains them all. You can also buy tip sheets recommending computer and expert picks. Each meet includes 14 races. You must be at least 18 years old to enter the betting area.

The moderately priced Pavilion Clubhouse Restaurant (lunch dishes are $5.95 to $9.95; dinner dishes, $11.95 to $17.95) has tiered seating, with big picture windows overlooking the track and TV monitors enhancing your view at higher tables. Tables are elegantly appointed with peach linen napery. At lunch you might order a Caesar salad or a Reuben sandwich. A typical dinner might consist of French onion soup and a main course of prime rib or shrimp scampi. There's a full bar. Reservations are suggested; request a window seat.

Admission: $1 adults (seniors 55 and over free at matinees); grandstand seating, 50¢–$1.75; restaurant, $2. Parking is free on the premises; preferred parking (closer to the entrance) is $1, and valet parking, $2.

Open: Night races usually Mon–Sat at 7:45pm (call before you go); matinees Mon, Wed, and Sat at 1pm. Doors and restaurant open an hour before post time.

DAYTONA INTERNATIONAL SPEEDWAY, 1801 W. International Speedway Blvd. (U.S. 92), at Bill France Blvd. Tel. 253-RACE for tickets, 254-2700 for information.

Opened in 1959 with the first Daytona 500, this 450-acre "World Center of Racing" is practically the raison d'être for Daytona Beach—certainly the keynote of the city's fame. It presents about eight weekends of major racing events annually, featuring stock cars, sports cars, motorcycles, and go-karts, and is also used for automobile testing. Its grandstand, a mile long, seats over 100,000.

Major annual races here include Speedweeks (16 days of stock- and sports-car racing in February, culminating in the Daytona 500 by STP), Bike Week (10 days of motorcycle events in early March), Daytona Beach Spring Speedway Spectacular (car show and swap meet featuring collector vehicles, in late March or early April), the Pepsi 400 (stock cars, in July), the AMA/CCS Motorcycle Championship (on a three-day weekend in mid-October), and the Daytona Beach Fall Speedway Spectacular (a car show and swap meet on Thanksgiving weekend). For further information, write to Daytona International Speedway, P.O. Box 2801, Daytona Beach, FL 32120-2801.

To learn more about racing, head for the **Visitors' Center** at the west end of the Speedway and NASCAR office complex. Open daily from 9am to 5pm, the center is also the departure site for entertainingly narrated 25-minute guided van tours of the facility that provide a close look at the high-banked 2.5-mile trioval and 3.56-mile road courses, the Winston Tower, the pit, and the garage area. Admission is $3 for adults, free for children 7 and under. Tours depart daily every 10 to 20 minutes between 9:10am and 4:10pm, except during races, special events, or car testing. Also at the Visitors' Center are a large gift shop; a snack bar; the Gallery of Legends, where the history of motorsports in the Daytona Beach area is documented through photographs and memorabilia; and the Budweiser Video Wall, presenting a continuous showing of racing in the Daytona Beach area, tracing its history from the "Birthplace of Speed" to the "World Center of Racing." You can "feel the thunder" while listening to a 20-minute Surround-Sound audio presentation called *The Daytona 500: From Dawn to Determination.* The center also stocks information on area accommodations, restaurants, attractions, and nightlife.

Admission: Auto events, $30–$80; motorcycle events, $10–$35; go-kart events, under $10. Big events sell out months in advance (the Daytona 500 at least a year in advance), so plan far ahead and also reserve accommodations well before your trip. Parking is free for grandstand seating; infield parking charges vary with the event.

Open: Daily. **Closed:** New Year's Day, Thanksgiving, and Christmas Day.

ECO-TOURS AT HONTOON LANDING RESORT & MARINA, 2317 River Ridge Rd., in DeLand. Tel. 734-2474, or toll free 800/248-2474.

Just a 35-minute drive from Daytona, this rustic resort on the St. Johns River offers two-hour nature cruises in open-air pontoon boats. Knowledgeable guides point out local flora and fauna—the latter including herons, egrets, American bald eagles, cormorants, osprey, white ibis, otters, manatees, turtles, alligators, and many other endemic species. You'll see an ancient Timucuan shell mound and the remains of stills that once flourished in the dense riverside marshlands. And there's a 15-minute stop at Blue Springs State Park to visit manatee- and alligator-viewing stations. Binoculars, which greatly enhance the experience, can be rented at the resort store. Pack a picnic lunch and make a day—or overnight stay—of it. In addition to moderately priced accommodations (call for details), Hontoon Landing offers a swimming pool, volleyball, boat rentals (jet skis, fishing boats, pontoons, ski/cruise boats, and houseboats), freshwater fishing (licenses, bait, gear, and tackle can be obtained on the premises), and many other resort activities. In addition, there are camping cabins, nature trails, and a riverside picnic area at the adjacent 1,650-acre Hontoon Island State Park (tel. 736-5309).

Admission: Eco-Tours, $12 adults, $10 children 5–12 and seniors 55 and over, free for kids under 5.

Open: Eco-Tours cruises depart daily at 10:30am and 1pm (call for reservations). **Directions:** Follow International Speedway Boulevard west until it ends; then turn left on Spring Garden Avenue (Fla. 15A), right on Fla. 44, left on Old New York Avenue, left on Hontoon Road, and left again on River Ridge Road.

GAMBLE PLACE, 1819 Taylor Rd., in Port Orange. Tel. 255-0285.

This 150-acre nature preserve, under the auspices of the Museum of Arts and Sciences (see below) and the Florida Nature Conservancy, occupies the former estate of Ivory soap king James Gamble (of Procter & Gamble). On pristine nature trails (ranging from a half to three miles), you can view hardwood swamp forest, longleaf pine sandhills, Spruce Creek (home to alligators and tortoises), a 1907 citrus-packing house, an azalea garden, ancient cypress trees, and hundreds of wildlife species. And you can also tour both Gamble's turn-of-the-century cracker-style house and the whimsical Snow White cottage, inspired by the Disney classic, which Judge Alfred Nippert (Gamble's son-in-law, who inherited the property) built for his nieces in

1938. Swamp safaris on pontoon boats are offered twice a month on selected Fridays (call for details). The best time to go is on Saturday, when you can participate in 9am nature and local-history programs and take guided tours of the Gamble house and Snow White cottage. Reservations are required.

Admission: Nature trails, free. Guided tours and Saturday programs, $3 for adults, $1 for children and students with ID, free for kids under 6.

Open: Wed and Sat 9am–4pm. Historical/environmental programs, Sat at 9am; house tours, Wed and Sat at 11am, noon, 1pm, and 2pm; Snow White cottage tours, Sat at 1pm. **Closed:** New Year's Day, Easter, Thanksgiving, and Christmas Day, except when there are special holiday programs. **Directions:** Take International Speedway Boulevard (U.S. 92) west to I-95 south; get off at County Road 421 (Taylor Road), head west for 1½ miles, and look for the Gamble Place sign on your left.

KLASSIX AUTO MUSEUM, 2909 W. International Speedway Blvd., at Tomoka Farms Rd., just west of I-95. Tel. 252-3800.

Opened with appropriate fanfare during 1994 Speedweeks—complete with special events at the Speedway and a parade of antique race cars, classic cars, and modern show cars on Ormond Beach—this exciting new museum showcases every Corvette model manufactured from 1953 to the present. Also on display are collector cars (including the car from the movie *Days of Thunder*), special-interest Corvettes (such as the Mako Shark, a mid-'60s prototype), historic Daytona race cars from all motorsports, motorcycles, and racing memorabilia, along with exhibits on the same. Interactive videos allow visitors to vicariously experience the thrills of car racing—an activity that will be further enhanced in the near future via virtual reality. A 1950s-style soda shop and gift shop are on the premises.

Admission: $8.50 adults, $4.25 children 7–12, free for kids under 7.

Open: Daily 9am–9pm. **Closed:** Christmas Day.

MUSEUM OF ARTS AND SCIENCES, 1040 Museum Blvd., off Nova Rd. Tel. 255-0285.

Housing both art and natural science exhibits, this eclectic museum dates to 1956, when Cuban dictator Fulgencio Batista donated his vacation home and art collection to the city. In 1971 the museum relocated to its present building, and over the years its holdings have increased in volume and scope. The Cuban collection—mostly paintings—spans two centuries from 1759 to 1959. "Master-works of American Art: 300 Years of American Culture" includes art and furnishings from the Pilgrim period, Abolitionist paintings, works by Gilbert Stuart and Samuel Morse, Federalist furnishings, and Tiffany silver. In the Karshan Center of Graphic Arts you'll view 18th- and 19th-century European prints, turn-of-the-century art nouveau posters, and lithographs by artists ranging from William Blake to Degas. A lobby gallery highlights fine and decorative arts from the Age of Napoleon. A prehistory of Florida section contains such artifacts as a million-year-old mammoth tooth and the skeleton of a Pleistocene giant ground sloth that roamed the Daytona coast 130,000 years ago. And the museum's most recent permanent installation, "Africa: Life and Ritual," documents African peoples from over 30 cultures in 15 countries. A contemporary sculpture garden and a one-mile nature trail are on the grounds. Permanent exhibits are complemented by an ongoing schedule of concerts, lectures, and changing shows. Planetarium shows take place at 1 and 3pm daily.

Admission: $3 adults, $1 children and students with ID, free for kids under 6; planetarium shows, $1.

Open: Tues–Fri 9am–4pm, Sat–Sun noon–5pm. **Closed:** New Year's Day, Thanksgiving, and Christmas Day. **Directions:** Take International Speedway Boulevard west, make a left on Nova Road, and look for a sign on your right.

PONCE DE LEÓN INLET LIGHTHOUSE, 4931 S. Peninsula Dr., Ponce Inlet. Tel. 761-1821.

Built in the mid-1880s, this is, at 175 feet, the second-tallest lighthouse in the United States. And you'll find out just how high that is if you climb the 203 steel steps that spiral up its interior. The present beacon, visible for 10 nautical miles, flashes every 10 seconds.

In the 1970s this brick-and-granite coastal sentinel and its original outbuildings were restored and added to the National Register of Historic Places. The head lighthouse keeper's cottage—which was used as a barracks during World War II and later served as the first town hall of Ponce Inlet—today houses a museum of exhibits on navigational aids, marine biology, deep-sea fishing, and ocean exploration. The first-assistant keeper's house is furnished to reflect turn-of-the-century occupancy. And other historic buildings contain a museum of tools and artifacts involved in keeping the light burning, a picture gallery of lighthouses of the world, and a theater, where a 12-minute video on the history of this particular lighthouse is shown continually throughout the day (visit it first). On display in the boatyard is the 46-foot oak-and-cypress *F. D. Russell* Tug Boat, built in 1938, which you can board and explore. A gift shop on the premises sells lighthouse- and Florida-related items. There's an adjoining playground and picnic area with tables and barbecue grills.

Admission: $3 adults, $1 children under 12.

Open: May–Aug, daily 10am–9pm; Sept–Apr, daily 10am–5pm (last admission an hour before closing). **Closed:** Christmas. **Directions:** Follow Atlantic Avenue south, make a right on Beach Street, and follow the signs.

SPECIAL EVENTS

In addition to races at the International Speedway, Daytona hosts the **Florida International Festival,** a major musical event taking place every other summer (see "Florida Calendar of Events," in Chapter 2, for details).

SPORTS & RECREATION

FISHING If you're interested in deep-sea fishing and/or whale-watching, contact **Critter Fleet,** 4950 S. Peninsula Dr., Ponce Inlet (tel. 767-7676), or **Sea Love Marina,** 4884 Front St., Ponce Inlet (tel. 767-3406).

You can also fish from the **Main Street Pier,** near the Marriott (tel. 253-1212). Bait and fishing gear are available, and no license is required.

GOLF There are a dozen golf courses within 25 minutes of the beach, and most hotels can arrange starting times for you. The **Daytona Beach Club,** 600 Wilder Blvd. (tel. 258-3119), is the city's largest, with 36 holes.

HORSEBACK RIDING **Shenandoah Stables,** 1759 Tomoka Farms Rd., off U.S. 92 (tel. 257-1444), offers daily trail rides and horseback-riding lessons between 10am and 5pm.

WATER SPORTS **Daytona Recreational Sales & Rentals** (tel. 672-5631) rents pontoons, fishing boats, and ski boats, delivering the craft at a designated point on the Tomoka River. For jet-ski rentals, contact **Daytona High Performance— MBI,** 925 Sickler Dr., at the Seabreeze Bridge (tel. 257-5276). See also the listing for **Hontoon Landing,** above.

Additional water-sports equipment, as well as bicycles, beach buggies, and mopeds, can be rented along the beach in front of major hotels. A good place to look is in front of the Marriott at 100 N. Atlantic Ave.

WHERE TO STAY

Daytona Beach hotels fill to the bursting point during major races at the Speedway and other special events, and whenever college students are on break. At these times room rates skyrocket, if you can find a room at all, and there's often a minimum-stay requirement. If you're planning to be in town at one of these busy times (see the "Florida Calendar of Events," in Chapter 2), reserve far in advance. All the accommodations listed below are on or near the beach and close to the Speedway.

AT THE BEACH
Expensive

MARRIOTT, 100 N. Atlantic Ave. (between Earl St. and Auditorium Blvd.), Daytona Beach, FL 32118. Tel. 904/254-8200, or toll free 800/228-9290. Fax 904/253-8841. 377 rms, 25 suites. A/C MINIBAR TV TEL

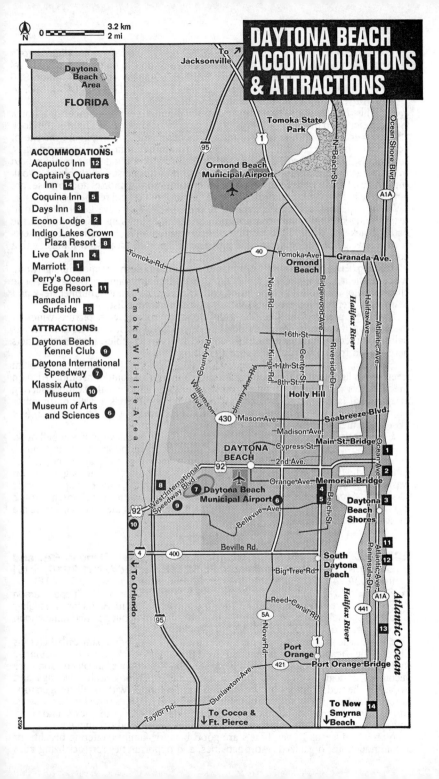

$ Rates: $149 single or double ($235–$250 during special events, when there's also a seven-night minimum stay); $198 single or double on the Executive Level ($250–$265 during special events); $250–$750 suite. Additional person $20 extra. Children under 18 stay free in parents' room. AE, CB, DC, DISC, MC, V. **Parking:** Free in lot across the street; valet parking $8 per night.

This is Daytona's most luxurious—and most central—beachfront hotel, designed so that every room offers a gorgeous ocean view. It's right at the clock tower and bandshell, and, in season, its beach and boardwalk are the site of concessions offering parasailing, bicycle rentals, motorized four-wheelers, pedal carts, surfboards, boogie boards, cabañas, and umbrellas. Accommodations are decorated in pleasing resort colors—mauve, peach, and light turquoise—with bleached-oak furnishings. Lovely watercolors of underwater scenes with seahorses and tortoises are a nice touch. In-room amenities include alarm-clock radios and remote-control cable TVs with Spectravision movie stations. Rooms on the Executive Level (16th floor) feature king-size beds, pullout sofas and armchairs, ceiling fans, VCRs, and, in the baths, black-and-white TVs, hairdryers, and extra phones. Executive Level guests receive a welcome gift on arrival and have use of a private ocean-view lounge with a console TV and games.

Dining/Entertainment: Coquinas is the hotel's plush premier dining room, with candlelit, peach-clothed tables amid massive oak columns, Louis XV–style chairs, and mirrored walls embellished with frosted-glass swans. Gourmet steak and seafood dinners are featured, and there's an extensive wine list.

The very pretty plant-filled Parkside Oceanfront Café, with picture windows overlooking the beach, serves moderately priced breakfasts, lunches, and dinners daily. Weather permitting, you can sit outside at umbrella tables. Early-bird dinners here, served from 5 to 7pm daily, are a great bargain.

Splash, an attractive poolside bar with Saltillo-tile floors, pots of ferns, and palm trees, serves light fare and specialty drinks; it has indoor and outdoor seating. Also on the beach is a complex of small restaurants with outdoor café seating, serving international fare—everything from tacos to souvlaki. There's a lively on-premises sports bar called Waves, and the sophisticated Clocktower Lounge offers live jazz (see "Evening Entertainment," below).

Services: Concierge, room service (7am to 11pm), free newspapers at bell desk.

Facilities: Indoor/outdoor swimming pool, two whirlpools, steam and sauna, kiddie pool, vast palm-fringed sun deck, sand volleyball court, playground, video-game arcade, full-service unisex hair and beauty salon (also offers massage), coin-op washer/dryers, complete health club, business services, florist, camera shop, an arcade of shops. Memorial Day to Labor Day, there are free activities for children 5 to 12 (arts and crafts, sports, etc.); a small amusement park adjoins the hotel, and there are cable-car rides on the pier.

Moderate

ACAPULCO INN, 2505 S. Atlantic Ave. (between Dundee Rd. and Seaspray St.), Daytona Beach, FL 32118. Tel. 904/761-2210, or toll free 800/874-7420. Fax 904/253-9935. 42 rms, 91 efficiencies. A/C TV TEL

$ Rates: $78–$100 single or double; $84–$116 efficiency. Additional person $6–$10 extra. Children under 18 stay free in parents' room. Rates may be higher during special events. Monthly rates available. Inquire about golf and honeymoon packages. AE, CB, DC, DISC, MC, V. **Parking:** Free.

One of six beachfront properties here under the auspices of a company called Oceans Eleven, the Acapulco Inn is fronted by festive Mayan symbols that comprise something of a local landmark when lit up at night. Resort-style balconied rooms are decorated in teal, mauve, and peach, with grasspaper-look wall coverings and tropically themed paintings on the walls. All are equipped with small refrigerators, in-room safes, and remote-control cable TVs with HBO, Spectravision pay movies, and tourist-information channels. Efficiency units offer ocean views and fully equipped eat-in kitchens. Higher rates reflect high season and ocean view.

Note: All Oceans Eleven hotels are good bets for families, offering beachfront accommodations, organized resort activities, and opportunities for socializing with your fellow guests. You can reserve at any of them via the above toll-free number, and the operator can tell you which best suits your needs. Their offerings run the gamut from standard rooms to ocean-view penthouse suites with full living and dining rooms. Guests at all properties receive coupon books offering discounts at local sports-equipment concessions, shops, and restaurants.

Dining/Entertainment: The many-windowed Fiesta Restaurant, which over-looks the ocean and offers outdoor seating at umbrella tables, serves all meals. Typical American fare is featured. Prices are reasonable, and there's a children's menu. In summer, the Fiesta offers poolside waiter service. The comfortable Sombrero Lounge adjoins.

Services: Complimentary newspaper in restaurant.

Facilities: Oceanfront swimming pool, two whirlpools, kiddie pool, shuffle-board, picnic area, coin-op laundry, gift shop, small video-game room, lobby lounge with TV and card tables. Like all Oceans Eleven properties, the Acapulco Inn offers an extensive daily activities program for adults and children.

PERRY'S OCEAN EDGE RESORT, 2209 S. Atlantic Ave. (between Moore and Bonner Aves.), Daytona Beach, FL 32118. Tel. 904/255-0581, or toll free 800/447-0002. Fax 904/258-7315. 204 rms. A/C TV TEL

$ Rates (including continental breakfast): $50–$120 single or double; $108–$242 suite (formed by combining rooms). Rate range reflects view and season. Additional person $10 extra. Two children under 12 stay free in parents' room. Rates may be even higher during major events, when there's also a four- to five-night minimum stay. Inquire about packages and weekly rates. AE, CB, DC, DISC, MC, V. **Parking:** Free.

Some people say that the secret of this family-run hostelry's popularity is the fresh-baked doughnuts served with your coffee, fresh fruit, and juice each morning. They certainly are a treat, but Perry's has more going for it than free frosted bear claws. Entered via an attractive knotty-pine–paneled lobby, it has a grassy palm-fringed garden beachfront—the prettiest in Daytona. The staff is extremely friendly and helpful. And the spacious rooms (75% of them with ocean views and private balconies or patios) are equipped with remote-control cable TVs, AM/FM alarm-clock radios, microwave ovens, coffee makers, and small refrigerators. Many units have full kitchens, living rooms, and dining areas, and most have hairdryers in the bath. Some rooms are furnished in wicker, others in knotty pine. A supermarket and 7-Eleven store are directly across the street.

Dining/Entertainment: The Smoke House Restaurant, a homey little coffee shop with curtained windows and hanging copper pots, is open for full American breakfasts and lunches daily. The above-mentioned doughnuts are served in two comfortable on-premises lounges equipped with pianos and large TVs. Guests gather for Monday-night football in the lodgelike South Tower lounge. There are year-round activities (Bingo, movies, tournaments, Monte Carlo nights, and more) for adults and children.

Facilities: Large free-form indoor pool with retractable roof, surrounded by a lushly planted garden sun deck; two large outdoor swimming pools; kiddie pool; whirlpool; shuffleboard; nine-hole putting green; horseshoes; bocci ball court; beach volleyball; coin-op washers/dryers; video-game room; car-rental desk; gift shop.

RAMADA INN SURFSIDE, 3125 S. Atlantic Ave. (between Van and Atares Aves.), Daytona Beach, FL 32118. Tel. 904/788-1000, or toll free 800/255-3838. Fax 904/756-9906. 102 rms, 17 suites. A/C TV TEL

$ Rates: $60–$90 single or double; $70–$100 efficiency; $85–$145 suite. Rate range reflects low and high seasons. Additional person $10 extra. Children under 19 stay free in parents' room. Rates may be even higher during major events, when there's also a five-night minimum stay. Inquire about packages. AE, CB, DC, DISC, ER, JCB, MC, V. **Parking:** Free.

This Ramada boasts a prime beachfront location, and all its rooms have ocean views and balconies. Accommodations are attractively decorated with oak furnishings, grasspaperlike textured wall coverings, burgundy carpets, and mauve shell-motif

358 • NORTHEAST FLORIDA

bedspreads and curtains. All offer remote-control cable TVs (with free HBO, Showtime movies, and visitor-information channels), AM/FM alarm-clock radios, and in-room safes; most have sofas. Families will appreciate the efficiency units with fully equipped eat-in kitchens and, in summer, the full schedule of free children's activities.

Dining/Entertainment: The very pleasant Sandcastle Restaurant, serving all meals and specializing in steak and seafood, has windowed walls overlooking the ocean and swimming pool; kids under 12 eat free. The adjoining Sundancer Lounge—which features complimentary happy-hour hors d'oeuvres, live bands for dancing weekends (Wednesday through Saturday in high season), and a blackjack machine at the bar—has the same beach view. It airs sporting events on a large-screen TV and serves a free halftime buffet during Monday-night football. A pool bar with umbrella tables on an awninged wooden deck serves fare and drinks from the restaurant and bar.

Services: Room service (during restaurant hours); guest services can arrange tours, transportation, fishing excursions, trips to Walt Disney World, and more.

Facilities: Large oceanfront swimming pool and sun deck, kiddie pool, oceanfront picnic tables, sand volleyball court, shuffleboard, video-game room, coin-op washers/dryers, snack machines, gift shop, activities for seniors October to February and in April and May.

Inexpensive

DAYS INN, 1909 S. Atlantic Ave. (at Flamingo Ave.), Daytona Beach, FL 32118. Tel. 904/255-4492, or toll free 800/224-5056 or 800/329-7466. Fax 904/238-0632. 188 rms, 8 efficiencies. A/C TV TEL
$ Rates: $35–$50 single; $45–$60 double; $55–$75 efficiency for one or two. During special events, $100–$125 single or double; $120–$145 efficiency for one or two. Additional person $6 extra. Children under 12 stay free in parents' room. AE, CB, DC, DISC, MC, V. **Parking:** Free.

At this recently renovated nine-story beachfront hotel, every room provides an ocean view. Pretty peach-and-teal rooms with oak furnishings offer remote-control cable TVs with HBO and visitor-information channels, in-room safes, and bed massagers. All have balconies, and some contain small refrigerators and microwave ovens. Large oceanfront efficiencies with fully equipped kitchens are ideal for families.

Facilities include a swimming pool/kiddie pool/sun deck overlooking the beach, an on-premises restaurant called the Tropical Tree serving breakfast only, and a video-game arcade. During summer, light fare is offered at a pool bar.

Days Inns nationwide offer a Super Saver rate of just $29 to $49 single or double if you reserve 30 days in advance via the second-listed toll-free phone number. This deal is, of course, subject to availability, but it's worth a try. If you can't get in here, there are three other Days Inns in town, all conveniently located beachfront properties.

ECONO LODGE, 301 S. Atlantic Ave. (at Broadway), Daytona Beach, FL 32018. Tel. 904/255-6421, or toll free 800/76-LODGE. Fax 904/252-6195. 100 rms. A/C TV TEL
$ Rates: $38–$78 single or double, $90–$150 during special events. Additional person $5 extra, $10 during special events. Children under 15 stay free in parents' room. AE, CB, DC, DISC, MC, V. **Parking:** Free.

This very centrally located Econo Lodge occupies a five-story beachfront building, with half of its rooms overlooking the ocean. The accommodations—standard motel units attractively decorated in peach and mauve—are equipped with cable TVs that offer visitor-information channels. A good deal for families are the reasonably priced suites (at the higher end of the rates quoted above) offering sizable living room areas with sofas in addition to bedrooms, plus small refrigerators and microwave ovens; some of these have private balconies.

Facilities include a very large swimming pool with a sun deck overlooking the beach (there's a pool bar in season, and a concession called the Tiki Hut vends beach accessories), a coin-op laundry, and a small video-game arcade. A casual hotel coffee shop called Time Out serves breakfast and lunch. Room service is available during restaurant hours (6am to 2pm daily). And a cozy on-premises pub called the Hole Bar is a popular local hangout featuring music (live or DJ) nightly, pool tables, dart boards, foosball, and video games; sporting events—including Monday-night football—are aired on large-screen TV.

A RESORT HOTEL

INDIGO LAKES CROWNE PLAZA RESORT, 2620 W. International Speedway Blvd. (between Williamson Blvd. and I-95), Daytona Beach, FL 32114. Tel. 904/258-6333, or toll free 800/874-9918. Fax 904/254-3698. 147 rms, 64 suites. A/C TV TEL

$ Rates: $70–$90 single; $85–$105 double; $90–$115 executive king room; $115–$155 one-bedroom suite. Additional person $10 extra. Children of any age stay free in parents' room. Inquire about golf, tennis, and honeymoon packages. AE, CB, DC, DISC, MC, V. **Parking:** Free.

This multifacilitied 250-acre resort is very close to the Speedway and a six-mile drive from the beach. The property is beautifully landscaped with verdant lawns and duck-filled lakes and lagoons spanned by arched bridges. Handsome accommodations, housed in two-story tan stucco buildings, are attractively decorated in earth tones with grasspaperlike wall coverings and dark-oak furnishings. Each room is equipped with an alarm-clock radio, coffee maker (and complimentary coffee), small refrigerator, and remote-control TV with HBO, Spectravision pay movies, an extensive roster of cable stations, and a tourist-information channel. All have patios or balconies. Large executive king rooms are especially luxurious and offer parlor areas. And gorgeous residential-style one-bedroom suites—many overlooking the golf course—offer fully equipped kitchens, baths with whirlpool tubs, and large, plushly furnished living/dining room areas.

Dining/Entertainment: Major Moultries is an elegant plant-filled golf-course restaurant with a wall of windows overlooking the greens and lagoons. It serves American regional fare at all meals. A bar/lounge adjoins, as does a snack bar with umbrella tables.

Services: Room service (7am to 11pm), complimentary newspaper daily, complimentary van to/from the golf course, tennis and golf instruction from resident pros, complimentary airport shuttle.

Facilities: Two swimming pools (one Olympic-size), 18-hole/par-72 Lloyd Clifton–designed championship golf course (ranked 19th in the state) with putting green and pro shop, volleyball, shuffleboard, horseshoes, basketball, 10 lighted hard-surface tennis courts with pro shop, 1½-mile jogging trail, extensive health and fitness center, ($5 a day charged for use), massage, business center, gift/sundry shop, coin-op washer/dryers, Budget car-rental desk.

BED & BREAKFAST

CAPTAIN'S QUARTERS INN, 3711 S. Atlantic Ave. (about a quarter mile south of Dunlawton Ave.), Daytona Beach, FL 32127. Tel. 904/767-3119, or toll free 800/332-3119. Fax 904/760-7712. 26 suites. A/C TV TEL

$ Rates (including full breakfast): $75–$95 suite for one or two; $110–$145 oceanfront penthouse suite. During special events, $90–$140 suite for one or two; $130–$195 oceanfront penthouse suite. Additional adult $5 extra. Children under 17 stay free in parents' suite. Lower rates available for weekly and monthly stays. AE, DISC, MC, V. **Parking:** Free.

This five-story beachfront inn offers large and lovely suites, most with ocean or river views. They have living/dining room areas, fully equipped kitchens, and country-look bedrooms furnished in oak antique reproductions. Residential decorator schemes utilize charming floral-print wall coverings and fabrics, balloon curtains, dried-flower wreaths, and framed botanical prints. French doors open onto balconies or patios furnished with wooden rockers.

Accommodations are equipped with clock radios, remote-control cable TVs (two per unit) offering HBO and another free movie station, and full VCRs (movies can be rented). Penthouse suites have fireplaces, spa tubs, and big picture windows overlooking the ocean. On-premises facilities include a country crafts/gift shop off the lobby, a heated swimming pool, coin-op washer/dryers, and the Galley Restaurant, which has an outdoor deck overlooking the ocean. Open for breakfast and lunch daily, it serves scrumptious fresh-baked cakes, cinnamon buns, and danish, as well as homemade soups, salads, and sandwiches on homemade breads. It's worth stopping by even if you're staying elsewhere. Other pluses: free transport to and from the airport, complimentary daily newspapers, wine and cheese at check-in, chocolate mints on your night table, and a full breakfast of eggs, bacon, grits or home-fries, juice, and coffee served each morning in your room or the Galley. Owner Becky Sue Morgan provides warm hospitality.

COQUINA INN, 544 S. Palmetto Ave. (at Cedar St.), Daytona Beach, FL 32114. Tel. 904/254-4969, or toll free 800/727-0678. 4 rms (all with bath). A/C

$ Rates (including full breakfast): $75–$105 single or double, $115–$140 during special events; $195 suite. Additional person $10 extra, $30 during special events. No children under 12 accepted. MC, V. **Parking:** Free.

This charming terra-cotta–roofed coquina and cream stucco house sits on a tranquil tree-shaded street half a block west of the Halifax River and Harbor Marina. Guests can relax before a working fireplace in a lovely parlor furnished with leather wing chairs, a comfortable sofa, and a baby grand piano. Baskets of magazines, books, games, and a TV are in the adjoining sunroom, which has terra-cotta-tile floors and cheerfully upholstered white wicker furnishings. An Oriental rug graces the highly polished oak floor of the dining room, which also features French doors, casement windows, and a crystal chandelier. Breakfast—elegantly served on Lenox and Rosenthal china—includes a main course such as eggs Benedict or French toast stuffed with cream cheese, bananas, and pecans; fresh fruit; fresh-ground coffee; and homemade breads and muffins. Classical music is played in public areas.

Each room is exquisitely decorated, most with area rugs strewn on oak floors and ceiling fans overhead. The Jasmine Room, painted adobe peach, features a working coquina fireplace and a canopied mahogany bed. In the Hibiscus Room, decorated in soft greens and pinks, a black iron bed embellished with gold leaf is made up with a pretty floral chintz spread. French doors lead to a private plant-filled balcony (pots of geraniums, hibiscus, gardenias, and hydrangeas) overlooking an ancient live oak draped with Spanish moss. Painted in raspberry with a floral frieze, the sunny Azalea Room has light streaming in from corner windows. Overlooking the patio garden, it's furnished with a mahogany waterfall bed (a Victorian teddy bear sits amid its throw pillows), white wicker chairs, and an antique Governor Winthrop desk. And the Magnolia Room, its mint stucco walls hung with framed botanical prints, contains a shell-shaped sink and a hand-carved mahogany four-poster bed and white iron day bed, both made up with beautiful floral chintz bedspreads and ruffled pillows. The Jasmine and Hibiscus Rooms can be combined to create a two-bedroom/two-bath suite. All rooms have clock radios and are provided with bubble bath and candles. Portable phones and TVs are available on request. Complimentary tea and sherry are served in the parlor throughout the day. Also gratis—10-speed bicycles and use of an Olympic-size pool at the nearby YWCA. During busy seasons, a two-night minimum stay is required.

LIVE OAK INN, 448 S. Beach St. (at Loomis Ave.), Daytona Beach, FL 32114. Tel. 904/252-4667. Fax 904/255-1871. 4 rms (all with bath). A/C TV TEL

$ Rates (including extended continental breakfast): $70 single or double Mon–Thurs, $95 Fri–Sun. Additional person $10 extra. Rates higher during peak events. Packages including dinner, golf, and other extras also available. AE, MC, V. **Parking:** Free.

Occupying a restored 19th-century house, its carefully tended front lawn enclosed by a white picket fence, this charming B&B is surrounded by centuries-old live oaks hung with Spanish moss. An inviting front porch with white wicker rocking chairs faces the street. The guest rooms—three with private sun porches or balconies—are exquisitely decorated. Yours might be painted pale peach with pristine white trim, furnished with an Eastlake bed and matching marble-top dresser. Or perhaps you'll get a Victorian sleigh bed with a patchwork quilt and a private plant-filled sun porch furnished with Adirondack chairs. Rooms look out on the Halifax Harbor Marina or a delightful garden. Baths have Victorian soaking tubs or Jacuzzis, TVs are concealed in old-fashioned radio and Victrola cabinets (you may find a VCR or cassette player as well), area rugs are strewn on highly polished oak floors, and wood-bladed fans whirr slowly overhead. Live plants, old family photographs, and baskets of potpourri add to the residential ambience. All rooms are stocked with books and magazines and equipped with alarm-clock radios.

The lobby bar is open throughout the day, and there's a lovely in-house restaurant serving American/continental fare at lunch and dinner. Comprised of two plant-filled dining rooms, with French doors opening onto an enclosed porch, it offers seating at elegantly appointed candlelit tables.

Other amenities include a croquet set on the front lawn, a washer/dryer and copy machine for guest use, a complimentary drink when you check in, a fruit basket and flowers in your room on arrival, terry robes, afternoon tea and cocktails, free transport to/from the beach, free airport shuttle, and room service during restaurant hours. Guests can also use an Olympic-size swimming pool at the YWCA four doors down. A delicious breakfast—fresh-baked muffins, cheeses, sausage, fresh fruit, juice, and French-pressed coffee—is served daily. The owners have purchased a similar 19th-century building next door and plan to add 12 more rooms. No smoking is permitted in the house.

WHERE TO DINE

EXPENSIVE

ALEXANDER'S CAFE, 123 W. Granada Blvd., between N. Ridgewood Ave. and U.S. 1. Tel. 673-5312.
   Cuisine: FRENCH/CONTINENTAL. **Reservations:** Recommended.
$ **Prices:** Appetizers $3.75–$5.50 at lunch, $6.75–$7.75 at dinner; main courses $5.20–$6.95 at lunch, $18.95–$23.95 at dinner; prix-fixe brunch $18.95. AE, MC, V.
   Open: Lunch Mon–Sat 11:30am–4pm; dinner Mon–Sat 5–9:30pm; brunch Sun 11:30am–3pm.

This charming innlike restaurant has a dark wood-beamed ceiling, multipaned windows, glossy pine floors, and seating in comfortable upholstered armchairs at tables clothed in white linen and lit (at night) by shaded candle lamps. Soft lighting also emanates from hunting-horn–motif brass chandeliers and sconces. The War Room—with green-and-sienna-striped wallpaper above pine wainscoting—is decorated with framed photographs of Civil War generals, a painting of Napoleon, battle scenes, and recruitment posters. The Bacchus Room offers a view of the wine cellar via a glass door. And in the third dining room a pianist plays standards (like Cole Porter) on a baby grand during dinner.

Though the menu changes frequently (owner John Cunningham likes to try new things), you can always count on French chef Christian Drouin for a superb meal. If it's available, order his tangy Cheddar soup spiked with sherry. On other visits, I've enjoyed appetizers of baked mushrooms stuffed with mild Italian sausage and spinach tortellini served atop fresh spinach in a light Alfredo sauce. Thick oven-baked pork chops in cranberry-orange-Dijon sauce was a memorable meat dish. Also excellent were large grilled sea scallops in a beurre-blanc citrus-cream sauce and a classic steak au poivre in brandy-cream sauce. All main courses are accompanied by a delicious salad, fresh vegetables, potatoes or rice du jour, and sorbets between courses; appropriate wines are recommended. Don't skip the desserts, which might include a very rich black velvet chocolate cake or a raspberry torte topped with butter-cream frosting and toasted almonds. The lunch menu lists sandwiches, salads, and a few main dishes, and brunch is an elaborate seven-course feast including a glass of champagne. Alexander's offers an extensive wine list, several dozen single-malt scotches, and 14 draft beers. The adjoining bar/lounge is deservedly popular (see "The Club & Bar Scene," below, for more details).

MODERATE

ANNA'S ITALIAN TRATTORIA, 304 Seabreeze Blvd., at Peninsula Dr., Tel. 239-9624.

Cuisine: ITALIAN. **Reservations:** Recommended.

$ **Prices:** Appetizers $4.25–$8; main courses mostly $8.50–$14; early-bird dinners (served 5–6:30pm) $5–$8. AE, MC, V.

Open: Dinner only, daily 5–10pm.

At this charming little trattoria, the Triani family, from Sicily, have created a homelike atmosphere enhanced by cheerful Italian music. Soft lighting emanates from brass oil lamps and sconces. Everything here is homemade—from the creamy Italian dressing on your house salad to the basket of hot crusty bread that accompanies all main courses. That bread comes in handy for soaking up the dressing (extra-virgin olive oil with pieces of celery, slivers of fresh garlic, lemon, parsley, and oregano) of a scungilli salad appetizer. An order of lightly breaded fried calamari with a piquant marinara sauce is also a good starter. Two irresistible pasta dishes are the fettuccine alla campagniola (pasta tossed with strips of sautéed eggplant and chunks of sausage in tomato-cream sauce flavored with a soupçon of crushed red pepper and romano cheese) and rigatoni siciliana (tubular pasta with sautéed broccoli, garlic, and pine nuts in a fresh tomato sauce). Nonpasta recommendables include salmon scampi (sautéed in garlic butter, mushrooms, sherry wine, and lemon). And risotto alla Anna is similar to a Spanish paella—a rice dish cooked with chunks of chicken, shrimp, green peas, and onions in a light tomato sauce.

Portions are hearty. If you like a heavy hand with garlic, as I do, tell your waiter. Main courses come with soup or salad and a side dish of angel-hair pasta or a vegetable. Take the pasta and order a vegetable side dish as well, perhaps asparagus, escarole, or broccoli rabe sautéed in oil and garlic. There's a nice selection of Italian wines to complement your meal. Both the tira misu and the homemade ricotta cheesecake make for excellent desserts.

There's free parking in a lot on Seabreeze Boulevard across Peninsula Drive.

AUNT CATFISH'S, 4009 Halifax Dr., at the west end of the Port Orange Bridge. Tel. 767-4768.

Cuisine: SOUTHERN/SEAFOOD. **Reservations:** Not accepted, but you can—and should—call ahead for priority seating (that means you get the first table available when you arrive).

$ **Prices:** Appetizers $2.90–$4.95; main courses $4–$8 at lunch, mostly $8–$13.50 at dinner; early-bird dinners $7–$10.50. Reduced prices for children and seniors. Sun brunch $9 for adults, $5.50 for children 4–12, free for kids under 4. AE, DC, DISC, MC, V.

Open: Mon–Sat 11:30am–9:30pm, Sun 9am–9:30pm (brunch Sun 9am–2pm; early-bird dinners daily noon–6:30pm). **Closed:** Christmas.

Aunt Catfish was the nickname of a gruff-voiced local character whom owner Jim Galbreath knew as a kid. She fished all day, drove around in a black Cadillac, and ate dinner every night in a restaurant owned by Jim's parents. Her namesake restaurant abounds in cozy southern-cracker ambience. Tables are topped with laminated horse-feed sacks, weathered-looking rough-hewn wood-paneled walls are hung with historic photographs of the Daytona Beach area, and decorative elements include antique clothes wringers and corn huskers. During the day, ask for a window seat overlooking the Halifax River.

The food is great, and there's plenty of it. No way will you finish everything you order. For one thing, all main courses include hush puppies, a chunk of watermelon, unbelievable yummy hot cinnamon rolls, a side dish (perhaps baked Mexican potato skins with melted Cheddar, salsa, and sour cream), and unlimited helpings from an extensive salad bar, which in addition to salads is laden with such down-home fare as cheese grits, cinnamon apples, fresh-baked cornbread, and hominy. A great main-dish choice is the Florida cracker sampler platter—a spit-roasted quarter chicken with cranberry-orange relish, crab cakes served in hollandaise sauce, fried shrimp, and fried catfish fingerlings. Lightly breaded fried oysters here are also highly recommendable. Beverage options include house wines, bar drinks, bottomless pitchers of iced tea, and fresh-squeezed lemonade. For dessert, split a boatsinker fudge pie with Häagen-Dazs coffee ice cream dipped in a coat of hardened chocolate and topped with whipped cream. Aunt Catfish's key lime and raspberry pies are also excellent.

Sunday brunch provides an unexampled opportunity for overindulgence. A buffet meal, it includes all the above-mentioned salad-bar items, plus an omelet station, pancakes, French toast, hot dishes, a carving station, fresh-baked muffins and pastries (even bananas Foster), and more—all for under $10! Lunch choices include burgers, sandwiches, and a soup and salad buffet in addition to ribs, chicken, and seafood dishes.

THE CHART HOUSE, 1100 Marina Point Dr., off Beach St. Tel. 255-9022.

Cuisine: CONTINENTAL/STEAK/SEAFOOD. **Reservations:** Recommended.

$ Prices: Appetizers $4.50–$8.95; main courses mostly $14.95–$21.95. AE, CB, DC, DISC, MC, V.

Open: Dinner only, Sun–Thurs 5–10pm, Fri–Sat 5–11pm.

The lushly plant-filled Chart House is of octagonal design, with palm trees growing toward a lofty skylit bamboo ceiling. Oak tables topped with laminated world maps, ship models, palm-frond–motif carpeting, and a service staff in Hawaiian shirts enhance the restaurant's tropical/marine ambience. And windowed walls overlooking the Halifax River and a boat-filled marina ensure every diner a water view. Consider having dessert or after-dinner drinks in the plush bar/lounge downstairs or on an open-air riverside deck with umbrella tables.

You might want to bypass appetizers here, since your main-course price includes a very extensive salad bar (including items such as caviar, artichoke hearts, and an array of fresh fruits), a basket of hot sourdough and seven-grain squaw bread (it's made with molasses), and a baked potato or Chart House wild rice cooked in chicken broth and tossed with slivered almonds, pineapple, pimento, and chives. For your main dish, select shrimp or chicken Santa Fe dusted with cumin, paprika, and cayenne, grilled in butter, and served with tangy bleu-cheese dip. Steak, prime rib au jus with creamed horseradish sauce, and surf-and-turf combinations are also options. Mud pie is the dessert of choice—coffee ice cream on an Oreo-cookie crust topped with real whipped cream and toasted almonds. The bar offers exotic tropical drinks, and an international wine list highlights American vineyards. Service is notably excellent.

MARKO'S HERITAGE INN, 5420 S. Ridgewood Ave., at Niver St. Tel. 761-9520.

Cuisine: SOUTHERN/SEAFOOD. **Reservations:** Not accepted, but you can—and should—call ahead for priority seating (that means you get the first table available when you arrive).

$ Prices: Appetizers $2.95–$6.95; main courses mostly $8–$13; early-bird dinners $5.95–$9.95. Reduced prices for children and seniors. Sun breakfast/brunch buffet $5.95 for adults, $3.50 for children 4–12, free for kids under 4. AE, DC, DISC, MC, V.

Open: Dinner Mon–Sat 4:30–9:30pm, Sun 11:30am–9pm (early-bird dinners served daily until 6pm); buffet breakfast/brunch Sun 8am–2pm. **Closed:** Christmas.

Like Aunt Catfish's (see above), Marko's is owned by Jim Galbreath. In fact, its 17,000-square-foot warren of cozy dining rooms encompasses the house in which he grew up and his parents' original Daytona Beach restaurant. Off the entrance you'll see large photographs of its 1950s interior, with Jim as a young lad tending the counter. It's all very southern and homelike. Overflow crowds wait for tables on a porch or in an antique-filled Victorian parlor, and there's an old-fashioned candy counter and bakery up front. Dining areas have windows with shutters or ruffled café curtains, walls paneled in knotty pine or whitewashed cypress lapsiding, hutches and shelves filled with display china, tables covered in pretty floral-print cotton cloths, and many hanging plants. One room even has a working fireplace.

Don't eat a big lunch the day you dine here. Your main-course price includes a complimentary bowl of Florida cracker-style clam chowder, salad (go for the fruit with creamy poppyseed dressing), an array of vegetables served family style (coleslaw, stewed apples, stringbeans, a jar of pickled beets), potato or scrumptious broccoli casserole, tangerine sherbet between courses, and a basket of fresh-baked oatmeal and cinnamon rolls. All of this bounty precludes the need for appetizers, but there are some great ones nevertheless: blackened mahi-mahi with hollandaise, buffalo shrimp with hot sauce, and buttery-garlicky chicken tenders prepared like escargots and served in mushroom caps. My favorite dish is the grouper Hemingway, sautéed in a crisp sesame crust. Other good choices include smoky barbecued baby back ribs and fried Maryland-style crab cakes. And desserts—such as a first-rate key lime pie, chocolate/peanut-butter pie, and funnel cake topped with macadamia-nut ice cream and hot fudge—are not to be missed. There's a full bar. After dinner, browse in the gift shop filled with charming country crafts.

SOPHIE KAY'S WATERFALL RESTAURANT, 3516 S. Atlantic Ave., at Raymond Ave. Tel. 756-4444.

Cuisine: CONTINENTAL/STEAK/SEAFOOD/PASTA. **Reservations:** Recommended.

$ Prices: Appetizers $3.95–$5.95; main courses $8.95–$23.95 (most under $15). AE, DC, DISC, MC, V.

Open: Dinner only, Sun–Thurs 4–10pm, Fri–Sat 4–11pm. (Bar, serving light fare, Sun–Thurs to midnight, Fri–Sat to 1am.)

Long-time Daytona restaurateur, cookbook author, and local television personality Sophie Kay has entertained dozens of celebrities—everyone from John Travolta (he celebrated his mom's birthday at Sophie's) to Carol Channing. Her newest restaurant venture—designed by talented son Dean, who also serves as maître d'—has an elegant plant-filled interior. The room centers on a rock waterfall that cascades into a goldfish pond. Stark-white stucco walls are hung with attractive abstract paintings and tapestries, while pottery and plants are displayed on rough stone ledges. Arched mirrors enhance the feeling of spaciousness, and full-size palm trees, candles aglow in peach frosted-glass holders, and soft piano music add romantic tropical nuance.

An order of half a dozen oysters Rockefeller bubbling with cheese, or lightly breaded crisp-fried shrimp scampi (the latter also available as a main course), makes an excellent beginning. Sophie is a great hand with pasta (she has written an entire book on the subject), and her primavera pasta—tossed with al dente chunks of broccoli, onions, carrots, yellow squash, zucchini, mushrooms, and sun-dried tomatoes in a delicate white sauce—is perfection. Also very good: baked seafood (shrimp, scallops, and filet of orange roughy) served en papillote in a creamy lobster béchamel sauce. And many people come here for items such as filet mignon, roast prime rib au jus with creamy horseradish sauce, or surf-and-turf combinations. Main courses include soup or salad, wild rice or baked potato, and a basket of fresh-baked bread and muffins. For dessert, don't pass up Sophie's delicious twice-baked cheesecake on a buttery graham-cracker crust—one of the best of its genre. After dinner, adjourn to the sophisticated piano bar for cocktails.

INEXPENSIVE

DOWN THE HATCH, 4894 Front St., Ponce Inlet. Tel. 761-4831.

Cuisine: SEAFOOD. **Reservations:** Not accepted, but call ahead for priority seating (that means you get the first table available when you arrive). **Directions:** Take Fla. A1A south, make a right on Beach Street, and follow the signs.

$ Prices: Appetizers $2.75–$5.95; main courses $7.95–$12.95; sandwiches $3.25–$5.25. Reduced prices for children. AE, MC, V.

Open: Daily 11:30am–10pm. **Closed:** Thanksgiving and Christmas.

Occupying a half-century-old fish camp on the Halifax River, Down the Hatch is a cozy, candlelit restaurant serving up fresh fish and seafood (note their shrimp boat docked outside). During the day, picture windows provide scenic views of a passing parade of boats and shore birds—blue herons, egrets, pelicans, and cormorants—and you might even see dolphins frolicking. At night, arrive early to catch the sunset over the river, and also to beat the crowd at this very popular place. Inside, rough-hewn cypress walls are hung with hundreds of photographs of the Daytona Speedway and the old fish camp, and the nautical ambience is enhanced by a clutter of mounted fish trophies, ship models, harpoons, hurricane lamps, and antique bottles. In summer, light fare is served outside on an awninged wooden deck.

Start your meal with an order of buffalo shrimp—tiny shrimp quick-fried in hot oil, finished with a piquant Louisiana hot sauce, and served with chunky homemade bleu-cheese dressing. Lightly breaded, deep-fried grouper fingers, served with tartar sauce, are also tasty. Ditto the raw oysters served with cocktail sauce and horseradish. Main courses include fried or broiled fresh fish such as red snapper or grouper, and there's an excellent crab Imperial—crabmeat broiled in a tarragon-mayonnaise sauce and garnished with chopped green peppers. If seafood isn't your thing, filet mignon and prime rib are aged on the premises. All main dishes are served with hush puppies and a choice of baked potato, salad, coleslaw, or fries. There's a full bar; desserts include mud pie, key lime pie, and cheesecake.

SOPHIE KAY'S COFFEE TREE FAMILY RESTAURANT, 100 S. Atlantic Ave., at Bosarvey Dr., Ormond Beach. Tel. 677-0300.
   Cuisine: AMERICAN. **Reservations:** Not accepted.
 $ Prices: Appetizers $1.95–$3.50; main courses $5–$9; breakfast items mostly under $5. Reduced prices for children and seniors over 55. AE, MC, V.
   Open: Daily 7am–10pm.

This casual coffee shop, with sunshine streaming in through numerous windows, is a cheerful spot for inexpensive meals. You can sit in a comfy booth or at a counter facing an open kitchen hung with copper pots. Food is served on colorful Fiestaware dishes.

The same menu—including breakfast fare—is served all day, with specials such as homemade meatloaf, lasagne, and stuffed cabbage offered at lunch and dinner. You might begin the day here with thick slabs of Texas-style French toast, Belgian waffles dusted with powdered sugar, or eggs Benedict. The rest of the day, choices include deli sandwiches, burgers, salads, and main courses ranging from fried shrimp to roast turkey served over sage dressing with cranberry sauce, either including coleslaw, mashed potatoes, and a fresh vegetable. For dessert, try the ultra-rich chocolate suicide cake. Everything is fresh and well prepared. This is food like Mom's.

SPRING GARDEN RANCH, 900 Spring Garden Ranch Rd., DeLeon Springs. Tel. 985-0526.
   Cuisine: AMERICAN. **Reservations:** Recommended. **Directions:** Take International Speedway Boulevard (U.S. 92W), turn right at Rte. 1792 (Woodland Boulevard), stay on your left, and take U.S. 17 to Spring Garden Ranch Road; look for the sign on your right and go to Gate 3.
 $ Prices: Breakfast fare $1.95–$6.95; breakfast buffet $4.95 for adults, $3.50 for children under 10; lunch fare $2–$5.50. MC, V.
   Open: Oct–May, daily 6am–2pm; June–Sept, Tues–Sun 7am–1pm. **Closed:** Easter, Thanksgiving, and Christmas.

This is more than a meal, it's an outing. Spring Garden Ranch is a 148-acre training center for harness-race horses, and from its trackside restaurant you can watch pacers and trotters being schooled through large picture windows. The verdant surroundings are scenic, and, all in all, this is nice way to start your day. After you eat, you can go look at the horses.

Breakfast choices include a hearty buffet—eggs, biscuits and gravy, pancakes, sausage patties and bacon, home-fries, grits, and citrus fruits. Or you might order steak and eggs à la carte. Lunch fare includes sandwiches, salads, burgers, and main dishes like southern fried chicken, with fruit cobbler à la mode for dessert. Ask for a window seat when you reserve.

EVENING ENTERTAINMENT
THE PERFORMING ARTS

At the 2,552-seat **Peabody Auditorium,** 600 Auditorium Blvd., between Noble Street and Wild Olive Avenue (tel. 255-1314), Daytona Beach's Civic Ballet performs *The Nutcracker* every Christmas and sponsors another ballet every spring. The Daytona Beach Symphony Society arranges a series of six classical concerts between December and April. During the same season, Concert Showcase features pop artists such as Liza Minnelli, Tony Bennett, Steve Lawrence and Eydie Gorme, and Frank Sinatra, as well as full Broadway-cast stage shows like *Cats* and *City of Angels*. And the London Symphony Orchestra has been performing here for over 25 years during the semiannual Florida International Festival.

Under the same city auspices is the **Oceanfront Bandshell** (tel. 258-3169), on the boardwalk next to the Marriott Hotel. The city hosts a series of free Big Band concerts at the Bandshell every Sunday night from early June through Labor Day. It's also the scene of spring-break concerts.

Prices at the Peabody vary with the performances. Bandshell concerts are usually free. Parking is $3 in a lot adjacent to the Peabody.

THE CLUB & BAR SCENE

In addition to the following, the piano bar at **Sophie's Waterfall Restaurant,** which offers a special bar menu (pizzas, potato skins, steak sandwiches), and the **Chart House** downstairs bar are elegant and simpatico nighttime settings. For details, see "Where to Dine," above.

ALEXANDER'S CAFE, 123 W. Granada Blvd., between N. Ridgewood Ave. and U.S. 1, in Ormond Beach. Tel. 673-5312.

The convivial bar/lounge of this upscale restaurant has a ski-lodgey ambience comprised of exposed-brick and pine-paneled walls and a cathedral ceiling. A sled called Rosebud behind the bar and a painting of Batman are among its whimsical adornments. The crowd comes for the music (live guitarists play oldies, and there's a primo jukebox stocked with Otis Redding, Bob Marley, Joe Cocker, and Springsteen tunes). Sporting events (most notably Monday-night football) are aired on three TV monitors. You can order from the extensive wine list, have an appetizer or dessert, try one of the café's many single-malt scotches (I recommend the smoky Lagavulin) or draft beers, even order up a fine cigar. The bar is cigar-friendly, but open windows keep the smoke level down. Open Monday through Saturday until somewhere between midnight and 2am, depending on the crowd.

CLOCKTOWER LOUNGE, in the Marriott Hotel, 100 N. Atlantic Ave., between Earl St. and Auditorium Blvd. Tel. 254-8200.

This sophisticated bar/lounge, with bamboo furnishings and palm trees growing toward a skylight ceiling, offers piano-bar music or live jazz Tuesday through Saturday from 8pm to midnight. There's a small dance floor, and in addition to drinks, you can order interesting light-fare items such as smoked-salmon mousse with crackers or black lobster ravioli in a light cream sauce. This is one of Daytona's most romantic settings. Make a night of it and dine earlier in Coquinas, the Marriott's elegant steak-and-seafood restaurant. It's open from 8pm to midnight. Parking is free in a lot across the street; valet parking is $3. See also Waves, below.

COLISEUM, 176 N. Beach St., at Bay St. Tel. 257-9982.

Heralded by a pedimented Doric colonnade, this upscale Roman-themed dance club occupies a converted movie theater. Inside, a raised dance floor is flanked by Ionic columns and Roman-style bas-reliefs and sculpture adorn the walls. A DJ plays alternative progressive dance music, with lapses into top-40 tunes; four big movie screens project music and ambience videos; and nightly laser shows are high-tech, utilizing 3-D and sophisticated graphic-arts effects. The crowd is mostly twentysomething with occasional glitterati (Tom Cruise partied here during the filming of *Days of Thunder*), rock musicians, and local athletes in attendance. During spring break there are live concerts and special events. The Coliseum is open from 10pm to 3am nightly from February to October, from 11pm to 3am Thursday through Sunday the rest of the year. Parking is free behind the club on Bay Street; usually there's ample street parking as well.

Admission: $5–$6.

RAZZLES, 611 Seabreeze Blvd., between Grandview and S. Atlantic Aves. Tel. 257-6236.

At this large and popular dance club, a DJ plays top-40 tunes and high-energy music till 3am nightly. The setting is archetypical, with lots of neon tubing, the requisite monitors flashing music videos, and sophisticated lighting effects over the dance floor. A magician frequently entertains in the lobby, there are four pool tables, a blackjack table, and a few video games. An awninged patio out front provides a place for quiet conversation. The crowd is young—early 20s. There's free parking behind the club on Grandview between Seabreeze and Oakridge Boulevards.

Admission: Before 10pm, $6–$8 with free drinks; after 10pm, $5 for 18- to 20-year-olds, $3 for those 21 and over.

701 SOUTH, in the South Beach Resort, 701 S. Atlantic Ave., at Revilo Blvd. Tel. 255-8431.

This is a high-energy club, with a big dance floor, two giant matrix (multiscreen) video walls, 13 bartenders (overseeing 8,000 square feet of bar area), and "shooter" girls in leotards proffering shots of a drink called Sex on the Beach—a mix of cranberry and orange juices, peach schnapps, and vodka—to willing customers. Monday through Saturday a DJ and live bands alternate playing progressive music and rock 'n' roll; Sunday there's a DJ only. Big-name acts have played here, among them Paula Abdul, Samantha Fox, the Red Hot Chile Peppers, Marky Mark, and Naughty by Nature. When you weary of dancing, you can play pool, darts, foosball, or air hockey. Light fare is available. Open nightly till 3am. Parking is free on the premises.

Admission: $6 for those aged 18–20, $4 for those 21 and over; higher when big-name bands play.

THE SPOT, 176 N. Beach St., at Bay St. Tel. 257-9982.

Under the same ownership as the above-mentioned Coliseum, the Spot shares its address and phone as well. Billing itself as a "premier sports bar," it has large-screen TVs in every corner, which, along with over 30 smaller monitors, air major worldwide sporting events via satellite. This cavernous club centers on a U-shaped Formica-topped bar trimmed in turquoise neon. The walls are decorated in a painterly collage of baseball cards, car-racing photos, sports paraphernalia, and American flags. And there's a comfortable seating area on a fire-engine-red vinyl sofa in front of a large TV. Less passive amusements include foosball, air hockey, video games, pinball machines, a one-on-one basketball court, eight regulation pool tables, dart boards, and bar games. Light fare is available. The Spot sponsors local rugby and pool teams. Monday-night football parties include raffles for tickets to local sporting events, and a DJ is on hand Tuesday nights. Open nightly till 3am. Parking is free behind the club on Bay Street; usually there's ample street parking as well.

WAVES, in the Marriott Hotel, 100 N. Atlantic Ave., between Earl St. and Auditorium Blvd. Tel. 254-8200.

An elegant sports bar on the hotel's boardwalk level, Waves airs continuous sporting events (via a four-dish satellite system) on two large screens and 23 additional monitors. Its main bar centers on a large aquarium of tropical fish. In addition to upholstered bamboo furnishings, there are comfy sofas in a quiet alcove with a large-screen TV. Bartenders and servers are dressed as referees. A DJ plays music for dancing nightly from 9pm. Other activities here include backgammon, QB1 interactive sports and trivia games, and electronic darts. Open nightly till 3am. Parking is free in a lot across the street; valet parking is $3.

Admission: Free, except during special events.

CHAPTER 11

NORTHWEST FLORIDA: THE PANHANDLE

- **WHAT'S SPECIAL ABOUT NORTHWEST FLORIDA**
1. **PENSACOLA**
2. **FORT WALTON BEACH & DESTIN**
3. **PANAMA CITY & PANAMA CITY BEACH**
4. **TALLAHASSEE**

A quick glance at a map shows why Northwest Florida is often called the Panhandle. Only a few miles of Florida separate the talcumlike beaches rimming the Gulf of Mexico from the adjoining states of Georgia and Alabama. Like its neighboring states, this handleshaped extremity offers the languid charm of the Deep South. The Panhandle is a land of graceful antebellum mansions, moss-draped little towns whose squares boast historic monuments, gardens brimming with azaleas and camellias, and plates piled high with local specialties like turnip greens and cheese grits. Gracious southern hospitality reigns supreme here, accented by words like *y'all*—which refers not to a sailboat but to all of you present, as in "*Y'all* want some more iced tea?"

That's not to say—in any accent—that Northwest Florida is all Deep South, for an influx of immigrants from other states and nations has been drawn to the Panhandle by its warm climate and relaxed atmosphere. Some came originally to serve at the huge military installations along the coast: the U.S. Naval Air Station at Pensacola, Eglin Air Force Base at Fort Walton Beach, and Tyndall Air Force Base at Panama City, all major contributors to the local workforce. Others came to take advantage of the growing sunbelt economy. For whatever reason they settled here, the expatriates have added cultural diversity to an already-interesting region.

Mother Nature certainly blessed the Panhandle with extraordinary beauty—countless acres of fragrant, green pine forests; crystal-clear rivers; spring-fed lakes and streams; soft white sand beaches with lacy, golden sea grasses.

Because the lifestyle is slow-paced, emphasis is on family activities in the great outdoors and enthusiastic participation in a variety of amusing annual festivals, such as the Boggy Bayou Mullet Fry in Niceville, the Watermelon Seed Spittin' Contest in the "watermelon capital" of Monticello, and the Wausau 'Possum Festival. It's fun to exit the region's only superhighway and explore the colorful towns and state parks along the way.

Fascinating history abounds in the Panhandle. Archeological sites and massive Native American mounds are interesting to tour. In the early 17th century, Spanish conquistador Hernándo de Soto set up camp one winter, before marching onward in his futile search for gold. During that time a Spanish mission was established to convert Native Americans, who seemed to be utilizing the Spaniards for target practice. The Seminoles were residents of the Panhandle for centuries until Gen. Andrew Jackson and early plantation owners greedily decided that all this rich farmland should be theirs. By hiding in the limestone cavern at Marianna, about 60 miles northwest of Tallahassee, many Seminoles were fortunate enough to escape the general's attacks, but they lost their land.

The wide diversity of the Panhandle, from the simplicity of peaceful rivers and

WHAT'S SPECIAL ABOUT NORTHWEST FLORIDA

Ace Attractions

☐ Fort Pickens, a spectacular setting in Gulf Islands National Seashore, where Apachee Chief Geronimo was imprisoned.

☐ Lake Jackson Mounds, Tallahassee, an 81-acre settlement dating to A.D. 1200.

☐ Seville Preservation District, Pensacola, with 10 historic buildings and museums, plus a shopping and dining complex.

Museums and Archives

☐ Black Archives Research Center and Museum, on the Florida A&M University campus, Tallahassee, with the world's second-largest collection on African American history.

☐ National Museum of Naval Aviation, at Pensacola U.S. Naval Air Station, one of the world's largest aerospace museums.

☐ Indian Temple Mound and Museum, Fort Walton Beach, with the world's largest collection of prehistoric southeastern Native American ceramics (6,000 + pieces).

Parks and Gardens

☐ Edward Ball Wakulla Springs State Park, near Tallahassee, one of the world's deepest freshwater springs.

☐ Alfred B. Maclay State Gardens, Tallahassee, with more than 300 acres of gorgeous magnolias, camellias, and azaleas, plus the restored Maclay House.

☐ St. Marks Wildlife Refuge and Lighthouse, south of Tallahassee, 64,000 acres with more bird species than anywhere else in Florida except the Everglades.

Architecture

☐ Seaside, east of Grayton Beach, a unique resort community built in 1981 and acclaimed one of the top U.S. architectural achievements.

☐ Eden State Gardens and Mansion, north of Grayton Beach, a restored 1898 Greek Revival southern mansion.

☐ Florida State Capitol, Tallahassee, a modern legislative center.

☐ Old State Capitol, Tallahassee, a restored 1902 white-columned American Renaissance building.

Beaches

☐ Gulf Islands National Seashore, mile after mile of dazzling white sand and rolling dunes, stretching from Perdido Key to Fort Walton Beach.

---

historic towns to the sophistication of Florida's capital city, makes this multifaceted area one of the most charming in Florida.

SEEING THE PANHANDLE

Northwest Florida is best visited by car, since public transportation is not available in most locales. Both I-10 and U.S. 98 link Tallahassee and Pensacola, some 200 miles apart. I-10 cuts through the rolling inland hills and is the fastest route, but the longer U.S. 98 is a scenic excursion in itself as it skirts the emerald waters of the gulf and passes through the major resort beaches at Pensacola, Fort Walton Beach, Destin, Panama City, and Panama City Beach. U.S. 98 becomes even more picturesque as it borders the broad bays around Apalachicola.

The resort beaches are no more than 90 minutes' driving time apart, so one can be an easy excursion from another. For example, you can stay in centrally located Fort Walton Beach or Destin and make easy day trips to Pensacola in one direction or Panama City in the other. The same is true of towns like Defuniak Springs, about equal distance from Fort Walton Beach or Panama City, and Apalachicola, halfway between Panama City and Tallahassee. Just because an attraction or excursion is included in one section of this chapter doesn't mean that it can't be easily seen or done from another nearby destination.

THE SEASONS   Since Panhandle winters can get downright cool, many beach facilities and restaurants are closed from November through February. The high season runs from Easter to Labor Day, when Georgians and Alabamians flock to the nearby beaches of Northwest Florida. Hotel or motel reservations are essential during this period. Room rates are highest from May to Labor Day, with premiums charged at Easter, Memorial Day, the Fourth of July, and Labor Day. There's another high-priced period in March, when thousands of raucous college students invade during spring break. Economical times to visit are April (except Easter), September, and October—the weather's warm, most establishments are open, and room rates are significantly lower than during the peak season.

1. PENSACOLA
200 miles W of Tallahassee, 375 miles W of Jacksonville

GETTING THERE   By Plane   The **Pensacola Regional Airport,** on 12th Avenue at Airport Road (tel. 904/435-1746), is served by American Eagle, Continental, Delta Connection, Northwest, and USAir.

By Train   Amtrak's *Sunset Limited,* which departs from Los Angeles and travels to Miami with stops along the way at Pensacola, Chipley, Crestview, and Tallahassee. Passengers can also connect from Jacksonville and New Orleans. Pensacola's Amtrak train station is at 940 E. Heinberg St., near the bayfront. For information and reservations, call Amtrak (tel. toll free 800/872-7245).

By Bus   The Greyhound terminal is at 505 W. Burgess Rd., in Pensacola (tel. 904/476-4800, or toll free 800/231-2222).

By Car   From the east or west take I-10, U.S. 90, or U.S. 98. From I-10, Exit 4 puts you on I-110, which terminates in downtown Pensacola. From the north, take Exit 69 off I-65 in Alabama and follow Ala. 113 to Formaton and Bluff Springs on the Alabama-Florida line, then U.S. 29 south to Pensacola.

Pensacola's turbulent past has all the elements of an exciting movie, but no Hollywood producer could ever imagine a scenario so complicated—the region has seen more than a dozen conquerors, and five different flags have been unfurled here.

It all began with the native tribes who lived in the area centuries ago and who left behind evidence of their sojourn in the pottery shards and artifacts discovered in the sand dunes. In 1559 King Philip II of Spain commissioned Tristan De Luna to colonize the coastal territory. But the ill-fated settlement survived only two years before De Luna and his settlers returned to Spain. Spain was more successful on the second try, when Capt. Jordan de Reina colonized Pensacola in 1698. Pensacola has had a long-time friendly feud with St. Augustine as to which city was the nation's first settlement—St. Augustine, founded in 1564, can claim to be the nation's first permanent settlement.

Important because of its strategic deep harbor, Pensacola was subsequently taken over by the French, the British, the United States, and the Confederacy. Pensacola's colorful history is just one reason why the city is so fascinating—it has the atmosphere of Old Spain, a romantic French influence reminiscent of New Orleans, and there remain the magnificent Victorian mansions built by the wealth of the lumber barons after Britain initiated that industry in the area.

Two of the Pensacola area's beaches are among America's top 10—Perdido Key, rated no. 3, and eastern Perdido Key, rated no. 7 by Dr. Stephen Leatherman of the University of Maryland's Laboratory for Coastal Research.

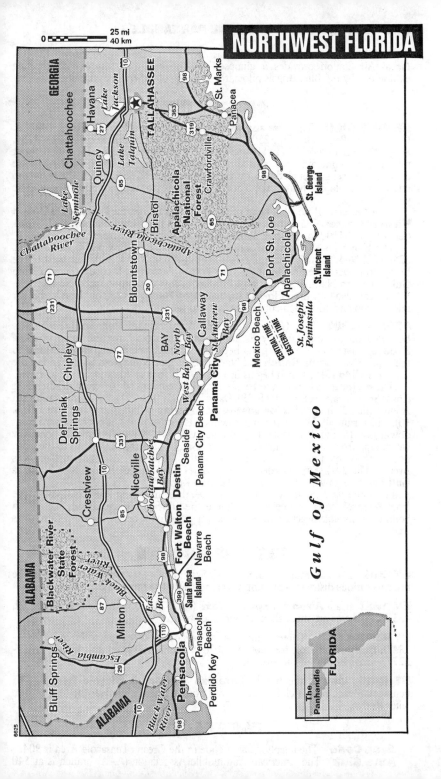

NORTHWEST FLORIDA

25 mi
40 km

GEORGIA

Chattahoochee
Havana
Quincy
TALLAHASSEE
St. Marks
Panacea

Lake Seminole
Lake Talquin
Lake Jackson

Chattahoochee River

Apalachicola River

Apalachicola National Forest
Crawfordville
St. George Island

Bristol
Port St. Joe
Apalachicola
St.Vincent Island
St. Joseph Peninsula

Blountstown
Callaway
Mexico Beach

BAY
North Bay
St. Andrew Bay
West Bay
Panama City

CENTRAL TIME
EASTERN TIME

Chipley
DeFuniak Springs

Panama City Beach
Seaside
Destin

Niceville
Choctawhatchee Bay

Crestview

Blackwater River State Forest
Black Water River

Fort Walton Beach
Navarre Beach

Santa Rosa Island

East Bay

Milton
Bluff Springs
Escambia River
Pensacola
Pensacola Beach
Perdido Key

Gulf of Mexico

ALABAMA

The Panhandle

FLORIDA

And there is yet another facet of Pensacola. A short drive from downtown, the U.S. Naval Air Station provides a glimpse into the high-tech future with thrilling exhibitions by the Blue Angels pilots, the epitome of expertise in the skies.

ORIENTATION

INFORMATION The **Pensacola Visitor Information Center,** 1401 E. Gregory St., Pensacola, FL 32501 (tel. 904/434-1234, or toll free 800/874-1234, 800/343-4321 in Florida; fax 904/432-8211), gives away helpful information about the Greater Pensacola Area, including maps of self-guided tours of the historic districts, and sells a detailed street map of the area for $1. Located at the mainland end of Pensacola Bay Bridge, the office is open daily from 8am to 5pm. It should be your first stop.

Near the Santa Rosa Island end of the Bob Sikes Bridge, the **Pensacola Beach Visitors Center,** 735 Pensacola Blvd. (P.O. Box 1174), Pensacola Beach, FL 32561 (tel. 904/932-1500, or toll free 800/635-4803), is open daily from 9am to 5pm.

The **Navarre Visitors Information Center,** P.O. Box 5337, Navarre, FL 32566 (tel. 904/939-2691, or toll free 800/480-7263), is on U.S. 98 just west of the bridge to Navarre Beach, about 20 miles east of Pensacola. It covers the area from Gulf Breeze to Navarre. By the way, Navarre is correctly pronounced Na-*var*.

You can also tune in to **Florida Information Radio** at 1230 on the AM dial for information and advertisements about what to see and do.

AREA LAYOUT The Greater Pensacola Area includes **Pensacola,** which is bordered on the mainland by Escambia and Pensacola Bays; the town of **Gulf Breeze,** on a peninsula jutting out between Pensacola and **Santa Rosa Island** to the south; **Pensacola Beach** and Navarre Beach, on Santa Rosa Island; and to the west, **Perdido Key,** which begins in Florida and ends in Alabama.

The **major north-south arteries** into Pensacola are I-110 (which dead-ends at Chase Street), Palafox Street (U.S. 29), Davis Highway (Fla. 291), 9th Avenue, and 12th Avenue (Fla. 295). The **major east-west arteries** include Cervantes Street (U.S. 90), which runs all the way through town. Chase Street runs one-way eastward from downtown to the Pensacola Bay Bridge (U.S. 98). Gregory Street is one-way westbound from the bridge into downtown. Garden Street (U.S. 98) runs to the west, becoming Navy Boulevard and leading to the U.S. Naval Air Station. Barrancas Avenue (Fla. 292) leaves Garden Street, crosses Navy Boulevard and then becomes Gulf Beach Highway, which leads to Perdido Key.

Heading east, U.S. 98 crosses the toll free, three-mile-long Pensacola Bay Bridge from Pensacola to Gulf Breeze. From there, the Bob Sikes Bridge crosses Santa Rosa Sound to Pensacola Beach; it costs 35¢ per car going to the beach, but the return trip is free.

GETTING AROUND

BY BUS The Escambia County Transit System (tel. 436-9383) runs buses on the hour to various districts—but not to the beaches. The fare is $1.

BY TAXI Call **Airport Express Taxi** (tel. 572-5555) or **Yellow Cab** (tel. 433-3333). Fares are more than $1 per mile.

BY RENTAL CAR Three major car-rental agencies—**Avis** (tel. toll free 800/831-2847), **Budget** (tel. toll free 800/527-0700), and **Thrifty** (tel. toll free 800/367-2277)—have booths at the airport.

BY BIKE Over at the beach, **Paradise Scooter & Bicycle Rental,** 715 Pensacola Beach Blvd. (tel. 934-0014), has both at its location near the foot of Bob Sikes Bridge.

FAST FACTS

Area Code The telephone area code in the Greater Pensacola Area is 904.
Auto Club The American Automobile Association (AAA) branch is at 540

Brent Lane, just east of Davis Highway (tel. 477-6860, or 477-3681 for emergency road service).

Doctor   If you need a doctor, call Sacred Heart (tel. 474-5700 Monday through Friday from 8am to 4pm) or MD Line (tel. 434-4080 Monday through Friday from 9am to 5pm), two physician-referral sources.

Emergency   In a life-threatening emergency, dial 911.

Tax   In addition to the statewide 6% sales tax, Pensacola adds a 3% tax on all hotel, restaurant, bar, and campground bills.

Time   The Pensacola area is in the central time zone, one hour behind the East Coast: When it's noon in Miami and New York, it's 11am in Pensacola.

WHAT TO SEE & DO

ATTRACTIONS

Downtown Historic Districts

Pensacola's intriguing past contributes to the atmosphere in the historic districts, where narrow streets are shaded by majestic live oaks and, in season, flowering magnolias. Old-world-style gaslight street lamps, wrought-iron balconies, and elaborate architecture recall the days when Pensacola was a prized pawn in the struggle between Spain and Britain. After Spain ceded western Florida and its capital, Pensacola, to Britain in 1763, the British carefully mapped out the city's streets. When Spain regained Pensacola in 1781, the British street names became Spanish again; for example, George Street, a main thoroughfare, became Palafox in honor of Spanish hero Gen. José de Palafox.

For **information** about the historic districts, call 444-8905. The Pensacola Visitor Information Center (see "Orientation," above) provides free walking-tour maps.

SEVILLE HISTORIC DISTRICT & HISTORIC PENSACOLA VILLAGE   One of your first stops should be the Seville Historic District, bounded by Government, Zaragoza, Adams, and Alcanz Streets. Listed on the National Register, this impressive district has some of Florida's oldest homes, along with charming boutiques and interesting restaurants.

Historic Pensacola Village, a living-history community, offers an interesting glimpse back into the past as you observe costumed "living history" characters go about their daily chores and demonstrate old crafts.

Among the landmarks to visit are the Museum of Industry, the Museum of Commerce, the French Créole–style Charles Lavalle House, the elegant Victorian Dorr House, the French colonial-Créole Quina House, St. Michael's Cemetery (land was deeded by the king of Spain), and Old Christ Church (one of Florida's oldest), housing the Pensacola Historical Museum. One of the most interesting sites is the **Julee Cottage Black History Museum,** 204 Zaragoza St. Built around 1790, this small house was owned by Julee Panton, a freed black slave, who ran her own business, invested in real estate, and loaned money to slaves so they could buy their freedom. Today the museum recalls her life and deeds, as well as the achievements of other African Americans with Pensacola associations.

A combination ticket to Historic Pensacola Village and the T.T. Wentworth, Jr., Florida State Museum costs $5.50 for adults, $4.50 for senior citizens and military, $2.25 for children 4 to 16, free for children under 4; $12.50 for families, $10 for couples. Tickets, good for two days, may be purchased at Tivoli House, 205 E. Zaragoza St., near Terragona Street, Monday through Saturday from 10am to 4pm.

THE PALAFOX HISTORIC DISTRICT   The Palafox Historic District, which runs up Palafox Street from the water to Wright Street, formerly Old Pensacola's harborfront and downtown commercial center, features beautiful Spanish Renaissance–style buildings. At one time the area had such outstanding hotels as the San Carlos, considered one of the South's finest. The Mediterranean Revival–style hotel at Palafox and Garden Streets remains, but has been closed for many years. In the good old days, more than a dozen foreign consulates were located here. Many structures, including the ornate Saenger Theatre, have been restored to their original beauty, including the New Orleans–style wrought-iron balconies.

The two-story Mission Revival building that once housed the Pensacola City Jail and City Court is now home to the Pensacola Museum of Art. Also located here is the T. T. Wentworth, Jr., Florida State Museum, a beautiful example of Renaissance Revival design and formerly Pensacola's City Hall (see "Downtown Museums," below).

Plaza Ferdinand VII, a National Historic Landmark and part of Pensacola's first settlement, is a Palafox district highlight. In a ceremony at the Plaza in 1821, Gen. Andrew Jackson formally accepted Florida into the United States, and his statue commemorates the event.

THE NORTH HILL PRESERVATION DISTRICT   The 50-block North Hill Preservation District, listed on the National Register of Historic Places, is just north of the Palafox Historic District and is bounded by Wright, Blount, Palafox, and Reus Streets. Descendants of early settlers still live in some of the more than 500 homes, and family backgrounds include Spanish nobility, timber barons, British merchants, French Créoles, buccaneers, and Civil War veterans. At one time, Spain and Britain had forts in this area; residents still occasionally find a cannonball or two, while working in their gardens.

The private homes are not open to the public, but are a bonanza for anyone interested in architecture. Various home designs include Mediterranean Revival, Queen Anne, Tudor Revival, neoclassical, art moderne, Victorian, Craftsman Bungalow, and more. The North Hill district includes Lee Square at Palafox and Gadsden Streets, where Union troops erected a fort in 1863. In 1891, Lee Square was dedicated to the Confederacy, complete with a 50-foot-high obelisk and sculpture based on John Elder's painting *After Appomattox*.

Downtown Museums

CIVIL WAR SOLDIERS MUSEUM, 108 S. Palafox St. Tel. 469-1900.
Founded by a local physician who grew up discovering artifacts at the Civil War battlefield near Antietam, Maryland, this storefront museum, in the heart of the Palafox Street business district, emphasizes how ordinary soldiers lived during that bloody conflict. As might be expected, a display of military medical equipment and treatment methods is especially informative. The museum's bookstore carries more than 500 titles about the war.
   Admission: $4 adults, $2 children 6–12, free for kids under 6.
   Open: Mon–Sat 10am–4:30pm. **Closed:** Major holidays.

PENSACOLA HISTORICAL MUSEUM, 405 S. Adams St., at Zaragoza St. Tel. 433-1559.
In the old Christ Church, built in 1823 and reminiscent of Bruton Parrish in Historic Williamsburg, Virginia, the museum has just about everything pertaining to the city's history, from Native American artifacts to a library with more than 2,000 volumes. It's in the heart of the Seville Historic District.
   Admission: $2 adults, $1 children 4–16, free for kids under 4.
   Open: May–Oct, Mon–Sat 9am–4:30pm; Nov–Apr, Mon–Sat 10am–4:30pm. **Closed:** Holidays.

PENSACOLA MUSEUM OF ART, 407 S. Jefferson St., at Main St. Tel. 432-6247.
A Palafox Historic District landmark (it was Pensacola's city jail from 1906 to 1954), the museum showcases permanent art and sculpture collections as well as art on loan. Shows range from avant-garde works by Andy Warhol to classic European masterpieces. The museum is a splendid building in itself.
   Admission: Free.
   Open: Tues–Fri 10am–5pm, Sat 10am–4pm.

T. T. WENTWORTH, JR., FLORIDA STATE MUSEUM, 330 S. Jefferson St., at Church St. Tel. 444-8586.
The museum houses exhibits of western Florida's history, and has a special hands-on Discovery Museum for children on the third floor. Located in the Palafox Historic District, the building is an architectural highlight.

Admission: Included in the ticket to Historic Pensacola Village, $5 adults, $4 seniors and military, $2 children 4–6, free for kids under 4.
Open: Daily 10am–4pm. **Closed:** Labor Day–Easter.

Nature Trails in Town

At the **Edward Ball Nature Walk,** located on the campus of the University of West Florida, there are 2½ miles of boardwalk around a shaded bayou—take along some dry bread to feed the turtles and fish. The nature trail is free and open daily. During the week, guided tours are offered by the Delta Tau Delta Fraternity (tel. 474-3000 or 474-2425). The trail is on the northwest side of the outstanding 1,000-acre campus, where the wetlands and woodland have been left in their natural state. The trail was named in honor of Edward Ball, a Florida millionaire who donated much of his fortune to preserving Florida's wildlife.

Bay Bluffs Park, at the corner of Scenic Highway and Summit Boulevard, offers rustic boardwalks and 20 acres of nature trails maintained by the city of Pensacola. This is part of the Scenic Highway, where U.S. 90 heads northeast to Tallahassee, an official Florida Scenic Route. The park's elevated boardwalk descends Florida's only scenic bluffs, a prehistoric formation dating back 20,000 years. From the unique, towering red bluffs, the views of Pensacola Bay can only be described as "breathtaking." The park is open daily from sunrise to 11pm.

Nearby Attractions

U.S. NAVAL AIR STATION   There's much to see west of Pensacola at the sprawling U.S. Naval Air Station, where pilots have trained since the U.S. Navy and Marine Corps began flying airplanes early this century. Accordingly, the highlight of any visit to Pensacola is the ✪ **National Museum of Naval Aviation,** where you'll see more than 100 aircraft dating from the 1920s to the space age. Both children and adults will get a kick out of sitting at the controls of a jet trainer. The museum is open from 9am to 5pm daily except New Year's Day, Thanksgiving, and Christmas. Admission is free. Call 452-3604 for information.

Also on the naval station, but now operated and meticulously restored by the National Park Service, the incredibly intricate brickwork of **Fort Barrancas** overlooks the deep-water pass into Pensacola Bay. The lower ramparts of this imposing structure were built by the Spanish in the 16th century; linked to them by a tunnel, the upper section was constructed by American troops between 1839 and 1844. Entry is across a dry moat, and you can walk all the way around the fort via an interior scarp gallery. The fort is open April to October, daily from 9:30am to 5pm; in winter, Wednesday through Sunday from 10:30am to 4pm. Guided tour schedules change from season to season, so call 934-2600 for the latest information. Admission is free.

Opposite Fort Barrancas stands the photogenic **Pensacola Lighthouse,** which has beaconed ships to the harbor entrance since 1825. The Lighthouse is not open to the public, but the nearby Lighthouse Point Restaurant (tel. 452-3251) offers bountiful, all-you-can-eat luncheon buffets and magnificent bay views for just $4 per person. It's open Monday through Friday from 10:30am to 2pm, and reservations are not required. Take the exit to Lighthouse Point off San Carlos Road. Keep going straight to the waterside eatery; to reach the Lighthouse, take an immediate right onto a dirt road.

Show the guards your driver's license to get a visitor's pass, either at the Main Gate at the south end of Navy Boulevard (Fla. 295) or at the Back Gate on Blue Angel Parkway (Fla. 173). Ask the guards for directions.

PERDIDO KEY   From the naval station, follow Fla. 292 to Perdido Key, which straddles the Florida-Alabama line about 15 miles west of Pensacola. This narrow barrier island has such wide, spectacular beaches of powdery, pure-white quartz that a road sign warns newcomers: RED CLAY IS PROHIBITED ON PERDIDO KEY. Stop for some swimming and sunning at the local section of **Gulf Islands National Seashore** (see "Santa Rosa Island," below), which occupies the totally undeveloped eastern third of the island. The Johnson Beach Day Use Area near the entrance provides restrooms and showers. The area is open daily from 8am to sunset. Admission permits, good for seven days, cost $4 per vehicle, $2 for pedestrians and bicyclists. Seniors and disabled persons can request a free pass.

Big Lagoon State Recreation Area (tel. 492-1595), on County Road 292A about 10 miles west of Pensacola on the way to Perdido Key, offers a bay beach for swimming, boating, picnicking, camping, and fishing. An observation tower provides panoramic views over the Big Lagoon and nearby bays and islands. The salt marshes attract great blue herons, brown thrashers, cardinals, and many other species of birds. The area is open daily from 8am to sunset. Admission is $3.25 for up to eight people in a vehicle, $1 for pedestrians or bicyclists.

SANTA ROSA ISLAND Stretching almost 35 miles to Fort Walton Beach, this skinny barrier island is best known as home to the resorts, condominiums, cottages, restaurants, and shops of **Pensacola Beach**—directly south of Pensacola—and **Navarre Beach,** some 20 miles to the east. But the highlight for beach lovers here is the local branch of ✪ **Gulf Islands National Seashore.** Jumping from island to island from Texas to Florida, this magnificent preserve includes mile after mile of undeveloped white beaches and rolling dunes covered with sea grass and oats. Established in 1971 to protect the beaches (it's against the law to pick the sea oats or remove any live shellfish), the national seashore is a natural environment for at least 280 species of birds. Visitors enjoy swimming, boating, fishing, scuba diving, camping, and ranger-guided tours and nature hikes. For specific information, contact the Gulf Islands National Seashore, 1801 Gulf Breeze Pkwy., Gulf Breeze, FL 32561 (tel. 934-2600).

The national seashore is home to the ruins of **Fort Pickens,** now standing silent guard in the dunes at the western end of Santa Rosa. Built in the 1830s to team with Fort Barrancas in protecting Pensacola's harbor entrance, this huge brick structure never saw combat but was the prison home of Apache Chief Geronimo from 1886 to 1888. The fort is open from 9am to 4pm daily except Christmas. A small museum featuring displays about Geronimo and the seashore's natural abundance is open from 8:30am to 4pm daily except Christmas. Admission permits to the Fort Pickens area, good for seven days, cost $4 per vehicle, $2 per pedestrian or bicyclist. Seniors and disabled persons can ask for a free pass.

After skipping over Pensacola Beach, the pristine national seashore resumes for 11 miles until reaching Navarre Beach. About 7 miles east of Pensacola Beach you'll find parking, restrooms, showers, a covered picnic facility, and a snack bar at the Santa Rosa Day Use Facility. It's open from 8am to sunset and is free.

EAST OF PENSACOLA Northwest Florida's answer to King Kong lives at the **Zoo,** on U.S. 98 about 10 miles east of Gulf Breeze, 15 miles east of Pensacola (tel. 932-2229). He's Colossus, one of the largest lowland gorillas in captivity. There are at least 600 other animals roaming freely in 50 acres of landscaped natural habitats, including two rare white tigers. Elephant shows, giraffe feedings, and a petting zoo are fun for young and old, who can see the animals up close from the Safari Line train. There's a lakeside restaurant and gift shop. Admission is $8.75 for adults, $5.25 for children 3 to 11, free for kids under 3. Open daily from 9am to 5pm during the summer months, from 9am to 4pm during the off-season.

On the way to the Zoo, stop off at the 1,378-acre **Naval Live Oaks Plantation** (tel. 934-2600), also on U.S. 98 a few miles east of Gulf Breeze. Ideal for shipbuilding, these super-strong trees have been protected from logging interests since the days of President John Adams in the early 1800s. Today the plantation is a place of peaceful primitive beauty. Artifacts discovered in the area indicate that prehistoric tribes lived here 10,000 years ago. Nature trails lead through the oaks to picnic areas and a beach; pick up a map at the headquarters building, which has a small museum and a gorgeous view through the trees to Pensacola Bay. Hours are 8:30am to 5pm daily during summer, 8:30am to 4:30pm daily during winter. Admission is free.

Also on U.S. 98, about 10 miles east of Gulf Breeze near the Zoo, the **Wildlife Rescue and Sanctuary** saves injured wildlife and birds so that after recuperation they can return to their natural habitats. Creatures unable to survive in the wild live happily ever after in the sanctuary. The facility is open Tuesday through Sunday from 10am to 4pm. Admission is free.

SPORTS & RECREATION

DOG RACING The **Pensacola Greyhound Track,** 951 Dog Track Rd. (tel. 455-8595), off U.S. 98 in West Pensacola, features races year-round at 7pm Tuesday through Saturday, and at 1pm on Saturday and Sunday. Admission is $1. For an excellent view of the action, there's a $2.50 charge for the Kennel Club, which also has a pleasant restaurant. Matinees are free for seniors, active military personnel, and tourists who show their hotel or motel key.

FISHING Red snapper, grouper, mackerel, tuna, and billfish are abundant. Anglers congregate along the Pensacola Bay Bridge Fishing Pier (which claims to be the world's longest), the Bob Sikes Bridge Fishing Pier, and also on the Fort Pickens Fishing Pier and Navarre Beach Pier. For information about the piers' hours of operation and fishing license information, contact the Visitor Information Center (tel. 434-1234).

Fishing charter services are offered by **Scuba Shack/Charter Boat** *Wet Dream,* 719 S. Palafox St. (tel. 433-4319). **AAA Charter Service,** at Pitt Slip Marina in downtown Pensacola's Harbour Village (tel. 438-3242), offers deep-sea fishing charters, sailing charters, sunset cruises, and more. *Chulamar,* on Pensacola Beach at the Bob Sikes Bridge (tel. 434-6977), features one of the area's best fishing boats and also makes arrangements for bottom fishing, trolling, and bay fishing. **Lo-Baby Charters** (tel. 934-5285), **Hooligan Charters** (tel. 968-1898), and **Rocky Top Charters** (tel. 432-7536) can make arrangements for deep-sea fishing, diving, sightseeing, and sunset excursions.

GOLF Among the 18-hole championship courses are **Creekside Golf Course,** 2355 W. Michigan Ave. (tel. 944-7969); **Marcus Pointe Golf Course** (site of the Ben Hogan PGA Tour, Pensacola Open, and American Amateur Classic), 2500 Oak Pointe Dr. (tel. 484-9770); **Perdido Bay Golf Resort,** One Doug Ford Dr. (tel. 492-1223); **Osceola City Municipal Golf Course,** 300 Tonawanda (tel. 456-2761); **Tiger Point Golf Course and Country Club** (36 holes!), 1255 Country Club Rd., overlooking Santa Rosa Sound (tel. 932-1330); and **Hidden Creek Golf Course,** 3070 PGA Blvd., in Navarre (tel. 939-4604). Reasonably priced golf packages can be arranged at local hotels and motels.

SAILING & SURFBOARDING The **Key Sailing Center,** 289 Pensacola Beach Rd., on the Quietwater Beach Boardwalk (tel. 932-5550), rents Hobie Cats, pontoon boats, waverunners, jet skis, and windsurfing boards.

SCUBA DIVING & SNORKLING Visibility in the waters around Pensacola can range from 30 to 50 feet inshore to 100 feet just 25 miles offshore. Although the bottom is sandy and it's too far north for coral, the battleship U.S.S. *Massachusetts,* submerged in 30 feet of water three miles offshore is one of some 35 artificial reefs where you can sight loggerhead turtles and other creatures.

Gulf Coast Pro Dive, 7203 U.S. 98 W. (tel. 456-8845), is the area's largest scuba specialist, offering rentals, all levels of instruction, and diving excursions. There's another branch in Gulf Breeze (tel. 934-8845). **Scuba Shack/Charter Boat** *Wet Dream,* 719 S. Palafox St. (tel. 433-4319), located at the waterfront, is Pensacola's oldest dive shop, offering rentals and NASDS classes. *Chulamar* (tel. 434-6977) at Pensacola Beach makes diving arrangements, and **Lo-Baby Charters,** 142 Highpoint Dr. (tel. 934-5285), also makes arrangements for diving excursions.

SPEED CAR RACING **Five Flags Speedway,** 7450 Pine Forest Rd. (tel. 944-0466), spotlights thrilling action Friday nights on one of the fastest half-mile tracks in the country. Top race-car drivers, such as Darrell Waltrip and Rusty Wallace, varoom around the course for the prize money. Admission fees are $7 for adults, $5 for active military, $4 for children 6 to 12, free for kids under 6. Call ahead for the schedule and program.

TENNIS The **Bayview Recreation Center,** 20th and Lloyd Streets, Pensacola (tel. 435-1788), offering six hard courts, is open free to the public daily from 9am to 5pm; **South Santa Rosa Recreation Center,** Sunset and Shoreline Drive in Gulf Breeze (tel. 934-5140 or 934-5141), with six hard courts, is also open free to the public, Monday through Saturday from 8am to 9pm and on Sunday from 1 to 6pm. **Scott Tennis Center,** Summit Boulevard at Piedmont, Pensacola (tel. 432-2939), is the area's largest tennis facility, and offers 18 hard courts at $3 per adult, $2.50 for children. It's open Monday through Friday from 8am to 10pm during the summer, from 9am to 10pm in winter; and on Saturday and Sunday from 9am to 6pm year-round. See "Where to Stay," below, for hotels and motels with tennis courts.

SPECIAL EVENTS

The **Fiesta of Five Flags** is Pensacola's annual June extravaganza. It combines with the DeLuna Landing Festival, commemorating the Spanish conquistador's arrival in 1559, and is celebrated with parades, a Spanish fiesta, a children's treasure hunt, a sand sculpture contest, a billfish tournament, and much, much more.

The **Blue Angels Air Show,** a thrilling, world-famous flight exhibition, takes place at the Pensacola Naval Air Station. It's usually scheduled in July and November.

First Spanish Settlement Walk is featured in October, and the **Christmas Walk in Old Seville** is a joyous, historic experience every December.

The **Frank Brown International Songwriters' Festival** brings country-music fans from far and wide to Perdido Key during the first week of November to hear the original writers and artists perform their hits.

WHERE TO STAY

In addition to the establishments recommended below, several well-known chains have motels on Plantation Road in the University Mall complex at I-10 and Davis Highway, about five miles north of downtown Pensacola. These include **Residence Inn by Marriott,** 7230 Plantation Rd. (tel. 904/479-1000, or toll free 800/331-3131), in which all rooms and apartments have kitchens and fireplaces; **Hampton Inn–University Mall,** 7330 Plantation Rd. (tel. 904/477-3333, or toll free 800/426-7866); and **Holiday Inn University Mall,** 7200 Plantation Rd. (tel. 904/474-0100, or toll free 800/465-4329). Also there are the budget-priced **Super 8 Motel,** 7220 Plantation Rd. (tel. 904/476-8038, or toll free 800/800-8000); **Red Roof Inn,** 7340 Plantation Rd. (tel. 904/476-7960, or toll free 800/843-7663); and **Motel 6,** 7226 Plantation Rd. (tel. 904/474-1060). The ZIP Code for all is 32504. To find Plantation Road, take Exit 5 off I-10 onto Davis Highway (Fla. 291) south. Turn right at the first stoplight south of I-10 into University Mall, then take the first right between the Hampton Inn and Red Roof Inn. There's an ample supply of inexpensive restaurants on Plantation Road and in the adjacent mall.

Sun worshipers can stay at either Pensacola Beach or Navarre Beach on Santa Rosa Island, or on Perdido Key about 15 miles west of Pensacola. **Pensacola Beach** is the largest, the closest to town, and the most extensively equipped with hotels, restaurants, bars, shops, and activities. **Navarre Beach,** about 20 miles east of town, is smaller and quieter, but it also has a more limited selection of rainy-day activities. **Perdido Key** compensates for its remoteness from Pensacola with several lively bars, which sprang up in the days before thirsty Alabamians could buy liquor by the drink at home.

Gulf Breeze offers more reasonable rates than the Pensacola Beach hotels, but is conveniently located on the peninsula between there and town.

There are at least as many **beach condominiums and cottages** for rent as there are hotel and motel rooms. Call the Pensacola Visitor Information Center (tel. 904/434-1234, or toll free 800/874-1234, 800/343-4321 in Florida) for its list of available town homes, condos, and vacation cottages.

PENSACOLA

Moderate

NEW WORLD LANDING, 600 S. Palafox St., Pensacola, FL 32501. Tel. 904/432-4111. Fax 904/435-8939. 14 rms, 2 suites. A/C TV TEL
$ Rates: $70 single; $80 double; $100 suite. AE, CB, DC, DISC, MC, V.

⭐ Near the scenic bay and in the historic district, this comfortable inn is enhanced by flower gardens adorned with splashing fountains. From the colonial-style lobby, a grand staircase leads to high-ceilinged, artistically decorated spacious rooms with interesting antiques. The lovely accommodations depict Pensacola's rich history; for example, four rooms flaunt Spanish decor, four rooms are très chic French style, four rooms portray Early Americana, and four focus on Olde England. The adjoining New World restaurant and pub is popular for local seafood.

PENSACOLA GRAND HOTEL, 200 E. Gregory St., Pensacola, FL 32501.
Tel. 904/433-3336, or toll free 800/348-3336. Fax 904/432-7572. 200 rms and suites. A/C TV TEL
$ Rates: $90–$100 double. AE, DC, DISC, MC, V.

⭐ On the site of the old L & N Railroad depot in the Seville Historic District at the end of I-10, this unique hotel incorporates the antiquated station into the grand lobby, the Lobby Bar, restaurants, lounges, meeting rooms, and the new library-museum area. It's well worth a visit to the beautifully restored lobby (especially if you're a railroad buff) just to admire the wealth of turn-of-the-century accoutrements: the ornate railroad clock, the original oak stair rails, the imported marble, the fancy ceramic mosaic tile floors, and the old-fashioned carved furniture. A two-story glass Galleria links the historic depot to the modern 15-story guest-room tower. On the 14th and 15th concierge floors, accessible by special elevator key only, guest rooms are provided with extra amenities and services. Should you not be a hotel guest, you're welcome to relax with a drink in the plush L & N Lobby Bar or dine in one of the interesting restaurants, such as The 1912.

Budget

DAYS INN DOWNTOWN, 710 N. Palafox St., Pensacola, FL 32501. Tel.
904/438-4922, or toll free 800/325-2525. Fax 904/438-7999. 150 rms, 2 suites. A/C TV TEL
$ Rates: $39–$50 double; $65 suite. Inquire about weekly rates. AE, CB, DC, MC, V.

A very convenient place to stay, this colonial-style motel at the corner of Palafox and Cervantes Streets has nicely decorated guest rooms, a restaurant, a cocktail lounge with a wide-screen TV, meeting facilities, a swimming pool, a free laundry, and movie rentals. Complimentary transportation is available to and from Pensacola Regional Airport.

Another 80-room Days Inn North is at 7051 Pensacola Blvd., U.S. 29 at I-10 (tel. 904/476-9090).

SEVILLE INN, 223 E. Garden St., Pensacola, FL 32501. Tel. 904/433-
8331, or toll free 800/277-7275. Fax 904/432-6849. 120 rms. A/C TV TEL
$ Rates (including continental breakfast): Summer, $50–$65 double. Winter, $30–$59 double. AE, DC, MC, V.

If you plan to do lots of sightseeing, shopping, and taking in evening entertainment, you couldn't do better than this two-story motel conveniently located at the entrance to the downtown Seville Historic District, across the street from the Civic Center, and about four blocks from the Saenger Theatre. Two swimming pools are on the premises. As part of the hospitality, guests receive complimentary airport transfers, local phone calls, and passes to the Pensacola Greyhound track.

PENSACOLA BEACH

Expensive

CLARION SUITES RESORT & CONVENTION CENTER, 20 Via de Luna
Dr., Pensacola Beach, FL 32561. Tel. 904/932-4300, or toll free 800/874-5303. Fax 904/934-9112. 125 suites. A/C TV TEL
$ Rates (including continental breakfast): Summer, $105–$135 suite Sun–Wed, $125–$155 Thurs–Sat. Off-season, $49–$100 suite Sun–Wed, $49–$109 Thurs–Sat. AE, DC, DISC, MC, V.

★ This tin-roofed, pastel-sided beachfront resort's 86 one-bedroom suites can accommodate up to four people, two in the bedroom and two on a convertible sofa. The attractively decorated accommodations include a living room with a dining area, bathroom (the 39 bilevel loft suites have 1½ bathrooms), and kitchen. It's nice to have two televisions—one in the living room, one in the bedroom—and two telephones. A complimentary continental breakfast is served every morning in the lobby. On the premises are a swimming pool, a fitness center, a children's play area, a beach pavilion, a dunes crosswalk, and a coin laundry.

HOLIDAY INN PENSACOLA BEACH, 165 Fort Pickens Rd., Pensacola Beach, FL 32561. Tel. 904/932-5361, or toll free 800/465-4329. Fax 904/932-7121. 150 rms. A/C TV TEL

$ Rates: Apr–Sept, $90–$110 double. Nov–Feb, $60–$90 double. Mar and Oct, $70–$80 double. Ask about senior citizen discounts. AE, DC, DISC, MC, V.

This gulf-front eight-story hotel boasts terrific views from the Penthouse Lounge and the Gulf Front Café. From Memorial Day to Labor Day, Beach Bunch children's programs are offered. Amenities include an electronic-game room, four lighted tennis courts, two racquetball courts, a volleyball area, a swimming pool, a beach bar (in summer), and rental boats. Arrangements can be made for fishing and surfing. The pleasant Casino Restaurant and Grille is open for breakfast, lunch, and dinner.

Moderate

BARBARY COAST MOTEL, 24 Via de Luna Dr., Pensacola Beach, FL 32561. Tel. 904/932-2233. Fax 904/932-0462. 24 rms and suites. A/C TV TEL

$ Rates: Summer, $70–$110 double. Winter, $45–$65 double. Monthly and weekly rates available. DISC, MC, V.

Although an older motel, the Barbary Coast has a great location on the beach. Guest rooms, recently refurbished with a tropical decor, are in cottagelike buildings with good cross ventilation. Some of the less expensive rooms do not have kitchenettes but the larger double rooms have cooking facilities. For families, suites will accommodate four to six people in two bedrooms plus the convertible sofa in the living room. In addition to the beach and swimming pool, the covered picnic area with a barbecue pit is fun. A very friendly atmosphere prevails here.

BEST WESTERN PENSACOLA BEACH, 16 Via De Luna Dr., Pensacola Beach, FL 32561. Tel. 904/934-3300, or toll free 800/528-1234. Fax 904/4366. 62 rms. A/C TV TEL

$ Rates (including continental breakfast): Summer, $90–$100 double. Winter, $50–$60 double. AE, DC, DISC, MC, V.

New on the gulf-front, this small, casual hotel is notable for bright, clean, and extra-spacious accommodations, complete with refrigerators, coffee makers, micro-waves, and wet bars. The best rooms face the beach; others can be devoid of views. The swimming pool and Cabana Bar are on the beachfront. Rental bikes are available to explore the scenic area. Inquire about the golf packages and deep-sea fishing trips.

THE DUNES, 333 Fort Pickens Rd., Pensacola Beach, FL 32561. Tel. 904/932-3536, or toll free 800/83-DUNES. Fax 904/932-3536. 140 rms and penthouse suites. A/C TV TEL

$ Rates: Mid-May to Labor Day, $75–$160 double. Labor Day to mid-May, $50–$108 double. Special vacation and golf packages available. AE, DISC, MC, V.

Local owners built this eight-story tower to replace a low-slung, beachside motel partially destroyed by Hurricane Elena in 1985. The two-story wing left standing still houses quite adequate—and lower-priced—motel-style rooms facing the beach. The spacious tower rooms have balconies with gorgeous gulf or bay vistas. The small but pleasant Gulf Front Cafe serves breakfast, lunch, and dinner. The kids can participate in the supervised "Beach Bunch" children's program from May to Labor Day. For $10 per child, the hotel will even take care of the kids so Mom and Dad can take Saturday night off. Facilities also include two swimming pools (one heated), a jogging trail, a bike path, and a volleyball area. The complex enjoys immediate access to an undeveloped dune preserve next door.

Budget

FIVE FLAGS INN, 299 Fort Pickens Rd., Pensacola Beach, FL 32561. Tel. 904/932-3586. Fax 904/934-0257. 49 rms. A/C TV TEL
$ Rates: Summer, $59–$69 double. Winter, $40–$59 double. MC, V.
This friendly motel looks like a jail from the road, but don't be fooled. Big picture windows look out to the swimming pool and gorgeous white sand beach, which comes right up to the property. Although the accommodations are small and the furniture is dated, every room has a view of the gulf—and the rates are a bargain.

SANDPIPER INN, 23 Via de Luna Dr., Pensacola Beach, FL 32561. Tel. 904/932-2516. 26 rms, 6 cottages. A/C TV TEL
$ Rates: Summer, $49–$120 double. Winter, $32–$89 double. Inquire about special weekly rates and other discounts. AE, DISC, MC, V.
Should you prefer preparing some of your meals, ask for one of the 10 rooms with kitchenettes at this bayside motel. The roadside swimming pool may be small, but the large private sun deck on the bay is delightful. Floor-to-ceiling picture windows make up for the rather small accommodations; however, every room is beautifully maintained. The highest rates apply to the six cottages, three of them on the bay. Restaurants and shops are conveniently nearby.

GULF BREEZE
Moderate

HOLIDAY INN–BAY BEACH, 51 Gulf Breeze Pkwy., Gulf Breeze, FL 32561. Tel. 904/932-2214, or toll free 800/HOLIDAY. Fax 904/932-2214. 168 rms. A/C TV TEL
$ Rates: May–Labor Day, $67–$110 double. Labor Day–Apr, $50–$71 double. AE, DISC, MC, V.
On a small bayside beach, this pleasant hotel offers complimentary coffee and newspaper with your morning wake-up call and complimentary drinks served Monday through Thursday evening in the special cocktail suite—a nice way to become acquainted with other hotel guests. There's a swimming pool plus a wading pool for the kids. Several bay-view rooms have refrigerators, which you may request. From the guest rooms, the scenic bay views are beautiful. The Bon Appetit Café serves breakfast, lunch, and dinner. Pensacola Beach is a short drive to the south via the Bob Sikes toll bridge.

Budget

GULF COAST INN MOTEL, 843 Gulf Breeze Pkwy. (U.S. 98), Gulf Breeze, FL 32561. Tel. 904/932-2222. 33 rms. A/C TV TEL
$ Rates: Summer, $38–$48 double. Winter, $28–$40 double. Weekly rates available. AE, DISC, MC, V.
This unpretentious motel is convenient to Pensacola Beach and is well maintained by its owners. Rooms have kitchenettes, and there's a small swimming pool open March to October. A Waffle House is next door.

NAVARRE BEACH

HOLIDAY INN THE TROPICS, 8375 Gulf Blvd., Navarre Beach, FL 32569. Tel. 904/939-2321, or toll free 800/465-4329. Fax 904/939-4768. 254 rms. A/C TV TEL
$ Rates: Apr to mid-Sept, $70–$120 single or double. Mid-Sept to Mar, $55–$100 single or double. AE, DC, DISC, MC, V.
Sitting among the sand dunes and on a tranquil white sand gulf beach, the resort is an excellent all-around vacation spot. For tennis buffs, four lighted courts await. The outdoor swimming pool is probably upstaged by a second pool inside the lush Holidome. Should you indulge in the Tropics Pizzaria, just work off the calories in the Health Spa. A restaurant, two bars, a movie theater, a games room, and a gift shop are also on the premises. During the summer, the Beach Brigade Children's Program keeps the kids entertained.

PERDIDO KEY

COMFORT INN, 13585 Perdido Key Dr., Pensacola, FL 32507. Tel. 904/492-2755, or toll free 800/221-2222. Fax 904/492-9587. 100 rms. A/C TV TEL

$ Rates (including continental breakfast): May–Labor Day, $54–$78 double. Labor Day–Apr, $49–$58 double. Family rates available. AE, DC, DISC, MC, V.

At this moderately priced motel, in addition to the beautiful white sand beach a short walk away, there's a swimming pool in the courtyard and an indoor hot tub. Since this motel is so family-oriented, another plus factor is the children's playground. The front desk will make arrangements for deep-sea fishing and other activities.

PERDIDO BAY GOLF RESORT, One Doug Ford Dr., Pensacola, FL 32507. Tel. 904/492-1214, or toll free 800/874-5355. Fax 904/492-1204. 37 rms in 9 cottages. A/C TV TEL

$ Rates (per person, including greens fees and golf cart): Nov–Dec, $59. Jan, $49.50. Feb–Apr, $69. May–Oct $58. Year-round nongolfer, $29. Two-night minimum stay required. AE, MC, V.

Pros like Jack Nicklaus and Lee Trevino made this resort a regular stop when the Pensacola Open was played here from 1978 to 1987. The 7,154-yard, par-72 championship course is open to the public, but the tennis courts are for guests only. The two- and four-bedroom cedar-and-brick cottages are clustered near the course. They can accommodate up to eight couples each, or you can rent individual rooms. There's a swimming pool and snack bar but no restaurant or cocktail lounge. The resort is on the mainland off Sorrento Road (Fla. 292), about three miles north of Perdido Key.

CAMPING

The **Fort Pickens** section of Gulf Islands National Seashore (tel. 904/934-2621 for recorded information) has 200 campsites (135 with electricity) in a pine forest about seven miles west of Pensacola Beach on the bay side of Santa Rosa Island. Nature trails lead from the camp through Blackbird Marsh and to the beach. A small store sells provisions. It's first-come, first-served, but you must register at the ranger station east of the campground. Sites cost $12 a night without power, $14 a night with it.

Big Lagoon State Recreation Area, Fla. 292A, Pensacola, FL 32507 (tel. 904/492-1595), near Perdido Key, is open from 8am to sunset year-round. Year-round rates are $10 with electricity, $8 without. See Perdido Key in "Nearby Attractions," above, for details. Gasoline, groceries, and a laundry are within a quarter mile of the park.

Mayfair RV Park, 4540 Mobile Hwy., Pensacola, FL 32506 (tel. 904/455-8561), at the intersection of Mobile Highway (U.S. 90) and Fairfield Drive, offers RV and tent camping. Sites for two people cost $12 with electricity, $9 without. The campsite is within walking distance of shopping malls and grocery stores and is close to restaurants, service stations, the naval air station, and the Pensacola Greyhound Track.

Timberlake, 2600 W. Michigan Ave., Pensacola, FL 32505 (tel. 904/944-5487), near Mobile Highway (U.S. 90), offers RV camping only, for $15 per day, or $206 per month from October to April, then $240 per month from May to September. Facilities include a swimming pool and clubhouse courts for tennis, basketball, and volleyball. There's also a lake for fishing and an adjoining golf course. The beach is less than a 15-mile drive away.

WHERE TO DINE

PENSACOLA

Expensive

JAMIE'S, 424 E. Zaragoza St., between Alcanz and Florida Blanca. Tel. 434-2911.

Cuisine: FRENCH. **Reservations:** Recommended.
$ **Prices:** Appetizers $7.50–$9; main courses $7.50–$8.50 at lunch, $17.50–$21.50 at dinner. AE, DC, MC, V.
Open: Lunch Tues–Sat 11:30am–2:30pm; dinner Mon–Sat 6–10pm.

⭐ Very intimate and chic, Jamie's is Pensacola's classiest and most romantic restaurant. In a restored Victorian home in the Seville Historic District, dinners are enhanced by glowing fireplaces, soft candlelight, gleaming antiques, and subdued background music. Popular with Pensacola residents who enjoy fine food or are celebrating a special occasion, Jamie's features a gourmet menu. Among the favorites are grilled lamb chops subtly laced with a fresh mint-mustard sauce, and broiled just-caught snapper lightly topped by a piquant herb-butter sauce and garnished with Brie. Freshly baked breads are irresistible, and try the authentic French onion soup. Among the luscious desserts, the white-chocolate Grand Marnier mousse is wonderful. The menu includes the chef's recommended wines for each course. Jamie's is consistently rated among Florida's Top 100 Restaurants.

Moderate

CAP'N JIM'S, 905 E. Gregory St., at Bayfront Pkwy. Tel. 433-3562.
Cuisine: SEAFOOD/STEAK. **Reservations:** Recommended.
$ **Prices:** Appetizers $2–$8; main courses $6–$13. AE, MC, V.
Open: Mon–Sat 11am–9:45pm.
Near the foot of Pensacola Bay Bridge, dim lighting emphasizes the scenic water views from this popular restaurant noted for a lengthy menu of deliciously prepared seafoods and crisp salads. The fried freshwater catfish and barbecued big shrimp are southern-style favorites. And kids enjoy making their own selections from the children's menu at this casual, family-oriented.

HALL'S, 916 E. Gregory St., near the Bay Bridge. Tel. 438-9019.
Cuisine: SEAFOOD. **Reservations:** Not accepted.
$ **Prices:** Appetizers $4–$7; main courses $9–$17. MC, V.
Open: Sun–Thurs 11am–9pm, Fri–Sat 11am–10pm.
At least seven all-you-can-eat seafood selections are on the menu at $13, and there are many other choices, such as freshwater catfish, broiled snapper, sautéed flounder, a variety of shrimp dishes, oysters on the half shell, hearty sandwiches, fresh salads, and grilled steaks—all at moderate prices. Senior citizens are given the choice of 21 all-you-can-eat platters for $6.

MCGUIRE'S IRISH PUB, 600 E. Gregory St. Tel. 433-6789.
Cuisine: AMERICAN/IRISH. **Reservations:** Not accepted.
$ **Prices:** Snacks, burgers, and sandwiches $5.50–$7; meals $6–$17. AE, DC, MC, V.
Open: Mon–Sat 11am–2am, Sun 11am–1am (11am–4pm for brunch).
Every day is a lively St. Patrick's Day here, with corned beef and cabbage, Irish stew, Irish seafood platters, and much more. In addition, there are such hybrids as Seafood O'Fettuccine. Super-size hamburgers, peppercorn steak, grilled fish, beer-batter shrimp, barbecued ribs, hearty bean soup, salads, nachos, and other treats are also on the menu. This is Pensacola's oldest brewery and produces great beer! (see "Evening Entertainment," below).

MESQUITE CHARLIE'S, 5901 N. "W" St., just north of Airport Rd. Tel. 434-0498.
Cuisine: STEAK. **Reservations:** Not required.
$ **Prices:** Appetizers $7; main courses $7–$15. AE, MC, V.
Open: Dinner only, Sun–Thurs 5–10pm, Fri–Sat 5–11pm.
There are lots of saddles and bridles—and even a stuffed moose—to get you in the mood for delicious Wild West grub at this barnlike steakhouse. Cowboy and cowgirl steaks are seasoned with Charlie's own blend of natural spices and grilled to order over mesquite charcoal. Chicken, seafood, and baby back ribs are also grilled over mesquite and basted with Charlie's secret sauce. Putting on the feedbag here is great

fun for little cowpokes too, who feel right at home on the range with the special children's menu.

NEW WORLD LANDING RESTAURANT, in the New World Landing Inn, 600 S. Palafox St. Tel. 434-7736.

Cuisine: CONTINENTAL/SEAFOOD. **Reservations:** Recommended.

$ Prices: Appetizers $3.50–$6.50; main courses $5.50–$7.50 at lunch, $13–$16 at dinner. AE, MC, V.

Open: Lunch daily 11am–2pm; dinner daily 5:30–9:30pm. **Closed:** Major holidays and often Sun.

Recalling the colorful historic past, this charming restaurant in an old brick building honors Spain with a Barcelona Room, spotlights French history in a Marseilles Room, and gives tribute to the city itself in the very special Pensacola Room. Sparkling chandeliers, antique furnishings, and rich wood paneling lend a very special atmosphere whether you're enjoying a casual lunch or a memorable dinner. Fresh seafood in wine or butter sauce is a specialty, but the menu also features excellent steaks, prime rib of beef, tender veal, and more. If you're a history buff, note the enlarged old photographs of Pensacola.

THE YACHT RESTAURANT AND LOUNGE, 600 S. Barracks St., at Pitt's Slip Marina, off Bayfront Pkwy. Tel. 432-3707.

Cuisine: SEAFOOD/STEAK. **Reservations:** Recommended.

$ Prices: Appetizers $4.50–$6; main courses $9–$17 (two-for-one 5–6pm). MC, V.

Open: Lunch Tues–Sat 11:30am–2:30pm; dinner Tues–Sun 5–10pm; brunch Sun 11am–2pm.

This 1929-vintage, 153-foot-long yacht is Pensacola's only shipboard restaurant. The spectacular panorama of Pensacola Bay adds to the enjoyable dining experience. Locally caught fish is prepared many delicious ways, from grilled to Louisiana-style blackened. Shrimp, prepared with tasty sauces or simply grilled, is a favorite. Tender steaks are broiled to your taste.

Budget

BARNHILL'S COUNTRY BUFFET, U.S. 98 E. at Oriole Beach Rd., three miles east of Gulf Breeze. Tel. 932-0403.

Cuisine: SOUTHERN. **Reservations:** Not accepted.

$ Prices: Lunch, $5; dinner $6.50. Discounts for seniors over 60; children 2–12 pay 40¢ times their age. No credit cards.

Open: Summer, Sun–Thurs 10:45am–9pm, Fri–Sat 10:45am–9:30pm. Winter, Sun–Thurs 10:45am–8:30pm, Fri–Sat 10:45am–9pm.

Pay when you enter any of Barnhill's Country Buffets, then proceed to attack seven food bars and eat all you can hold of such southern goodies as crispy fried catfish and chicken, turnip greens and collards, and banana pudding made with real 'Nilla Wafers. If you can't stomach southern-style vegetables cooked to smithereens in fatback, there's an ample supply of salad fixings. The one price includes beverage.

Two other Barnhill's Country Buffets are in Pensacola, one on North Davis Highway (Fla. 291) at Olive Road north of I-10 (tel. 477-5465), and another in West Pensacola on New Warrington Road (Fla. 295) at Entrance Road, just north of Navy Boulevard (U.S. 98) (tel. 456-2760). Prices and hours are the same at all three branches.

E. J.'S FOOD COMPANY & RESTAURANT, 232 E. Main St. Tel. 432-5886.

Cuisine: AMERICAN. **Reservations:** Not accepted.

$ Prices: Appetizers $2–$3.50; main courses $4–$5; buffet $5. MC, V.

Open: Lunch only, Mon–Fri 11am–2pm.

A long-time favorite with local residents, E. J.'s is conveniently situated in the Seville Historic District and was originally the First Southeastern Baptist Church Street (enter off Zaragoza Street between Tarragona and Adams Streets). A warm homey atmosphere is accented by lace curtains, paddle fans, and checkered tablecloths,

Favorite homemade specialties are the pecan-chicken salad sandwiches and the fried oysters-in-a-basket. In addition to a salad bar, a country-style buffet offers hot vegetables and meats. If you want to picnic in Seville Square or anywhere else, the restaurant will package your take-out order. No smoking is permitted.

HOPKINS' BOARDING HOUSE, 900 N. Spring St., at Strong St. Tel. 438-3979.
  Cuisine: AMERICAN. **Reservations:** Not accepted.
$ **Prices:** Full meals $6.50. No credit cards.
  Open: Breakfast Tues–Sat 7–9:30am; lunch Tues–Sat 11:15am–2pm, Sun noon–2pm; dinner Tues–Sat 5:15–7:30pm.

⭐ There's a delicious peek into the past when you dine at this Victorian boarding house in the heart of the North Hill Preservation District. Shaded by beautiful trees, the house is surrounded by a veranda with old-fashioned rocking chairs. Indoors, the parlor is decorated with all sorts of ornaments collected by the Hopkins family through the years. Lacy curtains on the windows are another touch of nostalgia. Everyone sits together to enjoy a real family-style meal. Platters are piled high with true southern-style food. Most vegetables and seasonal fruits are from nearby farms. The bountiful breakfast will "stick to your ribs" for a good part of the day—every Yankee should sample the grits. In true boarding-house fashion, guests are assigned the next available seat—and they bus their own dishes when they're finished eating.

MARINA OYSTER BARN, 505 Bayou Blvd., on Bayou Texas. Tel. 433-0511.
  Cuisine: SEAFOOD. **Reservations:** Not accepted.
$ **Prices:** Appetizers $3–$9; main courses $5.50–$11.50. DISC, MC, V.
  Open: Tues–Sat 11am–9pm.
At the Johnson-Rooks Marina, this rustic but clean restaurant has been a favorite with seafood lovers since 1969. As you'd expect, freshly shucked oysters are the delicious attraction. Locally caught fish is deliciously prepared, either broiled or fried. Daily luncheon specials are offered from 11am to 2pm. To get here, go east on Cervantes Street across the Bayou Texar Bridge, then left on Perry Avenue, and left again on Strong Street.

NORMA'S CAFE, 400 S. Jefferson St., at Zaragoza St. Tel. 476-3011, ext. 6140.
  Cuisine: AMERICAN. **Reservations:** Not accepted.
$ **Prices:** $4–$6. MC, V.
  Open: Lunch Mon–Fri 11am–3pm; snacks Mon–Fri 3–5pm.
With exposed brick walls soaring to skylights three very tall stories above, this pleasant café seems to be al fresco rather than in the air-conditioned atrium of the Pensacola Cultural Center. Norma offers a range of delightfully fresh sandwiches, salads, soups, and hot dishes such as crêpes, roast beef under gravy, and steamed vegetables in a pita pocket topped with melted cheese. This is a popular spot for the downtown lunch crowd, so come early.

PENSACOLA BEACH

Expensive

JUBILEE RESTAURANT, Via de Luna at Fort Pickens Rd. Tel. 934-3108.
  Cuisine: SEAFOOD/STEAK/POULTRY. **Reservations:** Not required.
$ **Prices:** Beachside Cafe, appetizers $4–$8; main courses $7.50–$16. Topside, appetizers $6.50–$12; main courses $13–$25. AE, DC, DISC, MC, V.
  Open: Beachside Cafe, Mon–Thurs 11:30am–10pm, Fri–Sat 11:30am–11pm, Sun 9am–3pm (champagne brunch); Topside, dinner daily 6–10pm.
At this beachside restaurant complex, complete with Island Bar and cocktail lounge, most dining is very casual, even in the five-star Topside Restaurant, where gourmet dinners are a highlight and the chef excels in the preparation of local fish and shellfish. Chicken De Luna, topped by sautéed fresh chunks of crabmeat, is deliciously different. Juicy steaks are mesquite grilled. Lunch is served in the Beachside Cafe,

offering a varied menu of fish and deli sandwiches, seafood combinations, just-shucked oysters, nachos, all sorts of great salads, chicken marsala, pastas, and more. On summer evenings there are live bands for dancing under the stars, and indoor entertainment year-round.

Moderate

FLOUNDER'S CHOWDER AND ALE HOUSE, Via De Luna at Fort Pickens Rd. Tel. 932-2003.
   Cuisine: SEAFOOD. **Reservations:** Not accepted.
$ Prices: Appetizers $3–$7; main courses $10–$18; burgers and sandwiches $6–$7. AE, DC, DISC, MC, V.
   Open: Daily 11am–2am (brunch Sun 11am–3pm).
Of course, the big specialty is flounder, baked and stuffed. Charcoal-broiled seafood and shrimp fettuccine are among the many selections on the menu. Since this is a fun place under the McGuire banner (McGuire's Irish Pub is a Pensacola favorite), you can expect a "bottomless" glass of champagne with your eggs Benedict during the sumptuous Sunday brunch. In addition to the scenic Santa Rosa Sound panorama, take notice of the stained-glass windows from an old New York convent and the confessional booth walls. At night, dance to live music on Flounder's beach.

Budget

CHAN'S MARKET CAFE, 16 Via De Luna. Tel. 932-8454.
   Cuisine: AMERICAN. **Reservations:** Not accepted.
$ Prices: Breakfast/lunch $3–$6; dinner $8–$11. AE, MC, V.
   Open: Breakfast Mon–Fri 7–10:45am, Sat–Sun 7–11:45am; lunch Mon–Fri 11am–3pm, Sat–Sun noon–3pm; snacks Mon–Fri 11am–9pm, Sat–Sun noon–9pm; dinner daily 5–9pm.
The aroma of pastries in the oven permeates this pleasant little café and bakery, which shares quarters with a liquor store virtually in the parking lot of the Best Western Pensacola Beach. It's the best place on the beach to have freshly baked croissants and bagels for breakfast, and a young chef was preparing excellent dinners recently when I feasted on his version of red snapper perfectly sautéed in butter and herbs. Lunches feature Blue Plate Specials of such favorites as meatloaf, smoked pork barbecue, and grilled amberjack, all served with a choice of southern-style veggies. Or you can order a heaping sandwich made with one of Chan's large, flaky croissants.

SHOPPING

Sightseeing and shopping can be combined in Pensacola's Palafox and Seville Historic Districts, where many shops are housed in renovated centuries-old buildings and are stocked with everything from artwork and antiques to fashions and unusual gifts.

A fun way to shop for fine art is on a **Gallery Night tour,** sponsored every month or so by the Downtown Arts District Association (DADA) and the Arts Council of Northwest Florida. They provide free bus transportation to more than a dozen galleries, with musical entertainment and refreshments along the way. Contact DADA, P.O. Box 731, Pensacola, FL 32594 (tel. 432-9906).

There were 37 **antiques dealers** in the area at last count. Get a complete list from the Pensacola Visitor Information Center (see "Orientation," above).

The city's two main suburban shopping centers are **Cordova Mall,** 5100 N. Ninth Ave., at Bayou Boulevard (tel. 477-7562), and **University Mall,** 7171 N. Davis Hwy., at I-10.

EVENING ENTERTAINMENT

Pensacola offers a surprisingly sophisticated array of entertainment choices for such a relatively small city. For a schedule of upcoming events, get a copy of **Vision,** a bimonthly newsletter published by the Arts Council of Northwest Florida, P.O. Box 731, Pensacola, FL 32594 (tel. 904/432-9906). Tickets for all major performances can be purchased by phone from Ticketmaster (tel. 904/433-6311, or toll free 800/488-5252).

THE PERFORMING ARTS

PENSACOLA CIVIC CENTER, 201 E. Gregory St., at Alcanz St. Tel. 433-6311.

This 10,000-seat multipurpose facility hosts a variety of entertainment: touring productions of Broadway plays and musicals, rock groups, famous bands, family shows, sporting events, and much, much more. Call ahead for the current schedule.

Admission: Tickets, $10–$25.

PENSACOLA JAZZ SOCIETY. Tel. 433-8382.

Jazz musicians are invited to perform at local venues and this organization is the primary supporter of the annual Jazz Fest, a major local event.

PENSACOLA LITTLE THEATER, 400 S. Jefferson St., at Zaragoza St. Tel. 432-2042.

For more than 50 years, the performances here have delighted audiences. Both drama and comedy are spotlighted in each season's nine productions. The Little Theater recently settled in its new home in the Pensacola Cultural Center. Incidentally, this is the Southeast's oldest continuing community theater. Call in advance for current schedules.

Admission: Tickets, $8–$12.

PENSACOLA SYMPHONY ORCHESTRA. Tel. 435-2533.

Considered the oldest continuous symphonic organization on the Gulf Coast, the Pensacola Symphony has performed for more than 65 years. Once a year there's a very special performance with the city's Choral Society. Call ahead to find out where the Symphony Orchestra is performing during the time you're in town.

SAENGER THEATER, 118 S. Palafox St. Tel. 444-7686.

A masterpiece of Spanish baroque architecture, this ornate theater has been lovingly restored, including the original bricks salvaged from the old Pensacola Opera House. The variety of presentations spotlighted here include the Pensacola Opera Company, the Pensacola Symphony, the First City Dance Company, visiting magician David Copperfield's astounding shows, and a 50th Anniversary showing of the great film classic *Gone with the Wind*.

Admission: Tickets, $5–$35.

UNIVERSITY OF WEST FLORIDA, on Campus Blvd. Tel. 474-2696.

A six-story center for fine and performing arts, the UWF Art Gallery presents University Theater performances. Theater experts conduct seminars and preside at discussions here. Call for information.

THE BAR SCENE

Pensacola

MCGUIRE'S IRISH PUB, 600 E. Gregory St. Tel. 433-6789.

If your mother comes from Ireland, you may want to leave an autographed dollar bill or an autographed drinking mug for the collection of more than 35,000 bills and 3,000 mugs contributed by customers who love the Irish fun here. Every night is party night during the summer; Saturday and Sunday evenings have live bands the rest of the year. The Irish entertainment makes any other pub green with envy. Open Monday through Saturday from 11am to 2am and on Sunday from 4pm to 1am.

SEVILLE QUARTER, 130 E. Government St., at Jefferson St. Tel. 434-6211.

★ Located in the Seville Historic District, this restored antique brick complex with New Orleans–style wrought-iron balconies is Pensacola's prime spot for dining and entertaining. The names of the establishments say it all: Rosie O'Grady's Goodtime Emporium, Lili Marlene's Aviator's Pub, Apple Annie's Courtyard, End o' the Alley Bar, Phineas Phogg's Balloon Works (a dance hall, not a balloon shop), and Fast Eddie's Billiard Parlor (which has electronic games for kids, too). The pubs all serve up libations, food, and live entertainment from Dixieland jazz to country and western. Open daily from 11am to 2am.

Pensacola Beach

THE DOCK, Via De Luna at Fort Pickens Rd. Tel. 934-3314.

There's plenty of live music at this lively pub on Casino Beach Boardwalk, the center of youthful surfside activity in Pensacola Beach (it's beside the water tank). Bands begin playing at 3pm daily during the summer, Wednesday through Saturday in winter, and continue until 2am. Year-round, Sunday sessions feature rum and reggae from 3 to 8pm. The bar is open daily from 10am to 2am the next morning. Snacks and meals are available.

FLOUNDER'S CHOWDER AND ALE HOUSE, Via De Luna at Fort Pickens Rd. Tel. 932-2003.

Dancing to a live reggae band on Flounder's beach keeps night owls happy until the wee hours seven days a week during the summer. For recharging the batteries, the special drink, Diesel Fuel (sipped from a Mason jar), keeps everyone in good spirits.

JUBILEE, on Quietwater Boardwalk, Via De Luna at Fort Pickens Rd. Tel. 934-3108.

Live entertainment is in the spotlight at the Beachside Cafe in this popular dining complex. When weather permits, there's dancing on the open-air deck. By the way, their beautiful Topside Restaurant is highly rated (see "Where to Dine," above).

Perdido Key

FLORA-BAMA LOUNGE, Fla. 292 on the Florida-Alabama line. Tel. 492-0611.

Country music sets the tempo at this slapped-together pub, famous especially during the special jam sessions from noon until way past midnight on Saturday and Sunday. Because original music is in the limelight, Flora-Bama sponsors the Frank Brown International Songwriters' Festival every November. And if you've never attended an Interstate Mullet Toss, catch the fun during the last weekend in April. The raw oyster bar is popular all the time. Take in the great gulf views from the Deck Bar. This is Pensacola's answer to the Grand Ol' Opry in Nashville. It's open seven days a week from 9am until the wee hours, and is on the gulf.

A COMEDY CLUB

COCONUTS COMEDY CLUB, in the Holiday Inn University Mall, 7200 Plantation Rd. Tel. 484-NUTS.

Different comedians appear Thursday through Saturday nights. The first performance is usually at 8:30pm, but the current schedule may change.
Admission: $4 Thurs, $5 Fri–Sat.

AN EASY EXCURSION

Less than an hour's drive northeast of Pensacola on U.S. 90, Milton, "The Canoe Capital of Florida," is a change of pace from the beach scene. The spring-fed wilderness streams of the Coldwater and Blackwater Rivers and Sweetwater/Juniper Creek meander through state forests and are perfect for canoeing, kayaking, tubing, rafting, and paddle-boating. The Blackwater River, at **Blackwater River State Park,** is considered one of the world's purest sand-bottom rivers and has retained its primitive beauty. Along the nature trails, plant life and wildlife can be closely observed.

Facilities for fishing, picnicking, camping, and cabin stays are provided. Blackwater is also Florida's largest state forest, with about 183,000 acres of oak, pine, and juniper.

Start your canoeing adventure at Milton. Once known as Scratch Ankle, Milton celebrates its heritage every year with the Scratch Ankle Festival in March, the Milton Riverfest in June, and the Blackwater Heritage Tour in December.

Adventures Unlimited, Route 6, Box 283, Milton, FL 32570 (tel. 904/623-9197), can make advance arrangements for canoeing, kayaking, rafting, and paddle-boating in Blackwater River State Park and surrounding rivers. Meandering along waterways surrounded by some of Florida's most gorgeous scenery is a memorable experience—special arrangements are made for novices.

Blackwater Canoe Rental, 10274 Pond Rd., Milton, FL 32570 (tel. 904/623-0235), also rents canoes, kayaks, floats, tubes, and camping equipment. Rates range from $11 for a short canoe trip to $26 for a three-day rental.

If you don't want to camp, Adventures Unlimited rents 14 cottages on Coldwater Creek. Rates range from $29 to $89, depending on facilities and size. Five of the cabins have fireplaces.

2. FORT WALTON BEACH & DESTIN

40 miles E of Pensacola, 160 miles W of Tallahassee

GETTING THERE **By Plane** Flights arriving at and departing from **Okaloosa County Air Terminal** (tel. 904/651-0822) actually use the field at Eglin Air Force Base. The terminal is on Fla. 85 north of Fort Walton Beach and is served by American Eagle, Delta Connection, Northwest Airlines, and USAir Express. Taxis wait outside the modern terminal.

By Train Amtrak's *Sunset Limited* transcontinental service stops at Crestview, 26 miles north of Fort Walton Beach. Call toll free 800/USA-RAIL for Amtrak information.

By Bus The Greyhound bus station is at 105 Chestnut Ave., in downtown Fort Walton Beach (tel. 904/243-1940, or toll free 800/231-2222).

By Car From east or west, take I-10 or U.S. 98. For Fort Walton Beach, exit I-10 at Crestview and follow Fla. 85 south for 24 miles. For Destin and the beaches of south Walton County, exit I-10 at DeFuniak Springs and follow U.S. 331 south to Santa Rosa Beach. You can avoid the beach traffic between there and Destin by leaving U.S. 331 at Freeport and taking Fla. 20 west to Villa Tasso, then Fla. 295 across the Mid Bay Bridge (there's a $2 toll). From the north, take U.S. 331 south through Alabama.

At the outbreak of the Civil War in 1861, a small Confederate contingent arrived in front of a large Native American mound on narrow Santa Rosa Sound and set up camp to guard the eastern approaches to Pensacola. Although the Rebels didn't stay long—they beat a hasty retreat when Yankee troops shelled their position from Okaloosa Island—the name they gave their little outpost has remained to this day: Fort Walton.

Back then the only settlement in these parts was Destin, a tiny fishing village on the banks of East Pass, which lets broad, beautiful Chottawhatchee Bay flow into the Gulf of Mexico. And even though the U.S. government established sprawling Eglin Air Force Base here in the 1930s, Fort Walton had just 90 residents as late as 1940. But then came World War II, when Eglin grew into a major Army Air Corps training base.

After the war, Southerners from neighboring states discovered the area's sugary white beaches and fabulous fishing. Fort Walton added "Beach" to its name in 1953, Destin turned into "The World's Luckiest Fishing Village" with Florida's largest charter fleet, and the area quickly grew into the diverse and vibrant vacation mecca you'll find today.

This is by no means a "Redneck Riviera" full of Southerners. Yes, you'll meet tanned fishermen born and bred in Destin (they call themselves "Fish Heads") and friendly old-timers who still speak with noticeable drawls and twangs. But there are thousands of air force officers and enlisted men stationed here, and many retirees from around the United States and Canada now call Fort Walton Beach and Destin home. All together, they make this area an interesting place to visit.

And one more thing: Take a look at the translucent gulf waters flowing through East Pass and lapping long, powdery beaches, and you'll see why residents proudly call their beautiful home "The Emerald Coast."

ORIENTATION

INFORMATION   For Fort Walton Beach and Destin, contact the **Emerald Coast Convention and Visitors Bureau,** P.O. Box 609, Fort Walton Beach, FL 32548 (tel. 904/651-7131, or toll free 800/322-3319; fax 904/651-7149). Once there, visit the **Okaloosa County Visitors Center,** a tin-roofed, beachside building on Miracle Strip Parkway (U.S. 98) on Okaloosa Island at the eastern edge of Fort Walton Beach.

The **Destin Chamber of Commerce,** 1021 U.S. 98E, Suite A (P.O. Box 8), Destin, FL 32541 (tel. 904/837-6241), opposite the Holiday Inn in Destin, also gives away brochures and maps pertaining to Destin.

For the beaches of south Walton County, which lie east of Destin and include Sandestin, contact the **South Walton Tourist Development Council,** P.O. Box 1248, Santa Rosa Beach, FL 32459 (tel. 904/267-1216, or toll free 800/822-6877). The **Walton County Chamber of Commerce Information Center** is at the intersection of U.S. 98 and U.S. 331 in Santa Rosa Beach (tel. 904/267-3511).

AREA LAYOUT   In Okaloosa County, on the western shore of the mainland, the city of **Fort Walton Beach** lies on the point where Santa Rosa Sound flows into Choctawhatchee Bay. **Eglin Air Force Base,** seven miles north, is linked to town by Eglin Parkway (Fla. 85)—the so-called Strip, bounded by scores of shops, grocery stores, gas stations, and fast-food restaurants.

Known in Fort Walton Beach as Miracle Strip Parkway, U.S. 98 runs from east to west along Santa Rosa Sound. It then continues eastward across the Brooks Bridge to **Okaloosa Island,** a narrow strip of sand separating Choctawhatchee Bay from the Gulf of Mexico. From Okaloosa Island, U.S. 98 then crosses East Pass to **Destin,** six miles east of Fort Walton Beach, and goes from there into Walton County. In Destin, this main drag is known as U.S. 98E, or as the locals call it, "Highway 98 East."

The huge **Sandestin Resort**—a virtual community unto itself—is in Walton County five miles east of Destin. Beyond Sandestin, County Road 30A leads to the low-key **beaches of South Walton:** Santa Rosa Beach, Dune Allen Beach, Blue Mountain Beach, Grayton Beach, Seagrove Beach, and Seaside.

To the north across Choctawhatchee Bay lie the small cities of **Valparaiso** and **Niceville.** Dating from the early 1900s, they are two of the earliest real estate developments in Northwest Florida.

Maps   For detailed street maps, the best local source is **Publishers Warehouse,** 255 Miracle Strip Pkwy., in the Manufacturers Outlet Center, on U.S. 98 near the mainland end of Brooks Bridge in Fort Walton Beach (tel. 904/243-0775; fax 904/244-1274).

GETTING AROUND

BY TAXI OR LIMO   For a taxi, call **Veterans Cab Co.** (tel. 244-666). **Continental Limousine** (tel. 651-5868) will drive you around in style.

BY RENTAL CAR   Area rental-car agencies include **Avis** (tel. toll free 800/831-2847), **Budget** (tel. toll free 800/527-0700), **Economy** (tel. 904/678-6223), **Hertz** (tel. toll free 800/654-3131), and **National** (tel. toll free 800/227-7368).

FAST FACTS

Area Code   The telephone area code is 904.

Doctor   For doctor referral, call the Humana Hospital in Destin (tel. 654-7680).

Tax   In addition to the 6% state sales tax, the local governments levy a 2% tax on all restaurant and hotel bills.

Time   The area is in the central time, an hour behind Miami and Orlando.

WHAT TO SEE & DO

ATTRACTIONS
In Fort Walton Beach

EGLIN AIR FORCE BASE, Eglin Blvd. (Fla. 189). Tel. 882-3933.

Five miles north of downtown Fort Walton Beach, this is the world's largest air force base, encompassing more than 700 square miles. Free tours include demonstrations of the world's largest environmental test chamber, McKinley Climatic Laboratory; a look into the 33rd Tactical Fighter Wing (the "Top Guns" of Desert Storm); and more. World War II's historic Doolittle's Tokyo Raiders trained at the base. Interesting bus tours of the base are offered in the summer months.

The **U.S. Air Force Armament Museum** (tel. 882-4189), the only U.S. museum highlighting air force armament, has 25 reconnaissance, flighter, and bomber planes, including the SR-71 Blackbird Spy Plane. The fighter-cockpit simulator spans developments from World War II through the Korean and Vietnam Wars to the Persian Gulf. Also exhibited are war films, photographs, rockets, bombs, missiles, and more.

The museum is on Fla. 85 west of the main gate. Bus tours depart from the Officer's Club parking lot.

Admission: Free.

Open: Museum, daily 9:30am–4:30pm (closed major holidays). Base tours given three days a week in summer at 9:30am; call for the schedule.

FOCUS CENTER, 139 Brooks St., one block south of Miracle Strip Pkwy., on the mainland. Tel. 664-1261.

This children's museum appeals to kids by stimulating the imagination with interactional fun and fantasy. It has such attractions as a reflecting Castle of Mirrors, an electrifying Illuma Storm, colossal bubble makers, and much more.

Admission: $2 adults and children over 2.

Open: Mon–Fri 9am–noon, Sat–Sun 1–5pm.

GULFARIUM, Miracle Strip Pkwy. (U.S. 98) on Okaloosa Island. Tel. 244-5169.

This is one of the nation's original marine parks. It features on-going shows with dolphin performers, and also shows off its California sea lions, Peruvian penguins, and Ridley turtles. There are at least 14 fascinating exhibits, including the Living Sea, with special windows that provide viewing of undersea life.

Admission: $12 adults (discounts for seniors), $8 children 4–11, free for kids under 4.

Open: Daily 9am–dusk. Shows given at 10am, noon, 2pm, and 4pm; additional show at 6pm in summer.

INDIAN TEMPLE MOUND AND MUSEUM, 139 Miracle Strip Pkwy., on the mainland. Tel. 243-6521.

This ceremonial mound, one of the largest ever discovered, dates back to A.D. 1200. The museum, located next to it, showcases ceramic artifacts from southeastern Native American tribes. The largest such collection, it contains at least 6,000 items. Exhibits depict the lifestyles of the four tribes that lived in the Choctawhatchee Bay region for 10,000 years.

Admission: 75¢ adults, free for children under 12.

Open: Oct–May, Mon–Fri 11am–4pm, Sat 9am–4pm; June–Sept, Mon–Sat 9am–4pm.

In Destin

DESTIN FISHING MUSEUM, Harborwalk Plaza, 35 U.S. 98E. Tel. 654-1011.

World-record trophies for red snapper to state-record trophies for blue marlin are displayed, as well as a variety of maritime memorabilia. There's also a hands-on tidal pool and a dry walk-through aquarium where the sand bottom exhibits sponges, sea fans, coral reefs, sea turtles, and other marine life.

Note: In 1995 the museum may move to a new marina complex on Destin harbor behind the Early Bird Cafe.

Admission: $1, free for children under 12.

Open: Tues–Sat noon–4pm, Sun 1–4pm.

In South Walton County

EDEN STATE GARDENS AND MANSION, Point Washington. Tel. 231-4214.

These splendid waterfront gardens and the Wesley Mansion should not be missed. The magnificent 1895 Greek Revival mansion has been lovingly restored and richly furnished. It stands overlooking scenic Choctawhatchee Bay, surrounded by immense moss-draped oak trees. The gorgeous gardens are resplendent with camellias, azaleas, and other typical southern flowers. Picnicking is allowed on the plantation grounds. The gardens and mansion are a short drive north of Seagrove Beach.

Admission: $1.50 for mansion and gardens.

Open: Gardens, daily 8am–sunset. Mansion, Thurs–Mon 9am–5pm (tours on the hour, 9am -4pm).

PARKS & BEACHES

FORT WALTON BEACH   Do your beaching here on the white sands of **Okaloosa Island,** where Santa Rosa Boulevard runs west of U.S. 98 through a strip of hotels, condominiums, and cottages until ending at U.S. Air Force property. East of U.S. 98, it dead-ends at "Shanty Town," a collection of 1950s-vintage buildings housing restaurants and lively pubs. Most resort hotels and amusement parks are grouped around the Gulfarium on U.S. 98 just east of Santa Rosa Boulevard. If you're not staying on the island, you can use the free facilities at **Beasley Park,** home of the Okaloosa County Visitor Center. Across the highway, the **Okaloosa Area, Gulf Islands National Seashore** has picnic areas and sailboats for rent on Choctawhatchee Bay.

DESTIN   Boardwalks at the 208-acre **Henderson Beach State Recreation Area,** just east of Destin on U.S. 98E (tel. 837-7550), allow easy access to the beach without endangering the fragile sea oats and other vegetation on the preserved white dunes. Swimming, sunning, surf fishing, picnicking, and seabird-watching are part of the fun. The area is open daily from 8am to sunset. Admission is $2 per vehicle.

SOUTH WALTON COUNTY   On County Road 30A, **Grayton Beach State Recreation Area** (tel. 231-4210) has a lovely gulf beach and 356 acres of pine forests surrounding scenic Western Lake. There's a boat ramp and campground with electric hookups on the lake. Get a self-guided-tour leaflet for the nature trail at the main gate. It's open daily from 8am to sunset. Admission is $3.25 per vehicle, with up to eight occupants, $2 per pedestrian or bicyclist.

SPECIAL EVENTS

The area celebrates more than 20 annual festivals, some of them outstanding. Call the **Emerald Coast Convention and Visitors Bureau** (tel. 904/651-7131, or toll free 800/322-3319) for information.

The **Fort Walton Beach Seafood Festival,** an annual April celebration, is a virtual seafood-eating frenzy.

The **Eglin Air Show,** an aviation spectacular at Eglin Air Force Base, Fort Walton Beach, varies in time from year to year, but often takes place in April.

The **Billy Bowlegs Festival,** an annual week-long party in June at Fort Walton Beach, is named for William Augustus Bowles, self-proclaimed King of Florida who became a notorious buccaneer known as Capt. Billy Bowlegs. A pirate flotilla, treasure hunts, fishing competitions, kids' contests, and amusing races are part of the fun.

The **Destin Fishing Rodeo,** celebrated annually all of October, proves why Destin is considered "World's Luckiest Fishing Village" and "Billfish Capital of the Gulf." The **Destin Seafood Festival** is also in October.

Other festivals in Destin are the **International Golf Tournament** in October, the **Boggy Bayou Mullet Festival** in October, and the **Christmas Boat Parade** in December.

The beaches of South Walton feature many cultural and fun events, including the annual **Grayton Beach Fine Arts Festival** in May; the **National and U.S. Open Water Ski Tournament** in August; the annual **South Walton Sportsfest Weekend** in November; the **PGA Pro Am/Pro-Pro Tournament** at the Sandestin Resort, also in November; and dazzling **Christmas celebrations** lighting up the entire area. Don't miss the annual **Winter Visitors' Appreciation Tea Dance,** usually held in February. For information, call the South Walton Tourist Development Council (tel. 267-1216, or toll free 800/822-6877).

SPORTS & RECREATION

BOAT RENTALS & CRUISES Hobie Cat and small craft rentals are available from many marinas, as well as from several beachfront resorts. **Paradise Water Sports** (tel. 664-7872) has six locations on U.S. 98. For sailing charters and excursions, contact the *Flying Eagle* (tel. 837-4986 or 837-3700), **Blackbeard Sailing Charters** (tel. 837-2793), or **Sailing South** (tel. 837-7245), all based in Destin. Rates are $25 for adults, $15 for children 3 to 10, free for kids under 3.

Party Pontoons, located dockside at the A. J. Seafood and Oyster Bar, just east of the Destin Bridge (tel. 837-2222), offer pontoon boats for a relaxing sojourn on the gulf; barbecue grills are available on board. Rates are $30 per hour, $110 for a half day, $175 for a full day.

The *Glass Bottom Boat II* (tel. 654-7787) offers a variety of daily sightseeing and nature cruises from Capt. Dave's Restaurant, 304 U.S. 98E, Destin.

CANOEING Canoeing lazily along crystal-clear rivers, bordered by scenic woodlands, is especially enjoyable in **Blackwater River State Park,** less than an hour's drive northwest of Fort Walton Beach (see "An Easy Excursion" in the Pensacola section for information.

FISHING Destin doesn't call itself the "World's Luckiest Fishing Village" for nothing. Almost every month, a different kind of fishing competition pays off with big money for the big ones. In fact, comedian Bob Hope won first prize with a big white marlin when he first visited the area.

Bottom fishing in the gulf offers grouper, amberjack, and snapper. **Inshore trolling** provides king and Spanish mackerel, cobia, and more. Serious sportfishermen hook sailfish, wahoo, tuna, and blue marlin. In the **bays and bayous,** you can catch trout, bass, sheepshead, bluefish, and buckets of blue crab. Less than an hour away, **freshwater fishing** is terrific in the Blackwater, Shoal, and Yellow Rivers, teeming with bass, bream, and catfish. The enormous Hurricane Lake in Blackwater River State Park abounds in large-mouth bass, catfish, bluegill, and more.

Destin also claims Florida's largest charter-boat fleet, with more than 140 vessels, many of them based at the marinas that line the north shore of Old Pass Lagoon, Destin's harbor along U.S. 98 just east of the high-rise bridge over East Pass. The **Destin Chamber of Commerce** (tel. 837-6241) provides a list of boats and captains. You can call them directly or visit one of several agents—such as **Pelican Charters** (tel. 837-2343)—who have booths on the boardwalk near A.J.'s Seafood & Oyster Bar, 116 U.S. 98E. Rates for the smaller vessels range from $300 to $800 per boat, depending on length of voyage. Or you can go on larger group-oriented boats such as the *Emmanuel* (tel. 837-6313) or the *Lady Eventhia* (tel. 837-6212) for about $35 per person.

For guided fishing excursions on the protected waters of Choctawhatchee Bay (groups up to six), contact **Elrod's Fish Camp,** on Mack Bayou Road (tel. 267-2318), about a five-minute drive west of Sandestin Resort.

Anglers also like to fish along the 1,200-foot **Okaloosa Pier,** which is illuminated at night. Over East Pass, the 3,000-foot **Destin Bridge Catwalk** is another popular fishing spot.

GOLF The area takes great pride in its 14 courses—more than 200 holes of golf altogether—designed by such well-known architects as Dye, Fazio, and Cupp. For advance information on all area courses, contact the **Emerald Coast Golf Association,** P.O. Box 304, Destin, FL 32540 (tel. 904/654-7086).

Open to the public, the **Fort Walton Beach Golf Course,** on Lewis Turner Boulevard (County Road 189) north of town (tel. 862-3314), is an 18-hole, par-72 course, complete with pro shop. The **Santa Rosa Golf & Beach Club,** off U.S. 98E (turn right on County Road 30A to Dune Allen Beach; tel. 267-2229), open to the public, offers a challenging 18-hole course through tall pines looking out to vistas of the gulf. The club has a pro shop, Beach Club restaurant and lounge, and also tennis courts. The **Sandestin Beach Resort,** on U.S. 98E (tel. 267-8000), offers 45 holes on two outstanding championship golf courses open to the public (see "Where to Stay," below). The **Seascape Resort & Conference Center,** 100 Seascape Dr. (tel. 837-9181), features an 18-hole course, where the public is invited to play. Another beautiful 18-hole public golf course is at the **Emerald Bay Golf Club,** 40001 Emerald Coast Pkwy. (tel. 837-4455). Nonguests may play golf (36 holes) or tennis (21 courts) at the **Bluewater Bay Resort** in Niceville (tel. 897-3613), only a 15-minute drive via the new Mid Bay Bridge. Call ahead for reservations and fees.

HORSEBACK RIDING The **Brand'n Iron Corral,** on County Road 1 in Santa Rosa Beach (tel. 267-2433), features guided tours on horseback (safe for inexperienced riders, too) on trails winding through Santa Rosa's forests and around Choctawhatchee Bay.

Fort Walton stables include **Sleepy Oaks** (tel. 863-2919) and the **Equestrian Center** (tel. 863-3295).

MINIGOLF/AMUSEMENT PARKS Several private parks combine various amusements with minigolf courses running through Disney-like fake mountains and waterfalls.

In Fort Walton Beach, **Lost Lagoon Adventure Golf,** 1306 Miracle Strip Pkwy. (U.S. 98) opposite the Gulfarium on Okaloosa Island (tel. 244-1612), has both minigolf and a short, par-3 regular course along the bay. The course at nearby **Magic Carpet Golf,** 1320 Miracle Strip Pkwy. (tel. 243-0020), features statues of kooky characters.

In Destin, the **Track Family Recreation Center,** 1125 U.S. 98E (tel. 837-3295), which includes Surfin' Safari Minigolf, is especially cool for kids, since it also offers a small Ferris wheel, plastic bumper boats in a shallow swimming pool, a track for tiny go-karts, and other activities designed for small tots. Next door, **Air Boingo Bungee Jump,** 1127 U.S. 98E (tel. 654-9306), lets adults dive head-first from atop a 75-foot-tall steel tower. **Big Kahuna's Water Park & Tropical Golf,** 1007 U.S. 98E, near the Holiday Inn Destin (tel. 837-4061), has eight water slides, a wave pool, various rides, and a dune-buggy race track out back.

All the parks are open daily from 10am to midnight in summer. Most, but not all, are open daily from noon to 5pm in winter. Prices vary depending on choice of activity.

SNORKELING & SCUBA DIVING At least a dozen dive shops are located along the beaches. Considered one of the best, **Scuba Tech Diving Charters** has two locations: at Capt. Dave's Marina, 312 U.S. 98E in Destin (tel. 837-1933), and 5371 U.S. 98E (tel. 837-2822), about a half mile west of the Sandestin Beach Resort. Beginner and advanced diving instruction classes are offered. Aboard the 45-foot dive boat *Sea Cobra,* a four-hour/two-tank reef or wreck dive (about 65 to 90 feet in depth) or one-tank night dive costs $40, a six-hour/two-tank reef or wreck dive (down to 110 feet in depth) costs $55, and the eight-hour/three-tank dive costs $65. Equipment is not included in these prices.

Kokomo Snorkeling Adventures, 500 U.S. 98E in Destin (tel. 837-9029), specializes in snorkeling only and takes you aboard the 50-foot custom-built *Kokomo* for 2½-hour excursions into the Gulf of Mexico and Choctawhatchee Bay. Gear is included for $20 per person.

TENNIS Have a smashing time at the **Fort Walton Beach Municipal Tennis Center,** 45 W. Audrey Dr., at Rogers Street (tel. 243-8789), featuring 12 lighted courts, a clubhouse, lounge, lockers, and showers. Rates are $2.50 per day. Open Monday through Thursday from 8am to 9pm, on Friday from 8am to 5pm, and on

Saturday and Sunday from 9am to 5pm. The **Sandestin Beach Resort,** U.S. 98E (tel. 837-2121), offers 16 courts open to the public, including hard, clay, and grass. *Tennis* magazine designated Sandestin as one of the nation's top 50 tennis resorts and the only ranked resort with natural grass courts. The **Seascape Resort & Conference Center,** 100 Seascape Dr. (tel. 837-9181), has eight courts open to the public. The **Destin Racquet & Fitness Center,** at 995 Airport Rd. (tel. 837-7300), provides six Rubico tennis courts. You have to phone ahead for reservations. Rates are $10 per person per day to play tennis or racquetball, or participate in the activities here.

WHERE TO STAY

Hotels, motels, beach cottages and resorts, and condominium apartments comprise more than 3,000 selections in the area. They're on the mainland shore of Santa Rosa Sound in Fort Walton Beach proper, or on the beaches of Okaloosa Island, Destin, and south Walton County.

If you don't mind not having daily maid service, many condominiums offer good value, especially for stays of a week or more. One example is **Venus Condos,** 885 Santa Rosa Blvd., Fort Walton Beach, FL 32548 (tel. 904/243-0885, or toll free 800/476-1885), a pleasant enclave on western Okaloosa Island. This three-story, 45-unit complex has been immaculately maintained since it opened in the early 1970s. Facilities include a guest laundry and a grassy courtyard with palm trees, swimming pool, lighted tennis court, and large barbecue pit. Each of the one-, two-, and three-bedroom units has a cable TV, fully equipped kitchen with microwave oven, telephone, and its own heating and air-conditioning unit. The beach is a short walk across the dunes. Rates are $85 to $135 daily between May and Labor Day, $50 to $90 the rest of the year. Weekly rates are available, and Discover, MasterCard, and VISA are accepted.

The tourist information offices (see "Orientation," above) will provide long lists of other condos and cottages for rent. The largest agent, **Abbott Realty Services** (tel. 904/837-4774 or 904/837-0805, or toll free 800/336-4853), will send a brochure of its many accommodations throughout the area.

FORT WALTON BEACH
Expensive

HOLIDAY INN, 1110 Santa Rosa Blvd., Fort Walton Beach, FL 32548. Tel. 904/243-9181, or toll free 800/732-4853. Fax 904/664-7652. 385 rms. A/C TV TEL

$ Rates: Summer, $95–$175 double. Off-season, $60–$115 double. Inquire about special vacation rates. AE, DC, DISC, MC, V.

A glass-enclosed elevator climbs up through a soaring atrium lobby to rooms with spectacular gulf views from a six-story building here, but the less expensive accommodations are found in the original motel-style units, most of which flank a courtyard with its own large outdoor pool and children's playground. There are two other pools, one under a glass roof, plus a beach bar and barbecue area, two lighted tennis courts, an exercise room, and a gift shop. JP's Cafe serves breakfast, lunch, and dinner, and there's live entertainment in the atrium bar nightly during summer.

RAMADA BEACH RESORT, Miracle Strip Pkwy. (U.S. 98), Fort Walton Beach, FL 32548. Tel. 904/243-9161, or toll free 800/447-0010. Fax 904/243-2391. 454 rms, 4 suites. A/C TV TEL

$ Rates: Summer, $95–$140 double; $200–$230 suite. Winter, $65–$90 double; $140–$170 suite. AE, CB, DISC, DC, MC, V.

Considered Fort Walton Beach's prime hotel, this big resort on Okaloosa Island boasts one of the most beautiful swimming pool–patio areas anywhere, with waterfalls cascading over lofty rocks and a romantic grotto bar, all surrounded by thick tropical foilage. Barbecue carried away from a shacklike structure can be eaten at thatch cabañas tucked away in this jungle. Most of the tastefully furnished rooms have beach or courtyard views from a six-story building, but the less expensive units overlook a parking lot from an older two-story structure next door. The Pelican's

Roost features casual seafood favorites, such as freshly shucked oysters, while the Lobster House specializes in just that. Calories can be worked off at the beach, on two lighted tennis courts, in two heated pools or a health club, or by dancing the night away in the gilded lobby bar.

SHERATON INN, 1325 Miracle Strip Pkwy. (U.S. 98), Fort Walton Beach, FL 32548. Tel. 904/243-8116, or toll free 800/874-8104. Fax 904/244-3064. 154 rms. A/C TV TEL

$ Rates: Summer, $95–$130 double. Off-season, $70–$90 double. AE, DISC, DC, MC, V.

Accommodations here on Okaloosa Island are very spacious, decorated with vivid, tropical colors and enhanced by beautiful views of the gulf and gardens. Many rooms have refrigerators and kitchenettes. Amenities include a heated swimming pool in a lush tropical garden with its own thatch-roofed Tiki Bar (open in summer only), whirlpool, exercise room, dining room, cocktail lounge, games room, and coin laundry. There's plenty of fun on the beautiful beach at this gulf-front resort.

Moderate

CAROUSEL BEACH RESORT, 571 Santa Rosa Blvd., Fort Walton Beach, FL 32548. Tel. 904/243-7658, or toll free 800/523-0208. Fax 904/244-4330. 105 rms. A/C TV TEL

$ Rates: Mar–Sept, $65–$120 double. Oct–Feb, $36–$85 double. AE, DC, DISC, MC, V.

At this friendly motel on western Okaloosa Island, families like the spacious accommodations. Rooms with kitchenettes cost more (usually $89 in summer for a beachfront view, but $80 for side view of the gulf); in winter, a standard motel room can be priced as low as $36. Rooms that have balconies overlook dunes on the sparkling white sand beach. Two swimming pools (one heated) are on the premises. Overlooking the shimmering green gulf waters, the fourth-floor Stowaway Lounge is a delightful oasis for cocktails. A good Italian restaurant is next door.

MARINA BAY RESORT, 80 Miracle Strip Pkwy. (U.S. 98), Fort Walton Beach, FL 32548. Tel. 904/244-5132. Fax 904/244-0491. 120 rms. A/C TV TEL

$ Rates: Summer, $50–$120 double. Off-season, $40–$91 double. AE, DC, DISC, MC, V.

On Santa Rosa Sound in town, this resort sports a dock, its own fishing pier and small beach, a volleyball court, a swimming pool, a whirlpool, a putting green, shuffleboard, and an exercise room and sauna. More than half the guest rooms are equipped with kitchenettes (request one, if that's your preference). The big bargain here is the special off-season $40 rate for accommodations with sleeper sofas. The best rooms face the sound.

Budget

HOWARD JOHNSON LODGE, 314 Miracle Strip Pkwy. SW (U.S. 98), Fort Walton Beach, FL 32548. Tel. 904/243-6162, or toll free 800/654-2000. Fax 904/664-2735. 138 rms, 2 suites. A/C TV TEL

$ Rates: Summer, $46–$51 single; $54–$75 double; $120–$140 suite. Winter, $33–$39 single; $36–$46 double; $85–$95 suite. AE, DISC, MC, V.

Beautifully located on Santa Rosa Sound in town, this pleasant hotel is only a two-mile drive to the beach. Majestic oak trees and lovely magnolia trees grace the courtyard. Here's a tip: Request a room that overlooks the courtyard with its large swimming pool; the outside units—even those facing the water—have parking-lot vistas. A Waffle House on the premises (now you know what to order for breakfast) is open 24 hours.

DESTIN

Expensive

HENDERSON PARK INN, 2700 U.S. 98E, Destin, FL 32541. Tel. 904/837-4853, or toll free 800/336-4853. 20 suites, 18 villas. A/C TV TEL

$ Rates (including buffet breakfast): Summer, $175–$210. Off-season, $90–$165. Special weekly, honeymoon, and family packages. AE, DISC, MC, V.

⭐ This shingle-sided, Cape Hatteras–style building is definitely a romantic, get-away-from-it-all hideaway (couples or singles only in the rooms, please). Nestled in a tranquil cul-de-sac on the undeveloped eastern edge of Henderson Beach State Recreation Area, the inn sports a beachside veranda complete with old-fashioned rocking chairs to sit in and admire the glorious sunsets. The adjacent villas are in a motel-style building next door. No two units, however, are alike. Several feature high ceilings, fireplaces, canopied beds, Victorian wicker furniture, and gulf views from the whirlpool baths. Every designer-decorated unit has a private balcony looking out to the scenic gulf.

Dining/Entertainment: All rates include complimentary daily buffet breakfast in the gulf-front dining room and cocktails at the nightly before-dinner social hour. Reservations are required for the gourmet-style dinners.

Services: Arrangements are made for golf, tennis, scuba, snorkeling, sailing, and fishing; children's programs available.

Facilities: Heated swimming pool, beachside sun deck, complimentary beach umbrellas and chairs, a beach gazebo, grills for barbecuing.

HOLIDAY INN OF DESTIN, 1020 U.S. 98E, Destin, FL 32541. Tel. 904/837-6181, or toll free 800/HOLIDAY. Fax 904/837-1532. 230 rms. A/C TV TEL

$ Rates: Summer, $88–$300 double. Off-season, $60–$275 double. Inquire about special vacation packages and discounts for seniors. AE, DISC, MC, V.

This attractive gulf-front resort features two swimming pools (one heated) and a wading pool for the kids. Although most rooms are in a round high-rise building, unfortunately an equally tall condo next door blocks some from enjoying what would otherwise be a spectacular view. Get a room facing south or east, however, and you're in for a visual treat. Rooms in an older, four-story building are more spacious than those in the tower; some of these older units open to an enclosed, fountained lobby sporting a comfortable mezzanine lounge with billiard, ping-pong, and foosball tables, plus a separate electronic-game room. Kids' and adults' recreation programs are offered during the summer. All rooms are nicely decorated. The Destin Cafe in the lobby serves breakfast, lunch, and dinner. There's entertainment in the adjacent bar during summers.

SANDESTIN BEACH RESORT, 5500 U.S. 98E, Destin, FL 32541. Tel. 904/267-8000, or toll free 800/277-0800. Fax 904/267-8197. 175 rms, 360 condos.

$ Rates: Summer, $120–$170 double; $170–$525 condo. Winter, $55–$85 double; $81–$260 condo. Ask about vacation packages. AE, DISC, MC, V.

⭐ A superstar resort, situated on 2,600 acres complete with a spectacular beach, Sandestin is a vacation wonderland five miles east of Destin. The array of handsomely decorated accommodations overlook the gulf or Choctawhatchee Bay, the golf fairways, lagoons, or a nature preserve—just state your preference. Hotel rooms are in the Inn at Destin, on the bay. All other accommodations—junior suites, condominium apartments, villas, and three-bedroom penthouses—are spread over the property and come complete with kitchen, living room, and patio or balcony. Don't worry about getting around the resort. Most amenities are a short walk or bike ride away. A tram shuttles around the resort and a tunnel runs under U.S. 98 connecting Sandestin's gulf and bay areas.

Dining/Entertainment: The dining delight here is the romantic Elephant Walk (tel. 267-4800), over on the gulf side a short walk from the Sandestin Hilton. The story behind this elegant house begins in Ceylon (now Sri Lanka), where in 1890 a defiant tea planter named John Whiley tried to prevent damage to his trees by building a huge home across an elephant herd's path to the river. When their thirsty stampede reduced his house to ruins, Whiley vowed never to return. He roamed for 30 years, buying treasures in all four corners of the world. Then he discovered Northwest Florida and settled here. His purchases are displayed in the Elephant Walk, designed to evoke his Ceylon mansion. The candlelit dining room features entirely different, gourmet-quality choices for dinner each evening. Other dining spots are the Sunset Bay Cafe, which serves breakfast, lunch, and dinner; and Chan's Market Cafe (see "Where to Dine," below, for more information).

Services: Free shuttle tram around the resort.

Facilities: Kids' Crew is the summer children's program for ages 3 to 13. For teenagers, the resort offers a junior's academy for both tennis and golf. Guests may rent bikes, boats, and water-sports equipment. Fishing is arranged in Sandestin's stocked lakes, abundant with large-mouth bass, or arrangements can be made for deep-sea-fishing charters from nearby Destin.

Sandestin's Baytowne Marina charters excursions or you can captain your own vessel. Eleven tennis courts offer hard and Rubico surfaces at the beach or bayside tennis centers, plus the Wimbledon-style grass tennis courts for a different experience; there's a tennis clinic also. Forty-five holes of championship golf include links along Choctawhatchee Bay: the Dunes (splendid gulf views), the Harbor, and the new Troon course with a unique island green. The fully equipped Sports/Spa & Clinic is highly acclaimed. There are nine swimming pools, three wading pools, a playground for kids, a conference center, and the Market at Sandestin with 30 shops (Chico's, Benetton, La Bonbonière with Godiva chocolates, Zoo Gallery, Islander's Surf and Sport, and Jamaica Joe's, to name just a few).

SANDESTIN BEACH HILTON GOLF & TENNIS RESORT, 5540 U.S. 98E, Destin, FL 32541. Tel. 904/267-9500, or toll free 800/HILTONS. Fax 904/267-3076. 400 suites. A/C TV TEL

$ Rates: Summer, $185–$260 suite. Off-season, $95–$165 suite. AE, CB, DC, DISC, MC, V.

Actually, this high-rise, family-oriented resort is nicely situated on the grounds of the Sandestin Beach Resort and features spacious accommodations, including a special area for childrens' bunk beds (kids love this set-up). Another family convenience is the dressing room with sink outside the bathroom (sink inside, too). And there's plenty of closet space, a wet bar, in-room refreshment center, refrigerator, and small hotplate. Balconies look out to splendid gulf views.

Dining/Entertainment: The multilevel Sandcastles Restaurant and Lounge in the lobby offers a moderately priced menu. In the summer season, the Beach Club Grill is enjoyable casual, and the Ice Cream Shop features sweet treats. For indoor or outdoor dining, the exotic Elephant Walk restaurant is nearby (see the Sandestin Beach Resort, above).

Services: 24-hour room service, guest services director, babysitting, summer program for children, youth program.

Facilities: Outdoor swimming pool, heated indoor pool, whirlpool spa and saunas, 16 tennis courts, 45 holes of USGA championship golf, sailing, windsurfing, charter fishing, games room, shops, meeting rooms.

Moderate

FRANGISTA BEACH INN, 4150 Old U.S. 98E, Destin, FL 32541. Tel. 904/654-5501. Fax 904/654-5876. 19 rms, 2 suites. A/C TV TEL

$ Rates: Summer, $90–$160 double. Off-season, $50–$80 double. Weekly and monthly special rates available. DISC, MC, V.

Located directly on the beautiful white sand gulf beach, this motel was built in 1939. The original owner was from Frangista, Greece, so the inn and its stretch of beach bear the unusual name. The inn was tastefully refurbished and renovated in 1989: The white stuccoed walls, terra-cotta-tile floors, and pastel prints combine the relaxed feeling of the Greek islands and the Caribbean. Most rooms have kitchenettes, and there's one two-bedroom suite and one three-bedroom suite. Ask if you prefer a room with a bathtub, as most units have only shower facilities. Definitely a delightful place to stay!

Budget

VILLAGE INN, 215 U.S. 98E, Destin, FL 32541. Tel. 904/837-7413, or toll free 800/821-9342. Fax 904/654-3394. 100 rms. A/C TV TEL

$ Rates: Memorial Day–Labor Day, $50–$60 double. Off-season, $40 double.

Weekly rates are lower. Children under 18 stay free in parents' room. AE, DC, DISC, MC, V.

Directly across the street from the charter fishing fleet, this friendly, two-story motel features oversize rooms with a choice of two queen-size beds or one king-size bed; some rooms have refrigerators. A swimming pool is on the premises. The drive to the gulf beaches is only five minutes; restaurants, shopping, golf, and some attractions are within a two-mile radius. Next door, a Waffle House restaurant is open 24 hours.

BED & BREAKFAST

A HIGHLANDS HOUSE, P.O. Box 1189, Santa Rosa Beach, FL 32459. Tel. 904/267-0110. 5 rms (all with bath). A/C

$ Rates (including breakfast): Mar–Nov, $83 single or double; $105 Carriage House. Dec–Feb, $55 single or double; $77 Carriage House. Additional person $10 extra. Children under 10 stay free in parents' room. No credit cards.

Beautifully situated where County Road 30A meets the gulf at Dune Allen Beach, A Highlands House was built in 1991 by Joan and Ray Robins, who are the proud innkeepers. Former residents of Beaufort, S.C., they reproduced the kind of luxurious 18th-century summer homes that Old South plantation owners once built for family beach vacations to escape the inland summer heat. The Robinses furnished their dream inn with four-poster "rice beds," comfy wingback chairs, and antique accoutrements. Wicker furniture inspires relaxation on the extra-wide porch. The formal parlor is lovingly decorated. In the cheerful dining room, delicious breakfasts are served—one favorite is the mile-high brandy-battered French toast, heaped with strawberries and cream. Joan's freshly baked coffee cakes are irresistible. Mother Nature provides delightful music in the sound of the gulf surf splashing against the sugar-white beach.

CAMPING

Emerald Coast RV Resort, on Dune Allen Beach (Rte. 1, Box 2820), Santa Rosa Beach, FL 32459 (tel. 904/267-2808, or toll free 800/232-2478), offers more than 140 campsites on 90 acres, shaded by beautiful trees. Secluded from heavy traffic, the resort is about a quarter mile off U.S. 98, on County Road 30A, east of the Sandestin Beach Resort. In addition to full RV hookups, the resort offers a putting green, fishing lakes, hiking and nature trails, a clubhouse, outdoor games area, a heated swimming pool, a tennis court, picnic facilities, a beach shuttle, and more. Of course, laundry rooms and cable television are provided. The landscaped site is guarded around the clock to ensure camping safety. Daily, weekly, and monthly rates are offered (rates are $25 a day in summer, $22 a day in winter). The office is open from 7am to 7pm daily. No tents or pop-ups are allowed.

Holiday Travel Park, 5380 U.S. 98E, Destin, FL 32541 (tel. 904/837-6334), on the gulf side of U.S. 98 near Sandestin Beach Resort, is the area's largest and oldest campground, offering 250 campsites, many right on the beach. In addition, the travel park has a bunkhouse that sleeps 40, three bath houses, picnic tables, a fishing pond, grocery store, and gift shop. Call or write for rates information.

Grayton Beach State Recreation Area, on Grayton Beach (Rte. 2, Box 6600), Santa Rosa Beach, FL 32459 (tel. 904/231-4210), offers hookups for camping vehicles as well as primitive campsites in this beautiful 356-acre park. Campfire interpretive programs are available to campers (call for the current schedule). Also request the free self-guiding leaflet for the Nature Trail. A boat ramp is available on the park's Western Lake. Swimming and surf fishing are permitted in the park; there are good picnic facilities, too. Camping fees are $14 from March to September, $8 from October to February.

About an hour's drive northwest of Fort Walton Beach, **Blackwater River State Park,** Rte. 1, Box 57C, Holt, FL 32564 (tel. 904/623-2363), provides campsites at a cost of $8 per night year-round. Blackwater River is terrific for canoeing, and swimming, fishing, boating, picnicking, and walking along nature trails are enjoyable here. See "An Easy Excursion," in the Pensacola Section, above, for details.

WHERE TO DINE

Not counting a plethora of fast-food eateries along Eglin Parkway and, so it seems, the full length of U.S. 98, there are more than 110 restaurants in Fort Walton Beach, Destin, and south Walton County. That's far too many to list here, but local publisher Sherry Babbidge has compiled all their menus in a loosely bound booklet, *Let's Eat Out!* Copies are available at local bookstores. It costs $25 at Publishers Warehouse (tel. 243-0775), in the Manufacturers Outlet Center on Miracle Strip Parkway (U.S. 98) near the mainland end of Brooks Bridge.

FORT WALTON BEACH
Moderate

LIGHTHOUSE RESTAURANT, 132 Miracle Strip Pkwy. (U.S. 98), on the mainland. Tel. 664-2828.
   Cuisine: SEAFOOD. **Reservations:** Recommended.
   $ Prices: Appetizers $2–$7; main courses $8–$18. AE, DC, DISC, MC, V.
   Open: Dinner only, Mon–Sat 4:30–9pm.
Most patrons arrive at this pleasant, sound-side seafood emporium between 4:30 and 7:30pm when most main courses are discounted 50% off their menu prices. Tops here are expertly charcoal-broiled yellowfin tuna and amberjack, but there's a wide selection of shrimp, scallop, oyster, crab, and fish dishes, plus prime rib, steak, ham, and chicken for landlubbers. For something cool to both fingers and palate, order the combination shrimp salad served with a third of a pound of chilled shrimp still in their shells.

PANDORA'S RESTAURANT, 1120 Santa Rosa Blvd., Okaloosa Island. Tel. 244-8669.
   Cuisine: STEAK/SEAFOOD. **Reservations:** Not required.
   $ Prices: Appetizers $2–$5; main courses $12–$17. AE, DC, DISC, MC, V.
   Open: Dinner only, daily 5–10pm (lounge open until 2am). **Closed:** Sun–Mon Sept–Apr.
Although Pandora gained its reputation as a steakhouse, freshly caught local fish and shellfish are among the seafood choices. But steaks remain the top favorite. The tender beef is cut on the premises and grilled to perfection. Pandora's setting is unusual; the front part of the restaurant is housed in a beached yacht. It's relaxing to sip a drink in the main-deck lounge before proceeding downstairs to the beamed-ceilinged dining room, aglow with lights from copper chandeliers. Delicious breads and pies are homemade. Because of the high quality of the steaks and seafood, Pandora's is the place to indulge in surf-and-turf combinations such as steak with lobster, crab legs, or gulf shrimp. Live entertainment and dancing are an added attraction in the lounge; call in advance for the current schedule.

PERRI'S ITALIAN RESTAURANT, 300 Eglin Pkwy. (Fla. 85). Tel. 862-4421.
   Cuisine: ITALIAN. **Reservations:** Not required.
   $ Prices: Appetizers $3.50–$10.50; main courses $9–$15.50. MC, V.
   Open: Lunch Tues–Fri 11am–2pm; dinner Tues–Sat 5–10pm. **Closed:** Mid-Dec to Jan.
For many, many years, the Perri family has maintained their restaurant's popularity with recipes that have been handed down for generations. A variety of veal dishes and sauces for pastas are lovingly prepared. Fettuccine replete with shellfish is a favorite with seafood lovers. This attractive restaurant also offers a children's menu. The wine list features good vinos from Italy.

THE SOUND, 108 Miracle Strip Pkwy. (U.S. 98), on the mainland. Tel. 243-2722.
   Cuisine: SEAFOOD. **Reservations:** Not required.
   $ Prices: Main courses $9–$20. AE, DC, MC, V.
   Open: Daily 11am–10pm. **Closed:** New Year's Day, Thanksgiving, and Christmas Day.

Just like dining in a friend's cozy waterside home, the Sound is notable for real southern hospitality—and, of course, deliciously prepared fish and shellfish. If you have rented a boat, dock alongside the private waterway wharf. Sensational views of Santa Rosa Sound are part of the enjoyable dining experience here. Local fish and seafood may be ordered simply steamed, broiled with lemon and butter, or combined with gourmet sauces. "Early-bird" dinners are featured at special prices. For the little ones, there's a children's menu. During the peak summer season, live entertainment is spotlighted in the cocktail lounge.

STAFF'S SEAFOOD RESTAURANT, 24 Miracle Strip Pkwy. (U.S. 98), on the mainland. Tel. 243-3526.

Cuisine: SEAFOOD. **Reservations:** Not accepted.
$ Prices: Appetizers $3.50–$7; main courses $10–$17.50. AE, MC, V.
Open: Dinner only, daily 5–11pm.

Considered the first Emerald Coast restaurant, Staff's is a 1913 barrel-shaped warehouse with the original pressed-tin ceiling. Among the display of memorabilia are an old-fashioned phonograph lamp and a 1914 cash register. All main courses are served with heaping baskets of hot, home-baked wheat bread from Pop Staff's 70-year-old secret recipe. One of the favorite main dishes is the Seafood Skillet, sizzling with broiled yellowfin tuna, shrimp, scallops, and crabmeat stuffing, drenched in butter and sprinkled with cheese. Tangy seafood gumbo and creamy oyster stew have also gained fame for this casual, historic restaurant. Many celebrities have dined here, including Hollywood's Bob Hope and the former First Lady Rosalyn Carter.

Budget

BARNHILL'S MARKET STREET BUFFET, 431 Mary Esther Blvd. (County Rd. 393), opposite Santa Rosa Mall. Tel. 243-0091.

Cuisine: SOUTHERN. **Reservations:** Not accepted.
$ Prices (including tax and beverage): Lunch $5.30; dinner $6.90. Children 3–12 pay 40¢ times their age. No credit cards.
Open: Lunch daily 10:45am–4pm; dinner daily 4–9pm.

Like its counterparts in Pensacola, this Barnhill's branch extracts your cash as you enter, then turns you loose to attack seven bars piled high with country-style meats, seafood, vegetables, and desserts. General Robert E. Lee's Confederate troops would have loved the fried okra and collard greens boiled in fatback. Yankees will find something here too, for the baked ham and fried chicken and catfish are excellent buffet fare.

HOSER'S, 1225 Santa Rosa Blvd., Okaloosa Island. Tel. 664-6113.

Cuisine: AMERICAN. **Reservations:** Not accepted.
$ Prices: Sandwiches and snacks $2–$7; main courses $10–$12. AE, DISC, MC, V.
Open: Mon–Sat 11am–4am, Sun noon–4am.

For those who dreamed of being firefighters when they grew up, this lively pub in "Shanty Town" near the Brooks Bridge is filled to the brim with firefighting memorabilia, from boots to hats and hoses to hydrants. Naturally, one of the most popular dishes on the menu is Three Alarm Chili, a spicy secret recipe garnished with jalapeños and grated cheese. If your taste buds catch fire, douse the flame with any of 80 imported cold beers, including Thai Singha, Mexican Chihuahua, German Bitburger, and English Oatmeal Stout, to name just a few. Super-size hamburgers, stacked-high sandwiches, and other favorites are on the menu. Night owls love to roost at Hoser's, where the action is nonstop.

To get here from Fort Walton Beach, turn right at the first traffic light east of the Brooks Bridge, then make an immediate right onto the service road; make a U-turn under the bridge, then turn left on Santa Rosa Boulevard. Coming from Destin, simply turn right onto Santa Rosa.

MARY'S KITCHEN, 575D N. Beal Pkwy. (County Rd. 189), at Mary Esther Cutoff. Tel. 863-1141.

Cuisine: BARBECUE. **Reservations:** Not accepted.
$ Prices: Sandwiches and salads $2–$5; barbecue plates $5–$7. No credit cards.

Open: Mon–Fri 11am–8pm.

Off the beaten tourist track, Mary Jones's storefront eatery is famous in these parts for husband Ray's barbecue slowly smoked in a brick pit in the middle of the dining room. Ray's beef can be on the dry side, but his pork butts and ribs are absolutely first-rate. Ask for the spicy sauce on the side, then apply as little or as much as your taste buds can tolerate. Daily specials feature fried chicken, chopped steak, and veal parmesean served with a host of country-style vegetables. Mary's homemade pies are both huge and delicious.

UPPER CRUST, 14 Racetrack Rd. (County Rd. 188), near Mooney Rd., on the mainland. Tel. 863-2143.

    Cuisine: AMERICAN. **Reservations:** Recommended.

$ Prices: $3.50–$5.50. MC, V.

    Open: Lunch only, Mon–Fri 11am–2:30pm.

    Ann Streit and Jeanne Riley have one of Fort Walton Beach's most popular lunch spots at this scenic location on a hill overlooking the still waters of Don's Bayou. They offer huge sandwiches and salads, and their chicken crêpes served with a congealed-strawberry salad with pretzel crust will leave memories as fond as the view. Don't go away without a licking your chops over a piece of Ann's homemade chocolate velvet pie.

DESTIN

Moderate

AJ'S SEAFOOD & OYSTER BAR, 116 U.S. 98E, Destin Harbor. Tel. 837-1913.

    Cuisine: SEAFOOD. **Reservations:** Not accepted.

$ Prices: Appetizers $3.50–$8; main courses $9–$13. MC, V.

    Open: Daily 11am–10pm (later on weekends).

On the picturesque Destin Harbor docks, where fishing boats unload the daily catch, tiki-topped AJ's is popular for fried blue crab claws, spicy steamed shrimp, fried seafood in baskets, charcoal-grilled local fish (and chicken, too), steamed Dungeness crab, hearty fish and seafood sandwiches, delicious seafood salads, Cajun crayfish fettuccine, and seafood gumbo. Yes, you can get a charcoal-grilled hamburger here too, and even buffalo hot wings. For the kids, there's a special menu. On the second level, Club Bimini, under a thatched roof, is a great place to slake a thirst. Live entertainment spotlights reggae music and limbo contests.

THE BACK PORCH, 1740 County Rd. 2378 (Old U.S. 98E). Tel. 837-2022.

    Cuisine: SEAFOOD. **Reservations:** Not accepted.

$ Prices: Appetizers $4–$7; main courses $8–$15. AE, MC, V.

    Open: Daily 11am–11pm.

A cedar-shingled seafood shack with glorious beach views, this popular restaurant originated charcoal-grilled amberjack (a favorite local fish). Additional charcoal-grilled varieties of fish and seafood are now on the menu, also charcoal-grilled chicken and juicy hamburgers. Seafood lovers go for the Commodore's Dinner (softshell crab, shrimp, scallops, fish, clams, oysters) or the Beach Party appetizer basket (crab claws, shrimp, scallops, smoked fish dip, plus a cup of soup). Great sandwiches, salads, and veggie platters, too! And there's a children's menu. Beer, wine, and cocktails are served. A favorite frozen libation is the Key Lime Freeze, a drink that tastes like key lime pie (best when sipped watching the spectacular sunset).

    Both the Back Porch and Scampi's (see below) are near the western boundary of Henderson Beach State Recreation Area. Turn toward the beach at the traffic light at U.S. 98E and Airport Road.

CAPTAIN DAVE'S ON THE HARBOR, 314A U.S. 98, Destin Harbor. Tel. 837-6357.

    Cuisine: SEAFOOD. **Reservations:** Not accepted.

$ Prices: Appetizers $2–$9; main courses $10–$18. MC, V.

    Open: Dinner only, daily 4:30–10pm.

While the movie *Jaws II* was being filmed on the photogenic beaches in this area, Captain Dave's was a mealtime rendezvous for the actors and film crew. The fishing fleet docks at the restaurant so you can be assured of the freshest seafood. In addition to a variety of fish and crustaceans, prepared just the way you like it, prime rib and chicken are also on the menu. Captain Dave's Oar Oyster Bar is right next door, serving lunch daily from 10am to 3pm (oysters and clams are the big favorites).

HARBOR DOCKS, 538 U.S. 98E, Destin Harbor. Tel. 837-2506.
 Cuisine: SEAFOOD. **Reservations:** Not accepted.
 $ Prices: Appetizers $3–$8; main courses $11–$18; burgers $7.
 Open: Lunch/dinner daily 11:30am to late night.
You can't miss the three tiki-style thatched roofs of this casual restaurant, where harbor views are spectacular from indoors or outdoors. The splendid hand-carved wood-and-marble bar dates back to 1890. Luncheon specialties include Gulf Coast seafood gumbo, red beans and rice, fried triggerfish, charcoal-grilled amberjack sandwich, and big hamburgers. Appetizers on the dinner menu include smoked yellowfin tuna with mustard sauce and shrimp nachos. Favorite main courses are charcoal-grilled filet of cobia in a delicate dill sauce, broiled filet of grouper stuffed with crabmeat, grilled filet mignon, and charcoal-grilled marinated chicken breast. For the kids, there's a special menu. Everyone loves Annie's homemade pies for dessert. Live entertainment every night and different bands weekly keep the action going on the outdoor deck. Harbor Docks delivers menu items: Call 678-FOOD.

MARINA CAFE, on the second floor of the Destin Yacht Club, 320 U.S. 98E. Tel. 837-7960.
 Cuisine: ITALIAN/LOUISIANNE. **Reservations:** Recommended.
 $ Prices: Appetizers $6–$9; main courses $8–$24. AE, MC, V.
 Open: Dinner only, daily 5–10pm (later on weekends).
Overlooking the multi-million-dollar fleet of the prestigious Destin Yacht Club and appropriately one of the town's finest, the Marina Café provides a classy penthouse atmosphere with soft candlelight, subdued music, and formally attired waiters. It's so pleasant to dine on the outdoor balconied deck, or perhaps sip drinks and nibble on crisply fried calamari prior to dining indoors, where the window wall looks out to the shimmering waters. Pastas are prepared with a special flair, especially the fettuccine combined with andouille sausage, shrimp, crayfish tails, and a piquant tomato-cream sauce. Among the chef's creative dishes is tender triggerfish sautéed with artichoke hearts, tomatos, and tarragon. Grilled prime steaks, sautéed veal medallions, grilled chicken, and crisply roasted boneless duckling are favorites always. Two people can save half between 5 and 6pm, when one main course comes free with the purchase of another of equal or greater value.

SCAMPI'S, 1741 County Rd. 2378 (Old U.S. 98E). Tel. 837-7686.
 Cuisine: SEAFOOD. **Reservations:** Not accepted.
 $ Prices: Appetizers $3.50–$9. Main courses $7–$13; sandwiches and burgers $3.50–$6. AE, MC, V.
 Open: Dinner only, daily 4:30–9:30pm.
Constructed from the historic pilings of the old Destin Bridge, this two-level restaurant is especially popular for the bountiful seafood buffet (priced daily at market rates). From an entire amberjack, stuffed and baked, to Louisiana Cajun étoufée, this is a veritable fish and shellfish "groaning board." From the regular menu, you can begin with just-shucked oysters (or crayfish in season). The steaming hot bowl of piquant seafood gumbo is almost a meal in itself, accompanied by freshly baked French bread. Just about all your piscine preferences can be satisfied in this casual, friendly restaurant. The lengthy bar and cocktail lounge are a local rendezvous. For directions, see the Back Porch, above.

Budget

BUSTER'S OYSTER BAR AND SEAFOOD RESTAURANT, in Delchamps Plaza, on U.S. 98E one mile west of the Sandestin Beach Resort. Tel. 837-4399.
 Cuisine: SEAFOOD. **Reservations:** Not required.

$ Prices: Appetizers $3.50–$9; main courses $7–$13; sandwiches and burgers $3.50–$6. DISC, MC, V.
Open: Lunch/dinner daily 11am–9:30pm.

A local favorite, Buster's claims that more than two million oysters have been shucked here. A fun place, Buster's likes to add something outrageous to the menu, such as "a toasted sea spider sandwich" (actually a softshell crab). Kids enjoy the Playground Menu and the family atmosphere. Fish and seafood dinners are deliciously prepared to order—and try the award-winning seafood gumbo. Cocktails are served here, also.

CHAN'S MARKET CAFE, 5494 U.S. 98E, in the Market at the Sandestin Resort. Tel. 837-1334.
Cuisine: AMERICAN. **Reservations:** Not accepted.
$ Prices: Sandwiches and salads $4–$6; meals $5–$11. MC, V.
Open: Jan–Labor Day, daily 7am–9pm. Labor Day–Dec, daily 7am–6pm.

This red-and-black–accented café draws scores of families vacationing at the otherwise expensive Sandestin Resort because—as the management likes to boast—they can "eat without taking a second mortgage on the Mercedes." The wide array of offerings here include freshly baked croissants and bagels at breakfast or wrapped around deli sandwiches at lunch, charcoal-grilled chicken and burgers, and meals featuring amberjack or yellowfin tuna grilled over coals. Seating is both indoors and outside on a shaded veranda beside a pond filled with lilypads.

THE DONUT HOLE, 635 U.S. 98E, Destin. Tel. 837-8824.
Cuisine: AMERICAN. **Reservations:** Not accepted.
$ Prices: $3.50–$6. No credit cards.
Open: Daily 24 hours.

No matter what the hour, breakfast is a special treat in this rustic "hole-in-the-wall." Who could resist luscious freshly made doughnuts and crullers, hot-from-the-oven breads and muffins, light-as-a-feather pecan waffles, southern-style cheese grits, fluffy omelets, or rich eggs Benedict? And there's nothing like a real good cup of just-brewed hot coffee to go with these goodies. In addition to the great breakfasts, hearty sandwiches on bakery-fresh bread are served for lunch, and country-style dinners are the evening specials.

By popular demand, there's a Donut Hole II Café and Bakery, also on U.S. 98E, 2½ miles east of the Sandestin Beach Resort (tel. 267-3239), but open only from 6am to 7pm in winter, 6am to 8pm in summer.

HARRY T'S, 320 U.S. 98E, Destin Harbor. Tel. 654-6555.
Cuisine: AMERICAN. **Reservations:** Not required.
$ Prices: Appetizers $3–$8.50; main courses $8–$15; sandwiches and burgers $6–$8.
Open: Daily 4pm–2am (lunch served certain months—check ahead).

The family of big top trapeze artist "Flying Harry T" opened this casual restaurant to honor his memory. Standing guard is Stretch, Harry's beloved giraffe, now duly stuffed for posterity. Circus memorabilia adorns this fun place. Also note the interesting items from the luxury cruise ship *Thracia,* which sank off the Emerald Coast in 1927. Harry T personally led the heroic rescue of the more than 2,000 passengers, and was presented the ship's salvaged furnishings and fixtures. The menu offers such taste-tempters as Mexican chimichangas, Cajun-style burgers, blackened grouper sandwich, Harry's Boathouse Salad, charcoal-grilled pork chops, and buffalo wings (Harry was a Buffalo native so the recipe is authentic). Key lime pie and strawberry cheesecake are two favorite desserts.

SOUTH WALTON COUNTY
Moderate

BAYOU BILL'S CRAB HOUSE, U.S. 98 at Santa Rosa Beach, and on County Rd. 30A, three miles east of Seagrove Beach. Tel. 267-3849 and 231-1400.
Cuisine: SEAFOOD. **Reservations:** Not required.

$ Prices: Appetizers $3–$6.50; main courses $10–$16.50. MC, V.
Open: Dinner only, Tues–Sun 5–10pm.

At two locations, Bayou Bill's features nightly chalkboard specials with a variety of chowders, salads, sandwiches, smoked dishes, buckets of steamed garlic crabs, steamed shrimp, combination seafood buckets, and charcoal-grilled and fried fish. The sautéed-alligator appetizer is an interesting choice.

The Santa Rosa Beach location is notable for rustic, tropical decor plus outdoor dining in the Garden Room. At the Seagrove Beach location, nestled in native hardwood hammocks, the restaurant features a covered walkway, where local artisans ply their special crafts. Inside, the colorful 12-foot-wide crab-and-lobster mobile adds fun to the decor. You'll find the same interesting menus at both locations.

CRIOLLA'S, 1267 County Rd. 30A, a quarter mile east of County Rd. 283, Grayton Beach. Tel. 267-1267.
    Cuisine: LOUISIANA CREOLE/CARIBBEAN. **Reservations:** Recommended.
$ Prices: Appetizers $7–$9; main courses $16–$25. MC, V.
    Open: Apr–Sept, dinner only, Mon–Sat 6–10pm; Mar and Oct–Nov, dinner only, Tues–Sat 6–10pm; Feb, dinner only, Thurs–Sat 6–10pm. **Closed:** Dec–Jan.

One of Florida's Top 10 Golden Spoon Award winners, this charming restaurant derives its name from the archaic word *criollo*, signifying persons of pure Spanish descent born in the New World. The attractive decor, combining New Orleans atmosphere with the Caribbean, features enormous potted palms, whirling ceiling paddle fans, and tropical island paintings on the walls. Many fish dishes carry the wonderful aroma of smoke from a wood-fired grill. Jerk-rubbed tuna combines both that and spicy Jamaican seasonings. Top off your meal with homemade sweets and plantation coffee.

GOATFEATHERS, County Rd. 30A at County Rd. 393, Santa Rosa Beach. Tel. 267-1273.
    Cuisine: SEAFOOD. **Reservations:** Not accepted.
$ Prices: Appetizers $2.50–$12; main courses $7–$14. DISC, MC, V.
    Open: Thurs–Tues 11:30am–9pm.

This casual small restaurant, upstairs over a seafood market and decorated with nautical antiques, offers a raw bar and indoor and outdoor dining (the outside deck and bar are covered). The gulf views are absolutely gorgeous. Try the tasty deep-fried scallops wrapped in shrimp and bacon—something different. The popular seafood platters are heaped high with shrimp, scallops, local fish, oysters, and more. No need to dress up here—cover-ups and cutoffs are permitted.

NENA'S SEAFOOD RESTAURANT, Kreig Rd. (inland off U.S. 98), Santa Rosa Beach. Tel. 267-3663.
    Cuisine: STEAK/SEAFOOD. **Reservations:** Recommended.
$ Prices: Appetizers $2.50–$5; main courses $8–$19. MC, V.
    Open: Dinner only, daily 5–9:30pm.

A romantic atmosphere prevails in this shingle-sided, tin-roofed restaurant, enhanced by a large fireplace and luxuriant plants in pretty clay pots. Nena is rightfully proud of her reputation for serving superior steaks, tender veal, and the freshest of seafood. Nena bakes her own tasty breads and tempting pies daily. The New York and Hollywood expression for complimenting food, "It's to die for," describes the irresistible Nena's Millionaire Pie, a luscious blending of pecans, chocolate, and caramel topped with rich ice cream. In one word, it's yummy.

SHOPPING

FORT WALTON BEACH   A free tram runs between the two branches of **Manufacturer's Outlet Center,** at 127 and 255 Miracle Strip Pkwy. (U.S. 98) near the mainland end of Brooks Bridge. Individual shops knock 30% to 50% off the prices of Levi's jeans, Jerzees and Russell athletic wear, Polly Flinders dresses, Bass shoes, and more. The city's main suburban shopping center is the **Santa Rosa Mall** (tel. 244-2172) on Mary Esther Cutoff (County Road 393), about three blocks north of Miracle Strip Parkway (U.S. 98) and three miles west of Brooks Bridge.

DESTIN   At the Sandestin Beach Resort on U.S. 98E, **The Market at Sandestin** features 28 upscale shops carrying elegant but casual clothing, jewelry, shoes, accessories, and keepsakes. There's even a Godiva Chocolates shop. Nearby on U.S. 98E, shops in the **Silver Sands Factory Stores** offer substantial discounts on upmarket designer fashions by such notables as Anne Klein, Donna Karan, J.Crew, and Jones New York.

EVENING ENTERTAINMENT
THE PERFORMING ARTS

The area is proud of its **Okaloosa Symphony Orchestra,** the **Stage Crafters Community Theater,** and the ballet and choral groups. Presentations are scheduled mostly in the winter months. Contact the individual beach chambers of commerce or inquire at your hotel for the current programs.

THE CLUB, MUSIC & BAR SCENE

Most resorts spotlight live entertainment during the summer season, including the Ramada Beach Resort, the Sandestin Beach Resort, the Sandestin Hilton, and the Seascape. It's a good idea to inquire ahead to make sure entertainment is scheduled when you plan to be at a particular lounge or restaurant, especially during the off-season months when things noticeably slow down at the beaches.

FORT WALTON BEACH   Country music and dancing fans will find a home at the **Seagull Restaurant and Lounge,** 1201 Miracle Strip Pkwy., virtually under the Brooks Bridge on Okaloosa Island (tel. 243-3413). Affectionately known as "The Dirty Bird" to generations of air force vets, the lounge here is often packed on Friday and Saturday nights when live bands play down-on-your-luck, tear-dropping tunes.

The young beach set is attracted to rock 'n' roll and reggae at two lively pubs in "Shanty Town" on the other Okaloosa Island side of Brooks Bridge: the **Hog's Breath Saloon,** 1230 Seibert St. (tel. 244-2199), and the neighboring **Hoser's,** 1225 Santa Rosa Blvd. (tel. 664-6113). Whichever has a live band draws the crowd. Shanty Town has been known to roar throughout many a summer night.

DESTIN   A terrific dance club, a rowdy saloon, and a Jimmy Buffet–style reggae bar are all under one roof at the acclaimed **Nightown,** 140 Palmetto St. (tel. 837-6448), near the harbor. The dockside **AJ's Club Bimini,** 116 U.S. 98E (tel. 837-1913), offers lots of live reggae on weekend nights. **Fish Heads,** 414 U.S. 98E (tel. 837-4848), features the Big Red Snapper, a lethal mixture of rum, vodka, and more. A somewhat older if not more sober crowd gathers at **The Deck,** on U.S. 98E at Harbor Docks, overlooking the harbor (tel. 837-2506). For a much more low-key evening, the Piano Bar at the **Marina Cafe,** in the Destin Yacht Club, 320 U.S. 98E (tel. 837-7960), is a popular rendezvous Wednesday through Saturday.

Out toward Sandestin, **Fudpucker's Beachside Bar & Grill,** 20001 U.S. 98E (tel. 654-4200), offers double the fun with two summertime stages, one on the bayside deck, the other in the Down Under Bar. There's another Fudpucker's at 108 Santa Rosa Blvd. on Okaloosa Island in Fort Walton Beach (tel. 243-3833).

EASY EXCURSIONS
SEASIDE

Less than a half hour's scenic coastal drive east of Destin (via County Road 30A), Seaside is one of the world's most beautiful beach towns, described as a "Downhome Utopia" by *Time* magazine, and "extraordinary" by Britain's Prince Charles. The American Institute of Architects has designated Seaside as one of the decade's top architectural masterplans because of its combination of creative architecture, urban planning, and ecological cooperation with Mother Nature. Yet despite its world fame, Seaside retains a slow-paced lifestyle beside its long stretch of gorgeous beach.

Built in the early 1980s on 80 acres of beach property, Seaside is inspired by Victoriana. Every individually designed home is painted in pastel sunrise colors and adorned with an old-fashioned porch, gazebo, and garden. Charming beach pavilions are gateways to the superb white sands splashed by the gulf's emerald waters. In addition to a Mediterranean-style open market, the village of Seaside is notable for interesting shops, fine art galleries, delightful restaurants, small hotels, and a postcard-size post office.

Seaside provides a memorable day trip, but should you wish to stay longer, fabulous homes and cottages may be rented by the day, week, or month and include the use of Seaside's swimming pool, tennis courts, croquet lawn, and more. Since Seaside was planned specifically for strolling around in the old-fashioned way, without a car, the village is a delight to explore on foot, or you may want to rent a bike from **Seaside Bike Rentals** at the Deck Pool, at the north end of Seaside Avenue. They cost $4 an hour or $15 a day.

Seaside also offers an eclectic schedule of **special events** throughout the year. In the Seaside Meeting Hall, the free architectural lectures are fascinating (tel. 231-4224 for information). In April, merchants usually sponsor a food, wine, and music festival, and there are always special Easter weekend activities. July 4th is celebrated with old-fashioned parades and fireworks. During September's concert series, international performers are in the spotlight. The Annual Wine-Jazz Festival is an October event. During the holiday season, Seaside is an extravaganza of Christmas lights. For information about Seaside's events and the current schedule, call 231-4224.

Where to Stay

JOSEPHINE'S BED & BREAKFAST, 101 Seaside Ave., Seaside, FL 32459. Tel. 904/231-1940, or toll free 800/848-1840. Fax 904/231-4196. 7 rms, 2 suites. A/C TEL TV

$ Rates (including gourmet breakfast): $120–$200 unit for two. Weekly rates available. MC, V.

Reminiscent of an elegant Virginia inn with its six large Tuscan columns framing the front entrance, Josephine's recalls the romantic Old South with mahogany four-poster beds, Battenburg lace comforters, rich furnishings, and fancy bathrooms with marble bathtubs; most guest rooms also have fireplaces. Enjoy your sumptuous breakfast beside the fireplace or on your private veranda or in the gracious dining room. It's nice to have some modern conveniences too, such as a wet bar, microwave, coffee maker, and small refrigerator neatly designed so as not to conflict with the nostalgic charm. Guest rooms are named for southern flowers: Peony, Marigold, Amaryllis, Lily, Narcissus, Chrysanthemum, Hibiscus. The Guest House offers two suites: Rose on the first floor and Dianthus upstairs with a gulf view (perfect for a honeymoon). Each lovely suite includes a living room, dining room, master bedroom with fireplace, kitchen, and full bath. Josephine's beautiful dining room is open to the public for dinner, by reservation only.

SEASIDE MOTOR COURT, County Rd. 30A, Seaside, FL 32459. Tel. 904/231-1320. Fax 904/231-5680. 6 rms. A/C TV TEL

$ Rates: $115–$210 double. MC, V.

Reminiscent of the one-story motels of the 1940s, the Seaside has standard rooms furnished with the tasteful Seaside designer decor. However, don't expect the usual porches and furbelows of Seaside's architecture. The motel rooms are perfect for staying overnight at an excellent rate for Seaside. The more expensive units have a kitchen and separate bedroom.

Long-Term Rentals

Whether you want to rent a beautifully furnished home or a hideaway cottage, contact the **Seaside Cottage Rental Agency,** P.O. Box 4730, Seaside, FL 32459 (tel. 904/231-1320, or toll free 800/635-0296). During the peak summer season, a three-day or one-week minimum stay may be required.

Where to Dine

Snacks are available in Seaside Town Square & Markets, which you can't miss as you enter the village on County Road 30A. **Sip & Dip** serves hearty sandwiches, freshly squeezed lemonade, and rich ice cream. **Dawson's Yogurt** serves it frozen atop homemade cones. Across the road in the beachside shops, the **Silver Bullet** offers ice cream and snacks.

BASMATI'S, at the Seaside Motor Court, County Rd. 30A. Tel. 231-1366.
Cuisine: ASIAN. **Reservations:** Recommended.
$ Prices: Appetizers $3.50–$9; main courses $12–$19. No credit cards.
Open: Dinner only, Thurs–Tues 5:30–10pm.
The cozy restaurant is owned by Charles Bush and his wife, Shueh Mei Pong. She is the talented chef and the cuisine reflects her Thai heritage. Among the specialties are honey-roasted duckling, piquantly spiced beef wrapped in Chinese pancakes, and curried chicken. Veggies Asian style take on new life. The house drink is an interesting blend of sake and plum wine. Or try the refreshing exotic juices, such as mango, papaya, and guava. Asian beers, such as Asahi and Tsing Tao, are also served. Since the restaurant seats only 22, a few outdoor tables are added in warm weather.

BUD AND ALLEY'S, on the beach at Seaside. Tel. 231-5000.
Cuisine: MEDITERRANEAN. **Reservations:** Recommended.
$ Prices: Appetizers $7–$10; main courses $14–$24. AE, MC, V.
Open: Lunch Wed–Mon 11:30am–3pm; dinner Sun–Thurs 6–10pm, Fri–Sat 6–9:30pm.
Still Number One to the steady patrons, this was Seaside's very first restaurant. The freshest of seafoods can be selected from the raw bar. Delicious pastas are a specialty, as well as osso buco and the crostini of chopped chicken livers combined with onion confit. You can dine indoors or outdoors on the screened veranda, where you hear the waves splashing against the white sands. Usually on weekends, jazz is in the spotlight. On New Year's Eve, everyone in town and from miles around celebrates in Bud and Alley's. No smoking is permitted.

JOSEPHINE'S DINING ROOM, 101 Seaside Ave. Tel. 231-1939.
Cuisine: GOURMET SOUTHERN/FRENCH. **Reservations:** Required.
$ Prices: Appetizers $4.50–$8; main courses $17–$22. MC, V.
Open: Dinner only, Wed–Sun 5:30–9:30pm.
In this southern plantation-style dining room in Josephine's Bed & Breakfast, with rich mahogany furniture and a wealth of period accoutrements, the stage is set for a romantic dinner. Glowing with candlelight, the intimate room seats only 20 people. Josephine's Maryland-style crab cakes are consistently delicious. Rhett Butler and Scarlett O'Hara would fall in love again if they dined here.

SHADE'S, Seaside Town Square & Markets, Seaside. Tel. 231-1950.
Cuisine: AMERICAN. **Reservations:** Not required.
$ Prices: Appetizers $2–$7; main courses $12–$16; sandwiches and burgers $4.50–$9. MC, V.
Open: Lunch/dinner Mon–Sat 11am–9pm, Sun 11am–3pm.
In another life, this was a rustic house built around the early 1900s in the small town of Chattahoochee. Over 70 years later the house was moved to Seaside's Town Square to be born again as quaint Shade's restaurant. Stacked-high sandwiches are popular for lunch and there are wings and hamburgers, too. At dinner, the bountiful fried seafood platter is a big favorite. In addition to reasonable prices, the service is very friendly.

DEFUNIAK SPRINGS

Noted for its well-preserved Victorian homes encircling a round, 60-foot-deep lake, DeFuniak Springs makes for an interesting sightseeing excursion from either the Fort Walton Beach or Panama City area. Founded in 1882 when the L&N Railroad built a station at the lake, the little town (pop. 5,100) came to prominence a few years later when the Chautauqua Society of New York decided to make its winter home here,

Built of clapboard in 1909, the impressively domed and columned **Chautauqua Auditorium** still overlooks the lake, as does the tiny building that houses **Florida's oldest library.** In addition to its books, the library holds a fascinating collection of medieval weapons and armor.

The town is still a hotbed of cultural activities, highlighted by the annual **Chautauqua Festival,** usually in late April, featuring sports activities, arts and crafts, and fireworks. On the first weekend in December, townsfolk are joined by visitors from all over to don period costumes at the annual **Victorian Ball,** which is accompanied by a homes tour earlier in the day.

GETTING THERE   From the beaches, take U.S. 331 about 35 miles north. Look for the HISTORIC DISTRICT sign about 2 miles north of I-10 and follow it along Live Oak Avenue to Circle Drive, which, appropriately, circles the lake. Main Street, the old train station, and the town's business district lie on the lake's north shore.

INFORMATION   Stop in at the **Walton County Chamber of Commerce,** in the Chautauqua Auditorium on the lakeshore (P.O. Box 29), DeFuniak Springs, FL 32433 (tel. 904/892-3191), for maps and booklets for self-guided tours, plus other useful information such as a list of local shops and antique dealers. The staff will know when the Chautauqua Festival, Victorian Ball, and other events are scheduled.

GUIDED TOURS   For a personalized guided tour, contact **Dianne Pickett** at the Chautauqua Shops and Welcome Center, 66 E. Nelson St. (U.S. 90), east of the junction with U.S. 331 on the north side of the lake, or call her at 904/892-5583. The shop is a cooperative effort by five local artists including Nell Baker, who is known for her handcrafted porcelain dolls.

For a horse-drawn historic tour, contact **Victorian Carriages, Inc.,** P.O. Box 49, DeFuniak Springs, FL 32433 (tel. 904/892-0226), at least a day in advance.

Where to Stay

Two of the historic district homes are now interesting bed-and-breakfast inns: John and Tricia Rauch's **Live Oaks Bed & Breakfast,** 405 Live Oak Ave., DeFuniak Springs, FL 32433 (tel. 904/892-0849); and John and Byrdie Mitchell's **Sunbright Manor,** 606 Live Oak Ave., DeFuniak Springs, FL 32433 (tel. 904/892-0656). In addition, there's a **Comfort Inn** (tel. 904/892-1333, or toll free 800/228-5050) and an **Econo Lodge** (tel. 904/892-6115, or toll free 800/553-2666) on U.S. 331 at the intersection with I-10, two miles south of the historic district.

Where to Dine

Among the friendly, small-town restaurants to choose from are **Mom & Dad's Italian Restaurant,** on U.S. 90 W. (tel. 892-5812), a relative of the very good Mom & Dad's in Tallahassee; **Mia's Cafe & Gourmet Market,** which overlooks the lake from Baldwin Avenue (tel. 892-6427); and **Edie's Cafe,** on North 9th Street (tel. 892-4847), which is open for lunch Monday through Friday from 11am to 2pm.

NEARBY ATTRACTIONS   Anyone interested in wines will enjoy a visit to **Chautauqua Vineyards,** at I-10 and U.S. 331 (tel. 892-5887), for free tours and wine tastings Monday through Saturday from 9am to 5pm and on Sunday from noon to 5pm. About 10 miles east of DeFuniak Springs via I-10, **Ponce de Leon State Recreation Area** includes the very deep Vortex Springs, site of a swimming beach, campground, lodge, and Florida's largest freshwater scuba-diving operation. For information, contact Vortex Spring, Inc., Rt. 2, Box 650, Ponce de Leon, FL 32455 (tel. 904/836-4979).

3. PANAMA CITY & PANAMA CITY BEACH

100 miles E of Pensacola, 100 miles SW of Tallahassee

GETTING THERE   By Plane   Delta Connection, Northwest Airlink, and

USAir Express commuter planes fly into the **Panama City/Bay County Regional Airport,** on Airport Road, north of St. Andrews Boulevard, (tel. 904/763-6751).

By Train Amtrak's *Sunset Limited* transcontinental service stops at Chipley, 45 miles north of Panama City. For Amtrak information, call toll free 800/USA-RAIL.

By Bus The Greyhound depot is located at 917 Harrison Ave. (tel. 904/785-7861 in Panama City, or toll free 800/231-2222).

By Car Interstate 10 runs east-west, 45 miles to the north. From I-10, take U.S. 231 or Fla. 77 south. U.S. 98, the gulf-hugging east-west artery, runs through both Panama City and Panama City Beach.

Centuries ago, Native Americans lived in this remarkably beautiful coastal area. In the 16th century, Spanish conquistadors sailed from the Gulf of Mexico directly into St. Andrews Bay and what is now Panama City, but their obsession for gold was not fulfilled here. Impressed by the strategic harbor, the British founded the first settlement at Panama City in 1765. During most of the ensuing centuries, Panama City was considered just a sleepy fishing village. How times have changed! Now this thriving city is one of the state's leading ports and an industrial center. Since boating and charter-boat fishing are favorite sports, the attractive city is fringed by a civic center and a 400-slip marina located where Harrison Avenue culminates at St. Andrews Bay.

For many years, Panama City Beach has attracted moderate-income vacationers from nearby southern states (at one time it was affectionately known as "The Redneck Riviera"). But now vacationers from every economic stratum and from around the nation flock to the miles of brilliant white sand beaches, splashed by the jewel-green gulf waters. Panama City Beach has also been compared to New York's Coney Island because of the razzle-dazzle amusement parks, with screaming crowds on the wild roller coasters. For vacationers who prefer lots of action, this is the liveliest vacation destination in Northwest Florida—and the most crowded, especially in summer.

The long, super-wide beach, rated among the nation's best, is notable for unbelievably white, soft sands attributable to a special variety of quartz washed down from the Appalachian Mountains, which has become very finely ground and polished through the centuries. There's exciting surf too, caused by offshore formations. The same phenomena have encouraged the abundant growth of exotic marine life, especially along the gulf's natural sand-bar system only a few miles offshore, which is excellent for snorkeling, spearfishing, lobstering, and shelling. And with many sunken wrecks, the gulf attracts many scuba divers.

Both Panama City and Panama City Beach radiate a very friendly, casual atmosphere. The southern hospitality is infectious, and the reasonable prices at many hotels, motels, and restaurants appeal to families. Newer, luxurious resorts, wonderful seafood, the sports activities, and fabulous beaches bring more and more vacationers and honeymooners to "discover" this lively area.

ORIENTATION

INFORMATION The **James I. Lark, Sr., Visitors Information Center,** 12015 Front Beach Rd., Panama City Beach, FL 32407 (tel. 904/234-3193), sits right on the beach across from Miracle Strip Park and provides recommendations on accommodations, restaurants, and attractions in Panama City Beach. The visitor information center is affiliated with the Panama City Beaches Chamber of Commerce (same address; same telephone number). Information is also supplied in advance by the **Panama City Beach Convention & Visitors Bureau,** 415 Beckrich Rd., Suite 205 (P.O. Box 9473), Panama City Beach, FL 32407 (tel. 904/233-6503, or toll free 800/PC-BEACH).

The **Bay County Chamber of Commerce** offers assistance to tourists interested in Panama City and is located at 235 W. 5th St., Panama City, FL 32407 (tel. 904/785-5206).

AREA LAYOUT   This is a land of peninsulas. On the mainland proper, Panama City sits on a broad peninsula hemmed by St. Andrews and East Bays to the south, and by West and North Bays in their respective directions. Along the coast, two long, narrow arms—along with skinny Shell Island between them—reach out like pincers to protect the city and its bays from the Gulf of Mexico. Tyndall Air Force Base claims all of the eastward peninsula, while Panama City Beach occupies the one to the west. The Panama City Beach arm is itself divided into two peninsulas by Grand Lagoon, which separates Bay Point and the Marriott from the resort area.

Panama City   U.S. 98 follows 15th Street through Panama City, although the main shopping strip is along **23rd Street** (County Road 368). To reach the St. Andrews Marina area, take Beck Avenue south from 15th or 23rd Street. For downtown, follow **Harrison Avenue** south to the waterfront.

   U.S. 98A (also called Business 98) is a scenic delight as it follows Beck Avenue, 9th Street, and the gorgeous Beach Drive along the waterfront from the Hathaway Bridge to downtown. The city's major north-south routes are **Harrison Avenue** and **Cove Avenue** (Fla. 77). The latter becomes Ohio Avenue in Lynn Haven before crossing the North Bay Bridge.

Panama City Beach   Panama City Beach forms an almost unbroken, 20-mile-long chain of hotels, motels, condos, cottages, restaurants, shops, and amusement parks along the gulf. From the west, U.S. 98 splits in two at the western end of the beaches. The north fork becomes the inland **Back Beach Road** (U.S. 98), the fastest route to the Hathaway Bridge linking Panama City Beach to Panama City. The south fork becomes **Front Beach Road** (U.S. 98A), which skirts the gulf shore through the resort area until turning inland and rejoining U.S. 98 just west of the Hathaway Bridge. **Middle Beach Road** (County Road 392) runs between these two arms of U.S. 98.

   On the eastern end of the beach, **Thomas Drive** (also County Road 392) loops south from the Front Beach/Back Beach intersection near Hathaway Bridge to St. Andrews State Recreation Area on the peninsula's point, then westward along the beach until intersecting Front Beach Road. Accordingly, **Front Beach Road** and Thomas Drive form the main drag along entire length of Panama City Beach. During the summer months, traffic often comes to a standstill on this busy route, so take Back Beach or Middle Beach Roads to get anywhere quickly. There are 14 crossing streets linking Back Beach, Middle Beach, and Front Beach Roads.

   Street numbers in Panama City Beach get higher—into the thousands—as you go west. When seeking directions, be sure to ask for the nearest cross street.

Maps   Detailed maps are available at **Alvin's Island Tropical Department Store,** 12010 Front Beach Rd. (opposite the James I. Lark, Sr., Visitors Information Center on Panama City Beach), and at the large Wal-Mart at the intersection of Back Beach Road, Front Beach Road, and Thomas Drive (near the beach end of Hathaway Bridge).

GETTING AROUND

BY TAXI   Call **Yellow Cab** (tel. 763-4691), which charges by the zone (rates vary).

BY RENTAL CAR   Rental-car agencies include **Avis** (tel. toll free 800/227-2847), **Budget** (tel. toll free 800/527-0700), **Hertz** (tel. toll free 800/654-3131), and **National** (tel. toll free 800/227-7368), all of which have booths in the Panama City/Bay County Regional Airport terminal.

FAST FACTS

Area Code   The telephone area code for the Panama City area is 904.
Doctor   To see a doctor, go to the Bay Walk-In Clinic, at 8811 Front Beach Rd.

(tel. 234-8511) on the beach, or at the corner of 23rd Street and Fla. 77 in Panama City (tel. 763-9744).

Tax   In addition to the 6% statewide sales tax, the local governments add a 2% tax to all hotel and restaurant bills.

Time   The Panama City area is in the central time zone, one hour behind Miami and Orlando.

WHAT TO SEE & DO

ATTRACTIONS

Museums

JUNIOR MUSEUM OF BAY COUNTY, 1731 Jenks Ave., at Airport Rd., Panama City. Tel. 769-6128.

An educational experience for young people and adults too, the museum displays Native American artifacts from nearby archeological digs (a life-size teepee can be explored, too). A re-created 1880s farm where chickens and ducks can be fed by visitors, a Nature Trail meandering through three Northwest Florida–type environments, puppet shows, science exhibits, concerts, and more offer a variety of interests for the entire family.

Admission: $1 donation.

Open: Tues–Fri 9am–4:30pm, Sat 10am–4pm. **Closed:** New Year's Day, July 4, Labor Day, Thanksgiving, and Christmas Day. Check ahead for special exhibits.

MUSEUM OF MAN IN THE SEA, 17314 Back Beach Rd., west of Fla. 79, Panama City Beach. Tel. 235-4101.

Owned by the Institute of Diving, this unusual museum exhibits relics from the first days of scuba diving, historical displays of the underwater world (dating back to 1500), and treasures recovered from shipwrecks, including artifacts from the Spanish galleon *Atocha* (a 25-minute video shows Mel Fisher discovering the *Atocha*). Visitors learn about marine life sciences, astronauts' training underwater, oceanography, and underwater archeology, and much more. Kids will enjoy climbing through a submarine and handling live sea life in a hands-on pool.

Admission: $4 adults, $2 children 6–16, free for kids under 6.

Open: Daily 9am–5pm. **Closed:** New Year's Day, Thanksgiving, and Christmas Day.

Amusement Parks

MIRACLE STRIP AMUSEMENT PARK, 12000 Front Beach Rd., at Alf Coleman Rd., Panama City Beach. Tel. 234-5810.

The exciting roller coaster, towering up to 200 feet high, defies the laws of gravity on the thrilling downward trip. This is just one of the 30 rides in the park. If you dare, ride the 40-foot-high Sea Dragon, designed like a Viking ship, which rocks passengers up to 70 feet in the air. Little ones love the traditional carousel. Marvelous at night, when everything is gaudily illuminated, this landmark amusement park is one of Florida's top 10 attractions. Nine acres of fun include nonstop entertainment and snackery with great junk food.

Admission (including all rides): Less than $20 adults, less than $15 children under 11. (You may pay a gate admission and buy a coupon rides booklet, but not that much is saved.)

Open: June–Labor Day, Mon–Fri 5–11:30pm, Sat–Sun 1–11:30pm; mid-Mar to May, Sat–Sun 1–11:30pm. **Closed:** Labor Day to mid-Mar.

SHIPWRECK ISLAND WATER PARK, 12000 Front Beach Rd., at Alf Coleman Rd., Panama City Beach. Tel. 234-0368.

Encompassing six landscaped acres of water rides and picnic areas, Shipwreck Island Water Park features the 1,600-foot winding Lazy River for tubing and the daring 35-m.p.h. Speed Slide. For adventure, try the Rapid River Cascades or the White Water Tube Trip. From young children to adults, there's a variety of fun things to enjoy in the water. Lounge chairs, umbrellas, and inner tubes are free, and a lifeguard is on duty.

Admission (including all rides): Less than $15 adults, around $11 children under 10.

Open: Apr–Sept, daily 10:30am–6pm. **Closed:** Oct–Mar.

More Attractions

GULF WORLD, 15412 Front Beach Rd., at Hill Ave., Panama City Beach. Tel. 234-5271.

This landscaped tropical garden marine showcase spotlights shows with talented porpoises, sea lions, penguins, and more. Not to be upstaged, parrots perform daily, too. Sea turtles, alligators, ducks, and other critters call Gulf World home. Scuba demonstrations, shark feeding, and underwater shows keep the crowds entertained.

Admission: $14 adults, $8 children 5–12, free for kids under 5.

Open: Summer, daily 9am–7pm.

ST. ANDREWS STATE RECREATION AREA, 4415 Thomas Dr., at the east end of Panama City Beach. Tel. 233-5140.

With more than 1,000 acres of dazzling white sand, topped by sand dunes that look like snowdrifts, this is beachcombers' heaven. Lacy, golden sea oats sway in the refreshing gulf breezes. Fragrant rosemary grows wild on the more inland dunes near pine-tree woodland. Picnicking is delightful on either the gulf beach or the Grand Lagoon. Showers are conveniently located to refresh yourself after a swim. For anglers, there are two fishing piers, jetties, and a boat ramp. Along the Nature Trail, it's fun to watch the wading birds and perhaps sight an alligator or two. Overnight camping is permitted. Take a look at the historic turpentine still on display; it was formerly utilized by lumbermen, who drew resin from the pine trees, then brewed it in the still to make turpentine and also rosin, important for caulking the old wooden ships.

Admission: $3.25 per car (maximum of eight people).

Open: Daily 8am–sunset.

ZOO WORLD ZOOLOGICAL & BOTANICAL PARK, 9008 Front Beach Rd., at Moylan Dr., Panama City Beach. Tel. 230-0096.

More than 100 species of animals live in re-created natural habitats. An active participant in the Species Survival Plan (SSP), which helps protect the world's endangered species with specific breeding and housing programs, Zoo World has many rare and endangered animals. Orangutans and other primates, big cats, reptiles, and other creatures provide an educational and entertaining experience here. Also included are a walk-through aviary and a petting zoo.

Admission: $9 adult, $8 senior, $6.50 children 3–11, free for kids under 3.

Open: Daily 9am–sunset.

A Day Trip to Shell Island

Accessible by boat only, Shell Island is a 7½-mile-long, 1-mile-wide barrier island off the coast of St. Andrews State Recreation Area. The uninhabited natural preserve is great for shelling, and also fun for swimming, suntanning, or just relaxing. Several cruise boats offer day-trip excursions to Shell Island from Panama City Beach marinas. Among the most popular are the *Capt. Anderson III* and the *Florida Queen,* both sailing from **Capt. Anderson's Marina,** 5500 N. Lagoon Dr., at Thomas Drive (tel. 234-3435). The *Island Queen* paddle wheeler departs from the pier at Marriott's Bay Point Resort, 4200 Marriott Dr., off Jan Cooley Road (tel. 234-3307, ext. 1816). The *Island Star* and *Island Runner* (tel. 235-2809) both leave from Hathaway Marina, on U.S. 98 at the west end of Hathaway Bridge. Costs range from $8 to $10 for adults, half that for children. Times vary by season and reservations are required, so call ahead.

SPECIAL EVENTS

The annual **Gulf Coast Offshore Powerboat Races** at St. Andrews Marina are the main event in April. In late June, the **Annual Ladies Billfish Tournament** is held at Bay Point Marina. The weekend after July 4, the **Bay Point Billfish Invitational** is one of the nation's most prestigious ($300,000 in cash prizes!).

Mid-September begins the **Annual Panama City Beach Fishing Classic,** which continues to the end of September; the annual **Treasure Island King Mackerel Tournament,** at Treasure Island Marina, is a late September event.

The annual **Indian Summer Seafood Festival,** in Panama City Beach, takes place in Aaron Z. Bessant Wayside Park (across from the Dan Russell Fishing Pier). Celebrated the second week of October, this is one of the South's top events, with continuous entertainment by famous performers, an amazing abundance of seafood to enjoy, and at least 100 arts and crafts vendors.

Important golf tournaments and sports competitions are also on the schedule. For current information, contact the visitors information center (tel. 234-3193).

In nearby Marianna, an important **Civil War battle** fought there in 1864 is reenacted, usually annually in October. For information, call 904/482-8061. From Panama City, take U.S. 231 north and follow the signs to Marianna.

SPORTS & RECREATION

The **Panama City Parks and Recreation Department** (tel. 872-3005) sponsors 20 tennis courts, 12 nature parks, and several community centers (including Noah's Ark, for activities-oriented senior citizen vacationers). Call for current information about these very inexpensive or free city-operated places.

BOAT RENTALS A variety of rental boats are available at the marinas near the Thomas Drive bridge over Grand Lagoon. These include the **Capt. Davis Queen Fleet,** based at Capt. Anderson's Marina, 5500 N. Lagoon Dr. (tel. 234-3435, or toll free 800/874-2415 from nearby states); the **Panama City Boat Yard,** 5323 N. Lagoon Dr. (tel. 234-3386); the **Passport Marina,** 5325 N. Lagoon Dr. (tel. 234-5609); the **Port Lagoon Yacht Basin,** 5201 N. Lagoon Dr. (tel. 234-0142); **Pirates Cove Marina,** 3901 Thomas Dr. (tel. 234-3839); and the **Treasure Island Marina,** 3605 Thomas Dr. (tel. 234-6533).

CRUISES The **Capt. Davis Queen Fleet,** based at Capt. Anderson's Marina, 5500 N. Lagoon Dr. (tel. 234-3435, or toll free 800/874-2415 from neighboring states), has daily sightseeing trips, including popular dolphin- and bird-feeding excursions, and dinner-dance cruises during the summer season. So do the **Island Star** and the **Island Runner** (tel. 235-2809), both at the Hathaway Marina on U.S. 98 at the west end of Hathaway Bridge. The **Glass Bottom Boat** (tel. 234-8944) offers underwater viewing cruises from the Treasure Island Marina, 3605 Thomas Dr., at Grand Lagoon.

The **Hydrospace Dive Shop,** also at the Treasure Island Marina (tel. 234-9436), takes snorkelers on three-hour boat excursions to the grass flats of Shell Island. The trips includes dolphin-viewing when porpoises are present.

DOG RACING You can bet on the puppies at **Erbo Greyhound Park,** on Fla. 20 west of Fla. 79 at Erbo, a 30-minute drive north of Panama City Beach. The track provides exciting live greyhound racing at 7:30pm daily from June through August, and Wednesday through Monday during March, April, May, and September. Saturday matinees start at 1pm from March through September; Wednesday matinees begin at 1pm during March, April, July, and August. The rest of the year, you can wager on races simulcast from other courses. General admission is $1. Children are welcome if accompanied by an adult. Snacks are available at trackside, and a dining room opens at 6pm. In the beach area, call 234-3943 for information, or 234-0500 for reservations.

FISHING Close to a quarter million visitors come just to fish in the bountiful waters for Spanish mackerel, flounder, redfish, bonito, sea trout, bluefish, amberjack, sailfish, marlin, and many more. Panama City Beach boasts three fishing piers—the **Dan Russell Municipal Pier** is the longest, stretching 1,642 feet into the gulf.

From March through November, charter-fishing-boat trips depart daily for trips of 4 to 12 hours (the longer the trip, the larger total catch and bigger the fish). A deep-sea fishing boat fleet operates from the **Capt. Anderson's Marina,** 5500 N. Lagoon

Dr., at Thomas Drive (tel. 234-3435). Charter-fishing boats are operated also from **Treasure Island Marina,** 3605 Thomas Dr. (tel. 234-6533).

GOLF   Thirty-six holes of championship golf are offered at **Marriott's Bay Point Resort,** 4200 Marriott Dr., off Jan Cooley Road, in Panama City Beach (tel. 234-3307), where the "Lagoon Legend" course challenges with "monster hazards." Greens fees range from $45 to $75, depending on the season and day of the week. Or tee off at the **Holiday Golf Course and Country Club,** 100 Fairway Blvd., Panama City Beach (tel. 234-1800), an 18-hole, par-72 course; **The Hombre,** 120 Coyote Pass, Panama City Beach (tel. 234-3573), where the 18-hole course is a venue for golf tournaments; the very flat **Signal Hill,** 9516 N. Thomas Dr., Panama City Beach (tel. 234-3218); or the **Edgewater Beach Resort,** 11212 U.S. 98A (tel. 235-4044). Reservations for tee times are recommended.

MINIATURE GOLF   A host of minigolf courses offer a fantasy of waterfalls, luxuriant landscaping, and such themes as pirate ships, jungle adventures, and medieval castles. Among those to choose from as you head west along Front Beach Road are **Pirate's Island Adventure Golf** (tel. 230-9900), **Coconut Creek Mini-Golf & Grand Maze** (tel. 234-2625), **Barnacle Bay** (tel. 234-7792), **Goofy Golf** (tel. 234-6403), **Hidden Lagoon Super Golf** (tel. 234-9289), and **Zoo-Land Carpet Golf** (tel. 234-3084). Hours and prices change with the seasons, so call ahead.

SCUBA DIVING & SNORKELING   Although the area is too far north for extensive coral formations, more than 50 artificial reefs and shipwrecks in the gulf waters off Panama City attract a wide variety of sealife. The **Hydrospace Dive Shop,** 3605 Thomas Dr., at Grand Lagoon (tel. 234-9463), takes divers to many of these spots on six fully equipped dive boats. The company's professionally trained staff also teaches short resort courses. Snorkelers can explore the grass flats off Shell Island; these three-hour trips feature dolphin viewing if any porpoises are around.

TENNIS & RACQUETBALL   **Sports Park,** 15238 Front Beach Rd., at Hill Avenue (tel. 235-1081), features tennis courts and racquetball courts and an indoor pool. Nautilus workout equipment, aerobics classes, a whirlpool, a sauna, and massages are offered in the fitness center. Daily and weekly passes cost $9 and $34, respectively. Open Monday through Friday from 7am to 9pm and on Saturday from 9am to 5pm.

Large resorts and hotels have excellent tennis programs for their guests. Call the **Panama City Recreation Department** (tel. 872-3005) for information about the municipal courts.

WHERE TO STAY

In the Panama City/Panama City Beach area, hotels, motels, and condominiums offer an extensive variety of accommodations, from luxurious suites to very reasonably priced places to stay. Rental condominium apartments can be a smart vacation buy. Most have recreation areas with tennis courts, swimming pools, games rooms, etc. Of the many agencies offering one-, two-, three-, and four-bedroom gulf-front, fully furnished condominium apartments, try **St. Andrew Bay Resort Management,** 726 Thomas Dr., Panama City Beach, FL 32408 (tel. 904/235-4075, or toll free 800/621-2462); and **Condo World,** 8815-A Thomas Dr. (P.O. Box 9456), Panama City Beach, FL 32408 (tel. 904/234-5564, or toll free 800/232-6636).

You can save by staying in Panama City, where room rates are considerably lower than at the beach—they don't exceed $65 for a double room, even in summer. One good choice, overlooking the bay at St. Andrews Marina, is the **Ramada Harbor View,** 3001 W. 10th St. (tel. 904/785-0561, or toll free 800/228-3344). Several other chain motels are located along U.S. 98 east of the Hathaway Bridge. These include the **Howard Johnson Lodge** (tel. 904/785-0222, or toll free 800/654-2000), which backs up to St. Andrews Bay; **Days Inn Central** (tel. 904/784-1777, or toll free 800/329-7466); and **Econo Lodge** (tel. 904/785-2700, or toll free 800/424-4777). Every room has a kitchenette at **Admiral Benbow Inn** (tel. 904/234-2114, or toll free 800/451-1986), on U.S. 98 at the west end of Hathaway Bridge.

PANAMA CITY BEACH
Expensive

EDGEWATER BEACH RESORT, 11212 Front Beach Rd., Panama City Beach, FL 32407. Tel. 904/235-4044, or toll free 800/874-8686. Fax 904/233-7599. 545 apts.

$ Rates: Summer, $95–$325 apt. Off-season, $50–$240 apt. Weekly rates available. AE, DC, DISC, MC, V.

One of the Panhandle's largest condominium resorts, the beautiful beachfront location and garden landscaping with palm trees conjures thoughts of Polynesia. The spectacular beachfront swimming lagoon with cascading waterfalls includes an island in the center.

Five towers stand by the beach; low-rise buildings are across Front Beach Road among ponds and golf greens. Tropically decorated, spacious one- to three-bedroom apartments feature fully equipped kitchens, living and dining areas, and the convenience of your own washer and dryer. Views from the towers look out to the gulf, swimming lagoon, or the fairway, whichever you prefer.

Dining/Entertainment: Breakfast is served in Bimini, a casual lunch in Palapa, and delicious dinners in the Upstairs Clubhouse, all on the premises. There's also a poolside bar.

Services: Shuttle service around the resort, children's program, airport transportation.

Facilities: Pool, whirlpools, 12 tennis courts (6 lighted); 18-hole Hombre Golf Club a quarter mile north; 9-hole par-3 course on premises; rental sailboats and bikes; arrangements for parasailing.

HOLIDAY INN BEACHSIDE, 11127 Front Beach Rd., Panama City Beach, FL 32407. Tel. 904/234-1111, or toll free 800/633-0266. Fax 904/235-1907. 342 rms. A/C TV TEL

$ Rates: Summer, $130–$160 double. Off-season, $70–$90 double. Weekly and monthly rates available; discount for seniors. AE, DC, DISC, MC, V.

Designed in a curve, this 15-story resort hotel has won architectural awards for its dramatic lobby with waterfall and tropical decor. Very attractive, spacious guest rooms feature private balconies and gulf views. Each has a full-size icemaker-refrigerator, which makes the accommodations suitable for a family vacation. The hotel is one of Holiday Inn's top 20 and has won the corporation's Quality Excellence and Torch Bearer awards.

Dining/Entertainment: Charlie's Grill, on the poolside deck, is enjoyable for lunch. For breakfast and dinner, the Blue Marlin features good food at moderate prices. A lively rendezvous, the Starlight Lounge serves drinks until late and usually offers entertainment during the peak summer season.

Services: Room service, guest laundry.

Facilities: Large swimming pool (with a waterfall surrounded tropical foliage and the Oasis Bar under a soaring thatch roof), whirlpool, exercise room, games room.

MARRIOTT'S BAY POINT RESORT, 4200 Marriott Dr., Panama City Beach, FL 32408. Tel. 904/234-3307, or toll free 800/874-7105. Fax 904/233-1308. 378 rms, suites, and villas. A/C TV TEL

$ Rates: May–Sept, $175–$195 double; $215 suite. Off-season, $125–$165 double; $165–$185 suite. Variety of vacation packages year-round. AE, DC, DISC, MC, V.

Ranked among the nation's top 25 golf and tennis resorts, this vacation mini-world spawls over 1,100 landscaped acres with 32 ponds and a beach on a tropical wildlife preserve peninsula bordered by St. Andrews Bay and Grand Lagoon (from Thomas Drive, take Magnolia Beach Road and follow the signs for three miles). The outstanding, multilevel, vivid coral stucco hotel is surrounded by gardens, palm trees, oaks, and magnolias. In the glamorous three-story lobby, the window walls look out to scenic water views.

Dining/Entertainment: No one will go hungry or thirsty here. The Terrace Court, in the Yacht Club overlooking Bay Point Marina, is the most expensive restaurant in town, but it's worth the splurge for a romantic, candlelit dinner. In the hotel itself and sharing its view of Grand Lagoon, Fiddler's Green serves breakfast, lunch, and dinner, plus a scrumptious Sunday brunch. In addition to its namesake, Stormy's Old Fashioned Ice Cream Parlor serves snacks and light meals all afternoon in the Club House adjacent to the hotel. From March to October, Teddy Tucker's Back Beach Club serves snacks and libations from its perch on the pier in front of the hotel and hosts day-long beach parties during the summer. Sports fans will find TVs going nonstop in the English-style Circe's Sports Bar off the lobby and in Dokker's Grill & Pub in the Bay Town Shops. Check with the guest services desk for a schedule of live entertainment during the summer months.

Services: Concierge, fax and secretarial services; the guest services desk will arrange excursions and scuba-diving trips.

Facilities: Together, the Bruce Devlin–designed Lagoon Legend (second most difficult in the U.S.) and Club Meadows courses offer 36 holes of championship play. Both have their own clubhouses, putting greens, driving ranges, clinic, and private instruction. The Bay Point Tennis Center has 12 clay courts (4 lighted), a tennis shop, clinics, and lessons. A long pier crosses a shallow bay in front of the hotel to a sandbar, where guests and nonguests alike can sun on a lagoonside beach, rent waverunners and boats from Teddy Tucker, and go waterskiing and parasailing during the season. The *Island Queen* paddle-wheeler departs the pier for sunset cruises and excursions to Shell Island. Three swimming pools (one indoor) sit in front of the hotel. Burn off the calories at two health clubs, and money at the Bay Town Shops, which have a deli and dry cleaners. Over at the marina, the Bay Point Billfish Invitational in July is one of the world's richest. To get around this wide-spread resort, rent a bike at the front desk. Note that guests must pay extra for most activities.

Moderate

DAYS INN BEACH, 12818 Front Beach Rd., Panama City Beach, FL 32407. Tel. 904/233-3333, or toll free 800/329-7466. Fax 904/233-9568. 188 rms. A/C TV TEL
$ Rates: Summer, $100–$110 double. Off-season, $50–$100 double. AE, DC, DISC, MC, V.

This recently refurbished hotel offers great views from its semicircular, high-rise building right on the beach in the heart of the resort district. Ironwork balcony railings lend a New Orleans flavor to the establishment, while cane furniture gives the rooms a tropical touch. Evoking the South Seas, waterfalls cascade down a craggy, seven-story-tall fake "volcano" into an odd-shaped swimming pool below. If you get the urge to tie the knot, there's even a wedding chapel embedded up in the rocks. The hotel shares dining facilities with the adjoining Ramada Beachside Resort, which was closed while undergoing a complete renovation when I was there recently.

FLAMINGO MOTEL, 15525 Front Beach Rd., Panama City Beach, FL 32413. Tel. 904/234-2232, or toll free 800/828-0400. 67 units. A/C TV TEL
$ Rates: Summer, $66–$124 unit. Off-season, $30–$70 unit. Children under 16 stay free in parents' room. AE, DISC, MC, V.

This friendly, family-owned motel takes great pride (and rightfully so) in the gorgeous tropical garden under its "dome"—actually a peaked wooden roof with skylights—an exotic paradise of palms, hibiscus, ferns, and flamboyant flowers that's cool for strolling in no matter how hot the summer's day. Bordering the garden, the heated swimming pool and large sun deck overlook the shimmering gulf. Brightly decorated rooms with kitchenettes sleep two to six people. Across the street from the beach, the kitchenette rooms accommodate six to eight. Budget-conscious families will like the low-priced rooms with small refrigerators, accommodating two to four. The famous Dan Russell fishing pier is only half a mile west of the Flamingo, and a casual seafood restaurant is also nearby. From a poolside lounge chair, you can sit back and admire a fabulous sunset daily.

GEORGIAN TERRACE, 14415 Front Beach Rd., Panama City Beach, FL 32413. Tel. 904/234-2144 or 904/234-8413. 28 apts. A/C TV TEL
$ Rates: Mid-May to mid-Sept, $70 apt for one or two. Off-season, $39–$44 apt for one or two. AE, DISC, MC, V.

A two-level apartment-motel right on the beach, the Georgian Terrace is family-owned and family-operated. All apartments overlook the beach and all have full kitchens, separated by room dividers. Cheerfully decorated, the rooms are cozily paneled with knotty pine. The homey decor is extended to private enclosed sunporches with each apartment. The enclosed heated pool area is exceptionally beautiful, containing a lush tropical garden and attractive lounge chairs.

HORIZON SOUTH, 17462 Front Beach Rd., Panama City Beach, FL 32413. Tel. 904/234-6663, or toll free 800/476-6458. 75 town houses. A/C TV TEL

$ Rates: Summer, $57–$114 town house for two. Off-season, $40–$60 town house for two. Weekly and monthly rates available. DISC, MC, V.

A short walk across the street from the wide expanse of gulf beach, most of these one-, two-, and three-bedroom town houses are equipped with washers and dryers, and all have full kitchens and cable television with HBO. Private patios or sun decks are a nice touch. The resort community features three swimming pools (one is heated), a wading pool for the kids, a whirlpool hot tub, lighted tennis courts, an 18-hole miniature golf course, and games and exercise rooms.

Horizon South II (tel. 904/234-8329) is part of this same resort community and offers one- and two-bedroom condominium apartments with higher rates.

Tip: When making reservations in this resort community, check to find out if your accommodations are located one or three blocks from the beach.

Budget

FIESTA MOTEL, 13623 Front Beach Rd., Panama City Beach, FL 32413. Tel. 904/235-1000, or toll free 800/833-1415. Fax 904/233-1677. 152 rms, 34 suites. A/C TV TEL

$ Rates: Summer, $50–$55 single; $70–$85 double; $90 suite. Off-season, $30–$50 single; $40–$55 double; $60–$70 suite. Children 17 and under stay free in parents' room. AE, MC, V.

A friendly beachfront motel, the four-story Fiesta offers neat rooms with wall-to-wall carpeting. Most have balconies or patios to enjoy views of the gulf. The furniture is dated, but the rooms are spacious at this price. The two-bedroom family suites have paneled-wood kitchens supplied with utensils. The palm-tree fringed swimming pool in a lovely lawn sits right next to an undeveloped stretch of beach.

LA BRISA INN, 9424 Front Beach Rd., Panama City Beach, FL 32404. Tel. and fax 904/235-1122, or toll free 800/523-4369. 60 rms. A/C TV TEL

$ Rates: Summer, $50–$62 double. Off-season, $26–$30 double. Weekly and monthly rates available. AE, DC, DISC, MC, V.

A good vacation buy for families, this motel has rooms with a king-size or two double beds, and many have kitchenettes. Cribs are supplied for the little ones. Every morning, complimentary coffee and doughnuts are served, and local telephone calls are free. This stretch of Front Beach Road is a 20-minute walk from the beach.

SUNSET INN, 8109 Surf Dr., Panama City Beach, FL 32408. Tel. 904/234-7370. 50 units. A/C TV TEL

$ Rates: Summer, $50–$95 unit. Off-season, $30–$70 unit. Weekly, monthly and family rates available. AE, DISC, MC, V.

This very well maintained, two-level inn is right on the gulf but away from the maddening crowds off Thomas Drive near the east end of the beach. It accommodates families in one- and two-bedroom carpeted units with kitchens or in motel rooms across the street. The inn sports a large heated swimming pool and a spacious sun deck overlooking the gulf.

SUGAR SANDS MOTEL, 20723 Front Beach Rd., Panama City Beach, FL 32413. Tel. 904/234-8802, or toll free 800/367-9221. Fax 904/234-3645. 50 rms, 4 suites. A/C TV TEL

$ Rates: Summer, $52–$83 double; $100 suite. Off-season, $28–$63 double; $50–$75 suite. AE, DISC, MC, V.

On a more family-oriented beach area, all but one of the Sugar Sands buildings are gulfside. The heated swimming pool is by the road, but a courtyard, complete with gazebo, is available for sunning by the beach. There's also a picnic area and grills to barbecue hot dogs or steaks. Volleyball and shuffleboard courts are on the premises. A grocery store and a gift shop are across the street. Three 18-hole golf courses are a short drive away.

BED & BREAKFAST

GULFVIEW INN, 21722 Front Beach Rd., Panama City Beach, FL 32413. Tel. 904/234-6051. 5 rms (all with bath), 1 suite, 1 apt. A/C TV TEL
$ Rates (including continental breakfast): Apr–Labor Day, $50–$60 double; $75 suite. Off-season, $40–$60 double; $55 suite. No credit cards.
In a residential neighborhood less than five miles west of the resort area, the unusually designed, two-story beach house is painted Cape Cod blue with cream-colored lattice trim. Guest quarters have private entrances. Hosts Raymond and Linda Nance invite you to enjoy breakfast on the upstairs sun deck, overlooking Gulf of Mexico views. The home-baked breakfast breads and homemade jellies are a treat. Beautiful Sunnyside Beach is just 200 feet across the road, and there are outdoor hot and cold showers to refresh yourself after a wonderful time on the beach. No pets, please.

CAMPING

The **St. Andrews State Recreation Area,** at the end of County Road 392 (tel. 904/233-5140), is beautifully located on the Gulf of Mexico. Encompassing 1,063 acres of dune-studded beach (some sand dunes are amazingly high), woodland, and marshes, the park offers one of the most outstanding camping sites anywhere. Park entrance fees are $3.25 for everyone in the car. From March to September, camping fees are $18.50 to $20.50 for waterfront sites, $16 to $18.50 for other sites. From October to February, rates drop to $8.50 to $11. The park is open year-round from 8am to sunset. For information, write to St. Andrews State Recreation Area, 4415 Thomas Dr., Panama City Beach, FL 32407.

The **Long Beach Camp Inn,** 10496 Front Beach Rd. (at Thomas Drive), Panama City Beach, FL 32407 (tel. 904/234-3584), is right on the gulf and offers almost 200 hookups for $25 to $40 per night.

The **Magnolia Beach RV Park,** 7800 Magnolia Beach Rd., Panama City Beach, FL 32407 (tel. 904/235-1581), enjoys great views of Panama City from an idyllic setting under magnolias and moss-draped oaks on the shores of St. Andrews Bay. Some 14 of the 94 sites are right on the water. The park has a boat ramp, fishing pier, pool, laundry, and recreation room, and all sites have cable TV hookups. There are no tent sites. Rates are $20 to $24 a night during summer, $14 to $17 off-season. The park is two miles from Marriott's Bay Point Resort. Take Magnolia Beach Road off Thomas Drive.

IN NEARBY MEXICO BEACH

Sitting on U.S. 98 some 30 miles east of Panama City, the little community of Mexico Beach seems like a peaceful world removed from the razzle-dazzle of its larger neighbors. And were it a few yards farther east, Mexico Beach actually would be in another time zone (the eastern/central zone dividing line runs along the town's eastern boundary). This is a land of homes and cottages, not high-rise condos and resorts. It's a lovely drive along U.S. 98, which for miles skirts a shoreline bordered by sea oats, not buildings.

DRIFTWOOD INN, 2105 U.S. 98 (P.O. Box 13447), Mexico Beach, FL 32410. Tel. 904/648-5126. Fax 904/648-8505. 15 rms, 4 cottages, 4 houses. A/C TV TEL
$ Rates (including continental breakfast): May to mid-Sept, $75–$130 double. Mid-Sept to Apr, $65–$85 double. DISC, MC, V.
Host Peggy Wood, Fred the Dog, and Joe the Parrot will welcome you to this comfortable little inn, which from the road looks like a lattice-trimmed clapboard train station left over from Victorian times. Befitting this outward image, the lobby contains a small shop brimming with antiques and gifts. Brightly painted with white and pastels, each with a sun room facing the beach, units in the two-story main building have the feel of small, old-fashioned beach houses. Two duplex, hexagonal

cottages on the beach and four Victorian-style houses across U.S. 98 complete the establishment. There is no pool, restaurant, or bar, but a beachside gazebo with Adirondack chairs makes a wonderful place to sip your own booze at sunset, and each unit has a kitchen. Breakfast sweet rolls and coffee are served in the lobby. This is a very popular inn, so reserve as early as possible.

EL GOVERNOR MOTEL, U.S. 98 (P.O. Box 13325), Mexico Beach, FL 32410. Tel. 904/648-5757. Fax 904/648-5754. 119 rms, 3 town houses. A/C TV TEL

$ Rates: Apr–Sept, $75–$120 double; $115–$125 town house. Oct–Mar, $55–$110 double; $100–$110 town house. DISC, MC, V.

The only tall building for miles, this five-story motel has spacious beachfront rooms complete with kitchenettes or full kitchens. The two- and three-bedroom town houses across the highway are exceptionally pleasant places to stay. There's a swimming pool with a bar, tiki huts for cookouts, and a gift shop and store to buy groceries, liquor, and other supplies. The Top of the Gulf Restaurant & Lounge is nearby.

El Governor Campground (tel. 904/648-5432), across the highway, has tent and camper sites, full hookups, showers, picnic tables, laundry facilities, and beach access at the motel.

WHERE TO DINE

In most restaurants, just-caught local fish and shellfish predominate on the reasonably priced menus. Most places are very casual, and just about every restaurant features a children's menu. Pay attention to the hours, for some are closed from October to April.

PANAMA CITY BEACH
Moderate

ANGELO'S STEAK PIT, 9527 Front Beach Rd., between Moylan Dr. and Thomas Dr. Tel. 324-2531.
  Cuisine: STEAK. **Reservations:** Not accepted.
$ Prices: Appetizers $4–$9; main courses $10–$18. AE, MC, V.
  Open: Mid-Mar to May and Sept, dinner only, Mon–Sat 5–10pm. June–Aug, dinner only, daily 4:30–10pm. **Closed:** Oct to mid-Mar.

You can't miss enormous super-steer Big Gus standing guard at family-owned Angelo's, one of the area's most popular restaurants since 1957. Western decor provides the colorful ambience for enjoying hickory-pit barbecued steaks, beef, and chicken—hearty portions for cowboys and cowgirls. A big baked potato accompanies your order, plus a choice of crispy salad or savory soup. Next door, the Longhorn Saloon is the place to belly up to the bar while you wait for a table.

BOAR'S HEAD RESTAURANT, 17290 Front Beach Rd., at Fla. 79. Tel. 234-2239.
  Cuisine: AMERICAN. **Reservations:** Recommended.
$ Prices: Appetizers $3–$9; main courses $13–$18. AE, DC, DISC, MC, V.
  Open: Dinner only, daily 4:30–10pm. **Closed:** Mon off-season.

This interesting restaurant and tavern with its impressively beamed ceiling, stone walls, and large shingled-roof looks like a resort from the road. Inside, the Merry Olde England decor, complete with fireplaces, presents a classy setting for a delightful dinner. Among the specialties are prime rib of beef, charcoal-grilled grouper, angel-hair pasta combined with shellfish and a delicate sauce, and tender baby back pork ribs. Wild game is featured during the winter months. The wine list has won awards. The Boar's Head is also notable for luscious desserts, such as macadamia nut cheesecake.

CAPT. ANDERSON'S RESTAURANT, 5551 N. Lagoon Dr., at Thomas Dr. Tel. 234-2225.
  Cuisine: SEAFOOD. **Reservations:** Not accepted.
$ Prices: Appetizers $4–$9; main courses $10–$25. AE, DC, DISC, MC, V.

Open: Mid-Jan to Oct, dinner only, Mon–Sat 4–10pm (or later). **Closed:** Nov to mid-Jan.

Overlooking the Grand Lagoon, this famous restaurant attracts early diners so that they can watch the fishing fleet unload the catch-of-the-day at the busy marina, home of cruise boats and fishing charters. For more than 25 years, Capt. Anderson's has been so popular that sometimes there's almost a two-hour wait for a table during the peak summer vacation time. But here's a tip: Just relax with a drink in the air-conditioned lounge or admire the views from the open-air top deck. Capt. Anderson's is noted for charcoal-grilled local fish, crabmeat-stuffed jumbo shrimp, a heaped-high seafood platter, and much more. The Greek salad accompanying dinners is a favorite (and there's also a choice of potato and home-baked rolls). Especially for the first-time visitor, Capt. Anderson's is a "must."

CAPT. DAVIS DOCKSIDE RESTAURANT, 5550 N. Lagoon Dr., at Thomas Dr. Tel. 234-3608.
   Cuisine: SEAFOOD/STEAK. **Reservations:** Not accepted.
$ Prices: Appetizers $3–$9; main courses $9–$25. MC, V.
   Open: Dinner only, Thurs–Tues 4–10pm. **Closed:** Oct–Apr.
If the wait's too long at Capt. Anderson's, head next door, where Capt. Davis features deliciously prepared seafood as well as grilled steaks and juicy prime rib of beef. A family atmosphere prevails and the kids are not the only ones who like to watch the waterfront action from the window walls. Cocktails are served, too.

HAMILTON'S SEAFOOD RESTAURANT & LOUNGE, 5711 N. Lagoon Dr., at Thomas Dr. Tel. 234-1255.
   Cuisine: SEAFOOD. **Reservations:** Not accepted.
$ Prices: Appetizers $3–$7; main courses $10–$18; early-bird specials $8–$10. AE, DISC, MC, V.
   Open: Summer, dinner only, daily 5–10:30pm. Winter, dinner only, Sun–Thurs 5:30–9:30pm, Fri–Sat 5–10pm.
Proprietor Steve Stevens continues in the tradition of his noted New Orleans restaurateur father, Gus, at this attractive, blond-wood and knotty-pine establishment on Grand Lagoon. For starters, try his blackened alligator bits. Baked oysters Hamilton—a combination of oysters, shrimp, and crabmeat—is another appetizer, but it could fill you up. Several other dishes are unique to Hamilton's, such as snapper étouffée and artichokes Irene, which comes with a crab stuffing. Mesquite-grilled fish and steaks also are house specialties. Arrive before 6pm to take advantage of the early-bird specials. Wait for a table at a long bar while listening to the recorded jazz background music.

JP'S RESTAURANT AND BAR, 617 Azalea St., at the west end of Middle Beach Rd. Tel. 234-7147.
   Cuisine: SEAFOOD/STEAK. **Reservations:** Recommended.
$ Prices: Appetizers $2–$9; main courses $8–$13; early-bird specials $7. AE, DC, DISC, MC, V.
   Open: Mon–Sat 11am–10pm. (Bar open later, especially on weekends.)
There's a gulf-view second-story deck at this lively, casual restaurant. The chef specializes in sautéed and Cajun blackened fresh fish and seafood. Thick, tender steaks are hand-cut and charcoal-broiled to your preference. Homemade pastas are delicious, especially the fettuccine combined with shellfish. Savory soups and chowders are home-style, great for lunch with a salad and home-baked bread. Delicious homemade pies are featured on the dessert list. Early-bird specials run from 11am to 6pm.

JP's has another restaurant and bar in Panama City, just a half mile east of the Hathaway Bridge at 4701 W. U.S. 98 (tel. 769-3711). Both locations spotlight live entertainment during summer.

Budget

ALL AMERICAN DINER, 10590 Front Beach Rd., just west of S. Thomas Dr. Tel. 235-2443.
   Cuisine: AMERICAN. **Reservations:** Not accepted.

$ Prices: Sandwiches and burgers $1.50–$4.50; main courses $8–$13; breakfast/lunch buffets $5 adults, $4 children. No credit cards.
Open: Daily 24 hours (breakfast buffet 6:30–11am; lunch/dinner buffet 11:30am–8pm).

This bright, 24-hour diner across the road from the beach is distinguished from a number of waffle shops in town by its 1950s memorabilia, including a now-antique jukebox which still plays rock 'n' roll hits from that era. The breakfast and lunch/dinner buffet bars are excellent value when compared to hotel prices. Regular meals feature diner-style fried seafood and grilled steaks and chicken.

BILLY'S STEAMED SEAFOOD RESTAURANT, 3000 Thomas Dr., between Grand Lagoon and Magnolia Beach Rd. Tel. 235-2349.
Cuisine: SEAFOOD. **Reservations:** Not accepted.
$ Prices: Sandwiches $2.50–$5; seafood $3–$8. AE, MC, V.
Open: Daily 11am–9pm.

More a lively raw bar than a restaurant, Billy's is famous for "the best crabs in town." These are the same hard-shell blue crabs we get from the Chesapeake Bay, and Billy prepares them Maryland style: steamed with lots of spicy Old Bay Seasoning. Unlike the crab houses in Baltimore, however, Billy removes the top shell, cleans out the "mustard" (intestines), and cuts them in two for you. All you have to do is "pick" the meat. If you don't know how, just ask the staff. Six crabs cost about $8, the same bargain price charged for frequent all-you-can-eat weekend specials. Other steamed morsels include shrimp (also with spicy seasoning), oysters, crabs, and lobster served with corn on the cob and garlic bread.

CAJUN INN, 477 Beckrich Rd., at Front Beach Rd. Tel. 235-9987.
Cuisine: LOUISIANA CAJUN. **Reservations:** Not accepted.
$ Prices: Appetizers $2.50–$5; main courses $8–$14; sandwiches $3.50–$6.
Open: Daily 11am–9:30pm.

In the Shoppes at Edgewater, this tiny restaurant brings the Big Easy to the gulf. If you liked the chicory café au lait and beignets in New Orleans, you'll love this strong, special coffee and the light-as-a-feather pastries. Louisiana's famous Cajun chef Paul Prudhomme would approve of the restaurant's Bayou Tèche jambalaya and the seafood étouffée. Overstuffed shrimp and oyster hoagie sandwiches, known as po'boys and muffalettas, are also specialties.

MONTEGO BAY SEAFOOD HOUSE & OYSTER BAR, 4920 Thomas Dr., near St. Andrews State Recreation Area. Tel. 234-8686.
Cuisine: SEAFOOD. **Reservations:** Not accepted.
$ Prices: Appetizers $2–$7; main courses $8–$14; sandwiches $3.50–$6. AE, DISC, MC, V.
Open: Summer, daily 11am–10pm. Off-season, Sun–Thurs 11am–9pm, Fri–Sat 11am–10pm.

This is the oldest of five Montego Bay restaurants, all popular for their $4 lunch specials and the dinnertime Captain's Catch Seafood Platter, stacked high with a variety of favorites and served with a savory hot gumbo and crisp salad, all for $10. This small, rather plain member of the local chain resides in a corner storefront at "the curve" of Thomas Drive.

The other Montego Bay restaurants are larger and sport tropical decor to create a more beachy atmosphere. They are in the Shoppes at Edgewater, Front Beach Road at Beckrich Road (tel. 233-6033); on the west end of the beach at Front Beach Road and Fla. 79 (tel. 233-2900); at the intersection of Thomas Drive, Front Beach Road, and Middle Beach Road (tel. 235-3585); and in Panama City on Cove Boulevard (Fla. 77) between 23rd Street and U.S. 231, opposite the Panama City Mall (tel. 872-0098).

PANAMA CITY
Moderate

HARBOUR HOUSE, in the Ramada Harbor View, 3001A W. 10th St., at Beck Ave. Tel. 785-9053.
Cuisine: STEAK/SEAFOOD. **Reservations:** Not accepted.

$ Prices: Appetizers $3–$6; main courses $9–$14; buffet lunch $5 Mon–Sat, $8 Sun. AE, DC, DISC, MC, V.
Open: Daily 6am–10pm (lunch buffet 11am–2pm). **Closed:** Christmas Eve and Day.

At picturesque St. Andrews Marina, the Harbour House is a long-time favorite for its sumptuous buffet lunch. During the usual dining hours, the menu highlights prime rib, charcoal-broiled steaks, and delicious gulf seafood. Usually, live entertainment is scheduled in the cocktail lounge, a friendly rendezvous. With great views, good food, and reasonable prices, the Harbour House has a winning combination.

Budget

THE HOUSE OF SEAFOOD, 6220 Ohio Ave. (Fla. 77), at the north end of Bailey Bridge, Lynn Haven. Tel. 265-8980.
Cuisine: SEAFOOD. **Reservations:** Not accepted.
$ Prices: Appetizers $4–$8; main courses $6–$17 (most $8–$10). DISC, MC, V.
Open: Mon–Thurs 10:30am–8pm, Fri–Sat 10:30am–9pm.

While visitors dine at the beach, local residents head for this country-style seafood house whose blue Formica-top tables enjoy lovely views of North Bay, about six miles north of Panama City. You have a choice of fried or broiled fish, shrimp, and oysters, or a combination thereof. Steamed whole Florida lobsters are offered in season. Landlubbers can order steaks or burgers. All meals come with a choice of potato or cheese grits, hushpuppies, and a salad. There's also a salad bar mounted in a skiff. This family establishment permits no alcohol or smoking.

SPECIALTY DINING

The Treasure Ship, at Treasure Island Marina, 3605 S. Thomas Dr., at Grand Lagoon (tel. 234-8881), must be seen to be believed, with its amazing two acres of ship space. The Treasure Ship claims to be the world's largest land-based Spanish galleon, a replica of the three-masted sailing ships that carried priceless loot from the New World to Spain in the 16th and 17th centuries. You can get anything from an ice-cream cone to peel-it-yourself shrimp to a sophisticated dinner on board in the various dining rooms and eateries. The Wharf Galley deli restaurant, for example, serves a nice lunch and sandwiches at reasonable prices from 11am to 5pm. Seafood specialties are highlighted in the Treasure Ship Dining Room, open Monday through Saturday from 4 to 10pm; dinner prices range from about $12 to $20. In the Captain's Quarters, live entertainment and dancing continue until the wee hours. Two cocktail lounges, games rooms, and boutiques are on board. Admission is free to the Treasure Ship, and take along your camera. It's a good idea to call ahead for current dining hours in the various restaurants, most of which close from October to April.

For a mini–Love Boat experience, **Captain Anderson's dinner-dance cruises** are romantic, available from Memorial Day through Labor Day. Boarding is at Capt. Anderson's Marina, 5550 N. Lagoon Dr. (tel. 234-5940), at 6:30pm Monday through Saturday. Steak dinners are usually featured, but check ahead. The ticket costs about $25 per adult, about $20 for children under 12 (tips are included). Live entertainment is always on the program. The triple-decker fun boat is so popular that it's a good idea to make reservations well in advance (weeks ahead, should you be celebrating a special occasion and want to make sure you can be accommodated).

EVENING ENTERTAINMENT
THE PERFORMING ARTS

Yes, there *is* life after the beach. The **Marina Civic Center,** 8 Harrison Dr., on the Panama City waterfront (tel. 763-4696), features a variety of performances throughout the year. Among the recent presentations were the musicals *The Buddy Holly Story* and *The Music Man,* performed by Broadway touring companies. The amazing magician David Copperfield was also in the spotlight, just one of the celebrities who stage special shows here.

The **Kaleidoscope Theater,** 201 E. 24th St., Panama City (tel. 265-3226), is a community theater that offers presentations of dramas, musicals, and comedies.

The James Lark Visitors Center on Front Beach Road (see "Orientation," above) distributes free copies of **"Bay Arts & Entertainment,"** a booklet published bimonthly by the Bay Arts Alliance, P.O. Box 1153, Panama City, FL 32402 (tel. 904/769-1217). It tells what's coming up on the arts and entertainment scene.

THE CLUB, BAR & MUSIC SCENE

The romantic lounges are in the limelight for both live entertainment and dancing at **The Treasure Ship,** 3605 S. Thomas Dr. (tel. 234-8881), and at **The Boar's Head,** 17290 W. U.S. 98A (tel. 234-6628). Call in advance for current schedules (hours vary according to season).

Good old-fashioned country comedy and country music are featured in the **Ocean Opry Show,** 8400 W. U.S. 98 (tel. 234-5464), starring the Rader family and a cast of 20. This is Panama City Beach's answer to Nashville and to Branson, Missouri. The air-conditioned theater, seating 1,000, is open year-round. Nashville country-music stars are usually spotlighted October through March; June through August, there's a show nightly at 7:30pm, but the schedule varies in other months. Popcorn, hot dogs, and soft drinks are sold at the theater. The two-hour show costs $13 for adults, about $5 for children (prices vary for special shows). The box office opens at 9am and reservations are necessary for the Opry Show, which is a long-time favorite.

For more than 20 years, **The Breakers,** 12627 Front Beach Rd. (tel. 234-6060), has been a popular night owls' roost. The nightclub recently was rebuilt with special tiered seating for better viewing of the terrific show (and the gulf). It's the place to dance all night, see a special show, and enjoy food and drinks.

The young late-night crowd likes open-air **Schooners,** 5121 Gulf Dr. (tel. 235-9074). Just-shucked oysters and grilled seafood are menu favorites. Every table has a gulf view, perfect for relaxing with a drink. There's good music for dancing, and Schooners describes itself as "the last local beach club." Gulf Drive parallels Thomas Drive near the east end of the beach.

Spinnaker, on the beach at 8795 Thomas Dr. (tel. 234-7882), is another action-filled restaurant-club, staying open until 4am. The band plays on and on for dancing and listening.

Pineapple Willie's Lounge, beachside at 9900 S. Thomas Dr. (tel. 235-0928), is open from 11am until the wee hours, serving Australian-style fun food, such as koala wings, and spotlighting live entertainment. Dancing includes everything from "Waltzing Matilda" to reggae.

Many establishments close from October to April, so call ahead.

GAMBLING

Local residents have good reason to call the *Star Dancer* the "Casino Boat." During the summer months, this floating Las Vegas makes day and night cruises more than nine miles offshore, where it's legal to wager your life's savings at the tables. Prices range from $20 to $60, depending on the length of the voyage. Call 233-7447 for details. Reservations are required.

AN EASY EXCURSION TO APALACHICOLA

Sometimes called Florida's Last Frontier, the relatively undeveloped gulf coast between Panama City and Tallahassee is a fascinating day trip for many visitors, a destination in itself for others. Vacationers can stay for weeks or months in beach cottages on **St. George Island,** one of the chain of skinny barrier islands that nearly enclose broad Apalachicola Bay, and on the long hook of **St. Joseph's Peninsula** to the west. The beaches here are long and gorgeous, the bays and estuaries are great for fishing and boating, and the seafood is as fresh and succulent as it can be.

The area also is rich in history, which makes a visit to the little town of **Apalachicola** (pop. 2,600) a highlight of any venture into this beautiful area. Strategically located at the mouth of the Apalachicola River, this charming community was a major seaport during autumns from 1827 to 1861, when plantations in Alabama and Georgia shipped tons of cotton down the river to the gulf. The town had a racetrack, an opera house, and a civic center which hosted balls, socials, and gambling. The population shrank during the mosquito-infested summer months, however, when yellow fever epidemics were likely to strike. It was during one of these outbreaks that Dr. John Gorrie of Apalachicola tried to develop a method of cooling his patients' rooms. In doing so, he invented the forerunner of the air conditioners and ice machines that make Florida tourism possible.

The Civil War put an end to Apalachicola's cotton boom, and although lumbering became important in the late 1800s, that industry found a home at Port St. Joe and its deep-water harbor some 30 miles to the west. From that time on, Apalachicola has made its living primarily from the water, starting with seine fishing for mullet, pompano, mackerel, blue fish, and trout. Sponge fishermen did a brisk business in the late 1800s. Today Apalachicola produces the bulk of Florida's oyster crop, and shrimping and fishing are major industries. The **Florida Seafood Festival** on the first Saturday in November is the area's biggest special event.

Apalachicola faces the estuarine marshlands from a point where the river flows into Apalachicola Bay. U.S. 98 leads west from town to the St. Joseph Peninsula and Port St. Joe, some 30 miles away. To the east, U.S. 98 departs town by the 3-mile-long Gorrie Bridge and then skirts the bay for some 27 picturesque miles. Offshore, St. George Island, Little St. George island, and St. Vincent Island separate the bay from the gulf. The road to St. George Island leaves U.S. 98 some 4 miles east of Apalachicola (the bridge to the island is now free). Little St. George and St. Vincent Islands can only be reached by boat.

The telephone area code for Apalachicola is 904. There are two banks in town but no automatic teller machines.

Note: Unlike the other Panhandle towns we have visited (Pensacola, Fort Walton, and Panama City), Apalachicola is in the eastern time zone, like Orlando and Miami.

GETTING THERE You'll have to drive to the Apalachicola area. The town is about 65 miles east of Panama City via U.S. 98, and about 80 miles west of Tallahassee via U.S. 319 and U.S. 98. From I-10, take Exit 22 at Grand Ridge, then follow Fla. 69 south to Bountstown, Fla. 71 south to Port St. Joe, and U.S. 98 east to Apalachicola.

INFORMATION The **Apalachicola Bay Chamber of Commerce,** 57 Market St., Apalachicola, FL 32320 (tel. 904/653-9419), supplies information about the area from its offices, which contain a small maritime museum. It's open Monday through Friday from 9:30am to 4pm and on Saturday from 10am to 3pm.

WHAT TO SEE & DO

HISTORIC DISTRICT Start your visit by picking up a map from the chamber of commerce (see above) and then taking a walking tour of Apalachicola's waterfront, business district, and Victorian-era homes. Along Water Street, several tin warehouses evoke the town's seafaring days of the late 1800s, as does the 1840s-era **Sponge Exchange** at Commerce Street and Avenue E. A highlight of the residential area, centered around Gorrie Square at Avenue D and 6th Street, is the Greek Revival–style **Trinity Episcopal Church,** built in New York and shipped here in 1837. At the water end of 6th Street, **Battery Park** has a children's playground and is the focus of the annual Florida Seafood Festival in November.

MUSEUMS Showpiece at the **John Gorrie State Museum,** Avenue D at 6th Street (tel. 653-9347), is a working replica of the doctor's cooling machine that accidentally produced ice. Open Thursday through Monday from 10am to 5pm; closed New Year's Day, Thanksgiving, and Christmas Day. Admission is $1.

The **Estuarine Walk,** at the north end of Market Street on the grounds of the Apalachicola National Estuarine Research Reserve (tel. 653-8063), contains aquariums full of fish and alligators, cages with snakes and tortoises, and displays of various other estuarine life. It's open Monday through Friday from 8am to 5pm. Admission is free.

In Port St. Joe, the **Constitution Convention State Museum** (tel. 229-8029) depicts the 34 days during which Florida's first constitution was drafted here in 1838. At the same time, the convention applied to the U.S. Congress for statehood. The museum is on Allen Memorial Way, off U.S. 98 about 30 miles west of Apalachicola. Open Thursday through Monday from 9am to noon and 1 to 5pm. Admission is $1.

PARKS   Countless terns, snowy plover, black skimmers, and other birds nest along the dunes and nine miles of beaches at **St. George Island State Park,** on the island's eastern end (tel. 927-2111). The wildlife can be viewed from a hiking trail and observation platform. The park has picnic areas, restrooms, showers, a boat ramp, and a campground with electric hookups. Entry fees are $3.25 per vehicle with up to eight occupants, $1 for pedestrians and bicyclists. Camping fees are $10 per night with electricity, $8 without. Primitive camping (take everything with you—including water) costs $3 a night per adult, $2 for children.

The beaches are even longer at **St. Joseph Peninsula State Park** (tel. 227-1327), at the end of County Road 30 about 35 miles west of Apalachicola. The peninsula is populated by cottages and a few shops around Cape San Blas, but beyond the park entrance it's totally preserved. Facilities include picnic areas, a marina with a boat ramp, campgrounds with electricity, and eight remote cabins. Admission and camping fees are the same as at St. George State Park, above, except that cabins rent for $70 a night during summer, $55 a night off-season.

There are no facilities whatsoever at the **St. Vincent National Wildlife Refuge** (tel. 653-8808), south of Apalachicola. This 12,000-acre barrier island is being left in its natural state by the U.S. Fish and Wildlife Service, but visitors are welcome to walk through its pine forests, marshlands, ponds, dunes, and beaches. In addition to native species like the bald eagle and alligators, the island is home to a small herd of sambar deer from Southeast Asia. Red wolves are bred here for reintroduction to other wildlife areas. Access is by boat only, usually from Indian Pass on County Road 30 about five miles west of Pensacola. The chamber of commerce (see above) will arrange to have a boat captain take you over. The refuge headquarters, at the north end of Market Street in town, has exhibits of wetland flora and fauna. It's open Monday through Friday from 8am to 4:30pm. The rangers conduct managed hunts for deer and wild hogs from November to January.

CRUISES   The **Governor Stone,** an 1877-vintage Gulf Coast schooner, makes morning, afternoon, and sunset cruises on Apalachicola Bay each day during the summer months, less frequently during the off-season. During its long life afloat, this fine old craft has been a cargo freighter, oyster buyer, sponge boat, and U.S. Merchant Marine training vessel. It departs the Rainbow Inn dock on Water Street. Call 653-8708 for schedule and reservations, which are recommended. The cruises cost $20 a person.

FISHING   Fishing is excellent in these waters, where trout, red fish, flounder, tarpon, shark, drum, and others abound. The chamber of commerce (see above) can help arrange charters on the local boats, many of which dock at the Rainbow Inn on Water Street. For guides, contact **Professional Guide Service** (tel. 670-8834) or **Boss Guide Services** (tel. 653-8139).

WHERE TO STAY

The dunes of St. George Island, about 10 miles east of town, are virtually lined with beach cottages and a few condominiums. These are available on a weekly or monthly basis. Among the rental agents are **Anchor Realty,** HCR Box 222, St. George Island, FL 32328 (tel. 904/927-2735, or toll free 800/824-0416); **Gulf Coast Realty,** HCR Box 90, St. George Island, FL 32328 (tel. 904/927-2596, or toll free 800/367-1680); and **Sun Coast Realty,** HCR Box 2, St. George Island, FL 32328 (tel. 904/927-2282, or toll free 800/341-2021).

GIBSON INN, 51 Ave. C, Apalachicola, FL 32320. Tel. 904/653-2191.
    25 rms (all with bath), 5 suites. A/C TV TEL
$ Rates: $65–$80 double; $110 suite. AE, MC, V.
Built at the turn of the century, this cupola-topped inn is such a brilliant example of Victorian architecture that it's listed on the National Register of Historic Inns. An

abandoned ruin, it was restored to its original splendor in 1985 by Michael and Neil Koun of Tallahassee. Guest rooms and suites are richly furnished with antiques to evoke Apalachicola's days as an important cotton port. Nonguests are welcome to wander upstairs and peek into unoccupied rooms (whose doors are left open) or partake of a sumptuous seafood meal in the comfortable dining room. Room and dining reservations are advised, especially on weekends, and rooms should be booked well in advance in summer and for the seafood festival in November. The dining room becomes a dinner theater on weekends during July and August. Grab a drink from the bar and relax in one of the high-back rockers on the old-fashioned veranda.

RAINBOW INN, 123 Water St., Apalachicola, FL 32320. Tel. 904/653-8139. 27 rms. A/C TV TEL

$ Rates: Summer, $49–$54 double. Off-season, $39–$49 double. AE, DC, DISC, MC, V.

From the street, this two-story inn's rough-hewn exterior timbers make it look like one of the neighboring waterfront warehouses, but inside are comfortable rooms with large windows overlooking the motel's own riverfront marina (leave the curtains open if you want a beautiful sunrise vista over the marshes of Apalachicola Bay). There's absolutely nothing fancy here, but the rooms are good value for the money. Those on the second floor are newer and better appointed than those at dockside. The inn's Riverfront Restaurant specializes in seafood dinners, but is also open for breakfast and lunch. The lively Rosetta Spoonbill Cocktail Lounge sits upstairs over the restaurant.

ST. GEORGE INN, HCR Box 927, St. George Island, FL 32328. Tel. 904/927-2903. 8 rms (all with bath). A/C TV

$ Rates: $50 single; $65 double. DISC, MC, V.

Although built in the 1980s, this comfortable inn has the look and feel of a Victorian boarding house. Entering from a double-decked, columned front porch, French doors open into a large central hallway with stairs leading to spacious and attractively furnished guest rooms. To one side of the hallway, guests dine in a colonial-style room with fireplace. To the other side, they gather in a comfortable bar and lounge.

WHERE TO DINE

APALACHICOLA SEAFOOD GRILL & STEAKHOUSE, 100 Market St., at Ave. E. Tel. 653-9510.

Cuisine: SEAFOOD/STEAKS. **Reservations:** Recommended in summer.

$ Prices: Appetizers $5–$7; main courses $7–$17. DISC, MC, V.

Open: Lunch Mon–Sat 11:30am–3pm; dinner, Mon–Sat 6–9pm. **Closed:** Jan.

With café curtains bedecking its storefront windows, this establishment looks like a typical small-town diner. It once was, but don't be fooled by outward appearances. Today's menu features southern-style pot pies and fried oysters, fish, and shrimp, but few places ever served such delicious daily specials as mixed seafood combined with a light cream sauce and linguine. Charcoal-broiled steaks run up to a full pound of sirloin.

BOSS OYSTER, 125 Water St. Tel. 653-9364.

Cuisine: SEAFOOD. **Reservations:** Not accepted.

$ Prices: Appetizers $4–$5; main courses $10–$15; sandwiches $4–$6. AE, MC, V.

Open: Mon–Thurs 11am–9pm, Fri–Sun 11am–10pm.

You've heard about the famous Apalachicola oysters and their reputedly aphrodisiac properties. Well, this simple, dockside eatery—which calls itself "Bivalvia"—offers them just about every way imaginable: raw, steamed, or under a choice of 30 toppings ranging from ham to jalepeños so spicy that they overpower the bivalves. They'll even steam three dozen of them and let you do the shucking. Not in the mood for oysters? Then try the steamed shrimp or fried seafood platters.

OLD TIME SODA FOUNTAIN & LUNCHEONETTE, 93 Market St. Tel. 653-2000.

Cuisine: SANDWICHES. **Reservations:** Not accepted.

$ Prices: $1.25–$2.50. No credit cards.
Open: Mon–Sat 10am–5pm.

The pharmacy that once occupied this store has long gone, but the soda fountain just keeps rolling along, a living relic of 1950s small-town Americana. Townsfolk still plop down on the round stools at the marble-top counter at lunchtime to order a ham sandwich and fountain-brewed Coca-Cola. Or they drop in while shopping for an ice-cream soda or a malted or milkshake spun to life by the green stirring machine. The sandwiches, hot dogs, brownies, and cookies are just like Mom used to make.

---

4. TALLAHASSEE

200 miles W of Jacksonville, 200 miles E of Pensacola,
250 miles NW of Orlando

GETTING THERE   By Plane   The **Tallahassee Regional Airport** (tel. 904/891-7800), 10 miles southwest of downtown on SE Capital Circle, is served by American Eagle, Delta, and USAir.

By Train   Amtrak's transcontinental *Sunset Limited* from Los Angeles through New Orleans to Miami stops in Tallahassee at 918 Railroad Ave. For information or reservations, call Amtrak (tel. toll free 800/USA-RAIL).

By Bus   The Greyhound bus depot is at 112 W. Tennessee St., at Adams Street (tel. 904/222-4240, or toll free 800/231-2222).

By Car   Four major highways lead to Tallahassee. From the east and west, highway access is Interstate 10 and U.S. 90. From the north and south it's U.S. 27 and U.S. 319.

Since 1824, Tallahassee has been the capital of Florida, selected for its midpoint location between St. Augustine and Pensacola, which were the state's major cities at that time. An Old South atmosphere prevails in this slow-paced area, dotted with lovingly restored antebellum mansions, plantations, beautiful lakes and streams, towering pine and cypress trees, richly scented magnolias, and colorful azaleas. In true southern style, tradition and history are highly important, and many of the city's historic homes and buildings have been preserved, especially along Park Avenue and Calhoun Street.

Nestled in what seems like an enormous forest, the environs of Tallahassee offer many picturesque drives. Majestic live oaks draped with Spanish moss canopy the old secondary roads—veritable green "tunnels" are formed by the leafy branches of trees joining together from both sides of the road. There are five official Canopy Roads (see "What to See and Do," below), lined with historic plantations, ancient Native American settlement sites and mounds, gorgeous gardens, quiet parks with picnic areas, and lakes for bass fishing. The blissful solitude is a rare experience in today's lifestyle. Indeed, Tallahassee is an unusual city, combining modernity with the elegance of a bygone era.

ORIENTATION

INFORMATION   For information in advance, contact the **Tallahassee Area Convention and Visitors Bureau,** 200 W. College Ave. (P.O. Box 1369), Tallahassee, FL 32302 (tel. 904/488-3990, or toll free 800/628-2866). Once in town, pick up brochures, pamphlets, and excellent street maps at the **Tallahassee Area Visitor Information Center** (same phone numbers as the bureau) in the West Plaza foyer of the New Capital Building, just inside the Duvall Street entrance. It's open Monday through Friday from 8am to 5pm, and on Saturday, Sunday, and holidays from 8:30am to 4:30pm. The Florida Welcome Center in the same foyer has information about the entire state.

The front pages of the Tallahassee telephone directory contain a list of annual events, city and campus maps, medical and human service facilities, and information about arts and entertainment.

CITY LAYOUT   Many of Tallahassee's main streets radiate outward from the Old Capitol like the spokes of a wheel. The east-west I-10 passes through the northern suburbs about 4½ miles from downtown. The main spokes from I-10 to downtown are North Monroe Street (U.S. 27) and Thomasville Road. The two join to become **Monroe Street,** the main north-south artery through downtown. **Apalachee Parkway** (also U.S. 27) begins at the Old Capitol and is the main drag to the east. **Tennessee Street** (U.S. 90) runs west from downtown and passes Florida State University. To the east, Tennessee Street becomes Mahan Drive. Although it's mostly a two-lane road, **Capital Circle** serves as a beltway by looping around the city's eastern, southern, and western sides.

GETTING AROUND

BY PUBLIC TRANSPORTATION   Built like an old-time streetcar, the free **Old Town Trolley** (tel. 891-5200) is the best way to see the sights of historic downtown Tallahassee. You can get on or off at any point, but the narrated tour begins at Adams Street Commons, at the corner of Jefferson and Adams Streets. The trolley runs at least every 15 minutes between 7am and 6pm Monday through Friday.

TALTRAN (tel. 891-5200) provides city **bus** service from its downtown terminal at Tennessee and Adams Streets. The fare is 75¢. Both the ticket booth there and the Tallahassee Area Visitors Information Center in the New Capitol Building have route maps and schedules for the Old Town Trolley and TALTRAN buses.

BY TAXI & LIMO   For taxi service call **Yellow Cab** (tel. 222-3070). **Capital Limousine** (tel. 574-4350) provides both taxi and limousine service.

BY RENTAL CAR   Major car-rental companies are **Avis** (tel. toll free 800/831-2847), **Alamo** (tel. toll free 800/327-9633), **Budget** (tel. 800/527-0700), **Dollar** (tel. toll free 800/800-8007), **Hertz** (tel. toll free 800/654-3131), and **National** (tel. 800/227-7368).

FAST FACTS

Area Code   The telephone area code for Tallahassee is 904.

Doctor   To see a doctor, Patients First Medical Centers has three branches (tel. 562-2010, 878-8843, or 688-3380).

Drugstore   The Walgreen's drugstore in the Parkway Shopping Center, on Apalachee Parkway at Magnolia Drive (tel. 877-3023), is open 24 hours a day.

Tax   In addition to the statewide 6% sales tax, Leon County imposes a 3% tax on all hotel and restaurant bills.

Time   Tallahassee is in the eastern time zone, like Orlando and Miami.

WHAT TO SEE & DO
ATTRACTIONS
The Capitol Complex

Number one on your must-see Tallahassee list should be the Capitol Complex, dominating the downtown area. The **New Capitol Building,** a $43-million skyscraper, was built in 1977 to replace the Old Capitol, which dates back to 1845. State Legislators meet in the New Capitol from February to April. The Chambers of the House and the Senate have public viewing galleries.

At any time of the year, the highlight is the spectacular view from the 22nd-floor **observatory.** On a clear day you can see from rolling green hills all the way to the sun-sparkled Gulf of Mexico.

The New Capitol is open Monday through Friday from 8am to 5pm (closed major holidays). Guided tours (tel. 488-6167) are scheduled on the hour, Monday through Friday from 9am to noon and on Saturday and Sunday from 1 to 4pm. Weekend visitors must take a guided tour.

Directly in front of the skyscraper, the strikingly white **Old Capitol,** with its majestic dome, is known as "The Pearl of Capitol Hill," and has been restored to its original beauty. An eight-room exhibit entitled "A View from the Capitol" portrays Florida's political history. Turn-of-the-century furnishings, cotton gins, and other artifacts are also of interest. The Old Capitol is open Monday through Friday from 9am to 4:30pm, and on Saturday, Sunday, and holidays from noon to 4:30pm. For information, call 487-1902. Admission is free to both the Old and New Capitols.

Facing the Old Capitol across Monroe Street are the twin granite towers of the **Vietnam Veterans Memorial,** honoring Florida's Vietnam veterans.

Historic Districts

You can take a self-guided tour of Tallahassee's historic districts. Use the Old Town Trolley map or get a copy of "Downtown Tallahassee Historic Trail" from the Visitors Information Center in the New Capitol.

The **Adams Street Commons,** 200 S. Adams St., at Jefferson Street, is a one-block winding brick and landscaped area, retaining an old-fashioned southern town-square atmosphere. Restored buildings include the Governor's Club, a 1900s Masonic Lodge, and Gallie's Hall. Florida's first five African American college students received their diplomas in Gallie's Hall in 1892, after graduating from Florida A&M University. Restaurants, shops, and Gallie Alley are also in the Adams Street Commons.

The **Calhoun Street Historical District,** affectionately called "Gold Dust Street" in the old days, was once a status-symbol address. The elaborate homes, built by prominent citizens on Calhoun Street between Georgia and Tennessee Streets, date back to the era between 1830 and 1880. Among the most outstanding are the Bloxham House, the Elizabeth Cobb House, the Bowen House, the Towle House, and the Randall-Lewis House. For tour information, call the Historic Preservation Board (tel. 488-3901).

The **Park Avenue Historic District** is a lovely promenade of beautiful trees, gardens, and outstanding old mansions to the east of Monroe Street. Park Avenue was originally named 200 Foot Street and then McCarty Street. However, it was renamed Park Avenue to satisfy a snobbish society matron's desire for a very sophisticated address to be imprinted on her son's wedding invitations.

Among the historic homes open to the public are the Knott House (see "Historic Sites and Buildings," below), the Murphy House, the Shine-Chittenden House, and the Wood House. For information about visiting these elaborate homes, call the Historic Preservation Board (tel. 488-3901).

The **Walker Library,** 209 E. Park Ave. (tel. 224-5012), was Florida's first library. The handsomely furnished library dates back to 1884. Admission is free, and it's open Monday through Friday from 9am to 1pm.

Historic Sites and Buildings

BROKAW-MCDOUGALL HOUSE, 329 N. Meridian, at Virginia St. Tel. 488-3901.

Constructed in 1856, this magnificent house with six impressive Corinthian columns is considered a superb example of Italianate and Classical Revival architecture. The landscaping is gorgeous and was designed when the house was built. The Historic Preservation Board is housed here, a perfect setting. It's also available for special meetings and tours.

Admission: Free.

Open: Mon–Fri 8am–5pm.

THE COLUMNS, 100 N. Duval St., at Park Ave. Tel. 224-8116.

The city's oldest surviving building, this beautiful mansion was the private residence of banker William "Money" Williams and his family of 10 children. The white-columned brick home was built in the 1830s on land purchased for $5 by Mr. Williams, who was president of the Bank of Florida. According to legend, there's a nickel embedded in every brick. The Columns now houses the Tallahassee Chamber of Commerce.

Admission: Free.
Open: Mon–Fri 9am–5pm.

FIRST PRESBYTERIAN CHURCH, 110 N. Adams St., at Park Ave. Tel. 222-4504.

Built in 1838, this is Tallahassee's oldest church. During the Seminole raids of 1838 and 1839, local residents sought refuge beneath the church steeple. The church is also important to African American history: Slaves were always welcome to worship here as independent members, with or without their "master's" consent.

FLORIDA GOVERNOR'S MANSION, 700 N. Adams St., at Brevard St. Tel. 488-4661.

Florida's First Family lives in this lovely Georgian-style mansion, enhanced by a portico patterned after Andrew Jackson's columned antebellum home, the Hermitage. Giant magnolia trees shade the landscaped lawns. Visitors are welcome to tour five of the rooms, furnished with 18th- and 19th-century antiques, and displaying such collectibles as the holloware from the battleship U.S.S. *Florida*. Paintings by Renoir, Modigliani, and other famous artists adorn the walls. A collection of books by Florida authors is also displayed.

Adjacent to the Governor's Mansion, the plantation home **The Grove** was home to Ellen Call Long, known as "The Tallahassee Girl," the first child born after Tallahassee was settled.

Admission: Free.
Open: Check ahead for current schedule, as it varies.

KNOTT HOUSE MUSEUM ["The House That Rhymes"], 301 E. Park Ave., at Calhoun St. Tel. 488-3901.

Adorned by a columned portico, this stately 1843 mansion is furnished with Victorian elegance and boasts the nation's largest collection of 19th-century gilt-framed mirrors. The most unusual feature is the eccentric rhymes written by Mrs. Knott and attached by satin ribbons to tables, chairs, and lamps. Her poems comment upon 19th-century women's issues, plus the social, economic, and political events of the era. The house is in the Park Avenue Historic District, and is listed in the National Register of Historic Places.

Admission (including a one-hour tour): $3 adults, $1.50 children under 18.
Open: Wed–Fri 1–4pm, Sat 10am–4pm.

OLD CITY CEMETERY AND EPISCOPAL CEMETERY, Park Ave. and Bronough St. Tel. 545-5842.

These adjacent cemeteries contain the graves of Prince Achille Murat, Napoleon's nephew, and Princess Catherine Murat, his wife and George Washington's grandniece. Also buried here are two governors and numerous Confederate and Union soldiers who died at the Battle of Natural Bridge during the Civil War. The cemeteries are important to African American history since a number of slaves and the first African American Florida A&M graduates are among those buried here. The Visitors Information Center in the New Capitol has maps of the cemetery.

UNION BANK, 295 Apalachee Pkwy., at Calhoun St. Tel. 487-3803.

The Union Bank with its columned portico is Florida's oldest surviving bank, built in 1841. The building is an excellent example of architectural restoration. Once a "planter's bank" for cotton plantation owners and then a Freedman's Bank for emancipated slaves, the bank now presents the history of territorial-period banking. The bank is only one block south of the Capitol Complex, directly across from the Old Capitol.

Admission: Free.
Open: Tues–Fri 10am–1pm, Sat–Sun and holidays 1–4pm.

Museums

BLACK ARCHIVES RESEARCH CENTER AND MUSEUM, on the Florida A&M University campus, at Martin Luther King, Jr., Blvd. and Gamble St. Tel. 599-3020.

Housed in the columned library built by Andrew Carnegie, this fascinating research center and museum displays one of the nation's most extensive collections of

African American artifacts as well as such treasures as the 500-piece Ethiopian cross collection. Most important, however, the archives contain one of the world's largest collections on African American history. It's interesting to listen to tapes of elderly people reminiscing about the past. There are also tapes of gospel music. The Florida Agricultural and Mechanical University (FAMU) was founded in 1887, primarily as a black institution. Today it's acclaimed for its business, engineering, and pharmacy schools.

Admission: Free. A visitor parking permit is available at the security office.
Open: Mon–Fri 9am–4pm. **Closed:** Major holidays.

FLORIDA STATE UNIVERSITY GALLERY AND MUSEUM, 250 Fine Arts Building, at Copeland and Call Sts. on the FSU Campus. Tel. 644-6836.

A permanent art collection features 16th-century Dutch paintings, 20th-century American paintings, Japanese prints, pre-Columbian artifacts, and much more. Every three or four weeks, touring exhibits are displayed.

Admission: Free.
Open: Mon–Fri 9am–5pm, Sat–Sun 1–4pm.

FOSTER TANNER FINE ARTS GALLERY, Florida A&M University, off Martin Luther King, Jr., Blvd. between Osceola and Gamble Sts. Tel. 599-3334.

The focus in this gallery is on works by African American artists, with a wide variety of paintings, sculptures, and more. Exhibits change monthly, with local, national and international artists in the limelight.

Admission: Free.
Open: Mon–Fri 9am–5pm.

LEMOYNE ART GALLERY, 125 N. Gadsden St., between Park Ave. and Call St. Tel. 222-8800 or 224-2714.

A restored 1852 antebellum home is the lovely setting for this collection of art. The building (known as the Meginniss-Monroe House) is listed on the National Register of Historic Places. The art gallery is named in honor of Jacques LeMoyne, a member of a French expedition to Florida in 1564. LeMoyne, commissioned to depict the natives' dwellings and map the sea coast, was the first artist known to have visited North America. Exhibits include permanent displays by local artists, traveling exhibits, sculpture, pottery, photography—everything from traditional to avant-garde. The gardens with an old-fashioned gazebo are spectacular during the Christmas holiday season. During the year, the schedule also includes programs of classical music combined with visual arts. Check in advance for the current schedule.

Admission: Free.
Open: Tues–Sat 1–5pm, Sun 2–5pm.

MUSEUM OF FLORIDA HISTORY, in the R. A. Gray Building, 500 S. Bronough St., at Pensacola St. Tel. 488-1484 or 488-1673.

Herman, a skeletal prehistoric mastodon, which originally weighed in at five tons (when he prowled around Wakulla Springs), is the museum mascot. Ancient artifacts from Native American tribes are exhibited, plus such relics from Florida's exciting past as the treasures of 16th- and 17th-century sunken Spanish galleons. Climb aboard a reconstructed steamboat (sorry, Herman cannot be a passenger) to recapture the good old days. Inquire about guided tours and educational programs. There's an interesting museum gift shop, too.

Admission: Free.
Open: Mon–Fri 9am–4:30pm, Sat 10am–4:30pm, Sun noon–4:30pm. **Closed:** Holidays.

TALLAHASSEE MUSEUM OF HISTORY AND NATURAL SCIENCES (formerly the Tallahassee Junior Museum), 3945 Museum Dr., off Lake Bradford Rd. Tel. 576-1636.

From tots to adults, there's something of interest here for all ages. Along a winding trail through a 55-acre natural woodland habitat, the wildlife includes alligators, red wolves, Florida panthers, and a variety of other animals. Farm animals roam around the re-creation of an 1880s farm. There are special programs demonstrating butter churning, syrup making, blacksmithing, sheep shearing, spinning, weaving, and quilt making. Other exhibits feature science and history displays, a restored one-room schoolhouse, a gristmill, an old church, and a railroad caboose. Bellevue, the restored plantation home of Princess Murat, was moved here in 1967 (100 years after her death) and is listed on the National Register of Historic Places. Special events are always scheduled, from arts and crafts shows to wildflower walks. Picnic facilities, a snack bar, and a gift shop are on the premises.

Admission: $5 adults, $4 senior citizens, $3 children 3–15, free for kids under 3.
Open: Tues–Sat 9am–5pm, Sun 12:30–5pm.

Archeological Sites

DE SOTO ARCHEOLOGICAL AND HISTORICAL SITE, 1022 DeSoto Park Dr., off La Fayette St. Tel. 922-6007 or 925-6216.

During the winter of 1539, Spanish conquistador Hernándo de Soto, his troops and friars, set up an encampment here before continuing their ill-fated search for gold. The friars celebrated the first Christmas mass in North America with de Soto and his entourage. An archeologist searching for Spanish mission ruins in 1986 discovered the de Soto encampment site. Rare copper coins, armor fragments, and a fossilized pig's jaw were unearthed. In the 1930s, when former Gov. John Martin built his English hunting lodge–style home at the site, he had no idea de Soto had camped here. His home is planned as a museum for exhibiting the artifacts. In December a colorful pageant-drama re-enacting the first Christmas is presented, beginning at 9am and continuing to 8pm. Check ahead for the exact date and program schedule. The admission is free.

Because the archeological site is being excavated and the home is under restoration, only the Christmas pageant is open to the public at present.

LAKE JACKSON MOUNDS STATE ARCHEOLOGICAL SITE, 1313 Crowder Rd., off N. Monroe St. north of I-10. Tel. 562-0042.

Artifacts discovered on this 18-acre excavation have revealed that native tribes settled on the shores of Lake Jackson centuries ago. (Could they have been lured by the lake's abundant bass? This is still one of the nation's best bass-fishing spots.) Evidently this Southeastern Ceremonial Complex flourished around A.D. 1200. You'll see six earth temple mounds and a burial mound. Part of the village and plaza area and two of the largest mounds are within the state site. The largest mound is 36 feet high with a base that measures 278 by 312 feet. If you'd like a guided tour, call the above number.

Admission: Free.
Open: Daily 8am–sundown.

SAN LUIS ARCHEOLOGICAL AND HISTORIC SITE, 2020 Mission Rd., off W. Tennessee St. Tel. 487-3711.

Located high on a hilltop west of downtown Tallahassee is this important Apalachee tribal settlement. A Spanish Franciscan mission was set up here in 1656. San Luís de Talimali, as it was called, soon included a tribal council house, a Catholic church, a Spanish fort, and many homes. In 1704 the inhabitants burned the town rather than submit to British invaders. The missions were destroyed and the Apalachees dispersed. Exhibits along the trails depict the San Luís story. Visitors are welcome to stroll around the area and to observe state archeologists uncover artifacts (in the spring season).

Admission: Free.
Open: Mon–Fri 9am–4:30pm, Sat 10am–4:30pm, Sun noon–4:30pm. Public tours Mon–Fri at noon, Sat at 11am and 3pm. **Closed:** Thanksgiving and Christmas.

The Canopy Roads

Graced by canopies of Spanish moss–draped oak trees and colorful flowers, the St. Augustine, Miccousukee, Meridian, Old Bainbridge, and Centerville Roads are the five official old canopy roads. Driving is slow on these winding, two-lane country roads, some of which are canopied for as much as 20 miles. Take along a picnic lunch; there are few places to eat in this tranquil setting. Here are highlights of each road.

The cotton harvest was piled on wagons, drawn by six-mule teams and transported along the **Centerville Road** to St. Marks to be loaded onto schooners. Plantation owners planted the majestic live oaks around 1800 to shade the mule teams. Stop at Bradley's Country Store for the area's best homemade sausage.

The only straight road in the group, the **Meridian Road** was built in 1825 according to a federal survey. However, the mule-drawn wagons made deep ruts and the packed clay on both sides created walls, now covered by lichen. From here, you can drive to Maclay Gardens or stop for bass fishing at Lake Jackson or at the picnic grounds on nearby Miller's Landing Road.

Originally, the **Miccousukee Road** was an early Native American trail. Driving north on Miccousukee, you reach the plantation town of Thomasville, Georgia, which has many beautiful antebellum homes as well as the All American Rose Test Gardens where 2,000 roses bloom from April to November.

The **Old Bainbridge Road** is considered the most scenic of the canopy roads. It leads to the Lake Jackson Indian Mounds State Archeological Site. Continuing on, about 15 miles north of Tallahassee you arrive at Havana, an old-fashioned typical southern town, known for good restaurants and antiques shops.

Other than the scenic beauty, and the pleasure of leisurely driving, there's not much to see or do along the **St. Augustine Road.** However, the road's history goes back to early Native American tribes and the subsequent Spanish invasion. Missions were established here in the mid-16th century by Spain's Franciscan friars, and according to records, about 15,000 Native Americans in this area were converted to Catholicism. Unfortunately, not one of the area's 20 missions remains—by the end of the 17th century they had all been destroyed in the battles between Spain and England.

For information and maps, contact the **Tallahassee Area Visitor Information Center** in the New Capitol Building.

Parks and Gardens

MACLAY STATE GARDENS, 3540 Thomasville Rd. (U.S. 319), north of I-10. Tel. 487-4556.

New York financier Alfred B. Maclay and his wife, Louise, began planting this floral wonderland on Lake Hall in 1923. The mansion was their winter home.

After her husband's death in 1944, Louise Maclay continued his dream of an ornamental garden to delight the public. In 1953 the land was bequeathed to the state of Florida. The more than 300 acres of flowers feature at least 200 varieties; 28 acres are devoted exclusively to azaleas and camellias. The beautifully restored home contains a camellia information center. The surrounding park offers nature trails, canoe rentals, boating, picnicking, swimming, and fishing. The high blooming season is from January to mid-April; the floral peak is mid- to late March.

Admission: Park and garden, May–Dec, $3.25 per vehicle with up to eight passengers; Jan–Apr, $3 adults, $1.50 children under 12.

Open: Park, daily 8am–sunset; gardens, daily 9am–5pm; Maclay House, Jan–Apr, daily 9am–5pm.

TALLAHASSEE–ST. MARKS HISTORIC RAILROAD STATE TRAIL, entrance on Woodville Hwy. (Fla. 363), just south of SE Capitol Circle. Tel. 922-6007.

Constructed with the financial assistance of wealthy Panhandle cotton-plantation owners and merchants, this was Florida's oldest railroad, functioning from 1837 to 1984. Cotton and other products were transported to St. Marks (see "Easy Excursions," below) for shipment to other cities. After the tracks were removed in recent years, the historic trail was improved along 16 miles for joggers, hikers, bicyclists, and horseback riders. A paved parking lot is at the entrance. Rental bikes are available (see "Sports and Recreation," below).

SPECIAL EVENTS

Springtime Tallahassee, celebrated from mid-March to mid-April, is the main local event, a four-week jubilee featuring parades, festivals, arts and crafts, sports competitions, and much more. The Natural Bridge Battlefield Re-Enactment takes place in March, as does the competitive Bike Tour of Tallahassee; and the Summer Swamp Stomp is in July. In September comes the Native American Heritage Festival, and in October the Greek Food Festival and the 11-day North Florida Fair. Winter Farm Days are celebrated in December, and the Winter Festival and Celebration of Lights marks the holiday season. The First Christmas Reenactment commemorates the first Christmas mass at Spanish Conquistador Hernándo de Soto's encampment on the De Soto Archeological and Historical Site.

For information about these and other area celebrations, call the Tallahassee Area Convention and Visitors Bureau (tel. 904/681-9200 or toll free 800/628-2866).

SPORTS & RECREATION

The football frenzy scores a touchdown when games are scheduled at **Florida State University** with their national-champion Seminoles team and at **Florida A&M University** when the Rattlers are cheered on by their high-stepping, world-famous Marching 100 Band. Both stadiums are packed to the rafters with the most enthusiastic fans in the football world. Hollywood star Burt Reynolds was a halfback at FSU in 1957; he's very proud of his alma mater. FSU also features a terrific **Flying High Circus** (tel. 644-4874), with annual shows (free) in April. Both FSU and FAMU have a seasonal schedule of sports events, including basketball, baseball, tennis, and track. Call for schedules and tickets (tel. 644-1830 for FSU, 599-3230 for FAMU).

Tallahassee features at least eight **city parks,** offering a variety of recreational facilities, including A. J. Henry Park (tel. 891-3905), Dorothy B. Oven Park (tel. 891-3915), Forest Meadows (tel. 891-3920), Hilaman Park (tel. 891-3935), Lafayette Park (tel. 891-3946), Lake Ella (tel. 891-3866), Myers Park (tel. 891-3866), and Tom Brown Park (tel. 891-3966).

On the 100-acre **Seminole Reservation,** 3226 Flastacowo Rd. (tel. 644-5730), the multipurpose recreational facility includes sailing, canoeing, and waterskiing on Lake Bradford (rentals available), a volleyball court, a playground for the kids, and a picnic area. It's open daily when FSU is in session.

BICYCLING   Cycleogical Bicycle Rentals & Touring, 4780 Woodville Hwy. (Fla. 363), just south of SE Capital Circle, at the entrance of the 16-mile Tallahassee–St. Marks Historic Railroad Trail (see "Attractions," above), offers a variety of rental bikes, off-road tours, cycling supplies, and in-line skate rentals (tel. 656-0001). Bike-rental rates are $9 for two hours, $14 for four hours, and various rates for three to five bikes' rental for families and groups. Guide maps and refreshments are also on hand. Cycleogical is open Monday through Friday from 10am to dark and on Saturday and Sunday from 9am to dark.

BOATING & CANOEING   Countless scenic waterways are enjoyable for boating and canoeing. Among the beautiful river recreation areas with boat and canoe rentals are **Three Rivers State Recreation Area** (tel. 482-9006), **Lake Bradford** at the Seminole Reservation (tel. 644-5730), the **Ochlockonee River** in Ochlockonee River State Park (tel. 962-2771), and the **St. Marks River** in the St. Marks National Wildlife Refuge (tel. 925-6121). All are within a 30- to 50-mile drive from Tallahassee.

FISHING   Bass abound in Tallahassee-area lakes. Record-size catches have been made in **Lake Jackson** and **Lake Talquin.** For a Tallahassee-area guide to fishing camps and lodges, contact the **Tallahassee Area Visitor Information Center** (tel. 681-9200, or toll free 800/628-2866).

In the nearby gulf, deep-sea-fishing excursions are available for grouper, snapper, and king mackerel. Check with the marinas at **Shell Point, Alligator Point,** and **Panacea** (also known as "The Blue Crab Capital of the World").

GOLF & TENNIS   Play golf and tennis at outstanding **Hilaman Park,** 2731 Blair Stone Dr., where the Hilaman Park Municipal Golf Course features 18 holes (par 72), a driving range, racquetball, squash courts, and a swimming pool. Rental equipment is at the club, and there's a restaurant, too (tel. 891-3935 for information and fees). The park also includes Jake Gaither Municipal Golf Course, at Bragg and Pasco Streets, with a 9-hole, par-35 fairway and a pro shop (tel. 891-3942). Open daily from 7:30am to 7:30pm, the park also has tennis courts, which are lighted for night play. Tennis courts are also available at Lafayette Park, Tom Brown Park, Myers Park and Forest Meadows (the latter two have lighted courts).

The leading golf course is at **Killearn Country Club and Inn** (tel. 893-2186, or toll free 800/476-4101), former home of the $750,000 PGA Centel Classic. Moss-draped oaks enhance the beautiful 27-hole championship course, which is for guests only. (See "Where to Stay," below.)

HIKING In addition to the 16-mile **Tallahassee–St. Marks Historical Trail** and numerous trails in state parks, the **Florida National Scenic Trail** meanders 110 miles through the Apalachicola National Forest and St. Marks National Wildlife Refuge. On the trail you'll encounter sink holes, the Bradwell Bay Wilderness Area, Confederate salt evaporation ponds, and more. Eventually, the trail will be extended to span 1,300 miles across Florida. For information, call 488-7326.

HUNTING In the 1800s, wealthy plantation owners invited friends on hunting expeditions. The custom is maintained at **Myrtlewood Plantation,** P.O. Box 32, Thomasville, GA 31799 (tel. 912/228-6232), about 35 miles from Tallahassee. Special arrangements can be made in season to hunt ducks, white-tail deer, pheasant, and quail. The 3,300-acre plantation also offers attractive, comfortable accommodations and meals. Largemouth bass and bluegill bream are abundant in the four fishing lakes. For plantation deer hunts arranged by **Big Pine Hunting,** call 912/226-2541 or toll free 800/841-0001. For the plantation quail hunt, contact **Southern Style Hunting Preserve,** P.O. Box 199, Thomasville, GA 31799 (tel. 912/228-0987). Myrtlewood also has a championship sporting clays marksmanship course (tel. 912/228-0987).

At the **St. Marks National Wildlife Refuge** (see "Easy Excursions," below), hunting is permitted only with such primitive weapons as cross-bows and muzzle-loading guns. For information, call 925-6121. The **Apalachicola National Forest** is one of only two areas in the state where the American black bear may be hunted. For information, call 926-3561, 681-7265, or 670-8644.

WHERE TO STAY

Hotels are often completely booked when the legislature is in session (usually between February and May) and during the very popular universities' football games on weekends from September to December. Rates go up, too, so reserve well in advance or you may have to stay far from the city. Just about every hotel offers excellent meeting/convention facilities.

Most hotels are concentrated in three areas: downtown Tallahassee, along North Monroe Street at Exit 29 off I-10, and along Apalachee Parkway east of downtown. In addition to those recommended below, the area along North Monroe Street at I-10 has several chain motels, including a **Comfort Inn,** 2720 Graves Rd. (tel. 904/562-7200, or toll free 800/228-5150); **Days Inn,** 2800 N. Monroe St. (tel. 904/385-0136, or toll free 800/325-2525); **Super 8,** 2702 N. Monroe St. (tel. 904/386-8818, or toll free 800/800-8000); and the rock-bottom **Motel 6,** 2738 N. Monroe St. (tel. 904/386-7878). There's a second Motel 6 at 1027 Apalachee Pkwy. (tel. 904/877-6171).

DOWNTOWN
Expensive

GOVERNORS INN, on Adams St. Commons, 209 S. Adams St., Talla-hassee, FL 32301. Tel. 904/681-6855, or toll free 800/342-7717. Fax 904/222-3105. 32 rms, 8 suites. A/C TV TEL
$ Rates (including continental breakfast and evening cocktails): $119–$135 single or double; $160–$220 suite. AE, DC, DISC, MC, V.

One of the most elegant hotels anywhere, the award-winning Governors Inn was opened in 1984 by the son of Gov. Lawton Chiles (at the time, he was a senator and then became governor). Actually, the hotel was named in honor of Andrew Jackson, Florida's first military governor, known for his appreciation of the good life.

On a brick-paved historic street, just half a block from the Old Capitol, the richly furnished hotel was a livery stable long ago and part of the building's original architecture has been preserved, including the impressive beams. Guest rooms are distinctive with four-poster beds, black oak writing desks, rock maple armoires, and antique accoutrements. The suites, each one named for a Florida governor, are sumptuous, some with whirlpool bath or loft bedrooms with wood-burning fireplace. Among the amenities are comfy robes.

Dining/Entertainment: The pine-paneled Florida Room is the perfect retreat for enjoying the complimentary continental breakfast elegantly presented with a silver service, fine china, sparkling crystal, and lovely linens. Early-evening complimentary cocktails are also served in this handsome room.

Services: Valet parking, airline reservations, European turn-down service, your choice of newspaper delivered daily to your door, same-day laundry service, shoeshines, room service, remote control TV with Movie Channel, airport transportation, health club privileges.

SHERATON TALLAHASSEE HOTEL, 101 S. Adams St., Tallahassee, FL 32301. Tel. 904/224-5000, or toll free 800/325-3535. Fax 904/222-9216. 246 rms, 7 suites. A/C TV TEL

$ Rates: $70–$130 single or double; $175–$300 suite. Also special Concierge Level rooms and suites. AE, DC, DISC, MC, V.

A favorite with politicians and lobbyists, this high-rise hotel is usually booked solid during legislative sessions. Not only is the hotel only a block from the Capitol Building but it's also notable for spacious, attractive guest rooms and beautiful public rooms. And, of course, the rooms are stocked with all the amenities, Sheraton style.

Dining/Entertainment: Café in the Court, with its skylight ceiling and lush greenery, is a favorite rendezvous for the power breakfast, lunch, or dinner. When the political celebrities aren't here, they're in Far Tuesday's Sports Bar.

Services: Room service, health club privileges, same-day laundry service, shoeshines, airport transportation, free or pay TV movies.

Facilities: Swimming pool (outdoor), beauty/barber salon, gift shop, garage, convention facilities.

Moderate

HOLIDAY INN UNIVERSITY CENTER DOWNTOWN, 316 W. Tennessee St., Tallahassee, FL 32301. Tel. 904/222-8000, or toll free 800/465-4329. Fax 904/222-8113. 174 rms. A/C TV TEL

$ Rates: $49–$79 double. Corporate and government rates available. AE, DC, DISC, MC, V.

Distinguished by its cylindrical 12-story design, this is one of two Holiday Inns in Tallahassee. At this location, you're convenient to FAMU, FSU, the State Capitol, and the Governor's Mansion. All guest rooms overlook the city panorama or the rolling hills. If you stay in the higher-priced rooms on the concierge level, there's a private rooftop lounge. Especially during the football season, the Tower Bar & Grill is very lively. An International House of Pancakes at street level is open 24 hours a day. The airport shuttle is complimentary.

RADISSON HOTEL, 415 N. Monroe St., Tallahassee, FL 32301. Tel. and fax 904/224-6000, or toll free 800/333-3333. 116 rms, 8 suites. A/C TV TEL

$ Rates: $83–$125 double. AE, DC, DISC, MC, V.

About half a mile north of the Capitol, the Radisson features cheerfully decorated guest rooms, a fitness facility with sauna, and facilities for the business executive. Complimentary airport transportation is provided. The pleasant Plantation Dining Room is open daily for breakfast, lunch, and dinner. The bar on the seventh floor is a friendly rendezvous.

Bed-and-Breakfast

RIEDEL HOUSE BED & BREAKFAST, 1412 Fairway Dr., Tallahassee, FL 32301. Tel. 904/222-8569. 2 rms (both with bath).

$ Rates (including breakfast): $65 double. No credit cards.

Surrounded by majestic live oaks, pines, magnolias, and flowers, this white-brick Federal-style, two-story home was built in 1937 for the Cary D. Landis family (he was a former Florida attorney general). Talented artist and art teacher Carolyn Riedel, the gracious innkeeper, now owns the elegant house. From the beautiful foyer, the spiral staircase leads to the upstairs art gallery and spacious guest bedrooms, both adorned with period furniture and antiques. The delicious continental breakfast is served in the lovely dining room overlooking terraced gardens. Located in the prestigious Capital Country Club area, the Riedel House is just minutes away from Florida State University and the Capitol, and within walking distance of public tennis courts and the club's golf course.

NORTH OF DOWNTOWN
Moderate

CABOT LODGE NORTH, 2735 N. Monroe St., Tallahassee, FL 32303. Tel. 904/386-8880, or toll free 800/223-1964. Fax 904/386-4254. 160 rms. A/C TV TEL
$ Rates (including continental breakfast): $55–$59 single; $61–$65 double. AE, DC, DISC, MC, V.

⑤ A clapboard plantation-style house with tin roof and wraparound, partially screened porch is the highlight at this friendly establishment just inside I-10. Guests can sit and relax southern fashion, either on straight-back rockers on the porch or on lots of comfy sofas and easy chairs by a fireplace in the living room. Although guest rooms in the two-story motel buildings out back don't hold up their end of the atmosphere factor, they're still quite satisfactory at these rates, and they give quick access to a swimming pool. Guests can graze a continental breakfast buffet, drink coffee and juice all day, and partake of free cocktails between 5:30 and 7:30pm daily.

KILLEARN COUNTRY CLUB AND INN, 100 Tyron Circle, Tallahassee, FL 32308. Tel. 904/893-2186. Fax 904/668-7637. 39 rms. A/C TV TEL
$ Rates: $55–$75 single; $65–$90 double. Golf and vacation packages available. AE, DC, DISC, MC, V.

In the Lodge, located in the Killearn development between Thomasville and Centerville Roads north of I-10, luxurious rooms include two double beds, a sitting area, and dressing rooms; some accommodations have a wet bar. Each room is individually decorated with attractive furnishings and spacious balconies overlooking the woodland-bordered golf course. To a basic large room with fridge, wet bar, and murphy bed, one to four bedrooms can be attached to make a suite, (at a higher price, of course).

Tallahassee's leading golf course is here, staffed with PGA professionals and former home of the $750,000 PGA Centel Classic. For tennis buffs, the resort offers four lighted hard courts and four soft courts; racquetball and handball courts are on the premises. The swimming pool is Olympic size. For keeping fit, there's a Hydra-Gym exercise facility plus miles of surrounding roads for jogging. Moderate prices prevail in the classy, beamed-ceiling Oak View restaurant. Live entertainment is spotlighted in the nightclub. This is one of the area's best resort bargains.

RAMADA INN TALLAHASSEE, 2900 N. Monroe St., Tallahassee, FL 32303. Tel. 904/386-1027, or toll free 800/228-2828. Fax 904/422-1025. 200 rms. A/C TV TEL
$ Rates: $75–$85 single or double. Two children under 18 stay free with existing bed space in parents' room. Special family rates available. AE, DC, DISC, MC, V.
On 13 landscaped acres just south of I-10, the Ramada Inn has the appearance of a modern suburban office park. An outdoor swimming pool and jogging trail help keep guests fit. The tropically decorated lobby bar with a waterfall is relaxing for a drink. Breakfast, lunch, and dinner are served in the new Monroe Street Grill. Dooley's Australian Nightclub is the fun place for comedy on weekends. For the executive, there's a business center and conference rooms (facilities for handling meetings up to 500 people).

Budget

HAMPTON INN, 3210 N. Monroe St., Tallahassee, FL 32303. Tel. 904/562-4300, or toll free 800/HAMPTON. Fax 904/562-6735. 92 rms. A/C TV TEL

$ **Rates** (including continental breakfast): $44–$49 single; $46–$51 double. Children stay free in parents' room. AE, DISC, MC, V.

Just north of I-10, this two-story inn with a beige stucco exterior offers comfortable rooms with convertible sofas in addition to beds. Local phone calls and daily newspapers are free, and a Waffle Shop next door is open 24 hours a day. The hotel has an outdoor swimming pool.

SHONEY'S INN, 2801 N. Monroe St., Tallahassee, FL 32303. Tel. 904/386-8286, or toll free 800/222-2222. Fax 904/422-1074. 112 rms, 26 suites. A/C TV TEL

$ **Rates** (including continental breakfast): $40–$53 single; $43–$58 double; $90 townhouse suite; $120 Jacuzzi suite. AE, DC, DISC, MC, V.

This attractive, Spanish-style inn has rooms, townhouse suites (especially a bargain), and suites with Jacuzzi pools. Guest rooms overlook pretty views of green lawns and moss-draped trees. A heated swimming pool is on the premises, also a Cantina cocktail lounge (restaurants are conveniently close by). Hospitality features complimentary cocktails from 5:30 to 10pm Monday through Friday. Complimentary airport shuttle service is offered from 7am to 9pm.

TALLAHASSEE MOTOR HOTEL, 1630 N. Monroe St., Tallahassee, FL 32303. Tel. 904/224-6183, or toll free 800/251-1962. Fax 904/224-6183. 88 rms. A/C TV TEL

$ **Rates:** $26–$28 single; $30–$38 double. AE, DC, MC, V.

A landmark for more than 60 years, this hospitable hotel, complete with swimming pool, has a lovely setting on five acres of lawn, shaded by Spanish moss–draped oak trees. Very small but pretty Lake Ella is across the way. For a better view, request the newer and more spacious accommodations in a the two-story building facing Lake Ella across North Monroe Street. The toll-free telephone number connects to the Master Host reservations system, so don't think that you have the wrong number when you call for reservations.

ON APALACHEE PARKWAY

Moderate

COURTYARD BY MARRIOTT, 1018 Apalachee Pkwy., Tallahassee, FL 32301. Tel. 904/222-8822, or toll free 800/321-2211. Fax 904/561-0354. 154 rms. A/C TV TEL

$ **Rates:** $74 single Sun–Thurs, $54 Fri–Sat; $84 double Sun–Thurs, $64 Fri–Sat. AE, DC, DISC, MC, V.

Just a mile east of the Old Capitol, this comfortable modern hotel encloses a landscaped courtyard with a swimming pool. About half the rooms face the courtyard; the others, the surrounding parking lots. All have sofas and rich mahogany writing tables and chests of drawers, plus nice little features like long telephone cords and extra hand-basin faucets dispensing piping hot water for tea and instant coffee, which are supplied. The lobby features a fireplace and dining area, which is open for breakfast only. Other facilities include an exercise room and indoor spa pool.

QUALITY INN, 2020 Apalachee Pkwy., Tallahassee, FL 32301. Tel. 904/877-4437, or toll free 800/253-4787. Fax 904/878-9964. 100 rms, 13 suites. A/C TV TEL

$ **Rates** (including continental breakfast): $60 single or double; $65–$85 suite. AE, DC, DISC, MC, V.

Reminiscent of an English country inn, there's more than just a touch of class here. Spacious, attractive guest rooms are tastefully furnished with sofas, wing chairs, king-size beds, desks, and night tables. The complimentary continental breakfast (delicious pastries!) is served in the cozy parlor, off the marble-lined lobby. Because the inn has no restaurant or cocktail lounge, the rates are lower than would be expected for such a pleasant place. Guests can partake of a complimentary wine bar from 5 to 11pm Monday through Saturday, and they receive free passes to the nearby YMCA, which has a pool. The owners were planning to add a pool and exercise room to the inn by 1995. The inn is located within a few yards of the Best Western Pride Inn and a Shoney's Restaurant (see above).

Budget

BEST WESTERN PRIDE INN, 2016 Apalachee Pkwy., Tallahassee, FL 32301. Tel. 904/656-6312, or toll free 800/827-7390. Fax 904/942-4312. 78 rms, 31 suites. A/C TV TEL
$ **Rates** (including continental breakfast): $39-$45 single; $44-$50 double. AE, DC, DISC, MC, V.
The friendly inn is within walking distance of the Governor's Square Mall for shopping and dining, and about two miles from the Capitol. Every evening, complimentary wine and cheese are offered. A small swimming pool and sunning patio are on the premises. Health club privileges can be arranged. Guests get a 10% discount at Shoney's Restaurant, just steps away at 2014 Apalachee Pkwy. (tel. 878-3979), serving budget-priced breakfasts, lunches, and dinners, with specials for children and seniors.

HOLIDAY INN PARKWAY, 1302 Apalachee Pkwy., Tallahassee, FL 32301. Tel. 904/877-3141, or toll free 800/465-4329. Fax 904/877-3141. 167 rms. A/C TV TEL
$ **Rates:** $40-$50 single or double. AE, DC, DISC, MC, V.
Pleasant guest rooms encircle landscaped lawns, a courtyard, and a swimming pool. About a mile from the downtown area, the inn also provides complimentary greens fees at a nearby course and complimentary passes to a nearby fitness facility. On site, the International House of Pancakes is open 24 hours with a varied menu. There's a cocktail lounge, too. Meeting facilities are available.

CAMPING

Bell's Trailer Park, 6401 W. Tennessee St. (U.S. 90) (tel. 904/575-5006), six miles west of the Capitol, offers 62 RV and tent campsites (there's a lake for fishing, too). Rates are approximately $15 per night, and weekly rates are available.

The **Tallahassee East KOA Kampground** (tel. 904/997-3890), about 20 miles east of Tallahassee, offers rustic camping under 100-year-old oak trees as well as 39 RV sites with full hookups and two furnished cabins with air conditioning/heat and electricity. The park has a swimming pool, fishing pond, playground, games room, general store, and shower/bathroom facilities.

The **Tallahassee RV Park,** 6504 Mahan Dr. (tel. 904/878-7641), features 66 RV campsites with full hookups in a scenic setting of rolling hills.

WHERE TO DINE
DOWNTOWN
Expensive

ANDREW'S 2ND ACT, 228 S. Adams St., in Adams Commons. Tel. 222-2759.
Cuisine: AMERICAN/INTERNATIONAL. **Reservations:** Recommended.
$ **Prices:** Appetizers $3.50-$7; main courses $11-$21. AE, MC, V.
Open: Lunch Tues-Fri 11:30am-1:30pm; dinner Mon-Thurs 6-10pm, Fri-Sat 6-11pm, Sun 6-9:30pm; brunch Sun 9:30am-1pm.

A consistent award winner, Andrew's 2nd Act is Tallahassee's premier restaurant, the dining rendezvous of gourmets, politicians, and lobbyists. In the labyrinth of intimate subterranean dining rooms, the old-world ambience is enhanced by stucco walls, paintings, and tiles. Tables are set with pretty linens, flowers, and candles. The tremendous wine cellar is notable for an amazing variety of wines; there's also a private wine-cellar room which diners may request. Favorites at lunch are stacked-high deli sandwiches, pastas, and seafood crêpes. Dinner specialties are superbly prepared, from puff pastry filled with escargots to succulent rack of lamb Dijon. Steaks, chops, veal, poultry, and seafood are always listed on the menu. Tableside cooking features steak Diane, expertly tossed Caesar salad, and flaming bananas Foster.

Moderate

CHEZ PIERRE, 115 N. Adams St. Tel. 222-0936.
   Cuisine: FRENCH. **Reservations:** Recommended.
$ Prices: Appetizers $3–$6; main courses $11–$17 (less than half that at lunch). MC, V.
   Open: Lunch Tues–Sat 11am–2:30pm; dinner Tues–Sat 5:30–9:30pm; brunch Sat–Sun 10am–2:30pm. Pastry shop, Tues–Sat 10am–4pm.
In this chic restaurant, you become an instant Francophile. Provincial French specialties are highlighted, such as pâtés, garlic-buttered escargots, onion soup, salade niçoise, croque monsieur sandwiches, just-baked croissants, and crusty French bread. Seafood lovers recommend crêpes fruits-de-mer, two light-as-a-feather crêpes filled with scallops, shrimp, and fish in a luscious lobster sauce. Roast duck and veal dishes are featured. French table wines are very moderately priced, and California house wines are also served. For dessert, the pastry tray, brought to your table, is an array of irresistible delights from Chez Pierre's pastry shop. And the delicious cheeses can also be purchased from their deli case.

Budget

ANDREW'S ADAMS STREET CAFE, 228 S. Adams St. Tel. 222-3444.
   Cuisine: DELI. **Reservations:** Not accepted.
$ Prices: Sandwiches and salads $2.50–$5. AE, MC, V.
   Open: Lunch only, Mon–Fri 11:30am–2pm.
Enjoy dining on a high-backed banquette amid a decor of brass and paneled wood walls. From the cafeteria-style selection, there's a delicious array of soups, salads, and sandwiches galore, including charcoal-grilled hamburgers and barbecued chicken. The outdoor café area is directly on the Adams Street Commons, delightful in warm weather.

ANDREW'S UPSTAIRS, A BAR AND GRILLE, 228 S. Adams St. Tel. 222-3446.
   Cuisine: NEW AMERICAN. **Reservations:** Recommended.
$ Prices: Appetizers $3–$7.50; main courses $6–$16. AE, DC, MC, V.
   Open: Lunch Mon–Fri 11:30am–2pm; dinner Mon–Thurs 6–10pm, Fri–Sat 6–11pm; champagne brunch Sun 10:30am–2pm.
Another in the trio of Andrew Reiss's famous Tallahassee restaurants, his Upstairs is especially popular with business executives. Steaks, chicken, and seafood from the mesquite grill are big favorites. The hot and cold all-you-can-eat lunch buffet is perfect for those in a rush. Blue Plate Specials are featured daily. The varied menu also lists pastas, salads, and pizzas. From the dining room, there's a nice view of the Capitol Complex. The Sunday brunch is a veritable "groaning board." Monday through Friday, the happy hour brings in the happy crowds for discounted cocktails and the complimentary hors d'oeuvres.

NORTH OF DOWNTOWN
Expensive

ANTHONY'S, in the Betton Place Shops, Bradford Rd. at Thomasville Rd. Tel. 224-1447.
   Cuisine: ITALIAN. **Reservations:** Recommended.
$ Prices: Appetizers $3–$6; main courses $10–$16. AE, MC, V.
   Open: Dinner only, Mon–Thurs 5–10pm, Fri–Sat 5:30–10:30pm, Sun 5:30–9pm.
Locals come to see and be seen at Dick Anthony's trattoria. Among the specialties are pesce Venezia, spinach fettuccine tossed in a cream sauce with scallops, crabmeat, and

fish. Chicken piccata and chicken San Marino are favorites. Of course, a thick, juicy steak is always popular with beefeaters. The wine list features choices from Italy and the United States. The dessert menu is highlighted by espresso pie.

Moderate

THE MELTING POT, 1832 N. Monroe St., behind Barnacle Bill's. Tel. 386-7440.
Cuisine: SWISS. **Reservations:** Recommended.
$ Prices: Appetizers $3.50–$10; main courses $8–$13. AE, MC, V.
Open: Dinner only, Sun–Thurs 6–10pm, Fri–Sat 6–11pm.

A romantic atmosphere prevails in this dimly lit basement, especially for loving couples enjoying the beef or seafood fondue for two (whoever inadvertently drops the food from the fork into the pot is supposed to kiss the person sitting next to them). The bubbling hot cheese fondue is always a favorite, with chunks of French bread for dipping (the same kissing rule applies). Chocoholics love the rich chocolate fondue with strawberries and fresh fruit to dip and "to die for."

ROOSTER'S, 2226 N. Monroe St. Tel. 386-8738.
Cuisine: STEAKS. **Reservations:** Not required.
$ Prices: Appetizers $3.50–$7; main courses $7–$21. AE, MC, V.
Open: Dinner only, Mon–Sat 5pm–10pm. (Bar stays open to 2am.)

At this country-style hangout, the grilled steaks are something to crow about, especially if you select the 32-ounce sirloin. Grilled chicken is also on the menu, but everything seems to be upstaged by the steaks. You can cook your own at the charcoal grill, or the chef will do it for you. Live bands are featured here starting at 9pm, attracting a lively crowd of night owls, who like to dance.

SILVER SLIPPER, 531 Scotty's Lane, one block south of the Tallahassee Mall behind Scotty's Hardware. Tel. 386-9366.
Cuisine: STEAK/SEAFOOD. **Reservations:** Recommended.
$ Prices: Appetizers $2–$17; main courses $10–$26. AE, DC, DISC, MC, V.
Open: Dinner only, Mon–Sat 5–11pm.

The oldest family-operated restaurant in Florida, the Silver Slipper has served thick, tender, juicy steaks to Presidents John F. Kennedy, Lyndon Johnson, Jimmy Carter, Ronald Reagan, and George Bush. As you would anticipate, the steaks are the very best Black Angus. From the award-winning menu, you can also select seafood dishes, lamb, veal, and quail; a dozen bacon-wrapped big shrimp are a meal-size appetizer. A favorite of politicians and lobbyists, the Silver Slipper is always packed to the rafters, especially the cocktail lounge, open to midnight Monday through Thursday and to 2am on Friday and Saturday. Should you prefer privacy, curtained booths can be requested, rather than the dining room.

Budget

BARNACLE BILL'S SEAFOOD RESTAURANT, 1830 N. Monroe St. Tel. 385-8734.
Cuisine: SEAFOOD. **Reservations:** Recommended.
$ Prices: Appetizers $3.50–$5; main courses $7.50–$10. AE, MC, V.
Open: Sun–Thurs 11am–11pm, Fri–Sat 11am–midnight.

There's always plenty of action here, especially when everyone is watching sports events on the big-screen TV. During summer, it's pleasant to dine outdoors and enjoy home-smoked fish and grilled or steamed seafood. For munchies, try the buffalo chicken wings. Freshly shucked oysters are served at the enormous tile-topped oyster bar. Among the menu favorites are the grilled fish platter, the shrimp Alfredo, and the Admiral (an enormous platter of oysters, shrimp, Alaskan crab, fish of the day, fresh corn, potatoes, and salad). Each night different specials are offered. In addition, there are specials for the kids and for senior citizens. At lunch, the Fit & Trim Menu and a variety of sandwiches are popular. From the bar, margaritas are usually priced at only $1. Every weekend, live bands play in the cocktail lounge.

FOOD GLORIOUS FOOD, in the Betton Place Shops, Bradford Rd. at Thomasville Rd. Tel. 224-9974.

Cuisine: AMERICAN/INTERNATIONAL. **Reservations:** Not required.
$ **Prices:** $3.50–$9. MC, V.
Open: Mon–Fri 11am–8pm, Sat 11am–7pm (full service Mon–Sat 11am–3pm).
Very unusual (but very healthy) sandwiches, salads, and pastas have made this deli/café the talk of the town. Items displayed in a cold case change daily, and could include such mouth-waterers as Tijuana lasagne, a tasty dish of layered baked polenta with piquantly spiced chicken, tomato-chile sauce, and a topping of Monterey Jack cheese. There's always a daily quiche and plenty of desserts featuring tempting pastries and cookies. Take-out food can also be ordered.

ON APALACHEE PARKWAY

Moderate

THE WHARF, 4141 Apalachee Pkwy., two miles east of Capitol Circle.
Tel. 656-2332 or 656-2395.
Cuisine: SEAFOOD. **Reservations:** Not accepted.
$ **Prices:** Appetizers $2.50–$5; main courses $5.50–$16; lunch $4–$16.50. AE, MC, V.
Open: Mon–Thurs 11am–9pm, Fri 11am–10pm, Sat 4–10pm, Sun 4–9pm.
Notable for southern hospitality and home-style cooking, the rough-hewn Wharf is often filled to its 400-seat capacity. Fried fresh mullet and hush puppies are undoubtedly the best ever tasted. Grouper stuffed with deviled crab and sizzled to perfection on a cast-iron skillet would please any Southerner. Other favorites include the savory seafood gumbo and the broiled or fried heaped-high combination seafood platters (served with real southern cheese grits, of course). Sweet tooths are satisfied by homemade desserts, such as key lime pie (only freshly squeezed juice is used) and rich chocolate–peanut butter pie. For the kids, there's a special menu. You may bring your own bottle of preferred spirits (many regular patrons keep their bottles in a special room at the Wharf).

Budget

LUCY HO'S BAMBOO GARDEN, 2814 Apalachee Pkwy. Tel. 878-3366.
Cuisine: CHINESE/JAPANESE. **Reservations:** Not required.
$ **Prices:** Appetizers $1.50–$5; main courses $5.50–$18. AE, DC, MC, V.
Open: Mon–Thurs 11:30am–10pm, Fri 11:30am–11pm, Sat 5–11pm, Sun noon–10pm.

This exotic restaurant and cocktail lounge is a popular rendezvous. Japanese specialties are featured at the Sushi Bar and the Japanese Hibachi Steak and Tatami Room. The luncheon buffet is a great Chinese-style smörgåsbord, highlighting Cantonese and Szechuan cuisines. The classy Lucy Ho, married to a University of Florida professor, runs several very successful restaurants.
Another Lucy Ho's is located at 1700 Halstead Blvd. (tel. 893-4112), near NE Capital Circle and Thomasville Road.

MILL BAKERY, EATERY AND BREWERY, 2329 Apalachee Pkwy. Tel. 565-2867.
Cuisine: AMERICAN. **Reservations:** Not required.
$ **Prices:** Appetizers $2.50–$6; main courses $6.50–$12; salads and sandwiches $2.50–$8. AE, DC, MC, V.
Open: Sun–Thurs 6:30am–11pm, Fri–Sat 6:30am–midnight.
Where else would you find all salads served in edible bowls? Not only is the restaurant ecology-oriented but also very nutrition-conscious. Sandwiches are prepared with home-baked breads; bran muffins are a specialty. If you don't care about splurging on calories, try the extra-special Mill Reuben sandwich. Pizzas are very popular, including the Mill Max (with everything) and the Veggie Max. Homemade soups, especially the veggie-chili soup, are very tasty. As you can note from the wonderful fragrance at the Mill, pastries are also baked on the premises. From their brewery, try GatorTail Ale. Don't miss the great breakfast buffet on weekends.
Another branch of the restaurant is at 2136 N. Monroe St. (tel. 386-2867).

MOM AND DAD'S ITALIAN RESTAURANT, 4175 Apalachee Pkwy., two miles east of Capital Circle. Tel. 877-4518.
Cuisine: ITALIAN. **Reservations:** Not accepted.
$ Prices: Appetizers $2.50–$6; main courses $7–$15. AE, DISC, MC, V.
Open: Dinner only, Sun and Tues–Thurs 5–10pm, Fri–Sat 5–11pm.

Diane Violante and Gary McLean have been making their own pastas and baking Italian breads at this popular, aroma-filled trattoria since 1963. A native of Abruzzo in Italy, Diane's specialty is "spaghetti a la Bruzzi"—a casserole of vermicelli, sautéed mushrooms, and tomato meat sauce topped with mozzarella and parmesan cheeses. She, Gary, and their son Gene make sure all plates are piled high, making the drive out here well worth the time.

SHOPPING

If you like antique-ing, you may find just what you're searching for in Tallahassee's antiques shops. Three downtown shops are clustered together: **Forget-Me-Not** and **Mid-Century Collectibles** are both at 1318 N. Monroe St. (tel. 222-4833 for both), and **Old World Antiques** is at 929 N. Monroe St. (tel. 681-6986). Hours are Monday through Saturday from 10am to 4pm. **SK's Antiques and Collectibles,** 317 E. Park Ave. (tel. 224-1838), is another good source. **Pedlers Antique Mall,** 600 Capital Circle NE (tel. 877-4674), is open Monday through Saturday from 10am to 5:30pm and on Sunday from 1 to 5pm. Some of the best antiques shopping is in Havana, 17 miles north on U.S. 27 (see "Easy Excursions," below).

Bradley's Country Store, on Centerville Road (tel. 893-1647), one of the historic Canopy Roads about eight miles north of I-10, sells more than 80,000 pounds of homemade sausage per year, both over the counter and from orders from around the country. Other country-style southern specialties produced and sold at Bradley's are coarse-ground grits, country-milled cornmeal, hogshead cheese, liver pudding, cracklings, and specially cured hams. On the National Register of Historic Places, the store is also a sightseeing attraction and everyone is welcome to stop in for a taste of the old-fashioned, friendly atmosphere. Open Monday through Saturday from 8am to 6pm.

EVENING ENTERTAINMENT
PERFORMING ARTS

The **Tallahassee-Leon County Civic Center,** 505 W. Pensacola St. (tel. 222-0400, or toll free 800/322-3602), features a Broadway play series, a concert series, performances by celebrity pop singers, and much more.

Special concerts are presented by the **Tallahassee Symphony Orchestra** at **FSU Ruby Diamond Auditorium,** College Avenue and Copeland Streets (tel. 224-0462). The **FSU Mainstage/School of Theatre,** Fine Arts Building, Call and Copeland Streets (tel. 644-6500), presents excellent productions from classic dramas to comedies. The **Tallahassee Little Theatre,** 1861 Thomasville Rd. (tel. 224-8474), is noted for exceptional presentations.

Check the "Limelight" section of Friday's *Tallahassee Democrat* for what's on.

THE NIGHTCLUB & BAR SCENE

Most hotel and restaurant cocktail lounges present a variety of entertainment. **Rooster's,** 2226 N. Monroe St. (tel. 386-8738), features live bands and dancing every night from 9pm until 2am. Entertainment is spotlighted in **Andrew's Upstairs** cocktail lounge (see "Where to Dine," above). In La Quinta Inn, **Julie's Place,** 2901 Monroe St. (tel. 386-7181), is popular as a late-night lounge. **The Moon,** an upscale nightclub at 1105 E. Lafayette St. (tel. 222-6666), showcases name performers with music from the '50s to rhythm and blues. **Club Park Avenue,** at 115 E. Park Ave. (tel. 599-9143), offers two dance floors (the DJ selects the music).

A downtown pub, **Clyde's & Costello's,** 210 S. Adams St. (tel. 224-2173), is very popular, featuring dancing to music from the '40s. You can play pool here, too. Another favorite billiard room, **Halligan's Pub-N-Pool,** 1700 Halstead Blvd. (tel.

668-7665), off Capital Circle NE at I-10, also serves snacks and beer. **Charley Mac's Restaurant & Lounge,** Oak Lake Village, on Capital Circle NE (tel. 893-0522), has a daily happy hour in the lounge from 4pm (5pm on Saturday) until the wee hours (good food here, too). **Dooley's Downunder** is a weekend comedy club in the Ramada Inn, 2900 N. Monroe St. at I-10 (tel. 386-1027). Entertainment, pool tables, and a big-screen television attract sports fans to the **Palace Saloon,** 1303 Jackson Bluff Rd. (tel. 575-3418).

EASY EXCURSIONS

WAKULLA SPRINGS

The 2,860-acre ✪ **Edward Ball Wakulla Springs State Park** (tel. 904/922-3632) is the location of the world's largest and deepest freshwater spring. Edward Ball was a financier who administered the DuPont estate, and he turned the springs into a preservation area.

Glass-bottom boats transport visitors around the remarkably clear waters and to the cavern site, 120 feet below, where mastodon bones were discovered (including Herman, now in Tallahassee's Museum of Florida History). Diver-explorers have found caves 250 feet below the springs, which have been known to dispense an amazing 14,325 gallons of water per second at certain times.

A free orientation movie is offered at the park's theater. You can hike or bike along the nature trails, and swimming is allowed, but only in designated areas. It's important to observe swimming rules—alligators can be very curious. A 30-minute wildlife-observation boat tour is also offered. The Tarzan movies, starring Johnny Weissmuller were filmed in this park.

The park is located 15 miles south of Tallahassee just east of the junction of Fla. 61 and Fla. 267. Both boat tours cost $4.50 for adults, half price for children. Entrance fees are $3.25 per vehicle with up to eight passengers, $1 for pedestrians and bicyclists. The park is open daily from 8am to dusk.

Where to Stay and Dine

WAKULLA SPRINGS LODGE AND CONFERENCE CENTER, 1 Springs Dr., Wakulla Springs, FL 32305. Tel. 904/224-5950. Fax 904/561-7251. 27 rms, 3 suites. A/C TV TEL
$ Rates: $55–$85 double; from $250 suite. MC, V.

On the grounds of Wakulla State Park, the lodge is distinctive for its magnificent Spanish architecture and ornate old-world furnishings, such as rare Spanish tiles, black granite tables, marble floors, and ceiling beams painted with Florida scenes by a German artist, supposedly Kaiser Wilhelm's court painter. High-ceilinged guest rooms are beautifully furnished and have marble bathrooms.

You don't have to be a lodge guest to dine in the lovely Azalea Dining Room, enhanced by arched windows and an immense fireplace. Meals are moderately priced. Dining hours are 7:30 to 10am for breakfast, noon to 2pm for lunch, and 6 to 8:30pm for dinner. For snacks and light meals, the coffee shop is open from 8am to 5pm (there's a 60-foot-long marble soda fountain for old-fashioned ice-cream sodas).

ST. MARKS AREA

Rich history lives in the area around the little village of St. Marks, 18 miles south of the Capitol at the end of both Fla. 363 and the Tallahassee–St. Marks Historic Railroad State Trail (see "What to See and Do," above).

After marching overland from Tampa Bay in 1528, the Spanish conquistador Panfilo de Narvaez and 300 men arrived at this strategic point at the confluence of the St. Marks and Wakulla Rivers near the Gulf of Mexico. Their only avenue back to Spain was by sea, so they built and launched the first ships made by Europeans in the New World. Eleven years later, Hernándo de Soto and his 600 men arrived here after following Narvaez's route from Tampa. They marked the harbor entrance by hanging banners in the trees, then moved on inland. Two wooden forts were built here, in 1679 and in 1718, and a stone version was begun in 1739. The fort shifted among Spanish,

British, and pirate hands until Gen. Andrew Jackson took the stone fort away from the Spanish in 1818. It has been in American hands since Spain ceded Florida in 1821.

Parts of the old Spanish bastion wall and Confederate earthworks built during the Civil War are in the **San Marcos de Apalache State Historic Site** (tel. 904/925-6216), reached by turning right at the end of Fla. 363 in St. Marks and following the paved road. A museum built on the foundation of the old marine hospital holds exhibits and artifacts covering the area's history. The site is open Thursday through Monday from 9am to 5pm; closed New Year's Day, Thanksgiving, and Christmas. Admission to the site is free; admission to the museum costs $1, free for children under 6.

DeSoto's men marked the harbor entrance in what is now the **St. Marks Lighthouse and National Wildlife Refuge.** Operated by the U.S. Fish and Wildlife Service, this 60,000-acre preserve occupies much of the coast from the Aucilla River east of St. Marks to the Ochlockonee River west of Panacea, and is home to more species of birds than anyplace else in Florida except the Everglades. The visitors center is off U.S. 98 about two miles east of St. Marks (turn south at Newport on County Road 59). Stop there for self-guided-tour maps of the roads and hiking trails through the preserve. Built of limestone blocks four-feet thick at the base, the 80-foot-tall St. Marks Lighthouse has marked the harbor entrance since 1842. The nearby beach is a popular crabbing spot.

Admission to the refuge costs $4 per vehicle, $1 for walk-ins and bicyclists. The refuge is open daily from sunrise to sunset; the visitor center, Monday through Friday from 8am to 4:15pm and on Saturday and Sunday from 10am to 5pm (closed all federal holidays). For information about seasonal tours and hunting, contact the refuge at P.O. Box 68, St. Marks, FL 32355 (tel. 904/925-6121).

In 1865, during the final weeks of the Civil War, Federal troops landed at the lighthouse and launched a surprise attack on Tallahassee. The Confederates quickly assembled an impromptu army of wounded soldiers, old men, and boys as young as 14. This rag-tag bunch fought the Federal regulars for five days at what is now the **Natural Bridge State Historic Site.** Surprisingly, the old men and boys won. As a result, Tallahassee remained the only Confederate state capital east of the Mississippi never to fall into Yankee hands. The historic site is on the St. Marks River halfway between Tallahassee and St. Marks (follow the signs from Fla. 363). It's open daily from 8am to sunset, and admission is free. For more information, contact the San Marcos de Apalache State Historic Site (see above).

APALACHICOLA NATIONAL FOREST

The largest of Florida's three national forests, this huge preserve encompasses 600,000 acres stretching from Tallahassee's outskirts southward to the Gulf Coast and westward to the Apalachicola River, some 70 miles away. Included are a variety of woodlands, rivers, streams, lakes, and caves populated by a host of wildlife. There are picnic facilities with sheltered tables and grills, canoe trails along the Sopchoppy and Ochlockonee Rivers, campgrounds with tent and RV sites, and a host of other activities, some of them especially designed for the physically disabled.

The **Leon Sinks Area** is closest to Tallahassee, 5½ miles south of Capital Circle on U.S. 319. Nature trails and boardwalks lead from one sink hole (a lake formed when water erodes the underlying limestone) to another. The trails are open daily from 8am to 8pm. The Hammock Sink Cave System beckons spelunkers.

The **Wakulla Area Ranger Station**, Rte. 6, Box 7860, Crawfordville, FL 32327 (tel. 904/926-3561), provides information about the forest and its facilities. The station is 20 miles south of Tallahassee off U.S. 319.

TORREYA STATE PARK

The sight of high bluffs along a bend in the Apalachicola River, some rising steeply to a height of 150 feet, help make this park special. The park takes its name from the rare Torreya tree, which grows only on the Apalachicola River bluffs, and which legend says grew in the Garden of Eden. Gen. Andrew Jackson's army crossed the river here in 1818 during the Seminole Wars. You can hike along a seven-mile loop trail, enjoy a picnic, or take a ranger-guided tour of the restored Gregory House, built in 1849 as the manor house of Ocheesee, a nearby cotton plantation. It was dismantled in 1935 and floated across the river to this site by the Depression-era Civilian Conservation Corps. It's furnishings are all vintage 1850s.

The park is about 50 miles west of Tallahassee on Fla. 12, between Greensboro and Bristol (take I-10 west to Exit 25, then follow the signs to Greensboro and Bristol). Open daily from 8am to sunset. Admission is $3.25 per vehicle with up to eight passengers, $1 for walk-ins. For more information, contact Torreya State Park, Rte. 2, Box 70, Bristol, FL 32321 (tel. 904/643-2674).

HAVANA

Any trip to Havana, 12 miles northwest of I-10 on U.S. 27, must be considered a shopping expedition. Havana used to make its living from shade tobacco, but when that industry went into decline in the 1960s, the town went with it. Things turned around 20 years later when downtown switched to art galleries and antiques, handcraft, and collectible shops. Today these interesting establishments are housed in lovingly restored, turn-of-the-century brick buildings along the little town's tree-lined commercial streets. Just drive into town on Main Street (U.S. 27), find a parking place when you get to Seventh Avenue, and start exploring. You'll have plenty of company on weekends, when Tallahasseeans flock here to add to their collections.

Where to Dine

NICHOLSON FARMHOUSE RESTAURANT, 15 miles north of Tallahassee, off Fla. 12 between Havana and Quincy. Tel. 904/539-5931.
   Cuisine: AMERICAN. **Reservations:** Recommended.
$ **Prices:** Appetizers $10; main courses $8.50–$23. MC, V.
   Open: Dinner only, Tues–Sat 4–10pm.

Talk to anyone in Tallahassee about where to dine and you will invariably be told, "You must have dinner at Nicholson Farmhouse." Built in 1828 by Dr. Malcolm Nicholson, the farmhouse has been occupied by succeeding generations. In fact, the current owner is the doctor's great-great-grandson. Varying only slightly from the original farmhouse, the hardwood floor, hand-hewn pine steps, front porch columns, and unusual curved ceiling are of architectural interest. The restaurant has been so successful that the outbuildings and two additional turn-of-the-century farmhouses have been converted into extra dining space. Especially aged steaks are a specialty (two ribeyes cut heart-shape are the popular "sweetheart steak"). Grilled chicken breasts, boneless grilled pork chops, shrimp "farmhouse style," and fish of the day are among the deliciously prepared dishes, served in hearty portions with salad, baked potato, and hot freshly baked bread. There's a children's menu, too. You may bring your own bottle of favorite spirits.

CHAPTER 12

THE TAMPA BAY AREA

Rimmed by the Gulf of Mexico in the heart of Florida's central west coast, the Tampa Bay area is often referred to as the "suncoast." The area not only boasts over 50 miles of white sandy beaches—from St. Petersburg, Treasure Island, Madeira, and Clearwater to Anna Maria Island, Longboat Key, Lido Key, and Siesta Key—but also a perpetually perfect climate, with temperatures averaging in the 70s and about 361 days of sunshine a year.

But the Tampa Bay area is more than sunshine, sand, and surf. It's also the cities of Tampa, St. Petersburg, Sarasota, and Bradenton—four historic and fast-growing urban centers.

First settled by Native Americans of the Tocobaga and Timucuan tribes, the Tampa Bay area was discovered by the Spanish in the 16th century when explorers Juan Ponce de León, Panfilo de Narvarez, and Hernándo de Soto came in search of gold but found a tropical paradise instead.

Travelers have been "discovering" the area's beauty ever since. In fact, in 1885, a prominent Baltimore physician presented a paper to the American Medical Society declaring the area "the healthiest place on earth."

The 1920s were boom years for Tampa and St. Petersburg. Henry B. Plant brought his narrow-gauge South Florida Railroad to the area and great hotels—the Tampa Bay Hotel, Belleview Biltmore, Don CeSar, and Vinoy—were built to accommodate the flow of movers and shakers who flocked to the area. Happily, all but the first have been restored to serve today's travelers (the Tampa Bay has been transformed into a university and museum). At the same time, south of the bay in Sarasota, circus-master John Ringling built a new winter residence, modeled after a Venetian palace and still standing today for the enjoyment of visitors.

Though they're united by a common history and a stretch of beautiful beaches, the Tampa Bay cities of Tampa, St. Petersburg, Sarasota, and Bradenton are different individually.

Tampa, the business hub of the quartet, is the home of Busch Gardens, the number-one visitor attraction on the west coast of Florida; Ybor City, an ethnic enclave rich in Spanish and Cuban architecture and tradition; and the new world-class Florida Aquarium.

St. Petersburg, long known as a haven for seniors but growing fast with new younger residents, offers such one-of-a-kind attractions as the Pier, an inverted pyramid of shops, restaurants, and attractions on the bay; the Thunder Dome, a new stadium that's the largest of its type in the world; and the Salvador Dalí Museum, repository of the world's largest collection of works by the Spanish surrealist painter.

Sarasota, home of the Ringling Museum Complex, is the cultural capital of Florida's west coast, with an array of arts and theatrical centers including the Van Wezel Performing Arts Hall and the Asolo Theater.

The sweet aroma of citrus fills the air at Bradenton, headquarters of Tropicana. This city offers a host of diverse attractions ranging from the South Florida Museum and Bishop Planetarium to Nick Bolletteri's Tennis Academy.

WHAT'S SPECIAL ABOUT THE TAMPA BAY AREA

Beaches
☐ From the fun-seeking water-sports activities at the St. Petersburg and Clearwater beaches to the sheltered "old Florida" ambience of Pass-A-Grille and the wide sandy strand of Treasure Island.
☐ Sarasota Keys, 20 miles of barrier island beaches, running from Longboat and Lido to St. Armands and Siesta Keys.
☐ Anna Maria Island at Bradenton, a 7.5-mile stretch of tree-shaded and sandy beaches.

Architectural Highlights
☐ The Pier, an "inverted pyramid" stretching out from downtown into Tampa Bay.
☐ The St. Petersburg Thunder Dome, a slant-roofed stadium that's the first cable-supported dome of its kind in the U.S. and the largest of its type in the world.
☐ Tampa's Hyde Park National Register Historic District, a showcase of American architecture from Colonial to Victorian.

Museums
☐ Salvador Dalí Museum in St. Petersburg, housing the world's largest collection of works by the surrealist Spanish artist.
☐ Ringling Museum Complex in Sarasota, one-time home of circus master John Ringling and now Florida's official state art museum.

☐ Museum of African-American Art in Tampa, the first of its kind in Florida and home of the U.S.'s foremost collection of African-American art.
☐ Museum of Science and Industry in Tampa, for a look at a simulated space shuttle operation, ham radio center, or weather station.

Events and Festivals
☐ Festival of the States, a winter celebration, with 17 days of parades, pageantry, and outdoor fun.
☐ Gasparilla Festival, Tampa's traditional annual frolic, with modern-day pirates, parades, concerts, and more.
☐ Florida State Fair, a two-week fest of all the best in Florida and Tampa.

Attractions
☐ Gamble Plantation, a 19th-century antebellum plantation home and now the oldest structure on Florida's southwest coast.
☐ Busch Gardens, for up-close views of 3,000 animals in natural settings, and thrilling rides and activities.
☐ The new $84-million Florida Aquarium.

Activities
☐ Swimming, sunning, shelling, or shore-walking along St. Petersburg's strip of sandy white beaches.
☐ Sailing aboard a ketch, sloop, yacht, or windjammer from St. Pete Beach or Clearwater Harbor.

1. TAMPA

200 miles SW of Jacksonville, 254 miles NW of Miami, 63 miles N of Sarasota

GETTING THERE   By Plane   Tampa International Airport, off Memorial Highway and Fla. 60, Tampa (tel. 813/870-8700), five miles northwest of downtown Tampa, is the gateway for all scheduled domestic and international flights. Most major airlines fly into Tampa, including Air Canada, American, America Trans Air, Cayman Airways, Canadian Airlines International, Continental, Delta, Northwest, TWA, United, USAir, and USAir Express.

Peter O. Knight Airport, Davis Islands, Tampa (tel. 813/251-1717), serves as a landing strip for private planes.

By Train   Amtrak trains arrive at the Tampa Amtrak Station, 601 Nebraska Ave. N., Tampa (tel. 813/221-7600).

By Bus   Greyhound buses arrive at the carrier's downtown depot at 610 Polk St., Tampa (tel. 813/229-2174).

By Car   The Tampa area is linked to the Interstate system and is accessible from I-275, I-75, I-4, U.S. 19, U.S. 41, U.S. 92, U.S. 301, and many state roads.

Sitting on the Hillsborough River and rimmed by Hillsborough Bay and Tampa Bay, Tampa is a city of many waterfront views and activities—a natural mecca for vacationers. This metropolis of nearly 300,000 people is also a major business hub on Florida's west coast and the seventh-largest port in the United States.

Although Tampa's number-one draw for visitors is the Busch Gardens theme park, the city also offers many other attractions, including the historic charm of Ybor City, a recently rejuvenated ethnic enclave that blends Spanish architecture, Cuban foods, flamenco music, and a Soho-style artistic ambience.

ORIENTATION

ARRIVING

Central Florida Limo (tel. 813/396-3730) operates van service between the airport and hotels. The fare is $7 to $15 for up to two passengers, depending on the destination (for most downtown hotels it would be $11).

Taxi service is provided by **Yellow Cab Taxis** (tel. 813/253-0121) and **United Cabs** (tel. 813/253-2424). The average fare from the airport to downtown Tampa is $10 to $12 and the ride takes about 15 minutes.

In addition, **Hillsborough Area Regional Transit Authority/HARTline** (tel. 813/254-HART) operates service between the airport and downtown on its no. 31 bus. This is not an airport express bus, but a local route that makes stops at the airport, between the hours of 6am and 8:15pm. Look for the HARTline bus sign outside each airline terminal; the fare is $1.

INFORMATION

For brochures and helpful advice about Tampa and hotel reservations before or during your visit, contact the **Tampa/Hillsborough Convention and Visitors Association, Inc. (THCVA),** 111 Madison St., Suite 1010, Tampa, FL 33602-4706 (tel. 813/223-2752, or toll free 800/44-TAMPA).

In addition, the THCVA also maintains unstaffed information/brochure centers at the Convention Center, on Harbour Island, and in Ybor Square.

A good source of on-the-spot information north of downtown in the Busch Gardens area is the **Tampa Bay Visitor Information Center,** 3601 E. Busch Blvd., Tampa, FL 33612 (tel. 813/985-3601). It offers free brochures about attractions in Tampa and other parts of Florida as well as a sightseeing tour-booking service.

CITY LAYOUT

Tampa's downtown district is laid out according to a grid system. **Kennedy Boulevard** (Fla. 60), which cuts across the city in an east-west direction, is the main dividing line for north and south street addresses; and **Florida Avenue** is the dividing line for east and west street addresses. The two major arteries bringing traffic into the downtown area are **I-275,** which skirts the northern edge of the city, and the **Crosstown Expressway,** which extends along the southern rim.

All the streets in the central core of the city are one-way, with the exception of pedestrians-only Franklin Street. From the southern tip of Franklin, you can also board the People Mover, an elevated tram to Harbour Island.

Neighborhoods in Brief

Downtown   The core of Tampa, this compact area is primarily a business and financial hub, where John F. Kennedy Boulevard (Fla. 60) and Florida Avenue intersect.

Ybor City   East of downtown, this is Tampa's Latin Quarter, settled for more than 100 years by Cuban immigrants. Today it's home to many Spanish and Cuban restaurants, as well as local artists and craftspeople.

Harbour Island   South of downtown, this small island is linked by an elevated People Mover to the mainland. It is the city's waterfront playground, with a marina and water-sports activities as well as a hotel, restaurants, shops, health center, and residential condominiums.

Hyde Park   West of downtown, this is the city's classiest residential neighborhood, Tampa's answer to Beverly Hills, with many of its homes part of a National Register Historic District.

West Shore   West of Hyde Park, this area runs from Tampa International Airport southward, particularly along Westshore Boulevard. It's a commercial and financial hub, with office buildings and business-oriented hotels.

Courtney Campbell Causeway   This is a small beach strip, running west of the airport, as Kennedy Boulevard (Fla. 60) crosses Old Tampa Bay. It's a prime tourist area, with waterfront hotels, restaurants, and sports activities.

Busch Gardens   North of downtown, this area surrounds the famous theme park of the same name. Busch Boulevard, which runs from east to west, is a busy commercial strip just south of the Busch Gardens entrance.

GETTING AROUND

BY PUBLIC TRANSPORTATION   By Bus   Hillsborough Area Regional Transit/HARTline (tel. 813/254-HART) provides regularly scheduled bus service between downtown Tampa and the suburbs. The service is geared mainly to commuters, although visitors staying at downtown hotels certainly can use a bus to get to the airport or major shopping centers.

Fares are $1 for local services, $1.50 for express routes; correct change is required. Many buses start or finish their route downtown at the Marion Street Transit Parkway, between Tyler and Whiting Streets. It provides well-lit open-air terminal facilities including 40-foot shelters with copper roofs, informational kiosks, benches, newspaper stands, landscaping, and 24-hour security.

The People Mover   This motorized tram on elevated tracks connects downtown Tampa with Harbour Island. It operates from the third level of the Fort Brooke Parking Garage, on Whiting Street between Franklin Avenue and Florida Street. Travel time is 90 seconds, and service is continuous, Monday through Saturday from 7am to 2am and on Sunday from 8am to 11pm. The fare is 25¢ each way.

BY TAXI   Taxis in Tampa do not normally cruise the streets for fares, but they do line up at public loading places, such as hotels, the performing arts center, and bus and train depots. If you need a taxi, call either **Yellow Cab** (tel. 813/253-0121) or **United Cab** (tel. 813/253-2424).

BY CAR   Although the downtown area can easily be walked, it's virtually impossible to see the major sights and enjoy the best restaurants of Tampa without a car. Most visitors step off a plane and pick up a car right at the airport for use throughout their stay. Five major firms are represented on the grounds of Tampa International Airport: **Avis** (tel. 813/396-3500), **Budget** (tel. 813/877-6051), **Dollar** (tel. 813/396-3640), **Hertz** (tel. 813/874-3232), and **National** (tel. 813/396-3782). Most of these companies also maintain offices downtown and in other parts of Tampa such as the Busch Gardens area.

In addition, many smaller firms and local companies have premises just outside the

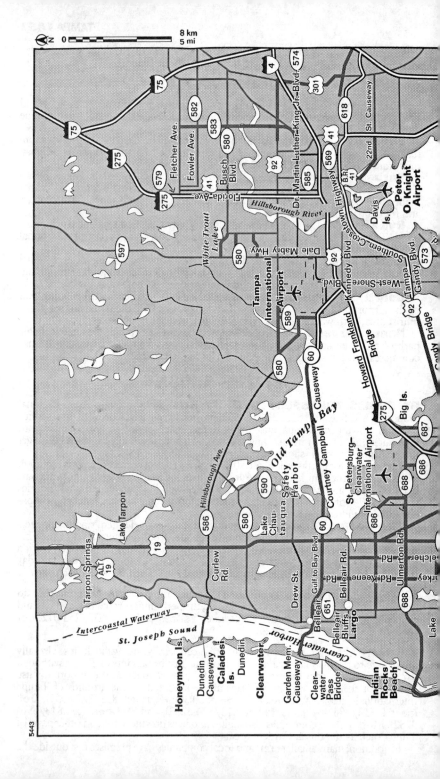

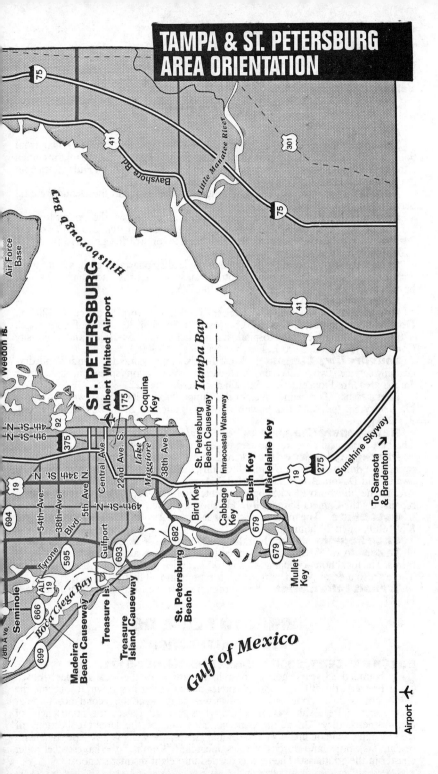

TAMPA & ST. PETERSBURG AREA ORIENTATION

75

41

Bayshore Rd.

Little Manatee River

301

75

41

Air Force Base

Hillsborough Bay

weedon Is.

ST. PETERSBURG

Albert Whitted Airport

Coquina Key

175

Tampa Bay

92

4th-St.-N.

4th-St.-N.

375

Lake Maggiore

Central Ave.

22nd Ave. S.

38th Ave.

St. Petersburg Beach Causeway

Intracoastal Waterway

19

4th Ave. N.

34th St. N.

Bird Key

Cabbage Key

Bush Key

Madelaine Key

19

275

Sunshine Skyway

To Sarasota & Bradenton

19

694

54th-Ave.

38th-Ave.

5th Ave. N.

49th-St.-N.

682

679

Blvd.

Tyrone

595

Gulfport

693

St. Petersburg Beach

679

Mullet Key

Seminole

ALT 19

666

Boca Ciega Bay

Treasure Is.

Madeira Beach Causeway

Treasure Island Causeway

699

8th Ave.

Gulf of Mexico

Airport ✈

airport. These firms, which provide van pickups to/from the airport and often post the most competitive rates, include **Alamo** (tel. 813/289-4323), **A-Plus** (tel. 813/289-4301), **Payless** (tel. 813/289-6554), **Thrifty** (tel. 813/289-4006), and **Value** (tel. 813/289-8870).

FAST FACTS

Area Code   Tampa's area code is 813.

Business Hours   Most businesses are open Monday through Friday from 9am to 5pm, with shops and stores open from 9am to 6pm or later. Banks are open Monday through Friday from 9am to 4pm; some banks are open on Friday until 6pm and others are open on Saturday morning.

Dentist   For information about dentists in the area, call the Dental Referral Service, Inc. (tel. 224-0073).

Doctor   Most hotels have a doctor on call; if not, contact the Doctor Referral Service of the Hillsborough County Medical Association (tel. 253-0471) or the 24-hour Ask-A-Nurse/Physician Referral Service of St. Joseph's Hospital (tel. 870-4444).

Drugstores   Eckerd Drugs is one of the leading pharmacy groups in the area, with over 35 stores throughout downtown and the suburbs, including a 24-hour branch at 11613 N. Nebraska Ave. (tel. 978-0775).

Emergencies   Dial 911.

Hospitals   If you need a hospital, try Transitional Hospital of Tampa, 4801 N. Howard Ave., Tampa (tel. 874-7575); St. Joseph's Hospital, 3001 W. Buffalo Ave. (tel. 870-4000); Tampa General Hospital, Davis Islands (tel. 251-7000); and University Community Hospital, 3100 E. Fletcher Ave. (tel. 971-6000).

Laundry/Dry Cleaning   Most hotels supply same-day laundry and dry-cleaning service. Two local chains, each with several locations spread throughout the Tampa area, are Pioneer (tel. 253-3323) and Sterling (tel. 221-8055).

Libraries   The main branch of the Tampa Public Library is downtown at 900 N. Ashley St. (tel. 273-3652), with a north branch at 8916 Boulevard N. (tel. 975-2111).

Newspapers/Magazines   The *Tampa Tribune* is the daily newspaper. The best periodical covering the area is *Tampa Bay*, a monthly magazine.

Photographic Needs   Eckerd Express Photo offers one-hour processing at over half a dozen convenient Tampa locations, including one in Hyde Park Village, at Swann and Dakota Avenues (tel. 251-2211), and another at 2750 W. Hillsborough Ave. in the Hillsboro Plaza Shopping Center (tel. 875-8665). For in-house camera repairs, try the Camera Barn, 100 E. Hillsborough Ave., Tampa (tel. 237-4935).

Post Office   The main post office is at Tampa Airport, 5201 W. Spruce St. (tel. 879-1600), open 24 hours daily.

Shoe Repairs   Try the Florida Shoe Hospital, 406 E. Zack St. (tel. 223-1020).

Taxes   A 6.5% sales tax is applied to all purchases and the cost of restaurant meals. The local hotel-occupancy tax is 10.5%, added to the cost of your hotel room. There's also a $6 airport departure tax for international flights.

Transit Information   For information on the local bus system, call 254-HART.

WHAT TO SEE & DO
THE TOP ATTRACTIONS

BUSCH GARDENS, 3000 E. Busch Blvd. Tel. 987-5171.

Founded 35 years ago as a hospitality garden for the local Anheuser-Busch brewery, this 300-acre family entertainment center has grown to become the most popular attraction on Florida's west coast—and the second most popular in the state (after Walt Disney World). Designed to reflect the atmosphere of turn-of-the-century Africa, the park contains one of the largest collections of free-roaming wild animals in the United States, as well as live entertainment, restaurants, shops, and dozens of rides, including "Kumba," the largest steel roller coaster in the Southeast. The park is divided into eight distinct sections:

Timbuktu is an ancient desert trading center with African craftsmen at work, plus a sandstorm-style ride, boat-swing ride, roller coaster, and electronic games arcade.

Morocco, a walled city with exotic architecture, has Moroccan craft demonstrations, a sultan's tent with snake charmers, and the Moroccan Palace Theater.

Serengeti Plain is an open area that's home to hippos, buffalos, impalas, gazelles, reticulated giraffes, black rhinos, elephants, and zebras, as well as antelopes, crocodiles, dromedaries (camels), flamingos, and ostriches.

Nairobi is home to "Myombe Reserve: The Great Ape Domain," a natural habitat for various types of gorillas and chimpanzees, and a baby animal nursery, as well as a petting zoo, reptile displays, and Nocturnal Mountain, where a simulated environment allows visitors to observe animals that are active in the dark.

Stanleyville, a prototype African village, has a shopping bazaar and live entertainment, as well as two water rides, the Tanganyika Tidal Wave and Stanley Falls.

The Congo features Kumba, the largest steel roller coaster in the southeastern United States, and Claw Island, a display of rare white Bengal tigers in a natural setting, plus white-water-raft rides.

Bird Gardens, the original core of Busch Gardens, offers rich foliage, lagoons, and a free-flight aviary for hundreds of exotic birds including golden and American bald eagles, hawks, owls, and falcons.

Crown Colony is the home of a team of Clydesdale horses as well as the Anheuser-Busch hospitality center. Questor, a flight simulator, is also located in this area.

In total, there are more than 3,700 animals, birds, and reptiles and many types of live entertainment. And the Anheuser-Busch brewery tour (self-guided) allows the visitor to observe the beer-making process and gives an opportunity to sample the famous brews.

To get the most from your visit, arrive early and allow at least eight hours. Start the day by taking one or more of the rides that circle the park (the monorail, open-air skyride, or train) to get your bearings and acquaint you with the location of things.

Admission: $31.90 adults, $25.50 children 3 to 9, free for kids under 3. Parking is $3.

Open: Daily 9am–6pm, with extended hours in summer and holiday periods.

Directions: Take I-275 northeast of downtown to Busch Boulevard (Exit 33), and go east two miles to the entrance on 40th Street (McKinley Drive).

FLORIDA AQUARIUM, 300 S. 13th St. Tel. 229-8861.

With a shell-shaped glass dome, this new $84-million aquarium stands out along the newly developing strip of waterside attractions between downtown and Ybor City. Slated to open in April 1995, it offers exhibits on over 4,300 animals and plants, with a focus on the state's wetlands, beaches, bays, sawgrass marshes, swamps, mangrove forests, and the Everglades. There's also a half-million-gallon Coral Reefs Exhibit.

Admission charges and opening hours were not final at press time, so call before you go. To get there, from the downtown Convention Center, turn east on Platt Street and go approximately half a mile to the aquarium.

GARRISON SEAPORT CENTER, Port of Tampa, 13th and Platt Sts. Tel. 248-1924.

Rising on the Tampa skyline adjacent to the Florida Aquarium, this facility is a new hub of waterfront activity for downtown Tampa. Slated for a spring 1995 opening, it is comprised of two new passenger cruise terminals serving the various lines that offer cruise trips from Tampa, including Holland America, Regency Cruises, OdessAmerica, Carnival Cruise Lines, and American Family Cruises. Entertainment also plays a large part at this new center, with a 16,000-seat music amphitheater, a music-themed restaurant, a comedy club, a nightclub, recording studios, a music super-store, music-oriented shops, and a food court.

Admission charges and opening hours were not final at press time, so call before

Tampa Area

Adventure Island ④
Busch Gardens ⑤
Florida Aquarium ⑫
Garrison Seaport Center ⑬
Henry B. Plant
   Museum ⑯
Lowry Park Zoo ⑦
Museum of African-
   American Art ⑭
Museum of Science
   and Industry ②
Seminole Indian
   Village ⑧
Tampa Bay Downs ③
Tampa Convention
   Center ⑰
Tampa Greyhound
   Track ⑥
Tampa Museum
   of Art ⑮
Tampa Stadium ⑨
University of Tampa ⑪
USF Art Museum ①
Ybor City State
   Museum ⑩

TAMPA AREA ATTRACTIONS

1 University of South Florida

Fowler Ave.

582

2

56th St.

Nebraska Ave.

ebaugh

5 **4**

Busch Gardens

Malcolm McKinley Dr.

Temple Terrace

Busch Blvd.

580

Florida Ave.

41

6

301

75

I-75

go River

275

Sligh Ave.

Sligh Ave.

8→

92

Hillsborough Ave.

I-4

4

Tampa

East Lake

574

Nebraska Ave.

22nd St.

Dr. Martin Luther King Jr. Blvd.

King Jr. Blvd.

BUS 41

585

Florida Ave.

Columbus Dr.

50th St.

10

Ybor City

Adamo Dr.

wntown

12 **11**

60

Crosstown Expwy.

60

13

BUS 41

Harbour Island

McKay Bay

Davis Blvd.

Davis Islands

Causeway Blvd.

14

DOWNTOWN

Peter O. Knight Airport

676

Tyler St.

15

Cass St.

Bayshore Rd.

Polk St.

Zack St.

Florida Ave.

Marion St.

Morgan St.

676A

Twiggs St.

Tampa St.

Franklin St.

Madison St.

Ballast Point

Kennedy Blvd.

41

16

Jackson St.

Washington St.

Hills-borough Bay

Whiting St.

Hillsborough River

Crosstown Expwy.

17

Ashley St.

Airport ✈

you go. To get there from the downtown Convention Center, turn east on Platt Street and go approximately half a mile.

HENRY B. PLANT MUSEUM, 401 W. Kennedy Blvd. Tel. 254-1891.

Modeled after the Alhambra in Spain, with 13 silver minarets and distinctive Moorish architecture, this landmark is a stand-out along the Tampa skyline. It was originally built in 1891 as the 511-room Tampa Bay Hotel by railroad tycoon Henry B. Plant, who filled it with priceless art and furnishings from Europe and the Orient.

Although it ceased to operate as a hotel in 1930, the building was saved by the University of Tampa and was declared a National Historic Landmark in 1977. Today the ground-floor rooms have been converted into a museum, filled with elegant displays of Venetian mirrors, Wedgwood china, Louis XV and XVI furniture, and other original art objects and fashions that hark back to the hotel's heydey.

Admission: Free; suggested donation, $3 adults, $1 children 12 and under.
Open: Tues–Sat 10am–4pm, Sun noon–4pm. **Directions:** Take Fla. 60 west of downtown.

MUSEUM OF AFRICAN AMERICAN ART, 1308 N. Marion St. Tel. 272-2466.

Touted as the first of its kind in Florida, this museum is the home of the $7.5-million Barnett-Aden collection, considered the country's foremost collection of African American art. More than 80 artists are represented in the display, which includes sculptures and paintings that depict the history, culture, and lifestyle of African Americans from the 1800s to the present.

Admission: $2 suggested donation.
Open: Tues–Sat 10:30am–4:30pm, Sun 1–4:30pm. **Directions:** Take Exit 26 off I-275; the museum is downtown, between Scott and Laurel Streets.

MUSEUM OF SCIENCE AND INDUSTRY (MOSI), 4801 E. Fowler Ave. Tel. 987-6300.

An educational attraction for all ages, this museum offers exhibits on industry, technology, and the physical and natural sciences, including the *Challenger* Learning Center, a space shuttle simulator and memorial to the seven *Challenger* astronauts who perished in 1986. Recent additions have included a permanent exhibit about water resources and conservation, an interactive butterfly garden featuring dozens of free-flying butterflies, and a 100-seat planetarium. As we go to press, MOSI is undergoing a $35-million expansion which will triple its size to become the largest science center in the Southeast. The centerpiece of the expansion will be a 350-seat, 85-foot domed Omnimax theater, Florida's first.

Admission: $5.50 adults, $2 children 3–15, free for kids under 3; planetarium admission is $1.50 per person additional.
Open: Sun–Thurs 9am–4:30pm, Fri–Sat 9am–9pm. **Directions:** Head north of downtown, one mile east of Busch Gardens.

TAMPA CONVENTION CENTER, 333 S. Franklin St. Tel. 223-8511.

Although not technically open as a public attraction, this is the city's focal point for conventions, meetings, and occasional concerts. Even if you're not attending a function inside, it's worth a look at the impressive exterior of this $140-million building owned and operated by the City of Tampa. Situated on a 14-acre site overlooking the Hillsborough River and Harbour Island, it has 2,000 feet of riverfront views and lush landscape. In the front of the center is a $1.7-million park with a spectacular six-ton fountain, *Shamayim—Fire & Water* by Yaacov Agam.

TAMPA MUSEUM OF ART, 601 Doyle Carlton Dr. Tel. 223-8130.

Situated on the east bank of the Hillsborough River, south of the Tampa Bay Performing Arts Center, this fine-arts complex offers seven galleries with changing exhibits ranging from classical antiquities to contemporary art.
Tours are given on Wednesday, Saturday, and Sunday at 1pm.

Admission: $3.50 adults, $3 seniors, $2 children 6–18, free for kids under 6; free for everyone Sat 10am–1pm.
Open: Tues, Thurs, and Sat 10am–5pm; Wed 10am–9pm; Sun 1–5pm. **Directions:** Take I-275 to Exit 25 (Ashley Street).

MORE ATTRACTIONS

ADVENTURE ISLAND, 4545 Bougainvillea Ave. Tel. 987-5600.

Adjacent to Busch Gardens, this is a separate 36-acre outdoor water theme park. A favorite with kids and teens, it has three swimming pools and water slides/play areas. There is also an outdoor café, picnic and sunbathing areas, games arcade, volleyball complex, and dressing-room facilities. Wear a bathing suit and bring towels.
Admission: $16.95 adults, $14.95 children 3–9; free for kids under 3; $1 for lockers.
Open: Mar–Oct, Mon–Fri 10am–5pm, Sat–Sun 9:30am–6pm; extended hours in summer. **Directions:** Take I-275 to Busch Boulevard (Exit 33); go east two miles to 40th Street (McKinley Drive), make a left, and follow the signs.

LOWRY PARK ZOO, 7530 North Blvd. Tel. 935-8552.

With lots of greenery, bubbling brooks, and cascading waterfalls, this 24-acre zoo aims to display animals in settings that closely resemble their natural habitats. The major attractions include a manatee hospital, aviary, wildlife center, and a building catering to rare and endemic nocturnal animals.
Admission: $6.50 adults, $5.50 seniors, $4.50 children 4–12, free for kids 3 and under.
Open: Apr–Oct, daily 9:30am–6pm; Nov–Mar, daily 9:30am–5pm. **Directions:** Take I-275 to Sligh Avenue (Exit 31) and follow the signs to Lowry Park.

SEMINOLE INDIAN VILLAGE, 5221 N. Orient Rd. Tel. 621-7349.

Located on Tampa's Seminole Indian reservation, this museum is designed to trace that tribe's history in the area. The structures include "chickees," thatched huts built just as they were 150 years ago, which shelter skilled Seminole craftspeople as they practice bead working, wood carving, basket making, and patchwork sewing. Other more lively demonstrations include alligator wrestling and snake handling.
Admission: $6 adults, $5 children 3–12, free for children under 3.
Open: Mon–Sat 9am–5pm, Sun 10am–5pm. Tours given every hour on the half hour, with the last tour at 3:30pm. **Directions:** Take I-4 northeast of downtown to Exit 5.

USF CONTEMPORARY ART MUSEUM, Building FAM 101, University of South Florida, 4202 E. Fowler Ave. Tel. 974-2849.

On the western side of the campus, this 10,630-square-foot facility spotlights artists and artworks from throughout the world. In particular, there are valuable collections of pre-Columbian and African artifacts, as well as contemporary prints from the southeastern United States.
Admission: Free.
Open: Mon–Fri 10am–5pm, Sat 1–4pm. **Directions:** Head one block north of Busch Gardens, between Fowler and Fletcher Avenues.

YBOR CITY STATE MUSEUM, 1818 Ninth Ave., Ybor City. Tel. 247-6323.

The focal point of Ybor City, this museum is housed in the former Ferlita Bakery (1896–1973), a century-old yellow-brick building. Various exhibits in the museum depict the political, social, and cultural influences that shaped this section of Tampa, once known as "the cigar capital of the world." You can take a self-guided tour around the museum, which includes a collection of cigar labels, cigar memorabilia, and works by local artisans.
Adjacent to the museum is **Preservation Park,** the site of three renovated cigar workers' cottages, furnished as they were at the turn of the century.

Admission: Museum, $1 adults and children 6 and up, free for children under 6; tours of cigar workers' cottages, $1 extra per person.

Open: Tues–Sat 9am–noon and 1–5pm. **Directions:** Head northeast of downtown, between 18th and 19th Streets.

ORGANIZED TOURS

BY BOAT   See the skyscrapers and other downtown highlights as you float across the waters of Tampa Bay and the lower Hillsborough River on an authentic 70-year-old, 30-foot-long gondola. Operated by ✪ **Gondola Getaway Cruises** (tel. 888-8864), these narrated trips last 35 to 45 minutes and the charge is $20 per couple, $5 each for additional passengers to a maximum of four. Gondola cruises depart from the Waterwalk dock on Harbour Island, beneath the Columbia Restaurant, Monday through Saturday from 6pm to midnight and on Sunday from noon to 9pm; other times, by appointment. Reservations are accepted daily from 9am to 7pm.

You can go on sightseeing and sunset cruises around Tampa Bay on a "downeast"–style 38-foot cutter-rigged sloop with Capt. Tom Kester at the helm. The charge is $70 per hour for a minimum of two passengers ($35 per hour for each additional passenger), or $400 for six hours. Departures are by appointment, and advance reservations are required: Contact **Sea Trader Cruises,** Harbour Island Marina, Harbour Island (tel. 286-8512).

BY BUS   Located opposite Busch Gardens, **Swiss Chalet Tours,** 3601 E. Busch Blvd. (tel. 985-3601), operates guided bus tours of Tampa, Ybor City, and environs. Four-hour half-day tours are given on Monday and Thursday, and cost $35 for adults and $20 for children. Eight-hour full-day tours are given on Tuesday and Friday, and cost $45 for adults and $35 for children. Reservations are required at least 24 hours in advance; passengers are picked up at major hotels and various other points in the Tampa/St. Petersburg area. Tours can also be booked to Sarasota, Bradenton, and other regional destinations.

ON FOOT   Led by enthusiastic local volunteer guides, ✪ **Ybor City Walking Tours,** Ybor Square, 1901 N. 13th St., Ybor City (tel. 223-1111, ext. 46), are the ideal way to acquaint yourself with the highlights of Tampa's Latin Quarter. The tours start at the Information Desk in Ybor Square, between Eighth and Ninth Avenues, and end at Preservation Park, covering over three dozen points of interest. These 1½-hour walking tours are free and depart on Tuesday, Thursday, and Saturday: from June to September at 11am and from October to May at 1:30pm. Reservations are suggested.

SPORTS & RECREATION
Spectator Sports

BASEBALL   About a half-hour drive from downtown Tampa, the **Plant City Stadium,** Park Rd., Plant City (tel. 752-7337), is the spring-training turf of the Cincinnati Reds. The season is from mid-February to April and admission is $4 to $7.

DOG RACING   **Tampa Greyhound Track,** 8300 Nebraska Ave. (tel. 932-4313), features 13 races daily, with eight dogs competing in each. Races are from July to December on Monday and Wednesday through Saturday at 7:30pm; on Monday, Wednesday, and Saturday at noon; and on Sunday at 1pm. It's closed the rest of the year. Admission is $1 to the grandstand, $2 to $3 to the clubhouse; free self-parking, $3 for valet parking.

FOOTBALL, SOCCER & MORE   Home to the Tampa Bay Buccaneers football team and the Tampa Bay Rowdies soccer team, ✪ **Tampa Stadium,** 4201 N. Dale Mabry Hwy. (tel. 872-7977), caters to sports events of all types, from the Super Bowl to horse shows, rodeos, motorcycle races, and tractor-pulling. Times and schedules vary. Admission ranges from $5 to $35 or higher, depending on the event.

HOCKEY The NHL's **Tampa Bay Lightning** is based at St. Petersburg's ThunderDome as we go to press. The franchise is scheduled to move back to downtown Tampa, starting with the 1995–96 hockey season (October to April). The team will be housed in a new $110-million, 20,000-seat arena located between the Tampa Convention Center and the new Florida Aquarium. For complete details at the time of your visit, contact Tampa Bay Lightning, 501 Kennedy Blvd., Tampa (tel. 229-8800).

HORSE RACING The only oval thoroughbred race course on Florida's west coast, ✪ **Tampa Bay Downs**, 11225 Racetrack Rd., Oldsmar (tel. 855-4401), is the home of the Tampa Bay Derby. The program features 10 races a day. Admission is $1.50 to the grandstand, $3 to the clubhouse; there is free grandstand admission for seniors on Wednesday and for women on Friday. Parking costs $1. From December to May, post time on Monday, Tuesday, Thursday, and Friday is 12:30pm; on Saturday and Sunday, 1pm. The track presents simulcasts June to November.

JAI-ALAI Similar to racquetball, the Spanish game of jai-alai is considered the world's fastest ball game (the ball can go over 180 m.p.h.). At **Tampa Jai-Alai Fronton,** 5125 S. Dale Mabry Hwy. (tel. 831-1411), professional players volley the lethal *pelota* with a long, curved glove called a *cesta*. Admission is $1 to $3 and parking is $1 or free. It's open year-round: Monday through Wednesday and Friday and Saturday at 7pm, with matinees on Monday, Wednesday, and Saturday at noon.

POLO Mallets swing at the **Tampa Bay Polo Club,** Walden Lake Polo and Country Club, 2001 Clubhouse Dr., Plant City (tel. 752-8731). Polo is played regularly at this sylvan site east of Tampa. Admission is $3; it's open mid-January to May, on Sunday at 2pm.

RECREATION

BOAT RENTALS Paddle downstream in a two-person canoe along a 20-mile stretch of the Hillsborough River amid 16,000 acres of rural lands in Wilderness Park, the largest regional park in Hillsborough County. The trips take two to four hours, covering approximately two to three miles per hour. **Canoe Escape,** 9335 E. Fowler Ave. (tel. 986-2067), charges $24 for two-hour trips, $28 for four-hour trips, and is open Monday through Friday from 8am to 5pm and on Saturday and Sunday from 8am to 6pm.

Club Nautico, The Waterwalk, Harbour Island (tel. 223-2107), lets you captain your own craft on the waters of Tampa Bay. This company rents powerboats and pontoons. Prices for half-day rentals are $99 to $179 for powerboats and $119 to $259 for pontoon boats. It's open daily from noon to 6pm or later, depending on the season.

Trident Boat Rentals, The Waterwalk, on Harbour Island (tel. 223-4168), rents small electric pedal boats and three-passenger electric boats to ply the waters of Garrison's Channel or the Hillsborough River around Harbour Island. Prices are $6 (two passengers) per half hour for pedal boats, $10 for electric boats. It's open on Friday from 6pm to midnight, on Saturday from 1pm to midnight, and on Sunday from 1 to 7pm.

FISHING Tampa's opportunities for casting a line are confined primarily to lakes, rivers, and bays. There's good freshwater fishing for trout in **Lake Thonotosassa,** east of the city, or for bass along the **Hillsborough River.** Pier fishing on Hillsborough Bay is also available from **Ballast Point Park,** 5300 Interbay Blvd. (tel. 831-9585).

GOLF Situated north of Lowry Park, the **Babe Zaharias Municipal Golf Course,** 11412 Forest Hills Dr. (tel. 932-8932), is an 18-hole, par-70 course. It has a pro shop, putting greens, and a driving range. Golf-club rentals and lessons are available. Greens fees run $14.50 to $18.50, $20 to $25 with a cart. The course is open daily from 7am to dusk.

You can literally step off the plane at the Tampa airport and play a round of golf at the 18-hole, par-72 course **Hall of Fame Golf Club,** 2222 N. Westshore Blvd. (tel. 876-4913). Facilities include a driving range and club rentals; lessons are also available. Greens fees, which include a cart, are $18 to $22; it's open daily from 7am to dusk.

The **Rocky Point Golf Municipal Golf Course,** 4151 Dana Shores Dr. (tel. 884-5141), located between the airport and the bay, is an 18-hole, par-71 course, with a pro shop, practice range, and putting greens. Lessons and golf club rentals are available. Greens fees are $20 to $25, including a cart, and it's open daily from 7am to dusk.

On the Hillsborough River in north Tampa, the **Rogers Park Municipal Golf Course,** 7910 N. 30th St. (tel. 234-1911), is an 18-hole, par-72 championship course with a lighted driving and practice range. Lessons and club rentals are available. Greens fees, including cart, are $22.50 to $25. It's open daily from 7am to dusk.

University of South Florida Golf Course, 4202 Fowler Ave. (tel. 974-2071), is just north of the USF campus. This 18-hole, par-72 course is nicknamed "The Claw" because of its challenging layout. It offers lessons and club rentals. The charge is $18, $30 with a cart. It's open daily from 7am to dusk.

RUNNING   Bayshore Boulevard, a 7-mile stretch along Hillsborough Bay, is famous for its 6.3-mile sidewalk. Reputed to be the world's longest continuous sidewalk, it's a favorite for runners, joggers, walkers, and cyclists. The route goes from the western edge of downtown in a southward direction, passing stately old homes, condos, retirement communities, and houses of worship, ending at Gandy Boulevard.

For more information on other recommended running areas, contact the **Parks and Recreation Department,** 7225 North Blvd. (tel. 223-8230).

TENNIS   The **City of Tampa Tennis Complex,** Hillsborough Community College, 4001 Tampa Bay Blvd. (tel. 870-2383), across from Tampa Stadium, is the largest public complex in Tampa, with 16 hard courts and 12 clay courts. It also has racquetball courts, a pro shop, locker rooms, showers, and lessons. Reservations are recommended. Prices range from $1.50 to $4.50 per person per hour. It's open Monday through Thursday from 8am to 9pm, and Friday through Sunday from 8am to 6pm.

On the water and overlooking Harbour Island, **Marjorie Park,** 59 Columbia Dr., Davis Islands (tel. 253-3997), has eight clay courts. Reservations are required. The price is $4.50 per person per hour and it's open Monday through Friday from 8am to 9pm and on Saturday and Sunday from 8am to 6pm.

Harry Hopman/Saddlebrook International Tennis School, 5700 Saddlebrook Resort, Wesley Chapel (tel. 973-1111, or toll free 800/729-8383), with its 45 tennis courts is a well-equipped school which caters to beginners as well as skilled players of all ages. A basic five-day/six-night package includes 25 hours (minimum) of tennis instruction, unlimited playing time, match play with instructors, audiovisual analysis, agility exercises, and accommodations at the Saddlebrook resort. Prices range from $630 to $1,035 per person, double occupancy.

At the north end of the University of Tampa, **Riverfront Park,** 900 North Blvd. (tel. 223-8602), offers 11 courts, and visitors are welcome to use it on a first-come, first-served basis, although reservations can also be made up to a day in advance. The courts are lit until 10pm. Prices are $2.25 to $4.50 per person per hour, and it's open daily from 7am to 10pm.

WHERE TO STAY

Tampa is a city of relatively new hotels, all built in the last 25 years or so. Unlike many major cities, the downtown section of Tampa is not flush with hotels. Instead, the greatest concentration of hotels is near Tampa International Airport, primarily along Westshore Boulevard and the Courtney Campbell Causeway. The next largest cluster of lodgings is north of downtown in the Busch Gardens area.

Price-wise, the high season is January through April, although rates don't vary dramatically throughout the year. The big price breaks come on weekends—all year long—when rates drop as much as 50%. The only exception to this rule is the Busch

Gardens area, where rates don't dip on weekends, and can even be slightly higher for holiday weekends or special events.

VERY EXPENSIVE

HYATT REGENCY WESTSHORE, 6200 Courtney Campbell Causeway, Tampa, FL 33607. Tel. 813/874-1234, or toll free 800/233-1234. Fax 813/870-9168. 445 rms. A/C TV TEL
$ Rates: $169 single; $195 double. AE, CB, DC, DISC, MC, V.
Situated a mile west of Tampa International Airport and overlooking Old Tampa Bay, this 14-story property is nestled on a 35-acre nature preserve, convenient to downtown and yet sequestered in a world of its own. Seashore colors and light woods grace the guest rooms, most of which provide expansive views of the bay and evening sunsets.
Dining/Entertainment: Armani's is a rooftop restaurant known for its fine Italian food and views. Behind the main hotel a 250-foot boardwalk leads to Oystercatchers, a Key West–style seafood eatery with indoor and outdoor seating overlooking the bay. For casual fare, there's Petey Brown's Café.
Services: Airport courtesy shuttle, 24-hour room service, concierge, babysitting, valet laundry.
Facilities: Two outdoor swimming pools, two lighted tennis courts, whirlpool, saunas, health club, nature walks and jogging trails.

SHERATON GRAND HOTEL, 4860 W. Kennedy Blvd., Tampa, FL 33609. Tel. 813/286-4400, or toll free 800/325-3535. Fax 813/286-4053. 350 rms. A/C TV TEL
$ Rates: $99–$129 single; $109–$139 double. AE, CB, DC, MC, V.
Located near the airport in the heart of the Westshore business district, this contemporary-style 11-story property is part of Urban Center, a financial office complex. In addition to a steady business clientele, it attracts vacationers who enjoy the panoramic views from the three glass elevators, and the bright atriums filled with greenery and cascading fountains. The guest rooms have soft-toned color schemes, traditional dark-wood furnishings, writing desks, easy chairs, full-length mirrors, built-in armoires, roomy closets, and marble-finished bathrooms. Rooms on the upper floors have views of Old Tampa Bay.
Dining/Entertainment: For continental recipes and fresh Florida seafood, try J. Fitzgerald's. There's also the Courtyard Café, for light meals in an indoor/outdoor setting, and the Grand Slam Sports Bar.
Services: Courtesy airport shuttle, 24-hour room service, concierge, valet laundry.
Facilities: Outdoor heated swimming pool, gift shop, florist, two banks, news/tobacco shop.

TAMPA AIRPORT MARRIOTT, Tampa International Airport, Tampa, FL 33607. Tel. 813/879-5151, or toll free 800/228-9290. Fax 813/873-0945. 296 rms. A/C TV TEL
$ Rates: $150 single; $160 double. AE, CB, DC, DISC, MC, V.
Wedged between the terminals, this is the only on-site hotel at Tampa's busy airport and a good specimen for those who thrive on the excitement of overnighting near the jetways. The guest rooms are well soundproofed, and decorated in contemporary style with dark woods and fabrics in cheery pastels.
Dining/Entertainment: An express elevator takes you to CK's, the hotel's revolving rooftop restaurant and lounge. On the lobby level is the Garden Café for light fare and the Flight Room for cocktails and a large-screen TV.
Services: Concierge, babysitting, valet laundry.
Facilities: Outdoor heated swimming pool, health club, gift shop.

WYNDHAM HARBOUR ISLAND HOTEL, 725 S. Harbour Island Blvd., Harbour Island, Tampa, FL 33602. Tel. 813/229-5000, or toll free 800/822-4200. Fax 813/229-5322. 300 rms. A/C MINIBAR TV TEL
$ Rates: $169 single; $189 double. AE, CB, DC, MC, V.

Tampa Area

Comfort Inn **3**
Courtyard by Marriott **13**
Crown Sterling Suites
 Hotel **14**
Days Inn–Bush Gardens/
 Maingate **5**
Days Inn-Rocky Point **8**
Hampton Inn **12**
Helnan Riverside Hotel **17**
Holiday Inn-Ashley
 Plaza **16**
Hyatt Regency Tampa **18**
Hyatt Regency
 Westshore **10**
LaQuinta–Airport **11**
Quality Suites–Busch
 Gardens **1**
Radisson Bay Harbor Inn **9**
Ramada Resort **2**
Red Roof Inn **4**
Sheraton Grand Hotel **15**
Sheraton Inn Tampa **6**
Tampa Airport Marriott **7**
Wyndham Harbour
 Island Hotel **19**

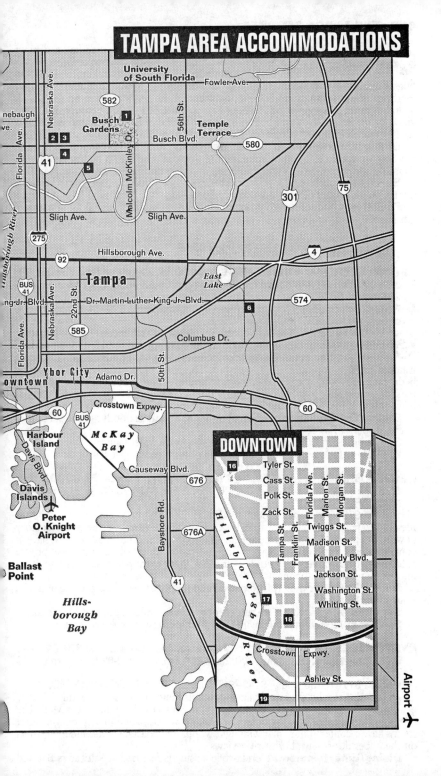

TAMPA AREA ACCOMMODATIONS

University
of South Florida

Fowler Ave.

582

Busch **1**
Gardens

2 **3**

4

41

5

Nebraska Ave.

56th St.

Temple
Terrace

Busch Blvd.

580

301

75

Malcolm McKinley Dr.

Florida Ave.

nebaugh
ve.

Sligh Ave.

Sligh Ave.

275

92

Hillsborough Ave.

4

Hillsborough River

Tampa

East
Lake

574

ng-Jr.-Blvd.

Dr.-Martin-Luther-King-Jr.-Blvd.

22nd St.

Nebraska Ave.

585

Columbus Dr.

6

50th St.

Florida Ave.

Ybor City

Adamo Dr.

owntown

Crosstown Expwy.

60

60

BUS
41

*McKay
Bay*

Harbour
Island

Davis Blvd.

Causeway Blvd.

676

Davis
Islands

Bayshore Rd.

676A

Peter
O. Knight
Airport

41

**Ballast
Point**

*Hills-
borough
Bay*

DOWNTOWN

16

Tyler St.

Cass St.

Polk St.

Zack St.

Florida Ave.

Marion St.

Morgan St.

Tampa St.

Franklin St.

Twiggs St.

Madison St.

Kennedy Blvd.

Jackson St.

Washington St.

Whiting St.

Hillsborough River

17

18

Crosstown Expwy.

Ashley St.

19

Airport ✈

★ If location is everything, then this 12-story luxury property has a distinct advantage—it's just a minute or two from the bustle of downtown, yet it sits tranquilly on Harbour Island, surrounded by the channels linking the Hillsborough River and Bay. It's likewise connected to the shops and waterside activities of the Harbour Island complex, and offers customers all the perks of living on the island, including guest privileges at the Harbour Island Athletic Club. The bedrooms, all with views of the water, are furnished in dark woods and floral fabrics, and each has a well-lit marble-trimmed bathroom, executive desk, and work area.

Dining/Entertainment: Watch the yachts drift by as you dine at the Harbourview Room, or enjoy your favorite drink in The Bar, a clubby room with equally good views. Snacks and drinks are available during the day at the Pool Bar.

Services: Courtesy airport shuttle, room service, concierge, secretarial services, notary public, evening turn-down service, valet laundry.

Facilities: Outdoor heated swimming pool and deck, 50 boat slips, newsand/gift shop.

EXPENSIVE

CROWN STERLING SUITES HOTEL, 4400 W. Cypress St., Tampa, FL 33607. Tel. 813/873-8675, or toll free 800/433-4600. Fax 813/879-7196. 263 suites. A/C TV TEL

$ Rates (including full breakfast and evening cocktail party): $99–$149 suite for one or two. AE, CB, DC, MC, V.

⑤ With an exterior of salmon-toned Spanish-style architecture, this eight-story building adds an old-world charm to the busy corridor beside the airport and Westshore Boulevard. The interior includes a plant-filled atrium with cascading waterfalls and a tropical garden courtyard. The guest units are suites with separate bedrooms and living areas, contemporary furniture, muted color schemes, and wet bars, and most have sofa beds, microwave ovens, coffee makers, and private patios or balconies.

Dining/Entertainment: Regional dishes and local seafoods are the specialties at the St. James Bar & Grill.

Services: Airport courtesy shuttle, room service, valet laundry.

Facilities: Indoor swimming pool, sauna, steam room, gift shop.

HELNAN RIVERSIDE HOTEL, 200 N. Ashley Dr., Tampa, FL 33602. Tel. 813/223-2222, or toll free 800/288-2672. Fax 813/273-0839. 285 rms. A/C MINIBAR TV TEL

$ Rates: $75–$85 single or double. AE, CB, DC, MC, V.

Ideally located on the Hillsborough River near the convention center, this six-story downtown property was formerly the Tampa Hilton. The guest rooms have a contemporary decor with blond woods and pastel tones; most units have private balconies with river views. Modern bathrooms have extra perks, such as a makeup mirror, hairdryer, and phone.

Dining/Entertainment: Choices include the River Deli for light fare and The Lounge for libations.

Services: Airport courtesy shuttle, room service, valet cleaning (weekdays).

Facilities: Heated outdoor swimming pool, exercise room, gift shop.

HYATT REGENCY TAMPA, 211 N. Tampa St., Tampa, FL 33602. Tel. 813/225-1234, or toll free 800/233-1234. Fax 813/273-0234. 518 rms. A/C TV TEL

$ Rates: $117–$150 single; $142–$175 double. AE, CB, DC, DISC, MC, V.

★ Standing out on the city skyline, with a striking mirrored facade, this 17-story tower sits in the heart of downtown adjacent to the Franklin Street Mall. The eight-story atrium lobby boasts a cascading waterfall and lots of foliage. Guest rooms have a contemporary flair with light woods and coastal colors, and many units on the upper floors have bay or river views.

Dining/Entertainment: Florida-style cuisine is featured at Saltwaters Bar and

Grille (lunch only). Light meals are on tap at Pralines, an all-day café with indoor/outdoor patio seating. For libations with piano music, take the escalator to Breeze's Lounge on the second floor of the atrium.

Services: Airport courtesy shuttle, 24-hour room service, concierge, valet laundry.

Facilities: Outdoor heated swimming pool, whirlpool, health club.

MODERATE

HOLIDAY INN–ASHLEY PLAZA, 111 W. Fortune St., Tampa, FL 33602.
Tel. 813/223-1351, or toll free 800/ASK-VALUE. Fax 813/221-2000. 311 rms. A/C TV TEL
$ **Rates:** $72.50–$92.50 single; $82.50–$102.50 double. AE, CB, DC, DISC, MC, V.

Perched along the Hillsborough River, this modern 14-story hotel is downtown, next to the Tampa Bay Performing Arts Center and within walking distance of most attractions. Guest rooms are spacious, with dark-wood furnishings, rose- or aqua-toned fabrics, and full-length wall mirrors. Most rooms on upper floors have views of the river.

Dining/Entertainment: The lobby level offers three choices: the Backstage Restaurant, for moderately priced meals in a theatrical setting; the Deli, for light fare; and the Encore lounge, for drinks and occasional live music.

Services: Airport courtesy shuttle, room service, valet laundry.

Facilities: Outdoor heated swimming pool, whirlpool, fitness room, coin-operated laundry, gift shop.

QUALITY SUITES HOTEL–USF/BUSCH GARDENS, 3001 University Center Dr., Tampa, FL 33612. Tel. 813/971-8930, or toll free 800/228-5151. Fax 813/971-8935. 150 suites. A/C TV TEL
$ **Rates** (including full breakfast and evening cocktail reception): $79–$155 suite for one; $84–$160 suite for two. AE, DC, DISC, MC, V.

This hacienda-style all-suite hotel sits directly behind Busch Gardens, although the entrance to the theme park is four blocks away. Each guest unit has a separate bedroom with built-in armoire and well-lit mirrored vanity area, a living/dining room with sofa bed, plus wet bar, coffee maker, microwave, and stereo/VCR unit. The decor relies heavily on art deco–style furnishings.

Services: 24-hour gift shop/food store, VCR rentals, valet laundry.

Facilities: Outdoor heated swimming pool, Jacuzzi, meeting rooms, coin-operated laundry.

RADISSON BAY HARBOR INN, 7700 Courtney Campbell Causeway, Tampa, FL 33607. Tel. 813/281-8900, or toll free 800/333-3333. Fax 813/281-0189. 257 rms. A/C TV TEL
$ **Rates:** $59–$99 single or double. AE, CB, DC, MC, V.

Situated on Old Tampa Bay, two miles west of the airport, this six-story property is one of the few hotels that actually has a sandy beach of its own. The guest rooms, all with views of the water, have a balcony or patio. The decor, which uses mostly sea-toned fabrics, reflects art deco influences.

Dining/Entertainment: Views of the water and food are the prime attractions at the lobby-level Damon's Restaurant and Lounge.

Services: Airport courtesy shuttle, valet laundry.

Facilities: Heated outdoor swimming pool, two lighted tennis courts, hair salons for men and women, gift shop.

RAMADA RESORT, 820 E. Busch Blvd., Tampa, FL 33612. Tel. 813/933-4011, or toll free 800/288-4011. Fax 813/932-1784. 255 rms. A/C TV TEL
$ **Rates:** $59–$99 single or double. AE, CB, DC, DISC, MC, V.

Attracting a business clientele as well as vacationers, this two- and four-story hotel is situated two miles west of Busch Gardens. The lobby leads to an enclosed skylit atrium-style courtyard with fountains, streetlights, benches, shops, café, bars, a pool, and other sports facilities. Guest rooms, which surround the courtyard, offer standard furnishings, enlivened by colorful, eye-catching fabrics.

Dining/Entertainment: Apricots Restaurant, off the lobby, features seafood dishes. Charades Nite Club offers live entertainment and the Atrium has a café, lounge, and coffee shop.

Services: Courtesy transport to Busch Gardens, concierge desk, secretarial services, valet laundry.

Facilities: Indoor and outdoor heated swimming pools, two Jacuzzis, sauna, four lighted tennis courts, tennis pro shop, exercise room, games room, coin-operated laundry, gift shop.

SHERATON INN TAMPA, 7401 E. Hillsborough Ave., Tampa, FL 33610. Tel. 813/626-0999, or toll free 800/325-3535. Fax 813/622-7893, ext. 246. 156 rms. A/C TV TEL

$ Rates: $95–$105 single; $105–$115 double. AE, CB, DC, MC, V.

Ten minutes from downtown, this two-, three-, and six-story property is situated off I-4 in a palm-tree–shaded setting, close to the State Fairgrounds and an hour away from Orlando-area attractions. Guest rooms, many of which surround a central courtyard and pool area, are contemporary in decor, with dark woods, brass fixtures, restful tones, and floral art. Most units have balconies or patios.

Dining/Entertainment: The lobby area has a lounge bar with an informal atmosphere; or follow a covered walkway to an adjacent building and the Cypress Landing Restaurant and Lounge.

Services: Airport courtesy shuttle, room service, valet laundry, secretarial services.

Facilities: Outdoor heated swimming pool, health club, gift shop.

INEXPENSIVE

COURTYARD BY MARRIOTT, 3805 W. Cypress St., Tampa, FL 33607. Tel. 813/874-0555, or toll free 800/321-2211. Fax 813/870-0685. 145 rms. A/C TV TEL

$ Rates: $49–$105 single or double. AE, CB, DC, DISC, MC, V.

With a fireplace glowing in the lobby, this contemporary four-story hotel is a quiet oasis tucked beside the busy Dale Mabry Highway, three miles from the airport. Like other properties of this chain, it follows the usual layout, with guest rooms surrounding a central courtyard. The rooms, which offer a choice of a king-size bed or two double beds, feature dark-wood furnishings and pastel-toned fabrics, and have in-room coffee makers. Facilities include a café/lounge, outdoor swimming pool, indoor whirlpool, exercise room, and guest laundry. The hotel offers complimentary airport transportation.

DAYS INN ROCKY POINT, 7627 Courtney Campbell Causeway, Tampa, FL 33607. Tel. 813/281-0000, or toll free 800/DAYS-INN. Fax 813/281-1067. 152 rms. A/C TV TEL

$ Rates: $50–$75 single; $55–$90 double. AE, DC, DISC, MC, V.

Set back from the main road two miles west of the airport, this motel-style property has a lovely waterfront setting on Old Tampa Bay, and a small strip of beach. The layout encompasses six two-story wings, surrounding an outdoor swimming pool with landscaped courtyard, so the bedrooms offer either bay-view or poolside views. The units have a cheery decor with basic light-wood furniture.

For dining or imbibing, try the Southern Exposure Waterfront Café and Sports Bar. Facilities include a heated outdoor swimming pool, two tennis courts, a shuffleboard court, horseshoes, badminton, a volleyball court, a children's playground, rentals for paddle boats, and a coin-operated guest laundry.

BUDGET

COMFORT INN, 2106 E. Busch Blvd., Tampa, FL 33612. Tel. 813/931-3313, or toll free 800/221-2222. Fax 813/933-8140. 50 units. A/C TV TEL

$ Rates: $36–$75 single; $41–$75 double; $45–$75 efficiency. AE, DISC, MC, V. Situated about half a mile west of Busch Gardens, this three-story motor inn offers a choice of accommodations. Most rooms are standard doubles, and some have only a shower instead of a full bath. In addition, there are larger rooms with king-size beds and full baths; and over a third of the units are efficiencies outfitted with small kitchenettes. Facilities are limited, but there's an outdoor heated swimming pool.

DAYS INN–BUSCH GARDENS/MAINGATE, 2901 E. Busch Blvd., Tampa, FL 33612. Tel. 813/933-6471, or toll free 800/DAYS-INN. Fax 813/931-0261. 179 rms. A/C TV TEL
$ Rates: $32–$59 single; $37–$64 double. AE, DC, MC, V.
Within walking distance of Busch Gardens, this two-story motel is popular with families. Although the registration office is just off the main thoroughfare, most of the guest rooms are set back in a quieter environment surrounding an outdoor swimming pool. Rooms offer colorful standard furnishings, mostly with two double beds. There are no dining outlets on the premises, but a full-service 24-hour restaurant is adjacent. In addition to the pool, on-site facilities include a children's playground and coin-operated laundry.

HAMPTON INN, 4817 W. Laurel St., Tampa, FL 33607. Tel. 813/287-0778, or toll free 800/HAMPTON. Fax 813/287-0882. 134 rms. A/C TV TEL
$ Rates (including continental breakfast): $52–$69 single; $62–$79 double. AE, DISC, MC, V.
This six-story property offers good value along the busy corridor within a mile of the airport. Guest rooms are decorated with dark woods, set off by pink, peach, and beige tones. Some units offer king-size beds and extra work areas, and 50% of the rooms are designated as no-smoking. Facilities are limited, but there's an outdoor swimming pool and a courtesy shuttle to the airport.

LA QUINTA–AIRPORT, 4730 W. Spruce St., Tampa, FL 33607. Tel. 813/287-0440, or toll free 800/531-5900. Fax 813/286-7399. 122 rms. A/C TV TEL
$ Rates (including complimentary continental breakfast): $53–$65 single; $60–$75 double. AE, CB, DC, DISC, MC, V.
Equally convenient to the airport and the Westshore business district, this two-story hacienda-style motel offers a homey alternative to the many sleek high-rise hostelries in this area. Guest rooms, which surround a central courtyard, are decorated in a contemporary southwestern motif, with light woods, pueblo art, and colorful fabrics. Public areas include a cozy lobby with a fireplace and a sun deck with sombrero-shaped umbrellas. There's a complimentary airport shuttle and an adjacent 24-hour restaurant.

RED ROOF INN, 2307 E. Busch Blvd., Tampa, FL 33612. Tel. 813/932-0073, or toll free 800/THE-ROOF. Fax 813/933-5689. 108 rms. A/C TV TEL
$ Rates: $26–$34 single; $44–$58 double. AE, CB, DC, DISC, MC, V.
Half a mile west of Busch Gardens, this two-story property is set back from the road in a well-landscaped, grassy setting. The layout consists of two adjacent wings with an outdoor pool and whirlpool in the center. The guest units are outfitted with bright, colorful fabrics and standard furnishings.

WHERE TO DINE

Tampa offers a wide variety of fine restaurants, with menus ranging from typically American fare to regional southern dishes or Cajun Créole cooking, as well as more exotic offerings from Spain, France, Italy, Germany, Mexico, and the Orient. Most of all, the Tampa area is outstanding for seafood—delights fresh from nearby gulf waters and beyond. The port of Tampa is home to one of Florida's largest shrimp-boat fleets. Other local favorites include grouper, pompano, snapper, stone crabs, rock shrimp, and crayfish.

VERY EXPENSIVE

BERN'S STEAK HOUSE, 1208 S. Howard Ave. Tel. 251-2421.
   Cuisine: AMERICAN. **Reservations:** Required.
$ Prices: Main courses $13.80–$45. CB, DC, MC, V.
   Open: Dinner only, daily 5–11pm.

✪ No visit to Tampa is complete without dinner at Bern Laxer's one-of-a-kind restaurant, an attraction in itself; indeed, many people make reservations weeks in advance. Started on a small scale in 1953, and still totally unpretentious on the outside, it has grown to a two-story, seven-room Tampa institution.

Above all, it's a temple of beef where the motto is "art in steaks"—you order a prime, well-aged steak according to the thickness and weight you prefer, which is then cut and broiled over charcoal to your specifications. If beef is not your fancy, perhaps the menu can tempt you with lamb or veal. Depending on the season, most vegetables served at Bern's are grown in the restaurant's own organic garden. All main dishes come with onion soup, salad, baked potato, garlic toast, and onion rings. (*Note:* Smoking is prohibited in six of the seven main dining rooms).

CK's, 8th Floor in the Tampa Airport Marriott, Tampa International Airport. Tel. 878-6500.
   Cuisine: CONTINENTAL/AMERICAN. **Reservations:** Recommended.
$ Prices: Main courses $16.95–$24.95. AE, CB, DC, MC, V.
   Open: Lunch Mon–Sat 11:30am–2:30pm; dinner Sun–Thurs 5–10pm, Fri–Sat 5–11pm; brunch Sun 10:30am–2:30pm.

✪ In the heart of the airport, this revolving rooftop restaurant is a one-of-a-kind in Tampa and an attraction in its own right. There's an ever-changing view from each table, spanning the adjacent jetways and more distant vistas of Tampa Bay and the city skyline. The extensive dinner menu ranges from local seafoods to prime ribs, steaks, and rack of lamb. Specialties include grilled marinated quail, roast half a smoked duck, smoked swordfish, and baked salmon. The "early bird" menu, available from 5 to 7pm, offers exceptional value.

DONATELLO, 232 N. Dale Mabry Hwy. Tel. 875-6660.
   Cuisine: NORTHERN ITALIAN. **Reservations:** Recommended.
$ Prices: Main courses $15.95–$24.95. AE, CB, DC, MC, V.
   Open: Lunch Mon–Fri noon–3pm; dinner daily 6–11pm.

With stucco arches, Italian tilework, and peach-colored linens, this romantic restaurant has a Mediterranean flair, artfully enhanced by soft individual table lighting, and an attentive tuxedoed waiting staff. Specialties include linguine with Maine lobster, breast of duck with Curaçao and orange sauce, veal "Dolce Vita" (with ham, mushrooms, and truffles), salmon Stromboli (with asparagus, shrimp, and creamy white wine sauce), and osso buco alla milanese.

EXPENSIVE

THE CASTAWAY, 7720 Courtney Campbell Causeway. Tel. 281-0770.
   Cuisine: AMERICAN/POLYNESIAN/SEAFOOD. **Reservations:** Accepted for dinner, with seating at the first available table at the time requested.
$ Prices: Main courses $13.95–$19.95. AE, CB, DC, MC, V.
   Open: Lunch Mon–Fri 11am–4pm, Sat–Sun 11am–4pm; dinner Sun–Thurs 5–10pm, Fri–Sat 5–11pm.

Situated beside the Ben T. Davis Municipal Beach, this nautically themed spot bills itself as Tampa's only beachfront restaurant. The building rests on stilts over the waters of Old Tampa Bay, making the views hard to equal, especially at sunset time. The menu is a blend of seafaring specials with a Polynesian influence. Choices range from seafood brochettes, bouillabaisse, and stir-fry dishes to coconut shrimp and scallops chardonnay. Non-seafood selections include Hawaiian chicken, pastas, and steaks.

SELENA'S, 1623 Snow Ave. Tel. 251-2116.
   Cuisine: CREOLE/SICILIAN. **Reservations:** Recommended.

$ Prices: Main courses $7.95–$17.95. AE, CB, DC, MC, V.
Open: Sun–Wed 11am–10pm, Thurs 11am–11pm, Fri–Sat 11am–midnight.
Step into this charming restaurant in the Old Hyde Park shopping complex and you'll feel like you're in the heart of New Orleans, whether you sit in the plant-filled Patio Room, the eclectic Queen Anne Room, or the outdoor café. Open the menu and you'll see an interesting blend of dishes, reflecting the owners' family backgrounds. Local seafoods, especially grouper and shrimp, top the menu at dinner, with many of the dishes served Créole style or blackened, as well as broiled and fried. Choices also include pastas, chicken, steaks, and veal. At night, jazz sounds enliven the proceedings, as musical groups perform in the upstairs lounge.

VILLANOVA BY LAURO, 4030 W. Waters Ave. Tel. 889-8800.
   Cuisine: ITALIAN. **Reservations:** Recommended.
$ Prices: Main courses $12.50–$21.50. AE, CB, DC, MC, V.
   Open: Lunch Mon–Fri 11:30am–2pm; dinner Mon–Sat 6–11pm.
With a classic decor, soft music, tuxedoed waiters, and a kitchen presided over by award-winning chef Lauro Medaglia, this restaurant is a little off the beaten track, but well worth a detour northwest of the airport, off the Dale Mabry Highway. The menu includes six different veal dishes; steak flamed in a cream sauce of brandy and green peppercorns; chicken breast with eggplant, mozzarella, and tomatoes; sweetbreads with prosciutto; and jumbo marinated grilled shrimp; as well as over a dozen freshly made pastas such as fettuccine Alfredo, cannelloni, tortellini, and gnocchi con Gorgonzola (potato dumplings with Gorgonzola cream cheese).

MODERATE

CAFE CREOLE AND OYSTER BAR, 1330 Ninth Ave., Ybor City. Tel. 247-6283.
   Cuisine: CREOLE/CAJUN. **Reservations:** Recommended.
$ Prices: Main courses $8.95–$14.95. AE, CB, DC, MC, V.
   Open: Mon–Thurs 11:30am–10pm, Fri–Sat 11:30am–11pm, Sun noon–4pm.
If you're curious about Ybor City history, the setting of this indoor/outdoor restaurant tells quite a tale. The building, dating back to 1896, was originally known as El Pasaje, the home of the Cherokee Club, a gentlemen's hotel and private club with a casino and a decor rich in stained-glass windows, wrought-iron balconies, Spanish murals, and marble bathrooms. During the Depression and the years following, the building was used variously as a political club, low-rent hotel, and WPA school of music, art, and dance. It was placed on the National Register of Historic Places in 1973 and new owners restored it in the 1980s.
   Specialties include Louisiana-style dishes—red beans and rice with andouille sausage, blackened catfish, seafood gumbo, grouper Bienville, crayfish étouffé, and jambalaya. During the crayfish season (January through June), there's a Louisiana "crayfish and shrimp boil" on Wednesday. The oyster bar also offers Bajou country oysters from New Orleans served half a dozen ways.

THE COLONNADE, 3401 Bayshore Blvd. Tel. 839-7558.
   Cuisine: AMERICAN/SEAFOOD. **Reservations:** Accepted only for large parties.
$ Prices: Main courses $7.95–$16.95. AE, DC, MC, V.
   Open: Sun–Thurs 11am–10pm, Fri–Sat 11am–11pm.
Overlooking Hillsborough Bay and nestled in Hyde Park's palm-shaded residential neighborhood, this restaurant was established in 1935, and it has since become a local institution, winning special acclaim for fresh seafood. Specialties include grouper in lemon butter, crab-stuffed flounder, wild Florida alligator, Cajun catfish, broiled Florida lobster, and half a dozen varieties of shrimp (from batter-dipped or crabmeat-stuffed, to pecan-fried or scampi). Prime rib, steaks, and chicken are also available.

THE COLUMBIA, 2117 Seventh Ave. E., Ybor City. Tel. 248-4961.
   Cuisine: SPANISH. **Reservations:** Recommended.

Tampa Area

TAMPA AREA DINING

University of South Florida

Fowler Ave.

582

Nebraska Ave.

Busch Gardens

56th St.

Temple Terrace

Busch Blvd.

580

41

Malcolm McKinley Dr.

301

75

Florida Ave.

Sligh Ave.

Sligh Ave.

275

Hillsborough River

Hillsborough Ave.

92

East Lake

4

Tampa

BUS 41

ng Jr. Blvd.

Dr. Martin Luther King Jr. Blvd.

574

Nebraska Ave.

22nd St.

585

Columbus Dr.

50th St.

Florida Ave.

Ybor City

Adamo Dr.

Downtown

14

15

16

Crosstown Expwy.

60

3

20

60

BUS 41

McKay Bay

DOWNTOWN

Tyler St.

Cass St.

Polk St.

Zack St.

Florida Ave.

Marion St.

Morgan St.

Harbour Island

Davis Blvd.

Causeway Blvd.

676

Twiggs St.

Tampa St.

Franklin St.

21

Davis Islands

Peter O. Knight Airport

Bayshore Rd.

676A

22

Madison St.

Kennedy Blvd.

Hillsborough River

Jackson St.

Washington St.

Whiting St.

Ballast Point

41

Hills-borough Bay

Crosstown Expwy.

23

24

Ashley St.

25

Airport

$ Prices: Main courses $10.95–$16.95. AE, CB, DC, DISC, MC, V.
Open: Daily 11am–11pm.

⭐ This is the Columbia that everyone talks about, dating back to 1905 and occupying a full city block in the heart of Ybor City. The decor throughout is graced with hand-painted tiles, wrought-iron chandeliers, dark woods, rich red fabrics, and stained-glass windows.

Ⓢ Among the tempting menu items are red snapper Alicante (baked in a casserole with Spanish onions and peppers, and topped with almonds, eggplant, and shrimp), filet mignon Columbia (wrapped in bacon, with mushrooms, ham, onions, peppers, in a tomato-and-burgundy sauce), traditional chicken and yellow rice, and three types of spicy paellas. All main dishes come with Cuban bread and yellow rice or potato. A favorite starter is the "Original 1905 Salad"—lettuce, tomato, smoked ham, Swiss and Romano cheeses, olives, and more, with a house garlic dressing. Monday through Saturday, there's also a flamenco show at 8:30pm ($5 extra).

A second location, with water views, is at 601 S. Harbor Island Blvd., Harbour Island (tel. 229-2992). Other branches are in downtown St. Petersburg, Clearwater, and Sarasota.

CRAWDADDY'S, 2500 Rocky Point Dr. Tel. 281-0407.

Cuisine: REGIONAL/SEAFOOD. **Reservations:** Recommended.
$ Prices: Main courses $3.95–$7.95 at lunch, $10.95–$17.95 at dinner. AE, CB, DC, MC, V.
Open: Lunch Mon–Fri 11am–3pm; dinner Sun–Thurs 5–10pm, Fri–Sat 5pm–midnight.

Overlooking Old Tampa Bay near the airport off the Courtney Campbell Causeway, this informal spot is named after Beauregard "Crawdaddy" Belvedere, a Roaring '20s tycoon. He owned a fish camp on this site and the decor has not changed much since—the seven dining rooms are all bedecked with Victorian furnishings, books, pictures, and collectibles. The "down home"-style menu ranges from beer-battered shrimp and fish camp fry (shrimp, scallops, and fresh fish, deep-fried in corn crisp and almond coating, with jalapeño hush puppies) to shrimp and chicken jambalaya, prime ribs, and steaks.

LE BORDEAUX, 1502 S. Howard Ave. Tel. 254-4387.

Cuisine: FRENCH. **Reservations:** Accepted only for parties of six or more.
$ Prices: Main courses $8–$16. AE, DC, MC, V.
Open: Lunch Mon–Fri 11:30am–2pm; dinner Mon–Thurs 5:30–10pm, Fri–Sat 5:30–11pm, Sun 5:30–9:30pm.

Ⓢ Located in a residential neighborhood, west of downtown near Bayshore Boulevard, this bungalow/bistro is a real find, with first-rate French food at affordable prices. The domain of French-born chef/owner Gordon Davis, it offers seating in a living room–style main dining area or a plant-filled conservatory. The menu changes daily, but you can count on homemade pâtés and pastries, and the specials often include salmon en croûte, pot au feu, veal with wild mushrooms, and filet of beef au roquefort.

LUCY HO'S BAMBOO GARDEN, 2740 E. Fowler Ave. Tel. 977-2783.

Cuisine: CHINESE. **Reservations:** Accepted only for parties of five or more.
$ Prices: Main courses $5.95–$19.95. AE, DC, DISC, MC, V.
Open: Mon–Sat 11:30am–10pm, Sun 11:30am–9pm.

A standout for Chinese cuisine, this restaurant is northwest of Busch Gardens, in the University Collection Shopping Center. The menu features a blend of Mandarin, Cantonese, and Szechuan dishes, such as Mongolian beef, cashew chicken, pepper steak, and whole fish Hunan style. Chinese alcohol and beer are also available.

MISE EN PLACE, 442 W. Kennedy Blvd. Tel. 254-5373.

Cuisine: AMERICAN. **Reservations:** Accepted only for parties of six or more.
$ Prices: Main courses $9.95–$16.95. AE, CB, DC, DISC, MC, V.
Open: Lunch Mon–Fri 11am–3pm; dinner Tues–Thurs 5:30–10pm, Fri–Sat 5:30–11pm.

With a fitting French name (meaning "everything in place"), this popular American bistro puts its emphasis on innovative cuisine that's beautifully presented and prepared with the freshest of local ingredients—all at moderate prices. It's conveniently located directly opposite the University of Tampa, an easy walk from downtown hotels. The menu changes daily, but main courses often include such choices as roast duck with Jamaica wild strawberry sauce, grilled swordfish with tri-melon mint salsa, rack of lamb with hazelnut parsliade, or grilled tournedos of beef with Gorgonzola in port-bordelaise sauce.

PARKER'S LIGHTHOUSE, 601 S. Harbour Island Blvd. Tel. 229-3474.
Cuisine: SEAFOOD. **Reservations:** Recommended for dinner.
$ Prices: Main courses $10.95–$20.95. AE, MC, V.
Open: Lunch Mon–Sat 11:30am–2:30pm, Sun 10:30am–2:30pm; dinner Mon–Thurs 5:30–10pm, Fri–Sat 5:30–10:30pm, Sun 5–10pm.

Overlooking the channels of the Hillsborough River and the Tampa skyline, this bright and airy Harbour Island restaurant is a favorite place to watch the boats go by and to enjoy cooked-to-order seafood in an indoor or outdoor setting. Choose a main course from an ever-changing selection that ranges from shark to swordfish, snapper to salmon, sheephead to Spanish mackerel, or yellowfin tuna to trout. Then decide how you'd like it prepared—sautéed, baked, broiled, or blackened—and with a choice of seasoned butters (from ginger-lime to chive-parsley or pine nut). The menu also includes lobster, steaks, pastas, and chicken.

RUMPELMAYER'S, 4812 E. Busch Blvd. Tel. 989-9563.
Cuisine: GERMAN/EUROPEAN. **Reservations:** Recommended.
$ Prices: Main courses $7.50–$17.50. AE, CB, DC, DISC, MC, V.
Open: Daily 11am–11pm.

Here's a little bit of Bavaria just eight blocks from Busch Gardens. The menu presents tasty and traditional dishes ranging from heringsalat (a cold plate of North Sea herring with red beets, apples, and onions), to assorted wursts, wienerschnitzel, sauerbraten, Hungarian stuffed cabbage, and Polish kolbassi. Seafood lovers take delight in the smoked mackerel from the North Sea, "Garnalen" (shrimp scampi with Moselle wine), and Dutch flounder sautéed in brown butter.

INEXPENSIVE

CRABBY TOM'S OLD TIME OYSTER BAR AND SEAFOOD RESTAURANT, 3120 W. Hillsborough Ave. Tel. 870-1652.
Cuisine: SEAFOOD. **Reservations:** Accepted only for parties of 10 or more.
$ Prices: Main courses $4.95–$15.95. AE, DISC, MC, V.
Open: Mon–Thurs 11am–10pm, Fri–Sat 11am–11pm, Sun 4–9pm.

Although this spot lacks waterside views and an impressive decor, the seafood lovers dining here don't seem to mind. Sit back, relax, and crack open a pile of stone crab claws, Alaska snow crab claws, or king crab legs. If you tire of crab, there's always a lobster from the tank or an array of other seafood, from grouper, flounder, and catfish to shrimp, scallops, and mahi-mahi, as well as clams and oysters on the half shell. Chicken, pastas, and ribs are also offered.

NATIVE SEAFOOD GRILLE, 238 E. Davis Blvd., Davis Islands. Tel. 254-9660.
Cuisine: FLORIDIAN/CARIBBEAN. **Reservations:** Accepted only for parties of six or more (preferred seating for smaller parties).
$ Prices: Main courses $7.95–$13.95. MC, V.
Open: Lunch Mon–Fri 11:30am–2pm; dinner Mon–Thurs 5–10pm, Fri 5–11pm; lunch/dinner Sat 11:30am–11pm, Sun 1–9pm.

Located directly across from Harbour Island, this indoor/outdoor restaurant exudes a tropical ambience, with Caribbean art, music, greenery, a herb garden, and a fresh fish market on the premises. The menu includes jumbo shrimp marinated in a Brazil- and macadamia-nut pesto, sautéed grouper with sliced bananas and rum sauce, grilled salmon with key lime marinade in watercress-dill sauce, crab cakes with mango-papaya salsa, smoked chicken with homemade jerk sauce and goat cheese, South American churrasco beef with chimichurri marinade, and a variety of fruit and vegetable salads.

BUDGET

CACTUS CLUB, 1601 Snow Ave. Tel. 251-4089.
   Cuisine: MEXICAN/AMERICAN SOUTHWEST. **Reservations:** Not required.
$ **Prices:** Main courses $5.95–$11.95. AE, MC, V.
   Open: Mon–Thurs 11am–midnight, Fri–Sat 11am–1am, Sun 11am–11pm.
Big and brassy, yet casual and comfortable, this sometimes-noisy café radiates southwestern pizazz in the heart of the Old Hyde Park shopping complex. It's the place to be if you're in the mood for fajitas, tacos, enchiladas, chili, hickory-smoked baby back ribs, Texas-style pizzas, blackened chicken, or guacamole/green-chili burgers.

CHA CHA COCONUTS, 601 S. Harbour Island Blvd. Tel. 223-3101.
   Cuisine: AMERICAN. **Reservations:** Not required.
$ **Prices:** Main courses $3.95–$7.95. AE, DC, MC, V.
   Open: Mon–Wed 11am–10pm, Thurs 11am–11pm, Fri–Sat 11am–1am, Sun noon–10pm.
With indoor/outdoor seating and lovely views of Hillsborough Bay and downtown, this informal Harbour Island eatery is billed as a tropical bar and grill. Ideal for lunch or a light meal, the menu is simple—burgers, grouper sandwiches, chowders and chilis, and finger foods such as peel-and-eat shrimp, oysters on the half shell, and chicken wings. Live music is often on tap, and all items on the menu are also available on a "to go" basis. Also located in St. Petersburg, Clearwater, and Sarasota.

FOUR GREEN FIELDS, 205 W. Platt St. Tel. 254-4444.
   Cuisine: IRISH/AMERICAN. **Reservations:** Not required.
$ **Prices:** Main courses $3.95–$8.95. AE, MC, V.
   Open: Mon–Thurs 11am–midnight, Fri–Sat 11am–1am, Sun noon–midnight.
   Closed: Mar 18.
Although this charming whitewashed and thatch-roofed cottage looks as if it belongs in the middle of Tipperary, it sits just one block west of the Tampa Convention Center. It's ideal for salads and sandwiches with an Irish flair or traditional dishes such as fish and chips, beef stew braised in Guinness, shepherd's pie, and corned beef and cabbage. There is Irish music on tap Tuesday through Saturday night.

THE LOADING DOCK, 100 Madison St. Tel. 223-6905.
   Cuisine: AMERICAN/DELI. **Reservations:** Not required.
$ **Prices:** Main courses $1.75–$4.95. No credit cards.
   Open: Mon–Fri 8am–8pm, Sat 10:30am–2:30pm.
As its name implies, this downtown eatery occupies a vintage Tampa building that was once the city's main loading dock for wholesale groceries. The menu conveys a loading-dock theme, with sandwiches such as the "union boss" (hot corned beef, Swiss, and sauerkraut), the "box car" (salami and provolone), and the "forklift" (all-beef knockwurst with sauerkraut and spicy mustard). Salads and soups are also featured.

MEL'S HOT DOGS, 4136 E. Busch Blvd. Tel. 985-8000.
   Cuisine: AMERICAN. **Reservations:** Not accepted.
$ **Prices:** Main courses $3–$6. No credit cards.
   Open: Mon–Sat 10am–10pm, Sun 11am–9pm.
   If you crave an old-fashioned Chicago-style all-beef hot dog before or after a foray into Busch Gardens, look no further. Considered "the big daddy" of hot-dog eateries, this informal place offers everything from "bagel-dogs" to bacon-, Cheddar-, or corndogs. All choices are served on a poppyseed bun and most come with french fries and a choice of coleslaw or baked beans. Even the decor is dedicated to weiners, with walls and windows lined with hot-dog memorabilia. And just in case hot-dog mania hasn't won you over, there a few alternative choices

(sausages, chicken breast, and burgers). And yes, there really is a "Mel" (Mel Lohn), who is usually on the scene, greeting guests, manning the cash register, or mingling among the tables.

SHELLS, 202 S. Dale Mabry Hwy. Tel. 875-3467.
   Cuisine: SEAFOOD. **Reservations:** Not accepted.
$ Prices: Main courses $4.95–$13.95. AE, MC, V.
   Open: Dinner only, Sun–Thurs 5–10pm, Fri–Sat 5–11pm.

Shells is a local institution, synonymous with fresh seafood at low prices. Founded in 1985, it has a simple formula for success—a fresh seafood menu, no frills, no reservations, and, above all, no strain on the budget. You may have to wait at least a half hour to be seated, and then you'll eat at picnic-style tables with paper and plastic utensils—but the food is worth it. The menu features Alaskan king crab legs and claws, Dungeness crab clusters, snow crab, scallops, shrimp, grouper, cod, and pasta combinations such as shrimp and cheese tortellini. There are also a few beef and chicken choices.

Other Tampa locations are at 14380 N. Dale Mabry Hwy. (tel. 968-6686) and 11010 N. 30th St. (tel. 977-8456). Also located in St. Petersburg and Bradenton.

SILVER RING, 1831 E. Seventh Ave., Ybor City. Tel. 248-2549.
   Cuisine: SPANISH/AMERICAN. **Reservations:** Not required.
$ Prices: Main courses $2.25–$4.95. No credit cards.
   Open: Mon–Sat 6:30am–5pm.

Operating since 1947, this place is now an Ybor City tradition. The walls are lined with old pictures, vintage radios, a 1950s jukebox, fishing rods, and deer heads. Most of all, it's *the* place to get a genuine Cuban sandwich—smoked ham, roast pork, Genoa salami, Swiss cheese, pickles, salad dressing, mustard, lettuce, and tomato on Cuban bread. Other menu items include Spanish bean soup, deviled crab, and other types of sandwiches.

SHOPPING

MALLS & MARKETS

OLD HYDE PARK VILLAGE, 1509 W. Swann Ave., Hyde Park. Tel. 251-3500.

Located in one of the city's oldest and most historic neighborhoods, this is Tampa's "Rodeo Drive," a cluster of 50 upscale shops and boutiques in a village layout. The selection includes Brooks Brothers, Crabtree & Evelyn, Godiva Chocolatier, Laura Ashley, and Polo Ralph Lauren. Open Monday through Wednesday and Saturday from 10am to 6pm, on Thursday and Friday from 10am to 9pm, and on Sunday from noon to 5pm.

THE SHOPS ON HARBOUR ISLAND, 777 S. Harbour Island Blvd., Harbour Island. Tel. 223-9898 or 228-7807.

Tampa's waterfront marketplace, on an island directly south of downtown, is well worth a day's outing. The 20 different shops include art galleries and fashion boutiques, as well as outlets for swimwear, sportswear, sunglasses, candies, collectibles, and Oriental treasures. Open Monday through Saturday from 10am to 9pm and on Sunday from 11am to 6pm.

YBOR CITY EUROPEAN MARKET, Centennial Park, Ybor City. Tel. 248-3712.

This is a colorful open-air farmer's market in the heart of Tampa's historic Latin Quarter, with a different seasonal theme each month. You might come away loaded down with fresh produce, pastries, flowers, wines, cheeses, coffee, antiques, or books. Open November through March, on the third Saturday of each month from 8am to 2pm.

YBOR SQUARE, 1901 13th St., Ybor City. Tel. 247-4497.

Listed on the National Register of Historic Places, this complex consists of three brick buildings (dating to 1886) that once comprised the largest cigar factory in the world, employing over 4,000 workers. Today it's a specialty mall, with over three dozen shops, selling everything from clothing, crafts, and jewelry to (of course) cigars. Open Monday through Saturday from 9:30am to 5:30pm and on Sunday from noon to 5:30pm.

SPECIALTY STORES

ADAM'S CITY HATTERS, 1621 E. Seventh Ave., Ybor City. Tel. 229-2850.
Established over 75 years ago and reputed to be Florida's largest hat store (with a mind-boggling inventory of more than 18,000 hats), this shop offers all types of headgear, from Stetsons and Panamas to top hats, sombreros, and caps. Open Monday through Friday from 9:30am to 5:30pm.

DEAN JAMES GLASS STUDIO, 1401 E. Seventh Ave., Ybor City. Tel. 248-3132.
Step inside this studio and watch artisans making decorative and functional art glass and handcrafted gifts. Open Monday through Saturday from noon to 6pm.

HEAD'S FLAGS, 1923 E. Seventh Ave., Ybor City. Tel. 248-5019.
Here you'll find colorful flags from all nations and all states, as well as banners, ethnic items, T-shirts, and hats. Open Monday through Friday from 9:30am to 5:30pm and on Saturday from 9:30am to 3pm.

MARTINEZ DE YBOR ART GALLERY, 2025 E. Seventh Ave., Ybor City. Tel. 247-2771.
Step inside this shop/studio and meet Arnold Martinez as he puts scenes of Tampa and Ybor City on canvas with his unique media—paints and acrylics made of Cuban coffee, tea pigments, and Tampa tobacco. Open Wednesday through Saturday from 11am to 4pm.

ONE WORLD GIFT SHOP, 412 Zack St. Tel. 229-0679.
Tucked into two rooms of the First Presbyterian Church, this downtown shop sells handcrafted clothes, jewelry, and gifts made by Third World artisans from Central and South America, Asia, India, and Mexico. Open Monday through Friday from 11am to 2pm.

THE PEN STORE, 404 Zack St. Tel. 223-3865.
The only store in the Southeast specializing in pens, this unique downtown shop stocks all the major brands of writing instruments, as well as desk sets and inks. Open Monday through Friday from 9am to 5pm and on Saturday from 10am to noon.

ST. FIACRE'S HERB SHOP, 1709 N. 16th St., Ybor City. Tel. 248-1234.
Named after the Irish monk who became the patron saint of gardeners, this unique shop stocks a wide array of fresh herbs, herbal products, fragrances, exotic teas, and books. Open Monday through Thursday from 10am to 6pm, on Friday and Saturday from 10am to 8pm, and on Sunday from noon to 5pm.

WHALEY'S MARKETS, 533 S. Howard Ave. Tel. 254-2904.
This store is a favorite source for Florida Indian River citrus fruit, marmalades, and other local foods, including gourmet picnic items. Open Monday through Saturday from 7am to 9pm and on Sunday from 7am to 8pm.

EVENING ENTERTAINMENT

Whether you're a fan of drama or dance, rock or reggae, comedy or the classics, chances are you'll find it in Tampa. To assist visitors, the Tampa/Hillsborough Arts

Council maintains an **Artsline** (tel. 229-ARTS), a 24-hour information service providing the latest on current and upcoming cultural events.

THE PERFORMING ARTS

Major Concert/Performance Halls

TAMPA BAY PERFORMING ARTS CENTER, 1010 N. MacInnes Place. Tel. 221-1045, or toll free 800/955-1045.

With a prime downtown location on a nine-acre site along the east bank of the Hillsborough River, this huge three-theater complex is the focal point of Tampa's performing arts scene. It presents a wide range of classical, orchestral, and pop concerts, operas, Broadway plays, cabarets, and special events.
Admission: Tickets, $12.50–$45 evenings, $4–$25 matinees.

TAMPA STADIUM, 4201 N. Dale Mabry Hwy. Tel. 872-7977.

Home of Super Bowls XVIII and XXV and many other sporting events, this giant 74,296-seat stadium is frequently the site of world-class concerts.
Admission: Tickets, $10–$35 and up, depending on the event.

USF SUN DOME, 4202 S. Fowler Ave. Tel. 974-3002, or 974-3001 for recorded information.

On the University of South Florida (USF) campus, this arena hosts major concerts by touring pop stars, rock bands, jazz groups, and other contemporary artists.
Admission: Tickets, $12–$25, depending on the event.

Theaters

MYSTERY CAFE, 725 S. Harbour Island Blvd., Harbour Island. Tel. 935-0846.

Audience participation is encouraged at this weekend murder-mystery dinner show, performed in the elegant setting of the Wyndham Harbour Island Hotel. It's on Friday at 8pm and on Saturday at 7pm.
Admission: Show and dinner, $29.95.

OFF CENTER THEATRE, Tampa Bay Performing Arts Center, 1010 N. MacInnes Place. Tel. 972-1200.

The Loft Theatre Production Company presents alternative and contemporary works at this 150-seat facility which is a showcase for aspiring bay-area creative talent.
Admission: Tickets, $10.

TAMPA PLAYERS THEATER, 601 Harbour Island Blvd., Harbour Island. Tel. 221-8587.

This 150-seat theater is a new and permanent home for the Tampa Players, a well-established local troupe known for performing innovative and contemporary plays. It's located on the upper level of the Shops on Harbour Island complex.
Admission: Tickets, $13–$17.

TAMPA THEATRE, 711 Franklin St. Tel. 223-8981.

On the National Register of Historic Places, this restored 1926 theater presents a varied program of classic, foreign, and alternative films, as well as concerts and special events.
Admission: Tickets, $5 adults, $3.75 seniors, $2 children 2–12; $3 adults and seniors on Tues and at weekend matinees. Some special events cost $15–$20 or more.

WAREHOUSE THEATER, 112 S. 12th St., Ybor City. Tel. 223-3076.

Located in the heart of the city's artsy Latin Quarter, this theater presents original scripts by contemporary writers, including mysteries and one-person shows.
Admission: Tickets, $10.50–$12.50.

THE CLUB & MUSIC SCENE
Comedy Clubs

THE COMEDY WORKS, 3447 W. Kennedy Blvd. Tel. 875-9129.
An ever-changing program of live comedy is on tap at this club west of downtown. Shows are Sunday and Tuesday through Thursday at 8:30pm and on Friday and Saturday at 8:30 and 10:45pm.
Admission: $5–$10.

SIDESPLITTERS COMEDY CLUB, 12938 N. Dale Mabry Hwy. Tel. 960-1197.
Located northwest of downtown, Sidesplitters presents professional stand-up comedians on most nights. Shows begin Tuesday through Thursday at 8:30pm and on Friday and Saturday at 8 and 10:30pm.
Admission: $6–$8.

Jazz/Blues/Reggae

BLUES SHIP, 1910 E. Seventh Ave., Ybor City. Tel. 248-6097.
With a mural of a ship adorning the wall, this club presents live blues, jazz, and reggae in an informal meeting-house atmosphere. Open from 5pm to 3am Tuesday through Sunday.
Admission: $2–$5.

BROTHERS LOUNGE, 5401 W. Kennedy Blvd. Tel. 286-8882.
A jazz haven for 20 years, this lounge concentrates solely on jazz, seven nights a week. Open on Monday from 8:30pm to 12:30am, Tuesday through Thursday from 9:30pm to 1:30am, on Friday and Saturday from 9:30pm to 2:30am, and on Sunday from 8pm to midnight.
Admission: $1–$3.

JAZZ CELLAR, 1916 N. 14th St., Ybor City. Tel. 248-1862.
Situated in the heart of the city's Latin Quarter, this place features the Jazz Cellar Underground Orchestra, drawing jazz fans from near and far. Performances are Thursday through Saturday from 9pm to 2am.
Admission: $2–$3.

SKIPPER'S SMOKEHOUSE, 910 Skipper Rd. Tel. 971-0666 or 977-6474.
This is a prime spot for live reggae or blues, and "zydeco," the Créole-blues-soul sound from New Orleans. Open on Tuesday, Wednesday, Saturday, and Sunday from 6:30 to 11pm, and on Friday from 8 to 11pm.
Admission: $3–$8; special events, $10 and up.

Dance Clubs/Discos/Rock and Top 40s Music

BRASS MUG PUB, 1441 E. Fletcher Ave. Tel. 972-8152.
This place features nightly music, from heavy metal to rock and top-40s. There's a jam session on Wednesday, and pool, darts, and video games are always available.
Admission: $5.

THE RITZ, 1503 E. Seventh Ave., Ybor City. Tel. 247-3319.
Housed in a former theater, this progressive dance club features live rock bands and groups playing the latest alternative hits for a youngish, mostly 20s crowd. Next to the main theater is a smaller room called Apocalypse, a dance club with a DJ who spins alternative music. Open Monday through Saturday from 9pm to 3am.
Admission: $5–$15 for live music, $1–$3 for DJ music.

YUCATAN LIQUOR STAND, 4811 W. Cypress St. Tel. 289-8454.
This is as close as you can get to a beach bar without actually being on a

beach—counters made of old surfboards, tiki-hut trim, mounted fish specimens, and tropically painted booths within. The music (live Wednesday through Friday) ranges from top-40s to reggae, country, or progressive. Open Monday through Thursday from 4pm to 3am, on Friday from 3pm to 3am, and on Saturday and Sunday from 6pm to 3am. Drinks cost $1 and up.

Admission: Free.

---

2. ST. PETERSBURG

20 miles SW of Tampa, 289 miles NW of Miami, 84 miles SW of Orlando

GETTING THERE   By Plane   Tampa International Airport, off Memorial Highway and Fla. 60 in Tampa (tel. 813/870-8700), approximately 16 miles northeast of St. Petersburg, is the prime gateway for all scheduled domestic and international flights serving the area (see the Tampa section for a list of airlines).

St. Petersburg–Clearwater International Airport, Roosevelt Boulevard/ Fla. 686, Clearwater (tel. 813/535-7600), is approximately 10 miles north of St. Petersburg. Although primarily a charter facility, it's served by scheduled flights operated by American Transair and Sun Jet.

Albert Whitted Municipal Airport, 108 Eighth Ave. S., St. Petersburg (tel. 813/893-7654), located downtown on the bayfront, serves as a landing strip for private planes.

By Train   Passengers heading for St. Petersburg arrive first at the Tampa Amtrak Station at 601 Nebraska Ave. N. in Tampa (tel. 813/221-7600), and are then transferred by bus to the St. Petersburg Amtrak Station, 33rd Street North and 37th Avenue North, St. Petersburg (tel. 813/522-9475).

By Car   The St. Petersburg area is linked to the Interstate system and is accessible from I-75, I-275, I-4, U.S. 19, and Fla. 60.

By Bus   Greyhound buses arrive at the carrier's downtown depot at 180 9th St. N., St. Petersburg (tel. toll free 800/231-2222).

Sitting on a sheltered curve of land between Tampa Bay and the Gulf of Mexico, St. Petersburg blends the pulse of a city with the heart of a resort. Sleek new office towers stand beside historic Spanish-style landmarks, and businesses hum while sailboats breeze by.

But St. Petersburg (pop. 238,629) is more than just a city—it's a city surrounded by some of the Gulf of Mexico's finest beaches. There's St. Petersburg Beach, a 7½-mile paradise of sun, surf, and sand, and the adjacent "Holiday Isles"—a cluster of a dozen other beaches, stretching from Treasure Island northward to Clearwater Beach. Altogether, the city plus its neighboring beach communities constitute this vibrant Gulf Coast resort.

ORIENTATION

ARRIVING

The Limo, Inc., 11901 30th Court N., St. Petersburg (tel. 813/572-1111, or toll free 800/282-6817), offers 24-hour door-to-door van service between Tampa International or St. Petersburg/Clearwater Airport and any St. Petersburg area destination or hotel. No reservations are required on arrival; just proceed to any Limo desk outside each baggage-claim area. The flat-rate one-way fare is $12 from the Tampa airport and

$10 from the St. Petersburg/Clearwater airport to any St. Pete or gulf beach destination.

Red Line Limo, Inc. (tel. 813/535-3391), also provides a daily 24-hour van service from Tampa International or St. Petersburg/Clearwater Airport to St. Petersburg or any other destination in Pinellas County. The cost is $10.75 from the Tampa airport and $9 from St. Pete/Clearwater, and reservations are required 24 hours in advance.

Yellow Cab Taxis (tel. 813/821-7777) line up outside the baggage-claim areas; no reservations are required. The average fare from the Tampa airport to St. Petersburg or any of the gulf beaches is approximately $25 to $35 per taxi (one or more passengers). The fare from the St. Petersburg/Clearwater airport is approximately $15 to $20.

TOURIST INFORMATION

For information on St. Petersburg, St. Petersburg Beach, and the neighboring "Holiday Isles," contact the **St. Petersburg/Clearwater Area Convention & Visitors Bureau,** Thunder Dome, One Stadium Dr., Suite A, St. Petersburg, FL 33705-1706 (tel. 813/892-7892, or toll free 800/951-1111 for an information guide or 800/354-6710 for advance hotel reservations).

Specific information about downtown St. Petersburg is also available from the **St. Petersburg Chamber of Commerce,** 100 Second Ave. N., St. Petersburg, FL 33701 (tel. 813/821-4069). There are also walk-in **visitor information centers** at The Pier in downtown St. Petersburg, and at St. Petersburg Beach, Treasure Island, Madeira Beach, Indian Rocks Beach, Clearwater, and Clearwater Beach.

CITY LAYOUT

St. Petersburg is laid out according to a grid system, with streets running north-south and avenues running east-west. **Central Avenue** is the dividing line for north and south addresses.

With the exception of Central Avenue, most streets and avenues downtown are one-way. Two-way traffic is also permitted on boulevards, usually diagonal thoroughfares west or north of downtown, such as Tyrone Boulevard, Gandy Boulevard, and Roosevelt Boulevard.

St. Petersburg's **downtown** district sits between two bays—Tampa and Boca Ciega. The major focus is on the section lining Tampa Bay, known as the Bayfront. Here you'll find The Pier, major museums, and most downtown hotels. Fanning out from the Bayfront, the city is composed of various residential neighborhoods.

St. Petersburg Beach, west of downtown and between Boca Ciega Bay and the Gulf of Mexico is a 7½-mile stretch of beach. **Gulf Boulevard** is the main two-way north-south thoroughfare, and most avenues, which cross in an east-west direction, have two-way traffic.

The **Holiday Isles,** north of St. Petersburg Beach and west of downtown, include Treasure Island, 3½ miles in length; Sand Key Island, a 12-mile island composed of Madeira Beach, Redington Beach, North Redington Beach, Redington Shores, Indian Shores, Indian Rocks Beach, and Belleair Beach; and Clearwater Beach.

GETTING AROUND

BY PUBLIC TRANSPORTATION   By Bus   The **Pinellas Suncoast Transit Authority/PSTA** (tel. 530-9911) operates regular bus service. The fare is 90¢.

BATS City Transit, 5201 Gulf Blvd., St. Petersburg Beach (tel. 367-3086), offers bus service along the St. Petersburg Beach strip. The fare is $1.

Treasure Island Transit System, c/o City Hall, 120 108th Ave. (tel. 360-0811), runs along the Treasure Island strip. The fare is $1.

By Trolley   The **Clearwater Beach Trolley** is operated by the PSTA (tel. 530-9911) in the Clearwater Beach area. The ride is free.

BY TAXI   Call either **Yellow Cab** (tel. 821-7777) or **Independent Cab** (tel.

327-3444). Along the beach, the major cab company is **BATS Taxi,** 5201 Gulf Blvd., St. Petersburg Beach (tel. 367-3702).

BY CAR   All major firms are represented at the airports and in the St. Pete area, including **Avis** (tel. 867-6662), **Dollar** (tel. 367-3779), **Hertz** (tel. 360-1631), and **National** (tel. 530-5491). Local car-rental companies include **Pinellas** (tel. 535-9891) and **Suncoast** (tel. 393-3133).

FAST FACTS

Area Code   St. Petersburg's area code is 813.

Business Hours   Most businesses are open Monday through Friday from 9am to 5pm; shops and stores are open from 9am to 6pm or later. Banks are open Monday through Friday from 9am to 4pm; some banks are open on Friday until 6pm and others are open on Saturday mornings.

Dentist   For 24-hour emergency services or referrals, call the Pinellas County Dental Society (tel. 323-2992).

Doctor   Most hotels have a doctor on call; if not, contact the Pinellas County Physician Information Line (tel. 585-PHIL) or the Bayfront Medical Center Doctor Referral Service (tel. 893-6112).

Drugstores   Eckerd Drugs is the leading pharmacy chain in the area, with many stores throughout downtown and the beaches, including a 24-hour branch at the Tyrone Gardens Shopping Center, 900 58th St. N. (tel. 345-9336).

Emergencies   Dial 911.

Hospitals   Two major facilities in St. Petersburg are the Bayfront Medical Center, 701 6th St. S. (tel. 823-1234), and St. Anthony's Hospital, 1200 Seventh Ave. N. (tel. 825-1100).

Laundry/Dry Cleaning   Most hotels supply same-day laundry and dry-cleaning service. Reliable local firms include Pillsbury Cleaners, 1800 4th St. N. (tel. 822-3456), and five other locations; and Rogers Cleaners and Laundry, 1700 Central Ave. (tel. 822-3869) and 2018 4th St. N. (tel. 894-0706).

Libraries   The St. Petersburg Main Library is at 3745 Ninth Ave. N., St. Petersburg (tel. 893-7724), with five branches spread throughout the city.

Newspapers/Magazines   The *St. Petersburg Times* is the city's award-winning daily newspaper; the best periodical covering the area is *Tampa Bay,* a monthly magazine.

Photographic Needs   Eckerd Express Photo Services offers one-hour processing at several St. Petersburg area locations, including 7900 Gateway Mall, St. Petersburg (tel. 579-4257); Dolphin Village, 4685 Gulf Blvd., St. Petersburg Beach (tel. 360-0818); and 467 Mandalay Ave., Clearwater Beach (tel. 796-1854). For general photographic- or video-equipment repairs, contact the Southern Photo Technical Service, 1750 Ninth Ave. N., St. Petersburg (tel. 896-6141).

Post Office   The main post office is at 3135 First Ave. N. (tel. 323-6516); it's open Monday through Friday from 8am to 6pm and on Saturday from 8am to 12:30pm.

Shoe Repairs   Two handy downtown locations are Bill's Shoe Service, 454½ First Ave. N. (tel. 822-3757); and Holmes Shoe Repair, 17 6th St. N. (tel. 898-7930).

Taxes   A 7% sales tax is applied to all purchases and the cost of restaurant meals. The local hotel-occupancy tax is 10%, added to the cost of your hotel room. There's also a $6 airport departure tax for international flights.

Transit Information   For information on the local transit system, call 530-9911.

Weather   Dial 976-1111.

WHAT TO SEE & DO
THE TOP ATTRACTIONS

THE PIER, 800 Second Ave. NE. Tel. 821-6164.

The focal point of the city, this festive waterfront sightseeing/shopping/entertainment complex extends a quarter mile into Tampa Bay. Dating back to 1889, it was originally built as a railroad pier, but over the years it was

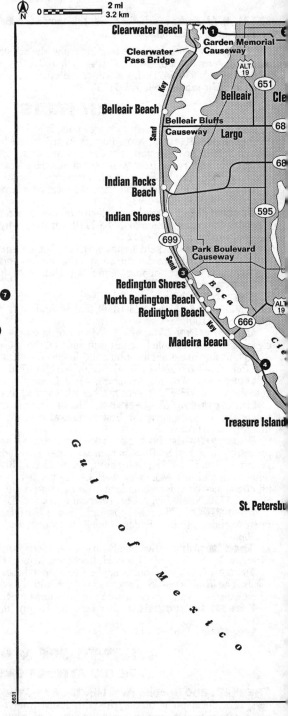

FLORIDA

St. Petersburg

0   2 mi
         3.2 km
N

Clearwater Beach ↑ ①

Garden Memorial
Causeway

Clearwater
Pass Bridge

Key

ALT
19

651

Belleair   Cle

Belleair Beach

Belleair Bluffs
Causeway

68

Sand

Largo

68

Indian Rocks
Beach

595

Indian Shores

699

Park Boulevard
Causeway

Sand

Redington Shores ③

North Redington Beach

Redington Beach

Boca

ALT
19

666

Key

Madeira Beach

④

Ciega

Treasure Island

Gulf of Mexico

St. Petersbu

6631

ST. PETERSBURG AREA ATTRACTIONS

To Tampa →

Courtney
Campbell
Causeway

O l d

St. Petersburg-
Clearwater
International
Airport

Howard Frankland
Bridge

T a m p a

92

Gandy
Bridge

B a y

Ulmerton Rd.

Pinellas
Park

694

74th Ave.

54th Ave.

49th St.

38th Ave.

Coffeepot
Bayou

Downtown

St. Petersburg

Treasure Island
Causeway

ALT
19

Central Ave.

375

S. Pasadena

Gulfport 22nd Ave. S.

175

Albert Whitted
Municipal Airport

St. Petersburg
Beach Causeway

Big Bayou

Lake
Maggiore

Coquina Key

B a y

Pinellas
Bayway

54th Ave. S.

Little Bayou

682

Bird
Key

I n t r a c o a s t a l
W a t e r w a y

Bush
Key

Cabbage
Key

Shell
Key

679

14

The
Reefs

Madelaine
Key

15

679

Mullett Key

T a m p a

B a y

Airport ✈

Long Key

each

Shell
Key

90

60

19

686

688

686

693

694

19

595

699

13

679

19

275

redesigned in various formats until taking its present shape of an inverted pyramid in 1988.

Today it's the city's prime playground, with five levels of shops and restaurants, plus an aquarium, tourist information desk, observation deck, catwalks for fishing, boat docks, a small bayside beach, miniature golf, water-sports rentals, and sightseeing boats. A free trolley service operates between The Pier and nearby parking lots.

Admission: Free to all the public areas and decks; donations welcome at the aquarium. Parking costs $1.

Open: Shops, Mon–Sat 10am–9pm, Sun 11am–7pm; restaurants, daily 11am–11pm; lounges, daily 10am–midnight or 1am; aquarium, Mon and Wed–Sat 10am–9pm, Fri–Sat 10am–1pm, Sun 11am–7pm.

ST. PETERSBURG THUNDERDOME, 1 Stadium Dr. Tel. 825-3100.

The skyline of St. Petersburg was dramatically changed in 1990 with the completion of this $110-million slant-roofed dome, built on a 66-acre downtown site to host major concerts, festivals, and sports events. The stadium's translucent roof is the first cable-supported dome of its kind in the United States and the largest of its type in the world.

Admission: $4–$30, depending on the event.

Open: Tours, available when events are not scheduled.

SALVADOR DALÍ MUSEUM, 1000 3rd St. S. Tel. 823-3767.

Nestled on Tampa Bay south of The Pier, this starkly modern museum houses the world's largest collection of works by the renowned Spanish surrealist. Valued at over $150 million, the collection includes 94 oil paintings, over 100 watercolors and drawings, and 1,300 graphics, plus posters, photos, sculptures, and objets d'art, and a 2,500-volume library on Dalí and surrealism.

Admission: $5 adults, $4 seniors, $3.50 students, free for children under 10.

Open: Tues–Sat 9:30am–5:30pm, Sun–Mon noon–5pm. **Closed:** New Year's Day, Thanksgiving, and Christmas.

MUSEUM OF FINE ARTS, 255 Beach Dr. NE. Tel. 896-2667.

Resembling a Mediterranean villa on the waterfront, this museum houses a permanent collection of European, American, pre-Columbian and Far Eastern art, with works by such artists as Fragonard, Monet, Renoir, Cézanne, and Gauguin. Other highlights include period rooms with antiques and historical furnishings, plus a gallery of Steuben crystal, and world-class rotating exhibits.

Admission: $5 adults, $3 seniors, $2 students.

Open: Tues–Sat 10am–5pm, Sun 1–5pm; third Thurs of each month 10am–9pm.

FLORIDA INTERNATIONAL MUSEUM, 101 3rd St. N.

As we go to press, it has been announced that the former Maas Brothers Department store, once an area landmark but standing idle for the past few years, has been earmarked for a $2-million renovation to convert it into a major cultural center. Slated for completion in early 1995, the new center will mark its inauguration with a major art exhibition from Russia, **"Treasures of the Czars"** (January 11–July 11, 1995), one of the largest collections of Russian royal family treasures ever to leave Russia. Details of hours, prices, and phone number are not final at press time; check with the St. Petersburg/Clearwater Area Convention & Visitors Bureau (see "Orientation," above) for the latest details.

ST. PETERSBURG HISTORICAL AND FLIGHT ONE MUSEUM, 335 Second Ave. NE. Tel. 894-1052.

Located on the approach to The Pier, this museum features a permanent interactive exhibition chronicling St. Petersburg's history. The thousands of items on display range from prehistoric artifacts to documents, clothing, and photographs. There are also computer stations enabling visitors to "flip through the past." Walk-through exhibits include a prototype general store and post office (ca. 1880) and a replica of the Benoist airboat, suspended "in flight" from a 25-foot ceiling and commemorating the first scheduled commercial flight in the world, which took off from St. Petersburg in 1914.

Admission: $4.50 adults, $3.50 seniors, $1.50 children 7–17, free for kids under 7.

Open: Mon–Sat 10am–5pm, Sun 1–5pm.

SUNCOAST SEABIRD SANCTUARY, 18328 Gulf Blvd., Indian Shores. Tel. 391-6211.

Of all the attractions outside the immediate downtown area, this one is well worth a detour or a special trip. Founded in 1971 by zoologist Ralph Heath, Jr., it's the largest wild-bird hospital in the nation, dedicated to the rescue, repair, recuperation, and release of sick and injured wild birds. At any one time, there are usually more than 500 sea and land birds living at the sanctuary, from cormorants, white herons, and birds of prey to the ubiquitous brown pelican.

Admission: Free, but donations are welcome.

Open: Daily 9am–dusk. **Directions:** Take I-275 north of downtown to Fla. 694 (Exit 15) west, cross over the Intracoastal Waterway to Gulf Boulevard, and turn left; the sanctuary is a quarter mile south.

MORE ATTRACTIONS

CLEARWATER MARINE SCIENCE CENTER AQUARIUM, 249 Windward Passage, Clearwater. Tel. 447-0980.

Nestled on an island in Clearwater Harbor, this facility is dedicated to the rescue and rehabilitation of marine mammals and sea turtles. The center also operates a turtle hatchery that releases more than 3,000 hatchlings each year in local waters.

Admission: $4.25 adults, $2.75 children 3–11, free for children under 3.

Open: Mon–Fri 9am–5pm, Sat 9am–4pm, Sun 11am–4pm. **Directions:** From the mainland, turn right at Island Way; the center is one mile east of Clearwater Beach on Island Estates.

FORT DESOTO PARK, 3500 Pinellas Bayway S. (Fla. 679). Tel. 866-2484.

One of the oldest sections of St. Petersburg, and used as a fort during the Spanish-American War, this is the largest and most diverse park in the area, made up of five islands south of the mainland, all nestled between the waters of Tampa Bay and the Gulf of Mexico. With a total of 900 acres, seven miles of waterfront, and almost three miles of beaches, the islands are all connected by roads and bridges. A public park for over 25 years, it also offers fishing piers; shaded picnic sites; a bird, plant, and animal sanctuary; and campsites.

Admission: Free, except for tolls totaling 85¢.

Open: Daily sunrise–sunset. **Directions:** Take I-275 south to the Pinellas Bayway (Exit 4) and follow the signs.

JOHN'S PASS VILLAGE AND BOARDWALK, 12901 Gulf Blvd., Madeira Beach. Tel. 391-7373.

Named after Juan (John) Levique, a 19th-century sea-turtle fisherman who lived here, this is a rustic Florida fishing village on the southern edge of Madeira Beach. It's composed of a string of simple wooden structures topped by tin roofs, all resting on pilings 12 feet above sea level, and connected by a 1,000-foot boardwalk. Most of the buildings have been converted into shops, art galleries, and restaurants. The focal point is the large fishing pier and marina, from which many water sports are available for visitors.

Admission: Free.

Open: Shops and activities, daily 9am–6pm or later; most restaurants, daily 7am–11pm. **Directions:** From downtown, take Central Avenue west via the Treasure Island Causeway to Gulf Boulevard; turn right, go for 20 blocks, and cross over the bridge; the entrance is on the right.

PORT ROYAL SUNKEN TREASURE MUSEUM, 5501 Gulf Blvd., St. Petersburg Beach. Tel. 360-4141.

Focusing on historic shipwrecks and adventures at sea, this new museum presents permanent exhibits and hands-on displays of sunken treasures. The objects include a replica of one of the first diving bells used to recover treasure from shipwrecks, as well

488 • THE TAMPA BAY AREA

as antiques and priceless valuables, such as Ming vases and gold and silver objects, recovered from the Sunken City of Port Royal. The museum also houses a collection of sand sculptures by Paul Dawkins.
Admission: $6.50 adults, $5 seniors and students, $3.50 children 6–12, free for kids under 6.
Open: Daily 10am–9pm.

SUNKEN GARDENS, 1825 4th St. N. Tel. 896-3186.

One of the city's oldest attractions, this seven-acre tropical garden park dates back to 1935. It contains a vast array of 5,000 plants, flowers, and trees. In addition, there's a walk-through aviary and over 500 rare birds and a wax museum depicting biblical figures.
Admission: $11 adults, $6 children 3–11, free for children under 3.
Open: Daily 9am–5:30pm.

SUNSHINE SKYWAY BRIDGE, I-275 and U.S. 19. Tel. 823-8804.

Spanning the mouth of Tampa Bay, this 4.1-mile-long bridge connects Pinellas and Manatee Counties and the city of St. Petersburg with the Bradenton/Sarasota areas. Built at a cost of $244 million over a period of five years (1982–87), this is Florida's first suspension bridge, soaring 183 feet above the bay.
Admission: $1-per-car toll each way.
Open: Daily 24 hours. **Directions:** From downtown, take I-275 south and follow the signs.

COOL FOR KIDS

GREAT EXPLORATIONS, 1120 4th St. S. Tel. 821-8885.

With a variety of "hands-on" exhibits, this museum welcomes visitors of all ages, but is most appealing to children, especially on a rainy day. Kids can explore a long, dark tunnel; measure their strength, flexibility, and fitness; paint a work of art with sunlight; and play a melody with a sweep of the hand, to name just a few of the activities.
Admission: $5 adults, $4.50 seniors, $4 children 4–17, free for children under 4.
Open: Mon–Sat 10am–5pm, Sun noon–5pm.

SPORTS & RECREATION
Spectator Sports

BASEBALL   The **St. Petersburg Thunder Dome,** 1 Stadium Dr. (tel. 825-3100), is St. Petersburg's sporting centerpiece. This $110-million domed stadium has a seating capacity of 43,000. As we go to press, this facility is still searching for a major-league baseball team. Exact details of schedule and prices will be announced when arrangements for a team are finalized.

The winter home of the Baltimore Orioles and the St. Louis Cardinals is **Al Lang Stadium,** 180 Second Ave. (tel. 822-3384). They are here for spring training each February and March. The crack of the bat can also be heard at other times, with major-league exhibition games in the spring, followed by the St. Petersburg Cardinals, a Class A minor-league team (April through September). Admission is $3 to $7.

The Philadelphia Phillies play their spring training season at the **Jack Russell Stadium,** 800 Phillies Dr., Clearwater. (tel. 442-8496). The season is mid-February to April. Admission is $7 to $8. **Grant Field,** 373 Douglas Ave., Dunedin (tel. 733-0429), is recently expanded, and is the winter home of the Toronto Blue Jays for a mid-February to April season. Admission is $6 to $8.

DOG RACING   Founded in 1925, **Derby Lane,** 10490 Gandy Blvd. (tel. 576-1359), is the world's oldest continually operating greyhound track, with indoor and outdoor seating and standing areas. Admission is $1 for adults, $2.50 for Derby Club level. It's open January to June, Monday through Saturday at 7:30pm. Monday, Wednesday, and Saturday races are at 12:30pm.

HOCKEY   For the 1994–95 season (October to April), the **Tampa Bay Lightning** hockey team is headquartered at the ThunderDome, One Stadium Dr. (tel. 825-3334).

Tickets range from $8 to $50. Note: For the 1995–96 season, the team will move back to Tampa into a new $110-million downtown arena (see "Sports and Recreation," in Section 1, above).

Recreation

With year-round sunshine and 28 miles of coastline along the Gulf of Mexico, the St. Petersburg area offers a wealth of recreational activities.

One of the newest developments, of benefit to walkers, bicyclists, joggers, and nature lovers, is the new **Pinellas Trail,** a 47-mile-long, 15-foot-wide path stretching from St. Petersburg to Tarpon Springs. So far, 23 miles of the trail have been completed, from Tarpon Springs to Seminole, with the remainder slated for completion by 1995–96. When fully open, it will be the longest linear recreation trail of its kind in the eastern United States. For more information and a brochure, contact the Pinellas County Park Department, 631 Chestnut St., Clearwater, FL 34616 (tel. 813/581-2953).

When visiting St. Petersburg, you can get up-to-the-minute recorded information about the city's sports and recreational activities by calling the **Leisure Line** (tel. 893-7500).

BICYCLING With miles of flat terrain, St. Petersburg is ideal for bikers. Among the prime biking routes are Straub Park and along the bayfront, Fort DeSoto Park, and Pass-a-Grille.

Beach Cyclist, 7517 Blind Pass Rd. (tel. 367-5001), on the northern tip of St. Petersburg Beach, offers several types of bikes, from a beach cruiser (allowed on the beaches at Treasure Island and Madeira Beach) to a selection of standard racing bikes. Prices are from $10 for 4 hours, $12 for 24 hours, $39 per week. It's open Monday through Saturday from 10am to 6pm.

Transportation Station, 645 Bayway Blvd. (tel. 443-3188), on Clearwater Beach, rents all types of bikes from single speed to racers, tandems, mountain bikes, and one- and two-passenger scooters. Helmets and baby seats are also available. Prices for bicycles are from $5 to $8 an hour, $14.95 to $21.95 for the overnight special, $44 to $66 per week; scooters are from $13 to $18 an hour, $39.95 to $54.95 for the overnight special, $109 to $169 per week. It's open daily from 9am to 7pm.

BOAT RENTALS If you can handle a boat yourself, **Boating Zone,** Slips 5 and 6, Clearwater Beach Marina, Clearwater Beach (tel. 446-5503), rents craft equipped with 70hp to 175hp motors. Sizes range from 17 to 20 feet, with capacities of three to seven people. Eight-foot mini-boats with 6hp engines, ideal for two people, can also be rented by the hour. Prices are $20 per hour; mini-boats are $14 an hour. It's open daily from 9am to 5pm.

Captain Dave's Watersports, 9540 Blind Pass Rd., St. Petersburg Beach (tel. 345-4336), offers waverunner and powerboat rentals, parasail rides, snorkeling trips, sailing, and shelling trips. Prices for waverunner rentals begin at $35 per half hour, $60 per hour; powerboat rentals are $50 and up for one hour, $70 and up for two hours, $135 and up per day; parasail rides are $30 to $35; snorkeling trips are $35; sailing and shelling trips, $25. Hours are daily from 9am to 5pm or later.

Fun Rentals, Municipal Marina, Slip 300, 555 150th Ave., Madeira Beach (tel. 397-0276), rents 22-foot pontoon boats (seating 10) for $90 for a half day and $150 for a full day to sightsee, fish, or play on the waters of the Intracoastal Waterway. It's open daily from 9:30am to 5:30pm.

A downtown facility, **Waterworks Rentals,** The Pier (tel. 363-0000), rents waverunners and boats from 12 to 22 feet. A second location is at 200D 150th Ave., Madeira Beach (tel. 399-8989). Prices for waverunners begin at $25 for a half hour; for boats, at $15 per hour. Daily hours are 9am to 6pm or later.

FISHING One of the largest party-boat fishing fleets in the area, Capt. Dave Spaulding's **Queen Fleet,** Slip 52, Clearwater Beach Marina, 25 Causeway Blvd. (tel. 446-7666), offers trips of varying duration. Bait is furnished, but rod rental is extra. Prices are $20 for a half day, $30 to $32 for three-quarters of a day, $5 extra for rods.

Capt. Kidd, Merry Pier, 801 Pass-a-Grille Way, St. Petersburg Beach (tel.

360-2263), takes passengers on half- and full-day fishing trips in the gulf. Rates, including rod, reel, and bait, are $24 for adults and $21 for children and seniors on a half-day trip; $33.50 for adults and $31.50 for children and seniors on a full-day outing. Half-day trips are scheduled Monday through Friday from 8am to noon and 1 to 5pm; full-day trips, on Saturday and Sunday from 8:30am to 4pm.

If you want a change from the usual fishing boat, try **Double Eagle's Deep Sea Fishing Boats,** Slip 50, Clearwater Beach Marina, 25 Causeway Blvd., Clearwater Beach (tel. 446-1653). They offer two catamarans, 83 feet and 65 feet in length. The vessels go 20 to 25 miles offshore into the gulf, on four- or seven-hour trips, with bait provided. Prices are $20 to $30 for adults, $16 to $25 for children, and $4 for tackle. The four-hour trip departs daily, 8am to noon and 1 to 5pm, and the seven-hour trip leaves daily at 9am lasting until 4pm.

Miss Pass-A-Grille, Dolphin Landings Charter Boat Center, 4737 Gulf Blvd., St. Petersburg Beach. (tel. 367-4488 or 367-7411), is conveniently docked in the heart of the St. Petersburg Beach hotel strip. This fishing boat offers daily trips into Tampa Bay and the gulf. Prices are $24.95 to $26.95 for four hours, $37.95 for seven hours. Sailings are scheduled on Tuesday, Wednesday, and Friday at 8am and 1pm, and on Thursday, Saturday, and Sunday at 9am.

GOLF Adjacent to the St. Petersburg/Clearwater Airport, the **Airco Flite Golf Course,** 3650 Roosevelt Blvd., Clearwater (tel. 573-4653), is an 18-hole, par-72 course, with driving range. Lessons and golf club rentals are also available. The price per person, including a cart, is $27. It's open daily from 7am to 6pm.

Bardmoor Country Club, 7919 Bardmoor Blvd., Largo (tel. 397-0483), is often the venue for major tournaments. This club offers an 18-hole, par-72 course, plus a driving range. Lessons and rental clubs are also available. Greens fees are $55 Monday through Friday, and $59 on Saturday and Sunday, including carts. It's open daily from 7am to dusk.

One of the top 50 municipal golf courses in the U.S., the **Mangrove Bay Golf Course,** 875 62nd Ave., NE (tel. 893-7797), hugs the inlets of Old Tampa Bay and offers 18-hole, par-72 play. Facilities include a driving range; lessons and golf club rental are also available. Prices are $18, $28 including a cart. It's open daily from 6am to 6pm.

SAILING **Annapolis Sailing School,** 6800 34th St. S. (tel. 867-8102, or toll free 800/237-0795), can teach you to sail or perfect your sailing skills. Various courses are offered at this branch of the famous Maryland-based school, lasting two, five, or eight days. Prices, depending on season and length of course, are $185 to $1,655 per person.

If you prefer to be part of the crew or just want to relax for 2½ hours, enjoying the views of the gulf waters, sail aboard a 54-foot windjammer or a 38-foot racing yacht at the **Suncoast Sailing Center,** Slip 10, Clearwater Beach Marina, Clearwater Beach (tel. 581-4662). Rentals of small sloops and sailing lessons are also available. Reservations are required. Prices range from $17.50 to $20 for adults, half price for children. The boats depart daily at 10am, 1:30pm, and 4:30pm.

TENNIS **Hurley Park,** 1600 Pass-a-Grille Way, Pass-a-Grille, St. Petersburg Beach, sports just one court, and is available on a first-come, first-served basis. The price is 25¢ for 15 minutes (quarters only). It's open daily from 8am to 10pm.

On a larger scale, with 15 Har-Tru courts, **St. Petersburg Tennis Center,** 650 18th Ave. S. (tel. 894-4378), provides lessons and clinics. Prices are $6.40 per person per hour. It's open daily from 8am to 9pm.

WATER SPORTS **Captain Dave's Watersports,** 9540 Blind Pass Rd., St. Petersburg Beach (tel. 345-4336), offers waterskiing lessons for $45 per half hour or $70 per hour.

BAY CRUISES

Shell Key Shuttle, 801 Pass-a-Grille Way, St. Petersburg Beach (tel. 360-1348), offers shuttle service to nearby Shell Island, south of St. Petersburg, via a 57-passenger catamaran. The ride takes 15 minutes, and you can return on any shuttle you wish.

Boats leave daily at 10am, noon, 2pm, and (summer only) 4pm, and prices are $10 for adults, $5 for children 12 and under.

Cruises around Boca Ciega Bay and the Gulf of Mexico are offered on *The Lady,* St. Petersburg Beach Causeway, 3460 Pasadena Ave. S. (tel. 367-7804). The three-deck boat operates at lunch and dinner times, with buffet meal service and dance music. On some evenings, cruises with special themes, such as Gospel music, are offered. Cruises take place from October to mid-May. The lunch cruises operate Tuesday through Friday and cost $14.50 for adults and $12.50 for children under 10. Dinner cruises are offered on Tuesday, Thursday, Friday, and Saturday from 7 to 10pm and cost $19.50 to $24.50 for adults, $12.50 to $14.50 for children; cocktails extra. Reservations are required.

The *Caribbean Queen* (tel. 895-BOAT) departs from The Pier, and offers one-hour sightseeing and dolphin-watching cruises around Tampa Bay. Sailings are daily at 11:30am, 1pm, 3pm, and 5pm, and cost $8 for adults and $5 for children 3 to 12; free for children under 3.

Captain Memo's Pirate Cruise, Clearwater Beach Marina, Slip 3 (tel. 446-2587), sails on the *Pirate's Ransom,* an authentic reproduction of a pirate ship. Swashbuckling two-hour daytime "pirate cruises" and evening champagne cruises are offered, under the direction of fearless Captain Memo and his crew. Cruises operate October to March, daily at 10am, 2pm, and 4:30pm; April to September, daily at 7pm. For adults, daytime cruises cost $25; evening cruises, $28; both daytime and evening cruises cost $18 for seniors and juniors 13 to 17, $15 for children 2 to 12, free for children under 2.

The *Sea Screamer,* King Fish Wharf, Treasure Island (tel. 367-2996), claims to be the world's largest speedboat. This 73-foot turbo-charged twin-engine vessel provides tow rides on one trip—an exhilarating spin in Gulf of Mexico waters and a leisurely narrated cruise around Treasure Island with opportunities to view birds and marine life along the way. Prices are $9 for adults, $6 for children 6 to 12. Sailings are Wednesday through Saturday at noon, 2pm, and 4pm. Sunday through Tuesday the *Sea Screamer* departs from the Clearwater Beach Marina, Slip 48, at 11am, 2pm, and 4pm; prices are the same.

WHERE TO STAY

The St. Petersburg area offers a great variety of accommodations, from posh resorts and chain properties to small family-run motels or bed-and-breakfasts. Above all, it also offers a choice of settings—downtown St. Petersburg, St. Petersburg Beach, or the "Holiday Isles," a cluster of a dozen neighboring beaches.

Price-wise, the high season is from December/January through April. The best bargains are available in May and September through November.

DOWNTOWN ST. PETERSBURG

Expensive

STOUFFER VINOY RESORT, 501 Fifth Ave. NE, St. Petersburg, FL 33701. Tel. 813/894-1000, or toll free 800/HOTELS-1. Fax 813/822-2785. 360 rms. A/C MINIBAR TV TEL

$ Rates: $119–$399 single or double. AE, CB, DC, DISC, MC, V.

With an elegant peach-toned Mediterranean-style facade, this sprawling seven-story world-class resort has greatly enhanced the downtown area. Dating back to 1925 and originally known as the Vinoy Park, it reopened in 1992 after a total and meticulous $93-million restoration and refurbishment. It overlooks Tampa Bay and is within walking distance of The Pier, Central Avenue, museums, and other attractions.

All the guest rooms, many of which enjoy lovely views of the bayfront, are designed to offer the utmost in comfort and include three phones, an additional TV in the bathroom, hairdryer, and more; some units in the new wing have individual Jacuzzis and private patios/balconies.

Dining/Entertainment: Marchand's Grille, an elegant room overlooking the bay, specializes in steaks, seafood, and chops. The Terrace Room is the main dining room for breakfast, lunch, and dinner. Casual lunches and dinners are available at the indoor-outdoor Alfresco near the pool deck and at the Clubhouse at the golf course on Snell Isle. There are also two bar/lounges.

Services: Concierge, 24-hour room service, laundry service, tour desk, child care, complimentary coffee and newspaper with wake-up call.

Facilities: Two swimming pools, 14-court tennis complex (nine lighted), 18-hole private championship golf course on nearby Snell Isle, private 74-slip marina, two croquet courts, fitness center (with sauna, steam room, spa, massage, and exercise equipment), access to two bayside beaches, shuttle service to gulf beaches, hair salon, gift shop.

Moderate

THE HERITAGE / HOLIDAY INN, 234 Third Ave. N., St. Petersburg, FL 33701. Tel. 813/822-4814, or toll free 800/283-7829. Fax 813/823-1644. 75 rms. A/C TV TEL

$ Rates (including continental breakfast): $49.50–$110 single or double. AE, CB, DC, MC, V.

With a sweeping veranda, French doors, and tropical courtyard, the Heritage is the nearest thing to a southern mansion you'll find in the heart of downtown. Dating back to the early 1920s, it was completely restored in the late 1980s. The furnishings include period antiques in the public areas and in the guest rooms.

Dining/Entertainment: The Heritage Grille offers a creative menu of "nouveau American" light regional cuisine.

Services: Room service, valet laundry.

Facilities: Outdoor heated swimming pool, Jacuzzi.

PRESIDENTIAL INN, 100 Second Ave. S. (P.O. Box 57306), St. Petersburg, FL 33701. Tel. 813/821-7117. Fax 813/821-7818. 30 rms. A/C TV TEL

$ Rates (including continental breakfast): $85–$130 single or double. AE, CB, DC, MC, V. **Parking:** Free adjacent covered self-parking.

Under the same management as the adjacent Hilton Hotel, this unique property occupies the fifth floor of a 12-story bayfront office complex. The bedrooms, each with a different view of the bay or city, are individually decorated with dark woods, silk wall hangings, and tasteful artworks; bathrooms offer separate phone extensions, and eight have private whirlpools. Guests have access to an on-premises living room–style lounge/reading room and to the Hilton Hotel's restaurants, room-service system, and laundry valet.

ST. PETERSBURG HILTON AND TOWERS, 333 1st St. S., St. Petersburg, FL 33701. Tel. 813/894-5000, or toll free 800/HILTONS. Fax 813/821-5943. 333 rms. A/C TV TEL

$ Rates: $84–$130 single; $94–$140 double. AE, CB, DC, MC, V.

Situated downtown on the bay, this 15-story tower is convenient to most major attractions. The spacious lobby reflects the tone of this hotel, with a rich decor of marble, crystal, tile, antiques, artwork, and potted trees and plants. The bedrooms are furnished with traditional dark woods, floral fabrics, a king-size bed or two double beds, and an executive desk; many have views of the bay.

Dining/Entertainment: Charmene's is a full-service restaurant specializing in continental cuisine and Eli's is a steakhouse. For light fare, try the First Street Deli, and for a quiet drink with a piano background, settle into Brandi's Lobby Bar; or for a lively evening, it's Wings, an aviation-themed lounge.

Services: Room service, concierge, valet laundry, babysitting.

Facilities: Outdoor heated swimming pool, patio deck, Jacuzzi, sauna, gift shop.

Inexpensive

DAYS INN MARINA BEACH RESORT, 6800 34th St. S., St. Petersburg, FL 33711. Tel. 813/867-1151, or toll free 800/DAYS-INN. Fax 813/864-4494. 157 rms, 11 lodges. A/C TV TEL

$ Rates: $49–$115 single or double; $99–$131 one-bedroom lodge; $148–$259 two- or three-bedroom lodge. AE, CB, DC, MC, V.

Located on the southern tip of the city, off I-275 on the approach to the Skyway Bridge, this sprawling two-story motel seems to have it all. Offering quick access to downtown, it sits in a tropical setting on 14 acres along the Tampa Bay shoreline. For good measure, it's also a year-round base of the Annapolis Sailing School. Guest rooms have an airy decor with light woods, pastel tones, ceiling fans, plants, and private balconies or patios; lodges also offer kitchenettes.

For dining there's a restaurant, a beach bar, a lounge, and a snack bar. Other facilities include a private bayside beach, two outdoor swimming pools (one heated), a Jacuzzi, seven tennis courts, a fishing pier, a marina, shuffleboard and volleyball courts, water-sports rentals, a games room, a children's playground, and a coin-operated laundry.

HOLIDAY INN–ST. PETERSBURG, 4601 34th St. S., St. Petersburg, FL 33711. Tel. 813/867-3131, or toll free 800/HOLIDAY. Fax 813/867-2025. 134 rms. A/C TV TEL
$ Rates: $49–$99 single or double. AE, CB, DC, DISC, MC, V.
Even though this basic two-story hotel is on the busy U.S. 19 corridor, it's set back from the main road in a convenient and quiet setting, across from a marina and south of downtown. Bedrooms are furnished in contemporary style, with dark woods, brass fixtures, and light pastel fabrics and carpeting.

Duke's is a country-western music lounge. Additional amenities include room service, valet laundry and dry cleaning, an outdoor freshwater swimming pool, a patio, shuffleboard, and a guest laundry.

Budget

BAYBORO BED AND BREAKFAST, 1719 Beach Dr. SE, St. Petersburg, FL 33701. Tel. 813/823-4955. Fax 813/823-4955. 4 rms (all with bath). A/C TV
$ Rates (including breakfast): $75–$85 single or double. MC, V.
Situated in a residential area a few minutes south of Bayboro Harbor, this three-story Victorian historical landmark overlooks the bay opposite Lassing Park and a small beach. An "Old South" ambience prevails here, with a wide veranda bedecked with rockers and cozy upstairs bedrooms, filled with antique beds and armoires, lace, and quilts. Breakfast is served in the dining room; wine and soft drinks are served in the afternoon.

BEACH PARK MOTEL, 300 Beach Dr. NE, St. Petersburg, FL 33701. Tel. 813/898-6325. 26 rms. A/C TV TEL
$ Rates: $35–$40 single; $40–$65 double. MC, V.
One of the few motels right in the downtown area, this is a well-maintained two-story property with views of the bayfront or The Pier. The guest rooms have one or two double beds, or a king-size bed, with a decor of light woods and bright Florida colors. Each has a small balcony or sitting area, and 11 have small kitchenettes.

SUNCOAST EXECUTIVE INN, 3000 34th St. S., St. Petersburg, FL 33711. Tel. 813/867-1111, or toll free 800/458-8671. Fax 813/867-7068. 120 rms. A/C TV TEL
$ Rates: $38–$60 single; $44–$85 double. AE, DC, MC, V.
An ideal choice for tennis buffs, this modern three-story hotel has nine championship tennis courts and an on-staff pro. Other facilities include an outdoor swimming pool, tropical courtyard, restaurant, and lounge. The public areas and guest rooms are furnished in contemporary style, with bright Florida colors and fabrics. Situated south of downtown along the U.S. 19 corridor, this hostelry also offers easy access to downtown or the beaches.

MANSION HOUSE, 105 Fifth Ave. NE, St. Petersburg, FL 33701. Tel. 813/821-9391. Fax 813/821-9754. 6 rms (all with bath). A/C
$ Rates: $60–$70 single or double. MC, V.
Reputed to have been the home of the first mayor of St. Petersburg, this cozy two-story bed-and-breakfast home is located downtown on a residential street, within walking

FLORIDA

St. Petersburg

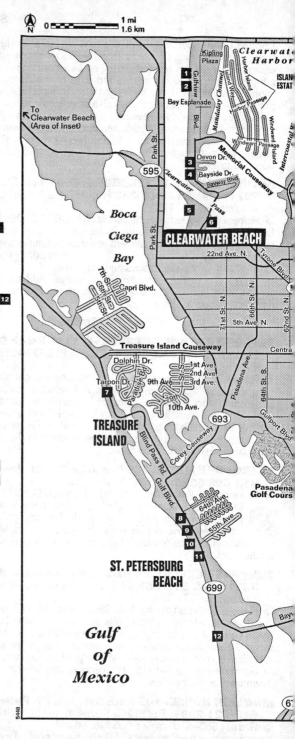

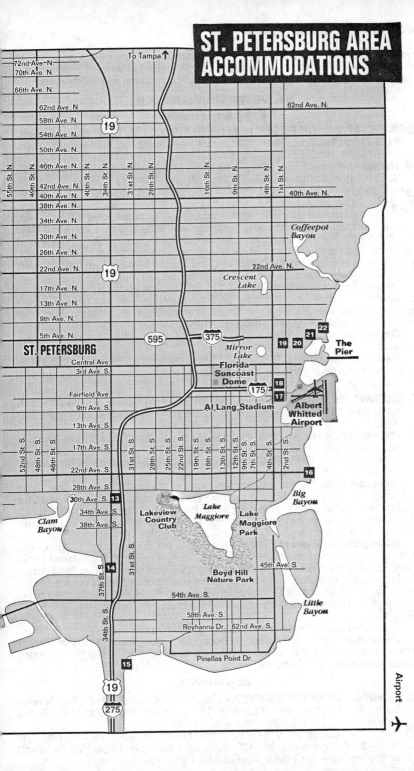

ST. PETERSBURG AREA ACCOMMODATIONS

To Tampa ↑

72nd Ave. N.
70th Ave. N.
66th Ave. N.
62nd Ave. N.
58th Ave. N.
54th Ave. N.
50th Ave. N.
46th Ave. N.
42nd Ave. N.
40th Ave. N.
38th Ave. N.
34th Ave. N.
30th Ave. N.
26th Ave. N.
22nd Ave. N.
17th Ave. N.
13th Ave. N.
9th Ave. N.
5th Ave. N.

62nd Ave. N.
40th Ave. N.

ST. PETERSBURG

Central Ave.
3rd Ave. S.
Fairfield Ave.
9th Ave. S.
13th Ave. S.
17th Ave. S.
22nd Ave. S.
26th Ave. S.
30th Ave. S.
34th Ave. S.
38th Ave. S.

45th Ave. S.

54th Ave. S.
58th Ave. S.
Royhanna Dr.   62nd Ave. S.

Pinellas Point Dr.

55th St. N.
49th St. N.
40th St. N.
34th St. N.
31st St. N.
28th St. N.
16th St. N.
9th St. N.
4th St. N.
1st St. N.

52nd St. S.
48th St. S.
46th St. S.
31st St. S.
28th St. S.
25th St. S.
22nd St. S.
19th St. S.
16th St. S.
13th St. S.
12th St. S.
9th St. S.
7th St. S.
4th St. S.
2nd St. S.
37th St. S.
34th St. S.

Coffeepot Bayou

Crescent Lake

Mirror Lake

Florida Suncoast Dome

Al Lang Stadium

Albert Whitted Airport

The Pier

Clam Bayou

Lakeview Country Club

Lake Maggiore

Lake Maggiore Park

Big Bayou

Boyd Hill Nature Park

Little Bayou

Airport ✈

19 20 21 22
18 17 16
13 14 15

595 375 175 19 275

distance of Beach Drive, The Pier, and other attractions. Rooms are decorated in southern turn-of-the-century style and a full English breakfast is served each morning. Public rooms include a screened-in porch, TV/library room, and sitting room.

ST. PETERSBURG BEACH
Very Expensive

DON CESAR BEACH RESORT, 3400 Gulf Blvd., St. Petersburg Beach, FL 33706. Tel. 813/360-1881, or toll free 800/637-7200 or 800/282-1116. Fax 813/367-3609. 277 rms. A/C TV TEL

$ Rates: May to mid-Dec, $140–$215 single or double. Mid-Dec to Apr, $235–$265 single or double. AE, CB, DC, MC, V.

Sitting majestically on 7½ acres of beachfront, the landmark "Pink Palace" dates back to 1928 and is a blend of Moorish and Mediterranean architecture, with an interior of classic high windows and archways, crystal chandeliers, marble floors, and original artworks. Restored and refurbished in the 1980s and again in 1993–94, it's listed on the National Register of Historic Places. Guest rooms, most of which offer views of the gulf or Boca Ciega Bay, are first-rate, with high ceilings, traditional furnishings, marble bathrooms, and a decor blending rich tones of rose, teal, mauve, and sea green.

Dining/Entertainment: The King Charles Restaurant is the place to splurge on a sumptuous Sunday brunch. Other outlets include the Maritana Grille for fresh seafood, Zelda's Seaside Café, the Lobby Bar, and the Beachcomber Bar and Grille for light snacks and drinks served outdoors.

Services: 24-hour room service, concierge desk, valet laundry, children's program.

Facilities: Beach, outdoor heated swimming pool, Jacuzzi, exercise room, sauna, steam room, whirlpool, resident masseuse, lighted tennis courts, volleyball, gift shops, and rentals for water-sports equipment.

TRADEWINDS, 5500 Gulf Blvd., St. Petersburg Beach, FL 33706. Tel. 813/367-6461, or toll free 800/237-0707. Fax 813/360-3848. 557 units. A/C TV TEL

$ Rates: Mid-Dec to Jan, $135–$190 single or double; $169–$239 one-bedroom suite. Feb–Apr, $175–$209 single or double; $245–$305 one-bedroom suite. May to mid-Dec, $115–$190 single or double; $147–$239 one-bedroom suite. AE, CB, DC, DISC, MC, V.

An oasis unto itself, this six- and seven-story resort sits amid 18 acres of beachfront property, sand dunes, and tropical gardens. The guest units, which look out on the gulf or the extensive grounds, have up-to-date kitchens or kitchenettes, contemporary furnishings, and private balconies. Two- and three-bedroom suites are also available on request, at higher rates.

Dining/Entertainment: The top spot for lunch or dinner is the Palm Court, with an Italian-bistro atmosphere; for dinner, there's also Bermudas, a casual family spot with a tropical atmosphere in a pastel gingerbread setting. Other food outlets include the Flying Bridge, a beachside floating restaurant in Florida cracker house–style; the Fountain Square Deli; and Tropic Treats. Bars include Reflections piano lounge; B.R. Cuda's, with live entertainment and dancing; and the poolside Salty's Beach Bar.

Services: Room service, valet laundry, children's program.

Facilities: Four heated swimming pools, whirlpools, sauna, fitness center, five tennis courts, racquetball, croquet, water-sports rentals, gas grills, guest laundry, video-game room, gift shops, hair salon.

Expensive

RADISSON SANDPIPER BEACH RESORT, 6000 Gulf Blvd., St. Petersburg, FL 33706. Tel. 813/360-5551, or toll free 800/237-0707. Fax 813/360-3848. 36 rms, 123 suites. A/C TV TEL

$ Rates: Mid-Dec to Jan, $75–$129 single or double; $119–$175 suite. Feb–Apr, $109–$174 single or double; $159–$229 suite. May to mid-Dec, $69–$99 single or double; $109–$149 suite. AE, CB, DC, DISC, MC, V.

A well-landscaped tropical courtyard separates the two wings of this six-story hostelry, set back from the main road. Decorated with light woods, pastel tones, and touches of rattan, most units have two double beds, some have a king- or queen-size bed, as well as coffee makers, toasters, small refrigerators, and wet bars.

Dining/Entertainment: Piper's Patio is a casual café with indoor/outdoor seating; and the Sandbar offers frozen drinks and snacks by the pool.

Services: Room service, concierge, valet laundry, child care.

Facilities: Beachfront heated swimming pool, enclosed heated swimming pool, two air-conditioned sports courts for racquetball, handball and squash, exercise room, volleyball, shuffleboard, games room, gift shop/general store.

Moderate

COLONIAL GATEWAY INN, 6300 Gulf Blvd., St. Petersburg Beach, FL 33706. Tel. 813/267-2711, or toll free 800/237-8918, 800/282-5245 in Florida. Fax 813/367-7068. 200 rms. A/C TV TEL
$ Rates: $67–$120 single or double. AE, CB, DC, DISC, MC, V.

Spread over a quarter mile of beachfront, this U-shaped complex of one- and two-story units is a favorite with families. The rooms, most of which face the pool and a central landscaped courtyard, are contemporary, with light woods and beach tones; about half the units are efficiencies with kitchenettes.

Dining/Entertainment: The White Horse Café is well known for its breakfast buffets, Etchings Lounge is a popular nightspot, and the Swigwam beach bar offers light refreshments.

Facilities: Outdoor heated swimming pool, kiddie pool, shuffleboard, games room, parasail and water-sports rentals.

DAYS INN ISLAND BEACH RESORT, 6200 Gulf Blvd., St. Petersburg Beach, FL 33706. Tel. 813/367-1902, or toll free 800/DAYS-INN. Fax 813/367-4422. 102 rms. A/C TV TEL
$ Rates: $79–$158 single or double; $89–$168 efficiency. AE, CB, DC, DISC, MC, V.

Located on the gulf beachfront, this two-story complex sits on five acres of tropical property. The guest rooms, furnished in light woods and pastel tones, have picture-window views of the beach or a central courtyard with the pool, lush greenery, and fountains. About half the units are efficiencies with kitchenettes.

Dining/Entertainment: Meals are available at Riddles, a family-style restaurant, and at Players Bar and Grille. Jimmy B.'s beach bar provides outdoor refreshment and evening entertainment.

Facilities: Outdoor heated swimming pool, volleyball, shuffleboard, games room.

Inexpensive

ISLAND'S END RESORT, 1 Pass-a-Grille Way, St. Petersburg, FL 33706. Tel. 813/360-5023. Fax 813/367-7890. 6 cottages. A/C TV TEL
$ Rates: $68–$99 one-bedroom cottage; $160 three-bedroom cottage. MC, V.

Nestled in the quiet southern tip of Pass-a-Grille where the Gulf of Mexico meets Tampa Bay, this is a resort well named and a good choice for those who want a nonhotel atmosphere. Six contemporary cottages enjoy a shady setting on the water's edge. Each cottage has a dining area, living room with sofa bed, kitchen, bathroom, and bedroom (one unit has three bedrooms), and a private pool. Facilities include a lighted fishing dock, patios, decks, barbecues, and hammocks; and a public beach is less than a block away.

THE HOLIDAY ISLES

Very Expensive

BELLEVIEW MIDO RESORT HOTEL, 25 Belleview Blvd. (P.O. Box 2317), Clearwater, FL 34617. Tel. 813/442-6171, or toll free 800/237-8947. Fax 813/441-4173 or 813/443-6361. 292 rms. A/C MINIBAR TV TEL

$ Rates: May–Nov, $85–$135 single; $130–$150 double. Dec–Apr. $135–$175 single; $150–$195 double. AE, CB, DC, DISC, MC, V.

Perched on a high bluff above Clearwater Bay, this massive multigabled white clapboard Victorian hotel sits amid lofty native pines, palms, and palmettos. Unlike most Clearwater hostelries, it's not on Clearwater Beach, but attracts a clientele who appreciate staying at a landmark—dating back to 1897 and listed on the National Register of Historic Places, it's the largest occupied wooden structure in the world. Although the exterior and much of the interior have been preserved over the years, there have also been modern additions, such as a futuristic glassy entrance and circular atrium-style lobby. The high-ceilinged guest rooms, for the most part, remain unchanged, decorated in Queen Anne style, with dark-wood period furniture.

Dining/Entertainment: The main restaurants are the informal indoor/outdoor Terrace Café for breakfast, lunch, or dinner; and Madame Ma's for gourmet Chinese cuisine. There's also a pub, lounge, and poolside bar.

Services: Room service, dry cleaning and valet laundry, nightly turn-down, currency exchange, transfer service from/to Tampa Airport, babysitting.

Facilities: 18-hole par-72 championship golf course, four red clay tennis courts, indoor and outdoor heated swimming pools, Jacuzzi, sauna, Swiss showers, workout gym, jogging and walking trails, access to a private Cabana Club on the Gulf of Mexico, bicycle rentals, fishing and sailboat charters, gift shops, art gallery, newsstand.

Expensive

CLEARWATER BEACH HOTEL, 500 Mandalay Ave., Clearwater Beach, FL 34630. Tel. 813/441-2425, or toll free 800/292-2295. Fax 813/449-2083. 157 units. A/C TV TEL

$ Rates: $90–$195 single or double. AE, CB, DC, MC, V.

Dating back 80 years but revamped and updated in 1988, this is one of the few Clearwater Beach properties with an old-world ambience. The complex, which sits directly on the gulf, consists of a six-story main building and two- and three-story wings. Rooms and rates vary, according to location—bay-view or gulf-view, poolside or beachfront; some have balconies.

Dining/Entertainment: The Dining Room offers views of the gulf, as does the nautically themed Schooner Lounge with entertainment nightly. Outdoor service is provided at the Pool Bar.

Services: Room service, valet laundry.

Facilities: Heated outdoor swimming pool.

NORTH REDINGTON BEACH HILTON, 17120 Gulf Blvd., N. Redington Beach, FL 33708. Tel. 813/391-4000, or toll free 800/HILTONS or 800/447-SAND. Fax 813/391-4000, ext. 7777. 125 rms. A/C MINIBAR TV TEL

$ Rates: May–Nov, $85–$140 single or double. Dec–Apr, $125–$185 single or double. AE, CB, DC, DISC, MC, V.

Surrounded mostly by private homes and condominiums, this six-story hostelry edges 250 feet of beachfront. Guest rooms are decorated in pastel tones, with extra-large bathrooms and full-length-mirrored closets. Each unit has a balcony with a view of either the gulf or Boca Ciega Bay.

Dining/Entertainment: Jasmine's Steakhouse offers outdoor and indoor dining, and the poolside Tiki Bar is popular each evening for its sunset-watching festivities.

Services: Room service, valet laundry.

Facilities: Outdoor heated swimming pool, sun deck.

RADISSON SUITE RESORT, 1201 Gulf Blvd., Clearwater Beach, FL 34630. Tel. 813/596-1100, or toll free 800/333-3333. Fax 813/595-4292. 220 suites. A/C MINIBAR TV TEL

$ Rates: May–Nov, $119–$195 suite for one or two. Dec–Apr, $160–$235 suite for one or two. AE, CB, DC, DISC, MC, V.

Opened in 1990, this 10-story all-suite hotel is an expansive $40-million seven-acre property overlooking Clearwater Harbor, with the Gulf of Mexico just across the street. Each suite has a bedroom with balcony offering water views, as well as a complete living room with a sofa bed, wet bar, video entertainment unit, coffee maker, and microwave oven.

Dining/Entertainment: The Harbor Grille specializes in barbecues and buffets, and the Harbor Lounge has a piano bar, while Kokomo's offers light fare and tropical drinks.

Services: Room service, laundry, free shuttle to the beach, child-care program.

Facilities: Outdoor heated swimming pool, sun deck, sauna, exercise room, waterfront boardwalk with a variety of shops and restaurants.

SHERATON SAND KEY RESORT, 1160 Gulf Blvd., Clearwater Beach, FL 33515. Tel. 813/595-1611, or toll free 800/325-3535. Fax 813/596-8488. 390 rms. A/C TV TEL

$ Rates: May–Nov, $88–$138 single; $98–$138 double. Dec–Apr, $88–$148 single; $98–$158 double. AE, CB, DC, DISC, MC, V.

Situated along 32 gulf-front acres, this nine-story resort overlooks a 650-foot beach and is a favorite with water-sports enthusiasts. Guest rooms currently offer standard beach-toned decor with light-wood furniture. All units have a balcony or patio with views of the gulf or the harbor.

Dining/Entertainment: Rusty's Restaurant serves breakfast and dinner; for lighter fare, try the Island Café, or the Sundeck or Gazebo Bar.

Services: Valet laundry, babysitting.

Facilities: Outdoor heated swimming pool, health club, Jacuzzi, three lighted tennis courts, volleyball court, newsstand, games room, children's pool, playground, water-sports rentals.

Moderate

BEST WESTERN SEA STONE RESORT, 445 Hamden Dr., Clearwater Beach, FL 34630. Tel. 813/441-1722, or toll free 800/444-1919 or 800/528-1234. Fax 813/449-1580. 65 rms, 43 suites. A/C TV TEL

$ Rates: $66–$79 single or double; $101–$168 suite. AE, CB, DC, DISC, MC, V.

Formerly two separate hotels, this is now one resort on the bayfront, connected by a pool and sun deck. The focus is on the Sea Stone Suites, a six-story building of classic Key West–style architecture containing 43 one-bedroom suites, each with kitchenette and living room. A few steps away, the older five-story Gulfview wing offers 65 bedrooms. Furnishings are bright and airy, with pastel tones, light woods, and sea scenes on the walls.

Dining/Entertainment: The Marker 5 Restaurant is on the lobby level of the suite complex, offering indoor and outdoor seating and a lounge.

Facilities: Heated outdoor swimming pool, Jacuzzi, boat dock, coin-operated guest laundry, meeting rooms.

PALM PAVILION INN, 18 Bay Esplanade, Clearwater Beach, FL 34630. Tel. 813/446-6777, or toll free 800/433-PALM. 26 rms, 4 efficiencies. A/C TV TEL

$ Rates: $49–$95 single or double; $64–$95 efficiency. AE, MC, V.

A stroll along the Clearwater beachfront is bound to draw your attention to this three-story art deco building, recently restored and artfully trimmed in pink and blue. The lobby area and guest rooms are equally art deco in design, with rounded light-wood and rattan furnishings, bright sea-toned fabrics, photographs from the 1920s–1950s era, and vertical blinds. Rooms in the front of the house face the gulf and those in the back face the bay; four units have kitchenettes. Facilities include a rooftop sun deck, beach access, and complimentary coffee.

Inexpensive

ALPAUGH'S GULF BEACH MOTEL APARTMENTS, 68 Gulf Blvd., Indian Rocks Beach, FL 34635. Tel. 813/595-2589. 16 rms. A/C TV TEL

$ Rates: $52–$74 single or double. MC, V.

A long-established tradition in the area, this family-oriented motel sits beside the beach with a grassy central courtyard area. The rooms offer modern furnishings, and each unit has a kitchenette and dining area. Facilities include coin-operated laundry, lawn games, picnic tables, and shuffleboard at each location.

There's a second Alpaugh's motel at 1912 Gulf Blvd., Indian Rocks Beach, FL 34635 (tel. 813/595-9421), with similar facilities and room rates, plus a one-bedroom cottage for $64 to $78 and some two-bedroom suites for $70 to $90.

CAPTAIN'S QUARTERS INN, 10035 Gulf Blvd., Treasure Island, FL 33706. Tel. 813/360-1659, or toll free 800/526-9547. 6 efficiencies, 3 suites. A/C TV TEL

$ Rates: $45–$70 efficiency for one or two; $65–$95 suite. MC, V.

This nautically themed property is a real find—offering well-kept accommodations on the gulf at inland rates. Six rooms are efficiencies with new mini-kitchens (including microwave oven, coffee maker, and wet bar or sink), and three units have a separate bedroom and a full kitchen. The complex sits on 100 yards of beach, an ideal vantage point for sunset-watching. Facilities include an outdoor solar-heated freshwater swimming pool, a sun deck, guest barbecues, a library, and a guest laundry.

PELICAN–EAST & WEST, 108 21st Ave., Indian Rocks Beach, FL 34635. Tel. 813/595-9741. 8 units. A/C TV

$ Rates: $35–$55 single or double at Pelican East; $55–$75 single or double at Pelican West. MC, V.

"P.D.I.P." (Perfect Day in Paradise) is the motto at this well-kept motel complex offering a choice of two settings, depending on your budget. The lowest rates are at Pelican East, 500 feet from the beach, with four units, each with bedroom and separate kitchen. Pelican West sits on the beachfront, offering four apartments, each with living room, bedroom, kitchen, patio, and unbeatable views of the gulf.

SUN WEST BEACH MOTEL, 409 Hamden Dr. S., Clearwater Beach, FL 34630. Tel. 813/442-5008. 4 rms, 10 efficiencies. A/C TV TEL

$ Rates: $40–$61 single or double; $48–$79 efficiency. DISC, MC, V.

Overlooking the bay and yet only a two-block walk from the beach, this well-maintained one-story motel has a heated pool, fishing/boating dock, sun deck, shuffleboard court, and guest laundry. All units, which face either the bay, the pool, or the sun deck, have contemporary resort-style furnishings. The four motel rooms have small refrigerators and the 10 efficiencies have kitchens.

WHERE TO DINE

From elegant candlelit dining rooms to panoramic waterfront restaurants or casual cafés, St. Petersburg has it all—especially outstanding seafood, fresh from gulf waters and beyond.

Like many Florida cities, St. Petersburg is a great exponent of the "early-bird dinner"—a three- or four-course evening meal at a set price, usually served between 4pm and 6 or 7pm. By being an "early bird," you can sample even the most expensive restaurants and rarely pay more than $10 for a complete dinner.

DOWNTOWN ST. PETERSBURG
Expensive

BASTA'S CANTINA D'ITALIA RISTORANTE, 1625 4th St. S. Tel. 894-7880.

Cuisine: NORTHERN ITALIAN/CONTINENTAL. **Reservations:** Recommended.

$ Prices: Main courses $13.95–$22.95. AE, CB, DC, MC, V.

Open: Lunch Mon–Fri 11:30am–3pm; dinner Mon–Sat 5–10pm.

Situated near the Dalí Museum, this classy little enclave is off the beaten track but worth a detour. The decor is a blend of art deco and Mediterranean influences, but the main attraction is the award-winning food. Specialties include seafood Porto Fino (lobster, shrimp, clams, scallops, and crab legs poached in white sauce over angel-hair pasta), and filet mignon Napoleone (filet of beef topped with mozzarella cheese, mushrooms, and herbs, and sprayed with brandy), as well as veal saltimbocca, shrimp scampi, lobster tails, steak Diane, and rack of lamb.

Moderate

APROPOS, 300 Second Ave. NE. Tel. 823-8934.
  Cuisine: AMERICAN. **Reservations:** Not accepted.
  $ **Prices:** Main courses $8–$15. CB, DC, MC, V.
  Open: Lunch Tues–Sat 11am–3pm; dinner Thurs–Sun 6pm–midnight; brunch Sun 8:30am–2pm.

Overlooking the marina and The Pier, this trendy art deco–style restaurant offers both air-conditioned seating indoors and patio-style seating on an outdoor deck. The menu, which features light foods spiked with fresh herbs, includes such dinner dishes as rosemary chicken, vegetarian platters, lamb chops, pepper steak, and fresh seafood.

THE COLUMBIA, 800 Second Ave. NE. Tel. 822-8000.
  Cuisine: SPANISH. **Reservations:** Recommended.
  $ **Prices:** Main courses $7.95–$16.95. AE, CB, DC, MC, V.
  Open: Mon–Thurs 11am–10pm, Fri–Sat 11am–11pm, Sun noon–10pm.

A branch of the Tampa landmark of the same name, this restaurant occupies the fourth floor of The Pier complex. Although it lacks the antique decor of the original Ybor City location, it excels by offering unequalled views of the Gulf of Mexico and the St. Petersburg skyline. A second location in this area is also on the water at 1241 Gulf Blvd., Clearwater Beach (tel. 596-2828). For a description of the menu, see "Where to Dine" in the Tampa section.

KEYSTONE CLUB, 320 4th St. N. Tel. 822-6600.
  Cuisine: AMERICAN. **Reservations:** Recommended.
  $ **Prices:** Main courses $8.95–$17.95. MC, V.
  Open: Lunch Mon–Fri 11am–2:30pm; dinner Mon–Thurs 5–10pm, Fri–Sat 5–11pm.

In a city that basks on fine seafood, this fairly new downtown restaurant prides itself on its beef, served in the clubby atmosphere of a Manhattan-style chophouse. Specialties include roast prime rib of beef, New York strip steak, and filet mignon, as well as lamb chops, calf's liver, chicken, and veal. Seafood also makes an appearance on the nightly special menu, with choices such as salmon filet with dill sauce, crab imperial, broiled grouper, and stuffed lobster tail.

LE GRAND CAFE, 247 Central Ave. N. Tel. 821-6992.
  Cuisine: CONTINENTAL. **Reservations:** Recommended.
  $ **Prices:** Main courses $10.95–$18.95. AE, DC, MC, V.
  Open: Lunch Mon–Sat 11:30am–3pm; dinner Mon–Thurs 6–10pm, Fri–Sat 6–10:30pm, Sun 1–9pm.

This stylish restaurant brings a little bit of Paris to the heart of downtown, with an art-filled bistro interior, French background music, and a sidewalk café outside. The menu blends classic with creative cooking, offering dishes such as pot au feu; pepper steak; filet of lamb with mushrooms, rosemary, honey, and herbs; roast duck with raspberry-shallot sauce; ground buffalo with chestnut sauce; and chicken breast with hazelnut liqueur, nuts, and cream. Salads, omelets, and sandwiches prevail at lunchtime.

LEVEROCK'S, 4801 37th St. S. Tel. 864-3883.
  Cuisine: SEAFOOD. **Reservations:** Not accepted.
  $ **Prices:** Main courses $6.95–$14.95. AE, CB, DC, MC, V.
  Open: Daily 11:30am–10pm.

Dating back to 1948 and synonymous with the freshest of seafood at affordable prices, Leverock's operates six fish houses along the Florida Gulf Coast (five in the St. Pete area and one in Bradenton). With the exception of the Pinellas Park site, all Leverock's restaurants offer lovely water views (this location, southwest of downtown, overlooks Maximo Moorings marina and Boca Ciega Bay). Menu selections range from 12 different shrimp dishes to sautéed snapper, grouper Florentine, salmon stir-fry, and crab cakes. Those with hearty appetites might opt for the "captain's platter" of shrimp, scallops, fish, crab legs, and petite lobster tails. Steaks, chicken Cordon Bleu, and baby back ribs round out the menu.

Other Leverock's locations in the area are at 7000 U.S. 19 at Park Boulevard, Pinellas Park (tel. 526-9188), north of downtown; 10 Corey Ave., St. Petersburg Beach (tel. 367-4588); 565 150th Ave., Madeira Beach (tel. 393-0459); and 551 Gulf Blvd., Clearwater Beach (tel. 446-5884).

LEVEROCK'S WATERFRONT STEAK HOUSE, 8800 Bay Pines Blvd. N. Tel. 345-5335.
   Cuisine: AMERICAN. **Reservations:** Not accepted.
 $ **Prices:** Main courses $6.95–$17.95. AE, CB, DC, MC, V.
   Open: Daily 11:30am–10pm.
   Northwest of downtown at the Lighthouse Point Marina, overlooking Boca Ciega Bay, diners can find choice western beef at affordable prices. The menu features three different cuts of prime rib, two sizes of filet mignon, and four types of steaks, plus chopped steak, beef kebabs, and four variations of surf-and-turf. Just for variety, there are baby back ribs, chicken, and two or three seafood items.

Inexpensive

NICK'S ON THE WATER, The Pier, 800 Second Ave. NE. Tel. 898-5800.
   Cuisine: ITALIAN/AMERICAN. **Reservations:** Recommended for dinner.
 $ **Prices:** Main courses $6.95–$14.95. AE, CB, DC, MC, V.
   Open: Sun–Thurs 11:30am–10pm, Fri–Sat 11:30am–11pm.
Located on the ground level of The Pier, this relatively new and informal restaurant offers expansive views of downtown St. Petersburg and the bayfront marina. The menu features a variety of pizzas and pastas, along with half a dozen veal dishes, seafood, and beef.

OLLIE'S GRILLE, 111 Second Ave. NE. Tel. 822-6200.
   Cuisine: AMERICAN. **Reservations:** Recommended.
 $ **Prices:** Main courses $5.95–$16.95. MC, V.
   Open: Lunch Mon–Fri 11am–2:30pm; dinner Mon–Thurs 5–9pm, Fri–Sat 5–10pm.
Situated on the mezzanine level of the Plaza Courtyard shopping complex on the approach to The Pier, this convenient restaurant is a local favorite at lunchtime. It offers a clubby bilevel interior with views of the city and seating under umbrellas overlooking a plant-filled courtyard. The menu features all-American favorites such as pot roast, lamb chop mixed grill, prime rib of beef, burgers, omelets, barbecued spareribs, jumbo beer-battered shrimp, lobster tail, and New York strip steaks. Lunch items also include sandwiches, soups, and salads.

Budget

CHA CHA COCONUTS, 800 Second Ave. NE. Tel. 822-6655.
   Cuisine: AMERICAN. **Reservations:** Not required.
 $ **Prices:** Main courses $3.95–$7.95. AE, CB, DC, MC, V.
   Open: Mon–Thurs 11am–midnight, Fri–Sat 11am–1am, Sun noon–10pm.
You'll feel as if you've been transported to the tropics when you enter this informal spot on the top floor of The Pier complex. While you dine, you can take in panoramic views of both the Gulf of Mexico and the St. Petersburg skyline. A second location in this area is also on the water at 1241 Gulf Blvd., Clearwater Beach (tel. 596-6040). For a description of the menu, see "Where to Dine" in the Tampa section.

FOURTH STREET SHRIMP STORE, 1006 4th St. N. Tel. 822-0325.
   Cuisine: SEAFOOD. **Reservations:** Not accepted.
 $ **Prices:** Main courses $4–$11. No credit cards.
   Open: Mon–Thurs and Sat 11:30am–8:30pm, Fri 11am–9pm, Sun noon–8pm.

Wedged on a busy street north of downtown, this is an Old Florida–style fish market and restaurant, offering no-frills seafood at rock-bottom prices. The tablecloths, utensils, and glasses are plastic and the plates are made of paper, but the seafood is the real thing—heaping servings of fresh grouper, smelts, or frogs' legs, shrimp of all sizes, oysters, and clams. Florida crab croquettes are a specialty.

PEP'S SEA GRILL, 7610 4th St. N. Tel. 521-1655.

Cuisine: SEAFOOD. **Reservations:** Not accepted.

$ Prices: Main courses $5.95–$12.95. No credit cards.

Open: Mon–Sat 4–10pm, Sun 11:30am–9pm.

Located north of downtown is this small, almost diner-style eatery, with a cheery art deco decor. It's known for serving fresh seafood at affordable prices. The menu items vary with the local catch, but specials often include salmon and snow crab, stone crabs, and a hearty one-pound shrimp feast.

Another branch is located in St. Petersburg Beach at 5895 Gulf Blvd. (tel. 367-3550). It's open Sunday through Thursday from 4 to 10pm and on Friday and Saturday from 4 to 10:30pm.

SHELLS, 1190 34th St. N. Tel. 321-6020.

Cuisine: SEAFOOD. **Reservations:** Not accepted.

$ Prices: Main courses $4.95–$13.95. AE, MC, V.

Open: Dinner only, Sun–Thurs 4–10pm, Fri–Sat 4–11pm.

Shells is a local institution. The first Shells opened in Tampa in 1985, and this location followed soon after, as have more than 20 other branches in Florida and beyond. For a description of the decor and menu, see "Where to Dine" in the Tampa section. Other branches in the St. Petersburg area area at 17855 Gulf Blvd., Redington Shores (tel. 393-8990), and 3138 U.S. 19 N., Clearwater (tel. 789-3944).

TED PETERS' FAMOUS SMOKED FISH, 1350 Pasadena Ave. S. Tel. 381-7931.

Cuisine: SMOKED SEAFOOD. **Reservations:** Not accepted.

$ Prices: Main courses $3.95–$11.95. No credit cards.

Open: Wed–Mon 11:30am–7:30pm.

Heading southwest of downtown toward the beach, the aromas of smoked fish tell you that you're approaching this rustic little roadside stand. The menu is limited, focusing primarily on smoked salmon, mackerel, or mullet, served with German potato salad. If you feel like something lighter, try a sandwich filled with smoked fish spread.

ST. PETERSBURG BEACH

Moderate

HURRICANE, 807 Gulf Way. Tel. 360-9558.

Cuisine: SEAFOOD. **Reservations:** Not accepted.

$ Prices: Main courses $6.95–$17.95. MC, V.

Open: Daily 8am–1am.

If you're a fan of Florida black grouper or even if you've never tasted it before, here's *the* spot to try it. Overlooking Pass-a-Grille beach, this informal, three-level indoor/outdoor restaurant is synonymous with grouper. Main courses range from grouper Florentine and grouper parmesan to grouper Oscar, grouper au gratin, or grouper amandine, to name a few. And if you crave something else, there's always crab legs and claws, shrimp, scallops, and swordfish, as well as barbecued ribs and steaks.

MULLIGAN'S SUNSET GRILLE, 9524 Blind Pass Rd. Tel. 367-6680.

Cuisine: SEAFOOD/AMERICAN. **Reservations:** Not accepted.

$ Prices: Main courses $8.95–$19.95. AE, MC, V.

Open: Daily 11am–11pm; brunch Sun 11am–3pm.

Overlooking the waters of Boca Ciega Bay at the north end of St. Petersburg Beach, this informal restaurant offers indoor and outdoor seating. The straightforward menu

FLORIDA

St. Petersburg

Apropos  **10**
Basta's Cantina d'Italia **9**
Cha Cha Coconuts
    at The Pier **11**
Columbia at The Pier **13**
Crabby Bills **7**
Fourth Street Shrimp
    Store **17**
Keystone Club **16**
Le Grande Café **14**
Leverock's, 37th Street **8**
Leverock's, St. Pete Beach **4**
Mulligan's Sunset Grille **2**
Nick's on the Water **12**
Ollie's Grille **15**
Pep's Sea Grill **5**
Silas Dent's **6**
Ted Peters Famous
    Smoked Fish **3**
The Waterfront
    Steak House **1**

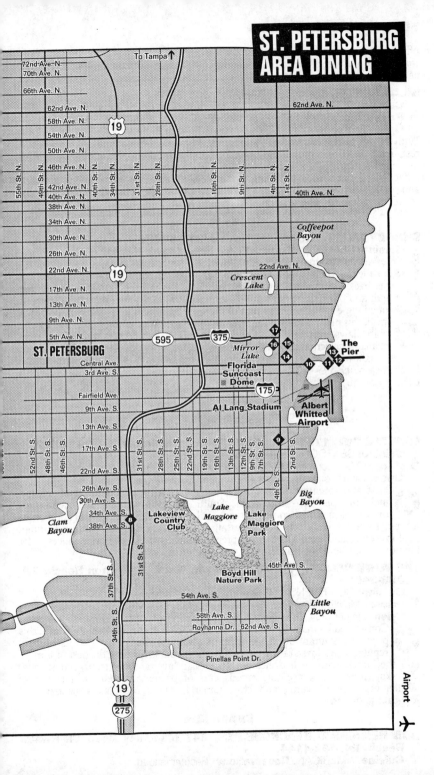

offers steamed seafood platters, stone crabs in season, and seafood combination pots for two people (with steamed oysters, snow crab, shrimp, corn on the cob, and more), as well as ribs, steaks, Southwest-style chicken, and pastas.

SILAS DENT'S, 5501 Gulf Blvd. Tel. 360-6961.
   Cuisine: REGIONAL/SEAFOOD. **Reservations:** Recommended.
$ **Prices:** Main courses $7.95–$18.95. AE, CB, DC, DISC, MC, V.
   Open: Dinner only, Sun–Thurs 5–10pm, Fri–Sat 5–11pm.
With a rustic facade of driftwood and an interior of palm fronds and cedar poles, this restaurant seeks to replicate the home of popular local folk hero Silas Dent, who inhabited a nearby island for many years early in this century. The menu aims to reflect Silas's diet of local fish using such ingredients as alligator, amberjack, grouper, and squid, along with such modern favorites as mahi-mahi, lobster tails, and scallops, as well as prime rib, filet mignon, and chicken Silas (with red bell pepper sauce).

Inexpensive

CRABBY BILL'S, 5100 Gulf Blvd. Tel. 360-8858.
   Cuisine: SEAFOOD. **Reservations:** Not accepted.
$ **Prices:** Main courses $3.95–$12.95. MC, V.
   Open: Mon–Thurs 11am–10pm, Fri–Sat 11am–11pm, Sun 1–10pm.
Set back from the main road, this beach house–style restaurant overlooks the gulf and offers great views amid a casual picnic table–style decor. An offshoot of a long-established restaurant of the same name about 15 miles up the beach strip, this place is known for its crabs—steamed blue crabs, garlic crabs, stone crab claws, soft-shell crabs, and crab cakes. In addition, there's an ever-changing selection of other fresh seafoods, from oysters, clams, and mussels, to shrimp, mahi-mahi, and catfish. The original Crabby's is at 401 Gulf Blvd., Indian Rocks Beach (tel. 595-4825), and nearly always has a line out the door. Come early to either location.

THE HOLIDAY ISLES
Very Expensive

LOBSTER POT, 17814 Gulf Blvd., Redington Shores. Tel. 391-8592.
   Cuisine: SEAFOOD. **Reservations:** Recommended.
$ **Prices:** Main courses $12.95–$27.95. AE, CB, DC, MC, V.
   Open: Dinner only, Mon–Sat 4:30–10pm, Sun 4–10pm.
First and foremost, this is a lobster house, with 22 variations of lobster, including specimens from Maine, South Africa, Florida, and Denmark—tails or whole, in sauces and au naturel—all sold at market prices. In addition to lobster, there's a wide selection of grouper, snapper, salmon, swordfish, shrimp, scallops, crab, and even Dover sole, prepared simply or in elaborate sauces. Filet mignon, steaks, and chicken round out the menu.

THE WINE CELLAR, 17307 Gulf Blvd., North Redington Beach. Tel. 393-3491.
   Cuisine: CONTINENTAL. **Reservations:** Recommended.
$ **Prices:** Main courses $11.75–$27.50. AE, CB, DC, MC, V.
   Open: Dinner only, Tues–Sun 4:30–11pm.
Considered by many locals to be the top choice in the St. Petersburg area, this popular restaurant doesn't even sport a view of the water. With its culinary reputation, it doesn't need views. The main courses present the best of Europe and the States, with such dishes as North Carolina rainbow trout, red snapper Waleska, frogs' legs provençal, various cuts of prime rib, weinerschnitzel, beef Wellington, rack of lamb, and chateaubriand. There are also vegetarian and low-calorie dishes.

Expensive

BOB HEILMAN'S BEACHCOMBER, 447 Mandalay Ave., Clearwater Beach. Tel. 442-4144.
   Cuisine: AMERICAN. **Reservations:** Recommended.

$ Prices: Main courses $10.95–$25.95. AE, DC, MC, V.
Open: Mon–Sat 11:30am–11pm, Sun noon–10pm.

Although it doesn't have water views, this restaurant has been popular for over 40 years. The menu presents a variety of fresh seafood, from Everglades frogs' legs to Maine lobsters, as well as Atlantic sole and the best of the local catch. Beef is also a specialty here, with aged steaks and prime rib much in demand. One of the most popular items on the menu is in a class by itself—"back-to-the-farm" fried chicken from an original 1926 recipe.

Moderate

FRIENDLY FISHERMAN, 150 128th Ave., Madeira Beach. Tel. 391-6025.
Cuisine: SEAFOOD. **Reservations:** Not accepted.
$ Prices: Main courses $7.95–$19.95. MC, V.
Open: Sun–Thurs 7am–10pm, Fri–Sat 7am–11pm.

At the southern tip of Madeira Beach, this waterside restaurant has become the centerpiece of John's Pass Village, an outgrowth of a busy fishing business launched over 50 years ago. The menu focuses on seafood, served smoked, steamed, fried, or broiled. Choices range from amberjack and mullet to stone crabs, shrimp, grouper, snapper, and flounder, as well as lobster tails, and four kinds of surf-and-turf.

SEAFOOD & SUNSETS AT JULIE'S, 351 S. Gulfview Blvd., Clearwater Beach. Tel. 441-2548.
Cuisine: SEAFOOD. **Reservations:** Recommended.
$ Prices: Main courses $6.95–$17.95. AE, MC, V.
Open: Daily 11am–10pm.

A Key West–style atmosphere prevails at this indoor-outdoor eatery across from the beach. And yes, there is a Julie (Julie Nichols), who is usually on the scene, and this is indeed a great vantage point for sunset-watching. Just to make sure no one misses this spectacular sight, sunset time is posted on a blackboard every day. The menu offers lots of seafood—Florida lobsters, stone crabs, conch, grouper and other fish (prepared charcoal-broiled, blackened, fried, or broiled), as well as steaks, surf-and-turf, and chicken.

SCANDIA, 19829 Gulf Blvd., Indian Shores. Tel. 595-5525.
Cuisine: SCANDINAVIAN. **Reservations:** Recommended.
$ Prices: Main courses $7.95–$19.95. AE, CB, DC, MC, V.
Open: Lunch Tues–Sat 11:30am–3pm; dinner Tues–Sat 3–9pm, Sun noon–8pm.

Unique in decor and menu along the gulf coast, this chalet-style restaurant brings a touch of Hans Christian Andersen to the beach strip. The menu offers Scandinavian favorites, from smoked salmon and pickled herring, to roast pork, sausages, schnitzels, and Danish lobster tails, as well as a few international dishes such as curried chicken, surf-and-turf, roast leg of lamb, and local seafood choices—jumbo shrimp, scallops, grouper, flounder, and more.

Inexpensive

OMI'S BAVARIAN INN, 14701 Gulf Blvd., Madeira Beach. Tel. 393-9654.
Cuisine: GERMAN. **Reservations:** Recommended.
$ Prices: Main courses $6.95–$13.95. DISC, MC, V.
Open: Wed–Mon 3–9:30pm.

This little restaurant is a small patch of Germany on the gulf, featuring such specialties as schnitzels, sauerbraten and schweinebraten (roast pork), chicken paprikash, beef goulasch, Bavarian bratwurst, and stuffed pepper. A variety of seafoods and steaks are also on the menu.

Budget

SUNSET BEACH CAFE, 9701 1st St. E., Treasure Island. Tel. 367-3359.
Cuisine: AMERICAN. **Reservations:** Not required.

$ Prices: Main courses $5.95–$9.95. CB, DC, DISC, MC, V.
Open: Daily 7am–9:30pm.

S Located across the road from the beach on the southern tip of Treasure Island, this family-run restaurant exudes a continental feeling, with reproduction art by Renoir and Monet. The wraparound windows add unmistakable Florida views on all sides. The all-day menu includes a variety of freshly prepared salads, burgers, sandwiches, omelets, Belgian waffles, pastas, and pizzas, as well as dinner choices of baby back ribs, steaks, scallops scampi, fried chicken, coconut shrimp, fried or broiled grouper, and stir-fry dishes.

SHOPPING
SHOPPING CLUSTERS

GAS PLANT ANTIQUE ARCADE, 1246 Central Ave. Tel. 895-0368.

Housed in a former gas plant, this four-story complex is the largest antiques mall on Florida's west coast, with over 100 dealers displaying their wares. Open Monday through Saturday from 10am to 5pm and on Sunday from noon to 5pm.

JOHN'S PASS VILLAGE AND BOARDWALK, 12901 Gulf Blvd., Madeira Beach. Tel. 391-7373.

Situated on the water, this converted fishermen's village houses over 60 shops, selling everything from antiques and arts and crafts to beachwear. There are also several art galleries, including the Bronze Lady, which is the largest single dealer in the world of works by Red Skelton, the comedian-artist. Open daily from 9am to 6pm or later.

THE PIER, 800 Second Ave. NE. Tel. 821-6164.

The hub of shopping for the downtown area, this five-story pyramid-shaped complex houses more than a dozen boutiques and craft shops. The Pier also leads to Beach Drive, one of the most fashionable downtown strolling and shopping streets. Open Monday through Saturday from 10am to 9pm and on Sunday from 11am to 7pm.

SPECIALTY SHOPS

EVANDER PRESTON CONTEMPORARY JEWELRY, 106 Eighth Ave., St. Petersburg Beach. Tel. 367-7894.

If you're in the market for some one-of-a-kind hand-hammered jewelry, it's well worth a visit to this unique gallery/workshop, housed in a 75-year-old building on Pass-a-Grille. Open Monday through Saturday from 10am to 5:30pm and on Sunday from 11am to 5pm.

FLORIDA CRAFTSMEN GALLERY, 237 Second Ave. S. Tel. 821-7391.

This is a showcase for the works of over 100 Florida artisans and craftspeople— jewelry, ceramics, woodwork, fiberworks, glassware, paper creations, and metal works. Open Tuesday through Saturday from 10am to 4pm.

GLASS CANVAS GALLERY, 233 Fourth Ave. NE, St. Petersburg. Tel. 821-6767.

Located just off Beach Drive, this modern gallery features a dazzling array of glass sculpture, tableware, art, and craft items, many of which have a sea, shell, or piscine theme. Open Monday through Wednesday and Friday from 10am to 6pm, on Thursday from 10am to 8pm, on Saturday from 10am to 5pm, and on Sunday from noon to 5pm.

HASLAM'S, 2025 Central Ave. Tel. 822-8616.

Although the St. Pete area has lots of bookshops, this huge emporium, established in 1933, claims to be Florida's largest, with over 300,000 books— new and used, hardcover and paperback, and electronic. Open Monday through Thursday and Saturday from 9am to 5:30pm, on Friday from 9am to 9pm.

P. BUCKLEY MOSS, 190 Fourth Ave. NE. Tel. 894-2899.

This gallery/studio features the works of one of Florida's most individualistic artists, best known for her portrayal of Amish and Mennonite people. The works include paintings, graphics, figurines, and collector dolls. Open Monday through Saturday from 10am to 5pm, and from September to April also on Sunday from noon to 5pm.

RED CLOUD, 208 Beach Dr. NE. Tel. 821-5824.

This is an oasis for Native American crafts, from jewelry and headdresses to sculpture and art. Open Monday through Wednesday and on Friday and Saturday from 10am to 6pm, on Thursday from 10am to 8pm.

SENIOR CITIZEN CRAFT CENTER GIFT SHOP, 940 Court St., Clearwater. Tel. 442-4266.

Opened about 30 years ago, this is one of the area's most unique gift shops—an outlet for the work of about 400 local senior citizens/consignors. The items for sale include knitwear, crochetwork, woodwork, stained glass, clocks, scrimshaw, jewelry, pottery, tilework, ceramics, and hand-painted clothing. It's well worth a visit, even though it's a little off the usual tourist track. Open June to August, Monday through Friday from 10am to 4pm; and September to May, Monday through Saturday from 10am to 4pm.

THE SHELL STORE, 440 75th Ave., St. Petersburg Beach. Tel. 360-0586.

This shop specializes in corals and shells and an on-premises mini-museum illustrates how they both live and grow. In addition, you'll also find a good selection of shell home decorations, shell hobbyist supplies, shell art, planters, and jewelry. Open Monday through Saturday from 9:30am to 5pm.

THE STRAW GOAT, 130 Beach Dr. NE. Tel. 822-4456.

This shop overflows with the work of American and European artisans, with particular emphasis on Scandinavian gifts and cooking utensils. Items range from crystal chandeliers and chimes to wall hangings and decorative stationery. Hours are Monday through Saturday from 10am to 5pm.

WINGS, 6705 Gulf Blvd., St. Petersburg Beach. Tel. 367-8876.

If you forgot your swimsuit or need a new one, this huge emporium is hard to beat, for price and selection. In addition to swimwear, you'll find hats, sunglasses, T-shirts, and more. Open daily from 9am to 10pm.

Other locations are at John's Pass Village, 12900 Gulf Blvd., Madeira Beach (tel. 392-9211); 400 Poinsettia Ave., Clearwater Beach (tel. 449-2710); and 646 S. Gulfview Blvd., Clearwater Beach (tel. 441-1042).

EVENING ENTERTAINMENT

THE PERFORMING ARTS

Major Concert/Performance Halls

BAYFRONT CENTER, 400 1st St. S. Tel. 892-5767, or 892-5700 for recorded information.

This is the city's waterfront showplace, with the 8,400-seat **Bayfront Arena** and the 2,000-seat **Mahaffey Theater.** The schedule includes a variety of concerts, Broadway shows, big bands, ice shows, circus, and sports.
Admission: Tickets, $5–$40, depending on event.

RUTH ECKERD HALL, 1111 McMullen-Booth Rd., Clearwater. Tel. 791-7400.

This 2,200-seat auditorium is a major venue for a varied program of Broadway shows, ballet, drama, symphonic works, popular music, jazz, and country music.
Admission: Tickets $10–$55, depending on the event.

ST. PETERSBURG THUNDERDOME, 1 Stadium Dr. Tel. 825-3100.

This giant arena has a capacity of 50,000 for concerts, but also presents a variety of smaller events.
Admission: Tickets, $15–$30, depending on the event.

Theaters/Dinner-Theaters

AMERICAN STAGE COMPANY, 211 3rd St. S. Tel. 822-8814.
This is St. Petersburg's resident professional theater, presenting contemporary dramas and comedies.
Admission: $12–$22.

ST. PETERSBURG LITTLE THEATER, 4025 31st St. S. Tel. 866-1973.
This is the city's community theater, presenting six plays or variety shows a year, from September through May.
Admission: $9–$10.

BELLS' SHOWBOAT DINNER THEATRE, 3405 Ulmerton Rd., Clearwater. Tel. 573-3777.
Designed with a vintage showboat facade, this inland theater presents a variety of Broadway comedies and musicals, with major stars, along with buffet meals.
Admission: $34.95 evenings, $27.90 matinees.

TIDES DINNER THEATER, 16720 Gulf Blvd., N. Redington Beach. Tel. 393-1870.
This facility presents Broadway musicals with performances by the local Seminole Players.
Admission: $30 evenings, $25 matinees.

THE CLUB & MUSIC SCENE
A Comedy Club

COCONUTS COMEDY CLUB, 6110 Gulf Blvd., St. Petersburg Beach. Tel. 360-NUTS, 360-6887, or 360-4575.
One of the oldest and best-known comedy spots on the beach strip, this club features an ever-changing program of live stand-up comedy acts. Shows are on Wednesday and Thursday at 9pm, and on Friday and Saturday at 9 and 11pm.
Admission: $7, plus a two-drink minimum.

Jazz/Blues/Reggae/Folk

THE HURRICANE LOUNGE, 807 Gulf Way, St. Petersburg Beach. Tel. 260-4875.
Long recognized as one of the best places for jazz, this beachside spot has a varied program of jazz on Sunday, Wednesday, and Thursday from 9pm to 1am and on Friday and Saturday from 9:30pm to 1:30am. Drinks run $2 to $4.
Admission: Free.

RINGSIDE CAFE, 2742 4th St. N., St. Petersburg. Tel. 894-8465.
Housed in a renovated boxing gymnasium, this informal neighborhood café has a decided sports motif, but the music focuses on jazz and blues (and sometimes reggae), on Friday and Saturday nights from 10pm to 2am.
Admission: $2 or more.

Dance Clubs/Discos/Top-40s Music

BEACH NUTTS, 9600 W. Gulf Blvd., Treasure Island. Tel. 367-7427.
This is a quintessential beach bar, perched atop a stilt foundation like a wooden beach cottage on the Gulf of Mexico. The music ranges from top-40s to reggae and rock. Open daily from 5pm to 1am. Drinks cost $2 to $4.
Admission: Free.

BIG CATCH, 9 1st St. NE. Tel. 821-6444.
This casual downtown club features live and danceable rock and top-40s hits, as well as darts, pool, and hoops. Open Thursday through Saturday from 9pm to 2am.
Admission: $3–$5.

CLUB DETROIT, 16 2nd St. N. Tel. 896-1244.
Housed in the landmark Hotel Detroit, this lively spot includes a lounge, Channel Zero, and an outdoor courtyard, Jannus Landing. Look for blues, reggae, and

progressive DJ dance music indoors and live rock concerts outdoors. Open daily from 9pm to 2am.
Admission: $2 and up indoors, $10–$18 for outdoor concerts.

GATORS ON THE PASS, 12754 Kingfish Dr., Treasure Island. Tel. 367-8951.
Located at Kingfish Wharf, on the northern tip of Treasure Island, this place claims to have the world's longest waterfront bar, with a huge deck overlooking the waters of John's Pass. The complex also includes a no-smoking sports bar and a three-story tower with a top-level observation deck for panoramic views of the Gulf of Mexico. There's live music, from acoustic and blues to rock, most nights from 7pm to 1am.
Admission: $2 cover charge for most acts.

JAMMIN'Z DANCE SHACK, 470 Mandalay Ave., Clearwater Beach. Tel. 441-2005, or 442-5754 for recorded information.
This nightclub offers a beachy atmosphere and a dance floor with state-of-the-art sound, light, video, and laser effects. A DJ spins top-40 tunes from 8pm to 2am daily.
Admission: $3–$5.

MANHATTANS, 11595 Gulf Blvd., Treasure Island. Tel. 363-1500.
Nestled on the beach strip, this club offers a variety of live music, from country to contemporary and classic rock, seven nights a week from 8pm until 2am.
Admission: Free.

Ballrooms

COLISEUM BALLROOM, 535 Fourth Ave. N. Tel. 892-5202.
Dating back to 1924, this landmark Spanish-style building is *the* place to go in downtown St. Petersburg for an evening of dancing to big-band, country, ballroom, and other kinds of music.
Admission: $4–$15.

JOYLAND, 11225 U.S. 19, Clearwater. Tel. 573-1919.
This is the area's only country-western ballroom, featuring live bands and well-known performers Wednesday through Sunday.
Admission: $3–$10.

3. SARASOTA

63 miles S of Tampa, 150 miles SW of Orlando, 225 miles NW of Miami

GETTING THERE By Plane Sarasota-Bradenton International Airport, 6000 Airport Circle, Sarasota (tel. 813/359-2770), is located north of downtown between U.S. 41 and U.S. 301. Airlines serving the airport include American, Continental, Delta, Northwest, TWA, United, and USAir.

By Train Amtrak trains arrive at Tampa station, with bus connections to Sarasota. For full information, call toll free 800/342-2520.

By Bus Greyhound buses arrive at the Sarasota depot at 575 N. Washington Blvd. (tel. 813/955-5735).

By Car From points north and south, Sarasota can be reached via I-75, U.S. 41, U.S. 301, and U.S. 19. From the east coast of Florida, use Fla. 70 or Fla. 72.

Often referred to as the "circus town," Sarasota is synonymous with circus legend John Ringling, who came to Sarasota in the 1920s and left quite an imprint. He built a palatial home, Ca'd'Zan, on the bayfront, acquired extensive real estate, erected a museum to house his world-class collection of baroque paintings, and moved the famed circus winter quarters from Bridgeport, Conn., to Sarasota, where it remained until 1957 when it moved farther south to Venice.

Known as the cultural center of Florida, Sarasota is home to the Florida West Coast Symphony, the Asolo Performing Arts Center, the Van Wezel Performing Arts

Hall, and many more artistic venues. A bright and thriving city of 50,000 people, Sarasota also boasts 20 miles of beach, and an average of 361 days of sunshine per year.

Like much of Florida, Hernándo de Soto is credited with being the first European to explore the area. Legend has it that Sarasota was named after de Soto's daughter, Sara, and hence "Sara Soto," or, eventually, "Sarasota."

ORIENTATION
ARRIVING

West Coast Limousine (tel. 813/355-9645) provides van transfers from the airport to hotels in the Sarasota area. Price depends on destination, but averages $6 to $10 per person. Taxi services include **Diplomat Taxi** (tel. 355-5155), **Green Cab Taxi** (tel. 922-666) and **Yellow Cab of Sarasota** (tel. 955-3341).

INFORMATION

For information about attractions, hotels, restaurants, events, and more, contact the **Sarasota Convention & Visitors Bureau,** 655 N. Tamiami Trail (U.S. 41), Sarasota, FL 34236 (tel. 813/957-1877, or toll free 800/522-9799).

CITY LAYOUT

Sarasota is divided into two sections. The **downtown** area on the mainland hugs the bayfront, with a modern and sleek urban skyline, edged by picturesque marinas, landscaped drives, and historic Spanish-style buildings. U.S. 41 runs through downtown Sarasota in a north-south direction.

An adjacent beach strip to the west, on the Gulf of Mexico, is composed of four islands or "keys," separated from downtown by Sarasota Bay. With white sandy beaches, lagoons, and lush vegetation, **Siesta Key** exudes a tropical ambience; the streets are narrow and shaded by overhanging branches draped with Spanish moss. The **Siesta Drive Causeway** and the **Stickney Point Road Causeway** link Sarasota with Siesta Key.

Lido Key is a lively and well-developed island with a string of motels, restaurants, and nightclubs. At the entrance to Lido Key is **St. Armands Key,** a tiny enclave named after Charles St. Amand (early spelling), a 19th-century French homesteader. It owes its development to circus-master John Ringling, who built the four-lane **John Ringling Causeway** that provides access to Lido, St. Armands, and to **Longboat Key,** a narrow, 12-mile-long island which is one of Florida's wealthiest areas.

GETTING AROUND

BY PUBLIC TRANSPORTATION Sarasota County Area Transit/SCAT (tel. 951-5851) provides a regularly scheduled **bus** service for the area. Standard fare is $1; exact change is required.

BY TAXI Taxi companies serving the Sarasota area include **Diplomat Taxi** (tel. 355-5155), **Green Cab Taxi** (tel. 922-6666), **Sarasota Cab** (tel. 366-0596), and **Yellow Cab of Sarasota** (tel. 955-3341).

BY CAR Rental-car companies with desks at the airport include **Avis** (tel. 813/359-5240), **Budget** (tel. 813/359-5353), **Dollar** (tel. 813/355-2996), and **Hertz** (tel. 813/355-8848).

BY TROLLEY For public transport between the mainland and beach strip, the **Siesta Key Trolley,** 110 Avenida Veneccia, Suite B, Siesta Key (tel. 346-3115), provides regular service Tuesday through Saturday. There are two routes: a South Trolley, which goes to major shopping areas, restaurants, and beaches from 10am to 8:30pm, November to September; and a North Trolley, which goes to downtown Sarasota, St. Armands Circle, Lido Beach, and major hotels and attractions, between 9:30am and 5:30pm, November to May. The trolleys start, finish, and interconnect their runs at the Best Western Siesta Beach Resort in Siesta Village. The fare is $1 per person.

FAST FACTS

Area Code   Sarasota's area code is 813.

Dentist   For emergency dental repairs, contact Dentist Information Services (tel. 951-1065).

Doctor   Most hotels have a doctor on call; if not, contact the Sarasota Physician Referral Center (tel. 957-7777).

Drugstores   Eckerd Drugs has over a dozen pharmacies in the downtown and beach areas, including one at the Crossroads Shopping Center, 3800 S. Tamiami Trail (tel. 955-3328), that's open until midnight.

Emergencies   Dial 911.

Hospitals   The Sarasota Memorial Hospital, 1700 S. Tamiami Trail (tel. 955-1111), and Doctors' Hospital of Sarasota, 2750 Bahia Vista (tel. 366-1411), are two prominent local facilities.

Library   Try the Selby Public Library, 1001 Blvd. of the Arts (tel. 951-5501).

Newspapers/Magazines   The *Sarasota Herald-Tribune* is published daily. *Sarasota Magazine* is a monthly magazine covering the area.

Post Office   The main post office is at 1661 Ringling Blvd. (tel. 952-9720).

Taxes   There's a 9% hotel tax, a 7% restaurant tax, and 7% general sales tax.

Transit Information   Dial 951-5851.

Weather   Call toll free 800/282-5584.

WHAT TO SEE & DO

THE TOP ATTRACTIONS

BELLM'S CARS & MUSIC OF YESTERDAY, 5500 N. Tamiami Trail. Tel. 355-6228.

This museum displays over 120 classic and antique autos, from Rolls-Royces and Pierce Arrows, to the four cars used personally by circus czar John Ringling. In addition, there are over 2,000 antique music machines, from tiny music boxes to a huge 30-foot Belgian organ.

Admission: $7.50 adults, $3.75 children 6–12, free for kids under 6.

Open: Daily 9:30am–5:30pm. **Directions:** Take U.S. 41 north of downtown and one mile south of the airport.

MARIE SELBY BOTANICAL GARDENS, S. Palm Ave., off U.S. 41. Tel. 366-5731.

A 17-acre museum of living plants, this facility is said to be the only botanical garden in the world to specialize in the preservation, study, and research of epiphytic plants ("air plants"), such as orchids, pineapples, and ferns. It is home to more than 20,000 exotic plants including over 6,000 orchids, as well as a bamboo pavilion, butterfly and hummingbird garden, medicinal plant garden, waterfall garden, cactus and succulent garden, fernery, hibiscus garden, palm grove, tropical food garden, and a native shore-plant community, plus a museum of botany and the arts.

Admission: $6 adults, $3 children 6–11, free for kids under 6 accompanied by an adult.

Open: Daily 10am–5pm.

MOTE MARINE AQUARIUM, 1600 Thompson Pkwy. Tel. 388-4441.

Part of the noted Mote Marine Laboratory complex, this facility focuses on the marine life of the Sarasota area. Displays include a living mangrove swamp and seagrass environment, a 135,000-gallon shark tank, loggerhead turtles and their eggs, starfish, lobsters, sea horses, and other inhabitants of both salt and fresh water. In addition, there are many "research-in-progress" exhibits on such topics as the red tide, aquaculture enhancement, cancer research in sharks, and the effects of pesticide and petroleum pollution on the coast. The aquarium is located on City Island, just south of Longboat Key.

Admission: $6 adults, $4 children 6–17, free for children under 6.
Open: Daily 10am–5pm. **Directions:** Take John Ringling Circle north to City Island Park, at the foot of the bridge between Lido and Longboat Keys.

MYAKKA RIVER STATE PARK, 13207 Fla. 72. Tel. 361-6511.

This is a 28,875-acre "Old Florida" preserve of wetlands, prairies, nature trails, birdwalks, and dense woodlands along the Myakka River. It includes an outstanding wildlife sanctuary and breeding grounds, home to hundreds of species of plants, trees, and flowers, as well as deer, alligators, and birds such as ospreys, bald eagles, and sandhill cranes. There are two ways to get an overview of the entire park, either via one-hour tram tours (seasonal) or a one-hour airboat ride (year-round).

Admission: $3.25 per car (up to eight passengers); airboat or tram tours, $6 adults, $3 children 6–12, free for children under 6.
Open: Daily 8am–sunset. **Directions:** Take U.S. 41 south to Stickney Point Road and go 15 miles east on Fla. 72.

PELICAN MAN'S BIRD SANCTUARY, 1708 Thompson Pkwy., City Island Park. Tel. 388-4444.

Situated next to the Mote Marine Aquarium is this shelter and rehabilitation center for injured pelicans and other wild sea birds. It's operated by Dale Shields, who has devoted his life to this cause, helping more than 22,000 birds and earning the unofficial title of "Pelican Man" from those who come to visit.

Admission: Free; donations encouraged.
Open: Daily 10am–4pm. **Directions:** Take John Ringling Circle north to City Island Park.

RINGLING MUSEUM COMPLEX, 5401 Bayshore Rd. Tel. 355-5101, or 351-1660 for recorded information.

The former estate of circus entrepreneur John Ringling, this 38-acre site overlooking Sarasota Bay offers four attractions. Foremost is the **John and Mable Ringling Museum of Art,** Florida's official state art museum, which houses a major exhibit of baroque art as well as collections of decorative arts and traveling exhibits. Next is the 30-room **Ca'd'Zan** (House of John), the Ringling winter residence, built in 1925 and modeled after a Venetian palace, and the **Circus Galleries,** a building devoted to circus memorabilia including parade wagons, calliopes, costumes, and colorful posters. The grounds also include the **Asolo Center for the Performing Arts,** a professional theater company, plus restaurants and shops.

Admission: $8.50 adults, $7.50 seniors, free for children 12 and under.
Open: Oct–June, Fri–Wed 10am–5:30pm, Thurs 10am–10pm; July–Sept, daily 10am–5:30pm. **Directions:** From downtown, take U.S. 41 north to De Soto Road, and turn left onto Ringling Plaza.

SARASOTA JUNGLE GARDENS, 37-01 Bayshore Rd. Tel. 355-5303.

Situated on the bayfront south of the Ringling Complex, this is a 10-acre preserve featuring jungle trails, tropical plants, exotic waterfowl, and reptiles in natural habitats. In addition, there is a petting zoo, bird shows, and a shell and butterfly museum.

Admission: $8 adults, $4 children 3–12, free for kids under 3.
Open: Daily 9am–5pm. **Directions:** From downtown, take U.S. 41 north to Myrtle Street, turn left, and go two blocks.

ART GALLERIES

A beacon for culture and the arts on Florida's west coast, Sarasota is home to more than 40 art galleries and exhibition spaces, all open to the public year-round, and including the world-famous **John and Mable Ringling Museum of Art** (see "The Top Attractions," above), Florida's official state art museum.

A convenient artistic starting point for visitors is the **Sarasota Visual Art Center,** 707 N. Tamiami Trail (tel. 365-2032), located next to the Sarasota Convention and Visitors Bureau information office. This newly renovated center contains three galleries, presenting the area's largest display of art by national and local artists, from paintings and pottery to sculpture, cartoons, jewelry, and enamelware. There are also art demonstrations and special events. Admission is free; hours are Monday through Friday from 10am to 4pm and on Saturday and Sunday from 1 to 4pm.

SPORTS & RECREATION
Spectator Sports

BASEBALL   Sarasota is the winter home of the Chicago White Sox who are at the **Ed Smith Stadium,** 2700 12th St., at Tuttle Avenue (tel. 954-7699), for spring training during March and April. East of downtown, this stadium seats 7,500 fans. Admission is $5 to $9.

DOG RACING   At the **Sarasota Kennel Club,** 5400 Bradenton Rd. (tel. 355-7744), you can "go to the dogs" and watch these sleek greyhounds in action. The club is located two blocks east of the Ringling Museum Complex, off De Soto Road. Admission is $1 per person and there are races December to June, Monday through Saturday at 7:30pm, with matinees on Monday, Wednesday, and Saturday at noon.

Recreation

With its flat, shady terrain beside the Gulf of Mexico and Sarasota Bay, Sarasota is natural turf for bicycling, walking, and many water sports.

BICYCLING   **Fun Rentals of Siesta Key,** 5254 Ocean Blvd. (tel. 346-0900), rents bicycles, ranging from standard models to 10-speeds, 18- and 21-speed mountain bikes, tandems, two- and four-passenger surreys, and duo cycles. Prices begin at $5 per hour, $18 a day, and $45 per week. Moped/scooters are also rented; prices are $15 per hour, $40 a day, $45 per week. It's open daily from 8:30am to 5:30pm.

Situated just east of downtown, the **Sarasota Bicycle Center,** 4084 Bee Ridge Rd. (tel. 377-4505), rents bikes of various types, from 3- to 10-speed, for $15 a day, $30 per week, or $50 for two weeks. It's open Monday through Saturday from 9am to 6pm.

BOAT RENTALS   **All Watersports,** Boatyard Shopping Village, 1504 Stickney Point Rd. (tel. 921-2754), rents personal watercraft (waverunners, jet boats, jet skis) for $45 to $65 per hour, as well as speedboats, runabouts, and bowriders beginning at $20 per hour. Parasail rides can also be arranged at $40 for 15-minute rides. Situated on the approach to Siesta Key, it's open daily from 10am to 7pm.

Cannons Marina, 6040 Gulf of Mexico Dr. (tel. 383-1311), on the end of Longboat Key, rents 14- to 24-foot runabout speedboats that cost $65 to $195 for a half day and $90 to $265 for a full day. Pontoons can be rented for $100 to $140 for a half day and $135 to $175 for a full day. Open skiffs are $40 for a half day and $55 for a full day. Waterskis are $25 for a full day. It's open daily from 8am to 5:30pm.

Mr. C. B.'s, 1249 Stickney Point Rd. (tel. 349-4400), is located beside the Stickney Point Bridge; 16- to 18-foot runabouts and 24-foot pontoons can be rented for bay fishing and cruising. Runabouts cost $75 to $90 for four hours, $110 to $130 for a full day; pontoons are $100 for four hours, $160 for a full day. Bicycles can also be rented, beginning at $10 a day. It's open daily from 7am to 6pm.

FISHING   **Capt. Joe Bonaro,** Midnight Pass Marina, Siesta Key (tel. 349-3119), takes small groups of up to six passengers for deep-sea fishing excursions aboard the *Rumrunner,* a 36-foot custom-built fishing boat, docked across from Turtle Beach. Prices are $50 per person for a half day and $80 for a full day. It departs daily, by reservation only.

For other fishing excursions, try the **Flying Fish Fleet,** Marina Jack's Marina, U.S. 41 at Island Park Circle (tel. 366-3373). Docked along the bayfront of downtown, these boats offer deep-sea fishing excursions—half-day, full-day, or six-hour trips. Bait and tackle are furnished. Prices for half-day trips are $20 for adults, $15 for seniors, and $12 for children; six-hour trips are $25 for adults, $20 for seniors, and $15 for children; all-day trips are $30 for adults, $25 for seniors, and $20 for children.

Monday through Saturday, half-day trips are scheduled for 8am to 12:30pm and 1 to 5:30pm; on Sunday, from 1 to 5:30pm. The six-hour trip is offered Sunday through Tuesday and on Thursday and Friday from 9am to 3pm. The all-day trip takes place on Wednesday and Saturday from 9am to 5pm, and the sunset trip is on Tuesday and Friday from 4 to 8:30pm.

GOLF The **Bobby Jones Golf Complex,** 1000 Azinger Way, off Circus Boulevard (tel. 955-8097), is Sarasota's largest public course, with two 18-hole championship layouts (par 72 and par 71) and a 9-hole executive course (par 30). Three-day advance tee times are accepted. Prices include carts and are $26 from November to April and $17 from May to October. It's open daily from 7am to dusk.

    Rolling Green Golf Club, 4501 Tuttle Ave. (tel. 355-6620), is an 18-hole, par-72 course with wide-open fairways. Facilities include a driving range, rental clubs, and lessons. Tee times are assigned two days in advance. Prices, including cart, are $30 arriving before noon, $24 arriving after noon. Open daily from 7am to dusk.

    The **Sarasota Golf Club,** 7820 N. Leewynn Dr. (tel. 371-2431), is an 18-hole, par-72 course that requires that tee times be arranged at least three days in advance. Facilities include a driving range, lessons, and club rentals. Prices, including carts, are $30 arriving before noon and $24 arriving after noon. It's open daily from 7am to dusk.

SWIMMING Sarasota's beaches are known worldwide for their fine white powdery sands and clear turquoise waters. Some of the most popular public beaches include Lido Beach, North Lido Beach, and South Lido Beach on Lido Key; and Siesta Beach, Crescent Beach, and Turtle Beach on Siesta Key.

TENNIS **Sarasota Civic Center Municipal Courts,** 901 N. Tamiami Trail (tel. 364-4605), is a downtown public facility with six Har-Tru tennis courts, available for play on a first-come, first-served basis. The price is $4.30 per person per hour. It's open daily from 8am to 9pm. Four other hard courts are located east of downtown at the **Forest Lakes Tennis Club,** 2401 Beneva Rd. (tel. 922-0660). A pro shop and lessons are available. The price is $4 per person for 1½ hours of play. It's open Monday through Saturday from 9am to 6pm.

WATER SPORTS Situated on the bayfront downtown, **O'Leary's,** Island Park Marina, Island Park Circle (tel. 953-7505), rents jet skis and offers sailing lessons and other water-sports activities by appointment. The price of jet skiing is $35 per half hour, $50 per hour. It's open daily from 8am to 8pm.

    Sweet Water Kayaks, 5254 Ocean Blvd. (tel. 346-0900), rents fully equipped sea kayaks and touring open-top kayaks for use in the gulf bays and Intracoastal Waterway. Prices range from $20 per hour for one person or $25 per hour for two people to $50 and $60 per day, respectively. It's open daily from 8:30am to 5:30pm.

BAY CRUISES

Le Barge, Marina Jack's Marina, U.S. 41 at Island Park Circle (tel. 366-6116), offers two-hour cruises around Sarasota's waterways aboard a 65-foot two-deck vessel from October to May. The hours for the sunset cruise change with the time of sunset, and leave Tuesday through Sunday between 5 and 7pm. The early-afternoon cruise departs daily, from 2 to 4pm. Both cruises cost $8.50 for adults and $4.50 for children 12 and under.

    The 41-foot, 12-passenger sailboat *Enterprise,* Marina Jack's Marina, U.S. 41 at Island Park Circle (tel. 951-1833), cruises the waters of both Sarasota Bay and the Gulf of Mexico. The three-hour half-day cruise departs daily at 8:30am and 12:45pm and costs $35; the two-hour sunset cruise departs daily at 4:45pm and costs $20.

WHERE TO STAY

Sarasota is a city of new hotels and motels, divided equally between the downtown area and the beach strip. Rates are at their highest from December to April and can be downright bargains from May to November. Rates are usually slightly higher along the beaches at all times, so bargain hunters flock to the downtown area and commute to the beach.

DOWNTOWN/MAINLAND
Expensive

HYATT, 1000 Blvd. of the Arts, Sarasota, FL 34236. Tel. 813/366-9000, or toll free 800/233-1234. Fax 813/952-1987. 297 rms. A/C TV TEL
$ Rates: $85–$205 single or double. AE, CB, DC, DISC, MC, V.

Located beside Sarasota Bay and boasting its own marina, this 10-story tower is the downtown area's centerpiece hotel. It sits adjacent to the Civic Center, the Van Wezel Performing Arts Hall, and the Sarasota Garden Club, and is within walking distance of downtown shops. The bedrooms, most of which have balconies and overlook the marina or bay, are decorated in contemporary style with soft beige and beach tones.

Dining/Entertainment: The main restaurant is Pompano Cay, known for seafood; the Boathouse offers casual fare and water views of the marina; and Tropics Lounge provides libations.

Services: Complimentary airport shuttle (6am to 10pm), room service, valet laundry.

Facilities: Heated outdoor swimming pool, patio, health club, marina.

Inexpensive

COMFORT INN, 4800 N. Tamiami Trail, Sarasota, FL 34234. Tel. 813/355-7091, or toll free 800/221-2222. Fax 813/359-1639. 72 rms. A/C TV TEL
$ Rates (including continental breakfast): $45–$80 single; $50–$90 double. AE, CB, DC, DISC, MC, V.

Just half a mile south of the airport, this two-story hacienda-style motel is set back from the main road in a palm-tree-shaded setting. The bedrooms have contemporary furnishings, with light woods, pastel tones, and mica accessories. Facilities include a coffee shop, heated outdoor swimming pool, and sauna.

HAMPTON INN, 5000 N. Tamiami Trail, Sarasota, FL 34234. Tel. 813/351-7734, or toll free 800/336-9335. Fax 813/351-8820. 97 rms. A/C TV TEL
$ Rates (including continental breakfast): $51–$64 single; $61–$74 double. AE, CB, DC, DISC, MC, V.

One of the closest downtown hotels south of the airport (a quarter mile away), this three-story hostelry sits on its own grounds in a quiet garden setting. The bedrooms, offering a choice of king-size or double beds, are decorated in pastel tones, with light-wood furnishings. Facilities include a heated swimming pool and a guest laundry.

WELLESLEY INN, 1803 N. Tamiami Trail, Sarasota, FL 34234. Tel. 813/366-5128, or toll free 800/444-8888. Fax 813/953-4322. 106 rms. A/C TV TEL
$ Rates (including continental breakfast): $40–$100 single or double. AE, DISC, MC, V.

Situated just north of the downtown district on the main thoroughfare, this imposing four-story hotel overlooks a marina and boatyard. A welcoming ambience prevails in the elegant lobby area, filled with plants and comfortable seating. The bedrooms are spacious with standard furnishings of light woods and pastel tones, many with views of the marina. Facilities include valet service, an outdoor heated swimming pool, and complimentary airport shuttle.

THE KEYS/ISLANDS
Expensive

AZURE TIDES, 1330 Ben Franklin Dr., Lido Beach, Sarasota, FL 34236. Tel. 813/388-2102. Fax 813/388-3015. 34 suites. A/C TV TEL
$ Rates: $105–$289 suite for one or two. MC, V.

Set on 160 feet of private beachfront overlooking the gulf, this two- and three-story Key West–style property offers one- and two-bedroom suites with fully outfitted kitchens, sleeper sofas, and videocasette recorders. Each unit has custom-designed art deco–style furnishings of light woods, pastel fabrics, mirrored closets, and batik wall hangings. Living/dining areas have airy skylit cathedral ceilings and each unit has a patio or balcony. Facilities and services include a heated outdoor swimming pool, deck, cabañas on the beach, a beach bar, concierge, valet service, and a VCR film library. Off-season specials dip as low as $49 per night.

CRESCENT VIEW BEACH CLUB, 6512 Midnight Pass Rd., Siesta Key, Sarasota, FL 34242. Tel. 813/349-2000, or toll free 800/344-7171. Fax 813/349-9748. 26 units. A/C TV TEL

$ Rates: $105–$195 efficiency; $150–$260 two-bedroom condo suite. AE, DISC, MC, V.

Enjoying a quiet setting on the gulf at Crescent Beach, this property is ideal for families or several couples traveling together. It offers two types of one- and two-bedroom apartments—condo suites facing the beach and gulf and efficiency units overlooking the pool or garden. All units are decorated in tropical teal tones with bright Florida fabrics and rattan furnishings; each has a living/dining area and a balcony. The smaller units have kitchenettes with microwave ovens and coffee makers; the condo suites have completely outfitted kitchens, with dishwasher. Facilities include a heated outdoor swimming pool and spa, picnic tables, barbecue grill, and a guest laundry.

HALF MOON BEACH CLUB, 2050 Ben Franklin Dr., Lido Key, Sarasota, FL 34236. Tel. 813/388-3694, or toll free 800/358-3245. Fax 813/388-1938. 85 rms. A/C TV TEL

$ Rates: Dec–Apr, $95–$225 single or double. May–Nov, $80–$150 single or double. MC, V.

Nestled in a quiet garden setting at the southern end of Lido Key, this two-story art deco–style hotel is right on the beach. The guest rooms, each of which has a patio or balcony with views of the pool or beach, are furnished with light woods, quilted fabrics, sea art and plants, and views of pool or beach. All units have a refrigerator and coffee maker, and some have kitchenettes with microwave ovens. Facilities include an indoor/outdoor restaurant, outdoor heated swimming pool, and volleyball and shuffleboard courts.

HOLIDAY INN, 233 Ben Franklin Dr., Lido Key, Sarasota, FL 34236. Tel. 813/388-3941, or toll free 800/HOLIDAY. Fax 813/388-4321. 140 rms. A/C TV TEL

$ Rates: May–Nov, $89–$149 single or double. Dec–Apr, $119–$219 single or double. AE, CB, DC, MC, V.

⭐ A stand-out along the beachfront, this modern seven-story hotel is directly across from Lido Beach and within walking distance of St. Armands Circle. Bedrooms, all of which have balconies and face the gulf or the bay, are furnished with light woods, pastel fabrics, and framed shell art.

Dining/Entertainment: For panoramic views of the Gulf of Mexico, try the rooftop Sand Dollar restaurant and lounge. Other outlets include the KoKoNuts Lobby Lounge and the casual Pool Bar.

Services: Room service, valet laundry.

Facilities: Outdoor swimming pool, sheltered crossover access to the beach.

HOLIDAY INN, 4949 Gulf of Mexico Dr., Longboat Key, FL 34228. Tel. 813/383-3771, or toll free 800/HOLIDAY. Fax 813/383-7871. 146 rms. A/C TV TEL

$ Rates: $108–$179 single; $118–$189 double. AE, CB, DC, DISC, MC, V.

This three-story hotel, sitting on a stretch of private beach, has a tropical ambience. Most of the guest rooms surround a central "Holidome" courtyard with a pool and recreation facilities. Many rooms also have views of the gulf. The decor emphasizes ˜ªl fabrics of raspberry, peach, and teal tones and light woods.

˜**ng/Entertainment:** Choices include the Crest Dining Room, specializing in , the Crest Café, for light fare overlooking the central Holidome; and the Beach ˜ormy's Lounge, and Crow's Nest Lounge for libations.

ervices: Room service, valet laundry.

Facilities: Outdoor and indoor heated swimming pools, private beach, whirlpool, sauna, massage/tanning salon, games room, four lighted tennis courts, pro shop, water-sports equipment rentals.

LONGBOAT KEY HILTON, 4711 Gulf of Mexico Dr., Longboat Key, FL 34228. Tel. 813/383-2451, or toll free 800/282-3046. Fax 813/383-7979. 80 rms, 20 suites. A/C MINIBAR TV TEL

$ Rates: May–Nov, $109–$209 single or double; $175–$275 suite. Dec–Apr, $159–$249 single or double; $235–$315 suite. AE, DC, MC, V.

Surrounded by lush foliage and gardens, this five-story property, which sits directly on the gulf, is the poshest of the chain hotels on Longboat Key. The bedrooms, accessible by computer-card keys, are furnished in a Florida-style decor, with light woods, pastel fabrics, and rattan touches. Most units have a balcony or patio.

Dining/Entertainment: The main restaurant is the Sunset Bay Grille & Lounge, offering great views of the gulf and seafood. Seascapes is a poolside bar for lunch or beverages.

Services: Room service, valet laundry, shuttle to St. Armands Key for shopping.

Facilities: Heated outdoor swimming pool, private beach, water-sports equipment rentals, tennis courts, shuffleboard.

Inexpensive

BEST WESTERN SIESTA BEACH RESORT, 5311 Ocean Blvd., Siesta Key, Sarasota, FL 34242. Tel. 813/349-3211, or toll free 800/223-5786. Fax 813/349-7915. 59 rms. A/C TV TEL

$ Rates: $79–$129 single or double. AE, CB, DC, DISC, MC, V.

Newly renovated in late 1992, this modern two-story motel is the only major chain affiliate on this island. Situated across the road from Siesta Beach, it is laid out in a two-building configuration, with 44 rooms in one and 15 in the other; each unit is decorated in pastel tones with light woods, and a few have kitchenettes. Facilities include a heated swimming pool, Jacuzzi, guest laundry, and shuffleboard court.

GULF SUN MOTEL, 6722 Midnight Pass Rd., Siesta Key, Sarasota, FL 34242. Tel. 813/349-2442, or toll free 800/653-6753. Fax 813/349-7141. 2 rms, 15 efficiencies. A/C TV TEL

$ Rates: $52–$95 single or double; $64–$135 efficiency. MC, V.

Nestled in a palm-tree-shaded garden setting, this well-kept motel is not on the gulf front, but within walking distance of Crescent Beach. Bedrooms have standard furnishings with queen-size beds and refrigerators; some units are efficiencies with kitchens. Facilities include a private swimming pool and barbecue equipment.

WHERE TO DINE

DOWNTOWN/MAINLAND

Expensive

BIJOU CAFE, 1287 1st St. Tel. 366-8111.
Cuisine: INTERNATIONAL. **Reservations:** Recommended.
$ Prices: Main courses $13.95–$21.95. AE, CB, DC, MC, V.
Open: Lunch Mon–Fri 11:30am–2pm; dinner daily 5–11pm. **Closed:** Sun June–Aug.

Situated in the heart of the theater district at the corner of Pineapple Avenue, this bistro-style restaurant is bright and airy, with crisp linens, brass fixtures, floral paintings, and leafy plants. The innovative menu includes prime veal Louisville (with crushed pecans and bourbon-pear sauce), sautéed red snapper, New Orleans crab cakes, charcoal-grilled swordfish, roast duckling with ruby port-orange sauce, and Black Angus peppered steak.

CARMICHAEL'S, 1213 N. Palm Ave., at U.S. 41. Tel. 951-1771.

Cuisine: AMERICAN. **Reservations:** Recommended.
$ Prices: Main courses $16.95–$19.95. AE, DC, DISC, MC, V.
Open: Dinner only, Mon–Sat 6–10pm.

Housed in a historic 1920s Spanish-style hacienda, in the heart of the art and theater district, this festive Florida-pink restaurant is filled with antiques. But the prime draw is the menu, which emphasizes regional cuisine and unique sauces blended from vegetable roux and natural fruit juices, free of butter, fat, and flour. The house specialty is filet of High Sierra buffalo, pan-braised with wild alpine mushrooms, lingonberries, and herbs. Other choices include Key West yellowtail snapper, Pacific Northwest salmon in a crust of herbal Wisconsin butter, and fettuccine with Colorado lamb and homemade pheasant sausage.

CHEZ SYLVIE, 1526 Main St. Tel. 953-3232.

Cuisine: FRENCH. **Reservations:** Recommended.
$ Prices: Main courses $16–$26. CB, DC, MC, V.
Open: Lunch Wed–Sat 11:30am–3pm; dinner Tues–Sat 5:30–10pm.

Under the careful supervision of Sylvie Routier, this shopfront bistro adds a touch of France to the downtown area. With classical music playing in the background and a French provincial decor, this restaurant offers an ever-changing menu ranging from rack of lamb, filet mignon, and free-range baby veal to jumbo sea scallops.

RISTORANTE BELLINI, 1551 Main St. Tel. 365-7380.

Cuisine: NORTHERN ITALIAN. **Reservations:** Recommended.
$ Prices: Main courses $12.95–$21.95. DISC, MC, V.
Open: Lunch Mon–Fri 11:30am–2pm; dinner Mon–Sat 6–10pm.

With a decor reminiscent of Venice, this midtown shopfront restaurant produces top-class cooked-to-order pastas and main dishes. In addition to universal favorites such as chicken cacciatore and saltimbocca, the menu includes such creative choices as scaloppine Bellini (veal topped with asparagus and mozzarella), roasted quail wrapped in bacon, breast of chicken topped with smoked salmon and mozzarella, and snapper sautéed with fresh tomato-basil olive oil.

Moderate

CAFE OF THE ARTS, 5230 N. Tamiami Trail. Tel. 351-4304.

Cuisine: INTERNATIONAL. **Reservations:** Recommended for dinner.
$ Prices: Main courses $10.95–$19.95. AE, MC, V.
Open: Breakfast daily 8–11am; lunch daily 11am–3pm; light lunch daily 3–5pm; dinner daily 5–9pm.

Situated across from the Ringling complex, this small cottage-style bistro/ bakery offers an artsy European ambience, with photos of entertainers and scenes of Europe on the walls, classical music in the background, and lots of leafy plants and flowers. Dinner dishes range from such signature dishes as breast of chicken of the arts (with Oriental sesame-seed sauce and roasted peppers) to duck à l'orange, veal francese, beef burgundy, steak Diane, rack of lamb, salmon Florentine, and bouillabaisse. Lunch offers choices with a French flair such as pastries, pâtés, quiches, croissant sandwiches, and cheese and fruit plates.

CARAGIULOS, 69 S. Palm Ave. Tel. 951-0866.

Cuisine: ITALIAN. **Reservations:** Not accepted.
$ Prices: Main courses $5.95–$13.95. CB, DC, MC, V.
Open: Mon–Thurs 11am–10pm, Fri–Sat 11am–11pm, Sun 4–9pm.

Housed in the historic MiraMar Hotel building in the downtown theater district, this informal street-level indoor-outdoor restaurant offers menu choices such as shrimp Fra Diavolo, chicken Florentine, veal piccata, and eggplant rollatini, plus gourmet pizzas, pastas, sandwiches, and salads.

COASTERS SEAFOOD BISTRO, 1500 Stickney Point Rd. Tel. 923-4848.

Cuisine: SEAFOOD. **Reservations:** Recommended.
$ Prices: Main courses $11.95–$18.95. AE, DC, DISC, MC, V.
Open: Daily 11:30am–1:30pm.

In the Sarasota Boatyard Shopping Village on the east side of the bay, this informal restaurant offers great water views and a variety of settings, from an indoor brasserie-style dining room to an outdoor sun deck and waterfront patio. The menu includes such choices as mustard grouper, conch fritters, Cajun scallops, baked stuffed shrimp, and baby lobster tails, plus beef and ribs, chicken, and pastas. The raw bar is particularly noteworthy.

JACK'S CHOPHOUSE, 214 Sarasota Quay. Tel. 951-2467.

Cuisine: AMERICAN. **Reservations:** Recommended.
$ Prices: Main courses $9.95–$19.95. AE, MC, V.
Open: Lunch Mon–Fri 11:30am–2pm; dinner Sun–Thurs 5–10pm, Fri–Sat 5–11pm; brunch Sun 11:30am–2:30pm.

Situated overlooking the Sarasota Bay marina, this restaurant offers expansive water views in a clubby, art deco, bilevel indoor setting and on an outdoor terrace. The menu offers culinary classics such as chateaubriand or rack of lamb, as well as such innovative choices as sesame-crusted Atlantic salmon; oak-grilled filet mignon; strudel pastry filled with shrimp, crab, scallops, and corn salsa in a lobster sauce; and boneless crispy duck dressed in pecan stuffing and seasonal fruit sauce. The downstairs bar is known for its jazz sessions.

JIM'S CAFE ST. LOUIE, 1258 N. Palm Ave. Tel. 955-8550.

Cuisine: AMERICAN. **Reservations:** Recommended.
$ Prices: Main courses $11.95–$21.95. AE, DC, MC, V.
Open: Dinner only, daily 4pm–midnight.

A theatrical atmosphere prevails at this chic downtown restaurant overlooking Coconut Avenue. The menu features prime rib, charcoal-grilled steaks, lamb chops, shrimp scampi, and surf and turf. After dinner, relax with a drink at the piano bar.

MARINA JACK, 2 Marina Plaza, Island Park. Tel. 365-4232.

Cuisine: SEAFOOD. **Reservations:** Recommended.
$ Prices: Main courses $8.95–$21.95. AE, MC, V.
Open: Lunch daily noon–3pm; dinner daily 5–10pm.

Overlooking the waterfront with a wraparound 270° view of Sarasota Bay and Siesta and Lido Keys, this restaurant is synonymous with seafood. The menu offers fresh native fish such as grouper, red snapper, swordfish, tuna, and dolphin, prepared charcoal-grilled, pan-seared, blackened, or sautéed. In addition, there are half a dozen shrimp selections, crab-stuffed roughy, and Caribbean lobster, as well as steaks, chicken, and pastas.

If you prefer to be on the water when you dine, this restaurant also operates the *Marina Jack II*, a paddlewheel sightseeing boat, offering lunch and dinner cruises. For information and reservations, call 366-9255 (October through August).

NICK'S ON THE WATER, 230 Sarasota Quay. Tel. 954-3839.

Cuisine: ITALIAN. **Reservations:** Recommended.
$ Prices: Main courses $5.95–$16.95. AE, DISC, MC, V.
Open: Lunch Mon–Sat 11:30am–4pm; dinner Mon–Thurs 4–10pm, Fri–Sat 4–11pm, Sun noon–9pm.

One of the many fine-dining choices in the Sarasota Quay complex, this indoor/outdoor spot is really two restaurants in one—a terrace overlooking the marina, and a wine bar with a vineyard ambience. The menu offers pizzas and pastas as well as such dishes as rigatoni à la vodka, calamari or shrimp marinara, sweet or hot scungilli, steak pizzaiola, osso buco, and Nick's "chef's special" of veal medallions with melted cheese, mushrooms, and prosciutto.

OLD HICKORY, 5100 N. Tamiami Trail. Tel. 355-8757.

Cuisine: AMERICAN. **Reservations:** Accepted only for parties of 10 or more.
$ Prices: Main courses $5.95–$12.95. AE, MC, V.
Open: Mon–Sat 11:30am–10:30pm.

Reputed to be Sarasota's oldest restaurant (established in 1949), this casual place is situated on the main thoroughfare, north of downtown. The menu focuses on steaks cut daily on the premises, as well as barbecued meats cooked on hickory wood producing a genuine smoked flavor, with choices such as ribs, and chicken, plus broiled fish, butterfly shrimp, and cornbreaded catfish. This restaurant is also known for its soup-and-salad bar, included with all main courses.

PATRICK'S, 1400 Main St. Tel. 952-1170.
  Cuisine: AMERICAN. **Reservations:** Not accepted.
  $ Prices: Main courses $10.95–$16.95. AE, MC, V.
  Open: Daily 11am–1am.

With a semicircular facade, this informal New York–style brasserie offers wide-windowed views of downtown at the corner of Main Street and Central Avenue. The decor blends brass fixtures and tiled floors with hanging plants and ceiling fans, plus a unique collection of sporting memorabilia, including sculptures of baseball players and referees. The menu offers steaks and chops, burgers, seafood, pastas, salads, sandwiches, and omelets, as well as such specialties as veal piccata, francese, or marsala; broiled salmon with dill-hollandaise sauce; shrimp de Jonghe; and sesame chicken.

Budget

MRS. APPLETON'S FAMILY BUFFET, 4458 Bee Ridge Rd. Tel. 378-1177.
  Cuisine: AMERICAN. **Reservations:** Not accepted.
  $ Prices: Lunch buffet $4.95; dinner buffet $6.95. CB, DC, DISC, MC, V.
  Open: Lunch Mon–Sat 11:30am–3:30pm; dinner Mon–Sat 4–8:30pm, Sun 11am–8:30pm.

A sumptuous rotating buffet is the big draw at this restaurant, particularly popular with seniors. The selection changes daily but usually includes carved roast beef, lamb, turkey, pork, corned beef, or ham; fried chicken; barbecued beef ribs; baked fish; and lots of vegetables and salads, as well as desserts and a sundae bar.

SHELLS, 7253 S. Tamiami Trail. Tel. 924-2568.
  Cuisine: SEAFOOD. **Reservations:** Not accepted.
  $ Prices: Main courses $4.95–$13.95. AE, MC, V.
  Open: Dinner only, Sun–Thurs 5–10pm, Fri–Sat 5–11pm.

Synonymous with fresh seafood at low prices, this restaurant is part of a Tampa-based chain. This branch is situated on the main thoroughfare two miles south of downtown. For a description of the menu, see "Where to Dine" in the Tampa section.

YODER'S, 3434 Bahia Vista St. Tel. 955-7771.
  Cuisine: AMISH. **Reservations:** Not accepted.
  $ Prices: Main courses $4.95–$9.95. No credit cards.
  Open: Mon–Sat 6am–8pm.

It's worth a slight detour about three miles east of downtown to sample this family-run award-winning eatery. The menu emphasizes made-from-scratch Amish cooking including home-style pot roast, meatloaf, baked and southern fried chicken, cabbage rolls, and country-smoked ham, as well as filet of flounder or prime rib. Burgers, salads, soups, and sandwiches are also available. Two dozen types of homemade pies are on the dessert list, including traditional cream pies and shoo-fly, strawberry rhubarb, chocolate peanut butter, and key lime.

THE KEYS/ISLANDS
Expensive

CAFE L'EUROPE, 431 St. Armands Circle, St. Armands Key. Tel. 388-4415.
  Cuisine: CONTINENTAL. **Reservations:** Recommended.
  $ Prices: Main courses $13.95–$29.95. AE, CB, DC, MC, V.
  Open: Lunch Mon–Sat 11am–3pm; dinner Mon–Sat 5–11pm, Sun 5–10pm.

As its name implies, a European atmosphere prevails at this popular restaurant, with a decor of brick walls and arches, dark woods, beamed ceilings, brass fixtures, pink linens, and hanging plants. The menu offers selections ranging from steak tartare, rack of lamb, wienerschnitzel, roast duckling with cherry-cognac sauce, and veal Frangelico to bouillabaisse marseillaise, sautéed sweetbreads with wild mushrooms, and whole Dover sole meunière.

CHARLEY'S CRAB, 420 St. Armands Circle, St. Armands Key. Tel. 388-3964.
   Cuisine: SEAFOOD. **Reservations:** Recommended.
$ **Prices:** Main courses $8.95–$24.95. AE, MC, V.
   Open: Lunch Mon–Sat 11:30am–2:30pm, Sun noon–2:30pm; dinner Sun–Thurs 5–10pm, Fri–Sat 5–10:30pm.
Live piano music adds to the lively atmosphere at this informal indoor/outdoor restaurant. As you might expect, the specialty of the house is crab—particularly lump crab cakes and crab claws. In addition, the menu includes lobster, yellowfin tuna, Lake Superior whitefish, Atlantic swordfish, sautéed walleye, and lake trout, as well as steaks, veal, pork, and chicken.

CHART HOUSE, 201 Gulf of Mexico Dr., Longboat Key. Tel. 383-5593.
   Cuisine: AMERICAN. **Reservations:** Recommended.
$ **Prices:** Main courses $15.95–$24.95. AE, DC, MC, V.
   Open: Dinner only, daily 5–10pm.
Situated overlooking the Gulf of Mexico on the southern tip of Longboat Key, this restaurant offers panoramic views and a menu concentrating on various cuts of steak and prime ribs. In addition, there's a wide selection of seafood, including lobster tails, swordfish, mahi-mahi, shrimp, salmon, and stone crab. All dishes include unlimited helpings from a sumptuous salad bar.

Moderate

THE COLUMBIA, St. Armands Circle, St. Armands Key. Tel. 388-3987.
   Cuisine: SPANISH. **Reservations:** Recommended.
$ **Prices:** Main courses $12.95–$21.95. AE, CB, DC, DISC, MC, V.
   Open: Mon–Sat 11am–11pm, Sun noon–10pm.
A branch of the highly successful restaurant of the same name that originated in Ybor City, this place has a distinctive Iberian ambience.
   Try the red snapper Alicante, baked in a casserole along with onions and peppers and topped with almonds, or the filet mignon Columbia. All main dishes include Cuban bread and rice or potato. For a complete description of the menu, see "Where to Dine" in the Tampa section.

HEMINGWAY'S, 325 John Ringling Blvd., St. Armands Circle, St. Armands Key. Tel. 388-3948.
   Cuisine: REGIONAL. **Reservations:** Recommended.
$ **Prices:** Main courses $10.95–$19.95. AE, MC, V.
   Open: Lunch daily 11:30am–4pm; dinner Sun–Thurs 4–10pm, Fri–Sat 4–11pm.
With an airy and plant-filled Key West atmosphere, this informal second-floor restaurant overlooks St. Armands Circle, with both indoor and outdoor seating. The menu offers choices such as Key West pepper steak, lobster, Key Largo chicken (with bacon, broccoli, and cheese on linguine), coconut fried shrimp, grouper Oscar, and surf and turf.

MOORE'S STONE CRAB, 800 Broadway, Longboat Key. Tel. 383-1748.
   Cuisine: SEAFOOD. **Reservations:** Not accepted.
$ **Prices:** Main courses $7.95–$19.95. MC, V.
   Open: Sun–Thurs 11:30am–9pm, Fri–Sat 11:30am–9:30pm. **Closed:** May 16–Oct 14.
Overlooking Sarasota Bay on the north end of Longboat Key, this popular 25-year-old seafood house began as an offshoot of a family seafood business established in 1927. Consequently, you'll hardly get fresher crab, since the restaurant still has its own boats and crab traps, and serves about 50,000 pounds of stone crab a year. The menu also features crab cakes and soft-shell crab as well as shrimp, scallops, Florida lobster, and other local fish. A few chicken and beef dishes round out the menu.

TURTLES, 8875 Midnight Pass Rd., Siesta Key. Tel. 346-2207.

Cuisine: AMERICAN. **Reservations:** Recommended.
$ Prices: Main courses $10.95–$15.95. AE, MC, V.
Open: Daily 11:30am–midnight.

Located across from Turtle Beach, this informal restaurant sits on Little Sarasota Bay, offering views of the water from tables both indoors and on an outside deck. The menu features dishes such as nut-crusted chicken breast, baked pink snapper, potato-crusted grouper, sautéed Dungeness crab cakes, and lobster and mushroom strudel, as well as rack of lamb and mango and ginger spiced ribs.

Budget

THE BUTTERY, 470 John Ringling Circle, St. Armands Key. Tel. 388-1523.

Cuisine: AMERICAN. **Reservations:** Not required.
$ Prices: Main courses $7–$10 at dinner. No credit cards.
Open: Daily 24 hours (dinner 5–10pm).

An ideal spot for breakfast, lunch, or a snack, this informal eatery also offers light dinner dishes such as petite sirloin or prime rib, mesquite-grilled breast of chicken, lime grouper, or lemon pepper catfish. Other items, available all day and night, include fruit-filled pancakes and waffles, omelets, burgers, sandwiches, salads, and finger foods.

Other branches are located at 5133 Ocean Blvd., Siesta Key (tel. 346-1343), open daily from 6am to 10pm; and 2833 Bee Ridge Rd. (tel. 923-5153), open 24 hours daily.

SHOPPING

Shopping in Sarasota is synonymous with **St. Armands Circle** on St. Armands Key, the "Rodeo Drive" or "Fifth Avenue" of Florida's west coast. Developed by John Ringling, it's a circle of more than 150 international boutiques, gift shops, galleries, restaurants, and nightspots, all surrounded by lush landscaping, patios, and antique statuary.

Downtown's main shopping focus is on **Sarasota Quay,** a new peach-toned and multilevel mixed-use facility housing shops and galleries amid a bayfront layout of piazzas and fountains.

Favorite shopping streets include historic **Palm Avenue** and **Main Street** downtown and **Avenue of the Flowers** off Gulf of Mexico Drive on Longboat Key. The area's largest enclosed mall is south of downtown at **Sarasota Square Mall,** 8201 S. Tamiami Trail at Beneva Road (tel. 922-9600). The city's largest and most interesting bookstore for browsers and shoppers alike is the **Main Bookshop,** 1962 Main St. (tel. 366-7653), open daily from 9am to 11pm.

EVENING ENTERTAINMENT

To get the latest update on what's happening during your visit, call the city's 24-hour **Artsline** (tel. 365-ARTS).

THE PERFORMING ARTS

Major Concert/Performance Halls

ASOLO CENTER FOR THE PERFORMING ARTS, 5555 N. Tamiami Trail. Tel. 351-8000.

Designated as the State Theater of Florida, this facility is home to the professional Asolo Theatre Company and the Conservatory for Professional Actor Training, the Sarasota French Film Festival, and Florida State University's Master of Fine Arts program in motion picture, television, and recording arts. The main stage is an attraction in itself—the former Dunfermline Opera House, originally constructed in Scotland in 1900 and transferred piece by piece to Sarasota in 1987. It replaced an earlier structure that had incorporated the original parts of an 18th-century Italian court theater. The Asolo presents a year-round program of plays, concerts, lectures, symposia, and art films. Free guided tours of the center are conducted Monday through Saturday at 10am, 10:30am, 11am, and 11:30am except from June to August and during technical rehearsals between plays; call in advance to check.

Admission: Tickets, $5–$40, depending on event.

VAN WEZEL PERFORMING ARTS HALL, 777 N. Tamiami Trail. Tel. 953-3366.

With a lavender seashell shape, this hall is visible for miles on the Sarasota skyline. It offers excellent visual and acoustic conditions, with year-round programs ranging from symphony and jazz concerts, opera, musical comedy, and choral productions to ballet and international performers. It's the home of the Florida West Coast Symphony, the Jazz Club of Sarasota, the Sarasota Ballet of Florida, and the Sarasota Concert Band.

Admission: Tickets, $12.50–$47.50.

Theaters

FLORIDA STUDIO THEATRE, 1241 N. Palm Ave. Tel. 366-9796.

Located downtown on the corner of Palm and Coconut Avenues, the Florida Studio Theatre presents innovative and experimental drama, Tuesday through Sunday year-round, and hosts a New Play Festival each May.

Admission: Tickets, $10–$25.

GOLDEN APPLE DINNER THEATRE, 25 N. Pineapple Ave. Tel. 366-5454.

This downtown theater presents cocktails, dinner, and a professional Broadway-style show, usually a musical, year-round daily except Monday.

Admission: Tickets, $26.50–$29 evening, $20.50 matinees.

THE OPERA HOUSE, 61 N. Pineapple Ave. Tel. 953-7030.

The Sarasota Opera performs here in February and March. Other companies including the Sarasota Ballet present their works during the rest of the year at this downtown venue.

Admission: Tickets, $15–$48.

THE PLAYERS OF SARASOTA, 838 N. Tamiami Trail. Tel. 365-2494.

Founded in 1930, this is Sarasota's longest-established theater, a community group presenting eight plays a year—a mix of comedies, musicals, and dramas—and a concert series featuring jazz, blues, and country music. The season runs from September through June, with evening performances Tuesday through Saturday and matinees on Sunday.

Admission: Tickets, $12–$15.

THEATRE WORKS, 1247 1st St. Tel. 952-9170.

Located downtown at Coconut Avenue, this professional non-Equity company presents musical revues and other works, year-round Tuesday through Saturday in the evening and matinees on Sunday.

Admission: Tickets, $7.50–$15.

THE CLUB & MUSIC SCENE

BUMPERS NIGHTCLUB, 1927 Ringling Blvd. Tel. 951-0335.

This club presents a variety of danceable pop dance music, with DJs spinning the tunes starting at 8:30pm Tuesday through Thursday. Live groups begin performing at 9pm on Friday and Saturday.

Admission: $3–$15.

DOWNUNDER JAZZ BAR, 214 Sarasota Quay. Tel. 951-2467.

Located at U.S. 41 and 3rd Street, this club is part of the innovative Sarasota Quay shopping and entertainment complex. It offers contemporary jazz, Sunday through Thursday from 9pm to 12:30am and Friday through Sunday from 9pm to 1:30am. Drinks run $2 to $4.

Admission: Free.

EMPHASIS CAFE & COFFEE HOUSE, 1301 1st St. Tel. 954-4085.

Situated opposite the Opera House, this bistro/gallery displays the work of well-known artists and craftspeople. In the evening it's a forum for contemporary poets and musicians, including the Sarasota Poetry Theater. Although it's open all day for food and drink, the evening gigs usually start at 8 or 9pm and run to 11:30pm Monday through Thursday, and until 12:30am on Friday and Saturday.
Admission: $5.

LIMERICK JUNCTION, 1296 1st St. Tel. 366-6366.

Situated around the corner from the Sarasota Opera House, this Irish-themed indoor/outdoor pub presents a variety of music (jazz, blues, rock, bluegrass, and more) Wednesday through Sunday, including authentic Irish music. Times vary, but performances usually run from 9pm to midnight or later.
Admission: $2–$3 for most music.

COCONUTS COMEDY CLUB, 8440 N. Tamiami Trail. Tel. 355-7771.

Well-known national and local comics perform at this club, north of downtown, at 9pm and 11pm on Friday and Saturday and 9pm on Sunday.
Admission: $7.

PATIO LOUNGE, St. Armands Circle, St. Armands Key. Tel. 388-3987.

One of the liveliest spots along the beach strip, the Patio Lounge features the Omni dance band performing high-energy dance music, Tuesday through Saturday from 9:30pm to 2am.
Admission: $3 on weekends.

PARADISE CAFE, 1311 1st St. Tel. 955-8500.

This popular downtown spot presents musical cabarets on Thursday, Friday, and Saturday at 8:30pm, and live piano music Tuesday through Saturday from 6pm.
Admission: $8 for cabaret; free for piano music.

---

4. BRADENTON

26 miles S of St. Petersburg, 41 miles SW of Tampa, 15 miles N of Sarasota

GETTING THERE   By Plane   Bradenton shares an airport with Sarasota. For full details on the Sarasota-Bradenton Airport, see the Sarasota section.

By Train   Amtrak trains arrive at the Tampa Amtrak station (see the Tampa section) and bus connections are provided to Bradenton.

By Bus   Greyhound buses arrive at the carrier's depot at 501 17th Ave. W., Bradenton (tel. 747-2984).

By Car   Bradenton is accessible from points north via the Sunshine Skyway Bridge (U.S. 19/I-275). Other north-south routes leading into Bradenton include I-75, U.S. 41, and U.S. 301. From the east, take Fla. 64 and Fla. 70.

Bradenton is a city edged by water—Tampa Bay, the Gulf of Mexico, and Intracoastal waters lie to the west, and the city is bordered on the north by the Manatee River, on the west by the Braden River, and on the south by Sarasota Bay. It's also a city of history, explored by the Spanish in the 16th century and eventually established over 100 years ago as the city of "Braidentown." It was named for the Braden brothers, Joseph and Hector, who settled the area in 1842. The superfluous "i" was added in error and remained in the name until 1903; 21 years later the "w" was dropped, giving the city its present name.

Although it has been touched by urban sprawl in recent years, this city still maintains some links with the past such as its historic "Old Main Street" (12th Street in today's city layout), and many Spanish-style buildings. Bradenton's star attraction, however, is Anna Maria Island, west of downtown. It's a 7½-mile stretch of sandy and tree-shaded beaches that rim the Gulf of Mexico. Legend has it that early Spanish settlers were so taken with the beauty of the island that they named it "Ana-Maria Cay," in honor of Mary, the mother of Christ, and her mother, Anne.

Today Bradenton is synonymous with the sweet aroma of fresh oranges in the air. As the home of Tropicana, this city of 40,000 people is a major producer of orange juice and citrus products, as well as other agricultural products such as tomatoes and ornamental plants.

ORIENTATION

ARRIVING

Van transport from the airport to hotels in Bradenton is provided by **West Coast Limousine** (tel. 813/355-9645). The price depends on the destination, but averages $10 to $15. Taxi companies in Bradenton include **Bruce's Taxi** (tel. 755-6070), **Checker Cab** (tel. 751-3181), and **Yellow Cab** (tel. 748-4800).

INFORMATION

For travel information about Bradenton, Anna Maria Island, and the surrounding Manatee County area, contact the **Greater Bradenton Convention & Visitors Bureau,** P.O. Box 1000, Bradenton, FL 34206 (tel. 813/729-9177, or toll free 800/4-MANATEE). The county also maintains walk-in **visitor centers** at the Civic Center, 1 Haben Blvd., off U.S. 301, Palmetto (tel. 813/729-9177) and at 5030 U.S. 301, Ellenton (tel. 813/729-7040).

CITY LAYOUT

Bradenton is laid out like a rectangle, with **U.S. 41** as a line of demarcation running through the center of the city in a north-south direction. All **"streets"** are numbered and run parallel to U.S. 41 in a north-south direction; and they are designated as "east" or "west" of that route.

"Avenues," which run east-west through U.S. 41, start at the Braden River and continue southward in ascending numerical order. Like the streets, avenues are also labeled as "east" or "west" of U.S. 41.

The basic core of downtown hugs the Manatee River near 12th Street. Originally known as Main Street, 12th Street (or "Old Main Street") today contains a row of historic old buildings leading to the Manatee River and a waterfront pier.

West of downtown is the **Intracoastal Waterway** and **Anna Maria Island.** The city is traversed in an east-west direction by two state roads—**Fla. 64** (also known as Manatee Avenue), crossing the north side of the city and **Fla. 684** (Cortez Road), crossing the southern sector. Two bridges, **Anna Maria Island Bridge** (on Fla. 64) and **Cortez Bridge** (on Fla. 684) connect Anna Maria Island to the mainland. Situated seven miles west of downtown between the Intracoastal Waterway and the Gulf of Mexico, this subtropical barrier island is 7½ miles long and a quarter of a mile to nearly 2 miles wide. It is composed of three island cities, Anna Maria to the north, Holmes Beach in the center, and Bradenton Beach to the south, and is accessible from the mainland via Fla. 64 and Fla. 684.

Cortez Island is on the east side of the Cortez Bridge, on the approach from the mainland to Bradenton Beach on Anna Maria Island.

GETTING AROUND

BY PUBLIC TRANSPORTATION [BUS] Manatee County Area Transit, known locally as **Manatee CAT** (tel. 749-7116), operates scheduled bus service throughout the area. The basic fare is $1 Monday through Friday and 50¢ on Saturday.

BY TAXI Taxi companies serving the Bradenton area include **Bruce's Taxi** (tel. 755-6070), **Dependable Cab** (tel. 749-0993), and **Yellow Cab** (tel. 748-4800).

BY CAR   Major rental-car companies maintain desks at the Sarasota-Bradenton Airport (see the Sarasota section).

FAST FACTS

Area Code   Bradenton's area code is 813.

Dentist   For emergency dental repairs, contact the Dentist Information Service (tel. 749-1472).

Doctors   Most hotels have a doctor on call; if not, contact Physician Referral Services at L. W. Blake Hospital (tel. 954-7445) or Manatee Memorial Hospital (tel. 745-7575).

Drugstores   There are at least half a dozen Walgreens Drug Stores in the Bradenton area, including one branch that operates a 24-hour prescription service at Cortez Commons, 5574 Cortez Rd. W. (tel. 792-3817).

Emergencies   Dial 911.

Hospitals   Try the Manatee Memorial Hospital, 206 2nd St. E. (tel. 746-5111), or L. W. Blake Hospital, 2020 59th St. W. (tel. 792-6611).

Library   The Central Library is located at 1301 Barcarrota Blvd. (tel. 748-5555).

Newspapers   The *Bradenton Herald* is published daily.

Post Office   The main post office is at 824 Manatee Ave. W. (tel. 746-4195).

Taxes   There's a 10% hotel tax, a 6% restaurant tax, and a local sales tax of 6%.

Transit Information   Call 749-7116.

WHAT TO SEE & DO

THE TOP ATTRACTIONS

ART LEAGUE OF MANATEE COUNTY, 209 9th St. W. Tel. 746-2862.
This gallery is Bradenton's downtown cultural hub. It offers an ever-changing program of art exhibits, shows, courses, workshops, and craft demonstrations.
Admission: Free.
Open: Mon–Fri 9am–4:30pm, Sat 10am–4pm, Sun 1–4pm.

DESOTO NATIONAL MEMORIAL PARK, DeSoto Memorial Hwy., 75th Street W. Tel. 792-0458.
Nestled on the Manatee River northwest of downtown, this park commemorates the Spanish explorer Hernándo de Soto's 1539 landing in Florida. Aiming to reflect the look and atmosphere you might have found here 400 years ago, it includes a restoration of de Soto's original campsite, and a scenic half-mile nature trail that circles a mangrove jungle and leads to the ruins of one of the first settlements of the area. From December through March, park employees dress in 16th-century costumes and portray the way the early settlers lived, including demonstrations of cooking and musket-firing.
Admission: Free.
Open: Daily 9am–5pm. **Directions:** Take Manatee Avenue (Fla. 64) west to 75th Street West and turn right; follow the road to its end and the entrance to the park.

GAMBLE PLANTATION, 3708 Patten Ave., Ellenton. Tel. 723-4536.
Situated northeast of downtown Bradenton, this is the oldest structure on the southwestern coast of Florida, and a fine example of an antebellum plantation home. Built over a six-year period in the late 1840s by Maj. Robert Gamble, it is constructed primarily of a primitive material known as "tabby" (a mixture of oyster shells, sand, molasses, and water), with 10 rooms, verandas on three sides, 18 exterior columns, and eight fireplaces. It is maintained as a state historic site, and includes a fine collection of 19th-century furnishings. Entrance into the house is by tour only, although the grounds may be explored independently.
Admission (including the tour): $2 adults, $1 children 6–12, free for kids under

Open: Thurs–Mon 9am–5pm; guided tours given at 9:30 and 10:30am, and 1, 2, 3, and 4pm. **Directions:** Take U.S. 301 north of downtown to Ellenton; the site is on the left at the juncture of U.S. 301 and Fla. 683 (Ellenton-Gillette Road).

MANATEE VILLAGE HISTORICAL PARK, Sixth Ave. E. and 15th St. E. Tel. 749-7165.

A tree-shaded park with a courtyard of hand-laid bricks, this national historic site features restored buildings from the city of Bradenton and the surrounding county. It contains the Manatee County Court House, dating back to 1860 and the oldest structure of its kind still standing on the south Florida mainland; a Methodist church built in 1887; a typical "Cracker Gothic" house built in 1912; and the Wiggins General Store, dating to 1903 and full of local memorabilia from swamp root and grub dust to louse powder, as well as antique furnishings and an art gallery.

Admission: Free; donations welcome.

Open: Mon–Fri 9am–4:30pm, Sun 1:30–4:30pm. **Closed:** Sun July–Aug. **Directions:** From U.S. 41, take Sixth Avenue East east to 15th Street East at the juncture of Manatee Avenue East.

SOUTH FLORIDA MUSEUM AND BISHOP PLANETARIUM, 201 10th St. W. Tel. 746-4131.

The story of Florida's history, from prehistoric times to the present, is told in exhibits including a Native American collection with life-size dioramas, a Spanish courtyard containing replicas of 16th-century buildings, and an indoor aquarium, the home of "Snooty," the oldest manatee (or sea cow) born in captivity (1948). The adjacent Bishop Planetarium features a 50-foot hemispherical dome with arcs above a seating area, for laser light shows and star-gazing activities.

Admission: $5.50 adults, $3.50 children 5–12, free for kids under 5.

Open: Tues–Sat 10am–5pm, Sun noon–6pm. **Directions:** From U.S. 41, take Manatee Avenue west to 9th Street West and turn right.

ANNA MARIA ISLAND MUSEUM, 402 Pine Ave., Anna Maria, Anna Maria Island. Tel. 778-0492.

Housed in a former 1920s ice house, this museum aims to present the history of Anna Maria Island. It contains memorabilia, maps, records, books, and photographs, plus collections indigenous to the island, such as shells, sand dollars, and a turtle display. It's situated adjacent to a historical landmark, the Old Anna Maria Jail.

Admission: Free.

Open: Sept–May, Tues–Thurs and Sat 10am–4pm; June–Aug, Tues, Thurs, and Sat 11am–2pm. **Directions:** Take Fla. 64 west to Fla. 789 (Gulf Drive) and turn right; continue north on Gulf Drive via Holmes Beach to Anna Maria, and turn right on to Pine Avenue.

PORT MANATEE, 13231 Eastern Ave., Palmetto. Tel. 722-6621.

Located north of downtown Bradenton on Tampa Bay, this is Florida's fourth-largest deepwater port, handling a wide variety of cargo, ranging from citrus concentrate and bananas to phosphate and petroleum. Tours are conducted by appointment.

Admission: Free.

Open: Year-round during business hours, by appointment.

ORGANIZED TOURS

BY BOAT The two-deck *Miss Cortez,* part of the Cortez Fleet, 12507 Cortez Rd., Cortez (tel. 794-1223), offers a 1½-hour narrated sightseeing cruise around Anna Maria Sound. It costs $6 for adults and $3 for children under 15, and departs Monday through Thursday at 3pm. There's also a 4-hour cruise along the Intracoastal Waterway to Egmont Key, a nearby tropical island where there's an opportunity to disembark for snorkeling and shelling. This cruise costs $12 for adults and $6 for children under 15, and departs Monday through Thursday at 10:30am.

Departing from Port Manatee, near the southern end of the Skyway Bridge north of Bradenton, **Regal Cruises,** Port Manatee, 13231 Eastern Ave., Palmetto (mailing address: 4199 34th St. S., St. Petersburg, FL 33711) (tel. 813/867-1300, or toll free 800/270-SAIL), offers six-hour cruises on the Gulf of Mexico aboard the eight-deck, 1,180-passenger *Regal Empress;* the cost begins at $29 per person. There are also overnight cruises (from $59 per person) and four-night trips to Mexico (from $299 per person).

BY TRAIN   See the sights of rural Manatee County northwest of Bradenton on a 1¼-hour narrated sightseeing tour on a 1950s diesel-engine train operated by the **Florida Gulf Coast Railroad,** 83rd Street East, off U.S. 301 in Parrish (tel. 776-3266). There's a choice of seating—in open-window coaches, air-conditioned lounge cars, or the caboose. Tickets, priced at $6 to $9 for adults, $4 to $5 for children 2 to 11, and free for children under 2—are sold on a first-come, first-served basis. Departures are on Saturday at 11am, 1pm, and 3pm; and on Sunday at 1 and 3pm.

SPORTS & RECREATION
Spectator Sports

BASEBALL   Located east of downtown, the 6,562-seat **McKechnie Field,** 9th Street and 17th Avenue West (tel. 748-4610), is the home of the Pittsburgh Pirates during its March-to-April spring-training season. Admission to games is $8 to $8.50.

POLO   The **Sarasota Polo Club,** 7550 Lorraine Rd., Bradenton (tel. 359-0000), a 26,000-acre ranching estate southeast of Bradenton, is the site of weekly polo matches November to April, on Sunday at 1pm. They're open to the public for an admission charge of $3.

Recreation

BOAT RENTALS   Situated on the east side of the Cortez Bridge, **Cortez Watercraft Rentals,** 4328 127th St. W. (tel. 792-5263), rents fishing, ski and pontoon boats, waverunners, and other equipment. Prices are $85 to $125 for fishing boats, $95 to $135 for ski boats, $105 to $155 for pontoon boats, and $25 to $45 per half hour for waverunners. It's open daily from 8am to 6pm.
   Captain's Marina, 5501 Marina Dr., Holmes Beach (tel. 778-1977), rents six-passenger 18-foot fishing boats, 10-passenger 21-foot pontoons, waterskis, and other watercraft. Fishing boats begin at $90 a half day and $135 for a full day; pontoons, at $115 for a half day and $155 for a full day. Waterskis are $20 per half day and $25 for a full day. It's open daily from 8am to 5pm.
   Five O'Clock Marine, 412 Pine Ave., Anna Maria Island (tel. 778-5577), rents fishing and speed boats of various sizes, accommodating two to seven passengers, for $50 to $100 per half day and $75 to $175 for a full day. As well, 10-passenger 28-foot pontoons begin at $80 per half day and $150 per day. It's open daily from 8am to 5pm.

FISHING   Whether you prefer to fish from a pier or a boat, Bradenton offers many opportunities. There is pier fishing at **Anna Maria City Pier** on the north end of Anna Maria Island, and at the **Bradenton Beach City Pier** at Cortez Road. Both are free of charge.
   For fishing in deep-sea waters, the **Cortez Fleet,** 12507 Cortez Rd., Cortez (tel. 794-1223), offers four-, six-, and nine-hour trips, departing from the east side of the Cortez Bridge. The boats are equipped with the latest in electronic fish finders, and rod, bait, and tackle are provided. Prices for a four-hour trip are $22.50 for adults, $20.50 for seniors, and $12 for children under 15; a six-hour trip costs $31.50 for adults, $28.50 for seniors, and $16.50 for children under 15; and a nine-hour trip is $38.50 for adults, $34.50 for seniors, and $20 for children under 15.
   Four-hour trips depart on Monday and Friday at 8am and 1pm; for six-hour trips, on Sunday, Tuesday, and Thursday at 9am; and for the nine-hour trips, on Wednesday and Saturday at 8am.

GOLF   The Greater Bradenton Convention & Visitors Bureau, P.O. Box 1000, Bradenton, FL 34206 (tel. 813/729-9177, or toll free 800/4-MANATEE) publishes a **"Golf Passport"** booklet to acquaint visitors with the particulars on area courses.

Available free of charge, the booklet also includes valuable coupons and discounts, valid from May to October, for playing golf at reduced rates or for buying golf equipment. Below are some golf courses that welcome visitors:

Situated just off U.S. 41, **Heather Hills Golf Club,** 101 Cortez Rd. W. (tel. 755-8888), operates an 18-hole, par-61 golf course on a first-come, first-served basis. There's a driving range and clubs can be rented. The price, including a cart, is $18.55 per person until 3pm and $12.75 after 3pm. It's open daily from 6:30am until dark. The **Manatee County Golf Course,** 5290 66th St. W. (tel. 792-6773), sports an 18-hole, par-72 course on the southern rim of the city and requires that tee times be set up at least two days in advance. They also have a driving range and golf clubs for rent. The price, including a cart, is $29 per person. It's open daily from 7am to dusk.

Located just north of Fla. 684 and east of Palma Sola Bay, the **Palma Sola Golf Club,** 3807 75th St. W. (tel. 792-7476), has an 18-hole, par-72 course which requires two-day advance booking for tee times. The charge is $30 per person, including a cart. It's open daily from 7am to dusk. The **River Run Golf Links,** 1801 27th St. E. (tel. 747-6331), set beside the Braden River, is another possibility. This 18-hole, par-70 course has lots of water in its layout. Two-day advance notice is required for tee times. Golf clubs can be rented. The price, including a cart, is $25 per person and it's open daily from 7am to dusk.

SWIMMING Swimming along safe and sandy beaches is a prime reason to visit the Bradenton area. There are four public beaches on Anna Maria Island: **Anna Maria Bayfront Park,** on Bay Boulevard at the northwest end of the island, fronting both the Intracoastal Waterway and the Gulf of Mexico; **Coquina Beach,** at the southwest end of Gulf Drive on Anna Maria Island, with a gulf and a bay side, sheltered by towering pines and palm trees; **Cortez Beach,** on Gulf Drive in Bradenton Beach, just north of Coquina Beach; and **Manatee County Public Beach,** at Gulf Drive, Holmes Beach, at the west end of Fla. 64.

TENNIS **Nick Bollettieri Tennis Academy,** 5500 34th St. W. (tel. 755-1000, or toll free 800/USA-NICK), is one of the world's largest tennis-training facilities, with over 75 championship courts, aerobic and sports training centers, video analysis, and a pro shop. Visitors can tune up on their tennis skills by enrolling in a one-day instructional program; three-day and one-week programs are also available for all age groups. The academy is open year-round and reservations are required for all activities. One-day instructional programs are $220 with overnight accommodations, $150 without boarding; a full day of play alone on courts is $75.

The **Walton Racquet Center,** 5512 33rd Ave. W. (tel. 749-7173), is a part of the county park system. The center has eight clay and eight hard courts. It's open Monday through Thursday from 8am to 9:45pm, on Friday from 8am to 7pm, and on Saturday and Sunday from 8am to 5:30pm. Prices are $2.40 per person for 1½ hours on hard courts, $4.40 on clay courts.

WHERE TO STAY

DOWNTOWN/MAINLAND

Moderate

HOLIDAY INN RIVERFRONT, 100 Riverfront Dr. W., Bradenton, FL 34205. Tel. 813/747-3727, or toll free 800/HOLIDAY. Fax 813/746-4289. 153 rms. A/C TV TEL

$ Rates: May–Nov, $79–$139 single or double. Dec–Apr, $115–$195 single or double. AE, CB, DC, DISC, MC, V.

Sporting a Spanish hacienda-style motif and overlooking the Manatee River, this five-story hotel stands out on the downtown skyline. The public areas also reflect an Iberian ambience, with dark woods, tile floors, and high beamed ceilings; an outdoor courtyard is full of palm trees, tropical flowers, lush foliage, and cascading fountains. Bedrooms are contemporary, with light woods and soft floral tones; all have balconies, with views of the river or the courtyard. Facilities include a Spanish-themed restaurant, a nautical-style lounge, a heated outdoor swimming pool, and room service.

Inexpensive

FIVE OAKS INN, 1102 Riverside Dr., Palmetto, FL 34221. Tel. 813/ 723-1236. 4 rms. A/C TEL
$ Rates (including breakfast): $55–$100 single or double. MC, V.

Across the Manatee River directly north of downtown, this stately Spanish-style bed-and-breakfast is surrounded by palm trees, oaks, and gardens overlooking the water. The bedrooms are individually decorated and named, offering a choice of king-size, queen-size, or twin-bed configurations. Guests enjoy use of a parlor with fireplace, and an enclosed wraparound solarium/sunporch filled with wicker and rattan furnishings.

PARK INN CLUB, 4450 47th St. W., Bradenton, FL 34210. Tel. 813/ 795-4633, or toll free 800/437-PARK. Fax 813/795-0808. 128 rms. A/C TV TEL
$ Rates (including continental breakfast): $55–$115 single or double. AE, DC, DISC, MC, V.

Nestled on its own well-landscaped grounds and set back from the main road along the busy Fla. 684 (Cortez Road) corridor, this three-story contemporary hotel is wrapped around a central courtyard with a patio and swimming pool. The spacious guest rooms are furnished in pastel tones with light woods. In addition to the pool, facilities include a lounge where guests are served breakfast and complimentary cocktails each evening.

ANNA MARIA ISLAND/BEACHES
Moderate

HARRINGTON HOUSE, 5626 Gulf Dr., Holmes Beach, FL 34217. Tel. 813/778-5444. 10 rms. A/C TV
$ Rates: $79–$159 single or double in the main house, $69–$159 single or double in the Beach House. MC, V.

In a tree-shaded setting on the beach overlooking the Gulf of Mexico, this three-story bed-and-breakfast exudes an Old Florida ambience. Built in 1925, it has been renovated and refurbished to the highest standard. The seven bedrooms are individually decorated with antiques, wicker, or rattan furnishings. Some units have four-poster or brass beds, and the higher-priced rooms have French doors leading to balconies overlooking the gulf. In addition to the bedrooms in the main house, three rooms are available in the adjacent Beach House, a 1920s captain's home recently remodeled and updated.

All guests enjoy use of the high-ceilinged living room with fireplace, an outdoor pool, patio, and complimentary use of bicycles, kayaks, and other sports equipment.

Inexpensive

CATALINA BEACH RESORT, 1325 Gulf Dr. N., Bradenton Beach, FL 34217. Tel. 813/778-6611. 31 rms. A/C TV TEL
$ Rates: $45–$99 single or double. AE, DC, MC, V.

Nestled in a shady spot across the street from the beach, this two-story Spanish-style motel offers well-kept rooms with modern furnishings and bright Florida colors, some with kitchenettes. Facilities include a restaurant, outdoor solar-heated swimming pool, barbecue grills, shuffleboard courts, guest laundry, fishing and boating dock, and water-sports rentals.

SAND & SEA MOTEL, 2412 Gulf Dr., Bradenton Beach, FL 34217. Tel. 813/778-2231. 30 rms. A/C TV TEL
$ Rates: $45–$95 single or double. MC, V. **Parking:** Free.

Situated directly on the beach overlooking the Gulf of Mexico, this modern two-story motel is surrounded by shady palm trees, with under-building parking. Bedrooms, which overlook the beach or the garden, are spacious, with standard furnishings and tiled bathrooms. Gulf-front rooms have balconies. Facilities include an outdoor heated swimming pool, Tiki-style beach umbrellas, lounge chairs, shuffleboard courts, and a guest laundry. Efficiency apartments are also available at higher rates.

WHERE TO DINE
DOWNTOWN/MAINLAND
Moderate

LEVEROCK'S, 12320 Manatee Ave. W. Tel. 794-8900.
   Cuisine: SEAFOOD. **Reservations:** Not accepted.
$ **Prices:** Main courses $5.95–$17.95. AE, CB, DC, DISC, MC, V.
   Open: Daily 11:30am–10pm.
   Overlooking Perico Harbor at the west end of the mainland, this trilevel restaurant is known for its great views as well as the freshest of seafood at affordable prices.
   Menu selections range from a variety of shrimp dishes to snapper, grouper, and crab to steaks, chicken, and ribs. For a full description of the menu, see the listing for Leverock's in the "Where to Dine" section in St. Petersburg.

THE PIER, 1200 First Ave. W. Tel. 748-8087.
   Cuisine: AMERICAN. **Reservations:** Recommended.
$ **Prices:** Main courses $9.95–$16.95. AE, DC, DISC, MC, V.
   Open: Mon–Fri 11:30am–9pm, Sat–Sun 11:30am–10pm.
With commanding views of the Manatee River, this restaurant is *the* place to dine downtown. It sits at the foot of 12th Street on Memorial Pier, housed in a stately Spanish-style landmark building. The menu offers such imaginative choices as golden snapper citron, shrimp tempura, blackened or charcoal-broiled grouper, and chicken Cordon Bleu or Oscar, as well as steaks and prime rib.

SEAFOOD SHACK, 4110 127th St. W., Cortez. Tel. 794-1235.
   Cuisine: SEAFOOD. **Reservations:** Not accepted.
$ **Prices:** Main courses $8.95–$19.95. AE, MC, V.
   Open: Sun–Thurs 11:30am–9pm, Fri–Sat 11:30am–10pm.
A tradition in the area for over 20 years, this informal spot sits on the marina, along the edge of the mainland beside the Fla. 684 bridge (Cortez Bridge) leading to Bradenton Beach. The menu offers many different seafood combinations and at least six different shrimp dishes (from scampi to stuffed), as well as freshly caught Florida lobster, stone crabs, grouper, and snapper. The "Shack specialty" is sautéed frogs' legs, and beef and chicken are also available.
   The Seafood Shack Showboat (tel. 794-5048), docked beside the restaurant, offers sightseeing cruises, priced at $10 to $14, which entitle participants to discounts off dinner dishes in the restaurant.

Inexpensive

MILLER'S DUTCH KITCHEN, 3401 14th St. W. Tel. 746-8253.
   Cuisine: AMERICAN. **Reservations:** Not accepted.
$ **Prices:** Main courses $4.95–$9.95. No credit cards.
   Open: Mon–Sat 11am–8pm.
   With a sprinkling of Pennsylvania Dutch recipes, this restaurant is an oasis of home-style cooking, nestled along a busy road known more for fast food. The menu includes Dutch casserole (noodles, peas, cheese, potatoes, beef, mushrooms, and chicken soup with croutons), pan-fried chicken, and cabbage rolls, as well as prime rib, stuffed flounder, veal parmesan, meatloaf, fried shrimp, barbecued pork ribs, lasagne, and spaghetti. To top it off, there are 17 varieties of freshly baked pies.

MRS. APPLETON'S FAMILY BUFFET, 4848 14th St. W. Tel. 758-9990.
   Cuisine: AMERICAN. **Reservations:** Not accepted.
$ **Prices:** Lunch buffet $4.95; dinner buffet $6.95. CB, DC, DISC, MC, V.
   Open: Lunch Mon–Sat 11:30am–3:30pm; dinner Mon–Sat 4–8:30pm, Sun 11am–8:30pm.
Situated in a shopping center half a mile south of Cortez Road (Fla. 684), this restaurant is short on views or setting, but offers an unbeatable value at its rotating buffet table. For a description of the food, see the listing in the "Where to Dine" section in Sarasota.

ANNA MARIA ISLAND/BEACHES
Expensive

BEACH BISTRO, 6600 Gulf Blvd., Holmes Beach. Tel. 778-6444.
  Cuisine: INTERNATIONAL. **Reservations:** Recommended.
$ Prices: Main courses $9.95–$28.95. MC, V.
  Open: Dinner only, daily 5:30–9:30pm.

One of the most creative restaurants on Anna Maria Island, this small 12-table culinary oasis sits right beside the beach, offering wide-windowed views of the gulf waters. The decor is bright and modern, with an overall elegance enhanced by crisp linens, sparkling crystal, and fresh flowers on every table. The menu presents such appetizers as smoked salmon Alfredo, and main dishes like salmon Benjamin with lime-dill butter in potato parchment, prime medallions of veal smothered in eggplant and provolone with a plum tomato and marsala wine sauce, chicken curry, veal Oscar, prime Angus beef filet, rack of lamb, duck au poivre, and bouillabaisse. The restaurant doesn't allow smoking.

Moderate

SANDBAR, 100 Spring Ave., Anna Maria, Anna Maria Island. Tel. 778-0444.
  Cuisine: SEAFOOD. **Reservations:** Not accepted on deck; "preferred seating" policy in main restaurant.
$ Prices: Main courses $8.95–$19.95. CB, DC, MC, V.
  Open: Lunch daily 11:30am–3pm; dinner daily 4–10pm.

"We are seafood" is the motto of this popular restaurant, perched on the beach overlooking the Gulf of Mexico, just off Gulf Drive. Established in 1979, it offers air-conditioned seating indoors and deck-style seating outside. The seafood choices change daily, depending on the local catch, but often include soft-shell crab and crab cakes, sautéed scallops, shrimp scampi, and stuffed grouper or flounder. Steaks, surf and turf, pastas, and chicken round out the menu.

Inexpensive

ROTTEN RALPH'S, 902 S. Bay Blvd., Anna Maria, Anna Maria Island. Tel. 778-3953.
  Cuisine: INTERNATIONAL. **Reservations:** Not accepted.
$ Prices: Main courses $6.95–$15.95. MC, V.
  Open: Daily 11am–10pm.

On the north end of the island overlooking the Anna Maria Yacht Basin, this casual Old Florida–style restaurant offers indoor and outdoor seating. The menu offers many seafood choices (from scallops and shrimp to crab cakes, snow crab, oysters, and grouper), as well as British-style favorites such as fish and chips and steak-and-kidney pie. Other choices include Danish baby back ribs, chicken pot pie, and Anna Maria chicken (marinated and grilled with a honey-mustard sauce).

Budget

SHELLS, Island Centre, 3200 E. Bay Blvd., Holmes Beach, Anna Maria Island. Tel. 778-5997.
  Cuisine: SEAFOOD. **Reservations:** Not accepted.
$ Prices: Main courses $4.95–$13.95. AE, MC, V.
  Open: Dinner only, Sun–Thurs 5–10pm, Fri–Sat 5–11pm.

Situated in a shopping center just south of the Fla. 64 bridge, this is a fairly new branch of the Shells chain, known for fresh seafood at low prices. For a description of the menu, see "Where to Dine" in the Tampa section.

SHOPPING

For discount shopping, the focal point of the Bradenton area is the **Gulf Coast Factory Shops** complex at 60th Avenue East, Ellenton (tel. 723-1150), about a 10-minute drive northeast of Bradenton, off I-75 at Exit 43. There are over 100 factory and outlet stores including names such as Bass Shoes, Corning Revere, Danskin,

Jockey, Levis, Nike, Aileen, AnnTaylor, Chaus, Donna Karan, Geoffrey Beene, Jones New York, Maidenform, Royal Doulton, Sony, and Van Heusen. Shops are open Monday through Saturday from 10am to 9pm and on Sunday from noon to 6pm.

EVENING ENTERTAINMENT
THE PERFORMING ARTS

ISLAND PLAYHOUSE, 10009 Gulf Dr. N., Anna Maria, Anna Maria Island. Tel. 778-5755.
For over 45 years, the Island Players, a community theater group, have performed from October through May.
Admission: Tickets, $9–$10.

MANATEE CIVIC CENTER, One Haben Blvd., Palmetto. Tel. 722-6626.
A community hub for meetings, conventions, and sports events, this huge circular building is also a popular venue for plays, concerts, and other types of entertainment. The box office is open Monday through Friday from 10am to 6pm, but the schedule of performances varies.
Admission: $6–$10, depending on the event.

RIVERFRONT THEATRE, 102 Old Main St. (12th St. W.). Tel. 748-5875.
Situated across from the Pier on the Manatee River, this community theater features the Manatee Players, a group established in 1948. They present musicals and dramas throughout the year, as well as a summer musical revue, band concerts, and a series of nontraditional works.
Admission: Tickets, $13–$15.

THE CLUB & BAR SCENE

ACES LOUNGE, 4343 Palma Sola Blvd. Tel. 795-3886.
Situated west of downtown on Palms Sola Bay, this lounge features a variety of live music, including karaoke on Saturday and Sunday, from 9pm to 1am. Drinks run $2 to $4.
Admission: Free.

CAFE ROBAR, 204 Pine Ave., Anna Maria, Anna Maria Island. Tel. 778-6969.
Located at the corner of Gulf Drive, this elegant place offers piano music and a sing-along bar each evening from 8pm until midnight. Drinks cost $2.50 and up.
Admission: Free.

D. COY DUCKS, 5410 Marina Dr., Holmes Beach, Anna Maria Island. Tel. 778-5888.
Wedged in the Island Shopping Center, this bar is known for its varied program of live Dixieland bands, jazz pianists, and guitar/vocalists. Music starts at various times (from 5 to 8pm) and usually continues until midnight or 1am nightly. Drinks go for $2 and up.
Admission: Free.

PEWTER MUG, 108 44th Ave. E. Tel. 756-7577.
Situated downtown one block east of U.S. 41, this lively lounge offers a blend of jazz bands or contemporary tunes, from 9pm until midnight Thursday through Sunday. Drinks cost $2 and up.
Admission: Free.

SCOREBOARD SPORTS PUB, 7004 Cortez Rd. W. Tel. 792-6768.
Bradenton's "only original sports pub" is an ideal place to watch football and other sports, from 8pm until midnight, depending on what's scheduled. Drinks are $2 and up.
Admission: Free.

CHAPTER 13

SOUTHWEST FLORIDA

- **WHAT'S SPECIAL ABOUT SOUTHWEST FLORIDA**
- **1. FORT MYERS**
- **2. FORT MYERS BEACH**
- **3. SANIBEL & CAPTIVA ISLANDS**
- **4. NAPLES**
- **5. MARCO ISLAND**

No tropical paradise would be complete without lots of balmy islands, and in Southwest Florida they come in every shape and size. In fact, there are so many islands in this beautiful corner of the state that when a research team tried counting them all, it gave up. Indeed, the promotion folks in Lee County have taken to calling themselves the Lee Island Coast, and neighboring Collier County even has an area officially known as Ten Thousand Islands.

The now-extinct Calusas lived on these islands when Juan Ponce de León discovered them in 1513. A relatively tall tribe of Native Americans, the Calusas discarded so many oyster and clam shells that they actually created a few new islets.

Ponce de León was so struck by the magnitude of seashells lying around that he named the entire area the Costa de Caracoles—the Coast of Seashells. The intricate waterways and winding rivers later came in handy for the notorious pirate José Gaspar, who used them as his hideaway. Gasparilla Island is named for him, and ancient pirate maps reputedly show his booty hidden on the islands. Today's visitors may not find Gaspar's loot, but they will discover a treasure among the exotic seashells washed up on the 50 miles of white, sugary beaches that line the entire length of Southwest Florida.

The natural beauty of this area has charmed rich folks for more than a century. The town of Naples was created in 1886 expressly as an enclave for affluent industrialists and their friends. Teddy Roosevelt and his buddies used to fish for tarpon between Boca Grande and Useppa Island; more recently, President George Bush came to Boca Grande to salve his wounds after his loss to Bill Clinton.

While Southwest Florida attracts its share of the rich and famous, it also lures the rest of us with its languid islands and great beaches, a broad spectrum of accommodations and restaurants, a dedication to controlled development, proximity to numerous wildlife sanctuaries including the Everglades, and the friendliness of the South and Midwest, from whence many of its permanent residents hail.

SEEING SOUTHWEST FLORIDA

From Fort Myers, it's only 42 miles to Naples, 53 miles to Marco Island, and 78 miles to the Everglades. This means that you can see much of Southwest Florida easily by car from one base of operations. Read the following sections with that in mind, for you can see and do a lot here during a week's vacation.

By air, most visitors arrive at Southwest Florida International Airport on the outskirts of Fort Myers and only 35 miles from Naples. Only commuter airlines use the much smaller Naples Municipal Airport.

By car, both I-75 and U.S. 41 run north-south through Southwest Florida, giving easy access from Tampa to the north and from Miami and Fort Lauderdale to the east. Also known as the Tamiami Trail, U.S. 41 is the main commercial strip through both Fort Myers and Naples.

WHAT'S SPECIAL ABOUT SOUTHWEST FLORIDA

Beaches
- ☐ Sanibel, Captiva, Cayo Costa, and Marco Island beaches—some of the world's best beaches for collecting seashells.
- ☐ Lover's Key, a hideaway beach, accessible by tram from the adjoining state park.

Wildlife Sanctuaries
- ☐ Ding Darling National Wildlife Refuge, encompassing more than 5,000 acres on Sanibel, with biking, hiking, canoeing, and driving trails for observing hundreds of species of birds and luxuriant Florida flora.
- ☐ Briggs Nature Center, in the Rookery Bay National Estuarine Research Reserve, with boat excursions for exploration, canoe rides, and a nearly mile-long boardwalk.
- ☐ Corkscrew Swamp Sanctuary, owned and operated by the National Audubon Society, 11,000 acres noted for the largest virgin bald cypress forest in the U.S. and woodstork migration.
- ☐ Babcock Wilderness Adventures, with excursions led by trained naturalists to observe alligators, bison, exotic birds, wild turkey, snakes, panthers, and wild hogs in Telegraph Cypress Swamp.

Regional Food and Drink
- ☐ Outstanding locally caught fish and seafood, locally grown citrus and tropical fruits and vegetables, as well as grapes for the regional wine produced at the Eden Vineyards and Winery.

Activities
- ☐ Abundant golf courses, some rated among the top in the nation.
- ☐ Excellent tarpon fishing—the waters between Cayo Costa and Gasparilla Island are considered among the world's best for this sport.

Buildings
- ☐ Seminole Lodge, winter home of inventor Thomas Alva Edison from 1886 to 1931, showing his talent for architecture, with Florida's first swimming pool.
- ☐ Mangoes, winter home of Henry Ford, next door to the Edison House, designed in the style of that era.

Shopping
- ☐ The Shell Factory in North Fort Myers, displaying zillions of seashells from everywhere in the world.

SEASONS   The climate is subtropical, which means that the high season is from mid-January to mid-April, when reservations are essential. Rates are always highest during this period, but since the hotels and resorts have myriad rate schedules, it's best to check ahead to find out exactly when their highest prices are in effect.

1. FORT MYERS

148 miles NW of Miami, 123 miles W of Fort Lauderdale,
142 miles S of Tampa, 42 miles N of Naples

GETTING THERE   By Plane   The **Southwest Florida International Airport,** on Daniels Parkway east of I-75, is served by Air Canada (tel. toll free 800/776-3000), American (tel. toll free 800/433-7300), Continental (tel. toll free 800/525-0280), Delta (tel. toll free 800/221-1212), TWA (tel. toll free 800/221-2000), and USAir (tel. toll free 800/428-4322).

The baggage-claim area has an information booth (with maps) and a board with advertisements and free phones to various hotels in the region. **Limousines** (actually multipassenger vans) are available at a booth across the street from the baggage claim.

You'll have to call **Yellow Cab** (tel. 352-1055) or **Aaron Limo & Taxi** (tel. 768-1898, or toll free 800/998-1898), both of which charge 10% to 15% less than the maximum legal fares. The maximum fares for one to three passengers are $20 to downtown Fort Myers, $25 to Fort Myers Beach, $30 to $36 to Sanibel Island, $46 to Captiva Island, $28 to Bonita Beach, $84 to Boca Grande, $38 to Naples, $60 to Marco Island, and $68 to Everglades City. Each additional passenger pays $8.

By Train Amtrak (tel. toll free 800/USA-RAIL) provides bus connections between Fort Myers and its nearest station, at Tampa.

By Bus The Greyhound bus station is at 2275 Cleveland Ave. (tel. 334-1011, or toll free 800/231-2222).

By Car To reach downtown from Tampa, take Exit 25 off I-75 and follow Palm Beach Boulevard (Fla. 80). From Naples or Miami, take Exit 23 off I-75 and follow Dr. Martin Luther King, Jr., Boulevard (Fla. 82).

It's difficult to picture this pleasant city with broad avenues along the Caloosahatchee River as a raucous cowtown, but that's exactly what Fort Myers once was. Thanks to the Spaniards who arrived in the 1500s, native Seminole tribes already had amassed huge herds of cattle by the time the U.S. Army built a fort on the river in 1844. Vast ranches sprang up after the Seminole Wars, and cowpokes drove steers by the thousands to boats tied up at the fort's long pier.

The army abandoned Fort Myers when the Civil War ended in 1865, but four permanent settlers arrived a year later. Others followed, attracted by the warm climate, good fishing, and land for farming and ranching. Included were horticulturalists from the Netherlands, Belgium, and Luxembourg, who turned the fledgling community into the "Gladiolus Capital of the World." By 1885 Fort Myers had 349 citizens and was second in size only to Tampa, on Florida's Gulf Coast.

Inventor Thomas Alva Edison arrived that same year. Then 38 and seeking warm temperatures in which to regain his health after years of incessant toil and the recent death of his wife, Edison liked the area so much that he built Seminole Lodge, a winter home and laboratory on the banks of the Caloosahatchee. In addition to the lush tropical gardens surrounding his own home, Edison planted royal palms along the part of McGregor Boulevard fronting his property. The palms now extend for more than a mile, leading to Fort Myers's other nickname: "The City of Palms."

Fort Myers may be the seat of vibrant and growing Lee County today, but downtown and the neighborhoods along the river still call to mind those slow-paced days when Edison and Ford arrived by steamship. It's a dignified, unprententious resort city whose riverfront downtown is undergoing a renaissance. You can stroll along the river, go sightseeing around town, play golf on challenging courses, shop at popular malls, and dine on excellent seafood in a variety of good restaurants. Inland, incredible numbers of wildlife wait to be observed in their river and swamp habitats. And all of this is only a few miles from Sanibel and Captiva Islands and Fort Myers Beach, where a plethora of islands and beaches wait to be explored.

ORIENTATION

INFORMATION For information in advance, contact the **Lee County Visitor and Convention Bureau,** P.O. Box 2445, Fort Myers, FL 33902 (tel. 813/338-3500, or toll free 800/237-6444; fax 813/334-1106). Once in town, drop by the **Fort Myers Chamber of Commerce Visitor Center,** 2310 Edwards Dr., Fort Myers, FL 33902 (tel. 813/334-6626), on the downtown waterfront, for brochures and other information. The chamber sells a detailed street map of the area for $2. Be sure to ask for a free trolley route map. Open Monday through Friday from 9am to 5pm.

AREA LAYOUT **Fort Myers** (pop. 44,000) lies along the south bank of the broad

FORT MYERS/NAPLES REGION

2 mi
0
3.2 km
N

Charlotte Harbor

Bokeelia

765

767

Pine Island

Pineland

Chiquita

Burnt Store Rd.

Pine Island Rd.

Pondella Rd.

Bay Shore Rd.

41

75

78

31

Olga

Beach Blvd.

Yacht
Basin
Park

Tice

Orange
River Blvd.

Orange
River

FORT MYERS

North Fort
Myers

Palm

Ortiz Ave.

80

78

Matlacha

Santa Barbara Blvd.

Del Prado Pkwy.

867

M.L. King Blvd.

Colonial Blvd.

Cleveland Ave.

Six Mile Pkwy

82

Commerce
Lakes Dr.

867

Pine Island Sound

Intracoastal Waterway

**Cape
Coral**

Cape Coral Pkwy.

Caloosahatchee River

McGregor Blvd.

College
Pkwy.
Cypress
Lake Dr.
Gladiolus
Dr.

Daniels Pkwy.

75

**Captiva
Island**

767

Punta
Rassa

San Carlos Blvd.

865

869

41

**Southwest
Florida
International
Airport**

867

**J.N. "Ding" Darling
National Wildlife Refuge**

Hendry
Creek

Alico Rd.

San Carlos
Park

Koreshan
State
Park

Estero

6

Sanibel

**FORT MYERS
BEACH**

Estero Blvd.

Estero

**Mound Key
State Park**

**Sanibel
Island**

7

Estero Bay

887

**Tamiami
Trail**

**Bonita
Springs**

75

865

**Bonita
Beach**

Bonita Beach Rd.

Gulf of Mexico

901

**Vanderbilt
Beach**

862

Cocohatchee River

846

951

8

Pine Ridge
Rd.

896

31

851

Golden Gate Pkwy.

41

9

**Naples
Municipal
Airport**

84

Airport

NAPLES

10

Davis Blvd.

951

41

11

N. Barfield Dr.

92

Collier Blvd.

Blue Eagle Dr.

Goodland

San Marco Rd.

Marco Island

Ten Thousand Islands

ATTRACTIONS:
Briggs Nature Center **11**
Collier County Automative Museum **9**
Calusa Nature Center **4**
Edison & Ford Winter Homes **2**
Fort Myers Historical Museum **3**
Lover's Key **7**
Old Naples **10**
Sanibel Lighthouse **6**
Shell Factory **1**
Six Mile Cypress Slough Preserve **5**
Teddy Bear Museum **8**

6626

Caloosahatchee River. On the opposite shore sit sleepy **North Fort Myers** and busy **Cape Coral,** a 116-square-mile, canal-laced city founded as a real estate development in 1957 and now the largest municipality between Tampa and Miami. **Lehigh Acres,** another sprawling development, lies east of Fort Myers. To the west of Cape Coral, **Pine Island** has a number of inexpensive "crab shack" restaurants and serves as a jumping-off point for cruises to Cabbage Key (see "Easy Island Excursions" in the Sanibel and Captiva Islands section, below). Across Pine Island Sound on Gasparilla Island sits Nantucket-like **Boca Grande** (see "An Easy Excursion to Boca Grande," below).

Edison's royal palm-lined **McGregor Boulevard** follows the river some 15 miles southwestward to **Punta Rassa** and the causeway to Sanibel and Captiva Islands. **San Carlos Boulevard** leaves McGregor and goes due south to Fort Myers Beach.

GETTING AROUND

BY BUS LeeTran (tel. 275-8726 for schedules) provides bus service throughout Lee County. One-ride fares are 75¢; one-day passes cost $2. Orange route 50 runs hourly between downtown and Fort Myers Beach via U.S. 41 and Summerlin Road and passes the Greyhound bus station.

BY TAXI Call **Yellow Cab** (tel. 332-1055).

BY RENTAL CAR Agencies at the airport are **Alamo** (tel. toll free 800/327-9633), **Avis** (tel. toll free 800/831-2847), **Budget** (tel. toll free 800/527-0700), **Hertz** (tel. toll free 800/654-3131), and **National** (tel. toll free 800/227-7368).

BY TROLLEY TOUR The narrated **guided tram tour** (tel. 275-8726) circulates daily among the Edison and Ford Homes, the Burroughs Home, and the Fort Myers Historical Museum (see "What to See and Do," below). The daily fare is $5, but a "Ticket to History" includes both rides and admission to the attractions for $13, a substantial savings. Purchase tickets at any of the attractions.

BY BICYCLE Rent from **Trikes, Bikes & Mowers,** 3451 Fowler St. (tel. 936-4301), or **Bike Route,** 14530 U.S. 41 S. (tel. 481-3376).

FAST FACTS

Area Code The telephone area code throughout Southwest Florida is 813.
Doctor Doctor referrals are provided by the Lee Memorial Hospital, 2776 Cleveland Ave. (tel. 332-1111).
Drugstore The pharmacy at Walgreen's Drug Store, College Parkway at Cleveland Avenue (tel. 939-2142), is open 24 hours a day.
Emergency To reach the police, report a fire, or call an ambulance, dial 911.
Tax In addition to Florida's statewide 6% sales tax, Lee County imposes a 3% tax on all hotel bills.

WHAT TO SEE & DO
ATTRACTIONS
Downtown

BURROUGHS HOME, 2505 1st St., at Fowler St. Tel. 332-1229.
All dressed up in 1918-vintage finery, sisters Mona and Jettie Burroughs lead "living history" tours through these riverside gardens and Georgian Revival mansion built in 1901 by cattleman John Murphy and later sold to their family. You must take a tour in order to visit the premises.
Admission: $3.20 adults, $1.05 children 6–12, free for children under 6. There's free parking in the Sheraton Harbor Place garage.
Open: Mon–Fri 10am–4pm; tours every 45 minutes Dec–Apr, on the hour May–Nov.

EDISON & FORD WINTER ESTATES, 2350 McGregor Blvd. Tel. 334-3614.

Thomas Edison and his second wife, Mina, brought their family to this porch-surrounded Victorian retreat, known as **Seminole Lodge,** from 1886 until he died in 1931. Mrs. Edison gave the 14-acre estate to the state of Florida in 1947, but it stands exactly as it did during Edison's lifetime. Made in the 1920s, some of his lightbulbs still burn in the laboratory where he and his staff worked on some of his 1,093 inventions. An avid amateur botanist, Edison experimented with the exotic foliage he planted in the lush tropical gardens surrounding the mansion (he used bamboo for lightbulb filaments and turned goldenrod into rubber). A museum displays some of his inventions, as well as his unique Model T Ford, a gift from friend Henry Ford. In 1916, Ford and his wife, Clara, built **Mangoes,** their bungalow-style house next door, so they could winter with the Edisons. Like Seminole Lodge, Mangoes is furnished as it appeared in the 1920s. Admission to the homes is by tour only.

Admission: Edison Home, $8 adults, $4 children 6–12, free for children under 6. Ford Home, $6 adults, $4 children 6–12, free for children under 6. Combination tickets, $10 adults, $5 children 6–12, free for children under 6.

Open: Mon–Sat 9am–4pm, Sun 12:30–4pm. Tours depart every half hour.

Closed: Thanksgiving and Christmas Days.

FORT MYERS HISTORICAL MUSEUM, 2300 Peck St., at Jackson St. Tel. 332-5955.

Housed in the restored Spanish-style depot served by the Atlantic Coast Line from 1904 to 1971, this interesting museum features exhibits depicting Fort Myers's history from the ancient Calusas and the Spanish conquistadors to the first settlers. There's even a picture of Colonel Myers, who never visited his namesake. For railroad buffs, the "Esperanza"—longest and last of the plush Pullman private cars—stands outside the museum.

Admission: $2.50 adults, $1 children under 12.

Open: Nov–Apr, Mon–Sat 9am–4:30pm, Sun 1–5pm; May–Oct, Mon–Fri 9am–4:30pm, Sun 1–5pm.

Nearby Attractions

BABCOCK WILDERNESS ADVENTURES, Fla. 31, 11 miles north of Fort Myers. Tel. 338-6367 for information, 489-3911 for reservations.

Experienced naturalists lead 90-minute "swamp buggy" tours through the Babcock Ranch, the largest contiguous cattle operation in the United States and home to countless birds and wildlife as well as domesticated bison and quarter horses. Mysterious Telegraph Swamp is a highlight, especially when alligators scurry from a bridge and lie motionless in the dark-brown waters as the buggies pass overhead. Visitors dismount to visit an enclosure where southern cougars stand in for their close cousins, the rare Florida panthers (which are tan, not black). Unlike most Everglades tours, this one covers five different ecosystems, from open prairie to cypress swamp.

Admission: $16 adults, $8 children under 12.

Open: Jan–Apr, daily 9am–3pm; May–Oct, Tues–Sun 9–11am; Nov–Dec, Tues–Sun 9am–3pm. Reservations are required, so call for tour times.

CALUSA NATURE CENTER & PLANETARIUM, 3450 Ortiz Ave., just north of Colonial Blvd. Tel. 275-3435.

Three nature trails wind through this 105-acre nature center so that visitors can observe Florida's flora and fauna. In addition, there's an aviary, a children's natural-history museum, a live-reptile exhibit, a 400-gallon saltwater aquarium, and a museum store. The planetarium features star and laser-light shows.

Admission: $3 adults, $1.50 children 3–12, free for children under 3. Extra admission to planetarium, depending on show.

Open: Mon–Sat 9am–5pm, Sun 11am–5pm. Guided walks, Sun at 12:15pm, Wed at 11am, Sat at 9:15am.

KORESHAN STATE HISTORIC PARK, U.S. 41, Estero. Tel. 992-0311.

This 300-acre landmark along the Estero River was the site of the Koreshan Unity Movement, a now-extinct 19th-century religious sect which believed that humans

lived *inside* the earth and—ahead of their time—that women should have equal rights. Cyrus Reed Teed and his followers from Chicago established a self-sufficient settlement here in 1894. Several of their buildings and gardens have been restored, and a museum is devoted to their beliefs. Nature and canoe trails wind through the settlement and downriver to Mound Key, an islet made of the Calusas' discarded shells. There is a picnic and camping area, where camping costs $17 per night December to April, $14 May to November.
Admission: $3.25 per vehicle with up to eight passengers, $1 pedestrians or bikers.
Open: Daily 8am–sunset.

SIX MILE CYPRESS SLOUGH PRESERVE, Penzance Blvd. at Six Mile Cypress Pkwy., between Colonial Blvd. and Daniels Pkwy. Tel. 338-3300.
A mile-long boardwalk leads through the wetland ecosystem of this 2,000-acre preserve, giving access to a wide variety of Southwest Florida's plants and wildlife. An amphitheater is on the premises. There are no organized tours, but you can pick up informative brochures at the entrance.
Admission: $2 per vehicle.
Open: Daily 8am–5pm.

CRUISES

J.C. Boat Cruises (tel. 334-7474) presents a variety of year-round lunch, brunch, dinner, sightseeing, and theme cruises on the Caloosahatchee River and its tributaries. The ticket office is at the downtown Fort Myers City Yacht Basin, Edwards Drive at Lee Street. The three-hour Everglades Jungle Cruise is a very popular way to observe waterfowl and other wildlife. They even have a full-day cruise up the Caloosahatchee to Lake Okeechobee and back. Prices range from $10 to $74. Schedules change and advance reservations are strongly recommended, so call ahead.

SPECIAL EVENTS

Fort Myers's most dazzling annual event is the **Edison Pageant of Light,** during the first two weeks of February. Arts and crafts shows, a five-kilometer marathon, pageants, and the spectacular finale, the Parade of Lights, attract thousands of visitors to Edison's winter home.
In March, nearby Pine Island celebrates with its annual **Seafood Festival.** In April, Estero hosts the unique **Koreshan Unity Lunar Festival.** May brings the **Concert in the Park** in Fort Myers and the **Tarpon Rodeo** in Cape Coral.
The Fourth of July sees a host of parades and fireworks in the area. August has music in the air at the **Riverfront Concert** in Fort Myers. In December, both the Edison and Ford homes are gloriously lighted for Christmas.

SPORTS & RECREATION

BASEBALL   The locals start counting balls and strikes when the Boston Red Sox and Minnesota Twins arrive in February to begin training for spring games in March. Seats are limited, so get your tickets early. The **Boston Red Sox** play at the 6,500-seat City of Palms Park, at Edison Avenue and Broadway (tel. 334-4700). The **Minnesota Twins** work out at the 7,500-seat Lee County Sports Complex, on Six Mile Cypress Parkway between Daniels and Metro Parkways (tel. 768-4270).

DOG RACING   The hounds race at the **Naples–Fort Myers Kennel Club,** at Old U.S. 41 and Bonita Beach Road in Bonita Springs (tel. 922-2411). Doors open at 6:30pm Tuesday through Saturday and at 1:30pm on Sunday, with races beginning one hour later. Four matinees are held each week; call for the schedule. Admission to the box seats costs $1. The Sky Region dining room has a view of the track.

GOLF & TENNIS   Public courses **in Fort Myers** are at the Fort Myers Country Club (tel. 936-2457), the Eastwood Golf Club (tel. 275-4848), the River's Edge Country Club (tel. 433-4211), and the Gateway Golf & Country Club (tel. 561-1010); **in North Fort Myers,** El Rio Golf Club (tel. 995-2204) and the Riverbend Golf

Club (tel. 543-2200); **in Cape Coral,** the Coral Oaks Country Club (tel. 283-4100) and the Cape Coral Golf and Tennis Resort (tel. 542-3191); **on Pine Island,** the Alden Pines Country Club (tel. 283-2179); **in South Fort Myers,** the San Carlos Country Club (tel. 267-3131) and Terraverde (tel. 433-7733); and **in Bonita Springs,** the Bonita Springs Golf & Country Club (tel. 992-2800). Call for tee times and greens fees.

Tennis buffs can play at **Fort Myers Racquet Club,** 4900 Deleon St. (tel. 278-7277), which has eight lighted courts.

HORSEBACK RIDING   Two stables in North Fort Myers offer riding: **D.J.'s Ranch,** 17840 Shelby Lane (tel. 543-4050), and the **Hancock Creek Riding Stables,** 865 Moody Rd. (tel. 997-3322).

MINIATURE GOLF/FUN PARKS   You might see the Boston Red Sox leftfielder at his **Mike Greenwell's Bat-A-Ball and Family Fun Park,** on Pine Island Road (Fla. 78) just east of Santa Barbara Boulevard in Cape Coral (tel. 574-4386). A round of golf costs $4.50 for adults, $3.50 for seniors and children 6 to 11, $2.50 for kids under 6. A turn at the plate in the batting cage costs $1 for 24 pitches. The park is open Sunday through Thursday from 10am to 10pm, and on Friday and Saturday from 10am to 11pm.

Fort Adventure, 1915 Colonial Blvd. (tel. 936-3233), between McGregor Boulevard and Cleveland Avenue, is Fort Myers's largest fun park, with something for all ages: a miniature golf course, bumper boats, batting cages, and a games arcade. Open from 10am to 10pm daily; closed Christmas Day.

TRAIN TOURS

It's fun to sightsee or have dinner in the old-fashioned dining car rolling along the **Seminole Gulf Railway** (tel. 275-8487), the original railroad between Fort Myers and Naples. Today its one train chugs as far south as Bonita Springs. Dinner trains usually depart at 6:30pm Monday through Friday. Sightseeing excursions usually leave at noon and 2:30pm on Wednesday, Saturday, and Sunday, and there's a Sunday brunch run. Schedules can vary with the season, so call ahead. Reservations are required for the dinner train. The trains depart Fort Myers from the Metro Mall Station, on Colonial Boulevard at Metro Parkway. The Bonita Springs station is on Old U.S. 41 at Pennsylvania Avenue.

WHERE TO STAY

In addition to the hostelries mentioned below, Fort Myers has several chain motels offering inexpensive accommodations. These include the **Budgetel Inn,** 2717 Colonial Blvd. (tel. 813/275-3500, or toll free 800/428-3438); **Comfort Inn,** 11501 S. Cleveland Ave. (tel. 813/936-3993, or toll free 800/228-5150); **Econo Lodge,** 13301 N. Cleveland Ave. (tel. 813/995-0571, or toll free 800/553-2666); **La Quinta Inn,** 4850 S. Cleveland Ave. (tel. 813/279-3300, or toll free 800/531-5900); **Motel 6,** 3350 Marinatown Lane (tel. 813/656-5544); and **Sleep Inn,** 13651 Indian Paint Lane (tel. 813/561-1117, or toll free 800/358-3170), which is actually on Daniels Parkway near I-75 and the international airport. For Boston Red Sox fans, the **Holiday Inn Central,** 2431 Cleveland Ave. (tel. 813/332-3232, or toll free 800/990-0466), is just four blocks from City of Palms Park.

EXPENSIVE

SANIBEL HARBOUR RESORT & SPA, 17260 Harbour Pointe Rd., Fort Myers, FL 33908. Tel. 813/466-4000, or toll free 800/767-7777. Fax 813/466-2150. 240 rms, 100 two-bedroom condo apts. A/C MINIBAR TV TEL
   Directions: Follow McGregor Boulevard to Punta Rassa Road, the last exit before the Sanibel Causeway toll plaza.
$ Rates: Winter, $230–$270 single or double; $285–$570 condo apt. Off-season, $105–$185 single or double; $145–$410 condo apt. Vacation packages available. AE, DC, DISC, MC, V.

⭐ A former Sonesta hotel, this sports-oriented, "casually elegant" resort overlooks San Carlos Bay from Punta Rassa, next to the Sanibel Causeway (it's
much closer to the islands than to downtown Fort Myers, 14 miles away). A
waterside cupola-topped pavilion in front of the 11-story hotel evokes the turn-of-the-
century resort that once stood on this point. Otherwise it's all modern and luxurious
inside. The spacious rooms are attractively furnished with dark or blond wood,
including armoires to hide the TVs. All rooms and most of the condo apartments have
wonderful water and island views from their balconies. This large property hosts
many conventions and groups.

Dining/Entertainment: There are four restaurants and lounges, including the
intimate Toucan Room and the casual, "calorie-conscious" Promenade; lounges with
entertainment during the winter season; and a sports bar.

Services: Complimentary shuttle to Sanibel Island three times a day; children's
activities program.

Facilities: Indoor and outdoor swimming pools with hot tubs and bars, 13
lighted tennis courts, 5,000-seat tennis stadium (host to Davis Cup matches),
40,000-square-foot fitness center (with spa, massage, and facials), marina with boat
and equipment rentals.

MODERATE

**COURTYARD BY MARRIOTT, 4450 Metro Pkwy., Fort Myers, FL 33901.
Tel. 813/275-8600,** or toll free 800/321-2211. Fax 813/275-7087. 149 rms.
A/C TV TEL
$ Rates: Winter, $110–$128 single or double. Off-season, $74 single or double.
AE, DC, DISC, MC, V.

⭐ This comfortable modern hotel at the corner of Metro Parkway and Colonial
Boulevard appropriately encloses a landscaped courtyard with a swimming
pool. About half the rooms face the courtyard; the others face the surrounding
parking lots. All have sofas and rich mahogany writing tables and chests of drawers,
plus nice little features like long telephone cords and extra hand-basin faucets
dispensing piping-hot water for tea and instant coffee, which are supplied. The lobby
features a fireplace and dining area which is open for breakfast and dinner. Other
facilities include an exercise room, indoor spa pool, and guest laundry. The Metro
Mall is across the street.

**SHERATON HARBOR PLACE, 2500 Edwards Dr., Fort Myers, FL 33901.
Tel. 813/337-0300,** or toll free 800/767-7777. Fax 813/337-1530. 240 rms.
A/C MINIBAR TV TEL
$ Rates: Winter, $119–$159 single or double. Off-season, $79–$139 single or
double. AE, DC, DISC, MC, V.

⭐ All rooms in this 25-story luxury hotel at the corner of Edwards and Fowler
Streets have spectacular views over the downtown waterfront and the
Caloosahatchee River. The more expensive versions are equipped with kitchen-
ettes and bookcaselike cabinets that divide the living and sleeping areas.

La Tiers restaurant, on the second floor, offers reasonably priced American and
Thai selections (the property is owned by Thai hoteliers). The indoor/outdoor Rum
Runners Bar is unique, surrounded by waterfalls and flaunting Florida's largest indoor
mural depicting an undersea fantasy world. The bar opens to both an indoor and
heated outdoor swimming pool. Nightly entertainment is offered on Friday and
Saturday evenings.

A BED & BREAKFAST

**DRUM HOUSE INN, 2135 McGregor Blvd., Fort Myers, FL 33903. Tel.
813/332-5668.** 6 rms (all with bath). A/C
$ Rates: Winter, $125 single or double. Off-season, $85 single or double.
It's a short walk from Shirley and Jim Drums' turn-of-the-century house at the corner
of McGregor Boulevard and Clifford Street to the nearby Edison and Ford Homes.
The Drums have lovingly restored this old wooden structure, originally built by a
lumberman in North Fort Myers, which was then literally out in the country. When

he died, his wife decided to move to town, so she cut the house in two, floated it across the Caloosahatchee, and nailed it back together (Jim will gladly point out the seam down the middle). Shirley has given each guest room a theme—lace, ruffles, rose, traditional Victorian, nautical, and honeymoon—and furnished them with a plethora of antiques and period pieces. There's a sitting room, music room, and library. Breakfast is served in the small sun room. Smoking isn't allowed in the house.

CAMPING

Campgrounds with tent sites as well as RV hookups include the **Fort Myers Campground,** 16800 Tamiami Trail S., Fort Myers, FL 33908 (tel. 813/267-2141; **Woodsmoke Camping,** 19251 Tamiami Trail S., Fort Myers, FL 33908 (tel. 813/267-3456); and **Shady Acres Travel Park,** 19370 Tamiami Trail S., Fort Myers, FL 33908 (tel. 813/267-8448). For a complete list, contact the Fort Myers Chamber of Commerce (see "Orientation," above).

WHERE TO DINE
EXPENSIVE

PETER'S LA CUISINE, 2224 Bay St. Tel. 332-2228.
Cuisine: CONTINENTAL. **Reservations:** Recommended
$ Prices: Appetizers $5–$11.50; main courses $20–$28.50; snacks in upstairs bar $8–$12. AE, DC, MC, V.
Open: Lunch Mon–Fri 11:30am–2pm; dinner Mon–Sat 5:30–9:30pm. (Upstairs Bar & Bistro, Mon–Sat 4:30pm–1am.)

Bavarian-born chef Peter Schmid masterfully blends European cuisine with local seafood, fruits, and vegetables. The dining room here has a refined ambience, while the Upstairs Bar & Bistro is more casual, with a light-fare menu and nightly entertainment.

THE VERANDA, 2112 2nd St., at Broadway. Tel. 332-2065.
Cuisine: CONTINENTAL. **Reservations:** Recommended.
$ Prices: Appetizers $4–$8; main courses $14–$23. AE, MC, V.
Open: Lunch Mon–Fri 11am–2:30pm; dinner Mon–Sat 5:30–11pm.

A romantic, gracious atmosphere prevails at this elegant turn-of-the-century boarding house, where dining is inside or al fresco in a courtyard with a small fishpond. The dinner menu is a gourmet delight, highlighting grilled Florida snapper. Complimentary accompaniments include sweet corn muffins, just-baked honey-molasses bread, and sassy pepper jelly. Evening entertainment in the cocktail lounge makes this a perfect watering hole.

MODERATE

THE CHART HOUSE, 2024 W. 1st St. Tel. 332-1881.
Cuisine: SEAFOOD. **Reservations:** Recommended.
$ Prices: Appetizers $4.50–$9; main courses $14–$22.50. AE, DC, DISC, MC, V.
Open: Dinner only, Sun–Thurs 5–10pm, Fri–Sat 5–11pm.

Attractive nautical decor is appropriate for this friendly, riverside restaurant with great views. Early birds get fine sunsets and a specially priced menu between 5 and 6pm. The lengthy salad bar is one of the best anywhere, with such gourmet choices as marinated palm hearts. Seafood selections include charcoal-broiled fish and Santa Fe–style shrimp. The luscious mud pie is a dessert not to be soon worked off.

THE PRAWNBROKER RESTAURANT AND FISH MARKET, in the Cypress Point Shopping Center, McGregor Blvd. at Cypress Lake Dr. Tel. 489-2226.
Cuisine: SEAFOOD. **Reservations:** Recommended.
$ Prices: Appetizers $3–$5.50; main courses $11–$17. AE, DC, MC, V.
Open: Dinner only, Mon–Sat 4:30–10pm, Sun 4:30–9pm. (Fish market, Mon–Sat noon–10pm, Sun 3–9pm.)

Really fresh fish and moderate prices provide enough bait for a drive to this very friendly restaurant. From peel-it-yourself shrimp to oysters crowned with caviar, it seems that everything from the briny deep is served here. Steaks are cooked to order for beef lovers. This restaurant and its popular sports bar are very casual and often crowded.

SMITTY'S, 2240 W. 1st St. Tel. 334-4415.
   Cuisine: STEAK. **Reservations:** Recommended in winter.
$ Prices: Appetizers $2.50–$6; main courses $8–$20. AE, MC, V.
   Open: Mon–Fri 11am–10pm, Sat 4–10pm.

Smitty's has been a favorite local steakhouse since 1958, and a sample of the perfectly prepared prime beef, roasted or grilled, will show why. The restaurant prepares its own peppercorn dressing and bakes yeasty rolls like Grandma's. The "Light & Lean" dishes are good value in the $8 to $12.50 range. Smitty's is a short stroll from the Edison and Ford winter estates.

BUDGET

EDISON'S PATIO, 2320 McGregor Blvd., at W. 1st St. Tel. 332-4674.
   Cuisine: SNACK BAR. **Reservations:** Not accepted.
$ Prices: $4–$5. No credit cards.
   Open: Breakfast daily 8–11am; lunch daily 11am–4pm.
Almost across the boulevard from the Edison and Ford homes' entry, this small clapboard cottage is the place to have breakfast before touring, or a relaxing lunch afterward. Order at the counter, then grab a seat on the screened porch or on the patio under the huge shade trees. The menu features soups, salads, and made-to-order sandwiches on a variety of breads, plus refreshing frozen yogurt.

FARMERS MARKET RESTAURANT, 2736 Edison Ave., at Crawford Ave. Tel. 334-1687.
   Cuisine: SOUTHERN. **Reservations:** Not accepted.
$ Prices: Breakfast $3–$5; sandwiches $2–$5; meals $5–$7. No credit cards.
   Open: Mon–Sat 6am–8pm, Sun 6am–7pm.
The retail Farmers Market next door may be tiny, but the best of the cabbage, okra, green beans, and tomatoes end up here at this plain and simple eatery frequented by everyone from business executives to truck drivers. The specialty of the house is thoroughly smoked beef and pork barbecue and other southern favorites like country fried steak, fried chicken livers and gizzards, and smoked hamhocks with a bowl of beans. Yankees can order fried chicken, roast beef, or pork chops, and they can have hash browns instead of grits with their big breakfast.

SHOPPING

An institution for more than 50 years, ✪ **The Shell Factory,** on U.S. 41 in North Fort Myers (tel. 995-2141), carries one of the world's largest collections of rare shells, corals, sponges, and fossils. One entire room is devoted to shell jewelry. Open daily from 10am to 6pm.

More than 800 booths carry antiques, crafts, fashions, and produce at **Fleamasters,** on Dr. Martin Luther King, Jr., Boulevard (Fla. 82), 1½ miles west of I-75. There are snack bars and entertainment, too. Open on Friday, Saturday, and Sunday from 8am to 4pm.

EVENING ENTERTAINMENT

For entertainment ideas and schedules, consult the daily *Fort Myers News-Press,* especially Friday's "Gulf Coasting" section.

THE PERFORMING ARTS

ARCADE THEATER, 2267 1st St. Tel. 332-6688.
   Originally a vaudeville playhouse which saw the likes of Jeanette MacDonald and

Nelson Eddie, this 1908-vintage theater in downtown Fort Myers has been completely renovated and now presents a variety of performances. Call for schedule and prices.

BARBARA B. MANN PERFORMING ARTS HALL, 8099 College Pkwy., at Summerlin Rd. Tel. 489-3033.

This $7-million arts center on the campus of Edison Community College features performances by world-famous celebrities, Broadway plays such as *Les Misérables,* and regular concerts by the Southwest Florida Symphony. Call for a brochure listing the season's offerings.

BROADWAY PALM DINNER THEATER, in Royal Palm Square, Colonial Blvd. at Summerlin Rd. Tel. 278-4422.

Broadway musicals and comedy hits such as *Annie* and *Steel Magnolias* are the attraction at this dinner theater in the upscale Royal Palm Square shopping mall. Evening performances usually begin with dinner at 6pm and the show at 8pm, a half hour earlier on Sunday. Matinees are normally staged four days a week. Call ahead for the schedule.

Admission: Dinner and show, $27 Sun–Fri, $30 Sat, $24 matinees; show only, $17.

HARBORSIDE CONVENTION HALL, 1375 Monroe St. Tel. 334-7637 for information, 334-4958 for the box office.

This 3,000-seat civic center on the downtown riverfront spotlights such entertainers as Ray Charles, the Oak Ridge Boys, and Liza Minnelli, as well as shows such as World Cup Champions on Ice and the Big Band Salute to Glenn Miller. Boat and auto shows also are featured. Call for upcoming events.

THE CLUB & BAR SCENE

Downtown has been enjoying a renaissance of late, with evening entertainment spotlighted at several restaurants and hotels. Entertainers perform nightly at the **Victoria Pier Restaurant & Pub,** 2230 Edwards St. (tel. 334-4881). Jazz and blues highlight evenings in the **Upstairs Bar & Bistro** of Peter's La Cuisine, 2224 Bay St. (tel. 332-2228). The lounge at the **Sheraton Harbor Place,** 2500 Edwards Dr. (tel. 337-0300), has entertainment during the winter months.

In the suburbs, **Bootleggers Saloon & Dancehall,** in the Metro Mall, Colonial Boulevard at Metro Parkway (tel. 275-4487), specializes in country and western music and often gives free dance lessons. Also in Metro Mall, **Flashback's Bar & Grill** (same phone number, too), has various country, western, disco, and dance-music nights.

AN EASY EXCURSION TO BOCA GRANDE

After he lost to Bill Clinton in 1992, a suddenly lame-duck George Bush went on vacation to Boca Grande (pronounced *Grand*). He chose well, for this charming village on Gasparilla Island is a president's kind of place. Legend says the infamous pirate José Gaspar lived in style on this seven-mile-long barrier island. So did the DuPont family, which founded Boca Grande in the 1880s. They were followed by the Astors, Morgans, and other rich clans, who still turn the island into a Florida version of Nantucket during their winter "social season."

In addition to the warm weather, the lure was some of the world's best tarpon fishing. Descendants of the watermen who were here first—and who guided the rich and famous—still work their 1920s-vintage marinas and live on streets named Dam-If-I-Know, Dam-If-I-Care, and Dam-If-I-Will. Their modest homes you can see, but high hedges hide the millionaires' mansions around 29th Street. Nevertheless, the quaint little village is a fascinating place to rub shoulders with the moneyed class.

GETTING THERE By car, take I-75 or U.S. 41 to Port Charlotte, then follow Fla. 776 and Fla. 771 to Placida and the Boca Grande Causeway ($3.20 toll). Give yourself two hours from Fort Myers. Captiva Cruises (tel. 813/472-5300) has day trips from Captiva Island (see "Easy Island Excursions," in the Sanibel and Captiva Islands section, below).

INFORMATION   Contact the **Boca Grande Chamber of Commerce,** 5800 Gasparilla Rd. (P.O. Box 704), Boca Grande, FL 33921 (tel. 813/964-0568). There's an unstaffed, walk-in **information booth** on Park Avenue at 4th Street in the heart of town.

GETTING AROUND   **Boca Grande Taxi & Limousine** (tel. 964-0455, or toll free 800/771-7433) will take you around. **Island Bike 'n' Beach,** 333 Park Ave. (tel. 964-0711), rents regular bikes, three-wheelers, tandems, and beach cruisers as well as chairs, umbrellas, boogie boards, snorkeling gear, and other beach items.

ESSENTIALS   There's no bank on the island. Doctors are available at the Boca Grande Health Clinic, at the corner of Park Avenue and 3rd Street (tel. 964-2276).

WHAT TO SEE & DO

ATTRACTIONS   The red-brick **Railroad Depot,** at the corner of Park Avenue and 4th Street, has been restored to its turn-of-the-century grandeur when it was Boca Grande's lifeline to the world. It now houses a cluster of classy boutiques and the Loose Caboose Ice Cream Parlor, where Katherine Hepburn once satiated her sweet tooth. Now a **bike path,** the bed of the old Charlotte Harbor and Northern Railroad begins at 1st Street and Railroad Avenue and follows Gasparilla Road north to the causeway.

The beautiful Spanish-style **Boca Grande Community Center,** at Park Avenue and 1st Street, originally was the island's school. **Banyan Street** (actually 2nd Street) is canopied with tangled banyan trees and is one of the prettiest places for biking or strolling.

To the north of town, the **Johann Fust Community Library,** at Gasparilla Road and 10th Street (tel. 964-2488), contains 15,000 volumes and the extraordinary **DuPont Shell Collection,** all gathered by Henry Francis DuPont during nearly 50 years of combing the island's beaches. Open December through April, daily from 10am to noon and 4 to 6pm; the rest of the year, daily from 4 to 6pm.

At the south end of the island, the **Boca Grande Lighthouse** began marking the pass into Charlotte Harbor in 1890 (the steel tower on Gulf Boulevard served as the light from 1966 to 1986, when the old building was restored). **Gasparilla Island State Recreation Area** around the lighthouse is open daily from 8am to sunset. Admission is $2 per vehicle.

WATER SPORTS   By far the biggest event here is the **World's Richest Tarpon Tournament,** usually the first weekend in July, when anglers try to reel in $100,000. Charter fishing and rental boats are available at **Miller's Marina** (tel. 964-2283) and at **Whidden's Marina** (tel. 964-2878), both on Harbor Drive. Miller's Marina also has backwater nature tours and parasailing. Beach access is limited by the expensive homes along the gulf, but there's a **public beach** just south of town on Gulf Boulevard.

WHERE TO STAY

You must rent a condo if you want to stay on the beach. One example is **Sundown Colony,** a group of 28 spacious, two-story, two-bedroom/two-bath town homes right on the beach about half a mile south of town. Rates range from $770 to $1,325 a week, depending on the season. Contact Boca Grande Real Estate, P.O. Box 686, Boca Grande, FL 33921 (tel. 813/964-0338, or toll free 800/881-2622; fax 813/964-2301).

GASPARILLA INN & COTTAGES, 5th St. at Palm Ave., Boca Grande, FL 33921. Tel. 813/964-2201. Fax 813/964-2733. 150 units. A/C TV TEL
$ Rates: Winter, $340–$400 single or double. Off-season, $148 single; $218 double. No credit cards. **Closed:** Mid-June to Nov.

Built in 1912, this architectural beauty with stately columns, southern-style verandas, and handsome wood floors is still the winter home for affluent socialites. So many return from one social season to the next that it's difficult to get a room or cottage from mid-January to April. In addition to its high-ceilinged, aristocratic dining room, the inn operates the more relaxed Pink Elephant Restaurant, nearby at 5th Street and Bayou Avenue (tel. 964-0100). Behind the inn, an 18-hole golf course stretches to the shores of Charlotte Harbor.

INLET ON THE WATERFRONT, 11th St. at Boca Grande Bayou, Boca Grande, FL 33921. Tel. 813/964-2294. Fax 813/964-0382. 32 rms and efficiencies. A/C TV TEL

$ Rates: Winter, $85-$125 double. Off-season, $75-$125 double. MC, V.
Owned and operated by the Gasparilla Inn (see above), this motel sits on Boca Grande Bayou. Rooms with this water view and kitchens are more expensive than the standard motel units. There's a swimming pool and marina on the premises, but no restaurant.

UNCLE HENRY'S MOTEL, 5800 Gasparilla Rd. (P.O. Box 1425), Boca Grande, FL 33921. Tel. 813/964-2300. Fax 813/964-2098. 16 rms, 2 suites. A/C TV TEL

$ Rates: Winter, $125-$195 double. Off-season, $95-$155 double. AE, MC, V.
Located in the Courtyard Shops, about 3½ miles north of Boca Grande near the causeway, this modern motel has spacious rooms, about half with views of an adjacent marina. The Casual Clam restaurant serves breakfast, lunch, and dinner, and has evening entertainment on Friday and Saturday. There's also a deli among the shops.

WHERE TO DINE

JAM'S ITALIAN RESTAURANT, Railroad Ave. at 5th St. Tel. 964-2002.
  Cuisine: ITALIAN. **Reservations:** Not accepted.
$ Prices: Pizzas $5-$16.50; pastas $5.50-$11; subs $6-$7. AE, MC, V.
  Open: Sun-Thurs 11am-9pm, Fri-Sat 11am-10pm.

While President Bush hobnobbed at the Gasparilla Inn, his White House staffers were at this inexpensive but pleasant joint scarfing down tons of excellent pizza and pasta while watching ballgames on three TVs (Jam's even has a plaque to prove it).

LIGHTHOUSE HOLE RESTAURANT, Harbor Dr. at Miller's Marina. Tel. 964-0511.
  Cuisine: SEAFOOD. **Reservations:** Not required.
$ Prices: Appetizers $3-$8; main courses $14-$18. DISC, MC, V.
  Open: Daily 11am-10pm.
The only restaurant in town on the water, this seafood emporium over Miller's Marina has a large screened porch overlooking Boca Grande Bayou and the mangroves along the opposite shore. The menu leans heavily on shrimp and grouper, but daily specials feature seasonal items like stone crab claws and Florida lobsters.

THE TEMPTATION RESTAURANT, Park Ave. between 3rd and 4th Sts. Tel. 964-2610.
  Cuisine: SEAFOOD/STEAK. **Reservations:** Recommended.
$ Prices: Appetizers $3-$7.50; main courses $17.50-$24; lunches $5.50-$10. MC, V.
  Open: Lunch Mon-Sat 11am-2pm; dinner Mon-Sat 6-9:30pm.
Along with the Theater Restaurant, this storefront establishment is very popular with locals. The regular menu offers fried grouper and shrimp and charcoal-grilled steaks, but the chef's nightly specials, such as mahi-mahi with yellow pepper and artichoke heart compote, are fit for a president.

THEATER RESTAURANT, Park Ave. and 4th St. Tel. 964-0806.
  Cuisine: CONTINENTAL. **Reservations:** Recommended.
$ Prices: Appetizers $3-$7; main courses $14-$22; lunches $5-$8. MC, V.
  Open: Lunch Mon-Sat 11:30am-2:30pm; dinner Mon-Sat 5:30-10pm.
  Closed: Aug-Sept.
The curtain goes up in this former theater turned into a mini-mall and restaurant with

delicious productions, starring roast pork tenderloin glazed with marsala wine and herb jelly, a mixture of seafoods tossed with fettuccine Alfredo, and steaks grilled over an open flame. The show-stealer is the large saltwater aquarium. Dine inside or on a screened porch.

2. FORT MYERS BEACH

13 miles S of Fort Myers, 28 miles N of Naples, 12 miles E of Sanibel Island

GETTING THERE   By Plane, Train, and Bus   See the Fort Myers section, above, for information about Southwest Florida International Airport, Amtrak's bus/train service, and Greyhound's bus station in Fort Myers.

By Car   From Fort Myers, take either McGregor Boulevard or Summerlin Road and turn left on San Carlos Boulevard (Rte. 865). From I-75 and the airport, follow Daniels Parkway due west, turn left on Summerlin Road, then left again on San Carlos Boulevard. From Naples, take either I-75 or U.S. 41 north to Bonita Springs, then go west on Bonita Beach Road (Rte. 865).

Often overshadowed by trendy Sanibel and Captiva Islands to the north and ritzy Naples to the south, Fort Myers Beach and Estero Island offer just as much sun and sand—and even more moderate prices—than their affluent neighbors.

Droves of young people are attracted to the busy intersection of San Carlos and Estero Boulevards, an area so packed with bars, beach apparel shops, restaurants, and motels that the locals facetiously call it "Times Square." But that Coney Island–like image doesn't apply to the rest of Estero Island, where old-fashioned beach cottages, manicured condos, and quiet motels beckon couples and families in search of an enjoyable vacation. In fact, local promoters now refer to Estero Island, not to Fort Myers Beach; it's their way of distinguishing their part of the island from noisy Times Square.

One thing is for sure: With miles of beach on one side and the peaceful waters of Estero Bay on the other, this barrier island playground has something for almost everyone.

ORIENTATION

INFORMATION   The **Fort Myers Beach Chamber of Commerce,** 17200 San Carlos Blvd., Fort Myers Beach, FL 33931 (tel. 813/454-7500, or toll free 800/782-9283; fax 813/454-7910), provides free information, sells a detailed street map for $1, and operates a visitors information center on the mainland portion of San Carlos Boulevard.

AREA LAYOUT   Fort Myers Beach lies partially on the mainland and on all of two islands: **San Carlos,** close to the mainland, and seven-mile-long, banana-shaped **Estero Island.** The high-rise **Skyway Bridge** over Matanzas Pass connects the two islands. **San Carlos Boulevard** crosses the Skyway Bridge and dead-ends at **Estero Boulevard** in the congested beach area locals call **"Times Square."** Estero Boulevard runs the entire length of Estero Island and continues south to beautiful, preserved **Lover's Key.** Seven miles farther south is the quiet resort area of **Bonita Beach.**

Street numbers start at the north end of Estero Island and get higher as you go south.

GETTING AROUND

BY TROLLEY   The free **Beach Trolley** runs along Estero Boulevard at frequent intervals. From November to April it goes all the way south to Carl E. Johnson State Park on Lover's Key. Ask your hotel staff or call LeeTran (tel. 275-8726) for details.

BY TAXI   Call **Local Motion Taxi** (tel. 463-4111).

BY RENTAL CAR **Avis** is at 6331 Estero Blvd. (tel. 813/463-6843, or toll free 800/831-2847), and **Budget** is at 19200 San Carlos Blvd., near the Skyway Bridge on San Carlos Island (tel. 813/463-5541, or toll free 800/527-0700). See "Getting Around" in the Fort Myers section, above, for information about other rental-car agencies.

BY BICYCLE Rental bikes are available at **Beach Cycle & Repair,** 1901 Estero Blvd. (tel. 463-8844), for $15 a day. (They also rent in-line skates.)

FAST FACTS

Area Code The telephone area code throughout Southwest Florida is 813.

Doctor Walk-in patients are welcomed at the Estero Island Medical Center, 6875 Estero Blvd. (tel. 463-5741).

Emergency To reach the police, report a fire, or call an ambulance, dial 911.

Tax In addition to Florida's statewide 6% sales tax, Lee County imposes a 3% tax on all hotel bills.

WHAT TO SEE & DO

ATTRACTIONS

BEACH PARKS The **Lynn Hall Memorial Park** features a fishing pier and beach right in the middle of Times Square, and a new county beach park equipped with showers and restrooms occupies the north end of Estero Island. But the key attraction in these parts is gorgeous **Lover's Key State Recreation Area,** on the totally preserved Lover's Key, south of Estero. Two wooden bridges lead from the parking lot to the beach, about half a mile away. It's open daily from 8am to 5pm. Admission is $2 per vehicle.

The equally pleasant **Carl E. Johnson County Park,** on the southern half of Lover's Key, has a tram shuttling from its parking area to the beach daily from 9am to 5pm. Admission to the park is $1.50 for adults, 75¢ for children 5 to 17 and free for children under 5. Neither park has a phone.

CRUISES The pontoon boats **Pelican Queen** (tel. 463-6181, ext. 246), **Miss Daisy** (tel. 463-4448), **Sand Dollar** (tel. 466-3600), and **Virginia Gentleman** (tel. 472-0982) all go on nature cruises in search of porpoises, manatees, and a multitude of birds out on Estero Bay, much of which is a state aquatic preserve. Prices range from $10.50 to $12 for adults, $6 to $8 for children. They also have sightseeing and sunset cruises. Reservations are recommended.

For sailing enthusiasts, the 72-foot topsail schooner **Island Rover** (tel. 765-7447) has morning, afternoon, sunset, and moonlight cruises on the gulf from its base under the Sky Bridge on Estero Island. Soft drinks, beer, wine, and champagne are available on board. At least two smaller sailboats go cruising on the gulf: the 36-foot **Quest** (tel. 334-0670) and the 42-foot **Sundance** (tel. 463-7333). Their schedules and rates change by season, so call ahead for information and reservations.

Gamblers can do some serious wagering on the **FunKruz** (tel. 463-5000), a floating casino that makes afternoon cruises several days a week and evening voyages Tuesday through Saturday. See "Evening Entertainment," below, for details.

SPECIAL EVENTS

The **Shrimp Festival,** in late February or early March, sees parades, races, a blessing of the fleet, and much eating of the sweet crustaceans. The **Fourth of July** features fireworks from the fishing pier at Lynn Hall Memorial Park. The **American Sandsculpting Championship,** in early November, is famous. Also in November, the **Offshore Power Boat Races** draw a crowd.

SPORTS & RECREATION

FISHING Anglers can surf-cast, throw their lines off the pier at Times Square, or venture offshore on a number of charter fishing boats which dock at marinas under both ends of the Skyway Bridge. Agents have booths there to take reservations even when the boats are out.

No reservations are required on the **Black Whale III** (tel. 765-5550), the **Miss Barnegat Light** (tel. 463-5665), and the **Island Lady** (tel. 936-7470), three large boats which take groups out daily from Fisherman's Wharf, virtually under the San Carlos Island end of the Skyway Bridge. In addition, the **Great Getaway** and **Great Getaway II** (tel. 466-3600) dock at Getaway Marina on San Carlos Boulevard about half a mile north of the bridge. They all depart about 8am, charge between $25 and $40, and have air-conditioned lounges with bars.

GOLF In addition to the plethora of nearby mainland courses, duffers can play at the **Bay Beach Golf Club,** 7401 Estero Blvd. (tel. 463-2064). It's open to the public daily from 7:30am to 5pm.

MINIATURE GOLF/FUN PARKS Two courses with waterfalls and other obstacles await on the mainland portion of San Carlos Boulevard: **Jungle Golf** (tel. 466-9797) and **Smugglers Cove Adventure Golf** (tel. 466-5855). Both are open daily. Rounds cost $5 for adults, $4 for seniors and children under 12.

WATER SPORTS Several locations are hotbeds of parasailing, waverunners, sailboats, and other beach activities. **Times Square,** at the intersection of San Carlos and Estero Boulevards, and the **Best Western Beach Resort,** about a quarter mile north, are popular spots on Estero's busy north end. Down south, activities are centered around the Holiday Inn and the nearby Carrousel Motel.

Scuba diving is available at **Seahorse Scuba** (tel. 454-3111). Two-tank dives cost $50. Snorkelers can go along for $25 each.

WHERE TO STAY

The hostelries recommended below are removed from the maddening crowds of Times Square, but two chain motels offer comfortable accommodations right in the center of the action: **Ramada Inn,** 1160 Estero Blvd. (tel. 813/463-6158, or toll free 800/544-4592); and **Days Inn,** 1130 Estero Blvd. (tel. 813/463-9759, or toll free 800/544-4592). The **Best Western Beach Resort,** 684 Estero Blvd. (tel. 813/463-6000, or toll free 800/336-4045), is just far enough north to escape the noise but still has a lively beach. The **Holiday Inn Fort Myers Beach,** 6890 Estero Blvd. (tel. 813/463-5711, or toll free 800/465-4329), is the center of activity about halfway down the island.

Fort Myers Beach has a number of condominiums and cottages which offer good value, especially for families or groups. For example, the **Santa Maria,** 7317 Estero Blvd., Fort Myers Beach, FL 33931 (tel. 813/765-6700, or toll free 800/765-6701; fax 813/765-6909), has 57 spacious condo units capable of accommodating up to six people. It's not on the beach, but every suite is beautifully furnished and flaunts a screened balcony, full-size washer/dryer, complete kitchen with microwave, a wet bar, and two TVs. There's a swimming pool, two Jacuzzis, and a sauna. Daily rates run $130 to $210 from February to April, $75 to $170 off-season. Weekly rates range from $860 to $1,390 during winter, from $485 to $825 off-season.

Santa Maria is managed by SunStream Hotels and Resorts, which also handles the **Seaside Suites Resort,** 4770 Estero Blvd., Fort Myers Beach, FL 33931 (tel. 813/463-4944, or toll free 800/723-4944), and the **Pointe Estero Island Resort,** 6640 Estero Blvd., Fort Myers Beach, FL 33931 (tel. 813/765-1155, or toll free 800/237-5141). Unlike Santa Maria, both are on the beach.

The **Fort Myers Beach Chamber of Commerce** publishes a complete list of condos and time-shares (see "Orientation," above).

DAYS INN AT LOVER'S KEY, 8701 Estero Blvd., Fort Myers Beach, FL 33931. Tel. and fax 813/765-4422, or toll free 800/325-2525. 75 studio apts. A/C TV TEL

$ Rates (including continental breakfast): Winter, $160–$190 studio apt. Off-season, $80–$150 studio apt. AE, DISC, MC, V.

The only building on Black Island, between Estero Island and Lover's Key, this 14-story, family-managed hotel offers a very quiet location and wonderful gulf, island, and bay views from its balconied apartments. Another highlight is a small, palm-fringed beach with lots of South Seas charm and canvas cabañas, powerboats, waverunners, and sailboats to rent. A coffee shop in a fully screened patio is open for breakfast and lunch. Guests enjoy free sundowner cocktails between 5:30 and 6:30pm.

THE OUTRIGGER BEACH RESORT, 6200 Estero Blvd. (P.O. Box 271), Fort Myers Beach, FL 33931. Tel. 813/463-3131, or toll free 800/749-3131. Fax 813/463-6577. 76 rms, 68 efficiency apts. A/C TV TEL

$ Rates: Winter, $90–$155 double. Off-season, $70–$125 double. DISC, MC, V.

The same friendly owners have maintained this clean, pleasant gulfside motel since 1965. Their "ranch efficiencies" in the original building offer bargain rates during the winter months; they're nothing fancy—cinderblock walls, shower-only baths, and kitchenettes—but they have the feel of small cottages, with excellent ventilation through both front and rear louvered windows. While some have views of the parking lot, most units in a newer, two-story building face a courtyard with swimming pool, large wooden deck for sunning, and beachside tiki (thatched-roof) bar which dispenses libations all day. The Deckside Cafe serves a breakfast buffet and is open for sandwiches and snacks until 8pm. A children's program keeps the kids busy.

PINK SHELL BEACH AND BAY RESORT, 275 Estero Blvd., Fort Myers Beach, FL 33931. Tel. 813/463-6161, or toll free 800/237-5786. Fax 813/463-1229. 175 units. A/C TV TEL

$ Rates: Winter, $155–$316. Off-season, $84–$236. AE, DISC, MC, V.

Quietly situated near Estero's north end, with frontages on both the gulf and Matanzas Pass, this family-oriented resort offers a variety of accommodations ranging from beach cottages to hotel rooms with or without kitchenettes. The one-, two-, and three-bedroom cottages on stilts make up for a lack of luxury with lots of 1950s-Florida charm, including tongue-in-groove paneling and ceiling fans. They are heavily booked during the winter months, so reserve early. Hotel rooms in a five-story building have lovely views of Sanibel Island from their balconies.

The gulf side of the property has a very broad beach with powdery white sand and water-sports equipment to rent. Two heated swimming pools and a kiddie pool sit by the beach. On the bay side, there's a marina (the *Pelican Queen* nature and sightseeing cruises leave here, and the *Island Rover* sailboat picks up guests for its cruises), a store for buying victuals, lighted tennis courts, and the Hungry Pelican Cafe, on a deck overlooking the channel (guests only can have breakfast, lunch, or dinner here).

SANDPIPER GULF RESORT, 5550 Estero Blvd., Fort Myers Beach, FL 33931. Tel. 813/463-5721. 63 suites. A/C TV TEL

$ Rates: Winter, $97–$114 suite for two. Off-season, $57–$75 suite for two. DISC, MC, V.

The units at this clean gulfside motel all are large enough to have dividers between the living and sleeping areas. They also have full kitchens, convertible sofas, and sun decks overlooking either the gulf or a courtyard with a heated swimming pool and hot tub. A wooden boardwalk leads from the bedecked pool to the beach. Some units are in two- or three-story buildings arranged in a U with flattened ends right on the beach; others are in the Sandpiper II, a palm-fronted high-rise with its own heated pool next door. All units are identical, but those facing directly on the beach are more expensive. Facilities include a coin laundry and gift shop. Restaurants are nearby.

CAMPING

Red Coconut RV Resort, 3001 Estero Blvd., Fort Myers Beach, FL 33931 (tel. 813/463-7200; fax 813/463-2609), has RV and tent sites right on the beach. On the mainland, **Gulf Air Travel Park,** 17279 San Carlos Blvd., Fort Myers Beach, FL 33931 (tel. 813/466-8100; fax 813/466-4044), and **San Carlos RV Park & Islands,** 18071 San Carlos Blvd., Fort Myers Beach, FL 33931 (tel. 813/466-3133), have RV and tent sites.

WHERE TO DINE
MODERATE

THE BRIDGE RESTAURANT, 708 Fisherman's Wharf, San Carlos Island, under the Skyway Bridge. Tel. 765-0050.
Cuisine: SEAFOOD/STEAK. **Reservations:** Recommended.
$ Prices: Appetizers $3.50–$7; main courses $10–$22; lunch platters $6–$9; sandwiches and salads $5–$9. AE, DC, MC, V.
Open: Daily 11am–11pm.

The emphasis is on seafood straight from the fishing boats that dock at this rough-hewn clapboard restaurant with fine water views. Specialties of the house are fresh fish, shrimp, and prime-grade steaks seared over a hickory fire. There also are broiled selections, plus seafood pasta dishes. The outdoor Hard Dock Cafe, at the water level, is a popular watering hole, especially during reggae parties from 4 to 10pm on Sunday.

CHANNEL MARK, 19001 San Carlos Blvd., at the north end of San Carlos Island. Tel. 463-9127.
Cuisine: NORTHERN ITALIAN. **Reservations:** Not accepted.
$ Prices: Appetizers $4–$8; main courses $14–$18; pastas $8.50–$13; sandwiches $6–$8. AE, DC, DISC, MC, V.
Open: Lunch daily 11am–4pm; dinner Sun–Thurs 4–10pm, Fri–Sat 4–11pm.

Nestled by the "Little Bridge" leading onto San Carlos Island's northern end, every table here looks out on a maze of channel markers on Hurricane Bay. Owners Mike McGuigan and Andy Welsh put a northern Italian spin on their seafood dishes, such as shrimp with cheese tortellini under tomato, pesto, or Alfredo sauce. Their American creations include grouper breaded in corn flakes and almonds. This is a nice spot for a romantic dinner, and the dock with palms growing through it is a relaxing place for waterside lunch.

GULF SHORE RESTAURANT, 1270 Estero Blvd., on the beach. Tel. 463-9951.
Cuisine: SEAFOOD. **Reservations:** Recommended.
$ Prices: Appetizers $4.50–$8.50; main courses $13–$22; early-bird specials $10. AE, DC, DISC, MC, V.
Open: Breakfast/lunch daily 7am–3pm; dinner daily 4:30–10pm.

Home of the Crescent Beach Casino back in the 1920s, this old clapboard building offers splendid views of the gulf and beach, especially of gorgeous young folk frolicking at the lively Lani Kai Resort next door. Breakfast is served until 3pm, so if a little hair-of-the-dog will help after a hard night at the Lani Kai, order "red beer" (tomato juice and suds) to wash down spicy eggs caliente or any of 16 different omelets. Lunch offers heaped-high sandwiches, salads, and seafood plates, while dinners provide a variety of seafood, prime rib, baby back ribs, and boneless chicken teriyaki. Lunches and light fare are also served in the Cottage Bar, perhaps the most infamous drinking establishment on the beach.

MATANZAS SEAFARE COMPANY, 416 Crescent St., under the Skyway Bridge on San Carlos Island. Tel. 463-3838.
Cuisine: SEAFOOD. **Reservations:** Not accepted.
$ Prices: Appetizers $3–$7; main courses $12–$16; sandwiches and light fare $6–$7.50. AE, DISC, MC, V.
Open: Mon–Fri 11am–10pm, Sat–Sun 7am–10pm.

Although it's right in the tourist district, local residents still frequent this casual, friendly restaurant with moderate prices. It sits right next to the Matanzas Marina, and you can dine on a dock by the boats or inside the dark-paneled dining room hung with ceiling fans. The seafare consists of fried, broiled, or charcoal-grilled seafood, with some Italian-accented selections such as grouper scampi. A light-fare menu offers shrimp salad, fish sandwiches, and hamburgers.

THE SKIPPER'S GALLEY, 3040 Estero Blvd., on the beach. Tel. 463-6139.

Cuisine: SEAFOOD/STEAK. **Reservations:** Not accepted.
$ Prices: Appetizers $3–$7; main courses $14–$20; early-bird specials $8–$13. AE, DISC, MC, V.
Open: Dinner only, daily 4:30–10pm.

Dine casually but elegantly at this fine restaurant whose every table has a view of the beach and gulf. Most selections here are breaded and fried or broiled, but the chef prepares tempting specialties such as pompano baked in parchment. There's prime rib, steaks, and chicken dishes for landlubbers. The early-bird specials between 4:30 and 6:30pm are a great value, especially since that's when the sun sets over the gulf.

SNUG HARBOR, 645 San Carlos Blvd., under the Estero Island end of the Skyway Bridge. Tel. 463-8977.
Cuisine: SEAFOOD. **Reservations:** Accepted holidays only.
$ Prices: Appetizers $3–$7; main courses $6–$10 at lunch, $11–$15 at dinner. DISC, MC, V.
Open: Lunch daily 11:30am–3pm; dinner daily 4:30–10pm.

This long restaurant is built on a pier, thereby giving diners views not only *of* water but *into* the water. The L-shaped building opens at one end to the thatch-covered Tiki Hut, which is the preferred place to wait for a table. The regular menu offers steamed, broiled, or fried shrimp, scallops, and grouper, but the best offerings here are the chef's excellent daily specials, such as fresh local snapper stuffed with crabmeat, shrimp, and spinach. There's a children's menu, too. Enjoy the view from the Shanty Bar upstairs.

BUDGET

GRECO'S ITALIAN DELI, in Villa Santini Plaza, 7205 Estero Blvd. Tel. 463-5634.
Cuisine: ITALIAN. **Reservations:** Not accepted.
$ Prices: Subs and sandwiches $3.50–$6; pizzas $12–$15; ready-to-cook meals $6–$7. No credit cards.
Open: Winter, daily 8am–8pm. Off-season, daily 8am–7pm.

Wonderful aromas of baking pizzas, calzones, cannolis, breads, and cookies have been wafting from Greco's since 1958. Order at the counter over a chiller packed with fresh deli meats, Italian sausage, and cheeses, then devour your goodies at tables inside or out on the covered walkway. You can also take "heat and eat" meals of spaghetti, lasagne, eggplant parmigiana, manicotti, and ravioli back to your hotel, apartment, or condo oven. Shelves are loaded with Italian wines, pastas, butter cookies, and anisette toast.

EVENING ENTERTAINMENT

THE CLUB & BAR SCENE The area around Times Square always seems active, but the real night owls and the 20-something crowd hang out at the **Lani Kai Resort,** 1400 Estero Blvd. (tel. 765-6500), where live rock and reggae bands roar virtually all night at the beachside tiki bar. A good vantage point to watch the action is from the **Cottage Bar,** at the Gulf Shore Restaurant next door (tel. 463-9951). Both establishments can become raucous late at night. Live bands and disk jockeys liven up the nights at the **Top O'Mast Restaurant & Lounge,** nearby at 1028 Estero Blvd. (tel. 463-9424).

Throngs head to San Carlos Island on Sunday when the **Hard Dock Cafe,** at the Bridge Restaurant on Fisherman's Wharf (tel. 765-0050), holds its reggae party from 4 to 10pm.

Down south in the more couples- and family-oriented part of the beach, the **Holiday Inn Fort Myers Beach,** 6890 Estero Blvd. (tel. 463-5711), has live music for dancing on Friday and Saturday from 9pm to 2am. Beyond Lover's Key, **McCulley's Rooftop,** at the foot of the bridge in Bonita Beach (tel. 992-0033), is another popular place to dine and dance.

GAMBLING CRUISES The floating casino *FunKruz* (tel. 463-5000, or toll free 800/688-7529) sails nine miles out into the gulf, where gambling is legal. Evening cruises depart Tuesday through Saturday at 6:30pm from Palm Grove Marina, 2500 Main St. on San Carlos Island, and return after midnight. Day cruises go out five days a week. In addition to craps and other tables, there's dining and dancing. Weekday cruises cost $40 per person; those on Friday and Saturday nights are $50. Women pay half on Friday.

3. SANIBEL & CAPTIVA ISLANDS

18 miles W of Fort Myers, 40 miles N of Naples

GETTING THERE   By Plane, Train, and Bus   See the Fort Myers section, above, for information about the Southwest Florida International Airport, Amtrak's rail/bus service from Tampa, and Greyhound's nearest bus station.

By Car   From Fort Myers, take McGregor Boulevard or Summerlin Road, which merges with McGregor, to the Sanibel Causeway ($3-per-car toll going over, free coming back). From I-75 and the airport, follow Daniels Parkway due west, turn left on Summerlin Road (Rte. 869), and proceed to the Sanibel Causeway.

Sanibel and Captiva seem a world removed from the neon signs, amusement parks, and high-rise condos that clutter many other beach resorts. Sanibel's main drag, Periwinkle Way, runs under a canopy of whispery pines, gnarled oaks, and twisted banyans so thick they almost obscure the signs for chic shops and restaurants. This wooded ambience is the work of local voters, who have saved their trees, limited the size and appearance of signs, and enacted tough zoning laws that keep all buildings below the top of the tallest palm. Furthermore, nearly 40% of the islands are preserved as wildlife refuges. All this makes Sanibel and Captiva one of the world's most visually pleasing and environmentally conscious beachside destinations anywhere.

Legend says that Ponce de León named the larger of these two barrier islands "San Ybel," after his queen, Santa Isabella of Spain. Another legend claims that Captiva's name is derived from infamous pirate José Gaspar's practice of keeping his kidnapped women prisoners there.

Nothing much happened on Sanibel and Captiva from Gaspar's time until 1892, when a few farmers settled here. In 1899 the Bailey family opened what is still Bailey's General Store. An early settler named Clarence Chadwick started an unsuccessful key lime and copra plantation on Captiva. Many of his towering coconut palms still stand, adding to the island's tropical luster.

Concluding that their terrific fishing grounds could be more profitable than their sandy soil, local residents soon switched from farming to fishing camps. Affluent anglers flocked to sleepy Captiva, first by private boat and then by ferry. The islands became accessible to everyone in 1963, when the Sanibel Causeway opened, but thanks to the zoning laws—and to wealthy settlers who built their luxury retreats back in the bush—both Sanibel and Captiva still have that hideaway feel the fishermen found here a century ago.

ORIENTATION

INFORMATION   The **Sanibel-Captiva Islands Chamber of Commerce,** P.O. Box 166, Sanibel Island, FL 33957 (tel. 813/472-1080; fax 813/472-1070), maintains a visitor center on the right-hand side of Causeway Boulevard as you drive onto Sanibel from Fort Myers. There are racks of free information, and the chamber sells an "Island Guide" for 55¢ and a detailed street map for $1.50 ($1.50 and $2.50, respectively, by mail). Other books are for sale, including comprehensive shelling guides and a helpful collection of menus from the islands' restaurants.

AREA LAYOUT   Sanibel is the larger of the two islands, about 12 miles long and 3 miles wide. The 6-mile-long Captiva is so narrow that you can walk across it in a few minutes. The bay sides of both islands give way to a maze of waterways and mangrove islands inhabited by alligators and other wildlife.

Causeway Boulevard (or Causeway Road) intersects **Periwinkle Way,** which runs inland from the eastern end of Sanibel to the commercial and governmental center in the middle of the island. This canopied main drag ends at **Tarpon Bay Road,** the north-south route between Tarpon Bay and the gulf. **Sanibel-Captiva Road** picks up there and runs along the J. N. (Ding) Darling National Wildlife Refuge (watch for the "Gator Xing" warnings) to Captiva, where it takes a hard right, becomes **Captiva Road,** and ends at the South Seas Plantation Resort & Yacht Harbour. The majority of Sanibel's hotels, resorts, and condominiums lie on **East, Middle, and West Gulf Drives.** Linked together, they parallel Periwinkle as they follow the beaches.

GETTING AROUND

BY TAXI Call **Sanibel Taxi** (tel. 472-4160).

BY RENTAL CAR **Avis** has an agent at 1015 Periwinkle Way (tel. 472-8180, or toll free 800/831-2847). **Budget** has a desk at the South Seas Plantation Resort & Yacht Harbour on Captiva (tel. 472-9600, or toll free 800/527-0700). See "Getting Around" in the Fort Myers section, above, for information about other rental-car firms.

BY BICYCLE Get a map of Sanibel's many bike paths from the chamber of commerce visitor center (see "Orientation," above) or from one of the island's bike-rental firms: **Fennimore's Cycle Shop,** 2353 Periwinkle Way (tel. 472-5577); **Island Moped,** 1470 Periwinkle Way (tel. 472-5248); and **Tarpon Bay Recreation,** at the north end of Tarpon Bay Road (tel. 472-8900). Bike rates range from $3 per hour to $12 a day. Both Fennimore's and Island Moped rent tandems, mopeds, and scooters, plus tricycles and four-wheelers with children's trailers attached.

BY TROLLEY From November through April, the **Sanibel Trolley** (tel. 472-6374) makes seven loops around the islands, starting at the chamber of commerce visitor center on Causeway Boulevard, proceeding along East, Middle, and West Gulf Drives, and returning via Periwinkle Way. You can flag it down anywhere except on Periwinkle Way, where it halts only at marked stops. Two trips go on to Captiva, passing the J. N. (Ding) Darling National Wildlife Refuge en route. The Sanibel portion costs $2 for adults, $1 for children under 5; double those fares for Captiva. Tickets are good all day, with free reboarding.

Loaded with history and local insights, the narrated **Trolley Tour** operates from November to April, with departures from the chamber of commerce at 10am and 1pm on Monday, Wednesday, Friday, and Saturday. Fares are $8 for adults, $4 for children under 5.

FAST FACTS

Area Code The telephone area code throughout Southwest Florida is 813.

Doctor Doctors are available at the Island Medical Center, 1648 Periwinkle Way (tel. 395-1130).

Emergency To reach the police, report a fire, or call an ambulance, dial 911.

Tax In addition to Florida's statewide 6% sales tax, Lee County imposes a 3% tax on all hotel bills.

WHAT TO SEE & DO

WILDLIFE PRESERVES

C.R.O.W. [CARE AND REHABILITATION OF WILDLIFE], Sanibel-Captiva Rd. Tel. 472-3644.

Professional rehabilitation specialists and volunteers staff this center devoted to the rescue and eventual return to the wild of sick, injured, and orphaned native and migratory wildlife. Some 1,800 "patients" from more than 300 species are treated annually. Wildlife shelters duplicate natural habitats.

Admission: Free.

Open: Oct–Mar, open house last Sun of each month 1–3pm; other months, by appointment only.

J. N. [DING] DARLING NATIONAL WILDLIFE REFUGE, Sanibel-Captiva Rd. Tel. 472-1100.

Named for the *New York Times* cartoonist who was a frequent visitor here and who helped create 330 other wildlife sanctuaries as head of the agency that became the U.S. Fish and Wildlife Service, this 5,000-acre refuge occupies nearly a third of Sanibel Island. Alligators, raccoons, otters, and hundreds of species of birds make their homes in its mangrove swamps and uplands. A boardwalk and a five-mile, one-way Wildlife Drive begin at the visitors center. If you do it yourself, stop at the visitors center first and watch videos about what you'll see. Tapes about the birds are shown continuously. A more comprehensive introductory program is shown at 10am, noon, 2pm, and 4pm. The best times for the drive are early morning, late afternoon, and at low tide (tables are posted at the visitors center). Give yourself at least an hour. Mosquitos and "no-see-um" sandflies are prevalent at dawn and dusk, so bring insect repellent.

An alternative is to take a two-hour narrated **tram tour** given by Tarpon Bay Recreation (tel. 472-8900), at the north end of Tarpon Bay Road. They cost $7 for adults, $3.50 for children under 13.

Admission: Visitors center, free; Wildlife Drive, $4 per vehicle, $1 for hikers and bicyclists (current Federal Duck Stamps, Golden Age, Golden Access, and Golden Eagle Passports accepted).

Open: Wildlife Drive, Sat–Thurs dawn–dusk. Visitor center, Nov–Apr, Sat–Thurs 9am–5pm; May–Oct, Sat–Thurs 9am–4pm. **Closed:** Federal holidays.

SANIBEL/CAPTIVA CONSERVATION FOUNDATION, Sanibel-Captiva Rd. Tel. 472-2329.

This nonprofit organization maintains a nature center, native plant nursery, and four miles of nature trails on a 247-acre wetlands tract along the Sanibel River. Environmental workshops, guided trail walks, beach walks, and a natural-history boat cruise help guests learn more about the islands' unusual ecosystems. Various items are for sale, including native plants.

Admission: $1, free for children under 12.

Open: Nature center, Jan–Apr, Mon–Sat 9:30am–4pm; summer, Mon–Fri 9:30am–3:30pm. Call for schedule of walks and cruises.

OTHER ATTRACTIONS

The **Sanibel Historical Village & Museum,** 950 Dunlop Rd., off Palm Ridge Road (tel. 472-4648), keeps expanding and now includes the pioneer-vintage Rutland home, the 1927–66 version of Bailey's General Store, and the old post office. Displays highlight the islands' prehistoric Calusa tribal era, old photos from pioneer days, turn-of-the-century clothing, and a variety of memorabilia. Special exhibits feature antiques in December and quilts in January. Open Wednesday through Saturday from 10am to 4pm; closed September 1 to October 15. Admission has been free, but that may change as the facility grows.

The **Sanibel Lighthouse,** at the east end of Periwinkle Way, has marked the entrance to San Carlos Bay since 1884. It's now operated by remote control and electricity, but the light keepers used to live in the cottages at the base of the 94-foot tower and climb the steps inside the cylinder every day to fill the giant lantern with oil and turn it on and off. The lighthouse itself isn't open to visitors, but the grounds are.

BEACHES Sanibel has five public beach-access areas with parking: the eastern point around **Sanibel Lighthouse,** which has a fishing pier; **Gulfside City Park,** at the end of Algiers Lane, off Casa Ybel Road; **Tarpon Bay Road Beach,** at the south end of Tarpon Bay Road; **Bowman's Beach,** off Sanibel-Captiva Road ($2 per vehicle to park); and **Thompson Beach,** at Blind Pass between Sanibel and Captiva, which is highly popular at sunset since it faces due west. All except Tarpon Bay Road Beach have restrooms.

On Captiva, the most popular beaches are the long stretch north of Blind Pass, where the houses are on the bay side of the road, and at the end of Captiva Road in front of the Mucky Duck Restaurant. Parking along these stretches, however, is scarce during the winter season.

CANOE TRIPS   A quiet canoe is an excellent way to paddle in close to the myriad birds that feed and nest along the quiet waterways and mangroves that line both islands' bay sides. A local resident for many years, **Mark "Bird" Westphal** (tel. 472-5218) leaves at dawn for trips on the Sanibel River and through the J. N. (Ding) Darling National Wildlife Refuge. **Michael Borma** does likewise, from Tarpon Bay Recreation (tel. 472-5900), at the north end of Tarpon Bay Road. The trips cost about $15 for adults, $5 for children under 12. Reservations are essential.

Do-it-yourselfers can rent canoes and kayaks from **Tarpon Bay Recreation** (tel. 472-8900), at the north end of Tarpon Bay Road on Sanibel; and at **Teddy's Kayak & Canoe Co.,** at McCarthy's Marina (tel. 395-0100), and at **'Tween Waters Inn Marina** (tel. 472-5161), both on Captiva.

CRUISES   **Captiva Cruises** (tel. 472-5300) goes out daily from the South Seas Plantation Resort & Yacht Harbour on Captiva to Cabbage Key, Useppa Island, Cayo Costa County Park, and Boca Grande (see "Easy Island Excursions," below, and "An Easy Excursion to Boca Grande" in the Fort Myers section, above). There are also nature and sunset cruises, which cost $25 per person. Reservations are required, since Captiva Cruises must arrange to have an entry permit waiting at the main gate to this exclusive resort.

SHELLING   Sanibel is considered one of the top three places in the world to collect seashells, with some 160 species found on its shores. December to February are the best months, but many beautiful specimens have been found at other times of the year. Low tide is the best time to look for whelks, olives, scallops, sanddollars, conch, and many more (the hotels post the tide tables). Florida law allows the taking of just two live shells per species per person, and the J. N. (Ding) Darling National Wildlife Refuge prohibits taking live specimens altogether. Nevertheless, tons of dead shells are washed ashore by the winds and tides.

With so many visitors hunched over in the "Sanibel stoop," you may have better luck on the adjacent shoals and nearby islands, such as Upper Captiva and Cayo Costa (see "Easy Island Excursions," below). At least 15 charter-boat skippers offer to take guests on shelling expeditions to these less-explored areas. Four of them operate from **'Tween Waters Inn Marina** (tel. 472-5161) on Captiva, including the guided tours led by **Capt. Mike Fleury** (tel. 472-1015 day or 994-7195 evenings). Others are based at **Jenson's Twin Palms Marina,** on Captiva (tel. 472-5800), and at the **Sanibel Marina,** on North Yachtsman Drive, off Periwinkle Way east of Causeway Boulevard on Sanibel (tel. 472-2723). They all distribute brochures at the chamber of commerce visitor center (see "Orientation," above) and are listed in the free tourist publications found there.

The new **Bailey-Matthews Shell Museum,** 2431 Periwinkle Way, Sanibel (tel. 395-2233), should be exhibiting its 100,000-plus collection in 1995.

SPECIAL EVENTS

The main event is the **Sanibel Shell Fair,** a four-day celebration beginning on the first Thursday in March. Exhibits include shells from around the world, and unusual shell art is for sale. Arts and crafts also are on the March schedule, featuring wood carving, weaving, stringing fish nets, and leather embossing.

The **Island Road Rally,** a treasure hunt on wheels, is held in July. October's highlight is the **Island Luau,** presented around the pool at the Dunes Golf & Tennis Club, 949 San Castle Rd. (tel. 472-3355). The Dunes also hosts the annual **Taste of the Islands,** a sampling of cuisines prepared by local eateries, in May and **Jazz-on-the-Green** in November.

One of the most spectacular sights is the **Luminary Trail,** the first weekend in

December, when thousands of candles in paper bags illuminate Periwinkle Way and Sanibel-Captiva Road. Shops and restaurants do a booming business.

SPORTS & RECREATION

BOATING & FISHING On Sanibel, rental boats and charter-fishing excursions are available from **The Boat House** (tel. 472-2531) and the **Sanibel Marina** (tel. 472-2723), both on North Yachtsman Drive, off Periwinkle Way east of Causeway Boulevard.

On Captiva, check with the **'Tween Waters Inn Marina** (tel. 472-5161), **Jenson's Twin Palms Marina** (tel. 472-5800), and **McCarthy's Marina** (tel. 395-0100), all on Captiva Road. Many charter-fishing captains leave free brochures at the chamber of commerce visitor center (see "Orientation," above), and they are listed in the free tourist publications found there.

Also based on Captiva, two sailboats take guests out on the waters: Mike McMillan's *Adventure* (tel. 472-7532) and Mic Gurley's *New Moon* (tel. 395-1782).

GOLF & TENNIS Golfers can tee off on the 6,000-yard, par-70, 18-hole course—and hackers can play tennis—at the **Dunes Golf and Tennis Club,** 949 Sandcastle Rd., Sanibel (tel. 472-2535). The **Beachview Golf Club,** 1100 Par View Dr., Sanibel (tel. 472-2626), has a 6,200-yard, par-71 course. Call a day in advance for a tee time. The **South Seas Plantation Resort & Yacht Harbour** has tennis courts and a 9-hole golf course, but for its guests only.

WATER SPORTS Both scuba divers and snorkelers can go along with **Redfish Dive Center,** 2330 Palm Ridge Rd., Sanibel (tel. 472-3438), which also rents equipment and teaches diving. **Yolo Watersports** (tel. 472-9656) offers parasailing and waverunner rentals on the beach in front of the Mucky Duck Restaurant, at the gulf end of Andy Rosse Lane on Captiva.

WHERE TO STAY

No budget-minded chain has a motel on either of these affluent islands. A local company, **Sanibel Resort Group,** 1539 Periwinkle Way, Sanibel Island, FL 33957 (tel. 813/472-1833 or 813/472-1001; fax 813/472-8131), manages six older motels and small apartment complexes on Sanibel, with rates ranging from $70 to $165 during winter, $40 to $90 off-season.

Two chains have comfortable resorts right on Sanibel's beaches. The **Best Western Sanibel Beach Resort,** 3787 W. Gulf Dr. (tel. 813/472-1700, or toll free 800/645-6559), has recently been renovated and has lovely grounds with palms, orange trees, and red and pink hibiscus. Rooms and apartments there range from $155 to $285 in winter, from $97 to $195 off-season. The **Ramada Inn Resort,** 1231 Middle Gulf Dr. (tel. 813/472-4123, or toll free 800/228-2828), has an equally pleasant beach setting around its rooms, efficiencies, and apartments, plus the popular J. Todd's Restaurant. Rates range from $168 to $215 during winter, $104 to $144 off-season.

The chamber of commerce's **"Island Guide"** contains a list of both condos and rental agents (see "Orientation," above), or you can contact two of the largest rental agents directly: **Priscilla Murphy Realty,** 1177 Causeway Blvd. (P.O. Box 5), Sanibel Island, FL 33957 (tel. 813/472-4883, or toll free 800/237-6008; fax 813/472-8995), and **VIP Vacation Rentals,** 1509 Periwinkle Way, Sanibel Island, FL 33957 (tel. 813/472-1613, or toll free 800/237-7526; fax 813/481-8477).

SANIBEL ISLAND

Very Expensive

SUNDIAL BEACH & TENNIS RESORT, 1451 Middle Gulf Dr., Sanibel Island, FL 33957. Tel. 813/472-4151, or toll free 800/237-4184. Fax 813/472-1809. 260 condo apts. A/C TV TEL

$ Rates: Winter, $235–$435 condo apt. Off-season, $153–$280 condo apt. AE, DC, DISC, MC, V.

⭐ Sometimes described as "Maui style," this award-winning, family-oriented resort stars an enormous, palm-studded, beachside pool and bar area that definitely has Hawaiian ambience. Very spacious accommodations with party-size balconies overlook the beach or tropically landscaped gardens from two- and three-story buildings (as high as they get on Sanibel). Beachside lanai units have screened porches and large patios. The apartments are individually owned condominium units, so the decor varies but is always tasteful. They have one, two, or three bedrooms, large living rooms, dining areas, and complete kitchens. Some even have an extra den.

Dining/Entertainment: The award-winning Windows on the Water dining room offers glorious gulf views at breakfast, lunch, and dinner (reservations not accepted). Master chefs put on a show as they prepare delicious steak, chicken, and seafood dishes right by your table in Noopie's Japanese Seafood & Steakhouse, where dinner reservations are required (tel. 395-6014). The Deli offers piled-high sandwiches, snacks, and picnic foods from early morning to midnight. Sprinkles Sweet Shop dishes up ice cream and pastries. Out by the pool, Crocodile's Patio Bar and Grille offers sandwiches, hamburgers, and salads for ravenous sun worshippers. The relaxing Sunset Lounge is the sunset-time venue for popular pianist and chanteuse Helen Skelton. A dance band then plays top-40 hits from 9pm until very late.

Services: Cold-food-only room service (until 10pm), grocery-shopping service (which stocks condos prior to arrival), babysitting and kid's recreation program (including tours of a small ecology center with touch tank), daily adult activities program, complimentary marine biology programs.

Facilities: 13 tennis courts, five swimming pools, jogging trail, fitness room, gift shop, convention facilities, games (board games and shuffleboard, croquet, putting green, and Ping-Pong equipment); bike, boat, movie, and VCR rentals. Golfers can play at the Dunes Golf & Tennis Club.

Expensive

CASA YBEL RESORT, 2255 W. Gulf Dr., Sanibel Island, FL 33957. Tel. 813/472-3145, or toll free 800/237-8906. Fax 813/472-2109. 114 apts. A/C TV TEL

$ Rates: Winter, $1,450–$2,500 per week apt. Off-season, $165–$200 per day apt. DISC, MC, V.

On the historic site of Sanibel's first beachfront resort, Thistle Lodge, the present-day Casa Ybel's turn-of-the-century central building houses a dining room, where both guests and nonguests can enjoy wonderful cuisine and gulf views. The spacious one- and two-bedroom apartments are bright with tropical rattan furniture, pastel carpeting, and ceramic-tile floors. The large landscaped swimming pool and bar area is a popular rendezvous. Children congregate in their special playground. Six tennis courts get plenty of action. The water-sports center has rental bikes, sailboats, Sunfish, and windsurfers.

GALLERY MOTEL, 541 E. Gulf Dr., Sanibel Island, FL 33957. Tel. 813/472-1400, or toll free 800/831-7384. Fax 813/472-6518. 32 units. A/C TV TEL

$ Rates: Winter, $160–$230. Off-season, $87–$120. MC, V.

Nestled in tall palm trees beside the gulf, the blue-and-green Gallery Motel has a tranquil location near the island's southeastern tip. All its motel rooms, efficiencies, cottages, and apartments have open-air balconies or porches, refrigerators, and (except for six motel rooms) full kitchens. The cottages are spacious and very brightly furnished. The swimming pool and suntanning patio are next to the wide expanse of white beach. Barbecue grills, shuffleboard, and rental bikes are available.

SANIBEL INN, 937 E. Gulf Dr., Sanibel Island, FL 33957. Tel. 813/472-3181, or toll free 800/237-1491. Fax 813/472-5234. 48 rms, 24 condos. A/C TV TEL

$ Rates: Winter, $225–$355. Off-season, $140–$200. AE, DISC, MC, V.

This beachfront inn includes two- and three-story buildings with attractively furnished rooms complete with mini-refrigerator and coffee maker. The elaborate condo units have separate bedrooms, living rooms, dining areas, and kitchenettes. The swimming pool area is tropically landscaped, and a boardwalk leads to the beach. There are two tennis courts, rental bikes, and a water-sports center. Portofino's, the inn's popular restaurant, is notable for northern Italian cuisine, as well as fresh seafood and steaks; it's open for breakfast and dinner. The poolside café is open for lunch.

Moderate

BEACHVIEW COTTAGES, 3325 W. Gulf Dr., Sanibel Island, FL 33957. Tel. 813/472-1202, or toll free 800/492-3224. Fax 813/472-4720. 32 cottages. A/C TV TEL

$ Rates: Winter, $100–$125 cottage. Off-season, $80–$150 cottage. Monthly rates less 15%. DISC, MC, V.

While modern resorts may try to re-create a South Seas island setting, this relic from Florida's recent past really does look as if it belongs beside the lagoon on Bora Bora. A narrow, unpaved lane runs from the road to the beach and is flanked by a row of palms, hibiscus, and old-fashioned wooden cottages. The shiplap houses date from the 1950s, so don't expect luxuries. They have screen porches off their knotty pine–paneled living rooms. Most are duplex units, and some have dividers instead of walls between the living and sleeping areas. There's no restaurant, but the West Wind Motel has one nearby. There is a small swimming pool, and a boardwalk leads to a beach pavilion equipped with old-fashioned wooden chairs and recliners. The cottages are often rented on a monthly basis during winter, so reserve early.

ISLAND INN, 3111 W. Gulf Dr., Sanibel Island, FL 33957. Tel. 813/472-1651, or toll free 800/851-5088. Fax 813/472-0051. 56 units. A/C TV TEL

$ Rates: Winter (including breakfast and dinner), $107–$191 single; $138–$191 double. Off-season (including breakfast), $82–$169 single; $89–$169 double. AE, DISC, MC, V.

Frankly, it's difficult to get accommodations here during the peak winter season, but it's worth trying, because this classic beach resort has been in business for 100 years. The central building houses a genteel dining room, a spacious lounge, and a library comfortably furnished with old-style bentwood and wicker sofas and chairs. It's the kind of place where guests dress up for dinner—coats and ties for men—during the winter season, when seating is assigned (some guests have had the same table for years). This old building looks through a South Pacific–like garden to the gulf. Although neither charming in the old-time sense nor luxurious by today's standards, the cottages and motel rooms (with or without kitchens) are modern and comfortable, and have screened porches or balconies. There's a small swimming pool, tennis court, and croquet area.

CAPTIVA ISLAND

Very Expensive

SOUTH SEAS PLANTATION RESORT & YACHT HARBOUR, P.O. Box 194, Captiva Island, FL 33924. Tel. 813/472-5111, or toll free 800/237-6000. Fax 813/472-7541. 600 rms, apts, cottages, town houses, and private homes. A/C TV TEL

$ Rates: Winter, $260–$275 double; $265–$660 apt, cottage, town house, or home. Off-season, $195–$245 double; $205–$530 apt, cottage, town house, or home. 16% gratuity added to all bills. DC, DISC, MC, V.

Many celebrities come here to unwind amid the 330 acres of tropical island beauty on Captiva's northern half (a free shuttle constantly carries guests the 2½ miles from one end of this narrow resort to the other). This was Clarence Chadwick's copra plantation during the late 19th century, and his coconut palms still wave above today's mega-million-dollar total retreat. There's a grand variety of accommodations, some with private pools and their own tennis courts. There are hundreds of gardenside and seaside villas; one-, two-, and three-bedroom condominium apartments; beach cottages on stilts with screened porches; and beach villas with two to four bedrooms. The least expensive units are "Harbourside" hotel rooms at the yacht basin and marina near the island's northern tip.

Except for Captiva Cruises (see "What to See and Do," above), the facilities beyond the main gate are restricted to guests only, and the resort has a no-cash, charge-to-your-room policy which effectively prevents gate-crashers from using them.

Dining/Entertainment: The elegant King's Crown, formerly the plantation worker's commissary, is open for dinner only; the handsome wood beams and impressive fireplace remain. Cap'n Al's Dockside Grill at the yacht harbor is a pleasant spot for al fresco breakfasts, lunches, and dinners. Uncle Bob's Ice Cream Parlor satisfies the sweet tooth. If you decide to prepare your own feast, C.W.'s Market & Deli and the Ship's Store Deli are on the premises.

Outside the main gate, the award-winning Chadwick's and Mama Rosa's Pizzeria are both open to the public.

Services: Babysitting, children's and teenagers' activities programs, free shuttle.

Facilities: Touring pro Virginia Wade presides over 22 tennis courts. The gulfside golf course is one of the best nine-holers anywhere. There are two marinas, one with Steve and Doris Colgate's Sailing School. There are 18 swimming pools, many with bars. A water-sports center arranges for parasailing, windsurfing, boat rentals, scuba diving, and more. Bikes can be rented. Reflections Dockside Boutique features resortwear.

Outside the main gate, Chadwick's Shopping Center includes high-fashion boutiques, jewelry stores, and gift shops, all open to the public.

Expensive

'TWEEN WATERS INN, 15951 Captiva Rd., Captiva Island, FL 33924. Tel. 813/472-5161, or toll free 800/223-5865. Fax 813/472-0249. 64 rms, 20 apts, 49 cottages. A/C TV TEL

$ Rates: Winter, $140–$260. Off-season, $85–$195. DISC, MC, V.

This was the regular haunt of cartoonist J. N. (Ding) Darling, and Anne Morrow Lindbergh spent a winter here writing *A Gift from the Sea.* Just as Ding Darling preserved the islands' wildlife, this establishment has saved the cottages he stayed in. These pink shiplap buildings capture Old Florida with simple white furniture and terrazzo floors. The modern hotel rooms and apartments are in a two-story building with screened balconies facing the gulf.

'Tween Waters is an appropriate name, for the property is wedged between the gulf and sound on one of Captiva's narrowest sections. The beach is just across Captiva Road, which skirts the gulf shore. On the sound side, charter captains dock at the full-service marina and are available for fishing, shelling, and sightseeing excursions, and canoes and bikes can be rented. There's a very large swimming pool complex, complete with bar and grill. Tennis courts are lighted for night play.

Casual meals, including good pizza, are offered at the bayside Canoe Club café and bar. The Old Captiva House restaurant appears very much as it did in Ding Darling's days (his cartoons adorn the walls) and offers breakfast, lunch, and dinner. The $14 fixed-price dinners are a bargain on this island. The Crow's Nest Lounge provides snacks and light evening meals, and has live entertainment from 9pm to 1am.

CAMPING

The islands' sole campground, **Periwinkle Trailer Park,** 1119 Periwinkle Way, Sanibel Island, FL 33957 (tel. 813/472-1433), is so popular that it doesn't even advertise. Call well advance to reserve a tent or RV site.

WHERE TO DINE

There are far too many restaurants on Sanibel and Captiva to mention them all here. The chamber of commerce visitor center (see "Orientation," above) and some bookstores sell the very helpful *Menu & Dining Guide to Sanibel & Captiva Islands,* a good $3 investment. It lists them all and reproduces the menus of many.

When it comes to dining, as with many other things, the words "budget" and "Sanibel" can seem to be mutually exclusive. For cheap eats, you'll find only two fast-food chain outlets: a **Dairy Queen,** 1048 Periwinkle Way (tel. 472-1170), and a

Subway, 2496 Palm Ridge Rd. (tel. 472-1155). For budget fare, try **Cheeseburger Cheeseburger,** 2413 Periwinkle Way (tel. 472-6111); the 1950s-motif **Ritz Diner,** 2407 Periwinkle Way (tel. 472-6882), which opens daily for breakfast at 7:30am; and **Sanibel Sam's Carry Out,** 2495 Palm Ridge Rd. (tel. 472-6327).

On Captiva, big deli sandwiches and picnic fare are available at the **Captiva Island Store,** Captiva Road at Andy Rosse Lane (tel. 472-2374), and **C.W.'s Market and Deli,** at the entrance to South Seas Plantation Resort & Yacht Harbour (tel. 472-5111).

One way to cut costs is to take advantage of **early-bird specials** between 5 and 6pm, when some main courses are discounted by as much as 40%. These are noted below.

Some restaurants close or take long vacations during the off-season, when it's wise to call ahead, even if an establishment doesn't accept reservations.

SANIBEL ISLAND
Expensive

JEAN-PAUL'S FRENCH CORNER, 708 Tarpon Bay Rd., near Sanibel-Captiva Rd. Tel. 472-1493.
   Cuisine: FRENCH. **Reservations:** Required.
$ Prices: Appetizers $6–$7; main courses $21–$25. $19 minimum per adult. MC, V.
   Open: Dinner only, Mon–Sat seatings at 6 and 8:30pm. **Closed:** May–Oct.

A favorite since 1979, this chic bistro is enhanced by large pots of beautiful flowers, French prints on wood-paneled walls, and terra-cotta floors. Candlelight on the tables and the recorded soft music of a French chanteuse provide the right romantic touches. There's nothing pretentious here, however, for the waiters are gracious and the atmosphere casual. If you're craving authentic French traditional cuisine, look no farther.

THE MAD HATTER, 6460 Sanibel-Captiva Rd., at Blind Pass. Tel. 472-0033.
   Cuisine: NEW AMERICAN. **Reservations:** Required.
$ Prices: Appetizers $6–$10; main courses $19–$28. AE, MC, V.
   Open: Dinner only, Mon–Sat 5–10pm.

This gulf-front restaurant has only 12 tables, but each has a glorious water view, which comes alive at sunset. Like the Mad Hatter in Lewis Carroll's *Alice in Wonderland,* the food is a fantasy of cuisines, based on California, the Southwest, and the South, with some exotic accents. For example, you might find skewered shrimp, scallops, and vegetables grilled with an orange-tequila and chive glaze and served with a key lime orzo and black-bean quesadilla. Or how about roast grouper served with green pumpkin-seed sauce.

Moderate

HARBOR HOUSE, 1244 Periwinkle Way. Tel. 472-1242.
   Cuisine: AMERICAN. **Reservations:** Not required.
$ Prices: Appetizers $2.50–$3.50; main courses $9–$19; early-bird specials $9. AE, MC, V.
   Open: Feb–Apr, lunch daily 11:30am–2pm; dinner 5–9:30pm (early-bird specials 5–6pm). May–Jan, dinner only, daily 5–9:30pm (early-bird specials 5–6pm).

Going back to 1948, this family-owned establishment is Sanibel's oldest seafood restaurant, and a comfortable Old Florida atmosphere prevails under the beamed ceilings of its paneled dining room. The seafood selections are down-home as well, with shrimp, scallops, and freshly caught fish either broiled or fried. Stone crab claws and Florida lobster are offered during their seasons. The early specials are a bargain. For dessert, by all means order the award-winning key lime pie, made with limes from the family's own trees.

THE JACARANDA, 1223 Periwinkle Way. Tel. 472-1771.
   Cuisine: SEAFOOD/PASTA. **Reservations:** Recommended.
$ Prices: Appetizers $3–$7; main courses $14–$19. AE, MC, V.

Open: Dinner only, daily 5–10pm.

Named for the Brazilian purple-flowered jacaranda tree, this friendly and casual restaurant features a raw bar and dining in a screened patio. Recipient of several dining awards, the Jacaranda is best known for expertly prepared fish and seafood, which the chef will bake, sauté, or blacken. A favorite pasta dish is linguine and a dozen littleneck clams tossed in a piquant red or white clam sauce. For dessert, try the gooey turtle pie—ice cream crowned with caramel, fudge sauce, chopped nuts, and whipped cream. The Patio Lounge holds a happy hour from 4 to 7pm and has dancing nightly.

MCT's SHRIMP HOUSE & TAVERN, 1523 Periwinkle Way. Tel. 472-3161.

Cuisine: SEAFOOD. **Reservations:** Not accepted.

$ **Prices:** Appetizers $3.50–$6; main courses $11–$17; early-bird specials $8. AE, DISC, MC, V.

Open: Dinner only, daily 5–10pm (early-bird specials 5–6pm). (Bar, to 12:30am.)

An Old Florida atmosphere prevails in the casual Shrimp House, where diners line up for the early-bird specials, served to the first 100 people who show up or until 6pm, whichever comes first. The selections include prime rib, steamed shrimp platters, barbecued beef ribs, seafood Créole, and fish and chips. If you can't be among the first 100, or want to dine later, try the all-you-can-eat shrimp-and-crab platters. There's a kids' menu. McT's Tavern, a popular watering hole in the rear of the building, offers a snack menu until closing. It features fried or steamed baskets and a variety of sandwiches.

THE QUARTERDECK RESTAURANT, 1625 Periwinkle Way. Tel. 472-1033.

Cuisine: AMERICAN. **Reservations:** Accepted for dinner.

$ **Prices:** Appetizers $3–$6; main courses $12–$16; breakfasts $3–$6; lunches $3.50–$7. MC, V.

Open: Breakfast daily 8am–noon; lunch daily 11am–2:30pm; dinner daily 5–9:30pm.

A sibling of the Lighthouse Café (see below), this family-style establishment offers such unique breakfast selections as San Francisco eggs, consisting of freshly ground beef, chopped spinach, and scallions sautéed with eggs and served with hash-brown potatoes and sourdough bread. The luncheon menu features flaky croissant sandwiches and soup-and-sandwich combinations. The lengthy dinner menu includes some surprisingly sophisticated choices for such an unpretentious eatery: baked Brie, fried calamari rings, seafood-stuffed mushrooms, quesadillas, and Cajun shrimp on a skewer.

THE TIMBERS, 703 Tarpon Bay Rd., at Palm Ridge Rd. Tel. 472-3128.

Cuisine: SEAFOOD/STEAK. **Reservations:** Not accepted.

$ **Prices:** Appetizers $4–$7; main courses $12–$20. AE, DISC, MC, V.

Open: Dinner only, daily 4:30–10pm.

A sibling of the Prawnbroker Restaurant & Fish Market in Fort Myers, this casual, upstairs restaurant is justly proud of consistently winning the Taste of the Islands award for its seafood and steaks. A new menu is printed every day and always features the freshest seafood available, be it snapper, grouper, yellowtail tuna, or pompano. If you want to know what's offered today, call the Fresh Fish Hotline (tel. 395-2722). The chef will charcoal-grill or blacken your choice. Not in the mood for fish? Try the tasty Captiva crab cakes. Even the steaks are aged and cut on the premises. The adjoining Sanibel Grill & Raw Bar, which serves as the Timbers' bar and shares its kitchen, is included in the "Inexpensive" section, below.

WIL'S LANDING RESTAURANT & LOUNGE, 1200 Periwinkle Way. Tel. 472-4772.

Cuisine: AMERICAN. **Reservations:** Not accepted.

$ **Prices:** Appetizers $3–$8; main courses $14–$18; early-bird special $10; lunches $6–$9. AE, MC, V.

Open: Lunch daily 11am–3pm; dinner daily 5–10pm (early-bird specials 5–6pm).

A native Virginian, Wil Schlosser used to operate a fish market here, and his lively restaurant still offers the freshest fish available—and cooked well enough to win a recent Taste of the Islands family restaurant award. Wil's keynote dish is shrimp lightly breaded in a coconut batter and served with a pineapple sauce for dipping. Snapper coated with cilantro-garlic butter and baked with vegetables in a paper bag is another specialty. About half a dozen main courses are offered as early-bird specials. Wait for a table at Sanibel's longest bar, which snakes around the lower level of this two-story eatery. Live bands play for dancing nightly from 8pm to 12:30am.

Inexpensive

CALAMITY JANE'S CAFE, in the Olde Sanibel Shops, Tarpon Bay Rd. at Periwinkle Way. Tel. 472-6622.

Cuisine: AMERICAN. **Reservations:** Not accepted.
$ **Prices:** Main courses $7–$11; early-bird specials $6–$8; breakfasts $4–$7; sandwiches and salads $4–$7. AE, DISC, MC, V.
Open: Breakfast Mon–Sat 7–11am; lunch Mon–Sat 11:30am–3pm; dinner Mon–Sat 5–9pm (early-bird specials 3–6pm).

A consistent award winner in the breakfast department, this cozy café offers a variety of eye-openers, including "Manhole Cover" pancakes that will blanket your plate. Great soups, salads, sandwiches, and burgers take the stage at lunch, followed by fried chicken, grouper, clam, and shrimp baskets for early birds and a limited selection of main courses for dinner. The homemade key lime pie is a close competitor of the Harbor House version in the annual Taste of the Islands competition.

THE LAZY FLAMINGO I AND LAZY FLAMINGO II, 1036 Periwinkle Way (near Causeway Blvd.), and 6520 Pine Ave. (at Sanibel-Captiva Rd., half a mile south of Blind Pass). Tel. 472-6939 and 472-5353.

Cuisine: AMERICAN. **Reservations:** Not accepted.
$ **Prices:** Appetizers $3–$7; sandwiches and main courses $5–$9. AE, DC, MC, V.
Open: Daily 11:30am–1am.

T-shirts and shorts or jeans are the dress code at these very casual, identical-twin pubs that always seemed packed by the young and young-at-heart, who are attracted to the reasonably priced food and wide selections of beers. Some of that beer is used to steam shrimp and a finger-stinging collection of oysters, clams, and spices known as "The Pot." It also serves conch fritters, conch chowder, and conch salad. The flamingo-pink menu has a wide array of sandwiches, burgers, fish platters, and very spicy "Dead Parrot Wings."

LIGHTHOUSE CAFE, 362 Periwinkle Way, east of Causeway Blvd. Tel. 472-0303.

Cuisine: AMERICAN. **Reservations:** Not accepted.
$ **Prices:** Appetizers $1.50–$6; main courses $8–$11; breakfasts $3.50–$6; lunches $4–$6. MC, V.
Open: Breakfast daily 7am–3pm; lunch daily 11am–3pm; dinner daily 5–9pm. **Closed:** Dinner May–Oct.

This casual storefront establishment near the Sanibel Lighthouse, a sibling of the Quarterdeck Restaurant mentioned above, dishes up breakfast omelets that are meals in themselves, especially the ocean frittata containing delicately seasoned scallops, crabmeat, shrimp, broccoli, and fresh mushrooms, crowned by an artichoke heart and creamy Alfredo sauce. Seafood Benedict is another delight. There's also an interesting lunch menu featuring a sweetly delicious croissant topped with shrimp, crabmeat, scallops, and melted Swiss cheese. Reasonably priced dinners are served only from November through April.

SANIBEL GRILL & RAW BAR, 703 Tarpon Bay Rd., at Palm Ridge Rd. Tel. 472-4453.

Cuisine: AMERICAN. **Reservations:** Not accepted.
$ **Prices:** Appetizers $3–$5; sandwiches, burgers, pizza, and baskets $5–$12. AE, DISC, MC, V.
Open: Lunch daily 11:30am–4pm; dinner daily 4pm–midnight. (Bar, Mon–Sat 11:30am–1am, Sun 11:30am–midnight.)

Adjoining the Timbers Restaurant & Fish Market, this casual eatery draws sports fans with its numerous TVs and reduced-price draft beer during games. The charcoal-grilled burgers are among the best on the island, and those same coals are used to fire up delicious pizzas. The overstuffed sandwiches are filling, especially the grouper Reuben on rye. Soups, salads, quesadillas, and shrimp baskets are luncheon or dinner choices. In addition to cut-rate drafts during games, there are two happy hours, from 4 to 7pm and again from 10pm to midnight.

CAPTIVA ISLAND

Expensive

THE BUBBLE ROOM, 15001 Captiva Rd., at Andy Rosse Lane. Tel. 472-5558.

Cuisine: STEAK/SEAFOOD. **Reservations:** Not accepted.

$ Prices: Appetizers $3.50–$6; main courses $18.50–$27; lunches $6.50–$7. AE, DC, DISC, MC, V.

Open: Lunch daily 11:30am–2:30pm; dinner daily 5:30–10pm.

The gaudy bubble-gum pink, yellow, purple, and green exterior is only a prelude to the '30s, '40s, and '50s Hollywood motif inside this restaurant amusingly decorated with puppets, statues of great movie stars, toy trains, thousands of movie stills, and antique jukeboxes that play Big Band–era tunes. The menu carries on the theme: Prime Ribs Weismuller, the Eddie Fisherman filet of fresh grouper, and the Henny Young-One boneless breast of young chicken. It's a fun place!

CAPTIVA INN, 11509 Andy Rosse Lane, off Captiva Rd. Tel. 472-9129.

Cuisine: CONTINENTAL/NEW AMERICAN. **Reservations:** Required for seven-course dinner, recommended otherwise.

$ Prices: Appetizers $4–$7; main courses $18–$23; fixed-price seven-course dinner $37.50. MC, V.

Open: Dinner only, daily 7–9:30pm. **Closed:** Sun May–Dec.

The tables here are elegantly adorned with crystal, lace, and linen, an appropriate setting for fine cuisine featuring fresh local seafood, aged beef, lamb, veal, duck, and pork. Guests are advised each evening of the day's specials. Reservations are required for a fixed-price, seven-course dinner including champagne crème cassis, a choice of appetizers, homemade soup, fresh salad with avocado dressing, fruit sorbet, main course, tempting desserts, and European coffee. They'll tell you the night's main-course offerings when you call.

Moderate

BELLINI'S OF CAPTIVA, Andy Rosse Lane. Tel. 472-6866.

Cuisine: ITALIAN. **Reservations:** Recommended.

$ Prices: Appetizers $4.50–$8; main courses $10.50–$25. AE, MC, V.

Open: Dinner only, daily 5:30–10pm. (Cocktail lounge, 7pm–late.)

"Bella, bella!" describes both the beautiful indoor dining room and garden courtyard of this large and very pleasant Italian restaurant. Whet your appetite with a frozen peach Bellini cocktail, a version of the world-famous Bellini served at Harry's Bar in Venice, Italy. For openers, the crabmeat manicotti with basil-cream sauce will do richly. Then select from a choice of excellent pasta, fish, chicken, veal, and beef dishes. Finish with a homemade pastry or Italian ice cream, then stroll over to the comfortable cocktail lounge for a drink and some live music.

THE MUCKY DUCK, Andy Rosse Lane, on the gulf. Tel. 472-3434.

Cuisine: SEAFOOD/PUB FARE. **Reservations:** Not accepted.

$ Prices: Appetizers $3.50–$8; main courses $9–$18; lunches $3–$9. AE, DISC, MC, V.

Open: Lunch Mon–Sat 11:30am–2:30pm; dinner Mon–Sat 5–9:30pm.

This lively, British-style pub is so close to the gulf that the views are great for sunset-watching. The owner makes the rounds and keeps everybody in good humor. If you don't get a window seat, he'll gladly roll a fake window over to appease you. The menu offers a selection of fresh seafood items, plus English fish and chips, steak-and-sausage pie, and a ploughman's lunch. There's a children's menu and a vegetarian platter. You probably will have to wait for a table, but there are worse places to idle time away than right on the beach.

SUNSHINE CAFE, in Captiva Village Square, Captiva Rd. Tel. 472-6200.
   Cuisine: AMERICAN. **Reservations:** Recommended.
$ Prices: Small platters $5–$9; large platters $18–$22; sandwiches $6.50–$7. No credit cards.
   Open: Daily 11:30am–9:30pm.

This friendly café has only 10 tables—five inside, five on the shopping center's porch—but the food is worth the wait. Specialties are charcoal-grilled steak and shrimp, tandoori chicken breast, po'boy sandwiches, and pasta Italian style. Delicious daily specials feature fresh seafood (especially good over linguine with fresh herbs, roasted garlic, and imported cheese). Or you can order light dishes such as a plate of black beans and rice or a Caesar salad. Various desserts are offered daily, with the white-chocolate cheesecake in an Oreo-cookie crust a constant favorite. Anything on the menu can be ordered to carry out.

EVENING ENTERTAINMENT
THE PERFORMING ARTS

THE PIRATE PLAYHOUSE, 2200 Periwinkle Way, Sanibel. Tel. 472-0006.

From December through April, professional actors perform Broadway dramas and comedies Monday through Saturday at 8pm in this state-of-the-art, 150-seat theater. Recent productions have included *Don't Dress for Dinner, The Hasty Heart,* and *Bus Stop.* Matinees usually are on Wednesday and Saturday.
   Admission: Tickets, $12.50–$20.

OLD SCHOOLHOUSE THEATER, 1905 Periwinkle Way, opposite the Pirate Playhouse. Tel. 472-6862.

Originally a one-room school built in 1896, and later used as the Pirate Playhouse before its new facility was constructed across the road, this theater compliments its neighbor by offering Broadway musicals and revues from December through April. During the summer, the local Off Beach Players take over. Call for the current schedule and prices.

THE CLUB & BAR SCENE

You won't find glitzy lounges or nightclubs on these islands, but night owls will enjoy fun places to roost at the resorts and restaurants mentioned above. Here's a brief recap:

On Sanibel, the Sundial Beach and Tennis Resort's **Sunset Lounge,** 1451 Middle Gulf Dr. (tel. 472-4151), features chanteuse Helen Skelton at the piano during sunset happy hour, then live bands for dancing from 9pm on. The **Patio Lounge,** in the Jacaranda, 1223 Periwinkle Way (tel. 472-1771), is another relaxed place to dance to live bands every night. The casual **Wil's Landing Restaurant & Lounge,** 1200 Periwinkle Way (tel. 472-4772), also has live dance music every evening. For pub-crawling, **McT's Tavern,** 1523 Periwinkle Way (tel. 472-3161), has darts, video games, and a large-screen TV for sports fans. The **Sanibel Grill & Raw Bar,** 703 Tarpon Bay Rd. (tel. 472-4453), specializes in sports, with numerous TVs and reduced-price drinks and drafts during games.

On Captiva, fine nightly entertainment is spotlighted at **Bellini's of Captiva,** 11521 Andy Rosse Lane (tel. 472-6866). **Chadwick's Lounge,** at the entrance to the South Seas Plantation Resort & Yacht Harbour (tel. 472-5111), has a large dance floor and music from 8:30pm on. Perhaps Captiva's number-one nightspot for dancing is the **Crow's Nest Lounge,** in the 'Tween Waters Inn, on Captiva Road (tel. 472-5161).

EASY ISLAND EXCURSIONS

Island-hopping is part of the fun during a Southwest Florida vacation, and Sanibel and Captiva are jumping-off points for boat trips to barrier islands and keys imbued with ancient legends and Robinson Crusoe–style beaches. You don't have to get complete-ly lost out there, however, for several islets have comfortable inns and restaurants. The trip across shallow Pine Island Sound is itself a sightseeing adventure, with playful dolphins surfing on the boats' wakes and a plethora of cormorants, egrets, frigate birds, and (in winter) scarce white pelicans flying above or lounging on sandbars between meals.

GETTING THERE As noted in "What to See and Do," above, **Captiva Cruises** (tel. 472-5300) has daily trips from the South Seas Plantation Resort & Yacht Harbor on Captiva. The *Lady Chadwick* goes to Cabbage Key and Useppa Island, where passengers disembark for lunch. The *Andy Rosse* goes to Boca Grande by way of Cayo Costa County Park. These day trips cost $25 per person and usually leave at 10:30am. Reservations are required. (For information about Boca Grande, see the Fort Myers section, above.)

The open-sided *Tropic Star* (tel. 283-0015) leaves Pine Island east of Fort Myers daily at 9:45am for Cayo Costa and Cabbage Key, where it waits until the afternoon return voyage. Fares are $17 for adults, $10 for children 6 to 12, $6 for children 2 to 6, and free for children under 2.

The **Cabbage Key Inn** (see below) operates its own launch twice a day Monday through Friday, once daily on weekends, from Pineland Marina on Pine Island.

The **Out-Island Water Shuttle** (tel. 395-0100) operates five times daily between McCarthy's Marina on Captiva and Grady's Waterfront Restaurant on Upper (North) Captiva Island. One-way fares are $15 per person.

Charter and rental boats are available at **Sanibel Marina** (tel. 472-2723) on Sanibel and at **'Tween Waters Inn Marina** (tel. 472-5161), **Jenson's Twin Palms Marina** (tel. 472-5800), and **McCarthy's Marina** (tel. 395-0100) on Captiva.

CABBAGE KEY

You never know who's going to get off a boat at 100-acre Cabbage Key and walk unannounced into the funky **Cabbage Key Inn**, a rustic house built in the 1920s by mystery novelist Mary Roberts Rinehart and her son. Ernest Hemingway liked to hang out here in the 1930s. Novelist John D. MacDonald was a frequent guest 30 years later. Today you could find yourself rubbing elbows at the bar with the likes of Walter Cronkite, Ted Koppell, Ed McMahon, or Julia Roberts. Singer and avid yachtie Jimmy Buffet likes Cabbage Key so much that it inspired his hit song "Cheeseburger in Paradise."

A path leads from the tiny marina through a South Seas–style lawn dotted with coconut palms to this white clapboard house sitting atop an ancient Calusa shell mound. Guests dine in the comfort of two screened porches and seek libations in Mary Roberts Rinehart's library-turned-bar, its pine-paneled walls now plastered with dollar bills. The straight-back chairs and painted wooden tables are showing their age, but that's part of Cabbage Key's laid-back, don't-give-a-hoot charm.

In addition to the famous thick and juicy cheeseburgers so loved by Jimmy Buffet, the house specialties are fresh broiled fish and shrimp steamed in beer. Lunches range from $5.50 to $9; main courses at dinner fall in the $16 to $20 range.

For overnight or longer, Cabbage Key Inn has six rooms and six cottages, all with original 1920s furnishings and their own baths, air conditioners, and screened porches. Four of the cottages have kitchens, and one room reputedly has its own ghost. Rates are $65 single or double for rooms, $145 to $200 for cottages. Reserve well in advance for major holidays and throughout the tarpon season from May to July.

For information, reservations, and transportation, contact Cabbage Key Inn, P.O. Box 200, Pineland, FL 33945 (tel. 813/283-2278; fax 813/283-1384).

USEPPA ISLAND

Lying near Cabbage Key, Useppa was a refuge of President Theodore Roosevelt and his tarpon-loving industrialist friends at the turn of the century. Today it's a "private membership resort," with more than 100 luxury homes. Other than by invitation from one of the members, the only way to visit it—and have lunch at the original **Useppa Inn**—is via the daily Captiva Cruises voyages from the South Seas Plantation Resort & Yacht Harbor (see "Getting There," above). The Useppa Inn is more expensive—and a great deal higher on the snoot scale—than Cabbage Key Inn.

UPPER (NORTH) CAPTIVA

Cut off by a pass from Captiva, its northern barrier island sibling is occupied by a real-estate development complete with its own airstrip. The Out-Island Water Shuttle comes over several times a day from Captiva (see "Getting There," above) and docks at **Grady's Waterfront Restaurant,** where visitors can have lunch before or after exploring the homes and beaches. For information, contact Islander Realty, P.O. Box 334, Pineland, FL 33945 (tel. 813/472-3000; fax 813/472-9635).

CAYO COSTA STATE PARK

You can't get any closer to a deserted tropical paradise than 2,132-acre Cayo Costa (pronounced *Key-oh Cos-tah),* an unspoiled barrier island with miles of white sand beaches, pine forests, mangrove swamps, oak-palm hammocks, and grasslands. The only permanent resident here is a lone park ranger.

Daytrippers can bring their own supplies and use a picnic area with pavilions. A tram carries visitors from the soundside dock to the gulf beach (50¢ round-trip fare). The state maintains 12 basic cottages and a campground on the northern end of the island near Johnson Shoals, where the shelling is spectacular. Cabins cost between $20 and $50 a day. Campsites are $13 a day between December and April, $10 a day the rest of the year.

The park is open daily from 8am to sundown. There's a $2-per-person honor-system admission fee. Overnight slips at the dock cost $5 a day.

For more information or cabin reservations, contact Cayo Costa State Park, P.O. Box 1150, Boca Grande, FL 33921 (tel. 813/964-0375). Office hours are Monday through Friday from 8am to 5pm.

---

4. NAPLES

42 miles S of Fort Myers, 106 miles W of Miami, 185 miles S of Tampa

GETTING THERE   By Plane   Most visitors arrive at the **Southwest Florida International Airport,** 35 miles north of Naples (see "Getting There" in the Fort Myers section, above). Air Limo (tel. 643-2148 or 775-0505) has scheduled bus service between Southwest Florida International Airport and Naples Municipal Airport.

Naples Municipal Airport, on North Road off Airport Road (tel. 643-6875), is served by American Eagle (tel. toll free 800/433-7300), Delta Connection (tel. toll free 800/221-1212), and USAir Express (tel. toll free 800/428-4322). Taxis await all flights outside the small terminal building, or call American Taxi & Limo (tel. 455-9157).

By Bus   Greyhound's bus terminal is at 2669 Davis Blvd. (tel. 774-5660, or toll free 800/231-2222).

By Car   From Miami, U.S. 41 (the Tamiami Trail) leads through the Everglades to Naples. A faster route is via I-75 ("Alligator Alley") from Miami and Fort Lauderdale. From Tampa and Fort Myers, take either I-75 or U.S. 41 due south.

From I-75, take Immokalee Road (Exit 17) for Vanderbilt Beach or Pine Ridge Road (Exit 16) for the Pelican Bay area north of downtown.

Only two families lived within the limits of present-day Naples in 1886. Then a group of 12 Kentuckians and Ohioans—including *Louisville Courier-Journal* publisher Walter Haldeman—bought 8,700 acres, laid out a town, and started selling lots. They built a pier and the 16-room Naples Hotel, whose first guest was President Grover Cleveland's sister Rose. She and other notables soon built a line of beach homes known as "Millionaires Row." Naples has been an enclave of the rich and famous ever since.

Naples remained a very small town, however, until 1946, when Ohio manufacturer Henry B. Watkins, Sr., bought the Naples Hotel and all the town's undeveloped land. He and his two partners laid out the Naples Plan, which created the environmentally conscious city you'll see today. While strict zoning laws preserve the old part of town, the Naples Plan blends development with the natural environment along the 10 miles of beachfront between U.S. 41 and the Gulf of Mexico.

Because its wealthy, well-traveled residents are accustomed to the very best, Naples is imbued with a special sophistication. Many of its boutiques and galleries would upstage those in Palm Beach or Beverly Hills, and some of its restaurants are among the finest in Florida. And yet Naples is not a snobbish city. An easy-going, friendliness prevails.

ORIENTATION

INFORMATION The **Naples Area Chamber of Commerce**, 3620 N. Tamiami Trail (U.S. 41), Naples, FL 33940 (tel. 813/262-6141; fax 813/262-8374), just north of the Ohio Drive/Anchor Rode Drive intersection, is open Monday through Friday from 8:30am to 5pm. Drop-in visitors can choose from a host of free brochures and other information. The friendly staff also sells a detailed street map for $2. By mail, they will send a complete Naples informational packet for $7 ($12 outside the U.S.) and the street map for $3.

AREA LAYOUT The original resort, **Old Naples,** lies on a peninsula formed by the gulf, Naples Bay, and the Gordon River. From there, a resort and residential area occupies the narrow strip between the gulf and U.S. 41 (the main drag named Tamiami Trail and 9th Street North but commonly called "41") to **Vanderbilt Beach,** 10 miles north. This manicured area includes large developments at **Pelican Bay** and **Venetian Bay.** East of U.S. 41, Naples changes character to a mix of working-class homes, shopping strips, and real-estate developments like those found elsewhere in Florida.

GETTING AROUND

BY TAXI Call **Yellow Cab** (tel. 262-1312), **Maxi Taxi** (tel. 262-8977), or **Naples Taxi** (tel. 775-0505).

BY TROLLEY The **Naples Trolley** (tel. 262-7300) clangs around 25 stops between Old Naples and Vanderbilt Beach from 8:30am to 5:15pm Monday through Saturday and 10:15am to 5:15pm on Sunday. Daily fares are $9 for adults, $4 for children 5 to 12, free for children under 5, with free reboarding. The main office is at 179 Commerce St., Vanderbilt Beach. Pick up a schedule there or at the chamber of commerce (see "Orientation," above).

BY RENTAL CAR Agencies in Naples are **Avis** (tel. toll free 800/831-2847), **Budget** (tel. toll free 800/527-0700), **Dollar** (tel. toll free 800/800-4000), **Enterprise** (tel. toll free 800/325-8007), **Hertz** (tel. toll free 800/654-3131), **National** (tel. toll free 800/227-7368), and **Thrifty** (tel. toll free 800/367-2277).

BY BICYCLE Rent a bicycle from **The Bike Route,** 655 N. Tamiami Trail (tel. 262-8373), at $12 for a half day, $18 for all day. For scooters, call **Good Times Rental,** 1947 Davis Blvd. (tel. 775-7529), which charges $50 a day.

FAST FACTS

Area Code The telephone area code throughout Southwest Florida is 813.

Doctor For a doctor, go to the Naples Medical Center Walk-in Clinic, 400 Eighth Ave. N. (tel. 261-5511).

Emergency To reach the police, report a fire, or call an ambulance, dial 911.

Tax In addition to Florida's statewide 6% sales tax, Collier County imposes a 2% tax on all hotel bills.

WHAT TO SEE & DO
ATTRACTIONS
Museums

COLLIER AUTOMOTIVE MUSEUM, 2500 Horseshoe Dr., off Airport Rd. near the Golden Gate Pkwy. Tel. 643-5252.

Even if you're not an aficionado of antique cars, it's fun to browse through the 75 models displayed in this beautifully landscaped museum just north of the Naples Municipal Airport. The collection contains the very first Ferrari and the late Hollywood star Gary Cooper's sleek Dusenberg SSJ.

Admission: $6 adults, $3 children 5–12, free for children under 5.

Open: May–Nov, Tues–Sat 10am–5pm, Sun 1–5pm; Dec–Apr, daily 10am–5pm.

COLLIER COUNTY MUSEUM, in the County Government Center, Airport Rd. just north of U.S. 41. Tel. 774-8476.

Artifacts and photos recount the major happenings in Collier County from the early Calusa settlements to Millionaire's Row. There's an antique steam locomotive and a re-created Seminole village. Native American festivities take place here during March and November (call for dates).

Admission: Free.

Open: Mon–Fri 9am–5pm.

PALM COTTAGE, 137 12th Ave. S. in Old Naples, between 1st St. and Gordon Dr. Tel. 261-8164.

Walter Haldeman, publisher of the *Louisville Courier-Journal* and a founder of Naples, built this gracious home in 1895 as a winter retreat for Henry Watterson, his chief editorial writer. After socialites Laurance and Alexandra Brown bought it in 1946, it became the scene of many gala functions attended by the likes of Hollywood stars Hedy Lamarr, Gary Cooper, and Robert Montgomery. One of the few remaining Southwest Florida houses built of tabbie mortar, a mixture made by burning sea shells, Palm Cottage today is a museum filled with authentic furniture, paintings, photographs, and other memorabilia.

Admission: Donation, $3 adults, free for children.

Open: Winter, Tues–Fri 2–4pm; off-season, varies (call ahead).

TEDDY BEAR MUSEUM, 2511 Pine Ridge Rd., at Airport Rd. Tel. 598-2711.

This entertaining museum contains 2,000-plus examples of stuffed teddy bears from around the world. They are cleverly displayed descending from the rafters in hot-air balloons, attending business board meetings, sipping afternoon tea, celebrating a wedding, even doing bear things like hibernating. There's a gift shop where you can buy your own bears.

Admission: $5 adults, $3 senior citizens and children 13–19, $2 children 3–12, free for children under 3.

Open: Wed–Sat 10am–5pm, Sun 1–5pm. **Closed:** New Year's, Thanksgiving, and Christmas Days.

Nature Centers

CORKSCREW SWAMP SANCTUARY, 16 miles northeast of Naples off Immokalee Rd. (Rte. 846). Tel. 657-3771.

Maintained by the National Audubon Society, this 11,000-acre wilderness is home to countless wood storks (which nest high in the cypress trees from November to April). Wading birds also are best seen in winter, when the swamp is driest and they congregate in pools near two miles of boardwalks and nature trails which lead through the largest bald cypress forest with some of the oldest trees in the country. Ferns and orchids also flourish.

The Collier County Audubon Society, P.O. Box 797, Naples, FL 33940 (tel.

813/455-8411), conducts programs and field trips here and elsewhere in Southwest Florida.

Admission: $6.50 adults, $5 full-time college students, $3 children 6–18, free for children under 6.

Open: Dec–Apr, daily 7am–5pm; May–Nov, daily 8am–5pm.

JUNGLE LARRY'S ZOOLOGICAL PARK & CARIBBEAN GARDENS, 1590 Goodlette-Frank Rd., at Fleischmann Blvd. Tel. 262-5409.

A family favorite for many years, Jungle Larry's features guided tram tours that meander around this 52-acre zoolike preserve to observe animals and birds, including primates living on an island without cages. The "safari" also includes the spectacular tropical gardens and boat tour. Visitors are captivated by the Wild Animal Show and the alligator lectures and feedings (call for the schedule). Kids get a kick out of the Petting Farm, elephant rides, and a playground. Picnic facilities are on the premises.

Admission: $11 adults, $7 children 4–15, free for children under 4.

Open: Daily 9:30am–5:30pm (last admission 4:30pm). **Closed:** Thanksgiving and Christmas Days.

NAPLES NATURE CENTER, 14th Ave. N. off Goodlette-Frank Rd. Tel. 262-0304.

One of two preserves operated by the Conservancy (the Briggs Nature Center near Marco Island is the other), this one includes a well-stocked serpentarium and an aquarium inhabited by stingrays, turtles, and all sorts of crustaceans. Outdoors, there are nature trails, a butterfly atrium, an aviary with bald eagles and other birds, and boat rides to observe lagoon wildlife. A Nature Store carries interesting gift items.

Admission: $3 adults, $1 children 7–17, free for children under 7.

Open: Mon–Sat 9am–4:30pm.

Historic Districts

Its history may only go back to 1886, but ✪ **Old Naples** still has the charm of that Victorian era. It's the part of town lying below Fifth Avenue South. The town docks are on the bay side, the glorious beaches along the gulf. Laid out on a grid, the uncurbed streets run between many houses—some, like Palm Cottage (see "Museums," above), date from the beginning—and along Millionaire's Row between Gulf Shore Boulevard and the beach. With these gorgeous homes virtually hidden in the palms and casuarinas, the Old Naples beach seems a century removed from the high-rise condos found farther north.

The **Naples Pier,** at the gulf end of 12th Avenue South, is a focal point of the neighborhood. Built in 1888 to let steamers land potential real-estate customers, the original 600-foot-long, T-shaped structure was destroyed by hurricanes and damaged by fire. Local residents have rebuilt it because they like strolling its length to catch yet another fantastic gulf sunset. The pier is now a state historic site. It's open 24 hours a day, but parking in the nearby lots is restricted between 11pm and 7am.

Just three blocks from the pier, **Third Street South,** at Broad Avenue, is another neighborhood focal center whose chic shops and fine restaurants equal those on Rodeo Drive in Beverly Hills.

Beaches and Parks

Beach access in Old Naples is at the gulf end of each avenue, although parking in the neighborhood can be precious (try the metered lots near the Naples Pier on 12th Avenue South).

Loudermilk Park, north of Old Naples on Gulf Shore Boulevard North at the end of Banyan Boulevard, has a pavilion, restrooms, showers, a refreshment counter, volleyball nets, and picnic tables. A few blocks farther north is a metered parking lot with beach access beside the Naples Beach Hotel & Golf Resort, 851 Gulf Shore Blvd. N, at Golf Drive.

Clam Pass County Park, at Pelican Bay, has a 3,000-foot boardwalk through mangrove swamps to the beach wrapping around Clam Pass. Entry is from a metered parking lot beside the Registry Resort at the end of Seagate Drive. A free tram runs from the parking lot to the beach. A refreshment center rents cabañas.

The **Delnor-Wiggins State Recreation Area,** at the west end of 111th Avenue North in Vanderbilt Beach (tel. 597-6196), has bath houses, picnic areas, and a boat ramp. Fishing from the beach is excellent. The area is open daily from 8am to sunset. Admission is $3.25 for vehicles with up to eight occupants, $1 for pedestrians and bikers.

Cruises

Tiki Islander Cruises (tel. 262-7577) offers two types of cruises from the Old Marine Marketplace at Tin City, Fifth Avenue South beside the Gordon River Bridge. The *Tiki Islander* goes sightseeing among the mansions lining Naples Bay at 11am, 2pm, and 4pm daily; the fare is $12 per person. The *Tiki II* makes half-day backwater fishing and shelling excursions. You can get off and shell on Keewaydin, an almost-undeveloped barrier island south of Naples, and catch the boat when it returns. This longer trip costs $25 per person.

Dalis Bouy One (tel. 262-4545) has an afternoon sightseeing cruise and a sunset cruise daily. Like Tiki Islander Cruises, it docks at the Old Marine Marketplace at Tin City.

The *Rosie* (tel. 775-6776), an old-fashioned, 105-foot-long paddlewheeler, has year-round lunch buffet cruises for $28.50 per person and sunset dinner cruises for $38.50 per person. You can take either cruise without the meal for $18.50. The *Rosie* docks at Rosie's Waterfront Cafe, 1444 Tamiami Trail E., east of the Gordon River Bridge. The open-air café is a pleasant place to have a "casual keys cuisine" meal or a cold libation.

Crazy Clam Fun Cruises (tel. 642-0061) has a "Naples at Night" dance cruise during the winter season. The *Crazy Clam* usually operates out of Marco Island, so the Naples schedule varies. Call for details and prices.

Nautilus Boat Tours, at Vanderbilt Beach 10 miles north of Naples (tel. 597-4408), has 1½-hour, narrated cruises daily through the Vanderbilt Lagoon to the Delnor-Wiggins State Recreation Area and the nearby Barefoot Beach Preserve. Call for times and prices.

SPECIAL EVENTS

Thanks to national television exposure, the best-known annual event is the **Swamp Buggy Races** in March and October at the 129-acre Swamp Buggy/Florida Sports Park (tel. 774-2701). The finish line is in mud six feet deep, and the slimy winner gets to escort the new Swamp Buggy Queen.

Naples Tropicool, during the first two weeks in May, is a fiesta of art shows, concerts, and a variety of special events. **July 4th** celebrations illuminate the skies with fireworks. **Seminole Indian Days** are celebrated in March and November at the Collier County Museum (tel. 774-8476). At Christmas, the brilliant **Festival of Lights** and **Fifth Avenue Christmas Walk** light up Old Naples's two shopping areas.

SPORTS & RECREATION

BOATING   Powerboat rentals are available from **Club Nautico,** at the Boat Haven Marina, 1484 Tamiami Trail E. (tel. 774-0100), on the east bank of the Gordon River behind Kelly's Fish House; the **Port-O-Call Marina,** 550 Port of Call Way (tel. 774-0479); the **Parkshore Marina,** 4310 Gulf Shore Blvd. N. (tel. 434-6964), in the Village Shops at Venetian Bay; the **Brookside Marina,** 2023 Davis Blvd. (tel. 774-9100); and the **Cove Marina,** 860 12th Ave. S. (tel. 263-7250), at the City Docks.

Sailing enthusiasts can line up a charter with **Sailboats Unlimited,** at the City Docks on 12th Avenue South (tel. 262-0139).

Good Times Rental, 1947 Davis Blvd. (tel. 775-7529), rents waverunners, windboards, skim boards, canoes, snorkeling gear, rafts, and other beach equipment. Hobie Cats and windsurfers can also be rented on the beach at the **Naples Beach Hotel & Golf Club,** 851 Gulf Shore Blvd. N. (tel. 261-2222).

DIVING   The **Under Seas Dive Academy,** 4125 Tamiami Trail E. (tel. 774-1234), rents water-sports equipment and teaches diver-certification courses.

FISHING   A number of charter boats go forth in search of snook, tarpon, redfish, trout, snapper, shark, and other game fish, both in the backwaters and in the gulf. Among them are *Dalis Bouy One* (tel. 434-0441), the *Capt. Marvel* (tel. 261-7159), the *Lady Brett* (tel. 263-4949), and the *Fish Finder* (tel. 597-2063), which operates out of Vanderbilt Beach. Two guides provide specialized services: **Capt. Steve Westervelt** (tel. 775-2003) and **Capt. Mark Ward** (tel. 775-9849).

GOLF   The Naples area boasts at least 35 golf courses. Nearby public courses include the **Lely Flamingo Island Club** (tel. 793-2223), **Boyne USA South** (tel. 732-5108), the **Ironwood Golf Club of Naples** (tel. 775-2584), the **Hibiscus Golf Club** (tel. 774-3559), and the **Riviera Golf Club** (tel. 774-1081).

The **Naples Beach Hotel & Golf Club** (tel. 261-2222) has an interesting 18-hole course for its guests. The Ritz Carlton Naples and The Registry Resort send their guests to **Pelican's Nest Golf Club.**

MINIATURE GOLF   **Coral Cay Adventure Golf,** 2205 Tamiami Trail E. (tel. 793-4999), at Commercial Drive, has two courses among waterfalls, streams, reefs, and caves. Open daily from 10am to 11pm.

TENNIS   Open to the public, **Cambier Park Tennis Courts,** 755 Eighth Ave. S. (tel. 434-4694), in Old Naples, offers 14 courts, 11 of them lighted. Play costs $5 per hour. Winter hours are Monday through Friday from 8am to 10pm, on Saturday to 5pm, and on Sunday to 4pm; off-season, Monday through Friday from 8am to 10pm, on Saturday to 5pm, and on Sunday to 1pm. Check with the pro in the middle of the courts.

Nonguests can arrange to play at the **Naples Beach Hotel & Golf Club,** 851 Gulf Shore Blvd. N. (tel. 261-2222), but call ahead.

WHERE TO STAY

Naples has several hotel chains from which to choose: the **Best Western Naples Inn,** 2329 9th St. N., Naples, FL 33940 (tel. 813/261-1148, or toll free 800/243-1148); the **Days Inn Naples,** 1925 Davis Blvd., Naples, FL 33942 (tel. 813/774-3117, or toll free 800/272-0106); the **Hampton Inn,** 3210 Tamiami Trail N., Naples, FL 33940 (tel. 813/261-8000, or toll free 800/732-4667); the **Holiday Inn Naples,** 1100 9th St. N., Naples, FL 33940 (tel. 813/262-7146, or toll free 800/465-6329); the **Quality Inn Gulf Coast,** 2555 Tamiami Trail N., Naples, FL 33940 (tel. 813/261-6046, or toll free 800/330-0046); and the **Super 8 Motel,** 3880 Tollgate Blvd., Naples, FL 33942 (tel. 813/455-0808, or toll free 800/800-8000).

In addition, the **Howard Johnson Lodge,** 221 9th St. S., Naples, FL 33940 (tel. 813/262-6181, or toll free 800/654-2000), has been given a complete facelift and enjoys a convenient location within walking distance of Old Naples. Rates there are $75 to $125 double in winter, $45 to $65 off-season.

VERY EXPENSIVE

EDGEWATER BEACH HOTEL, 1901 Gulf Shore Blvd. N., Naples, FL 33940. Tel. 813/262-6511, or toll free 800/821-0196. Fax 813/262-1234. 114 suites. A/C TV TEL
$ Rates: Winter, $205–$515 suite. Off-season, $100–$350 suite. AE, DC, DISC, MC, V.

Beautifully situated near the end of Millionaires Row north of Old Naples, this all-suite resort overlooks a ribbon of white sand gulf beach. Two pastel-pink older buildings and a newer seven-story tower overlook both the beach and a garden courtyard with luxuriant flora and a swimming pool. Tastefully decorated, the oversize suites are enhanced by Mexican tile floors and have kitchens with microwave ovens and coffee makers. Penthouse units have their own Jacuzzis and wide-screen TVs. Balconies in the two older wings are adorned with white grillwork and plantation shutters.

Dining/Entertainment: For dinner, both the lobby-level Crystal Parrot and the sixth-floor Penthouse Dining Room offer romantic candlelight and great gulf views (men must wear coats and ties). Live piano music accompanies libations in Mistral's

Lounge, which looks out to the gulf. The courtyard Fountain Café is delightful for breakfast and lunch. Flippers poolside bar specializes in juicy burgers and tasty salads.

Services: The friendly front-desk personnel will arrange sightseeing tours, fishing excursions, and other activities.

Facilities: Heated swimming pool and patio adjacent to the beach; water-sports equipment, cabañas, chairs, and umbrella rentals; guests can play on nearby tennis courts and golf course.

THE REGISTRY RESORT, 475 Seagate Dr., Naples, FL 33940. Tel. 813/597-3232, or toll free 800/833-8389. Fax 813/597-3147. 395 rms, 29 suites. A/C TV TEL

$ Rates (suites include continental breakfast): Winter, $275–$355 double; from $750, suite. Off-season, $110–$250 double; from $540, suite. AE, DC, DISC, MC, V.

In Pelican Bay, this handsomely designed 18-story luxury resort radiates elegance—but a more relaxed elegance than its chief rival, the Ritz Carlton Naples up at Vanderbilt Beach (see below). Vivacious celebrities like TV talk-show host Larry King like to stay here. The Registry is not directly on the beach, but the Clam Pass County Park shuttle passes every few minutes to take guests along the three-mile boardwalk through mangroves to the gulf (see "What to See and Do," above).

Dining/Entertainment: The magnificent Lafite dining room offers some of Naples's finest French cuisine (open nightly during winter, on Friday and Saturday evenings only from May to mid-December). Café Chablis is open for breakfast, lunch, and dinner and features a children's menu and moderately priced early-bird specials from 5 to 7pm. The Brass Pelican specializes in seafood, including a raw bar. The Palm Terrace serves poolside snacks, burgers, sandwiches, salads, and tropical drinks. Scoops Ice Cream Parlour and Pâtisserie soothes sweet tooths and has real Italian cappuccino. The multilevel Garrett's nightclub has dance music from 9pm until 2am Monday through Saturday during the winter, on Friday and Saturday off-season.

Services: Concierge, 24-hour room service, complimentary morning coffee, babysitting, children's activities program.

Facilities: Three heated swimming pools; whirlpools; bike, sailboat, catamarans, aquabikes, water-sports equipment rentals; putting green; horseshoes, putting, and shuffleboard equipment; Tennis Center with 15 courts (5 lighted); health club with sauna, massages, facials, body treatments; boutiques; hairdresser.

RITZ-CARLTON NAPLES, 280 Vanderbilt Beach Rd., Naples, FL 33963. Tel. 813/598-3300, or toll free 800/241-3333. Fax 813/598-6690. 463 rms and suites. A/C TV TEL

$ Rates: Winter, $300–$500 double; $800–$3,000 suite. Off-season, $130–$430 double; $550–$2,825 suite. AE, DC, DISC, MC, V.

This opulent 14-story Mediterranean-style hotel at Vanderbilt Beach is a favorite of affluent guests who like to be pampered. Most of the rich book suites on the top-level Ritz-Carlton Club floor, where the amenities are very special—and the rates just as high. The lobby is high luxe, from the imported marble floor with Oriental rugs to the sparkling Waterford crystal chandelier, which lend a royal ambience for the afternoon British-style high tea so loved by Ritz fans everywhere. The splendid collection of 18th- and 19th-century art adorning the walls has its own curator. All guest rooms look out to a gulf panorama, but not all have balconies. Four-poster beds with expensive quilted spreads add a traditional touch. Guests can relax in high-backed rockers on the verandas or unwind down by the heated swimming pool set in a landscaped terrace. They must walk through a narrow mangrove forest to reach the beach, however, for this stretch of sand is part of a public park. The hotel does have its staff out there to rent cabañas, boats, and other toys (only the towels and chairs are complimentary).

Dining/Entertainment: For dinner, you can literally "put on the ritz" in the wood-paneled Grill Room, reminiscent of a British private club, or in the Dining Room, notable for some of Naples's finest gourmet cuisine (be prepared to part with at least $160 for two people, including wine). The casual Beach Pavilion—actually by the pool, not the beach—serves breakfast, lunch, and dinner. There's full food and drink service (and a telephone) at the beach. Live music entertains guests by the pool during the afternoon, and bands play for dancing in the Club each evening.

Services: Let me put it this way: The Ritz is the epitome of service. Period.

Facilities: Heated swimming pool, six lighted tennis courts, fitness center; golf privileges at Pelican's Nest Golf Club.

EXPENSIVE

NAPLES BEACH HOTEL & GOLF CLUB, 851 Gulf Shore Blvd., Naples, FL 33940. Tel. 813/261-2222, or toll free 800/237-7600. Fax 813/261-7380. 239 rms, 34 efficiencies, 42 suites. A/C TV TEL

$ Rates: Winter, $165 double; from $375, suite. Off-season, $85 double; from $190, suite. AE, DC, DISC, MC, V.

Although Henry B. Watkins, Sr., bought the Naples Hotel along with the town's undeveloped land in 1946, he soon replaced that turn-of-the-century relic with this charming establishment, still owned and operated by his family. The beachside setting on Millionaires Row in Old Naples couldn't be better for carrying on the hallowed, Old Florida traditions of its predecessor. Improved over the years, the accommodations all have attractive and comfortable Florida-style furnishings. Their private balconies look out on the gulf and lush gardens below. Across Gulf Shore Boulevard, exotic orchids grow on the hotel's own golf course—and are often cut to decorate the premises.

Dining/Entertainment: Since the hotel predates Naples's strict zoning laws, it has the only two restaurants and bars directly on the beach. Overlooking this scene, the Everglades Dining Room offers moderately priced dinners. HB's on the Gulf is casual for breakfast, lunch, and dinner. The carefree Sunset Beach Bar is one of Southwest Florida's most famous beachside "tiki" bars (thatch roof and all) and is always crammed as the sun sets over the gulf. It's especially active on Sunday afternoons during the winter season, when live jazz and blues bands perform.

Over on the golf course, duffers can recharge at the Brassie Café or grab a cold one at the Tenth Tee Tent. Brassie's has live entertainment and dancing Tuesday through Saturday nights during the season.

Services: Activities desk, children's program.

Facilities: Olympic-size swimming pool, 18-hole par-72 championship golf course, four tennis courts, sailboat and water-sports equipment rental.

MODERATE

LA PLAYA BEACH & RACQUET INN, 9891 Gulf Shore Dr., Naples, FL 33963. Tel. 813/597-3123, or toll free 800/237-6883, 800/282-4423 in Florida. Fax 813/597-6278. 172 rms, efficiencies, and suites. A/C TV TEL

$ Rates: Winter, $125 double; from $340, suite. Off-season, $78 double; from $240, suite. AE, MC, V.

On Vanderbilt Beach, every room in this attractive resort has a gulf view. Some are in an older, motel-style wing; others are in a high-rise tower next door (rates depend on location and view). Pleasantly decorated in a variety of color schemes, every unit has sliding glass doors leading to a balcony or patio. There's plenty of action here, with six tennis courts, a volleyball court, shuffleboard, and two heated swimming pools. The Gulfside Café's screened dining patio is open for breakfast, lunch, and dinner. During the winter, La Casba serves French-style specialties, and the year-round La Tasca offers casual dining, deli-style carry-out, and patio bar.

PARK SHORE RESORT, 600 Neapolitan Way, Naples, FL 33940. Tel. 813/263-2222, or toll free 800/548-2077. Fax 813/262-0496. 156 suites. A/C TV TEL

$ Rates: Winter, $165–$190 suite. Off-season, $72–$152 suite. AE, MC, V.

Surrounding a man-made lagoon with waterfalls cascading on its own island, these attractive one- and two-bedroom suites offer much more space than hotel rooms. Guests can walk across a bridge to swim, order from the bar, and barbecue on the artificial island. The Island Club restaurant serves lunch and dinner, and there are plenty of restaurants in the nearby shopping centers along U.S. 41. The resort also has tennis, racquetball, volleyball, basketball, and shuffleboard courts, plus a whirlpool, laundry room, and a children's activities program. Although the address is on Neapolitan Way, the resort actually is at the south end of West Boulevard North.

VANDERBILT INN ON THE GULF, 11000 Gulf Shore Dr., Naples, FL 33963. Tel. 813/597-3151, or toll free 800/643-8654. Fax 813/597-3099. 147 rms, 16 beachfront efficiencies. A/C TV TEL
$ Rates: Winter, $127–$259. Off-season, $82–$189. AE, DC, DISC, MC, V.

Cheerful tropical decor in the accommodations and public areas sets the tempo for a casual, fun vacation at this motel-cum-inn right on Vanderbilt Beach—where guests can go parasailing and rent boats and water-sports equipment. A kidney-shaped, heated swimming pool surrounded by a brick terrace beckons those who want water but no salt or sand (there's a kiddie pool, too). The thatch-roofed Chickee Bar and Restaurant serves al fresco lunches and dinners and draws a crowd for sunset and happy hour day and on Saturday and Sunday afternoons when bands play. Also popular for lunch, the Seabreeze Lounge turns lively on Saturday nights when its band cranks up for dancing. The Jasmine Court serves breakfast and romantic candlelit dinners (early-bird specials from 5 to 7pm).

BUDGET

LIGHTHOUSE INN, 9140 Gulf Shore Dr., Naples, FL 33963. Tel. 813/ 597-3345. Fax 813/592-1518. 1 rm, 3 efficiencies, 11 apts. A/C TV
$ Rates: Winter, $80–$100. Off-season, $40–$59. MC, V.

A relic from decades gone by, this spotlessly clean, two-story motel sits across the street from other more expensive properties on Vanderbilt Beach. The efficiencies and apartments are simple, with freshly painted cinderblock walls, shower-only baths, and small kitchens. The one kitchenless room has a small fridge and coffee maker. A snack bar is on the premises, and the moderately priced Sea Witch Fish Market & Restaurant is a neighbor. Most guests take advantage of weekly and monthly rates during winter, when it's heavily booked.

THE TIDES MOTOR INN, 1801 Gulf Shore Blvd. N., Naples, FL 33940. Tel. 813/262-6196, or toll free 800/438-8763. Fax 813/262-3055. 35 units. A/C TV TEL
$ Rates: Winter, $70–$165 single; $75–$170 double. Off-season, $62–$120 single; $67–$130 double. AE, MC, V.

Little wonder that this immaculate two-story motel stays heavily booked during the winter months. It's right on the beach, two doors removed from the Edgewater Beach Hotel, and on the edge of Millionaires Row and Old Naples. Comfortable motel rooms, suites, and efficiencies are all tropically furnished and decorated. Each has a screened balcony or patio angled to face the beach across a courtyard with coconut palms and heated swimming pool. Suites and efficiencies must be reserved during winter for at least a month; otherwise, ask for a room and wait for a cancellation. It's certainly worth a try, for you can't stay anywhere else on a Naples beach for these rates.

THE TROPICS INN, 312 Eighth Ave. S., Naples, FL 33940. Tel. 813/ 262-5194, or toll free 800/637-6036. Fax 813/262-4876. 60 units. A/C TV TEL
$ Rates: Winter, $82–$165. Off-season, $42–$74. AE, DISC, MC, V.

In the heart of Old Naples, this dated but extraordinarily well-maintained "apartment hotel" is just two blocks from the beach and four blocks from the 3rd Street South shopping area (which more than makes up for the lack of an on-site restaurant). Its eclectic combination of rooms, efficiencies, and one- and two-bedroom suites are in three buildings occupying about 60% of a city block, but the tropical landscaping makes it seem smaller. Some of the bath and kitchen fixtures apparently date from the 1950s, but that only adds to the Old Naples charm. Otherwise, the units are comfortably furnished and immaculately maintained, and have excellent ventilation through louvered windows front and back. There are two swimming pools, laundry facilities, off-street parking, and maid service Monday through Saturday. This is another highly popular inn for long stays during winter, so reserve early.

BED & BREAKFAST

INN BY THE SEA, 287 11th Ave. S., Naples, FL 33940. Tel. 813/649-4124. 5 rms (all with bath). A/C
$ Rates (including continental breakfast): Winter, $108–$156 double. Off-season, $65–$85 double. MC, V.

Listed in the National Register of Historic Places, Cat McLeod's charming, be-porched home in the heart of Old Naples was built in 1937 and still has the original pine floors. Comfy wicker furniture and ceiling fans add to the Old Florida ambience. Cat has delightfully furnished her guest rooms with brass headboard beds covered with old-fashioned floral spreads. An interior decorator friend designed one bedroom's decor, and the art on the walls includes works by other friends and acquaintances. Cat likes to bake, so you'll have fresh muffins and breads for breakfast. Her house is two blocks to the beach, Palm Cottage, and the 3rd Street South shops.

CAMPING

Rock Creek Campgrounds, 3100 North Rd., Naples, FL 33942 (tel. 813/643-3100), at the corner of North and Airport Roads, has 200 RV-only sites for adults only. The **Naples R.V. Resort,** 10000 Alligator Alley, Naples, FL 33962 (tel. 813/455-7275), is a full-service RV resort at I-75 and Rte. 951 (Exit 15). The **Naples KOA Kampground,** 1700 Barefoot Williams Rd., Naples, FL 33962 (tel. 813/774-5455), is off Rte. 951 about 1½ miles south of U.S. 41.

WHERE TO DINE

Most fast-food and family-style restaurants are along the many incarnations of U.S. 41. The **Clock Family Restaurant,** 670 9th St. N. (tel. 261-6724), is open 24 hours a day. The **Black Tie Express** (tel. 352-0400) provides delivery service for many low- and moderately priced restaurants and publishes a compilation of their menus.

Some of the establishments mentioned below are two restaurants in one. Read the price listings carefully, therefore, since one half may actually belong in a less expensive category than I've placed it in.

VERY EXPENSIVE

SIGN OF THE VINE, 980 Solana Rd., off Tamiami Trail N., behind DeVoe Cadillac. Tel. 261-6745.
Cuisine: INTERNATIONAL. **Reservations:** Required.
$ Prices: Appetizers $7–$10; main courses $25–$38. AE.
Open: Oct–Apr, dinner only, Mon–Sat 6–10pm. Aug–Sept, dinner only, Fri–Sat 6–10pm. **Closed:** May–July.

Ever since owners/chefs Nancy and John Christiansen converted this gracious, old-fashioned house in 1985, their gourmet restaurant has been the kind of place Neapolitans go for special evenings like celebrating a wedding anniversary—or proposing a wedding in the first place. Flickering candlelight, a real wood-burning fireplace, fresh-flower bouquets, antique dinnerware, and hand-lettered menus presented in a silver picture frame create a romantic ambience perfect for such occasions. The Christiansens offer an international potpourri of selections, including such creations as Jack's lobster chunks with mushrooms and artichokes in a sassy Pernod-cream sauce accompanied by vegetable baklava. Nancy specializes in grandmother-style desserts like warm bread pudding with a whiskey-and-brown-sugar sauce.

EXPENSIVE

CHARDONNAY, 2332 Tamiami Trail N., at Mooring Line Dr. Tel. 261-1744.
Cuisine: FRENCH. **Reservations:** Recommended.
$ Prices: Appetizers $6–$16; main courses $16–$26. AE, MC, V.
Open: Dinner only, daily 5:30–10pm. **Closed:** Sun May–Nov.

⭐ "Tres chic" best describes this award-winning, glass-enclosed dining pavilion overlooking the pool and gardens of the Best Western Naples Inn. The dinnerware is Villeroy & Boch, the ambience is definitely romantic, and the men are wearing jackets (but not necessarily ties). The cuisine is gourmet French, with such delicious offerings as fricassé de homard St-Jaques au safran (lobster-and-scallop ragoût laced with saffron sauce). An outstanding green salad comes with the meal. Wines may be ordered by the glass or bottle from an extensive list. For dessert, try the baked-to-order luscious soufflés. Valet parking is provided, or sneak into the Best Western's lot.

THE CHEF'S GARDEN/TRUFFLES, 1300 3rd St. S. (actually faces 13th Ave. S.), in Old Naples. Tel. 262-5500.
   Cuisine: AMERICAN/INTERNATIONAL. **Reservations:** Recommended in the Chef's Garden.
$ **Prices:** Chef's Garden, appetizers $5–$9.50; main courses $17–$27. Truffles, appetizers $4–$7; main courses $11.50–$18; sandwiches and salads $7–$11. AE, DC, DISC, MC, V.
   Open: Chef's Garden, lunch Mon–Sat 11:30am–2:30pm; dinner daily 6–9:30pm. Truffles, daily 11am–11pm; brunch Sun 11am–2pm. **Closed:** Lunch at the Chef's Garden June–Sept.

⭐ This casual two-story eatery in the heart of the Third Avenue South shopping district actually is two restaurants in one. The more expensive Chef's Garden, downstairs, looks out on a screened tropical garden patio and is rated one of Naples's finest, with soft lighting and tropical foliage lending a romantic setting. Enjoy intriguing dinner selections like a mixed grill of jumbo shrimp and andouille sausage accompanied by ratatouille risotto and sun-dried tomato-basil butter.

Stairs at the entry lead to a mezzanine and the lively, publike Truffles, where you can order moderately priced pastas, a grand variety of sandwiches, interesting salads, light main dishes, and extraordinary desserts.

ST. GEORGE AND THE DRAGON, 936 Fifth Ave. S., at 10th St. S. Tel. 262-6546.
   Cuisine: STEAK/SEAFOOD. **Reservations:** Not accepted.
$ **Prices:** Appetizers $4–$12; main courses $10.50–$30. AE, DC, MC, V.
   Open: Lunch Mon–Sat 11am–4pm; dinner Mon–Sat 4–10pm, Sun 5–9pm.
   Closed: Christmas Day, and Sun Apr–Dec.
A favorite since 1969, this restaurant's clubby atmosphere is enhanced by exposed beams and a collection of marine antiques. Ships' lanterns provide dim lighting by which to enjoy the famous conch chowder, succulent prime rib, juicy steaks, and grilled filet of freshly caught fish. Jackets are required for men in the dining room after 4pm, but not in the cocktail lounge with its round bar surrounded by cozy tables. Valet parking is provided, or enter the lot directly from Sixth Avenue South.

MODERATE

BAYSIDE, A SEAFOOD GRILL AND BAR, in the Village on Venetian Bay, 4270 Gulf Shore Blvd. N. Tel. 649-5552.
   Cuisine: CONTINENTAL. **Reservations:** Required upstairs only.
$ **Prices:** Downstairs, appetizers $3–$9; sandwiches and light meals $6.50–$11. Upstairs, appetizers $4–$10; main courses $16.50–$25. AE, DC, MC, V.
   Open: Jan–Apr, downstairs, daily 2–11pm. Upstairs, lunch daily 11am–2pm; dinner daily 5:30–10pm. May–Dec, downstairs, daily 2–10pm. Upstairs, lunch daily 11am–2pm; dinner daily 5:30–9pm.
Like the Chef's Garden and Truffles (see above), this restaurant in the southern half of the Village on Venetian Bay shops is another two-level, eatery. Upstairs is more expensive and formal, with gorgeous water views enhancing traditional gourmet cuisine from the Continent. The casual downstairs specializes in Caribbean and Mexican dishes, such as spicy Jamaican jerk chicken. Both have sinfully delicious desserts like chocolate polenta cake laced with white-chocolate sauce. Entertainment is featured in the downstairs bar, nightly during the winter season and on weekends the rest of the year.

VILLA PESCATORE/PLUM'S CAFE, 8920 Tamiami Trail N., at Vanderbilt Beach and Hickory Rds. Tel. 597-8119.
Cuisine: ITALIAN/AMERICAN. **Reservations:** Recommended for Villa Pescatore, not accepted at Plum's Cafe.
$ Prices: Villa Pescatore, appetizers $3.50–$9; main courses $17–$23. Plum's Cafe, appetizers $3.50–$7.50; main courses $9–$17. AE, DC, DISC, MC, V.
Open: Villa Pescatore, dinner only, daily 6–10pm. Plum's Cafe, Mon–Sat 11am–11pm, Sun 5–11pm.

Yet another case of cuisine schizophrenia, these two highly acclaimed restaurants offer a choice of dining elegantly in Villa Pescatore or lightly and casually in Plum's Cafe. Plum's scrumptious and reasonably priced sandwiches, salads, and pastas are especially popular with local families. The recipient of numerous dining and wine selection awards, Villa Pescatore is noted for its Umbrian specialties such as spiedini mixt (grilled chunks of lamb, Italian sausage, pork, and chicken on a skewer and glazed with balsamic-vinegar).

BUDGET

THE DOCK AT CRAYTON COVE, 12th Ave. S., at the City Dock in Old Naples. Tel. 263-9940.
Cuisine: SEAFOOD. **Reservations:** Not accepted.
$ Prices: Appetizers $2.50–$8; main courses $11–$13; sandwiches $4–$9. AE, DC, DISC, MC, V.
Open: Mon–Sat 11:30am–midnight, Sun noon–midnight.

Right on the City Dock, brothers Phil and Vin De Pasquale's restaurant is a lively place for an open-air meal or a libation while watching the action out on Naples Bay. Their chow emphasizes local seafood, from hearty chowders to grilled swordfish, with Jamaican-style shrimp and snapper thrown in for spice. For something light, try the grilled Caesar salad. They have a good selection of sandwiches, hot dogs, and other pub-style fare. Unlike the De Pasquale's other establishment, the tourist-oriented Riverwalk Fish House at Tin City, this one is highly popular with local residents.

MICHELBOB'S RIB CAPITAL OF FLORIDA, 371 Airport Rd., at Progress Ave. Tel. 643-7427.
Cuisine: BARBECUED RIBS. **Reservations:** Not accepted.
$ Prices: Sandwiches $3–$7; platters $8–$19. AE, DC, MC, V.
Open: Sun–Thurs 11am–9pm, Fri–Sat 11am–10pm; brunch Sun 8am–1:30pm.
The name says it all about this winner of national and international cook-offs for the best ribs and barbecue sauces. The big specialty is the fall-off-the-bone baby back ribs, imported from Denmark (where the hogs reputedly are tulip-fed). The rack-and-a-half is not budget-priced at $16, but sliced pork or beef platters and sandwiches are, and there's a children's menu. The Sunday brunch presents an extensive buffet. The smoke aroma comes from the barbecue pit, not cigarettes (there's no smoking permitted).

SILVER SPOON CAFE, in the Waterside Shops at Pelican Bay, 5395 Tamiami Trail N., at Seagate Dr. Tel. 591-2123.
Cuisine: AMERICAN/ITALIAN. **Reservations:** Not accepted, but call ahead for preferred seating.
$ Prices: Appetizers $2–$5; main courses $7–$10; soups and salads $3–$8.50. AE, DISC, MC, V.
Open: Dec–Apr, Mon–Sat 11am–11pm, Sun 11am–10pm. May–Nov, Sun–Thurs 11am–10pm, Fri–Sat 11am–11pm.

Befitting the swanky Waterside Shops complex, this chic café flaunts sophisticated black-and-white high-tech decor and sports large window walls looking out to the mall action. Thick sandwiches are served either with french fries or black beans. The tomato-dill soup and the gourmet pizzas and pasta dishes are popular, especially with the after-theater crowds from the nearby Philharmonic Center for the Arts. The Silver Spoon doesn't accept reservations, but call ahead to get on the waiting list.

SHOPPING

Two blocks of **3rd Street South,** at Broad Avenue, are the Rodeo Drive of Naples, a glitzy collection of jewelers, clothiers, art galleries, and restaurants. The **Fifth Avenue South** shopping area is longer and a bit less chic, with stockbrokers and real-estate agents thrown into the mix of clothing boutiques and antiques dealers. Both areas make for fabulous browsing.

At the **Old Marine Marketplace at Tin City,** 1200 Fifth Ave. S., at the Gordon River (tel. 262-4600), historic boat- and warehouses have been restored to hold 50 interesting boutiques that sell everything from souvenirs to avant-garde resortwear and ornate imported statuary from Bangkok. Winter hours are Monday through Saturday from 10am to 9pm and on Sunday from noon to 5pm; off-season, Monday through Saturday from 10am to 5pm and on Sunday from noon to 5pm.

Two modern, upscale malls are worth a look. The **Village at Venetian Bay,** 4200 Gulf Shore Blvd., at Park Shore Drive (tel. 261-0030), evokes images of its Italian namesake, with 50 shops featuring high-fashion men's and women's clothiers and fine art galleries. Open Monday through Friday from 10am to 9pm, on Saturday from 10am to 6pm, and on Sunday from noon to 4pm. Ornate Mediterranean architecture and a tropical waterfall highlight the **Waterside Shops at Pelican Bay,** Seagate Drive at Tamiami Trail North (tel. 598-1605), where the anchor stores are Saks Fifth Avenue and Jacobsen's. Open Monday through Saturday from 10am to 9pm and on Sunday from noon to 5pm.

EVENING ENTERTAINMENT

For entertainment ideas, check the *Naples Daily News,* especially the Friday-morning edition.

THE PERFORMING ARTS

NAPLES DINNER THEATER, 1025 Piper Blvd., off Immokalee Rd. near Airport Rd. Tel. 597-6031.

Calling itself "Broadway by the Sea," this ornately decorated, turn-of-the-century–style theater features such shows as *Guys and Dolls, Carousel,* and *Second Time Around.* Candlelight buffets begin at 6pm Tuesday through Saturday, with curtain at 8:15pm. Matinee buffets begin on Thursday, Saturday, and Sunday at 11:15am with the show at 1:15pm. Men must wear jackets.

Admission: $27.25–$39, including buffet.

PHILHARMONIC CENTER FOR THE ARTS, 5833 Pelican Bay Blvd., at West Blvd. Tel. 597-1900.

✪ This impressive, mega-million-dollar center, one of the most impressive anywhere, is the home of the **Naples Philharmonic,** but its year-round schedule is filled with cultural events like the Bolshoi Ballet, concerts by celebrated artists and internationally known orchestras, as well as Broadway plays and shows aimed at children and families. Call ahead or pick up a copy of its seasonal calendar at the chamber of commerce (see "Orientation," above).

Admission: Varies with performance.

THE CLUB & BAR SCENE

Much of Naples's nightlife centers on the hotels and restaurants mentioned above. The beachside "Chickee Hut" bar and Brassie's at the **Naples Beach Hotel & Golf Club** (tel. 261-2222) are always popular and have live entertainment many nights. So is the beachside bar at the **Vanderbilt Inn on the Gulf** (tel. 597-3151), starting at sunset. A disc jockey spins dance tunes at Garrett's in the **Registry Resort** (tel. 597-3232). Among the restaurants, both the **Bayside Seafood Grille & Bar** (tel. 649-5552) and **The Chef's Garden** (tel. 262-5500) have pianists or jazz musicians. Since their schedules vary by season, it's always best to call ahead.

The **Old Marine Marketplace at Tin City,** the restored waterfront warehouses on Fifth Avenue South, on the west side of the Gordon River, comes alive during the winter when visitors flock to its shops and two lively pubs, the Riverwalk

Fish & Ale House (tel. 262-2734) and Merriman's Wharf (tel. 261-1811), both of which have live entertainment during the season.

At **The English Pub,** 2408 Linwood Ave. (tel. 774-2408), hospitable Brits Viv and Brian Stuart offer darts, English draft beers, and authentic pub meals like fish and chips, Yorkshire pudding, and steak-and-kidney pie. Their extraordinarily friendly establishment is east of the Gordon River, off Commercial Drive. Open Monday through Thursday from 11am to midnight and on Friday and Saturday from 11am to 2am.

The **Old Naples Pub,** 255 13th Ave. S. (tel. 649-8200), in the 3rd Street South shopping area, has a pianist from 7:30 to 9:30pm Monday through Saturday. This American-style pub serves soups, sandwiches, salads, burgers, and pizza after 4pm. Open Monday through Saturday from 11am to 12:30am and on Sunday from 11am to 10pm.

AN EASY EXCURSION TO EVERGLADES CITY

You won't be in Naples long—or anywhere else in Southwest Florida, for that matter—until you see advertisements for airboat rides in the Everglades. That's because Naples is only 36 miles from Everglades City, the "backdoor" to the wild and wonderful Everglades National Park.

Everglades City was the brainchild of Chicago advertising magnate Barron Collier, who by 1923 owned a million acres of Southwest Florida. To develop his holdings, Collier promised the state that if Lee County were split into two, he would put up the money to complete the Tamiami Trail across the Everglades from Miami to Naples. The state accepted, and the southern half of Lee County became—you guessed it—Collier County.

Collier dredged a channel through the Ten Thousand Islands, created a new island with the spoil, and laid out a town, which became the base from which he built the Tamiami Trail. He made Everglades City his new county seat and hoped it would someday become a metropolis. It did become a popular hunting and fishing spot for the rich and famous, but time and the highway passed it by, leaving the small backwater village with grid streets that we see today. In 1947, the Everglades National Park took in most of the land and bays around the town.

GETTING THERE   Take I-75 or U.S. 41 east to Fla. 29 and turn south to Everglades City. Florida 29 runs through town and then over a causeway along beautiful Chokoloskee Bay to Chokoloskee Island, an old Calusa shell mound that's the highest point in the Everglades. The Barron River forms the town's western boundary.

INFORMATION   The **Everglades City Area Chamber of Commerce,** P.O. Box 130, Everglades City, FL 33929 (tel. 813/695-3941; fax 813/695-3919), has a visitors information center at the intersection of U.S. 41 and Fla. 29.

GETTING AROUND   Everglades City is small enough to be seen on foot, but you can rent bikes during the winter months from the **Ivey House Bed & Breakfast,** 107 Camellia St. (tel. 695-4155).

WHAT TO SEE & DO

EVERGLADES NATIONAL PARK   Unlike the eastern side of the park (see "Easy Excursions from Miami" in Chapter 5, above), access to the maze of islands and swamps along this southwestern coastal area is by powerboat or canoe only. The **Wilderness Waterway** twists and turns for 99 miles between here and the Flamingo Visitor Center southwest of Miami. The waterway has primitive camping outposts for canoes and motor boats.

The **Gulf Coast Visitor Center,** on Fla. 29 at the south end of town (tel. 695-3311), has an interpretive center and is the jumping-off point for **National Park Boat Tours** (tel. 695-2591, or toll free 800/445-7724). The 1¾-hour narrated voyages depart every 30 to 45 minutes between 9am and 4:30pm during winter, less frequently off-season. The sunset cruise offers the best chance to observe the park's multitude of birds, which return to their rookeries at dusk The tours cost $10 for adults, $5 for children 6 to 12, free for children under 6.

The **E. J. Hamilton Observation Tower,** opposite the visitor center, is not part of the national park, but you can climb it for $1 and see for miles across the islands and sawgrass plains.

AIRBOAT RIDES   Other than fishing (two-thirds of Florida's stone crab claws are harvested by boats based in Everglades City), airboat rides are the town's major industry. These flat-bottom, airplane propeller–driven boats can take from two people to large groups speeding through the waterways.

The most advertised—and touristy—is **Wooten's Everglades Adventure,** on U.S. 41 east of Fla. 29 (tel. 695-2781, or toll free 800/282-2781). This large operation has airboat and swamp-buggy rides, a crocodile farm, gift shop, and snack bar. In town on Fla. 29, **Jungle Erv's Airboat World** (tel. 695-2805, or toll free 800/432-3367) has a large tour boat charging $12 a person, or private rides for $30 per person. **Eden's Jungle Boat Tours** (tel. 695-2800, or toll free 800/543-3367) has a nature tour by large pontoon boat as well as private airboat rides. A host of smaller operators offer private airboat rides for about $60 an hour. Pick up a list at the Everglades City Area Chamber of Commerce (see "Information," above).

CANOE EXCURSIONS   David Harraden and sons Jason and Jeremy of **North American Canoe Tours** (tel. 695-3299 or 695-4666; fax 813/695-4155) have been leading canoe expeditions into the Everglades every winter since 1978, offering trips ranging from one day to a week. The one-day trips cost $40 per person. The Harradens operate only from November to April.

Both the Harradens and National Park Boat Tours (see above) rent canoes and full equipment.

NATURE TOURS   Everyone raves about the narrated tours given by naturalists Frank and Georgia Garrett of **Majestic Everglades Excursions** (tel. 695-2777). They take up to six passengers on four-hour excursions through the islands on their covered deck boat and explain the bird, marine, animal, and plant life. The trips cost $50 per person, and reservations are required.

MUSEUMS   For a step back into pioneering days, visit **Ted Smallwood's Store,** four miles south of Everglades City on Chokoloskee Island. Established as a trading outpost in 1906, this waterfront clapboard store is now a museum dedicated to that period. If you read Peter Mathiessen's *Killing Mr. Watson,* you know that Ed Watson, reputed murderer of the notorious female outlaw Belle Star, was gunned down on the store's dock. Open daily from 10am to 5pm during winter, Friday through Tuesday from 10am to 4pm the rest of the year. Admission is by $2 donation.

SPECIAL EVENTS   The biggest annual event here is the **Seafood Festival** the first weekend in February, when the town is jammed with visitors cracking stone crab claws.

WHERE TO STAY

CAPTAIN'S TABLE LODGE & VILLAS, 102 E. Broadway (P.O. Box 530), Everglades City, FL 33929. Tel. 813/695-4211, or toll free 800/741-6430. Fax 813/695-2633. 26 rms, 4 suites, 24 villas. A/C TV TEL
$ Rates: Winter, $65–$88. Off-season, $45–$77. AE, DC, DISC, MC, V.
Located in the heart of town on Fla. 29, this collection of rooms, suites, and villas actually is a condo development, so the units are furnished and decorated in each owner's tastes. The rooms and suites are in a main building, while the villas are built on stilts and have a cottagelike feel to them. The old Spanish-style railroad station next door has been converted into a restaurant. A swimming pool sits by a canallike waterway running along the property's eastern flank.

IVEY HOUSE BED & BREAKFAST, 107 Camellia St. (P.O. Box 5038), Everglades City, FL 33929. Tel. 813/695-3299. Fax 813/695-4155. 10 rms (none with bath). A/C

$ Rates: $35–$45 single; $40–$50 double; $60 single or double during Seafood Festival (with a two-night minimum). MC, V. **Closed:** May–Oct.

During the 1920s, this wooden structure was operated by a Mrs. Ivey as a boarding house for men working on the Tamiami Trail. Today it's run during the winters by canoe specialist David Harraden (see "What to See and Do," above). A center hallway separates the simple rooms. Guests share separate men's and women's bathrooms. There's a deck and a large living room for relaxation. Cold breakfasts are served in a spacious kitchen at the rear of the house. Guests can smoke and drink on the deck, but not in the house.

ROD & GUN LODGE, Riverside at Broadway (P.O. Box 190), Everglades City, FL 33929. Tel. 813/695-2101. 17 rms (all with bath). A/C TV
$ Rates: Winter, $75 double. Off-season, $50 double. No credit cards.

This white clapboard house on the banks of the sleepy Barron River was built as a private residence in 1830, but Barron Collier turned it into a cozy hunting lodge during his Tamiami Trail days in the 1920s. President Herbert Hoover vacationed here after his 1928 election victory, and President Harry S Truman flew in to sign the Everglades National Park into existence in 1947. Other guests have included President Richard Nixon, actor Burt Reynolds, and rock star Mick Jagger. The public rooms are beautifully paneled and hung with tarpon, wild boar, deer antlers, sharks' teeth, and other wild trophies. Out by the swimming pool and riverbank, a screened veranda with ceiling fans offers a pleasant place for a libation. The rooms have lots of 1920s charm. The dining room serves breakfast, lunch, and dinner.

WHERE TO DINE

Everglades City has no gourmet restaurants, but you can get your fill of the freshest seafoods at the **Oyster House,** Fla. 29 opposite the national park visitor center (tel. 695-2073). Main courses range from $7 to $17; sandwiches are $3 to $4. Open daily from 11am to 9pm. Likewise at the **Oar House Restaurant,** 305 Collier Ave. (Fla. 29) in town (tel. 695-3535), where main courses range from $8 to $15, and sandwiches and seafood baskets run $2 to $8. Open daily from 6am to 9pm. Both establishments accept MasterCard and VISA.

5. MARCO ISLAND

15 miles SE of Naples, 53 miles S of Fort Myers,
100 miles W of Miami, 197 miles S of Tampa

GETTING THERE   By Plane   See the Fort Myers and Naples sections, above, for information about the Southwest Florida International Airport and the Naples Municipal Airport, respectively.

Brothers-in-Law Bus Co. (tel. 813/394-2257) shuttles between the Southwest Florida International Airport and Marco Island for $20 per person (two-person minimum). **Air Limo** (tel. 643-2148 or 775-0505) has scheduled bus service from both the Southwest Florida International Airport and the Naples Municipal Airport. **Classic Taxi** (tel. 394-1888) charges $50 from the Southwest Florida International Airport, $25 from the Naples Municipal Airport.

BY CAR   From either I-75 or U.S. 41, take Fla. 951 south directly to Marco Island.

Captain William Collier would hardly recognize Marco Island if he were to come back from the grave today. No relation to Collier County founder Barron Collier, the captain settled his family on the north end of this largest of Florida's Ten Thousand Islands back in 1871. He traded pelts with the Native Americans, caught and smoked fish to sell to Key West and Cuba, and charged fishermen and other guests $2 a day for a room in his home. By 1896 he was doing such a roaring tourist business that he built a proper inn.

Now a fine restaurant, his Old Marco Inn still stands, along with a few other turn-of-the-century buildings. But Collier would be shocked to find virtually every foot of Marco Island covered by resorts, condos, shops, restaurants, and homes. Indeed, Collier's little outpost has become a modern beach retreat for a broad spectrum of visitors, from the famous on down.

ORIENTATION

INFORMATION The **Marco Island Chamber of Commerce,** 1102 N. Collier Blvd., Marco Island, FL 33937 (tel. 813/394-7549, or toll free 800/788-6272; fax 813/394-3061), provides free information about the island. The chamber's visitors center is open Monday through Friday from 9am to 5pm, but a board outside the front door has brochures, an attractions list, and free phone connections to the local resorts.

AREA LAYOUT Florida 951 becomes **Collier Boulevard,** the main drag which crosses the island and passes the large resorts on the island's southwest corner. **Bald Eagle Drive** is the major route between the center of the island and **Old Marco,** Captain Collier's quaint settlement on the north end. The intersection of Collier Boulevard and Bald Eagle Drive is the commercial and administrative heart of the island. **San Marco Road (Fla. 92)** runs east-west through the center and leaves the island at **Goodland,** an old-fashioned fishing village on its eastern end.

GETTING AROUND

BY TAXI & LIMO Call **Classic Taxi** (tel. 394-1888) or **Kay's Executive Limo** (tel. 394-1033).

BY TROLLEY The **Marco Island Trolley** (tel. 394-1600) makes nine complete loops around the island from 9am to 4pm Monday through Saturday, five loops from noon to 4pm on Sunday, between the chamber of commerce visitor center and the Marriott. The conductors sell tickets and render an informative narration about the island's history. Daily fare is $9 per person, with free reboarding.

BY BICYCLE Rental bicycles cost $10 a day at **Beach Sports,** 571 S. Collier Blvd. (tel. 642-4282), opposite the Hilton, and at **Scootertown,** 855 Bald Eagle Dr. (tel. 394-8400), north of North Collier Boulevard near Old Marco. Scooters cost $30 for half a day, $45 for all day.

FAST FACTS

Area Code The telephone area code throughout Southwest Florida is 813.
Doctor For a doctor, go to the Community Treatment Center, 19 Bald Eagle Dr. (tel. 394-4600).
Emergency To reach the police, report a fire, or call an ambulance, dial 911.
Tax In addition to Florida's statewide 6% sales tax, Collier County imposes a 2% tax on all hotel bills.

WHAT TO SEE & DO
ATTRACTIONS
Beach Parks

TIGERTAIL COUNTY BEACH, Hernando Dr. Tel. 642-8414.
The 3½-mile-long, curving, sugar-white beach along Marco's western shore is a highlight of any visit here, and this delightful county park offers an undeveloped respite from the island's three big resorts and several high-rise condominiums that occupy its south end. A sandbar offshore creates a shallow lagoon safe for swimming and perfect for learning to windsurf. There are restrooms, cold-water outdoor showers, a children's playground, and volleyball nets. A concessionaire gives windsurfing lessons and rents cabañas, chairs, umbrellas, sailboats, windsurfers, and other toys. A display illustrates the shells you'll find lying on the beach. Todd's at

Tigertail (tel. 394-8828) has a fully screened patio where it serves inexpensive hot dogs, sandwiches, salads, and other snacks daily from 10am to 4pm.

Admission: Free.

Open: Daily dawn–dusk.

Nature Preserves

COLLIER SEMINOLE STATE PARK, 20200 Tamiami Trail, 12 miles east of Marco Island via U.S. 41 or Fla. 92. Tel. 394-3397.

This 6,423-acre preserve offers fishing, boating, picnicking, canoeing over a 13-mile loop with primitive campsites, regular tent and RV camping, and observing nature along hiking and nature trails. Many species of birds inhabit this mangrove forest. A "walking" dredge used to build the Tamiami Trail in the 1920s sits on U.S. 41 near the entrance. An interpretive center, housed in a replica of a Seminole Wars–era log fort, has information about the park. Narrated boat tours wander through the winding waterways (call for the seasonal schedule).

Admission: $3.25 per vehicle with up to eight occupants, $1 for pedestrians and bikers; boat tours, $8.50 adults, $5.50 children 6–12, free for children under 6.

Open: Daily 8am to sundown.

BRIGGS NATURE CENTER, Shell Island Rd., off Fla. 951. Tel. 775-8569.

Operated by the Conservancy and part of the Rookery Bay National Estuarine Research Reserve, this preserve has a half-mile boardwalk from which visitors can observe a great variety of birds in their natural habitat. Narrated pontoon-boat tours, at $20 per person, take place Tuesday through Saturday from December to April (call for the schedule).

Admission: $2 adults, $1 children 7–17, free for children under 7; interpretive center, free.

Open: Mon–Sat 9am–4:30pm.

Cruises

Marco is the major gateway to the Ten Thousand Islands along Florida's southwestern coast. **Sunshine Tours** (tel. 642-5415) and **Sea Excursions, Inc.** (tel. 642-6400), both offer backcountry fishing, shelling, sightseeing, and sunset excursions through these beautiful inland waterways. Their per-person prices are all the same: $15 for sightseeing, $20 for shelling, $30 for fishing, and $12 for the sunset cruise. Call for reservations, which are required.

O'Sheas' Casino Cruises (tel. 642-1001) has two daylight gambling cruises on the *Stardancer* daily during the winter, less often off-season. (See "Evening Entertainment," below.)

The 100-foot *Gulf Stream Falcon* (tel. 642-1166) goes all the way to Key West, a 4½-hour voyage. The boat departs at 8am and returns to Marco Island at 10pm. It stays in Key West from 12:30pm to 5:30pm, giving ample time to have lunch and a look around that fascinating island (see Chapter 6 for details about Key West). The round-trip fare is $75 per person.

SPECIAL EVENTS

January sees three popular events. The **Marco Island Art Festival** rings in the New Year at the San Marco Plaza on South Collier Boulevard. That's followed by the **Maritime and Seafood Festival.** Last, Stan's Idle Hour Seafood Restaurant (see "Where to Dine," below) hosts the ✪ **Goodland Mullet Festival,** a two-day bash the weekend before the Super Bowl featuring a "Men's Best Legs Contest" and the "Buzzard Lope" dance competition.

The entire island comes alive from late November through December for the annual **Christmas Island Style** street and boat parades, caroling, arts and crafts shows, and more.

SPORTS & RECREATION

BOATING & FISHING Sailing enthusiasts can slice the waters on **Captain Quinn's Catamaran Tours,** at Marriott's Marco Island Resort and Golf Club, 400

S. Collier Blvd. (tel. 642-2740), and on the *Sweet Liberty* (tel. 793-3525), a 53-foot catamaran based at Misfits Marina on the Isle of Capri, a development north of Marco Island.

Powerboats can be rented at the **Marco Island Marina** (tel. 394-2502), the **O'Sheas' Power Boat Rental** (tel. 642-7881), the **Factory Bay Marina** (tel. 642-6717), and **Marco Island Power Boats** (tel. 394-1006). All are on Bald Eagle Drive north of Collier Boulevard. The **Boat House Motel,** 1180 Edington Place in Old Marco (tel. 642-2400), rents pontoon boats.

Those same marinas are home to a number of **charter-fishing captains,** including Wally Valleau (tel. 394-2285); Jody Weis, Stephanie Weis, and Randy Hamilton (tel. 642-7269); Glenn Andrews (tel. 394-8959); and Phillip Ridge (tel. 642-7585). Call them at least a day in advance.

GOLF & TENNIS The closest golf courses are at the **Marco Shores Golf Club,** 1450 Mainsail Dr. (tel. 394-2581), and **Marriott's Golf Club at Marco** (tel. 353-7061), both in the marshlands off Fla. 951 north of the island (a sign at the Marriott's course ominously warns: PLEASE DON'T DISTURB THE ALLIGATORS).

Tennis courts are at the **Marco Island YMCA** (tel. 394-3144) and the **Collier County Racquet Club** (tel. 394-5454), both on San Marco Road, and at the **Tommie Barfield Elementary School,** Trinidad Avenue and Kirkwood Street (tel. 394-2611).

WATER SPORTS **Marco Island Jet Ski & Watersports,** at Marriott's Marco Island Resort and Golf Club (tel. 394-6589), rents jet skis, waverunners, bumper tubes, aqua-trikes, and windsurfers, and takes guests parasailing, waterskiing, and on Everglades trips via waverunner. **Beach Sports,** 571 S. Collier Blvd. (tel. 642-4282), opposite the Marco Island Hilton Resort, rents jet skis, windsurfers, snorkeling gear, skim boards, fishing equipment, tennis racquets, and other sporting goods. **O'Sheas' Power Boat Rental,** 1081 Bald Eagle Dr. (tel. 642-7881), also rents waverunners.

Scuba divers can take lessons, rent equipment, and go on dives with **Aqua Adventures,** 1079 Bald Eagle Dr. (tel. 394-3483), at Factory Bay Marina.

WHERE TO STAY

There are no chain hotels on Marco other than the Marriott, Hilton, and Radisson properties listed below, which stand in a row on the island's southwestern corner. On the other hand, the island is virtually loaded with condominium-style resorts. Ask the Marco Island Chamber of Commerce (see "Orientation," above) for its two-page list of condos and rental agents.

VERY EXPENSIVE

MARRIOTT'S MARCO ISLAND RESORT AND GOLF CLUB, 400 S. Collier Blvd., Marco Island, FL 33937. Tel. 813/394-2511, or toll free 800/438-4373. Fax 813/642-2672. 735 rms, 71 suites. A/C TV TEL

$ Rates: Winter, $240–$350 double; $520–$890 suite. Off-season, $130–$250 double; $325–$720 suite. Golf, family, and romance packages available. AE, DC, DISC, MC, V.

Often cited as one of the nation's top large resorts (it's the biggest on Florida's Gulf Coast), this deluxe establishment has two nine-story towers and two A-frame public wings forming beachfront courtyards with three swimming pools, bars, and water-sports center. Tropically furnished and decorated, the spacious accommodations range from hotel rooms to two-bedroom suites. All have balconies or patios with gulf views. It's a complete resort popular with couples, families, and groups.

Dining/Entertainment: Six restaurants and lounges offer a variety of cuisines and entertainment. The Marco Dining Room and Grille offers fine continental cuisine at dinner. Also for dinner, the Voyager specializes in charcoal-broiled steaks, seafood, and chicken. The casual Café de Sol serves breakfast, lunch, and dinner until midnight. The Pizzeria & Groceria provides convenience foods and snacks as well as ice cream and pizza and pasta to eat in or take to your room. The Tiki Bar & Grill and

Quinn's on the Beach (the latter named for Tahiti's most famous bar) both offer light meals and libations by the beach and swimming pools. The Lobby Lounge features piano music and views of the gulf.

Services: Concierge, room service, activities desk, valet and laundry, babysitting, children's activities program.

Facilities: Three swimming pools, 18-hole championship golf course (on the mainland), miniature golf course, lighted tennis courts and pro shop, health club, games room, boat and water-sports rental, mall with chic boutiques, beauty salon, conference facilities.

EXPENSIVE

MARCO ISLAND HILTON BEACH RESORT, 560 S. Collier Blvd., Marco Island, FL 33937. Tel. 813/394-5000, or toll free 800/445-8667. Fax 813/394-5251. 298 suites. A/C MINIBAR TV TEL

$ Rates: Winter, $172–$297 suite. Off-season, $92–$222 suite. Year-round, $800–$1,400 penthouse suite. Packages available. AE, DC, DISC, MC, V.

This 11-story tower overlooks the gulf, a courtyard with multi-angled swimming pool wrapped around four coconut palms, and a shingle-roofed public building noted for its large cage with colorful parrots. A boardwalk leads over to the beach with its own bar and water-sports-equipment-rental stand. The suites all have balconies angled to give water views, wet bars, refrigerators, and coffee/tea-making facilities. Four private penthouse units have their own saunas and whirlpool baths.

Dining/Entertainment: The Waterfront Dining Room serves dinner, while the adjacent Paradise Café provides indoor/outdoor seating for breakfast and lunch (both share the same moderately priced menu emphasizing seafood selections). The Beach Bar and Grill by the pool serves lunches, early dinners, and drinks. Sandcastles Lounge has a piano bar with nightly entertainment.

Services: Concierge, room service, activities desk, babysitting, laundry and valet.

Facilities: Swimming pool, whirlpool spa, three lighted tennis courts, fitness center (with saunas, steam rooms, massage therapy), gift shop, conference facilities.

RADISSON SUITE BEACH RESORT, 600 S. Collier Blvd., Marco Island, FL 33937. Tel. 813/394-4100, or toll free 800/333-3333. Fax 813/394-0419. 55 rms, 214 suites. A/C TV TEL

$ Rates: Winter, $185 double; from $450 suite. Off-season, $95 double; from $400 suite. AE, DC, DISC, MC, V.

The 11-story tower-on-stilts of this family-oriented resort seems like an overgrown motel, since entry to many rooms and suites is from outside walkways with bright-blue railings, rather than from interior hallways. The building partially encloses a landscaped courtyard with a swimming pool, from which a boardwalk leads to the beach. Suites face either the gulf or the courtyard, while most of the 55 "guest rooms" look out on the Hilton next door. All are comfortably furnished and decorated with bright spreads and drapes. The one- and two-bedroom suites have fully equipped kitchens and dining areas. Even the rooms have microwave ovens and coffee makers.

Dining/Entertainment: Mango Leoni's colorful restaurant specializes in moderately priced, Caribbean-accented cuisine. Perched next to the pool, Bluebeard's Beach Club Grill offers inexpensive lunches, early dinners, snacks, and drinks. Napoli Pizza Company sells just that, to take to your room or suite. A poolside bar provides libations.

Services: Concierge, activities desk, laundry, children's program.

Facilities: Heated swimming pool; whirlpool; tennis, basketball, and volleyball courts; exercise room; games room; children's recreation center; shop (with beachwear, sundries, and some groceries, beer, and wine); conference facilities.

BUDGET

BOAT HOUSE MOTEL, 1180 Edington Place, Marco Island, FL 33937. Tel. 813/642-2400. Fax 813/642-2435. 20 rms, 3 condos, 1 cottage. A/C TV TEL

$ Rates: Winter, $70–$90 double; $120–$165 condo or cottage. Off-season, $45–$65 double; $95–$150 condo or cottage. MC, V.

This comfortable little motel sits beside the Marco River in Old Marco, on the island's northern end. The rooms are in a two-story, lime-green and white building ending at a wooden dock with a small heated swimming pool and sporting lounge furniture, picnic tables, and barbecue grills. Two rooms on the end have their own decks, and all open to tiny courtyards. The one-bedroom condos next door open to a riverside dock. A two-bedroom cottage, named The Gazebo, is built right on the dock; its peaked roof is supported by umbrellalike spokes from a central pole. Facilities include a guest laundry, small library, and boat and bicycle rentals. Old Marco restaurants are a short stroll away.

CAMPING

There's no campground in the developed part of Marco Island. **Collier Seminole State Park,** 20200 Tamiami Trail E., Naples, FL 33961 (tel. 394-3397), has both tent and RV sites. So do **Mar-Good Resort Cottages & RV,** 321 Pear Tree Ave., Goodland, FL 33933 (tel. 813/394-6383), seven miles east on Fla. 92, in the fishing village of Goodland; and **Port of the Islands RV Resort,** 25000 Tamiami Trail E., Naples, FL 33961 (tel. 813/394-3101, or toll free 800/237-4173), at the Port of the Islands development on U.S. 41 about 13 miles east of the Fla. 951 intersection.

WHERE TO DINE

You won't go hungry here, for Marco Island has more than 35 restaurants, including a McDonald's on North Collier Boulevard. Every shopping center has at least two eateries, and most pubs offer light fare. The free *Marco Review* tourist publication, available from the chamber of commerce (see "Orientation," above) contains a complete list with descriptions.

For terrific and inexpensive eye-openers ranging from bacon and eggs to kippers to latkes, try **Breakfast Plus,** in the Town Center Mall, at the corner of North Collier Boulevard and Bald Eagle Drive (tel. 642-6900). It's open daily from 7am to 2:30pm. Also in Town Center Mall, **Kahuna's Restaurant** (tel. 394-4300) provides inexpensive family fare daily from 11am to 9pm. Neither establishment accepts credit cards.

KRETCH'S, 424 Royal Palm Dr., Old Marco. Tel. 394-3433.
    Cuisine: SEAFOOD/MEXICAN. **Reservations:** Recommended in winter.
$ Prices: Appetizers $4–$8; main courses $11–$22. DISC, MC, V.
    Open: Lunch Mon–Sat 11am–4:30pm; dinner Mon–Sat 4:30–9pm, Sun 5–9pm.
    Closed: Major holidays, and Sun Easter to Thanksgiving.

From the outside, this low-slung, tin-roofed, casual establishment in the heart of Old Marco looks like a fish market, but inside, noted pastry chef Bruce Kretschmer has created a sinfully rich seafood strudel by combining shrimp, crab, scallops, cheeses, cream, and broccoli in a flaky Bavarian pastry and serving it all under a lobster sauce. Cholesterol counters can choose from broiled or charcoal-grilled fish, shrimp, Florida lobster tail, steaks, or lamb chops. Bruce's popular "Mexican Friday" lunches feature delicious tacos and other inexpensive, south-of-the-border selections. Sunday is home-cooking night, with chicken and dumplings, Yankee pot roast, and braised lamb shanks.

OLDE MARCO INN, 100 Royal Palm Dr., Old Marco. Tel. 394-3131.
    Cuisine: INTERNATIONAL. **Reservations:** Recommended.
$ Prices: Appetizers $3.50–$9; main courses $13–$25; lunches $6–$10.50. AE, DC, DISC, MC, V.
    Open: Lunch daily 11:30am–2:30pm; dinner daily 5:30–10pm. **Closed:** Aug.

Built by Capt. William Collier in 1883 and fully restored to Victorian elegance by its present-day owner Marion Blomeier, this large clapboard building has several dining rooms and a pleasant veranda, all richly furnished (the huge crystal chandelier dominating the ballroom belonged to the late band leader Guy Lombardo). Seafood, beef, chops, and poultry are prepared with an international flair appropriate to Mrs. Blomeier's continental birth. Relax before or after dinner in the popular piano bar.

SNOOK INN, 1215 Bald Eagle Dr., Old Marco. Tel. 394-3313.
  Cuisine: SEAFOOD. **Reservations:** Not accepted.
$ **Prices:** Appetizers $3.50–$9; main courses $8.50–$15; sandwiches $6–$7.50. AE, MC, V.
  Open: Daily 11am–10pm.
On the scenic Marco River, this very casual establishment offers indoor and outdoor seating at lunch and dinner. Although seafood is the specialty, tasty steaks, chicken, burgers, and sandwiches are among the choices. The dockside Chickee Bar is a fun place, especially during sunset happy hour Monday through Friday and from 10pm to closing on Sunday. Live entertainment is featured during the winter season. There's free shuttle service from anywhere on Marco Island from 5pm to closing (call ahead).

STAN'S IDLE HOUR SEAFOOD RESTAURANT, Rte. 892, Goodland, seven miles east of Marco Island center off Fla. 92. Tel. 394-3041.
  Cuisine: SEAFOOD. **Reservations:** Not accepted.
$ **Prices:** Appetizers $3–$6.59; main courses $11–$13. No credit cards.
  Open: Tues–Sun 11am–9pm.
Owner Stan Gober, an Ernest Hemingway look-alike, is only one of the many characters who make this waterfront establishment so popular as a place to enjoy fresh but unpretentious seafood and have a lively time in the process. It's in the heart of Goodland, the Old Florida fishing village on the eastern edge of Marco Island, some seven miles—and at least 30 years—removed from the heavily developed part of the island. His place becomes one giant outdoor party from 1 to 6pm every Sunday, when barbecue grills are fired up, bands provide country music for dancing the "Buzzard Lope," and men compete to see who has the best legs. Stan's Goodland Mullet Festival, always the weekend before the Super Bowl, is the mother of all parties.

EVENING ENTERTAINMENT

THE CLUB & BAR SCENE   The lounges in the **Marriott and Hilton resorts** (see "Where to Stay," above) provide pianists every evening. The **Olde Marco Inn** and the **Snook Inn** both provide live entertainment nightly (see "Where to Dine," above).
  One of the most lively local spots is **La Casita Mexican Restaurant,** in the Shops of Marco, San Marco Road at Barfield Drive (tel. 642-7600), where owners Frankie Ray and Maryellen play a variety of Mexican, Irish, popular, and traditional music Monday through Saturday. On Sunday, the Gulf Coasters play 1950s and '60s dance music.
  Other establishments to check out are the **Purple Parrot,** in the Shops of Marco, San Marco Road at Barfield Drive (tel. 394-2222); **Konrad's** (tel. 642-3332) and **Rookies Pub & Grill** (tel. 394-6400), both in Mission de San Marco Plaza, South Collier Boulevard at Winterberry Drive; the **Windjammer,** 701 Bald Eagle Dr. (tel. 642-9998); and **Alan's Hideaway Piano Bar,** 23 Front St. (tel. 642-0770), where owner Alan Bogdan plays.
  The schedules vary by season, so call ahead.

GAMBLING CRUISES   O'Sheas' Casino Cruises (tel. 642-1001) sends the 157-foot long *Stardancer* nine miles offshore so patrons can legally wager at the blackjack, roulette, and craps tables and play stud poker and Bingo. There's also dining and live music for dancing on board. Evening cruises leave at 6pm Monday through Saturday and return at 12:30am. Cruises cost $53 per person (no one under 18 allowed on board). The ship departs from O'Sheas' Restaurant on Bald Eagle Drive in Old Marco.

Now Save Money on All Your Travels by Joining
FROMMER'S ™ TRAVEL BOOK CLUB
The World's Best Travel Guides at Membership Prices

FROMMER'S TRAVEL BOOK CLUB is your ticket to successful travel! Open up a world of travel information and simplify your travel planning when you join ranks with thousands of value-conscious travelers who are members of the FROMMER'S TRAVEL BOOK CLUB. Join today and you'll be entitled to all the privileges that come from belonging to the club that offers you travel guides for less to more than 100 destinations worldwide. Annual membership is only $25 (U.S.) or $35 (Canada and foreign).

The Advantages of Membership

1. Your choice of *three* free FROMMER'S TRAVEL GUIDES (any *two* FROM-MER'S COMPREHENSIVE GUIDES, FROMMER'S $-A-DAY GUIDES, FROMMER'S WALKING TOURS *or* FROMMER'S FAMILY GUIDES—plus *one* FROMMER'S CITY GUIDE, FROMMER'S CITY $-A-DAY GUIDE *or* FROMMER'S TOURING GUIDE).
2. Your own subscription to **TRIPS AND TRAVEL** quarterly newsletter.
3. You're entitled to a **30% discount** on your order of any additional books offered by FROMMER'S TRAVEL BOOK CLUB.
4. You're offered (at a small additional fee) our **Domestic Trip-Routing Kits.**

Our quarterly newsletter **TRIPS AND TRAVEL** offers practical information on the best buys in travel, the "hottest" vacation spots, the latest travel trends, world-class events and much, much more.

Our **Domestic Trip-Routing Kits** are available for any North American destination. We'll send you a detailed map highlighting the best route to take to your destination—you can request direct or scenic routes.

Here's all you have to do to join:

Send in your membership fee of $25 ($35 Canada and foreign) with your name and address on the form below along with your selections as part of your membership package to **FROMMER'S TRAVEL BOOK CLUB, P.O. Box 473, Mt. Morris, IL 61054-0473.** Remember to check off your *three* free books.

If you would like to order additional books, please select the books you would like and send a check for the total amount (please add sales tax in the states noted below), plus $2 per book for shipping and handling ($3 per book for foreign orders) to:

FROMMER'S TRAVEL BOOK CLUB
P.O. Box 473
Mt. Morris, IL 61054-0473
(815) 734-1104

[ ] **YES.** I want to take advantage of this opportunity to join FROMMER'S TRAVEL BOOK CLUB.
[ ] **My check is enclosed.** Dollar amount enclosed_____*
(all payments in U.S. funds only)

Name_____
Address_____
City_____ State_____ Zip_____
All orders must be prepaid.

To ensure that all orders are processed efficiently, please apply sales tax in the following areas: CA, CT, FL, IL, NJ, NY, TN, WA and CANADA.

*With membership, shipping and handling will be paid by FROMMER'S TRAVEL BOOK CLUB for the three free books you select as part of your membership. Please add $2 per book for shipping and handling for any additional books purchased ($3 per book for foreign orders).

Allow 4–6 weeks for delivery. Prices of books, membership fee, and publication dates are subject to change without notice. Prices are subject to acceptance and availability.

AC1

Please Send Me the Books Checked Below:

FROMMER'S COMPREHENSIVE GUIDES
(Guides listing facilities from budget to deluxe,
with emphasis on the medium-priced)

	Retail Price	Code		Retail Price	Code
☐ Acapulco/Ixtapa/Taxco 1993–94	$15.00	C120	☐ Japan 1994–95 (Avail. 3/94)	$19.00	C144
☐ Alaska 1994–95	$17.00	C131	☐ Morocco 1992–93	$18.00	C021
☐ Arizona 1993–94	$18.00	C101	☐ Nepal 1994–95	$18.00	C126
☐ Australia 1992–93	$18.00	C002	☐ New England 1994 (Avail. 1/94)	$16.00	C137
☐ Austria 1993–94	$19.00	C119	☐ New Mexico 1993–94	$15.00	C117
☐ Bahamas 1994–95	$17.00	C121	☐ New York State 1994–95	$19.00	C133
☐ Belgium/Holland/Luxembourg 1993–94	$18.00	C106	☐ Northwest 1994–95 (Avail. 2/94)	$17.00	C140
☐ Bermuda 1994–95	$15.00	C122	☐ Portugal 1994–95 (Avail. 2/94)	$17.00	C141
☐ Brazil 1993–94	$20.00	C111	☐ Puerto Rico 1993–94	$15.00	C103
☐ California 1994	$15.00	C134	☐ Puerto Vallarta/Manzanillo/Guadalajara 1994–95 (Avail. 1/94)	$14.00	C028
☐ Canada 1994–95 (Avail. 4/94)	$19.00	C145	☐ Scandinavia 1993–94	$19.00	C135
☐ Caribbean 1994	$18.00	C123	☐ Scotland 1994–95 (Avail. 4/94)	$17.00	C146
☐ Carolinas/Georgia 1994–95	$17.00	C128	☐ South Pacific 1994–95 (Avail. 1/94)	$20.00	C138
☐ Colorado 1994–95 (Avail. 3/94)	$16.00	C143	☐ Spain 1993–94	$19.00	C115
☐ Cruises 1993–94	$19.00	C107	☐ Switzerland/Liechtenstein 1994–95 (Avail. 1/94)	$19.00	C139
☐ Delaware/Maryland 1994–95 (Avail. 1/94)	$15.00	C136	☐ Thailand 1992–93	$20.00	C033
☐ England 1994	$18.00	C129	☐ U.S.A. 1993–94	$19.00	C116
☐ Florida 1994	$18.00	C124	☐ Virgin Islands 1994–95	$13.00	C127
☐ France 1994–95	$20.00	C132	☐ Virginia 1994–95 (Avail. 2/94)	$14.00	C142
☐ Germany 1994	$19.00	C125	☐ Yucatán 1993–94	$18.00	C110
☐ Italy 1994	$19.00	C130			
☐ Jamaica/Barbados 1993–94	$15.00	C105			

FROMMER'S $-A-DAY GUIDES
(Guides to low-cost tourist accommodations and facilities)

	Retail Price	Code		Retail Price	Code
☐ Australia on $45 1993–94	$18.00	D102	☐ Israel on $45 1993–94	$18.00	D101
☐ Costa Rica/Guatemala/Belize on $35 1993–94	$17.00	D108	☐ Mexico on $45 1994	$19.00	D116
☐ Eastern Europe on $30 1993–94	$18.00	D110	☐ New York on $70 1994–95 (Avail. 4/94)	$16.00	D120
☐ England on $60 1994	$18.00	D112	☐ New Zealand on $45 1993–94	$18.00	D103
☐ Europe on $50 1994	$19.00	D115	☐ Scotland/Wales on $50 1992–93	$18.00	D019
☐ Greece on $45 1993–94	$19.00	D100			
☐ Hawaii on $75 1994	$19.00	D113	☐ South America on $40 1993–94	$19.00	D109
☐ India on $40 1992–93	$20.00	D010	☐ Turkey on $40 1992–93	$22.00	D023
☐ Ireland on $45 1994–95 (Avail. 1/94)	$17.00	D117	☐ Washington, D.C. on $40 1994–95 (Avail. 2/94)	$17.00	D119

FROMMER'S CITY $-A-DAY GUIDES
(Pocket-size guides to low-cost tourist accommodations
and facilities)

	Retail Price	Code		Retail Price	Code
☐ Berlin on $40 1994–95	$12.00	D111	☐ Madrid on $50 1994–95 (Avail. 1/94)	$13.00	D118
☐ Copenhagen on $50 1992–93	$12.00	D003	☐ Paris on $50 1994–95	$12.00	D117
☐ London on $45 1994–95	$12.00	D114	☐ Stockholm on $50 1992–93	$13.00	D022

FROMMER'S WALKING TOURS
(With routes and detailed maps, these companion guides point out
the places and pleasures that make a city unique)

	Retail Price	Code		Retail Price	Code
☐ Berlin	$12.00	W100	☐ Paris	$12.00	W103
☐ London	$12.00	W101	☐ San Francisco	$12.00	W104
☐ New York	$12.00	W102	☐ Washington, D.C.	$12.00	W105

FROMMER'S TOURING GUIDES
(Color-illustrated guides that include walking tours, cultural and historic
sights, and practical information)

	Retail Price	Code		Retail Price	Code
☐ Amsterdam	$11.00	T001	☐ New York	$11.00	T008
☐ Barcelona	$14.00	T015	☐ Rome	$11.00	T010
☐ Brazil	$11.00	T003	☐ Scotland	$10.00	T011
☐ Florence	$ 9.00	T005	☐ Sicily	$15.00	T017
☐ Hong Kong/Singapore/			☐ Tokyo	$15.00	T016
Macau	$11.00	T006	☐ Turkey	$11.00	T013
☐ Kenya	$14.00	T018	☐ Venice	$ 9.00	T014
☐ London	$13.00	T007			

FROMMER'S FAMILY GUIDES

	Retail Price	Code		Retail Price	Code
☐ California with Kids	$18.00	F100	☐ San Francisco with Kids		
☐ Los Angeles with Kids			(Avail. 4/94)	$17.00	F104
(Avail. 4/94)	$17.00	F103	☐ Washington, D.C. with Kids		
☐ New York City with Kids			(Avail. 2/94)	$17.00	F102
(Avail. 2/94)	$18.00	F101			

FROMMER'S CITY GUIDES
(Pocket-size guides to sightseeing and tourist accommodations and
facilities in all price ranges)

	Retail Price	Code		Retail Price	Code
☐ Amsterdam 1993–94	$13.00	S110	☐ Montréal/Québec		
☐ Athens 1993–94	$13.00	S114	City 1993–94	$13.00	S125
☐ Atlanta 1993–94	$13.00	S112	☐ Nashville/Memphis		
☐ Atlantic City/Cape			1994–95 (Avail. 4/94)	$13.00	S141
May 1993–94	$13.00	S130	☐ New Orleans 1993–94	$13.00	S103
☐ Bangkok 1992–93	$13.00	S005	☐ New York 1994 (Avail.		
☐ Barcelona/Majorca/Minorca/			1/94)	$13.00	S138
Ibiza 1993–94	$13.00	S115	☐ Orlando 1994	$13.00	S135
☐ Berlin 1993–94	$13.00	S116	☐ Paris 1993–94	$13.00	S109
☐ Boston 1993–94	$13.00	S117	☐ Philadelphia 1993–94	$13.00	S113
☐ Budapest 1994–95 (Avail.			☐ San Diego 1993–94	$13.00	S107
2/94)	$13.00	S139	☐ San Francisco 1994	$13.00	S133
☐ Chicago 1993–94	$13.00	S122	☐ Santa Fe/Taos/		
☐ Denver/Boulder/Colorado			Albuquerque 1993–94	$13.00	S108
Springs 1993–94	$13.00	S131	☐ Seattle/Portland 1994–95	$13.00	S137
☐ Dublin 1993–94	$13.00	S128	☐ St. Louis/Kansas		
☐ Hong Kong 1994–95			City 1993–94	$13.00	S127
(Avail. 4/94)	$13.00	S140	☐ Sydney 1993–94	$13.00	S129
☐ Honolulu/Oahu 1994	$13.00	S134	☐ Tampa/St.		
☐ Las Vegas 1993–94	$13.00	S121	Petersburg 1993–94	$13.00	S105
☐ London 1994	$13.00	S132	☐ Tokyo 1992–93	$13.00	S039
☐ Los Angeles 1993–94	$13.00	S123	☐ Toronto 1993–94	$13.00	S126
☐ Madrid/Costa del			☐ Vancouver/Victoria 1994–		
Sol 1993–94	$13.00	S124	95 (Avail. 1/94)	$13.00	S142
☐ Miami 1993–94	$13.00	S118	☐ Washington, D.C. 1994		
☐ Minneapolis/St.			(Avail. 1/94)	$13.00	S136
Paul 1993–94	$13.00	S119			

SPECIAL EDITIONS

	Retail Price	Code		Retail Price	Code
☐ Bed & Breakfast Southwest	$16.00	P100	☐ Caribbean Hideaways	$16.00	P103
☐ Bed & Breakfast Great American Cities (Avail. 1/94)	$16.00	P104	☐ National Park Guide 1994 (avail. 3/94)	$16.00	P105
			☐ Where to Stay U.S.A.	$15.00	P102

Please note: if the availability of a book is several months away, we may have back issues of guides to that particular destination. Call customer service at (815) 734-1104.